Wrestling with God

Jewish Theological Responses during and after the Holocaust

GENERAL EDITOR

Steven T. Katz

ASSOCIATE EDITORS

Shlomo Biderman
Gershon Greenberg

OXFORD
UNIVERSITY PRESS
2007

Oxford University Press, Inc., publishes works that further
Oxford University's objective of excellence
in research, scholarship, and education.

Oxford   New York
Auckland   Cape Town   Dar es Salaam   Hong Kong   Karachi
Kuala Lumpur   Madrid   Melbourne   Mexico City   Nairobi
New Delhi   Shanghai   Taipei   Toronto

With offices in
Argentina   Austria   Brazil   Chile   Czech Republic   France   Greece
Guatemala   Hungary   Italy   Japan   Poland   Portugal   Singapore
South Korea   Switzerland   Thailand   Turkey   Ukraine   Vietnam

Library of Congress Cataloging-in-Publication Data
Wrestling with God : Jewish theological responses during and after the Holocaust /
general editor, Steven T. Katz; associate editors, Shlomo Biderman,
Gershon Greenberg.
     p. cm.
Includes some articles translated from French, Hebrew, and Yiddish.
Includes bibliographical references and index.
ISBN 978-0-19-530014-7; 978-0-19-530015-4 (pbk.)
1. Holocaust (Jewish theology)   I. Katz, Steven T., 1944–
II. Biderman, Shlomo.   III. Greenberg, Gershon.
BM645.H6W74   2006
296.3'1174—dc22   2006000070

9 8 7 6 5 4 3 2
Printed in the United States of America
on acid-free paper

CREDITS

Yissakhar Taykhtahl, "Second Preface: A Happy Mother of Children," from "Introduction," in *A Happy Mother of Children*, trans. Pessaḥ Schindler (Jerusalem: Ktav, 1999). Reprinted by permission of Ktav Publishing House, Inc.

Elie Wiesel, "God's Suffering: A Commentary." © 1994 Elirion Associates, Inc. Reprinted by permission of Elie Wiesel.

Michael Wyschogrod, "Faith and the Holocaust," from "Faith and the Holocaust: A Review Essay," by Michael Wyschogrod, originally published in *Judaism* (Summer 1971), reprinted by permission of the American Jewish Congress.

CONTENTS

PART II *Israeli Responses during and following the War*

PART III *European and American Responses during and following the War*

Wrestling with God

GENERAL INTRODUCTION
Steven T. Katz

I

This collection of Jewish theological responses to the Holocaust presents a wide-ranging selection of fundamental and important material. Indeed, it is the most complete anthology of its sort ever assembled. It is constructed in three sections, each the work of a different editor. Part I brings together for the first time a major selection of ultra-Orthodox responses to the Holocaust, written originally in Hebrew and Yiddish during and after the war. These writings show a profound, distinctive, religious sensibility that grew out of a deep commitment to the Jewish theological tradition. Though diverse, they all retain a commitment to the God of Israel and the Orthodox norms of Jewish life. Part II contains a substantial selection of essays written over the past half-century by Israeli authors. These essays were, for the most part, originally written in Hebrew, and they reflect both the subterranean and overt ideological influences operating in the rebuilt Jewish Zionist state. Compared to the selections in the first part, they also reveal a wider spectrum of theological opinion, ranging from staunch defenders of the Jewish tradition to those who affirm the non-existence of God. Part III collects a broad sampling of works originally written in English and French by American and European authors since the 1950s. These selections contain both defenders of the normative Jewish theological tradition and radical theological innovators. These views range from the claim that "God is dead," to those of conservative thinkers who attempt to respond to the Holocaust by re-cycling classical defenses of God, drawing on biblical models such as the "binding of Isaac," the "suffering servant" of the Book of Isaiah, and that offered by the Book of Job, among others. Taken in their totality, the highly diverse statements in the three sections of this collection represent just about every significant theological position that has been articulated by a Jewish thinker in response to the Holocaust.

To help readers find their way in the complex theological material that has been assembled here, the editor of each of the three sections has provided both an overall introduction to his section of this anthology, explaining therein what is special, notable, and valuable about the material selected for inclusion, as well as an introduction to each individual selection. Thus, readers can gain a broader contextual understanding of the material being studied as well as a more intimate biographical knowledge of the particular authors whose work is here represented. The introductions to the individual authors also conclude with a selected bibliography that provides material for further study. In addition, each of the three parts of the collection concludes with a selected bibliography. In consequence, students should find this anthology user-friendly, even though the issues it takes up are both emotionally and intellectually challenging.

II

The material in this collection deals with fundamental theological matters that arise as a consequence of reflecting on the genocidal assault on the Jewish people by the Nazi state and its collaborators. In the separate introductions to the three sections of this work, the many theological responses that have been put forward will be described and analyzed in more detail. Here, at the beginning of this anthology, I will only point out, in brief and schematic form, some of the most pressing methodological and philosophical questions to which students need to be sensitive when pursuing their study of this complex material. For example:

1. How does one weigh and evaluate good and evil as historical phenomena vis-à-vis theological judgments? Put another way, can one quantify good and evil?

2. What is the status of "history," of historical events, in Jewish thought? This is to ask: is Judaism a *historical* religion? And if yes, can historical events like the Holocaust disconfirm Judaism's basic theological affirmations? For example, does the existence of Auschwitz prove the non-existence of God? Or, contrarily, does the rebirth of the State of Israel "confirm" Judaism's basic theological claims?

3. How does one evaluate the *meaning* of Jewish and non-Jewish history? That is, do Jews and Jewish history, as well as history in its totality, embody some transcendent plan and purpose? And if so, how is this known, evaluated, responded to, by humanity?

4. Is Jewish history in any way singular? Does Jewish history operate under special rules that apply to it alone?

5. Is the Holocaust unique? And if it is, how, specifically, is it unique? That is, is it historically unique, or phenomenologically unique, or is it distinguished from other events by some special (im)moral qualities or characteristics? And again, does this uniqueness, once identified, matter philosophically and theologically?

6. What does it mean to speak of Divine Providence and of God's intervention into human affairs? Theologians, and more ordinary human beings, use these expressions all the time, but what they actually think they entail is not always clear. Moreover, to speak in this way carries further theological implications that require careful conceptual scrutiny.

7. What is the meaning of the term *revelation*? What is the meaning of the term *covenant*? Here I note that the essential need for precision in the use of such technical theological terms is often ignored by contemporary thinkers, even though the meaning of such terms is decisive in relation to claims made, for example, for the putative "revelatory" character of the Holocaust or, again, for the reborn State of Israel.

8. Recognizing the existence of a long Jewish (and non-Jewish) tradition of theological and philosophical reflection on the "problem of evil" and the nature of and character of God, by what limits, if any, are we bound in interpreting or reinterpreting God's character and attributes after Auschwitz?

9. What traditional biblical, rabbinic, and contemporary sources, if any, have authoritative status in this discussion? Or, alternatively, are all sources, classical and modern, equally open to criticism and equally significant?

10. Last but not least, theological conversation about the Holocaust raises a host of conceptual questions relating to the philosophical and theological meaning of the Land of Israel, Zionism, and the State of Israel. For example, is the reborn State of Israel God's compensation for the death camps? Is it the fulfillment of biblical

prophecy? Is it, as the prayer formulated by the Chief Rabbi of Israel claims, "the beginning of the dawn of redemption"? Or, alternatively, is there no real theological connection between the Holocaust and the State of Israel? And no special theological meaning to the rebirth of a Jewish state in the Land of Israel?

It should also be noted at the outset of this investigation that while the Holocaust raises the host of questions just listed and directly challenges almost all of the basic traditional Jewish theological categories, it does not necessarily falsify nor discredit them such that they require alteration, reformulation, or negation. Any argument in this direction that either asks for specific modifications or reformulations or, more radically, proposes total rejection of the Jewish theological tradition requires coherent and compelling reasons. And, let it be said clearly, to produce such reasons, such an argument, is not a simple matter. Alternatively, one cannot simply assume the correctness of the classical metaphysical assumptions that underlie the traditional theological responses to the world's evil. God's asserted existence, and His nature, have to be argued for by theists no less than God's asserted non-existence has to be argued for by atheists.

III

Readers should be aware that over the decades since the end of World War II—and even in the midst of the war—a number of Hebrew and English terms began to be used to describe the murder of European Jewry. The most common in English is the word *Holocaust*. Though it is unclear when it was first introduced to refer to the murder of European Jewry—Elie Wiesel used it early on and is often credited with its employment in this specific context—the word is drawn from a specific form of biblical sacrifice that involved an animal offering that was wholly consumed by fire. A second term that has become commonly used is *Shoah*, a Hebrew word meaning "catastrophe." This term is often preferred because it does not carry the religious, i.e., biblical, associations connected to the word Holocaust. A third term that is regularly used in Hebrew and Yiddish sources is the term *Ḥurban*. This is a term that has traditionally been used in Jewish sources to describe the destruction of the First and Second Temples as well as subsequent national tragedies. In the selections reprinted in this volume, students will encounter all three of these locutions as well as some others, e.g., the *tremendum*, coined by contemporary authors struggling to find what they feel is a still more accurate description of the tragic, overwhelming, at times seemingly incomprehensible events to which they are referring. Though these terms have different histories and different connotations, this diversity of nomenclature should not present a problem for readers. At the same time, however, readers should be sensitive to the alternative meanings these words carry, especially the deep religious associations carried by the terms Holocaust and *Ḥurban*.

IV

The abbreviation B.T. in the original texts here reprinted stands for Babylonian Talmud. The individual volumes of the Babylonian Talmud referred to in the texts are identified by the abbreviation B.T. followed by the name of the individual tractate of the Talmud being cited. For example, B.T. *Shabbat* refers to the tractate *Shabbat* in the Babylonian Talmud. The number following the name of the individual tractate indicates the relevant page number of the material being referred to. In addition, the page number given is followed by a small a or b. These small letters refer to either the front side of the page cited or the over side of the page being cited. So, for example, B.T. *Shabbat* 1a refers to the first side of the first page of the tractate *Shabbat*. A reference to B.T. *Shabbat* 1b would be a reference to the over side of the first page of the same tractate.

The abbreviation J.T. refers to the Jerusalem Talmud. The citation of texts from this classical rabbinic collection again indicates the name of individual tractates, for example, J.T. *Shabbat*, but the material being referred to is indicated by chapter and verse. So, for example, the reference J.T. *Shabbat* 1:1 refers to chapter 1, verse 1 of this tractate.

The Babylonian Talmud, which includes and is built upon the Mishnah—the first great code of Jewish law compiled by Rabbi Judah the Prince around the year 200 in the Land of Israel—is the most basic and authoritative source of Jewish law and lore after the Bible. It represents the collective wisdom—and normative legal decisions— of the Jewish Sages of Babylonia between the third and late sixth centuries CE. It received its final, edited form at the end of the sixth century CE.

The Jerusalem Talmud, also built on the foundation of the Mishnah, was compiled by the Jewish Sages in the Land of Israel between the third and late fifth, early sixth centuries. For complex historical reasons it did not achieve the authoritative status of the Babylonian Talmud. It received its final, edited form circa 500–530 CE.

It should also be noted that citations of the form, for example, Rashi *ad* Numbers 1:1, refer to the commentary of the medieval sage known by the acronym Rashi (Rabbi Shlomo Yitzchaki 1040–1105) to the biblical book of Numbers, chapter 1, verse 1. Sources cited in this form, for example, X *ad* Y, may also refer to the title of specific books that are commentaries on other, usually biblical, books, rather than to a specific author. So, for example, the citation *Metsudat David ad* Isaiah refers to the commentary by the title *Metsudat David* on the biblical book of Isaiah. Readers will be able to distinguish those citations referring to individual authors from those referring to the names of books (and commentaries) by the fact that the names of authors, for example, Rashi, are not italicized while those of books and commentaries, for example, *Metsudat David*, are italicized.

Citations from the major early rabbinic commentary on the Bible known as the *Midrash Rabbah* are identified in the following form, for example, *Midrash Bereshit Rabbah*, *Parashah* 1, *Siman* 1. The first three terms refer to the overall collection as well as the individual volume being referred to. That is, the form always followed is *Midrash ____ Rabbah* where the second word, here represented by the blank space, is the title of the specific volume of the collection being cited. So, for example, *Midrash Bereshit Rabbah* refers to the rabbinic commentary on *Bereshit* which is known as *Genesis* in English. The term *Parashah* following the title refers to the chapter cited, and the term *Siman* refers to the verse being cited. Thus *Midrash Bereshit Rabbah*, *Parashah* 1, *Siman* 1, refers to the midrashic commentary on Genesis, chapter 1, verse 1.

References to Maimonides (Rabbi Moses ben Maimon, 1135–1204) code of Jewish law known as the *Mishneh Torah* are introduced by the overall title of the work, *Mishneh Torah*, and then the individual volume being referred to. For example, *Mishneh Torah, Hilkhot Avodah Zarah* refers to the volume dealing with the "Laws of Idolatry" (*Avodah Zarah*) in the *Mishneh Torah*. This identification is followed by a number which refers to the specific chapter being cited. (Readers new to this material should note that the twelfth century *Mishneh Torah* of Maimonides and the late second, early third century *Mishnah* of R. Judah the Prince are two separate works.)

Three other works are cited a number of times in our original text. The first is Naḥmanides (Rabbi Moses ben Naḥman's 1194–1270) *Commentary on the Torah*. This is identified as, for example, Naḥmanides *ad* Numbers 1:1, indicating Naḥmanides commentary on Numbers, chapter 1, verse 1. The second is Baḥyah ibn Pakuda's (1040–late eleventh century) *Ḥovot ha-Levavot* (*Duties of the Heart*), a well-known medieval treatise on Jewish spirituality and ethics. And the third is Yehudah Halevi's (1075–1141) *Kuzari*, a philosophical defense of the special character and superiority of Judaism over other philosophical and religious traditions.

English translations of all of the rabbinic sources, biblical commentaries, and individual volumes here mentioned are available.

V

As the general editor of this volume, I would publicly like to thank my coworkers in this enterprise, Professor Gershon Greenberg of American University, who selected and translated the material for part I, and Professor Shlomo Biderman of Tel Aviv University, who selected the material in part II. Each undertook his work with diligence and a sense of responsibility worthy of the very serious topics under review.

I would also like to acknowledge the role played by Dr. Jerry Hochbaum, Executive Director of the Memorial Foundation for Jewish Culture, in this project. Dr. Hochbaum encouraged the creation of this collection and provided the financial support needed to assure that it became a reality. Without his unwavering commitment, this project would never have been begun, and it certainly would never have been completed.

This volume would also not have appeared were it not for the financial assistance generously provided by the Conference on Material Claims against Germany. The editors are very appreciative of this vote of confidence. I am also deeply indebted to Jessica Slobin and Shira Leibowitz, who translated the Hebrew selections in part II of this collection.

Closer to home, most sincere thanks are due to Ms. Pagiel Czoka, the administrative assistant at the Elie Wiesel Center for Judaic Studies at Boston University. Ms. Czoka undertook many different tasks in connection with the creation of this volume, and she did all that was asked of her and more with her usual commitment, efficiency, and cheerfulness. Also, I need to thank my wife, Rebecca, who, as always, has helped in many ways in the production of this anthology. Without her assistance, the volume would still be awaiting completion.

Last, I owe a profound thank you to Ms. Cynthia Read, senior religion editor at Oxford University Press, for her support of this project.

Part I

ULTRA-ORTHODOX RESPONSES DURING AND FOLLOWING THE WAR

INTRODUCTION
Gershon Greenberg

Prefatory Remark

As the Jewish communities in Europe were being shattered and those in Palestine and America were seized with shock and a sense of unspeakable loss, Jewish religious thinkers found a way to continue their activity, both within and around the Holocaust. The history of Jewish thought itself was not broken. But for two decades thereafter, the existence and path of wartime thought were overlooked by the historians, even denied. The situation began to change when Mendel Piekarz published his bibliography of wartime sources for religious thought in 1967; Pessaḥ Schindler wrote on wartime ḥasidic responses in the 1970s; Pinḥas Peli opened the window to the data in terms of religious language; and the journal *Sinai* (Jerusalem) identified theological dimensions to wartime *Responsa* literature. In the 1980s, Ephraim Shmueli wrote about Yitsḥak Menaḥem Danziger's response; Yitsḥak Herman placed Elḥanan Wasserman's reaction in the context of his predecessor, the Ḥofets Ḥayim (R. Yisrael Meir Hakohen), and his successor, R. Elazar Menaḥem Man Shakh; and Neḥemiah Polen researched Kalonymous Kalman Shapira's *Esh Kodesh* (*Holy Fire*) from the Warsaw ghetto. Toward the end of the 1980s, there were conferences at Bar Ilan and Yeshiva universities. In the 1990s, the research of Eliezer Schweid and Gershon Greenberg was published.[1]

What could account for the delay in integrating Holocaust era religious thought into the history of Jewish thought? To begin with, there was an overall paralysis in reacting to the trauma. Next, the sources were almost exclusively Orthodox (and in Hebrew and Yiddish), and they tended to be ignored by the non-Orthodox.[2] Orthodox scholars, for their part, were not inclined to study their intellectual history—perhaps because of a primary concern for religious practice. Also, leading religious philosophers of the Holocaust did not cite them. Emil Fackenheim, for example, wrote in 1970 that questions born of Auschwitz were so terrifying that "until a few years ago Jewish theological thought has observed a near total silence on the subject of the Holocaust. A well-justified fear and trembling, and a crushing sense of the most awesome responsibility to four thousand years of Jewish faith . . . has kept Jewish theological thought, like Job, in a state of silence." And Arthur A. Cohen likewise averred, though incorrectly, that the historical caesura identifiable with the Holocaust bore a theological silence which prevailed for two decades until "a new moment in the assimilation of the historical reality had begun."[3]

Hermeneutical Issues

The wartime thinkers expressed themselves from a variety of situations. Several were in occupied areas, ghettos, and camps. Of these, Avraham Yitsḥak Bloch, Wasserman,

Shapira, Unsdorfer, Ehrenreich, Tsevi Elimelekh Talmud, Avraham Grodzensky, and Shabtai Rappaport[4] were killed; Yehudah Layb Gersht and Ya'akov Kaplan survived.[5] Taykhtahl and Rokeaḥ offered their reflections from the border of the catastrophe in Budapest. Others escaped when it began and managed to find safe refuge: Jakob Rosenheim, Elberg, and Schneersohn.[6] Eliahu Botschko lived through the war in Montreux, Switzerland;[7] Eliahu Dessler resided in London and Gateshead, England;[8] Breuer, Reuven Katz, Amiel, Zalman Shragai, Sarna, and Tsimerman viewed the catastrophe from Palestine;[9] and Gedaliah Bublick, Aharon Petshenik, and Eliezer Silver spent the years in America.[10] In existential terms, those within the catastrophe were simultaneously subjects (observers) and objects (victims). Those who escaped became primarily subjects. Those in Palestine and America remained subjects throughout. However, as Eliezer Schweid has observed, all of these thinkers drew from traditional, transhistorical sources to justify God, to repair damaged faith, and to reestablish absolute commitment to God in the present. The classical sources provided a vital energy which helped the communities to endure. Insofar as faith was central, the process of interpretation and explanation may have enhanced the very desire to live.[11]

The theological writings of these Orthodox thinkers mingled historical and empirical terms with biblical and midrashic language. They also alternated their stances among history, metahistory (i.e., God's everlasting covenantal relationship with Israel over time), and what may be called "ontology" (the dramatic interplay among the metaphysical realities of catastrophe, redemption, and penitent return). Thus, divine intervention (metahistorical) was interpreted as a response to Jewish assimilation in the modern era in measure-to-measure fashion—for example, Nazi strictures against Jews' entering public places were seen as punishment for Jews having attended theaters. Or, the onset of the historical tragedy represented by Nazism was interpreted as the consequence of the decline in Torah observance (metahistorical) and indicated that a higher transition was under way from messianic calamity to messianic redemption (ontological). In his study of the *Esh Kodesh*, Neḥemiah Polen has shown how Shapira engaged in the study of the Torah text in order to transcend the horrific circumstances. So, for example, Shapira identified hints in Scripture that pointed to the contemporary situation, creating a reciprocal relationship between the biblical or rabbinic text and the current, horrific circumstance. The human situation prompted a search to uncover new meaning in the inherited text while a central textual idea bestowed significance upon the contemporary events. The metahistorical, that is, timeless, reality of Scripture framed the understanding of historical reality.[12]

Paradox and ambiguity pervaded this form of theological reflection. For example, God was described as free, transcendent, and omnipotent, but when the people of Israel sinned, He necessarily reacted by punishing them. Israel brought about divine reactions in history, but whether Israel's action was causal, coincidental, or evocative was left undefined. Were the people of Israel to atone to remove God's punishment, God's response would not be in kind (historical and metahistorical), restoring the status quo ante, but would shift into the framework of redemption (ontological). Again, while the Nazis were absolutely evil, seeking even to preempt God's role in the world, God, who is absolutely good, was said to employ them as His instrument. Note too, that the chaos of the Holocaust was attributed to the disregard of the Torah and its obligations, but the primary victims were those who observed Torah. God was all powerful, but once He delegated the punishment of Israel to the contemporary descendants of Esau,[13] He lost control over the punishment. Further, the Jews who were sinners were primarily responsible for the disaster, but the suffering of the righteous was disproportionately greater. Then, finally, it was expected that once there was total disaster, redemption would certainly follow, but redemption could not take place unless the people—whose sinfulness had brought about the calamity—performed *teshuvah* (penitent return). Remarkably, these and other paradoxes and ambiguities did not appear to overwhelm, to silence, the thinkers. They lived with them, demonstrating de facto that the ideas nevertheless functioned as viable components of religious life.

One needs also to note that, in the thought of these luminaries, central theological terms remained imprecise: "Israel" referred both to the corporate Jewish entity and to the spirituality of the nation. "Torah" referred both to the Pentateuch (the five Books of Moses) and to an undefined expanse of scriptural and rabbinic literature. *Geza* referred variously to racial (but nonbiological), cultural, or tribal legacies. Then, too, the relationship between symbol and reality remained unclear. Tsimerman, for example, invoked the sixteenth-century kabbalist Ḥayim Vital's notion that the souls of one generation could return to a later generation for punishment, and he averred that the Holocaust was the punishment for several earlier sinful generations. But did he believe this literally, or was this a desperately needed expression to explain the catastrophe without implying that God had lost control over the souls of Israel? Likewise, Schneersohn spoke of the imminent death of all of the non-Jews who did not bear the imprint of (the righteous) Noah, along with Jews situated outside the boundaries of the *teshuvah* refuge called Goshen. But did he really expect actual mass death, or was this his way of expressing his premise that God controlled the world's good and evil? Similarly, Amiel connected the rampant secularism of the emerging Jewish community [in Palestine] (known as the *Yishuv*, which came into being at the end of the nineteenth century and during the first several decades of the twentieth century) with the suffering of Jews in the diaspora at the hands of God's instruments of punishment. But did he really believe that punishment was so capricious that it touched millions who were innocent and bore no responsibility? Did he believe that the universe, irrespective of geography or causality, functioned in some Manichaean (dualistic) fashion under God? It should also be recognized that references to the Holocaust per se varied from symbolic, to direct, to implicit. Dessler, Ḥarlap, and Yehudah Ashlag wrote of massive suffering and the ascent of the realm of anti-being (the *Sitra Aḥra*), but rarely referred directly to the events of the war.[14]

Themes and Motifs

Wartime religious thinkers who responded to the catastrophe, almost all Orthodox (or ultra-Orthodox, as distinct from modern Orthodox), were steeped in rabbinic and kabbalistic traditions. These traditions provided a context for response that was unavailable to other (modern) forms of Judaism. Reform Judaism had no alternate, independent, that is, nontraditional, transhistorical layer to which theology could resort, when its ongoing, fundamental presumption that morality was inherent to human history was shattered by the events. Nor did Conservative Judaism, when its central principle regarding the organic development of Jewish history was cast into doubt. Orthodox Judaism, however, had roots in revealed Torah, that is, the claim that the Torah was given at Sinai by God to Moses, in divinely grounded morality, transhistorical drama, and the language of *midrash* (rabbinic interpretation of Scripture). The world having turned evil, Israel was forced off the stage of history, but there were other realms which remained intact and available to the reflective believer.

Beyond rabbinic and kabbalistic literature, the Orthodox stream of thought during the war years drew from great modern figures. R. Elijah of Vilna, known as the *Gaon* (genius) of Vilna (1720–1797), was a source for Harlap and Tsimerman.[15] Yisrael Lipkin Salant (1810–1883), the founder of the *Musar* (ethics) movement (1810–1883), influenced Sarna, Dessler, and Botschko. The Hatam Sofer's (R. Moses Sofer, 1762–1839) thought was present in the work of Unsdorfer and Ehrenreich; and both Sarna and Wasserman were students of the Hofets Hayim. The creator of modern neo-Orthodoxy in Frankfurt, Germany, Samson Raphael Hirsch (1808–1888), influenced Jakob Rosenheim and Yitshak Breuer. The responses of Avraham Grodzensky and Yitshak Ayzik Sher were rooted in the thought of Natan Tsevi Finkel (1849–1927), the founder of the *Musar* yeshiva in Slobodka, Lithuania. Tsimerman was indebted to Yehudah Leib Alter MiGur (the leader of the Ger sect of Hasidism in Poland, 1847–1905), Harlap to Rav Kook (kabbalist and first chief rabbi of modern Palestine, 1865–1935), Gersht to Nathan Birnbaum (1864–1937), and Amiel to Yitshak Nissenbaum (1868–1943).

While the religious stream of thought through the catastrophe was overwhelmingly Orthodox, there were different colorations. Six different schools may be discerned. Amiel and Shragai, who were associated with the *Mizrahi* (religious Zionist) movement's religious-nationalist thought, presumed the existence of a metaphysical-level alienation between the nation of Israel and all other nations, traceable to the struggle between Jacob and Esau in Rebecca's womb. The ongoing opposition, they argued, had to be accepted, and the best that could be hoped for was a "cold war" relationship. That would really be possible only when and if the people of Israel became isolated in their own Land of Israel. Having failed earlier to establish the required isolation, disaster inevitably followed. Should the people of Israel now be restored to the land, and steeped in a life of Torah, however, the present catastrophe would not only ebb but would even yield redemption. Wasserman, Gerst, Unsdorfer, Katz, and Elberg were associated with the Eastern European base of ultra-Orthodox *Agudat Yisrael*, the world rabbinical-political organization committed to *Halakhah* (Jewish law). They shared the view that the Holocaust came about because of and within the void left by the internal decline of Torah. They explained that when Torah was revealed at Sinai, the world became divided in a metaphysical way between Israel-of-Torah and nations who opposed it—leaving no neutral ground in between. While this opposition could have remained latent, Israel emptied itself of Torah and assimilated, and this brought the opposition to the surface. Inexplicably, the Holocaust had the form of an attack upon Torah from the outside by Israel's enemies. The hatred, however, could be contained again once Torah was restored—and even more, annulled upon redemption. Breuer, Rosenheim, and Botschko were affiliated with the *Agudat Yisrael* organization in Western Europe. For them, the Holocaust was connected to major historical changes. Rosenheim in New York tied it to unbridled quests for national sovereignty. Botschko, the head of the Ets Hayim yeshiva (Montreux), which he founded to join the regime of traditional talmudic academies in Eastern Europe with Western education, along with Breuer in Palestine, linked the Holocaust to Israel's turning away from its sacred metahistorical refuge of Torah and Messiah and turning toward the nations. It did so just as antagonism toward Israel was exploding. For Harlap and Yehudah Ashlag, devotees of kabbalah, the Holocaust belonged to an ontological apocalyptic drama. For Harlap, it was the dark threshold required for the entrance of redemptive light into the universe. Ashlag contended that the massive suffering represented by the Holocaust would ebb once the apocalyptic secrets of the *Zohar*[16] were comprehended. For hasidic thinkers, the

Holocaust belonged to a world-encompassing ontological process. Yosef Yitshak Schneersohn, the Lubavitcher rebbe (the leader of the *Ḥabad* sect of Hasidism), focused on the purification of the universe through penitent return to God (*teshuvah*) and the possible last-minute *teshuvah* and rescue of all Jews. Taykhtahl in Budapest focused on the divine mandate for return of the people to the Land of Israel; Shapira on the existential challenge to transcend the finite self and participate in God's infinite realm; and Rokeaḥ on God's concealing His face (the biblical idea known as *hester panim*) prior to entering the *Tsadik*'s (the holy righteous man's) historical life to redeem all Israel. For those of *Musar* background, the Holocaust constituted a challenge to penitent return (*teshuvah*), as understood in moral terms. Sarna placed the challenge within the context of the ontological triad of *Ḥurban* (catastrophe), *teshuvah* (repentance), and *geulah* (redemption). Dessler, who directed an institute for advanced rabbinic study (*Kollel Evrakhim*) in Gateshead, England, spoke in terms of overcoming the *teshuvah* loss, which was responsible for the evil of the Holocaust (a subjective reality), and drawing upon divine morality (an objective reality).

But the different schools also shared specific religious themes and concerns: silence toward God, belief in the divine participation in history, belief in the redemptive implications of suffering, a critique of assimilationist/secular Zionism, the evil of Amalek (Israel's traditional enemy; see Exodus 17), the power of *teshuvah*, [the metaphysical significance of the] suffering of the pious, the importance of the Land of Israel, past and future, and the coming of the Messiah.

The End of Explanation

Many of the religious thinkers were initially unable to respond to the catastrophe from the perspective of faith. In the first instance, they became intellectually paralyzed when the question confronted them: How could God have let it happen? The *Agudat Yisrael* leader Yitshak Meir Levin of Jerusalem became resigned to the fact that there was no theological or natural explanation for the sacrifice of millions of God's people. He turned within, looked to God, and only then could start to "understand."[17] Others focused on the incomprehensibility of the suffering of the righteous and, at least initially, fell into silence. But then they drew boundaries around the silence and discovered new ways to comprehend. Ehrenreich in Simleul Silvaniei, Transylvania, believed that silence rightly surrounded history-under-God. Redemption, however, would offer wisdom and access to that wisdom. He accordingly suspended verbal expression about the God of history until redemption. Meanwhile, he inspired his congregants to live according to Torah and to practice *teshuvah*, to pray and prepare to submit the soul to the point of sacrifice (*mesirut nefesh*). Unsdorfer in Bratislava suspended all questions about God's intentions. But then he turned to the depths within himself and apprehended a God outside history, who waited for the trusting Jew to leap to Him in faith. Once in God's presence, Unsdorfer accessed a higher, ontological source, an apocalyptic drama in which suffering and redemption belonged to a higher unity. Sarna could find no precedent to help him understand the calamities and, in his deep anguish, turned to God. God, he now argued, was crying over the tragedy, and this made it possible for the Jew to cry. Once the tears flowed, the threshold to ontological truths opened up. Elberg concluded that no language existed to understand, and no tears remained to break the psychological barriers to the flow of knowledge. But he began to "comprehend" after he accepted the suffering of the righteous as being central to Jewish identity through the ages, beginning with the *Akedah* (the binding of Isaac in Genesis 22). Others could make no sense at all of the tragedy initially, but then were able to find wisdom in rabbinic texts. Wasserman wrote that any attempt to understand by natural reason would drive a person insane. But there were explanations to be had, if one adhered relentlessly to the texts of Torah and the rabbinic tradition. Tsimerman—much of whose writings were dedicated to making a scholarly case for silence—and Katz both found means of expression in rabbinic literature as well. Harlap found it in kabbalah and the work of the Gaon of Vilna as its vessel.

History, Metahistory, and Ontology

The historical consciousness of our thinkers was characteristically elastic—transforming itself into different levels of apprehending reality. Some thinkers accepted historical reality as it was and responded to it. Some sublimated it into metahistory and/or ontology, and others ended up dismissing history categorically. Of those in the first group—where silence did not factor into the epistemology—Gersht explained the Holocaust as the natural long-term result of antimorality. Gersht was imprisoned in the Lodz ghetto until 1944 and then deported to Auschwitz. From there, he was moved to Kaufering, Landshut, Dachau, and Bergen-Belsen, and in 1947 he emigrated to the Land of Israel. The Sinai experience, he wrote, generated a hatred for morality and its bearers, the people of Israel, which grew larger until it finally exploded with Hitler. Gedaliah Bublick, wartime America's leading *Mizrahi* (religious zionist) ideologue, attributed the catastrophe to the assault of barbarism (i.e., Nazism) upon biblical (i.e., Jewish and nonracist Christian) civilization. Shragai, a *Mizrahi* leader who emigrated to the Land of Israel from Poland, was a member of the executive of the Jewish Agency in London in 1946 and toured German displaced persons (DP) camps in June 1948. He attributed the disaster to Hitler's evil, but blamed Jews for making themselves vulnerable to the evil by their landlessness and assimilation.

At the other end of the spectrum, that of the ontological mindset, Ashlag wrote that once the objective reality of redemption was achieved, through inner, kabbalistic comprehension of the apocalyptic universe, the historical sufferings would recede and history itself ascend to the realm of spirit. In Harlap's apocalyptic vision, history belonged to the dark threshold to redemption that served to channel the overwhelming light of redemption so the light would not burst into the world and destroy it. History reflected pollution (*tumah*) and would disappear in toto upon the appearance of the Messiah son of David. For Ashlag and Harlap, history's role was to express its own meaninglessness.

In between those who accepted history and those who rejected it, there were those who combined history, metahistory, and ontology. For Sarna, the ontological triad (*Hurban, teshuvah, geulah*) was reflected in Israel's metahistory—such that the Temple's destruction[18] implanted the potential for redemption, to be actualized with the Holocaust's evocation of *teshuvah*. Schneersohn also paired metahistory with ontology. After Israel failed to use the opportunity of exile to perform *teshuvah* as God intended, God imposed the choice of *teshuvah* or death through the Holocaust (metahistory). Along with this, the entities of *Hurban* (destruction) and *geulah* (redemption) interrelated dialectically through *teshuvah*; *teshuvah* connected one with the other (ontology). Israel's *teshuvah*, return to God, on the existential and anthropological level reflected the higher reality—and should the lower not be aligned with the higher in time, in the last chaotic moment God Himself would force the alignment. Unsdorfer discerned covenantal meaning in Israel's experience in history up until the calamity. At that point, he turned from metahistory to ontology. On the ontological level, darkness came with light, de facto resolving the crisis of faith brought on by suffering. In turn, the darkness-light dialectic became reflected in present troubles. Ehrenreich also discerned covenantal meaning in the past (meta-history). He silenced discussion about the present and awaited redemption (ontology). Shapira endeavored to transcend the realm of finite history with its physical and spiritual suffering and to touch the realm of the divine (metahistory). Wasserman, whose thought was rooted in metahistorical reality, treated historical events as re-flections thereof. According to his eschatology, the condition of Torah-lessness with its aspect of fratricide within Judaism (the internal Amalek) and the explosion of Nazism (the external Amalek) corresponded to a higher passage from catastrophe to redemption. The passage resembled the intense pains which give way to birth. Given Israel's failure to correct the loss of Torah below, Israel would soon be swept up in the apocalyptic passage. Finally, Botschko and Breuer bemoaned the fact that the people of Israel had turned away from metahistory and toward the history of nations. The Holocaust was now expelling them from history. But the Land of Israel provided for the restoration of Israel's metahistorical status, one within an appropriate historical context.

Divine Presence

Wartime thinkers addressed the matter of God's presence in different ways. Some expressed themselves individually and existentially. Aharon Rokeaḥ believed that God was manifesting Himself in Rokeaḥ's imminent escape via Budapest in early 1944 to the Land of Israel, and that God's *sefirot* (attributes) would bond with earthly reality in Rokeaḥ's very person after he arrived there. Sarna asserted that the idea that God's face was hidden (*hester panim*) was a subjective perception only, not an objective reality. God removed Himself only after, and to the extent that, man removed himself from God: "The punishment of *hester panim* above comes as measure-for-measure pun-ishment for our own *hester panim* below."[19] The (subjective) hiddenness of God's face, it followed, could only be removed by man. God remained present in the sorrow of those who did not turn from Him, weeping and helping them to perform *teshuvah*. Schneersohn went further, saying that God remained present whether or not the Jew was aware, calling the Jew to turn to Him in *teshuvah*. Still, the Jew had to be open to God as well as to the apocalyptic drama under way to know this.

Others thought in collective and metahistorical terms, focusing on God's pres-ence in the use of human instruments to carry out His will. Wasserman, citing his teacher the Ḥofets Ḥayim in the name of Yitsḥak ben Ḥayim of Volozhin, said that when Haman[20] oppressed the Jews, he was being used by God as a stick to beat Israel (see "O Assyria, the rod of My anger"; Isaiah 10:5). Fighting the stick was useless; it could always be replaced easily by God. Amiel and Levin averred that the current suffering was brought by God to undo assimilation and secular Zionism and to restore the people of Israel to their exclusive realm. They viewed the Nuremberg Laws positively, insofar as they served to restore the separation between Israel and the nations.

Several thinkers probed the issue of God's instrumental use of evil to achieve His good purpose. According to Unsdorfer, God entered history to restore Judaism to its preassimilated self and did so measure for measure. For example, when Jews aban-doned the use of *tsitsit* (ritual fringes), they were forced to wear Jewish stars. But Unsdorfer also condemned the persecutors for perversely citing divine authority for their evil deeds. Nor did the fact that God was using the persecutors mitigate against their evil. The fact that God related to the earthly persecutor did not imply that the persecutor had some sort of positive relationship to God. Addressing this issue, Ehrenreich pointed out that Israel's attackers would have hurt Israel with or without God's involvement. They were not at all interested in whether God might be using them to punish Israel so Israel would restore its authentic self. Shragai suggested that God chose Hitler only because he was already evil. Had there been no such evil, there would have been no Holocaust. Shragai also rejected the notion that Israel should atone in response to the assault; atonement was a matter of internal and direct relationship with God, not of responding to the enemy. Elberg wrote that while Hitler was an instrument of God, akin to Amalek and Haman, Hitler had no idea of this. To the contrary, Hitler perversely deified his own actions, sanctifying his slaughter and building gas chambers in the name of divinity (similar to Unsdorfer's argument). These thinkers refused to surrender God's presence in history, even in the form of persecution. But they still stressed that the persecutor's evil, in mind and deed, remained undiminished. To their mind, this preserved God's presence without compromising His goodness.

Assimilation and Secular Zionism

There were wartime thinkers who did not select any group of Jews for blame. Harlap, who regarded every Jewish soul as holy, did not blame any Jew or Jewish group for the catastrophe, and he attributed the tragedy solely to the polluted (*tumah*) character of the other nations. Gersht, who had opposed secular nationalism and godless *Haskalah* (modern rationalism and enlightenment) in the 1930s, dropped the attack once the war began. But many others did find Jews to blame: the assimilationists and secular Zionists.

Among the *Mizraḥi*, Amiel, the chief rabbi of Tel Aviv, asserted that the assimilationist legacies of Moses Mendelssohn and Theodore Herzl,[21] each of which removed a partition between Israel and the world, had actually set (*hekimah*) Hitler against the people of Israel. Amiel included assimilation in the secularist modern zionist community emerging in Palestine. When Jews sought to "be as the nations," he averred, God responded by asserting Himself against His people: "As I live" (Ezekiel 20:32–33). Shragai explained how by imbibing other cultures, the people of Israel defied the higher intent of exile, which was to instill the impossibility of survival outside the land into the descendants of the original sinners in the land, who had caused exile. In response, God had the nations thrust Israel back to its true identity.

For *Agudat Yisrael* thinkers, assimilation was a matter of Torah-lessness.[22] Once the Torah was diminished, those who lacked it became de facto part of another realm; there was no space in between Israel and not-Israel for anything else. Some spoke on an anthropological level. Elberg alleged that the Holocaust was the consequence of the sin of having made peace with the exilic world in exchange for autonomy and freedom. Hitler, for Elberg, crystallized what exile was all about. In America, Yosef Eliahu Henkin (*Agudat Yisrael*) wrote that inroads into the gentile world provoked persecution, because gentiles interpreted assimilation as an underhanded attempt to derive benefits from the Church while weakening Christianity.[23] Others spoke on a theological level. Wasserman and Unsdorfer elaborated upon measure-for-measure punishment from above. Levin attributed the chaos of the Holocaust to Torah loss among assimilationists, which dismantled the separation between Israel and the nations. He explained the release of the nations' pent-up hatred for Israel as an indirect means to restore Israel's chosen status. Ehrenreich's reaction to the unfortunate Jews passing through Simleul-Silvaniei with swastikas branded onto their faces and their fingers bitten off was to look to God—for such cruelty could not come from a human source. In response to assimilation, Ehrenreich explained to his listeners, God untied Esau's cruel hands. Once He did, Esau took control of managing divine indignation (see *Metsudat David ad* Isaiah 10:5).

The belief that secular Zionism was dangerous was so intense that after the catastrophe subsided there was still concern that it could bring even further disaster. Gersht, who had set discussion of assimilation and secular nationalism aside once the Nazi threat unfolded, returned to them after the war. In Lodz, he wrote that the internal threat of secular nationalism was overwhelmed by the Nazi external threat to Israel's very existence. After the Holocaust, he wrote that the threat could be devastating. Now, Israel's religious identity was inseparable from political, social, and economic life. Gersht, Shragai, and Levin were all furious about the desecration of the *Shabbat* at Kibbutz Daliah in May 1947. In the face of six million Jews who had been murdered, the desecrators danced and lit torches in a way reminiscent of Hitler's pogrom celebrations. *Agudat Yisrael* world president Rosenheim believed that if the secular Jews of the Land of Israel displaced the rule of Torah with political sovereignty, catastrophe would follow. A Torah-less commonwealth, he was convinced, would prepare the ground for a third Ḥurban.

Amalek

Ancient Amalek attacked the children of Israel in the wilderness and was condemned by God. Amalek's memory was to be blotted out from under heaven, and God would be at war with him through the ages (Exodus 17:14–16). At the same time, Amalek was regarded as an instrument to purge Israel of the sin at Refidim of questioning God's presence, in effect he was given birth and strength by Israel's heresy. In turn, this meant that evil Amalek, for all his evil, was indirectly under Israel's control (*Pesikta Rabbati* 13:1).

As the war progressed, there was a shift from a historical-dialectical approach to Amalek to an apocalyptic-dualistic one. The earlier thinkers (including Alexander Zysha Friedman of Warsaw; Levin and Unsdorfer from the *Agudat Yisrael* school; Yitshak Nissenbaum, Amiel, and Shragai from the *Mizraḥi*; and Ehrenreich independently) stressed Amalek's role in the course of divine action in history.[24] God used the evil Amalek as an instrument to turn the people of Israel back to their authentic selves of Torah and/or the Land of Israel in Torah, such that Amalek was simultaneously antithetical and not-antithetical to Israel. There was a positive purpose now to Amalek's work, and the issue of his punishment receded into the background. Wasserman, for whom Amalek was both the Nazi outside who was a divine instrument and anti-Torah Jews themselves (Jewish section of the Communist Party, the *Evsektsiia*, assimilationists, secular nationalists), did not mention Amalek's punishment.

Later, the instrumental interpretation yielded to a stark dualism between Israel and the enemy, and by the time the war ended the only connection between Israel and Amalek was solely the unbridled, homicidal assault upon Israel and the self-annihilation or cosmic destruction of Amalek as Israel was redeemed. For Elberg, Amalek built gas chambers in God's name. But the very chemicals manufactured from Jewish bodies would explode from the grave and destroy him. For Ḥarlap, the outburst of Amalek's evil in a final attempt to destroy Israel meant his self-annihilation— along with all of the history polluted by him. In the Ulm DP camp, Bentsiyon Firer wrote that Amalek was out to bring Esau's enmity to completion and to obliterate

Israel. But this was the era of the Messiah's birth, when the darkest point would yield to the emergence of light, and there was nothing more vital for Israel than to hate Amalek absolutely and to blot out his memory.[25]

Teshuvah

Teshuvah (repentance and return) was often regarded as the key to alleviating Israel's plight. Some believed that a human initiative of *teshuvah* could transform the catastrophic historical reality. For it meant the restoration of Torah, which would end the chaos and replace it with redemption. Eliezer Silver (president of the American *Agudat Yisrael*) admonished Jews to stop pleading to heaven about when their victimhood would end and turn to *teshuvah* instead. When a disaster occurred, Jews should look to change their conduct (see B. T. *Berakhot* 5ᵃ). Similarly, Ehrenreich told his congregation not to reflect upon whether or how the tragedies were divine judgments, but to leave all that to redemption and instead do *teshuvah* now as their forefathers had done in Egypt. Their own sins should be their focus—not the outer troubles and God's role. Dessler believed that as long as Jews did *teshuvah*, they would remain part of God's own moral realm, which was blended together with the objectively real universe. When they did not and instead turned to the nations, they descended into the chaos of the Holocaust (which was a subjective reality). By restoring *teshuvah* throughout the nation, Jews could bring the Holocaust to an end. At the other end of the spectrum, Shragai detached outer assaults from *teshuvah*. The torrents of blood were created by the nations and not Israel, he asserted. They were not a function of the presence or absence of Torah and *teshuvah*. *Teshuvah* belonged to Israel's internal relationship to God and was not a function of empirical history. *Teshuvah* was also outside the dynamics of history for Tsimerman—but on ontological grounds. As shown by the restored Land of Israel, redemption had been unfolding in the interwar period. *Teshuvah* was required for its completion, and when Israel failed to carry it out, it became necessary to impose *teshuvah* from above in the form of catastrophic suffering.

For Schneersohn and Sarna, *teshuvah* was two-tracked, unfolding below and above. It belonged to an ontological triad, along with catastrophe and redemption. But it also had to be enacted metahistorically and existentially. For this to take place, God entered into man's presence and called out for it. Schneersohn also believed that *teshuvah* would have an impact upon the historical scene. It would provide refuge from the storm in an invisible Goshen (Exodus 9:26) and even turn back the calamity and replace it with redemption.

Suffering by the Pious

While some were silenced by the suffering of the pious (Unsdorfer, Ehrenreich), others offered explanations. Several identified it with the *Akedah* ["the binding of Isaac," Genesis 22:1–19], but extended it from binding alone to actual sacrifice. Elberg spoke of the "*Akedah* of Treblinka," a holy event that brought sin to consciousness, atoned for all of mankind's sins, and fulfilled the need for the explosion of divine wrath at the apocalypse. Accordingly, only the holiest of Israel could serve, and they were the righteous Jews of Poland and Lithuania who were the very emanation of God. Their *Akedah* deaths even sanctified God ("Through those near to Me I shall make Myself holy"; Leviticus 10:3). Firer regarded the Holocaust as the final *Akedah* in Israel's self-sacrificial (*mesirut nefesh*) history—which could not be avoided if the people were to maintain the Torah amid hostile nations. Ḥarlap also identified the suffering of the righteous with the *Akedah*. For Ḥarlap, each victim, loving God with his entire soul as God took the soul (B. T. *Berakhot* 61^b), broke the bonds of finitude as he ascended to the infinite realm of redemptive light, and thus represented a form of the *Akedah*.

Some included the deaths of the pious in the drastic collective action which God took in order to reestablish the Jewish homeland. Tsimerman in Tel Aviv and Aharon Petshenik (a *Mizraḥi* ideologue and nephew of Mordekhai Rokeaḥ) in New York shared the notion that because the pious were involved in Israel's failure to return and restore the land, God let them be killed with the rest of the generation. That way, a fresh and courageous generation could arise—thus replicating what God did to the male Jews of the desert who were intimidated by Amalek and the Canaanites (see Abraham Ibn Ezra on Exodus 14:13). In Petaḥ Tikvah (Israel), Reuven Katz wrote that the pure souls were a burnt-offering sacrifice (*Olah*), given in sanctification of God and the Land of Israel.[26] By the strength of the ashes, he believed, God would fulfill His ancient promise of the land.

Others viewed the suffering of the pious in messianic terms. Wasserman, citing the Gaon of Vilna, wrote that there was no birth (redemption) without suffering (catastrophe), and that the closer the birth, the greater the suffering—as had been the case in Egypt (Exodus 5:16). The pious were included. Levin called the death of the six million a massive *Akedah*, which he identified with the birth pains of the Messiah. A different perspective about the suffering of redemption was offered by Shragai, Schneersohn, and Ḥarlap. They suggested that the imminence of redemption caused panic among the nations, for redemption came with Torah and this spelled their end. The nations sought to sabotage the process by attacking its vessel, the holy people of Israel. They were also going mad in the face of death and tried to destroy everything around them.

Most believed that God shared in the suffering—not only of the pious, but of all Jews. Shapira became overwhelmed by the suffering of God. As the believer transcended his finitude and the physical suffering which pervaded it to touch God's infinite pain and enter His omnipotent spirit, his physical suffering became absorbed by God. Sarna said that God was crying as He once cried when the First Temple was destroyed. Having entered Israel's tragic history then, the God who was eternal remained present for all tragedies to come—His eternity bonding with catastrophic time. Tsimerman wrote that God always shared in Israel's affliction (see Isaiah 63:9). He reminded his readers of the rabbinic teaching that when the Temple was destroyed, God wept bitterly and threatened to retreat to a place where the archangel Metatron could not enter, after Metatron tried to stop Him from weeping (*Midrash Eichah Rabba: Pesikta* 24). God suffered especially, Tsimerman pointed out, when the blood of the righteous was poured out (B. T. *Sanhedrin* 46^a).

Land of Israel: Issues of Past and Future

The issue of the relationship of the Land of Israel to the Holocaust constituted its own thread in the theologizing of the war years. For some, it was an issue anchored in the past; for others, in the future.

In terms of the past, some thought that initiatives taken to restore the land brought on the catastrophe. The Zionist revolt against the British, Ehrenreich believed, attempted to precipitate and force the settlement of the land, and incited God's judgment to "permit your flesh to be a prey like that of the gazelles and the hinds of the field" (B. T. *Ketubot* 111^a). To give money to *Mizraḥi* or *Agudat Yisrael* to develop the land amounted, in his judgment, to giving money to Haman to destroy the body and soul of Judaism. When it came to developing the land, God alone was to be relied upon (*Mishnah Sota*, end): "We must not be like those stupid people of the Zionist sect, who want to conquer and build the Land of Israel by their own power, without the Torah and the righteous messiah." But others, and they were in the majority, contended that the failure to take the initiative in restoring the land, and doing so in the name of the Torah, was directly or indirectly responsible for the Holocaust. For Petshenik and Tsimerman (speaking metahistorically), the responsibility was direct. Because the interwar generation failed to act, God destroyed it to make way for a new generation. Tsimerman, who attacked pious Jews for failing to sufficiently support the *Yishuv* (the Jewish community in Palestine), declared: "On account of this trespass specifically, that of not ascending to the land, the people of Israel have suffered to the point of their calamitous loss of a third of their number by annihilation."[27] Shragai asserted that the exile exposed the people of Israel to the ongoing hatred of the nations. Jews should have quickly sought refuge in the land— and done so with Torah, since Torah loss originally caused the exile—but instead they assimilated with the nations. The landlessness of the Jewish people, together with their intrusion into alien culture, precipitated the nations' violence. Botschko wrote that when the opportunity for messianic return to the land came—he did not say when or how—the Jews tragically turned instead to redemption in Western lands or secularism. Then Hitler appeared and stirred up long-latent hatred to the point of mass murder.

In terms of the future, Taykhtahl demonstrated on the basis of traditional sources that the Holocaust must be seen as divine instruction that the diaspora was now over and that the time for a massive initiative in restoring the land had begun. Once in the land, Jews would experience the manifestation of Divine Providence; the divine sphere of *Malkhut* (kingdom) would coalesce with the united people of Israel. Aharon Rokeah, believing that his escape to the land was an instance of divine presence in history, trusted that once he was there the divine spheres would bond through him with earthly reality, and redemption would reverberate from out of the land—even out to the *hasidim* (his pious followers) from whom he separated in Budapest. Schneersohn and Harlap, for whom catastrophe implied redemption, identified the Land of Israel as their vessel of transition. Schneersohn centered the passage in the land because it alone was Torah's true environment. Harlap believed that the movement from the Messiah son of Joseph[28] to the Messiah son of David could take place only in the land, for it was the unique vessel for life in God's image. Upon the destruction of the *tumah* (polluted) universe and its history, the Land of Israel would stand forth as the receptacle for redemption's holiness. He wrote that the purpose of the great suffering was to purify and sanctify the people into the holy nation on holy ground.[29] Juxtaposing the *Olah* (burned) sacrifice of the Holocaust with the prospect of a new state, Katz averred that the blood of the catastrophe, sacrificed in atonement for the (unspecified) crimes of the generation, brought freedom and political-religious redemption in the form of a Jewish state for the Jewish people ("And the blood shall be forgiven them"; Deuteronomy 21:18). In New York, Elberg rejected any "nationalizing" of the Holocaust, any attempt to juxtapose the murder of six million with the establishment of the state, as if the Holocaust were required for redemption in state form. Finally, Breuer looked to a future in which history and metahistory would come together in the land. According to Breuer, the people of Israel, who belonged essentially to a sacred metahistorical realm beyond the ravages of history, entered exile in order to draw the nations of the world toward the sacred realm. But, unfortunately, in the course of this process many Jews abandoned their metahistorical grounding and assimilated, and they did so just as sovereignty and racism crested. After the Holocaust, it was left to the people of Israel to retrieve their metahistorical identity. Recapturing this transcendent identity was now possible only in the Land of Israel, the only place where history would be able to receive and maintain it—as well as extend it to the wider world.

The Path to Redemption

Concepts of the path from the disastrous present to the salvational future differed according to the respective thinkers' time-space position. When the experience of tragedy was direct and the catastrophe was simultaneously subjective and objective, the attempt to verbally express the path was abandoned. Hoping for redemption, Ehrenreich and Unsdorfer imposed a silence upon theological inquiry into the present and its passage into the future. For them, stillness mediated Israel's past metahistory with its future ontology. Silence became the "language" that touched the threshold of the redeemed universe. Ehrenreich and Unsdorfer rooted their silence in that of Abraham at the *Akedah* and Aaron upon the death of his sons Nadav and Avihu (Leviticus 10). Confronted by the theological impossibility of catastrophe, they positioned themselves in the tradition of Israel's holiest, silent personalities and awaited the Messiah.

In Palestine and America, some thinkers gained wisdom about the passage from the present into the messianic future from kabbalistic revelation (Ḥarlap), God's compassionate presence (Sarna), and God's entry into history in the action of a *tsadik* (holy, charismatic leader; Rokeaḥ). Ḥarlap spoke of the souls of Israel's dead entering the realm of holy light on high and joining the process of redemption from the onset (Messiah son of Joseph) to completion (Messiah son of David). Sarna and Schneersohn paid attention to those still alive. They focused on *teshuvah* above in the divine triad and below in the triad's display in history as it proceeded toward redemption. Others discerned paths to redemption through *Da'at Torah* (all-embracing rabbinical authority) and the Torah-permeated Land of Israel. *Mizraḥi* and *Agudat Yisrael* thinkers believed that the way to redemption would begin in history and end in ontological redemption, and they identified the Torah and the land as the vessels of passage.

The Holocaust ended, but redemption did not come. Those who dealt with the issue through the war and survived did not modify their positions, choosing (implicitly) to wait anew. But those who began to write after the war allowed the path to redemption to disappear from their work. Tsimerman described an ontological process of redemption up to the Holocaust, with the Holocaust enacting the *teshuvah* it required. When redemption did not take place, he offered no suggestion about whether its onset could still be detected—nor did he invoke silence. Elberg contended that the Holocaust shattered the entire world of God's creation. It would be impossible to discern a path to redemption before a second creation, when a Torah-centered history would take place. Before redemption could even be conceived and insight about its path could be discerned, there had to be a new world history.[30]

Concluding Note

Wartime religious thinkers positioned themselves within their intellectual tradition and then extrapolated the truths of that tradition to console and lead their followers. While their orientations were different (*Mizraḥi*, *Agudat Yisrael*, *Musar*, kabbalistic, hasidic), they shared a metahistorical framework in which God related to Israel providentially; His Torah revelation was real; and His presence in the catastrophe was certain. Israel could reverse the catastrophe through *teshuvah* and transform the disaster into a sanctification of God. When this happened, Amalek and his polluted history would be annulled. Israel, abandoned by history, would achieve redemption, one now centered in the Holy Land.

In this tragic era, religious thought entered the interstice between life and death. There, religious thinkers staked their lives on their reflections. They integrated faith and ideas with their suffering and dying. They shared their reflections with others, offering consolation amid the agony and inspiring the lives of survivors with meaning. Their writings were existentially true, because they blended life and religious thought. They also provided life to the history of the Jewish religious mind as it met the present, and they provided a potential source for religious thinkers to come.[31]

Notes

1. The religious thought included in the rabbinical responsa literature of the Holocaust is not covered here. For more on these sources, see Esther Farbstein, *"Halakhah,"* in Esther Farbstein, *Beseter Ra'am: Halakhah, Hagut Umanhigut Bimei Hashoah* (Jerusalem, 2002), pp. 133–276; and Hirsch Jacob Zimmels, *Echo of the Nazi Holocaust in Rabbinic Literature* (New York, 1977).

2. Leo Baeck was the notable exception. See Eliezer Schweid, "From *The Essence of Judaism* to *This People Israel*: Leo Baeck's Theological Confrontation with the Period of Nazism and the Holocaust," in Eliezer Schweid, *Wrestling until Day-Break* (Lanham, Md., 1994), pp. 3–84.

3. Emil Fackenheim, "The Commanding Voice of Auschwitz," in Emil Fackenheim, *God's Presence in History* (New York, 1970), pp. 70–71; Arthur A. Cohen, *Thinking the Tremendum: Some Theological Implications of the Death Camps* (New York, 1974), pp. 4–5.

4. On R. Talmud, see Gershon Greenberg, "The Theological Letters of Rabbi Talmud of Lublin, 1942," in *Ghettos 1939–1945: New Research and Perspectives on Definition, Daily Life, and Survival* (Washington, D.C., 2005), pp. 113–128. On Rappaport, see Aliza Levanon, *Derashot Harav Shabtai Hakohen Rapaport Mipintchov*, in Aliza Levanon, *Derashot Shel Rabbanim Shenidrashu Bitekufat Hashoah Be'artsot Hakivush Hanatsi Bein Hashanim 1939–1945* (M.A. thesis, Touro College, 1993), pp. 56–64; and Esther Farbstein, *"Derashot Harav Mipintchov,"* in Esther Farbstein, *Beseter Ra'am: Halakhah, Hagut Vemanhigut Bimei Hashoah* (2002), pp. 448–452. On Bloch, see Gershon Greenberg, "Holocaust and Musar for the Telsiai Yeshivah: Avraham Yitshak Bloch and Eliahu Meir Bloch," in *The Vanished World of Lithuanian Jews*, edited by Stefan Schreiner, Darius Staliunas, and Alvydas Nikzentaitis (New York, 2004), pp. 223–261. On Grodzensky, see Gershon Greenberg, "God and Man in Slobodka Musar Theology: Avraham Grodzensky and Yitshak Ayzik Sher," in *Central and East European Jewry at the Crossroads of Tradition and Modernity*, edited by Lara Lampertiene (Vilnius, 2006), pp. 232–265.

5. On Gersht, see Gershon Greenberg, "Yehudah Layb Gersht's Religious 'Ascent' through the Holocaust," *Holocaust and Genocide Studies* 13, no. 1 (Spring 1999): 62–89. On Kaplan see Ya'akov Kaplan, *Les Temps D'épreuves: Sermons et Allocutions* (Paris, 1952); and Aliza Levanon, *Derashot Harav Ya'akov Kaplan Mitsarfat*, in Aliza Levanon, *Derashot Shel Rabbanim*, pp. 65–80.

6. On Rosenheim, see Gershon Greenberg, "Sovereignty as Catastrophe: Jakob Rosenheim's Ḥurban Weltanschauung," *Holocaust and Genocide Studies* 8, no. 2 (Fall 1994): 202–224. On the rescue of Schneersohn, see Bryan Mark Rigg, *Rescued from the Reich: How One of Hitler's Soldiers Saved the Lubavitcher Rebbe* (New Haven, Conn., 2004).

7. On Botschko, see Eliahu Botschko, *Die Spuren des Messias* (Montreux, 1937); and *Jiskaur!... Seelenspiegel ... Pro Leysin ... Sefer Sikaron* (Montreux, 1943). See also André Neher, *"Kavim Lidemuto Shel Moreinu Harav Rav Yeraḥmiel Eliahu Botschko z'l,"* and Simḥah Elberg, *"Yeshivat Ets Ḥayim Bemontreux, Shvayts,"* both in *Mimontreux Lirushalayim: Mi "Ets Ḥayim,"* in *Leheikhal Eliahu*, edited by Ḥayim Y. Ḥamiel (Jerusalem, 1956–1957), pp. 27–37 and 71–74.

8. On Dessler, see Eliezer Schweid, *"Vayehi Aharei Hahurban: Hatsdakat Ha'elohim Betorat Hamusar Shel R. Eliahu Eliezer Dessler,"* in Eliezer Schweid, *Bein Hurban Lishua* (Tel Aviv, 1994), pp. 155–192; and Schweid, "An Ethical-Theological Response to the Holocaust as It Was Evolving: The Teachings of Rabbi Eliahu Eliezer Dessler," *Henoch* 17 (1995): 171–195.

9. On Shragai, see Gershon Greenberg, *"Historiah Ugeulah: Bituyim Limeshihiyut Yehudit Ortodoksit Betom Milhemet Ha'olam Hasheniah,"* in *Holocaust and Jewish Historical Consciousness*, edited by Dan Michman (Jerusalem, 2005), pp. 181–210.

10. On Bublick, see Gershon Greenberg, "Jerusalem, Vilna, Chicago: Gedaliah Bublick's Wartime Dilemma," in *America and Zion: Essays and Papers in Memory of Moshe Davis*, edited by Eli Lederhendler and Jonathan Sarna (Detroit, Mich., 2002), pp. 255–275; and "Wartime American Orthodoxy and the Holocaust: *Mizrahi* and *Agudat Yisrael* Religious Responses," *Mikhael* 4 (2000): 59–94.

11. Eliezer Schweid, *Bein Hurban Lishuah: Teguvot Shel Hagut Haredit Lashoah Bizemanah* (Tel Aviv, 1994). Schweid speaks of the difference thusly:

> When the German army conquered and subjugated Poland and Lithuania [Dessler] was already settled elsewhere. In dealing with a theological response to such an unprecedented catastrophe as the Holocaust, this separation makes a significant difference which must be fully appreciated. First, it may explain how it was possible for him to develop a philosophically grounded theodicy during those years of ultimate distress and trial. But the most profound implication of which one needs to be aware is the qualitative difference in the existential challenge. Clearly there must be an essential difference between a response from the core of the *Hurban* itself—such as that of Rabbi Kalonymous Kalman Shapira, author of *Esh Kodesh*, who preached in his Beit Midrash in conquered Warsaw during the dark years of 1940–1943 as he tried to buttress the faith of his tortured *hasidim* in God Almighty—and that of Rabbi Dessler who was then situated in Gateshead near Newcastle.

Schweid, "An Ethical-Theological Response to the Holocaust as It Was Evolving: The Teachings of Rabbi Eliahu Eliezer Dessler," *Henoch* 17 (1995): 174.

12. Nehemiah Polen, *Holy Fire: The Teachings of Rabbi Kalonymous Kalman Shapira, the Rebbe of the Warsaw Ghetto* (Northvale, N.J., 1994).

13. Esau, the brother of Jacob with whom the biblical patriarch continually contended, is the symbol of Israel's traditional enemy. In classical Jewish thought, it was the term applied to the Roman Empire and then later to the Christian states that dominated and persecuted Jews.

14. See Eliezer Schweid, *"Hahitgalut Hago'elet: Hatsdakat Elohim Bemishnato Hakabbalit Shel Harav Yehudah Ashlag,"* in Eliezer Schweid, *Bein Hurban Lishuah*, pp. 193–215.

15. See Gershon Greenberg, "Ha'gra's Apocalyptic Expectations and 1947 Religious Responses to the Holocaust: Harlap and Tsimerman," in *The Gaon of Vilnius and the Annals of Jewish Culture*, compiled by Izraelis Lempertas (Vilnius, 1998), pp. 231–246.

16. The *Zohar* is a famous book in the Jewish mystical tradition. It is credited to R. Simeon bar Yohai (second century CE) by its devotees. Its secrets, however, are believed to go back to the revelation at Sinai.

17. On Levin, see Gershon Greenberg, "Ontic Division and Religious Survival: Wartime Palestinian Orthodoxy and the Holocaust (*Hurban*)," *Modern Judaism* 14, no. 1 (1994): 21–61.

18. This refers to the destruction of the Temple in Jerusalem in 70 C.E. by the Romans and the beginning of the long and terrible exile of the Jewish people from the Land of Israel.

19. Yehezkel Sarna, *Liteshuva Velitekumah: Devarim Shene'emru Bakinus Lemesped Uteshuvah Shehitkayem Ba'ir Biyeshivat Hevron-Keneset Yisrael Beyom 8 Kislev 5705* (Jerusalem, 1944), p. 22.

20. Haman is the villain of the biblical Book of Esther. The victory over Haman is celebrated yearly in the Jewish festival of Purim.

21. Moses Mendelssohn (1729–1786) was the leader of the so-called *Haskalah*—Jewish Enlightenment—who sought to bring Judaism into contact with modern science and philosophy. Theodore Herzl (1860–1904) was the leader of the modern political Zionist movement who created the World Zionist Organization in the 1890s.

22. On Torah and catastrophe, see Benyamin Brown, *"Doktrinat Da'at Torah: Sheloshah Shelavim,"* in *Derekh Haruah: Sefer Likhvod Eliezer Schweid*, edited by Yehoyada Amir (Jerusalem, 2005), pp. 499–563.

23. On Henkin, see Gershon Greenberg, "Assimilation and *Hurban* according to Wartime American Orthodoxy: Habad Hasidism," in *Jewish Assimilation, Acculturation, and Accommodation*, edited by Menahem Mor (Lanham, Md., 1991), pp. 161–177.

24. On Nissenbaum and Friedman, see Gershon Greenberg, "The Amalek of the Holocaust," in *Nuremberg Revisited: Bioethical and Ethical Issues*, edited by Jacques Rozenberg (New York, 2003), pp. 120–148.

25. On Firer, see Gershon Greenberg, "Religious Survival among Orthodox Jewish Displaced Persons," in *Thinking in the Shadow of Hell*, edited by Jacques Doukhan (Berrien Springs, Mich., 2003), pp. 45–60; and Greenberg, "From *Hurban* to Redemption: Orthodox Jewish Thought in the Munich Area, 1945–1948," *Simon Wiesenthal Annual* 6 (1989): 81–112. On Amalek, see Gershon Greenberg, *Amalek Bitekufat Hashoah: Mahshevet Yehudit Ortodoksit*, in *Mehkerei Yerushalayim Bemahshevet Yisrael 19: Derekh Haruah: Sefer Likhvod Eliezer Schweid*, pp. 891–913.

26. The identification of the catastrophe with the *Olah* sacrifice may be traced to Shlomoh Faynzilber in Kedainiai, when the tragedy was beginning to break forth. Faynzilber, *Hitna'ari Me'afar: Kollel Ha'emunah Vehabitahon Bashem Vekos Tanhumin Leaheinu Hameduka'im Be'et Hazot* (Kedainiai, 1940). See Gershon Greenberg, "The Vilnius Torah Conference, 19–21 June 1939: Messianism at the Onset of Catastrophe," in *Jewish Intellectual Life in Pre-War Vilna*, edited by Lara Lampertiene (Vilnius, 2004), pp. 87–107.

27. Hayim Yisrael Tsimerman, *"Tamin Pa'alo": She'elot Uteshuvot Bidevar Hahashmadah Haiyumah Shel Shishah Milyon Hayehudim, Hashem Yinkom Damam* (Jerusalem, 1947), p. 25.

28. The idea of the Messiah son of Joseph is found in rabbinic tradition. It refers to the notion that at the beginning of the messianic era there would appear a messianic figure descended from the patriarch Joseph. He would be killed during the wars that are part of the struggle to bring on the final and complete redemption marked by the arrival of the Messiah son of David. For more on these doctrines, see Joseph Klausner, *Hara'ayon Hameshihi Beyisrael* (Jerusalem, 1927); and Joseph Heinemann, "The Messiah of Ephraim and the Premature Exodus of the Tribe of Ephraim," *Harvard Theological Review* 68 (1975): 1–16.

29. See Dov Schwartz, *"Erets Vesod: Harav Ya'akov Mosheh Harlap,"* in *Erets Hamamashut Vehadimyon: Ma'amadah Shel Erets Yisrael Behagut Hatsionut Hadatit* (Tel Aviv, 1997), pp. 82–100.

30. See further, Gershon Greenberg, "Between Holocaust and Redemption: Silence, Cognition and Eclipse," in *The Impact of the Holocaust on Jewish Theology*, edited by Steven T. Katz (New York, 2005), pp. 295–335; and Greenberg, *Historiah Ugeulah*.

31. On postwar Orthodox reflections, see Gershon Greenberg, "Ultra-Orthodox Reflections on the Holocaust: 1945 to the Present," in *Contemporary Responses to the Holocaust*, edited by Konrad Kwiet and Jürgen Matthäus (New York, 2004), pp. 82–121; and "Ultra-Orthodox Jewish Thought about the Holocaust since World War II: The Radicalized Aspect," in Katz, *The Impact of the Holocaust on Jewish Theology*, pp. 132–160.

Within the Catastrophe

Elḥanan Wasserman

Elḥanan Wasserman (1875–1941), regarded in Lithuanian yeshivah circles as the successor to his teacher the Ḥofets Ḥayim (Yisrael Meir Cohen of Radin, 1838–1933), headed the Baranowicz (Poland) yeshiva. He first responded to signs of catastrophe (which included anti-*Sheḥitah* [kosher ritual slaughter] legislation) during the years 1931–1936. He maintained then that the simultaneous oppression of Torah (meaning both Scripture and the rabbinic tradition) from within by Jews themselves and from without by the persecutors implied the onset of the Messiah. The suffering could be relieved by *Da'at Torah*. However, should suffering increase to the point of Israel's becoming a persecuted victim (Ecclesiastes 3:15), God would come to the rescue. During his 1937–1938 travels to America to raise funds for his yeshiva, Wasserman composed the *Ma'amar Ikvetah Dimeshiḥah* (*Tractate: The Onset of the Messiah*)—with editorial input from his son Elazar Simḥah Wasserman. Now he expressed little hope that Jews could or would relieve the suffering through *Da'at Torah* (all embracing rabbinic authority). He rather resigned himself to the view espoused by the Vilna Gaon (1720–1797) that when the Messiah arrived, Israel would have proven itself unworthy in terms of *teshuvah* and Torah observance. Having failed to blend the restoration of Torah below with the higher process of redemption and its revelation, Wasserman reasoned, Israel would purify itself through suffering. At the extreme end, however, at the very entrance to redemption, a rapport between Israel and Torah would emerge from the realms above and below.

By the spring of 1939, Wasserman was back in Europe. He attended the June 1939 Torah conference in Vilnius, traveled to Telsiai during the months following, and by November of that year moved the Baranowitch yeshiva to Vilnius. In July 1941, he was in Kaunas (Kovno), where he was taken from the home of the *Musar* movement leader Avraham Grodzensky and killed at the Ninth Fort nearby—although Eliahu Botschko believed that he might still have been alive in 1943–1944.

SELECTIONS

In the selections below from the *Tractate: The Onset of the Messiah* (New York, 1938), translated from the Yiddish by Gershon Greenberg, Wasserman described the deterioration of Israel's religion in terms of the decline of scholarship and assimilation to foreign culture. God, Wasserman averred, responded to the decline by thwarting assimilation and punishing the people to change their minds. The punishment included massive wandering and poverty, global animosity, and intellectual and emotional turmoil. All of this belonged to the onset of the Messiah—which explained the unprecedented speed of historical events and the fact that there was no place to which Jews could escape.

In Wasserman's "The Afflictions Will Establish You (*Hayesurin matsivin etkhem*)," *Yidisher Lebn* 7, no. 261 (21 June 1940): 2, and "Torah Advice for All Times (*Torah*

Etsot far ale Tsaytn)," *Yidisher Lebn* 7, no. 262 (28 June 1940): 2, the last pieces he published before he was killed, he wrote that the sufferings were those which preceded the coming of the Messiah. In order to be rescued from them and emerge whole, the Jew had to remain firm. That meant engaging in Torah and deeds of loving kindness. In themselves, the sufferings were God's instrument to punish the Jews. The sufferings of those who trusted in God would be eased by His loving kindness. Wasserman was certain that the sufferings were related to redemption. God embraced those who suffered, and since the current sufferings were the worst of the exile, God's embrace would be that of redemption.

TRACTATE: THE ONSET OF THE MESSIAH

Deeds of the Fathers

...4. What is the correct meaning of the word "Torah"? Torah means teaching. Every word of the Torah contains instruction. Otherwise it would not be contained in the Torah. The question is, which teachings are contained in the Torah's stories of the past and their details? We have been given a key for this: "The deeds of the ancestors are a sign for their descendants" [see B. T. *Sotah* 34ª]. The whole of Jewish history, from the beginning until the end of days, is wrapped in these stories. The situation of Israel among the nations is alluded to in the Torah portions of *Vayishlah* [Genesis], which discuss Jacob and Esau. The first chapter of *Vayishlah* is the "portion of exile" [Nahmanides *ad* Genesis 32:4]. That passage indicates what the behavior of Jews should be while in exile amidst the descendants of Esau.

The Gaon of Vilna writes [in his *Even Shelemah*] that the second chapter of *Vayishlah* is the chapter of the "footsteps of the Messiah." When Jacob returned from his exile, it says: "And he put the handmaids and their children foremost" [Genesis 33:2]. The Gaon says: This shows that in the [era of the] "footsteps of the Messiah" the "mixed multitude" will lead the Jews. Maimonides writes in his *Letter* [*to Yemen*]: A promise exists, that: "And may also believe thee forever" [Exodus 19:9], meaning that Jews will always be believers in the Torah. However, we see that there are unbelievers among us. It is known that "Their ancestors did not stand at Mount Sinai" [B. T. *Nedarim* 20ª], that they are descendants of the "mixed multitude" and not of the seed of

Israel. When we see that unbelievers are now our leaders, it confirms the words of the Gaon that they are of the "mixed multitude." "And Leah and her children after" [Genesis 33:2]. This shows that the majority of ordinary Jews [the pious ones] will be under the "mixed multitude"; that is, the "mixed multitude" will rule over them. We see this now in the red land [i.e., Soviet Russia] and another place [Germany?] where the "mixed multitude" are in power and oppress pious Jews. "And Rachel and Joseph hindermost" [Genesis 33:2]. These are the Torah scholars, the lowest of all. Everywhere there still remains a remnant of Torah scholars, one sees how they are demeaned and debased.

5. It is written further: "And there wrestled a man with him" [Genesis 32:25]. Jacob is the pillar of Torah. The "man" is Samael (satan). This means that in the [era of the] "footsteps of the Messiah" impurity will wage war against the study of Torah (ignorance is alive and well). "And the hollow of Jacob's thigh was wrenched" [Genesis 32:26]. Jacob's thigh alludes to the small children, the young schoolchildren, who were the foundation of the existence of the nation for thousands of years. They will be fractured during the [era of] "footsteps of the Messiah" by all kinds of agents, both internal and external. This has taken place throughout the Jewish diaspora. The great majority of Jewish children are being raised as complete gentiles.

6. A second meaning of "Jacob's thigh" is: Support of the Torah. This is the strengthening of Torah, the support of those who study Torah, and making provisions for studying Torah in

peace. This is something that existed among Jews since they became a nation (the tribes of Yissakhar and Zevulun). It becomes fractured during [the era] of "footsteps of the Messiah." One sees this everywhere now, even in those lands where at present Jews are still able to give money. They give for everything, but leave only pennies for Torah. In the best case they are indifferent to Torah. This is quite natural, because the new generation is completely estranged from the Torah and does not understand at all why Torah is needed. The result is disrespect for the [religious] schoolchildren and disrespect for the strengthening of Torah, and one leads to the other. How does Heaven respond to this? For the sin of disrespect for Torah, with sword and destruction. As it is written, "And I will bring a sword upon you, that shall execute the vengeance of the covenant" [Leviticus 26:25]. The covenant is the Torah, as it is written, "If My covenant be not with day and night, if I have not appointed the ordinances of heaven and earth" [Jeremiah 33:25], therefore, annulling Torah will be punished with sword and plunder, for it states, "I will bring a sword of vengeance over you, the vengeance for My covenant." Covenant means the Torah. As it says, "Were it not for My covenant, I would not have made day and night, or established heaven and earth in nature" [*Mishnah Shabbat, Perek 2, Bameh madlikin*]. In one city—Vienna—Jews have been robbed of almost forty million dollars. "Woe to those people who have contempt for the Torah" [*Mishnah Avot 6:2*].

"We Will Be as the Nations"

7. Ezekiel prophesies that in the [era of] "footsteps of the Messiah" a solution will be proposed among Jews: "We will be as the nations" [Ezekiel 20:32]. The actualization of the prophecy began with the Berlin Enlightenment (*Haskalah*), almost 150 years ago. Its proponents masked what they were doing with the words, "Be a Jew in your home and a person in public." The fruits of this approach quickly ripened. Their children apostasized. Their slogan amounted to an undermining of the foundations of the Torah. The Torah had warned that Jews should be separated from the nations in their whole lifestyle. "And

have set you apart from other peoples, that ye should be Mine" [Leviticus 20:26; see Maimonides, *Mishneh Torah, Hilkhot Avodah Zarah*, ch. 11]. The *Maskilim* came and said exactly the opposite: "Be only like the nations." God said about this: "In that ye say: We will be as the nations . . . shall not be at all." "Surely with a mighty hand, and with an outstretched arm and with fury poured out" [Ezekiel 20:32–33]. It will begin with "a mighty hand." If that does not help, the "outstretched arm" will come. If this also does not help, then there will be a "fury poured out." We cannot know in which of the three processes we now are. The near future will show us. In any event, it is clear that the prophecy of "shall not be at all" will be realized. The nations are driving us away from them in a murderous way. It is said, that it is difficult to be a Jew. A wonder has occurred in recent times. It is increasingly difficult to become a gentile. The gentiles are driving us back.

It is said in the name of the *Gaon* [dean of scholars Yosef Dov Ber Soloveichik], the author of *Beit Halevi*, of blessed memory: It is written, "He who separates between light and darkness and between Israel and the gentiles" [*Havdalah* service at end of sabbath]. There is a specific distance between light and darkness [twilight]. One cannot change the distance, lengthen or shorten it. It is the same between Israel and the gentiles. There is a specific distance as to how far they should be one from the other. If the Jews approach too closely, the gentiles push them back. From this one can understand why the more the Jews have approached the gentiles, the more severely the Jews have been repelled. We see this now in the lands where Jews have completely assimilated, how horribly the gentiles push back. It was also this way in Egypt when the servitude became difficult. The Jews began to emulate the Egyptians, thinking that through this their situation would become easier. What did God do? "He turned their heart to hate His people" [Psalms 105:25]. The more they wanted to assimilate with the Egyptians, the greater the animosity of the gentiles toward them. When the Jews realized their mistake, the redemption came. The same will be with us. "If you are separated from the nations, you are Mine. If not, you are with Nebuchadnezzar and his friends" [Rashi *ad* Leviticus 20:26].

The Shepherds

8. In Ezekiel [ch. 34] there is a clear picture of the generation of the "footsteps of the Messiah" and its shepherds. The generation is divided into five classes [regarding spirituality]: (1) weak ones, (2) sick ones, (3) ones with broken limbs, (4) those led astray, (5) lost ones. This is all in relation to Judaism. The last three categories refer to various sorts of heretics—those who separate themselves from the community of Israel by not yielding to the discipline of one or more commandments of the Torah. The Gaon of Vilna says [in *Sefer Mishlei ad* Proverbs 33:2]: A heretic with regard to one commandment is one who lacks a limb in his soul [he is crippled]. There are two sorts of heretics to all of Torah: The denier is the same as an apostate, but the denier is still together with Jews. These are the ones led astray. A second kind is one who has mixed with gentiles. These are the lost ones. Nobody knows any more that they are from the seed of Israel. The shepherds who make a living from the sheep—"Ye did eat the fat, and ye clothed you with the wool" [Ezekiel 34:3]—are supposed to watch over the sheep, but they do not. Instead of feeding the sheep they feed themselves. The sheep go astray over all the hills and hillocks to be eaten by all kinds of animals. Nobody is concerned about them. "And there was none that did search or seek" [Ezekiel 34:6]. Therefore God says, I will remove the shepherds and I will become the shepherd of my sheep. What will I do? (1) "I will seek that which was lost"; (2) "And will bring back that which was driven away"; (3) "And I will bind up that which was broken" [Ezekiel 34:16]. Here we have to notice the ordering of the three events. The very first: "I will seek that which was lost." Those whose grandfathers and grandmothers converted 120–130 years ago will be sought out. It will be discovered that they are not Aryans. They will be beaten over the head: Know that you are Jews and that is what you must remain. In a country where there are thousands of gentiles for every Jew, the lost Jews will be sought and found. At the moment we are at that point. The process is not at an end. It is still going on and spreading quickly from one land to other lands. When this will end, all the lost ones will be found. Then the second events will come: "And will bring back that which was driven away." The formerly lost ones will also be incorporated into those gone astray. Then the third: "And I will bind up that which was broken," etc.

. . . 9. There is more to note concerning the expression in the prophecy "My sheep wandered" [Ezekiel 34:6]. This prophecy indicates that those of the generation in general—excluding the shepherds—are thought of in heaven as unintentional sinners. For whenever the people sinned unintentionally, it turns out that it would not have been difficult to bring the Jews back to the Torah had the shepherds not acted as a steel wall between Israel and their Heavenly Father. The teachers, the leaders, the writers, the party leaders, let no ray of light from the Torah penetrate among Jews. They have *their* Torah, *their* Torah sages, *their* leaders of the generation. They darken Jewish minds and hearts with a new Torah and new commandments. It is noteworthy that on the rare occasion when Jews do have the opportunity to hear true Torah thoughts, they swallow them like people parched with thirst. However, the shepherds give them stones instead of diamonds. Instead of Torah thoughts, the readers and listeners are given heretical thoughts. In the most fashionable circles one reads and hears jokes and idle gossip mixed with profanity. These are the shepherds that the prophet prophesied about for our times.

10. The prophecy mentions a category of sheep, "The fat and the strong" [Ezekiel 34:16]. Such are many of our modern wealthy people. They meet to give money to all those things to which we should not donate. Where they should give, where the Torah tells us to give, they are nowhere to be found. They are surrounded by guards who do not let them be approached. The prophecy describes: What remains of your food you trample with your feet and then the weak and poor receive it [see Ezekiel 34:19]. When one looks at the relationship of our modern wealthy people to Torah scholars, who are the weakest of the weak and the most forlorn of the forlorn, one can understand how clear a picture the prophecy provides. What will become of the wealthy people? The same as what will become of the shepherds. The prophecy, "And I will leave in the midst of thee an afflicted and poor people" [Zephaniah 3:12] will be fulfilled.

11. In recent times we can observe: Wherever one comes to be among Jews, one finds that they have come or flocked together from the most diverse areas. In the past it was not like this. Each area had its own Jews. It did not happen that a city had a large number of Jews from distant areas. What is different? Concerning this, there was a different prophecy for our times: "And I will sift the House of Israel among all the nations, like as corn is sifted in a sieve" [Amos 9:9]. Jews will be scattered like wheat kernels which are sifted. The Hofets Hayim, of blessed memory, used to say: Inside the sieve one kernel falls closer and one further, but none remains in its original place. So it will be with Jews in the "footsteps of the Messiah." He reported in the name of Rabad (R. Abraham ben David) [of Posquieres c. 1125–1198, *ad Mishnah Eduyot* 8:7] that before the Messiah comes, Jewish families will be separated. The parents will be in one land and each of the children in another land, and they will not be able to come together until Elijah will come "And He shall turn the heart of the fathers to the children, and the heart of the children to their fathers" [Malachi 3:24].

12. Another noteworthy phenomenon: The whole world today is in an agitated state. We find ourselves as in a forest among agitated wild animals. One nation against the other, and in the same country one ethnic group against another, and in the same group one party against the others, etc., a development which is unprecedented on such a worldwide scale. This was foretold concerning the [era of] "footsteps of the Messiah" in the prophecy, "For I set all men every one against his neighbor" [Zechariah 8:10].

13. "In the generation that the son of David will come, the face of the generation is like the face of the dog" [*Mishnah Sota* 9:15, and B. T. *Sanhedrin* 97a]. The habit of a dog is to run in front of its master. It looks like the dog is going where it wants and that the owner looks where the dog is going and follows along. But we know that the opposite is the case. The owner goes where he needs to go and the dog runs ahead to where the owner wants to go. If the owner turns around, the dog also turns and runs before him. When Jews conduct themselves according to the Torah, the face of the generation [i.e., the Torah scholars] is the guide. The face of the generation considers where we need to go and the genera-

tion follows it. In the [era of] "footsteps of the Messiah" the authority of Torah will be broken. The generation will go according to what it understands by itself. The face of the generation will watch where the generation wants to go and will run ahead of it like a dog (in the name of the sage Rabbi Yisrael Salanter, of blessed memory). We see now how rabbis run with the "street" to show their "democracy"; and they run downhill, down to the abyss.

The Hofets Hayim of blessed memory used to give a second meaning to "the face of the dog" (in the name of the sage Rabbi Yitshak ben Hayim Volozhiner, author of *Nefesh Hahayim*, of blessed memory). The nature of a dog is that if one throws a stone at it, the dog runs to bite the stone. When a Haman arises against Jews, we need to know that it is only a stick with which Jews are being punished from Heaven. "O Asshur, the rod of Mine anger" [Isaiah 10:5]. There is no sense in waging war with the stick, since there is no shortage of sticks in Heaven. There are "many messengers to the one God" [*Midrash Bamidbar Rabbah, Parashah* 18, *Siman* 18]. We need rather to employ measures so that Heaven will not cast the stick. However, in the [era of] "footsteps of the Messiah" there will be no knowledge. We will run like the dog to bite the stick. We see this now, when our modern [Jewish] leaders have declared war on the mightiest nations in the world. What is our strength and what is our power? We take shots with articles in Jewish newspapers? With what result? It only incites the snakes further against the Jews. The leaders only see the stick. They do not want to know who is hitting with the stick. "Yet the people turneth not unto Him that smiteth them" [Isaiah 9:12].

14. "In the [era of] footsteps of the Messiah, arrogance will increase (*yisge*)" [*Mishnah Sota* 9:15]. Another meaning of *yisge* is greatness (*gedulah*). To be one of the leaders of the generation in earlier times demanded learning, piety, and wisdom. In the [era of] "footsteps of the Messiah" a "leader" will be one who possesses arrogance. The more arrogant he is, the greater the leader he is. We see it now among the political leaders whose only qualification for leadership is arrogance.

15. "And there is no rebuke" [B. T. *Sanhedrin* 97a]. There were always "preachers of rebuke"

among Jews who used to travel from city to city, preaching rebuke. In addition, there was one in every city who used to rebuke the local rabbi. A hundred years ago [the preacher] the Dubno Magid [Ya'akov Kranz] was famous. The Gaon of Vilna would send for him so that he would speak words of rebuke to him—the Gaon of Vilna. More recently, there was the Magid [preacher] of Kelme [Mosheh Yitshak Darshan]. With his fiery sermons he turned many people to repentance. We see in the *Responsa* of the medieval authorities (e.g., the Rashba, and the Rivash) that every city had "sin clarifiers" whose task it was to rebuke sinners. Now we no longer have any preachers of rebuke. There are more than enough speakers, but they do not speak words of rebuke. They do not cite any words of Torah.

Who are these speakers? Hired party agitators with the job of putting the audience to sleep with sweet dreams about the "redemption" that their party will bring for Jews—the nationalists—or for the whole world—the internationalists. Even though everyone sees that the dreams will melt away. All the idols that people had hoped for are being unmercifully broken and smashed. However, the false prophets are not being silenced. When the biblical spies uttered lies they threw in a bit of truth, because something that is completely false is not fulfilled [Rashi *ad* Numbers 13:27]. However, the current liars are not concerned about their lies being fulfilled. If one lie is invalidated they already have thirty other lies ready under different names.

Ordinary people who are estranged from the Torah are unable to differentiate between indigo and blue (*tekhelet*). [As they say] "Falsehood has no legs," it cannot walk by itself, cannot stand, and someone has to carry it. What carries the current prophets of falsehood? The [act of] forgetting of the Torah, the ignorance. The Hofets Hayim used to say: "The Torah enlightens the eyes; it gives a brightness to the eyes. But without the Torah one has a cataract." [As is said], "They see and don't know what they are seeing." There is darkness and when it is dark all kinds of animals creep out. "Wherein all the beasts of the forest do creep forth" [Psalms 104:20]. "If there is no knowledge, from where will differentiation come?" [J. T. *Berakhot* 5:2]. "'For she hath cast down many wounded; Yea a mighty host are all her slain'

[Proverbs 7:26]. This refers to a disciple who has attained the qualifications to decide questions of law and does not decide them" [B. T. *Sotah* 22ª]. This applies to individual questions about kosher and unkosher, [so how much more so] to questions that affect the whole nation of Israel! Who are our guides today with regard to these questions? Empty and reckless people who do not possess the slightest knowledge of Torah, worthless people who are ready to sell all of Judaism for a mess of pottage. They set the tone for the leaders of the generation. The prophecy, "And babes shall rule over them" [Isaiah 3:4] is being fulfilled.

16. [In the generation in which the son of David will come,] there will be prosecutions against the scholars [B. T. *Ketubot* 112ᵇ]. The ancient heretics said: "What do we have from the Torah scholars? When they study it is good for them" [B. T. *Sanhedrin* 99ᵇ]. The ancient heretics [at least] understood that it is good for one who studies Torah. The current heretics speak differently. [According to them,] the Torah scholars make themselves and the world unhappy. Another interpretation is that the rebuke [of the heretics] has been internalized among the scholars themselves: They rebuke one another.

17. "All the sinners of My people shall die by the sword" [Amos 9:10]. The Hofets Hayim said in the name of the *Zohar* that the decree of the sword has been transformed into poverty. Before the redemption, Jews will become poor. "And the afflicted [or poor] people Thou dost save" [2 Samuel 22:28]. The Hofets Hayim used to say: "Those who still have money should not think that the money will remain with them. What Jews have will be taken away from them. If they would have the sense to understand this, they would know what to accomplish with the money while they had it." It is more than twenty years since the Hofets Hayim said this. Since then, his words have been fulfilled for the majority of Jews. This was prophesied in the Talmud: "The Son of David will not come until a coin will not be found in the purse" [B. T. *Sanhedrin* 97ª].

18. The Hofets Hayim said another thing. Soon, changes will occur in a short time that used to take hundreds of years. We see the wheel of time turning with extraordinary speed. "What has God done to us?" Why is it different now

than before? The Ḥofets Ḥayim said: Accounts have accumulated in Heaven since the creation of the world until now. All of these accounts must be straightened out before the Messiah comes. After that, the evil inclination will become nullified. The result will be that the entire worldly business consisting of a battle of the inclinations will close down. Each soul must pay what it still owes Heaven. Since the time before the Messiah is short, this must occur quickly. [In the period] since the Ḥofets Ḥayim, of blessed memory, said this—twenty years ago—until today, the rush of time has increased. Today, things happen literally overnight which in the past used to take whole generations. One sees that time flies as if someone is chasing it: "Run faster." Every thinking person can understand from this that we are living in an extraordinary time. It will bring tremendous changes in the situation of the whole world. According to the reckoning, we will not have to wait long. With every day the tremendous rush of time accelerates. The time of many centuries runs its course within a single year.

19. "And thou shalt teach them diligently unto thy children" [Deuteronomy 6:7]. Teaching children Torah has constituted the foundation upon which Judaism has been maintained in the course of thousands of years. The ideal for Jewish parents was for their children to be great in Torah and piety. What about earning a living? They knew: "One who has life will have sustenance" [see B. T. *Ta'anit* 8^b]; the one who lives well will be given life. In recent generations, having lost their faith, people have also lost their trust in God. Parents must provide for their child's material needs. How do they provide for them? They have the child study [secular subjects]. So the child will be provided for, for all of life. This would [allegedly] be a salvation for the whole nation of Israel as well. If we have a lot of educated people, we will be respected. Recent times show how much we have provided for the individual and for the whole nation of Israel when it comes to our chasing after [secular] studies. This is providing materially. But how have children been provided for spiritually? We have raised complete gentiles, nationalists and internationalists. What measures are taken by Heaven against this spiritual plague? "And thy backslidings shall reprove you" [Jeremiah 2:19].

Students and intellectuals are the primary oppressors of Jews in most countries today. Jewish students are being driven by their "friends" with iron sticks. Instead of sacrificing themselves for the study of Torah as Jews used to do, today Jews sacrifice themselves for the honor of sitting on the same bench with wild scoundrels.

20. "Rejoice not, O Israel, unto exultation, like the peoples" [Hosea 9:1]. Jews should not look for the same amusements as the nations of the world. The gentiles have idle time. When a gentile finishes his work he has nothing to do. So he must find various games and amusements to spend the time. A Jew does not have any idle time. When he finishes work, he has another obligation: the study of Torah. If he is not able to study alone he should find a teacher to study with him. In the time which remains he should be engaged in fulfilling commandments and good deeds, engage in charitable acts according to his ability. The Torah demands this type of lifestyle from Jews: "You shall be holy" [Leviticus 19:2]. Jews should be holy, the Jewish home should be holy, and every Jewish heart should be holy. [God said,] "You should be separated from the gentiles in everything, then you will be Mine." "And have set you apart from the peoples, that ye should be Mine" [Leviticus 20:26]. "If you are separated from the nations then you are Mine." In recent times, as people stopped studying Torah, they were left with idle time. What do they do? Jews fill up all the places of amusement and theaters. They return home from these places infused with impurity. As a result, Jewish homes become impure. How does Heaven respond to this? Jews are now being chased from the amusement places like one chases away lepers. "Jews out!" "This is not your place!" And this is the truth. The place for Jews is the study house, studying or reciting psalms. This is what we have been warned: "If you are separated from the nations, you are Mine. If not, you are with Nebuchadnezzar and his friends" [Rashi *ad* Leviticus 20:26].

21. There are two primary false gods whom Jews serve and to whom they offer sacrifices: socialism and nationalism. The "torah" of modern nationalism consists of [the] words: "We will be as the nations" [Ezekiel 20:32]. To be a Jew, it is enough to be nationally [Zionist] minded. One

needs no more. Just pay a *shekel* [as dues] and sing [the national anthem] *Hatikvah*. This absolves one from all the commandments of the Torah. It is quite clear that such a system, according to the Torah, is idolatry. The hearts and minds of the whole of Jewish youth are darkened by these two false religions. Each false religion has an entire headquarters of false prophets in the form of writers and speakers who are committed to their work. A miracle has occurred: In Heaven these two false religions have been combined into one. A terrible stick of wrath to punish Jews murderously in all corners of the land, national-socialism, has been created from the mix. The same impurities that we worshipped are now punishing us. "And thy backslidings shall reprove you" [Jeremiah 2:19].

22. The prophets prophesied that there will be a time of troubles for [the people of] Israel, such as they never had since becoming a nation. The Gaon of Vilna writes [in *Even Shelemah*]: In the passages of Scripture, the travails of the entire exile are similar to the pregnancy of a woman. The birth pangs of the Messiah (*ḥevlei mashiaḥ*); [see B. T. *Sanhedrin* 97–98 and Rashi *ad* Isaiah 26:17] are like the throes of birth. Just as the anguish of pregnancy cannot be compared to the anguish of giving birth, so too, the troubles of exile cannot be compared to the troubles of the birth pangs of the Messiah. There is a specific order as to how the troubles of exile are to [unfold]. The order was established in the "chapter of the exile" [the beginning of *Parashat Vayishlaḥ*]. It is written there: "The camp which is left shall escape" [Genesis 32:9]. When Jews were being persecuted in one country there was always a second place to which to escape. During the Spanish expulsion, Turkey and Poland were open to Jews and later Holland. During the birth pangs of the Messiah, it will not be this way. Jews will be persecuted and they will have nowhere to escape. They will be pursued everywhere and admitted nowhere.

23. "Every drove by itself" [Genesis 32:17]. In the travails of exile there is an interval between one evil decree and the next one. In the [era of] "footsteps of the Messiah" the travails "flow like a river" [see Isaiah 59:19]; they will be uninterrupted. Aside from this, every day will be worse—"In the morning thou shalt say, Would it were even!" [Deuteronomy 28:67]—i.e., the

evening before [Rashi *ad* Deuteronomy 28:67]. An even greater difference between previous times and today is that in previous generations Jews were not forlorn. They knew that they had a Father in Heaven, a guardian of Israel who told them: "And yet for all that, when they are in the land of their enemies, I will not reject them, neither will I abhor them" [Leviticus 26:44]. They knew that they suffered because of their allegiance to God and that they were preparing themselves for an eternal life in a place where no ordinary creature could stand [see "No creature can attain to the place in heaven assigned to the martyrs of the Roman government"; B. T. *Baba Batra* 10[b]]. This made it easier for them to suffer the persecutions. However now, because the Torah has been forgotten, faith is disappearing from among a large number of Jews. As a result, they are the most forlorn people in the world. They do not know why they suffer and they have no one to ask for help. They are terribly disappointed and confused. They see no way out other than suicide.

"The Afflictions Will Establish You" [Rashi *ad* Deuteronomy 29:12]

We offer a statement in the name of the sanctified author of the text *Ḥofets Ḥayim*, may his memory be blessed. The passage states, "Many are the sorrows of the wicked. But he that trusteth in the Lord, mercy compasseth him about" [Psalms 32:10]. The author of the text *Ḥofets Ḥayim* commented that when a person is given medicine for a stomach sickness, although it is sour and bitter to swallow, it provides a cure. But science came up with a capsule to be swallowed, curing the illness without the sour and bitter taste. So it is with the suffering for the evil one. The pains inflicted upon the sinner provide a cure, although it is bitter. The person with trust in God receives a cure enclosed in a capsule of loving kindness. The person swallows the capsule, surrounded by loving kindness. The person's trust in God diminishes the bitterness.

Rashi wrote about "Ye are standing this day all of you" [Deuteronomy 29:10], that the sufferings make you firm and maintain you. The sufferings set you on your feet and maintain your existence. His interpretation follows his comment on "None hath beheld iniquity in Jacob" [Numbers 23:21]. Rashi writes that the passage "The Holy One Blessed be He does not look for deceits by Israel" means that He does not see the Jewish perversities. What does this mean? Our sanctified sages say, "All who say that the Holy One Blessed be He is indulgent is renunciated from the world" [B. T. *Baba Kamma* 60ᵃ]. That is: Anyone who thinks that God forgives gratuitously will not be forgiven for anything. Both are true: The Holy One Blessed be He does not look for deceits by Israel. But there is a machinery in place, whereby [as is said] "Anyone who trespasses once, acquires one prosecutor." The prosecutor is not silent. He relates everything, pointing to particulars. The prosecutor rejects the plea of the trespasser. Nothing deters the accuser, because "The king by justice establisheth the land" [Proverbs 29:4]. The king of the world maintains the world with justice.

In the kingdom on earth, when an informer, a complainant, points to the one accused and judged as having done something, and there is evidence, clear, black-and-white proof, the judge will follow the law even if the judge is a friend of the accused. The same applies to the kingdom of heaven. When a prosecutor takes a firm position against the congregation of Israel, God forbid, and shows what should happen to Israel according to the laws of heaven, Israel may not tell the Holy One Blessed be He what to do. In one respect, one must not listen passively to the accuser; in another there is the promise: "For I the Lord change not. For ye, O sons of Jacob, are not consumed" [Malachi 3:6]. I, says the Holy One Blessed be He, have not changed My word and you, children of Israel, will not be doomed. What does the Holy One Blessed be He, do? A Haman is set up in some country to persecute the Jews with the most terrible venom. The Jews are persecuted, and this is their rescue. For among the attributes of the Holy One Blessed be He is, "And God seeketh that which is pursued" [Ecclesiastes 3:15]—even when an evil person is being persecuted by the pious. The Holy One Blessed be He becomes involved with the persecuted person even if the person is evil and the persecutor is pious. The Holy One Blessed be He stands on the side of the persecuted. In this way,

the Holy One Blessed be He has a proper answer for the accuser: I must, so to speak, embrace the persecuted one. The result is that the harsher the persecution of the Jew, the greater the ground for the rescue. As the persecution of the Jew now is at a terrible level, unprecedented, the Holy One Blessed be He must embrace the persecuted— which we are. It states: "Shall I bring to the birth, and not cause to bring forth?" [Isaiah 66:9]. That is, at the time the Jews will be in the greatest crisis of exile, the birth will come. Clearly, we are currently in crisis. It is to be understood from this that the birth [of redemption] is near.

Torah Advice for All Times

What should a person do during a difficult period? Is there any advice at all for the difficult day? There certainly is. It is the advice of Torah for all times: "Rabbi [Eliezer's] students asked him: What should a person do to be rescued from the pangs of the Messiah? He said to them: Become engaged in Torah and deeds of loving kindness" [B. T. *Sanhedrin* 98ᵇ]. Torah, together with loving kindness, could be helpful even with the pangs of the Messiah. The Ḥofets Ḥayim, may his memory be blessed, said that "Become engaged" meant to conduct oneself as one does in business. In business, a person acts with his whole heart and all his energy, and so one should act in terms of Torah and loving kindness when there are pangs of the Messiah. This would help the person.

In exile, Jews were like the single sheep among seventy wolves. The best thing the sheep could do was to act in such a way that the wolf would not even notice it. The healthiest situation for the Jews is one in which the nations are so involved with other interests that they do not even think about the Jews. It was the most dangerous for Jews when the nations talked routinely and without respite about the Jews.

The angels asked: "What shall we do for our sister, in the day when she shall be spoken for?" [Song of Songs 8:8]. That is: What should be done for our sister the Jewish nation, in the day when nations speak about her? An answer came from the mouth of [God's] power (*gevurah*); [see 1 Chronicles 29:11]: "If she be a wall, we will build upon her a turret of silver" [Song of Songs

8:9]. That is, if Jews remained as firm as a wall in their faith, not bowing to any wind in the world, then "we will build upon her a turret of silver." [As is said] "This silver goes into the fire and comes out whole. But Israel enters into the kingdoms and comes out whole." Silver emerges whole, even from fire. The same with Jews. Israel will emerge whole from all the sufferings under different regimes. Israel will be in the fire and come out whole: "The bush burned with fire, but the bush was not consumed" [Exodus 3:2]. But "If [Israel] is a door"—a door which turns on its hinge—"we will enclose [Israel] with boards of cedar" [Song of Songs 8:9] (which is liable to decay). If [the people of Israel] want to be like a door, letting themselves turn in all directions, i.e., letting themselves be influenced by every ephemeral movement of the mind which blows for a moment in the world, then "we will enclose her with boards of cedar," which spoils when left in dampness. This advises us how to act in the most difficult time, and this advice is permanent: We should be firm in our faith, like a wall, and not bow to the world. How is this possible? The answer is: "I am a wall; this is Torah" [B. T. Pesaḥim 87ᵃ]. Torah, and Torah alone, can discipline us and make us like steel.

Thousands of years of Jewish history demonstrates that with Torah's power, Jews have remained intact, through fire and water: "When thou passest through the waters, I will be with thee. . . . When thou walkest through the fire, thou shalt not be burned. Neither shall the flame kindle upon thee" [Isaiah 43:2]. In different words, this is also found in "Tell me, O thou whom my soul loveth, where thou feedest, where thou makest thy flock to rest at noon" [Song of Songs 1:7]. Noon, midday, is the most difficult time for shepherds; it is very hot. Israel asked its shepherd, the blessed God: How will You graze Your sheep when the most difficult time, that of exile, comes? When the sheep will wander and not know the way? The answer is: "If thou know not, O thou fairest among women, go thy way forth by the footsteps of the flock" [Song of Songs 1:8]. When you see different ways before you and you do not know which way to go, you have a clear sign from [God]: Go behind the sheep. Look at the footsteps of your parents, and follow them. You should not follow a new path, one not taken by your parents. "All paths contain danger" [Midrash Kohelet Rabbah, Parashah 3, Siman 3]. New paths are dangerous for you.

Which paths have our parents followed? The path of Torah. That path contains clear instructions about how we should conduct ourselves and the means we should use to defend ourselves.

Kalonymous Kalman Shapira

Kalonymous Kalman Shapira (1889–1943) was born in Grodzisk, Poland. He served as rabbi in Piaseczno outside Warsaw, where he founded the Da'at Mosheh yeshiva to help revitalize Ḥasidism. He authored *Ḥovat Hatalmidim* (*The Students' Responsibility*, 1932), which addressed the spiritual development of his students. During his internment in the Warsaw ghetto, he offered material and spiritual sustenance to Piaseczno's refugees. Shapira's son was killed on 26 September 1939; his mother died shortly thereafter; and his daughter was taken to Treblinka on 14 August 1942. During the winter of 1942–1943, he collected the Shabbat and festival sermons he had delivered in the ghetto and buried them in a milk can. He was deported in April or May 1943 to the Trawniki labor camp in the Lublin district and was shot to death by Waffen SS soldiers in 1943. After the war, the manuscripts were discovered by a construction worker, along with a cover letter asking that they be sent to his brother Rabbi Yeshayahu Shapira in Tel Aviv.

Shapira sought to transcend his limited consciousness to the point of comprehending God's unlimited suffering and crying over Israel's troubles. If the human ego could be diminished to the point of touching God's infinite suffering, the Jew could submerge his finitude into God's infinite presence. God would then fill all, alleviating the pain which seeped through the finitude.

SELECTIONS

Our selections are from *Esh Kodesh* (Jerusalem, 1960), translated from the Hebrew by J. Hershy Worch. On the Sabbath, 16 August 1941, when the Torah portion *Ekev* was read, Shapira asked how faith remained possible despite the suffering. While the spirit should be strong enough to elevate the body, physical pains were in fact debilitating spirit and soul. The physical pain even affected worship, bringing on a spiritual turmoil caused by the inability to pray. Shapira responded by seeking God's help. Through God, he was certain, the pain could and would be diminished, and this would enable the Jew to serve God once again. That is, by submerging the physical pain into a relationship with God and His infinitude, Shapira's pain, as finite, could be erased. If mediated by the soul which sought to worship God, physical pain could be transformed into its own impetus for becoming subdued. During Ḥanukah (15–22 December 1941), Shapira spoke of a divine spark that each Jew had to assure a process in which the trouble would be overcome through God and Torah. The Jew had to awaken the spark, despite the onslaught, so as to be able to draw from the divine substance the strength to reach the level of overcoming physical suffering. On the Sabbath of 14 February 1942, when the Torah portions *Mishpatim* and *Shekalim* were read, Shapira invoked the experience of R. Yose as related in the tractate *Berakhot* of the Babylonian Talmud.

R. Yose entered the ruins of the Temple to pray, and by doing so internalized the historical destruction. His ego became dissolved, allowing R. Yose to hear God's tormented voice. As Israel suffered over the destruction, so did God (Isaiah 63:9), and as God was without limitation, so was His suffering. Shapira also assured that God's apparent absence did not mean that He had abandoned His people. Rather, God's distress was so great that He had to remove Himself lest the world be destroyed by His tears. If the Jew contemplated God's unlimited suffering, his individual pain would fall away.

HOLY FIRE

Ekev 9 (Deuteronomy 7:12 through 11:32), 16 August 1941

It will come to pass when you listen to these judgments, safeguarding and keeping them, that God your Lord will keep and guard the covenant and the kindness with which He made an oath to your fathers.

—Deuteronomy 7:12

We learn in the Talmud [B. T. *Zevaḥim* 53^b], R. Levi b. Ḥama said in R. Ḥama b. R. Ḥanina's name: "A strip of land issued from Judah's tribal territory and penetrated Benjamin's tribal territory, whereon the Temple altar was situated. The pious Benjamin grieved over it every day, wishing it were in his domain, as it is written, 'Fretting over Him, all day long' [Deuteronomy 33:12]. Therefore Benjamin was privileged to become a host to the Holy One, blessed be He; the Holy of Holies was situated in his territory, as it is written, 'And between his shoulders He dwells'" [ibid.].

Because Benjamin experienced longing, and because his desire to be a part of the holiness of the Temple was so powerful that he suffered pain, he attained his desire. Through the power of his yearning, he became a host to the holiness. We know from the sacred literature that it is a Jew's desire that draws holiness down from heaven. The Hebrew word *ratson* (desire) comprises the very same letters as the Hebrew word *tsinor* (conduit). The pious Benjamin's longing was so powerful, causing him so much pain, that he was able to draw the holiness down. This is how he became host to the *Shekhinah*, the Indwelling Presence of God [in the world].

It is also possible that it was not just a more powerful desire—one that caused him pain—that made Benjamin successful. More likely the cause was twofold: Desire and pain both produced separate, complementary effects that together resulted in the drawing down of holiness. While desire connects with and draws down the love and the light, the pain of longing overcomes any withholding or judgments that block, hide, restrict, or prevent the flow of holiness from heaven. The longing is for the flow and connection to the light, while the pain is at the absence of this flow.

Therefore, a Jew's ability to draw down the holiness of God upon himself is determined equally by both the measure of his desire to worship God—to be sanctified with His holiness—and the measure of the pain he feels when he finds defects in himself that are not sanctified. These two aspects determine his ability to eliminate any withholding and restrictions from inside himself, so that he can truly draw God's holiness upon him.

Extrapolating from this it is possible to understand, even at our level, the answer given by R. Akiba to his students [B. T. *Berakhot* 61^b]: "While his flesh was being raked with iron combs he recited the *Shema*. When they asked him, 'Our Teacher, thus far?' R. Akiba answered them, 'All my days I have been at pains over this verse in the *Shema* [Deuteronomy 6:5] "And thou shalt love the Lord thy God with all thy soul, and with all thy might." When will I ever have the opportunity of fulfilling it properly? I asked myself. But, right now, I have the opportunity to love God with all my soul. Should I not realize it?'"

We need to understand: What did R. Akiba's students mean when they asked him "Our Teacher, thus far?" Were they suggesting he had brought the whole calamity upon himself, and that it was his fault? What could R. Akiba possibly have done to change anything? Was there anything he could do to prevent the unfolding of his martyrdom? If his dying was to atone for the selling of Joseph by his brothers [Genesis 37] as is proposed in kabbalistic literature, then surely it was impossible for him to have prevented the events from unfolding. If he was being killed for teaching Torah in public and his students were asking whether teaching Torah is worth going "thus far," R. Akiba was still powerless to effect any change because he was being punished for something that had already happened. We know that from the time of his imprisonment and interrogation by the Roman authorities R. Akiba was no longer teaching Torah, as he had refused to teach even R. Simeon b. Yoḥai Talmud [B. T. *Pesaḥim* 112ª]: "R. Simeon b. Yoḥai said to R. Akiba while in prison, 'Master, teach me Torah.' 'I will not teach you,' he replied. 'If you will not teach me,' said he, 'I will tell my father Yoḥai and he will turn you over to the state.'"

We are forced to conclude that when the students asked "Our Teacher, thus far?" they were not referring to the matter of R. Akiba's death at all. We learn in the Talmud [ibid.] that R. Akiba was meditating on the word "One" [in the *Shema* prayer] ["Hear O Israel, God the Lord, God is One"] when he died. The students were watching him submit to the yoke of heavenly dominion, even while he was dying. They were not asking him a question at all, but were wondering aloud how it was possible for R. Akiba to concentrate on reciting the *Shema*, accept upon himself the yoke of heaven, and meditate on the word "One" in the midst of such agony, while his flesh was being raked with iron combs.

He answered them, "All my days I have been at pains over this verse in the *Shema*.... 'When will I ever have the opportunity of fulfilling it properly?' I asked myself...." R. Akiba was saying, "Not only did I desire to fulfill this commandment properly, I was also in pain at being unable to fulfill it." Therefore, "it was both my desire and my pain," says R. Akiba, "that brought down so much Divine Light that even under torture I am not disconcerted. I am able to don the yoke of heavenly dominion while concentrating and meditating."

We also need divine mercy and an outpouring of light and holiness upon us in order that our pain

and anguish not impede our worship of God, and especially to prevent our minds and our hearts from becoming flustered. This we can only bring about when we live at the level of "All my days I have been at pains," as we said before. It is exactly the Jew's measure of desire and longing to worship God truthfully, without allowing difficulties to deter him, and the measure of pain he feels upon finding himself nowhere near the level of holiness and worship that he desires, that determine his success. We are not talking just about the desire and pain that we had before all the troubles began. Even now, the desire a Jew feels for himself and all Israel to worship God without interference, and the pain he feels over the destruction of our bodies and souls, have the effect of removing the hindrances and clearing away all difficulties. As we said earlier, pain defeats the judgments and restrictions, and when this happens we will find ourselves worshipping God amid joy, salvation, and goodness.

Who can avoid pain when seeing such suffering of body and spirit? Who is it whose heart does not break when he sees the lack of schools and yeshivas—no places of Torah and no gathering of students to learn Torah? This is not just pain over the current situation, and it is not just now that the houses of God are destroyed. What is happening now will affect the future, because from now on there will be a shortage of young men to learn Torah. How many of them are gone, incomprehensibly murdered or starved to death, may the Merciful One protect us? How many have been forced to concentrate only on their physical survival? Where will we find young men to learn Torah in the future if they do not learn now? How many of them have been unable to withstand the test, and have been driven by hunger to go out on the *Shabbat* to do business in the marketplace? What can we expect of the children and young men who spent years in the markets and on the streets doing business, knocking at doors, begging for crumbs of bread during the week and on the *Shabbat*? Will they take advantage of the opportunity to return to the schools and yeshivas, and will everything be as it once was?

Everyone knows that for a number of years before the advent of the current trouble, many children of observant families were heartbreakingly distanced from Torah and from the ways of their parents, becoming freethinkers, may the Merciful One protect us. To balance this, however, God put into the hearts of children from unobservant families the desire to come closer to the Torah, and these newcomers withstood tests, because all they wanted was to be pious children of Torah. These young people who came from outside filled the spaces that were left by those who had abandoned the homes of the observant and the camp of worshippers of God.

This is not the case now. There are many young people who, out of pain and poverty are distancing themselves, but not even a single young person from an unobservant family is taking their places. The reason for this is simple: We no longer have any places or people left for gatherings of Torah scholars. The study houses and *Shtiblah* (prayer houses), which used to draw and arouse the children of the unobservant to Torah, worship, and *ḥasidut* (piety) are gone. It is self-evident that the cause of people's abandoning Judaism at this time is the bitter, almost unbearable trouble that has fallen upon us, may the Merciful One protect us.

So when God does have mercy and saves us, with whom will we be left? God forbid, there won't be anyone remaining to fill up the schools, and there won't be enough students left to make the founding of a yeshivah worthwhile, and the congregation of those who tremble at the word of God will be, God forbid, pitifully small. It is not just the mass of ordinary Jews, young people, and children learning Torah who will be missing. All of Jewry, even great Jews, will be damaged by this.

In the book *Toldot Ya'akov Yosef* [published in 1780] [by Ya'akov Yosef of Polonoye, 1704–1794] we learn two interpretations of the verse from Psalms 12:2, "Save me O God, for the pious have ceased to be; the believers have disappeared from among the children of man." One interpretation is that simple people have stopped believing because the pious have disappeared. The leaders of the Jewish people have been damaged, and this has caused the simple people to fall away from their spirituality. The second interpretation is that the pious have disappeared because the belief of the simple people has been damaged. The fact that people in general have lost faith has caused the disappearance of the great spiritual leaders.

For a deeper understanding of this idea, we will examine a passage from the Talmud [B. T. *Moed Katan* 17ᵃ], "The lips of the *kohen* guard knowledge. They should seek the law at his mouth, for he is an angel of the Lord of Hosts" [Malachi 2:7]. This has two aspects: "Only if the teacher resembles an angel of the Lord of Hosts," says the Talmud, "should we seek the law at his mouth. But if not, we should not seek the law at his mouth."

With that talmudic dictum in mind, let us examine what it says elsewhere in the Talmud [B. T. *Shabbat* 25ᵇ]: "This was the practice of R. Judah b. I'lai. On the eve of the Sabbath a basin filled with hot water was brought to him; he washed his face, hands and feet; and then, wrapping himself in fringed linen robes, he sat, looking like an angel of the Lord of Hosts."

It would appear from the theme of this quote that R. Judah b. I'lai resembled an angel only on the eve of the *Shabbat*, when he had finished his ablutions. What about all the other days of the week, and especially when he was learning with his students? Did he not then also need to resemble an angel?—because "If the teacher resembles an angel of the Lord of Hosts, then we should seek the law at his mouth, and if not . . . ," then not.

It appears that the meaning of the Talmud quoted above is this: Even when a teacher does not always resemble an angel, but only does so from time to time, we should still seek Torah from his mouth even during those times he does not resemble an angel. If, however, he never resembles an angel, we should not learn Torah from him. Why is it that even if the teacher only rarely resembles an angel, his students should ask him to teach them Torah? Why must they request the Torah from him at those times?

They need to request the Torah from him then, because when the teacher does resemble an angel, he is already a messenger of God and students do not need to ask anything of him; as an angel, his job is to teach them Torah. However, when he does not resemble an angel, then his students have to ask him for Torah so that the level of angel, which is dormant in the teacher, will reveal itself. If the students do not ask the teacher for Torah then the teacher suffers damage, because he is not aroused to teach. In addition, it is even possible for the degree of angel in the teacher to be dulled, and to disintegrate.

This is what the verse [Psalms 12:2] quoted above means when it says, "The pious have ceased to be; the believers have disappeared from among the children of men."

When Jews contemplate their physical and spiritual destruction, and the annihilation of the Torah and the Law that will result from all of this, God forbid, obviously their pain is great. But, through our longing for Torah and worship, and with the pain we feel at the destruction and the withholding of Torah and worship, we can sweeten all judgments and bring about a connection that constitutes a spiritual and physical salvation and a total redemption for all Israel. But this will only happen if people, even at this time, remain resolute and continue to worship God and study Torah with all their capability.

True, at a time when every head is sickened and every heart is breaking, it is difficult to study or pray as we ought to. On the other hand, it must be admitted, there are people today who make too much of the troubles, doing nothing but wasting time and words all day. Is it too much to demand that they use their spare time to learn things that do not require too much concentration, or at least to recite psalms?[1]

Returning to the original quote: "It will come to pass when you listen to these judgments, safeguarding and keeping them, that God your Lord will keep and guard the covenant and the kindness with which He made an oath to your fathers" [Deuteronomy 7:12]. *Ekev tishm'un*— When you listen to these laws. The Hebrew word *ekev*, "when," also translates as "heel." Thus, when you hear and comprehend how the

Torah and the Law are being crushed and ground beneath the *ekev* [heel] of judgment and decree; when you suffer pain as a result of that realization; and if you can keep bright the hope, "guarding" it in your hearts [see Genesis 37:11: "Jacob 'guarded' the matter"] and longing for the day when you will be able to worship God and fulfill His commandments, then "God your Lord will keep and guard the covenant and the kindness with which He made an oath to your fathers. He will love you and bless you ... " because it is through this process that you will sweeten all the judgments and decrees, bringing down the flow of goodness and salvation for Israel.

Ḥanukah, 15–22 December 1941

In the days of the Hasmonean high priest, Mattityahu b. Yoḥanan, and his sons—when the evil Hellenic empire conquered Your people Israel, compelling them to neglect Your Torah and stray from Your desired statutes—at that time of distress, You in Your great mercy stood up for them. You took up their grievance, avenging their wrong. You delivered the strong into the hands of the weak and the many into the hands of the few. You put the corrupt into the hands of the undefiled, the wicked into the hands of the pious, and the savage into the hands of diligent students of Your Torah, making Yourself a great, holy name in Your world. For Your people Israel, You wrought great victory and salvation as clear as the day. So Your children went into the holy sanctuary, cleansing and purifying the Temple, and kindling lights in Your holy

---

1. [This note was added by the author in 1943.] The above was said and written in 1941. Then—however bitter were the troubles and suffering, as is apparent from the text above—it was at least possible to lament, to find words to describe a handful of events, to worry about the survivors, and to grieve for the future—how will they rebuild the schools and yeshivas, etc.? We still had the wherewithal to admonish, and inspire those who remained, with the desire for Torah and worship. This is no longer the case, now at the end of 1942, when the holy congregations have been annihilated in a radical excision. Those individuals who survive, pitiful and few, are broken in slavery and Egyptian bondage, downtrodden and terrified for their lives. There exist no words

with which to lament our woes. There is no one to admonish, and there is no heart to awaken to worship and to Torah. How many trials must one undergo as the price of a prayer, and how many tests must be withstood, just to observe Sabbath, even for those who genuinely long to observe it? There is certainly no spirit or heart left to grieve for what the future holds, or to plan reconstruction of the destroyed edifices at such time as God will have mercy on us and save us. Only God, He will have mercy and save us in the blink of an eye. As for the rebuilding of all that has been destroyed, that will only happen with the final redemption and the resurrection of the dead. God, alone, can build and heal. Please, O God, have mercy; please do not delay rescuing us.

courtyard. They fixed these eight days of Hanukah as a festival to express appreciation and to praise Your great Name.

—From the Hanukah liturgy

Let us try to understand: When the evil Hellenic empire was compelling Jews to neglect the Torah, it was not just the Jews who were in trouble. It was also, so to speak, God's problem. So why do we say, "You in Your great mercy stood up for them," when God was really standing up for Himself?

Let us try to understand at least a little, with our limited intelligence, why, when speaking of the faith of Abraham the patriarch, the Torah says, "Abraham believed in God, and He considered it righteousness" [Genesis 15:6]. Why was it that with our father Abraham, faith was considered an act of righteousness, while the faith of the Jews who were in Egypt was not considered righteousness, though the verse says [Exodus 4:31], "The people believed and heard that God had remembered the Jewish people"? This is even more difficult to comprehend when we consider that for the Jews in Egypt, faith was more challenging than it was for Abraham. God did not speak directly to them, nor did they even know God's name. Moses said to God [Exodus 3:13], "When they ask me what Your name is, what shall I say to them?" The Jews of Egypt were in such pain and distress that, as it is written, "Because of their broken spirit and the hard work, they could not listen to him" [Exodus 6:9].

It may perhaps be understood as follows: It is often taught in sacred literature that faith is not simply confidence substituting for certainty. Faith is the light and holiness of God inside the Jew. This inner light resonates to the holiness of God's brilliance and is tied and bound to it. Faith is intrinsic to Jews; it is an inheritance passed down to us from our ancestors, and therefore we say in our prayers, "God, our God, God of our Fathers, God of Abraham, Isaac and Jacob . . . " [from the silent Amidah (the standing benediction)]. The fact that He is our God and that we believe in Him has nothing to do with reason or logic. He is God, our God, because we are tied to Him through our ancestry. Only Abraham the patriarch did not inherit faith, and so of him it is said, "Abraham believed in God, and He considered it righteous-

ness." It is not said of the Jews of Egypt that their faith was considered an act of righteousness because faith was already instilled inside them as an inherited trait. Even for our patriarch Abraham, the Torah tells us, it was only his faith that was considered an act of righteousness. It is not written that God considered his meeting other challenges, such as the Akedah (binding of Isaac), [as] acts of righteousness. Even though the Akedah was the sternest of tests, it depended on the level of Abraham's faith. The greater and more powerful the faith, the stronger and more capable of self-sacrifice is the worshipper. Only Abraham's faith was remarkable, and considered a righteous act. His sacrifice of Isaac in the Akedah was nothing more than the natural consequence of his faith.

Because worship depends on faith, a Jew's faith must be wholehearted; for it is only total, selfless faith that enables Israel to give its life for God. If the faith is flawed, and only halfhearted, how can it empower anyone to self-sacrifice? Total, selfless faith means continuing to believe in Him even in times of hester panim (concealment of God's face) with faith that everything comes from Him, that everything is beneficial and just, and that all the agony and anguish is filled with God's love for the Jewish people.

To our grief, we see that even among those whose belief was always wholehearted, there are now certain individuals whose faith has been damaged. They question God, asking, "Why have You forsaken us? If we are being tortured in order to bring us closer to Torah and worship," they argue, "then why, on the contrary, is the Torah and everything holy being destroyed?"

Now if a Jew utters these words in a form of prayer or supplication, as an outpouring of his heart before God, it is a good thing. But if, God forbid, he really is questioning—even if not God directly but his internal faith, God forbid—then may God protect us!

Faith is the foundation of everything. If the faith of a person is, God forbid, damaged, then the person is torn asunder and distanced from God. Souls condemned to Gehenna (hell) emerge purified and cleansed after having repented. We hope to God that all those suffering these tortures now will rise, cleansed, purified, and closer to Him. But the soul of someone whose faith is damaged is like a soul enduring Gehenna while continuing to add offenses to its sins. After a time, upon examining itself, the soul sees the situation and asks itself, "What have I achieved with all this suffering, if I am just as sullied now as I was before?"

In all honesty, what room is there, God forbid, for doubts or questions? Admittedly, Jews endure suffering of the sort with which we are currently afflicted only every few hundred years. Still, how can we expect or hope to understand these, God's actions, and then allow our faith to be damaged, God forbid, upon finding that we cannot understand them? If one blade of grass created by God is beyond our understanding, how much more unfathomable is the soul; and if we do not understand a soul, how much less do we understand an angel, and how much less even than this can we understand the mind of God? How could we possibly expect to grasp with our mind what God knows and understands?

What excuse does a person have to question God and have his faith damaged by this prevailing suffering more than all the Jews who went through suffering in bygone times? Why should a person's faith become damaged now, if it was not damaged when he read descriptions of Jewish suffering from antiquity to the present day in Scripture, the Talmud, or Midrash? Those who say that suffering such as this has never befallen the Jewish people are mistaken. There was torture comparable to ours at the destruction of the Temple and at Betar, etc.[2] May God have mercy and call an end to our suffering; may He save us now, immediately, forthwith and forever.

The reason why today's suffering can damage someone's faith more so than it did in the past is only because he is more self-centered than he used to be. His pain affects him more than it once did. If someone says he flinches only at seeing the torture of others, it may in fact be true that he is feeling compassion for his fellow Jews, but the truth is also that deeper down, inside himself, his compassion is really terror of being forced to go through such terrible torture himself. It is this that damages his faith and feeds his doubts, God forbid. As we have already said, a person must relinquish his life, his self-centeredness, and his bias, for only then will his faith be undamaged. He will be able to continue affirming with perfect faith that everything happening is just and a manifestation of God's love for the Jewish people. With our limited perspective, we suggest that there may be a hint of this in the Talmud [B. T. *Berakhot* 61[b]]: "R. Akiba was reciting the *Shema* ['Hear O' Israel, the Lord is One'] while his flesh was being raked with iron combs. His students asked, 'Our Rabbi, thus far?' He answered them, 'All my days I have been at pains over this verse in the *Shema* [Deuteronomy 6:5] "Love God with all your heart, with all your soul, and with all your might." "When will I ever have the opportunity of fulfilling it properly?" I asked myself. But right now, I have the opportunity to love God with all my soul. Should I not grasp it?'"

If we approach this at the simple level, then the well-known question arises, why would the students of R. Akiba—who were themselves remarkable for their individual piety—have asked, "Our Rabbi, thus far?" They were well aware that every Jew is prepared to give his life for God. Furthermore, why did R. Akiba answer them by referring to himself when he might have answered more directly by simply quoting the verse "Love God with all your heart, with all your soul," even if God demands your soul?

With what we have said above, this can perhaps be explained in a way that teaches us something about our own plight. The terrible tortures R. Akiba endured caused such great suffering in his disciples that they were provoked to ask the same question that was asked by Moses when he was shown this same event [B. T. *Menaḥot* 29[b]]: "Is this Torah and this its reward?" The disciples were afraid that, God forbid, they might have doubts, however fleeting, as a result of their emotional and visceral response, and that their faith might be damaged. They wanted their

---

2. [Note added by author on the eve of the holy Sabbath, *Kislev* 18, 27 November 1942.] The torment that was endured until the middle of 1942 had transpired previously in history. The bizarre tortures and the freakish, brutal murders that have been invented for us by the depraved, perverted murderers, solely for the suffering of Israel, since the middle of 1942, are, according to my knowledge of the words of our sages of blessed memory, and of the chronicles of the Jewish people in general, unprecedented and unparalleled. May God have mercy upon us, and save us from their hands, in the blink of an eye.

teacher, who was so powerful in his faith, to speak of his belief, so that his faith might inundate them. When they asked, "Our Rabbi, thus far?" they were saying, "Can you be our teacher thus far, even into the circumstances of this terrible death?" Perhaps they did not articulate their question fully, or make it more specific, but merely hinted at it in order to avoid invoking the response that the Talmud [ibid.] says had already been given to Moses: "Be silent."

R. Akiba understood that the students were not questioning God but rather begging him to bestow upon them some of his faith, and so he told them something about himself and his own aspirations to faith: "All my life I was in pain over this verse. . . . Right now I have the opportunity to love God with all my soul. Should I not grasp it?"

At that time, in R. Akiba's epoch, when the divine decree was against only the ten martyrs who were put to death by the Roman emperor, the students sought a bolstering of their faith through the words of R. Akiba. Now, however, when the decree of martyrdom is upon the whole Jewish people, God forbid, we must look to strengthen our faith by looking at the decree of martyrdom itself.

It is a well-known teaching from the Rav [R. Shneur Zalman of Liadi, *Tanya*, I.25] that even the least sincere Jew, who commonly finds himself unable to resist the urge to sin, is nevertheless prepared to give his life for God when tested. This is because when his enemies try to extinguish the spark of his soul with their heresy, may the Merciful One protect us, the tiny spark burns into flame and grows stronger and more powerful, as is well known.

If only people would bear in mind that it is not because we robbed or did anything wrong to anyone that we are being persecuted, but because we are Jews—children of Israel, bound to God and to His holy Torah. First, it would explain why our enemies are not satisfied with just killing us or extinguishing the divine spark inside us but feel they have to annihilate simultaneously both [the] body and soul of the Jew. Then, if we could only bear it in mind, our faith and our cleaving to God and to the Torah would, on the contrary, burgeon and strengthen. But because we tend to feel only our physical pain and not the spiritual pain, and because we fail to remind ourselves that what we

are enduring is actually a war upon God and the Torah, therefore there are certain individuals who experience a weakening of their faith.

The Hellenes in Hasmonean times also tried "compelling them to neglect Your Torah and stray from Your desired statutes." They did this with the torture and oppression of Israel, as is recorded in the writings of Josephus, and through the spread of Hellenic culture among the Jews. It reached a point where they said to Jews, "Write upon the horn of your ox that you have no portion in the God of Israel," as is known from the *midrash* [*Tanḥuma, Tazria, Perek* 11]. At that time the Jews knew that the purpose of all the physical suffering was to make them forget the Torah, to make them "stray from Your desired statutes." This is what they worried about; it was the chief cause of their pain; and so their faith grew stronger and God's salvation came to them in merit of their faith. Thus the liturgy reads: "At the time of distress, You in Your great mercy stood up for them. You took up their grievance, avenging their wrong." The distress of the people of Israel was not at their physical pain but at the efforts of the Hellenes to destroy God's Torah and worship. That is why "You stood up for them, and You saved them."

Mishpatim (Exodus 21:1–24:18), 14 February 1942

And these are the judgments that you must set before them.

—Exodus 21:1

We learn in the Talmud [B. T. *Berakhot* 3ª], R. Jose said: "I was once traveling on the road, when I entered into one of the ruins of Jerusalem in order to pray. Elijah the Prophet, of blessed memory, appeared and waited for me at the door until I had finished my prayer. Whereupon, he said to me, 'Peace be with you, son, why did you enter this ruin?' I replied, 'To pray.' . . . He said to me, 'My son, what sound did you hear in this ruin?' I replied, 'I heard a Divine Voice, cooing like a dove, saying "Woe to Me, that I razed My house, burned My temple, and exiled My children among the Gentiles!"' He said to me, 'By your life and by your head! It is not only now that God exclaims thus, He does so thrice each day!

And even more than that, whenever Jews go into synagogues and study houses and respond, "May His great name be blessed!" the Holy Blessed One nods His head and says, "Happy is the king who is thus praised in his house! Woe to the father who banishes his children, and woe to the children who are banished from their father's table!" ' "

We have previously discussed why R. Jose heard the Divine Voice only when he was praying amid the ruins, even though the Holy Blessed One speaks thus three times every day. For behold! A Jew, tortured in his suffering, may think he is the only one in pain, as though his individual, personal pain, and the pain of all other Jews, has no effect above, God forbid. But, as the verse [Isaiah 63:9] says, "In all their pain is His pain," and as we learn in the [Babylonian] Talmud [*Ḥagigah* 15^{b}] in the name of R. Meir, "When a person suffers, to what expression does the *Shekhinah* (Divine Presence) give utterance? 'O Woe! My head, O woe! My arms.' " In sacred literature we learn that God, as it were, suffers the pain of a Jew much more than that person himself feels it.

Possibly because God is infinite—and hence unknowable in the world—His pain at the suffering of Jewish people is also infinite. Perhaps it is not just impossible for any human to feel such immense pain, it is impossible even to apprehend the level of God's pain, to know that He bears it. Just to hear God's voice saying, "Woe to Me, that I razed My house, burned My temple, and exiled My children among the Gentiles!" is impossible, because it is beyond the boundaries of human comprehension. It was only when R. Jose entered into the devastation of one of the ruins of Jerusalem, letting go somewhat of his self-centeredness, that the boundaries restricting his perception were also destroyed and he was able to hear the voice of God. Even then, he heard only a little of the voice, for, as he said, "I heard a Divine Voice, cooing like a dove," while we know from the verse [Jeremiah 25:30] "God roars, howling over his city," that God roars, as it were, like a lion, over the destruction of the Temple.

And so, the world continues to exist steadfast; it is not obliterated by God's pain and His voice at the suffering of his people and the destruction of His house, because God's pain never enters into the world. This could explain the teaching in the *midrash* [*Eicha, Rabbah*: Intro. 24]: "At the hour of the destruction of the Temple, God wept, saying, 'Oh! Woe to Me, what have I done? I brought My *Shekhinah* (Divine Presence) down to dwell below, for Israel's sake, and now I am retreating to My original position, to be the laughingstock of Gentiles, reviled among creatures.' At that moment the angel Metatron appeared, and falling upon his face he begged, 'Master of the Universe, allow me to cry, and then You need not cry.' God replied, 'If you do not leave Me to cry now, I will go somewhere you have no permission to enter, and I will cry there, as it is written [Jeremiah 13:17]: "For if you listen not, My soul will weep in *mistarim* (concealment)." ' "

In the *midrash* [*Tanna Debe Eliahu Rabbah* 17] we learn: "Why does God weep in private? Because it is unseemly for a king to cry in front of his subjects." If the only reason the angel Metatron asked leave to cry in God's stead was because it is unseemly for God to cry publicly, the angel could simply have left God's presence, leaving God to cry privately. But with what we have said above, it may be explained thus. What the angel meant is that it is a shame for his subjects that their king should have to cry at all. But since His pain is, as it were, infinite—pain greater than the world can discern—and consequently cannot enter the world, so the world does not even tremble at it, the angel made his proposal, saying, "Allow me to cry, and then You need not cry." Although angels are messengers of God, through whom God performs His acts, this is why this angel wanted to be allowed to do God's weeping, as it were, to introduce it into the world, so that God, as it were, would not have to cry; because, no sooner would the world listen to the sound of God's crying, as it were, then it would hear and explode! If but a single flash of God's pain, as it were, would enter the world, all His enemies would be scorched. At the Red Sea, the Holy Blessed One said to the ministering angels [B. T. *Megillah* 10^{b}], "My handiwork drowns in the sea, and you want to sing?" And now, when the Jewish people are drowning in blood, the world continues to exist? "Allow me to cry," said the angel, "and then You need not, because Your crying would no longer be necessary."

At the time of the destruction of the Temple, God wanted to atone for the sins of the Jewish people, but it was not yet a time of salvation. So, He said to the angel, "I will go somewhere you have no permission to enter, and I will cry there." Now, the pain is so great, the world cannot contain it; it is so far beyond the world. God's pain and suffering have increased so greatly, they are beyond even the angel's ability to perceive it; even he cannot see God's pain. We learn in the Talmud [B. T. Ḥagigah 5ᵇ]: "The Holy Blessed One has a place for weeping. It is called *mistarim*. . . . Is there such a thing as weeping before God; has not R. Papa said, 'There is no grief in the presence of the Holy One, blessed be He'? There is no contradiction; *Mistarim* refers to inner chambers, while R. Papa is referring to outer chambers." The Maharsha [ibid.], in his commentary, teaches that the "inner chambers" refer to the *sefirah* (divine attribute) of *Binah* (understanding). It is understandable according to what was said earlier, because the *sefirah* of *Binah* is described in the book of the *Zohar* [Intro., 1ᵃ] as "open to inquiry but closed to comprehension." Because it is beyond the capacity of the mind to comprehend, God's pain is, as it were, hidden from the angel and from the rest of the world.

This, though, is the difference. We spoke last week about the Torah, which, before it was given on Sinai, was referred to as a "hidden treasure," not as a precious object in a treasure house. We explained that it was incomprehensible, hidden by its own greatness. At the time of the destruction of the Temple, even though God's pain was, as it were, hidden even from the angels and from the whole world, it was not incomprehensible due to its immensity. Note the word "chambers"—how the text uses the phrase "inner chambers," because everything exists here in this world, in the Torah. Since, as we explained last week, the Torah was given on the Sabbath because everything had to be compressed and constricted for the sake of the Jewish people, it means that through the Torah absolutely anything can be revealed in the world. This includes even what has been concealed within "chambers," hidden by the vessels containing it.

We learn in the *Mishnah* [*Ta'anit* 2:1]: "What is the order of service for fast days? The ark, which houses the Torah scroll, is taken out into the open space of the city." In the holy *Zohar* [III.71ᵃ] we learn that in times of trouble, may

the Merciful One protect us, the Torah scroll was even taken out of its ark. Besides the reason given in the Talmud, to publicize the fast, it may be hinting at what we have said above. Through the Torah we are capable of revealing even the most sublime and concealed light, even that which is usually hidden from the world because it is so exalted. It can even reveal God's pain and His weeping, as it were, over the pain of the Jewish people. Then, as it is written [Psalms 94:4], "All who have wrought evil will crumble," and our salvation will be revealed swiftly, immediately, and forthwith.

It is possible that this is the meaning of the verse [Psalms 22:2] "My God, my God, why have You forsaken me, so far from me, my salvation, the words of my pleading?" Of course, we believe that You will save us, that You have not forsaken us completely, God forbid. But, in feeling "forsaken," we refer to our salvation that is so far away and the suffering that just goes on and on. The psalm continues, "You are holy; You dwell in the supplications of the Congregation of Israel."

We learn in the teachings of the holy Rav, R. Shneur Zalman of Liadi, of blessed memory, that *kadosh* [holy] is an expression of separateness and distinction, as in [Deuteronomy 22:9] "Do not plant different species in your vineyard . . . lest the yield of both the crops be *tukdash* (condemned)." Meanwhile, as Rashi explains on the verse [Genesis 38:21] "There was no *kedeshah* (prostitute) here"; *kedeshah* means separated and distinguished for a single purpose.

This, then, is the meaning of God's *kedushah* [holiness]: that He is separate and distinct from all worlds. Thus, the verse reads, "Why have You forsaken me . . . You who are holy [i.e., separate and distinct]?" But the truth is, "You dwell in the supplications of the Congregation of Israel." You are to be found in Torah and in the prayers of Jews, which are called "the supplications of the Congregation of Israel." But how can You bear the humiliation of the Torah and the pain of the Jewish people, who are being tortured only because they observe the Torah?

Therefore, it is incumbent upon us, the Jewish people, to grasp the Torah, wherein is the Holy Blessed One. By entering into the Torah, by learning it and observing its commandments, we are actually entering into God's presence. Then His weeping and His voice, as it were, which laments our suffering, will be revealed, and all evil, like smoke, will just disappear. It is true that in times of suffering it is very difficult to learn, and there are Jews who find it difficult to observe certain commandments. But the Jewish people have been skilled at suffering for ages, and have never slackened their observance of Torah and its commandments. Speaking generally, the Torah was not given to us on condition that when things go well for us, we will observe it, and when things are bad for us, God forbid, we will abandon it, God forbid. God is always our God, and we will always learn His Torah and observe His commandments.

Let us return to our previous discussion. Through the Torah that we learn and observe, God's voice, roaring over the destruction of the Temple and the Jewish people, will be revealed and salvation will come hurriedly and swiftly. For He, God, and His voice, which are in *mistarim*—concealment, at the level of "My soul shall cry in *mistarim*"—will be revealed through the Torah, because although the Torah was once a "hidden treasure," nonetheless it was revealed to the Jewish people. All the holiness of heaven can, likewise, be revealed through the Torah. Furthermore, Torah not only brings about a revelation of God and of His weeping, it also sweetens all the pain and judgments. At the simplest level, the sweetening of judgments is the reward for learning Torah, as is promised [Leviticus 26:3]: "If you follow My laws and are careful to keep My commandments, I will provide you with rain at the right time."

Aside from that, as we learn in sacred literature, sin does not just draw *din* (judgment) down in retribution; sin and *din* are intrinsically connected. Similarly, the good brought about by observing Torah and *mitsvot* (commandments) is not just a reward; goodness is intrinsically and essentially a fact of Torah and *mitsvot*. For example, in the book *Sha'arei Orah* [intro.], we learn that anyone who knows how to concentrate upon the meaning of his prayers has the keys to open all the gates of heaven in his hands. Since the flow and revelation happen through the letters and the names of God, when a person knows how to combine them, he is able to repair the conduit and restore the flow of

abundance. Similarly, with Torah and *mitsvot*, good does not come only by way of a reward, but happens intrinsically. So it is with this. Aside from the rewards it brings with it, the Torah unifies all the voices into one voice, which is the voice of the Torah.

We learn in the Midrash that God's voice at the giving of the Torah went from one end of the world to the other. We also learn that the Jewish people heard God's voice coming from all directions—east, west, north, and south. Besides the literal explanation, this hints to us that we should not think the physical world too distant from and antithetical to the Torah, for this is not so. We can hear the Torah coming from everywhere in the world because the world was also created at the word of God. His word is the very essence of the world. It seems otherwise only because people utilize the world evilly, destroying thereby the world that was created with ten divine statements. But he who uses the world to do good finds himself being assisted by the world in his Torah and in his worship.

In the Talmud [B. T. *Baba Kamma* 72[b]] we learn, R. Naḥman said to Rava: "The reason why I did not tell you this in the morning was because I had not yet eaten beef." Through eating meat, his knowledge of Torah increased. The simple reason for this is, as everyone understands, the living soul dwells inside the body, while the human mind, which is the seat of the soul, reposes in the brain. When a person's brain is starved, it is difficult for him to acquire Torah, but when he eats as much as he needs, his mind is strengthened and gains the power to comprehend, and it becomes easier to increase his knowledge of Torah. Thus it seems that bread and meat can enable a person to hear the Torah. But at the time of the revelation of the Torah, the voice of Torah was heard from the whole world. Even now, a person can still hear the voice of Torah coming from everywhere in the whole world—not just from those parts of the world that merge with him and become a part of his body, as through eating and drinking, but also from the world that is external to himself.

The world was created at the word of God, and the Torah is the word of God. Truly, He, God, is One, and His word is One. The whole Torah was included in the Ten Commandments, and the Ten Commandments were uttered in one word, as is written in the midrash [*Yalkut Shimoni* 250]. Likewise, God's word at the creation of the world and God's word at the giving of the Torah are the same, one word. With *hishtalshelut*—the process of becoming physical in this world—the word of God separates into two elements, two manifestations of speech. For the world, God's word becomes the *mitsvot* [commandments] to be observed by mankind and commands to the created world to come into existence. At God's decree the sun shines by day and the moon at night, and so forth. For the Jewish people, God's word becomes the Torah and *mitsvot* that sustain them and the world.

When examined at a higher level, the Ten Commandments are one word and the ten statements of creation are one. On the first day, everything was already created, as Rashi explains [Genesis 1:1]. When examined at a still higher level, the word of the ten statements and the word of the Ten Commandments are also one word, because He and His word are One. Just as He is One, so all of His words are also One.

A person who is elevated and united with the single voice of God in the Torah can hear the voice of the Torah from everywhere in the world—from the twittering of the birds, from the lowing of cattle, and from the voices and cacophony of people. Out of all of these, he hears the voice of God in the Torah. At the revelation of the Torah, it is written [Deuteronomy 5:18], "They heard a great Voice that did not cease." Rashi [ibid.] says that the voice giving the Torah never ceased and can always be heard. Because it goes on forever and can be heard from everything, thus all evil is elevated to good. All the evil speech and evil doctrines spoken by the enemies of Israel are transformed into the voice of the Torah, because they also exist in the world. Their vitality is drawn from the voice of God in the Torah, which has branched out into evil words.

It is simply that the words of admonishment to be found in the Torah have become physical and manifest to the point where the enemies of Israel—these ones or those ones—can talk of physically beating and inflicting pain on a Jew, God forbid. When everything is unified with the Torah, they also are elevated to become the voice of Torah, and all evil is sweetened.

To return to the verse with which we opened this chapter, "And these are the judgments that you must set before them," Rashi [ibid.] explains that wherever the phrase "And these" is used in a sentence, it adds something to the previous subject, in that it forms a continuation of it. Here, the phrase "And these" adds these laws to the previous ones. Just as the previous ones, the Ten Commandments, were given at Sinai, so these too are from Sinai. With Torah, we can fix those words that are judgments, as is written [2 Kings 25:6]: "And they spoke judgments to him."

The judgments must be set before the people according to their needs, and not, God forbid, in opposition to them. For these judgments also are from Sinai, and they are also the voice of God. It is just that they have branched out into *Din* [judgment], into words, and even into the evil deeds of the enemies of Israel. In the midrash [*Tanḥuma, Ki Thissa, Perek* 5] we learn: "Moses said to God, 'But once I am dead, I will not be remembered.' God replied, 'I promise you: Just as you are standing here now, elevating them and teaching them the chapter of the *shekels*, so every year as they read the chapter of *shekels* before Me, it will be [as] though you were standing right here elevating them.'" The midrash explains that this is why the verse in the Torah does not say "count/raise their heads" but rather "you will count/raise their heads" [Exodus 30:12]. When, God forbid, there is fear lest there be a plague due to the census, their heads can be lifted through reading the Torah, because everything may become Torah, and everything can be sweetened into good.

Shlomoh Zalman Unsdorfer

Shlomoh Zalman Unsdorfer (1888–1944) of Bratislava (Slovakia) began his study at the nearby Galantar yeshivah under Yosef Tsevi Dushinsky, who later headed the separatist Orthodox community in Jerusalem. He continued at the Bratislava yeshiva under the Da'at Sofer (Akiva Schreiber), the great-grandson of the yeshiva's eminent founder, the Ḥatam Sofer (Mosheh Schreiber), an outspoken opponent of Reform. He served as rabbi of Bratislava's Weidritz Alley congregation, helped to establish the *Ḥevrah Mevakshei Derekh*, a study group for working youth, and headed the burial society (*Ḥevrah Kadishah Digemilut Ḥasadim*). During the war, Unsdorfer made his way regularly to the nearby displaced persons camps in Patronka and Ratenbriken to offer consolation to the interned Jews. In mid-September 1944 he fled to Marienthal Internirungslager, a refuge for Jews with American papers eligible for prisoner exchange. In early October, the Nazis discovered his false papers, and he was taken to Auschwitz, where he was killed upon arrival. However, his son Simḥah Bunem survived Auschwitz, returned to Bratislava, and found the manuscripts of his father's sermons and diary notes in the ruins of their house. After conferring with the Da'at Sofer (by then in Jerusalem), Simḥah Bunem's brother Shmuel Aleksander in Montreal translated the sermons from Yiddish to Hebrew and published them with the title *Siftei Shlomoh* (*The Lips of Shlomoh*).

Unsdorfer presumed the presence of latent hatred against Israel through the line of Esau's successors. The hatred was activated by God when Jews surrendered Torah and emulated the nations. But Unsdorfer could not understand why pious Jews were being caught in a fire which was set for assimilationists. He drew a categorical distinction between God's knowledge and man's and then fell into silence. But he also envisioned a metaphysical process under way from catastrophe to redemption. Unsdorfer urged Jews to trust in that higher drama and, remaining silent about God's ways, act with the piety and trust of Abraham at the *Akedah* (binding of Isaac).

SELECTIONS

In *Vayeḥi: Erev Shabbat Kodesh Lesidra Vayeḥi Shenat 5702* ("*Vayeḥi*: Eve of the Holy *Shabbat* of the Torah Portion *Vayeḥi* [Genesis 47:28–50:26]" [Prepared 2 January for 3 January 1942 delivery]), Unsdorfer stated that given the enormity of the troubles it may be inappropriate to rebuke trespassers. But he would at least affirm that the troubles had to be measure-for-measure punishments which were administered ultimately by God. In *Parashat Va'era: Or Leyom 6 Erev Shabbat Kodesh Va'era Shenat 5703* ("Torah Portion *Va'era* [Exodus 6:1–9:35]: Friday, the Day before the Eve of the Holy Sabbath *Va'era*" [Prepared 8 January for 9 January 1943 delivery]), Unsdorfer stipulated that human knowledge was limited and time bound while God's was unlimited. It was impossible to explain the sufferings of the pious; their meaning was held by God alone. But Abraham's experience could serve as a paradigm. When ordered to take Isaac as a burnt offering,

Abraham did not question God's intention. Instead he proceeded as God ordered (Rashi *ad* Genesis 21:12). When Abraham was unable to find a burial place for Sarah in the very land promised to him by God, he purchased a spot. In *Re'eh Anohi 5703* ("[Torah Portion] *Re'eh* [Deuteronomy 11:26–16:17]" [Prepared 27 August for 28 August 1943 delivery]), Unsdorfer asked why, if observance of God's commandments brought blessings (see Deuteronomy 12:26–28), the pious were now in anguish. He was aware that once God's fury was released in flames, the pious could not be protected (see Exodus 22:8) and that once He authorized the nations to act out His anger they acted at will and without a sense of justice (*Metsudat David ad* Isaiah 10:5). Unsdorfer also recognized that by dying at this point in time, the pious would be spared the comprehensive destruction yet to come and that the pious bore the brunt of Torah trespassers because the pious guaranteed at Sinai that Torah would be observed (*Or Hahayim ad* Exodus 22:6). But these midrashic-type explanations could not subdue the religious turmoil (Unsdorfer, *Siftei Shlomoh*, Brooklyn, 1972, pp. 81–89, 308–310, 141–144). Selections have been translated from the Hebrew by Gershon Greenberg.

Vayehi: Eve of the Holy *Shabbat* of the Torah Portion *Vayehi* [Genesis 47:28–50:26] [Prepared 2 January for 3 January 1942 Delivery]

[Historical notation] Friday of *Parashat Vayehi* (Genesis 47:28–50:26) 1942, in a time of great trouble, heaven forbid. In this last week the old age home in Patronka, where the aged were brought several days earlier, was completely burned. The old people gathered in great fear and confusion in the dining room. It is possible that the pious woman, the daughter of R. Zalman Spitzer, may his merit protect us, may have been among those burned. In the same day, the evil ones, may their memory be obliterated, came to the synagogues, Temimei Derekh synagogue and others, and beat the Jews who were praying there. May God have mercy.

"'And Jacob lived in the land of Egypt seventeen years' [Genesis 47:28]. Why is the section [of *Vayehi*] completely closed [and without the usual space between it and the preceding section]? Because when Jacob our father died, the eyes and hearts of Israel were closed because of the affliction of the bondage with which the Egyptians began to enslave them" [Rashi]. My teachers and masters: To my great sorrow, my head and heart have not been there to prepare the sermon as is appropriate before this dignified community. This is because of the anguish of the servitude. But the mercies of God have not been exhausted. Precisely in a time of troubles such as

this, we need to strengthen our study of Torah in public. As the rabbinic Sages taught about the biblical passage, "Also my wisdom stood me in stead" [Ecclesiastes 2:9]: "Of all the Torah which I learned, there remained with me in my old age only what I acquired through the blows which my teacher gave me in anger" [*Midrash Kohelet Rabbah, Parashah* 2, *Siman* 15]. "Unless Thy law [Torah] had been my delight, I should then have perished in mine affliction" [Psalms 119:92].

The portion concerning the death of Jacob our patriarch, of blessed memory, is called by the name, "He lived." The years when the teacher in the *heder* (Hebrew school) taught us the portion with enthusiasm and a special melody are still in my memory. Particularly, "And as for me, when I came from Paddan" [Genesis 48:7], "Assemble yourselves, and hear, ye sons of Jacob," etc. [Genesis 49:2]. All of the blessings that Jacob bestowed before his death, every word, was a prophecy for the future. More than three thousand years have passed. But the holy testament of our patriarch Jacob still lives with us and within us. Particularly in a time of trouble like that of today, we need these holy words as a remedy for our broken hearts and as a consolation for the travails of our servitude even more.

"And he set Ephraim before Manasseh" [Genesis 48:20]. This is because Ephraim alludes to a time of trouble. That is to say, "God has made me fruitful in the land of my affliction" [Genesis 41:52]. We strengthen ourselves with faith and trust in God even in the land of our affliction, even in a time of great troubles, heaven forbid. "God has made me fruitful" indicates that God has taken us out to freedom. "And it is a time of trouble unto Jacob. But out of it shall he be saved" [Jeremiah 30:7] is explained in the holy writings to mean that we will still be worthy to see that the trouble itself will be our salvation, that "God has made me fruitful in the land of my affliction" [Genesis 41:52]. If we advance in [this understanding] we will be worthy of "For God hath made me forget all my toil" [Genesis 41:51]. In the future the joy will increase and we will forget all the days of trouble. But for now we are in a time [of] terrible trials. Heaven forbid that we should forget that everything is under the supervision of divine providence from Heaven.

The Talmud alludes to this: "If one omits to say the [prayer] 'True and firm' (*Emet veyatsiv*) in the morning and the 'True and trustworthy' [prayer] in the night, he has not performed his obligation. For it is written, 'To declare Thy loving kindness in the morning, and Thy faithfulness in the night seasons'" [Psalms 92:3; B. T. *Berakhot* 12ᵃ]. Night alludes to the darkness of the exile. Day alludes to the redemption. If in a time of troubles one truly believes that everything is from Heaven and for one's good, then one will be worthy to see the "True and firm," the "To declare Thy loving kindness in the morning" revealed, which is the day. On the condition of "Thy faithfulness in the night seasons" [Psalms 92:3].

The portion is called "And Jacob lived" because this lesson lives with us through all generations, to strengthen us in the time of troubles and servitude. "By thee shall Israel bless, saying: God make thee as Ephraim and as Manasseh" [Genesis 48:20]. This is the blessing for all future generations, which is alluded to in the names of Ephraim and Manasseh, as mentioned above.

From this we can understand what Jacob said, "The angel who hath redeemed me from all evil, bless the lads" [Genesis 48:16]. It would seem difficult for Jacob to say, "The angel who hath redeemed me from all evil." Who suffered as many troubles as Jacob? He testified about himself, "Few and evil have been the days of the years of my life" [Genesis 47:9] and "I was not at ease, neither was I quiet, neither had I rest" [Job 3:26] and "When I came from Paddan, Rachel died" [Genesis 48:7]. How could he say about himself, "The angel who hath redeemed me from all evil?" [Genesis 48:16]. The word *all* (*kal*) can also mean "completely whole." Jacob said [in effect], "Command our hearts to know that even when I was in very great trouble, I had faith and trust within me that the trouble would not be complete, heaven forbid. In the midst of my troubles I saw the light of God's word." This is "The angel who hath redeemed me from all evil" [Genesis 48:16]. "The angel" means faith in God's divine providence. The holy Ḥayim Ibn Attar, author of *Or Haḥayim*, also explained the term *angel* that way. The trust that the evil would not be complete [is what] redeemed [us] from all evil. Namely, the trust that we would not fall and not break under the heavy burden of misfortunes and severe suffering during a time of trouble. Rather, we would hope and pray to God that He would still save and redeem us. "Bless the lads" [Genesis 48:16] is the true blessing for future generations and a great source of strength for them.

Therefore, Jacob said to Joseph, "If now I have found favor in your sight...bury me not, I pray thee, in Egypt" [Genesis 47:29]. The meaning is, if the previously mentioned things found favor in your eyes. That is, if you truly accept your father's ethics, then you bequeath the attribute of faith and trust to your children after you, from generation to generation, from fathers to children, teaching them the ways of God that are hidden from us. "A brutish man knoweth not, neither doth a fool understand this" [Psalms 92:7]. But "The righteous shall flourish like the palm tree" [Psalms 92:13] in his faith "To declare that the Lord is upright, My Rock in whom there is no unrighteousness" [Psalms 92:16]. [The meaning of Jacob was], if you, Joseph, will fulfill this testament, then you will not bury me in Egypt and I will not remain here, heaven forbid, between the impure straits. Then when I lie down with my fathers, I will know clearly that through you I too will be established in the doctrine and holy tradition of the faith of our ancestors.

After Joseph promised Jacob, "I will do as thou hast said" [Genesis 47:30], that is, to fulfill the testament and teachings of his father, Jacob called all of his children to his bed and said, "Assemble yourselves and hear, ye sons of Jacob, and hearken to Israel your father" [Genesis 49:2]. Jacob wished to reveal the "end of days" to his sons, and when he did the *Shekhinah* (Divine Presence) departed from him. Said he, "Perhaps, Heaven forbid! There is one unfit among my children" [B. T. *Pesaḥim* 56a]. According to the midrash,

> When the patriarch Jacob was departing from the world, he called his twelve sons and said to them: "Is the God of Israel in heaven your Father? Maybe in your hearts ye wish to break away from the Holy One, blessed be He?" His sons replied, "'Hear O Israel the Lord is our God, the Lord is One' [Deuteronomy 6:4]. As there is no desire in thy heart to break away from God, so is there none in our hearts, but 'The Lord is our God, the Lord is One.'" He too [Jacob] thereupon made utterance with his lips, saying, "Glorious kingdom forever and ever." [*Midrash Bereshit Rabbah, Parashah* 98, *Siman* 3]

This is also a teaching for the future and for our own days, when we are living in "a time of trouble unto Jacob" [Jeremiah 30:7], heaven forbid, when many are posing problems and seeking to understand the ways of God which remain hidden from us. There is also, heaven forbid, controversy over the Holy One Blessed be He. There was strength in our patriarch Jacob's complete faith in the unique unity of His blessed name. "The Lord is our God, the Lord is One." The interpreters explain that beyond *Adonai*'s attribute of mercy and *Elohim*'s attribute of judgment, all is of one God of absolute mercy. We will see God's salvation before our eyes.

Woe is me if I speak! Woe is me if I do not speak! The time for words of rebuke is not when there is "trouble for Jacob" [Jeremiah 30:7]. The afflictions certainly purge the sins of man [B. T. *Berakhot* 5ª]. Still, perhaps it is our obligation to awaken ourselves about the contemporary events, about the evil decrees that are repeated every day [and to recognize that] "Unto thee, O Lord, belongeth righteousness but unto us confusion of face" [Daniel 9:7]. Many of the evil decrees which we see with our senses are measure for measure [in character]. The *Haftarah* [prophetic portion] of this week describes the testament of King David to his son Solomon. It deals with how Solomon should behave with Joab ben Zeruiah, repaying him according to his acts [1

Kings]. The same with Shimei ben Gera. "Shimei the son of Gera . . . cursed me with a grievous curse in the day when I went to Maḥanaim" [1 Kings 2:8]. "Now therefore hold him not guiltless, for thou art a wise man" [1 Kings 2:9]. "But show kindness unto the sons of Barzilai the Gileadite, and let them be of those that eat at your table; for so they drew nigh unto me when I fled from Absalom thy brother" [1 Kings 2:7]. God "recompenses men with kindness according to his deed; He places evil on the wicked according to his wickedness" [*Yigdal Elohim Ḥai* hymn].

An evil decree was issued, according to which we are permitted to take no more than one hundred and fifty crowns a week of our money from the bank. This is not enough even for meager bread and water. Because of our many sins, how miserly we have been in giving charity, heaven forbid, from the money we had in the bank. It was "capital," not to be touched when it came to a religious command. How miserly we were when it came to paying the wages of those who worked for us. Their salary was minimal while the householders had much. On the beginning of the Christian new year, called *Neu Jahr*, they forbade us to leave our houses. Because of our many sins, during peaceful times we also celebrated and rejoiced according to the calendar of the nations. What did we have to do with their impure holidays? Israel, do not rejoice in the New Year like the nations! "For I the Lord am holy, and have set you apart from the peoples, that ye should be Mine" [Leviticus 20:26]. We have, thank God, the holy festival of *Rosh Hashanah* [New Year]. There are thousands of contrasts to be made. Everything good for them is bad and abominable to us. Their schools are forbidden to us, they closed the doors of their universities to us. This was measure-for-measure [retaliation] toward us. How much have our written and oral Torah and all the moralistic books warned us to distance ourselves from their apocryphal wisdom, which is full of heresy and atheism? They forbade us to have a radio in the house. What do we have to do with [the nations'] entertainment and evil desires? With their instruments of destruction, which destroy and confuse the hearts and minds of the holy children of Israel, pure boys and girls, making their hearts and minds impure with obscene language and mockery, heaven forbid? Our holy Torah has warned us, "And that ye go not about your own heart and your own eyes, after which ye used to go astray" [Numbers 15:39]. They forbade us to visit their theaters. What need do we, the holy seed and the children of the living God, have of these houses of prostitution? We need to get beyond bowshot distance from the stinking dead animal, from these houses which provoke and arouse all evils. They are the exact opposite to the knowledge of our holy and pure Torah, and to the will of God who created us for His glory to serve Him with a pure heart and with joy for His holy Torah and commandments.

They have taken away our livelihoods. All Jewish stores have been closed or given over to gentile owners. We work for them. They have forbidden us from having gentile servants in our homes. Who knows how much we have sinned toward His Blessed Name, by having gentile servants who supervised the cooking and the food in the house? They ordered us to wear *gele Tsaykhen* (yellow insignia) [to announce] that we are Jews. Because of our many sins, how ashamed we were of our Jewish garments and names, of our fringes and of the *mezuzah* on our doorposts, when it was our obligation to have everyone who saw us recognize that we were the seed of the blessed God, when it was our obligation not to transgress, heaven forbid, the strict sin of shaving the beard with a razor! Out of shame before the gentiles, we did not want to be recognized at all by the sidelocks of the head. Now, as over-against this, the evil ones have decreed that everyone should recognize that we are Jews. Therefore they have decreed that each of our shops display a prominent sign indicating that it is a Jewish shop.

We have no income, not even enough for a loaf of bread. Because of our many sins, how much we have spent on evil luxuries and worthless pleasures! They have forbidden ritual slaughter. Because of our many sins, how much did we trespass with forbidden foods! In peaceful times we were obsessed about our apartments. We were afraid to bring poor people into our homes, lest they dirty the carpets on the floor. A decree went out to hand over to the authorities all the valuable objects in the house. Whoever had a fur garment had to turn it over to the authorities. [Why?] Because in peaceful times we kept everything. We did not share with the needy who came and asked for our help. [For my

part], I will ask the good God that He forgive me. It is not my intention, heaven forbid, to awaken accusations against the holy Jewish people. The worst among us is a thousand times better than the best among the gentiles. However, perhaps through the reflections of penitent return, it will arise in the will of the Blessed Name to lighten our burden. Perhaps His mercy and unconditional *hesed* (lovingkindness) for us will be aroused. As we say in the *Selihot* (penitential prayer), "Turn to the hardships and not the sins. From this day forward each one of us will improve his ways. Just let God have mercy on us" [see *Peneh na* in *Selihot*].

Of the things that happened this week, the worst and most horrific decree of all, heaven forbid, was the terrible fire in the old age home. Old men and women, sick and feeble, fled for their lives into the cold, without clothes, in fear and confusion. This terrible evil decree and trouble befell us, in my opinion, because of [the message of this metaphor:] There was this wicked person. His elderly father, a widower, was living in his house. In a moment of anger, the arrogant son grabbed his father and threw him from [near] a table in the outer room and out the door into the street. When the old man reached the door, he grabbed the doorposts. He would not let his son throw him into the street. He said to his son,

> Until now I let you do this evil. I let you throw me from the table and the room because I remember that many years ago I did the same to my father. I was an evil person like you. However, I did not throw my father out into the street, only to the door. I let you throw me to the door. It was only just that what I did should be done to me, measure for measure. But no more.

Lord of the universe, we have sinned greatly and have been evil. All justice is with You, and there is no injustice to the just and righteous. It is measure for measure. However, have we sinned so much before You, that [You] judge old men and women to flames and to panic? Lord of the Universe, heaven forbid that we should question Your attributes and the justice of Your judgments. But please be merciful as a father to his children. Have mercy on us, out of Your great mercy and out of Your love of the world and the great love with which You loved us. Because of our lack of understanding we do not have the strength and perception to reciprocate to You as would be appropriate for us. Please do not turn us away from You empty-handed.

In the blessing of Judah [see Genesis 49: 8–12], the [Hebrew] letter *Zayin* is missing, although it contains the Holy Name. This is a hint to us that we do not need to fear any weapons (*klei zayin*), "Some trust in chariots, and some in horses. But we will make mention of the name of the Lord our God" [Psalms 20:8]. Only our trust in God will "gather us together and deliver us from the nations, that we may give thanks unto Thy holy name" [1 Chronicles 16:35]. [The name] Judah [spelled in Hebrew *Yod*, *Hay*, *Vav*, *Dalet*, *Hay*] contains within it the holy Tetragrammaton, Blessed be He, and the letter *Dalet* within it. It indicates that even in a time of our poverty (*daluteinu*) and degradation, God will save us out of His mercy for us.

We will conclude with a prayer of the poor person to God. I ask You, God, to protect us always—enlighten my eyes lest death overtake me. There is a parable attributed to the Magid [Preacher] of Dubno, of blessed memory. A father left behind a lone daughter. He left all of his belongings to her in the care of a guardian, with the provision that the guardian give her a third of the money, but only when she became married. He did so. At one point the daughter contracted a terrible illness, heaven forbid. Her relatives and friends came to the guardian so he would provide the money for remedies to save her from death. He insisted that he should not give the money until she married. They said to him, "Who are you going to bring under the marriage canopy if you do not heal her first?" Similarly, we believe with complete faith that all the afflictions are for our good. We believe all the words of the true prophets, that the time of our redemption and

salvation of our souls will come, and that the community of Israel will enter under the bridal canopy with God. We will have eternal joy. But we pray until then,

Protect us always God, enlighten our eyes lest death overtake us. Redeem and save us whenever there is someone to save, so that our enemies should not overcome us, heaven forbid, to destroy us. Save us, our Lord and Savior, for Your name. In our days, and even more so until Shiloh comes, "And unto him shall obedience of the peoples be" [Genesis 49:10]. That is, the coming of the just redeemer speedily in our days, amen.

Rashi asks, Why is this Torah portion closed [and without the usual space between it and the preceding section]? This can be explained by an allegory. When the world proceeds for ordinary people in a way that all their time is of power and strength, and the sun of success shines on them, they make the insignificant into the important. They forget their true purpose in this world, which is to complete themselves through Torah and the commandments and to prepare themselves in this vestibule [to the world to come]. Only in their old age, when their strength wanes and the day of death approaches, if they are worthy they regret their sins and begin another chapter in their lives, where they awaken to penitent return. The God who acts mercifully accepts them. However, this is not the true path. The path of the righteous and upright of heart makes no distinction between ages. From their youth, they are ready to serve and worship God. Happy is their youth that does not embarrass their old age. Therefore, in this Torah portion concerning the death of Jacob our patriarch, may peace be upon him, the end of his life in this world is undefined vis-à-vis the previous Torah portions [about his life]. Because there is no difference between the portions. They are equally good.

Torah Portion *Va'era* [Exodus 6:1–9:35] [Prepared 8 January for 9 January 1943 Delivery]

An awakening to faith and trust in a time of terrible trouble and war. May God have mercy.

"And God spoke unto Moses, and said unto him: I am the Lord; and I appeared unto Abraham, unto Isaac, and unto Jacob, as God Almighty, but

by My name YHWH I made Me not known to them" [Exodus 6:2–3]. For Rashi, "He spoke with Moses sternly, because Moses was severe in speaking and saying, 'Wherefore has Thou dealt ill with this people?'" [Exodus 5:22].

Our times provide explanation about the plea of Moses our teacher, of blessed memory, concerning his mission to redeem Israel. As a faithful shepherd, when Moses first saw the burning bush he pleaded, "Who am I, that I should go unto Pharaoh, and that I should bring forth the children of Israel out of Egypt?" [Exodus 3:11]. All of the commentaries, in their own ways, tried to find the reason why Moses [sought to] decline this mission at a time of trouble and servitude in Egypt. His heart was burning with his love for Israel. He saw their affliction and sacrificed himself in killing the Egyptian to save one Jewish soul. Now when the redemption of Israel depended upon him, he [sought to] refuse the mission?

Moses our teacher, of blessed memory, pled in two ways. [First], if this is now the time of the complete redemption and the redemption of the world, it is not possible that it would take place through the mission of a human being. Only God Himself [could] redeem. [Second], as Scripture says, "O Israel, that art saved by the Lord with an everlasting salvation" [Isaiah 45:17]. Only if there is salvation through God Himself will there be salvation everlasting.

"Who am I?" [Exodus 3:11] means, "You promised Jacob our father, of blessed memory, when he went down to the exile of Egypt, 'I will bring you up." Where is the "I"? Everlasting redemption is impossible, except through God Himself. If, heaven forbid, the time for complete redemption does not arrive, Moses argued, the Israelites will complain out of impatience and lack of knowledge. "And that I should bring forth the children of Israel out of Egypt?" [Exodus 3:11] means, "Of what [value] will it be for them to be brought forth from here? Let them remain in Egypt, only redeemed from servitude and hard labor. Should everything return to what it was in the past, a time of peace, why should they leave? Let Pharaoh and the evildoers leave and have us stay here." This resembles what we hear today, when people pray for a return to the years of normalcy.

However, God responded to him, "I will be what I will be" [Exodus 3:14]. That is, "This is not yet the final exile, nor the eternal redemption. [At this point] I need a messenger for this: 'When thou hast brought forth the people out of Egypt, ye shall serve God upon this mountain'" [Exodus 3:12]. The purpose of the exodus from Egypt was to receive the Torah. The exodus was

to purify the Israelites and bring them to the worship of God through receiving the Torah and commandments. That is why they needed to leave that impure place. What benefit would there be in remaining in Egypt, even if the Israelites were to be freed from their troubles? They would then return to idol worship, to impurity and base urges. This was no salvation for them. To the contrary, they would lose their eternal souls. They were a holy seed, the children of the living God, descendants of Abraham, Isaac, and Jacob. "I" wanted to raise them to a high level of holiness and purity. They needed to leave the foulness of the shell of Egypt so they could be brought to Mount Sinai, the place chosen for receiving the Torah for true and eternal life.

After Moses received his mission from God he went to Pharaoh. Scripture says, "And the people believed" [Exodus 4:31]. They all [let themselves] think that with the first meeting of Moses and Aaron with Pharaoh, their salvation and redemption would come immediately. This was because it was already difficult for them to endure the poverty and troubles. They wanted to see their salvation immediately. In fact, they saw the opposite. After Moses spoke to Pharaoh in the name of God, the work burden for the [already] harshly enslaved people increased beyond what it was previously. The evil [slave masters] complained: "Ye are idle, ye are idle" [Exodus 5:17]. "You are lazy. And your falsehoods will not save you."

In our day we can well imagine what the result of a mission like this was, a mission to people who were wounded and sick from the burden of work and troubles. They complained, "Ye [Moses and Aaron] have made our scent to be abhorred in the eyes of Pharaoh" [Exodus 5:21]. "Why did the salvation not come immediately? We have no more patience. We want salvation now. We see the opposite: renewed harsh decrees, the new ones worse than the original ones." Moses, the faithful shepherd, returned the people's words to God, "Wherefore hast thou dealt ill with this people?" [Exodus 5:22]. The Holy One responded, "I am the Lord; and I appeared unto Abraham, unto Isaac, and unto Jacob, as God Almighty" [Exodus 6:2–3]. "My thoughts are not your thoughts" [Isaiah 55:8]. "It is impossible for a human to understand the ways of God, 'For man shall not see Me and live'" [Exodus 33:20]. His Blessed Name knows literally the hour and minute of the salvation. As is written in the story of Genesis, "On the seventh day God finished the work" [Genesis 2:2]. Ten things were created even during twilight. Because His Blessed Name knows the moment when the seventh day, the holy *Shabbat*, began.

Therefore, in all actions of His Blessed Name, whether universal or particular, everything is precisely calculated. He created His world with boundaries. He said to His world, "Enough." He said to the sea, "You come until here." It is similar with all the lights of the firmament. It is similar even, heaven forbid, with evil decrees. Everything has its time and hour, its specific day, and specific hour and minute. Contrary to what you think and say, nothing is accelerated. There is an intended calculation for everything. Therefore, God said to Moses, "I appeared unto Abraham, unto Isaac, and unto Jacob as God Almighty" [Exodus 6:2], meaning, if you study and contemplate the story of the patriarchs you will see the boundaries and the precise times of God's just calculation.

With regard to Abraham our patriarch, God saved him from Ur Kasdim, from the hand of the evil Nimrod. But he did so at the very last moment, when Abraham [according to the midrash] was being thrown into the burning oven. Abraham could have complained about this, "I know that my salvation is near. Why did I have to wait in fear and dread and until I was thrown into the burning oven? [Why did salvation] not come earlier?" But Abraham our patriarch went on to be righteous in faith and innocence, and You found his heart to be true before You. He did not question the ways of God. This is because he knew the aspect of the Almighty, who said to His world, "Enough," at the exact moment He intended to be a time of favor.

It was similar with our patriarch Isaac, of blessed memory, when he went for the *Akedah*.

Throughout the three-day journey, and even as he was already lying on the altar of God, it was not made known to him that he would be saved. Nothing intervened at all, not until the very last second when his throat was outstretched. Abraham reached for the knife to slaughter him. Then the decree came from Heaven, "Lay not thy hand upon the lad" [Genesis 22:12]. In their holy and pure faith, father and son did not question the ways of God. In their going and in their returning, they were like raw material in the hands of the creator of all the worlds. The creator told His world, "Enough" at the hour and moment He desired, may His name be blessed.

Similarly with Jacob our father, of blessed memory. After all his trials—the last, when he lost his beloved son Joseph, being the worst—it was still not enough. Simeon was taken away from him. This was not enough. He was forced against his will to send Benjamin [away], adding agony to his agony and to his pain. What did Jacob say when he parted from Benjamin and his other sons, filled with great pain and anguish? "And God Almighty give you mercy before the man" [Genesis 43:14]. He believed with complete faith in the attribute of *El Shaddai* [a God of mercy]. He believed that there was a time and hour for everything, and that was when it arose in the divine will, may His name be blessed. Jacob did not despair or complain.

This is the greatness of the merit of our holy ancestors. They bequeathed to us as an inheritance for all generations until the present day, not to fall into despair, heaven forbid. Certainly, God in His mercy will save us. He will benefit us in the end with true and eternal life, in a complete redemption through our righteous Messiah, speedily in our days, amen.

[TORAH PORTION] *Re'eh* [DEUTERONOMY 11:26–16:17] [PREPARED 27 AUGUST FOR 28 AUGUST 1943 DELIVERY]

"Behold, I set before you this day a blessing and a curse: The blessing, if ye shall hearken unto the commandments of the Lord your God, which I command you this day; and the curse, if ye shall not hearken unto the commandments of the Lord your God" [Deuteronomy 11:26–27]. The holy Torah speaks in the language of seeing. That is, it is within one's power to see blessing if one obeys, and to see curse if one does not obey. But there seems to be difficulty. Does not human freedom of choice [take place] without a person's seeing the blessing and curse with the senses? [For example], sometimes the righteous have troubles and the evil do well.

Our current trials provide explanation of the matter to us. When there is a pouring out of wrath, heaven forbid; when God's wrath goes forth, heaven forbid, and we eat stalks and grains; when the righteous and evil are condemned together and we all have one fate, we do see a great difference with our senses. We see instances every day of evil ones, who did not know God and were estranged from faith and trust, committing suicide, heaven forbid. They have nothing to rely upon. They abandon hope and possibility, having lost everything and having lost their love of life. Not so with the righteous, who fulfill God's commandments and trust in God with all their heart and soul. They do not get depressed. They strengthen themselves through every attribute that He extends to them. They put themselves under the protection of the Blessed Creator in every respect, to the point that they are prepared to sacrifice their body and soul should that be His will. They have no true anguish, because they have faith about what is prepared for them in the world to come. This is the true blessing.

We find in our tradition that "Happy is everyone that feareth the Lord. That walketh in His ways" [Psalms 128:1]. Happy is the God fearer who desires His commandments, since "Behold, surely thus shall the man be blessed that feareth the Lord" [Psalms 128:4]. Happy are the righteous who fear God all the time. They walk in His paths and desire His commandments, since the person who fears God will be blessed. This is the blessing [received by the one] who fears God and cleaves to God's commandments, who does not turn to arrogance and false foolishness and all the world's vanities. To such a person, they are all vanity and falseness. He considers them transitory, vain, and empty, as insignificant as the dust of the earth. The purpose of the human being in the world is to cleave to God with all his heart and soul, and that is the only blessing for him. All his possessions have no value and all worldly transactions are insignificant to him.

"Ye are the children of the Lord your God" [Deuteronomy 14:1]. We know about the extra fondness because we are children to God and He is our father. Similarly, a discerning son loves his father all the time, even if the father chastises him with a rod. Because he knows that a father does not hate a son. He loves him always and only wants what is good for him. We find in the Talmud, "It is as clear to thee as the sun that it is not a matter of life or death; it would be a matter of a father [who has compassion for] his son" [B. T. *Sanhedrin* 72[a,b]]. Clearly, a father does not wish to harm his son. This should indicate to us that with everything that happens to us, all is of His goodness toward us. We also need to conduct ourselves like children toward Him and not question His ways, heaven forbid. For justice is with Him. "Righteous art Thou, O Lord, and upright are Thy judgments" [Psalms 119:137]. "How be it Thou art just in all that is come upon us" [Nehemiah 9:33]. In turn, this will awaken the mercies of our Father toward us to save us publicly. Then all the nations of the world will see that all of us [children of Israel] have one Father and that we are under heavenly providence.

This is like the story of a king during a war. He wanted to test his servants to see if they trusted in him, loved him, and were tied to him with bonds of love. He came to a certain large city. The king's army was stationed there and they went out to greet him with great joy, with drums and dances. The king was very happy with this, because he saw that they attended to his words. But one wise minister told him that this was no proof. The army lacked for nothing from the king's house and they ate off the bounty of the land. Why should they not love him? Go to the battlefield, [he continued], and look at the beaten and the ill, who were wounded and sickened by the war, rolling in blood and terrible misfortune, heaven forbid. All this because they were fighting for you. You will see what they will say about you, and whether they are happy with you and accept everything gracefully. If so, this would be a sign of true love for you and of the readiness to sacrifice life for you.

The meaning is obvious. In times of peace and quiet, plenty and pleasantness, it is easy for a person to say that he loves God. Things are good for him and all the desires of [the] heart are given to him. But now we are at a time when we are in trouble. We have been given over to killing and derision among the nations, to punishment and shame. The nations whip and exile us, etc. Now we are required to show extra love for God, lest we be called complainers, heaven forbid. Rather, we should accept God's decrees with love. With this we show our love, like a son for the father. Therefore, the rabbinic Sages said that the Blessed One did not find a better attribute for Israel than poverty [B. T. *Hagigah* 9ᵇ]. For then one saw the good attributes of Israel, as believers who were children of believers. As we find in the *Tanhuma*, "Thine eyes are as doves" [Song of Songs 4:1]. . . . Through this God will have mercy on us like a father has mercy on his child [*Tanhuma*, (ed. Warsaw), *Tetsaveh*, *Perek* 5].

"At midnight I will rise to give thanks unto Thee because of Thy righteous ordinances" [Psalms 119:62]. The Talmud says, "Rabbi Aha bar Bizana said in the name of R. Simeon Hasida, 'A harp was hanging over David's bed. When midnight came a northern wind stirred it and it played by itself. He immediately arose and occupied himself with Torah until dawn'" [B. T. *Berakhot* 3ᵇ]. David, king of Israel, anointed of God, endured a series of persecutions from youth on. From within and without, he was persecuted. Others conspired to kill him. However, with his great trust in God he strengthened himself whenever there was trouble and he did not despair. On the contrary, he was always happy. "A psalm of David when he fled from Absalom his son" [Psalms 3:1]. "Thy statutes have been my songs in the house of my pilgrimage" [Psalms 119:54]. As a result of this, in the end all of his enemies were disgraced while David, king of Israel, lives forever. This is the meaning of the talmudic passage: "When midnight came" alludes to the darkness of the troubles and misfortunes. "A northern wind stirred it" alludes to the spirit of God calling to David, "You are of the children of the Lord our God, completely trusting that everything will be for your good, magnifying His name and raising the horn of His messiah." The harp played by itself, meaning that it was impossible for sadness to enter David's heart and that he was always happy. David always cleaved to God and His commandments. He occupied himself with Torah until dawn, then the sun shone on him, its light broke through and he went from darkness to a great light. This is the true blessing "Which I command you this day" [Deuteronomy 11:27]. The essence of this is to listen and hearken to the words of our holy

Torah and the words of rebuke for the people. The little portion upon which the whole Torah depends is "Hear O Israel" [Deuteronomy 6:4]. If the people listen to and understand what God asks, it will go well for the nation and it will be blessed. In the Talmud, Raba said, "If he made the other deaf, he must pay for the value of the whole of him" [B. T. *Baba Kamma* 85ᵇ]. For whoever does not listen is lost completely and has no hope. It is a curse not to listen.

This is the moral of "Behold, I set before you this day a blessing and a curse" [Deuteronomy 11:26]. Four years ago, on this [very] holy Sabbath, *Parashat Re'eh*, in the year 1939, the troubles began in our community. They publicly destroyed the great synagogue here and destroyed and desecrated holy books and Torah scrolls. From then until now, because of our many sins, we have had no peace or respite from trouble after trouble, decree after decree, heaven forbid, one order rushing after the other. May God have mercy. Therefore, the verse reads, "Behold, I set before you this day a blessing and a curse" [Deuteronomy 11:26]. That is, "Do not forget that He resides in heaven, sees everything, and that in the end of time He will repay those who lit the conflagration, measure for measure." "The wicked is snared in the work of his own hands" [Psalms 9:17]. Do not despair, heaven forbid, "For My salvation is near to come, and My favor to be revealed" [Isaiah 56:1]. The *Haftarah* [prophetic portion of the week] states, "O thou afflicted, tossed with tempest, and not comforted" [Isaiah 54:11]. That is, we have no comfort around us. Our poverty thrashes about like a stormy sea. So many troubles, evil acts, and fears. However, [God speaks:] "Here I am, do not forget Me, I am He, I am the Lord. I have not changed and you are the children of Jacob. You are not finished." Especially not in the days of mercy and forgiveness, the days of *Ellul* [the month of the New Year holiday and the Day of Atonement], when we will be strengthened through prayer and supplication before God. "And bring your youngest brother unto Me, so shall your words be verified, and ye shall not die" [Genesis 42:20]. This alludes to the month of *Ellul*, which is the youngest month and the last month in the year. May *El Shaddai* give you mercy. May we be worthy of the complete redemption, speedily in our days, amen.

Shlomoh Zalman Ehrenreich

Shlomoh Zalman Ehrenreich (1863–1944) was educated by his maternal grandfather, the Kol Aryeh (Avraham Yehudah Hakohen Schwartz), a student of the hasidic dynasty founder Mosheh Teitelbaum (Ujkeli, Hungary). He served first as rabbi in Ceaba, Romania, and then for nearly a half century in Simleul-Silvaniei, Romania. Persecution of the Jews of Simleul-Silvaniei began with Hungarian control in 1940. It culminated in early May 1944, when the town's Jews were collected outside Ehrenreich's synagogue and then force-marched five kilometers to the Cehu-Silvaniei ghetto. In the ghetto, when he was caught praying, Ehrenreich was strung up on a tree until he became unconscious; his beard and *Peot* (side curls) were cut off; and the manuscript of his extensive interpretation of *Pirkei Avot* (*The Ethics of the Fathers*) was burned in front of him. At the end of May 1944, he was transported to Auschwitz. He was murdered upon arrival along with eighty percent of the ghetto's Jews, who were too debilitated to be taken for forced labor. According to the former rabbi of nearby Cluj, Mosheh Carmilly-Weinberger, the rest of Ehrenreich's manuscripts were preserved by a local gentile family.

Ehrenreich initially interpreted the suffering as a matter of God's using the nations to force Jews away from assimilation and Zionism. God then destroyed the nations, and this elicited sanctification of His name in the world. But Ehrenreich realized that he could not comprehend why the pious suffered, and in the tradition of Aaron (Leviticus 10:3) he became silent. The explanation still existed, he believed, but it could be expressed only with redemption. He stressed that in the meantime, piety had to fill the Jew's life. Torah study could reduce suffering, to the extent that it precipitated the in-gathering of exiles; while penitent return (*teshuvah*) could elicit divine compassion. Self-sacrifice and the risk of life brought Torah study and *teshuvah* to their most intense level.

SELECTIONS

In *Mah Shedarashti Beyom Alef Parashat Tetsaveh 7 Adar 5699* ("What I Preached on Sunday [of the Week of] the Torah Portion *Tetsaveh* [Exodus 27:20–30:10], 26 February 1939," in *Derashot Lehem Shelomoh*, Brooklyn, 1976, pp. 283–285), Ehrenreich explained that since the torture of Grosswardein's (Oradea's) Jews was of nonhuman character, a human enemy alone could not be responsible. He traced the torture to the fact that German and Austrian Jews had stopped the voice of Torah. God, he averred, responded by transferring His indignation over to Esau's cruel hand—whereupon Esau acted at will. At the same time, Ehrenreich stressed, man should not reflect upon God's judgment—which could and would be clarified only with the Messiah. In *Mah She'amarti Besimhat Torah Shenat 5703* ("What I Preached on [the Festival of] Simhat Torah, 4 October 1942," in *Derashot*, pp. 149–151), he stated that divine administration over history indicated the existence of an ultimately positive outcome to the nations' assaults. The nations would be destroyed by God. Then, His name would be sanctified in the world because He destroyed the enemy of His people. For a nation to serve as God's instrument and be destroyed in a process which served sanctity, it must have manifested at least some spark of goodness. In *Mah Shedarashti Beshabbat Hagadol Shenat 5703* ("What I Preached on the Great *Shabbat* [preceding Passover], 17 April 1943"; *Derashot*, pp. 212–216), Ehrenreich explained that silence toward the present historical suffering would be filled by the wisdom to come with redemption. Selections have been translated from the Hebrew by Gershon Greenberg.

What I Preached on Sunday [of the Week of] the Torah Portion *Tetsaveh*, 26 February 1939

On a Day When a Communal Fast Was Declared Because of Israel's Troubles

Gentlemen, today is the seventh of *Adar*, the anniversary of the death of Moses our teacher, of blessed memory. We have gathered in the synagogue to pray and to recite Psalms, because the troubles of Israel have increased greatly. A communal fast day has been declared today for the whole country. It is elucidated in the holy books concerning the words of King David, of blessed memory, in Psalms 106:2, "Who can express the mighty acts of the Lord, or make all His praise to be heard?" that whoever wants to annul and abrogate the evil decrees or crush and smash them so that they do no damage should "make all His praise to be heard." That is, recite the whole book of Psalms and thereby destroy the evil decrees.—We also remember the rabbis and sages who died since the last seventh of Adar: Rabbi Menaḥem Brody, of blessed memory, rabbi of Kalov (Nagykallo); Rabbi Naftali Teitelbaum, of blessed memory, of Nyirbator; Rabbi Benyamin Ze'ev of Monostor; Rabbi Benyamin Shenfeld, *Av Beit Din* [head of the religious court] of Mihaifalav (Ermihalyfalva) [all of Hungary]. I had loving friendships with them. We should shed tears for them and cry ceaselessly for this group of holy sages who have left us to our wretched plight.

The rabbinic Sages said that when a scholar dies, he has no replacement [*Midrash Bereshit Rabbah, Parashah 91, Siman 11*]. We need to clarify. When it says "He has no," should it not say, "We have no" substitute? We should explain this according to what our teacher, the Ḥatam Sofer [Mosheh Schreiber], may his merit protect us, explained in his introduction to [the talmudic] tractate *Ḥullin*. We [Jews] follow the rule that the day follows the night. For the nations of the world, the night follows the day. But when it comes to sacrifices, we follow the rule that the night follows the day, as do the nations of the world. This should be explained. It seems that for us, this world is called night. What is essential is the world to come. One hour of contentment in the world to come is more pleasant than all of life of this world. Therefore the rule is that the night is first and the day follows. However, among the nations of the world this world is primary. As long as they live in this world, this world is day for them and the world to come is night for them. For the nations, the day precedes the night. Now when it comes to sacrifice, the important thing for the rabbinic Sages is to serve God. This is not so in the world to come, where the dead are free of the commandments. In this respect the primary category becomes this world. For one hour of repentance and good deeds in this world is better than all the life in the world to come. If so, this world is the day and the world to come belongs to the category of night and is secondary. Accordingly, when it comes to sacrifices the night follows the day. Up to here, the holy words of the Ḥatam Sofer.

I have discussed this at length elsewhere.—As such, the primary aspect of the life of the sage is to occupy himself with the Torah, to investigate, innovate, argue, and enjoy Torah in this world. This world is more precious in his eyes than the world to come. Even though the sage would enjoy the spiritual pleasures in the world to come, the pleasure of repentance and good deeds [here] are more important to him than all the life in the world to come. When he dies and enjoys the pleasures of the world to come, they are no substitute. This is because the pleasure of his worship in this world is more precious to him. Let this be understood.—As such, how much is there to mourn over the loss of the great sages who were taken from us?

But at this time the words of Jeremiah the prophet are being fulfilled, "Weep ye not for the dead, neither bemoan him; but weep sore for him that goeth away, for he shall return no more, nor see his native country" [Jeremiah 22:10]. So it is at this time. Thousands of Jews have been expelled from Germany and Austria. Everything has been taken from them and they suffer immeasurable troubles. They have nowhere to turn. They are not allowed to enter the Land of Israel or America. They are betwixt heaven and earth. There is more to mourn over this than over the loss of pious ones who have gone to their eternal rest. Thousands of Jews are sighing. They have been expelled from their homeland and their home to become wanderers. The Holy One will not do anything unjust. It is forbidden for us to question the Holy One, heaven forbid. As the tribes [i.e., Joseph's brothers] said, "We are verily guilty concerning our brother, in that we saw the distress of his soul, when he besought us, and would not hear; therefore is this distress come upon us" [Genesis 42:21]. They did not pin it on accident, but said [the distress] was of the hand of God. We can only do penitent return (*teshuvah*). Every person should become embittered in his heart and say, "Woe, what have I done? I have sinned, I have transgressed, I have done wrong, I have not behaved as a Jew. I wanted to be Mr. Herrschaft. That is why these troubles have come upon us. It was [the resultant] jealousy toward us which caused it." [Yitshak] Abravanel writes that this is what caused the exile from Spain and Portugal. Every person should say, "I will go and repent" [source uncertain]. The purpose of the troubles is that we do penitent return.

In the Torah portion *Shemot* it is written, "And the children of Israel sighed by reason of the bondage, and they cried, and their cry came up unto God by reason of the bondage. And God heard their groaning, and God remembered His covenant with Abraham, with Isaac, and with Jacob. And God saw the children of Israel, and God took cognizance of them" [Exodus 2:23–25]. Rashi comments: "He paid attention to them and did not avert His eyes." Indeed, it says in *Targum Yonatan* that God saw the penitent return that they had done secretly, where a person did not know about his friend. This is the meaning of "And God took cognizance." Only God knew [of the penitent return], not the people. In my humble opinion, one could say that this is alluded to again in the words of the verse. It is noteworthy that first it says, "their cry" and later it says, "their groaning." In my humble opinion, we can say that "their cry" means that they cried out from their physical troubles. "Their groaning" refers to the turmoil in their hearts. They said in their hearts, "Woe, what I have done, I have sinned, I have transgressed, and I have done wrong, for I did not live my life like my ancestors and the tribes." This was in every heart secretly. No one knew about his friend. This is the meaning of, "God heard their groaning."

At this time there are unheard-of troubles for Israel. The people who passed in a transport through Grosswardein (Oradea) had swastikas [branded into] their faces and their flesh. Some had no fingers; the evil ones bit them off. There were those whose fingernails were torn out and other such things. Things which wild animals do. Some think this is an accident. In Germany the people are educated. How could such cruelty be found among people? Expelling people and taking their wealth to the last penny? With such great troubles? [No.] It is the hand of God, on account of the greatness of the sins that were done in Germany. [The Jews in Germany] assimilated among the gentiles. For several generations they married non-Jewish wives. A certain rabbi expelled from Germany was told that God was right in His judgment against them. The rabbi told about hundreds of divorce decrees which he wrote for people who came from Russia and Poland to live in Germany. They sent the divorce decrees to their wives and they all married gentile women. Similarly, in Vienna there was no end to the sins committed by Jewish daughters who came from Poland, including daughters and granddaughters of rabbis and ḥasidic *Rebbes*. They sat in their houses on the third floor while their daughters, wives, and granddaughters went to the theater, and on and on.

There were still Jews in Vienna who were pious and God fearing, but as the rabbinic Sages said in B. T. *Baba Kamma* 92ª, "They are also taken out to be punished." It says in the Torah portion *Beshallaḥ* [Exodus 13:17–17:16] that there were evildoers who went out to collect manna on the Sabbath, and God said to Moses, "How long refuse ye to keep My commandments and My laws [Torah]?" [Exodus 16:28]. It is difficult to understand why He would punish the innocent. But one cannot question this. It is God's judgment. When God will help us and redeem us, we will understand all this. In the meantime, heaven forbid that we should open our mouths to speak evil or to question Him. We should repent as our ancestors did in Egypt. Most certainly the Holy One will save us and the salvation will be very soon. But everything depends on the gravity of our transgressions. Moreover, the sins and iniquities should pain us more than the troubles.

We find in the midrash for the Torah portion *Toldot* [Genesis 25:19–28:9], that Isaac our patriarch says, "The voice is the voice of Jacob, but the hands are the hands of Esau" [Genesis 27:22]. Eunomos of Gedera was a great sage among the nations of the world. The people of the nations came and asked him if they could mate with Israel, heaven forbid, in order to cause Israel evil and troubles. He said to them:

Go and look at the synagogues and study houses. If the children are raising their voices [studying Torah] then you can do nothing against them. If not, then you can prevail against them. For their patriarch assured them saying, "The voice is the voice of Jacob. As long as the voice of Jacob is in the synagogue and study house, the hands of Esau will not prevail." [*Midrash Bereshit Rabbah, Parashah* 65, *Siman* 20]

We need to understand how the rabbinic Sages derived their understanding of the verse. It seems

that the word *kol* (voice) is written [the] first time without the *vav* and the second time with the *vav*. This is the point that they emphasized in the midrash. In my humble opinion, it may be said that our holy Torah is divided into two parts, the written Torah and the oral Torah. The written Torah is the Five Books of the Torah. The oral Torah consists of the six orders of the *Mishnah*. The first *kol* is written without a *vav*, as *hay* (5) *kol*, indicating the written Torah. The second is written with a *vav* (6), indicating the oral Torah [*vav* being the sixth letter]. That is, when the voice is the voice of Jacob and the written Torah and the oral Torah are being studied, the hands of Esau have no power over us. This is excellent, blessed be God.

As over against this we need to understand the statement, "But the hands are the hands of Esau" [Genesis 27:22]. Does it mean, heaven forbid, the contrary? [Ephraim Misudylkow], the author of the holy book *Degel Maḥaneh Ephraim*, has already discussed this. However, in my humble opinion, we need to see what is written in Isaiah 10:5, "O Asshur, the rod of Mine anger. In whose hand as a staff is My fury." Rashi writes, "I have made Assyria the rod of My anger to subdue My people with it and the staff is My anger in the hands of the Assyrians." David Ahtschuler, the author of *Metsudat David*, comments that the anger present when God is angry over Israel, is [materialized] in the hands of the Assyrians as the staff. Through it, God punishes Israel according to His will. If so, when the nations of the world rise up against us, it is the staff of the Holy One that is rising up. It is not their [own] hands. From their hands we have nothing to fear. As King David said in Psalms 119:161, "Princes have persecuted me without cause. But my heart standeth in awe of Thy words." Holy texts have commented on this: "When princes persecute me without reason, it is in vain and does nothing for them. But my heart fears Your word. That is, my fear is that You command them to do this and that it comes from Your word" [source uncertain]. If so, there is nothing for us to fear except if the hands of Esau are the hands of the Holy One, the rod of His wrath. Surely, if Israel observes the Torah and the voice of Jacob is heard in the synagogue and the study house, then the hands will remain the hands of Esau and not those of the Holy One. Obviously they will not be able to have power over us. Let this be understood.

Therefore, we need to do penitent return. This is the essence of the fast: to repair and to remove the obstacles, as the rabbinic Sages said. It is the same in the *Shulḥan Arukh*, *Oraḥ Ḥayim*, *Siman* 576:15. If we take it upon ourselves to observe the holy Sabbath, the laws of family purity, and not to eat nonkosher meat or other forbidden foods and to strengthen the holy Torah, then God will certainly hear our voices and will have mercy. He will relate to us mercifully and redeem us from our troubles. Our enemies will wither away and His holy name will be sanctified in the world.

The rabbinic Sages said in B. T. *Ḥagigah* 9[b], "The Holy One did not find an attribute for Israel as good as poverty." The reason is contained in the explanation of Rabbi Ḥananel: In order that we should have a broken heart, He sends us troubles and poverty. If we already have a heart broken into pieces as we do today, it is appropriate for the Holy One not to conduct Himself with us with this good attribute any longer. I said [in my sermon] that this is alluded to in the words of our rabbinic Sages in tractate B. T. *Megillah* 10[b], "The place of the ark is not a full unit." [Ya'akov ben Asher,] the author of the *Turim*, writes in his commentary to the Torah portion *Terumah* [Exodus 25:1–27:21] that it is written that the ark was two and a half ells, its width was one and a half ells and its height was one and one-half ells. All of the ells were fractional by half. We do not find this regarding the other objects in the Tabernacle. Even the poles and the table were once only a fraction of an ell. The author of the *Turim* writes that this teaches that everyone who studies Torah needs to break himself

into pieces. [We find ourselves in] the place of the ark. Where the ark is, the heart is broken into pieces. The [good] attribute does not apply. God does not need to conduct Himself with the good attribute by sending us troubles to break our hearts. Because in our day we [already] have a broken and depressed heart. God should [rather] have mercy on us. He should bring down and destroy our enemies before our eyes and before those of the whole world. He should sanctify His great name in the world, and send us our righteous Messiah, speedily in our days, amen.

Concerning that which I wrote above, it would seem that we can interpret what King David, of blessed memory, said in Psalms 51:19, "The sacrifices of God are a broken spirit; a broken and a contrite heart, O God, Thou wilt not despise." We have to understand that King David said first that a contrite spirit is a sacrifice to God, like an offering. Do not turn around and despise it, saying that it is much less than a sacrifice. Do not despise it.—It would seem that David's enemies despised him and said despicable things about him and shamed him. King David, of blessed memory, asked: "Is not the reason for the troubles, that I should have a contrite heart and a broken heart, which is as precious in Your eyes as a sacrifice? My heart is certainly [already] broken within me." Concerning this, King David said, "The sacrifices of God are a broken spirit" [Psalms 51:19]. That is, "Whoever has a broken heart is as precious in Your eyes as a sacrifice. Therefore, I ask out of a broken and contrite heart: 'Master of the universe, Do not allow the one who has a broken heart to be despised and do not allow me to be despised.'" Let this be understood.

WHAT I PREACHED ON [THE FESTIVAL OF] *Simḥat Torah*, 4 OCTOBER 1942

There is a way to explain the connection of the end of the Torah to its beginning. Concerning the verse, "And in all the mighty hand (*yad haḥazakah*)" [Deuteronomy 34:12, the last verse of the Torah], Naḥmanides, of blessed memory, explained that

this refers to the splitting of the sea, as is written in the Torah portion *Beshallaḥ*, "And Israel saw the great work (*yad hagedolah*) which the Lord did upon the Egyptians" [Exodus 14:31]. Avraham Ibn Ezra explained it similarly. However, we need to understand why it says *yad hagedolah* in the Torah portion *Beshallaḥ* [Exodus 13:17–17:16] and *yad haḥazakah* in [Deuteronomy 34:12]. [To shed light on *yad hagedolah*] let us humbly introduce what I explained [in my address] about the verses "I will sing unto the Lord, for He is highly exalted (*ga'oh ga'ah*); the horse and his rider hath He thrown into the sea" [Exodus 15:1] in the Torah portion *Hashirah* [Exodus 15:1–15:19]. *Targum Onkelos* explained it as "He triumphed over their arrogance." Rashi wrote similarly. "Triumphed (*ga'ah*) is written twice, because the Egyptians were full of arrogance, and are therefore called the most arrogant." And Pharaoh said, "Who is the Lord that I should hearken unto His voice?" [Exodus 5:2]. God triumphed over them and threw and cast them and their horses into the sea.

In my humble opinion, we can explain why in the Torah portion *Vayigash* [Genesis 44:18–47:27] Joseph says to his brothers, "And ye shall tell my father of all my glory in Egypt" [Genesis 45:13]. We need to understand: Was Jacob happy about the excessive glory that came with becoming a king? [No.] His primary source of joy was that he remained a God fearer and did not turn arrogantly and follow [Egyptian] ways. If so, the important thing was the brothers' telling Jacob that he still maintained his purity and piety. It is written at the end of the holy text *Kedushat Levi* [by Levi Yitshak of Berdichev] that a great matter is being alluded to here. We know that the enemies of Israel will arise in every generation to destroy us. The author of the [Passover] *Haggadah* writes, "In every generation they arise to destroy us, but the Holy One saves us from them." This was so with Pharaoh and Haman. When the Holy One helps us and the enemies of Israel are removed from the world and defeated, the name of Heaven is sanctified because of [the] great sanctification of God's name in the world. Everyone recognizes and knows that the Holy One [destroyed Israel's enemies]. Through this, the name of the Holy One will be magnified. As Scripture testifies, through this, "The people feared the Lord; and they believed in the Lord and His servant Moses" [Exodus 14:31]. Similarly, the name of Heaven was sanctified with Haman. The whole world saw how the Holy One saved Israel and fear fell upon the nations. And Israel fulfilled and accepted the Torah anew.

As the rabbinic Sages said, "They fulfilled what they had already accepted" [B. T. *Shabbat* 88ᵃ].

Sometimes the evil of the enemy is so great that the enemy is [absolutely] unworthy. It is inappropriate for the name of God to be sanctified through such an enemy, because it is completely evil. Such an enemy does not have the privilege of being a factor in the sanctification of His great name in the world. For this, very great worthiness is required. The whole world was only created for the holy Torah [and for Israel and for the sanctification of God's name]. It is written, "In the beginning [*bereshit*]" [Genesis 1:1]. The rabbinic Sages and Rashi, of blessed memory, said [the world was created] for the sake of Israel, which is called *reshit* [first, beginning], and for the sake of the Torah which is also called *reshit*. That is, by means of the holy Torah and its commandments Israel will sanctify the name of God and publicize His great name in the world. God's name will be sanctified in the world when the enemies of Israel suffer a great defeat. The enemy will have achieved something great, because the world was created for His name to be sanctified. One needs to be most worthy for this [role]. If so, how did Pharaoh and his people become worthy enough for the name of God to be greatly sanctified in the world through their disaster? Pharaoh honored Joseph and made him the viceroy. Through this Pharaoh became worthy, with his people, of suffering a catastrophe and having God's name sanctified through them.

Jacob knew that Israel would be in Egypt. The Holy One said to Abraham our patriarch, of blessed memory, "Know of a surety that thy seed shall be a stranger in a land that is not theirs, and shall serve them; and they shall afflict them four hundred years" [Genesis 15:13]. Jacob received this tradition from Abraham. He knew that it would be impossible for the Israelites to leave Egypt by normal means, since it would be impossible even for a slave to escape from there. However, Jacob believed in what God had promised. Afterward they left with a great fortune. That is miraculously whereby the name of God would be greatly sanctified. Jacob was worried that Pharaoh and his people would be so evil that they would not be worthy for the name of God to be sanctified through them. If so, the

Israelites would be stuck there, heaven forbid. Therefore, Joseph said that they should tell Jacob about his [Joseph's] glory in Egypt. Through this, their honoring him, Pharaoh and his people would have the merit of suffering defeat in the sanctification of His name through great miracles. And so it truly was.

The author of the *Kedushat Levi* wrote that when it is written, "And Israel saw the great work (*yad hagedolah*) which the Lord did upon the Egyptians" [Exodus 14:31], *gedulah* is called *ḥesed* (loving kindness). As is written, "Thine, O Lord, is the greatness (*gedulah*), and the power [*gevurah*], etc." [1 Chronicles 29:11]. Therefore, the kabbalists called the attribute of *ḥesed* [one of] *gedulah*. It would appear that God's vengeance upon Egypt came entirely from the attribute of stern justice. It was an incomparable catastrophe. However, the truth is that this [catastrophe] was a great [act of God's] *ḥesed* for the Egyptians. They were worthy; and through their defeat the name of God was sanctified among [the people of] Israel who [now] believed in God. The name of God was sanctified as well among all the nations. As it is written, "The peoples have heard, they tremble; pangs have taken hold on the inhabitants of Philistia" [Exodus 15:14]. Israel understood that this was an immeasurable [act of God's] *ḥesed* for the Egyptians. Therefore it is written, "And Israel saw the great work (*yad hagedolah*)," [i.e.,] the great *ḥesed* that God had done to the Egyptians. These are the contents of [Levi Yitshak of Berdichev's] sweet words. I have elaborated on this in my book [*Tiyul Bepardes*], in the section on the Torah portion *Bo* [Exodus 10:1–13:16].

There is a *midrash* (rabbinic explanation), that when the Egyptians were drowning the heavenly angels wanted to sing praises. God said, "My creatures are drowning in the sea and you want to sing praises?" [B. T. *Megillah* 10^b]. From this we see that one does not sing praises when people, even evil ones like the Egyptians, are drowning and dying. If this is so, how could the Israelites sing praises? The Israelites understood that the Egyptians' drowning in the sea was not bad for the Egyptians. On the contrary, it was good and a great merit to be worthy of having the name of the Holy One sanctified through them. It is written, "And Israel saw the great work" [Exodus 14:31], the

great [act of] *ḥesed* that God did for the Egyptians, that through them, "And the people feared the Lord; and they believed in the Lord, and in His servant Moses" [Exodus 14:31]. There is no greater good than this, and therefore "Then sang Moses and the children of Israel this song, etc." [Exodus 15:1]. They were able to recite songs of praise. And this should be understood.

Pharaoh and his people, who were called arrogant, were very boastful in their lifetimes. In truth they had nothing to boast about. Particularly the generation that lived after the death of Joseph and which persecuted the Israelites and killed and pillaged them. It was despicable and contemptible in terms of human attributes. They were boastful about nothing, for they had no positive attributes about which they could boast. Now, because through them the name of God was greatly sanctified, they had something to boast about. Regarding this it is written, "I will sing unto the Lord" [Exodus 15:1]. We are able to recite praises even though God's creatures were drowned and died, because their death and drowning was a great good for them. Through them the name of God was sanctified, as mentioned above. Concerning what is written, "for He is highly exalted (*ga'oh ga'ah*)" [Exodus 15:1]. The triumphal ones [i.e., the Egyptians] now had something to be triumphant about. They could be triumphant [over the fact] that "The horse and his rider hath He thrown into the sea" [Exodus 15:1]. For they were worthy of something great, that of having the name of God sanctified through them. Let this be understood. One must add further that the meaning of "thrown into the sea" is that they were exalted through the sea, that they were made great and lofty through the sea. They were so worthy that God's name was sanctified through them. Therefore we can recite praises, because this was a great good. It was not something bad. It was excellent indeed, with God's help.

There is a superb association between "The mighty hand" and the splitting of the sea. Indeed, Israel also understood that the "mighty hand" was [an act of God's] great *ḥesed* for the Egyptians. They were drowned in the sea because they were worthy of having God's name sanctified through them. There is no greater merit. The world was created for this. As is written, "In the beginning God created" [Genesis 1:1] for the sake of the Torah, which is called first (reshit), in order that the name of the Holy One should be publicized in the world through the Torah and its commandments. In this way, their drowning attained the purpose for which the world was created. It is something excellent.

Indeed, the creation of the world was an act of ḥesed by the Holy One. As it is written, "The world will be built on [an act of] ḥesed." The name [of God] Elohim is one that refers to stern judgment. Nonetheless, the Torah begins with the name Elohim. [Ḥayim Ibn Attar, the author of] Or Haḥayim writes that in the verse [Genesis 1:1] the attribute of the name Elohim was also positive. When it says, "In the beginning Elohim created" [Genesis 1:1] the name Elohim is positive. God created the world so He could be merciful and good to the inhabitants of heaven and earth. There is no greater mercy than this, etc. See the beginning of the Torah portion Bereshit, verse ten [Genesis 1:10]. This is the [profound] association. The Torah ends with the "mighty hand (hayad haḥazakah)" [Deuteronomy 34:12], which is the splitting of the sea, an attribute of judgment. Even here, it is called the "great work (yad hagedolah)." This is because the attribute of judgment itself is ḥesed. It was a great [act of] ḥesed for the Egyptians, for the name of the Holy One to be sanctified through them, as mentioned above. For this reason, the creation of the world, which is also an [act of] ḥesed, is also written along with the name Elohim, as the Or Hayim writes. Let this be understood.

I said [in my address] that the evil Haman had a great merit. This is because the name of God was sanctified through him, for through his evil Israel did penitent return. The rabbinic Sages say, "The removal of [Ahasuerus's] ring accomplished more for [the people of] Israel than the forty-eight prophets and seven prophetesses of Israel" [B. T. Megillah 14ª]. This is because through Haman, Israel did penitent return completely. Therefore, Haman was worthy. Through Haman's fall there was a great sanctification of God's name. Now too, if because of the troubles we take matters to heart, redemption will be easy. Through this the enemies of Israel will gain great merit. For through their disasters the name of God will be sanctified. I have talked at length [in my address] about morality. Indeed, the Holy One who examines hearts knows that now, as a result of the great darkness and travails and because of the great hiding [of the divine], as if great stones were laying on our heads and hearts, it is difficult for us to concentrate our minds and leave our evil ways. However, when the Holy One will help us and redeem us from the troubles and the exile, we will no longer walk in the [evil] path we have followed. We will listen to parents and teachers. The Holy one will certainly save us soon. Our forlorn hearts will rejoice. There will be an end to our troubles and we will grasp the joy of all Israel, speedily and soon, amen.

WHAT I PREACHED ON THE GREAT *Shabbat* [PRECEDING PASSOVER], 17 APRIL 1943

The *Haggadah* (Passover narrative) says,

The Torah speaks about four sons, one wise, one evil, one simple, and one who does not know how to ask. What does the wise one say? "What do the testimonies, and the statutes, and the ordinances mean, which the Lord our God has commanded you?" And you instruct him in the precepts of Passover [specifically], "One may not eat after the *afikomen*."

The question is not understandable. The answer is even less understandable. Also when it says, "The precepts of Passover": There are laws and precepts concerning Passover which are more precious and necessary than the one [about the *afikomen*, the piece of *matzah*, unleavened bread, eaten at the end of the meal], ones which are from the Torah.

In my humble opinion it would be proper to explain, with the help of God, why it is called

Passover. The Torah explains the name, "For that He passed over the houses of the children of Israel in Egypt, when he smote the Egyptians" [Exodus 12:27]. That is, He leaped over or spared the houses—as Rashi and *Targum Onkelos* write. Rabbi Yitshak Luria, of blessed memory, said that there was another intention. The word [*PeSaH*] was composed of two parts, *Peh* and *Samekh-Het*, for speech was in exile [and not unified]. His words are very profound. However, the simple meaning [can be seen from this:] Today we see that the hatred of Israel is increasing greatly. When, heaven forbid, some Jew does or says something reckless, the punishment is very great. Immediately there are witnesses who [claim to have] seen or heard that so-and-so spoke against the government. Or because of some insignificant thing, they say that some Jew is a secret agent and wants to hand over the country to the enemy. They call him a "spy." One needs to be very careful not to utter anything at all regarding the war or the government. It is very dangerous. Someone might see or hear something and twist it for evil. One needs to keep one's mouth closed. It was similar in Egypt. Because of the great hatred, [the children of Israel] had to keep their mouths closed and say nothing, lest their words be twisted and they be severely punished. After the Holy One redeemed them, they were free of the Egyptians and the Egyptians received their punishment, they could open their mouths and speak. For then they would no longer be afraid. Therefore it is called *Peh Samekh-Het*, because then the mouth (*peh*) would be able to say (*sah*) what it wants.

Furthermore, we see today how the enemies of Israel rise against us and torment us with all sorts of persecutions. They remove every source of livelihood from us. Many thousands and tens of thousands of Jews are exiled from their country and land. How many tens of thousands have been killed by the evildoers for no reason? How many have been buried alive, they, their wives, their sons, and their daughters? The reckless among us will open their mouths, asking questions and doubting God: "Why did God do this to pious and good Jews?" They will actually ask, "Where is your God?" But we remain silent and closed. For we are unable to answer these people at all until God has mercy on His people and sends us our

redeemer and takes us out of this dark and long exile. It was the same in Egypt. There were evil people who asked, as mentioned above. We had nothing with which to answer them. But after the Holy One helped us we could respond and answer all the questions which the reckless ones raised and asked. Therefore it is called *Pesah, PeSaH*. They were then able to tell [the reckless ones] that the troubles and servitude were necessary for the purpose of the redemption. Our rabbinic Sages said that the children of Israel were not worthy of attaining the redemption from Egypt, the giving of the Torah, and the Land of Israel, except through suffering [B. T. *Berakhot* 5ᵃ]. So we say and ask on the Days of Awe, "And free speech to those who yearn for Thee" [*Amidah, Musaf Lerosh Hashanah*, the standing, silent benediction for the additional service for the New Year]. And if today, heaven forbid, one should forget oneself and question the Holy One and ask why the pious ones of Israel suffer? [The answer is that] God knows what He does. Undoubtedly there is a need for the suffering; our great sins caused it. Just as they said, "Because there were no graves in Egypt, hast thou taken us away to die in the wilderness?" [Exodus 14:11]. Moses our teacher, of blessed memory, answered them, "Fear ye not, stand still, and see the salvation of the Lord. The Lord will fight for you, and ye shall hold your peace" [Exodus 14:13–14]. That is, "Watch yourselves and do not say anything, heaven forbid, to question the Holy One." Undoubtedly justice is with Him, may He be blessed. We are unable to resolve all the problems now. But when the Holy One will help us and send us our Messiah and Elijah the prophet with him, Elijah will resolve all our problems concerning the Holy One. In any case, Elijah will respond to all the uncertainties, problems, and difficulties. As it says, *Teiku*. This is an acronym for "*Tishbi* [Elijah] will resolve problems and difficulties (*Tishbi yitarets kushiyot ve'iba'ayot*). And he will answer here."

[In my sermon] I alluded to the Torah portion *Vayehi*, "The scepter shall not depart from Judah. Nor the ruler's staff from between his feet, as long as men come to Shiloh (*ad ki yavo Shiloh*) (i.e., the Messiah, the king, for the kingdom is his [Rashi *ad* Genesis 49:10]); and unto him shall the obedience of the peoples be" [Genesis 49:10]. [Ya'akov ben Asher], the author of the *Turim*, writes that "come [to] Shiloh" has the same numerical value as

"Messiah." Rashi writes that "obedience" means the gathering of the nations. Rashi cites the verse from Proverbs 30:17, "The eye that mocketh at his father, and despiseth the wrinkles of his mother." It refers to the gathering of the folds of the mother's face which accrued because of her age [Rashi *ad* Genesis 49:10].... They will pour out before the Messiah all their problems concerning the Holy One. The Holy One and Elijah will resolve everything and there will be no more problems. "Obedience" is derived from the same root as "problem," as explained above. Let this be understood. Therefore, each person should be guarded and be very careful not to speak or to think, heaven forbid, against the Holy One. Though we do not understand, the Holy One knows. Justice is with Him, and He knows how He needs to behave. The Kedushat Levi, may his merit protect us, said about himself, that Levi Yitshak [of Berditchev] would be a fool to worship someone to whom he needed to give advice. How precious are his holy words.

[In my sermon] I explained this by what is written in Job 36:3, "I will fetch my knowledge from afar, and will ascribe righteousness to my Maker." It is stated in *Midrash Rabbah: Parashat Tazria*, "Rabbi Nathan said, we value the name of Abraham who came from afar, as it says 'Abraham lifted up his eyes, and saw the place afar off'" [Genesis 22:4] [*Midrash Vayikra Rabbah, Parashah* 14, *Siman* 2]. An explanation is needed. It seems that we have to be precise about what is written, "Abraham lifted up his eyes, and saw the place afar off" [Genesis 22:4]. That "Abraham lifted up his eyes" would seem to be superfluous. I have explained elsewhere that this tells of the greatness of Abraham's yearning. It is similar to a student who spent several years studying in yeshivah. He did not go home at all since he left. After several years, out of great yearning, he traveled home to see his father and mother. He constantly looked up to see if the city where his parents live was already in sight. Similarly, with Abraham our father, of blessed memory. Out of his great yearning to bring his son as a sacrifice on Mount Moriah, he lifted his eyes to look for the place so that he might see it. From what is written, "Abraham lifted up his eyes, and saw the place afar off," we see how great Abraham was and how he yearned to do the will of the Creator, may His name be blessed.

At the beginning of the Torah portion *Va'era*, Rashi writes that Abraham did not question God. God rebuked Moses for being so emboldened as to speak against God, "Wherefore hast thou dealt ill with this people?" [Exodus 5:22], while Abraham did not question God. That which is written, "I will fetch my knowledge from afar" [Job 36:3], refers to Abraham's coming from afar. That is, how great Abraham was because he came from afar. It implies how much he yearned to do the will of God to sacrifice his only son. Abraham did not question His attributes and did not ask any questions or investigate into why the Holy One told him to do this. That is, "'And will ascribe righteousness to my Maker' [Job 36:3] even if it seems to me that the Holy One should not behave this way. I will not question and will instead justify Him. Justice is with Him." Let this be understood. (See my book *Tiyul Bepardes* [II], part 6 section 200, which I am presently editing.) One may express an intention to question the Holy One, as to why the merit of our holy patriarch Abraham does not protect us: Why should the descendants of that holy man suffer such troubles? Nonetheless, I do not question and "will ascribe righteousness to my Maker" [Job 36:3]. This is why it says that we value the name of Abraham. He came from afar. Despite all, "And will ascribe righteousness to my Maker."

There is another explanation of *Peh* [and] *Samekh-Het*. I explained it in my book on the Torah [Torah portion *Matot*] concerning what King David, of blessed memory, said in Psalms 17:3, "Thou hast tried my heart, Thou hast visited it in the night; Thou hast tested me, and findest not that I had a thought which should not pass my mouth." I said, based on the words of [Bahyah Ibn Pakudah, author of] the *Hovot Halevavot* (*Duties of the Heart*), that hidden things should be more than what is revealed. It said, "You have tried me and searched me very well. Look. You will not find anything amiss in me. My thoughts will not transgress, and my mouth will not exceed my thoughts." Let this be understood.

There is proof for this from the speaking mouth. The power of speech has five parts. They are united until speech emerges. They are the lips, teeth, tongue, palate, and throat. The letters that come from the lips are *Bet, Vav, Mem, Peh*. Letters from the teeth are *Zayin, Samekh, Shin, Resh, Tsaddi*. Letters from the tongue are *Dalet*,

Tet, Lamed, Nun, Tav. Letters from the palate are *Gimel, Yud, Khaf, Kuf.* Letters from the throat are *Alef, Ḥet, Hay, Ayin.* Some [are] with the lips open, or teeth partially open, or partially closed. We find at the beginning of [the tractate] *Baba Kamma,* "The spoliator indicates tooth" [B. T. *Baba Kamma* 3ᵇ] where a little is revealed. As it is written, "How are his hidden places sought out!" [Obadiah 6]. The tongue is hidden because it is improper to stick the tongue out. The palate is hidden completely, and similarly the throat is hidden completely. We find that most of speech is closed and hidden, that only a small part of it is open. Thus, the hidden is more than the revealed. So it should be with the worship of God. There should always be more that remains hidden in the heart than is revealed with the limbs. Then there is worship with integrity. What is written [under *Tefillah*] in the holy text *Kehilat Ya'akov: Otsar Shemot, Pealim Vekhinuyim Umafteaḥ Nifla Betorat Shimon bar Yoḥai Vekabbalat Ha'ari* [by Ya'akov Tsevi Jolles], [is] that *tefillah* (prayer) is an acronym for *tenu peh le-yud-heh-vav-heh* (give your mouth to God). From what I wrote [in my book on the Torah], it may be understood that prayer needs to be like a mouth, where what is hidden is greater than what is revealed. Let this be understood.

In 1 Samuel 17 it says that David heard [that] Goliath the Philistine "taunted the armies of the living God" [1 Samuel 17:26].

> And David said to Saul... "Thy servant will go and fight with this Philistine." And Saul said to David, "Thou art not able to go against this Philistine to fight with him; for thou art but a youth, and he a man of war from his youth." And David said unto Saul, "This servant kept his father's sheep, and when there came a lion or a bear and took a lamb [*zeh* = it] out of the flock, I went out after him and smote him, and delivered it out of his mouth. And when he arose against me, I caught him by his beard and smote him, and slew him. Thy servant smote both the lion and the bear; and this uncircumcised Philistine shall be as one of them, seeing he hath taunted the armies of the living God." [1 Samuel 17:32–36]

The written text states, "and took (*zeh*) out of the flock," but we read it as "took a lamb (*seh*) out of the flock." In the text *Toldot Adam* by (Yehezkel Fayvel ben Ze'ev Volf about] the sage R. [Shelomoh] Zalman of Vilna, may his merit protect us, the author [cites a *midrash* found by the Gaon of Vilna which] explains that after David reflected, he saw that it was a great miracle for him to be saved from the lion. He made a small garment from the skin of the lamb that he always wore, to always remember God's [act of] *ḥesed* for him. Therefore it is written, "and took it (*zeh*) out of the flock." This alludes to the garment that he wore. The reading is *seh*, that it was a lamb (*seh*); [*Toldot Adam, Perek 9,* Jerusalem, 1986, p. 143].

When a person receives something good, let alone a miracle from the Holy One, that person needs to always be thankful, to praise the Holy One and never forget. Thus, when the Israelites went out of Egypt and saw the miracles of God and His great favors, they took it upon themselves to serve the Lord with all their hearts and souls, and never to forget the good and miracles that the Holy One did for them. They took it upon themselves to serve Him with a pure worship, one that was more hidden than revealed. Therefore, it is called *PeSaḤ* to indicate a mouth that speaks where what is hidden is greater than what is revealed. Thus, they took it upon themselves to serve God. Similarly with the paschal lamb which they slaughtered and ate, as God had commanded them. What was hidden was more than what was revealed with the limbs.

From this, we can understand the question of the wise one and the response of the rabbinic Sages [B. T. *Pesaḥim* 119ᵇ]. It states: "One may not eat after the Passover *afikomen.*" Rabbi Ovadiah Bertinoro explained on the basis of the term "to utter," that one does not ask for sweets after the Passover meal as one does after other meals. This is in order that the taste of the Passover meal remain in the mouth. We need to understand why the rabbinic Sages did not say [explicitly] that we do not eat after the Passover meal. However, one could say that the Passover meal should be eaten with such holiness and purity that, given the great holiness, it would not enter the minds of the rabbinic Sages to ask for sweets to be brought. Concerning the statement "One may not eat after the Passover *afikomen,*" [the rabbinic Sages] wanted to say that such a thing would not even enter their minds. Because of the great holiness in the hearts of the rabbinic

Sages, what is concealed is greater and more important than what is revealed. Let this be understood.

There were these two sinners. Someone informed on them, that they had done such and such. They were in police custody for several months and suffered greatly. Afterward, the court imposed a serious penalty on them. Then a miracle happened. The king passed through and ordered them to be freed. They recognized that this was a miracle from heaven. One of them said to his friend, "From this day forward I will pray every day, morning and evening, and I will fulfill the commandment of washing the hands before eating and reciting the grace after meals." His friend said to him, "What is this as compared to the great goodness that the Holy One has done for us? I take it upon myself never to forget, even for a second, the loving kindness of God. I will serve Him always with all my heart and soul, until what is hidden in me will be much greater than what is revealed."

The wise son is the one who understands the greatness of the miracles and the favors that God did for us, when He took us out of Egypt. The wise son understands that the commandment of the Passover festival, the *matzah*, and the cups of wine return the favor, which we acknowledge, and they reciprocate to the Holy One. And the wise son asks, "What are the testimonies, etc.?" That is to say, "What are they as compared to the great favors that we received from the Holy One? They are nothing as compared to the great good that He has done for us. And you also tell him about the laws of Passover." That is, according to the order and according to the matter of the *PeSaH*. Just as when the mouth speaks, the hidden is greater than what is revealed, so when I perform the rituals and the other commandments of the night of Passover, the hidden is greater than the revealed. (We find that it says, "His goings are as of old" [*Habakkuk* 3:6]. The rabbinic sages say, "Do not read it as routes (*halikhot*) but as laws (*Halakhot*)" [B. T. *Megillah* 28ᵇ]. Likewise, *Halakhot* are like *halikhot*, [i.e.,] like the *halikhot* of the *PeSaH*.) That is, I am filled with thanks and holiness. I want to serve the Lord all my days, with all my heart and soul, such that the hidden should be much greater than what is

revealed. It says "One may not eat after the Passover *afikomen*" to indicate that I want to serve the Lord such that the hidden would be so great that I would not think of saying, "Bring me sweets after the Passover meal," given the great holiness of eating the Passover meal and the other commandments. Let this be understood.

Thus, we must take it upon ourselves to serve the Lord and to turn from the path of evil which we have followed until now. We should raise our sons and daughters in the ways of Torah and faith. [In my sermon] I went into moralistic themes at length. May God have mercy on us and hasten our redemption and the delivery of our souls. May He send us our redeemer, so our eyes will see the salvation and joy of Israel speedily in our days, amen.

There is more to say about *PeSaH*. Today, because of our sins, there are reckless people who would open their mouths and question the Holy One. They would speak irately and angrily about the Holy One. I do not want to cite their words. Similarly, there were reckless people in Egypt before the Holy One brought the plagues. They looked upon their great troubles, which were exacted from the Egyptians and, as is written in the Torah portion *Shemot* [Exodus 1:1–6:1], they spoke against the Holy One. And if Moses our teacher, of blessed memory, said, "Why did You bring harm upon this people?" [Exodus 5:22], it was because of the great anguish of Israel. He also watched his tongue. It does not say "he said," but "he asked" the Lord, [which is] the language of [the] recitation of blessings. Concerning this as well, God spoke to him justly. However, the reckless ones spoke arrogantly. Indeed afterward, when they saw God's redemption, they greatly regretted that they had spoken harshly against God. Therefore, it is called *PeSaH*, a reminder that their mouths spoke improperly. When they eat the Passover meal they should remember that they sinned with their mouths, with *peh saḥ*.— Indeed, it is not God's will to embarrass them and so He gave another reason, "That ye shall say: It is the sacrifice of the Lord's Passover, for that He passed over the houses of the children of Israel" [Exodus 12:27]. But they themselves were very embarrassed when they ate the Passover meal. Let this be understood.

At the Border of Catastrophe

Yissakhar Taykhtahl

Yissakhar Taykhtahl (1885–1945) was born in Nagyhalasz, Hungary. He headed the Moriah yeshiva in Piestany (Slovakia) and authored a volume of *Responsa* (1924). He made his way in October 1942 from Nitra (Slovakia) to Budapest, where he wrote *Em Habanim Semeḥah* (*A Happy Mother of Children*, published by Katzburg in December 1943). German armies entered Hungary in March 1944. In January 1945, traveling on a train of Auschwitz inmates to Bergen–Belsen, he was killed by a Ukrainian prisoner.

In *Em Habanim Semeḥah* Taykhtahl reversed his earlier anti-Zionist position and identified the catastrophe as a call for mass emigration to the Land of Israel. The Holocaust, he demonstrated, was in fact a declaration from above that the people had no life any more in the diaspora. It had been a mistake to rely on miraculous intervention in the past before moving to the Land of Israel. Now, when divine intent was manifest, Jews had to take every possible initiative to correct the earlier error. Successful reestablishment of the Land, Taykhtahl was convinced, would precipitate redemption. The role of the secular Jew in the process was laudable—so much so that such a Jew deserved more respect than the pious Jew who stood apart from the process.

SELECTIONS

In the second preface to the book (translated here from the Hebrew by Pessah Schindler), Taykhtahl observed that the current suffering was unprecedented, at least since Haman, insofar as now there was no way to escape. Why did the darkness increase without any sign of light? Because God was inciting the gentiles to make it impossible for Jews to survive in the diaspora and to force Jews to return to their Land. The fact that the Land was already being rebuilt meant that the time for massive in-gathering and the messianic advent had arrived.

SECOND PREFACE: A HAPPY MOTHER OF CHILDREN

Dejected, I perceive the ruin of my people [Lamentations 3:11] overwhelmed in these times in their exile. We are as captives in prison. *There* is the reality of all suffering. As it is written: "Those destined for death shall die; those by the sword, shall be put to the sword; those by famine, shall starve; and those meant for captivity shall be made captive" [Jeremiah 15:2]. Each is more extreme than the next (as elaborated in the talmudic tractate B. T. *Baba Batra* 8). All forms of suffering are included [within the punishment of] captivity [see Rashi *ad* B. T. *Baba Batra* 8[b]]. The glory of all Israel has been cut down. Never in all of Israel's history has there been such misfortune. True, there have been difficult periods in the past. But these were spaced during different periods and places which permitted our forefathers alternate sites for refuge. The massive and comprehensive form of the current destruction of this European continent (which had heretofore been a center of Jewish life from which emerged many of the great personalities and sages during recent centuries) is now characterized by complete imprisonment with no opportunity for escape. Everything is being destroyed. Every nation has shut its gates before us.

"Strip her, strip her, to its very foundation!" [Psalms 137:7]. "And they were entirely enclosed. No one could leave or enter" [see Joshua 6:1]. This has not occurred since the time of Haman the evil one. He too decreed the destruction of the entire Holy people. He also shut before them the gates of the nations, as the Midrash explains [see *Midrash Ester Rabbah, Parashah* 7, *Siman* 23]. And now that so much daily life is without pleasure [see Ecclesiastes 12:1] and my mind is preoccupied with the suffering of this generation I am unable to concentrate on regular study as is my habit. The study of *Halakhah* requires concentration. To make matters worse, due to the storms of exile which have assaulted us, the yeshivas and houses of study have been eliminated. On that bitter day when the pogroms of the people broke out in all their fury and trampled under them all that was holy, yeshivah students were evicted from their schools. I remained alone, absorbed in my thoughts of the destruction of the people and communities of Israel. . . . Why did the Lord do such a thing? [Deuteronomy 29:23]. Why the extraordinary anger? [Deuteronomy 29:3].

Hence, I decided to examine the 2,000-year chronicles of our people during their exile and persecutions among the nations. True, I never before dealt with questions of this sort. After all I was always trained in the House of God and resided in the world of *Halakhah* and Responsa literature. I was privileged to learn and to teach. I published works in the field which were well received and praised by the scholars, thank the Almighty. (See the endorsements of the great masters in my *Mishneh Sakhir*, part one, published in the year 5684 [1923–1924]. See also the letter

to me from the holy person of Ostrowtza [Meir Yeḥiel Halevi Halstuk] published in my volume *Tov Yigael* in the year 5686 [1925–1926].) I never took the time to be concerned with matters affecting the welfare of our holy nation, since the mitzvah could be left to others with the claim that "all of your goods cannot equal her" [Proverbs 3:15]. I did not believe that the study of Torah should be neglected on its account (as elaborated in *Moed Katan* and the legal ruling in *Shulḥan Arukh: Yoreh Deah, Hilkhot Talmud Torah, Siman* 246:18).

During the present upheaval, however, it is impossible to limit oneself to the teachings of Abaye and Raba and other complex legal matters. My students have been forcibly removed from me. No one remains with whom I can engage in halakhic study. Thus I have been stimulated to question as in the Book of Daniel: "How long until the end of these awful things?" [Daniel 12:6]. Are we not as yet close to the eve of the sixth day? As it is written, "at evening time there shall be light" [Zechariah 14:7]. Note Rashi's commentary: "Prior to the completion of the millennium the shining light shall appear" [Rashi *ad* Zechariah 14:7].

See the *Piyyut* [liturgical poem] for the second day of Rosh Hashanah, which gives a similar time, "when the sun tends to the west, two-thirds of an hour from darkness. Light for the upright will shine before evening." It would seem that we have already reached this time. (I also found this in the commentary on [*Midrash*] *Tanna Debe Eliyahu, Tosafot Ben Yeḥiel*, at the beginning of chapter 2.)

Nevertheless the son of Yishai has not come. There must surely be some restraint upon us which delays our redemption. We are, therefore, compelled to identify and understand this obstacle so that it is removed from our midst. Clear "the highway" [see Isaiah 62:10] for our righteous Messiah, who will surely and speedily rescue us from distress in our own day and raise the *Shekhinah* [the Divine Presence in the world] from the dust. With the help of He who favors man with knowledge [see "Eighteen Benedictions," daily prayer], I decided to investigate this area as much as my limited abilities would allow me. Further, I recalled the statement of our sages of blessed memory cited in "The Chapter on Judges," *Reshit Ḥokhmah* [by Eliahu ben Mosheh de Vidas], as follows: "One who is decent and fears sin should be involved in the needs, burdens, and sufferings of Israel." Indeed such a person sustains the entire world, as it is written: "By justice a king sustains the land, etc." [Proverbs 29:4]. But one who refrains from sharing their burden, from mending their broken fences, and acts as if he were a priestly offering set aside from the dough [see Numbers 15:18–21], it is as if he tramples upon the world and destroys it, as it is written: "But a fraudulent man tears it down" [Proverbs 29:4].

This is the extent to which our sages insisted that we be concerned with the plight of the Jew even during times of normalcy and tranquillity in the world. Certainly this is incumbent on every Jew when the Jewish people are disgraced [see Lamentations 2:3], when they writhe in their own blood and are utterly abandoned as fish in the sea. Then he must, to the best of his God-given knowledge . . . seek a way in which they may be extricated from their distress. Our master Rabbi Mosheh Cordovero in his work *Tomer Devorah* (seventh chapter) observes that one must entertain positive thoughts on behalf of all of Israel, for their benefit. Note the comment of *Ya'arot Devash* [by Yehonatan Eybeschutz] (part two) discussing the blessing, "O Lord return our judges" ["Eighteen Benedictions," daily prayer]. There, as well, the responsibility for directing constructive thoughts toward Israel is placed upon the leadership.

According to the author, the suffering which befalls Israel is due to bad leaders. . . . I dared to survey and research [the literature] devoted to the continued persistence of the exile. I proceeded to compose this work, with the help of God, in which I publicly express my views in order to advise my people as to what should be done to advance redemption speedily in our day. . . . After some respite following my arrival here in the capital, fulfilling my vow, I began work on the volume devoted to the rebuilding of our Holy Land; to raise it from the mounds of dust [see Nehemiah 3:34]; to stimulate love and affection in the hearts of our Jewish brethren, old and young, so that they would endeavor to return to our Land, the Land of our forefathers, and not remain here in the lands of exile. As expounded in the [*Midrash Bereshit Rabbah, Parashah* 39, *Siman* 10]: "It is preferred that one lives in the deserts of *Erets Yisrael* and not live in palaces outside the Land."

Furthermore, the purpose of all of the plagues with which we were assailed during our periods of exile were mainly intended to stimulate us to return to our Holy Land. As it is explained in *Midrash Tehillim, Perek* 17, *Siman* 4 concerning King David during the time of the pestilence, the Holy One, blessed be He, sent to him Gad the prophet, as it is written: "Gad came to David and said to him 'Go and set up an altar to the Lord'" [2 Samuel 24:18]. This may be compared to one who strikes his son and the son doesn't know why he is being struck. After the beating he [the father] addresses him as follows: Go and discharge that which I have ordered you to do today, and in days past, but which you have neglected to act upon. Thus was it with the thousands who were slain in David's day merely because they did not demand the building of the Temple. From this we can argue the following: If these who neither witnessed the building of the Temple nor its destruction were destined to be punished in this fashion because they did not insist on building the Temple, we who witnessed its destruction and nevertheless do not mourn, nor receive compassion, how much more so [are we deserving of punishment]? Rashi in Hosea [3:5] quotes the following: "Rabbi Shimon b. Menassiah said: 'The Jewish people will not be shown a good omen until they repent and seek the Kingdom of Heaven, the Kingdom of the House of David and the building of the Temple as it is written: "Afterward the children of Israel shall return and seek the Lord their God and David their King, etc."'"

Now included in our plea to return to *Erets Yisrael* are these very three conditions. "Whoever resides in Erets Yisrael may be considered to have a God" [B. T. *Ketubot* 110[b]]. The building of the Temple will also be realized with our return, and with the help of God, as explained in B. T. *Megillah* [17[b]–18[a,b]]. Thereafter the Messiah will come. This is the [fulfillment] of the House of David. . . . First and foremost, however, we must endeavor to return to *Erets Yisrael* and then with the help of God all three conditions will be fulfilled.

The Tosefta in *Avodah Zarah* (chapter 5) remarks upon the verse: "And I will faithfully plant them in this land" [Jeremiah 32:41]. "[Whenever] they shall be on the land they will be as if I had planted them before me, faithfully, with all my heart and soul, [but if they] not be settled upon her, they will not be planted before me faithfully, neither with my whole heart nor soul." It is indeed startling for the Holy One, blessed be He, to declare that when Israel is not in its land they are not at one with Him in heart or soul. What has befallen us in our time and the limited degree of evident [divine] providence should not astonish us, since He is not faithfully linked to us with His entire heart and soul. We are after all in the land of other nations. When we shall attempt to return to her, then we will immediately cleave to Him with all our heart and soul. As it is explained [by Yehudah Halevi] in the *Kuzari* [2:14] ... the *Shekhinah* [God's Presence] descended upon Ezekiel despite the qualification of our sages of blessed memory that the *Shekhinah* does not rest outside the Land of Israel [*Mekhilta: Bo*, 2]. Since, however, he prophesied in regard to *Erets Yisrael* the *Shekhinah* rested [upon him] outside the Land of Israel. ...

Primarily, God expects us to assume the initiative and yearn to return to our Land. We should not wait until He Himself brings us there. Therefore, we are told, "I will faithfully plant them in this land" [Jeremiah 32:41]. That is to say, we are consciously to strive and yearn for this purpose, faithfully, and with all our abilities. Then He will successfully complete the task for us.

In this spirit, the *Zohar* [Noah] writes concerning Solomon's Temple. Although it was prefabricated, nevertheless the Holy One, blessed be He, waited in expectation for our handiwork. Then did God complete the building. So must it be with us in the settling of *Erets Yisrael*. ... I came upon a similar lesson with regard to David in 1 Chronicles 13:2, where he first consulted with [the people of] Israel. It is stated: "If you approve, and if the Lord our God agrees, let us send far and wide to our remaining kinsmen throughout the territories of Israel." One should

take note of David's partiality toward Israel, prefacing "If you approve, and if the Lord our God agrees."

This [reversal of order] is prohibited as noted toward the close of *Yadayim* [*Mishnah Yadayim* 4:8]. Rashi's commentary [1 Chronicles 13:1] is revealing: "David said to them: You have now achieved [placing a king at your helm] for your benefit [so that he may help you]. Now you should devote yourself to paying homage to God." David's plan to return the Ark to Jerusalem involved some act in honor of God. This is why he did not refer to God first, but to Israel, so that he would motivate them.

That which related to the reverence for Heaven should rightfully emanate first from them and not from above. ... We learn from this that all which is of divine concern requires first the human act. Thereafter, the individual is assisted by Heaven.

I emphasize that my writings are intended for the Jew who is interested in learning the sober truth emanating from the discussions of *Halakhah*. Redemption is also a subject for *Halakhah* as taught by our sages in B. T. *Shabbat* 138[b] and *Tanna Debe Eliahu*. "The word of the Lord is this *Halakhah*. The word of the Lord, this is *hakets*" [see B. T. *Shabbat* 138b]. Thus they taught that all which concerns redemption lies within the realm of *Halakhah* and requires [the] legal discussion of scholars. ...

However, one who is thoroughly predisposed to a particular view will never be objective and admit to our viewpoint. No amount of evidence will suffice. They are blinded by their partiality. They go as far as denying the obvious. Was there anyone more fit for a mission than the spies [sent by Moses]? [Numbers 13:1–16]. But since their ambition for authority was firmly rooted within them, as elaborated in the *Zohar, Helek* 3, *Shelah Lekha* 158b and the *Shelah* [Yeshayah ben Avraham Halevi Horowitz, *Shenei Luhot Habrit: Parashat Shelah*, part II, 68a], they were afraid that should they come to *Erets Yisrael* they would lose their positions of authority. They turned against this lovely land and deceived others as well, thereby causing this exile, as elaborated by our sages [*Midrash Bamidbar Rabbah, Parashah* 16, *Siman* 20]. Joshua and Caleb challenged [their fellow leaders] in order to demonstrate the trustworthiness of Moses and his Torah, saying, "Let us go up at once and occupy it!" [Numbers 13:30].

They elaborated upon their arguments [in defense of Moses and the Land] insisting that they could succeed [despite the threatening inhabitants] as Rashi indicates [Numbers 13:30]. Nevertheless, their efforts at persuasion did not succeed since the spies suffered from a deeply rooted bias because of selfish motives. The current situation is similar even among rabbis, *Rebbes*, and their *ḥasidim*. This one has a good rabbinic post; another is endowed with a lucrative *Rebistve*. This one owns a profitable business or factory, or is appointed to a good and prestigious position offering great satisfaction. They are frightened now that should they move to *Erets Yisrael* their status will be shaken.... Note the comments of the *Divrei Ḥayim* [by Ḥayim Halberstam of Zans (Nowy Sacz)] on Ḥanukah. A person perceives what he wishes to perceive....

Also, that man of God, the Ḥatam Sofer, in the sixth volume of his *Responsa* [responsum 59] writes in a similar vein, "...but not merely the ignorant and the multitude. The learned as well, even rabbis who do not utter the truth that is in their heart or embody decency and righteousness, or keep a distance from them and do not walk in their paths."

If they wrote thus in their generation which was yet, truly, a learned generation, what shall we say in our generation?... Truly, the movement of *aliyah* [settlement in the Land of Israel], to ascend and return to *Erets Yisrael*, is not new. Great and saintly sages responded in the past as I indicated above. Since, however, that period was one of emancipation for Jews and they resided in the lands of exile in peace and tranquillity, no one paid attention to what was said with divine inspiration.

Note Rashi's observation [B. T. *Kiddushin* 69[b]] concerning the return of Ezra [to *Erets Yisrael*] with only the poor and the hard-pressed, while those who had lived in comfort in exile did not join him. See *Seder HaDorot* [by Yehiel Halpern] which cites our master the *S'M'A'* [*Sefer Me'irat Einayim* by Joshua Falk], who in turn makes reference to the following which he read in the *Sefer Ma'aseh Nissim*, of our Rabbi Eleazer of Worms, the author of the *Rokeaḥ*. Ezra

sent letters to all the communities of the exile requesting them to ascend with him to *Erets Yisrael*. One such communication was received in the city of Worms in Germany where Jews resided at the time.

They replied: "You may live in Great Jerusalem. We shall dwell here in *Little Jerusalem*." (Since at that time they were considered to be distinguished among the lords and gentiles.) [Besides] they were very wealthy. They dwelt there at ease and in peace.... Because of this, major and difficult decrees befell the Jews of Germany, and Worms particularly. During the destruction of the First Temple they had settled there. After the completion of the seventy years [of exile] Ezra wrote and beseeched them to join him. They did not ascend.

Indeed, as we know from our people's history, all the suffering and punitive decrees emanated from the Germanic countries, as presently in our day.... So it has always been throughout Israel's tranquil periods in exile. They refused to respond to *aliyah*....

Now, however, the prime Advisor, Planner, and Mover of all that is formidable and awe inspiring, has seen fit to cause all of our gentile neighbors to persecute us with oppressive decrees. It is no longer possible to remain here among them. Every Jew would now consider himself fortunate if he could return to our Holy Land. He would surely respond to the summons for *aliyah* with love and affection.

This may have been the sense of the interpretation of the *Midrash of the Song of Songs* verse "Draw me to you, we will run after you" [Song of Songs 1:4]. Because you have incited my evil neighbors against me [*Midrash Shir Hashirim Rabbah*, Parashah 1, Siman 4]. That is to say, for some time now we have lived with our gentile neighbors on good and amicable terms. Suddenly, they have been transformed into enemies and evil neighbors who hound us. But this is only because they have been incited against us by a particular Source. This impulse emanates from the profound purpose of God, in order that "we will run" to ascend to *Erets Yisrael*, since *Erets Yisrael* instantaneously follows God [in rank] (as explained in the holy book *Tseror HaMor* [by Avraham ben Ya'akov Saba] in the reading of *Mas'ei*)....

The *Midrash Tanḥuma* (ed. Warsaw), *Tetsaveh*, *Perek* 13, states as follows:

> When [the people of Israel] were exiled to Babylon what did Ezra say to them? "Ascend to *Erets Yisrael*." They did not respond. So it was Ezra who replied: "You have sowed much and brought in little, you eat without being satisfied; you clothe yourselves but no one gets warm and he who earns anything earns it for a 'leaky purse . . .'" [Haggai 1:6]. Similarly it is written in Zephaniah: "And I will punish the men who rest untroubled as would wine on its sediment, who say to themselves 'The Lord will do nothing, good or bad.' Their wealth shall be plundered and their homes laid waste. They shall build houses, but will not dwell in them. They shall plant vineyards, but not drink their wine." [Zephaniah 1:2–13]

This is precisely what has occurred in our time in nearly all of the European nations. This has come about due to their being remiss and not ascending to *Erets Yisrael* (as explained previously in the *Midrash Tanḥuma*).

Indeed the great Yavets [Yaakov ben Tsevi Emden] in the preface to the *Siddur* [prayer book] *Sulam Beit El* grieves over our neglect to return to and dwell in *Erets Yisrael*. We continue to live calmly outside the Land as if we have discovered another *Erets Yisrael* and Jerusalem. That is the reason for the tragedies which have befallen the Jews when they dwelled in comfort in Spain and other countries. Once again they were expelled.

Not a Jew remains in that country. Righteous indeed is God [see Lamentations 1:18], since their exile has made them lose their mind entirely as they assimilated among the nations. All this has befallen us because "we abandoned the glorious Land" [see Daniel 11:16].

This explains what is happening to our people in these countries. "My beloved is calling" [Song of Songs 5:2] in order to awaken in us the desire to return to our land. Surely, after all that is occurring to us during these difficult days there is no doubt that our words will fall upon fertile ground. They will surely ponder on the [merit of their] conduct here in exile. All their pursuits are in vain. The fruits of their toil benefit Esau. Not alone does he plunder their assets and property, but, as is evident in Europe presently, he robs

their bodies, their very life. During such times they will surely listen to me.

I further discovered in the volume *Hon Ashir* (by [Immanuel Ḥai ben Avraham Riahi] the author of *Mishnat Ḥasidim*) expounding upon the *Mishnah* at the close of the tractate *Sota*, "The Galilee will be destroyed" [*Mishnah Sota* 9:15] in which he writes as follows:

> The homes shall be laid waste as it is written "And your cities shall be made waste" [Leviticus 26:33]. When I was privileged by the Almighty to ascend to *Erets Yisrael*, here in Safed (may it be speedily rebuilt and established in our days, Amen), in the year 5478, this being Galilee. [The city was] filled with homes in ruins, the result of our many sins. "My eyes beheld this, and no one else" [Job 19:27]. Thank Heaven, I was happy to be present during these past two years and witness their daily rebuilding. I claim this to be an indication of the coming of the redeemer (speedily in our day), since should he come while all is in a state of desolation, there would be no space to accommodate the in-gathering of the exiles. So it was with the "First Coming."

Our rabbis commented:

> The Holy One, blessed be He, purposefully delayed Israel in the wilderness for forty years in order to allow the land to be restored following the destruction of its trees and houses which were uprooted by the Amorites during the exodus from Egypt. They had thought that Israel would enter the land immediately and find it in a state of destruction. It was only when the land was eventually restored that He brought them in. So it will be with God's help with the coming of our Messiah, speedily in our day, and be revealed first in this land, as is mentioned in the *Zohar*.

I was astounded with this discovery. I interpreted this to be a response from Heaven to the question which I posed earlier—how much longer [must we wait] for the wondrous end of days? It is God, blessed be He, who sustains the exiles until the time when *Erets Yisrael* is rebuilt, as indicated by these holy words written by one imbued with the Holy Spirit and who received the revelation of the prophet Elijah, as is known. . . . Who, after all, are we in this day and age to dispute his views? Presently, and especially in recent years, when a significant portion of the Land is being rebuilt and transformed into a productive land, the words of the holy kabbalist should indeed direct us to recognize [this process] as an indication of redemption. . . .

One is astonished, therefore, as to why some of these who fear God's word should oppose this. The subject [of returning to *Erets Yisrael*] is practically one of abhorrence and loathing for them. This can only be explained by what we quoted previously from the holy teachings of R. Elijah of Greiditz. It is the force of the *kelipah* [the "shells" of evil matter] which compels them to delay [redemption]. It [the *kelipah*] knows that with the building of the Land her existence comes to an end. It may also be their own self-interest which accounts for their remaining here as it was with the spies. . . .

I have consequently proven to all my Jewish brethren in exile that the present time is the most opportune moment to do all within our means to leave the *Erets Ha'amim* [the lands of the nations], to return to our Holy Land, and to attend to its restoration. By these means we shall bring closer the coming of the messiah, speedily in our day.

I entitled this volume *Em Habanim Semeḥah* [Psalms 113:9], based on the Jerusalem tractate of *Berakhot* (toward the close of the second chapter) which portrays *Erets Yisrael* as the mother of Israel and the lands of exile as the stepmother [J.T. *Berakhot* 2:8]. Our sages describe our mother of Zion who weeps and laments when we are in exile. She awaits our return to her bosom. "In my own flesh I behold God" [Job 19:26], when in the year 5702 before Passover a terrible decree was issued in Slovakia by the cursed villains. Young Jewish women from the age of sixteen were forcibly transported to a distant place and to an unknown destination. To this very day we do not know what occurred to the thousands of innocent Jewish souls who were deported. May God avenge them on our behalf.

The Jewish community was in a state of great panic. I knew a person who sought to rescue his young daughters from this evil trap. He tried to cross the border with them. This happened during the intermediate days of Passover. He promised to send his wife a telegraphed confirmation that he had arrived safely together with

his daughters at the predesignated point. The mother waited at home with great anticipation for the good news. As it happened they seized the father together with his daughters before they crossed the border. They were arrested and interned in a prison near the border. The rest of the Passover festival was spent in jail. They were now in great danger of being immediately deported to an unknown destination of doom. This was the anticipated penalty for violating the laws of illegal departure. Those caught for this offense were given a harsher sentence than the other prisoners.

We can imagine the bitter disappointment of the mother when she realized what had actually transpired. The initial joy turned into grief. The holiday [of Passover] was transformed into an occasion of mourning for her husband and daughters. . . . She understood the fate which awaited them. We must now recall with praise the dedicated and valiant efforts . . . of the *Gaon* [genius], *tsadik* [holy, righteous man], and *ḥasid*, our master R. Shmuel David Ungar, may he be blessed with a long and good life, the senior *Dayan* [judge] of the holy community of Nitra. He did not rest or relent until he had ransomed the three captives with a considerable sum. They were set free and returned safely to their home. One can well imagine the reaction of the unfortunate woman when she was informed by telephone that her husband and daughters were free, safe from the clutches of the enemy. From that moment on she waited with yearning for their return. The following day she could no longer be contained. She sat near the entrance of the courtyard with great anticipation waiting for the moment of their return.

Immediately upon seeing them she burst into tears and poured out all the emotions of her heart. Her excitement was so intense that she was unable even to express words of thanks to the Holy One, blessed be He, for the great miracle which transpired for her and for her family. . . . Those who did not witness this reunion, the tears, the emotions of happiness of a joyous mother [reunited] with her children, never were privileged to have witnessed genuine joy. . . .

I imagine that such would be the experience of joy of our Mother *Erets Yisrael* at the time when we shall return to her after a terrible captivity such as in our present time. I have, therefore, called my volume *Em Habanim Se-mehah* [*A Happy Mother of Children*]. May the Lord grant me the privilege of utilizing my book for the purpose of returning the children to their Land [see Jeremiah 31:10] and thereby fulfilling speedily in our day [the hope of] a joyous mother of children [Psalms 113:9]. May we ascend to Zion in gladness [see Isaiah 35:10] speedily in our day. Amen.

The second preface is now completed in the fifth millennium of the weekly portion: "I have also heard the cries of the children of Israel" [Exodus 6:5] on the new month of *Shevat*... the year [5]703 in the city of Budapest.

Aharon Rokeaḥ

Aharon Rokeaḥ (1880–1957) was born in Belz, Ukraine. He was the son of Yissakhar Dov, the leader of the Belz *hasidic* dynasty, who was known for his anti-Zionism. With the outbreak of World War II, he escaped first to Sokol (Ukraine) and then to Przemysl (Poland)—where thirty-three family members were murdered. He was imprisoned in the ghettos of Vizhnitsa (Ukraine), Cracow (Poland), and Bochnia (Poland); was deported to Kaschau, Hungary, at the end of 1942; and from there made his way to Budapest. He escaped from Budapest in November 1943 with his brother Mordekhai of Bilgoraj (Poland) to the Land of Israel, where he arrived in 1944. In his address prior to leaving, delivered for him by Mordekhai, he articulated his belief that God, who until then was hidden, was manifesting Himself in history in the act of their imminent escape. Once in the Land of Israel, he continued, the heavenly attributes of God (the *sefirot*) would bond with earthly reality in his (Aharon's) individual person. This would initiate redemption and with it the recession of the Holocaust. The metahistorical process would also bring relief to his followers left in Hungary. He was also convinced that tranquillity would prevail for his followers remaining in Hungary until that point.

SELECTION

The address selected here was published originally as *Haderekh: Derashat Peredah* (*The Path: Parting Sermon*) in Budapest in 1944. The version used here, translated from the Hebrew by Gershon Greenberg, is found in Betsalel Landau and Natan Ortner, *Harav Hakadosh Mibelza* (Jerusalem, 1961), pp. 151–159, and in Mendel Piekarz, *Hasidut Polin* (Jerusalem, 1990), pp. 424–434. Rokeaḥ described the unprecedented satanic cruelty, which he blamed on assimilationist Jews, their egoism, and their activities contrary to Torah. Hungarian Jews were still alive only because Jews murdered elsewhere constituted a "heifer" sacrifice for their (unspecified) sins. Rokeaḥ believed that this was the era of messianic birth pains (*hevlei mashiah*; see B. T. *Sanhedrin* 97–98; Rashi *ad* Isaiah 26:17). Now, evil Jews would be punished and pious Jews redeemed. Their own (the two brothers') imminent miraculous escape, he continued, belonged to the messianic process. He agreed with Taykhtahl's point in *Em Habanim Semehah*, which he cited, that there had to be some form of declaration of salvation prior to its unfolding (although he rejected Taykhtahl's interpretation that Zionist action needed to take place in exile for the redemption, with the Land of Israel as its vessel, to begin). Their escape, he averred, was that form. They were not leaving to avoid the suffering. Rather, they were taking action to awaken a spiritual vitality in the world below and thereby precipitate a parallel awakening in the world above. In the Land, they would help to establish a spiritual center which would enhance the onset of redemption. By believing in the miracle of the brothers' rescue, the ḥasidim left behind in Hungary could participate spiritually (and therefore actually) in the awakening.

PARTING SERMON

...Since "culture" has [allegedly] illumined the whole world, it has not done so actually but only euphemistically. That is, since the egotistical culture of might-is-right has spread and eclipsed the luminosity of personal freedom in all lands of the dispersion, the eyes of Israel have been darkened from the troubles of their servitude. The privileges have turned into tears. Justice has turned into an outcry [at its absence]. The wicked have ruled with a strong hand. They have abrogated all the laws of righteousness and justice. They have uprooted and destroyed the institutions concerning the love of man and even more so the love of strangers, about which our holy Torah warns us some thirty-six times [see B. T. Baba Metsia 59ᵇ]. Tyrants have now abrogated the institutions. They have thrown the pure flag of love of man to the ground. They have trod underfoot the flag of freedom for the inhabitants of the land, [whereby there was] one law and one judgment for both citizen and stranger. Since this false civilization, this metamorphosis of vanity has spread, people here attacked and destroyed their fellow men without pity and compassion and "The earth was corrupt before God" [Genesis 6:11]. This false culture [may be characterized with:] "For she hath cast down many wounded; Yea, a mighty host are all her slain" [Proverbs 7:26].

From [the time this false culture began] until now, the pain inflicted by the persecution by our enemies has been severe. Our ability to tolerate this captivity has wavered. There is no recovery to be had at the hands of the enemies of Israel. "But if we had been sold for bondmen and bondwomen, I had held my peace" [Esther 7:4]. Rather, "We are accounted as sheep for the slaughter" [Psalms 44:23], to be killed, destroyed, beaten, and to be shamed, at the hands of every cruel barbarian. There has been no refuge. We have seen all these things ourselves, how the evildoers have killed and murdered thousands of Jews with terrible cruelty. They struck the [life]

blood of brothers and sisters, the [life] blood of tsadikim (righteous ones) and ḥasidim (pious ones), the [life] blood of fathers and children, in the countless thousands. We saw with our eyes how they took young children and burned them with gas and fire. Lord of vengeance, avenge before our eyes, "Let the avenging of Thy servants' blood that is shed [be made known among the nations in our sight]" [Psalms 79:10].

Our hearts are sick over this. Our eyes have darkened over the victims of our people who have fallen by the sword, over the millions of our pure and holy ones, from infants nursing at the breast to old and venerable ones, who have died as martyrs. There was nearly no one whose pure Jewish blood was not poured. In addition to the victims of the sword, tens of thousands succumbed to famine. Our calamity "is great as the sea" [Lamentations 2:13]. Lord, who will heal us? Who will provide the watery source for tears, so I may cry day and night over the terrible and overwhelming shattering of the house of Israel, a shattering that will never be mended, a great loss for which there is no replacement, a loss for which there is no compensation? Look and see if such a thing ever happened in the world, if such as this ever happened to any nation in the world. And why? Why and until when? Look and see if there is any pain like our pain. My heart is hot, my thoughts burn with a fire. I am depressed. "Hear, O heavens, and give ear, O earth" [Isaiah 1:2], "the world, and all that dwell therein" [Nahum 1:5]. Do not cover their blood [see Job 16:18].

To our great sorrow, not even "one of a city and two of a family" [Jeremiah 3:14] has been left. Only the tiniest number of remnant individuals who hide in the forests and between hills and valleys, between heaven and earth, between the earth and the abyss. The world is dark for them. Their life is no life, only fear and panic, from hunger and thirst. We are certainly obligated to try, exerting all our strength and more to save them from death and sustain them in the face of hunger, to save them from the sword and plague in the land of *Gehenna* (hell). Those who have not been sentenced to captivity, and who have barely escaped with their lives, their lives are in danger of the oppressor every moment. A person could give all of the wealth of his household with love and desire, spend all his riches with joy and happiness [to rescue the victims], and still he would not fulfill his obligation. We are obligated to work even harder for their welfare, day and night, and do so with self-sacrifice. It is a great and holy obligation to help our fellow Jews, the tiniest number of Jews who have escaped and reached this land after meeting terrible dangers. They hunger for bread but nobody feeds them. They are naked without any clothing but nobody clothes them. It is hard to find a place to sleep, but they are not properly welcomed. They turn to the right and nobody helps, to the left and find no one upon whom to rely. Everyone pushes them away with both hands. There is no support and no assistance. Truly, they need to be accepted with every bit of love and respect, with overwhelming affection and with a receptive countenance, strengthening their weak hands, and supporting their shaking knees. We need to worry about them and to share in their troubles. "All those who mourn over the anguish of Israel will be worthy to see their consolation and salvation" [see B. T. *Ta'anit* 30[b]]. In a situation of this [intensity] the rabbinic Sages did not speak of spending only a fifth [of our income]. For it is a matter of saving the lives of Israel. A person should give everything he has for the life [of another]; a person should try everything to save a Jewish life, to save the other from death and destruction. At every moment at every hour, each of us needs to be our brother's help and support. One is obligated to do more, to the [ultimate] extent of one's ability. This means even going to solicit and beg at the doors of the wealthy, to open the closed hearts of people, to arouse people to help the unfortunate refugees who left their homes and lost their families and everything they had. They have been left with nothing, exiled, to wander in a strange land. God should have mercy on the refugees, so few of whom are left, "that a child may write them down" [Isaiah 10:19]. They are thought of as

nothing, while they once [constituted] a great community.

"I seek my brethren" [Genesis 37:16]. Tell me where the shepherds are. "Unto you, O men, I call" [Proverbs 8:4]. I raise my voice openly for volunteers from among our people: Do it for our eminent brethren. Do it for the families who have gone through fire and water for the sanctification of God's name. Holy ones of Israel, do it, volunteer, consider helping them, arise and go to help Israel. Come and help the people, help the people! With what? Do not ask—just act with intensity, with all your heart and soul. With whom? Do not scrutinize—everyone should donate. For whom? Do not investigate—for everyone who has been persecuted, for every refugee, and without questions and without preconditions. In times of danger one does not investigate. As to those who object, saying that this is disgraceful, that not everyone who ran away escaped, and not everyone who asks is needy: [Put all this aside]. Save lives! Rescue families. Work for their welfare, without exception, and without reservations. Every offering is desired, every self-sacrifice will be accepted. And every hour counts. O for those who are gone and cannot be replaced. Awaken, awaken, to give life to souls in a desolate desert. Awaken, awaken to give life to the many people in the land. Wake up from your sleep! Leave your love of money, money which is like a passing shadow and a fleeting dream. Do not get involved in doing what you need to do to accumulate wealth, collect money, to make a fortune. What good will it do, when blood is being spilled in the streets? Rend your hearts and your garments, open your hands and extend aid. Be mutually supportive. The crumb does not satisfy the lion, and the pit cannot be filled [unless you all] fulfill your obligations faithfully. Help by donating seven times what you can. We are obligated to go and knock on doors to help these unfortunates.

Though there is no testimony for this, there are references in two sources about when a person is obligated to spend all his fortune and even beg door to door. The first is in regard to honoring one's father and mother. The law requires a person to beg door to door [when necessary] to honor one's parents appropriately. This is explained in Maimonides' *Mishneh Torah, Hilkhot Mamrim*, 8, and in *Shulḥan Arukh, Yoreh Deah, Siman* 240:5. The second is in regard to Ḥanukah candles. One is obligated to beg door to door [when necessary] to light the candles to publicize the miracle [of Ḥanukah], as explained in *Shulḥan Arukh, Oraḥ Ḥayim, Siman* 671:8. A pauper who lives off charity should borrow or sell his garment [when necessary] to get oil to light the candles. The law is the same regarding the four cups [of the Passover *Seder*]. Rabbi Mosheh Schick explained that the rationales were equal: Honoring one's father is a matter of recognizing the father who raised and educated [one]. One is obligated to even beg door to door to repay the obligation to one's father. Similarly, publicizing the miracle acknowledges the miracles and wonders that God did for us. Here too we need to beg door to door [when necessary] to publicize the miracle and salvation. Nor does this mean that someone who wanted to carry this out but was prevented from doing so did, in effect, carry it out. Good thoughts are not enough. We need to actually act in order to repay the debt and to [thereby] acknowledge God's many kindnesses and mercies [Schick, *Oraḥ Ḥayim, responsum* 331].

How much more so is it a good, multiplied many times over, in our place in this land. Here [in Hungary], thank God, the guardian of the remnant of Israel does not rest or sleep. Surely and justifiably we are under obligation in the two respects [of honoring and publicizing]. We should even beg door to door to repay the kindness that God has bestowed on us, the goodness and mercy that He has done to save us from the hand of the enemy who lies in wait to destroy. This is in respect to recognizing the goodness. Every person has the additional obligation to declare and publicize the miracles and wonders that the Creator, blessed be His name, has done. Honor God with your wealth. Give praise and thanks to the Father of Mercy and publicize His many wonders.

We find in the Torah portion *Shoftim* [Deuteronomy 11:18–21:9],

If one be found slain in the land which the Lord thy God giveth thee to possess it, lying in the field, and it be not known who hath smitten him, then thy elders and thy judges shall come

forth, and they shall measure unto the cities which are round about him that is slain. And it shall be, that the city which is nearest unto the slain man, even the elders of that city shall take a heifer of the herd, which hath not been wrought with, and which hath not drawn in the yoke. And the elders of that city shall bring down the heifer unto a rough valley, which may neither be plowed nor sown, and shall break the heifer's neck. There in the valley . . . and all the elders of that city, who are nearest unto the slain man, shall wash their hands over the heifer whose neck was broken in the valley. And they shall speak and say: "Our hands have not shed this blood, neither have our eyes seen it. Forgive, O Lord, Thy people Israel, whom Thou hast redeemed, and suffer not innocent blood to remain in the midst of Thy people Israel." [Deuteronomy 21:1–8]

The explanation of these words is that someone from the city nearest the corpse probably killed the person. Therefore, the elders and magistrates [of the city] are obligated to bring a sacrifice of the heifer with the broken neck to expiate [the murder]. Indeed, sometimes it is possible for the murderer to be from one city and the corpse to be from another city. In order that the matter not become known and to avoid suspicion, it is possible that the murderer took the corpse and dragged it near the city where it was found. If so, why are [those of the neighboring city] obligated to bring a sacrifice of expiation? The issue is this: The corpse was found in the neighborhood of a certain city. Surely, the [ultimate] cause was the [divine] cause of all causes. Surely some evil against His countenance [was committed by those in the city], heaven forbid. Some decree of murder was issued against the inhabitants of this city. They were absolved of the punishment of this decree through this victim. One soul was ransomed for another. Through this victim, the inhabitants atoned [vicariously] for the decree that was decreed against them and the punishment was abrogated. Therefore, the elders and magistrates were obligated to offer the heifer with a broken neck. Through this they would be [completely] atoned.

Our brethren of this country are near the slain, near the countries upon which the troubles and persecutions of apostasy and destruction, heaven forbid, have been brought. Your eyes should look at all of this as if, heaven forbid, there was a decree against you. Heaven save us. These holy ones in the lands close to us were sacrificed as an atonement and ransom. Through them you will be forgiven. Through them all the terrible and difficult decrees [against you] will be abrogated, and you will be saved from all punishments, all evil attacks, and diverse decrees. Out of gratitude [and in the manner of expiation with the heifer] we are obligated to spend all our wealth and stand at the side of the refugees and the unfortunate orphans who have been left like a ship adrift at sea. We should endeavor to help them. But this alone does not discharge our obligation to them. We are obligated even to beg door to door [in recognition of God's kindness and to publicize the miracle of our survival] in order to support the families of the holy ones who fell by the sword. Heaven forbid that the children of Abraham our patriarch, who have endured terrible trials and life-threatening dangers, heaven forbid, should still have to suffer hunger and thirst, oppression and want. We need to worry about them and improve their situation. Every person should extend his hand, a full and broad hand. Each should awaken the other, lest there be sin [on our part]. The hour [of opportunity] should not be missed; there should be no delay. Let there be no need for one to say to the other, "They said to one another, Alas, we are being punished on account of our brother, because we looked on at his anguish, yet we paid no heed as he pleaded with us" [Genesis 42:21].

We need to try to rescue them, with more than money. Those going through deserts and forests are in danger. There should be no delay, not for a moment. Satan prosecutes in time of danger and so there is the obligation to be zealous [at such times] in saving souls. See B. T. *Sanhedrin* 73[a] on the verse "Neither shalt thou stand idly by the blood of thy neighbor" [Leviticus 19:16]. One is obligated to save one's friend's life and fortune. See also B. T. *Baba Batra* 8[b], that the rescue of captives is obligatory because of "Neither shalt thou stand idly by the blood of thy neighbor" and also because of "Thou shalt not rule over him with rigor" [Leviticus 25:43]. Maimonides writes similarly in his *Sefer Hamitsvot* [*Book of the Commandments*]. We have this obli-

gation in respect to publicizing the miracle, involving the obligation to beg door to door. Anyone with a brain in his head will understand the many miracles and great wonders that have been done for us during these years of war. "We need to praise the Lord of all, to give praise to the Creator of the world, who has not made us [in this country] as [with] the nations [in the surrounding] countries" [*Aleinu* prayer], where they caused destruction to the house of Israel, heaven forbid. He has not made our portion here like theirs and our fate is not like theirs. With the help of God we have been saved until now. God will help us in the future as well to be saved from all trouble and oppression and will speedily redeem and save us.

It is our responsibility to publicize the miracle by going beyond our ability for the benefit of the refugees. Through this we show gratitude to the Lord for the wonders in the past and in the future. We show that we are most trusting in God's salvation in the blinking of an eye, and in His being with us, as if salvation has already come. Jews are believers and the children of believers, and in their eyes it is as if redemption has already come, according to the rabbinic Sages' statement "In the future the righteous will sing songs of praise for the future" [see *Midrash Shemot Rabbah, Parashah* 23, *Siman* 5]. [Yeshayah ben Avraham Halevi Horowitz, author of] the holy *Two Tablets of the Law* (*Shenei Luḥot Habrit*), explains that the people of Israel would be so strong in their faith and trust in the redemption that in their eyes it would be as if redemption had already come. They will sing songs of praise in advance about the future to come, although it is not proper to sing songs and praises unless salvation is already complete. With a new song, the redeemed people offered praise for the future salvation. Thereby it will actually take place: The Rock of Israel will come to the aid of Israel and will redeem His people, the house of Israel, and will lead us upright to a restored Land of Israel.

It is told that in a dream our holy rabbi, the noble Shalom [Rokeaḥ] of Belz, may his merit protect us, asked the holy rabbi [Elimelekh of Lyzhansk, d. 1786], author of the *Noam Elimelekh,* may his merit protect us, the meaning of the verse in the Torah portion *Beshallaḥ,* "Wherefore criest thou unto Me? Speak unto the children of Israel, that they go forward" [Exodus 14:15]. There was nothing surprising about asking, "Wherefore criest thou unto Me?" The people of Israel were in great trouble then; the sea was before them, the Egyptians behind them, and snakes and scorpions on all sides. If so, what else could Moses our teacher, the leader of Israel, do, if not cry out to God to help them? It is also difficult to understand why the sea had not yet split. And how could Moses tell them to go forward? Rabbi Elimelekh, may his merit protect us, answered with a story (mentioned in the book *Em Habanim Semeḥah* by Yissakhar Taykhtahl, page 239, in the name of the *Tiferet Yonatan, Parashat Lekh Lekha* [Genesis 21:1–17:27]) about a king who had an only daughter. She had all the positive attributes appropriate to a king's daughter. The daughters of the land were jealous of her and wished her harm. When she grew up, she got married. As her pregnancy was coming to an end and she was about to give birth, the doctors became extremely concerned. For she suffered terribly and the birth process placed her in great danger. A certain wise man came. He said that he had a remedy for her that would allow her to give birth peacefully and unobstructed. He ordered everyone to leave the room, so that except for himself and the king, no one would see or observe the birth. When they were alone, the wise man asked the king to go out and declare that a child had been born to his daughter. He should command that the good news be publicized immediately in every city. The proclamation was made throughout the land. While the king was surprised that the wise man sought to publicize the birth before it happened, the wise man ordered him to quickly fulfill his request, so the problems would immediately disappear and she would give birth quickly and easily. What would a father not do for the good of his only daughter? He went and proclaimed that his daughter had given birth, God willing. The king commanded messengers to publicize it in all the lands of his kingdom. Immediately the difficulties were transformed into lovely joy, for she gave birth to a son. The king was very happy that the remedy worked and healed his daughter, and he rejoiced over the son born to her. He asked the wise man to explain the matter to him. Why had he asked to proclaim the good news before the birth actually took place? He answered

that the king's daughter had many enemies. Witches cast many spells to stop the birth of the child and cause such hardships that she would even die in childbirth. Therefore he commanded that it be proclaimed that the child was already born healthy and wholesome. When it would be proclaimed that the child was already born, the witches would give up hope and would stop their incantations and spells against the mother. It was as the wise man explained.

It was also so in Egypt. Egypt was full of magicians and sorcerers who took pains themselves to disrupt the exodus of the Israelites from Egypt. The rabbinic Sages said, "Why is sorcery called *keshafim* (bewitching)? Because it overrules the decree of the heavenly council" [B. T. Ḥullin 7ᵇ]. In such a way the redemption was held back from arrival. In addition, there were many accusers and denouncers, and they accused Israel of not being ready to be redeemed. When Moses cried out to God, God said to him,

> "Wherefore criest thou unto Me?" [Exodus 14:15]. You defeat your own purpose. On account of your crying out the accusers will judge that the rescue of Israel has not been completed. [The accusers] will see that the heavenly guardian of Israel has not been victorious, and they will accuse even more. Therefore, it is best for you to be quiet and not cry out further. Instead, speak to the Israelites about going, as if "The rugged shall be made level" [Isaiah 40:4], and as if "The deeps were congealed" [Exodus 15:8] and "The mighty waters" [Exodus 15:10] have already dried up, and had already "maketh a way in the sea and a path in the mighty waters." [Isaiah 43:16]

[So God spoke.] When the accusers saw that Moses had commanded the Israelites to go forward and walk into the sea, they assumed that a decision had been reached above, that Israel prevailed, and that the miracle of the splitting of the sea would occur. They stopped their accusations. Immediately, all the sorcerers and enemies were neutralized; as the rabbinic Sages said, "The Israelites were redeemed solely through the merit of their faith" [see *Midrash Bereshit Rabbah, Parashah* 56, *Siman* 2]. The people of Israel had faith even before the miracle came about and even before salvation arrived. Therefore they were

worthy to be redeemed. Up to here [has been] the
answer of our teacher, the Noam Elimelekh [R.
Elimelekh of Lyzhansk (d. 1786)], who responded
in a night vision to the rabbi, the noble Shalom
[Rokeaḥ] of Belz, may his merit protect us.

The current situation of Israel is similar. We
have reached a crisis. There is no strength to
[endure the labors of] birth. This is because the
accusers stand against us from all sides, poised to
retard the redemption. [In this situation] it is
advisable to "Speak unto the children of Israel,
that they go forward" [Exodus 14:15]. They
should not be distracted by the exile. [They
should act] as if all the troubles have ended, as if
the redeemer were already standing there, as if
the redemption were rising and coming, and as
if salvation had come. [If they go forward, then
indeed] all the accusers will be abrogated and
redemption will truly come.

There is a matter of *Halakhah* (law) to tell you
about. I [Mordekhai Rokeaḥ] am sharing this
halakhic ruling as we part from one another. I do
so in the name of my brother [Aharon Rokeaḥ],
the holy sage, our teacher. May God be with him
and render him effective, and may God be with
him as he teaches the *Halakhah* properly. My
brother, the holy sage, may he have a long life,
states, as a ruling of *Halakhah*, that one is obligated to spend more than one-fifth [of one's
wealth] and to expend more money than the
value of those redeemed [see B. T. *Ketuvot* 52^b].
My brother concluded and said that he was not
speaking out of piety or out of fear of heaven.
This was a ruling of *Halakhah*. With these words
of [my brother] the holy one, I fulfill, with you,
the words of the rabbinic Sages: "A man before
taking leave of his fellow should not finish off
with ordinary conversation . . . but with some
Halakhah" [B. T. *Berakhot* 31^a]. You too will
fulfill the last part of this *Halakhah*. Through this
you will remember him. I will repeat and repeat
again my question and request. Remember this
Halakhah well, in theory and in deed.

*There is something else which I [Mordekhai Ro-
keaḥ] want to say, about which I want to awaken your
hearts and enlighten your eyes. It has to do with my
hearing many utterances [to the effect] that there are
many who are greatly afraid, fearful, anguished, trembling, and travailed [see Job 4:14]. They say that our
departure is very difficult for them. They are deeply*
*concerned about the future. They say that perhaps, God
forbid, danger lurks over this land. [They allege] that
my brother, a tsadik [righteous one] of the generations,
may he live long and happily, sees the events to come
and therefore is proceeding with his journey to the Land
of Israel. For there God has commanded the blessing,
"I will give peace in the land" [Leviticus 26:6]. [They
allege] that he is going to a place of peace and calm,
abandoning us to lamentation. [They wonder:] Who
will be responsible for us? Who will defend us? Who will
rescue us? Who will supplicate on our behalf? Who will
make attempts on our behalf? It is therefore my obligation to let you know the beautiful truth, my dear and
precious ones, scholars of Hungary. Anyone close to my
brother [Aharon], great among the rabbis, may he live
long and happily, anyone who stands near him, surely
knows that he is not taking flight. He is not rushing and
hurrying. It is not as though he wants to flee and get out
of here. Rather, it is a matter of his longing and desire to
ascend to the Holy Land, a land sanctified with ten
sanctities [i.e., the attributes of God]. I know that this is
the great time, when he yearns very much for the Land of
Israel. He has a tremendous desire. His holy soul longs
to ascend to the city of God. [Why?] To awaken there
[God's] compassion and will for the entire congregation,
so that our sorrow will end, so a camp of refuge remains as
a refuge, so that quickly "All the horns of the wicked also
will I cut off; but the horns of the righteous shall be lifted
up" [Psalms 75:11].*

*And this is indicated in the passage [in the Torah
portion Vayeḥi], "For he saw a resting place that it was
good. And the land that it was pleasant; and he bowed
his shoulder to bear, and became a servant under task
work" [Genesis 49:15]. Rashi interprets, "And became to all his brethren of Israel 'a servant under task
work' to adjudge for them the teachings of Torah"
[Rashi ad Genesis 49:15. This is surprising. What
was Rashi after in this interpretation?]. The intention
of "For he saw a resting place" appears [for us] to be
that the Tsadik [Aharon] sees that rest and peace will
prevail here [in Hungary] for the residents of the
country, that it is good [here]. The Tsadik sees that it is
good, and completely good. And good and mercy will
even pursue and grasp our brethren of this land, the
children of Israel.*

And I [Mordekhai Rokeaḥ] am eager to settle
in the Land of Israel and ascend to it, because the
land is lovely. Because supernal loveliness prevails
there. "A land flowing with milk and honey"
[Deuteronomy 6:3]. It is lovely, pleasing, and

sweet, spiritually and materially. In his home in the early days [Aharon] spoke about his journey to the Holy Land. The longing arose in his heart to go to the Land of Israel. Mighty waters could not quench the love, his love and desire for the Land of Israel. This is a sign for you that the journey of our rabbi [Aharon], may he live long, is not for the purpose of becoming prosperous or finding rest or improving his situation or position. Our rabbinic Sages said: "The Land of Israel is acquired through suffering" [see "The Holy One Blessed be He gave Israel three precious gifts. All of them were given only through suffering. These are Torah, the Land of Israel, and the world to come"; B. T. *Berakhot* 5ᵃ]. Surely the meaning is about the [spiritual] holiness of the Land of Israel. When it comes to the material aspects of the Land, eating its fruits and enjoying its bounty: Why should it have to be acquired with any more suffering than other lands? It is possible to travel to the United States or other countries overseas without suffering. Why, then, is it not possible to travel to our land in peace and serenity without suffering? Certainly, the meaning of the rabbinic Sages was that it was as impossible to attain holiness in the land without suffering, just as it was to attain Torah and the world to come without suffering.

And so his pure soul was replete with many troubles bound together, before he reached the stage of being worthy to ascend to the Land of Israel and see the loveliness of higher splendor. The sufferings will demonstrate that what he seeks is to gaze upon the loveliness of God and visit His sanctuary. . . . With this our rabbi, may he live long and happily, will come to the sanctity of seeing the sublime loveliness, of pleading there on our behalf for our salvation and imminent redemption. This is the "and the land that it was pleasant [lovely]" [Genesis 49:15]. The journey to the Land of Israel is for the holy loveliness in it. "He bowed his shoulder to bear" [Genesis 49:15] the suffering of the ascent; "and became a servant under task work" is the proof that he will be the messenger to all our brethren, the children of Israel, to apportion to them instruction of Torah. For it is a time of grace. The time of complete redemption is coming. For the Land of Israel is the place which is capable of instruction. As written in the Torah portion *Shofetim*, "Then

shalt thou arise, and get thee up unto the place which the Lord thy God shall choose" [Deuteronomy 17:8]. The rabbinic Sages explain, "This teaches that the place has an influence" [B. T. *Sotah* 45ᵃ]. The rabbinic Sages said, "Why is it called Mount Moriah? For from it went out instruction (*hora'ah*) to Israel" [B. T. *Ta'anit* 15ᵃ]. "For out of Zion shall go forth the law [Torah] and the word of the Lord from Jerusalem" [Isaiah 2:3]. In our Holy Land, the *Tsadik* [Aharon] will have superior power to instruct according to *Halakhah*, such that the Holy One Blessed be He will save us right away and immediately in a salvation which is forever. The statement of the rabbinic Sages is "It is righteous: For I make a decree and he may annul it" [B. T. *Moed Katan* 16ᵇ]. This is the *Halakhah*. The Land, which is holier than all others, is able to bring the Holy One to do the will of the *tsadik*. Also, there is no authorized religious court (*Beit Din*) except in the Land of Israel. "O that the salvation of Israel were come out of Zion" [Psalms 14:7].

Before I end my words, I want to give my thanks and blessings to our brethren, the children of Israel, who inhabit this country [Hungary]. May God preserve and protect them and keep them alive for all the good and kindness they have extended to us. With all their might and property, they have fulfilled the commandment of hospitality for guests. In particular the [Jewish] inhabitants of this city [of Budapest], who are known for their special love in fulfilling "Love ye therefore the stranger" [Deuteronomy 10:19] [have done so]. We have seen how Abraham our patriarch was perfect in the attribute of loving kindness [Torah portion *Va'era*; Exodus 6:2–9:35]. He was the only one in his generation to be hospitable to strangers. When the angels came to him he said, "And I will fetch a morsel of bread, and stay ye your heart; after that ye shall pass on" [Genesis 18:5]. This is very remarkable. Is the way to be hospitable to strangers to say to them, "Eat and then go on your way"? To the contrary, the way of love and affection would be to ask the guests to stay another day or two. Texts explain that Abraham was [indeed] perfect in the fulfillment of the commandment of hospitality for strangers. [Only] after he understood that the angels did not want to stay with him, he said reassuringly, "Then go on." That is, he would not delay them or deter them from going on their way. You [Jews of Budapest] have done similarly with us. After you learned that it was the will of the *Tsadik* [Aharon] to travel to the Holy Land, you did not deter him from our path. Also with this, I thank you for all the help and assistance you extended in preparing for the journey and ascent to the Land of Israel without trouble or pain. May God bless your strength. May the work of your hands be accepted. May you be blessed with children, life, and bountiful income. May you succeed in all your endeavors now and forever. May you be worthy to see the complete redemption and eternal freedom, to see the loveliness of God and visit His sanctuary, to ascend to Zion in joy and celebration, in all kinds of salvations and consolations.

I heard my father and teacher [Yissakhar Dov Rokeaḥ], the holy sage, may his merit protect us, explain the text of the *Kaddish* [prayer in praise of God], "Beyond all song and psalm, beyond all tributes that mortals can utter." It was remarkable, he said. Granted that [God is] "Beyond all song and psalm, beyond all tributes." And it is

understood well that God has no boundary. If so, how can a person bless or praise Him? A person can do so, because the praise is without boundary. But what about our saying that He is "beyond all consolation"? Does not the kind of praise need to be explained? [Yissakhar Dov Rokeaḥ] said that sometimes a person had so much pain and anguish that it was beyond human ability to console him. But the Holy One could do anything. When it comes to the mourning, anguish, and great and terrible destruction [which we are experiencing], it is impossible for people to console others. The Blessed Creator alone can offer consolation: "Comfort, comfort ye My people, sayeth your God" [Isaiah 40:1]. This is the "beyond all consolation." A person cannot console. Only God can console. Only God can heal our brokenness and bind our wounds. Only God can transform everything from anguish to joy, from darkness to light, from deprivation to abundance, from servitude to redemption. May the Blessed Creator bring to reality all the salvations and consolations of prophecy, speedily and in our days.

The Land of Israel

Reuven Katz

Reuven Katz (1880–1963) was educated in the yeshivas of Mir and Radun in Belarus and in the Slobodka yeshiva in Lithuania and participated in Ḥayim Ozer Grodzensky's study circle in Vilna. He held a variety of rabbinical positions in Eastern Europe until 1933, when he settled in Petaḥ Tikvah. He interpreted the Holocaust as punishment by God, for whom all of history concentrated into a single moment, for past, present, and even future Torah loss. The Holocaust was also the ultimate expression of transmission of the soul in terms of self-sacrifice and risking life (*mesirut nefesh*) and an *Olah* (whole sacrificial offering) of atonement, the ashes of which would evoke divine mercy in the form of restoration of the Land of Israel. Lest the *Olah* be in vain, Jews had to fill the Land with Torah—the only land where the life of Torah could be comprehensive.

SELECTIONS

In *Pidyon Shevuyim Vehatsalah* ("Redemption and Rescue of Prisoners") of December 1943–January 1944, Katz declared that the Jews of the *Yishuv* (the settlement in the Land of Israel) had to take responsibility for rescue. The *Yishuv* was the "camp" which was left as the first "camp" was threatened (see Genesis 32:8). Katz pointed out how David used the Temple's treasury for sustaining the poor, because their rescue was more important even than maintaining the *Shekhinah*'s (God's presence in the world) abode (2 Samuel 21:1). In *Kiyemu vekiblu* ("The Jews Ordained, and Took It upon Them"; Esther 9:27) of May–June 1944, Katz stated that in the time of Haman, Jews could not rescue themselves. But by declaring a fast in the name of *teshuvah*, Mordekhai and Esther evoked God's miraculous intervention. Now with Hitler, Jews had to assert Torah in the name of *teshuvah*—whereupon God would erase the new Amalek and bring redemption. In *Amalek Begilgul Hadorot* ("Amalek's Transmigration over the Generations") of February–March 1945, Katz declared that Amalek (personified by Hitler) was out to annihilate all Jewry. Assimilated Jews, however, were incapable of believing that German culture would allow it. The Torah, to the contrary, had commanded Israel not to forget Amalek nor his unchanging destructive impulse—and Amalek now meant Germany. Further, only in the Land of Israel, seeped in Torah, could the Jewish people protect themselves from Amalek's polluted (*tumah*) power (*Sha'ar Reuven: Davar Be'ito*, Jerusalem, 1952, pp. 216–222, 132–135, 150–153). In *Parashat Beḥukotai, Sevel Yisrael Ugeulato* (Torah portion *Beḥukotai*, "Israel's Misery and Israel's Redemption"), written shortly after the end of the war, Katz identified the Holocaust as a collective *Akedat Yitsḥak* ["Binding of Isaac"], but now one that had progressed from binding-for-sacrifice to actual murder. It was an atonement by the entire nation which God desired. By the strength of the ashes, God was fulfilling His promise to remember the Land, to break the yoke of exile, and to bring the people of Israel en masse to the Land for the freedom, independence, and political sovereignty needed in order to establish His presence among the people. It was now left to the Jews of the Land to draw God's presence toward them through Torah (*Duda'ei Reuven*, vol. 2, Jerusalem, 1954, pp. 72–78). Selections translated from the Hebrew by Gershon Greenberg.

Redemption and Rescue of Prisoners, December 1943

Redemption of captives takes precedence [even] over supporting and clothing poor people. There is no *mitsvah* greater than the redemption of captives, since captivity includes the categories of the hungry, thirsty, and naked and is life threatening. The one who averts his eyes from ransoming the captive transgresses, "Neither shalt thou stand idly by the blood of thy neighbor" [Leviticus 19:16] and "Thou shalt not rule over him with rigor" [Leviticus 25:43]. There is no commandment greater than that of ransoming captives [*Mishneh Torah, Hilkhot Matanot Aniyim* 8, *Halakhah* 10].

1

With these concise sentences and few strong utterances, Maimonides defined the shocking and tragic condition of captivity. It includes hunger, thirst, nakedness, and is life threatening. The situation implies the highest obligation, higher even than of sustaining and clothing the poor. With all our strength and ability we must turn to fulfilling the great commandment of ransoming captives and saving those doomed to death.

This definition is apt in evaluating realistically the terrible fate of captivity in normal times and times of normal and "humane" war, more or less. But when it comes to the murderous government which rules in this war, with Jewish captives in the hands of an enemy who despises people and destroys the image of God, not even Maimonides' incisive words cover the suffering and pain which is expected and fated for the captives. The greatest human oratory lacks the power to come even close to describing the punishments and the cruelties done every day and every hour to our brethren, the children of Israel. They have been abandoned to savage wrath and murder in the land of trouble and conquest.

2

In our long history, there have been countless instances of confronting a situation of ransoming captives and saving those condemned to death. However, we have never confronted such a terrible catastrophe (*Shoah*), so large in scope and as murderous as today's. This is the first time in our history that there is so much blood. A whole nation is committing all its powers to promulgating governmental "laws" to illegally obliterate Jews from the face of the earth. In this period of terrible persecution, we are witnessing a tragic reality. It confirms without a shred of doubt that the redemption of captives in our day is not [only] a question of lives in danger. It is a question of literally saving life, of saving our brothers who are being led to slaughter and death.

The help and rescue from our side needs to be as comprehensive and as great as is the disaster. We need to gather immediately and without any delay all the strengths that are latent in our people. We need to enlist all the means and abilities currently available in our nation, in order to deal with the many tasks and deeds with full responsibility and impetus. As much as it is possible, we need to immediately rescue the greatest number of our suffering brothers who still remain alive and take them out of the valley of slaughter of Europe which is rolling in Jewish blood. We have to use all means to save [those of] our brothers who can still be rescued from the teeth of the murderous animals which bring devastation in the vineyard of the house of Israel.

It is the fraternal obligation and command of the hour for the institutions of the *Yishuv* [the Jewish Community in Palestine] and the leaders of Israel, of all groups and [political] parties, to place the great and holy task of ransoming captives and rescuing brothers who are being led to slaughter at the top of all discussions and daily activities. In this terrible hour, we need to forget all the personal frictions and political differences that divide the leaders of the Jewish community all the year long. The agonized cries of our brothers in the claws of death in vanquished lands should awaken the conscience of the nation to readiness and rescue work. They should mobilize the nation to great actions and deeds of sublime strength. Warmhearted and active individuals who belong to help and rescue organizations have the obligation to utilize immediately all means at their disposal toward the holy task of rescuing the captives. We may not neglect any means, nor undermine any opportunity that comes our way. We should be ready to accelerate rescue and liberation of the suffering unfortunate ones. We are obligated to know and to teach that "Whoever saves one Jewish life, it is as if he saved a whole world" [*Mishnah Sanhedrin* 4:5].

The *Yishuv* is morally obligated to take to heart that the cruel invader stands at the gates of this Land of Israel. The *Yishuv* will not be saved through its own merit, but by the merit of our brothers in the exile which is drenched in blood. The grace of God has strengthened His people and our land, and we [here] will be rescued from the hands of the enemy and his soldiers of prey. This is in order that we be able to save the remnant that has remained in the lands of blood.

Jacob our patriarch teaches us about this in his command: "If Esau come[s] to the one camp, and smite[s] it, then the camp which is left shall escape" [Genesis 32:9]. The intention is not to say that by splitting the camp into two, the camp which is left could flee and save itself from the danger that surrounds the first camp. Rather, the words mean that the camp which is left would become a place of refuge for the camp that is attacked. Those who are saved would be support, help, and rescue for saving the camp that has fallen, the camp over which the decree of death and destruction hovers at every moment.

3

The Jewish *Yishuv* in [the Land of] Israel is obligated to be and should be in the vanguard of the redemption to save the afflicted camp. We are obligated to be instilled with the fundamental recognition that God has sent us to support and to liberate. He has sent us to sustain the firebrands which were saved from the worldwide abomination which embroils the camp of Israel. There are wondrous words by the rabbinic Sages, which touch to the depths of the soul, as to how and in what manner the nation is obligated to rise up to rescue at a time when part of the nation is drenched in suffering and crying out for liberation and redemption.

Scripture explicitly says: "Thus all the work that King Solomon wrought in the house of the Lord was finished. And Solomon brought in the things which David his father had dedicated, the silver, and the gold, and the vessels, and put them in the treasures of the house of the Lord" [1 Kings 7:51]. The words would seem to be remarkable, astonishing. How much exertion and effort was expended by King David before he was able to collect the great treasure that was needed for the building of the house of the Lord, to prepare the *Beit Hamikdash* (Holy Temple), the place of the *Shekhinah* (Divine Presence) in Israel! King David said about himself, "Now I have prepared with all my might for the house of my God the gold for the things of gold, and the silver for the things of silver, and the brass for the things of brass, the iron for the things of iron, and wood for the things of wood; onyx stones and stones to be set" [1 Chronicles 29:2–3]. What did Solomon do with all this? Solomon brought the many treasures and objects of beauty that David gathered with holy devotion over many years to the treasury of the house of the Lord. That is to say: Solomon placed them in storehouses. He used other treasure, other gold, and other vessels for worship in the Temple.

How was it that Solomon ventured to decide to store the life work of his father, King David? [The midrash says]:

"And there was a famine in the days of David for three years" [see 2 Samuel 21:1]. And David had—who knows how many?—treasures piled up with silver and gold which he had prepared for building the Temple, treasures all of which he should have spent to keep people alive; but he did not do so. God said to him: "My children are dying of hunger, and thou pilest up riches wherewith to build a building. With such riches thou shouldest have done nothing other than keep people alive. Yet thou has not done so. As thou livest, Solomon will find no need to take any of it." And Solomon brought in the things (which David his father had dedicated) . . . and put them into the treasuries of the house of the Lord. [*Pesikta Rabbati, Piska* 6:6]

Shishak, the king of Egypt, came up against Jerusalem, and he took away the treasures of the house of the Lord and the treasures of the king's house [see 1 Kings 14:25].

These penetrating words should serve as a paradigm and stir the hearts of our brothers living in peace in the land of our ancestors, as to how great the obligation is to come to the aid of the survivors and extend help and rescue to them. The building of the Temple served as a foundation for the unity of Israel. It was designated for the atonement of sins. The building of the Temple was the first commandment for the kingdom of Israel. Nevertheless, Solomon did not sympathize with the efforts and the work which David expended in accumulating the wealth, so that from the labors of amassing treasure the house of God would be built. Why is this so? Because of the famine during the days of David. David should have spent the treasure to feed the poor of Israel. David did not do so. He continued to guard the treasure for the holy and exalted goal of [building] the Temple. Therefore God said to him: "As thou livest, Solomon will find no need to take any of it" [*Pesikta Rabbati, Piska* 6:7]. This was to teach you that saving the people of Israel stood on a higher level, even higher than that of building the Temple which is the abode of the *Shekhinah* and the glory of the nation.

4

This important teaching should remain before the eyes of the leaders of Israel in light of the present danger to the remnants of our people who are captives of the enemy. All who avert their eyes from the terrible danger to the remnant of the slaughter transgress the "Neither shalt thou stand idly by the blood of thy neighbor" [Leviticus 19:16] and other prohibitions enunciated by Maimonides in the above-mentioned *Halakhah* (legal ruling).

The leaders of Israel are obligated to open the treasures of the people in this hour and to spend all the treasures of the nation to save the people of Israel and for their redemption. For what is not included in the category of captivity? It includes hunger and thirst, nakedness, disgrace, and threat to life. The whole *Yishuv* is called upon to give its all to save the refugees. The task of rescue needs to be the primary desire of the *Yishuv*. It needs to be its primary national and moral obligation in this fateful hour. As we know, Mordekhai and Esther gave their lives and their all to save Jews from the hands of those who wanted to destroy them. Whoever participates in the troubles of the community will be worthy to see the consolation of Israel.

We need to know in these fateful hours that we are dependent on the mercy of heaven, even in the Land of Israel. The cry for help from our brothers being slaughtered in the conquered lands needs to resound in our ears like the verse "For if thou altogether holdest thy peace at this time, then will relief and deliverance arise to the Jews from another place, but thou and thy father's house will perish; and who knoweth whether thou art not come to royal estate for such a time as this?" [Esther 4:14].

We work and expend our energies on governmental matters. But in the meantime, we neglect and abandon the obligation to save the remnant. We are oblivious to the fact that without a people of Israel, there is also no government of Israel. Without the root—Judaism of the diaspora and its branches—even our revival in the Land will evaporate and lose its power to exist.

Therefore, let us rise to God and His people! We must accelerate our help and extend rescue to the refugees! We must throw off the bonds of servitude and captivity from the remnant of the slaughter and destruction! We must increase our work for our brothers who are being brought to slaughter in the lands of blood! May God be our help in increasing our efforts. As we know from the words of the rabbinic Sages: "Said

R. Phineḥas: Five times in the first Book of Psalms does David petition the Holy One, blessed be He, to rise. . . . Said God to him: 'My son, David, even if thou petitionist me to rise many times, I will not rise. But when will I rise? When thou seest the poor, oppressed, and the needy sighing'" [*Midrash Bereshit Rabbah, Parashah* 75, *Siman* 1].

"The Jews Ordained, and Took It upon Them" [Esther 9:27], May–June 1944

1

When "a time of trouble" [Jeremiah 30:7] came to Jacob, and Haman decreed the destruction of the Jews from young to old, children and women, Mordekhai and Esther announced the observance of a three-day fast. It was to atone for the sin of having bowed down to an image and having enjoyed the banquet of that evildoer. God then accepted their penitent return and annulled the intentions of the enemy. "The Jews ordained, and took it upon them, and upon their seed" [Esther 9:27]. The rabbinic Sages interpreted: [After God annulled the intentions of the enemy,] they ordained what they already accepted—that is, they accepted the Torah voluntarily, as is explained in the talmudic tractate *Shabbat* 88ᵃ.

These words would appear remarkable. Why did the people of Israel delay accepting the Torah voluntarily until the time that God saved them from their enemies and they emerged with a great victory? Why did they not accept the Torah during the [three-day] fast, during a time of tears and mourning? That would have been a more appropriate and proper time for accepting Torah voluntarily, since accepting Torah is one of the ongoing definitions and principles of penitent return. Why did they delay accepting the Torah until the rescue [actually] came?

In my opinion, the explanation is as follows: It was a time when danger loomed in the air. A single step remained between the people and death. Even the righteous Mordekhai sought natural methods to abrogate the decree, through Esther's intervention before the king. But Esther said, "Go gather together all the Jews" [Esther 4:16] to do penance, to fast, and to afflict their souls. Esther believed less [than Mordekhai] in

the natural solution of intervention before the king. Even though she too believed that it was in the hands of the king to abrogate the decree, penitent return and fasting were the means to prepare for "And so will I go in unto the king" [Esther 4:16].

Esther was afraid to go to the king improperly and feared that the king would deny her request to overturn Haman's plan. However, she was certain that if she only succeeded in [actually] reaching the king without being turned away, he would extend the golden scepter to her. And it was within the ability and authority of the king to abrogate the decree, so the rescue of Jews would be assured. After Esther reached the king and he extended the golden scepter and asked, "Whatever thy petition, it shall be granted thee; and whatever thy request, even to the half of the kingdom, it shall be performed" [Esther 5:6], his sleep was disturbed. A miracle took place, where Haman was forced to lead Mordekhai on the king's horse through the streets of the city and call out, "Thus shall it be done unto the man whom the king delighteth to honor" [Esther 6:11]. This began the sequence of events leading up to the hanging of Haman, [including] the transformation of the intention of Haman, who wanted to destroy the Jews. But at this point it was also revealed that it was not in the hands of the king to recall the documents of the decree to destroy the Jews. For whatever was written by the king and sealed with his ring could not be recalled [see Esther 8:8].

In order to save the Jews from the decree, this suggestion surfaced: Write the Jews that the king gave them permission to gather and defend themselves, to kill all those who would threaten them and be avenged on their enemies. That is,

Jews alone and by their own powers would need to fight to free themselves from their enemies [see Esther 8:13]. Salvation and rescue would thereby come to them.

2

We need to reflect a little about this point. If the rescue came solely through the Jews' efforts, it is relevant to ask: What really prevented the Jews from doing this before the many miracles occurred? Not even Haman's decree denied the Jews permission to defend themselves, to battle their enemies, and to defend their lives with the stratagems of war. However, it was clear to the Jews that by their own strength they would not succeed in meeting the great challenge of standing against the many armies of their enemies. A miracle from heaven was needed to save them from this conflict, enabling them to stand against their enemies and vanquish them.

In the end, the Jews saw that they needed a miracle from heaven in order to be saved from the claws of Haman's decree, a miracle where fear of Jews would fall upon the enemy and the Jews would dominate the enemy. The miracle certainly did not delay the pace [of events]. The Jews gathered in their cities to attack those who sought their downfall. Nobody opposed them. In fact, they killed seventy-five thousand of the enemy and abrogated Haman's decree.

When the Jews were convinced that the hand of God alone had done this, they realized their mistake. They understood now that the course of events had a completely different explanation [than they thought]. For all this time, the Jews were inclined to believe that Haman's decrees were intended against them because they were Jews. [The decrees came, they believed,] because Mordekhai did not agree to kneel and bow to Haman: "But it seemed contemptible in his eyes to lay hands on Mordekhai alone; for they had made known to him the people of Mordekhai" [Esther 3:6]. Accordingly, the Jews saw the Torah and religion as the cause of the separation between them and their neighbor nations. They imagined that Judaism was the primary reason for the decrees, and even under the decrees they were not disposed to accept the Torah

voluntarily. In fact, their feeling was the opposite, namely, that the Torah and the religion of Israel were the cause of the evil that was afflicting them. Thus, the penitent return carried out by Israel was done only under compulsion. It was done so that God would have mercy on them and save them. In their inner souls, they did not understand that they had to accept the Torah voluntarily [and in the knowledge] that only Torah protected them and saved them from disaster.

There was a change in the situation in favor of the Jews. There was a change in the king's attitude, the hanging of Haman, the ascendancy of Mordekhai, and the announcement that Esther was of Jewish descent. Nevertheless, it was not these things which deterred the enemy from waging war against the Jews, and their rescue came only with a miracle from heaven. It became obvious that the foul hatred was not on account of their Judaism. It was rather a natural hatred, the hatred of a person against his friend. The hatred was generated when the weak did not yield to the desire of the strong to dominate the weak. It was generated when the weak desisted from bowing and kneeling before the stronger and more ruthless. This is one of the great disasters that has descended on the world. It is a plague which has dominated all humanity. Every nation wants and tries to dominate its peers, to oppress and humble its neighbors, if it only has the power to do so. The people of Israel have always been "the fewest of all peoples" [Deuteronomy 7:7] and the weakest. Therefore it has been easiest to degrade them, to humble them, and to dominate them. It is only by miracles from heaven that we have withstood the attacks of our enemies. The power of Torah alone has preserved the spirit of the nation, so as to stand courageously against the wicked and not to mix or assimilate among the nations.

3

This idea continues to be repeated in the reality of contemporary life, in all its ramifications and implications. To our great misfortune, the words of the rabbinic Sages are being fulfilled among us: "He placed a harsh king like Haman over them and returned them to the good" [B. T. *Sanhedrin* 97^b]. The evil Haman of our era also decreed to kill and annihilate all Jews. What the first Haman did not accomplish, his heir the second Haman did. He annihilated the Jews of Europe, destroyed the widespread, deeply rooted Jewish communities of the diaspora. True, we trust in the eternal Rock of Israel not to abandon His people and not to forsake His legacy. True, Haman/Hitler will fall under the weight of his own evil. Still, his schemes continue to be realized in many parts of the world which have been the abodes of Israel's spirit and life from time immemorial. Let us not repeat the mistake made in the days of the first Haman. Let us not wait to accept the Torah until after redemption and rescue come. Let us all accept the Torah already now, voluntarily and knowingly, in such a way that penitent return and Torah acceptance are joined together. For in Torah and penitent return lie the secret of Israel's rescue, now as in all generations and eras.

We see that the Haman of our generation plots not only against the Jews. He also plots against all nations which do not want to subordinate themselves to his discipline or submit to his political juggernaut. Strong and powerful countries, among them France, have fallen under the yoke of his tyranny. How much more so our weak and poor nation, which can rely only upon our Father in Heaven. If the greats of the world are imbued with the recognition that the rescue of the whole world can only come through the intervention of divine providence, how much more does this eternal truth need to be recognized absolutely and comprehensively by the people of Israel, the nation first to recognize the Creator of the world and to view Him as the ruler of creation.

We must draw the obvious conclusions from the events of the present and fulfill "The Jews ordained, and took it upon them" [Esther 9:27]. From now on, we must repair our way of life and understand that the Torah is the basis of our existence. We need to use all our strength to inculcate this recognition into the whole house of Israel. Namely, that with voluntary acceptance of the Torah the Holy One will eradicate the memory of the Amalek of this generation. The light of redemption will penetrate the land and its inhabitants. As Maimonides cites in his "Laws of Repentance": "Israel will not be redeemed except through penitent return. The Torah has already promised that when Israel will finally do penitent return, their exile will end and they will be redeemed immediately" [*Mishneh Torah, Hilkhot Teshuvah* 7, *Halakhah* 5].

It is clear that this is the period of the end of the exile. If we are instilled with the true will to speed up the redemption and liberation, we must strengthen ourselves in the protection of the Torah, to fulfill "The Jews ordained, and took it upon them" [Esther 9:27] voluntarily. We are to go back to the right path, to return the Torah to its original splendor, to strengthen and fortify those who fortify the Torah, the great centers of Torah learning, the yeshivahs in Israel which have remained refuges from the flood of blood.

AMALEK'S TRANSMIGRATION OVER THE GENERATIONS, FEBRUARY–MARCH 1945

1

For many, it is surely difficult to understand the depths of the Torah's command: "Remember what Amalek did unto thee" [Deuteronomy 25:17]. Why should it matter whether we preserve the memory of Amalek's deeds when we left Egypt or shift our attention away from them completely? Moreover, the Amalek of that generation has already disappeared from the world and time. [Since then,] "Sennacherib came and mixed up the nations" [Rashi *ad* B. T. *Sotah* 9^a], and we do not know who is or is not a descendant of Amalek. Even if we did, what benefit is there to keep remembering over generations the despicable deeds of Amalek in a generation which is no more? In every generation, particularly in this generation, Amalek-like bugs and insects proliferate in every place and land. They plot to destroy Israel. Why is memory of the deeds of the first Amalek of greater weight than [any] other?

Now comes the Amalek of this generation. He adequately provides the correct [object for the] meaning of the command of the Torah and the great value of the memory. It is clear and obvious that the explicit and fundamental evil design of this enemy of the Jews, Hitler, which he made public in his venomous program and speeches, was the complete destruction of the Jews. At the time, Jews certainly did not believe nor attach any importance to the words of the credo of this cruel gentile, namely, that he was indeed prepared to carry out the terrible decision to murder and destroy the Jews without fear or hesitation, once he had the power to do so.

Had the Jews believed in the seriousness of the frequent pronouncements of this cruel gentile, they would not have cared about their fortunes and valuables. They would have left the land of bloodshed immediately. That is the problem. The Jews did not believe. The Jews could not imagine that anyone walking on two legs could be so cruel and [capable of] such terrible ways of arousing horror, let alone that he would have the power he needed to do so. The Jews imagined that such an explicit warning from a wild beast was mere boasting and arrogance. The Jews calmed themselves with soothing fables, namely, that even if the desire to destroy was the core belief of that evildoer, the [German] nation as a whole [was different]. It was a nation of splendid culture, one which attained the highest and most magnificent levels of culture and science. It was a nation, so Jews were inclined to think, which was incapable of perverting God's image, of desecrating it by a sin as abominable as destroying a whole people, including the elderly and infants. In particular, [it was incapable] of destroying a people that gave the world the unity of God, the splendor of ethics, and the foundation of philosophy.

The chairman of the refugees, Mr. [James E.] McDonald, traveled to Germany to check on the accuracy of Hitler's threats concerning his plans for the future of the Jews. When he returned, he shouted at the top of his lungs that it was clear to him that the barbaric nation had definitely decided to exterminate the whole Jewish nation.

People laughed and ridiculed him. Normal human thought could not accustom itself to such an awful idea, that it was possible, particularly in the twentieth century, to erase a whole nation from the face of the earth and that nobody would raise any objection.

Because of this innocent and naive thought, the vast majority of the Jewish people remained in place in the diaspora until the great Ashmodai came and exterminated the vineyard of Israel, killing, slaughtering, and offering up six million brothers and sisters, elders and children. The [Jews'] belief in the humanity and the justice of that lawless nation was so great that when there was distress in areas of Russian conquest in terms of livelihood and food, hundreds and thousands of Jews left these areas for the area of German conquest.

2

That is why our holy Torah has the absolute command, "Remember what Amalek did unto thee" [Deuteronomy 25:17]. Then too, in the generation of the first Amalek, Amalek surprised you on the road. You apparently did him no harm. You did not plot against him. You did not attack him. You did not scheme to murder him. You did not intend to steal his money or inherit his wealth. Nevertheless, "And smote the hindmost of thee, all that were enfeebled in thy rear" [Deuteronomy 25:18]. In every way, Amalek tried to destroy and erase the name and memory of the Jews from the world. This is because the urge to destroy is an inseparable part of the existence and nature of Amalek.

The command of the Torah transmits an important declaration for Jews over the generations: They need to remember well and believe what Amalek says. If the gentile warns and proclaims that he will attack and slaughter you, you should believe him with all your soul and without any reservation or hesitation.

Another thing we need to learn from this instructive Torah portion concerns erasing [the memory of] Amalek. In general, we have a [self-] destructive weakness when it comes to remembering well the conditions of life in the diaspora. It is almost natural for Israel to have repeated feelings of comfort and longing [in the manner of] "We remember the fish, that we were wont to eat in Egypt for nought" [Numbers 11:5]. In no way can any Jew erase the land of Egypt from his heart once and for all—the very land that tormented the people of Israel and made them do hard labor. At times, a hidden desire even exists in the heart to return to Egypt and begin life there afresh.

Against all those with short memories, three times the Torah explicitly warns us not to return to Egypt. The Torah teaches the Jew to uproot any hesitation and notion from his thought and comprehension about returning to that land—a land without mercy, where there was killing without compassion. Egypt was a land in which you lived and for whose advance and welfare you worked. If Egypt could be so terribly cruel to Israel to kill children and wash in their blood, you have no permission or authority to return to this land. Nor to imagine that what happened in the past would not happen again today.

The land of Egypt is not a matter of one time and place. The rule that the Torah ordained at the time against Egypt must be applied now with redoubled force and strength against the Germany of today. For the nature of Amalek has not changed. There was still a need to impose a ban of excommunication not to return when the people of Israel were exiled from Spain. When it comes to Germany, there is no need for an explicit ban. For when it comes to Germany, the original Torah command not to return to Egypt remains in full force and authority: Do not return to Germany. The Jewish foot is forbidden by Torah to set foot on the soil of impure Germany. The whole nation is a nation of murderers. It is a nation which washed its hands in pure Jewish blood. It willingly participated in the extermination of a whole nation, the murder of a people in a torment which freezes the blood.

Yes, this is the identity of all the Amaleks. This was also the correct identity of the Polish Amaleks. With the help and support of the Polish Amaleks, the chief of the butchers [Hitler] was able to implement the work of exterminating our whole people. We are forbidden, under all sanctions of the law, to return there, to return to a people like this and a land like this. It is a land soaked with the blood of martyrs. [The Polish Amaleks] rejoiced over the blood they spilled. It is forbidden to forget. It is forbidden to put out of mind the savage belligerence of those who aided and abetted the murder or those who stood aloof from it. It is proper to engrave into the memory of our nation the bitter recognition of what the Poles, "the noble ones," were ready and able to do when given the opportunity.

3

"Remember what Amalek did unto thee" [Deuteronomy 25:17]. We are obligated to carry this command in the memory of the nation under all circumstances and possibilities. We will believe with complete faith in the threats of the gentile. Do not listen to the falsely seductive words that the nation of murderers will improve its ways and will uproot from its soul the roots of destruction and extermination. Amalek will remain Amalek through all his transmigrations and in all his situations.

"Therefore it shall be, when thy Lord thy God hath given thee rest from all thine enemies" [Deuteronomy 25:19]—only in the Land of Israel can the people of Israel find a place of endowment and growth—"that thou shalt blot out the remembrance of Amalek" [Deuteronomy 25:19]. Israel is required to exert all strength to remove from its mind and thought any inclination or any yearning for the impure lands under the control of Amalek. Remember and do not forget! We need to remember and learn this living truth well. To our great misfortune, this reality of life was deleted from our memory. The nation of Israel paid a terrible price in blood for this blunder. The terrible destruction in the diaspora, so strictly methodical, should open the eyes of Israel to see the truth of life from now on. We have to believe the gentiles' words of accusation and threat. On the other hand, we need to know that there is no renewal and place of rest for the people of Israel other than in the Land of Israel. Only in the land, the home of Jewish life, are we able to build a life of the present and for the future.

But emigration to and settlement of the Land of Israel is still not the only goal and end to Israel's path. Indeed, the rabbinic Sages determined, "In the land which you conquer you inherit" [source uncertain]. In the land of the Amalekites, there is no permanent conquest or inheritance to be had. At the same time, Judaism must clearly and honestly recognize that the essence of the aspiration and goal of the settlement in the Land of Israel needs to be aimed at building a life of Torah and Judaism to the full extent of, and deference for, their concepts.

We have been convinced countless times that "not by might nor by power" [Zechariah 4:6] is the path of Israel. Not by force of arms alone was the *Yishuv* saved when it was exposed to serious danger. The *Yishuv* was saved by the mercy of divine providence. The spirit of God hovers over Israel. It watches over Israel so that Israel remains a light and a remnant in the land of the patriarchs. Let us recognize and know the power of the existence of the nation. And let us establish the Torah as the authority for the life of Israel!

Torah Portion *Behukotai*: Israel's Misery and Israel's Redemption [Written Shortly after the War's End]

"If ye walk in My statutes and keep My commandments" [Leviticus 26:3]. I might think that this refers to the fulfillment of commandments. But when it says, "And faithfully observe My commandments," then the fulfillment of the commandments is already stated. How then shall I explain "If you follow my statutes"? That you shall toil in the study of Torah [Rashi *ad* Leviticus 26:3].

1

In the Torah portion [*Behukotai* (Leviticus 26:3–27:34)] it then says, "And I will set My tabernacle among you, and My soul shall not abhor you. And I will walk among you, and will be your God, and ye shall be My people. I am the Lord your God, who brought you forth out of the land of Egypt, that ye should not be their bondmen; and I have broken the bars of your yoke, and made you go upright" [Leviticus 26:11–14].

Among the commentaries about these verses and their explanations, we find insightful and wonderful things in this compilation:

"And I have broken the bars of your yoke" [Leviticus 26:11–14]. There was a parable: To what can this be compared? To a householder who had a plow ox which he lent to someone for plowing. That person had ten sons. One came and plowed and returned it and another came and plowed and returned it. The furrow was long and the ox lay down. All the oxen came home, except for that ox. When the owner saw that the ox did not come home, he was inconsolable. He immediately grabbed and broke the yoke and tore up the harness. Such is [the nation of] Israel among the nations of the world. One government comes and subjugates Israel and then goes on its way. Another government comes and subjugates Israel and goes on its way. When the end comes, the Holy One does not say to the nations, "So have you done to my son." He immediately breaks the yoke and cuts the harness. As it says, "The Lord is righteous; He hath cut asunder the cords of the wicked" [Psalms 129:4]. He lowered them so that no human being would fear them. [*Sifra: Behukotai* 3:6]

At the end of this portion, in which the blessing and the curse are designated, it says: "Then will I remember My covenant with Jacob; and also My covenant with Isaac and also My covenant with Abraham will I remember; and I will remember the land" [Leviticus 26:42]. About this verse, Rashi cites *Midrash Rabbah*: "Why was 'remembering' not stated in the reference to Isaac? Because the ashes of Isaac appear before Me, heaped up and resting on the altar" [*Midrash Bereshit Rabbah, Parashah* 94, *Siman* 5; Rashi *ad* Leviticus 26:42].

In the Talmud it says, "'This is an ordinance forever to Israel' [2 Chronicles 2:3]. Rabbi Gidel says in the name of Rav, this is the altar that was built and the great lord Mikhael stands and offers a sacrifice on it" [B. T. *Menaḥot* 110ᵃ]. The *Tosafot* [medieval commentators] comment:

> The *midrashim* disagree. There are some who say that [the sacrifices] are the souls of the righteous. There are some who say lambs of fire. We recite in the *Shemoneh Esrei* (the silent, standing prayer), *Avodah* section, "Speedily accept with love and favor the fire offering and prayer of Israel." There are those who say that the fire offering belongs to the previous passage, "And restore the service to the Holy of Holies of Your Temple and the fire offering of Israel." [*Tosafot ad* B. T. *Menaḥot* 110ᵃ]

The words of the Talmud and *Tosafot* require explanation. When does the fire offering of Israel refer to the former part of the *Shemoneh Esrei* and when to the latter part [along with prayer]? The explanation is the same for those who say the fire offering is the souls of the righteous and those who say the lambs of fire.

In order to comprehend the passages that are unclear, we will explain the fundamental matter of the death of the righteous and the expiation it carries for Israel. In the Torah portion *Shofetim* it says:

> If one be found slain in the land which the Lord thy God giveth thee to possess it, lying in the field, and it be not known who hath smitten him; then thy elders and thy judges shall come forth, and they shall measure unto the cities which are round about him that is slain.... And all the elders of that city, who are nearest unto the slain man, shall wash their hands over the heifer whose neck was broken in the valley. And they shall speak and say: "Our hands have not shed this blood, neither have our eyes seen it. Forgive, O Lord, thy people Israel, whom Thou hast redeemed, and suffer not innocent blood to remain in the midst of Thy people Israel." And the blood shall be forgiven them. So shalt thou put away the innocent blood from the midst of thee, when thou shalt do that which is right in the eyes of the Lord. [Deuteronomy 21:1–2, 6–9]

The midrash says about this matter of the heifer whose neck is broken and the removal of the innocent blood: "and suffer not innocent blood to remain in the midst of Thy people Israel" [Deuteronomy 21:8]. The Holy Spirit always answers, "So shalt thou put away the innocent blood from the midst of thee, when thou shalt do that which is right in the eyes of the Lord" [Deuteronomy 21:9; see B. T. *Sotah* 46ᵃ]. These words are enigmatic and hidden. The implication is that there is a controversy between the elders of the city and the Holy One. The elders of the city argue and say to God, "Suffer not innocent blood to remain in the midst of Thy people Israel" [Deuteronomy 21:8]. In response, the Holy Spirit answers and puts the blame on Israel itself, "So shalt thou put away the innocent blood from the midst of thee, when thou shalt do that which is right in the eyes of the Lord" [Deuteronomy 21:9].

The core of the Torah portion about the heifer whose neck is broken [requires] shedding light on the term "innocent blood" and explaining "innocent blood." We have to understand the meaning of the biblical verse "And the blood shall be forgiven them (*venikhpar lahem hadam*)" [Deuteronomy 21:8]. According to accepted interpretation, it should have said, "And they shall be forgiven for the blood (*venikhpar lahem al hadam*)." For the heifer is the atonement for the blood [of the slain man]; the blood itself was not the atonement.

Thus it is also appropriate for us to discuss the explanation for the continuation of this verse. "And they shall speak and say: 'Our hands have not shed this blood, neither have our eyes seen it. Forgive, O Lord, Thy people Israel'" [Deuteronomy 21:7]. The question is clear. If "Our hands have not shed this blood, neither have our eyes seen it," why is absolution needed? The rabbinic Sages responded to this and said: "The heifer whose neck is broken comes about because of their bidding farewell to the one who was killed without food and without accompaniment" [see Rashi *ad* Deuteronomy 21:7 and B. T. *Sotah* 45ᵇ–46ᵇ]. If so, then the meaning of the statement is thus: The elders say, "Our hands have not shed this blood, neither have our eyes seen it" [Deuteronomy 21:7]. Our eyes did not see to guarding the life of the one who was killed in advance. We did not give him food or accompany him, such as to prevent the calamity.

Because the elders contributed to the murder by not keeping an eye on the stranger, the Torah commanded them to bring the heifer whose neck was broken and to atone for the blood.

In order to understand the meaning of innocent blood thoroughly and comprehensively, I will employ a parable. The son of a distinguished person traveled to a distant land on business. On the way he felt ill. The physicians who examined him prescribed medicines and told him to conduct himself in certain ways. They warned him that as long as he followed their instructions he would have nothing to worry about, but that if he violated their instructions he would endanger his life. The son did not listen to their instructions. He became very sick and needed a difficult surgical operation. The alarmed parents called expert physicians to perform the surgery. The danger did not subside after the surgery, and the mother told the expert physicians that they should [continue to] have concern for her son's life lest the blood spilled during the surgery be in vain. The experts responded and explained to her that their primary task ended with the surgery and that the patient's condition from then on depended upon the son and physicians who were expert in continuing his care. If he would listen to instructions of the caring physicians, he would certainly recover his health completely. If not, his condition was liable to get worse and the danger to his life would become imminent.

Let us return and understand properly the meaning of the verses concerning the heifer whose neck is broken. The Holy One has commanded and taught man how to establish his manner of life for good and success. "If ye walk in My statutes and keep My commandments" [Leviticus 26:3], "And dwell in your land safely" [Leviticus 26:5], "I will cause evil beasts to cease out of the land, neither shall the sword go through your land" [Leviticus 26:6]. "But if ye will not hearken unto Me," etc. [Leviticus 26:14]. Later it says: "If one be found slain in the land which the Lord thy God giveth thee to possess it, lying in the field, and it be not known who hath smitten him" [Deuteronomy 21:1]. If someone slain is found lying in the open, this is not some accident that has nothing to do with the specific place. It is clear that the deed was connected with the specific place. The people

who were close to the corpse needed to be completely absolved, for surely they did not observe the path of God and the Torah as was their obligation. The elders of the city were to go out, "And they shall speak and say: Our hands have not shed this blood, neither have our eyes seen it" [Deuteronomy 21:7]. Thus, the sin was that "neither have our eyes seen it." The eyes were required to see that the stranger not be sent on his way without food and someone to accompany him. Since they did not worry about the stranger's needs, they [indirectly] caused his being killed. That is why they are obligated [to bring] the heifer with the broken neck.

However, the elders prayed and pled that the heifer whose neck was broken would be accepted favorably, and "Suffer not innocent (naki) blood to remain in the midst of Thy people Israel" [Deuteronomy 21:8]. "Innocent" in the sense that the sacrifice should not be for nought and in vain. The rabbinic sages used the term naki in another context: "As one says to a fellow man, 'That man went clean (naki) of his possessions,'" that is, with nothing [B. T. Baba Kamma 41ᵃ]. If the sacrifice is not accepted, the result would be that the blood will have been shed in vain. But to that, the Holy Spirit answers and says: "So shalt thou put away the innocent blood from the midst of thee" [Deuteronomy 21:9]. [That is,] you will ask of the Holy Spirit that the absolution be accepted and desired so that the blood which was spilled would not have been in vain. It would be better for you to worry about repairing what needs repair in yourselves and around you, since the calamity resulted from your deeds. The corpse found on the ground is not an accident that could have happened anywhere. It happened in your neighborhood, and the corpse that was found was the result of defective action by the inhabitants of your city. The people of the city need absolution because they contributed to the murder by averting their eyes. Therefore, "so shalt thou put away the innocent blood from the midst of thee" [Deuteronomy 21:9], in order that the blood should not be naki (in vain). This does not depend on God. The person himself is obligated to do the just and the good. Obviously, no affliction or misfortune should befall the whole community of Israel.

2

The core of all these words is that every victim of Israel is a result of the damaging acts of the community. Therefore the blame for guilt rests on each and every individual. We will arrive at the principle underlying several hidden and closed points. This idea is embodied in the verse "That the righteous are taken away from the evil to come" (*mipnei hara'ah ne'esaf hatsadik*); [Isaiah 57:1] because the righteous are taken from the world in order to atone for the trespasses of the generation. Through the meaning of this concept, we come to an explanation of the rabbinic passage [B. T. *Menaḥot* 110ᵃ] and the *Tosafot* cited above.

"There are those who say that [the sacrifice] is the souls of the righteous and there are those who say that [the sacrifice] is lambs of fire" [*Tosafot ad B. T. Menaḥot* 110ᵃ]. Why the souls of the righteous? When the righteous die for the sins of the generation, this belongs to the aspect of the [sacrificial] altar, which atones for Israel. Why the lambs of fire? When schoolchildren who never tasted of sin die and are killed, they are an absolution and atonement for the whole generation. As we say in the *Shemoneh Esrei* [the silent, standing prayer], "And speedily accept with love and favor the fire offering and prayer of Israel." When the Holy One takes the righteous and just, who in their deaths are to serve as [sacrificial] altars in order to atone for the sins of the generation, we plead and ask that "the fire offering of Israel" [be accepted with love and favor]. We plead and ask that these sacrifices which God took, and [the prayers] ("And accept their prayers with favor," *Shemoneh Esrei*) will be the desired atonement for the sins of the generation, such that the nation should not, heaven forbid, need additional sacrifices of the righteous and children. There are those who say that [the fire offering] belongs to the previous passage, "And restore the service to the Holy of Holies of Your Temple and the fire offering of Israel," for we ask that the service be returned to the sanctuary of the Temple, when the fire offering of Israel sacrificed would be that of bullocks. As is written, "Then will they offer bullocks upon thine altar" [Psalms 51:21]. At that time, we will have no need for human sacrifices of the righteous ones and children. As long as the nation of Israel is not yet worthy to attain the level

where their sacrifices would be of bullocks, we pour out our hearts so that the sacrifices of the righteous and the children that we offer up will be accepted with love and favor. Those sacrifices should be [as the sacrificial] altar that atones for the generation, so that the generation will be saved from all trouble and calamity.

Accordingly, *Midrash Rabbah* explains, "Then I will remember My covenant with Jacob" [Leviticus 26:42]. "It was because He saw Isaac's ashes, as it were, heaped up upon the altar" [*Midrash Vayikra Rabbah, Parashah* 36, *Siman* 5]. When does Israel need to be remembered before the Holy One? When the ashes are not piled up and resting on the altar. When the sacrifices of man are not of such merit as to ask that the memory of Israel ascend to the throne of mercy and justice. However, when the sacrifices of man and their ashes are piled up and resting on the altar, when the multitudes of Israel have been offered up as burnt offerings, and when their ashes are piled up and resting on the altar of the great *Akedah* [sacrifice] there is no need to explicitly mention the *Akedah* ["binding of Isaac"]. Their ashes bear testimony and raise the merit [of the sacrifice] before the Creator of all. Isaac does not need to be mentioned explicitly, since his ashes are piled up and resting on the altar. Accordingly, the ashes of his children and grandchildren which are piled up on the altars of the world are enough to awaken the mercies of heaven over the terrible situation of the nation to accelerate the redemption and the deliverance of worlds.

The *Akedah* of Isaac, of multitudes upon multitudes of the children of Israel, was created in our generation before our very eyes. This generation was a unique witness to a terrible Holocaust (*Shoah*), [and] "Upon earth there is not his like" [Job 41:25]. To our misfortune, angry chastisements, in awful and incredibly harsh measure, have poured down upon the head of Israel. The ax of destruction has swung over the inhabitants of the lands of the diaspora. It has killed six million brothers and sisters without any pity for the beauty of Jacob. More than a million children and babies among them. Since the destruction of the Temple, Israel has had no *Olah* (burnt) offering [see Genesis 22:3] of so many *Akedah*s, dying in the purity of sanctification of God and land.

This Holocaust (*Shoah*) placed the piled-up ashes of the greatest and noblest of the Torah on the altar of the righteous of the generation, the cedars of Lebanon, holy and pure Jews whose souls yearned to liberate Israel and yearned for the redemption of its land. Through the merit of these ashes which were resting on the altar by themselves, the greatest memory of Israel has been awakened before the throne of mercy. For that calamity agitates for the flight of the supplication and the outcry up to and before the Holy One. "And suffer not innocent blood to remain in the midst of Thy people Israel" [Deuteronomy 21:8]. The destruction and annihilation of the Jewish victims should not be in vain. It should be used as a desirable absolution for the whole nation.

Indeed, the power of the ashes that were piled up and rested on the altar raised the memory of the children of Israel before God. The Holy One fulfilled the promise, "Then will I remember My covenant with Jacob, and also My covenant with Isaac, and also My covenant with Abraham will I remember; and I will remember the land" [Leviticus 26:42]. All the nations of the world were knowing accomplices in the Holocaust of Israel, whether they were direct, active partners with the murderous nation, or stood by coldly at the [spilling of] blood and the slaughter and did not prevent it. All the nations of the world fulfilled the words of King David regarding Israel, "The plowers plowed upon my back; they made long furrows" [Psalms 129:3]. Therefore it says and was fulfilled regarding all of them, "And I have broken the bars of your yoke" [Leviticus 26:13].

All the nations dominated over Israel. In every land and every country of the gentiles, the nations maltreated us. They cut off limb after limb of the living physical and national body of Israel. This rule and this slavery had already assumed terrible dimensions. It ended up with the Holocaust of the slaughtering of a third of the nation. "When the owner saw that the ox did not come home, his mind would not be consoled. He immediately grabbed and broke the yoke and tore up the harness" [*Sifra, Parashat Behukotai* 3:6]. When the Holy One saw that Israel was almost exterminated from the world, heaven forbid, He immediately broke the yoke and led Israel upright and erect, to a life of freedom and independence.

The people of Israel have earned a country and a life of sovereignty and freedom, with the power of the destiny of courage and the promise of "Unto thy seed will I give this land" [Genesis 12:7]. However, the great memory that ascended up before God was that of the ashes of the children of Israel, the martyrs of the *Akedah*. On account of the conciliation [provided by the blood] of the Holocaust of Israel (*mishum hapiyus al hashoah shel Yisrael*), God "tore up the harness" [*Sifra, Parashat Behukotai* 3:6], i.e., the bonds of servitude placed on the throat of Israel. But freedom and independence are not a goal in themselves. They are means designed to lead Israel to the great promise of "And I will set My tabernacle among you. And I will walk among you and will be your God, and ye shall be My people" [Leviticus 26:11–12]. Freedom and liberty are required to be instruments which bring Israel to a life of holiness and to be a chosen people.

"If ye walk in My statutes, and keep My commandments" [Leviticus 26:3] and "I will give peace in the land, and ye shall lie down, and none shall make you afraid" [Leviticus 26:6]. Many dangers still lie in wait for the country. There are still many great and awesome tasks and objectives remaining in stabilizing the legacy and achieving complete security. However, it has been promised to the country that if the people "shall toil in the study of Torah" [Rashi *ad* Leviticus 26:3], if they establish the country and its way of life on the foundations of Torah and the heritage of Israel, then "And I will establish My covenant with you" [Genesis 9:11]. The country which began in trouble will survive and thrive to be a source of life and light for the world.

"And the blood shall be forgiven them" [Deuteronomy 21:8]. It is not that the absolution is separate from the blood. It is not that the absolution is for the blood. The blood itself is the absolution for Israel. The blood of the holy ones and heroes who brought Israel freedom and the country itself. The blood of the righteous functions as the desired conciliation for the sin of the generation.

May the Holy One keep for us and what concerns us, the "And I have broken the bars of your yoke" [Leviticus 26:13]. However, at this hour it is for us to fulfill the verse "So shalt thou put away the innocent blood from the midst of thee"

[Deuteronomy 21:9], according to its midrashic meaning. We are responsible. The matter has been placed in our hands, for the blood that has been shed not to be in vain. Our deeds will determine the destiny of our life and the revival. If we will fulfill the Torah according to "If ye walk in My statutes," then we are assured the "And make you go upright" [Leviticus 26:13]. That is, upright in a life of eternal redemption, upon the arrival of the righteous Messiah, amen and amen.

Yitshak Breuer

Yitshak Breuer (1883–1946) was born in Papa, Hungary, the son of Solomon Breuer and grandson of Samson Raphael Hirsch. He studied at his father's Frankfurt am Main yeshiva and then pursued philosophy, law, and history at various German universities. He settled in Jerusalem in 1936 after the Nazi rise to power and became founding president of the *Poalei Agudat Yisrael* (workers' division of *Agudat Yisrael*). His works include *Messiasspuren* (1918), *Judenproblem* (1922), *Wegzeichen* (1923), *Das jüdische Nationalheim* (1925), *Die Welt als Schöpfung und Natur* (1926), *Elischa* (1928), *Eliahu* (1929), and *Der neue Kusari* (1934).

Carrying forward his grandfather's themes, Breuer argued that the people of Israel were rooted in God's two eternal creations, nature and Torah. They had a metahistorical dimension in terms of a timeless covenantal relationship to God and were to draw the rest of the nations up to this height. For this purpose, Israel went into exile. The nations, obsessed with sovereignty, resisted. In the modern era, just as Jews in Western Europe were abandoning the refuge provided by their metahistorical dimension to mix with the nations, thereby becoming vulnerable to them, the nations' sovereignty and racism exploded into attacks. The goal of raising the nations' history up to Israel's metahistory sank into oblivion. It was now left to the people of Israel to establish their own historical context, one which related to metahistory. This was possible only in the Land of Israel. Once history and metahistory related in the Land, it would be possible for the people to resume their worldwide historical mission.

SELECTIONS

In the selections below from *Moriah: Yesodot Hahinukh Haleumi Hatorati* (*Moriah: Foundations of National Torah Education*), translated from the Hebrew by Gershon Greenberg, Breuer wrote that Israel's place was not in general history, with its sovereignties. It was in sacred, creative history, i.e., metahistory. Once in exile, however, Israel became enmeshed in general history. Eventually, this involved confrontation with Germany. Germany's war against the Jews verified that Israel inevitably resided in history as well. The war also established the limit to emancipation. The confrontation in Europe reached apocalyptic and messianic proportions, pitting power, fury, and tyrannical sovereignty against righteousness, judgment, and man-as-God's-image; and pitting racial doctrines against the unity of mankind. Ultimately, it set in opposition Nazism/*Sitra Ahra* against Torah/God. Following the calamity and once in the Land of Israel, Breuer averred, the people of Israel must transcend the exilic mindset which made metahistory secondary to history. Jews in the Land also had to resist any attempt to create any sort of history which drew from the exile, in effect replacing the exile with exile-defined history. In the Land, non-exilic history was to be instilled with Israel's metahistory. Drawing on the ideology of *Agudat Yisrael* world president Jakob Rosenheim, Breuer envisioned the organization, centered in the Land, as providing definition and leadership for world Jewry (*Moriah*, Jerusalem, 1944–1945).

Moriah: FOUNDATIONS OF NATIONAL TORAH EDUCATION

Israel Has No Place in General History

The most fundamental principle of Judaism is to know that Israel has no place in general history. "Know of a surety that thy seed shall be a stranger in a land that is not theirs, and shall serve them; and they shall afflict them four hundred years" [Genesis 15:13]. Enslaved and afflicted as strangers in a land not theirs: This is the fate of the seed of Abraham in general history up to the present day. "'And also that nation, whom they shall serve' [Genesis 15:14]—this includes the four kingdoms" [Rashi *ad* Genesis 15:14]. The exile of Egypt was the "iron crucible" in which the seed of Abraham felt, in body and soul, the nature of the sovereign state. Pharaoh thought that there was national advantage to oppressing the children of Israel. In the name of the state, as the supreme will of the state, he proclaimed laws against the children of Israel. The whole purpose was to kill and destroy them. Were these laws lawful? In a formal way, [they were] without question, for they were the compelling authority of Egyptian society. But in truth they were but terrible wrath. They were not intended to be fair. They were to serve a political purpose, which was the supreme vision of the sovereign nation. In the iron crucible of Egypt, the seed of Abraham learned that an unbridgeable, threatening abyss had opened between the sovereign state and humanity. The seed of Abraham would not forget this teaching until the present day, not even if their deeds became alien to their Father in Heaven. This teaching, the heritage of their fathers, even beats in the hearts of the Jewish "revolutionaries," albeit without their knowledge—such that none is able to recognize the state as a goal in itself.

It also teaches, "We were Pharaoh's bondmen in Egypt" [Deuteronomy 6:21]. The Egyptian exile was the school in which to learn not only the grievous curse of sovereignty in terms of relations between nations. [But] also [to learn] the grievous curse it has been in relations between people, in internal social relations. The societal question, no less than the international one, burns around the cradle of the nation of Israel. In Egypt, our fathers experienced all the poverty and servitude of the worker and the slave who is denied property and is exploited by those who dominated to the last penny. God promised Abraham, of blessed memory, to avenge the social injustice as well as the national injustice: "And afterward shall they come out with great substance" [Genesis 15:14]. "And they despoiled the Egyptians" [Exodus 12:36]: That is, they exploited the exploiters! In Egypt, the seed of Abraham acquired feelings of justice and righteousness, feelings of pity and loving kindness, of moral pathos in the face of social injustice. Until the present day it beats in the heart of the Jewish revolutionaries, even though their deeds have been estranged from their heavenly Father.

The nation [of Israel] was a decidedly poor nation, amid a large and dominant nation. It had the status of workers with no rights amid a successful society of cruel exploiters. Two problems arose at the beginning of Jewish history, and general history has not found a solution to them even to the present day. Namely, problems of right and justice. One needs to guard the path of God to do justice and right, since justice and right belong to God. In general history, that of the history of sovereign states, the nation of Israel remains a small nation to the present day, decidedly poor amid large and strong nations. Israel's situation is that of workers with no rights, amid a society of cruel exploiters. Therefore, until the present day Israel has no place in general history.

The Exodus from Egypt: The Entrance of Israel into Metahistory

The exodus of the seed of Abraham from Egypt and the exodus of Abraham, may peace be upon him, from Ur of the Chaldees parallel each other completely. The deeds of the fathers are a portent for their descendants [see B. T. *Sotah* 34ᵃ]. Abraham, may peace be upon him, and his descendants exited from general history—Abraham, may peace be upon him, as an individual, and his descendants as a familial group. Miraculously, [with Egypt], His Blessed Name took the father and his family out of general history, with the former acquiring the human being for Himself, and with the latter the family. With ten new utterances of creation—"Let there be"—the Creator removed the veil of nature, thereby breaking the bonds of general history founded upon nature. Creation arose against nature in strengthening created history over natural history. The exodus from Egypt was the primary foundation of all of Judaism. "That thou mayest remember the day when thou camest forth out of the land of Egypt all the days of thy life" [Deuteronomy 16:3]. It was also the exit from natural general history, where Israel had no place. The exodus from Ur of the Chaldees was the return of the human being to the pure and holy [history of] humanity. The exodus from Egypt was the return of the human family to the holy and pure history of humanity. This exodus was also not an end in itself. It was the necessary precondition for entry into created history, which we call "metahistory." From the day that the seed of Abraham, of blessed memory, left Egypt, every single Jew has been forever obligated to leave Egypt, that is, to separate himself from general history and enter the history of his nation, to enter metahistory where only his people and his God are found. The exodus from Egypt testified both to metahistory and to metaphysics, to the history of createdness and to creation itself—"Let there be" for the former and "Let there be" for the latter—to the *Shabbat* of the creation and to the *Shabbat* of history: "A reminder of the exodus from Egypt" [see Nahmanides' *ad* Exodus 21:2].

History and Metahistory

There is a *Shabbat* in history as there is a *Shabbat* in creation. "Remember the day of *Shabbat*, to keep it holy" [Exodus 20:8]. "For in six days the Lord made heaven and earth ... and rested on the seventh day" [Exodus 20:11]. This is the *Shabbat* related to creation. Creation exited the aspect of "Let there be" and entered the aspect of "And it was thus." Creation clothed itself in the robes of *Shabbat*, which covered the whole secret of creation. The human mind is able to recognize the creation and prevail over it only in the form of nature. The *Shabbat* of creation was the necessary assumption for the six days of human activity. The *Shabbat* of creation is, surely, the spatial and temporal connection, the undisturbed connection between cause and effect. Nevertheless, the whole essence of nature is solely that of creation. The laws of nature are the will of the Creator, the Creator who rested from the seventh day on, since from then on He used the laws of nature in His rule over the whole world. And as the laws of nature were His will alone, the Blessed Name truly "Renews His creation with His goodness every day" [*Berakhot Keriat Shema, Shaḥarit Leḥol*]. Each and every week, when the day comes when the *Shabbat* of creation began, the people of Israel are commanded to remove the covering of nature from creation and to conduct themselves with creation as if creation belonged to the category of "Let there be." For then, given the prohibition of work, it is impossible for the human being to dominate creation: Whoever works on the *Shabbat* denies creation and asserts belief in the eternality of nature. The nation of Israel is the nation of creation, the nation of metaphysics.

"Observe the day of *Shabbat* to keep it holy" [Deuteronomy 5:12]. "That thy man-servant and thy maid-servant may rest as well as thou. And thou shalt remember that thou was a servant in the land of Egypt, and the Lord thy God brought thee out thence by a mighty hand and by an outstretched arm" [Deuteronomy 5:14–15]. This is the *Shabbat* which relates to history and not even a hint of creation is found here. With the rebellion of Adam and the rebellion of the generation of the flood, the earth filled with sovereign nations and sovereign people. All of them think of themselves as God, knowers of good and evil, of justice and injustice, and He who sits in heaven smiles and lets them. "And the flaming sword which turned every way" [Genesis 3:24]— social wars internally, and international wars externally, of which there is no end in the course of the history of human sovereignty—and the two cherubim guard the path to the tree of life. Not the "Let there be" of the Creator, Blessed be He, but the "Let there be" of the tyrants is realized with history. It appears that the strong always overcome the weak. This is the *Shabbat* of history. With this *Shabbat*, the [divine] King of the world contracts Himself, leaving room for the tyrannical sovereignty of people and their nations. Despite this, the King of the world remains the King of the nations. The tyrannical sovereignty itself, with all its evolutions, continues in its mission to be a master who performs all things, who hires fools and transients [see Proverbs 26:10]. The [divine] king of the nations rules over history as the Creator of the world rules over nature.

The nation of Israel alone has no sovereignty. The nation of Israel is the historical creation of the Blessed Name. This creation remains a creation without a natural covering. It remains in terms of the aspect of the "Let there be" of the Creator. The nation of Israel is a "nation within a nation." Its history is a history within history. Each and every week, when the [*Shabbat*] day comes on which the nation of Israel testifies about the creation of the world, the nation of Israel testifies to its own creation. The prohibition of work of [the aspect of] "remember" says: Nature is a creation, and it is completely for the sake of the Blessed Name. The prohibition of work of [the aspect of] "observe" states: The nation of Israel is a creation and is completely for the sake of the Blessed Name. Every *Shabbat*, the nation of Israel returns nature in its totality to its Creator. Every *Shabbat*, the nation of Israel returns itself completely to its Creator. It is also said to the nation of Israel: "Subdue it." Indeed, "subdue it," according to the will of God. The "work" is a symbol of the subduing. The *Shabbat* of "remember" says: The subdued is for God. The *Shabbat* of "observe" says: The subduer is for God. Everyone who works on the day of *Shabbat* denies the creation of the nation of Israel and

believes that the nation of Israel is like the families of nations. Metahistory is the history of the historical "Let there be" of the Blessed Name. It realizes itself indirectly within general history and realizes itself directly in the history of the nation of Israel. The nation of Israel is the nation of metaphysics and the nation of metahistory.

Rest itself symbolizes freedom. The nation of Israel did not acquire freedom for itself. With a strong hand, the Blessed Name took Israel out of the house of bondage to be His nation. Anyone who rests on the *Shabbat* as he wishes, and not according to the will of the Blessed Name by abstaining from prohibited work, once again denies the exodus from Egypt. "Your children will recognize and will know that their rest is from You." The Friday evening prayer is of "remember." The *Shabbat* afternoon prayer is of "observe." "That thy man-servant and thy maid-servant may rest as well as thou" [Deuteronomy 5:14]. Compare [this with]: "Thou shalt love thy neighbor as thyself" [Leviticus 19:18].

The War of Nazism against the Nation of Israel

The League of Nations glorified justice and right as the highest social values of humanity. Therefore, the failure of the League of Nations and of its vision meant the failure of justice and right in societal life. Indeed, the obvious contradiction between the vision of the League of Nations and the sovereign states, and the obvious contradiction between the League of Nations and the peace agreement it was assigned to keep, awakened all the enemies of justice and right. They provided the enemies with an excuse for tremendous propaganda against the vision itself, saying that it only protected the strong and the victorious. The failure of the League of Nations infinitely degraded the vision of justice and transformed it into a scarecrow among the nations. The terrible degradation of the feeling for justice and right spread throughout the whole world. This prepared the ground for all the evil powers slumbering forever in the hearts of man. It is obvious that the degradation of justice and the spread of the evil impacted first of all the nation whose whole existence depended on justice and on justice alone.

The Messianic Character of This War

The war of Nazism against the Jewish people was the introduction to World War II. The world war began in 1939. The beginning of the "Jewish war" was in 1933. When Nazism took control of Germany, it officially declared war against the whole Jewish people. Not only against the Jews of Germany, but against all the Jews in the world. [This is] another step forward in the movement of national emancipation: Germany will fight against the Jewish people, thereby recognizing precisely that the place of the Jewish people is—in history.

A strange war, a war that has no parallel, a messianic war. Not army against army, not power against power, not might against might. Rather, strength against justice, wrath against right, tyrannical sovereignty in its ultimate persistence against the fundamental vision of humanity: the person in the image of God. Never in the course of history has the human character of the Jewish people been as pronounced as in this war. The destiny of the Jewish people, and the destiny of justice and of the vision of humanity itself, and also the destiny—as it were—of the Holy One in the world have become one. Never have the people of Israel been elevated to such a degree in history. Surely, they paid a terrible price.

With great perceptiveness, Nazism recognized that its most menacing enemy in the world was the Jewish people, the people of the Torah. There is no place in the one world for [both] Nazism and Judaism. One of the two must certainly go to the grave. And this is the importance of the Jewish nation.

Nazism is the most extreme rebellion against God and His Messiah. Nazism is the unbounded tyrannical sovereignty of bestial society. Race is a bestial concept. It is the rule of "And it was thus" and not the concept of "Let there be." The doctrine of racism is the deification of the beast. The individual beast and bestial society are in truth "sovereignty" for they recognize only their own purpose, and their purpose is the supreme [goal]. For Nazism, race is the foundation of the person and of the nation. Nazism denies the unity of humanity with all its strength. Race is the basis for the state. It is the ethical basis and the religious basis. "You shall have no other gods before race!" To the individual racist, it is the foundation of faith; for the racist nation, it is the foundation of law. What is useful for racism is good and just. What damages racism is bad and sinful. Therefore, Nazism is literally the creation of the *Sitra Aḥra* [the evil side]. The war of Nazism with the people of Israel is the war of the *Sitra Aḥra* with the Holy One. This is the glory of the Jewish people. The period of national emancipation continues and advances. "Thou art a mighty prince" [Genesis 23:6] against the minister of materiality.

"Jacob Was Left Alone" [Genesis 32:25]

This war broke out in 1933, a war of Nazi Germany against the people of Israel. With one stroke, social emancipation in Germany was abrogated. The doors of justice and right were locked to the Jewish person, and the whole Jewish nation was condemned to destruction and extermination. The League of Nations was silent, and all the democratic powers remained silent as well. It was then in their power to squash Nazism like a bug, but they did nothing. After all, Germany was a sovereign nation. Therefore, its "internal" matters could not be interfered with. Justice and right were "internal matters" for each nation. The nations did not realize that right and justice tolerated no division, and that denial of right and justice in any particular context meant denial of justice and right in general. The Second World War was a direct result of this error.

When the "Jewish" war broke out, the Jewish people found not one ally in the world. When Germany attacked the Jewish people, it also attacked justice and right. Know and do not forget: Justice and right as well found not a single ally. "Jacob was left alone"! [Genesis 32:25]. Like "For His name alone is exalted" [Psalms 148:13], there's "alone" in the former and "alone" in the latter. The people of Israel's only ally is God. And God has no other ally in history than the people of Israel. In the era of national emancipation, the people of Israel had the status of a nation among nations. Precisely because of this, their aloneness was visible to all. Metahistory within history. "It is a people that shall dwell alone, and shall not [be] reckoned among the nations!" [Numbers 23:9]. Not even Zionism will abrogate the promise of the Torah.

The European Catastrophe

"Jacob was left alone" [Genesis 32:25] further after the Second World War was added to the war against the Jews. Jacob was also left alone after the democratic powers finally decided to "fight for justice and right." Today, there are two wars in the world: the separate war against the Jews and the separate world war. The democratic powers are beginning to win, and the trumpet call of their strength fills the land. The sound of our nation's cry bursts out and ascends to the firmament, and the nation's blood is spilled every day like water. There is no model for the Jewish catastrophe, either in all of Jewish meta-history or in all of general history. What took hundreds of years to build was destroyed in Europe in a few short months. The wrath of our King, the King of the nations! A number of times, our King passed over the entrance to His land. He did not allow the destroyer to come to His land and smite it! The intelligent person remains silent in such a time! What is this? Why is this? Because the people of Israel did not understand the voice of God? Who knows if it was not by the merit of the holy ones slaughtered in Europe that we live in the Land of Israel? Who knows whether it is because of our sins here in the Land of Israel that holy ones are being slaughtered in Europe? Our King passed over the threshold of our land. He allowed the destroyer to go to the diaspora. Will the people of Israel understand the second call of our King?

The War of Nazism against the Allies

The whole world is once again burning in fire. Once again, all human culture has been abrogated. The powers of destruction rule the face of the whole world. Once again, general history shows its original face. The Allied powers are the standard bearers of "justice and right." Indeed, where is the naïve person who today thinks that this terrible war is—the last one?

The Messianic Character of This War

How long, O Lord, shall I cry, and Thou wilt not hear? I cry out unto Thee of violence, and Thou will not save. Why dost Thou show me iniquity, and beholdest mischief? And why are spoiling and violence before me? So that there is strife, and contention ariseth. Therefore the law is slacked, and right doth never go forth; for the wicked doth beset the righteous; therefore right goeth forth perverted. Look ye among the nations, and behold, And wonder marvelously. For, behold, a work shall be wrought in your days, which ye will not believe though it be told you. For, lo, I raise up the Chaldeans, that bitter and impetuous nation, that marches through the breadth of the earth to possess dwelling places that are not theirs. They are terrible and dreadful; their law and their majesty proceed from themselves. Their horses are swifter than leopards, and are more fierce than the wolves of the desert; and their horsemen spread themselves; Yea, their horsemen come from far. They fly as a vulture that hasteth to devour. They come all of them for violence. Their faces are set eagerly as the east wind; and they gather captives as the sand. And they scoff at kings, and princes are a derision unto them. They deride every stronghold, for they heap up earth and take it. Then their spirit doth pass over and transgress, and they become guilty. Even they who impute their might unto their god. Art not Thou from everlasting, O Lord my God, my Holy One? We shall not die. O Lord, Thou hast ordained them for judgment, and Thou, O Rock, hast established them for correction. Thou that art of eyes too pure to behold evil, and that canst not look on mischief, wherefore lookest Thou, when they deal treacherously, and holdest Thy peace, when the wicked swalloweth up the man that is more righteous than he; and makest men as fishes of the sea, as the creeping things, that have no ruler over them? They take up all of them, with the angle they catch them in their net, and gather them in their drag; therefore they rejoice and exult. Therefore they sacrifice unto their net, and offer unto their drag; because by them their portion is fat, and their food plenteous. Shall they therefore empty their net, and not spare to slay the nations continually? I will stand upon my watch, and set me upon the tower and will look out to see who He will speak by me, and what I shall answer when I am reproved. And the Lord answered me, and said, "Write the vision, and make it plain upon tables, that a man may read it swiftly. For the vision is yet for the appointed time, and it declareth of the end, and doth not lie. Though it tarry, wait for it; because it will surely come, it will not delay." [Habakkuk 1:2–2:3]

This [current] war too is messianic. "Thou hast ordained them for judgment, and Thou, O Rock, hast established them for correction." God raised up the Nazi nation, "that bitter and impetuous nation, that marches through the breadth of the earth to possess dwelling places that are not theirs." A "terrible and dreadful" nation, "they come all of them for violence," and "they gather captives as the sand." Their power is their god, and they sacrifice to his "drag" and they make offerings to his "net," and then his laws come from their god. For power is their god, and their laws come from their god.

It is impossible to describe more succinctly the character of tyrannical sovereignty. It is the root of all the wars and all the tragedies of human history. The double rebellion of the generation of the flood: Nazism drew the final conclusions. This [current] war is the destructive eruption of all the material powers found in people, which are vehemently opposed to the plan of creation. Only divine justice and divine right are able to restrain these powers. Even the teachings of democracy are not enough. A little bit of Nazism slumbers in every sovereign people, in every sovereign state. All sovereign states and sovereign peoples can recognize themselves in Nazism as in a mirror. To the question that is being asked today: How is it possible that a cultured people like the Germans descended to the deepest abyss? To this question there is only one answer: From ancient times until the present, tyrannical sovereignty and the nationalization of justice and right have been thresholds for extreme barbarism. The insane exaggeration of the doctrine of sovereignty, which is Nazism, is the satanic and public denial of justice and right and the image of God, and of the plan of creation and the Creator Himself. This war is the war of the allies against the historical evil inclination, against the national evil inclination which burns in the hearts of—all

sovereign states and peoples. It is no accident that the people of Israel have no allies in the Jewish war. The nation that denies sovereignty stands alone in history. Until when? Read what is written on the tablets! "For the vision is yet for the appointed time, and it declareth of the end, and doth not lie. Though it tarry, wait for it; because it will surely come, it will not delay" [Habakkuk 2:3].

The Atlantic Charter and the Jewish People

The period of iron will come after the war. God will grant victory to the Allies. This time, people will not trust any more in the League of Nations. The name of the League of Nations is not even cited in the Atlantic Charter. People will trust in their tremendous power. They will not allow the enemy to disturb the peace of the world for another half century. The charter stands with two feet on the ground of reality. A peace will come that will recognize only victors and vanquished. And woe to the vanquished! You should know and not forget! The second messianic war will not be the last messianic war! The period of national emancipation of the people of the Torah has not yet ended! God has not yet come to judge the earth: "He will judge the world with righteousness, and the peoples with equity!" [Psalms 98:9]. Be strong and of good courage, because you have the messianic mission!

The Messianic Mission: The Conflict between History and Metahistory Is the Characteristic of Our Age

Metahistory is the history of the plan of creation. General history is the history of sovereign humanity, of nations and sovereign states. General history is also the history of the conflict between the sovereign will of the Creator Blessed be He and the sovereign will of people. Therefore there is a strong and permanent connection between history and metahistory, just as there is a strong and permanent connection between physics and metaphysics.

In the Whole World

This conflict between the sovereign will of the Creator and the sovereign will of people is stormier in our age than it has been in any other age. The wealth of cultured humanity is great and magnificent, based upon its visions and its experiences. Despite this, its societal life is disorganized. Its eruptions are ever more awesome and terrible. These eruptions imperil the whole culture. They evidently show that justice and right is the vision of visions. Without them, all other visions have only relative value. And that is the trouble. The nationalization of justice and right, that is to say, the revolt against the God of right, destroys the whole vision of justice and right as a supreme value, as an absolute value. Internally, the state can overcome crude violence in the name of national and political right because internally it is stronger than the individual. Externally however, in relations between states, the barbaric relation of earlier days has remained without any development for the good. Further, internally, the social differences continued to be exacerbated, without any solution. Finally, totalitarian states were created in our age. They oppress the private individual and completely confuse the boundary between acknowledged benefit and right, as well as between right and violence. Indeed human society, with all its nations and states, is fatally ill. Only between wars does human society have a little tranquillity. Particularly in our age, we recognize the deep contradiction between human culture which is excessively individualistic, and nationalism and politics which swallow individuality and grant no private sphere. The exaggerated individualism is the source of the first rebellion, the rebellion of "Ye shall be as God, knowing good and evil" [Genesis 3:5]. The nationalism and politics are the source of the second rebellion, "And let us make us a name" [Genesis 11:4]. Who in our age is still so simple as to believe that humanity and states and nations will of themselves one day find the remedy for the human illnesses? Anyone who will but look has already seen that the prophets of Israel are prophets of truth, that our age is the last age of conflict between the king of the nations and the nations. And "Though it tarry, wait for it; because it will surely come, it will not delay" [Habakkuk 2:3].

Let us sit and cry over the catastrophe of our nation in this age. Truly, despair did not make me afraid, and I was not paralyzed by shock. Did not our prophets and ancestors transmit to us that this age would be the most difficult and awful of all? Read and read again the books of the prophets of Israel. Pay attention to the traditions of your fathers. Then you will attain understanding of every terrible trouble of the age. Then you will no longer ask, "Why and what for?" but you will ask, "What does the Lord our God demand of us today?"

The movement for social emancipation was just the prelude for the movement for national emancipation. These two movements brought the people of Israel into the witches' cauldron of general history. There, the nation of Israel is found today, throughout all its dispersions. Even after the war, this will not change. The pangs of revival for the whole Jewish people in the whole world are birth pangs and not death throes. They are the birth of "Thou art a mighty prince" [Genesis 23:6] in the aspect of "My covenant with Abraham" [Leviticus 26:42].

Particularly in the Land of Israel

These two movements [the social and national emancipations], the metahistory within the history, which led the nation of Israel into the witches' cauldron of general history, caused the nation incalculable damage, brought the nation inestimable trouble, and caused the nation incalculable shame and degradation, were the very movements which blazed a new trail for the nation to its land, to build its national home there. How much is our era full of contradiction. And how much can we understand it! Surely "Thou art a mighty prince" [Genesis 23:6], Honor the Lord of *Urim* (flames).

The whole characteristic of our age is the confrontation between metahistory and history. There is no place in the world where this confrontation is so direct and violent as it is in the Land of Israel. Precisely in this era, which has manifested for all the fatal disease of general history, secular Zionism arose and paraded about with the phrase: "We will be as the nations" [Ezekiel 20:32]. When all of society is sighing under the burdens of tyrannical sovereignty, and general history is already on its last legs, secular Zionism knocks at its gates and entreats and says, "Open the gate for me when the gates are closing, so that I may come through your gates!" Secular Zionism also built the national home on the foundation of general history with its double rebellion: national sovereignty and individual sovereignty. Secular Zionism thinks that a national home like this can be the end of the Jewish exile. It does not see, or does not want to see, that a national home like this only converts exile into exile: the exile of the Jews into the exile of the nations.

It is really like a blind man in the dark. This is the issue: We endured the Jewish exile, the metahistorical exile, for two thousand years. We could not endure the exile of the nations, the historical exile, even a single era. Upon whom should we rely? On our "friends" among the nations? Did you learn nothing from our historical experience? The voice of the blood of our brothers and sisters cries out to you from the earth! [see Genesis 4:10]. You say there is no trust except the evil trust in your power and the strength of your hands, in the manner of the sovereign nations? Please do not get drunk on patriotic phrases. Please do not sound the trumpet of megalomania! The nation of Israel in the Land of Israel is a very small nation, and the weapons of violence in the messianic age are incomparably strong and ingenious. Do you want to perish in an act of courage and fight to the last man, so you may be remembered forever in heroic epics? You could have done that two thousand years ago. And do not deceive yourselves. Because in this era as well, a new Rabbi Yoḥanan ben Zakkai will arise, in order to continue the metahistory of the nation of Israel! Therefore, whoever has eyes to see and ears to hear [see Deuteronomy 29:3] will be enlightened and understand that only on the foundation of metahistory can the nation of Israel build a national home in the Land of Israel. Only the divine rule of justice and right can protect it. The metahistory will be victorious in the history. The metahistorical national home will be established forever.

Zionism and Agudahism as History and Metahistory

There is an individual evil inclination and there is a national evil inclination. Every evil inclination has a great and important task, since it [relates to] the "dignity" of the human being and the nation. It is the desire of the evil inclination to rule over the human being and the nation. In this destructive era, the era of national emancipation, by strength of the national inclination, secular Zionism has been awakened amid the holy nation. It is up to the holy nation to overcome this inclination, in order to be worthy of redemption. Zionism and Agudahism relate to each other as history to metahistory. Therefore the war between Zionism and Agudahism is a messianic war.

Messianic Mission: The Establishment of the People of the Torah in the Land of Israel, the Messianic Task

Agudat Yisrael did not understand the age and did not ascend to the fourth [historical-metahistorical] level. The nation of Torah did not appear on the stage of history such as to assume a mandate in the metahistorical sense. Or to prepare its [metahistorical] self and its [historical] land, such that together they would be worthy and qualified for the loving kindness of God, which would, thirdly, unite them into a state of Torah. "And the earth was filled" [Genesis 6:11] with impurity. The Second World War broke out and devoured European Judaism; lovingly [related] in their lifetime, [Europe and Judaism] were unseparated in their death. The King of the nations passed twice over His land despite all the land's impurity and did not let it be destroyed. God "had compassion on His people" [2 Chronicles 36:15] in His land. With His great compassion, He still awaited the nation to establish and build the national home for His holy Torah. And after all these things, what is our mission?

[Our mission is] the establishment of the nation of Torah! To raise world *Agudat Yisrael* to the fourth level, the historical-metahistorical, such that *Agudat Yisrael* will itself be the organized nation of Torah. The nation of Torah was distorted as long as it did not return to the land of

Torah, as long as God did not reveal the glory of His kingdom upon the land; until He appeared and reigned over it before the eyes of all; and until the nation was one which heard the voice of God speaking amid society, a nation which accepted with self-sacrifice the great and difficult mission of building the national home for God and His Torah. The establishment of the nation of Torah! Only from the Land of Israel can the initiative and incentive go forth to the whole world, because the Land of Israel is the primary place for the movement of national emancipation, for the violent confrontation between history and metahistory. Only there can matters be decided.

[We seek] the establishment of the people of the Torah through the national organization of the nation of the Torah, the national organization of the nation of the Torah which identifies completely with the nation of the Torah itself, just as the national state identifies completely with the nation. A national organization of the people of the Torah in the land of the Torah! Not an organization of "guardians of the faith" and certainly not an organization of those who "leave the community of Israel"! It is an organization that does not have even a hint of a political party. It does not receive its character and form from anything negative. Rather through the nation of the Torah itself, without any contraction or any limitation. It is a nation of the children of Israel. The organization that carries the name of the Jewish people needs to be a national organization from the sole of the foot to the head.

It is self-evident that this organization is not an end in it self, but a means to a goal. The nation of Israel is not sovereign. The state of the Jewish people is not sovereign. Indeed the nation of Israel is a historical phenomenon. It has a unique historical mission. The mission of the national organization of the nation of Torah is the mission of the people of the Torah itself! The place of the national organization: history! The nation of Torah has no mission in history, other than to unite itself with the land of the Torah into the state of the Torah!

Mosheh Avigdor Amiel

Mosheh Avigdor Amiel (1883–1946) studied in the Tels (Lithuania) yeshiva and in Vilna under ayim Soloveichik and ayim Ozer Grodzensky. He served as rabbi in Grajewo, Poland, and in Antwerp, and in 1936 he became chief rabbi of Tel Aviv. Amiel authored texts of *Halakhah* (*Darkhei Mosheh: Hamidot Leḥeker Hahalakhah*) as well as sermons (*Derashot el Ami, Hegyonot el Ami*). His thought was structured according to concentric circles. At the center was the reality of the divine, which was expressed directly in Torah. The Jewish people were rooted in Torah, and the Land of Israel and the Hebrew language were Torah's vessels. Outside this sacred construction, the world remained profane. To the extent that the people or land diluted the Torah, Jewish life itself became unsanctified and lost its power. God stepped in to restore the structure, and did so through punishment. Amiel blamed the Enlightenment and Zionism, both expressions of assimilation which diminished Torah, for the Holocaust. The catastrophe was at once a manifestation of the void left by Torah's absence, divine punishment, and a means for Israel's self-restoration. The severity of the chaos generated by Israel was such that Israel could no longer be entrusted to remain sacred in history. But it could and would remain sacred in the realm of redemption as centered in the Land of Israel.

SELECTIONS

In the portions from *Am Segulah: Haleumiyot Veha'enoshut Behashkafot Olamah Shel Hayahadut* (*A Treasured Nation: Nationality and Humanity according to Judaism's World View*, Tel Aviv, 1942–1943), Amiel wrote that Judaism was a national-racial entity which began with Sinai and that the Nuremberg Laws confirmed what had long existed. But Judaism was racial in the cultural, not biological, sense and remained committed to the welfare of the whole world. After generations of attempts to have a positive influence on the world, beginning with Abraham, the people were now drowning in a flood of blood and tears. But the intensity of the darkness also implied the onset of dawn. The assimilationists' attempt to tie Jewish destiny to the diaspora and blending with gentiles, which proved to be disastrous, would now be transcended by Israel's destiny in the Land of Israel. Instead of focusing on contributing to the nations and awakening compassion among them, Israel's mission would now be conditioned primarily by life in its own land.

In the portions from *Linevukhei Hatekufah: Perek Histaklut Bemahut Hayahadut* (*To the Perplexed of the Era: A Chapter of Observation about the Essence of Judaism*; Jerusalem, 1943, published partly in *Hayesod* 12, no. 388 [12 May 1943]: 2; see Avraham Drimer, *Linevukhei Hatekufah*, *Bamishor* 4, nos. 174–175 [28 September 1943]: 13), Amiel divided the recent era of non-Orthodox Jewish history into two realms:

assimilation and secular nationalism. The ultimate goal of both were equal rights, the first in individual and the second in national terms. The quest for equal rights resulted in an unprecedented eruption of evil across the diaspora, with its ghettos and slaughterhouses. Israel's separate existence in exile always involved suffering, but it did not turn into a terrible curse until Jews burst out of their realm for the sake of equality among the nations. Still, for every disaster in the world, God created a cure. The antidote for Israel's exile had been the ability to assert spiritual identity and dignity. This, however, was annulled by the quest for approval by others. For that, the antidote was nationalism based on Torah and holiness. Amiel rejected nationalism of race and land—which he identified as the basis for both the White Paper and the Red Paper of blood poured by Hitler. Selections translated from the Hebrew by Gershon Greenberg.

A Treasured Nation: Nationality and Humanity according to Judaism's World View

What is Judaism's world view about the problems of nationality and humanity which divide the world? And because of which all the nations of the world—literally "All ye inhabitants of the world, and ye dwellers on the earth" [Isaiah 18:3]—are fighting? And because of which we see a flood of blood and tears everywhere we turn? In modern terms, the problems are Nazism and fascism on one side and democracy, internationalism, liberalism, and universalism on the other. In our language, they come under the names of nationality and humanity.

1. It would seem that it is possible to respond with complete certainty that Judaism exists on the basis of a radical and consequential national-racial (*giza'it*) world view. Long before the Nuremberg Laws were issued, the laws of Mount Sinai—by contrast—were issued. The well-known evildoer [Hitler] did not innovate anything when he forbade intermarriage between [the people of] Israel and the nations. The Torah forbade it more than four thousand years ago. And when it came to a chosen race, the first to decree was also not the evildoer. We heard at Mount Sinai: "Ye shall be Mine own treasure from among all peoples" [Exodus 19:5]. We repeat this and always say to God: "You have chosen us from all peoples" [*Kiddush* (benediction) for festivals]. Before the German anthem *Deutschland, Deutschland über alles*, above the

whole world, the words of the God of Israel were heard explicitly in very clear words: "And to make thee high above all nations that He hath made, in praise, and in name, and in glory" [Deuteronomy 26:19]—"And thou shalt be above only, and thou shalt not be beneath" [Deuteronomy 28:13].

We have always kept a distance. We not only assumed, as said, that we were the race which was specially chosen. We totally excluded others from the human community. And we said, "You are called a human being and the foreigners of the world are not called human beings" [B. T. *Baba Metsia* 114[b]]; or there is the well-known statement "Abide ye here with the ass" [Genesis 22:5]—the nations being compared with an ass [see B. T. *Ketubot* 111[a]]. In the *Halakhah* [Jewish law] we often find discrimination in the [relationship] between Israel and the nations of the world. For example, the prohibition about interest applies to Israel. But "Unto a foreigner thou mayest lend upon interest" [Deuteronomy 23:21]. According to the theory of Maimonides, this is not only an authorization but a positive commandment [*Mishneh Torah, Malveh Veloveh* 5, *Halakhah* 1]. Or, a law which is a matter of boundary applies only to Jews, and not to the nations of the world. The prohibition of fraud relates only to Jews, and not to the nations of the world. Only the children of Israel are acceptable witnesses, not the strangers. There are other such things.

The enemies of Israel have issued really difficult and belligerent decrees against us in the lands of the diaspora. They have confiscated all of our goods there and put us into ghettos, etc. But we ourselves were not accustomed to anything different when we related to them. We said that gentiles had no right to own land in the Land of Israel [B. T. *Gittin* 47ᵃ]. We declared gentiles to be impure, not only concerning the earth of the nation's land but even about the atmosphere. We forbade their bread, their oil, and their wine. In this way, long before we were put into ghettos, we organized our own ghettos. We erected an iron wall around those ghettos so gentiles would have no access to them.

Add to this the sayings "Converts are as difficult for Israel as psoriasis" [B. T. *Yebamot* 47ᵇ]; "A Jew, even though he sins, remains a Jew" [B. T. *Sanhedrin* 44ᵃ]. There is also the way in which we praise the uniqueness of the God of Israel, and even say, "Israel, the Torah, and the Holy One are all one" [see *Zohar, Helek* 3, *Aharei Mot* 73ᵃ]. Surely it is obvious that Judaism has an extreme national racial perspective.

2. On the other hand, it is possible to cite much evidence to the contrary. Namely, that Judaism's world view is one of pure, even radical internationalism. Ultimately, our history does not begin with our patriarchs but precisely with *the first human being*. It is true that Rashi asked the question "Why does the Torah not begin with 'This month shall be unto you'?" [Exodus 12:2] out of nationalistic innocence. He explained what he explained. But ultimately, "A verse cannot depart from its plain meaning" [B. T. *Shabbat* 63ᵃ]. Our Torah is not satisfied with strict nationalism. It sees the whole world before itself. Our patriarchs were preceded by humanity as a whole. According to the tradition, God went with His Torah in His hand to each and every nation before He revealed Himself to Israel, and He wanted just Israel to accept the Torah. Even when the nations were unwilling to accept it, the Torah was given in seventy languages, not just in our national language.

There's also this: All of our festivals, including the *Shabbat*, have not only national character, but also general human character. The festivals are based not only on national historical events, but on nature, which is common to all inhabitants of the

world. Their names testify to this: the spring festival, the festival of first fruits, the fall harvest festival. The Torah itself provides two reasons for the Sabbath: a national reason relating to the Exodus from Egypt, and a human reason, that "For in six days the Lord made heaven and earth," etc. [Exodus 20:11]. Our new year festival is not, essentially, for our own new year, which is on the first day of *Nisan*. It is for the nations' new year, as in "The kings of the nations of the world count from the first day of *Tishrei*" [source uncertain].

Also Abraham, our first patriarch, himself did not find spiritual satisfaction in the fact that God made a covenant with him and his descendants after him. Rather, [he found satisfaction in] only God's promise to him that "And thou shalt be the father of a multitude of nations" [Genesis 17:4]— "And in thee shall all the families of the earth be blessed" [Genesis 12:3]. When King Solomon built the Temple, he did not build it only for his nation. He prayed explicitly: "Moreover concerning the stranger that is not of thy people Israel" [1 Kings 8:41]—"Hear Thou in heaven Thy dwelling place" [1 Kings 8:43]. Our final goal in the messianic era is to see "And all nations shall flow unto it" [Isaiah 2:2]—"For My House shall be called a house of prayer for all peoples" [Isaiah 56:7]. As long as the Temple stood, they sacrificed "seventy bulls for seventy nations" [B. T. *Sukkah* 55ᵇ] until the Holy One came to remind us through *Shemini Atseret* that "You should sacrifice for yourselves" [*Midrash Bereshit Rabbah, Parashah* 21, *Siman* 24] and not exist only according to the aspect of "They made me keeper of the vineyards; But mine own vineyard have I not kept" [Song of Songs 1:6]. Our prophets felt that they were prophets not only for Israel. They knew that their task was to be "I have appointed thee a prophet unto the nations" [Jeremiah 1:5]—"See, I have this day set thee over the nations and over the kingdoms" [Jeremiah 1:10], etc. They felt the troubles of every nation: "Wherefore my heart moaneth like a harp for Moab" [Isaiah 16:11]. They considered it an obligation to awaken any nation which turned from its path to evil [back] to penitent return, like the dove that traveled with self-sacrifice to awaken Nineveh to penitent return, and the like.

More than what prophets of truth and justice did when the Temple stood, the children of the prophets did when the Temple was already destroyed. As the rabbinic Sages said, "God did not exile Israel among the nations except that they should gather converts to themselves" [B. T. *Pesaḥim* 87ᵇ]. Rabbi Yehudah Halevi used this passage in order to give a winning response to the Khazar king's question: "If God truly chose the people of Israel to be His chosen people, why are they [the] lowest and most despised of all the nations in the world?" [see *The Kuzari* I.95–113]. Yehudah Halevi's answer was the analogy of sowing precisely the very best and praiseworthy seeds into the ground in order to grow the best crop—even though the seeds go through many troubles and actually decompose deep in the earth, to the point that they sink and decompose into the abyss. Rabbi Yehudah Halevi did not think of this as just a legend, of which we say, "We do not learn from legends." Rather, it teaches our world view. The exile of two thousand years pushed us into a really deep depression. It destroyed us not only materially but spiritually. It decreased us not only quantitatively—according to the statisticians, were it not for the exile, we now would be a nation of one hundred and thirty million, and more—but also qualitatively. God brought all this upon us so we could take on proselytes [see B. T. *Pesaḥim* 87ᵃ], even though what was left from the exile was only "a brand plucked out of the fire" [Zechariah 3:2]. And now, even this brand is being destroyed, heaven forbid. . . .

In short, Abraham did much to raise the spiritual level of humanity collectively. He "made the soul (*nefesh*)." He discovered the soul (*neshamah*), the divine soul found in the heart of every human being. If scholars of the ancient world and seekers of ancient treasures were to come and some of them show that even before the Torah was given to Israel many laws and rules (*ḥukim umishpatim*) of the Torah were known to the nations of the world, this would not contradict our faith. On the contrary, this would strengthen our faith in "And the souls that they had gotten in aran" [Genesis 12:5].

Abraham our patriarch was a pillar of loving kindness and mercy. This is the principle essence of Judaism and its root [in its identity] as an innovation in the world. Noah was also commanded about judgments. Those [of his day] also knew about the attribute of justice, even though they were not scrupulous at all about it, and they did not have the slightest idea about the attribute of mercy. Precisely Abraham our patriarch was an eyewitness to the rebellion at Sodom and Gomorrah. From the language of the Torah and from rabbinic tradition, it does not appear that [the inhabitants of Sodom and Gomorrah] violated the attribute of justice. Their entire sin was not behaving according to the attribute of mercy and opposing it completely. In their eyes, behaving according to the attribute of mercy was considered a great sin. They were not suspected of stealing. On the contrary, they were extremely careful, saying: "What's mine is mine and what's yours is yours." It was precisely because of this that they received a punishment more severe than did the generation of the flood, about whom it is said: "For the earth is filled with violence through them" [Genesis 6:13]. In the generation of Abraham, we only see the rebellion of Sodom and Gomorrah and not the rebellion of the rest of the world. We learn from this that in the rest of the world, they ultimately knew the attribute of mercy. This is so, even though before Abraham our patriarch, we find no mention of this. All of this certainly came from "And the souls that they had gotten in Haran" [Genesis 12:5]. . . .

13. On an apparent level, it is clear that all of our blood, spilled like water from the time of the destruction of the Temple until today; all the lives sacrificed over generations only in order to get souls [*la'asot nefashot*] to keep, as we said, "And the souls that they had gotten" [Genesis 12:5], was all for nothing and in vain. Humanity is now returning to the condition in which there were "two millennia of abyss" [B. T. *Sanhedrin* 97ᵃ], to the condition of the generation of the flood, a flood of blood and tears. Apparently, in place of our mission to add proselytes—as the rabbinic Sages of blessed memory said, "The Holy One, blessed be He, did not exile Israel among the nations save in order that proselytes might join them" [B. T. *Pesaḥim* 87ᵇ]—we [now] have added only evildoers. There have been no such evildoers in any generation or time, even in the most terrible times. The great evildoer [Hitler] of this generation decided to destroy by fire the good inclination of the human being. Not, as we thought in the days of Ezra and Neemiah, to destroy by fire the evil inclination in man, as the rabbinic sages, of blessed memory, said.

Things appear today like the days of crisis for the sick person before the scale is tipped [one way or the other]. These are the moments when "even darkness . . . may be felt" [Exodus 10:21], before dawn and sunrise, in the aspect of the seed that lies in the ground and decomposes completely as it begins to sprout anew. Indeed, this is the mistake that the assimilationists made. They based our mission only on the diaspora. Our "final goal" was assimilation among the nations. They completely forgot how all our prophets emphasized that the mission for which we were most qualified was to fill the Land of Israel. The blessings "And in thee shall all the families of the earth be blessed" [Genesis 12:3], "And thou shalt be the father of a multitude of nations" [Genesis 17:4] related specifically to our return to the Land of Israel.

Our golden age, the days of David and Solomon and the days of the last Hasmoneans, of King Yannai and Queen Shlomzion, were days when the promise of "And all nations shall flow unto it with joy" [Isaiah 2:2] [and] "Come ye, and let us go up to the mountain of the Lord" [Isaiah 2:3], etc., began to be realized. Our era is the transitional period between the end of our mission in the diaspora and the beginning of our mission in our land. It is hard to imagine that we still have any place in Europe—where we dwelled for a thousand years and where our cultural influence was essential. We must "renew our days as of old" [Lamentations 5:21] and in the ancient lands which were the cradle of our birth. In the diaspora we were influenced by the "Let Israel be poor" [B. T. Ḥagigah 9ᵇ]. We did so through the feeling of pity which we aroused among the nations. We did so through being "a kingdom of priests" [Exodus 19:6] which expressed itself only in this, "And when they went about from nation to nation, from one kingdom to another people" [Psalms 105:13], in the name of God. Here in the Land of Israel we should influence all of humanity through "And nations shall walk at thy light, and kings at the brightness of thy rising" [Isaiah 60:3]; through "That the mountain of the Lord's house shall be established as the top of the mountains, and shall be exalted above the hills, and all nations shall flow unto it" [Isaiah 2:2]. Let us hope that we are approaching the days of the prophetic promise, which tells us: "In that day shall the Lord be One, and His name one" [Zechariah 14:9]—for all of humanity.

To the Perplexed of the Era: A Chapter of Observation about the Essence of Judaism (1943)

The last era, extending from Mendelssohn until today, is divisible into two parts. The first part is the movement of assimilation; the second is the movement of secular nationalism. They had common sociological roots. It can be shown that they also shared the dimension of the aim toward equal rights. For both of them, for both the movement of assimilation and the nationalist secularist movement, that aim was the final goal. But while assimilation thought of equal rights in terms of each and every individual human being, secular nationalism yearned for national equal rights, for Israel as *one nation* among the nations of the world.

It was as if the assimilationist movement forgot that there were nations in the world and not human beings [per se]. [For them,] "The foreigners of the world are not called human beings" [B. T. *Baba Metsia* 114ᵇ]. There was no human being who was just a human being, only the human being as connected to some nation. Rights were not rights if they encompassed only the human being, and not national life. The assimilationists thought that if the Jew received all citizen rights in the land in which the Jew resided, the Jew would be equal to all the citizens of the nation. They forgot that ultimately the Jew was not equal to the citizens of the other nations at all. Because the non-Jew (*nokhri*) had his own language, his history, and his land, etc., and the Jew did not share them. The Jew [according to their view] needed and had to assimilate, while the non-Jew had no need at all to assimilate. The Jew had to campaign for equal rights while the non-Jew did not. [For secular nationalism,] equal rights needed to come about in a different way. As each and every nation had its own land, its own history, we too needed all these instruments. This was the position of the secular nationalist movement.

The secular nationalist movement, were it consequential in its thinking, would reach the conclusion that we should not seek equal rights at all in the diaspora. Because in the diaspora we remained completely foreign subjects. There are no examples like this among the gentiles, where human beings belong at once to *two nations simultaneously*. The gentile can go from nation to nation, leave his land, abandon the citizenry of his nation, and become a citizen of another land. Every nation has a right to an identifiable land. But no nation may presume [to belong] both to its land and any [other] land. But generally, there are few who think consequentially. It is always easy to say, "It is good that thou shouldest take hold of the one; yea, also from the other withdraw not thy hand" [Ecclesiastes 7:17], and to be oblivious to the fact that "this" and "that" are contradictory.

To be sure, there were some secular nationalists who thought consequentially and felt that it was possible to choose one of the two, but not both simultaneously [i.e., to belong to two nations simultaneously]. Max Nordau, for example, sought to have children of Israel everywhere become subjects of the Land of Israel and to yield all claims to equal rights in diaspora lands. And on the other hand there was Professor [Simon] Dubnow who sought the opposite, namely, the rights of national minorities in all the diaspora lands, and who yielded the Land of Israel (if not explicitly, then in principle. See his "Our Claim to the State of Israel" [source uncertain]). As stated, there were few consequential thinkers. The majority did not want to probe the matter in depth. They even sought contradictory things when the matter touched upon rights. And the more rights, the better.

What emerged from all this, in terms of equal rights in the diaspora? Evil unfolded from Berlin, the cradle of secular enlightenment and assimilation. It was an evil without comparison in all our history. It spread over most of the diaspora lands. The ghettos were reinstated. The ghettos became slaughterhouses. We became "as a lamb that is led to the slaughter" [Isaiah 53:7], abandoned to beating and abuse. Do not throw salt on the wounds. Even the greatest preacher of all generations, the prophet Jeremiah, would not recite his "words of Jeremiah" [Jeremiah 1:1] about this. He would rather sit on the ground and recite "lamentations":

> How is the gold become dim! How is the most fine gold changed! The hallowed stones are poured out at the head of every street. The precious sons of Zion, comparable to fine gold, how they are esteemed as earthen pitchers. The work of the hands of the potter! [Lamentations 4:1–2]

It would be more correct to recite the asidic phrase "Do not act *thusly* toward the Lord your God." You should not always say *thusly* even to the act of your God. And if your actions are so evil, then you should plead at such times as Moses, "Why have these evils come upon this nation?" [*Midrash Shemot Rabbah, Parashah* 5, *Siman* 22]. The words "So that thou shalt be mad for the sight of thine eyes which thou shalt see" [Deuteronomy 28:34] were realized. This is the most terrible and horrifying curse. And the question is asked in every era: Why did God do so? And why this great fury? If we go a bit deeper, we will see that to a certain extent we can say: "The foolishness of man perverteth his way; and his heart fretteth against the Lord" [Proverbs 19:3]. In truth, the catastrophe (*Ḥurban*) did not begin in the present, when the foundation for everything is already ruined and destroyed and the entire area of our settlement in Europe is transformed into a cemetery. Rather, our catastrophe began with the movement for equal rights itself. Equal rights itself has wounded us, and in a shocking and terrible way.

It is impossible for an equilibrium to exist at all between us and the nations. God decreed this one thing: "And to make thee high above all nations that He hath made, in praise and in name and in glory" [Deuteronomy 26:19]; "And thou shalt be above only, and thou shalt not be beneath" [Deuteronomy 28:13]. I use the words "God decreed this one thing" intentionally because these blessings also contain a decree from heaven to us. The decree comes in order that we keep forever the words of God: "Then ye shall be Mine own treasure from among all peoples" [Exodus 19:5]. That is, whether or not you want to be [this treasure]. And when it comes to [the issue of] equality, obviously we rise above. There is no equality, for one is above and the other is below. And it is in the nature of man that God did not create him to exist below in order to be enraged because his fellow existed above, or to hate the fellow above out of jealousy, or for the hatred to transform him at times into an animal of prey.

Our entire existence in exile was possible because we were *ivrim*, which meant, according to the rabbinic Sages: "Why is he called *ivri* [other]? Because the entire world is from 'the side' of materiality and we are from 'the other side' of spirituality" [*Midrash Bereshit Rabbah, Parashah 42, Siman* 8]. For everything which the Holy One Blessed be He created in His world, He created a countermeasure over-against it. When God created the evil inclination, He created the Torah as countermeasure. When He created the plague, He created medicine as countermeasure to it. There is nothing more evil in the world than exile. A countermeasure was created over-against it, namely, our power to annul it. At times this power was balanced over-against all the powers of the world, which were out to obliterate us from the face of the earth. If any other nation could not exist in exile, this was not on account of *physical* torment, which can be overcome, but rather on account of torments of the *soul*. It was because a nation could not bear the shame of being viewed by every other nation as on a lower level, as some sort of contemptible creature, as a creature devoid of all status. The name *human being (adam)* came from the name *earth (adamah)*. A person who did not have earth was not called a human being. He was not considered a human being, and he himself did not look upon himself as a human being.

The countermeasure to our exile, as said, was the power to annul it. [That is, to be able] to recite [the prayer] "All leaven in my possession which I have not seen, as well as which I have not removed, may it be annulled and considered as the dust of the earth" [*Bedikat Ḥamets*] not only on the eve of Passover but on all 365 days of the year, evening, morning, and afternoon. And if our enemies and those who hate us have caused us injury and trouble in all the years of our exile,

shame, etc., in practice they have caused nothing [to happen to] us. It is said, "Everything is according to the one who shames and the one who shames oneself" [B. T. *Baba Kamma* 86ᵃ], and "these who shame" are not considered as those who shame [by the one who is shamed]. Just as the human being is not shamed by the bite of the snake, even though the venom causes much pain, we have not been shamed by the snakes who walk on two [feet]. We have looked upon them below from high above, as upon wretched creatures whom we pity. It is similar to what the youngest of Hannah's seven sons said to her: "Pity upon you, Caesar, pity upon you" [*Midrash Eichah Rabbah, Parashah* 1, *Siman* 50]. It is not only that we exist in terms of "Those who suffer insults but do not inflict them, who hear themselves reviled and do not answer back" [B. T. *Gittin* 36ᵇ]. Rather, we were not insulted at all, and we were not reproached at all. This is because we considered the reproach itself to be the greatest honor.

There were many times when we sent intermediaries to the gates of the kings and to the courts of the tyrants in order to remove the decrees. We even let ourselves flatter the evil ones. Our authoritative basis came from Jacob, who told Esau, "For as much as I have seen thy face, as one seeth the face of God, and thou wast pleased with me" [Genesis 33:10]. But at the same time we despised those tyrants and regarded them as dust of the earth. We have tried to remove their evil decrees. But we never asked for their approval. For we too are human beings. Their approval would have been a great disgrace for us, just as their mockery would have been considered a great honor. We were the *gaon* (exalted one). The *gaon* was not esteemed in public opinion. Were public opinion to be identified with him, he would start to reconsider his actions and views. We have become the *gaon* among the nations.

In short, in all exiles, and not just in the Egyptian exile, we observed the wonder about which the rabbinic Sages said:

When the Egyptians noticed them, they went to kill them; but a miracle occurred on their behalf so that they were swallowed in the ground, and [the Egyptians] brought oxen and plowed over them, as it is said, "The plowers plowed upon my back" [Psalms 129:3]. After they had departed, the Israelite women with their babes broke through the earth and came forth like the herbage of the field, as is said, "I cause thee to increase, even as the growth of the field" [Ezekiel 16:7]. [B. T. *Sotah* 11^b]

So it was in all exiles. From the gentiles' perspective, we were swallowed in the ground. But among ourselves we always budded forth.

Indeed, there were those who were surprised at how we could maintain the contradiction within us. From the outside we were easy to trample upon, and we had no respect for ourselves. From within, there were trivial disputes—about some honor in the synagogue; about being assigned the third and sixth *aliyah* [person called to recite the blessing over the Torah]; or having an important seat in the eastern section. About acquiring descriptions like "our teacher" and "teacher of our teacher." Thus, truly, "the prosecutor was silent and the defender took its place" [source uncertain]. But as a matter of fact, this was the basis of existence. In truth, the human being's honor is that *he is a human being*. There is nothing worse than for a person to be humiliated in his own eyes. But, we never humiliated ourselves. As a matter of fact, we are more sensitive about the attribute of honor than others. The proof is the disagreement among us about the honor due something [in particular]. While we could humiliate ourselves a lot externally, vis-à-vis others, this only testifies to the [in]tense feeling of pride which survived internally, to the extent that we said that others were in no position to shame us at all, for everything was a function of the one who *shames oneself*.

Our *Halakhah* says: "With the idolatry of the idolaters, then just an annulment would have sufficed" [B. T. *Avodah Zara* 53^b]. For if we needed to burn up all the idolatry in the world, we would be unable to do so. Before all the idolatry in the world would be destroyed, the idolatry would destroy us. "Let the owner of the vineyard himself [God] come and weed out the thorns" [B. T. *Baba Metsia* 83^b]. We are satisfied, when it comes to idolatry, with merely annulling it. And the matter is so easy that it need not even be spoken about. Annulling in the heart is enough.

Therefore, on the one hand, [having] equal rights did not liberate us from the exile. On the other hand, we were deprived of the antidote provided by equal rights which gave us the possibility of existing. Our power of annulling was thereby annulled. Instead of annulling others, we annulled ourselves in the eyes of ourselves. Mediation with tyrants was transformed into our disgrace. But along with this, we began to seek approval. Like paupers begging at the doorpost, we sought approval from each and every tyrant for the fact that we too were human beings. We were happy, overjoyed, when the very worst tyrant praised us. We sounded the cymbals loud enough for the whole world to hear.

And so it happened: We began to dream about *nationalistic* equal rights. Before this, we had not dreamed about this. We did not doubt that "For thou art a holy people unto the Lord thy God: The Lord thy God hath chosen thee to be His own treasure, out of all the peoples that are upon the face of the earth" [Deuteronomy 7:6]. We never asked ourselves whether or not the gentiles recognized us as a nation. We did not exist in their terms. But when we began to dream in terms of nationalistic equal rights, we also became perplexed about [our existing in our own terms]. And the pursuit of approval began again. And from one end of the universe to the other, we sounded the trumpets when some leader gave us the nod, saying that we too were among the nations. We were greatly distressed, without reprieve, if God forbid one of the nations denied this and told us: It is absolutely untrue.

The era of Hitler, may his name be erased, who blotted out, God forbid, a large portion of the nation of Israel, began ten years ago [in 1933]—with the Nuremberg Laws. We still remember the mourning and the moaning about these decrees which arose from all the camps of Israel everywhere. But essentially, what was new about the Nuremberg Laws? They brought nothing new at all. They implemented decrees which we ourselves would have decreed. These eighteen decrees [of the Nuremberg Laws] were also agreed upon [in principle] by Beit Shammai and Beit Hillel:

For when R. Aḥa b. Ada came from Palestine he declared in the name of R. Isaac: "They decreed against heathens' bread on account of their oil." But how is the oil stricter than bread! Rather should the statement read that they made a decree against their bread and oil on account of their wine, and against their wine on account of their daughters, against their daughters on account of another matter and against this other matter on account of still another matter. [B. T. *Avodah Zarah* 35[b]]

Not only the contented assimilationists but also radical nationalists cried over the eighteen decrees [of the Nuremberg Laws]. Even those with fear [of God], who were attentive to both easy and weighty commandments, cried over the great disgrace. The disgrace was that Hitler annulled the agreements made with us by others. According to them, we were human beings like all human beings. We too were a nation like all other nations.

Unintentionally, we are reminded of the rabbinic Sages' statement about "And all the congregation lifted up their voice, and cried, and the people wept that night" [Numbers 14:1]. The rabbinic Sages added:

> Israel had wept on the night of the ninth of *Av*, and the Holy One blessed be He, had said to them: You have wept a causeless weeping before Me. I shall therefore fix for you a permanent weeping for future generations. At that hour it was decreed that the Temple should be destroyed and that Israel should be exiled among the nations. [*Midrash Bamidbar Rabbah, Parashah* 16, *Siman* 20]

This was the weeping of "She weepeth sore in the night" [Lamentations 1:2]. It was the weeping for the destruction of the First Temple and the Second Temple, both of which were on the ninth of *Av*. For then too they wept in advance, and only on account of the "And we were in our own sight as grasshoppers, and so were we in their sight" [Numbers 13:33]. That is, the gentiles looked upon them as grasshoppers and that upset them a great deal. Our crying over the laws of Nuremberg, was it not the sort of crying involved in "And so were we in their sight" [Numbers 13:33]?

In earlier generations of exile, surely there were Hitlers, and in the tens and hundreds. But then we did not cry about what they said. We

carried out Jacob's testament that in this world it was permissible to flatter the evil ones [see Genesis 33:10]. We did not consider this a disgrace, any more than it would be a disgrace to be injured by some malicious animal. The emancipation was not able to annul the exile. But it was able to annul our power of annulling, which was the antidote against exile. It was the cure to the disease, the instinctive feeling of each and every creature which recognizes the power of its existence. Once that feeling was annulled, we had no possibility of existing in exile.

And so the first portion of our last era was completed, the portion of simple assimilation, the assimilation which ruled the roost for about a hundred years. To be sure, it passed away in "blood, and fire, and pillars of smoke" [Joel 3:3]. The victims who died because of it were without number. There are still individuals—even after all this, there still are—who assimilate among the nations. But as a system, as a world view of Judaism, assimilationism will not be revived.

In our day, we see "God lives" [Namanides *ad* Genesis 2:7] as the eternal response to that system. I have in mind what the prophet said:

> And that which cometh into your mind shall not be at all; in that ye say: We will be as the nations, as the families of the countries, to serve wood and stone. As I live, sayeth the Lord God, surely with a mighty hand, and with an outstretched arm, and with fury poured out, will I be king over you. [Ezekiel 20:32–33]

But the second portion of the era, that of secular nationalism, still continues, the second edition of "And that which cometh into your mind shall not be at all; in that ye say: We will be as the nations, as the families of the countries" [Ezekiel 20:32]. "The nations" is not meant in the *personal* sense of foreigners, rather in the national sense. We will be national as all are national. There are many positive aspects of this nationalism. It is not only shadow, but also light—as with "May You shine a new light upon Zion" ["*Le'el barukh*," in *Shaharit Lehol*, the weekday morning prayers]. To a recognizable extent, nationalism realizes the third section of the commandments of Torah, which [covers the relation] of the Israelite to his nation. But the one who is aware of consequences will see that the secular nationalist part of the era cannot continue for long. Not only because "As I live, saith the Lord God" [Ezekiel 20:33] applies to "We will be as the nations" [Ezekiel 20:32] in the second context, that of secular nationalism, as it does in the first context, that of assimilation. But because the world view of secular nationalism among us is *perverted of itself.*

The emphasis of *holy* applies to *holy nation, holy land, holy language, holy Torah, holy Shabbat.* We do not emphasize holy when it comes to the rest of the commandments specified in the Torah. We do not say, for example, holy *mezuzah,* holy *tefillin,* holy *sukkah,* etc., even though all of these are instruments of holiness. Why? Because all these other commandments of Torah have no sense of the secular, only of the holy. Even without any special emphasis of holiness, there would be no mistaking [them for secular]. This is not so with the former, all of which could be comprehended in a completely secular way. Someone who says we are a holy nation could also say a nation like all others. Even more so with land or language. Other nations have larger, more important lands than ours—which is but 400 by 400 parasangs in size. Each nation has its special language, some richer in terms of numbers of words than ours. The other nations do not say that their lands or their languages are holy. Why do we have to sanctify our land and language with special holiness? The same applies to Torah—which is our history and culture. Every nation has a special history and culture. Every nation considers it a national possession, but not a holy possession. All nations have a sabbath, understood as a weekly day of rest. That we determine that the day of rest is on the seventh and not the first day should make no difference. We particularly emphasize the holiness: holy nation, holy land, etc., to remove error from the heart.

Certainly the relation of the holy to the secular is not two hundred to one, of which it says, "On the principle that in the total of two hundred the sum of a hundred is included" [B. T. *Baba Batra* 74ᵃ]. This is because holiness contains a deficit vis-à-vis the secular. The deficit is that it is possible to make the secular holy by sanctifying it. But if holiness contains some sort of physical holiness, in no way can it become secular. And if the [physical] holiness is blemished, what is

sanctified becomes defective, and it may not be enjoyed.

The *holy nation* means a nation which cannot, in any way, be changed into a secular nation. If its holiness is removed, it would be a matter of the sanctified's being defective. It would be forbidden to enjoy it. It is the same with holy land, holy language, etc. The holiness is in the substance. We would never be able to make the nation of Israel like other nations. We would never be able to make the nation of Israel in the Land of Israel into a nation like all nations in their lands.

According to the trustworthy witness of our history, we were not successful in war when the war was not for religious purpose. Our golden ages of the First and Second Temples were only during times of sublime holiness. So it was in the Davidic and Solomonic eras of the First Temple, and in the Hasmonean era of the Second Temple. That is what we meant by saying that holiness also contains the deficit, that it can in no way be transformed into the secular. The Israelite nation as an international pillar among the nations, the Land of Israel as a geographic pillar among all lands, do not leave the impression that we could become a secular nation or that the Land could become a secular land. There are nations and lands which are smaller than the nation of Israel and the Land of Israel. Nevertheless they exist. And this [is] owing to the fact that the larger lands which surround them do not have a single opinion about their relation to the smaller ones. This is not so when it comes to the nation of Israel and the Land of Israel. All the nations have a single opinion and one relation to [it]. It is a relation of hatred since the day we stood at Mt. Sinai when hatred toward us descended upon the nations [B. T. *Shabbat* 89ᵃ]. We have no right to exist, except as a holy nation. Our land has no right to exist, except as a holy land.

With regard to the holy language: From the first great era of our patriarchs until the end of the destruction of the First Temple, only holy Scripture has remained for us. This is so, even if in this entire lengthy era much more than the twenty-four books [of Scripture] have been written. From the whole era between the Second Temple and the end of the Babylonian era, only the Talmud has remained. It appears that the language, the holy language, takes in only what is holy with permanent absorption. Not what is secular. Should the secular enter into the language, it is "in and out." Currently, there is a great deal of secular literature. But it must always be modern, for as soon as it gets old, its rationale decays and its impact is dissolved. Who reads the literature written a hundred and eighty years ago? Our sacred literature *will always* have readers and interested students.

The *Yishuv* [Jewish Community] of the new Land of Israel made an experiment, one which was truly not forever, to secularize even the holy Torah and the holy *Shabbat* into the profane, to teach the *Tanakh* [Hebrew Bible] itself not as holy Scripture but as culture, to observe the *Shabbat* not as a holy day but as a day of rest. What became of the experiment? Wherever the holiness of the *Shabbat* stopped, the resting on the *Shabbat* also stopped. The satisfaction of modern educators themselves, who teach the *Tanakh* not on the basis of holy Scripture but as cultural writing, is well known.

The difference between the assimilationist movement and the secular nationalist movement in our most recent era consists in the following: The first has left but the smallest trifle of Judaism, unrecognizable leftovers. But what it did leave was in terms of the holy. The latter, secular nationalism, removed much of Judaism: a third of the commandments, namely, those commandments between the Israelite and the nation. But it emulates the holiness, even the holiness of the commandments. Thus, not only the past demonstrates that it is impossible to transform all the sanctities of nationalism into secular properties; the present too is beginning to bear witness to this.

[The 1939 British White Paper and the Nazi Red Paper]

The most recent White Paper regarding our national homeland in the Land of Israel has been forgotten, because of the Red Paper. "Red," as in the blood of millions of our brethren who have been killed, slaughtered, and buried alive in diaspora lands. Still, there is a value to opening up this White Paper from time to time. Much ink has flowed about it. Many pens have been broken

over the poison it contained. But very few who comprehended the White Paper's "evil root," namely, the term *Palestinian nation* instead of the *nation of Israel in the Land of Israel* of which the Balfour Declaration speaks. On the surface, this is only a name change. But the change in name brings not only a practical change but a substantial one. It tears away the entire root of the Balfour Declaration, to which so much hope was attached. All the decrees of the White Paper, such as the decree which limited *aliyah* (Jewish immigration) to a minimum, the decree about areas of land—all of these were but particular ramifications of this name change. For if there is Israel and there is a Land of Israel in the world, such a fact obliges a great deal. In these names we feel the necessity of pairing pairs, namely, the nation of Israel with the Land of Israel. What is principally new in the Balfour Declaration is not essentially the definition of the national homeland, but the definition of the nation of Israel. Not only that there are communities of Jews in the various lands, and that by itself each community is an atrophying limb. Rather, that all these communities belong to one nation, which is of itself complete. And as there is no such thing as something without a place, this nation *must* have a place. This place certainly needs to be the place with our definite article: And this is the Land of Israel.

If in actuality we are a minority in the Land of Israel, this means nothing. It is not the a posteriori which determines but the a priori. The whole nation of Israel, which has the right to settle in the Land of Israel, will certainly become the majority. It is obvious that this whole ideological structure collapses if it is determined that there is only a *Palestinian* nation. In this manner, the principle is who it is who settles in Palestine. Jews settled in different lands do not come into question; they no more belong to the Palestinian nation than they belong to the Iraqi nation, or the nation of Egypt, or the like. The criterion is whether or not something helps or hinders the Palestinian nation. Since *aliyah* [Jewish immigration] and sale of land could hinder the interest of the majority of the Palestinian nation, fair judgment obliges limiting both *aliyah* and sale of land to zero. In short, the White Paper not only limits the possibility of realizing the national homeland in the Land of Israel. It totally annuls

Zionism, not only in practice but in theory. There is also no need for a *national* home. For in principle, there is no Israeli nationalism. If only a Palestinian nation exists in the Land of Israel, then surely there is only a Polish nation in Poland. Jews are but a small part of that nation. If so, in which place is there Jewish nationalism?

Surely there is no one among the children of Israel who would say "justice is done" when it comes to the White Paper. It darkens the face of the nation of Israel, disgracing it. The fact is, justice is impossible without acknowledging that the words "When the arrow maker is slain by his own arrows, he is paid with the clue which his own hand wound" [B. T. *Pesaḥim* 28ᵃ] are taking effect among us. Ultimately, it is up to us to seek some sort of basis for our nationalism. If we drain every drop of holiness from this nationalism, every drop of spirituality, then we end up establishing our nationality on the basis of race (*geza*) or the basis of land. The corrupted nations under the influence of Hitler establish nationality on the basis of race. Out of this comes all the persecution of Jews. Even Jews settled for generations in the diaspora are considered marginal to the principal race settled in the particular place. The reformed ones among those nations establish nationality on the basis of land. A member of the nation and a citizen of the land are, for them, synonyms. A person who becomes a citizen of the Land automatically belongs to the nation of the land.

Those who established Judaism solely as secular nationalism, who were evasive when it came to Jewish nationalism both in exile and in the Land of Israel, and "made him ride on two harnessed horses" [B. T. *Ketubot* 55ᵇ], held to both nationalism of race and nationalism of land. They therefore thought of themselves as members of a single nation in the diaspora as well. For we are of one race—even though there is no connection at all between one Jew and another in terms of our spirituality. For in principle, [according to them,] we do not have spirituality. Likewise, our nationalism is stronger in the Land of Israel, because here there is also the land basis. But out of this it emerges, God forbid, that we provide justification for the [Nazi] Red Paper in the diaspora, which came about on the basis of our united race. [We provide] justification also for the White Paper in the Land of Israel, which

comes about on the basis of the nation of the land. For the meaning of the nation in the land is that whoever has the majority in the land *is* the nation of the land.

If we ask that they give us free right over the land, so that we become the majority of the land, there is something here in respect to a statement with its contradiction. For in such a way it is possible to annul all the nationalism of all the nations and to tell every nation: What did you envision? That you were the nation of the land because you have the majority in the land? That through immigration another nation could be the majority of the land?! We will feel the contradiction even more when we are truly worthy of a Jewish state. The question will be: Who is to be called a Jew? Once, the definition was "Anyone who denies idolatry is called a Jew" [B. T. *Megillah* 13ᵃ]. Now this is also denied. It is possible to be a total idolater and to be called a Jew. It will be impossible to establish Judaism on the basis of race, as already explained. To be sure, in the diaspora there is another criterion for the name Jew, which is the hatred by the gentiles. But we hope that through a "Jewish state" this hatred will cease. If so it will be necessary to call anyone a Jew who belongs to the Jewish state, that is, anyone who is a citizen of this state. Certainly this would apply to those who are right-minded. Citizen rights will be granted to anyone settled in the land and who fulfills his citizen obligations. It would be impossible to establish the criterion of being Jewish as a matter of language, as to whether or not one speaks Hebrew. For then, surely, the foreigners settled in the Jewish state would also speak Hebrew. Second, again, this criterion would not apply to those who are right-minded, were such a franchise qualification to be enforced. Because in all right-minded nations, no such limit is set. And the result would be that all residents of the land would change into Jews. Even those who belong to other nations, even idolaters in general. And all the Jews who remain outside the land—and surely the great majority will remain there for a long time—would become gentiles. Because they would have no connection to "the Jewish state." Because they would be citizens of other lands.

We have a clear criterion for being part of the Israelite nation, that of Saadia Gaon: "Our nation is a nation solely of Torah" [*Emunot Vedeot* 3:7]. But what will the deniers do with this? That is what I said: We are called "the holy nation" [Deuteronomy 7:6] both in a positive and in a negative sense. Holiness has the advantage over the secular. But there is also the deficiency, that holiness cannot be changed in any way into the secular. Anyone who wants to establish Israel on secular foundations alone will become irretrievably tangled up in endless opposition and contradictions.

We still do not see the end of the era, at least in terms of the secular nationalism which longs for the equal rights of the nation as a nation. But anyone aware of consequences can see that the chapter is nearing its close. Even the heads of this movement will say in the end: "Let us search and try our ways, and return to the Lord" [Lamentations 3:40]. That is, if they would only search out their paths, which are so distant from the paths of God, and seek them out properly, they would finally say, "And return to the Lord" [Lamentations 3:40].

This era is terrible, very terrible! Who will bring it to conclusion? Even for the pious it is clearly difficult to say, "Justice has been done." The thought is also terrible, that the entire catastrophe came solely for the sake of Israel [B. T. *Baba Batra* 8ᵃ]. For the primary reason for all catastrophes which have [now] come to the world has been the hatred for Israel by the known tyrant of tyrants [Hitler]. But that obliges us precisely to show to all the world not only that the whole catastrophe came solely for the sake of Israel, but that all the blessings came only for the sake of Israel as well. God promised to our patriarch Abraham alone that "In thee shall all the families of the earth be blessed" [Genesis 12:3]. And we will achieve this only if we will adhere to "The Lord thy God hath chosen thee to be His own treasure, out of all peoples that are upon the face of the earth" [Deuteronomy 7:6]. By lifting ourselves to the highest moral level, we will also lift all the nations to at least a minimal moral level. We are to be a nation of the *extra soul* also during weekdays, so that other nations become at least bearers of the single soul. We are to reach the level of "Thy people also shall be all righteous" [Isaiah 60:21] in order that at least remnant individuals will be found among others, the righteous among the nations. We are to keep all 613 commandments so that the others, the nations of the world, will keep at least the Noaide commandments. We need to be a *holy* nation, so that others will at least be ordinary people and behave correctly. In short, in place of a *perplexed generation*, a generation of knowledge will come. As is said: "For the earth shall be full of the knowledge of the Lord, as the waters cover the sea" [Isaiah 11:9].

Yeḥezkel Sarna

Yeḥezkel Sarna (1889–1969), born in Gorodok (Belarus), studied in the Keneset Yisrael yeshiva in Slobodka under the *Musar* leaders Natan Tsevi Finkel and Mosheh Mordekhai Epstein. When the yeshiva was transferred to Kremenchuj, Ukraine, upon the outbreak of World War I, Sarna had the opportunity to study with the Ḥofets Ḥayim. He returned to Slobodka with the yeshiva after the war, taught there, and then moved with it to Hebron (1924). He became head of the yeshiva in 1927 and continued in this position after it moved to Jerusalem in 1929.

Sarna responded to the Holocaust in a eulogy address at the yeshivah in Jerusalem on 4 December 1944. He assured his listeners that God was not hidden, but present among the anguished remnant at the yeshiva as He was always present amid catastrophe. God's weeping enabled Jews to cry and begin to console themselves. Moreover, the metaphysical realities of redemption (*geulah*), penitent return (*teshuvah*), and disaster (*ḥurban*) were displayed across Israel's metahistorical line of development such that redemption was imminent. Redemption's onset, however, was conditioned by Israel's existential *teshuvah*. The tragedy was so severe that it paralyzed even the individual effort for *teshuvah*, but God entered into history to make that *teshuvah* possible.

SELECTIONS

In the selections from *Liteshuvah Velitekumah: Devarim Shene'emru Bakinus Lemasped Uteshuvah Shehitkayem Ba'ir Biyeshivat Ḥevron-Keneset Yisrael Beyom 8 Kislev 5705* (*Toward Penitent Return and Restoration: Words Said at the Gathering for Mourning and Penitent Return in the City [of Jerusalem] in the Ḥevron-Keneset Yisrael Yeshiva on 4 December 1944*), Sarna stated that the shock was so great that even crying was impossible. But as God cried over the destruction of the First Temple, He was also crying now. This made it possible for the human being to cry and, once this took place, to reflect upon the catastrophe. Sarna spoke of a higher, metaphysical relationship among *ḥurban*, *teshuvah*, and *geulah*, where each implied the other. *Ḥurban*'s purpose was *teshuvah*, and *teshuvah* carried the promise of *geulah*. In turn, *geulah* evoked preparatory suffering (*ḥurban*), and *ḥurban* brought on *teshuvah*. The dynamic included the Holocaust, as the resolution of tension between potential and actual *geulah*. The higher triadic structure displayed itself metahistorically. Trespasses in Babylon prevented the Messiah's coming there as intended. But the seed for the end of days, the potential for *geulah*, was planted at that point. God entered Israel's tragic history when the First Temple was destroyed, to remain present for all future tragedies. Future *teshuvah* was also assured. When the suffering of the Holocaust broke the human being with such intensity that it became impossible to initiate *teshuvah*, God opened a point in the heart for *teshuvah* to begin. The point would expand into a threshold for *teshuvah* suitable to redemption (see *Midrash Shir Hashirim Rabbah*, *Parashah* 5, *Siman* 3). These selections have been translated from the Hebrew by Gershon Greenberg.

Toward Penitent Return and Restoration

1. The Anguish Above

"The Lord, the God of hosts, call[s] to weeping and to lamentation" [Isaiah 22:12]. There is a weeping whose depth and degree neither prophet nor angel can understand. It is a weeping, a mourning for which God Himself in all His glory calls. It was so during the destruction of the Temple, and so it is with our destruction in our day. In our gathering today, in the city that is the stronghold of Torah, to weep and to wail over the terrible catastrophe that has come as a Holocaust (*Shoah*) on our nation, we must bend our ears to heed the voice that calls us from heaven to weeping and lamentation. For there is no one to summon us to such weeping and lamentation aside from the Holy One Himself. When the Holy One calls us, He is not just calling us to weep and to lament. The calling is [also] for weeping and lamentation above. We are called, because in hearkening to this terrible calling, we also are made into an example of what is [transpiring] above.

All of the laws of mourning that were established by the rabbinic sages for us and which we observe on the ninth of *Av*, are a kind of example of what is [transpiring] above. As it says:

The Holy One called the ministering angels and said to them, "If a human king had a son who died, what is customary for him to do?" The angels said to Him, "A sackcloth is hung at his door." The Holy One said to them, "I will also do so." As it is written, "I clothe the heavens with blackness and I make sackcloth their covering" [Isaiah 50:3]. He asked them again, "What does a human being do when mourning?" They replied, "He extinguishes the lamps." He said to them, "I will also do so." As it says, "The sun and the moon are become black, and the stars withdraw their shining" [Joel 4:15]. He asked, "What

does a human king do?" They replied, "A human king overturns his couch." He said, "I will also do so." As it says, "Till thrones were placed, and one that was ancient of days did sit" [Daniel 7:9], the thrones, as it were, were overturned. He asked, "What does a human king do?" They replied, "A human king walks barefoot." He said, "I will also do so." As it says, "He travels in whirlwind and storm, and clouds are the dust on His feet" [Nahum 1:3]. He asked, "What does a human king do?" They replied, "A human king rends his purple garments." He said, "I will also do so." As it says, "The Lord hath done that which He devised; He hath performed His word" [Lamentations 2:17]. What means, "What He has purposed (*bitsa emrato*)?" He rent (*bitsa*) His purple garments. He asked, "What does a human king do?" They replied, "A human king sits and is silent." He said, "I will also do so." As it is stated, "Let him sit alone and keep silence" [Lamentations 3:28]. He asked, "What does a human king do when he is in mourning?" They replied, "He sits and weeps." He said to them, "I will also do so." As it says, "The Lord, the God of hosts, call[s] to weeping, and to lamentation, and to baldness, and to girding with sackcloth" [Isaiah 22:12]. [*Midrash Eykhah Rabbah*, *Parashah* 1, *Siman* 1]

All the laws and customs that we observe on the ninth of *Av*—[including] extinguishing candles, overturning the couches, taking off one's shoes, removing the curtain from the holy ark, sitting silently, the weeping and lamentation, etc.—are also, as it were, an example of what is [transpiring] above. All the manifestations of anguish and mourning on the part of the person are according to that person's ability. And they are nothing in comparison to the catastrophe. Jeremiah the prophet already entreated before his

Maker: "Oh that my head were waters, and mine eyes a fountain of tears, that I might weep day and night for the slain of the daughter of my people" [Jeremiah 8:23]. That is to say, God should create Jeremiah as a new creature, with a head of water, and eyes a fount of tears. Because tears, according to laws of nature, do not express the anguish. Not even the tears of Jeremiah the prophet, each of which split the heavens.

God counts every tear that a person sheds and deposits it into His treasure house. As the rabbinic Sages already said:

"And given them tears to drink in large measure" [Psalms 80:6]. Rabbi Elazar said that Esau shed three tears. The verse does not read *shalosh* [the usual word for "three"] but *shalish*. Therefore, taught R. Berechiah, Esau shed only a third of a tear, for the exact meaning of *shalish* is one-third—hence only a third of a tear. The community of Israel said before the Holy One, "For the merit of the three tears that the evil one [Esau] shed, You gave him dominion over the whole world and gave him prosperity in this world. How much more, then, wilt Thou do for us when Thou comest to see that we are humiliated and that we pour out our very souls in weeping?" [*Midrash Tehillim, Perek* 80, *Siman* 4]

The tears of Esau, the evil one, were also counted, measured, and weighed. Esau received his reward for them in this world and through them he rules in the world. [Could you imagine what] the value and weight of the tears of Jeremiah the prophet are in God's eyes? Despite all this, Jeremiah did not receive satisfaction from them, and they were too small to contain and express his anguish and lamentation. If it were thus with Jeremiah the prophet, then how much more so with the ordinary person?

This is the principle. We are commanded to walk in the ways of God and imitate His attributes. As the rabbinic Sages said: "As He is merciful, you should also be merciful; as He is compassionate, so you too should be compassionate" [B. T. *Shabbat* 133[b]]. Though there is no comparison between human mercifulness and divine mercifulness, we have [nevertheless] been commanded to have our attributes resemble His attributes to the extent that it is possible for us. We have also been commanded to walk in His ways with regard to the anguish and mourning over the destruction of the Temple. As He walks barefoot, as it were, so we are to walk barefoot. He overturns His throne, as it were, and sits on it overturned, so we are to overturn our couch. And as He cries, so are we to cry. The value of all our deeds is according to the value of our understanding and the depth of our thought concerning the anguish above. When we overturn our couches, we must consider and place before our eyes the terrible image of the divine throne overturned [above] because of Israel's anguish. When we weep, we must contemplate the terrible anguish of "My soul shall weep in secret for your pride" [Jeremiah 13:17], because the pride of the people of Israel was taken from them. Only in this way will our tiny deeds have value. For walking should be in His paths and imitating should be of His blessed attributes. Through this, our deeds will also be raised and elevated to the greatest heights.

2. The Revelation of the Anguish [Transpiring] Above

After the destruction of the First Temple, they sat and wept by the rivers of Babylon. The rabbinic Sages said that they merited that the anguish above would be revealed to them in all its depth and greatness, sharing their trouble, and in God's eternal love for them. [According to the *Zohar*,] Rabbi Simeon began by citing "The word of the Lord came expressly unto Ezekiel," etc. [Ezekiel 1:3]. Ezekiel was a faithful prophet. One must ask: How did he reveal everything he saw? Does the person whom the king brings into his palace reveal all the secrets that he sees? [Yes], Ezekiel was certainly a faithful prophet. He revealed what he revealed because he had the permission of the Holy One.

[According to the *Zohar*] Rabbi Simeon said, "Whoever is used to suffering anguish, though a period of anguish comes to him, he bears his burden. He is not afraid [and] does not feel the pain. But whoever is not used to anguish and has spent his whole life in pleasure and being pampered, when he has anguish, it is complete anguish and there is [really] something to weep about." Thus, when the children of Israel descended to Egypt, they were used to anguish, for all the days of Jacob their father were in anguish. Therefore they bore the suffering of the exile as needed. But the exile of Babylon was complete anguish, one which those above and those below cried over. The ones above, as it is written, "Behold, their valiant ones cry without" [Isaiah 33:7]. The ones below, as it is written, "By the rivers of Babylon, there we sat down, we wept," etc. [Psalms 137:1]. They all wept over the Babylonian exile. What is the reason? Because, as it is written, they had enjoyed the pleasures of kings: "The precious sons of Zion," etc. [Lamentations 4:2]. Now they were descending into exile with collars around their necks and their hands tied behind their backs. When they were in the Babylonian exile, they thought that they had no chance to exist in the world, for the Holy One [had] left them and would never watch over them.

"It has been taught," Rabbi Simeon [continued] to say: "At that time, the Holy One called His whole family, all the holy chariots, His whole army, and His camp, his generals and whole hosts of heaven and said to them: 'What are you doing here? My beloved children are in the Babylonian exile and you are here. Arise and descend all of you to Babylon and I will be with you.'" As it is written, "Thus sayeth the Lord, your redeemer, the Holy One of Israel: For your sake I have sent to Babylon, and I will bring down all of them as fugitives" [Isaiah 43:14]. "For your sake I have sent to Babylon" refers to the Holy One. And, "I will bring down all of them as fugitives" refers to divine chariots and camps. When they descended to Babylon, the heavens opened and the spirit of prophecy rested on Ezekiel. He saw all that he saw, and he said to the Israelites: "Your Lord is here and all the hosts and chariots of heaven who have come dwell among you." They did not believe Ezekiel, and he had to reveal everything he saw: "I saw this and I saw that." If he revealed more than what he should have revealed, it was [because it was] necessary. When the children of Israel saw this, they rejoiced. When they heard the things from Ezekiel's mouth, they were not fearful at all about their exile, since they knew that the Holy One had not left them [*Zohar, Ḥelek* 2, *Shemot* 2^b].

The rabbinic Sages revealed to us a great secret and most wondrous things. All the revelations of the event of the chariot that God revealed to Ezekiel were none other than the revelation of prophecy about the secrets of the chariot. God really revealed His descent to Ezekiel, as it were, with His chariot to Babylon. He descended in order to be with the children of Israel in their troubles and console them and mitigate the anguish of their difficult exile, after they had become accustomed to the pleasures of kings. He descended to instill in their hearts that He had not left them and would never leave them. He is with them in their anguish. God revealed all this to Ezekiel. This was not to teach him the secrets of the chariot. It was in order that Ezekiel should reveal the reality of these things to the Israelites. It was in order that they should be consoled. Indeed, they were consoled, and they rejoiced to the point that they did not fear the exile at all.

Although in our exile and trouble, we are not worthy of God and that His chariot be revealed to us, matters are the same now [as in Babylon]. When we study and read the section concerning the chariot of Ezekiel, we must imagine this wonderful image in our souls: the revelation on the river Chebar and the joy of the Israelites there. We should participate in their joy. This is a doctrine that we need. And we are obligated to learn from this esoteric chapter, whose secret is only for the elect. Not only that. The anguish above is the greater, because we are not worthy of seeing with our eyes the exile of the *Shekhinah* (Divine Presence) of God with us in our exile. As it is written: "In all their affliction, He was afflicted (*lo tsar*)" [Isaiah 63:9]. It is written "not" [*lamed alef*] but read "His" [*lamed vav*]. For the greatest affliction before God, as it were, is the "no" [concerning God's] affliction. That is to say: It is impossible to reveal before us "His" affliction, and this afflicts Him greatly. Instead of envisioning with our own eyes the "I will be with him in trouble" [Psalms 91:15] in His descent with the whole host of heaven and His whole chariot, all that is before us [is] only the terrible and awesome hiding of His face. Therefore, from our side, we need to plumb the depths and look with penetrating observation. We need to remove the misty covering until we too become worthy to discern and understand a little of that truth as it is. This secret is concealed in the laws of mourning for the destruction of the

Temple. Namely, to plumb the depths of the ways of God, His trouble, and the trouble of Israel, and to walk in His paths. To plumb the depths concerning: As He mourns so we also mourn; as He weeps so we also weep. Then, together with the expression of mourning, our souls will also find profound consolation.

3. The Terrible Catastrophe

It is written: "And I will make it as the mourning for an only son, and the end thereof is a bitter day" [Amos 8:10]. "As the mourning for an only son" is our mourning. There is no other [prior] example of this mourning in the world, in any nation or language, even in our nation. Even the parables provided by our ancients to reflect the trouble of Israel in the days of our exile are not adequate. (Concerning what David said, "Nay, but for Thy sake are we killed all that day; we are accounted as sheep for the slaughter" [Psalms 44:23]. The intention here is not to describe the greatness of the trouble but rather the peace of mind of the Israelites who gave their souls in sanctification of God's name, as the earlier commentaries explain about this verse.) We are thought of "as sheep for the slaughter" [Psalms 44:23]. Has the world ever seen even sheep brought to such a terrible slaughter? For years, brought to slaughter in trains in the tens of thousands as the ultimate tyrant has brought our brethren? Was there ever another example of such cruel slaughtering? Woe to us, for our disaster! During the destruction [of the Temple,] our nation was also destroyed, and from a nation of many millions only tens of thousands were left, as explained at the end of the Book of Jeremiah. But there were battle[s] and heroism also from our side and tens of thousands of our enemy also fell dead. This is unlike the slaughtering and killing [now], slaughter like slaughtering mosquitoes, without the possibility of opposition. The deaths have been wicked. Fathers together with children, mothers together with children, old and young. In their tearing apart and trampling, the animals of humankind exceeded [what is done by] animals of prey. Animals of prey have their customs and bounds. Some rip apart but do not trample, and some trample but do not rip apart. These evil

[human] animals ripped apart and trampled and had no compassion. There were those who were murdered at Betar. It was a terrible catastrophe for a whole city which was important to God. But along with their catastrophe, they were worthy of a great good in terms of an open miracle from heaven. Until this very day and forever, the entire community invokes the blessing of gratitude for the good, the blessing, "Who is good and beneficent (*Hatov Vehametiv*)" for being brought to burial. But the millions of our dead, "The slain of the daughter of my people" [Jeremiah 8:23], did not have even that privilege. Woe to us!

The rabbinic Sages tell [us] that after the destruction of the [First] Temple, Jeremiah the prophet went and collected fingers which had been cut off. He embraced, fondled, and kissed them [*Midrash Eichah Rabbah*, Proem 34]. We did not have even this privilege. Where are the beloved bones? Who will give them to us to embrace and kiss? They have turned into dust and ashes in ovens and flames of fire. In the thousands and tens of thousands, they are in the black streets of the enemy. Our mourning is "as for an only son" [Jeremiah 6:26]. How can we imagine it? There is nothing like it. How can we compare it?

The scope of the catastrophe is so terrible, and our disaster is "great like the sea" [Lamentations 2:13], that it cannot be absorbed by our ideas. It is not grasped in our thoughts. We stand before it in shock. We are like an infant during a terrible calamity in the house. It sees mournful faces before it. Grief and mourning surround it. Its mind cannot comprehend all the anguish and the pain surrounding it. What it feels most of all at the time of the event is how it does not receive its food as usual and that its needs are not being attended to as usual. We are like that today.

Therefore the appropriate advice in this matter is as it is written: "Make thee mourning, as for an only son" [Jeremiah 6:26]. That is to say: It is impossible to encircle the mourning entirely, because it is greater than our intellect's grasp and deeper than our normal feelings. Therefore each of us must contract ourselves into our own corner, each to his own mourning. For there is not one person in Israel who does not have a share in the catastrophe. It is his share. This one mourning over his father or mother, this one mourning over his brother or relatives, this one mourning for his teacher or student, and this one over his friend and loved ones. Let each person take his portion and do his singular mourning. Then perhaps he will grasp a little, and then he will mourn. . . .

5. From Catastrophe to Penitent Return

However, there also is a purpose to the catastrophe. The purpose to the catastrophe is penitent return. The scroll of Lamentations, in all of its chapters and laments, has a purpose. It is the verse that ends the scroll: "Turn Thou us unto Thee, O Lord, and we shall be turned; renew our days as of old!" [Lamentations 5:21]. None of the catastrophes that have happened to Israel have been accidental, heaven forbid. All of them have a source in the "These are the words of the covenant" [Deuteronomy 28:69] of our holy Torah. Scripture is full of the decrees and catastrophes to be poured out upon us during the footsteps of the Messiah: "In thy distress, when all these things are come upon thee, in the end of days, thou wilt return to the Lord thy God, and hearken unto His voice" [Deuteronomy 4:30]. As is explicit in this verse, "All these things," so too the purpose of all these things is explicit. It is, "return," etc. This is to say, there is but one unique purpose for all these things. It is penitent return. Therefore, in this generation, when all these things happened to us, we are commanded one specific commandment, to return to God. Every day for us is as Yom Kippur (Day of Atonement). Just as the commandment of Yom Kippur is penitent return, so the commandment for every day which passes for us is penitent return. For so we have been commanded in the commandment of "Thou wilt return to the Lord thy God" [Deuteronomy 4:30].

Certainly, there is a difference between the commandment of penitent return for Yom Kippur and the commandment of penitent return [to be carried out] after all these things have taken place. Even the commandment of penitent return on Yom Kippur is a commandment left to the person's choice. If the person wants to do penitent return, he has atoned. If he does not want to, on Yom Kippur he has the complete choice to deviate and to add rebellion to his sins, to the point that God would not want to forgive him and he dies with his sins.

But the commandment of penitent return in our day is different. Besides the commandment itself, the commandment has a promise. The commandment of penitent return is connected with the promise of redemption. Therefore, to that extent it is also a promise, as our rabbinic Sages wrote: "Rabbi Eliezer said, if Israel repents they will be redeemed, and if not they will not be redeemed. Rabbi Joshua said to him, if they do not repent they will not be redeemed, but the Holy One will put over them a king whose decrees will be as difficult as Haman's and Israel will repent and return to the right path" [B. T. Sanhedrin 97[b]]. In the Jerusalem Talmud, the version is that Rabbi Eliezer responded thus to Rabbi Joshua, saying that it is indeed so that Israel will not be redeemed except through penitent return. However, it is certain that the redemption will come, since the Holy One has already promised it. Similarly, it is also certain that penitent return will come at the end of days, since it too was promised [J. T. Ta'anit 3[a]]. Maimonides, of blessed memory, writes:

> All of the prophets commanded penitent return. Nor will Israel be redeemed except through penitent return. The Torah has already promised that the people of Israel will do penitent return at the end of their exile and they will be redeemed. As it is written, "When all these things are come upon thee . . . and shalt return unto the Lord thy God . . . then the Lord thy God will turn thy captivity." [Deuteronomy 30:1–3; Mishneh Torah, Hilkhot Teshuvah 7, Halakhah 5]

It is written: "As I live—sayeth the Lord God—surely with a mighty hand, and with an outstretched arm, and with fury poured out" [Ezekiel 20:33]. There is an apparent contradiction. We say in the prayers, "And brings a redeemer to their children's children for the sake of His name with love" [Shemoneh Esrei (the silent, standing benediction)]. That is, redemption should come with love and not with overflowing fury. But both are true. For it continues to say: "And I will cause you to pass under the rod, and I will bring you into the bond of the covenant" [Ezekiel 20:37]; "With your sweet savor will I accept you" [Ezekiel 20:41]. That is, the overflowing fury will indeed come first. It involves the rise of a king as severe as Haman. But from this will come the penitent return which will return [God's] love. Thus, the overflowing fury comes out of love and guides to love. For it is also written there: "And ye shall know that I am the Lord, when I have wrought with you for My name's sake" [Ezekiel 20:44]. That is, for the sake of His name with love. As Rabbi Naḥman says: "Even with such fury let the Merciful rage against us, but that He redeems us" [B. T. *Sanhedrin* 105ᵃ]. Rashi, of blessed memory comments, "That which He gives and brings upon us, is the anger. 'I will reign over you . . . with overflowing fury.' And He will redeem us against our will and will rule over us" [Rashi *ad* B. T. *Sanhedrin* 105ᵃ].

This great question pierces at our brain: How is it possible for a perverse and obstinate generation, a poor and orphaned generation, a broken and dejected generation, miserable and dejected in spirit, to be worthy of returning in penitent return on a level that previous generations of greats could not attain? The answer to this question is the secret of heavenly assistance.

6. Heavenly Assistance

It is written: "Thou turnest man to contrition"—to spiritual dejection—"and sayest: 'Return, ye children of men'" [Psalms 90:3]. Spiritual dejection does not deter from penitent return. On the contrary, it causes penitent return, both individually and communally. In addition, spiritual dejection is the great awakener to penitent return. For the "In thy distress" [Deuteronomy 4:30] opens the threshold in the heart of the individual and in the hearts of the community until it brings them to the "thou wilt return" [Deuteronomy 4:30]. In addition, the "In thy distress" [Deuteronomy 4:30] contains a deep secret. It is heavenly assistance.

There is no comparison between the attribute of heavenly assistance which helps and assists one who remains unconcerned and sits under his vine and fig tree and the heavenly assistance to the one who is in exile and wanders and is dejected because of poverty and lacking in everything. This is so with the individual and even more so with the community since the many mercies of heaven are stopped from providing material welfare be-

cause the attribute of stern judgment rules the world. But they are strengthened in all their power, in their spiritual influence, by heavenly assistance with penitent return. The more the attribute of stern judgment is strengthened and the more it rules, the more is heavenly assistance with penitent return strengthened. In the end of days, when all these things happen to Israel and wrath intensifies in the world, the attribute of stern judgment rules and the wrath rules us. Precisely then, the mercies of heaven are awakened with a great effulgence and help with penitent return. Every needle eye [turns into a] threshold which opens as to a great hall, of a dimension impossible to attain in good and tranquil days [see *Midrash Shir Hashirim Rabbah, Parashah* 5, *Siman* 3].

The promise itself, which God Himself promised concerning penitent return in the end of days, stands at the right hand of those who return. It helps them and brings them to the return. As it says:

Rabbi Yoḥanan says, If you see a generation where many travails come upon you like a river, as it is written, "For distress will come in like a flood, which the breath of the Lord driveth" [Isaiah 59:19]; this is followed by: "And a redeemer will come to Zion" [Isaiah 59:20]. Rabbi Yoḥanan says, the son of David will not come until the generation is completely righteous or completely guilty. In a generation that is innocent, as it is written, "Thy people also shall be all righteous; they shall inherit the land forever" [Isaiah 60:21]. [Rashi: That is, redemption.] In a generation that is completely guilty, as it is written, "And he saw that there was no man, and was astonished that there was no intercessor" [Isaiah 59:16], and it is written, "For Mine own sake will I do it" [Isaiah 48:11]. [B. T. *Sanhedrin* 98ᵃ]

That is, [let us imagine that] all ends have been exhausted and that no person has been awakened to attach himself to the Lord. The generation is completely guilty. Then, "For Mine own sake will I do it" [Isaiah 48:11]. [That is,] for the sake of the promise that God promised them concerning the redemption and penitent return, God will pour a spirit from on high upon them [see Isaiah 32:15]. "And the spirit of God will pine for them until they return to Him" [Rashi's second comment on the verse in Isaiah]. And then, "A redeemer will come to Zion" [Isaiah 59:20]. That is, the designated redemption will come together with the penitent return which is promised.

7. Penitent Return after the Ḥurban

After the catastrophe, it will be demonstrated that this generation was able to correct, in thought and deed, what earlier generations before the catastrophe were unable to correct. We find in the Talmud:

> R. Yehoshua bar Levi asked: Why were they called the men of the Great Assembly? Because they returned the crown [of divine attributes] to its ancient completeness. Moses came and said, "The great God, the mighty and the awful" [Deuteronomy 10:17]. Then Jeremiah came and said, "Strangers are destroying His sanctuary. Where are His awful deeds?" He omitted the attribute "the awful." Daniel came and said, "Strangers are enslaving His sons. Where are His mighty deeds?" He omitted the word "mighty." Then the men of the Great Assembly came and said, "On the contrary, His mighty deeds lie in His suppressing His wrath, extending long suffering to the wicked. Therein are His awful powers. Were it not for the fear of the Holy One, blessed be He, how could one nation survive among the nations?" [B. T. Yoma 69ᵇ]

On the face of it, why should it be asked, "Why were they called the men of the Great Assembly?" Are they not the ones who established the Torah and the worship, which is prayer? [see Mishnah Avot 1:1; and B. T. Megillah 17ᵇ]. However, from the response, it appears that by this action they transcended all their [other] greatnesses with regard to establishing the Torah. The greatness which transcends all of that is the returning of the crown to its ancient completeness. What is this return of the crown? They returned the crown of God's praise to its former completeness. Moses said, "The great God, the mighty [or strong] and the awful [or awesome]" [Deuteronomy 10:17]; Jeremiah came and did not say awful; Daniel came and did not say mighty. Then the men of the Great Assembly came and said, "On the contrary, 'His mighty deeds...His awful powers.'" But

what is the greatness concealed in this? The greatness by means of which they were worthy to be called the men of the Great Assembly?

Essentially, the matter seems to be this: Moses uttered the praise of the mighty and awful in a period when the might and awfulness of the Holy One were known to all. Not only to Israel, but even to the nations of the world. As it is written: "The peoples have heard, they tremble," etc. [Exodus 15:14]. For it was a shining era among the eras and "The right hand of the Lord is exalted! The right hand of the Lord doeth valiantly" [Psalms 118:16]. Therefore, Jeremiah and Daniel thought that the praise which Moses uttered was known to all. Therefore, in a time of catastrophe when strangers destroy, [Jeremiah asks, "Where is His awfulness?"]. When strangers are enslaving His children, [Daniel asks, "Where is His strength?"], meaning that the praises that Moses uttered were not manifest. Therefore Jeremiah and Daniel did not recite the praises of mighty and awful in their prayers. For they were not manifest in their time. Jeremiah and Daniel did know that the might lay in His suppressing His inclination and His awfulness lay in the [ongoing] existence of one nation among the nations. But in the opinion of Jeremiah and Daniel, this was not the ultimate praise which Moses recited and not equivalent to the might and awfulness that were known to all. The principle is to recite in prayers only those praises of God which Moses recited. As it says, "We only recite the three [that is to say, the great, the mighty, and the awful]. If Moses had not recited them in the Torah and the men of the Great Assembly had not come and established them in the prayers we would not be able to recite them" [B. T. Berakhot 33ᵇ]. Maimonides, of blessed memory, writes that it is not within the power of man to achieve an ultimate praise of God. Rather, one says [only] what Moses our teacher, of blessed memory, said [Mishneh Torah, Hilkhot Tefillah 9, Halakhah 7]. Therefore, Jeremiah and Daniel did not recite the praises of the mighty and the awful in their prayers. Rashi, of blessed memory, writes similarly there: Daniel did not include the term mighty in his prayer [Rashi ad B. T. Yoma 69ᵇ]. Concerning Jeremiah, Scripture explicitly says, "I prayed unto the Lord," etc. [Jeremiah 32:16]. In his prayer, he did not say awful. This is the question of the rabbis and the Talmud. "How could they do this and uproot the principle that Moses established?" [B. T. *Yoma* 69[b]]. That is to say, the rabbis did not ask about how they allegedly diminished the praises of God. For it did not cross their mind at all, heaven forbid, that Jeremiah and Daniel would diminish the praises of God. Rather the question was: "How did they do this and establish the custom not to recite these terms in prayer?" Even if the might and awfulness were not known in their time as in the time of Moses, Moses already said it and it was the praise of God. Why did they not say it on the principle that Moses had already said it? The response to this question is: Rabbi Eleazar said, "Because Jeremiah and Daniel knew that God insists on truth, they would not ascribe false things to Him." That is, in the prayer, which is the service of the heart, one is to enunciate only the praise which one feels. The Holy One, who sees into the heart, will recognize the truth in the heart of the person who recites it. However, if one recites the praises and there is a place in one's heart to ask, "Where is God?" this is not a recitation of the truth. "Because Jeremiah and Daniel knew that the Holy One is truthful" [B. T. *Yoma* 69[b]]. (Rashi agrees with the truth and hates falsehood [Rashi *ad* B. T. *Yoma* 69[b]]. "Therefore, they did not lie to Him" [B. T. *Yoma* 69[b]].) They did not recite the praises in their prayers, even though Moses had said them. This is not uprooting the rule that Moses had established.

But, the men of the Great Assembly came and said: On the contrary, this is His might and His awfulness. That is to say: It does not exhaust the praises of God to say that He is mighty and awful. Moses said that He is the might and awfulness that are known to all through the manifest miracles of the exodus from Egypt and the splitting of the sea, etc. On the contrary, the primary praise of God in Moses' praise is the might of overcoming His will and extending long suffering with regard to evildoers. This attribute is not seen when the might of God is known, when all the nations of the world fear Him and tremble because God's terror and fear fall upon them. On the contrary, [it is seen] precisely when strangers shout and dance in His sanctuary and enslave His children, as Rashi, of blessed memory, wrote:

"His strength is that He suppressed His will all those years when His children were enslaved and He was long suffering when it came to all the decrees imposed upon His children. This is His awesomeness, that were it not for His fear, etc." [Rashi *ad* B. T. *Yoma* 69[b]]. Rashi, of blessed memory, interpreted: "From the day of the destruction [of the Temple] you learn of His awesomeness. All the nations were gathered to destroy all the children of Israel, and the children of Israel outlasted them" [Rashi *ad* B. T. *Yoma* 69[b]]. You do not learn the ultimate praise about God's might and awfulness from the exodus from Egypt, from the splitting of the sea. Rather, [you learn it] precisely from the day of the destruction, when the whole nation was destroyed and only a small number of tens of thousands remained, as explained at the end of the Book of Jeremiah. From this you also learn about His awfulness. Even though all the nations gathered to destroy the children of Israel. But nothing at all would remain of Israel's enemies. Israel nevertheless outlasted them. This is what they said: The men of the Great Assembly came and returned the crown to its previous glory. And they established the praises of might and awfulness in the prayers, as Moses our teacher had established them. The greatness is the return of this crown, to the point that it transcends all the [other] great things done by the men of the Great Assembly. With this, they returned the praise of God and His honor everywhere and in every situation. Had the Israelites gone into an exile full of troubles, decrees, and conversions without recognizing this profundity, they might not have continued to exist, heaven forbid. For they would have come to reflect on His attributes and to ask the question: Where is His might and awfulness? Not like Jeremiah and Daniel, but as one who asks out of resentment in his heart. It would be like Bar Daroma, who said, "Hast not Thou cast us off, O God? And Thou goest not forth, O God, with our hosts" [Psalms 108:12; B. T. *Gittin* 57[a]]. Not as a matter of surprise and prayer as David said, but out of complaint and grumbling. Bar Daroma's end was bitter. Everyone who does the same is likened to one who has no God. Without God there is no Torah or worship. Therefore, had the men of the Great Assembly not returned the great crown to its former glory, there would, heaven forbid, be no continued existence for the establishment of Torah and worship which they had accomplished. The return of this crown alone returned the children of Israel to their heavenly Father. It established everything in His name. That is why it is great. Only because of this were they worthy to be called the men of the Great Assembly.

8. The Crown of Israel's Praise

Not only that. The return of this crown was twofold. When the men of the Great Assembly returned the crown of the praise of God, they thereby returned the crown of the praise of Israel. The essence of the treasuredness of the people of Israel and their chosenness from among the nations is that they are ever connected to God's love—through suffering and tranquillity, in exile and in the Land of Israel. Naḥmanides, of blessed memory, wrote:

> "The Lord did not set His love upon you, nor choose you, because ye were more in number than any people—for ye were the fewest of all peoples—but because the Lord loved you, and because He would keep the oath which He swore unto your fathers, hath the Lord brought you out with a mighty hand, and redeemed you out of the house of bondage, from the hand of Pharaoh king of Egypt" [Deuteronomy 7:7–8]. [Naḥmanides:] No other reason is needed for God's choosing us and favoring us [besides this]: That we are suitable to be loved by God and chosen for love by Him because we know to endure with our love for Him through everything which comes upon us from him. [Naḥmanides ad Deuteronomy 7:7–8]

Indeed, the Holy One is certain of our enduring love for Him. It is written in the Torah portion Ha'azinu:

> I thought I would make an end of them, I would make their memory cease from among men, were it not that I dreaded the enemy's provocation, lest their adversaries should misjudge, lest they should say, "Our hand is exalted, and not the Lord hath wrought all this." [Deuteronomy 32: 26–27]

The argument against the attribute of judgment's having dominion over Israel is not out of dread that Israel would misjudge and say things. Heaven forbid. There is nothing to fear and nothing to be afraid of when it comes to the people of Israel. They will always remain with their eternal love for Him, whether [the love be] of the staff or of loving kindness. [There is only the fear of] "Were it not that I dreaded the enemy's provocation" [Deuteronomy 32:27]. That is, lest their adversaries misdeem, lest they say, "Our hand is exalted." For this is the way of the nations of the world. They know to love only when the love is obvious to them and only when they are satisfied. If there were to be a famine, they would become angry and curse their king and their God. This is the trait which differentiates the nation of Israel from the nations. It is the secret of the existence of the nation of Israel and its eternality. For "Thy rod and Thy staff—they comfort me" [Psalms 23:4]; "I will sing of mercy and justice" [Psalms 101:1]. Just as the people will sing [in times of] loving kindness to God for His loving kindness, so they will sing in [times of] justice. Only a member of the chosen people of Israel is fit to wear the garments of Sabbath and stand with joy before his Maker and sing with love and longing, "They smote me, they wounded me, the keepers of the walls took away my mantle from me" [Song of Songs 5:7] and, when the troubles increase, to call out of the depths to God. They stand like sinners before their Maker, like a son who sinned before his father. As the rabbinic Sages said:

> "Hearken unto Me, O Jacob, and Israel My called" [Isaiah 48:12]. God calls out to those who are killed, and they call out in His name. As it says, "Nay, but for Thy sake are we killed" [Psalms 44:23]. Job says similarly, "Thou He slay me, yet will I trust in Him" [Job 13:15]. . . . Those generations said to Him, "Lord of the universe." The first generation had patriarchs and the merit of the patriarchs stood by them. [When they said,] "We are become orphans and fatherless," etc. [Lamentations 5:3] . . . God said to the early generations, "Do penitent return and I will heal your afflictions." As it is written, "Return, ye backsliding children, I will heal your backslidings"

[Jeremiah 3:22]. And it is written, "I will heal their backsliding, I will love them freely" [Hosea 14:5]. [That is, God says], "I love you with an unending love.... As much as the nations try to place hatred between Me and you they will not be able to...." Not only that. Some nations kill Israel in order to turn them from God. The congregation of Israel says to them, "I cannot deny God." As it is written, "And my heart was moved for him" [Song of Songs 5:4].... [God says,] "The nations of the world hate Me because of My children and beyond all nations My children love Me. I give My children one hundred worlds full of the love with which I love my children. The nations will disgrace My children." As it says, "If a man would give all the substance of his house for love, He would utterly be condemned" [Song of Songs 8:7]. [*Midrash Aggadat Bereshit, Parashah* 84, *Siman* 2]

This conversation of love between the Holy One and the congregation of Israel continues throughout all the generations. It continues even in our generation, although we do not hear it. But we must incline our ears and hearken to the voice of the Holy One who calls to His downtrodden children with the longing of a merciful father: "I love you with unending love." We must also incline our ears and hearken to the voice of the congregation of Israel, which knows how to endure with love through everything which comes upon us from Him. It is the voice which responds to the nations of the world, which kill the people of Israel and which try to turn them from the Holy One: "I cannot deny Him. For my soul heard what He said on Sinai and my heart longs for Him. For I am lovesick." Every stain on this crown [of the praise of Israel] would stain the treasured character of Israel, heaven forbid. It would jeopardize Israel's whole existence through this long and bitter exile, full of trials and tribulations. Only through the return of the crown by the men of the Great Assembly, who returned it to its former splendor, did the people of Israel go into exile like a hero, armed with their love for the Holy One, with a love that would never separate Israel from Him. They would walk in His path securely, until God would have mercy on us and redeem us for the sake of His name with love.

9. The Annulling of the Evil Inclination of Idolatry

The men of the Great Assembly were worthy to return the crown to its original splendor after the destruction of the Temple, something of which they were not previously worthy. Likewise, they were worthy of the merit of annulling the desire for idolatry. The rabbinic Sages said:

"And cried with a loud voice unto the Lord their God" [Nehemiah 9:4]. What was said? Rav said, and some say that it was Rabbi Yoḥanan, "Woe, woe" [Rashi: a term of crying out and complaint] [to see the evil inclination of idolatry] which has destroyed the sanctuary, burnt the Temple, killed all of the righteous and drove all of Israel into exile and is still dancing around us! You have surely given [the evil inclination of idolatry] to us so that we may receive reward through it. We want neither it nor reward through it. [Rashi, of blessed memory, comments about this destruction: They ask for mercy because the evil inclination of idolatry was given over to them. About receiving reward: We will subdue it and receive a reward.] Thereupon a tablet fell down from heaven for them upon which the word truth was inscribed [Rashi: That is to say, I agree with you]. [B. T. *Yoma* 69[b]]

Go and learn: The generations before the destruction of the Temple struggled with the urge for idolatry. All the words of the prophets were full of words of rebuke against this severe sin. The kings of Judah and Israel were tested through this trial. To some extent the kings were able to extirpate idolatry. But none of them succeeded in uprooting it. Finally it was what destroyed the Temple. It burned the sanctuary, killed all the righteous, and exiled the people of Israel from their land. This is when they were indeed able to completely uproot it and completely annul it. This was the greatest level of penitent return. It is the level of penitent return for which we hope in the days of the Messiah. Naḥmanides, of blessed memory, wrote about the verse "And the Lord thy God will circumcise thy heart," etc. [Deuteronomy 30:6]: "The circumcision cited in this verse is that of the lust and desire of the foreskin of the heart. Circumcising the heart means not to lust and not [to] desire"

[Naḥmanides *ad* Deuteronomy 30:6]. The generation after the destruction of the Temple was worthy of the merit of the high level of penitent return, that of annulling the evil inclination, which is promised for the future, because it annulled the evil inclination of idolatry. The great generations before the destruction of the Temple were not worthy, despite their great attributes.

The tablet that fell from heaven to [the generation after the destruction] reveals to us the root of the matter. The generation was worthy of the attribute of truth in their penitent return, the sort of attribute which would come to them in the days of the Messiah. But in the days of the Messiah the entire evil inclination will be annulled, while at that time they were worthy only of annulling the evil inclination of idolatry. And it was also possible for them to annul the inclination to sin [per se] as well. As it is said there. But the world could not exist were the evil inclination to be completely annulled. Therefore they left it, albeit weakened in its powers. As to the two serious sins of idolatry and incest, which had caused Israel to stumble and because of which the First Temple was destroyed: As it says, "Why was the First Temple destroyed? Because of three things that existed then: idolatry, incest, and shedding of innocent blood" [B. T. *Yoma* 9ᵇ]. (Of course, not in their ordinary meaning but according to their elevated status and according to the claims of the Torah.) After the destruction, they were able to annul the first [idolatry] completely and at least weaken the second [incest]. All [of this happened] on account of the attribute of truth of which they were worthy, such that a tablet fell from heaven on which was written "truth."

We also find such an enlightening phenomenon in the days of Mordekhai and Esther. As the Talmud says, "'And they stood at the nether part of the mount' [Exodus 19:17]. This teaches us that God hung the mountain over them" [B. T. *Shabbat* 88ᵃ]. Nonetheless, they reaccepted it in the days of Aḥasuerus. As it is written, "The Jews ordained, and took it upon them" [Esther 9:27]. That is, they confirmed what they had accepted long before to do. [Rashi comments: in the days of Aḥasuerus, out of love for the miracle that was done for them; Rashi *ad* B. T. *Shabbat* 88ᵃ.] Thus, the reception of Torah on the part of Israel was still in the language

of the Torah, although from the aspect of reception, out of fear. When did Israel merit to accept the Torah out of love? After the destruction of the Temple in the days of Mordekhai and Esther, out of love for the miracle that was done for them. Why was it so? The rabbinic Sages already revealed the secret of the matter and said:

> The removal of the ring was more efficacious than the forty-eight prophets and seven prophetesses that prophesied to Israel. For all these were not able to turn Israel to better courses, and the removal of the ring did return them to better courses. [Rashi: They decreed fasts for penitent return. As it is written, "and fasting and weeping, and wailing; and many lay in sackcloth and ashes"; Esther 4:3]. [B. T. *Megillah* 14ᵃ]

And in the midrash: "The removal of Aḥasuerus's ring was better for Israel than the sixty myriads of prophets who prophesied in the days of Elijah because what the prophets did not do, the travails accomplished" [*Midrash Eichah Rabbah, Parashah* 4, *Siman* 27].

The most fortunate of all generations, the one worthy of the pinnacle of success, of seeing the future during its lifetime, which spoke to God spoke face to face, and over which the clouds of glory hovered, accepted the Torah out of fear. The unfortunate generation, which was in terrible danger of death, slaughter, and destruction and for which God's face was in hiding, was worthy of receiving the Torah out of love. While it's possible that by standing at Mount Sinai we are worthy to receive the Torah out of fear, through suffering we are worthy to receive it from love.

10. The Promise of Penitent Return

Essentially, the ability to transcend all preceding generations, whether in regard to annulling the evil inclination or accepting the Torah, was [a matter of] heavenly assistance with penitent return. It is hidden in the promise of "Thou wilt return" [Deuteronomy 4:30]. This promise is also for the end of days. But Naḥmanides already wrote about this verse: "In thy distress, when all these things are come upon thee, in the end of days, thou wilt return to the Lord thy God, and hearken unto His voice" [Deuteronomy 4:30], which alludes to the redemption from Babylon. There, the generation returned to God and confessed before Him and listened to the voices of the prophets whom God appointed for Israel. Therefore God promised them that He would not annihilate them and would not forget His covenant with their forefathers [Nahmanides *ad* Deuteronomy 4:30]. The end of days is very far away. It began upon the destruction of the First Temple. The reason for this is seen from what is said:

> The [the book the] *Tanna debe Eliahu* teaches: The world is to exist for six thousand years. In the first two thousand there was desolation; two thousand years the Torah flourished; and the next two thousand years is the messianic era. [Rashi: After the two thousand years of Torah, the judgment is that the Messiah will come and end the reign of evil and abrogate Israel's servitude.] [B. T. *Sanhedrin* 97ª]

The entire two thousand years are the years of the Messiah. By right, the Messiah should have come right at the beginning. But there were consequences to our many sins. Rashi, of blessed memory, comments: "The Messiah did not come at the end of the four thousand years and the consequences were such that he is still prevented from coming" [Rashi *ad* B. T. *Sanhedrin* 97ᵇ]. Therefore, the promise of penitent return began immediately upon the destruction of the Temple. Only through the heavenly assistance hidden in this promise was the generation after the destruction of the Temple worthy of learning from the day of destruction what it was not worthy of learning from the prophets.

If so, then our spirits should not fall on account of the decrees and devastations. Nor on account of the weakness and pettiness of the generations. Heaven forbid that we despair of

penitent return and heaven forbid that we despair of redemption. For faith in the redemption and faith in penitent return are one. As we have been promised redemption by a true promise from the mouth of God and His prophets, and not one of His words remains unfulfilled, so we have been promised with the promise of penitent return. Since the end of days is the secret of the promise, the fact is that the more the end of days is delayed, the more the mercies of heaven increase. One cannot compare the mercies with which God had mercy for His nation after the destruction of the First Temple—when there still were prophets and Torah sages among the people and the realm of spirit ruled in all the generations after the destruction—to the mercy for [our] orphaned generation about which it is said: "When He seeth that their stay is gone, and there is none remaining, shut up or left at large" [Deuteronomy 32:36]. The Talmud says,

> Were it possible to say, Israel had neither supporter nor helper. [Rashi: as if they could complain against heaven. There is no helper or supporter for Israel that they would be humiliated to the extreme and say, Neither helper nor supporter, etc.] [B. T. *Sanhedrin* 97ª]

There is no one to rely on except our Father in heaven. We should believe that this generation, which has really drunk the cup of bitterness of the birth pangs of the Messiah in the end of days, this generation for which will be fulfilled: "When all these things are come upon thee" [Deuteronomy 30:1], is also suitable to, and worthy of, the realization of the promise: "And shalt return unto the Lord thy God, and hearken to His voice according to all that I command thee this day, thou and thy children, with all thy heart, and with all thy soul" [Deuteronomy 30:2].

Ya'akov Mosheh Ḥarlap

Ya'akov Mosheh Ḥarlap (1883–1951) was born in Jerusalem and studied kab-balah under Tsevi Mikhael Shapiro. He served as rabbi of the Sha'arei Ḥesed district of Jerusalem and directed the Ets Ḥayim yeshiva in the city. A principal disciple of Rav Kook, he succeeded him as head of the Merkaz HaRav yeshiva in Jerusalem.

Ḥarlap's writings are filled with a sense of imminent redemption. He envisioned two stages. In the first, that of the Messiah son of Joseph, darkness enveloped the light of redemption. The darkness had to accompany the light, lest an overwhelm-ing entry of the light destroy the universe. The tension between the light and dark was also explosive. The explosion took place in the form of the assault of the nations (darkness) upon the people of Israel (light), i.e., the Holocaust. This did not have to happen. Israel's light had been available to the nations and they could have accessed the sacred through the people of Israel. Instead of transcending their pro-fane existence, however, they turned away from Israel and back to dark profanity. By the late 1930s, redemption became imminent. Fearing devastating consequences to the profane reality, the nations sought to undermine the entry of redemption by destroying the people of Israel who served as its vessel. For the people of Israel, there was also a positive meaning to the explosion. Every Jewish soul, Ḥarlap wrote, struggled to release itself from the darkness which enveloped it. The darkness included the physical body. As the bodies of Aaron's sons were once destroyed as they neared the holy fire in the Temple (Leviticus 10:1–2), the bodies of pious Jews were destroyed in the Holocaust as their souls ascended with, and toward, the pure light of the second stage of redemption, that of the Messiah son of David.

SELECTIONS

In *Mei Merom: Mima'yenei Hayeshua* (*Waters Sublime: From the Sources of Salvation*), written in the course of the war, Ḥarlap described the elements of the apocalyptic drama. In the section entitled "Secret of the Era of Transition," he stated that damage and destruction to the body testified to the soul's intensified holiness. Thus, Aaron's sons Nadav and Avihu were destroyed physically. The tribe of Levi, which en-countered the *Shekhinah* (Divine Presence) in the Tabernacle (*Torat Kohanim*, *Sifra* 8:23), was small in number. In "The Aspect of Silence," Ḥarlap observed that now, in the era of the onset of the Messiah, silence was required. Only by silencing the senses was it possible for the human being to receive the wisdom of God's drama. In "The Substance of the Binding of Isaac," Ḥarlap stated that the command to love God with the entire heart and soul was absolute. The love for God was inexhaustible and would endure, even should the soul of the entire nation be taken, that is, should there be a collective *Akedah* (Jerusalem, 1981–1982, pp. 115–118, 173–174, 205).

In his 3 October 1946 response to Barukh Yeḥiel Duvdevani in the Saint Cesarea DP camp in Italy, entitled "Behold, it says, 'Comfort ye, comfort ye My people' [Isaiah 40:1]" (held at the Beit Zevul-Ḥarlap archives in Jerusalem), Ḥarlap wrote that when redemption would finally come, the value of past suffering for Israel's soul would be clarified. At the present moment, he could assure that current suffering involved the presence of the *Shekhinah*, and as such should be a source of joy. Even more, the souls of the murdered Jews were souls from the realm of the chaotic void, as had been conceptualized by Rav Kook. These souls were able to perceive the realm of light, which transcended both the destructive realm of darkness and the tension between light and dark which characterized the era of the Messiah son of Joseph. The moment of murder, of the end to physical existence, coincided with entry into the threshold of the infinite realm of the light of redemption, a point where profane filled history ended and eternity began. Each such soul, Ḥarlap believed, was its own *Akedah* ("binding of Isaac"), while all of Israel was potentially a collective *Akedah*. In his essay "Towards the Era of Love" of December 1947–January 1948, citing the Gaon of Vilna, Ḥarlap described the destruction and building of the Messiah son of Joseph's era and the redemption of the era of the Messiah son of David. At the end of history, the Messiah would appear as a cosmic vessel which was dark outside and light within, and which then would shed its darkness. For their part, the nations would seek to attack Israel, oblivious to the fact that this destroyed their exclusive access to existence (*Sinai* 11, nos. 4–5 [December 1947–February 1948]: 126–138). Selections translated from the Hebrew by Gershon Greenberg.

WATERS SUBLIME: FROM THE SOURCES OF SALVATION

Secret of the Era of Transition

The selection by which God chose His holy people and the selection by which His holy people chose Him, may His name be blessed, "For the Lord hath chosen Jacob for Himself, and Israel for His own treasure" [Psalms 135:4], are eternal selections. No change will come to them, heaven forbid, "For I the Lord change not; And ye, O sons of Jacob, are not consumed" [Malachi 3:6]. What does the *Shekhinah* [Divine Presence] say, even during her wanderings from her place, following the wanderings of the people of Israel, when they are expelled, when their enemies stand over them to swallow them? "My head is heavy, my right hand is heavy" [B. T. *Ḥagigah* 15ᵇ]. The *Shekhinah* is with them in their trouble, "I will be with him in trouble" [Psalms 91:15]. Here, all the revelations of the *Shekhinah* are radically contracted. Her glory, splendor, and majesty are deeply concealed. This is the greatest trouble for her,

that she is not able to reveal her holy glory, her splendid beauty, and the majesty of her kingdom. Even then, "For I the Lord change not." The same "I" of "I am the Lord thy God who brought thee out of the land of Egypt" [Exodus 20:2] is that of "And I will surely hide My face in that day" [Deuteronomy 31:18]. God's mercy and truth are always and forever with us, "Even from everlasting to everlasting, Thou art God" [Psalms 90:2]. "Verily Thou art a God that hidest Thyself, O God of Israel, the Savior" [Isaiah 45:15]. Also, "And ye, O sons of Jacob, are not consumed" [Malachi 3:6]; with all of their falls and descents, they remain worthy of their holy name: children of Jacob, seed of Israel, His servants, His chosen children of Jacob. Really, with all of her contraction and disappearance of her light, the *Shekhinah* does not produce any change, heaven forbid, in her essence, "For I the Lord change not" [Malachi 3:6]. Similarly, the children of Israel, with all of their contractions and disappearance of their holy light, are always holy and pure in character, from then and forever, "And ye, O sons of Jacob, are not consumed."

Enclosed in their essence, in the innermost recesses of the people of Israel, the chosen ones of God, there is a holy fire; "A very flame of the Lord" within them [Song of Songs 8:6]. "My soul yearneth, yea, even pineth for the courts of the Lord" [Psalms 84:3]. Even the final path, that of descent and decline, is not some aspect of loathing the holy, heaven forbid. Rather, even the descent comes about primarily in the wake of the reverence which is internal to the people, who praise and tremble mightily before God's countenance. Due to this, the body is unable to proceed at all. After the flash of the soul, the body recoils backward, divided and broken. Indeed [the soul] will not rest or relax "Until I find out a place for the Lord, a dwelling place for the Mighty One of Jacob" [Psalms 132:5], so as to be purified and sanctified both internally and externally.

"And they shall wander from sea to sea, and from the north even to the east; they shall run to and fro to seek the word of the Lord, and shall not find it" [Amos 8:12]. "The word of the Lord, this is Halakhah (Jewish law). The word of God, this is the end time. The word of God, this is prophecy" [B. T. Shabbat 138[b]]. The entire goal [of the souls of Israel], their ambition and fervent wish, is to find the complete word of God in all its luminous aspects. "The word of the Lord, this is Halakhah" [B. T. Shabbat 138[b]]. This is to say that, in all the days of their life, in all their times, hours, and minutes, in their entire way of life, and in every foothold, [indeed] everywhere, they will be surrounded, both at home and outside, with the Halakhah of the Torah, with the Torah of the living God. The Halakhah will be clear and without any doubts. "The word of God, this is prophecy" [B. T. Shabbat 138[b]]. This is to say, [they are] to be found constantly in the atmosphere of holiness and the sanctuary of the light of His holiness, to benefit from His emanation and from the manifest appearance of the splendor of His holiness, by means of [the presence of] God's word with them. Not only in [discontinuous]

sections, but as prophecy of continuous clear sight, similar to the love of God for His holy people, who longs for His children to be seated around His pure table and to rejoice with them forever—like the rejoicing of the Holy One blessed be He with His Torah before the creation of His world. "The word of God means the end time" [B. T. Shabbat 138[b]]. This is the revelation of the teachings of the Messiah. As the midrash says, "Our Torah is insignificant in comparison to the Torah of the Messiah" [Midrash Kohelet Rabbah, Parashah 11, Siman 7]. The Torah will not change, heaven forbid. When the profundity of Torah's holy secrets will be revealed, all the concepts of the present will become insignificant in comparison to the concept revealed in the Torah through the light of the Messiah.

In general, the revelation of the end time is also [a matter of] awakening from sleep and slumber, such that there will no longer be a need to taste sleep, which is a sixtieth of death. It means attaining the level of Jacob our patriarch, with the wonders of his understanding when he awoke from sleep, "And Jacob awaked out of his sleep, and he said: 'Surely the Lord is in this place'" [Genesis 28:16]. This is in contrast to what he saw in his dream: "A ladder set up on the earth, and the top of it reached to heaven; and behold the angels of God ascending and descending on it" [Genesis 28:12]. When he awoke from his sleep, he saw and grasped not only the negative conception [that of distance], but also the positive conception [that of nearness], "Surely the Lord is in this place" [Genesis 28:16]. Not only [was there] the stairway to ascend. Not only "Its top reached to the sky," and not only were "the angels of God ascending and descending on it." Rather precisely here below, in the holy land on Mount Moriah, the place of the holy of holies, there was the gateway to heaven, where heaven and earth touched each other. Here, below, it was not angels who were ascending and descending. Jewish people were entering the holy of holies: "'There shall be no man in the tent of meeting' [Leviticus 16:17]. Not even angels whose faces are as the face of man" [see Ezekiel 1:10; J. T. Yoma 7:2].

There should be nothing surprising about dwelling upon the profound secrets of the transitional period of the children of Israel. [This is] the onset of the Messiah, [taking place] amid terrible troubles and a most shocking decline of the nation. Precisely because of the grandeur of their holiness and because their faces are turned upward to adhere in true devotion to the living God, which they do within their innermost selves, they wander around in search of the word of God in its fully glory, the *Halakhah*, prophecy, and revelation of the end time. Because of this, the people have the aspect of the Levites who carried the Ark of the Covenant. The midrash said:

> You will find that the whole tribe of Levi were the fewest. Why were they the fewest? They saw the face of the *Shekhinah* often, and because of this they were the fewest. When they left the exile, they were sought and not found, as it is written, "I reviewed the people and the priests, but I did not find any Levites there" [Ezekiel 8:15]. The Holy One said that in this world those who saw His glory were destroyed, as it is written, "For man shall not see Me and live" [Exodus 33:20]. [God said,] "In the future when I return to Zion I will reveal My glory for all of Israel and they will see Me and live forever," as it is written, "For they shall see, eye to eye, the Lord returning to Zion" [Isaiah 52:8]. Not only that, but we will be shown with a finger, as it is written, "For such is God, our God, forever and ever; He will guide us eternally" [Psalms 48:15] and it is written, "And it shall be said in that day: 'Lo, this is our God, for whom we waited, that He might save us. This is the Lord, for whom we waited. We will be glad and rejoice in His salvation'" [Isaiah 25:9]. Similarly, all of Israel will atrophy, since their souls yearn "to behold the graciousness of the Lord, and to visit early in His Temple" [Psalms 27:4], though they grow fewer. [*Tanḥuma* (ed. Warsaw), *Bamidbar, Perek* 17]

There are consolations for us from the mouth of the Holy One. He tells us, "Be tranquil my children. Do not inquire into My attributes" [Rashi *ad* Exodus 6:1]. Please know that [now] in the end of days, after all the purifications from the lengthy darkness of the days of exile, you are now as spotless as clean corn. "Comfort ye, comfort ye My people, sayeth your God. But Jerusalem take heart, and proclaim unto her, that her time of service is accomplished, that her guilt is paid off; that she hath received of the Lord's hand double for all her sins" [Isaiah 40:1–2]. Behold, you are all now at the level of Nadav and Avihu who drew near to God and died. As [God] then spoke: "Through them that are nigh unto Me I will be sanctified, and before all the people I will be glorified" [Leviticus 10:3]. And Moses said to Aaron, "Aaron my brother, I knew the sanctuary would be sanctified by the friends of God. I thought that it would be me or you. Now I see that they are greater than you and I" [*Torat Kohanim, Sifra* 8:23]. [That is], "Now all of you have arisen to this level. All of you have been diminished by the ark [in the tabernacle?] that destroyed them. All of this is in this world. In the world to come, I will reveal Myself to all of Israel and you will all see Me and live forever."

In truth, our ultimate consolation comes when we know why we have been stoned and killed. It is because our souls have been annihilated in order to see our King: "When the Lord hath built up Zion, when He hath appeared in His glory" [Psalms 102:17]; "And it shall come to pass in that day, that a great horn shall be blown; and they shall come that were lost in the land of Assyria, and they that were dispersed in the land of Egypt; and they shall worship the Lord in the holy mountain at Jerusalem" [Isaiah 27:13]; "For I the Lord thy God hold thy right hand, who say unto thee: 'Fear not, I help thee. Fear not, thou worm Jacob, and ye men of Israel; I help thee,' sayeth the Lord, and thy Redeemer, the Holy One of Israel" [Isaiah 41:13–14].

The Aspect of Silence

Why is silence a fence around wisdom? Not only not to fall into any of the sins of speech. The essence of silence is that one silences the sense of speech and all the other senses and clears a place for wisdom. This wisdom pursues and seeks a place in which to prevail and have effect over speech. Through the silence, wisdom appears and prevails over speech.

The phenomenon of the reception of the Torah by Israel took place by means of the silence of all the winds. "No bird chirped, no bird flew, no donkey brayed" [see *Midrash Shemot Rabbah, Parashah* 29, *Siman* 9]. Every phenomenon of sublime wisdom appeared and came about solely by means of the silencing of all the senses. The senses stood prepared for the phenomenon. "Indeed ye indeed speak as a righteous company" [or "Indeed in silence speak righteousness"; Psalms 58:2]. What should be a man's pursuit in this world? He should be silent, which he could be even with regard to the words of the Torah. It says therefore, "Speak righteousness" [see B. T. *Ḥullin* 89ᵃ]. Even the speech of the Torah needs to come from the side of heavenly power. With Torah speech, one should feel as if one's mouth is being opened from above, moving the tongue and lips. With this, speech also has the aspect of [initial] silence. This is the aspect of Torah for its own sake. It is not at all its own cause, [rather] everything comes solely by the power of the command from above to utter with the mouth. "For they are life to those who find them—to him who utters them with his mouth" [B. T. *Eruvin* 54ᵃ].

The miracle of the splitting of the Red Sea took place in terms of this aspect: "The Lord will fight for you, and ye shall hold your peace" [Exodus 14:14]. The leap into the sea also took place with such a feeling; the Higher Power had the people leap and led them into the sea. By means of this [Higher Power], their mouths were opened and they recited the song.

Similarly, the onset of the Messiah is interpreted to have the aspect of silence. From our side, we are to feel, in every activity and conflict, that the power of God alone is at work within us and is awakening us. With this, all the holy names are united and the names of *YHVH* and *Adonai* are completely joined. It is revealed that "The Lord is a man of war, the Lord is His name" [Exodus 15:3]. The greats of the generations are called upon to work toward this unity [of names]. They are to silence all the desires and senses within themselves so that this wisdom will take effect within them. They will, thereupon, extend this power as well to all who work on the field of redemption, so they too feel the power of God at work in them. From their side, the greats remain silent and still.

In all the different sufferings endured by the people of Israel, the profane ones [*refaim*; see *Zohar, Ḥelek* 1, *Bereshit* 25ᵇ] burst out, rioting and circulating the question, "Where is their God?" [Psalms 79:10]. They incited difficulties and different heresies. But the righteous sat and remained silent. They accepted the sufferings of silence upon themselves. Thereby, they silenced all the mouths which spoke rebellion. The faith which is in the hearts of the righteous spreads and brings consolation to the multitudes, and the name of heaven is praised and elevated by them.

The Substance of the Binding of Isaac [*Akedah*]

The commandment "To love the Lord with all your heart and all your soul, even though God takes your soul" [B. T. *Berakhot* 61ᵇ] needs to be fulfilled at the current time. Not only individually, but collectively as well. Even, heaven forbid, if the soul of the entire nation were to be taken, the love of God will not be restrained. This was the content of the binding of Isaac [*Akedah*]. Nothing is known on an individualistic level about the patriarchs. They are called patriarchs because their lives were lives of fatherhood [in the collective sense of the whole nation]. When Isaac accepted the risk to his life, he did so on behalf of the whole nation. During the onset of the messiah, this trial will be actualized collectively. Nonetheless, the love [for God] is not weakened in the slightest. On the contrary, it becomes stronger and stronger. All of Israel seeks what Isaac our patriarch sought, namely, that Abraham our father would bind him so that the sacrifice would not be flawed. This is the secret of the saying "Exiles are not gathered in, except by the merit of Isaac" [see B. T. *Shabbat* 89ᵇ]. All of them are elevated to the capacity and level of Isaac. When Isaac was born, the Holy One added to the light of the sun and moon [*Tanḥuma* (ed. Buber), *Va'yera, Perek* 37].

Letter to Barukh Yeḥiel Duvdevani in Saint Cesarea, Italy, DP Camp, 3 October 1946 [Two Days before *Yom Kippur*]

I received your letter [of 12 September 1946]. May it be His will that our prayers for His lofty glory be accepted. Your merit is very great. God will surely be with you. May you see the consolation of Israel and the deliverance of Israel's salvation.

It is written, "Comfort ye, comfort ye My people, sayeth your God" [Isaiah 40:1]. There is nobody who can console Israel to the extent of the terrible distress. There is no mouth that could express words of consolation. Only the blessed God Himself, who Himself said, "Comfort ye, comfort ye My people," could do so. Surely, the consolations that were uttered by the mouth of His blessed name cannot be retracted. To comprehend these consolations and to be able to compare the value of their sweetness and the pleasure of their paradise [means to know that] the time of consolation spoken of by Him, may His name be blessed, will come. We will see with our eyes that it was worth enduring all the difficult and bitter sufferings, if only to attain the supernal, glorious pleasantness and holiness borne by those consolations. How sublime and pleasant will that time be, when we will hear the mouth of God saying to us consolingly: "My people." Each individual in Israel will become a nation and a nation of God. Through this [suffering], God distills, refines, and purifies each individual, as gold is distilled and silver is purified. They will be qualified, such that each individual in Israel will become [as] a holy nation upon the Holy Land, and for this alone the [stern] judgments [must be seen] as great. The time has now arrived for each individual to be tested and to raise the individual into a nation which is faithful to God. Happy are those who, despite everything, divert their attention from their individuality and who sense and feel the whole community. They are sensitive and yearn to share in the troubles of the community, and they sacrifice themselves to save their community and to accelerate salvific deliverance and the refuge for the bodies, spirits, and souls. [The salvation] will pour the dew of revival upon the community, the refreshing light of the

Torah and the commandments, bringing the community closer to the *Shekhinah*, which cries and weeps over the community's troubles. "In all their affliction He was afflicted" [Isaiah 63:9]. This period [now] is only the transitional period. It is the hour in which our traditional love of God, His Torah, and His land will be discerned.

"Hide thyself for a little moment, until the indignation be overpassed" [Isaiah 26:20]. This is the indignation of the powers which feel their descent and being at the edge of total and utter annulment. "And the unclean spirit to pass out of the land" [Zechariah 13:2]. Therefore, the [dark] powers will not rest and will not be quiet. With every strengthening [of deliverance] they attempt to darken the light of Israel and to hunt down the many souls to destroy and kill them. But all this will not help them. They are like ephemeral smoke, while "also the glory of Israel will not lie nor repent" [1 Samuel 15:29]. We must overcome them. We must not become ensnared, heaven forbid, into "inquiring into the intentions of the Holy One Blessed be He" [Rashi *ad* Exodus 6:1]. We are now participating in the anguish of the *Shekhinah*, an anguish whose dimensions we cannot estimate. We are [called upon] to diminish the anguish [of the *Shekhinah*] and declare in a great voice that we are content in suffering, ready to ascend the altar in sanctification of His name, and that we will not abandon His Torah and His faith. On the contrary, we will become stronger. We will make a greater effort to love Him and show everyone that we do not serve for the sake of reward. Further, we will [demonstrate] that we would not turn away from God, even should we actually receive paradise for a trespass and Gehenna for carrying out a commandment. This is not an issue of calculation. For there is nothing that brings joy to the above, like the joy and pleasure [that comes] when the Holy One blessed be He can praise Himself and say, "Look what kind of child I have in My world." Of themselves, all the [stern] judgments become lessened while the light of God's delight proceeds to be revealed in all the power of His holiness and wonders of His glory. Therefore, despite all the travail and the entire [terrible] episode [extending over] past and present, we must envelop ourselves in the fire of courage and power. "Is not my word like a fire?" [*Jeremiah* 23:29]. We should fulfill the will of God Blessed be His name with the flame of the fire of God. With this we will shut the mouths of the accusers. They will be destroyed and sink into oblivion. And you [Israel] shall stand.

The sacred strength which is revealed is one where each Jewish individual assumes the dimension of the nation. Truly, each one will be expanded into a multitude, where the [collective] strength of the people of Israel never amounts to less than 600,000. The chaotic void advanced this sacred strength. Each individual who ascended the pyre, who was killed, starved, choked, and burned, who ascended the altar [of Isaac], became a nation, a whole people. The souls from the realm of the chaotic void are very great. The whole universe can barely contain them and their ascent to heaven. They are of a [realm] close to God which not even ministering angels may enter [see B. T. *Nedarim* 32ª]. The chaotic void advanced the mending (*tikkun*) with great immediacy, and behold we stand already at the threshold of redemption. "For it is time to be gracious to her, for the appointed time is come" [Psalms 102:14]. The fire of one's love for God will burn and destroy all the barriers. And behold we are all holy to God. We are happy at how good our portion is, how pleasant our fate, and how beautiful our heritage.

The thoughts flow, but because of the holiness of the great day, the day of *Yom Kippur*, I am required to stop. Let us hope that God's mercies will not cease. For in the near future we will be worthy of the complete revelation of His manifold mercies, penetrating totally, and of the sublimity of the strength of the Messiah and the building of the Temple. I am your friend who recognizes your good works. Please convey my greetings and friendship to all of the refugees and our friends who are taking part in the work of rescue. Happy are they and happy is their portion. Likewise to all of our dear brothers, the remnant of the dispersion, the brands plucked from the fire, may the blessing of Zion be on them. May they enter its gates with thanks and "The voice of rejoicing and salvation is in the tents of the righteous" [Psalms 118:15]. May "The right hand of the Lord is exalted; the right hand of the Lord doeth valiantly" [Psalms 118:16] be fulfilled with them.

Towards the Era of Love [December 1947–January 1948, Sinai]

"And I have put My words in Thy mouth, and have covered thee in the shadow of My hand, that I may plant the heavens, and lay the foundations of the earth, and say unto Zion: 'Thou art My people'" [Isaiah 51:16].

There are shadows that come from the hidden dimension which are out to hide the light, and there are those shadows which come in order to be of benefit to the light. This is because without the shadow it is impossible to grasp the light, on account of the greatness of its splendor. As it says: "And God saw the light, that it was good" [Genesis 1:4]. God saw that the world was not worthy of the light, and He arose and concealed it. The world could not grasp the light without its sheath. This relates to what is said concerning Betsalel. Moses said to him, "First the vessels and afterward the tabernacle." Betsalel said to him, "It is customary to build the house first and then put the vessels into it." Moses responded, "Thus have I heard from the Holy One." Moses said to Betsalel, "You were in the shadow of God (*Be'tsal El*)" [see Rashi *ad* Exodus 38:22]. The issue is this: From the perspective of thought, the deed comes last and the thought first; first the purpose arises and then the method of attaining it. Moses, who was included in the thought of the Holy One, first intuited the making of the vessels. Even though he heard from the mouth of the Holy One Blessed be He about the construction of the tabernacle, which was a dimension of deed, he spoke in terms of the thought. For this reason he said to [Betsalel]: "You were in the shadow of God [i.e., of the deed]." In truth, were it not for the shadow of God, it would have been possible for the deed to also be according to the order of thought. But from the aspect of [stern] judgment, the world is not worthy [for deeds to be according to the order of thought]. Because of this, things [in the world] come about according to the order of deeds. This order involves the participation of the attribute of mercy, so that deeds can receive their light.

Similarly with the redemption, upon whose threshold we are standing:

> It was destined that of the Israelites that only "one of a city and two of a family" [Jeremiah 3:14] would leave the exile, given that they were judged in terms of power. The world was to return to primordial chaos, but because of Moses' [earlier] prayer, the Israelites merited compassion. The left hand of God [which extends power] rejected them, such that they would not leave the exile, but the right hand of God, which extends mercy, embraced them. [*Tikkunim Mi-Zohar Ḥadash* 27ᵃ]

The Gaon of Vilna explained:

> During the period of its destruction the world is called *Tohu*, chaotic. . . . When it is not *Tohu*, the world is a fitting home for the *Shekhinah*. . . . The era of the first Messiah is that of the Messiah son of Joseph . . . emanating from the left side. . . . Through the 974 pre-Adamite generations, God constructs and destroys the world. For each person is a world upon which light is shed. In the 26 generations from Adam to the giving of the law, there was chaos: 2,000 years of chaos [(974 + 26) × 2 = 2,000] and 2,000 years of Torah and 2,000 years of the Messiah [B. T. *Sanhedrin* 97ᵃ]. . . . Most of the 974 generations are alive again at the end of days. Insolence abounds. . . . "But with great compassion will I gather thee" [Isaiah 54:7]. That is, they will leave [the exile] by means of the right dimension. But the events will be initiated first through the left dimension: "Let his left hand be under my head" [Song of Songs 2:6]. The emanation of the left dimension prevailed until the days of Cyrus and the era of the Second Temple when the nation did not leave the Land of Israel. Only then was the right dimension awakened. . . . At first God considered [creating the world] in terms of the quality of judgment. But

he saw that the world could not take hold [in this way]. So he included the quality of mercy, i.e., redemption [at] the time of the world's construction. But until that time, God constructs and destroys the world repeatedly. [*Beur ad Tikkunim mi-Zohar Ḥadash* 27ᵃ]

The redemption's flashing light is immensely vigorous, and the world is not yet worthy to receive and grasp it. Because of this, events will be initiated through the left dimension, the secret of "His left hand was under my head." It is the shadow. But the redemption is hardly complete. Events will thereupon be initiated through the right dimension, "And his right hand should embrace me" [Song of Songs 8:3]. Then it will be possible for the sublime light of the redemption to penetrate into us. We will also grasp the light. We will no longer need to go out, according to "And I will take you one of a city, and two of a family" [Jeremiah 3:14]. The Holy One acts with mercy with His holy people. They are able to present themselves before God [see Job 1:6] and His goodness, to benefit from His light, the concealed light which emerges from its sheath as does the sun. "Arise, shine, for thy light is come; and the glory of the Lord is risen upon thee" [Isaiah 60:1].

In any event, to our great sorrow, even after the obvious shadows, there were to our regret [other hidden, higher shadows] and many who fell dead, and our blood was spilled like water. All of this happened because of the flash of the light that penetrates through the web [of darkness].

This is what is written: "And I have put My words in thy mouth, and have covered thee in the shadow of My hand" [Isaiah 51:16]. In order for you to be able to stand with the good which is concealed and receive it with love, things will come as they are of the mouth and not as they are of thought. [The way of the mouth] is also the way of the shadow: "In the shadow of My hand." All this is for the sake of setting heaven and establishing the earth, such that heaven and earth will touch and tell Zion, "You are my nation."

The [lower] shadows grow before the coming of the messiah in order to hinder the light. They are removed by the higher shadows on behalf of the penetration of light. When they see the shadows like them above, the [lower] powers want to hinder the flash and penetration. But the work [of the lower shadow] is then weakened, its power removed. The evil powers are dissolved and abrogated. This is what happened with respect to Joseph, the antagonist of Esau [see Rashi *ad* Genesis 30:25]. The whole aim and desire of Esau [the lower shadow] is to hinder the light. The aim of the [higher] shadow of Joseph is to have the light penetrate. Esau errs and thinks that the shadows are in favor of helping him so the light will not be dispersed. In truth, they [serve as] a flame on behalf of the house of Joseph, for the house of Esau [is] to be [burned] as straw.

From here on, we will consider the matter of the two messiahs: the Messiah son of David and the Messiah son of Joseph. It is impossible to receive the light that shines from the Messiah son of David without a sheath. Therefore, the light of the Messiah son of Joseph, who is the secret of higher [and hidden] shadows, advances before him: "And have covered thee in the shadow of My hand" [Isaiah 51:16]. The divine visitation— that is to say, the hidden [and higher] shadow— will perhaps come by means of the nations, which will be the ones to agree to and authorize the people of Israel to return to the land of their heritage, to come and possess it [see Joshua 21:41]. Do not be surprised by this. For this was the order from the onset and forever. The Second Temple came about through Cyrus [who represented the higher shadow which served on behalf of the light]. As it is written: "Thus said the Lord to His anointed, to Cyrus" [Isaiah 45:1]. It seemed that by the third year of Aḥasuerus's reign, which was after the first proclamation of Cyrus, it already appeared that Israel's hope had come to nothing. Aḥasuerus mistakenly thought that the seventy years had already passed. It seemed to him that from then on he would sit securely on the throne. He made a feast for all of his nobles and servants. He took out all the vessels and utensils of the Temple and he dressed himself in the garments of the high priest [source uncertain]. Concerning this, the disciples of Rabbi Simeon bar Yoḥai said, "The enemies of Israel are condemned to destruction" [B. T. *Ta'anit* 7^{b}], because they enjoyed the feast of that evildoer. That is to say, there were those who despaired of redemption. They imagined that they would find their place by

becoming citizens in the exile. Therefore the decree was issued "To destroy, to slay, and to cause to perish, all Jews, both young and old, little children and women, in one day" [Esther 3:13] and to plunder them. This was so they would know that there was no rest and revival for Israel except in their Holy Land.

This was at the root of all redemptions. With the redemption from Egypt, the Holy One did not take the people of Israel out of Egypt, only for Pharaoh to send them out and declare, "You are on your own, you are free people." Rather, on one hand, the exodus was to benefit the Egyptians, who would be worthy of relating the glory of God, "But in very deed for this cause have I made thee to stand, to show thee My power, and that My name be declared throughout the earth" [Exodus 9:16]. On the other hand, should they not want to submit to the holy nation of Israel, this would of itself be calamitous for them; they would choke themselves. [As representatives of the higher shadow,] Cyrus delayed [the return] and Pharaoh made things difficult.

[Today, shadowy] nations of our generation have divided the land. There would be protest regarding "And divided My land" [Joel 4:2], in particular regarding the holy city of Jerusalem— Jerusalem which is completely sacred for heaven— which was not to be touched by the hand of any nation. Jerusalem is given to us directly by the higher hand, with no intermediary. [Avraham Azulai] wrote that the window of the sky is wide below, representing the whole Land of Israel, and small above, representing Jerusalem and the Temple [*Ma'ayan* 3, *Nahar* 3, in *Ḥesed Le'avraham*].

This is also a wonder of wonders, "The wondrous works of Him who is perfect in knowledge" [Job 37:16]. For in the end of days all the leading ministers of the nations will feel that the end is near and "That the Lord will punish the host of the heaven on high" [Isaiah 24:21]. They will set their eyes on Jerusalem and will want to grab a piece of the holy city. They will seem to appropriate the funds of the altar and thereby hinder the redemption of Israel. "Though they were not present, their guiding stars were present" [B. T. *Shabbat* 146^{a}] refers to the leaders who were out to make Jerusalem into a city among nations. During [the original]

Hanukah, we were worthy to purify and rescue the Temple from the enemies who sought to attack the sanctuary of God. The [Maccabees] entered the Holy of Holies, cleared Your sanctuary, and purified Your holy place, and lit the candles in the courtyards of Your sanctuary. Now in the end of days, from the perspective of the intuition of Israel, the day of the Lord which burns like an oven is near. It sets aflame all the evildoers who devoured Jacob and destroyed his habitation, ate our flesh, and spilled our blood like water for two thousand years. It appears that the evil one will succeed in removing the good from the world. In the name of doing so, other gods will be called upon. It appears that with this, [the evil ones] will, heaven forbid, clog up the original source [of light] from which divine emanation comes and shines upon Israel. But the enemies will become ridiculous; their eyes will be covered from seeing; and they will neither know nor understand. They will walk in darkness. For without Israel and the fullness of its abundant holy emanation, there will be no revival for them. Only when Israel will remove their yoke from their necks and they glorify the name of God will everything be complete and the idols vanish totally. There will be no hope for the nations unless they will accept the supremacy of Israel and all the nations will say, "O house of Jacob, come ye, and let us walk in the light of the Lord" [Isaiah 2:5]. We will be instructed by His ways and walk in His paths.

We must understand the words of holiness, the words of truth. The order of redemption is also revealed once revelation begins on its path. Should the beginning be according to nature, nature will not be lowered but raised. Nature will be raised and established at the height of its majestic value and at the high level of its sublime splendor. For it is a principle of the order of creation that all growth comes from the sowing. The seed is buried in the bowels of the earth and the earth swallows it. Out of this, the seed grows and sprouts and grows larger. Indeed, according to the current order, after the growth of sin ends and sin is pulled from the ground, the ground remains as before. In truth, according to the order which prevailed before the sin, in particular before the sin of the land whereby the land changed and brought forth a tree making fruits

instead of a tree of fruit, the tree would also bear fruit. The earth in which the tree grew was also transformed into something of fruit and growth. It was not the cause of the fruit and growth, but more or less of the fruit and the growth. And as it is with materiality [in terms of nature], so it is with spirituality. The order of every higher revelation is like sowing, where the seed is buried in the bowels of what is hidden. From there, it emerges and develops. The righteousness and greatness of its cause are universally acknowledged. In the material [or natural] respect, there are different time lengths spent in the womb before birth. With spiritual revelations, there are different time lengths to concealment, to the secret of "pregnancy" and the development.

According to the higher wisdom of the divine will, in order to be revealed, some revelations need to be hidden for all six thousand years, and some need to be hidden less. When the time comes for the birth, for the revealing, in order for the revelations to be exalted and disclosed their hiding place [in nature] is exalted with them. The wondrous revelation is concealed in the treasure house of nature until the time comes for God's glory to be revealed. Then nature [itself will be] unchained; [it will be of] the glorious name. It will also become a mighty, awesome, and great revelation, with the capacity of Him, His life, and His cause as one. Therefore, in the days of Mordekhai and Esther the miracle took place through the channel of nature. Concerning this, the rabbinic Sages said, "The story of Esther is the last of all miracles" [B. T. *Yoma* 29[a]], implying that until then there was revelation of miracles alone. This did not affect nature, such that it too would ascend. [But] from then on, in the days of Mordekhai and Esther, nature did indeed begin to awaken and to rise. It too was a miracle. They said: "The story of Esther is the last of all miracles," indicating the capacity of being the means between miracle and nature and of their joining together.

[The rabbinic Sages ask,] "But there is Hanukah—we refer to those included in Scripture" [B. T. *Yoma* 29[a]]. [Yosef Caro] cites the question, "Why did they establish eight days?" The oil in the flask was enough for one night, and there was a miracle for seven nights only. [Yosef Caro] explains that they divided the oil in the flask into eight parts, and every night they put one part into the candelabra and it burned until morning. Or, after they poured the appropriate amount of oil into the candelabra, the flask remained full as at the beginning. It was recognized as a miracle even on the first night. Or, because on the first night they used all the oil in the candelabra. It burned all night. In the morning, they found the candelabra full of oil. It was the same every night [Yosef Caro, *Siman 670, ad Orah Ḥayim, Hilkhot Ḥanukah* by Ya'akov ben Asher]. The first explanation is difficult [to understand]. Since we do not rely on miracles, how could they divide the oil into eight parts and burn the eighth part until morning? The last explanation, that it was lit every night and that only an eighth burned is difficult. It is accepted that the residue was removed at the same time as the wick was removed [see B. T. *Menaḥot* 88[b] and Ephraim Eliezer Tsevi Ḥarlap, *Hod Tehilah: Al Hilkhot Ḥanukah*, no. 20].

We do not rely on miracles only when miracles and nature are separate. When nature is elevated and disclosed in its miraculous beauty and splendor, one should rely on the nature revealed in holy splendor rather than on the hidden nature. In the days of Ḥanukah, after Esther, the last of all miracles [see B. T. *Yoma* 29[a]], there was the epoch of the elevation of nature to [the level of] miracle. Thus, since the amount of half a *Lug* was only enough for burning through the whole night, and it was recognized that the oil which was by nature an eighth would also burn the whole night, they could rely on this [as a miraculous disclosure]. At that time, this was not of the principle of not relying on miracles. Likewise, the way in which an eighth was lit and remained as full as before was a great miracle. For the wick and the oil remained in the candelabra. As for its not being lit at all and the wick and oil residue not being removed, this belonged to the association of the oil and wick

with what they were previously. Not so, regarding the nature of the oil and wick in terms of their revelation regarding the degree to which the splendor changed into another nature. There is no place at all to debate this because the oil and the wick were cleaned out.

The Talmud states, "We refer to those written in Scripture" [B. T. *Berakhot* 58[a]]. This is according to what is said: Prophecy that was intended for the generations was written, and prophecy not intended for the generations was not written. It is similar in the matter of the elevation of nature and its harmony with the orders of miracles. If the order of revelation of the oil and the wick was to continue also for the future, it would have been written down. Since this order did not continue and was not established in the whole order of nature, even though it was a revealed miracle, it was not written down.

With this, we consider the matter of the prohibition of using the light. If it is extinguished, there is no need to relight it. For the whole revelation of the complete harmony between miracle and nature took place only then. From then on, the radiant paths of that harmony were revealed only in flashes. They return and disappear immediately, in the manner of back and forth. We are not worthy to benefit from this glowing light. Therefore the rule is that it is forbidden to utilize the light. Also, this revelation is revealed only at the point of the kindling, and then it goes back and disappears. Therefore, if it is extinguished, there is no need to relight it. Not so in the future, when this wondrous revelation will return to be permanent. Then, in truth, if it will be extinguished, it will be necessary to light it. We will be worthy of utilizing its light, of warming ourselves by the holy light, and of drawing from it, from the wells of wisdom. These wells pour out in an incessant stream of Eden's waters, endlessly and limitlessly.

Ḥayim Yisrael Tsimerman

Ḥayim Yisrael Tsimerman (1901–1967?), who was born in Kosov, Poland, studied at the Beit Yisrael yeshiva in Sokolov-Podlaski (Poland) under the Rebbe of Sokolov, Yitsḥak Selig Morgenshtern. Morgenshtern was a descendant of the ḥasidic master Menaḥem Mendl of Kotsk and son of the Rebbe of Pilov (Ḥayim Yisrael), a ḥasidic pioneer in Palestine. Tsimerman continued at the Novogrodok *Musar* yeshiva in Warsaw, and settled in Palestine in the late 1920s. There he served as rabbi of the Sokolover *ḥasidim* synagogues in Tel Aviv, which had been established by the Rebbe of Sokolov. He belonged to the Ateret Yosef *Kollel*, a *Musar*-oriented institute for advanced rabbinic study, and published biblical, talmudic, and halakhic commentaries.

In the summer of 1947, Tsimerman published *Tamim Pa'alo* (*His Work is Perfect* [Deuteronomy 32:4]), in response to persistent questions about how the merciful and righteous God could let the Holocaust happen. After introducing sources to justify intellectual silence on the matter, Tsimerman turned around to offer explanations in terms of the revealed tradition. As shown from the growth of the Land, redemption had begun before the war. But for redemption to be fulfilled, Jews had to do *teshuvah* (repent) for all sins, and they had failed to do so. Tsimerman cited the failure on the part of pious Jews to put an end to the trespasses of others and to sufficiently support the restoration of the Land of Israel. *Teshuvah* was therefore imposed upon them in the form of massive suffering, i.e., the Holocaust. Tsimerman also believed that the Holocaust purified Israel's sinners from earlier eras. The sudden growth in the Jewish population over the preceding generation indicated that the kabbalistic vision in which sinful souls returned to be purified in later generations was being comprehensively and conclusively realized.

SELECTIONS

In the selections from *"Tamim Pa'alo": She'elot Uteshuvot Bidevar Hahashmadah Ha'iyumah Shel Shishah Milyon Hayehudim, Hashem Yinkom Damam* (*"His Work Is Perfect"*: *Questions and Responses concerning the Terrible Destruction of Six Million Jews, May God Avenge Their Blood*, Jerusalem, 1947), Tsimerman wrote of the transgressions by the pious. According to the rabbinic Sages, a pious Jew who did not even attempt to stop a household member from sinning was culpable (B. T. *Shabbat* 54[b]–55[a]), and according to Maimonides a pious person was guilty of trespass if he allowed an evil person to do as he wished (*Mishneh Torah, Hilkhot Deot* 6, *Halakhah* 7). In many German Orthodox and ḥasidic homes, no attempt was made to stop mixing with gentiles, and assimilation was even rationalized as a source of income. In Warsaw, the *Shabbat* was violated by store owners and newspaper publishers. Tsimerman cited Yitsḥak Luria's student Ḥayim Vital concerning the transmigration of souls (*Sefer Ḥezyonot* [*Book of Visions*] and *Sha'ar Hakavanot* [*Chapter of Intentions*]): Adam's single soul multiplied over the centuries to 600,000 souls, which were either pure or had to be purified over the generations. According to the *Mizraḥi* newspaper *Hatsofeh* (edited by *Mizraḥi* leader Meir Bar Ilan), there was a Jewish population explosion during the century before the war. The Holocaust was the final purification of all Jewish sinners; all their unnatural and cruel deaths were according to measure. Selections translated from the Hebrew by Gershon Greenberg.

"HIS WORK IS PERFECT": THE LOFTINESS OF GOD AND HIS RIGHTEOUSNESS

The Question

The question about the six million Jews who were killed in sanctification of God's name (*Al kedushat Hashem*) throughout Europe and all the other places, dying every sort of death in the world, is the principal question of the day. It is a painful and agonizing question, one which penetrates into the inner depths of the heart. It upsets the entire nation of Israel, from the small to the great, from regular folk to the pietist (*ḥasid*). Everyone, without exception, is posing this quandary: Why did God do this to the nation? It is a disaster (*Ḥurban*) unlike anything since the world came into existence, a disaster of six million Jews of our nation. It included those who feared God, who were perfect; geniuses; scholars; pious ones; pure pietists. It included people of good deeds engaged in holy Torah day and night, [and those] who never stopped for a moment to speak of Torah. It included the center of religious Judaism, the yeshivas with its rabbis, deans, and *yeshivah* heads. It included the students, great and small, who studied in them, their instructors and tutors, and schoolchildren who studied in their schools.

This was a destruction of cities and villages and states and communities which left not a trace. They were eradicated from the face of the earth. "Then the Lord caused to rain... brimstone and fire" [Genesis 19:24] upon all the lands in which Jews lived. God sent a flood of fire from above, upon all the parts of Europe as well as other places, and all four deaths [see B. T. *Sanhedrin* 49^b] were decreed. All kinds of different deaths in the world. Poison gases and all sorts of sadistic tortures. "And wonder marvel-

ously" [Habakkuk 1:5]. It was incredible, inconceivable. Woe, that we have come to such a time, hearing things which neither our forefathers nor we could have ever imagined. God poured his fury out upon His people, and the bitter cup has been emptied out upon them. The spinal cord of the nation of Israel has been broken, throughout the exilic dispersion. Only the brand plucked from the fire remains, and along with it troubles upon troubles and sufferings upon sufferings. There is "no rest for the sole of her foot" [Genesis 8:9]; people wander naked and barefoot, in cold and in heat, in starvation and thirst. They wander from city to city and from country to country and from camp to camp. Given nothing, risking their lives at every step. Day and night they ask: Why did God do this to these lands? You will hear such questions and quandaries when you meet with your neighbors, in the synagogue, in the street, on the bus, in your home, and in your neighbor's home. Anywhere you speak with someone, you are immediately asked the question: Why? It brings on confusion, anxious heart, and, God forbid, heresy.

Even today, two years after the world has turned to peace, the question does not stop. Everyone passes over the question in silence. There is no response, no answer. No one dares to contradict [the question, let alone] breathe a word to excuse the Sovereign of the universe [in an attempt] to silence the question, lest the blessed name of the Holy One be desecrated. [At some point], I thought to myself that I should "turn aside" [Exodus 3:3] and probe the ways of God and His conduct with the children of man in each generation; I would probe the Talmud and other holy books in order to explain and respond to questions that come to mind. After looking and reflecting about the holy books, I thought it over and saw that it was generally possible to divide the answers to the above questions into five sections: (1) the answer to one who is a pietist and has true fear of God; (2) the general answer to the nation, an inquiry into the ways of God; (3) sins and trespasses; (4) the sin of protest; (5) the answer provided by *Sha'ar Hakavanot* (*Chapter of Intentions*) by Yitshak Luria, may his memory be for a blessing. And with God's help we will explain each in turn.

Answer One

One who is a pietist and truly has awe for God would not pose such questions and quandaries. He knows what is written in Torah: "Thou shalt be wholehearted with the Lord thy God" [Deuteronomy 18:13]. Everything will be of perfection; there will be no questions or difficulties. A person who is a pietist and truly has awe for heaven knows that "Out of the mouth of the Most High proceedeth not evil and good" [Lamentations 3:38]. Evil is only from you, for not having taken the path of Torah and [the] commandments. You alone are to blame for this: "The foolishness of man perverteth his way; and his heart fretteth against the Lord" [Proverbs 19:3]. When a man sins, he ruins his path, which is of itself not blemished. Then he angrily makes claims against God, saying: "Why did this affliction happen to me?"

We find that God said to Abraham: "Walk before me, and be thou wholehearted" [Genesis 17:1]. As the *Targum* [Aramaic translation] translates it, "Worship before Me; attach yourself to My service." "Be perfect in all My tests" [Rashi *ad* Genesis 17:1].

If we think and reflect upon the innocence of Abraham our father, we remain greatly astonished, not understanding or comprehending: How is it possible for a human being to achieve such great perfection? A perfection to the point of being infinite? Abraham, and he alone, can be called by the name "father." For I have something to learn from him, a lot to learn from him. A father such as this leaves a legacy (*toldot*). Not in vain does God say to Abraham, after the final

test [of the *Akedah*, "the binding of Isaac"]: "Now I know that thou art a God-fearing man" [Genesis 22:12]. God did not say this before, when He sent Abraham to Ur Kasdim and Abraham committed himself (*masar nafsho*) to faith in God. For when a person wishes to die in sanctification of the name and decides in his mind to do so [as with the *Akedah* in terms of Abraham's son], this is a once-and-for-all [decision].

As we found, Rabbi Akiva said to his disciples: "All my days I have been troubled by this verse, 'With all thy soul' [Deuteronomy 6:5], which I interpret 'Even though He takes thy soul.' I said: 'When shall I have the opportunity of fulfilling this? Now that I have the opportunity, shall I not fulfill it?'" He prolonged the word "one" until he expired while saying it [B. T. *Berakhot* 61b].

Naḥmanides says that the issue of "And when he saw that he prevailed not against him" [Genesis 32:26] was all about Jacob's generations. There would be a generation of the seed of Jacob which would be overcome by Esau. Esau would come close to destroying that generation completely, God forbid. This was one of the generations in the days of the *Mishnah* sages, in the generation of Yehudah ben Baba and his friends. As it says in the midrash about "I adjure you, O daughters of Jerusalem" [Song of Songs 3:5]:

> R. Ḥiyya b. Abba said: If one should say to me, "Sacrifice your life for the sanctification of God's name," I am ready to do so, on condition only that they slay me at once. But I could not endure the tortures of the great persecution. What did they formerly do in the generation of the great persecution? They brought iron discs and made them red-hot and put them under their armpits till they expired. Or they brought needles and stuck them under their nails, till they expired [and there are other generations where they did more evil to us]. And we endured all of this which happened to us. [*Midrash Shir Hashirim Rabbah*, *Parashah* 2, *Siman* 7] [Naḥmanides *ad* Genesis 32:26]

While Abraham was called holy, he was not worthy of "fear of God" status until he passed the test of the *Akedah*. Toward the end of his life, God promised Abraham that he would give him a son by Sarah. He waited and persevered until he was one hundred years old, and it [finally] happened. At that point Abraham became worthy of God's keeping His promise, and his request was fulfilled. A single son, Isaac, was born to him from mother Sarah. How much laughter and joy, how much amusement and gaiety, how much enjoyment and pleasure Abraham our patriarch had: "And Abraham made a great feast on the day that Isaac was weaned" [Genesis 21:8]. "Listen everybody: Isaac is mine!" Then Abraham heard the command and the call: "Take now thy son, thine only son, whom thou lovest, even Isaac, and get thee into the land of Moriah, and offer him there as a burnt offering" [Genesis 22:2]. Had that happened to any other person, that person would have died from a heart attack. He would have died from hearing such a thing. This was not so with Abraham our patriarch, who did everything perfectly and efficiently and with total love. He did so without any questions or quandaries, even though he did have plenty to ask.

R. Bibi, Abba said in the name of R. Yohanan:

> "Said Abraham before the Holy One, blessed be He, 'Lord of the Ages! It is self-evident to You that when You told me to offer up Isaac, my son, I had a good answer to give You: Yesterday You said to me, "Let it not be grievous in Thy sight because of the lad, and because of thy bondwoman; in all that Sarah sayeth unto thee, hearken unto her voice; for in Isaac shall your descendants be named" [Genesis 21:12]. "'And now You tell me: "Take now thy son, thine only son, whom thou lovest, even Isaac, and get thee into the land of Moriah; and offer him there for a burnt offering upon one of the mountains which I will tell thee of" [Genesis 22:2]. "'But I, God forbid, I did not [give you that answer] but I overcame my impulse and did what You wanted. Now may it be pleasing to You, O Lord my God, that when the children of Isaac, my son, come to a time of trouble and will have no one to speak in their behalf, You will speak in their behalf.'" And Abraham said, 'God will provide Himself the lamb for a burnt offering, my son." So they went both of them together' [Genesis 22:8]. You remember in their behalf the binding of Isaac, their father, and have mercy upon them" [J. T. Ta'anit 2:4].

Abraham our patriarch was the father of the quality of loving kindness (ḥesed). He committed

his life with great suffering. On the third day after his own circumcision, he received guests, feeding and giving them drink. He obtained much throughout his life in terms of the attribute of loving kindness. Let us remember the holy texts concerning the passage "And be thou a blessing" [Genesis 12:2]:

> Lest it be inferred that we must conclude the benediction [in the *Shemoneh Esrei* (silent benediction)] with all of them ["Blessed art Thou . . . God of Abraham, Isaac, and Jacob"], Scripture [stipulates] "And be thou a blessing," thus telling Abraham: With your name they will conclude the blessing, saying, "The shield of Abraham." [*Midrash Bamidbar Rabbah, Parashah* 11, *Siman* 2]

The end [of the benediction in the *Shemoneh Esrei*], the "In the days of the Messiah," includes the attribute of loving kindness. And such a thing is done to Abraham's only son, his sole hope that the world would be built with faith in God! Is there anything crueler than this? Anything [from what we can see] comparable to this: for Abraham to take the knife and to stretch out his arm to slaughter his son? To annul all his human feelings, his feelings of love and mercy for the sake of God's will? Nothing transcends such power. In this way, Abraham became truly and properly worthy of the fear-of-God status. "Now I know that thou art a God-fearing man" [Genesis 22:12], and not before this. [Apart from this], fear of God in truth and with complete and perfect heart cannot conceivably exist in reality.

After all this, after Abraham stood the test of the *Akedah*, Sarah died on him. He went to purchase a place to bury her. He remained patient. With respect, openness, and with perfection and clarity he spoke with the "children of Ḥeth" [Genesis 23:3]. He spoke with Ephron [the son of Zohar; see Genesis 23:8]. He ingratiated himself before the regular folk. And he paid a great fortune of four hundred silver *shekels* to the merchant. He was not distressed, excited, or angry, even though God promised to give him this land and told him "I am the Lord that brought thee out of Ur of the Chaldees, to give thee this land to inherit it" [Genesis 15:7] to proclaim His affection to Abraham, who had endured everything. And Abraham did not inquire into God's attributes [Rashi *ad* Exodus 6:1]. Subsequently we find: "And God spoke to Moses" [Exodus 6:2]. God judged Moses. Matters became difficult for Moses and he said, "Lord, wherefore hast Thou dealt ill with this people?" [Exodus 5:22] and God said, "'I am the Lord' [Exodus 6:2] of mercy and I appeared to the patriarchs as God almighty. I gave promises which I did not keep. Nevertheless, the patriarchs did not inquire into My attributes. I promised Abraham that I would give him the land. But when Abraham needed a place to bury Sarah, he had to purchase the land with a great sum of silver. However, he did not inquire into My attributes. I told Isaac and Jacob that I would give them the land. I did not give it to them, and they had to purchase it. They were not permitted to dig wells. But they did not inquire into My attributes." "Alas for those who are lost and are not found" [see Rashi *ad* Exodus 6:9 and Rashi *ad* B. T. *Sanhedrin* 111ᵃ]. And Moses asked, "Lord, wherefore hast Thou dealt ill with this people? [Exodus 5:22]. "Therefore see now what I will do to Pharaoh. Look now, and do not look at the war of the thirty-one kings" [see Joshua 12:9–24]. Moses was punished on account of this, even though it was a time of trouble for the nation of Israel, the trouble of the harsh slavery as found in the passage "And moreover I have heard the groaning of the children of Israel, whom the Egyptians keep in bondage" [Exodus 6:5]. "And the children of Israel sighed by reason of the bondage and they cried, and their cry came up unto God by reason of the bondage" [Exodus 2:23]. [That is,] "I [God] also know [about the evil done] to the nation. Do not create difficulties. You have only to entreat and pray to God to rescue Israel from the slavery. Nothing more."

And we will speak further about this later, if God wills and with His help: "Go thy way by the footsteps of the flock" [Song of Songs 1:8]. That is, in the footsteps of our forefathers. Go and learn from them about the path of perfection. It was the path our patriarchs took from [the] early days on. Whatever it was, and in whatever manner, there was no straying from this path. There always was love and affection for God. As the pietists say, "His joy is in his face." We truly see the conduct of the pietist in the text [of Bahyay Ibn Pakudah], where it says, in the name of an individual pietist:

If He afflicts her, she will suffer patiently and will only increase her love for Him and trust in Him. As it is said of one of the pietists, that he was wont to rise at night and say, "O my God, Thou hast made me suffer hunger, left me naked, set me in the darkness of the night and Thou hast shown unto me Thy might and greatness. If Thou were to burn me in the fire, it would only increase my love for Thee!" [*Ḥovot Halevavot, Sha'ar Ahavat Hashem*, ch. 1]

This is similar to what Job said: "Though He slay me yet will I trust in Him" [Job 13:15]. The wise Solomon hinted at this sentiment when he said, "My beloved is unto me as a bag of myrrh, that lieth betwixt my breasts" [Song of Songs 1:13]. Our rabbinic Sages explain homiletically as follows: "Though my life be distressed and embittered, yet my love lieth betwixt my breasts" [B. T. *Shabbat* 88ᵇ]. Similarly the prophet Moses says, "Thou shalt love the Lord thy God with all thine heart, and with all thy soul, and with all thy might" [Deuteronomy 6:5]. He thought to himself and imagined even worse sufferings. Still, he did not remove his love from the Blessed One. [To those who question,] I say that only someone called a pietist, called a righteous one, the one with fear of God, is entitled to ask questions.

The proof may be found with Aḥer at the end of B. T. *Ḥullin*:

R. Yosef said, "Had Aḥer interpreted this verse [which promises happiness and length of days to him that performs the commandments; see Deuteronomy 5:16] as R. Ya'akov, his daughter's son, did, he would not have sinned." What actually did he see? Some say, he saw such an occurrence. [Where a person engaged in the performance of a precept met with an accident and was killed. This incident made him doubt the truth of the Torah, and he turned into an unbeliever.] He saw the tongue of Rabbi Ḥutzpith the Interpreter lying on a dung heap, and he explained, "Shall the mouth that uttered pearls lick dust!" But he knew not that the verse "That it may go well with thee" [Deuteronomy 5:16] refers to the world that is wholly good, [while] "and that thy days may be long" [Deuteronomy 5:16] refers to the world that is wholly long. [B. T. *Ḥullin* 142ᵃ]

Aher took an evil course and became a heretic. Had he sought a biblical teacher like Rabbi Ya'akov bar Bartiya, he would not have sinned. He did not know what was good for him in a world which was entirely good. He did not know how to lengthen his days in a world which was quite lengthy. The single difficulty is the alternate question: How is it possible for a man [like Aher], who sits in the synagogue all the time and learns the wisdom of Torah with all the scholars and feels that the Torah of God is perfect and refreshing; a man for whom Torah is delightful, sweetened by the choicest honey, and illuminating, who will say "Let me go forth and enjoy this world" [B. T. Ḥagigah 15ᵃ] to have any greater joy? How is it possible that upon seeing the tongue of Rabbi Ḥutzpith, Aher removed himself from the wisdom of Torah? Even though he did not know what was good for him in a world which was entirely good? Even though he heard the echo from heaven, "Return O backsliding children" [Jeremiah 3:14]. Aher, as cited in Ḥagigah, immersed himself in vulgar and crude appetites which even a simple person would find unattractive [B. T. Ḥagigah 15ᵃ]. According to this explanation, he did not take an evil course because he saw the tongue hanging in the garbage, moving him to create difficulties, whereupon he went into the street. Certainly not. To the contrary, he wanted to enter an evil course long before this. Tosafot brings this into B. T. Ḥagigah 15ᵃ. According to B. T. Ḥagigah 15ᵇ sectarian books fell from his breast. Rashi says that before Aher abandoned himself to an evil course, that incident brought him to ask questions to a degree which removed him [from Torah]. If you begin to ask questions, this is a sign that things are not in order with you, and that you are leaving the realm of the pietist and righteous ones [Rashi ad B. T. Ḥagigah 15ᵇ].

Do not veer from the path of perfection. Do not ask any questions. Instead, everything should be perfect. All that God does will teach you whatever [you need to know], both about what happens to you individually and about what happens to the community. The question of the community depends upon the question of the individual, in terms of manner and substance. [It is up to the individual to compose himself.]

R. Abba b. Zabda also said in the name of Rab, "A mourner is bound by the obligation of Sukkah (tabernacle)." Is this not obvious? I might have said that R. Abba b. Zabda said, in the name of Rab, that he who is in discomfort is free from the obligation of Sukkah and that this mourner should be exempt since he also is in discomfort. Therefore R. Abba b. Zabda informs us that this applies only to discomfort over which there is no control and not to that experienced by a mourner. Since it is he himself who is the cause of his discomfort, it is incumbent upon him to compose his mind [B. T. Sukkah 25ᵇ].

. . . Answer Four: Protest

You have now reflected about the ways of God and have pondered your questions about [divine] behavior. From previous descriptions and, generally, from what has been clarified up to this point, [it is self-evident that] everything is contained in the knowledge and wisdom [of Torah]. According to the knowledge of Maimonides, all is according to sins and transgressions. This leaves us to clarify and explain the matter of protest. It is said that [in a situation] where all are perfectly righteous and without sin, without blame for the punishment received, this one sin was sufficient: When a righteous person sees others committing sins, there is a great obligation to protest and shout. One must not lend a free hand, allowing sinners to do freely what their heart desires and wants. There is a great obligation not to let an evildoer [carry out] the desires of his heart to the extent possible and to the extent of his ability. Assuming this, that those who are righteous are obligated in terms of protest, [when they fail to do this] they are seized on account of the trespass of others.

As we find,

whoever can forbid his household to sin, but does not, is seized for the sins of the household; if he can forbid his fellow citizens, he is seized for the sins of his fellow citizens; if the whole world, he is seized for the whole world. "The Lord will enter into judgment with the elders of His people, and the princes thereof" [Isaiah 3:14]—if the princes sinned, how did the elders sin? But say, He will bring punishment upon the elders because they do not forbid the princes. . . . "And set a mark (taw) upon the foreheads of the men that sigh and that cry for all the abominations that be done in the midst thereof" [Ezekiel 9:4]. The Holy One, blessed be He, said to Gabriel, Go and set a *taw* [last letter of the alphabet] of ink upon the foreheads of the righteous, that the destroying angels may have no power over them, and a *taw* of blood upon the foreheads of the wicked that the destroying angels may have power over them. Said the attribute of justice before the Holy One, blessed be He, "Sovereign of the universe, Wherein are these different from those?" "Those are completely righteous men, while these are completely wicked," replied He. "Sovereign of the universe," it continued, "They had the power to protest but did not." [Replied He], "It was fully known to Me that had they protested they would not have heeded them." "Sovereign of the universe," said he, "if it was revealed to Thee, was it revealed to them?" Hence it is written, "Slay utterly the old man, the young man, and the maiden, and little children and women; but come not near any man upon whom is the mark" [Ezekiel 9:6] [B. T. *Shabbat* 54ᵇ, 55ᵃ].

Rashi says: "This was at the beginning: 'But come not near any man upon whom is the mark.' At the end of the verse it is written, 'Begin at My sanctuary' [Ezekiel 9:6]. 'At My sanctuary God praises the accuser, the attribute of justice [or judgment] and turned away from the good'" [Rashi *ad* B. T. *Shabbat* 55ᵃ].

As it is written, "Then they began at the elders that were before the house" [Ezekiel 9:6].

It is not written, "And begin the slaughter at My sanctuary" [see Ezekiel 9:6], which, R. Yosef learned, should not read "My sanctuary" but "My sanctified ones," namely, the men who fulfilled the Torah from *Alef* to *Taw*. There too, since it was in their power to protest against the wickedness of the others, but they did not protest, they are not regarded as thoroughly righteous [B. T. *Avodah Zara* 4ᵃ].

The Tosafists [medieval commentators] emphasized that if it were doubtful that they would be heeded, they would be punished and seized for not protesting; while if it were certain that they would not be heeded, they would not be punished [*Tosafot ad* B. T. *Avodah Zarah* 4ᵃ]. However, let us agree with the words of *Tosafot*. If they were punished so severely, it would be attributable to not protesting, if doubt remained as to whether they would have been heeded. And so the slaughter still begins with them, "Begin with My sanctified ones."

I looked at [the book] *Imrei Shafer* [of Shlomoh Kluger] concerning the verse "Ye have sinned a great sin; and now I will go up unto the Lord, peradventure I shall make atonement for your sin" [Exodus 32:30]. Apparently, we need to understand why Moses spoke thusly now, but not before. It appears that in truth, the primary sin of the calf was committed by the mixed multitude, as the rabbinic sages said [*Tanḥuma* (ed. Warsaw), *Ki tissa*, *Perek* 21]. [Secondarily], the people of Israel were punished because they did not rebuke the mixed multitude. Thus, as long as Moses did not say, "Whoso is on the Lord's side, let him come unto me" [Exodus 32:26], their trespass was not so great. For it was possible that they were afraid to protest. But here, when Moses said, "Whoso is on the Lord's side, let him come unto me" [Exodus 32:36] and they heard and did not gather around him, their sin grew—except for the tribe of Levi, which gathered to protest while the others did not. We find the same concerning King Solomon, of blessed memory. Because he did not protest, he is cited as if he committed the sin himself. Moses our teacher, of blessed memory, decided the matter himself. For if he had not said, "Whoso is on the Lord's side, let him come unto me" [Exodus 32:36] and the tribe of Levi had gathered around him, then the rest of Israel would not have committed the sin of not protesting. The sin was drawn to them only through Moses. Therefore, Moses said to God, "Oh, these people have sinned a great sin, and have made them a god of gold" [Exodus 32:31]. Because they did not protest, they were ascribed with sin as if they did it themselves. Therefore, "Yet now, if Thou wilt forgive their sin—; and if not, blot me, I pray Thee, out of Thy book which Thou hast written" [Exodus 32:32] because Moses caused this by his statement "Whoso is on the Lord's side, let him come unto me" [*Imrei Shafer Al Hatorah*, vol. 1, p. 255].

Think and reflect about how the younger generation in these countries [of Poland and Germany] was educated and how it was distanced from the Torah and Judaism. In terms of religion, "There was not a house where there was not one dead" [Exodus 12:30]. We heard that in the period before the war in the city of Warsaw, several newspapers appeared publicly on the *Shabbat*. From time to time, the number of Jewish stores that were open on the *Shabbat* increased. There were houses where the son, the father, and the grandfather, three generations together, left God and were completely estranged from the Jewish religion. There were great [scholars] who said that they once visited Germany and they saw with their own eyes how the Jews there mixed with the gentiles and learned from their deeds, [and they concluded that] Germany had to be destroyed. We are witnesses that this happened. There were many in Orthodox and ḥasidic households who looked upon the Jews who were mixing with indifference or politeness, and said nothing. Some even [rationalized] that they were earning money and giving it to their households. Sometimes the father protested. But the mother was happy that her son was modern. She hid him behind her apron lest the father's pinkie touch him. Many of them did not protest at all. Some were happy and supported those who mixed monetarily, in order to satisfy their own urges and desires. There is much to be considered when it comes to this. It teaches that God is very strict when it comes to the righteous.

[Further:]

> "And over the sea affliction shall pass" [Zechariah 10:11]. Rabbi Joḥanan said, this is the sculpted idol of Micah. We read in a *Baraita* [an earlier teaching], "Rabbi Nathan said, from Garab to Shiloaḥ was three *mils* and the smoke of the altar and that of Micah's statue intermingled. The ministering angels wished to thrust Micah away, but the Holy One, blessed be He, said to them, "Let him alone, because his bread is available to wayfarers." [B. T. *Sanhedrin* 103[b]]

The Israelites did not protest the idol of Micah and because of that the people involved with the concubine of Gibeah fell into the hand of the Benjaminites, who killed forty thousand of them. The fact that his bread was available to wayfarers deceived the men of Israel in the incident of the concubine of Gibeah. They did not protest the idol of Micah, and because of this they were punished and forty thousand of them were killed.

> The Holy One said to them, "For my honor you did not protest, but for the honor of a human being you did protest?" [B. T. *Sanhedrin* 103[b]]

On the same page [B. T. *Sanhedrin* 103[a]], we read that the Holy One blessed be He desired to hurl the world back into chaos because of Zedekiah's generation. But he gazed at Zedekiah and His mind was appeased. Zedekiah was so worthy that the world was not destroyed due to his merit. But it is still written, "And he did that which was evil in the sight of the Lord" [2 Kings 24:19]. This is because he could have stemmed the evil of those of his generation—all the righteous were already exiled—but did not [B. T. *Sanhedrin* 103[a]].

Therefore, given all the proofs and evidence and clarifications we have provided up to this point in what we have written, we find that all the questions, difficulties, and doubts concerning the behavior of the Creator have been completely annulled. They have been disintegrated and dissolved, and they have disappeared.

The Birth Pangs of the Messiah

Rav said, "All the predestined dates have passed and the matter depends upon penitent return and good deeds. If all Israel does penitent return, the Messiah will come. If not, he will not come" [B. T. *Sanhedrin* 97[b]]. [Rashi: Samuel said, "It is sufficient for a mourner to keep his period of mourning."] It is enough for God to stand several days with His right hand behind Him. That is to say, if Israel will not repent, God will not remain mourning forever. But there is certainly an end date to the matter. Another explanation of "It is sufficient for a mourner" is that the anguish of exile is sufficient for Israel. The people of Israel will be redeemed even without penitent return [Rashi *ad* B. T. *Sanhedrin* 97[b]].

According to Shemuel Eliezer Edels [known as the Maharsha]:

> Rav said, "All the predestined dates have passed." [That is, there is no end date to the matter.] For the matter depends upon penitent return and good deeds, that is, on the people of Israel returning on their own. It is not in the hands of God. For all is in the hands of heaven except the fear of heaven. Samuel said, "It is sufficient for a mourner to keep his period of mourning." That is to say, it is sufficient for the people of Israel to return from their mourning. There is an end date to the matter.

When the time for redemption comes, the Holy One blessed be He will establish a king as harsh as Haman for the people and this will return them to the right path, such that they do penitent return. Rabbi Eliezer said, "If Israel does penitent return." This is serious penitent return, on their own. As it is written, "Return, O backsliding children" [Jeremiah 3:14], then "I will heal their backsliding" [Hosea 14:5]. Rabbi Yehoshua responded to him that the verse refers to compulsory penitent return. As was said previously, He will establish for them a king as harsh as Haman and will return the people to the right path. [Maharsha *ad* B. T. *Sanhedrin* 97^b]

According to Raphael ben Yekutiel Süsskind Kohen and the teachings of the rabbinic Sages, redemption will come in one of two ways: (1) If the people of Israel do penitent return, they will be redeemed immediately. Then, "In quietness and in confidence shall be your strength" [Isaiah 30:15]. (2) [Redemption will come] by means of travails and the birth pangs of the Messiah [*Da'at Kedoshim* 42^b and B. T. *Sanhedrin* 98^a]. According to the definition of Samuel Eliezer Edels of blessed memory, either through serious penitent return or through compulsory penitent return. God will raise up a king as harsh as Haman and will return the people to the right path. Or perhaps by means of the path of purity. As in the statement "The son of David will not come except in a generation which is completely innocent," i.e., by means of serious penitent return. "Or in a generation that is completely guilty," that is, by means of compulsory penitent return by means of a king as harsh as Haman [Maharsha *ad* B. T. *Sanhedrin* 97^b, 98^a]. The words of the Gaon of Vilna of blessed memory, in his *Tikkunei HaZohar* commentary, are splendid. When he cites the statement "In a generation which is completely innocent or in a generation that is completely guilty" [B. T. *Sanhedrin* 98^a], he comments in these words: "It will certainly be in the second way" [*Beur Le Tikkunei HaZohar* 126^a].

If the people of Israel do not do penitent return on their own by the time redemption is to come, then "It is sufficient for a mourner to keep his period of mourning" [Maharsha *ad* B. T. *Sanhedrin* 97^b]. It is sufficient for God to remain for several days with His right hand behind Him. That is, He

does not remain in mourning forever. There is a definite end date to the matter. God will raise up a king as harsh as Haman and will return the people to the right path. This is the secret of the birth pangs of the Messiah. On account of our many sins the birth pangs have reached their climax. We look forward hopefully to God's salvation, its coming really soon, to its speedy arrival and to our being redeemed and saved with eternal salvation.

In order to understand everything which has happened to us in these terrible years, the awful and menacing catastrophe in which a third of our people have been annihilated and slaughtered with cruel and violent deaths, we have found it necessary to cite the words of Rabbi Yitshak Luria, of blessed memory, from the *Sha'ar Ha-kavanot*, page 1 [according to Hayim Vital]. This is what it says.

We need to know what the Talmudic Sages wrote, "It is enough for the Holy One, in His mourning, it is enough for Israel in their mourning" [B. T. *Sanhedrin* 97b]. This statement can be understood in a single introduction. Prior to the generation of the flood and the generation of the dispersion, the Holy One emanated 600,000 holy souls. The generation of the flood was so corrupt that God chose to annihilate it and refine it through Noah and his children, as will be explained later. Similarly with the generation of dispersion. Holy souls were emanated collectively. Then they became blemished with the sin of the tower [of Babel]. The Holy One divided them into seventy nations, and selected Israel for Himself: "For the portion of the Lord is His people" [Deuteronomy 32:9]. Then the people of Israel entered the land [of Israel]. There were 600,000 souls. Over the generations they blemished their souls severely, with sins of idol worship, bloodshed, sexual relations, etc. God sent His prophets to Israel to rebuke them and have them repent, so there would be no need to refine their souls with sword, famine, etc. But the sins became overwhelming and they did not want to repent. In His wisdom He found it necessary to refine them in a conclusive way. It would no longer help for them to die in a natural way and then return through transmigration. For the sins were as overwhelming as those of the generation of the flood. So the

[First] Temple was destroyed. You say that those who had killed Zechariah during the [First] Temple did not receive their punishment because they had already died? Not so. The Holy One let them be killed in order for them to transmigrate. Those who worshipped idols in another generation, or those who had killed Zechariah, transmigrated in order to receive their punishment with the destruction of the [Second] Temple. Each one received punishment according to the respective sin. There were those who took little pleasure in their sin, and they were killed with little pain and died quickly. There were those who took much pleasure, who had many sexual encounters and the like. Such a person was stabbed or lived for days in hunger and lacking all. He would see his children slaughtered before his eyes, Heaven forbid. All this according to measure and balance. Each was cleansed according to the sin. Those Israelites who remained after the destruction [of the First Temple were as Noah and his children and] constituted a crucible of purification, which refined all the killed souls. Therefore the people increased greatly in the days of the Babylonian exile and the Second Temple. [*Sha'ar Shishi*, in *Sha'ar Hakavanot*, vol. 1, p. 1]

We need to delve deeply into these holy things. They will illuminate our eyes with the light of the refined faith. We see that there is no refuge or hope for the person who sins. Either he will do penance or he will be refined through terrible suffering by means of transmigrations in order to cleanse his sins. "When the sins became overwhelming and they did not want to repent, He saw in His wisdom that He needed to refine them in a comprehensive manner. It would no longer help for them to die in a natural way and to return in transmigration" [*Sha'ar Hakavanot*]. He needed to return them in transmigrations in order to refine them through violent deaths. The hair on our head stands on end when we contemplate such words. What are the results and conclusions in the laws of heaven that make them obstinate and they don't want to repent? The second fundamental [concept] in the words of Yitshak Luria, of blessed memory, which enlighten our eyes, is that the people increased greatly in the days of the Babylonian exile and the

Second Temple. All were the souls who had worshipped idols or had killed Zechariah. They were transmigrated in order to receive their punishment in the destruction of the Temple. In light of the words of Yitshak Luria, of blessed memory, whose words are enlightening and a warning concerning our situation, [I have the following to say:] The numbers of our compatriots, before and after the catastrophe, recorded in several places, are most instructive:

A hundred years ago we reached approximately four and a half million Jews. In the course of a hundred years, we grew fourfold and at the outbreak of the war we reached seventeen million and perhaps more than this. Even though this century also did not excel in love of Israel. Even though there were also many bad years of assimilation, spiritual apostasy, and physical apostasy. Now we have retreated greatly, a fateful final retreat, and we again stand at the level we were at fifty years ago, at the beginning of this century—at eleven million souls. [*Hatsofeh*, 10 January 1947]

These facts, namely, the great population increase in the last centuries, and the great and terrible catastrophe in which a third of our nation was destroyed, illuminate and warn us as a force of heaven as to the purity of the holy words of Yitshak Luria, of blessed memory, concerning the birth pangs of the Messiah. In a clear light he reveals to us everything that has occurred to us, and everything that will happen to us for good in the coming days. We should remember these holy words. We and our children should study them.

...All of the cruel and violent deaths were according to measure and balance. There is no accident, heaven forbid. Everything is according to a just and precise calculation and everything is for the good of the sinner in order to cleanse his sin. "The Rock, His work is perfect. For all His ways are justice, a God of faithfulness and without iniquity" [Deuteronomy 32:4]. "To declare that the Lord is upright, my Rock, in whom there is no unrighteousness" [Psalms 92:16]. As the million terrible troubles and the birth pangs of the Messiah have been fulfilled, similarly all the promises of the prophets concerning the end of days will be completely fulfilled. "[It is] sufficient for [the Holy One] to keep [His] period of mourning. It is sufficient for [the people of Israel] to keep [their] period of mourning" [Maharsha *ad* B. T. *Sanhedrin* 97[b]]. Surely there is an end to the darkness. He does not stay in His mourning forever. There is certainly an end to the matter and an end to Israel's anguish of exile. We will be redeemed speedily and the Messiah will appear. "O Israel, that art saved by the Lord with an everlasting salvation" [Isaiah 45:17]. Amen.

Teshuvah and the Suffering of the Pious

Yosef Yitshak Schneersohn

Yosef Yitshak Schneersohn (1880–1950), of Lubavitch, Russia, was the son of the Lubavitcher hasidic movement ("Habad") leader Shalom Dov Ber Schneersohn (1866–1920). He directed Habad's Tomkhei Temimim yeshiva and became the movement's leader after his father's death in 1920. Denounced by the *Evsektsiia* (Jewish section of the communist party), he was arrested briefly in 1927. He moved to Riga (1928), traveled to America and the Land of Israel (1928–1929), then moved to Poland (Warsaw and Otwock) in 1934. He escaped after the Nazi occupation in the fall of 1939 and arrived on 19 March 1940 in New York.

Schneersohn responded to the Holocaust in the belief that, given the dimension of the disaster, redemption must be imminent. He founded in 1941 *Mahaneh Yisrael* (camp of Israel), an eschatological movement intent upon stopping the growing catastrophe by means of total religious commitment. Massive penitent return (*teshuvah*), he was convinced, would halt the calamity and bring about redemption. He explained that Israel's harsh exile was originally intended by God to bring penitent return. But sin increased instead, evoking proportional divine punishment. The Holocaust, which was the ultimate punishment, confronted Israel with the either-or choice of *teshuvah* or death. Blending ontological and anthropological dimensions, he was absolutely certain that Israel could never die and that penitent return must take place, and simultaneously that *Mahaneh Yisrael* must also bring about penitent return.

SELECTIONS

Schneersohn issued four proclamations (*Kol Kore*) about the crisis (*Kol Kore fun'm Lubavitsher Rabin* [26 May 1941], *Hakeriah Vehakedushah* 1, no. 9 [June 1941]: 15–16; *Tsvayter Kol Kore fun'm Lubavitsher Rabin* [11 June 1941], *Hakeriah Vehakedushah* 1, no. 10 [July 1941]: 9–11; *Driter Kol Kore fun'm Lubavitsher Rabin* [8 July 1941], *Hakeriah Vehakedushah* [August 1941]: 5–7; and *Ferter Kol Kore fun dem Lubavitsher Rabin Shlita* [11 September 1942], *Hakeriah Vehakedushah* 3, no. 25 [October 1942]: 12–13).

In the first proclamation (26 May 1941), he spoke of God's presence, confronting Jews with a life-or-death choice (Ezekiel 16:6) and warning them to awaken and turn to Him lest the compassion He had for the surviving remnant until then turn into punishment. Schneersohn pleaded with Jews to choose life and do penitent return, so as to diminish the *hevlei mashiah* (the "birth pains of the Messiah") and participate in the rapidly approaching redemption. If they did not become aware of the messianic onset and need for penitent return, they would be killed by the angel of destruction. The bleak situation, however, persisted. While the body of the Jewish nation was being burned in Europe, the soul was being destroyed in America. Focused on democracy's response to the war, American Jews left no room for faith. The death of the pious in Europe led them to falsely conclude that as God was not present there, piety in America was meaningless. They were blinded, exiling themselves within the exile. In the second proclamation (11 June 1941), Schneersohn described the choice as one between being abandoned by God in a desert or penitent return—where God would stop Amalek. It was also one between being burned to death for profaning the holy or sharing in a collective movement of penitent return, which would have the storm abate and the enemy become impotent. In any case, all the ignorance concerning the final juncture of Israel's metahistory, that between exile and redemption (the rabbinic Sages identified the ignorance as an ingredient of the prelude to the Messiah), was about to be shattered. In the third proclamation (8 July 1941), Schneersohn beseeched Jews to join *Mahaneh Yisrael* (the camp of Israel) in its spiritual Goshen (see Exodus 9:26). There they would share in the secret knowledge of the apocalypse, help to change the world through penitent return, and be protected within while God punished the trespassers outside (see Isaiah 26:20–21). Schneersohn stressed that with the *hevlei mashiah* well under way, it was imperative to act immediately. He declared that if the Messiah did not come in the next moments, the arrival would not be delayed for long. In his fourth proclamation (11 September 1942), he reiterated the life-or-death choice (see Deuteronomy 30:19) and blamed the failure to comprehend it and respond to his call on assimilation. He averred that military strategy and world leadership were ultimately in the hands of God and that the destruction was under His direction. Now he predicted that redemption would take place within the year, and then the enemy would be annihilated and Israel would be redeemed and become a holy nation of benefit to all the world.

In his statement of 11 September 1942 under the heading "Let Our Masters Teach Us" ("*Yelammedeinu Rabbeinu*," *Hakeriah Vehakedushah* 3, no. 25 [October 1942]: 2–3), Schneersohn spoke of how Jews, sunk in materiality and assimilation, would surely recognize their Jewishness amid the turmoil of the eve of redemption. They would participate in penitent return and the messianic return to Jerusalem, and the Jewish nation would be purified of its filth. At the final, undefinable moment when Israel's experience in time would touch the apocalyptic threshold, when Israel's relationship to God in historical terms would rise to a transhistorical level, the question of existential penitent return on the anthropological level would be reconciled with penitent return on the metaphysical level. In the statement of 29 October 1943 ("*Yelammedeinu Rabbeinu*," *Hakeriah Vehakedushah* 4, no. 39 [December 1943]: 2), Schneersohn explained how at the very end, amid the precipitous decline of exilic reality, the imminent defeat of Amalek, and the messianic onset, the choice to do penitent return would be inspired by a divine call from above (Jeremiah 3:14, 22). Once the penitent return mindset was in place, it would overwhelm the Jew's entire being. The Land of Israel also had to be restored primarily in terms of penitent return, so as to prepare for the Messiah's advent. Selections translated from the Yiddish by Gershon Greenberg.

First Proclamation: 26 May 1941

Immediate Redemption!

A fire is now sweeping over the whole Old World, threatening to annihilate, heaven forbid, more than two-thirds of the Jewish people. Nobody can guarantee that the fire, heaven forbid, will not leap over even here in the New World! The call of the local spiritual leaders for penitent return, prayer, and fasting, though in and of itself correct, is in the current circumstances not enough and of little value. The worst is that the call is insignificantly small. The reason for the insufficient response is twofold: Those who are called are deaf, and the call is, unfortunately, not as it should be!

The Two Fires

A stormy fire burns in the Old World which destroys, heaven forbid, the Jewish body. Here in America, a silent fire burns which destroys the Jewish soul. The customary coldness and indifference of the local Jews to Torah and faith is indeed on account of the fire in the Old World. [That fire] is transformed here into a quiet fire of apostasy, which rages no less than the Old World fire. The terrible catastrophe (*Ḥurban*) of Judaism in Europe has turned local Jews against the faith, heaven forbid. They do not see that the Sovereign of the universe is standing by the community of Israel. They are instilled with a single hope, that the Jewish people will be saved through the victory of world democracy. They see that even with the help of world democracy, things are not going well. [But they continue] to contribute toward the victory of democracy with all their talents, with money, and with a Jewish army. They go on thinking this way. But they do not want to hear about penitent return and prayer. They argue falsely that if the Lord of the universe does not help Torah-true Judaism in Europe, it is certainly a waste for American Jews to seek help by becoming more pious than local spiritual leaders demand of them!

The Call of Truth

Therefore, the ones who are called remain deaf to the call for penitent return and prayer. This deafness is indeed the result of the [fact that] local spiritual leaders have until now neglected to respond to the call of truth about which the rabbinic Sages wrote concerning such troubled times. Namely, the call of "Troubles have come to the world, look for the footsteps of the Messiah!" The

spiritual leaders neglected to tell the Jewish masses that one of the fundamentals of Judaism is the [doctrine that] "I believe in the coming of the Messiah." Also, that before the Messiah comes, one must expect such troubles as the present ones. And that in any event, it is possible that [what is happening now] are the birth pangs of the Messiah before the Jewish redemption! In truth this [messianic expectation] is no longer a pious hope and empty consolation. It is a fact. The Jewish people are suffering the birth pangs of the Messiah. The complete redemption stands behind our backs. The Jews of this country are completely distracted, [and] as the rabbinic Sages foretold, the Messiah of David will come when the people's attention is diverted, completely unexpectedly! [see B. T. *Sanhedrin* 97ª].

In the finest Jewish homes of this country, faith in the coming of the Messiah is considered to be an old wives' tale. In the synagogues, it is the same. After removing the prayer shawl and phylacteries, Jews discuss the world catastrophe in light of press reports about the battlefield situation. They do not even consider whether these times might be the days of the Messiah. The small number [of people] who do mention this are laughed at. They are helpless against the general stream of heresy! This is the situation with the *Shul* Jew. What all other Jews think about the coming of the Messiah is superfluous to cite here! For the last nine months we have warned the Jewish world in our monthly journal, *Hakeriah Vehakedushah*, that we are definitely living in the period of the birth pangs of the Messiah. Our call has unfortunately remained without a proper response from the local spiritual leaders. Ultimately it was unable to reach the larger Jewish masses in sufficient measure.

The American Jews do not believe in the whole theme of exile and redemption. They thereby deny the fundamental principle of Judaism. They have accepted the greatest heretical idea, that Jews are like all the nations. We suffer together with all nations (This itself is incorrect. We suffer ten times more!) and together with them we will be helped by the victory. Once "I believe in the coming of the Messiah" is denied, all the other "I believes" can have little meaning. So heresy truly rages here, heaven forbid. In general, and in all the corners of local Jewish life in particular! The Jewish troubles have now reached such a dangerous level that it would have been difficult to convince previous generations that this was some era other than that of the birth pangs of the Messiah. Here in America, it is a disgrace to mention that *perhaps* we are at the beginning of the redemption! The current callers to penitent return, with their old-fashioned style, have [come too] late. This style is now completely played out. People are already used to ignoring it, and it does not address the current moment. It lacks what is fundamental—the call [for] "immediate redemption!" This is the only true call in this time!

The Jewish people are now experiencing the birth pangs of the Messiah. For the last few decades, we have delayed the footsteps of the Messiah era. Now we need to do penitent return, having failed to do penitent return earlier, and also for having brought the birth pangs of the Messiah upon ourselves. The birth pangs will become much worse, heaven forbid, if we fail to correct the error!

Another Time, Other Obligations!

Now it is not enough to end sermons with the cold and dry "And a redeemer will come to Zion" [Isaiah 59:20]. This expression depends on "And unto them that turn from transgression in Jacob" [Isaiah 59:20]. It must be explained to the Jewish masses that without penitent return one cannot expect the redemption! Now is the end of the onset of the redemption (*ithalta digeulah*). Now we have a different duty, a different concept of penitent return. The angel of destruction has come to obliterate everything that is bad and traitorous in the world. The destroyer cannot be allowed to find among us Jews the old type of traitorous deeds and the old neutral style of calling for penitent return! Now the call must demand a fiery awakening to welcome the Messiah. Now we must stop hiding under the cloak of neutral piety, neutral faith, and neutral Torah parties. We must plant new centers [of Torah] in the exile! We must now have an awakening in the name of purity of heart, purity

of thought, purity of the house, purity of the yeshivah, and purity of family in the sense of bringing back the children who have been born to the Torah and to faith! Now we must tell the young generation about the new festival for the Lord and "We will go with our young and with our old" [Exodus 10:9]. And every Jewish house that does not want to be visited by the angel of destruction, heaven forbid, must be purified of all forty-nine gates of impurity and filled with authentic holiness!

Without such an authentic spiritual "Wash you, make you clean" [Isaiah 1:16], our weapons of penitent return, prayer, and fasting are worthless. Without the readiness of the majority of the whole Jewish people to become the only holy people, to go out to greet the Messiah, we will, heaven forbid, not be any better in the eyes of the angel of destruction than any other nation. We must explain this to our children, tell them the meaning of "immediate redemption!" We must also awaken in them the fiery will to be ready for the complete redemption!

The Responsible Ones Must Awaken

The first ones who must respond are the believers and also those children of believers who still remember what Judaism meant for their parents. You and we are responsible for all the other Jews, and you and we must be the first to awaken ourselves and to awaken others!

"Immediate redemption!" The imminent redemption of Israel is the only true response to the secular catastrophe and all other Jewish troubles! It is the eve of the redemption. We are paying the price for having allowed our Jewish soul to fall asleep, for having forgotten that we are in exile, and for having given up our "I believe in the coming of the Messiah!" "Immediate redemption!" must be the point of our penitent return and prayer, of our hopes and deeds. All other hopes and deeds are empty dreams. All national "isms" will soon be broken. The situation of the community of Israel will not be improved by them, but they—the "isms"—will cease! And we say this with absolute certainty! The point of our penitent return should be "immediate redemption!" by God. God is not silent. He reminds us, awakens us, wants to save us. In his mercy, He has until now protected the remnant of the dispersion in this country. What happens in the future is in our hands!

"In Thy Blood, Live" [Ezekiel 16:6]

"Choose life" [Deuteronomy 30:19]; "In thy blood, live" [Ezekiel 16:6]. The Jewish blood which has been spilled everywhere is for the [sake of the] Jewish people's coming to life again. It is for the sake of each individual's selecting for himself, between the "blood" or the "live." And His Blessed Name told us, "Choose life!" Let us bring this divine appeal into our houses, synagogues, yeshivas, into our shops and offices, into the whole Jewish environment! Let us greet each other with the words "immediate redemption!" Declaring to the unknowing what these words mean—that they are the response to the world catastrophe and the Jewish catastrophe. We must prepare ourselves to be worthy of enjoying the imminent redemption! Let us carry on tremendous self-sacrifice to show that we will truly rectify our betrayal until now of Torah and faith. Then God will accept our penitent return and

regret, and protect us from the birth pangs of the Messiah!

Our Appeal and Warning

"Immediate redemption!" is our appeal. Because this is the appeal of the current time. This is not only to comfort the despondent. This is our good news of a factual "salvation soon to come." We must prepare in heart and soul to greet the true redeemer. We call on all Jews to join the camp of Israel (*Mahaneh Yisrael*), which is, with God's help, being organized for this task! "Immediate redemption!" Be prepared for the imminent redemption. It is coming with quick steps though you do not see it. "Behold, he standeth behind our wall" [Song of Songs 2:9]. The true redeemer is already behind the wall. The time for preparing to meet him is very short! The community of Israel will be blessed with the complete redemption very speedily in our day. With this outcry we intend only to warn every Jewish individual that he should not, heaven forbid, be an exception! "Immediate redemption!" is our heartfelt wish for every Jew and our appeal and warning! And to those [Jews] who listen, greetings and, God willing, may the blessings of redemption come to them!

SECOND PROCLAMATION: 11 JUNE 1941

To the Indifferent

"What does the simple one ask [at the Passover *Seder*]? What is this?" [*Haggadah Shel Pesah* (narrative read at Passover *Seder*)]: You have heard our appeal concerning the imminent coming of the Messiah. You have also heard our call for sincere penitent return to avert the coming birth pangs of the Messiah, heaven forbid. And you remain indifferent. Completely indifferent, ignoring our proclamation as if it were an announcement about a shop's merchandise on sale for possibly cheaper prices! You believe that it is natural for a *Rebbe* to call Jews to penitent return in every time of trouble and to comfort them with the

good old hope in the coming of the Messiah! You already have your old opinion about such things that it is idle talk. Your response is to discuss it with a wave of the hand. You believe that it is silly and useless even to talk about it! You have ignored it. Some with angry, nervous disparagement, others with a humorous smile! We expected this. Regrettably, precisely this has also been foretold by the prophets and the rabbinic Sages! They foresaw that at the end of the exile the majority of Jews would ignore the "I believe in the coming of the Messiah." They would only awaken to the [messianic coming] through the birth pangs of the Messiah, heaven forbid. Not through faith in the speech of their own Jewish awakeners! Before they would feel the true pain, heaven forbid, like the simple one, they would ask about the troubles, "What is this?"

To the indifferent ones who ignore our appeal we say:

1. You think that we are making a mistake in our appeal and warning "immediate redemption!" So, study the developing world news and the changes in the Jewish situation in this land. Convince yourselves slowly, whether they both agree more with our appeal and warning or with your own groundless hopes, on account of which you feel justified in ignoring our proclamation!

2. You think that by ignoring our call, you are at most neglecting penitent return and failing to become more steadfast in Judaism in time. However, you will soon understand that you are also neglecting your economic and physical existence, your businesses, factories, work, and every other possibility for existing. It is either the "proclamation" or "in the wilderness" [Isaiah 40:3]. By ignoring our proclamation, the "wilderness" will remain for you. But this is wilderness without manna, without a pillar of clouds, without a pillar of fire, without a Moses with a divine staff in hand. It is with a new "Then came Amalek" [Exodus 17:8] in the form of the cruel anti-Semitic wave, heaven forbid, the likes of which has never before existed!

3. You think that we know as little about the concept of redemption as you do and that we are using it in accord with the non-Jewish concept of "the ends justify the means!" That is, that we are fooling you with false tidings so that you should do penitent return. You will find out, faster than you think, that our means are holy and true. Both our announcement of the imminent coming of the redemption and our call for sincere and speedy penitent return are based on pure truth. To ignore them, as you are doing, means to pay, heaven forbid, the most terrible price for a foolish frivolity.

4. You think you are right. But you will find out that you are wrong. You will find this out, heaven forbid, too late! You will find out through hatred of Israel by strangers, how foolish it was to ignore our appeal, an appeal that comes to you from love of Israel, from a friend!

To the Opponents and Crusaders

"Answer a fool according to his folly" [Proverbs 26:5]: You came out with the ridiculous but terrible argument against our call and warning of "immediate redemption!" that it was missionary stuff! What has happened to you? What is your concept of Judaism? What do you believe? You commit a terrible and tremendously foolish mistake! One of our articles of faith, the main principle of Judaism, is the belief in the coming of the Messiah. You give it away to the nations of the world, because they also preach this belief in their own way! Would you also give up the Sabbath, family purity, phylacteries, fringes, and similar Jewish sanctities, if Christian missionaries started to preach about them in their own way? Don't you know that faith in the coming of the Messiah is one of the primary principles of our holy Torah, the foundation for all our holy prophets and the rabbinic Sages? Do you really want to persuade the Jewish masses so they no longer believe in the coming of the Messiah, as you [in fact] are doing? Declaring to them that this is a contaminated matter, because [Christian] missionaries also preach about a messiah in whom Christians believe? Will you ever be able to redeem yourselves and repent for the terrible sin of making the belief in the coming of the Messiah loathsome to the Jewish masses, on the false and foolish ground that you suggest?

Nadav and Avihu, the two sons of Aaron the high priest, brought an alien fire onto the Jewish altar. They were burned because of this. They received the greatest punishment, heaven forbid, because they brought a foreign fire, an alien fire, where there should have been only a divine holy fire. The Torah says about this, "Through them that are nigh to Me I will be sanctified" [Leviticus 10:3]. This is a warning that when there is such a sin, not even such holy worthies as Nadav and Avihu, the two sons of Aaron, are spared! Now you, regrettably, do the same. You seek making the holy fire of our faith in the coming of the redeemer loathsome by offering your foreign fire! Do you want to bring the terrible punishment of burning of the soul and death of the body upon yourself, heaven forbid? Don't you believe that the Messiah must come, *our* Jewish Messiah who was foretold by *our* prophets in *our* Tanakh

[Hebrew Bible], and by *our* rabbinic Sages in *our* holy Talmud? As *we* now say to the community of Israel in the name of the prophets and in the name of our rabbinic Sages, of blessed memory?

To these opponents and crusaders against us we must answer according to the statement of the man wiser than all others [King Solomon], "Answer a fool according to his folly" [Proverbs 26:5]:

1. You think and you hope, and now you must already hope this way, namely, that our words will be proven false and that the Messiah will indeed not come soon. For then you can remain the wise men and the pious ones to whom Jews should listen in the coming days as well. You will be terribly disappointed. Besides, you must already be ashamed of your opposition to our proclamation. No sensible person will believe you that you asked the Blessed Creator to send the king Messiah soon. You will thereby be associated with the shame of having contested those who knew the truth better than you!

2. You are dispersing the false, criminal, and ridiculous thought that to inform Jews about the coming of the Messiah is missionary stuff. Soon you will have to stamp the last true messenger as a missionary, namely, Elijah the prophet, who will, with the help of God, soon confirm our proclamation. You will not ask Elijah how he knows [about the Messiah], just as you did not ask us. And he himself will certainly not come to you before he comes to the community of Israel!

3. You think that your battle will bring you a good name as pious, smart, and practical leaders. But your illogical conduct, as already said, has demonstrated that you are the opposite. In your heart, you cannot want the Messiah to come soon, because that would make you look foolish. About your piety, there is not much to say. Because you did not calculate things before you undertook this battle, your wisdom and practicality are also of little value. The prophet's words "Many shall purify themselves, and make themselves white, and be refined" [Daniel 12:10] are being fulfilled. Many will show themselves in their true image. And if you say that our appeal is missionary stuff, you demonstrate

very clearly how much scholarship, fear of heaven, and wisdom you lack!

4. You put yourselves forward as the spiritual leaders of Jews. But your words are like those of the greatest misleaders. In the future you will be judged, and you will bring upon yourself the greatest punishment, heaven forbid, unless you take on a penitent return immediately which is commensurate with revoking your sinful talk and admit that you committed a grave error, sinning by trespass!

To the Believers and to the Uncertain Ones

"Unto you, O men, I call" [Proverbs 8:4]. To you who believe in our proclamation, and to those who are uncertain about it, because so-called pious Jews leave them cold, we call: We do not need to preach to you and to use sharp language with you. This is not our way. We have used this sharp tongue only against our will, to oppose those who are completely indifferent and who oppose us. To you we speak with brotherly and heartfelt words. These words come out of love of Israel. The hour has come! The time of grace has come. We await God's redemption of us from exile. Now we must also stop acting like exile Jews, by our own will. We must become redemption Jews in order to be worthy of "immediate redemption!"

Join our camp of Israel (*Maḥaneh Yisrael*). It does not come to compete with any movement. It is not for anyone's personal interest. Help us to enlarge the camp and do the work needed at this time for the community of Israel! The camp of Israel has already quietly accomplished the greatest holy things. We have already saved many Jewish souls, pulling the nails of apostasy out of them, heaven forbid. We have saved them from falling into a life of shame. We have been demonstrably able to remake them into dear and holy Jewish souls. In secret we have gathered dreadful facts about networks to mislead Jewish children. We have tens of documents which demonstrate what we have already accomplished. We have various plans about what must be done to rescue many thousands of victims! We have implemented the strongest measures and powers to combat the poison and fire of the impurity, heaven forbid, which have imposed themselves on the local Jews in order to change their minds and their minds about their Creator. They are helpless to combat alone. We are in contact with political leaders, who are ready and willing to help us, because we have convinced them how necessary it is to help us! The work is holy, the biggest and the most difficult. But it must be done. It must reach into all corners of the country. It can and will bring great results! At the very center of our work stands the work of awakening the Jews to the thought of "immediate redemption!" It is already more than a distant hope. With God's help, it will be a fact which is soon realized.

We have spent much money to awaken the Jews here in our monthly publication, *Hakeriah Vehakedushah*. We have advertised in the *Morning Journal*, offering free copies for everyone. We have received thousands of responses. We have published a large number of twenty-four-page editions of our publication in Yiddish and in English. We have hired extra people and spent a whole week sending out copies, whole truck-loads, free to everyone who requested them. We have advertised our proclamation in the *Morning Journal* and have disseminated it over nine months in our *Hakeriah Vehakedushah*—the call of "immediate redemption!" This is because we know that the local Jews are lying in a lethargic sleep. By our awakening them, we want to protect them from the angel of destruction, heaven forbid. If you wait until the angel of destruction, heaven forbid, starts waking you, you will find yourself, heaven forbid, in the greatest danger. His awaking is without mercy. Praying and screaming will not help you. Pouring out tears and bitter sobbing will not help you!

Remember, we must awaken the mercies of heaven to avert the terrible troubles that have hit all of Judaism in Europe like a thunder! You cannot rely on your [own power] or on the uprightness of the enemies. The English press of this country is already [talking about] the "Jewish problem." Christian liberals are expressing themselves openly and with concern that the same thing will happen to the Jews here as in Europe. What are the sleeping Jews waiting for? Why wait until it is too late? When you will not even have the putrid excuse that nobody warned you? The events in Europe are warning you. The

local English[-language] press warns you. Our prophets warn you. Common sense warns you. All of this is brought out in our warning to you. Our warning is your good luck, your life insurance. Our life and death lie in the balance; our life hangs on a single shift one way or the other. We say to you, "Choose life." Choose for yourself life, salvation, and consolations!

Every Jew should join our *Maḥaneh Yisrael*. Together we will become a strong fortress. Through our unity we will influence God to shackle our enemies. We call to every Jew, every man or woman, young and old, in every corner of America, no matter which party or movement anyone belongs to. Come closer to sincere Judaism! Awaken in yourself the fire of holiness. Throw away the alien fire of impurity that is devouring your souls! Only in this way, with God's help, will we be worthy of the complete redemption and without having to suffer the terrible birth pangs of the Messiah. They are unavoidable, if you do not embrace our appeal with total seriousness! Our united work in the *Maḥaneh Yisrael* will help and benefit all other Jewish activities; it will benefit all those working in all other Jewish areas. We will create a living, conscious, and strong Judaism. We will organize ourselves into a great mass "that bore the ark of the covenant of the Lord" [Deuteronomy 31:25]. Then, no oncoming storms, heaven forbid, can touch us. The "Then were the chiefs of Edom affrighted" [Exodus 15:15] will be fulfilled for us. Our enemies will become dumb and lame before they can carry out any of their putrid actions!

We ask all the important ḥasidic leaders and rabbis who spoke during the last *Shavuot* [Festival of Weeks] about our appeal and are preparing to talk about it, to let us know who they are. They should join our call as equal participants and confer privileges on the multitudes. Then the verse "And they that turn the many to righteousness as the stars forever and ever" [Daniel 12:3] will be fulfilled for them. We ask all the synagogue presidents and the conscious, sincerely pious householders to display our appeal in the synagogues. You and your families should read and think about it. You should look into the occurrences of our time and realize how correct our appeal is and how important it is to listen to our voice! We ask every reader of the *Morning Journal* to cut out and save this proclamation and to look at it from time to time. The true value of this proclamation will become increasingly self-evident in the coming months. You will learn the meaning of our words later. More, perhaps, than you can learn now.

The Gravity of the Commandment of the Moment!

Jews and brothers, be serious! Give up all petty things and all personal insignificant ambition! It is an altogether new time. It is a time of emergency, when nothing will come of all personal ambition! We do not want to encroach on anyone's boundaries. We do not want to hinder anyone. Nor will we impugn anyone's honor. We want to awaken, wake up, and live to see how you wake yourselves and others up! We could not remain sitting with folded hands, watching what is happening and remaining silent. We found ourselves forced to become the force that pushes, which pushes the Jewish community onto the right path. We have also shown you the direction. Let it now become yours! We have established a constant awakener, the [the monthly periodical] *Hakeriah Vehakedushah*. It should be yours! We have begun the work of creating a *Maḥaneh Yisrael*. Let this become your work! Come and help build, with serious commitment to the task and to the community of Israel! Come and take on the only position where you can, with God's help, remain firm and do wonders. For all other positions are as good as lost. All other fortresses are as good as broken into pieces! We warn you that this is the truth. It is to your good fortune to believe us, a short time before you perceive it yourself. It is, heaven forbid, to your misfortune to doubt our

words until you are convinced that you were delayed in perceiving the truth in time! The commandment of the moment is of gravity. Pettiness was always a silly thing. Now it is literally a danger to life!

"Immediate redemption!" is not a fantasy. It is not only a pious hope, not now. It is the call of the time. The redemption is behind our backs. It comes with quick footsteps. Fortresses will fall like splinters. Nations and lands will be overturned overnight. The whole earth will be shaken apart, "The word of our God shall stand forever" [Isaiah 40:8]. In our generation, God's word through his prophets will be fulfilled! Let us be worthy to remain alive with the generation! To remain whole with the better part of humanity. As Jews, we can attain this only through immediate, sincere penitent return, through earnestly believing in God's word, awaiting the true redeemer, and through being worthy to greet him! Believe, and you will thank us and live to attain salvation and consolation! Believe and follow our call, and you will, with God's help, avoid all the birth pangs of the redemption! Believe, and you will be worthy of the redemption! "Immediate redemption!" is now also, thank God, "immediate truth!" You will not have to wait long for the whole world to know that this is true!

"Immediate redemption!" should be the call that you must now transmit to your children. Tell them that God has remembered His suffering people and that He is going to redeem them from exile and the troubles of exile. The terrible suffering of Judaism everywhere is the last warning of God to His children, that they should do penitent return and become Torah-true Jews again—as it should be! "Immediate redemption!" is now our greeting to the community of Israel. It is our wish to live to see it with all Israel, our brothers. Amen!

THIRD PROCLAMATION: 8 JULY 1941

To Those Who Think They Do Not Believe in the Coming of the Messiah

History and psychology testify that nonbelievers only convince themselves that they do not believe. In general, there are no nonbelieving Jews. There are only those who have convinced themselves and think that they do not believe.

"One shall say, 'I am the Lord's,' and another shall call himself by the name of Jacob, and another shall subscribe with his hand unto the Lord and surname himself by the name of Israel" [Isaiah 44:5].

The Old Prophetic Warning

Brother Jews of all nonbelieving camps! In our earlier two proclamations, which appeared in the *Morning Journal* and in the *Chicago Courier* and in other Yiddish and Anglo-Jewish American newspapers and elsewhere, we have provided you with the prophetic warning about the current time, "Come, my people, enter thou into thy chambers, and shut thy doors about thee; hide thyself for a little moment, until the indignation be overpassed. For, behold, the Lord cometh forth out of His place to visit upon the inhabitants of the earth their iniquity" [Isaiah 26:20–21]. The prophet Isaiah warns us against getting in the way of the nations of the world when they are being hit with punishment for their sins. Except for the duty that Jews must perform for the lands of exile as citizens and individuals, the prophet warns us that as a community we should go into our own Jewish chambers. We should wash our hands of our own sins, dust off *our own* neglected Jewish faith and *our own* Jewish hopes. Only in this way can we avoid the punishment of the inhabitants of the earth when God leaves his place to wash away the sinners!

All the uninvited mixing by Jews into nationalistic wars will come crashing down on our heads, heaven forbid. Even when we are doing nothing, we are accused of being warmongers, as opponents of [peace] and as the ones solely responsible for all troubles. Even more so when we actually do mix in! The prophet warns us to protect ourselves. Not to intrude where we ought not, not to get involved with the alien world. We should rather confine ourselves to our own four corners. We should do the only thing that we can do to avoid the general world: penitent return with hope for our own redemption! More than any previous time, it now looks as if God has left His place to punish all the inhabitants of the earth for the sins they have committed. More than at any previous time, Jews

need to lock themselves in their own chambers and not get in the way of others. Besides these words of the prophet, we also reminded you in our proclamations. Every Jew can understand how timely and necessary the prophet's words are for all of us. However, it is also a fact that our warning about the forthcoming birth pangs of the Messiah and the redemption which soon follows is right on time! The prophet spoke more than certainly about the current time. Our heart bleeds seeing how everything that the Jews here do and say is exactly opposite to what the prophet advises them!

We Have Fulfilled Our Responsibility!

You say that you are not compelled to believe that we know more than others about the nearness of the coming of the Messiah. You want more evidence, facts, and thorough persuasion. That way, everyone could see the truth, that we are situated at the threshold of the redemption, as we assert! As patriotic Americans, would you also want the government to supply all of its secrets? Are you not rather ready to trust it blindly? Before it pours out everything it knows just to satisfy your curiosity? Including those elements which should not be accessed lest they be used to harm the state's interests? Why should you demand of us that we should give out more information than what we find necessary? Our warning cannot be given as anything other than a pure religious belief. We do not want to win over the whole world to recognize the truth of our words. We do not even want all Jews here to agree with us. Because the prophet said about this, "And shut thy doors about thee" [Isaiah 26:20]. [That is], at the right time one should discuss the complete redemption only behind locked doors. Unfortunately even among our pious Jews there are those who do not want to know, and are not allowed to know, the full truth as *it is*. We have already risked telling you more than enough!

We intended to draw in only those steadfast and seriously thinking Jews. Thank God, we have drawn them near from all camps. We have truly carried out everything we intended. The whole Jewish press has directly and indirectly made our warning and appeal about the imminent redemption known. Similarly, all the local Jewish leaders have expressed, directly or indirectly, their agreement with or opposition to our announcement about the "imminent redemption." With this, we have carried out our task completely. We have no more to say about the matter of the coming of the Messiah. The near future will speak for us!

FOURTH PROCLAMATION: 11 SEPTEMBER 1941

Rejoice in the Festival of Redemption: The Third Front!

The year 5703 is approaching. It is the year of exaltation about which we say, "May your kingdom be exalted, Lord!" and "May the tabernacle of David which has fallen" [Amos 9:11] be exalted!—through the true redeemer, who will bring complete redemption for the Jewish people! The free countries are working for a second front and for a victory. As human beings, they do the best they can under the circumstances. However, now everyone sees clearly that the Blessed Name is directing the true war strategy from above and on many fronts. The secular leaders no longer lead. They are being led, often not knowing to where. They have been assigned as the emissaries of God to precipitate complete Jewish redemption. They will be successful in this mission. Therefore, not overlooking the fact that our Jewish people is receding in blood, heaven forbid, we say to the community of Israel: "In thy blood, live!" [Ezekiel 16:6]. Through your current bleeding you will come to life again! And "Rejoice in the festival of redemption!" [source uncertain]. No matter how terrible our suffering is, we cannot forget the joy with which we are approaching the complete redemption and what a great role the coming year of 5703 will play in this!

In the coming year, through many newly opened fronts, the greatest front of all, the third, will open: the redemption front for the Jewish people and for all of humanity. This will obviously not happen according to the previously calculated strategy of the military leaders. Nor according to the predictions of experts in the press and on the radio. This will happen according to divine providence from heaven. It will happen according to the predictions of our holy prophets in the holy Scriptures and of our rabbinic Sages, of blessed memory, in the Talmud and midrash. So it *is* and *so will it be*. Whether you believe our words or not! The complete redemption is nearer than near and our call "Rejoice in the festival of redemption" is more serious than serious.

No Change in the Situation!

Our call, "immediate repentance, immediate redemption!" which we put out two full years ago, was meant exactly as we then explained. We called the Jews to penitent return for the sake of the imminent redemption. In no way, as certain circles tried to interpret it, did we, heaven forbid, use "immediate redemption!" solely as a means for the call to "immediate penitent return!" Since then, we have not given up the call. We have not changed it. We have constantly strengthened it through our monthly periodical, *Hakeriah Vehakedushah*, month after month and year after year. Twenty-four issues in two years, comprising a total of hundred of thousands of copies, were sent to all the corners of the world. Several articles in each issue repeatedly emphasized the necessity of penitent return for the sake of "immediate redemption!" This cannot be considered anything other than a call of great seriousness! Today, as before, we repeat the same *shofar* call of the ram's horn, with the same three voices: We need to do penitent return in time in order to avoid, or at least make easier, the birth pangs of the Messiah. We should not despair if the times become, heaven forbid, unbearable. We should constantly keep in mind the consolation of the imminent, complete redemption!

World events since our first proclamation have not invalidated our call; they have only justified it more powerfully. Things have not improved, either for the Jewish community in general or for the local Jewish community. America was dragged into the war and therewith the local Jewish youth. In the meantime, the enemy of the world has not been defeated. This will require more and more victims. Nobody can know how many more victims there will have to be!

The government of wickedness will finally lose, and in a repulsive manner. This will lead, we believe, to the Jewish redemption. It is clear that we Jews will suffer more than all others, actually living through the period of the birth pangs of the Messiah. This was and is the special Jewish worry. Our call of "immediate repentance, immediate redemption!" comes on account of the birth pangs and for their sake. We are now repeating the call, adding "Rejoice in the festival of redemption!" because it is already, thank God, closer to redemption than further from redemption!

Today as then, much is said and done on the American Jewish street to weaken our call. Much is said and done to support the impression among the Jewish masses that [eventually] everything will remain as it was, only improved on account of the victory of the democratic nations. But this is the false hope of "We will be as the nations" [Ezekiel 20:32]. The prophet Ezekiel said about it: "[It] shall not be at all" [Ezekiel 20:32]. Our Torah and prophets have other plans for the Jewish people. These are the plans of complete redemption. We claim with certainty that this complete redemption is on the way. The Jewish leaders, unfortunately, disparage these plans in all sorts of ways, open and concealed.

It is still the same opposition and the same means of combating our threefold call [i.e., do penitent return, resist despair, be mindful of consolation]. Because it is the same call! We have not [changed] and do not want to change the call. The last two years demand no change, and our opponents do not want to change! There is no change in the situation, except that the troubles of Israel get worse, heaven forbid. The redemption is now closer. The continued ignoring of our call for "immediate repentance, immediate redemption!" is now more foolish and more harmful!

Our "You Have Chosen Us" Status and the Harm in Ignoring It!

The root cause as to why the belief and hope in Jewish redemption must drag after the worldly wagon is the denial of the Jewish "You have chosen us." This is connected to the denial of our Torah and prophets. This denial leads to ignoring what the Torah and prophets tell us about the Jewish redemption. The denial brings so much harm to us! The denial of our "You have chosen us" status has, on account of our many sins, become the sign of progress. Although in fact it is the sign of simple ignorance, of spiritual descent to the point of accepting the falsehoods of the enemies of Israel, of cowardice, and finally of ignoring a fact that stabs into the eyes of its deniers.

More than fifty billion people have lived in the world since our Jewish history began. The current civilization has collected together the spiritual work of all generations. Among them, our holy *Tanakh* (Hebrew Bible) stands like an elephant among fleas! More than fifty billion people have produced not a single true prophet whom the world could use. The small Jewish people of but a few million have produced scores of grand prophets. No nation can boast of prophets who supposedly foretold the nation's future thousands of years ago with precision. This is [in fact] the case with our Jewish people. This is the cause for the worldwide jealousy [and] hatred toward us. It is also the cause for the worldwide fear the nations have about having to account for the hatred. If this does not mean being the chosen people among the nations, then the Nazis, who place the spirit below raw brutal power, are indeed right.

Our Torah and prophets are truly the richest heavenly gift which the Creator of the world has given humanity. God, may He be blessed, gave the gift to humanity through the Jewish people; our "You have chosen us" status is no idle boasting. Not to mention that we are the only nation which has been attacked for thousands of years by the whole world, and the mightiest enemies could not annihilate us. They themselves become annihilated through their battles against us!

Our "You have chosen us" status goes far deeper than this. Having the Torah and prophets, we do not have to grope blindly inside all the worldly catastrophes. Our Torah and prophets, being God-like, give us the clearest answers to all the most difficult world problems. But if one ignores the Jewish chosenness, and no longer believes in the holiness and divinity of the Torah and prophets, one indeed becomes, because of this, as the other nations. That is, in the sense that [for this person] the future for Jews becomes as blind as the future is for others. One drags after the worldly wagon, believing and hoping in the same way that other nations believe and hope! This is the factual damage that we suffer from ignoring our "You have chosen us" status, namely, from not knowing the truth. As if we do not have the Torah and prophets, when the fact is that we *indeed* have them. When they *indeed* provide us with the correct answer about the worldwide and Jewish question, "What is to be done?" The answer would be "immediate penitent return! immediate redemption!" This has been our appeal since 5701!

Not wanting to know the truth which the Torah and prophets have to tell us concerning our near future, one risks, heaven forbid, having to find out afterward how any other hope for continued Jewish existence will be completely excluded. This too is not our own warning. It is what the Torah, the prophets, and the rabbinic Sages have given us, so that we should not be led into this situation. By ignoring our "You have chosen us" status, we lose the privilege for which the whole world should envy us, namely, the possibility of seeing the future clearly instead of groping in the dark like all the others. This is really a great harm, which is powerfully regretted!

"Choose Life!"—You Must Choose Life Yourself!

Our Torah and prophets give us the clearest answer regarding the current world catastrophe and the best advice about what to do to survive it intact. They, the Torah and prophets, would not be god-like if they did not give us this clearest answer. But they give it to us in a sealed package which one must accept unopened! The Torah and prophets promise us the complete redemption on condition of [our] prior complete penitent return and com-plete faith, because they are the original condition on which the Torah itself was given to us!

"I call heaven and earth to witness against you this day, that I have set before thee life and death, the blessing and the curse; therefore choose life, that thou mayest live, thou and thy seed" [Deuteronomy 30:19]. The Torah is an elixir of life and a blessing for those who choose it without questions and without turning up their noses. It becomes a poison and a curse for those who question it to find out first if it is worth accepting! If those in doubt do not find convincing evidence in the Torah that it gives them life and blessing, this is not because the Torah does not have the evidence. It is because the Torah does not want to give it to those in doubt. The Torah reveals its proofs only to those who choose the Torah without doubt and without reluctance. Heaven and earth bear witness. For there to be the "That thou mayest live" [Deuteronomy 30:19], there must be the "Choose life!" Paradise in heaven and the complete redemption on earth are too precious to be offered to someone by first showing that person a piece thereof. One must already have the dignity to comprehend that the Torah is divine and that one must have the fullest trust in God. Only through choosing the Torah and following Torah's commandments without prior proof can one earn eternal life in heaven and blessing on earth. Only then will one also be convinced, and indeed here in this life, that one made a fortunate choice!

Ultimately, the complete redemption must realize the building of the truly Jewish "a kingdom of priests and a holy people" [Exodus 19:6]. The Sovereign of the world does not want the new Dathans and Avirams to jump on the redemption wagon with the new Koraḥs [Numbers 16:1–35]. He, may He be blessed, wants Jews who are already observing the commandments. Or at least Jews who have the strength to return in penitent return through purification and suffering. Such Jews earn the redemption and the redemption needs to have them. Such Jews, if they are also scholars, can even find out where the secret of the redemption is hidden in the Torah and prophets. Really, to the point that they know the day on which redemption will come. However, such fortunate discoverers [also] discover the secret that they cannot reveal the secret to others.

The Sovereign of the world has safeguarded the secret such that the finders will not be able to do so. Those who want to reveal the secret of redemption do not know it. Those who know it are forced to remain silent!

Not the patriarch Jacob, not Moses our teacher, and not the other true prophets could reveal the secret of the redemption. The holy spirit is supposed to have left them, but the thought implied is that they perceived that it was not the Creator's will for it to be revealed and that all they could do was to talk about the necessity of penitent return prior to redemption. "In thy distress...thou wilt return" [Deuteronomy 4:30]. When things become very bitter, the advice is "immediate penitent return!" Because it means "immediate redemption!" They could not say more than this, no matter how powerfully they wanted to! Those who want proof from us for the "immediate redemption!" before they take on the "immediate penitent return!" are unjustified in demanding that proof. The redemption package must remain sealed. It must be accepted and paid for by unconditional return to Torah Judaism. Only fools can demand that specially closed packages which are on sale be opened for them! There is good reason that the Jewish redemption can only be mentioned with a hint!

The argument about how all of our rabbis and Torah scholars still do not know about the "immediate redemption!" and are silent about our call is also foolish. Nowhere in the written or oral Torah is there any statement that, at the time of the end, Jewish leaders will know of the end and publicize it. It is the exact opposite! It says explicitly that they will not know of the end or not want to know it. Precisely because of this [not-knowing or not wanting to know], the birth pangs of the Messiah must come! The prophet Daniel, who foresaw the current time, became sick from suffering when he perceived how the Jewish leaders of the [final] generation would be blind and not understand what was happening! He says about this: "And I was appalled at the vision, but understood it not" [Daniel 8:27]. That is, "I became despondent because of a vision where nobody would understand when the end would actually come about. Where, due to this, Jewish leaders would not console those who were suffering and would not call them to penitent return

with the call of 'immediate redemption!' when only such an appeal would be able to awaken those suffering ones!"

The redemption, like the Torah itself, is a sealed package. It guarantees life and blessing to every Jew who accepts redemption and Torah without question, solely due to their god-like status. Demanding prior proof is out of order, according to the conditions with which Torah and revelation were given to us. We can also call out "immediate penitent return!" only with the additional consolation that it is for the sake of "immediate redemption!" But we do so without proofs and even without declaring whether we ourselves have the proof. This is because penitent return due to the belief that the *one who calls* has proofs is also not correct penitent return. Penitent return needs to be solely for the sake of the divine advice "Choose life!" The one who calls is only the one who reminds and explicates the verse!

The Same Circumstances, the Same Results!

Our holy prophets called themselves "seers." This is not the place to explain how they became such lucid seers. It is enough that we now know from Jewish history that they saw correctly and that all of their words were fulfilled precisely. They foresaw the destruction of the Land of Israel. The exile implemented all the biblical rebukes [see Deuteronomy 28:15–68] as foreseen and, exactly as foreseen, the Jewish people have not, thank God, been doomed. They have survived many mighty enemies.

We know from their own descriptions that when the prophets preached their visions, they took no pleasure from them. Beyond the pain of knowing that Jews were bringing the most terrible destruction upon themselves, they were not certain about their own lives. They were treated terribly and endured plenty of suffering. We can imagine how they were ridiculed by the false prophets, how they were ridiculed and mocked by the idlers! The result was that the prophets of truth were not heard and not followed. The masses used to imitate those who misled them with, "The prophet is a fool, the man of the spirit is crazy" [Hosea 9:7].

LET OUR MASTER TEACH US: 11 SEPTEMBER 1942

An Essay of Holy Writing

With the help of heaven, "And it shall come to pass in that day, that a great horn shall be blown; and they shall come that were lost in the land of Assyria, and they that were dispersed in the land of Egypt; and they shall worship the Lord in the holy mountain at Jerusalem" [Isaiah 27:13]. This is the prophecy that the prophet Isaiah uttered in the name of God about the end of days of the final redemption. As it says in the previous verse, "And ye shall be gathered" [Rashi: from the exile], "one by one, O ye children of Israel" [Isaiah 27:12]. In the time of exile, the people of Israel were spread out in all the corners of the earth. As it says, "For I have spread you abroad as the four winds of heaven, sayeth the Lord" [Zechariah 2:10]. When the time of the redemption comes, there will be Jews in different, even faraway corners of the earth, in far, distant small islands. Even in places where there will be a few isolated Jews, all will be gathered up and brought into the community of Israel.

The small number of Jews, particularly those isolated ones in different, distant corners of the earth and the islands of the sea, will certainly be very ignorant and immersed in worldly things and estranged from Judaism in general. They will not want to leave their well-established homes to follow the Messiah to the Land of Israel, and they will not want to hear at all about the fortunate redemption from exile by the Messiah today. How, then, will God Blessed be He keep the promise, which Isaiah said in the name of God? According to Isaiah, when the time of redemption approaches, a number of Jews, for various reasons, including bad friends or bad leaders, will become very ignorant and will be mixed into the populations of the lands where they find themselves. Some will forget or not want to know about their Jewish descent. How will they return to their people? Concerning this, the [second] prophecy says that the sound of the great ram's horn will be heard and it will terrify everyone. The [first]

prophecy is that on the eve of the redemption God will shake up the world with such a strong shaking that all of humanity will be stirred. The extraordinary stirring-up will make humanity recognize that even the forgotten Jews are Jews. The [second] prophecy is that the great ram's horn will awaken even the lost and banished ones, so that they also will have the desire to bow before the holy divinity in Jerusalem.

Summary

On the eve of the redemption, God will stir up the whole world. Then even the most estranged Jews will recognize that they are Jews. The great ram's horn will awaken the point of Judaism even among the lost and banished Jews. Here we have to understand the issue of the great ram's horn.

It is written, "And the Lord (*Adonai*) God (*YHVH*) will blow the horn and will go with whirlwinds of the south" [Zechariah 9:14]. This verse is also a prophecy by Zechariah the prophet concerning the end of days, of the final exile. What is the problem with the great ram's horn? The issue is that the prophecy "And the Lord God will blow the horn" concerns the ram's horn of war, which must destroy the lands which have greatly sinned in general and warred against the people of Israel in particular. And this is the meaning of "and will go with whirlwinds of the south." The sound of the *shofar* of "my Lord God will blow the horn" is the sound of the horn of war of the "and will go with whirlwinds of the south," which proceeds to destroy the sinful lands. In the prophecy, two names of God are mentioned, the name *Adonai* and the name *YHVH*. The name *Adonai* is the name for strict justice [or judgment] and the name *YHVH* is the name for mercy. Though the matters of destruction and war are matters of strict justice, in truth the justice is mercy.

In addition, through the destruction, the sinful ones are washed clean of their sins. Thus, the war, with its stormy shake-up, is a prerequisite and preparation for the complete redemption through the messiah. This is the sound of the great ram's horn which will awaken the point of Judaism in every Jew. Each, according to his level and situation, should become better and higher in the Jewish life of Torah and the commandments. The Messiah will come soon and the scriptural passage "And ye shall be unto Me a kingdom of priests, and a holy nation" [Exodus 19:6] will be fulfilled. The birth pangs of the Messiah will cleanse the people of Israel of their accumulated dirt. The great ram's horn will awaken everyone to hear the divine holiness. This includes the lost and banished who have become completely estranged from the people of Israel and have affiliated with strange nations. It includes even those who have been pushed away so far and fallen so low that they are ashamed of the name Jew. They get angry when anyone reminds them of their Jewish descent and do everything possible to separate themselves from Jews and Judaism. The sound of the ram's horn and the stormy tempest will also make them recognize that they are Jews. We see in reality that the birth pangs of the Messiah have affected everyone powerfully. To a certain extent, they brought them closer to Judaism and will bring them even closer. However, all these are the sufferings of the pains of the birth pangs of the Messiah. The great ram's horn, however, is God's fatherly call which brings people near. It will reach all Jews, even the lost and banished Jews.

Summary

"My Lord God shall sound the ram's horn" is the war sound of the ram's horn, which "advances in a stormy tempest." It destroys the sinful world and brings the estranged Jews back to the community of Israel. *Adonai* is strict justice—the birth pangs of the Messiah. *YHVH* is mercy—the preparation for the complete redemption. The "shall sound the ram's horn" is the divine call to all Jews to come near with penitent return.

The divine call for drawing closer with penitent return, which will take place after the birth pangs of the Messiah, will be very strong. Aside from awakening Torah students and observant Jews with an extraordinary longing for godliness and superhuman devotion to the fulfillment of the commandments and study of Torah, it will awaken a strong desire to grow in fear of God, in love of the Creator Blessed be He, and in love of Israel in terms of virtue. The divine call for drawing closer with penitent return will reach even those who have fallen low and immersed themselves in worldly lustful filth, [evoking] "the strayed who are in the land of Assyria and the expelled who are in the land of Egypt." That is, even those embedded in the deepest swamp, abandoned to lustful desires which lead to the worst murderous deeds. The divine appeal for drawing close with penitent return will also reach even these. It will also "awaken the desire in them for the Jewish life of Torah and the commandments." Their inner longing will be to bow down to the divine holiness in Jerusalem. This means "the strayed who are in the land of Assyria and the expelled who are in the land of Egypt shall come."

General human sins are divided into two parts with two different types of qualities. One is cold, deliberate pleasure and the other is a fiery, stormy devotion. These two types of qualities have two separate sources. The source for the cold and deliberate pleasure of physical desires is essentially intellectual. The source for the fiery, stormy devotion to physical desires is essentially ethical. When we say that the source is essentially intellectual and essentially ethical, the meaning is that while in both cases the primary essence is the pleasure of physical desires, there is a difference now as to how this pleasure in physical desire is expressed. When it comes to cold and deliberate pleasure or fiery, stormy, devotional pleasure, the difference is that the cold and deliberate pleasure satisfies the person. The satisfaction draws him in more and more until he drowns in the pleasure. This is "the strayed who are in the land of Assyria." Assyria means pleasure and luck. The one who surrenders to the desire for pleasure is the one who is "the strayed who are in the land of Assyria." The fiery, stormy devotion to physical pleasures creates a greater thirst in the person for these desires, until he becomes immersed in the deepest swamp of crime, which is "the expelled who are in the land of Egypt." Egypt means the lowest swamp of crime.

First come the birth pangs of the Messiah of the "My Lord God shall sound the ram's horn" to shake up Jews in general and the alienated Jews in particular. Then there will be "the great ram's horn will sound," the god-like, fatherly call for drawing closer with penitent return which awakens the point of Judaism in all Jews in general [and] in particular among those who were "the strayed" and "the expelled" of Judaism. Very soon, all will go with the Messiah to bow to God on the holy mountain in Jerusalem.

Summary

After the terrible, fearful birth pangs of the Messiah, a very strong divine call for drawing closer with penitent return will come. It will affect all Jews, even the radically alienated who are given over to the lowest carnal desires, whether in a coldly deliberate or in a fiery, stormy way. They will also turn to a life of Torah and the commandments. The Messiah will very soon take them all along with him to the thoroughly cleansed Land of Israel.

LET OUR MASTER TEACH US: 29 OCTOBER 1943

With the help of heaven, "And a redeemer will come to Zion, and unto them that turn from transgression in Jacob" [Isaiah 59:20]. The redeemer will come to Zion and to those drawn back away from sin, those who do penitent return who were with Jacob, God said. This verse relates to the previous verses. The prophet prophesied in the name of God Blessed be He, that God would see that in the bitter time of exile the Jews will become corrupted. Sins will become like a wall between God and the Jews. The Jews will be horribly punished for their bad behavior and their sins. God, Blessed be He, will see to it that there will be no *tsadik* of value to rise up and pray for Jews, whose prayers would be accepted by God. God, as it were, is astonished that the nations do not grasp the Jewish troubles, and He Himself will severely punish all the nations who have mistreated the Jews. Even those nations which live in the distant islands will be severely punished. All will recognize that by divine direction, there will be a diffusion of the enemy, coming into all lands, like the overflow and flooding of a lake. Finally, the divine mood will devour the enemy. The divine holy name will be feared because of everything that is happening in the West. The divine holy honor will overwhelm everyone because of what will happen in the East.

The Jews will do penitent return. Then "And a redeemer will come to Zion, and unto them that turn from transgression in Jacob, sayeth the Lord" [Isaiah 59:20]. Rashi says, "As long as Zion remains in ruins, the redeemer will not arrive." We need to understand the interpretation "As long as Zion remains in ruins, the redeemer will not arrive." What is the meaning of this? It is an obvious fact which everyone understands, that the primary task of the redeemer is to rebuild all the ruins. With his leadership and strength, he brings the proper assurance that there will be no more destruction and that matters will remain as is. What is new in what Rashi tells us with his comment? The first impression one gets is that this comment is something simple, superfluous. No, the meaning of this comment is profound, and everyone needs to know it. The Talmud says:

> Great is penitent return. For it brings about redemption. As it says, "And a redeemer will come to Zion, and unto them that turn from transgression in Jacob" [Isaiah 59:20]. Why will a redeemer come to Zion? Because of those in Jacob who turn back from sin. [B. T. *Yoma* 86ᵇ]

The sinful ones in Jacob will return, and through their penitent return the redeemer will come. For Rashi, this means you should not be fooled. Even when the Land of Israel is being physically built, the redeemer still does not come. The buildings are all ruins, for all matters of faith are in ruins. The criminals of Israel are in power, which is opposite to the truth of "those in Jacob who turn back from sin." Everything that is already built and is being built is equivalent to ruins, heaven forbid. This is because the redeemer needs to come through "those who turn back from sin."

Summary

This explains that "And a redeemer will come to Zion" is a continuation of the previous verses. They explain the corruption of the Jewish exile and the punishments that one receives for it. Also the punishment of all the nations that have done evil to the Jews. All of this will bring the Jews to penitent return. The commentary of Rashi explains that as long as the sinners of Israel are the leaders of the Land of Israel, all the physical buildings are ruins.

The Jerusalem Talmud [J. T. *Ta'anit* 1.1] and the midrash say:

Rabbi Eliezer said, when Israel was redeemed from Egypt, they were redeemed through these five things: through trouble, through repentance, through the merit of the patriarchs, through mercy, and through the end, etc. Even in the future they will be redeemed through these five things, as it is written, "In thy distress, when all these things are come upon thee" [Deuteronomy 4:30]. This is through repentance. "For the Lord thy God is a merciful God" [Deuteronomy 4:31]. This is through mercy. "He will not forget the covenant of thy fathers which he swore unto them" [Deuteronomy 4:31]. This is through the merit of the patriarchs. "In the end of days thou wilt return to the Lord thy God" [Deuteronomy 4:30]. This is through the end of days. [*Midrash Devarim Rabbah, Parashah 2, Siman* 23]

The final redemption will come through five things, as was so in the first redemption when God redeemed the Jews from Egypt. The five things are:

1. The troubles that Jews, in whichever countries they may be, will feel as they are persecuted and oppressed. Even those who are well off in terms of wealth and human pleasures. Even those who temporarily have access to and various honors from the authorities—which attract people for their own use when they need to. Even those whom the authorities appear to love, when they are of benefit and when they can be used, feel this oppression and persecution.

2. Penitent return. The harsh hand of the divine punishes with the greatest rebukes, as foretold. This punishment will and must finally result in Jews doing penitent return. As the Talmud says, God will raise up a ruler whose decrees will be as bad as Haman's and this will return the Jews to the right path to do penitent return and be redeemed [see B. T. *Sanhedrin* 97[b]]. Why does penitent return come in two ways? This can be explained by means of a parable about how a father treats a badly behaved child. At first, the father guides the child by trying to bring him near. If that does not help the child to forsake bad behavior, behave appropriately, take the straight path, and listen to and behave as the father wishes, the father punishes the child with the greatest severity. He does so until the child regrets its bad behavior and behaves as its father instructed. It is superfluous to explain the moral of the parable at length. Everyone knows that it is only necessary to mention and warn those who, thank God, have not yet been punished bitterly—themselves, their families, and their wealth. They should not think that they are already saved and they do not need to do penitent return. Maimonides said that all the prophets warned about penitent return because Jews will be redeemed through penitent return, and the Torah assured that the end will be that the bitter exile will bring Jews to penitent return and then they will be redeemed [*Mishneh Torah, Hilkhot Teshuvah* 7, *Halakhah* 5].

3. Merit of the patriarchs. Though the essential thing is penitent return, one must have the matter of the merit of the patriarchs.

4. Mercy. Aside from the merit of the patriarchs, one must have mercy.

5. From out of the end. In the end of days, Jews must be redeemed. This takes place only through penitent return and the merit of the

patriarchs with great mercy. The meaning of all the troubles is that through penitent return comes the "From out of it shall he be saved" [Jeremiah 30:7]. And this is "He will come as redeemer to Zion, to those in Jacob who turn back from sin."

Summary

The Jerusalem Talmud [*Ta'anit* 1:1] and midrash [*Midrash Devarim Rabbah, Parashah* 2, *Siman* 23] explain which things will bring the complete redemption:

1. Troubles. All Jews without exception in all lands will feel oppressed and persecuted.
2. Penitent return. When the father's drawing a badly behaved child near does not help it become better, strong punishment helps. Also, those who are, thank God, not punished need to do penitent return.
3. In the end of days, the merit of the patriarchs and
4. the mercies of heaven will awaken so that the Jews will understand the meaning of the troubles and they will do penitent return and
5. that will bring the righteous redeemer.

The issue of penitent return is not, as the world thinks, a matter of penitent return only for sin, that is, only for the one who has transgressed positive commandments, did not don phylacteries, did not observe the *Shabbat*, etc., or the person who was a sinner, desecrated the *Shabbat*, ate nonkosher food, did not observe family purity, etc., had to repent. Observing family purity, donning phylacteries, observing the *Shabbat*, eating kosher, etc., are not the ways. Penitent return means making good on that which one did not do but should have done, and on what one did but should not have done. Certainly, the sinner needs to do penitent return and stop doing what is forbidden by the Torah and needs to do what one should according to the Torah. But not only this. Restoring what one spoiled by not fulfilling the positive commandments and making good what one damaged by transgressing the negative commandments is the full sense of penitent return. The literal translation of the word is to turn around, to turn around to be what one should be according to the Torah. But the meaning of penitent return is to be better. Words of praise which declare the virtue of a thing contain two expressions, "good" and "better." The concept of penitent return is not only a matter of "good" but a matter of "better." Compared to "better," "good" is not the most complete achievement. The reason that the movement of penitent return comes about is the divine call, a spirit from above.

Four reasons bring about a movement of penitent return:

1. Awakening of one's soul which is in heaven. It is awakened when it hears the proclamation which is called out in heaven, "Return, O backsliding children" [Jeremiah 3:14]. The heavenly soul influences the branch soul, and this animates the movement of penitent return. We see this happen when a person suddenly becomes dominated by thought of penitent return and he becomes truly good in everything, according to Torah.
2. The penitent return that comes through reflection. The person thoughtfully considers the path of his life. He [realizes] that he is very weak in Torah and the commandments and that he has become ignorant of ethics. He thinks deeply about the meaning of his life and how he spent most of his years on physical needs. This reflection awakens a movement to penitent return. He changes his way of life and becomes very observant and sets time for Torah study.
3. The person draws near to heaven and is given great success and great abundance in children, health, and livelihood. The great drawing close to heaven awakens a movement of penitent return.
4. The penitent return that comes through troubles and suffering, heaven forbid. Whatever reasons bring about the movement of penitent return, it is not only a matter of penitent return for sin. It is also a matter of becoming better than good. This is the good preparation for welcoming the countenance of our righteous Messiah very soon.

Summary

This explains that although penitent return is also restoring what has been spoiled, in terms of observing the positive commandments and transgressing the negative commandments, the significance of penitent return is becoming better. Compared to "better," "good" is incomplete. Four things awaken a person to penitent return:

1. the awakening of one's heavenly soul through proclamations
2. reflecting about the meaning of one's life
3. drawing near to heaven
4. heavenly punishment

Constantly becoming better is a good preparation for welcoming the countenance of our righteous Messiah.

Simḥah Elberg

Simḥah Elberg (1908?–1995) studied at Warsaw's Emek Halakhah yeshiva, where his main teacher was the ḥasidic rabbi Natan Spigelglas. He edited the *Emek Halakhah* journal there, as a means of combating *Haskalah* (Enlightenment). Elberg continued his study at the Montreux yeshiva (1935–1936), founded by Eliahu Botschko, after which he went to Paris to serve as a correspondent for the religious press and to write religious poetry. He also enrolled at the Sorbonne—where, after the war, he would defend a dissertation on the problem of slavery among the Jews of antiquity. Soon after he returned to Warsaw in August 1939 for his sister's wedding, the Nazis invaded. But he was able to flee, made his way through Poland and Lithuania into Russia, and sailed from Vladivostok to Japan and then Shanghai (September 1941). He left Shanghai in 1946 and settled in Brooklyn, New York. Elberg's parents, brother, and sisters and Natan Spigelglas were murdered in Treblinka and Auschwitz.

Elberg's *Akaydas Treblinka* (*The Akedah of Treblinka*, 1946) began amid intellectual paralysis over the catastrophe. He found himself strangled by contradictions—for example, if Hitler personified absolute evil, how could he be the educational instrument with which Israel's enemies were traditionally identified? He distilled the confusion into a single question, one posed from Moses to Job: Why did the righteous suffer and the evil ones prosper? Or, how could six million Jews die when God promised never to bring an end to Israel (see Jeremiah 5:18)? With this transcending question, the paralysis began to ease. The *Akedah* (binding for sacrifice) of Mount Moriah, Elberg wrote, remained with the people, and the slaughter of the death camps, where binding blended with murder, was its ultimate manifestation. The *Akedah* of Treblinka (i.e., of all death camps) was also the greatest of atonements, one for which the sacrifice of the holiest Jews, those of Poland and Lithuania, was required. With their cries of *Shema Yisrael* ("Hear O Israel") they fulfilled their atoning act. Elberg believed that with the Holocaust, history as a collective entity was categorically destroyed. But the Torah remained, and with it God could create a new universe, a universe where redemption would again be possible. As a metaphysical entity, *Akedah* remained as well. As late as 18 May 1984, in the journal *Hamodia* in Tel Aviv, Elberg spoke of its ongoing existence—and of his awaiting a new creation.

SELECTION

In *The Akedah of Treblinka* (Shanghai, 1946), Elberg described the continuity of the *Akedah* from Mount Moriah [Genesis 22:1–18] to Treblinka, despite their dramatic differences, as an internal reality which identified and sanctified the Jewish people. The Treblinka *Akedah* was the atonement for sins of the generations, an ultimate atonement which required the holiest of Jews. It was also the final definition and translation of the meaning of exile. The catastrophe, however, also implied redemption. Because world history was now totally and irretrievably polluted, a new creation would have to take place before redemption could unfold. Selections translated from the Yiddish by Gershon Greenberg.

The *Akedah* of Treblinka

The *Akedah* of Isaac and the *Akedah* of Treblinka, the first for an individual and the second for a people. Both sanctified our history, our existence. Treblinka is the culmination of Mount Moriah. The *Akedah*-of-Isaac-nation has survived the test. The wretched voices of millions [have been] ripped forth from the flaming red fires. A voice split the heavens by calling out, "Hear O Israel." Never before have the heavens seen so much sanctification-of-God's-name Jews. I think that Isaac, the eternal Jew, was never taken down from the *Akedah*. Mount Moriah has always been transferred from one land to the other, from Spain to France, from France to Germany, to Poland. Jewish history began with the episode of the *Akedah*, and it will continue even after the giant *Akedah* of Treblinka. Isaac was led to the *Akedah* solely by God's order. God's will was effectual in this way at the *Akedah* of Treblinka.

At Isaac's *Akedah* a merciful angel called out at the last minute: "Lay not thy hand upon the lad" [Genesis 22:12]. Isaac was placed on the *Akedah* for a short time. But the six million burned in the flames of *Akedah* for years. The divine call which thundered, "Lay not thy hand" [Genesis 22:12] was not heard. An Abraham led Isaac to the *Akedah*. How joyfully does one proceed to the *Akedah* when an Abraham is leading the way! But who were the emissaries for the six million? Human cannibals! And that pains us. Precisely because Abraham was the one who led him to the *Akedah*, Isaac did not perish. Wherever the emissary is an Abraham, not even a single Jew can perish. And who were the evil emissaries for the *Akedah* of Treblinka?

*Akedah*s do not frighten us. With the *Akedah* of Isaac, God showed Abraham that His "great nation" [Deuteronomy 4:7] would, by its historical destiny, be an *Akedah* nation, that it would unfold upon the fires of the *Akedah*. The only thing that

tortures us is this: Who were the evil spirits who assumed the role of being our annihilators? We have always had days of destruction. But we consoled ourselves with the fact that the intermediaries of our punishment were a Moses, or a Jeremiah. Today, Hitler has spoken in the name of God. For us, that is the bitterest punishment of all. We were punished not only with death, but also by whom our terrible executioner would be. How lowly, how worthless we are, for Germans to be chosen as the messengers of death, as our judges.

Six million people perished upon new *Akedah*s. How did the people possess such superhuman strength as to be able to endure so much suffering? It is naturally not important whether every individual endured the test and remained standing at the proper ethical level. In the course of many years, the totality, the six million as an interlocked community, transformed itself into a sanctification-of-God's-name era. From where did this community derive so much heroism? So much faith? The physical strength to endure all the fires of *Gehenna* (hell) over the several years? And without a moment to breathe?

I only want to make sure of what I am saying. I am trying to concentrate all my spiritual energies. I want to understand the psychological situation of a Treblinka Jew, which manifests itself in his actions regarding what was beyond nature. I doubt whether I or thousands like me would be able to raise ourselves to the level of holiness attained by the six million. From where did the six million get the strength to be able to accept death with such tranquillity? Even, possibly, with such inner spiritual satisfaction? From what source did they draw, in their last moments when with radiant hope they took leave of the cruel world?

It seems to me that any person selected by Providence to accomplish a great task is endowed with a special, specific power enabling him to easily carry out the task. It is much easier for the person who is designated to be the sacrifice to endure all the unbearable suffering than it is for the deeply compassionate outside observer. Only the human sacrifice is raised to the highest degree of that which is beyond nature. The role which is placed upon the sacrificial victim induces him to the highest possibility beyond nature. The sacrificial victim, as the object for a great act, is overwhelmed by an unimaginable bravery. The observer, who is only compassionate, will have no means to be able to penetrate, psychologically, the deepest chambers of the human sacrificial victim's soul. The human being and the human sacrificial victim are two separate creations. They cannot be measured by the same standard. We, who only have compassion with Treblinka, and who have never found ourselves in a life-and-death struggle, will never feel the metaphysical power in ourselves which transforms the person into a supernatural being above nature.

With the *Akedah* of Isaac, Abraham was put to the test. Not Isaac. Why? Because Isaac, as the sacrificial victim, was endowed with spiritual power, giving him strength to stretch out his neck for the slaughter with love. It was different for Abraham, who did not have to be the sacrificial victim. He only had to lead his child to the *Akedah* and be present when his child perished. It is hard to bear such pain, and the trial is therefore great. The mother did not suffer the pains of *Gehenna* when she was the sacrificial victim and went to the gas chamber. Then, carrying out the role of innocent sacrificial victim, she lived in another, heavenly atmosphere, and this sweetened her suffering. Instead, the mother struggled convulsively when she was condemned to be the observer of her child's demise. The father did not suffer the travails of Job when he was buried alive. Then, in the shadow of danger, a new strength was born in him, a strength that nourished him until the last moment. It gave him the strength to endure all the suffering. Instead, the father certainly only suffered when he observed his child or wife struggling in agony. The *Akedah* of Isaac and the *Akedah* of Treblinka—both have sanctified our history, our existence.

Poland

[Jewish] Poland. Who possesses enough holiness to be able to write the holy word, Poland? After seven immersions, Rabbi Mosheh Pshevarsker, the holy scribe of the Baal Shem Tov, wrote the five glowing letters—*P-O-L-I-N* [Poland]—with a trembling hand. I will not profane your holiness, Poland, even with boiling tears. Tears are created to quiet human suffering. Your disaster, Poland, is beyond the human, beyond nature. I am mute, my tongue is lopped off. I can say nothing about you, Poland. Let all the millions who perished rise with mouths open from their graves and let them tell what happened to them in those dark days. I am mute. What can I, a poor little person, say about you, Poland? Each speck of dust should cling to another speck of dust; let all the little specks of dust of ash of the millions who perished become great mountains, and let the mountains relate and speak out, so the whole world is terrified from screaming.

Jerusalem has become a widow. And what are you, Poland? "The *Shekhinah* (Divine Presence) is in exile." We felt the exile much more in Poland than we did in other lands. We were persecuted in Poland much more than in other lands, even in the idyllic times. However, we were given a temporary reward for this hard exile. Our daily sufferings were recompensed with [the presence of the] *Shekhinah*. As intense [as] the exile of Poland was, the impact of the *Shekhinah* was even more intense. It lightened our destiny, enabling us to persevere and endure. In the difficult years of exile, in Poland, we consoled ourselves with the *Shekhinah* [in exile]. And we had a lot of *Shekhinah* in Poland. The holy trembling of hundreds of years, the holiness of generations filled the air there.

Today we are being sent to new lands, into much freer and more democratic countries. It is true, perhaps, there is less exile, that exile is physically much easier. But who knows if we will be able to endure the quiet exile, when so little [of the presence of the] *Shekhinah* has remained? In Poland, one feels the "That I may dwell (*ve-shakhanti*) among them" [Exodus 25:8] with the touch of the finger. We have continued to remain in exile, but without the holy exile-Jews of

Poland and Lithuania, Jews who built a nest for the *Shekhinah* in their hearts. Poland with its thirty-six *tsadikim* (righteous ones), its hidden holy men and kabbalists is gone.

The nation (*Am*) of Israel and the community (*keneset*) of Israel are two separate concepts that should not be identified with one another: The community of Israel is the emissary of the nation of Israel. In all difficult moments, the nation argues with the Creator of the world. The community of Israel speaks to the Sovereign of the universe. The community of Israel is the representative of the nation of Israel. The beloved, holy, noble Jews of Poland and Lithuania, who used to argue things out with the Sovereign of the universe, are no longer here. Where else but in Poland did Jews pray and plead so much? Where else did Jews argue things out with the Sovereign of the Universe in such an intimate way? As did the thirty-six *tsadikim*, the holy Baal Shem Tov's fellowship, and all the children and students of the Baal Shem Tov, of the Rabbi Ber [from Mezhiritsh], of [Menahem Mendel] from Kotsk, of [Yitshak Kalish] from Warka in Poland?

The question bores a hole in the mind: Why Poland? Poland, a dwelling place for angels on earth, was the first to be brought to trial. The strongest wrath was poured on this Poland, the Poland of hundreds of years of purified prayers. The eternal Poland has become an abyss. Son of man, understand what has happened here. It seems that precisely because Poland, Jewish Poland, was purified over the many generations, that it was condemned to be the sacrifice for the sins of humanity. "Through those near Me I show Myself holy" [Leviticus 10:3]. "Through the deaths of those close to Me I will be made holy"—says God. This is the deep meaning of the catastrophe of Poland. This holy community fell first, because it carried in itself what was purely noble, profoundly humanitarian, and purely ethical. Therefore it became the "Them that are nigh unto Me" [Leviticus 10:3], the ones close [to God] from whose violent deaths the nations should learn. This is the deep meaning of the catastrophe (*Hurban*) of Poland.

I ask myself: Have we at least properly mourned our most dearest and best, who perished so tragically? Have we at least mournfully

lamented their painful deaths? How many tears would we have shed in quiet times, if a father, a mother would have left us in a natural death, after a fullness of years and pleasures? Today, having learned of the great catastrophe, we have not even poured many tears. The pain strangles us, and we cannot cry. It is one of the greatest punishments for a person to be unable to lament his misfortune. Our tear ducts have been dried up, so that the tears cannot even calm us for a while. We must remain forever in the grip of anguish, without the consolation of shedding tears.

Ezekiel warned us about the terrible moment of not being able to cry over the most tragic events. This moment has come. We are witnesses to "I take away from thee the desire of thine eyes with a stroke; yet neither shalt thou make lamentation nor weep" [Ezekiel 24:16]. The most precious thing is being taken away from [before] your eyes, and you cannot even express your anguish in tears.

By the Waters of Poland

We sat down by the waters of Poland. It sounds like a sad elegy now, a new poem for catastrophe (*Hurban*). By the waters of Poland. And my right hand should be forgotten, should I forget you, Poland. I understand, yes. I understand the death of the holy ones, of the six million, more than I understand why we were those selected to remain alive. Whom has God punished? Those burned in gas chambers or we, those who remained alive? Which is the punishment: their martyrs' death or our meaningless life? I regard our gift of life not so much as a privilege as a deep, furious punishment. But the greatest punishment for a nation is when the criterion for judging between punishment and privilege is taken away. And how is it for the person who substitutes punishment for privilege? How tragic is the human being's position, when life for him is a punishment?

In a flaming rage, the prophet Ezekiel warned us about the bitter hour of "fury poured out": "With fury poured out, will I be king over you" [Ezekiel 20:33]. Treblinka and Auschwitz have given the tragic moment of "fury poured out" a deep explanation. We have paid dearly for the "fury poured out." Therefore the properly earned reward, the prophet's promise of "will I be king over you," should be delivered to us. The "I will rule" should indeed be in proportion to the "fury poured forth." I think that if the "fury poured forth" has already reached its culmination point, the hour of divine revelation should already be arriving for all humanity. And this is our real mission: to redeem the world with our blood.

Our rabbinic Sages say: When Haman had thrown lots to murder the Jews [*Esther* 3:7], each particular day protested. Each day placed a complaint before the Sovereign of the world: How can you murder Your people Israel? Each day sought out rights for itself and to protect itself from becoming a date of sadness. Today, Hitler has slaughtered on Sunday, burned on Monday, buried alive on Tuesday. Quiet, be still. All of nature has approved. No one reckoned with it. No one protested. As if everything were natural. How should we understand that chaos, other than as [a form of] payment for the "fury poured out"? And how else can one understand the world's abandoning us?

Six million Jews have been slaughtered. The violence! From where does one draw such a power for murdering? All murders in all of world history have surely been [collectively] rehabilitated today. Cain was the first to bring forth the power of murder to exist in creation. That is why the Torah brought an eternal curse upon him. But Cain made only the commitment of individual murder possible. Hitler brought forth a new demonic power of murder into humanity, a transnatural power, a power beyond human intellect. Hitler surely procured a new creation, one of the murder of an entire nation of millions. That demonic power of mass murder would carry out its destructive role further. It would place its stamp on God's creation. This was the first time in world history when creation was so terribly stained, so terribly polluted. Can humankind still, at some point, be mended [*tikkun*] and cleanse itself of the sin of murder against creation? I think not. The world has descended into the deepest void, into the abyss of holocaust [*Umkum*], of chaos [*tohu vavohu*].

A new formation (*yetsirah*) must come, a new six days of creation (*bereshit*). A new formation-creation, however, can only come when the Torah becomes the light for the nations, when the hour of "And nations shall walk at thy light" [Isaiah 60:3] will be struck. The death of those murdered is painful. Killing, the potency of murder which exists and which has become intelligible to that "sincere democratic world" which relates so sentimentally to the "noble" German nation, is even more horrifying. How much killing is hidden in the democratic world's "compassion"? The judgment of Nuremberg, as strong and merciless as it was, will offer no satisfaction to us. We do not expect any justice to be dictated by judges under oath. [Rather,] "And also that nation, whom they shall serve, will I judge" [Genesis 15:14]. The moment of the "I will judge" will quiet our boiling blood. Until today we did not know that a single person could be the incarnation of all evil, of original malice and wrongdoing. What sort of demonic power must a single human being possess, to be able to poison the human feeling of millions? [However], as hypnotizing as the power of *evil* is, the effect of the *good* is even stronger. All positive, effective elements can be incarnated in a single human being who will reconstruct the world from out of the destruction. And perhaps such a human being is already standing behind our backs, with words of redemption in his mouth.

How deeply Hitler translated the "hatred of the world toward the eternal nation" [Maimonides, *Igeret Teiman* (*Letter to Yemen*)] for us. We thought that this hatred expressed itself in jealousy, in competition. We have, obviously, misunderstood. Hatred means Treblinka, Auschwitz. But we have found consolation in the world's hatred, as strong as it might be. The hatred of the world is the barometer of the eternal nation. The eternal nation has power in exact proportion to the power of the world's hatred. Hatred has no limits, no obstacle. The eternal nation is wealthy in terms of the same elements. The eternal nation is even more powerful. In the historical sense, it is the victor.

We want to console ourselves with the Jews or the *She'erit Hapeleitah* (saving remnant). But it is such a poor *She'erit Hapeleitah*. Each Jew who survived is precious. Each Jew who survived because of a thousand miracles should be treasured as gold. But one should not be deceived that anything has remained. Our [nation's] holdings have become too lavish for us, the *She'erit Hapeleitah*, to be considered the inheritors.

The *She'erit Hapeleitah* should not imagine itself as having been placed upon the *Akedah* of Treblinka, as having been purified by a thousand lowly deaths, as having been sanctified through suffering, misery, and pain. With those of Treblinka, the [rabbinic Sages'] "suffering removes the trespasses of man" [B. T. *Berakhot* 5ᵃ] has taken place. The *She'erit Hapeleitah* has been physically and morally enslaved no less than our predecessors in Egypt. And what are we? What is our value? What does all our misery and our experience over the years amount to, compared to that of a single Jew in Treblinka for a single hour? "The act of Your hands is drawing in the sea and you are singing?" [B. T. *Megillah* 10ᵇ]. When God's work was threatened with destruction, the angels were not allowed to sing. Why did Jews sing, "I will sing" [Exodus 15:1]? Because the Jews had suffered. They bore on their backs the suffering and pain of 210 years. Then came the joy of victory. One cannot restrain the joy of a nation, which ripped away the chains of slavery after many long years, despite the fact that the overall circumstances still remain tragic enough. At the moment of liberation, the joy of someone who had been in pain is infinite. But angels did not feel the yoke of Egypt. Why then was their enthusiasm so great when a portion of God's creation was killed? The Treblinka Jews are one thing. We of the *She'erit Hapeleitah*, those with deep compassion, are another. With what are we left? Who is left with us? We are left with a larger, cruel world and an emptiness in our own camp. Misery, loneliness—again and again.

Exile and Redemption

For thousands of years, we have been situated between exile and redemption. Since we have lost our Holy Land we have waited daily for redemption. We were told precisely how long the Egyptian exile and the desert exile would last: 210 years in Egypt, and 40 years in the desert. For the last, difficult exile, we were issued no specific time. "God sought to reveal the end" [Rashi *ad* Genesis 49:1]. But God did not express it. In the nonexpression lies our fateful existence. Because by not knowing that the exile would last 10,000 years, Jews could hope, even in the first day of exile, that liberation would come at any moment. The exile was viewed as a short, temporary appearance liable to disappear any day. Each dark day in exile was regarded as the last. One believed deeply that the morning would already be blessed with the joy of liberation. Only each and every day has lasted a thousand years. It is good that no one told us that the longer path of suffering could last a thousand years. The Jewish people might not have passed the difficult exile exam, had they known at the onset of the diaspora that they would be homeless in exile for the great period of a thousand years.

One cannot learn from the richest history of nations as much as one can learn from the exile history of the Jewish people. It shows that a nation can exist when all it possesses is a "spiritual grounding." Hitler went into battle against exile history. He denied our conception about exile-nation-power. He wanted to show that the thousand-year exile history must end with the doom of those who created history. His motto about this was: Away with the Jewish people, and thereby away with their exile history. But the history of exile is more powerful than a Hitler. In a deeper sense, Hitler did not achieve his aim. Our potential power does not lie in numbers. There have been epochs when the Jewish nation has blossomed among the nations, although it was smaller than it is even today after the great national catastrophe. We have continued to remain a living nation, which rebuilds its spiritual ruins. Powerful people make glorious history. With us Jews, it is the other way around: Glorious history makes the Jews into a powerful nation.

We have found nothing comparable to the contemporary tragedy. Contemporary events resemble what we read about quietly with the two rebukes [see Leviticus 26:14–45 and Deuteronomy 28:15–68]. Rebuke punishes the living with unbearable sufferings. Today, punishment has come for whole generations, generations which disappeared long ago. They have shouted "proud Jews" into the graves. And still, who ever said that when the rebuke would be realized, even in its strongest form, exile would end? The time of rebuke, manifest even in all its horrors, lasts for only a small period in the long exile. But exile is far from ending at that point. The rebuke is only a bitter lesson. It is a deep explanation to have us understand what is so awful about exile and the consequences which it brings.

One wonders about understanding Hitler's "personality." From whom, one ponders, did he inherit so much bestiality? From which filthy sources did he draw his doctrine of murder and destruction? One wants to explain the evil phenomenon literally. Hitler is supposed to have gone through an entire school [of thought] before growing to his demonic height. From the metaphysician Fichte up to Nietzsche—all of them [allegedly] poisoned [Hitler's] morality. The first [Fichte] was the teacher of Hitler's chauvinism. The second [Nietzsche] was the source of Hitler's Jew hatred, of his sadism. Nietzsche's doctrine of slaughter and murder hovered over the German nation like a holy spirit, whose prophet was *Nietzsche*. Hitler merely brought Nietzsche's new "morality" into real life.

Such was the academic solution for the difficult Hitler problem. I could swear to you that all of Germany's cannibals, all the horrible sadists among its politicians and generals taken together, from the bloodthirsty General Bernady [i.e., Friedrich Adam Julius Bernhardi, 1849–1930] to the dreamy philosopher Nietzsche, would not want to be involved, not one percent, in the bestiality demonstrated by Hitler and his helpers. As much as ancient human morality was, for Nietzsche, a slave morality contrary to "nature," Nietzsche would not have allowed one day of Treblinka.

Hitler did not learn about murder from anyone, any more than Cain had anyone from whom to learn about murder in the ideal world of his time. Hitler is an original. You ask: How is such human bestiality possible? One answer consists of one word: exile. Hitler is the deeper translation of exile. We have leveled out the deep meaning of exile and its tragic consequences. We have made too much peace with exile. We have not reckoned with being accused of generations of sins and [the

fact] that at any minute the exile could demand what is due for our guilt. We have not properly understood the deep tragedy of exile. We have sweetened the exile with some small amount of autonomy and the right to speak. At no time have we failed to understand the tragedy of exile as much as we have today. We have known that exile was the greatest punishment of a people. But it was Hitler who showed us in what a harsh form the punishment [could] manifest itself. We were being punished with exile, and now we have been sentenced with a Hitler. "And among those nations shalt thou have no repose" [Deuteronomy 28:65]. We have paid for that.

In the Zionist circles today, one speaks a great deal about the negation of the exile, about redemption. Something should be said about this. Hitler has shown what a tragic punishment exile is for us. This is something which we perhaps did not learn over the course of our two-thousand-year exile. But in no way may one see the end of exile in the current *Ḥurban*. Exile has not been dissolved with the holocaust (*Umkum*) of six million exile Jews. We are still in exile. This is even clearer in the Land of Israel than in other countries. Even the entry of a hundred thousand Jews does not liberate the Land of Israel from exile. More than ever, one must be on guard not to let the concept of redemption, in its historical and religious sense, be inked over. The natural striving of tens of thousands of Jews of the *She'erit Hapeleitah* for the Land of Israel has grown into a holy ecstasy. But the ecstasy should not be transformed by sectarian dreamers into a source for believing that the true redemption has already come to the fields of Zion. It must be learned once again that we are situated between exile and redemption. Today, we should understand more deeply how terrible the exile is for us, in order to [be able to] bring the redemption closer to us through our deeds. We have become living witnesses to the "For a small moment have I forsaken thee" [Isaiah 54:7]. Perhaps we will have the good fortune to experience the moment of "But with great compassion will I gather thee" [Isaiah 54:7].

BIBLIOGRAPHY

Amiel, Mosheh Avigdor. *Am Segulah: Hale'umiut Veha'enoshut Behashkafot Olmah Shel Hayahadut* (*A Treasured Nation: Nationality and Humanity according to Judaism's World View*) (Tel Aviv, 1942–1943).

Bacon, Gershon C. "Birth Pangs of the Messiah: The Reflections of Two Polish Rabbis on Their Era," in *Jews and Messianism in the Modern Era: Metaphor and Meaning*, edited by Jonathan Frankel (Jerusalem, 1991), pp. 86–99.

———. "*Da'at Torah Vehevlei Mashiah: Lishe'elat Ha'idiologiah Shel Agudat Yisrael Bepolin,*" *Tarbits* 52, no. 3 (1983): 497–508.

Baumel, Judith Tydor. "*Esh Kodesh, Sifro Shel Admor Mipiatsetchna, Umekomo Behavanat Hahayim Hadati'im Bageto Varshah,*" *Yalkut Moreshet* 29 (Spring, 1980): 173–187.

Breuer, Yitshak. *Das jüdische Nationalheim* (Frankfurt am Main, 1925).

———. *Der neue Kusari* (Frankfurt am Main, 1934).

———. *Die Welt als Schöpfung und Natur* (Frankfurt am Main, 1926).

———. *Judenproblem* (Frankfurt am Main, 1922).

———. *Messiasspuren* (Frankfurt am Main, 1918).

———. *Moriah: Yesodot Hahinukh Haleumi Hatorati* (Jerusalem, 1944).

Brown, Benyamin. "*Doktrinat 'Da'at Torah': Sheloshah Shelavim,*" in *Derekh Haruah: Sefer Likhvod Eliezer Schweid*, edited by Yehoyada Amir (Jerusalem, 2005), pp. 499–563.

Ehrenreich, Shlomoh Zalman. *Derashot Lehem Shelomoh* (Brooklyn, 1976).

Elberg, Simhah. *Akaydas Treblinka* (Shanghai, 1946).

Elior, Rachel. "The Lubavitch Messianic Resurgence: The Historical and Mystical Background, 1939–1996," in *Toward the Millennium*, edited by Peter Schäfer and Mark Cohen (Leiden, 1998), pp. 383–408.

Greenberg, Gershon. "An Active Messianic Response during the Holocaust: *Mahaneh Yisrael-Lubavitch,*" in *Bearing Witness: 1939–1989*, edited by Alan Berger (Lewiston, Maine, 1991), pp. 141–163.

———. "Assimilation as *Hurban* according to Wartime American Orthodoxy: *Habad Hasidism*" in *Jewish Assimilation, Acculturation, and Accommodation*, edited by Menahem Mor (Lanham, Md., 1991), pp. 161–177.

———. "Elhanan Wasserman's Response to the Growing Catastrophe in Europe: The Role of Ha'gra and the Hofets Hayim upon His Thought," *Journal of Jewish Thought and Philosophy* 8, no. 1 (2000): 1–34.

———. "Holiness and Catastrophe in Simhah Elberg's Religious Thought," *Tradition* 25, no. 5 (November 1991): 39–64.

———. "Holocaust and Musar for the Telsiai *Yeshiva*: Avraham Yitshak Bloch and Eliahu Meir Bloch," in *The Vanished World of Lithuanian Jews*, edited by Stefan Schreiner, Darius Staliunas, and Alvydas Nikzentaitis (New York, 2004), pp. 223–261.

———. "The Holocaust Apocalypse of Ya'akov Mosheh Harlap," *Jewish Studies* 41 (2002): 100–107.

———. "*Le'alter Liteshuvah* for Yosef Yitshak Schneersohn and *Mahaneh Yisrael,*" in *The Habad Movement in the Twentieth Century*, edited by Mosheh Halamish and Yitshak Krauss (Ramat Gan, forthcoming).

———. "Mosheh Avigdor Amiel's Religious Response to the Holocaust," in *Proceedings of the Eleventh World Congress of Judaic Studies*, edited by David Assaf (Jerusalem, 1994), pp. 93–100.

———. "A *Musar* Response to the Holocaust: Yehezkel Sarna's *Liteshuvah Velitekumah* of 4 December 1944," *Journal of Jewish Thought and Philosophy* 7, no. 1 (December 1997): 101–138.

———. "Ontic Division and Religious Survival: Wartime Palestinian Orthodoxy and the Holocaust (*Hurban*)," *Modern Judaism* 14, no. 1 (1994): 21–61.

———. "Redemption after Holocaust according to *Mahaneh Yisrael-Lubavitch*, 1940–1945," *Modern Judaism* 12, no. 1 (February 1998): 61–84.

———. "The Religious Response of Shlomoh Zalman Ehrenreich (Simleul-Silvaniei, Transylvania) to the Holocaust, 1940–1943," *Studia Judaica* 9 (2000): 65–93.

———. "Sect of Catastrophe: *Maḥaneh Yisrael Luba-vitch* 1940–1945," in *Jewish Sects, Religious Movements, and Political Parties*, edited by Menaḥem Mor (New York, 1992), pp. 165–184.

———. "Shlomoh Zalman Unsdorfer, Disciple of the Ḥatam Sofer: With God through the Holocaust," *Yad Vashem Studies* 31 (2003): 61–94.

———. "Sovereignty as Catastrophe: Jakob Rosenheim's *Ḥurban Weltanschauung,*" *Holocaust and Genocide Studies* 8, no. 2 (1994): 202–224.

———. "*Tamim Pa'alo*: Tsimerman's Absolutistic Explanation of the Holocaust," in *In God's Name: Religion and Genocide in the Twentieth Century*, edited by Omer Bartov and Phyllis Mack (Oxford, 2001), pp. 316–341.

Ḥarlap, Ya'akov Mosheh. *Mei Marom: Mima'yenei Hayeshua* (*Waters Sublime: From the Sources of Salvation*)(Jerusalem, 1963).

———. "Le'et Dodim," *Sinai* 11, nos. 4–5 (December 1947–February 1948): 126–138.

Horowitz, Rivkah. "Exile and Redemption in the Thought of Isaac Breuer," *Tradition* 26, no. 2 (Winter 1992): 77–98.

———. *Yitsḥak Breuer: Iyunim Bemishnato* (Ramat Gan, 1988).

Katz, Reuven. *Duda'ei Reuven*, 2 vols. (Jerusalem, 1954).

———. *Sha'ar Reuven: Davar Be'ito* (Jerusalem, 1952).

Landau, Betsalel, and Natan Ortner. *Harav Hakadosh Mibelz: Perakim Letoldot Ḥayav Vehalikhotav Shel Harabi Hakadosh Rabi Aharon Mibelza* (Jerusalem, 1961).

Lebovitsh, Menaḥem Aharon (ed.), *Haderekh: Kollel Derekh Tsadikim* (Budapest, 1944).

Mittleman, Alan. *Kant and Kabbalah: An Introduction to Isaac Breuer's Philosophy of Judaism* (Albany, N.Y., 1990).

Piekarz, Mendel. *Ḥasidut Polin: Megamot Ra'ayoniyot Bein Shetei Hamilḥamot Uvigezerot 700–705* (Jerusalem, 1990), pp. 424–434.

———. *Hateudah Haḥasidit Hasifrutit Ha'aḥironah Al Admat Polin: Divrei Harabi Mipiasetchna Bageto Varshah* (Jerusalem, 1979).

———. "Harabanit Mistropkov Al Havtaḥat Harabi Mibelz Ushetei Hashkafot Sotrot Al Lekaḥ Hagezerot," *Kivunim* 24 (August 1984): 59–73.

———. "Hashkafato Shel R. Mordekhai Rokeaḥ," in *Sifrut Ha'edut Al Hashoah Kimekor Histori, Veshalosh Teguvot Ḥasidiyot Be'artsot Hashoah* (Jerusalem, 2003), pp. 163–177.

Polen, Neḥemiah. "Divine Weeping: Rabbi Kalonymous Shapiro's Theology of Catastrophe in the Warsaw Ghetto," *Modern Judaism* 7, no. 3 (October 1987): 253–269.

———. *Holy Fire: The Teachings of Rabbi Kalonymous Kalman Shapira, the Rebbe of the Warsaw Ghetto* (Northvale, N.J., 1994).

Rakeffet-Rothkoff, Aaron. "Rabbi Reuven Katz: Spiritual Leader on Three Continents," *Tradition* 35, no. 3 (2001): 24–33.

Rokeaḥ, Mordekhai, "Ve'dah Hadevarim *Asher Diber Bekadsho Lifnei Benei Yisrael*" ("These Are the Things Spoken in Holiness before the People of Israel"), in Betsalel Landau and Natan Ortner, *Harav Hakadosh Mibelza: Rabbi Aharon Mibelza* (Jerusalem, 1961).

Sarna, Yehezkel. *Liteshuvah Velitekumah: Devarim She-ne'emru Bakinus Lemasped Uteshuvah Shehitkayem Ba'ir Biyeshivat Ḥevron-Keneset Yisrael Beyom 8 Kislev 5705* (*Toward Penitent Return and Restoration: Words Said at the Gathering for Mourning and Teshuvah in the City [of Jerusalem] in the Ḥevron-Keneset Yisrael Yeshiva on 4 December 1944*) (Jerusalem, 1944), pp. 3–18.

Schindler, Pessaḥ. Introduction to *Em Habanim Semeḥah: Restoration of Zion as a Response during the Holocaust* (Hoboken, N.J., 1999).

———. "Rabbi Yissakhar Teichthal [*sic*] on *Ḥurban* and Redemption," *Tradition* 21, no. 3 (Fall 1984): 63–79.

———. "*Tikkun* as Response to the Tragedy: *Em Habanim Semeḥah* of Rabbi Yissakhar Shlomoh Teichthal [*sic*], Budapest, 1943," *Holocaust and Genocide Studies* 4, no. 4 (1989): 413–433.

———. "Tsiduk Hadin Mitokh Hashoah," *Petaḥim* 55–56 (1981): 42–52.

Schneersohn, Yosef Yitshak. "Kol Kore fun'm Lubavitsher Rabin," *Hakeriah Vehakedushah* 1, no. 9 (26 May 1941): 15–16.

———. "Tsvayter Kol Kore fun'm Lubavitsher Rabin," *Hakeriah Vehakedushah* 1, no. 10 (July 1941): 9–11.

———. "Driter Kol Kore fun'm Lubavitsher Rabin," *Hakeriah Vehakedushah* 1, no. 11 (August 1941): 5–7.

———. "Ferter Kol Kore fun dem Lubavitsher Rabin Shlita," *Hakeriah Vehakedushah* 3, no. 25 (October 1942): 12–13.

Schwartz, Dov. "Erets Vesod: Harav Ya'akov Mosheh Ḥarlap," in *Erets Hamamashut Vehadimyon: Ma'amadah Shel Erets Yisrael Behagut Hatsiyonut Hadatit* (Tel Aviv, 1997), pp. 82–100.

Schweid, Eliezer. "Hasneh Bo'er Ba'esh-Vehasneh Einenu Ukal? Derashot 5700–5702 Shel Ha'admor Mipiasetchna," in *Bein Ḥurban Lishuah* (Tel Aviv, 1994), pp. 105–154.

———. "Hatsad Hanegdi Shel Hamatbea Hahareidit: Hafiḥat-Halev Hatsiyonit Shel Harav Taykhtahl," in *Bein Ḥurban Lishuah* (Tel Aviv, 1994), pp. 89–104.

———. "Hatsdakat Elohim Halakhtit: Ha'idiologiah Hadatit Ha'apokaliptit shel R. Elḥanan Bunem Wasserman," in *Bein Ḥurban Lishuah* (Tel Aviv, 1994), pp. 15–29.

———. "Nes Hahatsalah Shel Harabi MiBelz," in *Bein Ḥurban Lishuah* (Tel Aviv, 1994), pp. 65–88.

———. *"(Siḥat) Hapurim Shel Ha'admor Milubavitch,"* in *Bein Ḥurban Lishuah* (Tel Aviv, 1994), pp. 39–64.

Shapira, Kalonymous Kalman. *Esh Kodesh* (Jerusalem, 1960).

Teichthal, Yissakhar Shlomoh. *Em Habanim Semehah: Restoration of Zion as a Response during the Holocaust* (Hoboken, N.J., 1999). [Note: The name "Teichthal" has been spelled in the previous readings "Taykhtahl" following the principles of translation employed.]

Tsimerman, Ḥayim Yisrael. *"Tamim Pa'alo": She'elot Uteshuvot Bidevar Hahashmadah Ha'iyumah Shel Shishah Milion Hayehudim, Hashem Yinkom Damam* (*"His Work Is Perfect": Questions and Responses concerning the Terrible Destruction of Six Million Jews, May God Avenge Their Blood*) (Jerusalem, 1947).

Unsdorfer, Shlomoh Zalman. *Siftei Shlomoh* (Brooklyn, 1972).

Wasserman, Elḥanan. *Ma'amar Ikvetah Dimeshiḥah* (*Tractate: The Onset of the Messiah*) (New York, 1938).

Part II

ISRAELI RESPONSES DURING AND FOLLOWING THE WAR

INTRODUCTION

Shlomo Biderman

I

Is the Holocaust an "unprecedented event"? Eliezer Schweid, in his essay "Is the *Shoah* a Unique Event?" republished in this anthology,[1] stresses the persistence of this question and argues very convincingly that everyone who studies the *Shoah* should refrain from seeing the extermination of European Jewry as comparable to other accounts of murder or genocide. Schweid identifies a number of elements that establish the uniqueness of the *Shoah*. These include the intent to extirpate a people by the physical slaughter of every one of its members, down to the very last individual; the systematic planning of the destruction; the unparalleled extent of the killing, even when compared with attempts at genocide of other peoples; the total dehumanization of the victims; and the intent to commit genocide not for any specific material, political, or territorial advantages but rather because of the victimized group's putative racial identity.[2] Seconding this view, Pinchas Peli, in an essay also reprinted in this collection, outlines the uniqueness of the Holocaust clearly and sharply, relying on the thought of Emil Fackenheim. He claims that the *Shoah* was unique not only because it was the embodiment of the ugliest, most iniquitous evil in the Western world, but also because it overturned a number of hitherto accepted historical, philosophical, sociological, and anthropological assumptions.[3]

As these two essays suggest, any philosophical or theological discussion of the Nazis' annihilation of European Jewry should lead not only to an examination of the nature of evil as such but also to a revision of the regular ways of speaking about evil, as these have found expression in the annals of Western thought. The more one contemplates the monstrous dimensions of the plan to destroy the Jewish people, the harder it is to miss the uniqueness of these evil deeds, even against the background of other acts of evil. But I believe that Schweid, and Peli before him, both neglect a highly important feature of the uniqueness of the Holocaust. I refer here to the complex and morbid combination, second to none, of capricious arbitrariness and minute design, happenstance and planning, chance and ideology present in the destruction of European Jewry.

On the one hand, the Nazis demonstrated incomprehensible randomness in their Jew killing. One image that indicates this randomness is provided, for example, in a terrifying scene in Roman Polansky's film *The Pianist*. A German SS officer encounters a gang of Jewish prisoners on their way to forced labor. Spontaneously, he orders them to kneel down, and while they obey, he pulls out his pistol and shoots them, head by head, one after the other. He takes no visible pleasure in the deed and has no particular motive; he just kills them for no reason. This randomness—which reflects the actual happenstance of the *Shoah*—was only possible, of course, because of the process of total dehumanization that the Jews underwent in the eyes of the

German. Yet, paradoxically, the annihilation of the Jews revealed consistent pre-meditation, from its abstract ideological basis (in the Nazi racial *Weltanschauung*), down to enforcement on the most individual level. A tight thread ran from Hitler's paranoid preoccupation with "international Jewry" and Himmler's speeches morally justifying the right to kill Jews to the punctilious attention to the schedules of the trains operated by the German railway system, which governed the "shipments" to the death camps.

From a philosophical viewpoint, this apparent inconsistency, these apparent contradictions, highlight the unique feature of the evil that was the *Shoah*. In a way similar to other historical instances of collective brutality, the Germans deprived their victims of their status as human beings; but unlike these other acts of dehumanization, Hitler's negation of the humanity of the individual Jew was invariably intertwined, in the most horrendous manner conceivable, with the attribution of degeneracy to the Jewish people in its entirety. That is, every individual Jew, by virtue of his or her racial character—the "blood" in Nazi parlance—was subhuman. Thus, while the Nazi evil deprived Jews of their status as human beings, it did not invalidate their possession of a distinct, inferior self-identity. The Jew was thus both a subhuman object and an autonomous subject. This double negation was actually vital to the Nazis because it served to justify the annihilation itself, at various levels of abstraction. As such, while the Holocaust is, of course, a "modern" event, it still retains a hidden religious way of thinking: Jews must be exterminated because they all belong to an ethnic group that by virtue of its essential (dangerous, racial) character not only deserves but demands extermination. The "Jew" constructed by Hitler's racial doctrine is both dangerous to the whole of humanity as well as subhuman, belonging to a different order of nature toward which the normal moral obligations that obtain vis-à-vis humankind do not apply.

II

There is no denying that Israeli philosophers and religious thinkers found these bizarre doctrines and beliefs difficult to understand and assimilate. From the time of the establishment of the State of Israel in 1948 until the last decade of the twentieth century, one can sense the severe difficulty felt by Israeli intellectuals in confronting the epistemic and moral problems embodied in and generated by the *Shoah*.[4] The source and nature of this difficulty, however, were not intellectual nor conceptual but rather psychological. Indeed, to follow the philosophical and religious reaction to the *Shoah* in Israel during that period is to learn a lesson in the mechanics of repression.

This repression stemmed from Zionist ideology as understood, interpreted, and implemented during the early decades of Israel's existence as an independent, sovereign country. Zionist ideology, in its various classical forms, sought to establish a unique Israeli identity based on a dialectical synthesis of two opposing factors: traditional Jewish identity, on the one hand, and a vague image of what it understood to be the secular "man of enlightenment," on the other hand. But, in truth, one has good reason to doubt whether Zionism, in practice, ever successfully realized the incarnation of this dialectic pattern. The Zionist principle of the "negation of the diaspora," i.e., the need to end the situation in which Jews lived outside the land of Israel, a dogma taught by classical Zionist thought, was supposed to lead to a sort of Hegelian *aufhebung* (overcoming and synthetic transformation), which would culminate in a new Israeli Jew. In actuality, however, Zionist ideology based the image of the Israeli upon a simple process of negation. If anything, it established the new Israeli primarily through the methodical deconstruction of Jewish history.

Take, for example, the attempt to base Zionist Judaism on a somewhat synthetic version of biblical Judaism, while ignoring the historical authenticity of the diaspora and the two-thousand-year Jewish experience of exile. Consequently, Zionism, as it was cultivated in Israel, essentially recognized the new Israeli Jew as the consummate negation of the "diaspora Jew," and nothing else. It characterized the diaspora Jew as passive, submissive, and wholly at the mercy of circumstances beyond his control. And then, almost stereotypically, it constructed the image of the modern Israeli as the total opposite of what it took to be the traditional image of the diaspora Jew. As Alan Mintz has succinctly put it, "the new kind of Jew ... consciously defined his stance toward the world of power and the question of self-defense as the antithesis of the passive creatures stigmatized in Bialik's *In the City of Slaughter*."[5]

The *Shoah* seems to have supplied cruel support for both the negation of the diaspora Jew and the establishment of the alternative Zionist paradigm of what it is to be an Israeli. Zionist ideology described the *Shoah* as merely another punishing event in the lives (and deaths) of Jews who were unable, untrained, or unwilling to alter the historic and existential reality in which they found themselves. There is no need to go into detail in recalling the intense difficulties of integration that *Shoah* survivors experienced in the Land of Israel. Many survivors felt that Israelis who had not experienced the *Shoah* strongly repressed the entire subject. Indeed, while it was going on, they were involved in building the new Israeli experience. The *Shoah* was seen as a tragedy better left unmentioned, for any discussion would readily lead to recognition of the contrast between the active Israeli Jew, solely responsible for the reality he was building and maintaining, and his polar opposite, the diaspora Jew who, afflicted and subjugated, was carried along by the tide. Some survivors saw no choice but to cooperate with the repressors. The most shocking example of this was that some survivors attempted to remove the tattooed numbers imprinted by the Nazis from their arms. Others were obsessively careful to wear long sleeves, hiding the tattoos from native Israeli eyes.

Repression was not limited to the strange relationship between survivors and older, more-settled Israelis; the sovereign institutions of the emerging State of Israel also declared it openly. The term *Shoah*, used to describe the events in Europe in the 1940s, stems from biblical language: "What will you do about the day of retribution, about catastrophe [*shoah*] that comes from afar?" (Isaiah 10:3), and "There will come upon you suddenly a catastrophe [*shoah*], such as you have never known" (Isaiah 47:11).[6] This word describes misfortune that visits a people from a truly distant place, "from afar," and that falls upon them "suddenly." This adversity comes upon a people (as retribution) without their knowledge of its timing. And it is inevitable. What is more, the *Shoah* was "bequeathed" to the young country's citizens largely through the emphasis on an ethos of heroic acts performed by a small number of Jews in the ghettos and death camps of Europe who, in contrast to the majority of Jewish victims, who were said to have been passive in the face of death, acted as heroes through their active, physical, military opposition to Nazi persecution.

This identification represented more than a scathing denial of the status of European Jews as victims; it also appropriated the Holocaust and identified it with the underground activities of struggle and vigorous opposition. This move created a common bond between those Jewish fighters in Europe and their Israeli counterparts, who at that same time were organizing their own undergrounds and paramilitary frameworks to fight the British and, later, the Arabs. Reflecting on this connection, Dan Laor has noted the analogy between "the miracle of heroism manifested during the uprising in Europe, and the values of bravery and staunch defiance expressed during the War of Independence."[7] And he has called attention to the distinctive formulation of the law adopted by the Knesset, the Israeli Parliament, for the national Memorial Day that was designated as *Yom Hazikaron LaShoah u'La-Gevurah* (Day of Remembrance for the Destruction and the Resistance [to the Nazis]). Regarding this legislation he reminds us that:

> According to a Knesset decision in 1951, each year the 27th day of *Nissan* will be declared a national day of unity with the six million. On this date, between Passover and Israel's Independence Day, inhabitants of the Warsaw ghetto declared their uprising. The choice of this day for remembering the Holocaust, and the conjunction of the terms "Holocaust" [*Shoah*] and "heroism" [*gevurah*], clearly reflects the collective wish to emphasize the place and the value of armed resistance during the *Shoah*. . . .
>
> The connection between the Jewish reality [of the underground that fought the Nazis] in the diaspora and the present-day reality of Israel has strengthened the by-now familiar rejection of the passivity, submissiveness, and surrender associated with the Jewish masses and the official leadership of their communities.[8]

The inner dynamics of these repressive symptoms represent an inability to accept the identity of the Jew as that of a victim, as happened throughout Jewish history in the diaspora, climaxing in the Nazis' destruction of European Jewry. Israeli identity must never again be based on being a victim. A victim cannot be a subject. If most of those killed in the *Shoah* behaved with complete passivity (in other words, if most of the murdered were simply "victims"), then the best way of responding to their plight was avoidance, an ignoring of their situation. Thus, philosophers and intellectuals who accepted the Zionist ethos avoided discussion regarding the question of evil during the Holocaust. Turning Nazi evil into a *Shoah* and then immediately neutralizing this evil through the semantic maneuver of turning the term *Shoah* into "Holocaust and heroism"—the latter term obscuring the former—preempted such a needed discussion and denied the status of subject to those who were destroyed. The Zionist concept of the *Shoah* awarded that position, i.e., the dignity of being a subject, only to those who demonstrated activity, who fought and took fate into their own hands.

Even a cursory glance at these attempts at repression reveals that they were usually followed by an aggressive reaction of moral condemnation. I refer here, in particular, to all those debates, polemics, accusations, and denunciations that branded *Shoah* victims as "sheep taken to the slaughter." Granting esteem to those few who fought the enemy was supposed to facilitate the avoidance of specific reference to the overwhelming majority of European Jews who had seemingly placed their necks on the chopping block. This act of denial, however, did not always succeed. The accusing questions then arose, sometimes indirectly and discreetly but very often so aggressively as to be vulgar: Why did you go like sheep to the slaughter? The rhetorical formulation of this question, as well as the tone in which it was put forward, made it a question that was impossible to answer, especially within the mainstream of the new Israeli society, which essentially maintained a secular way of life. Answering this painful and difficult question was, thus, left to the ultra-Orthodox thinkers, most of whom were also committed ideologically to an anti-Zionist or non-Zionist religiopolitical position.

III

A typical religious justification of the Holocaust that speaks specifically to this issue is given in a significant theological work by Rabbis Yoel Schwartz and Yitzchak Goldstein[9] (excerpted below, pp. 263–273). For them, the proper way to deal with this implied or overt criticism of the Jews of Europe is to stress that the term "victim" is inappropriate in light of what occurred and should be changed to the religious term "sacrifice." This change of terminology radically alters our conception of the situation of those who were murdered and removes the blame and the shame implied in the phrase "like sheep to the slaughter." The deaths of the six million Jews were not meaningless but, rather, had profound religious significance. Those individuals who died should be understood to have given their souls "in sanctification of the Divine name." Utilizing the biblical story of the binding and near-sacrifice of Isaac (as recorded in Genesis 22)—a tale of overwhelming and steadfast religious faith—as their theological model, Schwartz and Goldstein transform the mass murder that occurred into a religious sacrifice of the "slaughtered lamb."

This pattern of justification has been well known and well practiced throughout Jewish history. Recall, for example, the reaction of the Jews of medieval Germany to the brutal demand of the Crusaders that they convert to Christianity or die. According to the Jewish chronicles of that age, whole communities of Jews slaughtered themselves—which included killing their children—in preference to renouncing their Jewish faith. In these chronicles, these actions were not considered suicide. Instead, they were understood to be acts of religious martyrdom.[10] Employing this martyrological explanatory paradigm, Schwartz and Goldstein entitle the section of their book reproduced in translation here " 'Like Sheep to the Slaughter' or '*Kiddush Hashem*'?" (death as a sanctification of God's name). And given this theological presupposition, they go on to conclude their book with the judgment:

> We cannot understand the deeds without relating them to the whole. We must see them against the backdrop of Jewish history, as a direct continuation of the sacrifice of Isaac and the many other sacrifices throughout the ages. . . . Jews have been martyred due to their uniqueness as Jews. The fact that the people of Israel exist in the world enables the Divine presence and the influence of holiness to persist. When a Jew is killed and persecuted just because he is a Jew, this emphasizes the special existence of the people of Israel in the world, and glorifies God's great name.[11]

Given religious explanations such as this, which give religious meaning to the evil manifest in the *Shoah*—and which preserve the traditional Jewish world view—Eliezer Schweid, among others, has argued[12] that the ultra-Orthodox stood up well under the theological test to which they saw themselves subjected. As Schweid tells us:

> Their answers were consonant with the fundamental concern of all theology that justifies the existence of God. This concern is: to derive from the annihilation some assuaging truth that would create renewed energy for belief and hope, and also to show the way along a path of norms and obligations which would rebuild the religious way of life after the annihilation.[13]

And this argument is suggestive, for theology does serve, at least in part, as apologetics and for the purpose of encouraging belief in the face of realities that appear to contradict the basic articles of faith. However, at the same time, one should ultimately treat this claim with caution because it is not certain that Schweid is justified in his estimation of the persuasive power of the ultra-Orthodox theological position, especially because the yardstick he used to measure success or failure is not at all clear. Put as a more general question, Schweid's remarks raise the critical issue: What conditions are necessary and sufficient in order to establish a successful theodicy?

The subject of theodicy reappears with a vengeance in the heated debate, here reproduced, over God's role and presence during the Holocaust, carried on between Alexander Donat, Moshe Unna, and Yehuda Bauer. In contradistinction to Schwartz and Goldstein and other believers, Donat, whose skeptical argument sparked off an intense theological dispute in Israel, concluded that despite all the attempts to maintain a belief in the traditional God of Israel during and after the Holocaust, belief in God's existence is intellectually dishonest. If, Donat argued, there is a God who possesses the traditional attributes ascribed to Him, i.e., He is omnipotent, omniscient, and moral, then He would have stopped the murder of European Jewry. In that He did not, it must be concluded that He does not exist. This radical judgment was passionately opposed by Moshe Unna and was upheld by Yehuda Bauer. Unna defended God's existence and justice—despite the carnage—through recourse to the "free-will defense," i.e., God gives human beings real freedom of action, and this entails its possible misuse as in the Holocaust. Thus, the death camps reflect very badly on human beings rather than on God. In contrast, Bauer sharpened the attack against religious belief, going so far as to describe God as Satan, given what had transpired. In critically evaluating each of these three positions, I would say that each is provocative; none is definitive.[14] As a wise man once noted: To the believers, there are no questions; to the skeptics, there are no answers.

Moreover, whatever the merits of the religious reinterpretation of the Holocaust, such an understanding was not a possible option for most Israelis, who were irreligious and deeply suspicious of traditional religion and its metaphysical claims. For these secular "new Jews" living in the first decades of the essentially secular State of Israel, the "sheep," i.e., the murdered Jews of Europe, lacked the status of subject and had no religious standing. They were simply sheep—a flock whose slaughter created no identity for them and whose fate was, in fact, determined (and perhaps even decreed) because they were a flock of sheep. In particular, the question "Why did you go like sheep to the slaughter?" phrased so aggressively in the secular realm, left no room for a philosophical or theological answer. In fact, it prevented meaningful debate on the profound ontological and moral questions that the annihilation of European Jewry raised. Indeed, it may well be argued that this was one of the main reasons, perhaps even *the* central one, for the resounding silence vis-à-vis the annihilation of European Jewry on the part of the majority of philosophers and theologians active in the intellectual life of the State of Israel. In addition, psycho-sociological explanations of this silence claimed that the proximity to the events prevented discussion: Temporal distance was required in order to deal with the horrors in a more abstract, general, and perhaps even objective fashion. Such explanations carry a certain persuasive power, but nevertheless they are insufficient. They ignore the fact that serious conceptual debate could not take place as long as Israeli theologians, philosophers, and spiritual leaders shared a rigid ideology concerning the characters of both the new Israeli Jew and the diaspora Jew.

The exceptions to this overall consensus bear witness to its power. The most outstanding of these was the poet Natan Alterman, who was, ironically, one of the chief architects of the new Israeli identity. Alterman, despite his Zionist outlook, is the one who dared, as early as nine years after the end of the Second World War, to suggest a minority opinion regarding the meaning of the Holocaust. At that time, his point of view was almost, if not actually, subversive. As readers will see in the selection of his writing republished in this volume, Alterman questioned the moral legitimacy of the accusation "like sheep to the slaughter" directed at the victims. Furthermore, in dealing with this sensitive issue, Alterman chose to focus on the most extreme manifestation of supposedly passive Jewish behavior during the *Shoah*: Jews who went "like sheep to the slaughter" and while doing so were dragged into active cooperation with the Nazis. The Jews he had specifically in mind were the members of the Jewish councils, or *Judenräte*, who had to assist the Nazis in running the ghettos and who, ultimately, had the terrible, overwhelming task of participating in the selection of those Jews slated for deportation to the death camps.[15]

Alterman, in framing his defense of the members of the Jewish Councils, both repudiated the accusations made against them and distanced himself from the prevailing myth of the *Shoah*, which idealized the ghetto fighters' heroism. Instead of calling for absolution for—or providing a narrow defense of—the *Judenräte* members, he demanded a more general conceptual and terminological change in reference to the *Shoah*. His motivation for doing so was to undermine the popular dichotomy, then much in evidence, that divided the Holocaust "into two very different and opposing viewpoints—the *Shoah* (by which is meant resignation) versus the *Gevurah* (by which is meant the uprising); victimhood versus heroism." With his sharp linguistic sense, Alterman recognized that to assign the word "uprising" to what had taken place in several Polish and Russian ghettos was, given the situation in which the ghetto Jews found themselves, to sever this term from its standard context and regular usage and thus from its ordinary meaning. Likewise, those who apparently went "like sheep to the slaughter," or even collaborated with the Nazis, given the coerced situation in which they found themselves, need to have their actions described in a new and different way. And this is because those who condemned the victims, as well as their leaders, did not sufficiently take into account that all these individuals "were forced to make decisions that were outside of human ken and beyond the scope of their authority."[16]

Alterman's dissent, however, was a voice in the wilderness. In the mid-1950s, few supported his call to dispense with the accusation of passivity and collaboration. His was a brave attempt to echo the voices of the survivors, as well as of the victims, not by supplying some justification for their passivity and cooperation but rather by repudiating the accusations as totally unfounded. It took another seven years, until Adolf Eichmann, one of the main Nazi officials responsible for the Holocaust, was apprehended in Argentina and brought to justice in Jerusalem in 1961, for the voices of the survivors to be loudly heard by the Israeli public. During the Eichmann trial,[17] testimonies of *Shoah* atrocities started to become important in and of themselves in the minds of Israeli society. Now they were no longer seen merely as addenda to testimony on acts of heroism, opposition, and revolt.

Yet even then, the theological and philosophical discussion of the fundamental issues raised by the *Shoah* remained largely abandoned. Was it mere happenstance that Alterman was not a theologian or a philosopher, but a poet? I think not. Most of the discussions in Israel dealing with the Holocaust—trying to decode its uniqueness and to evaluate the victims' moral status—have essentially been conducted by poets, novelists, and dramatists. Indeed, the plethora of references to the *Shoah* in the Hebrew literature of the last decades is very well known. Hebrew works of literature, understood in its broadest sense, that center around the *Shoah* by now constitute quite a substantial body of work. Of the many viewpoints from which the *Shoah* can be studied, not a single one remains unexpressed in the totality of modern Hebrew literature. Victims' testimonies, the nature of post-Holocaust life, the manner in which survivors relate to those who perished, the relationships between survivors and the next generation (their children and families), and ethical conflicts in the victims' relationships to their hangmen—e.g., the role of the *Judenräte*, the behavior of Jewish policemen, and the actions of Jewish *kapos* in concentration and death camps—are all subjects found in contemporary literary sources. The last forty years of Hebrew literature treat all of these themes in abundance, and this preoccupation shows no sign of waning. In this way, Hebrew literature serves as a faithful mirror of the deep changes and altered spiritual perspectives that have taken place in the way Israeli society relates to the annihilation of European Jewry. Furthermore, this literature has worked to actively effect and determine these changes, with the emphasis gradually shifting from public to private, from heroic to conflicted, from pathos to ethical considerations, and from ideology and religion to psychology and memory.

Recently, however, encouraged by a project called Jewish Faith after the Holocaust, which is funded by the Memorial Foundation for Jewish Culture—interestingly located in New York City—two major conferences were held in Israel, which have led to a number of important, new contributions by significant Israeli thinkers to this theological debate. Four of these are republished here. The first of these is by Yehoyada Amir. In the opening section of his essay, he explains that theological investigation is meant "to explore the possibility of developing a vocabulary that will enable us to ask questions regarding the significance of our existence in view of the Holocaust and that will provide us with tools to examine what we are obligated to do as educators, as people of culture, and as Jews." To accomplish these goals, he undertakes an original philosophical analysis of the meaning of *Galut*, the traditional Hebrew term for personal and national exile, in the hope that this will provide a helpful way of approaching the conceptual and existential problems posed by the *Shoah*. That is, he feels that the Holocaust needs to be understood as pointing beyond itself to a cosmic-ontological condition of exile that involves even God Himself. This metaphysical alienation, which defines our existence as well as the nature of the universe we inhabit, is inescapable. It can, however, be opposed. In practice, such opposition means struggling against the harsh, even cruel, realities of exile: injustice, poverty, ignorance, and the meaningless suffering of others. Undertaking such activity does not, once and for all, destroy the exile of history and nature, but it makes it possible to live a meaningful human life with dignity.

A second substantive contribution is provided by Yosef Achituv. In his learned essay, he reviews the different theological understandings of the Holocaust expounded in religious Zionist circles over the past six decades. More specifically, he examines how, according to a variety of religious Zionist thinkers, one can still maintain belief in God's presence in human history in the face of the Holocaust. He points out that, in particular, two markedly different, even opposing, analyses of this issue have been given by different groups within the religious Zionist camp. One of these he associates with the (Jerusalem) Merkaz HaRav yeshiva community, which bases its views on the teachings of Rabbi Abraham I. Kook, the mystical first chief rabbi of modern Palestine (who died in 1929), and his son R. Yehuda Zvi Kook. This group responded to the theological challenges posed by the *Shoah* with a "messianic faith and a mystification of Israeli nationalism." For them, Israel's extraordinary victory in the 1967 war with its Arab neighbors, which led to the reunification of Jerusalem under Jewish control and territorial expansion of the State of

Israel, was an unmistakable, overt, sign that God was still at work in contemporary Jewish history and that all of this remarkable military and political activity was leading to the messianic era. The second, alternative, religious Zionist understanding rejects (or mutes) this messianic interpretation of events and, instead, shifts the center of the problem from God to man and emphasizes that human beings, not God, created the death camps, and therefore the Holocaust does not destroy a belief in Divine Providence. Achituv clearly sets out the nature and meaning of these alternative positions while leaving the reader with the obligation to decide for him- or herself which makes the more persuasive case.

The third Israeli conference essay reprinted here was written by Warren Zev Harvey, professor of Jewish philosophy at the Hebrew University of Jerusalem and a well-known scholar of medieval Jewish rationalism. In it, he considers anew the issue of the source of evil and its bearing on the analysis of the murder of European Jewry. In his analysis, he stresses, in the tradition of Maimonides and medieval rationalism, the human and (ir)rational character of evil. Evil, on this reading, is due to human ignorance. In this connection, Harvey has very acute things to say about—and in criticism of—those religious and philosophical thinkers who, in contradistinction to a rationalistic explanation of events, appeal to a mystical view of evil that reifies evil into an independent metaphysical reality. Most important, he correctly points out that the kabbalistic-mystical view holds that evil is not primarily the result of human action but, rather, of uncontrollable negative cosmic forces, and therefore this view leads necessarily "to a severe diminution of human responsibility." While there may be something comforting in this mystical denial, or attribution, of responsibility, this comes at a high price, for it then follows that we can do little or nothing to combat or control it.

Our fourth and last Israeli contribution comes from Shalom Rosenberg, who has recently (2005) retired as professor of Jewish philosophy at the Hebrew University. Like Warren Zev Harvey, he is also a distinguished student of medieval Jewish thought. However, Rosenberg takes a very different approach to the Holocaust. For him, what defines the *Shoah* is its metaphysical mysteriousness and its resistance to philosophical analysis. In particular, he stresses that "the Holocaust means faith in meaning beyond the absurd." In subtle fashion and with wide-ranging erudition, Rosenberg supports this view, emphasizing repeatedly that it is not God and His attributes that should be the focus of our attention after Auschwitz but, rather, the special character and destiny of the Jewish people. In other words, he puts the question of the meaning of Jewish existence—and the continued existence of Judaism—during and after the Holocaust at the very center of his (and our) theological concern. And this is not an inconsequential matter given that the *Shoah* was, in Hitler's terms, about the *Endlösung*, "the final solution to the Jewish problem."

IV

Though I have given a prominent place to the evasion of the issues raised by the *Shoah* by Israeli theologians and philosophers, I would like, with not a little irony, to conclude by noting that in evaluating this subject one needs to remember that the small, new political entity of Israel was home to hundreds of thousands of Holocaust survivors. And for all the active and passive repression of their experiences, their presence and their memories could not be totally ignored. Despite different techniques of evasion, everyone in the country, whether survivor or veteran Israeli, lived in the presence of the long, dark shadow cast by Auschwitz and Treblinka. And everyone in Israel understood that Hitler—with his partner in mass murder, the Grand Mufti of Jerusalem, Hajj Amin Al-Husseini[18]—had intended that the Jews of Palestine no less than the Jews of Europe should be exterminated. Thus, while the Holocaust has not always been a topic taken up publicly by Israeli thinkers—as a consequence of their Zionist ideological presuppositions, among other causes—it in fact provides one of the abiding, unavoidable, repercussive subtexts in almost all areas of life, including most assuredly religious life, in the Jewish state.[19]

Notes

1. Eliezer Schweid, "Is the *Shoah* a Unique Event?" *Iyyun* 37 (1988): 274 [Hebrew]. See pp. 219–229 in this volume.

2. Schweid, "Is the *Shoah* a Unique Event?" p. 276.

3. Pinchas Peli, "Searching for a Religious Language of the *Shoah*," in *Jerusalem: Literary and Philosophical Essays*, edited by A. Zemach and Z. Brameir (Jerusalem, 1976), pp. 105–125 [Hebrew]. See this volume, pp. 245–262.

4. Until the Eichmann trial in 1961, writers of Hebrew literature (both prose and poetry) faced a similar difficulty in their reaction to the *Shoah*. On this, see Alan Mintz's important work *Hurban: Responses to Catastrophe in Hebrew Literature* (New York, 1984). Presenting this difficulty, Mintz quotes the Israeli writer A. B. Yehoshua, who finds it "astonishing to note how persistently Hebrew literature has avoided the subject of the Holocaust, particularly in the decade after the war" (p. 157). But, as we shall see, the Holocaust became a prominent subject in Hebrew literature from the 1970s onward.

5. Mintz, *Hurban*, p. 160.

6. Also "You will not fear sudden terror, nor the catastrophe of the wicked [*shoat reshaim*] when it comes" (Proverbs 3:25). The English expression "Holocaust" has a different meaning, derived from the terminology of biblical ritual. It indicates a sacrificial offering that is completely burned on the altar.

7. Dan Laor, Afterword to Natan Alterman's *On Both Paths: Memos from the Notebook* (Tel Aviv, 1989), p. 118 [Hebrew].

8. Laor, Afterword, pp. 117–118.

9. Yoel Schwartz and Yitzchak Goldstein, *The Shoah: An Anthology on the Destruction of European Jewry, 1939–45, from a Torah Perspective* (Jerusalem, 1987) [Hebrew].

10. Jewish liturgical poetry and histories from the Crusader period contain specific comparisons between the killing, raping, and suicides of that period and the sacrifices of Isaac and of the burnt offerings in the Temple. See A. M. Haberman, *Crusader Decrees* (Jerusalem, 1946) [Hebrew].

11. Schwartz and Goldstein, *The Shoah*, p. 199.

12. Eliezer Schweid, "The Holocaust at the End of the Twentieth Century, from a Theological and Research Perspective," *Madaei ha-yehadut* 39 (1979): 35–49 [Hebrew].

13. Schweid, "The Holocaust at the End of the Twentieth Century," p. 37.

14. I refer readers to Steven T. Katz's critical observations regarding Richard Rubenstein's skeptical position in his introduction to part III of this volume. His observations, with suitable contextual refinement, would also apply to the negative positions articulated by Donat and Bauer.

15. Indeed, in 1955, the District Court of Jerusalem found a Hungarian Jewish leader, Rezso (Rudolf) Kastner, guilty of "cooperating with Satan." He had negotiated with Eichmann regarding the rescue of the Jews of Budapest. For more on this highly controversial trial, see A. A. Biss, *A Million Jews to Save: Check in the Final Solution* (Cranbury, N.J., 1975); Yehuda Bauer, *American Jewry and the Holocaust: The American Joint Distribution Committee, 1939–1945* (Detroit, Mich., 1981); and Rezso (Rudolf) Kastner, ed., *Der Bericht des jüdisches Rettungskomitees aus Budapest, 1942–1945* (Budapest, 1946).

16. Alterman, *On Both Paths*, p. 24.

17. Adolf Eichmann was one of Heinrich Himmler's crucial subordinates in the Nazi murder of European Jewry. For more on Eichmann, his capture by Israeli intelligence agents in Buenos Aires, and his trial in Jerusalem, see Hannah Arendt, *Eichmann in Jerusalem: A Report on the Banality of Evil* (New York, 1964); Israel Harel, *The House on Garibaldi Street* (New York, 1975); Gideon Hausner, *Justice in Jerusalem* (New York, 1966); Moshe Pearlman, *The Capture and Trial of Adolf Eichmann* (New York, 1963); Jacob Robinson, *And the Crooked Shall Be Made Straight: The Eichmann Trial, the Jewish Catastrophe, and Hannah Arendt's Narrative* (Philadelphia, 1965); and Jochen Von Lang, ed., *Eichmann Interrogated* (New York, 1983).

18. The Grand Mufti, Hajj Al-Husseini, entered into a political and ideological pact with Hitler to destroy the Jewish people. He visited Berlin in the spring of 1943 to seal this arrangement. He even asked Hitler to bomb Tel Aviv in late 1942 and 1943 and provided Arab soldiers to fight in the SS. For more on this significant issue, see M. Pearlman, *Mufti of Jerusalem: The Story of Haj Amin el-Husseini* (London, 1947); F. Nicosia, *The Third Reich and the Palestine Question* (London, 1985); and J. B. Schechtman, *The Mufti and the Fuehrer: The Rise and the Fall of Haj Amin el Husseini* (New York, 1965).

19. For a fuller examination of this issue, see Tom Segev's *The Seventh Million: The Israelis and the Holocaust* (New York, 1993).

Eliezer Schweid

Eliezer Schweid was born in Jerusalem in 1929. After high school, he served in the Israeli Defense Force during the War of Independence in 1947 and 1948. After Israel achieved independence in 1948, he joined Kibbutz Tzorah in 1949 and lived as a member of the kibbutz until 1953 when he started his studies at the Hebrew University of Jerusalem majoring in Jewish philosophy, mysticism, and history. In 1962, he received his Ph.D. from Hebrew University for a thesis on medieval Jewish philosophy. He then became a member of the faculty of Hebrew University and also, between 1976 and 1986, taught at the Kerem Institute for Teacher Training, an innovative program that emphasized both Jewish and humanistic values. He has also held several visiting appointments, at Stanford University in 1982, at Oxford University in 1989, and at Yale University in 1992–1993. In 1994, Schweid was awarded the Israel Prize, Israel's highest public academic honor.

A prolific author, he has published numerous books and essays on the history of Jewish culture, the history of Jewish thought from biblical to modern times, Jewish national and Zionist philosophy, the social philosophy of the Jewish labor movement, modern Hebrew literature, and the philosophy of education. In addition, he has been one of the few Israeli philosophers to address the philosophical challenge posed by the uniqueness and significance of the *Shoah*, and to study Jewish theological responses to the *Shoah*.

SELECTIONS

In the first of the two essays by Eliezer Schweid included here, "Is the *Shoah* a Unique Event?" he offers an extended critique of Emil Fackenheim's presentation of the Holocaust as an unprecedented and exceptional event that stands apart philosophically from other genocides in its creation of "another planet." Though he agrees with Fackenheim that we need to study the *Shoah*, Schweid takes issue not only with Fackenheim's findings but, in particular, with his philosophical methodology. Schweid notes that Fackenheim asserts that the *Shoah* was a "*refutation* of the history of Western culture" in that, based on the "understanding of culture and history" preceding the destruction of European Jewry, the events that followed were unexpected, even unthinkable. However, this only means that our understanding of the historical realities were incorrect because, logically speaking, the *Shoah* can only have been a product of its culture. For Schweid, Fackenheim's findings are invalid because they emerge from the same "groundless philosophy" as those which he attempts to critique. Alternatively, Schweid emphasizes that the *Shoah* does not represent "another planet" entirely separate from and unrelatable to our own—although its victims may have experienced it as such—but is, rather, an extreme (and perhaps in some aspects unique) event that can and must be compared to other historical genocides using the same methods of study and evaluation.

In his second essay, "Does the Idea of Jewish Election Have Any Meaning after the Holocaust?" Schweid engages the elemental yet problematic issue of Jewish "chosenness," i.e., Israel's having been selected by God for some type of special spiritual mission, in a post-Holocaust reality. He sees this issue as being especially significant because he considers it "the root of the insoluble dispute" regarding anti-Semitism and Jewish otherness.

Schweid begins his substantive discussion of "chosenness" by noting that prior to the Holocaust many Jews in the modern era focused on working for their cultural and political acceptance within the majority culture—although this did not work, hence the "failure of humanism"—and viewed this effort as "itself a struggle for the realization of the universal mission of the Jews to humankind." Coinciding with this struggle for political and cultural inclusion in the nations of the diaspora, Zionism, in its own way, also emerged as another, distinctive form of Jewish mission but one which, after the Holocaust, dealt a massive blow to the goal of assimilation and "united the survivors of the Holocaust into a 'covenant of destiny' marked by the establishment of the State of Israel." Interestingly, in Zionism—at least for secular Zionists—the particular mission of the unique Jewish people was simply that of normalization. Yet normalization is a goal that, as Schweid notes, makes itself obsolete upon completion. (Parenthetically, for Schweid, the success of Israel during the Six Day War in 1967 proved that the process of the normalization of the Jewish people envisioned by Zionist thinkers was successful.) Moreover, in becoming "a nation like all other nations," the Jewish people was losing sight of its "covenantal values" and special mission. Despite this, Schweid contends that the Jewish people do indeed still have a "covenant of destiny" as a chosen people, and he advises the State of Israel to try to "preserve its identity as a Jewish state," meaning both a state in which Jews are the majority population and one that reflects Jewish values and traditions. Even today, even after Zionism's success in creating a Jewish state, total normalization is not the true Jewish mission. Indeed, if normalization is carried forward completely and successfully, it will cause the disappearance of the Jewish people. Therefore, the Jewish people need to revitalize the special theological (covenantal) message that has provided and energized their unique self-identity over time.

The first article by Eliezer Schweid reprinted here has been translated especially for this collection. It originally appeared in the Israeli philosophy journal *Iyyun* 37 (1988): 271–285. To date, the article by Schweid is one of the few articles discussing the *Shoah* to appear in *Iyyun*. The second essay being republished was prepared for a conference on Jewish Theology after Auschwitz, sponsored by the Memorial Foundation for Jewish Culture and held in Ashkelon, Israel, in 1999.

Selected Bibliography

Books and Articles by Eliezer Schweid

Israel at the Crossroads (Philadelphia, 1973).
The Solitary Jew and His Judaism (Tel Aviv, 1974) [Hebrew].
Israel's Faith and Culture (Jerusalem, 1976) [Hebrew].
A History of Jewish Thought in Modern Times (Jerusalem, 1977) [Hebrew].
The Land of Israel: National Home or Land of Destiny (Rutherford, N.J., 1985).
"Justifying Religion in Light of the *Shoah*," *Yehadut Zmaneinu* 5 (1988): 3–24 [Hebrew].
"The *Shoah* at the End of the Twentieth Century: A Theological and Research-Oriented
    Perspective," in *Madei Ha-yehadut* 59 (1998): 35–49 [Hebrew].

Articles about Eliezer Schweid

"The Thought of Eliezer Schweid: A Symposium," *Immanuel* 9 (Winter 1979): 87–102.

Oppenheim, Michael. "Eliezer Schweid: A Philosophy of Return," *Judaism* 37 (Winter 1986): 66–77.

———. "Paths of Return: The Concept of Community in the Thought of F. Rosenzweig and E. Schweid," in *Community and the Individual Jew: Essays in Honor of Lavy M. Becker*, edited by Ronald S. Aigen and Gershon D. Hundert (Philadelphia, 1986), pp. 171–183.

———. "The Relevance of Rosenzweig in the Eyes of His Israeli Critics," *Modern Judaism* 7 (May 1987): 193–206.

———. "Eliezer Schweid," in *Interpreters of Judaism in the Late Twentieth Century*, edited by Steven T. Katz (Washington, D.C., 1993), pp. 301–324.

Is the *Shoah* a Unique Event?

Since the end of the Second World War, witnesses and researchers have made massive efforts to collect detailed information about the *Shoah*, to study it from every possible angle, to describe its contributing causes, to analyze the motivations of individuals and groups involved, and even to draw conclusions. Researchers from many fields of the social sciences and humanities have taken part in these efforts: historians, sociologists, jurists, political scientists, and psychologists, as well as writers, poets, and artists. For some of these individuals, the *Shoah* is the focus of their thought, research, and creative endeavors. Questions that might otherwise not have been articulated have been raised and addressed from a philosophical perspective, and professional philosophers have certainly taken part in the conversation. But as is typical of the approach of methodical, precise

philosophical analysis, studies of the *Shoah* are characterized by particularly strong inhibitions,[1] even while they reveal a disproportionate focus on theodicy, questions of faith, and analysis of the role of religion in these historical events.

For any topic that demands a focusing of philosophical analysis, internal struggle will mark the beginning of creativity. This also holds true in the case of *Shoah* studies, where internal conflicts surface as inhibitions. Therefore in order to provide a basis for philosophical study of this subject, analysis must start with the inhibitions. What deters methodical philosophical study of the *Shoah*? Here the topic in question must be taken into consideration. The various disciplines of the social sciences and humanities all base their research on philosophical assumptions. But philosophical study worthy of the name on a specific historical

---

1. Inhibition is expressed first and foremost in the fact that theoretical responses of philosophers to the *Shoah* began many years after World War II. Of course, it is not difficult to find philosophers who dealt with the *Shoah* outside philosophical theory, but it is highly significant that Jewish philosophers and theologians who were at the height of their creative activity during the *Shoah*, and who were definitely involved personally in the events of the *Shoah*, such as Buber, Heschel, Strauss, Levinas, and Soloveitchik, did not relate to the *Shoah* as a unique topic for philosophical and theological study. Thus, the most illustrative example is that of Emil Fackenheim, a Holocaust survivor. Today, as I shall argue below, the *Shoah* is at the center of his philosophical theories, although his treatment of the topic began twenty years after the end of the Second World War. Those were not twenty years of silence. During

that period, Fackenheim persevered in formulating a theological-philosophical doctrine on neo-Kantian and neo-Hegelian foundations, in other words, on the foundations of a philosophical-idealistic school which he later argued was refuted by the *Shoah*. Finally, Fackenheim's example, while it is especially remarkable, is not exceptional. Today we can count a sizable number of philosophers and theologians for whom the *Shoah* stands at the center of their philosophical and theological interest, such as Richard Rubenstein, Eliezer Berkovits, Andre Nehar, Ignaz Maybaum, Yitzhak (Irving) Greenberg, Jean Amery, Arthur Cohen, Steven T. Katz, and a long and respectable list of Christian theologians, especially in the United States. All of these, however, came to the study of the *Shoah* after the twenty-year mark and after focused study of other topics.

topic requires an accumulation of knowledge in various disciplines as well as enough mental distance to provide perspective while still permitting some connection to the events. The deep involvement of the *Shoah* generation clearly precludes their having the necessary distance.

Possibly, members of that generation do not allow themselves the perspective of distance since they perceive personal involvement as an absolute moral duty imposed upon them.[2] In taking the first steps toward viewing the *Shoah* as a non-unique event, inhibition rears its head immediately, resulting in two opposite philosophical formulations with identical results: (a) The *Shoah* is exceptional in an absolute way; it is so unprecedented and unique that it cannot be compared to any other previous event, and therefore it cannot be scrutinized according to philosophical generalizations and distinctions;[3] (b) despite its being exceptional and unique, the *Shoah* does not raise any unique philosophical or theological questions.[4]

From the philosophical point of view, an especially typical expression of this is Hannah Arendt's famous declaration regarding the "banality of evil."[5] This is a clever attempt to equate paradoxical depth with a banal response. But the great storm of philosophical reflection that followed may indicate that philosophical depth may be present behind this retreat into banality due to failure to discover significance in "absolute evil." The same conclusions could be reached, and were reached after the fact, from events less exceptional and less terrible. Thus exceptionality, even when it is total, does not add meaning to what is already known, and its lack of unique meaning is the reason behind insistence on its banality. This is the rule in the responses of fundamentalist theologians who write from a *ḥaredi* [ultra-Orthodox] viewpoint. In their view, the *Shoah*, for all its unprecedented terrors in the troubled history of the Jews, raised no theological question that had not been raised and resolved already.[6]

2. The conflict between the need to feel a direct link with the Holocaust that should not be severed and the need for distancing oneself in order to gain the perspective necessary for creativity is also recognized as a difficult problem by artists who deal with the *Shoah* in their work. The question of whether and how it is possible to give artistic/aesthetic expression to the *Shoah* occupies the artists and their critics to a great extent. See Alvin H. Rosenfeld, *A Double Dying: Reflections on Holocaust Literature* (Bloomington, Ind., 1980); Elie Wiesel, "Art and Culture after the Holocaust," in *Auschwitz: The Beginning of a New Era?* edited by Eva Fleischner (New York, 1977); Laurence L. Langer, "The Writer and the Holocaust Experience," in *The Holocaust: Bureaucracy and Genocide*, edited by Henry Friedlander and Sybil Milton (New York, 1980).

But in the realm of artistic creation, the problem is solved within the process of creation itself and through the unique methods of expression that the artist creates. This is not only because of the unmediated drive to create and the liberating and revivifying therapeutic value embodied in the process, but also because the struggle to find an appropriate means of expression is an inseparable part of the process of expression itself. Therefore the emotional conflict is solved by the creative achievement that enables the artist to be deeply and directly involved while at the same time allowing for the distance necessary for creativity. This avenue seems blocked to the scientist and philosopher. The depth of the problem is apparent when we observe that a phi-

losopher such as Fackenheim, who placed the *Shoah* at the center of his attention, attempted to propose a solution that parallels that of artists through his unique methodology of philosophizing from within a position of involvement. See Emil Fackenheim, *To Mend the World* (New York, 1982), pp. 1–31.

3. Alan Rosenberg was the first to identify the pitfalls of this position. See his "The Philosophical Implications of the Holocaust," in *Perspectives of the Holocaust*, edited by Randolph Braham (The Hague, 1983), pp. 1–19.

4. David Sidorsky, "Secular Theodicy and Historical Evidence," *Holocaust and Genocide Studies* 1 (1986): 265–277.

5. Hannah Arendt, *Eichmann in Jerusalem* (New York, 1983). This book aroused strong repercussions and wide argument. It demonstrates to a large degree the challenge to the awakening of a philosophical discussion on the *Shoah*, following Eichmann's trial. See also Gershom Scholem's response, "Letter to Hannah Arendt: 'Is There Anything to It?'" in his *Devarim be-go* (*Explications and Implications*), ed. Abraham Shapira (Tel Aviv, 1975), pp. 91–96.

6. There is a spectrum of Orthodox views. But the differences are all within the framework of traditional theological views, ranging from "hiding His face" to the determination that the *Shoah* was a punishment for the sins of the majority of Jews. Lately, the argument has been advanced that the *Shoah* brings no new challenge to theology. See Immanuel Jakobovits, "Religious Responses to the Holocaust," *L'Eylah* 25 (April 1988): 2–7.

In any case, these two positions invite philosophical reflection because they communicate, in either an overt or implied manner, that it is unnecessary or superfluous to wrestle with the question. The second explicitly says that we have examined the issue and arrived at the conclusion that no unique problem stands before us for philosophical study. The first admits of the possibility that the topic requires philosophical confrontation, but evades it, saying that we do not have the tools for philosophical discussion of a phenomenon that is sui generis and deviates so completely from everything previously known to us. It is clear that if the assertion of the banality of evil is a conclusion whose opponents are the only ones who can be drawn into philosophical reflection about it, then the first argument can serve as the initial step in a dialectic process, whether through a new philosophical "breakthrough" or through reexamination of the argument that the *Shoah* was a completely aberrant, unprecedented, and incomparable event. This assertion is the first subject that requires philosophical study based on scientific findings, and the answer to this question will determine whether the study should continue, and if so, on what topics and in what areas.

We will begin by citing a fact obvious to all readers of the wide-ranging literature on the *Shoah*: Philosophers have no monopoly on the question of whether the *Shoah* was a completely aberrant, unprecedented event that cannot be compared with any other historical or contemporary occurrence, or whether it can be discussed together with other attempts at genocide, especially with contemporary outbreaks of mass killing. Almost everyone who studies the *Shoah* addresses this question seriously,[7] for several reasons. First, studying the details of this event put all who attempt to confront it through the severest of emotional and intellectual tests. Second, the unmediated response of *Shoah* witnesses and survivors, who saw and suffered acts that could not be predicted and whose substance could not be digested in their consciousness, is transferred to researchers and students who did not experience the *Shoah*. Finally, many attempts have been made to blur and evade responsibility by placing the *Shoah* into a "framework" of "war crimes" which are considered "normal," and *Shoah* witnesses and researchers are justifiably sensitive to such attempts. Their sensitivity is vehement and expressed through passionate opposition to attempts at blurring and evasion, as well as to honest attempts at theorizing. This is because putting the *Shoah* into a comparative framework, even if the comparison is with the gravest and most shocking of crimes, can be seen as willingness to understand, accept, or acknowledge the Holocaust as "human," or even to forgive. For the victims, and for those researchers who adopt their point of view, the only legitimate response is complete refusal to consider these acts as within the range of human behavior, or included in what is called "humanity." The perpetration of these acts means that the borders of humanity, as known to us throughout history, were breached by something foreign, and we humans lack the tools to understand it.

7. This was a convention that was practically self-evident for Jewish researchers of the *Shoah*. It expressed the feeling of the generation of *Shoah* survivors that what happened exceeded the worst evil that could have been expected from humanity, even considering that the history of the Jews was full of calamity and disaster. The writings of Shaul Asch, one of the first researchers on the *Shoah*, are characteristic of this view. He emphasized the unique methodological difficulties connected to scientific research on the *Shoah* and took into consideration such issues as research tools and problems of emotional involvement. See his *Iyyunim Beḥeker Hashoah Veyehadut Zmanenu* [*Studies in Research on the Shoah and Contemporary Judaism*] (Jerusalem, 1973). Most *Shoah* researchers repeat such assertions and caveats in the introductions to their books. The approach of non-Jewish researchers is somewhat different. They understand the *Shoah* first as one of the subtopics in historical research on the Second World War, or on modern totalitarianism in general and the Nazi regime in particular. In this way, conflict arises between the approaches of researchers whose basic assumptions differ in their starting points and purpose. Certainly, those who consider the Second World War and Nazi totalitarianism as background to the *Shoah* assume the centrality of the Holocaust as well as its conspicuousness as an aberrant event that cannot be subsumed as a component within a wider historical process. On the other hand, those who consider the *Shoah* as one result of the Second World War and Nazi totalitarianism assume that the Holocaust is not central and place it among the crimes that are usually committed during war by tyrannical regimes. See Lucy S. Davidowicz, *The Holocaust and the Historians* (Cambridge, Mass., 1981).

We can argue that philosophical discussion is both necessary and impossible,[8] especially because of the last factor, which presents the *Shoah* as unprecedented and unique in an absolute sense. If the factors we indicated in the beginning form an assertion that is tested empirically, this last factor presupposes vis-à-vis the empirical test a certain assumption about the reality that is being empirically described. Again, we will be unable to accurately interpret the facts if we cannot decipher that unique reality called "absolute." At any rate, those who raise this question must first confront it on the empirical-scientific plane, mainly because of the last factor.

Undoubtedly, the *Shoah* was the execution of a plan for the murder of an entire people in the most exhaustive manner. As such, did the *Shoah* deviate from the category of "genocide," as some claim? To address this question, we must first examine whether and how the *Shoah* deviated from all other such plans, which are acknowledged as not uncommon in the history of mankind; the history of Western civilizations and modern times proffer numerous examples.[9] First and foremost, this examination is scientific, empirical, and comparative, although it certainly includes the possibility of concluding that the *Shoah* is significantly different in every aspect.

Those who consider the *Shoah* to be an aberrant and unprecedented event in an absolute sense point to the following facts:[10] (1) During the Holocaust, there was an intent to murder by undermining the foundations of the Jewish people's existence as well as physically destroying all of its individuals, down to the very last one. (2) During the *Shoah*, a systematic, exacting, and comprehensive plan was implemented in order to carry out this intent. (3) Implementation of this plan reached a stage so advanced that the result was aberrant in the quantitative sense as well; witness the colossal number of victims. (4) As far as the underlying motivation is concerned, the *Shoah* differs from all other plans for genocide. This was a plan to destroy the Jewish people as Jews. The Nazis murdered the Jews not for material interest or as part of a struggle for survival, usual pretexts for nations to destroy their enemies, and not because of their religious views, the usual pretext for religious organizations to destroy competitors or heretics. During the *Shoah*, Jews were murdered not for their deeds or omissions, not for their beliefs, and not because of competition between them and their murderers, but only due to the fact of their Jewish origin. In summary, genocide took place during the *Shoah* out of "purely" ideological motivations. (5) Prior to the methodical attempt to murder their victims, the Nazis tried to destroy their humanity by making them victims of the cruelest and most degrading torment possible.

Cautious and critical researchers who claim that the *Shoah* was an aberrant and unprecedented event (such as the historian Yehuda Bauer in his later work) admit that some of the above elements

---

8. See Alan Rosenberg's article, "The Philosophical Implications of the Holocaust," already cited.
9. A variegated body of literature has appeared since the Second World War on the phenomenon of genocide, especially dealing with twentieth-century examples. The numerous examples of genocide represent a major problem central to modern history, an inseparable part of the syndrome of modernity, which the family of nations must cease evading and must confront. First and foremost among the philosophers who have studied the significance of the *Shoah* against this background is Richard L. Rubenstein, who finds the root of the problem deep in the foundations of Western civilization and its Judeo-Christian ethos. He even tries to describe what appear to him as forms of sociopolitical organization and the ethos associated with them, which lead to the phenomena of destruction of whole population groups, not by foreign governments but by the governments of those very populations. Rubenstein is not alone in that view, but he is the most extreme proponent of the historical-philosophical premises underlying it. See Richard L. Rubenstein, *The Cunning of History* (New York, 1975); Rubenstein, *The Age of Triage* (Boston, 1983); Rubenstein, "Anticipation of the Holocaust in the Political Sociology of Max Weber," in *Western Society after the Holocaust*, edited by Lyman H. Legers (Boulder, 1982); Henry Friedlander and Sybil Milton, eds., *The Holocaust: Ideology, Bureaucracy, and Genocide* (New York, 1980); Leo Kuper, *Genocide: Its Political Use in the Twentieth Century* (New Haven, Conn., 1981).
10. Yehuda Bauer, *The Holocaust in Historical Perspective* (Seattle, Wash., 1978); Bauer, "On the Place of the Holocaust in History," *Holocaust and Genocide Studies* 2 (1987): 209–220; Raul Hilberg, "The Anatomy of the Holocaust," in Friedlander and Milton, *The Holocaust*, pp. 85–94; and idem., "The Significance of the Holocaust," pp. 95–104.

are common to other attempts at genocide. But these characteristics appear in their most concentrated, exclusive, and distilled form only in the Nazis' attempt to destroy the Jewish people on the basis of Nazi ideology. If we can postulate a continuum of plans for genocide that have taken place throughout history, the *Shoah* would be located at the end of this continuum, as the most extreme embodiment of the meaning of the term "genocide" vis-à-vis its planning and execution. Therefore the Holocaust must be described as aberrant and unique even on this continuum.

Indeed, we can place this last assertion on the border of philosophical reflection whose role is not only to state the facts but also to evaluate them. It seems that the argument made by philosophers, which also relies on those empirical considerations, is presented in a different manner from the outset. I will discuss below a contention proposed by the philosopher Emil Fackenheim. According to him, not only does the *Shoah* demand philosophical inquiry, but it is also a "philosophical event," or an event requiring fundamental analysis and perhaps a complete revolution in the discipline of philosophy, as it has developed in Western culture up until the Second World War.[11]

Fackenheim develops his argument in three stages. In the first stage, he uses accumulated historiographic data as "scientific" proof for the determination that the *Shoah* cannot be compared to any previous event of mass murder or genocide. The *Shoah* is "unprecedented" and an absolute "exception," and from this viewpoint it is a category unto itself among historical events. Yet Fackenheim does not attempt to use this bold assertion to remove the *Shoah* from the continuity of historical developments in Western civilization. On the contrary, for him, this unprecedented exception becomes a central historical event that forces us to go back and examine the fundamentals of history in their entirety, both because an "exception" that took place can repeat itself, and also because this exception took place against the background of all that preceded it in Western history. If so, we have here an exception that proves the rule, and this assertion contains a problematic tension.

In the second stage of his argument, Fackenheim claims that the *Shoah* as a historical event is a form of *refutation* of the history of Western culture. The exceptionality of the *Shoah*, which is undoubtedly related to core elements of the social fabric in the European states and in Western culture, contradicted everything that the creators of culture and leaders of history knew about themselves, including the culture they represented and at whose helm they stood. Everything that society and Western culture before the *Shoah* thought about itself was revealed to be fundamentally refuted, because the *Shoah* occurred in opposition to everything expected according to the self-consciousness of that culture. Herein lies the depth of significance of the above-mentioned expression that the *Shoah* was a "philosophical event." The fact that the *Shoah* occurred refutes the philosophy that developed beforehand in Western culture. On the one hand, philosophy did not predict the *Shoah* and did not take into account the possibility of its happening as an outgrowth of Western cultural history; but on the other hand, it did not make the *Shoah* truly preventable. Such a philosophy, claims Fackenheim (and this is a most radical and explicit assertion) cannot be true, and his statement can be interpreted as placing some of the blame on Western philosophy of the past. In other words, philosophy's guilt is in its refutation. If so, we need another philosophy that incorporates the lesson of the *Shoah* into the depths of Western culture and that formulates a culture in which an event like the *Shoah* will no longer be within the realm of possibility.[12]

11. Emil L. Fackenheim, "Holocaust," in *Contemporary Jewish Religious Thought*, edited by Arthur A. Cohen and Paul Mendes-Flohr (New York, 1987). In its Hebrew translation, the title of this article reveals his underlying assumption: *Hashoah Keirua Haser Takdim Behistoria, Bephilosophia Ubeteologia* ["The *Shoah* as an Unprecedented Event in History, Philosophy, and Theology"], *Da'at* 15 (5745): 121–129. [Selections from Emil Fackenheim's work appears in part III of this collection.]

12. The assertion that the *Shoah* is a general refutation of the foundations of philosophy (and religion) is developed in Fackenheim's concluding work, *To Mend the World*. In this book, he also makes the statement that one criterion for any philosophy possible after the *Shoah* is the transformation of events like the *Shoah* into

The third step is implementation of the conclusion, or searching for a starting point beyond the history of the refuted philosophy, in order to develop a different philosophical method that is suitable for its purpose. Fackenheim tried to formulate such a position in his concluding work on the topic of the *Shoah*, *To Mend the World*. Of course, at this point the problem latent in the preceding steps arises in the fullness of its severity: We cannot anchor a philosophical method which is to serve as a true cultural conscience on the basis of the refuted pre-*Shoah* philosophy. Neither can we base a new philosophy on the *Shoah*, because it is exceptional, incomprehensible, and a complete negation of morality and culture. Therefore, we certainly cannot derive any positive philosophy from within it. So we find ourselves dependent in our research and philosophical study on the future that has yet to be created and for whose creation we need the guidance of a new philosophy in the here and now. This is the question that Fackenheim has great difficulty facing in the introduction to his above-mentioned book: What will be the positive basis and method of the philosophy that is to replace that which he believes was refuted?

Clearly, the way that Fackenheim as a philosopher interprets the assertion of the *Shoah*'s uniqueness is different from the way that historians such as Yehuda Bauer interpret that assertion. This is already recognized in Fackenheim's method of argument on the historiographic-scientific plane. They do overlap insofar as they identify the facts that, in his opinion, set the

Shoah apart from every previous attempt at mass murder or genocide. But his manner of argument is remarkably different, as revealed in the philosophical assertion of the second stage. Fackenheim describes the targeted attempt to destroy the Jewish people on the sole basis of its biological origin, by destroying all of its elements and through a preliminary process of dehumanization that magnified the murder and denied the victims the final human right to die their own deaths.[13] He shows how this process transformed the political, social, cultural, and individual psychological reality of Germany and the occupied countries into "another planet." To a known extent, this "planet" also included the other Western countries that cooperated with the Nazis by abstaining from active objection to murder. In other words, Fackenheim's assertion as a philosopher is that the *Shoah* created a *comprehensive* human reality. In its completeness, purpose, and modes of behavior, this reality was totally different from everything we knew as part of human reality before the *Shoah*. Indeed, it was the *total opposite* of everything known to us previously about human reality. Human culture, with all its faults and failures, is directed toward life and its creation, but the *Shoah* created a comprehensive reality all of whose components were directed to the opposite purpose: creating death.[14]

This assertion of total uniqueness and complete separateness grounds the philosophical assertion of the *Shoah* as a philosophical event. Fackenheim shrinks from the possibility of applying to the Nazi regime a philosophy of its own,

impossibilities. In this context, what Fackenheim calls the "614th commandment," ensuring the existence of the Jewish people in order to prevent Hitler from victory after his failure and death, he understands as an ethical-religious *mitzvah*, as well as the basis of his new philosophical methodology. In his eyes, it seems to be equivalent to Descartes's *cogito*; see especially the seventh section of the introduction of *To Mend the World*.

13. During his search for that which most clearly and decisively expresses the unique dimension of the *Shoah* that completely differentiates it from every previous case of mass murder, Fackenheim identified distinctions between methods of killing, marking the degree of cruelty and extent of the murder as well as the significance of death itself. Beyond the dehumanization of victims before their murder, Fackenheim identifies the phenomenon of the *Muselmann* as a

completely "original contribution" of the Nazi. This is a person who has died a spiritual death before his physical death, one whose humanity has died, and whose physical death therefore takes place in the absence of his individuality as a person. He was denied the natural right given every creature to die "his own death" (in other words, to relate to the fact of his death when it occurs, even when death arrives by an external factor). As such, at Auschwitz even death took on an unnatural and completely unique dimension. Yet we must admit that the significance of the phrase "the right to die his own death," from the subjective point of view of the victim, remains far from clear.

14. As will be recalled, Fackenheim asserts that the entire Nazi machine worked toward one goal: the creation, maintenance, and operation of death camps for the creation of death. As demonstrated in the previous

a "conscience of the cultural planet" that they created. To him, the term *philosophy*, like the term *culture*, is too positive and honorable a term to use regarding the Nazis. At most, he thinks, they had an "ideology," which also bears witness to inferiority and intellectual worthlessness. The description of "planet Auschwitz" as being a total environment with its own methodology leads to the conclusion that it represents "antihuman reality" or "antihuman culture," directed by a comprehensive and consistent way of thinking in a specific manner that can be defined in this terminological continuum as "antiphilosophy." In other words, Nazi ideology was a type of thought that reverses the characteristics and methods of philosophy and serves as their parallel in the negative.

At the foundation of this conception lies the assumption that for every cultural-historical reality there is a spiritual infrastructure defined by a comprehensive world view, expressed by philosophy at its highest level. Alternatively, historical reality in its formation identifies this world view with the history of the spirit, and philosophy, according to this method, is the spirit that knows itself.[15] This view clearly leads to the conclusion that the *Shoah* was an event in the history of the spirit. It was an antispiritual type of spiritual reality, the historical embodiment of complete spiritual perversion. In this is located its uniqueness as "another planet": For the first time in the history of the human race, the *Shoah* realized a spirituality of antispirituality, a culture of anticulture, and a philosophy of antiphilosophy. It is the perfect antihumanity, and that is its true uniqueness. This clarifies the intent of the asser-

tion that the *Shoah* was a philosophical event. In its essence, the *Shoah* is a problem that philosophy must solve within itself, if we are to free ourselves from it and create a new world in which it is avoidable.

Of course, we can agree with such an assertion only if we accept Fackenheim's understanding of the nature of philosophy and the nature of the relationship that exists between philosophy, culture, and history. His understanding is ostensibly a classic idealistic view, in the tradition of the German, especially Hegelian, schools of philosophy. Paradoxically, if we accept this view, then we cannot accept his argument that the *Shoah* disappointed or completely refuted the philosophy that developed in the period preceding it. This is because the body of his argument is grounded, in method and in substance, on the basic assumptions of that same groundless philosophy. Close examination will show that this fact is the source of the philosophical trap into which Fackenheim places himself with his radical assertion that the *Shoah* as a philosophical event refutes the philosophy preceding it. How can we transcend this assertion to create a new foundation for a different philosophy, if we assume that the philosophical foundation for refuting all of philosophy is also groundless? Such a complete refutation leaves no foundation for any kind of philosophical creation! In retrospect, in order for Fackenheim to succeed in creating a foundation for a new philosophy, one of *tikkun olam* [mending the world], he had to correct (although he did not completely admit it) his radical stance. He had to reformulate the foundations of the philosophical and idealistic world view he held

footnote, [this type of] death was also different, in an existential sense, from all natural death. Of course, in this description, he does not present the act from the point of view of Nazi ideology. That ideology held that its goal was "purification" of the German people from foreign and undesirable elements, to further its national/racial success. Creation of death is the purpose embodied in the operation of the mechanism, and of course it is interpreted as such by the victims.

15. Fackenheim proposes in fact that there is a philosophical infrastructure underlying his views, when he describes his development as a philosopher before and after the *Shoah* in the introduction to his methodological and concluding work, *To Mend the World*. It is revealing that

in this summary, he fails to mention that his confrontation with the renewal of the foundations of Jewish belief against a background of neo-idealistic philosophy did not take place, chronologically, before the *Shoah*, but rather afterward. In the first stage of his development as a philosopher, he worked on resolving differences created in philosophical and theological thought through modern philosophical and theological criticism entirely unconnected to the *Shoah*. Afterward, he used the philosophical methodology as he had formulated it to examine the *Shoah*, and this explains well why he could not repeal his previous method when he decided to make the *Shoah* the focus of his study. To him, it was not a starting point, but a continuation.

before the *Shoah*, after finding support for this in the lives, thoughts, and actions of *Shoah* survivors.[16]

These distinctions are enough to enable us to identify the overgeneralization and the excessively methodical approach that cause Fackenheim's argument to fail. Possibly, this conclusion is understandable against the background of German idealism. If we indiscriminately accept the idealistic view of the nature of history and the role of philosophy in culture, we conclude that the Nazi regime, and the *Shoah* as its quintessential product, are complete contradictions of the historical-cultural vision of idealism. At the same time, they are also products of that history for which idealism saw itself as guide and foundation. If so, the *Shoah* refuted idealistic philosophy according to its own self-understanding, yet within its own parameters it is possible that the *Shoah* can be understood as its product. Fackenheim implies this in his writing. But if this is the case, an immeasurably more reasonable philosophical alternative exists, and that is to accept the philosophical criticism of idealism and of the understanding of culture and history that was articulated well before the *Shoah*. Then we understand differently both the role of philosophy and its method, as well as the relationship between philosophy and historical events. This means that the *Shoah*, like every other historical event, is not, and cannot be, a philosophical event in the sense that Fackenheim intends. Events in philosophy can only include the propounding of philosophical ideas great and small. All other historical events do not take place within philosophy, but are objects of its contemplation, comment, and analysis, whether accepted and influential or unaccepted and noninfluential. We can also argue that historical events can affirm or refute certain philosophical views (those relating to history), or that certain philosophical views are among the factors influencing the occurrence of events. But this does not justify the assertion that those events or historical processes (wars, revolutions, social and governmental institutions) take place within philosophy. Therefore, even if we find that these events have an influence on philosophy, we cannot reach the radical conclusion that they entirely refute it. The fact that Fackenheim refused to give up his idealistic philosophy that predated the *Shoah* led him to this overgeneralization and its internal philosophical trap.

But in order to establish this conclusion, we must go back and examine its basis in the arguments regarding the uniqueness of the *Shoah* in the empirical-historiographic realm. Examining Fackenheim's statements in the first stage of his argument reveals that the overgeneralization is already found there, although it is partially based on fact. First of all, regarding the distinction between the *Shoah* and other attempts at mass murder and genocide: Even without denying the assertion that what happened in the *Shoah* had unprecedented proportions, all the motives that found their expression in a methodical and extreme manner in the *Shoah* were already present in previous attempts to hound, repress, and destroy the Jewish people, or peoples of other nations and religions.[17] Therefore, the argument that the *Shoah* cannot be legitimately compared to such antecedents is unfounded. On the contrary, the comparison is required, to identify both similarities and differences (in retrospect, the argument that the *Shoah* is unprecedented is made on the basis of comparisons to "similar" events).

But more important and fundamental is the second criticism: Even without denying the assertion that the *Shoah* was the most extreme revelation of evil imaginable, we cannot factually prove the argument that the *Shoah* was a "total reality" in the way that Fackenheim presents it, in that it stands apart from all previous realities, past or present, whose existence we recognize.

16. In order to overcome the dilemma created by refuting philosophy when confronted with the unique case of the *Shoah*, Fackenheim arrived at a conclusion that he had to "go back to school," or learn from the ways of life of *Shoah* survivors and find in them the foundation for a philosophy of the future. He describes this process in section 6 of his Introduction to his above-mentioned book. Clearly, the significance of this step, from many viewpoints including the philosophical, is the return to the normal trajectory of life. Just as the survivors rebuilt their lives, Fackenheim actually rebuilt after the *Shoah* the foundations of the philosophy he had previously formed.

17. See bibliography in n. 9, above.

Of course, to the victims and, in a parallel and opposite manner, to those who perpetrated the *Shoah*, while it was *taking place*, the *Shoah* was a total reality apart from all that were previously known. Ka tzetnik's expression "another planet" was completely justified, in its reflection of what happened from the point of view of the victims and as an expression of their feeling that whoever was not with them cannot imagine or grasp what happened to them.[18] In other words, a completely different total reality was created in the *Shoah*, for the victims and for the direct perpetrators. Also, we can identify the characteristics of this reality, although we admit that the ability to comprehend and internalize the existential significance of such characteristics is beyond the ability of ordinary humans who did not experience such acts. What happened in the *Shoah* is characterized on the one hand by complete isolation of the victims from the social and cultural environment of all other humans (to the extent that the Nazis succeeded in accomplishing this, their success was quite considerable), and on the other hand by planned, focused nullification (a nullification that was disciplined and institutionalized) of all moral restraints, such that every act that would torture, humiliate, desecrate, and destroy the victims, body and soul, was not only considered permissible but was required.

Complete isolation is what justifies, therefore, the assertion that a separate planet was created, and the planned and institutionalized invalidation of all moral restraints justifies the assertion that an alternative reality was created from a "human" point of view. In previous attempts at destroying the Jewish people, or other peoples, the abolition of restraints was an expression of disorder, even an organized disorder. In previous attempts, moral restraints were not abolished, although they were knowingly violated as an act of revolt. But in the *Shoah*, all restraints were breached, not as manifestations of disorder, but rather in complete abolishment of them regarding the victims, so as to enable the creation of a norm of torture,

humiliation, desecration of human dignity, and murder. During previous attempts at genocide, humane characteristics may have remained in the reality that was created and may have survived beyond the malice and evil. But in the reality created during the *Shoah*, no positive humane dimensions remained, except those that the victims succeeded in preserving among themselves despite all that was done to them, and in those few who attempted to break out of the isolation through acts of assistance and rescue. To formulate the issue more precisely: In the domain in which the *Shoah* took place, a reality was created in which the worst incarnations of crime were made the ruling law that shaped it in its entirety. This law was applied to victims because of the mere fact of their origin, without any relationship to their deeds. Their origin was the pretext for the crime against them. Such a reality should be defined as absolute evil, and as such, it has no precedent.

But now, we must present this assertion for close examination from the point of view of those who were not directly involved in the *Shoah* - either as victims or perpetrators and of those who were partially or indirectly involved through omission more than through action. Beyond this, we must put it to the test of those who look at what happened in the *Shoah* from a historical point of view, i.e., a perspective that understands the *Shoah* within the wider context of the reality before, during, and after the war. From those two vantage points, does the *Shoah* look like an event that created another planet?

When we examine the implications of Fackenheim's argument in answering our question, we meet with ambiguity. Together with the assertion that the concentration camps and ghettos were what created the other planet, Fackenheim claims that the *Shoah* was unique in that it transformed all of Germany and the occupied countries into another planet. The best of the national resources was dedicated to the goal of creating death. Also pressed into service for this

---

18. This idea, expressed in his testimony at the Eichmann trial, is the basis for most of Ka tzetnik's literary-documentary works. (Yeḥiel Dinur chose this name for himself out of complete identification with his role as a witness, and not as an ordinary pen name.)

However, for our purposes, it is important to note that in his last book, which documents his healing process, he arrived at the conclusion that the *Shoah* was not on another planet and that we are morally required to recognize that it took place on our planet.

goal were the institutionalized and noninstitutionalized systems of state and society: economy, transportation, justice, administration, education, military, and others. This means that the other planet is the entire society in which the *Shoah* served as its highest expression of purpose, and this assertion can be widened to include all of Europe, which unfortunately enabled the *Shoah* to take place through intentional omission. Can we therefore validate both senses of the expression "another planet," as two understandings that complete one another? The answer, it seems, is in the negative, because if we see all of Germany, or all of Europe, as the planet of Auschwitz, then Auschwitz is again not isolated within it, and the significance of the assertion that this is another planet is again blurred. If it is another planet, from what other planet does it differ?

But the main criticism of Fackenheim's argument is directed at its central contentions. First, those who were not directly involved in the *Shoah* as victims and perpetrators, or those whose involvement was partial or indirect, saw the *Shoah* as a reality that was, on the one hand, defined and differentiated from the reality in which they themselves lived. But on the other hand, the infrastructure of their own culture was a function of the same framework of economic, social, and political rule that those caught up in the *Shoah* inhabited, so that those not directly involved nevertheless shoulder some responsibility for the complete isolation of the *Shoah* victims and the crimes against them. What happened in those precincts touched by the *Shoah* did not apply to those marginally affected, at least not directly. Yet the latter did have contact with and were involved in the social and governmental institutions with whose resources the aberrant activities of the *Shoah* were carried out. Second, those who were not involved in the *Shoah*, or whose involvement was partial or indirect, lived in a multifaceted reality. As individuals and groups, they had many variegated goals, some negative and some positive. Even while the *Shoah* was taking place, the general cultural milieu of Europe, or even that of Germany, was not defined by the *Shoah* alone. To be exact: Fackenheim was correct that the *Shoah* was unique in that the German state made the "final solution" one of its supreme national goals. It

recruited enormous national resources for that purpose and saw to it that almost all the state systems contributed toward it. Fackenheim was also correct in his statement that the cooperation or nonintervention of other nations contributed actively to implementation of the "final solution." But even the German regime had additional goals, and most of the German people lived and functioned in other fields of endeavor, ignoring or distancing themselves from what happened during the *Shoah*. All the more so can we say this about the non-Germans, and it most certainly applies to those who fought against the Nazis. Even so, the way that the Germans lived and acted, even those with positive aspirations, contributed directly or indirectly to the events of the *Shoah*. From these standpoints, therefore, can we argue that the *Shoah* is perceived as happening on another planet?

No. From this point of view, the *Shoah* occurred in a dichotomously separate sector, but nevertheless well within the same planet. This is certainly so when we examine the events from a historical perspective that takes into account the full continuum of the various facets of reality during that time and during the periods preceding and following the *Shoah*. With all the emotional difficulty involved, it is a moral obligation to recognize the fact that it took place on this planet. The *Shoah* took place in the context of the history of Europe; it was not an ahistorical event. It is located on the continuum of European social, political, cultural, and spiritual/religious developments, not beyond them. We have before us the same planet, the one that was inhabited before the *Shoah*, and the one that continues to exist afterward, the planet that created and supported the *Shoah*, and the one that carries within it, as demonstrated, the potential for such an event to happen on it. After the *Shoah*, we see clearly that this planet embodies within it a very extreme dichotomy, more extreme than imagined before the *Shoah*. It is extreme to the point of creating a reality of total evil on its surface, as an articulation of the threatening potential contained within.

How are such dichotomies created on the same human planet, within the same history and culture? That is one of several great questions that must be asked against the background of the *Shoah*. We must confront this question with the tools of the social sciences and humanities, including philosophy. This is so that we can learn from the *Shoah* not only about the *Shoah* itself and about the historical reality that followed, but also about humankind, society, and its culture in general.

DOES THE IDEA OF JEWISH ELECTION HAVE ANY MEANING
AFTER THE HOLOCAUST?

The very posing of the question of the significance of the election or chosenness of the Jewish people in our time illustrates the emotional and intellectual difficulty involved in discussing this issue after the Holocaust. This difficulty indicates a deep crisis in the historical continuity of the very identity of the Jewish people. Throughout the ages, the Jewish people's consciousness of being chosen as "a kingdom of priests and a holy nation" or as "the special people" of the one and only God of the universe, by whose means He made Himself known to all peoples as their king, has marked them both in their relationship to other, neighboring peoples and in the shaping of its way of life. This consciousness seems to have become institutionalized close to the time of the destruction of the kingdom of Judah and its Temple [586 BCE] and the exile of the people, known from that time by the name "Jewish," into Babylonia. Historians know that the debate regarding the election and its meaning continued within the people, and between them and the peoples of the Persian and Roman empires, and later on with the Christian and Islamic empires, throughout the entire period between the first and second returns to Zion. Indeed, the debate created by the unique religious character of the Jewish people and its extraordinary fate under the rival religions which subjugated it and which derived from it their own original inspiration was to become the focus of the collective identity that united its various factions so long as they did not separate from one another. Even those who rejected the idea of chosenness but remained Jewish, retained it willy-nilly, even if turning its meaning about.

Thus, were we to ask whether, following the Holocaust, there are any Jewish groups that accept the notion of the election of the Jewish people as a dogmatic principle, the positive answer would be accepted de rigueur. All of the Orthodox movements are committed to this principle, just as they are committed to the principle of the Torah having been revealed from heaven. But they are not alone. Both the Reform and Conservative movements are committed to this idea, albeit to a different reading, as are to some extent the secular Zionist movements. Yet adherence to this principle as a time-honored axiom, whether by dint of tradition or as a historical-cultural memory, is not commensurate with a fundamental belief that shapes practical, contemporary orientation in the world. Does this consciousness define the goals that these movements strive to realize? Is it a factor in the debates being conducted today in Israel and in the diaspora regarding Jewish identity? Does this consciousness determine a definite mission that the Jewish people is called upon today to fulfill? This last question would seem to reveal the gist of the problem. Chosenness implies a mission, so that the deeper question confronting us today is: Following the Holocaust, do the Jewish people have a mission of universal meaning? Does the continued existence of the Jewish people in the world that rose upon the ashes of the Second World War entail any value-oriented message that demands realization and that serves as the reason for which this people persists in maintaining its existence in the face of the threats of still-existing enemies and increasing temptations to assimilate?

A survey of the topics on the agenda of all of the movements active among the Jewish people today suggests a negative answer. For the religious movements, the consciousness of the Jewish people being a chosen people, with a land and state, is consciously intertwined with their political positions which, on the one hand, relate to the status of religion in the State of Israel and, on the other, to that of the non-Jewish minorities within its borders. On the other hand, we find those movements which consider such attitudes immoral and hence criticize the underlying idea of chosenness as such. Many of the representatives of these movements argue that, in light of their experience in the Holocaust, Jews should reject any and all forms of "consciousness of superiority" as racist and as indicative of an unequal and unfair attitude toward minorities within the State of Israel. Does this imply that those adhering to such a critique demand that their people view as their mission in the post-Holocaust world their divesting themselves of national and religious egotism? While such an option does theoretically exist, such a pretense is in fact generally viewed as a kind of self-righteous superiority. It has nothing to do with mission, but with drawing a lesson from the Jewish people's experience as a minority for so many generations. Thus, the conclusion is that both those who accept the idea of chosenness as a dogmatic belief, as well as those who criticize it, prefer to avoid serious discussion of the issue. This is so almost as a matter of course, because in the eyes of the generation that matured after the Holocaust, the idea appears incompatible with the reality experienced and still being experienced by the people, both from a religious/theological standpoint (God's relationship to His people) and from a humanistic standpoint (the attitude of humankind to the Jewish people). From either perspective, the idea of chosenness seems to be mired in absurdity. Or, to formulate the issue in existential terms: It would appear that the post-Holocaust generation has not extrapolated from the life tendencies of its people any sense of it being chosen in the sense of a goal or destiny.

The questions that need to be examined for the sake of the future of the Jewish people are the following. First of all, what brought about this situation? Second, what are its implications for the future identity of the Jews as a people? Finally, is it possible, after the Holocaust—or, more aptly, as a result thereof—to find, in the continued existence of the Jewish people, some positive message of universal import by which its uniqueness is expressed? A thoughtful examination of these questions demands an assessment of the change engendered regarding the subject of chosenness during the founding period of the

various movements that currently divide the Jewish people, in which are rooted both the causes of the Holocaust and the responses to it.

The roots of the movements which currently divide the Jewish people—including the ultra-Orthodox movements—are based upon the crisis of Emancipation. The complex and ambivalent turnabout in the attitude of the Christian nations toward the Jewish people, and the concurrent change within the Jewish people in relation to them, raised the issue of the concept of election as the focus of a new and different sort of dispute, both externally and internally. In this manner, the problem became even more acute than it had been in the Middle Ages, both because of the more complex division within the Jewish people and because of the internalization by the Jews themselves of the negative attitude toward Judaism and Jewry on the part of both Christianity and European nationalism.

Underlying this dispute were several points of agreement. Jews and non-Jews agreed that Jewish collective existence—regardless of how defined, whether in national, ethnic, class, or religious terms—was unique in relation to its environment. All agreed—even those Jews who had internalized the environment's attitude toward them—that their uniqueness led to a problematic otherness when expressed in sociopolitical contexts within which the Jews constitute a minority group. The modern European nations found it more difficult to assimilate them than did the kingdoms and religions in ancient times and the Middle Ages; all agreed that the difficulty in accepting Jews as citizens of the modern states, particularly that entailed in integrating them with their special identity within the general society, distorted the relations between the Jewish minority and the majority society within which it was tolerated. The dispute focused upon the questions of who was at fault and how the problem was to be resolved. In any event, the hatred which slid into violence provided both sides with self-justifying arguments, on whose basis there was a consensus that, at the root of the insoluble dispute was the Jews' identification as the chosen people vis-à-vis the peoples who competed over the status of chosen religion or nationality.

In all these agreements, there should be emphasized the ambiguity asserted on both sides of the dispute. Over the course of many generations, from the very beginning of the consolidation of European nationhoods, the Jewish people posed the challenge of differentness upon which their religious identity was shaped. Jew hatred was exacerbated due to this ambiguity. The Jews' presence at the very heart of the spiritual life of the European peoples was a reminder of the traumatic conflict implicit in the depth consciousness of the cultural-religious identity, both of the Jews and of those peoples united under Christianity as a victorious religion. Indeed, on both sides there was an ambivalent love-hate relationship which explains why, despite the mutual repulsion, existence side by side persisted for so many generations.

Yet, in light of the problematic reality catalyzed by the processes of secularization during the modern age, an essentially consistent attitude toward Jews and Judaism took shape in most of the national, class, and religious movements in Europe. From each of these three standpoints—religious, national, or class—the Jews' consciousness of chosenness was seen as an expression of their inferiority. This was explained in different ways. One may not overlook the importance of the differences between them in terms of the policies taken regarding the Jews, but in terms of the attitude implied toward Jewish beliefs, they were negligible. At best, they explained the inferiority of Judaism as the consequence of the unfortunate circumstances of the Jewish people's history, as a people shaped under conditions of slavery, that remained subjugated throughout most of its history. The result was that they became an ignorant, narrow-minded, and stubborn people, full of animosity toward their oppressors, filled with the desire for revenge, and tending to compensate for their suffering by a consciousness of their chosenness and superiority. Furthermore, a people who had transformed the hatred directed toward them into a source of instinctive strength, by which to withstand this animosity and to protect their distinct identity. It should not be surprising that the Jewish obstinacy in rejecting the dominant religions in the lands where they lived and in insisting upon the exclusivity of their faith was regarded thus by non-Jews. Of greater significance is the fact that the theological and philosophical formulation deeming Judaism as an inferior faith was carried out by two personalities of Jewish origin: Paul, at the beginning of the founding of Christianity, and Spinoza, at the beginning of the modern era.

At worst, the Jews' inferiority was interpreted in organic terms: as an inborn spiritual turpitude or inherited inadequacy. In either case, the notion of chosenness was seen as an expression of the despicable nature of the Jewish people and the reason for its tragedy. Since there was a tangible connection between its plight and its situation in the life of its host peoples, these peoples viewed this narrowness as the main reason for the internal and external troubles experienced by the Jewish people. During the Middle Ages, the Jews were made the scapegoat for every disaster befalling their hosts: plagues, economic collapse, wars, and revolutions. In the modern age, the Jew was held accountable for the socioeconomic ills deriving from the industrial revolution and the consequent process of secularization. Modern nationalism brought about a profound identity crisis among the European peoples. The Jews' otherness stood out, as a disruptive factor against the formation of new national identities that liberated themselves from the authority of religion and which sought a unity beyond it.

One must admit that the Jews' insistence upon maintaining the antiquated mother religion from which Christianity was derived, and their sharp rejection of the daughter religion, at a time that the new European elites were trying to become liberated from the daughter religion that had shaped their cultural identity, turned the Jews' separatist collective existence within the Christian majority into an intolerable challenge—all the more so because, on the basis of the link between the mother faith and the daughter, the Jews claimed equal partnership in the creation of Western culture, some even considering this as a fulfillment of their mission as the chosen people.

From the Jewish side, these things were stated out of a sense of pride and from the aspiration to demonstrate a relevant creative contribution to the modern age. But, from the standpoint of Christian society, such a claim was viewed as expressing singular impertinence, exposing the traumatic rift within the self-awareness of the European peoples. Christianity had been imposed upon them in order to unite them within an imperial-political framework from which they now sought to free themselves, but ex post facto it had shaped their cultural identity for so many generations that it was impossible for them to become free of its influence without incorporating it within a new, secular national synthesis.

The fact that Judaism which had spawned Christianity continued to reject it made it, in this context, insufferable. And this both in the eyes of those who continued to maintain their Christian faith, as well as in the eyes of Christians who had rebelled against their religion in the name of the universal humanistic values inherited from Greece and Rome. Indeed, even those who had rejected Christianity in favor of the archaic pagan values of the European peoples prior to the Christian conquest were hostile to the continued existence of Judaism as a form of life. From all three perspectives Judaism, which had stubbornly maintained its claim to be the only true religion for humankind, was perceived as a factor fanning the flames of controversy that had ruptured Europe's cultural identity and, as such, was an obstacle to the creation of the redeeming synthesis. This was particularly so in light of the fact that Jewish advocates of Emancipation were not satisfied with demanding that their heritage be recognized as a legitimate component of the new cultural synthesis, but insisted that it be acknowledged that Judaism had actually fulfilled its mission through a universalist contribution to all aspects of modern national cultures, impressive both in scope and in level.

The tragic dialectic embodied in both the extraordinary success and the extraordinary failure of the Emancipation throughout the nineteenth and the first half of the twentieth centuries follows from this: The more the Jews tried to appear as a missionary, universalist, integrative factor in Western civilization, the more they were seen as a disintegrative, particularistic, domineering factor from which it was imperative to be liberated. Hence, the condition of the Emancipation of the Jews from the social and political discrimination directed against them, as that of the liberation of the host peoples from their intolerable otherness, was the demand that they renounce their identification as the chosen people, that they recognize their cultural inferiority

and irrelevance to the modern age, relinquish all separatist characteristics as a group, internalize the culture of their environment in good faith and with a cognizance of its superiority, and thereby disappear now solely as individuals within the general culture.

There was also another option: that those Jews wishing to preserve their uniqueness would withdraw as an organized group and constitute an independent nation. This was the ironic (or tragic) common basis of consensus for both anti-Semitism and Zionism. The third option was the "final solution" that was to be implemented in the Holocaust.

Be that as it may, in the modern age the Jewish people were "chosen" to be the atoning sacrifice for the twisted paths of the national and cultural identity of European peoples. The Jews' involvement with the elites that led the social, political, and cultural revolutions, on the one hand, and the increasing hatred toward them because of that same involvement, on the other, created the background for the renewed consciousness of chosenness within modern Jewish movements, even among secularist ones. If God had not chosen Israel, they had in any event been destined for a special mission by their extraordinary historical fate. Indeed, all of the movements in the Jewish people discovered this truth, willingly or not, from which derived the sharp controversy among them concerning the essence of that mission.

The debate which developed within the Jewish people against the background of the alternative presented by Emancipation initially revolved around two parallel issues. First, are the unique fate and cultural identity of the Jewish people of the order of an "election" deriving from a mission and indicative of an exalted spiritual/moral quality, or are the other nations correct in interpreting them as a kind of inferiority? Second, what is the special mission of the Jewish people in the modern age (if the chosenness is in fact a mission), or alternatively, what is the organic defect that sets the Jewish people aside in the modern age (if their chosenness is a sign of inferiority)?

But the ambivalence in the attitude of the European nations toward the Jews is also expressed in the answers given to these questions by all of the movements in Judaism. Those who rejected the idea of chosenness because they had internalized the attitude of the nations later re-affirmed it as a kind of reaction to the oppression and injustice caused to the Jews, while those who advocated the idea of chosenness internalized the demand of the nations to assimilate and relinquish their separate collective identity. Either way, the idea of chosenness and the consciousness of the universal mission of the Jewish people be-came the central axes that shaped Jewish identity throughout the entire period preceding the Ho-locaust.

The harbinger of the negative attitude toward the idea of the chosen people during the modern age was Spinoza [1632–1677]. He articulated this message while resigning from his people and adopting the Christian-Protestant view of them, though he did not convert because he preferred Protestantism solely for political reasons. His pantheism placed him in a vantage point beyond the existing organized religions, albeit he accepted their existence for pragmatic reasons because, to his mind, they satisfied a psychological need found among the masses, which the state should seek to satisfy if only for its own reasons. In any event, it is clear that according to scientific truth there was no transcendent God and therefore no entity that could select for itself a chosen people. On the other hand, all nations, whatever they may be, are by nature equal to one another, and none may argue that it is by nature chosen, unless we state that all are chosen in their own eyes.

The distribution of the peoples and their po-litical organization as nations is, according to Spinoza, a natural process. The same holds true for the emergence of religions. Those religions which claim a revelation of a transcendental God also have a natural source: ignorance, instinct, fears, and delusions; illusory and misleading imag-ination; and the lust for power. The rationale at the base of these religions is, according to Spi-noza, the universal aspiration of all living things for power. The differences among peoples and religions in this respect are thus the result of causal determinism becoming embodied in their history as particular groups.

From this standpoint, the Jewish people are like all other peoples. Like them, they were united by their historical fate. Like them, they

established and shaped their national and religious identity and their unique strategy for its preser-vation. Spinoza had a scientific explanation as to why the Jews considered themselves the chosen people. To his mind, this was clearly a self-election whose efficacy could be justified, so long as it in fact benefited the worldly interests of the people. Did the Jewish people have a universal mission? Though Spinoza was imbued with a sense of personal mission, as a prophet of secular ethics and democratic political theory, he re-jected the idea of mission. All beings in nature operate, according to him, only out of the ne-cessity of their nature, and if they are intelligent, they operate through the necessity of their in-telligence in accordance with their degree of er-udition and their cognitive abilities. But, of course, this does not prevent those lacking in developed intelligence to consider themselves as imbued with a mission. Moses' law thus ex-presses a subjective consciousness of a religious mission of universal import. However, upon examination of the reasons which brought this about, its manner of implementation, and its re-sults and using scientific tools, we discover that the sense of mission served particular national interests, such as the desire to settle in their land, to unite in order to defeat their enemies, and to flourish materially.

One might therefore say that, so long as the consciousness of chosenness effectively served those interests, it was verified—in the eyes of the Jews, as well as by those of the nations they de-feated. The question which follows from this is, until what point did this consciousness continue to justify itself from the perspective of the Jewish people and its environment? For Spinoza, fol-lowing the initial success of Moses' law, it bore more failures than success[es], both from the perspective of Israel's sociopolitical organization in its land, as well as in the array of forces be-tween itself and the surrounding peoples. In the end, its state was destroyed, the Temple ruined, and the people exiled from their land.

All this evinces, according to Spinoza, that their chosenness had to all intents and purposes been abrogated and its objective justification lost. The insistence upon maintaining this idea only served to preserve the existence of the people under conditions of inferiority. This should not be understood, according to his view, as deriving from the system itself, but as a result of their inferiority per se, as expressed in besieged ignorance and religious zealotry. Spinoza succeeded as a private individual in leaving this state of besiegement by virtue of his scientific education and philosophical acumen, and he drew the necessary conclusions: He rejected the principles of his religion, abandoned the practice of its religious precepts, and left his community and his people. But he knew his people and [knew] that most of them would refuse to follow his lead. He therefore prophesied that the political changes occurring in the lands of their residence, especially in terms of the relationship between state and religion, would leave them no choice but to return to their land and to establish their state there according to the Torah of Moses, thereby once again proving that they were the chosen people. [See his 1670 Theological-Political Treatise]

By virtue of his ironic rejection of the doctrine of election, Spinoza was deemed by the Jews to be, first of all, a prophet of the concept of Jewish nationalism and, as such, a harbinger of political Zionism. Yet one could argue that, by dint of his individual decision to withdraw from his people in the name of a personal-political mission as a secular-democratic prophet, he became the prophet of a renewed consciousness of chosenness and the mission among those modern Jewish religious movements which aspired to emancipation sans conversion. In retrospect, Spinoza's heresy was internalized in all modern Jewish movements and first and foremost in the secular-national movement that developed out of the [19th C.] Eastern European Haskalah [Enlightenment] and which strove in the direction of political Zionism while sharply rejecting the idea of chosenness.

Spinoza assumed, as mentioned, that the Jews would return to their land in order to establish their state out of loyalty to their religion and the idea of their chosenness. However, his influence was by and large absorbed by pro-Emancipation and pro-Haskalah Jews such as himself, whose identification with Judaism as a nation and not as religion derived from their desire to be free of the burden of exile and isolation, not by abandoning their own people, but by altering their situation among the nations. In other words, for the secular Maskilim (enlightened intellectuals), the national self-definition of Judaism expressed a desire for normalization. They defined this as a return to "normality," internalizing the criticism drawn against the Jewish people from the standpoint of the "natural" peoples they sought to emulate. Spinoza's disciples, the Maskilim, internalized the outlook according to which the consciousness of chosenness expressed an exilic inferiority, which they blamed for the people's betrayal of their original and authentic identity as a natural people, the destruction of their kingdom, and their separation from their land in order to wander among the peoples. The "negation of exile" derived from these evaluations. It entailed a negation of all the unnatural characteristics of Jewish existence that found expression, to their mind, in their religion. How did they see the continuance of their national identity as Jews? In the premonotheistic heritage upon which, to their mind, the Israelite kingdom had been founded in biblical times, as was later the Hasmonean kingdom during the time of the Second Temple. This was, according to them, a heritage shared with the other cultures neighboring upon Israel. The prophets and the sages had succeeded in overcoming and suppressing it, but its remnants survived and continued to live, even in exile, in the ethnic existence underlying the rabbinic layers. It can therefore be uncovered and rehabilitated in a modern, secular spirit.

But the paradox was that precisely the heroic desire to return to a natural national existence, once placed in the crucible of actualization, led to the rebirth of the idea of election. Two motivations dovetailed to bring about this upheaval. The first was the profound gap between the gravity of the task of returning the people to their land and the resources at their disposal. This might also be described in terms of the contradiction between the necessity discovered in the modern age to return to the Land of Israel and the conditions of life in exile, which made a mass exodus virtually impossible. In order to overcome this contradiction, a superhuman effort was required. Hence there was needed not only a cognizance of the compelling circumstances, but also an intensely idealistic motivation.

Second, the true normalization of the Jewish people "like all of the nations" could not be achieved simply by emulating other national societies and cultures as they were. The travail of the Jews in those countries which underwent the processes of nationalist modernization stemmed from the as-yet-unresolved severe social and national problems engendered by modernity. Thus, a return to normalcy depended upon finding a solution to the social and national problems with which European society was grappling and which were as yet without a solution. Thus, in retrospect, the Jews needed to solve in their own land the national, social, and political ideals that the European peoples were struggling unsuccessfully to realize. The paradoxical conclusion of this was that, due to their inferior condition among the nations, the Jews needed to make extraordinary efforts and to be the chosen people in order to accomplish in their own land the model solution to the unrealized social and national problems of the European peoples.

This dialectic appeared in all of the ideologies that shaped the secular Jewish nationalist movements. Among the central personalities who led these movements were Herzl and Jabotinsky in political Zionism; Moses Hess, Nachman Syrkin, Ber Borochov, Martin Buber, and A. D. Gordon in social Zionism (which bore the brunt of building the country); and Aḥad Ha'am and Chaim Naḥman Bialik in spiritual Zionism.

But the same dialectic also appeared in the modern movements which sought Emancipation in the lands of the diaspora. Notwithstanding the fact that the ideology defined by the negation of exile and the desire for normalization was specific to the Zionist movement, it should be emphasized that all those movements that favored Emancipation negated the exile as personified by the "ghetto" and advocated normalization of Jewish existence based upon the standard of enlightened civil society in the lands of the diaspora. It is therefore clear that, like Spinoza, the advocates of Emancipation rebelled against the idea of chosenness as delineated by rabbinic Judaism. Indeed, the rebellion against the idea of chosenness, à la Spinoza, was unequivocally expressed in extremist movements that sought to realize the demand of non-Jewish society to educate the Jews to total assimilation. In France, this pattern was expressed in the individual behavior of most Jews, who had no other real alternative. In Germany, and to a certain extent in England, it

found expression in extreme religious Reform (à la Samuel Holdheim, 1806–1860), which viewed itself as a path toward total assimilation, while in Eastern Europe it found expression in joining the general social democratic revolution, whether directly or through the Bund, which from the outset had also sought total assimilation.

The dialectic turning the idea of election into the main means of realizing Emancipation was glaringly exposed in those movements that refused to relinquish a certain degree of Jewish collective identity, which they considered the necessary degree of tolerance to be demonstrated by the absorbing society. Here, too, there was a confluence of two factors. First, the need to define the parameters of Jewish identity in terms of the liberal-humanist society which facilitated Emancipation. As noted, Jews who wished to be accepted as citizens with equal rights, without giving up all aspects of their collective identity, justified their demand for tolerance with the claim that Judaism was a major component of the European cultural synthesis. More than that: The sources of the humanistic ideals underpinning the liberal basis of the Emancipation were to be found in prophetic Judaism. The Jews were therefore entitled to view their acceptance as citizens with equal rights not as a favor, but as the fulfillment of their mission among the nations.

Second, a yawning chasm separated the Jews' aspiration to be accepted and the obligation in principle of liberal society to accept them and the resistance on the part of non-Jewish society to receiving them into its midst in practice. The more the assimilating Jews pressured to be accepted, the greater the resistance of Christian society and the more repulsive the image of the Jews became. The assimilating Jews, who had already become integrated within the surrounding society and even saw it as their own culture, reacted sharply to this, on the basis of the universal values of their common culture. They were, in their own eyes, the authentic representatives of the "general" society that the non-Jewish society, despite a pretense of enlightenment, had yet to truly internalize. In actuality, by rejecting those who had contributed it, the larger society was betraying its own values. Thus the conclusion (argued for by Jews) that the struggle for the acceptance of the Jews into the general society was in itself a struggle for the realization of the universal mission of the Jews to humankind.

This consciousness, which developed particularly in [19th C.] Reform Jewish theology and, later, to varying degrees in Conservatism and modern Orthodoxy as well, reached its peak in the crisis of humanism beginning in the last decades of the nineteenth century. Confronting the failure of humanism expressed in increasing anti-Semitism, the leadership of the modernizing movements in Judaism reacted by turning away from the pattern of assimilation and toward a strengthening of Jewish selfhood, with a growing cognizance that Judaism was the only bastion of humanism and that only through a return to the ethical monotheism of the prophets might it be possible to realize humanist values within Western society as a whole. In this context, I would mention the names of Hermann Cohen, Martin Buber, Franz Rosenzweig, Leo Baeck, Nehemiah Nobel, and even Isaac Breuer, as spokesmen of an increasingly strict modern Orthodoxy.

On the eve of the Holocaust, all the movements in the Jewish people beat with the consciousness of a universalist messianic mission that sprang from the depths of their traditional national or religious identity, on the one hand, and from the age-old historical fate of the Jewish people, on the other. This is demonstrated by the literature written during the course of the war, while struggling with the actual occurrence of the Holocaust. The consciousness of mission was the spiritual resource drawn upon by Jews in all the movements—including now even the radically antireligious Bund—to withstand the dehumanization instituted by the Nazi regime immediately upon its coming to power. Different ideological explanations were proffered in accordance with the original ideology of those movements that fractionalized the people, but the common denominator was the understanding that the main enemy against which Hitler had declared war was the Jewish people. Hitler, who raised the Aryan race to the level of the "super man," viewed the Jewish people, with its consciousness of universal missionary chosenness, as the epitome of the negation of his vision. With apocalyptic madness, he conducted a mythological war against Jews and Judaism. In the eyes of Jewish humanists of all movements, World War

II was the war of a man who had created himself in the image of Satan against that of man created in the image of God, a war of antimorality against morality, of the lie against the truth, of the self-deification of human egotism against the recognition that man is subject to the authority of transcendent truth and morality. This was a war of paganism, as embodied at that time at the height of its viciousness and depravity in Nazi Germany, against the belief in the uniqueness embodied in the image of the degraded and destroyed Jewish people.

This consciousness united the survivors of the Holocaust into a "covenant of destiny" marked by the establishment of the State of Israel. It would appear that in no other period in its history was the Jewish people as united as it was during the two decades following the Holocaust. The rifts between the different parties which had deepened on the eve of the Holocaust were not healed, but the lesson learned from the isolation of the Jewish people during the Holocaust superseded all differences in ideas and conflicts of interest. For the majority of the Jewish people, the establishment of the State symbolized the true victory over what Nazi Germany had symbolized in its war against humanity.

The philosopher Emil Fackenheim has expressed the consciousness of mission that unified the Jewish people after the Holocaust in theological terms. He defined it in the context of the establishment of the State of Israel as a "614th mitzvah (commandment)," whose content was "not to grant Hitler any posthumous victory." Couched in positive terms, the sense was to do whatever was necessary to prevent a repeat of the Holocaust. Thus, all the resources of Jewish individuals had to be invested and all possible help mobilized from the Jews who recognized their obligation toward the Jewish people, toward its physical rehabilitation, and especially to fortifying the Jewish people's ability to defend itself and deter its enemies.

For Fackenheim, this task was the enterprise in which all of those peoples who had learned the lessons of the Holocaust had to participate. The general directive to humankind was, to his mind, to create a world in which another Holocaust would be impossible. Notice how his words were formulated: Fackenheim, in defining the objective of humankind after the Holocaust, expressed his disappointment in idealistic humanism and in all of the derivative secular messianic movements which had, in the final analysis, led to the world war and to the Holocaust, rather than to a realization of their diametrically opposed visions. The 614th precept is thus a conclusion drawn from the disappointment with humanism and is aimed at a different form of *tikkun olam*, of repairing the world: a realistic one, built not upon illusions regarding the nature of man and upon futile dreams of an ideal world that would rise as a result of the intrahistoric and transhistoric dialectic, but one which strives for a just balance of interests and solidarity among peoples, so as to avoid sliding back into the turpitude and apathy reached by humanity in World War II.

Fackenheim tried to emphasize this, in the expectation that those nations that had participated in the war would help the Jewish people to become rehabilitated and to become as one of them. This was not only their moral obligation toward the people whose blood they had allowed to be shed, but part of their own interest in the efforts to rebuild the ruins of the war in such a way that there would be international guarantees to prevent its recurrence. In this context, Fackenheim insisted that the Holocaust was not only an unprecedented event in human history, but also that it was a consequence of the unique status of the Jewish people among the peoples, due both to its unusual mission and to the unusual weakness which was a product of that mission. Genocide from ideological motives could be contemplated only with regard to the Jewish people. Hence, the establishment of a world in which such a Holocaust would never be repeated requires a correction of the distortion in the relations between the Jewish people and Western culture.

The practical conclusion was the strengthening of the State of Israel. The fact that it needed to confront the threat of annihilation from the very moment of its founding obscured even to Fackenheim, who was not a Zionist until the Six Day War, the full revolutionary implication of his interpretation of the idea of Jewish election in light of the Holocaust. The Holocaust, as an unprecedented event in human history, had, to his mind, refuted the idealistic philosophies through which Jewish religious philosophers—

himself included—had succeeded in imparting rational meaning to the myth of Sinai and the belief in Divine providence in history. Henceforth, to continue to rely upon Divine guidance in history, in any form, would be an act of shocking irresponsibility.

The necessary conclusion was the realization that humanity alone carries full responsibility for its fate, as does each individual people. The idea of "the final solution" could be conceived by an insane leader and executed by an insane state only because the Jewish people did not possess the means to defend itself. It relied upon God or upon humanity. This conclusion relates to his "614th commandment." To wit, the mission to be derived from the lessons learned from the fate of the Jewish people in the Holocaust was the internalization of their self-responsibility and its application in practice: Each people must be concerned about its leadership. It is forbidden to harm another people. But an interdiction no less severe is that against enticing the aggressor by demonstrating weakness. It is therefore forbidden to rely upon Divine providence, international solidarity, or the laws of historical progress. International solidarity may only be relied upon when nations capable of defending themselves enter into obligatory mutual pacts among themselves.

This lesson of the Holocaust penetrated Fackenheim's consciousness after the Six Day War, which also explains why it was only then that he grasped its meaning as an unprecedented event. Only then did he become a passionate political Zionist. In the Six Day War, the Jewish people once again faced the danger of a Holocaust; it once again confronted the phenomenon of international isolation. All of Israel's putative "allies" looked on from afar and let Nasser realize his threat. But this time, Israel had learned the lesson of the Holocaust and assumed full responsibility for its fate. According to Fackenheim, this had profound international meaning. The amazing victory demonstrated that even a small people, isolated and surrounded by enemies, could by itself repel an attack if it mobilized all of its strength and resourcefulness. Fackenheim saw in this lesson a proof that Zionism was justified in its day. It alone had foreseen the encroaching disaster and provided the only solution. If the entire people would have united behind it, and if the democratic nations would have lent a hand, the Holocaust could have been avoided. What is the significance of adopting the theory of "catastrophic Zionism," of the school of Herzl, Nordau, Borochov, and Jabotinsky, after the establishment of the State, namely, that of turning political Zionism's concept of "normalization"— that the Jewish people should be "a nation like all other nations"—into a universal mission? If such a turnabout is not diametrically opposed to the mission established at Sinai, it is in any event exactly opposite the interpretation given it by all the religious movements before the Holocaust.

Fackenheim himself emphasized the radical implications of his intent when he voiced sharp criticism of the disapproval of leftist circles in Israel and in the world about the way the State of Israel was fighting Arab terror. These latter claimed that, against the background of Jewish history and against the background of its teachings, the Jewish state was expected to abide by different norms of war morality, loftier than those of its attackers and loftier than those adopted by ordinary democratic states when in similar situations. Fackenheim quite properly considered such demands as not only hypocritical, but also as camouflaged anti-Semitism. He argued that the abandonment of the Jewish people by the nations that had fought against Hitler denied them any moral right to preach morality to a State of Israel defending itself against a second Holocaust. But his argument went further: To his mind, the Jewish people was not only permitted to defend itself in an effective manner, but obligated to do so, commensurate with its enemies' ethics of war and in exactly the same manner. From the standpoint of Israel's enemies, maintaining loftier norms of war would be a demonstration of weakness, which would be exploited to endanger Israel. A demonstration of weakness in the face of aggression, he argued, was not a manifestation of morality. It would be a severe transgression that would invite further immorality.

As noted, when Israel defended itself on its own against seven Arab states, it sent an authentic universal message for humanity. Internally, however, the simple significance of this was that Israel needed to focus, like all "normal" states, upon developing its physical strength: military, economic, and political. Until such time, it must not become mired in dreams of a model state realizing sublime moral values, as such a state could not survive in our world. It needed to invest maximum resources and resourcefulness in strengthening itself until all of its neighbors would understand that they would do better to strive for cooperation with it rather than seek its destruction.

Of course, apart from their philosophical and religious formulation, there was nothing new here after the Six Day War. The enthusiastic response to Fackenheim's words, both in Israel and in the diaspora, derived from his elevating the Zionist consensus that had united the Jewish people about the State of Israel since its establishment to a philosophical level. Even ultra-Orthodox Jewry had actually accepted this consensus, notwithstanding its tendency to oppose Zionist ideology. Typical from this standpoint was the support of the non-Zionist Ḥabad (Lubavitch) Hasidic movement for the State of Israel, especially for the Israeli Defense Forces. But even some of the anti-Zionist ultra-Orthodox changed their policy from what it was before World War II. Instead of rejecting all worldly, political, social, and economic initiatives to ameliorate the condition of the people, including that of the ultra-Orthodox movements themselves, because they viewed such initiatives as a kind of sin of turning the Jewish people into a nation like all nations, after the war they adopted the religious Zionist idea that in order to further salvationist Divine intervention in the fate of the Jewish people, one must first engage in initiative from "below." By this, they referred to the political, social, and economic initiative needed to rehabilitate the ultra-Orthodox movements that had suffered crippling blows in the Holocaust. In retrospect, they utilized the political and economic achievements of the hated modern movements and thereby gradually became integrated to all intents and purposes as secular parties in Israeli politics and American Jewish politics. In retrospect, the rationale for their activity was secular and mundane, and their attack on the secular movements was no more than a kind of dogmatic entrenchment against their harmful influence while at the same time exploiting their achievements in a manipulative manner.

The example of the ultra-Orthodox movements is significant because the glaring paradox therein exemplifies a similar internal tension within all of the religious movements. None of them recanted their definition of the universal goal of the chosen people in terms of *tikkun olam*, "reparation of the world," on the one hand, or in terms of "Divine service," on the other. However, the rationale for practical activity was security: demographic, socioeconomic, and political normalization. It would therefore seem that in the final analysis all the modern religious movements within the Jewish people supported Spinoza's contention that the idea of chosenness only developed in order to advance the worldly interests of the Jewish people: settling its land, unification, victory over its enemies, and economic prosperity.

In this context, we would do well to take note of two salient facts: Upon the establishment of the State of Israel, a gradual retreat began in the realization by socialist Zionism of its utopian social goals; spiritual Zionism retreated from the goal of establishing a "spiritual center" in the Land of Israel, even though it was much spoken of; and even religious Zionism focused its efforts upon bolstering its sectoral strength, rather than its initial effort to build a bridge between the secular/nationalist public and the ultra-Orthodox religious public, so as to create a common spiritual denominator to unite religious Zionism and secular Zionism.

This pattern was even more striking after the Six Day War. Religious Zionism focused its efforts upon settlement in Judaea and Samaria, with the clear goal of capturing the position of leadership that had previously been denied it in the concrete enterprise of settling the Land of Israel. A parallel pattern became visible within the Jewish diaspora. It united around financial and political support for the State of Israel, while at the same time completing its integration in the lands of its residence from the standpoint of economic, political, and cultural security. This can only be interpreted as normalization in terms of the civic standards of their countries of residence.

As we have noted, so long as a great voluntary effort was required to close the gap between the desire for normalization and the concrete reality, it was possible to define the striving for normalization as a mission of universal significance. But once the process of physical rehabilitation had achieved its goals at a reasonable level, and once it

was understood that no actual threat of a Holocaust hung over any part of the people, the meaning of things underwent a change. Normalization is not an infinite ideal. Once achieved, it ceases to be an ideal and ipso facto ceases to function as a unifying factor. Instead, it became a catalyst for competition among individuals, groups, and parties, groping for benefits from achievements in the here and now. In other words, presenting normalization as a goal after its having been achieved (the Six Day War was in retrospect an achievement demonstrating that the full rehabilitation of the people from the Holocaust was nigh) served as a kind of affirmation of egotistical competition as a basic value, rather than of the covenantal values upon which Israel had been established as the state of the Jewish people.

This has been the general feeling in the Jewish people in the past decade [the 1990s]. It now encompasses most of the Jewish public in Israel and the diaspora and is expressed in the shaping of the policy of the state's institutions and movements, including the areas of education and cultural creativity. The memory of the Holocaust still plays a role in shaping the consciousness of Jewish identity, but its meaning is undergoing a process of universalization, whose goal is to integrate the Jewish people into the family of nations rather than to set it apart from them. At the same time, the consciousness of "the covenant of destiny" that united the people after the Holocaust is breaking down. Within the State of Israel, this fact is expressed in the strengthening of the ideology of an "Israeli" identity, based upon citizenship in the State of Israel, while playing down the overall identity with the Jewish people, both in terms of historical continuity connecting Judaism to the exile and its creations, and that of connection to the Jews of the diaspora. The latter are seen as a resource for economic and political strength, but not as a partner in overall national responsibility.

As a result of that, there are increasing reservations about the Zionist definition of the State of Israel as the state of the Jewish people, or as a Jewish national state. The argument is that these definitions cannot be reconciled with the accepted contemporary definitions of a normal democratic state. Normalization necessitates the adoption of the liberal definition of "a state of all its citizens," with all that implies with regard to diaspora Jewry, the attitude toward the significant non-Jewish minorities within the State of Israel, and the constitutional rulings shaping the Jewish characteristics of the State of Israel.

Within the Jewish diaspora, this normalization is expressed first of all in an accelerated process of assimilation; second, in a declining level of existential identification with the State of Israel; and third, in a greater emphasis upon the local interests of each Jewish diaspora, with the tendency being the full integration and identification of the Jews of each diaspora with their specific countries. But this also applies to the relations that have developed among the rival movements within the Jewish people in Israel and in the diasporas. Normalization led to the breakdown of the covenant of destiny that united the people after the Holocaust, replaced by a *Kulturkampf* on many levels. All of the rifts that have deepened in the Jewish people from the time of the Emancipation until the Holocaust have reappeared, laden with violence and hatred. The question has been asked as to whether the Jewish people is still one people, and whether it has a common cultural language and cultural creativity. But these questions are superseded by one that is even more relentless: Can the fissures still be healed, or is fractionalization already an unalterable fact?

This is the meaning of the previous statement, that the generation within the Jewish people that was educated and matured after the Holocaust did not internalize from its immediate life experience the sense of belonging to *Klal Yisrael*, the community of the Jewish people, as an overall entity not concentrated in one country and with an age-old spiritual/cultural identity created mainly in *Galut* (exile). This means that, from the concrete existence of the Jewish people in all of its centers, the consciousness of a unifying covenant based upon a universal mission of a chosen people has not been internalized. Indeed, one can state that the generation that came of age after the Holocaust internalized a contrary message, and, since we are dealing with internalized life experience (as opposed to ideological indoctrination), it follows that the universal missionary message was not realized and therefore disappeared from the life reality of the Jewish

people in our generation. As such, it fits well into the mode defining "postmodernism" in Western culture.

As a matter of course, the problematic implications of this change for the unity of the Jewish people, and regarding the patterns of assimilation which are predominate therein, entered within consciousness well before the awareness of the spiritual change that had occurred on a deep level, for the spiritual and political leadership that engendered it did not intend for these implications to come about and is now much concerned about them. But if the dissolution of the Jewish people's identity still worries most of those identified as Jews, and if they understand that the State of Israel cannot exist as an independent state if it does not preserve its identity as a Jewish state—both from the standpoint of its being the state of the Jewish people and from that of being a state bearing constitutional, social, and cultural characteristics expressing its own tradition—they must reexamine the question of the normalcy of the Jewish people in its State and in the diaspora.

There is need for a deeper examination of the concept of normalization. Its imprint within political/Zionist ideology is not only the result of an anomalous national state of being, but also one of its expressions. No people that considers itself normal set the parameters for its collective life as an objective requiring fulfillment, but accept it as a factual datum. In this respect, normality means the acceptance by the people of itself as it was in the past, as it is now, and as it shall be in the future. For this reason it is impossible to present a model to demonstrate what a normal nation is. It is only possible to construct a theoretical model based upon characteristics common to most nations. I say "most" of them because there is no nation that does not differ from such a model in one or another of its characteristics, and each one certainly includes certain characteristics that make it unique. All of which goes to show that the concept of normal nationhood makes the Jewish people unique against the background of the consciousness of anomaly that has emerged within it in the modern age.

The great problem that follows from this statement is that the application of the terms of normalcy to the Jewish people, according to a comparative theoretical model suited to most peoples of Western culture in the postmodern period, would force it to relinquish its unique historical memory, including its religious and moral values; the pattern of its social, family, and community institutions; and its way of life and symbols that identified and made it unique throughout the generations. It should be noted that this does not mean that the Jewish people is totally unlike all other peoples. On the contrary, in terms of the basic definition of the concepts of ethnicity and nationalism, the Jewish people was throughout the generations a natural people. It also defined itself as a nation within its own legal framework. Furthermore, despite the salient differences between itself and the peoples among whom it resided, it always strove to be like them and even identify with them in the universal parameters of its culture. However, the ways in which it attempted to participate in the cultures of other peoples in itself set it apart from them. It absorbed influences, not in order to assimilate, but rather to strengthen its own selfhood and to grant itself universal validity.

This is the reason that normalization, as defined by Zionism, was understood both by its supporters and by those who opposed it as a deviation from the traditional parameters of normalcy of the Jewish people, to the extent that its application was understood as turning it into another people. The question was whether such a change could be made in the identity of the Jewish people while preserving its very existence as a nation among the nations. There have been many fierce arguments around this issue both within the Zionist movement and between it and its opponents. Today, when the goal of political/Zionist normalization is being realized within a large section of the people, one may unequivocally state that the answer is negative. Like all other peoples, the Jewish people cannot exist if it breaks with its historical memory, with the institutional patterns that united it and set it apart among the nations, and particularly with the basic elements of the covenant that has united it despite its dispersion, despite the revolutionary cultural changes it has undergone as a result of its encounters with the cultures of other nations, and despite the great disputes relating to the very consciousness of its mission.

The question that arises today against this background is: In light of the reality that has taken shape since the Second World War and the Holocaust, can one revive the unique universal sense of mission which underlies the covenant which established and maintained the Jewish people throughout the generations as *Klal Yisrael*, the community of Israel? Does the Torah that the Jewish people received as the basis and purpose of its existence among the peoples still have a vital, true message for itself and for humanity? Can this message be revitalized as a living *Halakhah* (religious law) formative of a culture and way of life?

These questions return us to the implications of the Holocaust for the relationship of the Jewish people to the missionary Torah heritage that united it throughout the generations. Is it possible, after all that the Jewish people and humanity experienced in the Holocaust and in the reality subsequently created, to return to the myth of the Sinai covenant—even on the basis of a new *midrash* [homiletical exposition of Scripture]? Fackenheim, who during the course of his intellectual development grappled with these questions as well, proposed a postmodern *midrash* that would maintain the Sinai myth in reverse, through its very refutation. But it would appear that the task he undertook, by its very definition, generated a negative answer: A *midrash* that assumes existential absurdity as part of its very essence cannot serve as the basis for a faith that unites a people. This is confirmed by reflection upon the state of mind that has actually shaped the views of Jews in our time.

The ultra-Orthodox and Orthodox movements do indeed adhere to a fundamentalist interpretation of the myths of Exodus and Sinai and, upon listening to their theological declarations, one may see that not only was their belief in Divine providence being revealed in the history of the Jewish people not refuted by the Holocaust, but it was actually strengthened. However, a comprehensive view of the positions that have guided all of the members of the Jewish people demonstrates that the Holocaust irreparably undermined the basis for a belief in Divine providence. First of all, such has been the feeling of most of the Jews actively involved in shaping the contemporary Jewish life experience of the non-Orthodox and nonreligious movements.

A realization of the implications of World War II and the Holocaust in the reality that was subsequently created led them to an existential certainty: It was impossible to discover in the life experience of humanity any "fingerprint" of Divine providence, any program, any orientation determined by an authority beyond the conflicting wishes of different individuals and human groups. Hence, reliance upon any sort of belief in providence seems to most members of contemporary Western culture, both non-Jews and Jews, as not only blind, but also as irresponsible. This feeling has also been expressed by some Orthodox thinkers, such as Yeshayahu Leibowitz and Yitzḥak Greenberg, who internalized the postmodernist attitudes and who today have quite a few disciples.

However, the entrenchment of most of the Orthodox movements in fundamentalist definitions regarding the issues of "providence" and "revealed Torah" is itself a self-refuting testimony. Fundamentalism means an automatic refusal to think in critical terms because of the foreknowledge that critical thinking would undermine faith. One can easily see that a belief that needs to be defended in such a manner is internally flawed and in need of outward-oriented zealotry so as to strengthen it from within. To my mind, this implies that the sense of reality of most Orthodox thinkers is no different from that of the majority of Jews in our time. Indeed, if belief is judged not by declarations, but by behavior that relies upon it, then the change in the position of the ultra-Orthodox movements toward political activity and worldly interests after the Holocaust speaks volumes.

Fackenheim is thus correct in his claim that the Holocaust refuted the philosophical myth of idealistic humanism, which identified Divine providence with human reason legislating human progress toward messianic goals. One might say that in this respect the Jewish people and the peoples of Western culture are in overall agreement, namely, that the experiential and philosophical underpinnings upon which modern religious movements based their theology of mission have been undermined. The same holds true for the secular social and national movements founded during the prewar period, which are likewise based upon inner historical laws of progress that have been refuted.

The inevitable conclusion is that, in the social, cultural, and political reality of the post-Holocaust era, there has been undone the experiential and intellectual hold of the myth of the chosen people as conceived in the Bible and its commentaries through the generations: the God who chose Himself a people and gave it the Torah so that they might testify to His Kingship. But if Fackenheim was correct in his third statement—namely, that humanity, including the Jewish people, carries the burden of responsibility for what happened in the Holocaust and that they are obligated from here on to act with the knowledge that it alone bears responsibility for what may happen in the future if its lessons are not implemented—then the necessary conclusion is, not normalization of the Jewish people according to the standard of the life of other nations, particularly as they define themselves within their states in the postmodern period, but rather denormalization of the internal and external relations of all peoples in accordance with the notion of the covenantal mission established in the ancient law of the Torah of Moses, which has been repeatedly interpreted in the Torah enterprise and in the efforts of the Jewish people to bring it to fruition.

A basis for this statement may be found in the contemporary condition of the Jewish people: We have seen above that its process of normalization, particularly in terms of its integration within the postmodern tendencies in the areas of interpersonal morality, society, state, international relations, and the shaping of human existence in terms of its deep memory and its spiritual meaning, leads to its disintegration and disappearance. These things are so tangible that they can no longer be doubted. Jews, for whom integration into postmodern existence is not only a matter of being swept up by what is seen as an unavoidable stream, but a chosen goal, express this explicitly by the statement that, even though they are Jews by origin, they neither possess Judaism nor want it.

The conclusion that follows from all this is that the continued existence of the Jewish people is dependent upon a sea change of missionary significance. It needs to unite itself around a different conception of realizing the moral responsibility incumbent upon human individuals, societies, and peoples—for their own future as individuals, as nations, and for that of humanity as a whole. This concept is indeed embodied in the Sinai covenant in its ideological, moral, legal/constitutional, and cultural aspects. From the standpoint of the Jewish people, this is once again a fateful juncture at which the covenant needs to be renewed: A decision needs to be taken between being swept up in the stream, which from the standpoint of the present it is convenient to connect with, but leads to oblivion, or to stand up against it through attention to the national human destiny. Concerning such matters, the Jewish people was commanded at all of its decisive junctions throughout its history: "Therefore you shall choose life."

But is there any basis in reality for the implementation of such a change? Can it be applied, and in what way can it be applied? These questions require a separate discussion. In general, one might answer that the change is not one of "religious return" or "revival" in the ultra-Orthodox sense that has by now become common coin—that is, return to a mythological-utopian point of reference in the past. Rather, it is a continuation toward a future based upon the fullness of a living heritage that renews itself in every generation, including our own generation, in all of the movements which have fractionalized and renewed the Jewish people. As noted, this process has continued in the modern age, and it has been partially surveyed above. A broad basis has been constructed for the renewal of Jewish life based upon the foundations of the covenant, not only in books, but also in living social and cultural creativity upon which were laid the foundations both for the establishment of the State of Israel

and for Jewish life in the diaspora. Upon this foundation, it will be possible to establish the ongoing creation, even though this clearly means going against the current, and this is an arduous task that cannot be realized without dedicated pioneering leadership.

I will conclude by mentioning the covenant that was renewed with the establishment of the State of Israel, as expressed in the Scroll of Independence: to establish a Jewish state, a state that will be the state of the entire Jewish people, that will realize the goal of its redemption throughout the generations, and thereby a state that will realize through its laws and practical policies the universal values of Judaism. In both these contexts, the Scroll of Independence fused responsibility for the ongoing existence of the Jewish people together with responsibility for the future of humankind, relying upon the "eternal book of books," upon the yearning of all of the generations to be redeemed, upon the Zionist enterprise, on the one hand, and upon the Universal Declaration of Human Rights of the United Nations, on the other. It was upon these foundations that the founding fathers of the State of Israel pledged to establish a state "based upon the principles of freedom, justice, and peace in light of the vision of the prophets of Israel."

These statements, although general, are not empty rhetoric. They embody an entire theory that was implemented in the pioneering endeavor that laid down the social and national-cultural foundations for the establishment of the State. This document is, therefore, a promissory note which the Jewish people must redeem in its state and in its diaspora, both for itself and for humanity.

Pinchas Peli

Pinchas Peli (1930–1989) was born in Jerusalem to a distinguished rabbinic, ḥasidic, that is, ultra-Orthodox, family. After receiving a strong traditional Jewish education in his youth, he went on to receive a B.A. in Jewish history and Talmud at Hebrew University and to become a strong supporter of the religious Zionist cause. Already at the age of sixteen he began to publish poetry in the Israeli newspaper *Davar* under the pseudonym Peli (= wonder) because he was afraid to use his real name (Hacohen) given that his family lived in Meah Shearim, the ultrareligious quarter of Jerusalem. He thereafter adopted this as his actual name. Also, while still a student, he became the editor of *Panim el Panim* (*Face to Face*), a weekly magazine published by Mosad Harav Kook, a major religious publishing house.

After his initial academic appointment in Israel, Peli served as professor at Yeshiva University in New York from 1967 until 1971. There he became a friend and disciple of Rav Joseph B. Soloveitchik. While in New York, he wrote his doctoral dissertation under the supervision of R. Abraham Joshua Heschel of the Jewish Theological Seminary. In 1971, he accepted a call to become professor of Hebrew literature and Jewish studies at the new Ben Gurion University in Beersheva, Israel. From 1979 on, he was the incumbent of the university's chair for Jewish values. A regular visitor to American universities, he taught as a visiting professor at the Jewish Theological Seminary of America, Yeshiva University, Cornell University, and Notre Dame. In addition, he was a visiting professor at the Makuya Bible Seminary in Japan and the Seminario Rabbinico in Buenos Aires, Argentina. He was also an active participant in Jewish-Christian dialogue, representing the State of Israel at Vatican conferences.

His first publication was a Hebrew book of poetry entitled *Five Springs*, published in Jerusalem in 1950. He then went on to publish numerous articles in the fields of Jewish thought and Hebrew literature, as well as on social and ideological issues. In addition, starting in 1986, he wrote a weekly column for the *Jerusalem Post* newspaper dealing with the biblical portion of the week that is read each Sabbath in the synagogue. The erudition and charm of these columns made him a widely recognized figure both in Israel and abroad. Many of these columns were eventually collected under the title *Torah Today* (1987). Nine of his major articles were published after his death in the Hebrew book *Perakim be-machshevet medinat Israel* (*Chapters in Jewish Thought in the Land of Israel*).

SELECTION

In his essay "Borderline: Searching for a Religious Language of the *Shoah*," Pinchas Peli explored the need for unique linguistic and conceptual tools through which to address appropriately the uniqueness of the *Shoah*. His basic premise was that while we may never be able to answer the question "Where was God during the *Shoah*?" we certainly need to try to understand the Holocaust as an event of human and religious significance. Moreover, Peli argued, in so doing, it is essential to remain "in dialogue" with God. Indeed, on a topic as serious as the *Shoah*, "God cannot remain outside of meaning."

Peli outlined a wide range of Jewish responses to the murder of European Jewry, summarizing a number of theological arguments and offering a reasoned critique of each. Among the positions he engaged are different reward and punishment models—here he included arguments regarding Zionism, opposition to Zionism, and assimilation—as well as the classical theological "free choice" arguments, the argument for silence, and the death-of-God theology. While Peli may have indicated his own preference for certain of these responses as being more persuasive, it was not his goal in this essay to select the "correct" answer. Rather, he stressed that because we must say something in response to "What happened during the *Shoah*?" we need to develop an appropriate religious language that will help us grapple with this urgent Jewish and human conundrum.

This essay originally appeared in the Hebrew journal *Yerushalayim* 11–12 (1977): 105–125.

Selected Bibliography

Books by Pinchas Peli

Editor of *On Repentance in the Thought and Oral Discourses of Rabbi Joseph B. Soloveitchik* (New York, 1980).
Torah Today (Washington, D.C., 1987; reprint, Austin, Tex., 2005).
Chapters in Jewish Thought in the Land of Israel (Bet-El, 1990) [Hebrew].
The Jewish Sabbath: A Renewed Encounter (1991) [New York, Hebrew].

BORDERLINE: SEARCHING FOR A RELIGIOUS LANGUAGE OF THE *Shoah*

The *Shoah* is unprecedented in the annals of Jewish history, if not in the scope of its destruction (in absolute or relative terms), then certainly in the advance planning and public enunciation of its goals. From the viewpoint of humanity in general, the *Shoah* also demonstrated an entirely new combination involving the use of advanced technological methods which were among the magnificent achievements of modernity, together with nefarious characters with abysmally evil intentions and a capacity for cruelty such as we have never known nor have wanted to know. We dis-covered the existence of a dark underside to humanity, among those considered "enlightened" as well as those who are considered "primitive." The huge number of human beasts of prey with their perfected machines of destruction who arose from deep chasms of evil did not appear out of primeval forests, but from within the walls of universities and cultural institutions.

The *Shoah*, as many claim,[1] stands out in its uniqueness and singularity, and not only because it is the incarnation of the fiercest and ugliest evil to raise its head in modern times. It refutes several

1. See Emil L. Fackenheim, *God's Presence in History* (New York, 1970), pp. 69–70. People of other nations and races perished in the Second World War, and their numbers even exceed that of the Jews who were murdered. But those wartime deaths, and even the destruc-tion of peoples during and after the war, are different in substance from the planned and ideological destruction of the Jews. This began, during the rise of Nazism, in "scientific" literature and research that drew on "traditional" anti-Semitic sources, and its implementation

accepted historiosophical, sociological, and anthropological assumptions, so that these disciplines and others are only just beginning to deal with this period as an object of study. Here and there, a few begin to penetrate the topic, out of horror and the urgent need to comprehend and understand it, and not only in order to prevent its repetition, if that is possible.[2] All agree that confronting the conundrum of the Holocaust is difficult, depressing, and deterring. Yet the lack of desire or ability to confront this challenge does not diminish the obligation or its urgency. Just as crucial for the believer, and for faith in general, is the difficult confrontation with one particular issue which, simply formulated, is: Where was God during the *Shoah*?

When thusly expressed, this unsophisticated and banal question is not as trivial as it sounds. It also implies the following:

a. What part did God play before and during the *Shoah*? Was He involved in the decision that it would take place ("Man does not lift a finger below without His declaration from above")?[3] And if so, why?

b. During the *Shoah*, was He there, in the midst of the horror of the most awful of awful tortures? If so, how can this be, if He is the "merciful and gracious God"?[4]

c. After the *Shoah*, the world returned to its routine concerns, and Jews to synagogues and keeping *mitzvot* (commandments) as before, as if nothing had happened to undermine our belief in Him from time immemorial ("Our God and God of our forefathers").[5] How could this be?

Many attempts have been made to get around these questions in all their simplicity and complexity and to reject their urgency by transferring them to "another planet,"[6] in place as well as time. Some have maintained that because the existential and emotional impact of the *Shoah* makes it difficult to comprehend, conceptually or cognitively, therefore we must push away, repress, or transfer the entire period between 1938 and 1944[7] to metahistory or metageography. The use of the very expression *Shoah* or "Holocaust"[8] even further removes those years from the standard course of events in normative human history.

sometimes went against the interests of the destroyers themselves. Other holocausts, such as forced-labor camps in Russia, the bombing of Hiroshima and Nagasaki, the butchery in Indonesia and Bangladesh, all demonstrate significant differences from the *Shoah*, even though similarities and connections (some obvious, others subtle) can also be found. See Shaul Friedlander, *Mashmauta Hahistorit Shel Hashoah* [*The Historical Significance of the Shoah*], *Molad* (Spring 5735): 243–244, 328–340; Norman Lamm, "Teaching the Holocaust," *Forum* 1 (1976): 57ff.; the anthology *Out of the Whirlwind*, edited by Albert R. Friedlander (New York, 1968), pp. 462ff. For a non-Jewish point of view, see Marcel R. Dubois, "Christian Reflections on the Holocaust," in David Burrell and Yehezkel Landau, eds., *Voices from Jerusalem: Jews and Christians Reflect on the Holy Land* (New York, 1992), pp. 4–5.

2. Among the few serious attempts in this direction was the four-day symposium at St. John's Cathedral in New York, organized in June 1972 by Professor Irving (Yitzhak) Greenberg, director of the Jewish studies program at City College of New York, on the topic "Auschwitz: The Beginning of a New Era." [The papers given at this conference have been edited by Eva Fleischner (Hoboken, N.J., 1977).] A similar conference took place at the same time sponsored by Hebrew University's Institute of Contemporary Judaism.

3. B.T. *Hullin* 7[b].

4. Two of the thirteen attributes in which the God of Israel reveals Himself. See Numbers 34:6; the Prophets (Joel 2:13; Jonah 4:2); the Writings (Psalms 86:15 and 103:8; Nehemiah 9:17; 2 Chronicles 30:9; and elsewhere); and the prayerbook.

5. Biblical expression appearing frequently in prayers. See, for example, Deuteronomy 26:7.

6. The *Shoah* as taking place on "another planet" was described by the Holocaust survivor and author Katzetnik in his testimony at the Eichmann trial in Jerusalem.

7. The organized aggression against Jews began openly with *Kristallnacht* (9 November 1938), while the anti-Jewish laws had begun years earlier, as soon as the Nazis rose to power.

8. The source of this expression is in the Bible (Proverbs 3:25; Isaiah 10:3 and 47:11), where it means a sudden natural disaster. It was first used by historian Yoav Gelber in Israel, while the expression "destruction" (*hurban*) was at first popular in Europe. In the letters of the Gerrer Rebbe, one of the first refugees of Warsaw who arrived in the Land of Israel, he calls what happened in Poland *hasha'aruya* which in modern Hebrew means "the scandal" but connotes the Holocaust when used by the Gerrer Rebbe and others (see *Holy Letters* [Tel Aviv, 5720/1959], p. 64). Holocaust, the accepted translation for *Shoah*, comes from the sacral language as the translation of the term for a burnt offering which is completely consumed on the altar.

This repression into the subconscious, and recently even in the consciousness of the Germans, Austrians, and their confederates, has enabled many to observe with equanimity of spirit the green grass sprouting in the fields of Theresienstadt and Treblinka.

Metaphysics and theology are also invoked and facilitate the use of expressions borrowed from metahistory and metageography. There are those who speak of the "demonization"[9] of the *Shoah* and other forms of temporary or permanent release of God from responsibility for what happened during that period. These attempts may provide temporary escape from the painful confrontation with the problem that continues to grip the Jew who believes or wants to believe, as long as he approaches his Creator in prayer or fulfillment of *mitzvot* (commandments). But sooner or later he will feel the folly of pretense, since he who prays to the Holy One knows that He is truth and rejects falsehood, and therefore the believing Jew cannot lie to Him.[10] He will recall again and again that the entire Torah and writings of the prophets are a reminder to "Remember the days of yore, understand the years of generation after generation."[11] Despite the difficulty and painfulness, the Jew is obliged to search beyond simplistic theological speculations for the significance of the events he participates in and witnesses. He is commanded, and stands to learn and draw conclusions[12] from what happens before his eyes, as in the verse "You have seen" (Exodus19:4).

We are not always granted the ability to arrive at an acceptable explanation for what happens. On the contrary, the greater the impact of a historical event, the more it remains "an unsolvable mystery" to all except the One who "proclaimed the generations from the beginning"[13] and for whom all mysteries are solved. But if there is no satisfactory explanation, there is a meaningful response[14] and an attempt to learn something of significance. This significance is not outside God or history and certainly not outside the ability of language to provide tools to deal with the questions.

So we arrive at the problem that will serve as the focus of this discussion: the use of religious language in understanding the *Shoah*.[15] I should immediately emphasize that I do not mean

9. See especially the Jewish scholar Richard L. Rubenstein, who makes the *Shoah* the basis for "radical Jewish theology" in the style of Christian theology concerning the death of God, in his book *After Auschwitz* (Indianapolis, 1966), especially pp. 153–154; compare with Professor Yirmiyahu Yovel's *Hashoah Kemarkiv Betoda'ateinu Ha'atzmit* ["The Shoah as a Component of Our Self-Awareness"], *Ha'aretz*, 4 August 1975; and Haim Shetzker, *Megamot Betfisat Hashoah Behevra Hayisraelit* ["Directions in Israeli Society in Understanding the Shoah"], *Ha'aretz*, 4 August 1975. [Selections from Richard L. Rubenstein's work are republished in part III of this collection.]

10. B.T. *Yoma* 69[b]: "Because they know that the Holy One, blessed be He, is true [Rashi: [He] accepts the truth and abhors lies], therefore they do not lie to Him." This refers to the rendering of the prayer service into a permanent format.

11. Deuteronomy 32:7. This idea that God directs the world and regulates history appears throughout the Torah, prophets, writings of the sages, and the prayerbook.

12. When we draw conclusions, the problem of evil in the world becomes evident to a certain extent. Rabbi Joseph B. Soloveitchik clarifies this and bases it on sources in his cautioning essay *Kol Dodi Dofek* [*Listen My Beloved Knocks*, ed. Jeffrey R. Wolf, trans. David Z.

Gordon (Jersey City, 2006)]. He divides the evil of human existence into two types. The first is fatalistic, compulsive existence, in which humanity is dumbfounded by evil and cannot comprehend it. Some are completely paralyzed by this, in thought and action. The other type is purposeful existence, in which humanity attempts to face evil, confront it, and draw conclusions regarding its purpose. See the entire essay in *Besod Hayehid Vehayehad* [*In Aloneness, in Togetherness*], a selection of Hebrew essays by Rabbi Soloveitchik, edited by Pinchas Peli (Jerusalem, 5736/1975), especially pp. 333–347.

13. Isaiah 41:4. This is also the feeling that the Book of Job tries to impart by silencing Job when he demands "explanations." Regarding this, see below.

14. An anthology of religious responses to the *Shoah*, some of which appear later in this article, was published as *Readings for Religious Responses to the Holocaust* by the School of Overseas Students of the Hebrew University (Jerusalem, 1973), edited by Pinchas Peli.

15. The problem of "religious language," central to classical theology and the philosophy of religion, has attracted attention in contemporary times in both empiricist and analytical philosophy. See the interesting anthology *Words about God*, edited by Ian T. Ramsey (New York, 1971), and his book *Religious Language* (New York, 1963).

theodicy. Every attempt in this direction (and such attempts exist, as will be seen below) responds to the three questions raised above, which are included in the simplistic phrasing of the question of God's role or presence in the *Shoah*. Furthermore, it seems that every attempt toward theodicy on our part (we who were not with those in the furnaces) includes a certain amount of conceit, sometimes bordering on self-righteous cruelty. This contradicts the spirit of Jewish prayer[16] and Israel's nature as expressed by the sages in the phrase "merciful sons of merciful ones."[17] Every justification of God places blame of some kind on the Jews, but the empathy we have for the *Shoah* victims hinders us from accepting this easily.[18] In this search for a religious language of the *Shoah*, I will attempt neither to explain nor to legitimize. In truth, I do not mean sacred language, but rather descriptive language in the field of religion that describes the *Shoah*, to differentiate, for example, from the field of quantitative measurement of statistics or qualitative historical-political evaluation. With such language, we can perhaps arrive at the question that J. L. Magnes asked in a lecture at the Hebrew University at the inauguration ceremony of the

1944–1945 (5705) school year. This is one of the most penetrating statements of theology of the *Shoah*, spoken as the full extent of the European vale of tears began to unfold when the war drew to a close.[19] Magnes purposely attributed the statement to the great defender of the people of Israel, Rabbi Levi Yitzhak of Berditchev:[20] "I do not ask you, Master of the universe, to reveal to me the secrets of Your ways—I could not endure them. I do not desire to know why I suffer, only whether I suffer on Your behalf."

This "on Your behalf" seems too strong for a vocabulary appropriate for the immense terrors of the *Shoah*. In my opinion, it would be better if we rewrote the end of Rabbi Levi Yitzhak's statement: "I do not desire to know why I suffer… but only whether You know that I suffer."

In other words, we want to know whether and how reciprocal Divine-human communication exists regarding this event. Can we continue to speak to each other in an "I-Thou" or "I-Him-You" relationship,[21] as Jewish tradition had taught us up until the *Shoah*? In religious life, we cannot accept Wittgenstein's logical prohibition against metaphysical sentences that are not descriptive.[22]

---

16. See Abraham Joshua Heschel, *Man's Quest for God* (New York, 1954); Jacob J. Petuchowski, *Understanding Jewish Prayer* (New York, 1972); and Joseph Heinemann, *Tfila Bamahshevet Hazal* [*Prayer in the Thought of the Sages*] (Jerusalem, 5720/1959). Unlike Christian prayer in which the main principle is "Thy will be done," our forefather Abraham is not willing to justify His verdict by saying "righteousness is Yours," but rather asks difficult questions.

17. B.T. *Yevamot* 79[a]; and B.T. *Beitza* 32[b].

18. See the introduction to Eliezer Berkovits's book *Faith after the Holocaust* (New York, 1973), pp. 3–6, and see below regarding his legitimate reservations. [Selections from this work appear in part III of this collection.]

19. J. L. Magnes, *Ki Aleikha Huragnu Kol Hayom* ["For You Were We Killed Daily"], in his book *B'mvukhat Hazman* [*In Confusing Times*] (Jerusalem, 5705/1944), pp. 43–50.

20. The figure of Rabbi Levi Yitzhak of Berditchev, known in the popular hasidic tradition as a lover and defender of Israel before God, appears often in literature of the *Shoah* period. See also Itzik Manger, *Berogez* ["Angry"], in *Leid Un Ballade* (Tel Aviv, 5704/1943), p. 459; Uri Zvi Greenberg, *Beketz Hadrakhim Omed Rabbi Levi Yitzhak MeBerditchev Vedoresh Tshuvat Ram* ["Rabbi Levi Yitzhak of Berditchev

Stands at the End of the Road and Demands a Loud Reply"], in *Rehovot Hanahar* (Tel Aviv, 5711), pp. 271–275.

21. The dialogue between God and humanity in Jewish tradition is always in terms of "You" ("One praying should view himself as if the *Shekhinah* [Divine Presence] were before him"; B.T. *Sanhedrin* 22[a]). Some maintain that it is a direct "I-Thou" relationship, such as Franz Rosenzweig and Martin Buber describe. See Buber's *Ani Veata* (*I and Thou*), translated by Z. Wiselevsky (Jerusalem, 1959); and the booklet *Giluyim Letoldot Hithavot Hasefer "Ani Veata" Shel Martin Buber* [*On the History of Martin's Buber's Book "Ani Veata"*] by Rivka Horwitz (Jerusalem, 5735/1974), regarding Rosenzweig's role in formulating this terminology. Some hold that the relationship between man and God is not direct but passes first through a stage of fear that precedes love, or "I-Him-You." See J. B. Soloveitchik, *Ish Haemunah* [*The Lonely Man of Faith*] (Jerusalem, 1968), p. 28, in the original, "The Lonely Man of Faith," *Tradition* 7, no. 2 (summer 1965): 5–67.

22. As quoted in Yosef Shechter, *Yahadut Vehinukh Bazman Hazeh* [*Judaism and Education in Modernity*] (Tel Aviv, 5726/1965), pp. 28–29. See also *Yehadut: Mikra'ah* [*Judaism: A Reader*], edited by Yosef Bentwich (Tel Aviv, 5728/1967), p. 7.

The believer, at least in the Judaism of prayer, Torah, and *mitzvot* that constantly brings a Jew to stand before God, overturns Wittgenstein's sentence and insists that it is essential to speak of that about which we cannot speak! But these words cannot be nonsense or gibberish. This is speech before God, and the Jew must "place his soul in His palm" before beginning.[23] If man has no descriptive language, he must exert himself to obtain it; he must excavate the quarries of religious language and extract it from there. This, therefore, lends urgency to the search for a religious language appropriate for the *Shoah*. The existence and continuation of the Divine-human dialogue depends on this language, for language, since biblical times, is at the crux of the Jewish experience.[24]

This language must be refined so that it relates to the events as they took place. These events are incontrovertible facts, whose existence cannot be doubted. They are facts of human history and facts before God, which seem to involve Him in the unfolding of the events, whether His participation was active or passive.

According to a Jewish understanding, it cannot be that God stepped out, whether for an hour or an eternity, from world history, for this is the very world that He created and with whose life and destiny He is connected.[25] The need for a religious language appropriate to the *Shoah* derives from the assumption that it was not a random incident, not a political-historical coincidence, as in "what was, will be,"[26] but that it had significance before God, all-seeing and all-knowing (even if He "hid His face," willingly or under compulsion). God cannot remain outside of meaning, or at least outside of the human language into which this meaning or its absence is translated.

This meaning is not synonymous with justification. Meaning can also be negative. It seems that today, the question remains open whether Job was truly convinced, whether he accepted the verdict and was reconciled after hearing God's speech from within the whirlwind.[27] The Bible, however, relates that the speech took place, since this means that God remained present, beside Job, whether Job was right or wrong. From here we arrive at our question: In what language did God speak, or what language do we use to speak to and about God from within the Jobian whirlwind of 1938–1945, or 1933–1948?

Both during the war and afterward, attempts were made to fathom the religious significance of the *Shoah*.[28] We can group these attempts into categories which are based on Jewish sources, especially the Bible, which naturally serves as the basis of religious thought in everything relating to understanding God and His ways. These categories might even be of help in the search for a religious language that is suitable for relating to the *Shoah*. The common denominator of these attempts at a typology of the *Shoah* is that they search for theodicy, in other words, justification of God or of the *Shoah*, and they do not limit themselves to the descriptive language that is our goal.

23. B.T. *Ta'anit* 8ᵃ: "Man's prayer is not heard until he places his soul in His palm."
24. Regarding the difficulties of religious expression in general, see Maimonides, *Moreh Nevukhim* [*Guide of the Perplexed*], part 1, end of sec. 3.
25. Compare Abraham Joshua Heschel, *God in Search of Man* (New York, 1955), pp. 235–248 and 412.
26. In contrast to Yeshayahu Leibowitz in *Yehadut, Am Yehudi Vemedinat Israel* [*Judaism, the Jewish People, and the State of Israel*], ed. Eliezer Goldman, trans. Eliezer Goldman and Yoram Navon (Cambridge, Mass., 1995)] (Jerusalem and Tel Aviv, 5736/1975), pp. 410ff. See also p. 92: "Historical events, for humanity in general and the Jewish people in particular, are in themselves neutral from the perspective of any religious value or meaning."
27. For different solutions to the riddle of the figure of Job from various viewpoints (Jewish, Christian, and literary), see *The Dimensions of Job*, edited by Nahum Glatzer (New York, 1969).
28. See the writings of Fackenheim, Berkovits, Rubenstein, and several chapters from the anthology edited by Peli mentioned above. Also, in *Understanding Jewish Theology*, edited by Jacob Neusner (New York, 1973), see the chapter "Implications of the Holocaust" by Neusner, pp. 177–194. A selected bibliography on *Mashmaut Hashoah Beaspeklaria Datit* ["The Significance of the *Shoah* from a Religious Perspective"] can be found at the end of the anthology *Ani Ma'amin* [*I Believe*], expanded version, edited by Mordekhai Eliav (Jerusalem, 5729/1969). [Selections from Fackenheim, Berkovits, and Rubenstein also are republished in part III of this collection.]

Aside from those who give up on some sort of solution,[29] or who declare that the *Shoah* "proved" that there is no God,[30] there exists a wide variety of religious responses. These responses are grouped into categories as follows.

Model 1: The First Man

The formula here is simple: transgression and punishment. Man defies God's word and is banished from Eden and punished. This is a classic model that appears frequently in the Bible (although it is not a monolithic explanation for all evil, and related to it is the classic problem of "the suffering of the righteous").

Several frequent objections to this model are

1. Can there be a sin that is so terrible that it would justify the killing of six million individuals? They were transported to the camps from various countries for the purpose of murder solely because they shared an identity as Jews. The sin that brought in its wake such punishment upon them must be connected to what they had in common: their Judaism.
2. If some of the condemned individuals sinned, they could not all have committed the same sin. They included religious and secular, believers

and *apikorsim* (cynical nonbelievers), men and women, elderly and young, nationalists and assimilated, hasidim and their opponents—a wide variety of types of people. Could it be that all were punished for the same sin? There must have been innocents; why were they also punished?

The religious and rabbinical literature of the last generation has clear and articulate responses to these two sets of questions and has a rationale for applying the sin-punishment approach to questions about the *Shoah*. These answers are not vague generalizations such as the admission of our culpability that we make to God on Yom Kippur (The Day of Atonement), "because You are righteous in all [suffering] that has come upon us, while we have caused wickedness."[31] Rather, these responses point clearly to the nature of the sin that caused the destruction. The responses in this category repeatedly refer to citations from the Bible, writings of the Sages, and the literature of Jewish religious thought. The second critique, that the innocent were punished together with the guilty, is unfounded, since it is an accepted principle that when punishment is meted out to the nation, the righteous are stricken along with the wicked,[32] and individual righteous persons are judged together with their fellow citizens or the

---

29. For example, Rabbi Yissachar Yakobson (*Deot*, Spring 5722/1962, pp. 26–28) thinks that

> regarding the problem of the *Shoah*, we must give up on an intellectual solution, in order to remain faithful, God-fearing, observant, and altruistic.... Job taught us to believe in God, to trust a Divinity who is not congruent with our human sense of morality. Perhaps we can use an adaptation from the words of Rabbi Shlomo Ibn Gavirol [C. 1021–C. 1058] in *Keter Malkhut*: "I flee from You, to You." In other words, I flee from You, the Divinity whose ways I do not comprehend, to my unquestioning faith in the Blessed One.... Our generation requires a *difficult* [emphasis in the original] faith, one that demands much from the believer. Human intelligence does not comprehend the disaster and the fate of one-third of our people, yet our belief in God remains unshaken, as Job demonstrated to his generation and subsequent ones.

30. A collection of material in this vein appears in Alexander Donat's article *Kol Mitokh Haefer: Masah Nedu-*

dim Behipus Ahrei Haelokim ["Voice from the Ashes: Wanderings in Search of God"], *Yalkut Moreshet* 21 (Sivan 5736/1976): 105–138, excerpts from which also appear in this volume. See also Moshe Unna's response, *Mi Yirpeh Lekha* ["Who Can Heal You?"], *Yalkut Moreshet* 22 (Kislev 5737/1976): 63–68, which also is reprinted in this volume.

31. From the *vidui* [confession] said on the Day of Atonement. Although it is followed by a listing of specific sins in the prayer *ashamnu* ["We have become guilty"] and *al het* ["For the sin that we have sinned before You by . . . "], this acceptance of God's judgment [*tziduk hadin*] does not exempt us from searching for the sins that led to the verdict. The identification of sins leads to acceptance of the declaration that *hatzur tamim poalo, ki kol drakhav mishpat* ["The Rock—perfect is His work, for all His paths are justice"].

32. See B.T. *Baba Kamma* 92[a] ("Together with the thorn the cabbage is smitten," i.e., the good are punished with the bad); *Mishnah Negaim* 12:6 ("Woe to the wicked one and woe to his neighbor"); and B.T. *Sukkah* 56[b].

sinful public.[33] Three sins are usually mentioned in this context:

1. The sin of Zionism. This means the attempt to "force the end" [*lidḥok et haketz*], to make *aliya* (emigration) to the Land of Israel en masse in preparation for the coming of the messiah. This sin violates the oaths that, according to a talmudic tradition, the Holy One made Israel take "not to storm the wall" and "not to rebel against the nations" during their years in exile.[34] Violation of these oaths on Israel's part is what caused Divine protection to be withdrawn. Rabbi Yoel Teitelbaum, the [ḥasidic] Rebbe of Satmar, develops this idea at length with great fervor.[35] In his writings, he is adamant that because the Jews attempted to terminate the diaspora before the appointed end of time, the diaspora terminated them as punishment for forcing the end. Thus, he argues:

> Behold, when times of trouble visited the house of Jacob over the generations, they sought for some meaning or explanation, and searched within the nation of Israel to ascertain what sin had caused this situation. They would take notice, mend their ways, and return to the Blessed Name, as we see in the Bible and the Talmud. . . . Now in our generation, we do not have to search for the sin that brought this woe upon us, because it is quite explicit in the writings of our sages. In their

interpretation of the Bible they have told us that because of our violation of the oaths not to storm the wall and not to force the end, God forbid, "I will permit your flesh as prey like the deer or the gazelles of the field." Our multitude of sins was such that the heretics and skeptics made all kinds of attempts to violate these oaths and to "storm the wall" by creating their own government and declaring their own freedom before the right time. This is "forcing the end," and they attracted the hearts of most of the people of Israel to this defiled idea. . . . No wonder that this provoked God's great anger and fury. . . . In the hour of destruction, the supremely righteous were also killed because of the crimes of these sinners and instigators, and due to our many sins, His wrath was very great.[36]

According to the Rebbe of Satmar, the punishment for the sin of forcing the end extended beyond the *Shoah*, and continued with the establishment of the State of Israel and the victory of the Six Day War. In this, the Satmar Rebbe is not alone, even if he seems alone in his interpretation of the connection between the *Shoah* and the State of Israel, which he sees as the continuation of God's punishment and testing of the Jews. Accordingly he contends that:

---

33. See Maimonides, *Mishneh Torah*, Laws of Repentance 83:1–2, and comment of *Leḥem Mishneh*; the source for the ruling is in B.T. *Kiddushin* 40[b]. It may be that this concept is referred to by Rabbi Akiva in Mishnah *Avot* 3:18: "Everything is predicted but freedom of choice is given, and we will be judged according . . . to the [behavior of the] majority" (I owe this source to a comment by Professor Gerald Blidstein).

34. B.T. *Ketuvot* 111[a]:

> Rabbi Yosi said in the name of Rabbi Hanina: "What are these three oaths [written in the Song of Songs]? One, that Israel should not storm the wall [Rashi interprets: forcefully]. Two, the Holy One made Israel take an oath not to rebel against the nations of the world. Three, the Holy One made the nations vow that they would not enslave Israel too harshly" Rabbi Eliezer said, "The Holy One said to Israel: If you fulfill the oaths, things will go well for you; and if not, I permit your flesh as prey like the deer or the gazelles of the field."

35. Yoel Teitelbaum, *Vayoel Moshe: Explaining the Laws of the Three Oaths . . . Which I Collected and Gathered*

from Reliable Sources, May God Take Pity upon Me, in the Merit of My Forefathers and Holy Rabbis, 2d ed. (Brooklyn, 5721/1961). This book caused an uproar in religious circles because of its extreme language, which borders on hatred of his fellow Jews and enmity toward Zionism. Among the many responses and critiques of this book are Ḥaim Lieberman, *Der Rebbe Un Der Satan* [*The Rabbi and Satan*] (New York, 5709/1950); Shmuel Hacohen Weingarten, *Hishbati Etkhem: Iyunim Vebirurim Beinyan Shalosh Hashevuot* [*I Have Sworn You to This: Studies and Analyses of the Three Oaths*] (Jerusalem, 5736/1975); Rabbi A. H. Zimmerman, *Beinyan Shalosh Hashevuot* [*Regarding the Three Oaths*], *Hatzofeh*, 10 Elul 5733 [7 September 1973]. After the appearance of critiques and debates on the book and after the stunning victory of the Zionists in the Six Day War, the Rebbe of Satmar again sounded the battle cry and published *Al Hageula Ve'al Hatmura* [*Of Redemption and Consequences*] (Brooklyn, 5727/1967), which repeats his thesis regarding Zionism's direct causal connection to the *Shoah*. [See also the Hutner selection in part III; and part I, pp. 33–34.]

36. Teitelbaum, *Vayoel Moshe*, p. 5.

The remainder of the people of Israel that the Holy One spared, in fulfillment of his vow that their seed would not die out, were also given a difficult and bitter punishment, in the success of the satanic deed of the heretical reign that tests the people of Israel with a monumental trial.... We still do not realize that all the troubles and hardships that have come upon us were because of these evildoers.... Now anyone who has a brain in his skull can recognize the truth, that it is the sin of those who promote the defiled idea of Zionism, and who work for the fulfillment of this defiled idea, that has led to all our troubles and hardships.[37]

Even after the Six Day War, when many observers considered Israel's military miraculous, the Satmar Rebbe remained firm in the sin-and-punishment view.

Because of our many sins, this abomination continues even now in Israel. Some think the recent events are akin to the miracles and wonders performed by God in Egypt of yore. They do not notice that this increases the power of the defiled Zionists, who are a thousand times worse than the worshippers of the Golden Calf. There has never been such a total heresy as Zionism.[38]

Aside from the identification of Zionism as the sin which justified the Shoah retrospectively, and which continued to fester afterward, the model of transgression and punishment sometimes identifies another sin, which is the opposite of the first, as the cause of the tragedy:

2. The sin of opposing Zionism. In this view, there was a time when Israel was remembered on high and called upon to exit the diaspora and make aliya (emigrate) to the Land of Israel. But most of the nation did not awaken to the signs of impending redemption. They remained in exile and did not return to the Land of Israel. This argument says that because the people did not want to terminate the exile, the exile came and terminated them. Rabbi Yissakhar Taykhtahl expresses this position harshly in Em Habanim Semeḥah [A Happy Mother of Children (which is excerpted in part I, pp. 75–82, of this volume)]. He published this work in 1944 at the height of the devastation,[39] years before the post-Shoah publication of the book by the Rebbe of Satmar. As he notes on the book's title page, "In the Vale of Gloom," Rabbi Taykhtahl expresses his painful and tortured tziduk hadin (acceptance of God's judgment), wherein he searches for a reason that would justify the suffering, in the hope that the Shoah will not be implemented in its entirety and that a "window of hope" still remains for salvation and exodus from the gloomy valley.[40]

Rabbi Taykhtahl's argument for justifying the Shoah is clear and well documented with numerous references from the midrashic and traditional literature:

After I present to you, dear reader, the words of my revered and holy predecessors, you will see that more than eighty years ago the Holy Spirit awakened.... We were encouraged to return to the bosom of our motherland rather than remain

37. Teitelbaum, Vayoel Moshe, p. 8.
38. Teitelbaum, Al Hageula Ve'al Hatmura, p. 19.
39. The book Em Habanim Semeḥah is based on the liberation and redemption of our souls from the final exile after doing everything that our God and the God of our forefathers, the Creator of all worlds, has requested of us and commanded us to do regarding the hastening of the redemption.... Composed by myself, least among Israel's thousands, Issachar Taykhtahl.... I began arranging the manuscript of the present book on the third day of the Va'era portion in the year 5703 [January 1943], in the above-mentioned capital city in the Vale of Gloom [emphasis in the original] during the terrible birth pangs of the Messiah, and the suffering surrounding us during the years of the present Second World War. May God enable us to find ourselves at war's

end at the threshold of an opening for hope [Petaḥ Tikva]. We should speedily envision Israel's salvation and its glorification, "when God will return the captivity of Zion" speedily and in our days, amen. (Budapest, 5703/1943), p. 113, n. 39 [an English translation under the title Eim Habanim Semeichah: On Eretz Yisrael, Redemption and Unity, trans. Moshe Lichtman, was published in Brooklyn, N.Y., in 2000]

40. During the printing in 1944, the author added a "second introduction" that, when compared to the first, deeply evokes the feeling of approaching dread as the noose tightened around the necks of Hungarian Jewry. See Yissakhar Taykhtahl, Em Habanim Semeḥah. An English translation of this "second introduction" is in part I, pp. 75–82, of this collection.

in the embrace of gentile lands. We should contribute our strength, our wealth, and our property in order to build up our Holy Land, to raise it up from dust, and to improve it and glorify our kingdom. . . . [He commanded us] to awaken our brothers, the children of Israel, to buy land within the Land of Israel from the hands of the Ishmaelites [Muslims]. Then came the hour of strength. The [Turkish] sultan desired to make war and needed funding. He expressed his desire to sell land in the lands of Israel, the land beyond the Jordan River, and Syria for practically nothing. The holy one [Rabbi Hillel of Kolomiya] saw this as a good sign. He called out forcefully to the Jews, appealing to their hearts that they should hurry to redeem our kingdom from the hands of strangers. . . . But in our great sinfulness, his words fell on deaf ears. His words disappeared into thin air and found no resting place in the hearts of our Jewish brothers, because the zealots [*haredim*] in the Orthodox world maintained silence. They preferred to sit and do nothing, as has always been their attitude. The free-minded radicals [*hakitzonim hahofshiim*], on the other hand, were tempted by the new age that brought unfettered freedom to the world. They planned to settle down in gentile lands, after receiving full citizenship. After comparing the Emancipation to the privilege of living in the Land of Israel, they decided to make their home in the lands of the diaspora. They abandoned our holy mother, the Land of Israel, leaving her to wallow in the dust of her ruins. They made her eyes fill with tears; she wailed and cried that we remained in the diaspora without desire or longing to return to her bosom and rebuild her house.[41]

Here Rabbi Taykhtahl goes into a historical analysis of the modern anti-Semitism that arose and developed together with the Emancipation, of which it was part and parcel. He combines theological and historiosophical arguments to prove that the refusal to move to the Land of Israel in the modern age, when the time came to do so, caused the rise and spread of anti-Semitism until it developed into Nazism.

If the Orthodox zealots had lent their hand to those who participated in the holy mission [of returning to Zion] sixty, fifty, or even forty years ago, and had encouraged the people of Israel to participate in this grand endeavor, our settlement in the Land of Israel would have expanded and many thousands of Jews would have settled there. They would have been saved from death, and by this would also have fulfilled the precept to save lives. But they opposed it and not only did they oppose *aliya* (emigration), they caused antipathy for building up the land to arise in the hearts of the simple Orthodox Jews. If one of the latter opens his mouth to speak enthusiastically about building our land, he is detested and abominated, and so the anti-Zionists have truly caused loathing and repulsiveness toward our beautiful land. . . . Their sin is similar to the sin of the biblical spies, about whom it is said, "they grumbled against their God" and despised our lovely land. What happened to the spies in the end? They caused weeping for many generations and torrents of tears. So we have arrived at a situation today where we find the house of Israel drowning in torrents of tears and crushed under terrible forces of utter destruction. All this happened because they despised our beautiful land.[42]

He describes with heart-wrenching pathos the horrors of the *Shoah* transpiring before his eyes while his book is being printed. He abandons analysis of the past and focuses on the present, continuing his train of thought and argument:

Today we children of Israel are in terrible straits, may God save us quickly. New troubles entwine themselves around our necks from day to day and from hour to hour. If I try to recount them, I will run out of pages, so I leave that story for future writers. . . . In my opinion, the main thing to remember [is] that we are in great trouble, God save us, and every day brings a curse greater than its predecessor. Therefore, we now need the merit of our Holy Land to protect and guard us, to save us from troubles and extract us from this plight. . . . In the merit of our Holy Land may we

41. Taykhtahl, *Em Habanim Semehah*, pp. 13–14.

42. Taykhtahl, *Em Habanim Semehah*, pp. 16–17.

be delivered speedily to salvation and mercy, because we can no longer stand the suffering.[43]

The two theses outlined above within the model of sin and punishment are diametrically opposed to each other. Yet both the Rebbe of Satmar and Rabbi Taykhtahl rely on authoritative sources from *halakhah* (Jewish law) and legend, moral literature (*musar*), and scriptural interpretation. Interestingly, both were learned rabbinical scholars, who grew up in the same social and cultural environment of Hungarian Jewry. Both wrote out of deep spiritual motivation, after witnessing the *Shoah* with their eyes and in their flesh, which perhaps reduces what might seem to outsiders as the cruelty involved in the act of *tziduk hadin*.[44] The polar opposition between these two conceptions of the sin that caused the *Shoah* casts doubt on the theological assumption that underlies the model of transgression and punishment. Even so, this model serves as a starting point for other explanations. Aside from the above two sins, other offenses have been suggested as causes of the *Shoah*.

3. The sin of assimilation. Those who see the basis of the Holocaust in this sin see a direct connection between the processes of heresy and renunciation of Judaism that European Jewry underwent, beginning with the Enlightenment, and the annihilation of European Jewry in the *Shoah*. Proof for this connection is also taken from ancient sources as well as attempts at theologizing sociological processes. This theory even sees

the Divine principle of compensation, "measure for measure," being played out in the fact that the annihilation decrees came from Germany, which was also the source of the European Jewish Enlightenment [the *Haskalah*]. Here sin and punishment are organically connected. Rabbi Menaḥem Emmanuel Hartum, a proponent of this view, tells us, for example, that:

From the Jewish point of view, this heresy [abandoning the principles of Judaism] deserves severe punishment, measure for measure. Yet Judaism also holds that the Holy One, blessed be He, does not strike at once, but is slow to anger. He gives the sinner ample time to repent. In this case as well, Hashem (God) was slow to anger. As our sages recount, the first rains of the biblical deluge came down gently, in the form of rains of blessing, out of the hope that humans would repent and the rains would serve as a last warning. So did Hashem first bring light calamities upon the assimilated Jews, sometimes with positive results [such as the establishment of the Zionist movement following anti-Semitic outbreaks in France]. But the small and relatively limited persecutions did not inspire the people of Israel to repent and give up their illusions regarding equal rights, assimilation, and other ideas. So the drops of rain became a flood.[45]

Apparently, Hashem purposely used the German people to reprove and strike his people hard. It was in that country that assimilation reached its

43. Taykhtahl, *Em Habanim Semeḥah*, p. 22. He relies there, as do others (such as A. Aviḥail in his essay *Mashmaut Hashoah Batfisat Haemunah* [*The Significance of the Shoah from the Perspective of Faith*; Jerusalem 5729]) who see the neglect of the Land of Israel as the sin that caused the *Shoah*, on Rabbi Yaakov Emden (known as the Yabetz, 1697–1776), who wrote in his prayerbook:

The sin of our forefathers caused generations of woe, and [paraphrasing the Passover *Haggadah*] it is this same sin which has stood over us in our exile. It was not that someone rose up against us, but rather that in every generation we kept silent and we forgot our home in the Land of Israel. Not one in a thousand awakens to try to grasp at it. In our settled life in the diaspora, we have already found the Land of Israel and another Jerusalem as good as the original. Therefore all these evils came upon us while Israel lived in Spain and other countries.

44. Rabbi Taykhtahl died during the Holocaust. "He died for sanctification of the Name [*kiddush Hashem*] on 10 Shvat 5705 [24 January 1945] may God avenge his blood" (addendum to the second edition, photocopy, New York, 5729/1968). Despite his strong yearning to go to the Land of Israel, Rabbi Taykhtahl did not merit this. But his anti-Zionist colleague, the Rebbe of Satmar, was saved from the killing fields by the Zionists and left Hungary on Rudolph Kastner's famous train [containing Jews Himmler allowed to escape]. He went to the Land of Israel, where he lived for a few years, from the end of the Second World War until the beginning of Israel's War of Independence. At that time he moved to the United States. There he established a rabbinical court and a ḥasidic community of hundreds [now thousands] who served as a significant center of opposition to Zionism and the State of Israel.

45. *Deot* (Winter 5722/1962).

greatest dimensions, where there was complete and total equality between the Jews and other citizens of the country. There the Jews penetrated most deeply into all facets of local life; there the Jews achieved the apex of identification with their host country and abandonment of their own homeland. But it was Germany that reminded Jews in the most extreme and cruel manner that despite their assimilation, despite their heretical rejection of the main precepts of Judaism, despite their acceptance of a foreign culture, and the acceptance by some of a foreign religion, despite the sacrifices they made honestly on behalf of their country of residency, they were a foreign body in that country, a body that must be purged and annihilated.

To a certain extent, this argument overlaps with the two previous ones, since it posits the diaspora as having the power to destroy those within it, whether through suppression or acceptance. The assimilation argument differs, however, in its expression, since it says that if the *Shoah* had not caused the total destruction of the Jews, they would have been condemned anyway to spiritual destruction. The *Shoah* therefore anticipated a situation, and perhaps worked in a sense to the "benefit" of the victims, since during the Holocaust Jews died (be it unwillingly) qua Jews, whereas in the case of assimilation they, their children, and grandchildren continued to live but as non-Jews.

I include this argument by the Italian Rabbi Hartum, who wrote a few years after the *Shoah*, in order to draw conclusions for the present. However, it should be noted that there were others who had adopted this line of reasoning before the *Shoah*. One of the great Lithuanian yeshiva heads, Rabbi Elhanan Wasserman (who was killed during the Holocaust) writes in the name of the *Maggid* (Preacher) of Kelm that "for the sin of the *Shulhan Arukh* (Reform *Code of Jewish Law*) of [Abraham]

Geiger [one of the fathers of the Reform movement], a new *Shulhan Arukh* will arise against the people of Israel. In it will be written, Heaven preserve us: The greatest of the Jews have been killed, the greatest of the Jews have been killed! May Hashem preserve and save us."[46] Even at the beginning of the *Shoah*, when no one anticipated its dimensions, the well-known Vilna scholar, Rabbi Haim Ozer Grodzinski, in the introduction to his book *Responsa of Ahiezer*, connects the decrees of the Nazis who were in political ascent and the burning of synagogues with the fact that these were taking place in the same countries in which "the reform took root."[47] This same stand is taken in the work of another great Lithuanian scholar, Rabbi Yaakov Israel Kanievsky, known in the yeshiva world as the Steipeler or "the *ilui* [prodigy] of Steipel," who lived in Bnei Brak. He writes: "We see in this the finger of God, that the beginning of 'throwing off the yoke' and abandonment of Judaism in an organized manner, God save us, and the decree to destroy all the Jews, God save us, originated in the same evil country."[48]

Here it is interesting to note that this *tziduk hadin* does not remain in the theological realm, but is also heard as a popular and even secular sociological argument.

So we find echoes of this reasoning in the argument of one Leible Brodeski, a simple villager, who stands on *Kol Nidrei* night (the eve of the Day of Atonement) in the ghetto's temporary synagogue and says:

Jews, tell me, what would have been if Hitler had given the Jews the choice that the enemies of Israel were given throughout the ages: convert or be destroyed? Would the heretical Jews of our generation, the nonbelievers, have stood the test, as the previous generations did? Only a few, a small number, would sanctify the Name in public and

46. Rabbi Elhanan Wasserman, *Ikvata Bemeshiha* [*Footprints of the Messiah*] (Tel Aviv, 5702/1942), p. 61 [See excerpts part I, pp. 28–36 above]. The Maggid of Kelm was Rabbi Moshe Yitzhak Darshan (1828–1899), a famous itinerant preacher and follower of Rabbi Israel Salanter (1810–1883), founder of the Musar movement. See for more on him Shai Gliksberg, *Hadrasha Beyisrael* [*The Jewish Homily*] (Tel Aviv, 5700/1940), pp. 453–456.

47. *Responsa Ahiezer*, vol. 3 (Vilna, 3 Sivan 5699/21 May 1939).

48. *Hayei Olam: Likutei Amarim Lehazek Halevavot Le'emuna Shleima Ve'avoda Tamah, Avodat Haboreh* [*Everlasting Life: An Anthology of Sayings to Strengthen Hearts toward Complete Faith and Simple Worship of the Creator*] (Rishon Lezion, 5732/1972).

prefer death to conversion. This time we are not speaking of religion, but "blood," "race." There is no room here for evasion. Believer, *apikoros* [cynical nonbeliever], assimilated Jew, third-generation apostate, Jews who have forgotten their origins, Jews who hate their own people, gentiles who do not know that they were of Jewish descent—all pay the debt in blood. Everyone serves the sentence. The people of Israel are responsible for one another. Is God's hand absent in this racism run amok? Is it only coincidence?[49]

Another expression of *tziduk hadin* that actually excludes the religious content is found in the writings of Yitzhak Tabenkin, a secular Zionist-socialist ideologue, who said at the Twenty-Sixth Zionist Congress:

I was afraid there was a Holocaust coming upon us, and I saw that it was inevitable. I am more afraid of assimilation. Is there anything more terrible than the destruction of Jews? Assimilation is part of the destruction of Jews. A Jew who is destroyed will not assimilate.[50]

This argument, and those preceding it, invite several objections. Did the punishment achieve its goal? Did assimilation cease, or did it possibly increase after the *Shoah*? Did not the Jews experience even more spiritual dilution after the *Shoah*?

In addition, every such argument according to the model of transgression and punishment puts us in the strange situation that Eliezer Berkovits defines in the introduction to his *Faith after the Holocaust*:[51]

How can we, who were not there inside the hell of destruction, justify the verdict? Some of those present did not do so. If some of those present accepted and justified it for themselves, they are permitted to do so, but we are not, since "I am not Job, I am only Job's brother." Job's brother is not allowed to speak as if he were Job himself, neither in defiance nor in defense.[52]

This is perhaps one of the reasons that some among the searchers for a theodicy of the *Shoah* are not satisfied with the model of "the first man," which implies a search for reason and provocation in the cycle of sin and punishment; instead they suggest other models in its place.

Model 2: Cain Kills Abel

God gave humans free choice; they can either choose life and goodness or opt for death and evil. This choice is articulated by Maimonides: "Every man is given the choice of directing himself to the path of good and being a righteous man. The choice is his. If he wants to direct himself to the path of evil and to be an evil man, the choice is his."[53] God is not responsible for what happened in the *Shoah*; rather, those responsible are the people who used for the purpose of evil the unlimited possibilities that God gave them. Man banished from his midst the God of righteousness and mercy, then crowned himself king of the world. The terror of the *Shoah* took place in this kingdom of man alone. God calls out after Cain kills his brother, "What have you done?" But Cain evades responsibility, feigns innocence and answers, "Am I my brother's keeper?" The *Shoah* is therefore not God's problem, but rather that of man who rebels against God's word and refuses to take responsibility for his own actions. Abraham Joshua Heschel searching for the origins of the *Shoah* in the human domain writes:

Our world is like a snake pit. It was not in 1939 that we fell into this pit, and not even in 1933. We descended into it generations ago, and the snakes injected their poison into the arteries of humanity, to silence us gradually, to murder us nerve by nerve, to dim our wits and darken our sight.... The war did not break out suddenly, it came as the expected result of extensive spiritual decline.[54]

Here, Heschel is faithful to his view that the Bible is not human theology, a book by man about

49. From *Ani Ma'amin* [*I Believe*], expanded version, edited by Mordekhai Eliav (Jerusalem, 5729/1969), p. 28.
50. *Proceedings of the Twenty-Sixth Zionist Congress* (Jerusalem, 1965).
51. (New York, 1973).

52. Berkovits, *Faith after the Holocaust*, pp. 3–5.
53. Maimonides, *Mishneh Torah*, Laws of Repentance 85:1.
54. "The Meaning of This Hour," in *Man's Quest for God* (New York, 1954), pp. 147–151.

God, but rather an anthropological study by God.[55] The Holocaust is merely another chapter, dark and sad, in this work. Man fails again! Cain and Abel come into the world and are given free choice to build up man's seed, to build the world and multiply life and goodness. But instead: "Cain rose up against Abel his brother and killed him." The fault is completely Cain's.

However, the sages were not willing to accept this argument as such. They wrote many *midrashim* (biblical interpretations) about this incident of the first murder in the world. "Why does Cain kill Abel?" they asked. In attempting to understand, they answered: because of conflicts over property, arguments about religion, disputes over women, and so forth.[56] But if Cain is guilty (and accepts his punishment), what is the sin of the murdered Abel? Why he? If the Nazis used their free choice for evil, why did it have to be the Jews who were their victims? To that, Heschel would reply, because the Jews are "witness" to the Creator's direction of His world, and therefore they are first in the line of fire against all who would conspire against His providence.[57] However, the sages are not willing to accept these arguments without some protest. They refuse to absolve God of responsibility for Cain's act of "free will." Thus we read in a *midrash*:

So said Cain: "Am I my brother's keeper? You, Lord, are the guardian of all creatures and You ask me about him?" To what can this be compared? To a thief who stole vessels at night but was not caught. In the morning, the guard caught him and said, "Why did you steal the vessels?" The thief replied, "I am a thief and continued to perform my job. But if your job is to guard the gate, why did you not perform your job properly?" Cain even said, "I killed him, but You

created the evil inclination within me. You guard everything but You allowed me to kill him? You are [indirectly] the one who killed him!"[58]

Model 3: The Sacrifice of Isaac

There are many other models taken from the Bible and from works of Jewish thought over the ages that we can use in our attempt to anchor the *Shoah* in some understandable framework. On close inspection, however, the differences between the models and the *Shoah* are greater than their similarities... The image of the sacrifice of Isaac, for example, is often used in *Shoah* literature[59] and appears in eyewitness accounts of those on their way to die. Yet with all the threads of empathy drawn between "Please take your son, your only one, whom you love" and the *Shoah* victims whom we loved—how great is the difference! Can we possibly conceive that God is the one who commanded this sacrifice of six million? And to whose ear was the command directed? Did Hitler's soldiers hear what Abraham heard? And finally, where was the angel who cried out at the last minute: "Do not stretch out your hand against the lad nor do anything to him" (Genesis 22:12)?

The story of the sacrifice of Isaac, according to its plain meaning and its midrashic interpretation, cannot be compared to the *Shoah*, neither from Abraham's point of view, nor from Isaac's. The use of linguistic images from this story to describe situations in the *Shoah* is not new. It has a long tradition in the history of those who died for *kiddush Hashem* [sanctification of the Name = martyrdom], in *piyutim* [religious poetry] about mass tragedies in Jewish history, and descriptions of acts of sacrifice by Jews for their faith.[60] Yet in

55. Heschel, *God in Search of Man* (New York, 1955), p. 412.
56. See for example, *Genesis Rabba* 22:7.
57. This leads to the idea of the "servant of God" who suffers on behalf of all, as in "but in truth, it was our ills that he bore, and our pains that he carried" (Isaiah 53:4), which is referring to Israel among the nations.
58. *Sefer Ha'agada* 1, 19:101, based on *Midrash Tanḥuma*, (Genesis), *Bereshit* (Genesis) *Rabba* 22, and *Shmot* (Exodus) *Rabba* 31.
59. This image also appears in many eyewitness accounts of the *Shoah*. See for example, *Ani Ma'amin*, pp. 45, 62, and elsewhere.
60. Some fascinating material on this topic has been collected by Shalom Spiegel from a broad range of sources in his article *Me'agadot Ha'akeda* ["From the Legends of the Sacrifice of Isaac"], in *Jubilee Book in Honor of Alexander Marks*, Hebrew section (New York 5710/1950), pp. 471–547. An expanded version of the article by Spiegel appeared as a book in English, *The Last Trial* (New York, 1967).

this aspect, every comparison of the sacrifice of Isaac with the *Shoah* supports the assumption made at the beginning of this article, that the *Shoah* stands out in its uniqueness in Jewish history and the history of Jewish martyrdom. The sacrifice of Isaac, with all its mystery and all the variety of interpretations given it, will always remain a world apart from the *Shoah*.

Model 4: Job

Another biblical model, seemingly self-evident and widely used, is that of Job. This model can be interpreted several ways (I have already noted its disqualification on the grounds that we are "Job's brothers" and not Job himself). But beyond the Book of Job's conflicts over the central problem of God's seeming injustice and unfairness, its point is that God convinces Job that the human attempt to "understand" His ways is useless. In light of this fact, man should keep silent ("Behold, I am deficient; what can I answer You? I place my hand against my mouth"; Job 40:4). The only one who is able and permitted to ask questions is God. He asks man, but not the contrary ("Gird your loins like a warrior! I will ask, and you answer Me"; Job 40:7). Man must be satisfied with incomprehension of the ways of God ("Therefore I declared, yet I understand nothing. It is beyond me. I shall not know"; Job 42:3) and comforted by contact with God ("I had heard of You through hearsay, but now my eye has beheld You"; Job 42:5). We know of no such contact during the period of the *Shoah*. The voice of God was not heard from within the whirlwind.

Model 5: Silence

Silence in the face of an incomprehensible and unfathomable situation is a legitimate religious response. The power of the question and the imperative of a respectful attitude toward the victims obligate us, some contend, to silence. But in order for this silence to have significance, it cannot be a silence of complete astonishment that

leads to the paralysis of thought, but rather a silence expressed verbally and articulated fully, followed by a self-imposed silence. Such was Job's silence, a silence that comes after speech and not instead of it.

Such a silence, a roaring silence, was Aaron's after the death of his two sons when "they brought before God an alien fire" (Leviticus 10:1). A talmudic *midrash* discusses silence thusly:

> Because Aaron's sons died, Moses said to his brother: Aaron my brother, your sons died for the sanctification of the Name of the Holy One, blessed be He. Because Aaron knew that his sons were known to the Omnipresent, he kept silent and was rewarded, as it is written "and Aaron was silent" (Leviticus 10:3). To David, He says, "Wait silently for [the salvation by] God and wait longingly for Him" (Psalms 37:6); although he takes many casualties from your midst, you keep quiet. To Solomon, He says, "a time to be silent, and a time to speak" (Ecclesiastes 3:7); sometimes one is silent and receives reward for that silence; sometimes one speaks and receives reward for that speech.[61]

Such silence cannot ease pain or bring tranquillity to the struggling soul. On the contrary, it incorporates the valor of suffering. The following verse in the song of praise to God following the crossing of the Red Sea (Exodus 15:11) is interpreted in this way: " 'Who is like You among the heavenly powers [*elim*], God!' means to ask rhetorically: Who is like You among the mute [*ellemin*]! And 'Who is like You, O mighty One, God?' (Psalms 89:9) implies, who is like You, mighty in self-restraint, that You hear the reviling and abuse of that evil one, but remain silent?"[62] It is as if God Himself imposes silence upon Himself, as He imposes silence upon those who love Him when they come before Him with difficult questions.

> When Moses went up to the heavens, they took him before God, who was sitting and tying crowns onto the letters [of the Torah]. Moses said to Him, Master of the universe, who is delaying You? God said to him, in the future there will be a man at the end of several generations, named

---

61. B.T. *Zevahim* 115[b].

62. B.T. *Gittin* 56[b].

Akiba ben Yosef. For each and every dot, he will interpret many, many *halakhot* (laws). Moses said to Him, Master of the universe, show him to me. God said to him, turn around. Moses went and sat eight rows back [in the study house of Rabbi Akiba], and did not understand what they were saying. He felt weak. When Rabbi Akiba arrived at a certain point, his students said to him: Rabbi, how do you know that? He replied: It is *Halakhah* (Jewish law) from Moses at Sinai. Moses' confusion was dispelled. He returned and stood before the Holy One, blessed be He, and said: Master of the universe, you have such a man [as Akiba] and yet you will give the Torah through me? God said to him: Be silent, this is part of my plan! Moses said to Him: Master of the universe, you have shown me his Torah, now show me his reward! God said to Moses: Turn around. He did so, and saw that they [the Romans] were tearing [Rabbi Akiba's] flesh with the rake. Moses said to God: Master of the universe, this is Torah and this is its reward? God answered him: Be silent! This, too, is part of my plan.[63]

Here we have silence that comes not out of amazement and wonder, and not out of inability or unwillingness to ask. On the contrary, this silence comes as the response to wonderment and the answer to a question asked. Silence comes here as the crown of the powerful mystery embodied in both the giving of the Torah and the seeming injustice of Rabbi Akiba's cruel end.

This solution, silence, is the hardest of all. From the frontiers of silence, tongues of doubt crawl out and protrude. Yes, I must remain silent. But is this truly part of the plan? Can it be? Is there anyone in our time who has clearly heard this command that was given to Moses, "Be silent"? Is there a Moses in our time who will take it upon himself to tell the bereaved Aaron who remained silent, "Your sons died for sanctification of the Name of the Holy One"? Is there anyone today who recognized what Aaron did,

who can say that "my sons are known to the Omnipresent"?

If the answer to these questions is negative, or doubtful, then silence is not silence. The original question stands: Where was God during the *Shoah*?

Model 6: The Hidden Face of God

The seekers sought and found an answer: God hid His face. The period of the *Shoah* was a period of "the hiding of God's face" [*hester panim*]; in Buber's modern phrase, an "eclipse of God,"[64] like a solar eclipse. This model is also based on a biblical archetype. Either it can be seen as a theological mystery that one of God's characteristics is to hide and reveal Himself, or it can be understood as a punishment for humanity's sins.

So says the prophet Isaiah (45:15): "Indeed, You are a God who conceals Himself," while in the Book of Deuteronomy, God describes to Moses what will happen when the people of Israel will go astray.

My anger will flare against them on that day and I will forsake them; and I will conceal My face from them and they will become prey, and many evils and troubles shall befall them, so that they will say on that day, "Is it not because my God is not in my midst that these evils have come upon me?" But I will surely have concealed My face on that day because of all the evil that they perpetrated, for they have turned to gods of others. (Deuteronomy 31:17–18)

The same feeling of terror that man has during the time of concealment of God's face is expressed powerfully in many passages in the Book of Psalms, especially 44:24–25: "Awaken, why do You seem to sleep, O Lord? Arouse Yourself, forsake not forever! Why do You conceal Your face, do You forget our affliction and oppression?"

Without entering the theological maze of "God hiding" from His essence or "because of

63. B.T. *Menaḥot* 29[b].
64. See Martin Buber, *Man's Face* (Jerusalem 5726/1966), pp. 221–321 [Hebrew], on "the eclipse of God's light"; also Buber's English volume *Eclipse of God: Studies in the Relation between Religion and Philosophy*,

trans. Maurice Friedman (New York, 1952) [For more see the Buber selections in part III below], and see Emil Fackenheim, "On the Eclipse of God," in *Quest for the Past and Present* (Boston, 1968), pp. 229–243.

our sins"[65]—there is something within us that rebels against use of these expressions for the *Shoah*. This terminology does not help us to avoid the penetrating question: Where was He? If the answer is, He was hiding, then the problem remains unsolved. Why did He hide just when we needed Him more than ever? Did those murdered and tortured accept His disappearance in that hour? Could they accept the fact of His not being there with philosophical and theological equanimity of spirit?

Below is a selection translated from document PS 2999, the account of a German submitted to the International Military Tribunal at Nuremberg.

I, Hermann Friedrich Graebe, declare under oath: From September 1941 until January 1944 I was manager and engineer in charge of a branch office in Sdolbunow, Ukraine, of the Solingen building firm of Josef Jung. In this capacity it was my job to visit the building sites of the firm. Under contract to an army construction office, the firm had orders to erect grain storage buildings on the former airport of Dubno, Ukraine. On 5 October 1942, when I visited the building office at Dubno, my foreman Hubert Moennikes of 21 Aussenmuehlenweg, Hamburg-Haarburg, told me that in the vicinity of the site, Jews from Dubno had been shot in three large pits, each about 30 meters long and 3 meters deep. About 1,500 persons had been killed daily. All of the 5,000 Jews who had still been living in Dubno before the pogrom were to be liquidated. As the shootings had taken place in his presence he was still much upset. Thereupon I drove to the site, accompanied by Moennikes and saw near it great mounds of earth, about 30 meters long and 2 meters high. Several trucks stood in front of the mounds. Armed Ukrainian militia drove the people off the trucks under the supervision of an SS man. The militiamen acted as guards on the trucks and drove them to and from the pit. All these people had the regulation yellow patches on the front and back of their clothes, and thus could be recognized as Jews. Moennikes and I went directly to the pits. Nobody bothered us. Now I heard rifle shots in quick succession from behind one of the earth mounds. The people who had gotten off the trucks—men, women, and children of all ages—had to undress upon the orders of an SS man, who carried a riding or dog whip. They had to put down their clothes in fixed places, sorted according to shoes, top clothing, and underclothing. I saw a heap of shoes of about 800 to 1,000 pairs, great piles of underlinen and clothing. Without screaming or weeping these people undressed, stood around in family groups, kissed each other, said farewells, and waited for a sign from another SS man, who stood near the pit, also with a whip in his hand. During the 15 minutes that I stood near the pit, I heard no complaint or plea for mercy. I watched a family of about 8 persons, a man and woman, both about 50 with their children of about 1, 8, and 10, and two grown-up daughters of about 20 to 24. An old woman with snow-white hair was holding the one-year-old child in her arms and singing to it, and tickling it. The child was cooing with delight. The couple were looking on with tears in their eyes. The father was holding the hand of a boy about 10 years old and speaking to him softly; the boy was fighting his tears. The father pointed toward the sky, stroked his head, and seemed to explain something to him. At that moment the SS man at the pit shouted something to his comrades.... Then I heard a series of shots. I looked into the pit and saw that the bodies were twitching or the heads lying already motionless on top of the bodies that lay before them.[66]

The German's testimony continues in minute detail. For our purposes, we would have been interested to hear what the father said to his ten-year-old son as he stroked his hair and pointed to the sky. Did he say that there is a powerful God in heaven who knows what is happening down here and who has just gone out for lunch but will

65. For clarification of the theological issue of the hidden God, see sources in the previous note and also Berkovits, *Faith after the Holocaust*, p. 94ff.; and Andre Nehar, *Beḥol Zot [Despite All]* (Jerusalem 5737/1977).

66. *Encyclopaedia Judaica*, 1st ed. (Jerusalem, 1971), *s.v.* "Holocaust," 8:867.

soon return? Did he explain to him the complicated expression *Deus absconditus*, the hidden God, and why He was hiding just at that moment?

The SS officer's order to fire prevents us from knowing exactly what the father said to his son when he pointed his finger to heaven. The words fell, together with the father and the rest of the family, into the pit on the outskirts of Dubno, a pit thirty meters long and three meters deep.

Model 7: The Death of God

The theory of the "hidden God" branches into another theory, more extreme in expression, which speaks of the "death of God." This argument, as it should be understood, does not exclude the possibility of the existence of God or His revelation to humanity and Israel. This is not an argument for the rule of anarchy (*leit din v'leit dayan*: "there is neither law nor judge"). This is not the case of the fool in the first line of Psalm 14 who says in his heart, "There is no God." These are also legitimate arguments, but they are found outside the framework of religious language within which we are working. The theology of the dead God that found expression in Christianity,[67] and to a lesser extent in Judaism,[68] says that God really was alive and existing, but at a certain moment He stopping being and is permanently hiding His face.

All Christian theology that refers to the death of God, whose basis is in the declaration by the insane character in Nietzsche's work,[69] is diametrically opposed to the historical "living God" of Judaism. Thus, Emil Fackenheim[70] has interestingly proposed that we should accept the possibility of the death of God as a *midrash* and not as a solution or final answer.

But even if this response does relate to God at the one terrible moment of the *Shoah*, then we have answered only one out of three parts of the question, while the two remaining parts, i.e., where was God *before* and *after* the Holocaust, remain unanswered. If "our God" is dead, what happens to "the God of our forefathers"? The well-known *midrash* about the intervention before the throne of God by the forefathers and foremothers on behalf of Israel during the destruction of the Temple[71] challenges the possibility of a Jewish view of God from the point of view of a particular individual or a particular historical hour. The name of the God of Israel (YHWH) implies all the tenses: past, present, and future. The God of the Jews, Creator and Master of the universe, who made the covenant with Abraham, Isaac, and Jacob, must always remain if not within history, then above it. Even when He hides His face, He remains alive and we can "arrive at Him" beyond the obscuring clouds with which He surrounds Himself. He is the God of our forefathers in the past, and our living redeemer of the future. He is connected (against His will!) to the people Israel. He is present among the Jewish people, whose children continue to act and create as Jews, who continue, or want to continue, to stand before Him in prayer as Jews, even after Auschwitz.

Therefore, even though it is possible that we will never arrive at a justification of the *Shoah*—or an understanding—this resignation does not exempt us from the urgency of finding appropriate terms to enable us to speak of it with the meaning it deserves in the treasury of religious language, the esoteric private language of believers, like an esoteric language between two lovers. This is not the language of the marketplace, that can express everything. Thus when such language is eventually found, silence will still be a part of it.[72] Unlike

67. See *The Meaning of the Death of God*, edited by Bernard Mortschland (New York, 1967).
68. See Richard L. Rubenstein, *After Auschwitz* (Indianapolis, 1966). [See excerpts in part III below.]
69. F. Nietzsche, *Fröhliche Wissenschaft* (Chemnitz, 1882).
70. See Fackenheim, *God's Presence in History*, p. 77, where he gives as an example a story about God hanging, as it were, on the gallows in the image of a Jewish boy, from Elie Wiesel's book *Leilah* [*Night*] (Tel Aviv 5726/

1966), pp. 82–83 in the Hebrew version. The first English version of *Night*, trans. Stella Rodway, was published in New York in 1960. A new translation by Marion Wiesel appeared in New York in 2005.
71. *Petiḥta l'Eikha Rabati, Sefer Ha'agada* 1, 87:6.
72. On the multisignificant role of silence in Jewish religious language from the Bible to the *Shoah*, see Andre Nehar, *L'exil de la Parole* (Paris, 1970), and his *Bekhol Zot* [*In Any Case*].

the language of science and informative communication, religious language is full of meaningful silences, as in "To You, silence is praise" (Psalms 65:2). Silence as part of the conversation, yes; silence that contains within it the relationship term "to You" from this psalm, yes; but not a silence that kills all dialogue and removes all meaning.

True, when we look for explanations or answers to the question of why, it seems we have no choice but to wrap ourselves in quiet, to decree silence upon ourselves. But the reality is that the *Shoah* is an extant experience, a dynamic in our lives today, and we cannot pass over it or blur it with muteness. We have no choice but to reach those layers of language that will give us the possibility of answering the question "what." What happened during the *Shoah*? How can we attempt to describe it in the metaphysical and religious sphere, beyond the language available to us in the fields of statistics, history, sociology, and politics?

This question is asked in the religious sphere, but remains essential beyond that arena. It touches on the roots of our experience as Jews, upholders of an age-old tradition, of which language is, and has always been, one of the main supporting pillars.

Yoel Schwartz and Yitzchak Goldstein

Rabbi Yoel Schwartz and Rabbi Yitzchak Goldstein both live their lives within the orbit of the Israeli ultra-Orthodox Jewish world. As youths, they both received traditional Jewish educations and then went on to do advanced rabbinical studies. Rabbi Schwartz has been a student at several of Israel's most prestigious *yeshivot* (advanced rabbinical academies) including the Mir yeshiva in Jerusalem and the Ponevitz yeshiva in Bnei Brak. He now is a member of the teaching faculty at Yeshiva D'var Yerushalyim in Jerusalem. He has published very widely on ethical issues in the Jewish tradition and has produced commentaries on biblical and rabbinic texts. In addition, he has addressed contemporary theological subjects in a variety of publications. For example, he has written about the issues surrounding conversion to Judaism; the issues of peace, materialism, and spirituality; and the holiness of the human body, as seen from an ultra-Orthodox perspective. He is also the author of a book in Hebrew entitled *Zechut Avot* (*Merit of the Fathers*). Rabbi Goldstein did his rabbinic studies at Yeshiva Yoesodei Ha-Torah in Jerusalem and now teaches at the Ithri yeshiva. He is the author of a number of articles for the important *Encyclopedia of the Talmud* published in [Hebrew] in Jerusalem.

SELECTION

Rabbis Schwartz and Goldstein address the familiar but difficult question of the passivity of Jews during the *Shoah* from a *halakhic* (religious-legal) perspective. They ask: Was that passivity, whether real or imagined, an act of shameful cowardice or proper martyrdom? In asking this question, they are especially concerned with the recurrence—particularly within the Jewish and Israeli communities—of the accusation that, among Hitler's many victims, only the Jews went "like sheep to the slaughter." Why, they ask, does this myth still exist? In order to answer this question, they turn to an examination of the Zionist movement with its ideological emphasis on independence and, for them, "vulgar" (antireligious) slogans, such as "our fate rests in our hands only" and "Israel has no Messiah." That is, they argue that the accusation "like lambs to the slaughter" is a consequence of Zionist ideology which is, as they understand it, rooted in values drawn from "foreign cultures" that devalue true Jewish martyrs and "turn the Jewish value system topsy-turvy."

In opposition to the Zionist narrative and its norms, Rabbis Schwartz and Goldstein make two pertinent suggestions. The first is that, "the Jewish hero ... conquers his own base instincts, behaves with restraint and is slow to anger." This heroism does not seek to express itself in "external might" but rather in "superior internal strength." War and physical exploits, though employed by Jews and the Jewish people when necessary, are not the ideal of Jewish behavior. Moreover, the notion that one "die honorably" is "far removed from the language of the

Torah." The notion of "honor," i.e., of dying with honor, has, they contend, no *halakhic* status. The only meaningful criterion is saving life, one's own and those of others. Pursuing "honor" at the cost of one's life or the lives of others is, from the *halakhic* perspective, impermissible.

Second, Rabbis Schwartz and Goldstein define the murdered Jews of Europe not as "victims" but rather as "sacrifices," since they died solely because they were Jews. This change of understanding totally alters the equation regarding their behavior and any judgments subsequently made about it. Furthermore, given this reformulation—and Rabbis Schwartz and Goldstein's distinctive, traditional value system—they conclude that from a Torah perspective the very question "Why like lambs to the slaughter?" is altogether illegitimate and even absurd.

The key to the analysis of proper *halakhic* action regarding compliance versus revolt during the Holocaust lies—they argue—in the individual circumstances of each case and the determination in each instance as to which sort of action would save the most Jewish lives.

The present selection is taken from the original Hebrew edition of *Shoah: A Jewish Perspective on Tragedy in the Context of the Holocaust* (Jerusalem, 1988).

Selected Bibliography

Book by Yoel Schwartz

Zion Today: Torah Perspective (Jerusalem, 1986) [Hebrew].

Books by Yoel Schwartz and Yitzchak Goldstein

A Light unto the Nations, translated by Mordecai ben Aharon and edited by Yirmeyahu Bindman (Jerusalem, 1988).

Shoah: A Jewish Perspective on Tragedy in the Context of the Holocaust, translated by Shlomo Fox-Ashrei (New York, 1990).

The *Shoah*: From a Torah Perspective

"Like Sheep to the Slaughter" or "*Kiddush Hashem*"?

This chapter will discuss the question "How could an entire people allow itself to be annihilated?" but with a slight change in formulation. The Jewish people did not "allow itself" to lose one-third of its members. This third was murdered in the cruelest manner by other peoples. The victims were civilians, not soldiers. They were members of a people scattered and dispersed among other nations and without a homeland. The defenseless Jews were murdered by police and armed forces. This was no war between equal powers. The behavior of the murdered would not have changed anything about the acts of murder.

The question presented here is how, or in what way, did the Jewish people behave during the terrible destruction, and what can we learn from this behavior? Did our martyrs[1] go to their death "like sheep to the slaughter"? Was their death in itself an act of *kiddush Hashem*,[2] or has it no such significance? Looking back through the millennia, did the generation of the *Shoah* behave

---

1. Translator's note: here the author[s] used the term *kadosh* [holy one] rather than the term *korban* [victim, sacrifice].

2. Literally, "sanctification of the name," meaning martyrdom.

like our forebears during other dreadful periods such as the destruction of the Temple and the Crusades? Should we see the *Shoah* as one more addition to a series of evil edicts and massacres, or is this a new phenomenon, a new type of decree and Jewish response? This chapter will address all these and additional questions related to "where was the Jew?" during the *Shoah*.

The question is often posed: Why did the *Shoah* victims not resist the acts of murder? The prosecutor during [Adolf] Eichmann's trial [in Jerusalem in 1961] also raised this question, repeatedly demanding of the witnesses, "Why did you not resist?" Israeli youth almost always raise this question during discussions on the *Shoah*. Sometimes this question arises not out of pure astonishment, but rather as an accusation of cowardice, weakness, and perhaps stupidity, the bestial dumbness of sheep brought to slaughter with no resistance whatsoever.

This accusation was originally made during the days of the *Shoah* by the Zionist leader Yitzhak Greenbaum, who said that the Jews died "like rags" and not like human beings. The indictment was repeated by historians, including significant ones (for example, Raul Hilberg, in his book *Destruction of European Jewry* [Chicago, 1961]). According to them, the traditional Jewish policy not to oppose oppressors led to a lack of resistance to the Nazis and the *Judenrat*'s cooperation with them. The Zionist expression for this was *galut* [exile/exilic] mentality: self-abasement and submission to foreign authority. This led Israeli youth to refuse to commemorate the *Shoah*, out of shame for the *galut* behavior of the martyrs that was responsible for everything.

This phenomenon caused embarrassment among public leaders in Israel and is the main reason for the great emphasis our Israeli historians place on acts of armed resistance to the Nazis. Yad Vashem is the government's Holocaust Martyrs' and Heroes' Remembrance Authority, and 27 Nissan was made Holocaust Martyrs' and Heroes' Remembrance Day, [*Yom Hazikaron LaShoah u'LaGvurah*] as if the two concepts are equal in weight: *Shoah* (of *galut* mentality Jews) and *Gvurah* (heroism of Jews who resisted). This date was purposely chosen because it commemorates the Warsaw ghetto uprising, a symbol of valor and courage, and this is the context in which we should remember the Holocaust of our people.[3]

Lately, historical research in Israel on this topic has changed direction. Researchers focus more and more on the *Shoah* and less on "heroism." Slowly, they have come to recognize that other types of spiritual bravery, unrelated to armed resistance, might be included in the "heroism" category. But we cannot know if this shift will correct the educational and historical damage already done.

Interestingly, the question of "like sheep to the slaughter" did not arise so intensely among the religious public. Of course, many wondered how so few SS men managed to guard thousands of Jews on their last journeys, as in "how could one pursue a thousand, and two cause a myriad to flee, if not that their Rock had sold them out, and Hashem had delivered them" (Deuteronomy 32:30). But this incredulity is only at the size of the disaster and the profundity of Divine judgment, and certainly not an accusation of our martyrs. Because despite the faintheartedness and desperation they exhibited (if they did indeed exhibit this—see below), all was in the hands of God, and that itself was part of the dreadful Divine decree. The *tokhaha* [literally "admonition," a biblical list of punishments that God will bring if Israel does not heed His commandments] says, "I will bring weakness into their hearts in the lands of their foes; the sound of a rustling leaf will pursue them" (Leviticus 26:36). Fearfulness itself was one of the *tokhaha*'s curses.

Rabbi Abraham Ibn Ezra (1089–c. 1167) wrote the following regarding the children of Israel's fear of the pursuing Egyptians upon their departure from Egypt:

> We must wonder how a great camp of six hundred thousand people feared their pursuers, and why they did not fight for their lives and for their children. The answer is because the Egyptians were masters over Israel. The generation that left Egypt had learned from its youth to suffer the yoke of Egypt, and its soul was downtrodden. How could they now fight their masters, while they were weak and untrained for

---

3. The date always follows exactly one week after Israeli Independence Day.

war? Remember that Amalek came with a small force, yet were it not for the prayers of Moses, they would have dominated Israel. God alone does great works. "[Men's] deeds are taken into account by Him" (1 Samuel 2:3): He caused all the Israelite males who left Egypt to die, because they did not have the strength to fight the Canaanites. Then a new generation arose, the generation of the desert that had not experienced exile and had a proud spirit. (Rabbi Abraham Ibn Ezra's *Commentary on the Torah*, Exodus 14:13 and 2:3)

We can therefore identify both a spirit of *galut* that is "downtrodden" and succumbs to its foreign master and the "proud spirit" of those who did not experience exile, which the Israelites needed to conquer the Land of Israel. But all this is included in the decree of exile, and the subjugated and defeated spirit is not the true nature of Israel. On the contrary, Israel is the strongest of all nations (see B.T. *Beitza* 25). Its strength is a gift from Heaven and not in the hands of human beings. We should not read into Ibn Ezra more than what has already been said, that the decree of exile includes faintheartedness. He also adds that even after the exodus from Egypt, the generation that had lived there remained of defeated spirit. Far removed from Ibn Ezra's view is the superficial secular outlook that "my strength and the might of my hand" (Deuteronomy 8:17) is all-powerful, of "taking our destiny into our own hands" and of the power of human prowess in general. To Ibn Ezra, the attitude that "Hashem is the God of thoughts, and [men's] deeds are taken into account by Him" (1 Samuel 2:3) determines both weakness and courageousness of spirit, since all is in the hands of Heaven except for the fear of Heaven.

Yet it seems that the issues run much deeper than this, for the accusation of faintheartedness and admiration of heroism is based on error and rooted in foreign cultures. Failure of spirit is not moral injustice, for which one can blame someone. It is a characteristic like all others, and recognized in the Torah as a legitimate reason for exemption from military service. Weak people do exist. They should not be blamed for this, but rather given special consideration. The origin of the attitude of contempt for "cowards" is in the culture of power that admires the mighty (in body and spirit) and scorns the weak. How dreadful it is that discussion on the *Shoah* uses moral standards adopted from the culture that gave birth to the Nazis! How appalling to judge the murdered according to the standards of the murderers! For it was the murderers who first used such terms as "rags" and "weaklings," and they who relied solely on brute physical force.

The Jewish hero, on the other hand, conquers his own base instincts, behaves with restraint, and is slow to anger. This is not external might but superior internal strength. The Jewish hero does not need physical exploits and implements of war. He does utilize these when needed, but he does not see them as an ideal in and of themselves. Occasionally, they are even defective, since they are seen as descending to the enemy's level, as stooping to means that are not appropriate for those whose forefathers stood at Sinai. The Jewish hero does not want to react to terror with terror, to murder with murder, because of the fear that he himself may turn into a shedder of blood. Sometimes he has no choice and must use the principle of "if someone comes to kill you, kill him first" (B.T. *Berakhot* 58ᵃ), but he finds no heroism in such an act.

The demand to "die honorably" is far removed from the language of the Torah. It encompasses the assumption that all hope for living is lost, and that death must come anyway, as in "Let my soul die with the Philistines" [Judges 16:30; Samson's declaration when he pulls the building down on top of himself and the enemy]. But this gloomy despair is not of Jewish origin. The Jews always knew that "even if a sharp sword is placed on a man's neck, do not despair of calamity" (B.T. *Berakhot* 10ᵃ). In the darkest days of the concentration camps, Jews with true spiritual strength taught themselves and others that "God's salvation is imminent." And let us not forget that this strength-giving, deep faith and hope saved many from certain death.

But the concept "like sheep to the slaughter" is groundless not only from our point of view. Historians and secular thinkers also have proved that this question has no basis in fact. Journalist K. Shabbtai (Shabtai T. Keshev) does so in a most convincing manner in his book *Like Sheep to the*

Slaughter? (Bet Dagan, 1963), and we will discuss his main points below.

First, Shabbtai rejects the argument that the *galut* mentality of the Jews is relevant in this case. Many non-Jews were also murdered by the Nazis in a manner similar to the Jews. These included four to five million Russian prisoners of war, trained soldiers who cannot be accused of faint-heartedness, and one million Poles. Not one of them rebelled. Yet many Jews participated in partisan operations against the Germans and fought heroically. In the Red Army, more Jews received medals of bravery than [did soldiers of] any other nationality. Many *Shoah* survivors made *aliya* (emigrated) to the Land of Israel and fought heroically in the War of Independence, as if they were transformed in a moment into *tzabarim* [native Israelis], proud of stature and free of the so-called *galut* cowardice, which thus is obviously not an intrinsic characteristic of Jews.

Still, why did the millions who were annihilated not rebel against a system of destruction that comprised only thousands or tens of thousands? This is a very superficial question. These thousands were a marvelously organized army, equipped with arms and enjoying freedom of movement, while the millions were disorganized citizens interned in ghettos and camps. The murderers were young and healthy, while the millions of victims included elderly, women, and children who were the hungriest people in Europe. (Even if the Nazis had not destroyed European Jewry in the concentration camps and mass murder campaigns, the Jews would have died rapidly of starvation in the ghettos.) Above all, the murderers included not only those who killed directly, but the citizens and civilians of Germany and of other nations who were anti-Semites. Even the partisans who fought against the Germans included virulent anti-Semites. Often Jews would manage to run away from the Germans into the forests, only to be murdered by the partisans.

The destruction was perpetrated with state-of-the-art psychological methods, using deceit and illusion. Because this organized and methodical destruction of a people had never before taken place in human history, no one believed such a thing could happen. No one believed either that such a cultured and advanced people as the Germans would descend to such a moral nadir.

And because the purpose of the destruction was kept highly secret by the Nazis, many did not believe that they were about to be annihilated. The Nazis also exploited the hope that is natural to every human being. They hinted that not everyone would be sent to the camps and that not all the Jews were "extraneous" to them. The *aktions* and "selections" were often sprung on the Jews, allowing no time for planned responses. Overall, the Nazis used advanced methods of terror and intimidation that paralyzed will and thought, well before they began the actual murder.

About 1.5 million (some say 2 million) Jews were killed during mass murders [by the *Einsatzgruppen*] in territories conquered by the Germans from the Soviet Union in lightning raids. Because previously the Soviet Union had been Germany's ally, the Russians abstained from publicizing the Germans' persecution of the Jews, and so the Jews were completely unaware of the Germans' intentions toward them. The murders were usually carried out with no advance preparation. One fine day a delegation of practiced killers would appear and announce that all the Jews had to gather in one place (such as the town square or synagogue). Almost all the Jews naively responded to the order. From there they were taken outside the city in trucks and shot into mass graves. How could such carnage have been prevented?

In addition, the Nazis used collective punishment. A village in which a rebellion against them took place was completely torched and its inhabitants executed. When a German was killed in an underground uprising in the areas of German conquest, the Nazis would immediately take some hundred hostages and threaten to slay them all if the underground leader were not turned over to them. In the ghettos, they would murder the entire family of one who had fled to join the partisans. Understandably, many refrained from any act that might harm family members or bring disaster upon the entire community.

Those who were caught by the Nazis for rebellious acts were executed using various types of unusual tortures. The survivors tell about all kinds of strange and horrible deaths conceived by the Nazis' sadistic imagination. Even those who were certain of impending death refrained from endangering themselves with such dreadful suffering.

Rabbi Yehoshua Moshe Aharonson wrote the following in his diary while interned in a German concentration camp:

> Before I begin, I would like to respond to the question that future researchers will ask: why did we not defend ourselves and take revenge against the angels of death who came to take us to the valley of the shadow of death?
>
> The answer: (1) Firstly, many did not believe they were being taken to death like sheep to the slaughter. They believed what they were told, that we were traveling to do light work or to the hospital. (2) Even the minority who understood what was happening did not want to take responsibility for the entire public. (3) After living under their authority for four years and in slavery for 16–25 months, we were so weakened in spirit and body that we did not have the strength to resist. We were drained of the necessary energy and might, bravery and stamina. The Warsaw ghetto uprising was an exception to this. (4) The guarding was extremely careful, and everything was done suddenly, in the blink of an eye. (5) Many were already worn down by the life of slavery. They felt that death had been chosen for them; they awaited the opportunity to die and anticipated the angel of death. They saw it as the angel of salvation from their terrible afflictions, from the tortures inflicted by an enemy in the full sense of the word. (*Ani ma'amin* [*I Believe*], ed. Mordekhai Aliav [Jerusalem, 1969], pp. 81–82)

Dr. Hillel Zaidman, also a survivor, writes in his *Warsaw Ghetto Diaries* (Buenos Aires, 1947; E.T., trans. Yosef Israel [Southfield, Mich., 1997]):

> How could it take place? Why did we allow them to lead us like sheep to the slaughter? Was resistance impossible? . . . First of all, it was not clear that the Nazis had planned from the beginning to annihilate us, that this was their intention when they put us in the ghetto. I saw the poverty. I observed their evil schemes closely the entire time. I cannot say that their plan was premeditated. It did not seem that there was one single plan, because the treatment of the Jews took various directions.
>
> . . . It could be that at the time that Hitler and his entourage were discussing the annihilation of European Jewry, they meant it literally, but the Jews could not imagine such a thing, that the Germans really intended to kill and destroy them. We thought that "to destroy" meant what was happening every day: to starve, torment, persecute, harass, rob, occasionally incite pogroms, but not to uproot everything totally.
>
> . . . All throughout the expulsions, the Jews still deceived themselves. Almost everyone thought that he would be exempt. In the 22 July expulsion order, the Germans enumerated so many categories of exceptions that everyone believed he would fall under of these categories. Some were community officials (there were ten thousand who thought they would be the lucky ones) or joint officials (another ten thousand thought they would be under this rubric), or factory workers inside or outside the ghetto. In theory, the expulsion affected only a small portion of the Jewish population. They thought that their identity cards, work cards, and passports would save them. They thought that the destruction would not touch everyone, otherwise why all the factories and selections? They thought that at least a small number would be saved, and everyone believed that he would be among that minority.
>
> They believed, hoped, and dreamed. Was there any other choice?
>
> They believed in something else: in the world, in the world's conscience. What happened here would become known to the free world—for despite the complete communication blockade, news filtered out of the country—and the world would be shocked. When the terrible cruelty became known, how could any person in the world with a soul remain silent? Would not walls be breached, the world shaken in order to save the survivors?
>
> How? No one asked this. They were certain that the strong and mighty world with its enormous spiritual and material resources would find a way to stop the slaughter. They would punish the Germans or use legal methods; neutral nations

would come to their defense; the International Red Cross or the Pope would intervene. The Jews would be recognized as foreign citizens or granted foreign passports. In any case, how could we, imprisoned in this jail, give the world advice on methods to free us? Weren't there numerous Jewish organizations, businessmen, politicians (such as Morgenthau, Baruch, Rosenson, Hore-Belisha, and others for whom the Nazis hold us responsible), lawyers, and diplomats? They will find ways to save us.

And if so, is it worth immediately abandoning the lives of our loved ones, our children, parents, brothers, and sisters, in order to begin a hopeless, impossible struggle against the power dominating most of Europe that has yet to be beaten by another army?

Are we the ones who should have fought? We the starved, the tortured, the untrained, with our wives, children, sick, and elderly? There were concentration camps for Russian military prisoners. Did rebellion or uprising break out in even one of those camps? (*The Warsaw Ghetto Diaries*, pp. 264–268)

We could elaborate on this topic, but there is no need to go on. All who study these issues in depth and who seriously learn the history of the *Shoah* will arrive at the only possible conclusion. As expressed by a well-known French writer, the question of why the Jews did not rebel is "the most foolish of this century's questions."

The true question that arises from examining this topic is: What is the root of the accusation "like sheep to the slaughter," and why does it return again and again in such intensity, when it has no valid historical basis? One of the most well-known contemporary researchers on the *Shoah*, Professor Yehuda Bauer, conjectures the following:

This is the major question arising in every discussion on the *Shoah*, in every unit of soldiers, every school class and university seminar. It is distilled in the expression "like sheep to the slaughter." This phrase is interesting in that it appears only among the Jews. About twenty million Russians, Ukrainians, and other citizens of the Soviet Union were murdered, many more than the number of Jews, of course without a sign of resistance. This leads us to ask: Did

anyone in the Soviet Union ever ask why those twenty million went like sheep to the slaughter? Did anyone ask this about the 2.5 million Soviet prisoners who were murdered by the Nazis, without any resistance whatsoever? Was this asked about the three million Poles who were murdered, or the many thousands of other nationalities who opposed the Nazi regime? I have not found any historical book, lecture, or document, in which a non-Jew asks whether the other tens of millions of people who died in the Second World War went like sheep to the slaughter. This question is uniquely Jewish. It seems to be an expression of self-hate, of a demand from ourselves to be superhuman, heroic, completely supernatural.

The fact that this question is asked at all regarding the Jews, and that it is asked passionately and sometimes with tremendous hostility, demands a response. Apparently, the answer is found in the uniqueness of our particularly self-destructive and self-critical attitude toward ourselves as Jews, although we are forgiving toward others. (*Jewish Reactions to the Holocaust* [Tel Aviv, 1983] [Hebrew], pp. 164–165)

But Professor Bauer's answer—that the source of the question is in the Jews' "particularly self-destructive and self-critical attitude"—is neither satisfactory nor true. If there were room for criticism, perhaps the Jewish people would excel in criticism of itself, but when the critique is groundless in principle, one wonders about its roots.

The true answer is not beyond us and we need not delve too deeply into the obscurities of the unique Jewish psyche in order to find it. For the last hundred years, generations of children and adults have been educated according to Zionist ideology, which attests in vulgar articulation that "our fate rests in our hands only," because "only we can save ourselves" and because "Israel has no Messiah." We have had enough of the *galut* policy of our forefathers, who relied on heavenly grace. We can trust only our own power, the only thing that will bring salvation. The source of the whole long exile and the troubles of the Jews is that they did not take responsibility for saving themselves.

A generation educated to view the martyrs of the Crusades (beginning 1096) and the Chmielnitzki massacres[4] (1648–1649) as having been led "like sheep to the slaughter"—how could they not view the martyrs of 1939–1945[5] as such?

Those who were taught to believe that man holds his fate in his hands, and in his hands only, how could they comprehend a reality in which man stands powerless against forces greater and stronger than he?

Those who learned to scorn the diaspora and the diaspora Jews—how could they identify with the fate of their fellows?

Those who were trained to admire power and physical heroism, those Israeli youth who grew up in an atmosphere that emphasizes military prowess, can never put themselves in the place of millions of Jews, unarmed citizens, women, the elderly, and children, who were murdered without defense or hope for salvation.

About eighty years ago, after a pogrom in the Russian town of Kishinev, the national poet of Israel, Ḥayyim Naḥman Bialik, wrote a poem called "In the City of Killing" ("Be'ir Ha-Haregu," in Ḥayyim Naḥman Bialik, *Collected Poems* [Tel Aviv, 1997], pp. 350–360), in which he describes the pogrom as a terrifying and heart-wrenching experience. But he also criticizes the victims, "great-grandchildren of those whom the *Av Haraḥamim* prayer describes as stronger than lions to do their Creator's will, descendants of holy martyrs" who "fled a fleeing of mice and hid a hiding of fleas, and will die a dog's death there where they are discovered." With equal harshness, he heaps his wrath on the survivors, whom he compares to a flock of weak-hearted paupers, and calls to them: "To the cemetery, beggars! You shall dig the bones of your forefathers.... And with a parched throat you will sing a beggar's song of yourselves, and call for the mercy of states and pray for the compassion of nations. As you held out your hands, so shall you hold them out, and as you begged, so shall you beg." No more, no

less! How could a generation brought up on this poem possibly avoid scorning our *kedoshim*, our holy martyrs?

The question of "like sheep to the slaughter" is the natural conclusion that follows from the myth created by "Zionist" education (quotation marks used purposely), and the absurdity of this question is the final refutation of the ideology which underlies this myth.

One of the most important components of this myth is the story of Masada, still taught to tens of thousands of youth. Again and again the story is told how the zealots [in 73 CE] took their own lives in order to avoid being captured by the Romans, because "We shall die before serving as slaves to those who despise us, and remain free men by leaving the land of the living" (Elazar Ben Yair, commander of the zealots, according to Josephus). Admiration for the zealots' heroism inspired the slogan "Masada shall not fall again." In other words, we, with our own strength and bravery, will not allow another defeat to occur.

But the Masada story is another example of the extent to which this whole ideology is groundless. First, it proves that even Masada can fall. Even heroes can arrive at a desperate situation in which they cannot save themselves, as described by the prophet, "And the bold-hearted among the mighty will flee naked on that day" (Amos 2:16). Second, it reflects the problematic aspect of the expression "heroism," rendering the heroism in the act of Masada dubious. We would not exist today if, God forbid, the residents of Jerusalem and the Galilee during Roman times had behaved like those Jews at Masada, committing mass suicide in order to avoid surrender to the Romans. Was it not greater heroism to confront the life of difficult slavery that awaited them under the Romans in order to continue living and keep the Jewish people alive, instead of dying "as free men"?

I will not relate to the suicides of Masada from a *halakhic* (Jewish law) point of view, but there

---

4. The Chmielnitzki massacres are known in Hebrew as the decrees of *taḥ v'tat*, a reference to the Hebrew years 5408–5409 (1648–1649).

5. Here the author used the Hebrew dates *taf-shin* to *taf-shin-hey*, 5700–5705.

seems to be a reason that their names are missing from our sages' legends of the destruction [of the Second Temple]. The sages do describe youths who committed suicide after being prosecuted for observing *mitzvot* that had been outlawed by non-Jewish rulers. To the sages, martyrdom, dying for *kiddush Hashem*, was defined as giving one's life for the sake of Torah and *mitzvot*. They did not consider as *kiddush Hashem* the choice of death in order to escape from slavery or torture; that could perhaps be judged as an act done under compulsion, but not as martyrdom or heroism.

As a chapter in Zionist education, Masada has become a symbol of heroism that is an aspiration, while the suicides during the Crusades, committed to avoid conversion to Christianity, do not merit a similar status. This reveals the extent to which Zionism confuses issues and turns the Jewish value system topsy-turvyp. In this framework, the Jew who gives his life for his faith is considered a submissive *galut* Jew, while the rebels against the Romans who committed suicide for the sake of their honor are considered national heroes. What an upside-down world!

One of the components of the Zionist legend is the belief in an almost miraculous change in the nature of the *galut* Jew upon joining the Zionist enterprise in the Land of Israel. Immediately upon making *aliya*, he stands heroic, willingly risks his life against his enemies, and even prevails over them. How much more so are the *tzabarim*, native-born Israelis, like lion cubs, heroes by [their] very nature. Shabtai B. Beit-Tzvi tells how much real damage this belief caused during the *Shoah* period:

> The story of the paratroopers sent from Eretz [Land of] Israel to Europe at the end of the war is summarized by Professor Yehuda Bauer as follows:
>
>> Those who study the history of the Jewish paratroopers have to admit that the entire enterprise did not achieve the hoped-for success. Most of the fighters were taken prisoner by the enemy. Seven were killed in action, and many did not act until the Russian conquest or afterward. The great plans—organizing an anti-Nazi Jewish underground, preventing the murder of Jews, active war against the German conquerors—were not implemented, mainly because of the limited number of soldiers and their delay.
>
> I accept this reliable concluding statement, except for one issue. I do not believe that the lack of success was caused mainly by the limited number of paratroopers and their belatedness. I think that *if many more paratroopers had been sent, and at an earlier date, when the Russian front was still far off, the failure could have reached catastrophic proportions. This applies to the number of casualties among the paratroopers and also to the pogroms that could have afflicted the Jews in the lands of the paratroopers' missions.* The stories and legends told of the paratroopers' heroic acts and sacrifices are justified. This was a band of young idealists who risked their lives in order to fulfill a life-and-death mission. . . . But things are different regarding those responsible for sending them. When Ben-Gurion and Sharett point to the paratrooper mission as proof that the pre-state *Yishuv* [Jewish community in pre-State Palestine] came to the assistance of European Jewry, their statement has mere formal validity. Doubtless, the paratroopers were sent to help. But the principal type of aid they meant to give was not the sort that was needed. Armed resistance—if achieved— would have meant destruction for many more Jews in Romania, Budapest, and elsewhere.
>
> . . . The psychological background for the paratrooper mission stemmed from a belief widespread throughout the *Yishuv* that the Jews of the Land of Israel, or at least the young pioneers among them, were of better character than the diaspora Jews. On the basis of this belief, they assumed that two or three paratroopers arriving at their destination in a given European country could train the local Jews in what to do and how to behave. In fact, the Jewish leadership in Bucharest, Budapest, and Bratislava carried out activities for which the paratroopers' training was unnecessary. (*Post-Ugandan Zionism during the Holocaust Crisis* [Tel Aviv, 1977], pp. 375–377)

All of the above is not intended to detract, God forbid, from the admiration of the heroism and sacrifice of those few who succeeded in striking an occasional blow at the murderers. They deserve honor and respect, but this must not lead us to

castigate the vast majority who could not participate physically in the war against the enemy. The
lack of proportion in the comparison between
Shoah and "bravery" has as its source the false
ideology that continues to be implanted in many,
and against this we must warn. Failure to rectify
this great injustice to the memory of our *kedoshim*
(holy ones) would be a terrible historical error.
The mistake would be moral as well as national,
because it would imply severing them (us!) from
the continuous chain of generations and denying
the memory of our ancestors. After all, we are the
inheritors who continue in their footsteps.

In conclusion, I must admit that I have not
found in the writings of our generation's great
Torah scholars a clear response to the question of
whether the Jews should have revolted. It seems
the issue depends on the individual circumstances. The main question they ask is: Would
revolting have led to saving Jewish lives or, God
forbid, to the opposite? Certainly this is no issue
of "honor." Various responses on similar issues
appear already in the writings of the sages, and
certainly the question is addressed in later periods. Regarding the *Shoah* period, one story documented was that of the Rebbe of Radzin, may
God avenge his death. He organized an armed rebellion in the forests among the partisans and
was executed for this (details are found in *Ani
ma'amin* [*I Believe*], pp. 69–70, along with a section of a poem by the secular poet Yitzhak
Katzenelson, "Poem of the Rebbe of Radzin,"
glorifying this incident). Similarly, Dr. Hillel
Zeidman tells about Rabbi Menahem Zemba,
may God avenge his death:

Then Rabbi Menahem Zemba said with great
gravity:

There are different ways to become a martyr. If
today they forced the Jews to convert, and we
could be saved by converting, as in Spain or during
the Crusades, then our death[s] would be considered martyrdom [*kiddush Hashem*]. The Rambam
(Maimonides) says that when a Jew is killed because

he is a Jew, this is martyrdom, and the *Halakhah*
(Jewish law) follows his opinion. But today, the
only way to become a martyr is active armed resistance. (*The Warsaw Ghetto Diaries*, p. 221)[6]

On the other hand, we know that a representative of *Agudat Israel* (the Orthodox religious
party) in the Warsaw community, Rabbi Zisha
Friedman (author of *Ma'ayana Shel Torah* [*Well-
springs of Torah*]), may God avenge his death,
strongly opposed the Warsaw ghetto uprising. He
saw it as an act of desperation, anathema to any
Jew who believed in "Divine salvation in the
blink of an eye" (see citation in Lucy Davidowicz,
Hamilhama Neged Hayehudim [*The War against the
Jews* (New York, 1986)], p. 317).

Similarly, Rabbi Moshe Blau, may his memory be a blessing, leader of the ultra-Orthodox
Agudat Israel in the Land of Israel, wrote at the
height of the uprising:

Only those who have despaired of life are able to
rebel under such conditions, where all hope for
victory has been lost. It cannot be denied that the
situation in Poland may cause Jews to despair of
life. It may drive the youth to their wits' end,
and cause them to commit acts that hasten death.
But clearly this is insanity, and only those capable
of concluding insanity can make that decision.
To die a hero's death for its own sake—this has
no basis in Jewish faith, even if it does not endanger others. Certainly it has no basis when it
endangers the lives of others who greatly value
even one hour of life, and who, even in the most
desperate situation, do not cease hoping for the
salvation of He whose ways are wonderful and
which can arrive in the blink of an eye.

Believing Jews do not pursue hastening their
own death[s], and certainly not the death[s] of
others, merely because their situation is difficult. Others who do so have lost faith; they pass
judgment according to the laws of nature. Such
people are capable of any kind of insanity, even
this kind, and are undeterred even by the fear
that their act of suicide can harm the lives of

---

6. In his article *Mered Hagetaot Lefi Hahalakhah . . .* ["The
Ghetto Rebellions in *Halakhic* Perspective . . ."], *Hamodia* (15 Sivan 5744/Spring 1984), Rabbi Simha Elberg categorically denies that Rabbi Menahem Zemba
supported the Warsaw ghetto uprising. He relies on his

personal acquaintance with the rabbi to make this assertion. In addition, Rabbi Zemba's memoirs from that
period do not offer the slightest hint that he supported
the uprising.

others. (*Kitvei Rabbi Moshe Blau* [*The Writings of Rabbi Moshe Blau*] [Jerusalem, 1983], p. 241)

Many Torah scholars throughout our history took a similar position regarding rebellion against the non-Jewish rulers, although we cannot know whether they would have preferred surrender to rebellion in such extreme circumstances. The issue demands further study and clarification.

Alexander Donat

Alexander Donat (1906–1983) was born in Warsaw. After completing his schooling, he became a journalist and eventually became the publisher and editor of the Polish daily newspaper *Ostatnie Wiadomosci* (*The Latest News*). When the Nazis conquered Poland, beginning World War II, in September 1939, he, like most of the Jews in Poland, was forced into a ghetto. For Donat, this meant the Warsaw ghetto. Here he participated in the Jewish resistance movement. After the Warsaw ghetto uprising, begun on the eve of Passover (19 April 1943), and then the defeat of the ghetto fighters and the total liquidation of the Warsaw ghetto in the late spring of 1943, Donat was sent to the Maidanek death camp which, by a turn of fate, he survived, and then to Dachau concentration camp. After the war, along with his wife, who had also managed to survive, and his son, who had been hidden in a Catholic orphanage during the war, he emigrated to New York City. Here he again became a journalist and published several Holocaust-related works.

SELECTION

In the present essay, Alexander Donat, writing as a witness to and survivor of the Holocaust, rejects God. His testimony, as he tells us, is neither "theological discourse" nor philosophical argumentation but rather a personal response to the evil he personally witnessed. He writes, as he describes it, "from the top of the smokestack [of the crematorium]," in evaluating the various responses to the question of God's whereabouts during the *Shoah*.

The famous, oft-repeated theological explanation regarding Divine behavior and justice given in the biblical Book of Job—that we do not and cannot know God's ways—is unsatisfactory for Donat. Also intellectually and morally unacceptable is the hasidic response that everything, even suffering or death, comes from God and should be embraced as good, and the explanation that the Holocaust was a necessary part of some larger plan of God's (perhaps as a punishment for sin), using the Nazis as His agents. Donat likewise rejects the "free will" argument that the *Shoah* reflects primarily human actions and belongs to the human realm and thus does not indict God. He believes that "[t]here must be rules, limitations to evil" that even God Himself respects and enforces. That is to say, God, as our Creator, either helps us from going too far in the direction of evil or, by failing to do so, "God is made a partner to evil." Therefore, upon careful, if personal, reflection, Donat concludes that he cannot find any explanation to excuse the inaction of traditional Judaism's assertedly benevolent, omnipotent, historically active God during the *Shoah*. And so he rejects Him, i.e., His existence, outright, allowing no half-measures.

Donat, however, retains hope in Judaism (and the Jewish people) without God for he believes that Judaism (as distinct from the "Jewish religion") represents a "sublime concept of personal and social justice and is also a source for the ideals and noblest aspirations of all peoples throughout all history." Thus, by fighting for a strong State of Israel and the continued existence of the "Jewish people and Jewish culture," one serves not only "the basic tenets of Judaism" but also "the affirmation of life, love, justice, freedom, and truth."

Donat's article, "Voice from the Ashes," began as a lecture that he gave in 1975 in New York City at a conference entitled "The *Shoah*: One Generation Later." In 1976, it was translated into Hebrew and appeared first in full in *Yalkut Moreshet* 21 (June 1976), and then in an abridged Hebrew form in *Machshavot* 46 (1977), under the title "A Voice from the Ashes: Wandering[s] in Search of God." Despite the fact that Donat is not an Israeli, we have chosen to include his article in its abridged form here, together with Israeli responses to his piece, because of the intense reaction it provoked among Israeli philosophers and *Shoah* researchers. His article inspired replies from a number of distinguished Israeli thinkers that were published in *Yalkut Moreshet* between 1977 and 1979. Among those responding to Donat were Moshe Unna, Yehuda Bauer, Avraham Korman, Ya'akov Rabi, and Israel Gutman.

The two very different responses by Moshe Unna and Yehuda Bauer to Donat's essay are also reprinted below, pages 287–292 and 293–296.

Selected Bibliography

Books and Articles by Alexander Donat

"Armageddon: Twenty Years after the Warsaw Uprising," *Dissent* 10, no. 2 (Spring 1963): 119–132.
"Revisionist History of the Jewish Catastrophe," *Judaism* 12, no. 1 (Spring 1963): 416–435.
Jewish Resistance (New York, 1964).
Our Last Days in the Warsaw Ghetto (New York, 1964).
Holocaust Kingdom: A Memoir (New York, 1965).
"Voice from the Ashes: Wanderings in Search of God," *Yalkut Moreshet* 21 (June 1976): 105–138 [Hebrew].
The Death Camp Treblinka: A Documentary (New York, 1979).

Voice from the Ashes: Wanderings in Search of God

I Believe
Do I have the choice not to believe
In the living God, who slays me for reasons that
    I cannot decipher,
And who, after He has burned my flesh to ashes,
Awakens me to renewed life?
And when I rage and revolt against Him,
He causes the blood to flow from my wounds,
While my lament is his praise.

—Aaron Zeitlin

The *Shoah* occupies a central position in the history of our generation and in all of Jewish history. The focus of the *Shoah* is the search for God.

Anyone who experienced the ghettos and camps remembers the God syndrome that prevailed there. From morning to night we cried out for a sign that God was with us. From the depths of our disaster, amid the hangings, the gas chambers, and the incomprehensible manifestations of evil, we shouted: "Omnipotent God, merciful and compassionate One, where are you?" We searched for Him, but we did not find Him. The maddening and humiliating feeling of the absence of the Divine accompanied us constantly. The experience is eternal, unforgettable.

I have no personal claims against God. I am one of the lucky handful who survived the torturous path from the Warsaw ghetto to Maidanek and Dachau. My wife also survived her wanderings from Warsaw to Maidanek, Auschwitz and Ravensbruck. My son, then five years old, was saved by non-Jewish friends two weeks before the final razing of the Warsaw ghetto. Eventually, after indescribable suffering, he was taken in by a Catholic orphanage, where we found him after the war.

On the other hand, I do not have the feeling that I was "bribed" by my miraculous salvation, as many of my survivor friends do. They feel a personal obligation to serve as faithful and captive servants of the Lord, who chose them to be saved. Therefore there is no personal dimension to my claims against God. Mine are not the accusations of Job. I am speaking as a witness to the calamity that befell my people.

I do not pretend to be a theologian, and those who expect a theological discourse will be disappointed. The permanent, fixed archetypes are not found here, wrapped in the cryptic professional dialect of the shaman or mandarin who attempts to hide triviality under a torrent of words. Disappointment also awaits those who expect a flood of proclamations from a former believer who has abandoned his faith, desecrated His Name, and profaned the sacred.

I will not make the superficial atheistic claims of the thinkers and dialecticians of the eighteenth and nineteenth centuries. I will not search for contradictions and discrepancies in the sacred writings, nor will I discuss the incompatibility of religious dogma and modern science.

We cannot logically prove God's existence or absence; it is a matter of faith and therefore occupies a completely different realm. There are well-known scientists who believe in God and reject Pierre Simon Laplace's answer to Napo-

leon, that the scientific explanation of the universe does not require the assumption of God's existence. I intentionally overlook the problem of God and the conflict between religion and science. That topic, while fascinating in itself, is outside the realm of this statement.

My argument is based on moral revulsion against the total evil that was done to us, that cannot be justified with any excuse, not even considerations derived from the recent advances of science. . . . In this essay on the implications of the Shoah for religion, I do not intend to reopen the age-old argument between believers and agnostics. My role is more modest. While witnesses and researchers reconstruct and preserve how these events happened, I will try to penetrate the question: How could they have been allowed to happen? I want to know why they happened. Where was God? What is the reason—if one exists—for our inexpressible suffering? Many years ago, I began the quest for an answer, a religious response to the Shoah. The following is the report from my extended journey.

I looked for answers in every possible source and attempted to evaluate them. In trying to understand these explanations, I examined them with the test I thought conclusive: How do they look from the top of the smokestack [of the crematorium]? This test is extreme and harsh but infallible, incorruptible, and lucid.

To prevent semantic confusion and dispute, I should explain that when I use the word "God," I refer to the popularly accepted, traditional image of the biblical God: compassionate and merciful, omnipotent, good and beneficent. I mean the God who is King, Judge, Father, Shepherd, Teacher, Healer, and Redeemer; the God of Abraham, Isaac, and Jacob. The believing Jew trusts in Him and prays to Him.

The presence of God in history is the cornerstone of traditional Judaism. God not only created the universe, He also manages it and directs the course of its events. He is the God of nature and history. No wonder that during the period of the Shoah and afterward, we have continued to ask, where is God? This question has become a trauma and a burden, and continues to trouble our generation.

"Where is God?" asks Abraham Joshua Heschel in his book Man in Search of God. "Why did you not stop the trains, stuffed with Jews taken to slaughter? It is so difficult to raise a child, to nourish and teach him. Why did you make it so easy to kill?"...

1. The Sacrifice of Miriam

The poet Hirsch Leiwick presents the same question in a different manner. In his speech before the Ideological Congress in Jerusalem on 15 August 1957, he told the following story from his childhood:

> We were studying with our rebbe the Torah portion *Vayera* [Genesis 22], which includes the story of the sacrifice of Isaac. In the story, Abraham and his son Isaac go to Mount Moriah, where Abraham binds Isaac to the altar.
>
> My heart cries out with pity for Isaac, and when Abraham brandishes the knife, my heart is silenced in fear.
>
> Suddenly the voice of the angel is heard: "Abraham, Abraham, do not raise your hand against the youth and do not cause him harm! It was only God's test."
>
> Then I burst out in tears. "Why are you crying now?" asked the rebbe, continuing, "Isaac was not sacrificed."
>
> In tears, I answer, "What would happen, rebbe, if the angel were late?"
>
> The rebbe comforted me, "Please calm down. The angel cannot be late."

Leiwick concludes his story with the comment: "We all saw six million Isaacs lying under knives and axes, in flames and in gas chambers, and they were sacrificed. The angel of God *was* late."

I would like to tell you about another sacrifice, not of Isaac but of Miriam. The setting was not Mount Moriah of four thousand years ago, but Warsaw, capital of Poland, Tuesday, 26 Elul 5702 [8 September 1942], during the last stage of the big Warsaw ghetto pogrom. After six weeks of manhunts, transports, and murders, the pogrom reached its height in what was called the "vat" *Aktion*, in which an SS officer would determine life or death for the lines of Jews who passed in front of him. The remnants of the Jews in the ghetto, those few who remained alive after the pogrom, were concentrated in a square area of a few clusters of houses.

There they underwent the final "selection," in which all had to pass through the mouth of the large vat-shaped structure. Daily, the columns would march back and forth as they were gradually thinned by the Nazis' systematic murders. Husbands were separated from wives, parents from children, brothers from sisters. Frightened parents abandoned their children in the middle of the street. Other parents chose to accompany their children to the gas chambers even though they were offered temporary clemency for their own lives.

When the turn came for the Jews of the Eleventh Military Supply Detail to pass the SS officer, a contemporary Abraham (his real name) stood in a row with his wife on Wilenska Street. They were young and healthy, "useful Jews," and their safe passage seemed certain. In a sack on his shoulder, Abraham carried a few clothes, some food, and live baggage—his daughter, Miriam, two years old, who had been put to sleep with a few sleeping pills. The line advanced slowly, while the SS officer in his magnificence determined right or left, who would live and who would die. Suddenly, the tense silence was interrupted by a baby's cries a few lines in front of Abraham. The SS officer froze, and a thousand men and women held their breath. A Ukrainian policeman hurried up and stuck his bayonet into the sack from which the cries emitted. Immediately, it began to run with blood.

"You poisonous pig!" shouted the SS officer furiously, striking his whip across the face of the deceiver who had dared to try to save his child's life. The Ukrainian shot the father, which was an act of mercy since he had gone out of his mind. Now the policemen began to "check" all the sacks with their bayonets.

Only three lines separated Abraham and the SS officer. Abraham's face was white as chalk, but his wife was stronger than he was, or perhaps weaker. She whispered to him, "Put down the sack!" He did so as one hypnotized, and without losing his place. He moved to the end of the row of marchers and lowered the sack carefully onto the edge of the sidewalk. The deed was done in a moment, and he returned to his original place, his eyes bewildered. That was the sacrifice of Miriam. She was two years old.

I ask a simple, unsophisticated question: Where was the angel of God? Why was the angel late? Why were six million angels late? Was this a rebellion of the angels, or God's command? Or perhaps there were no angels and no God? Why did God allow the creation of a situation in which a father must make such a choice? ... The journalist Gershon Jacobson said:

> The question of where God was during the Holocaust of the Second World War is intensifying. Until now, rabbis and religious leaders did not feel it necessary to answer or explain, or give their opinion as to how Divine Providence could allow the destruction of six million Jews.... Recently, the Lubavitcher Rebbe approached the problem in a thorough and straightforward manner. This was the first time, to my knowledge, that a person of standing discussed the subject. He asserted that *Hashem* [God] is true and righteous in all His ways and deeds. This is the fundamental basis of faith that is repeated clearly and decisively many times in the Bible, the *midrashim* (biblical commentaries), and other sources. Moses and the prophet Jeremiah asked the age-old question of punishment of the righteous and reward of evil. The Talmud and *midrashim* discuss it endlessly.

2. We Do Not Know

This basic answer to Auschwitz is perhaps neither relevant nor obvious, yet it is honest and consistent. What is its significance?

A. The *Shoah* is a contemporary event, yet its problem is ancient and discussed many times in the holy Scriptures. "Why do the righteous suffer while the wicked succeed?" "Why is man born to evil?" The Bible answers this question.
B. The ways of God are inscrutable. They are beyond our ability to comprehend.

This point of view is expressed by a wide range of religious thinkers, who offer various types of interpretations and conclusions. Some see the *Shoah* as the last in a long chain of evil occurrences that may differ in the quantity of evil, but not in quality. As Dr. Robert Gordis writes: "At what point is evil expressed: when the number of victims reaches six million, five million, or one million? Is not the death of one

child a tragedy in the eyes of God?" ("A Cruel God or None: Is There No Other Choice?" *Judaism* 21, no. 3 [Summer 1972]: 278–79; reprinted in this volume, pp. 491–496).

Professor Emil Fackenheim sharply disagrees with those who compare the *Shoah* to previous disasters in Jewish history. He believes that the *Shoah* has no precedent. "The Book of Chronicles is full to the bursting with unjust suffering; but its description cannot approximate what happened at Auschwitz." ...

The idea that God's ways are unfathomable finds expression in Isaiah 55:9:

> But as the heavens are high above the earth,
> So are My ways high above your ways
> And My plans above your plans.

This answer, however ancient, is not enough. I cannot accept the death of 1.5 million Jewish children with the answer: It is too complicated for you to understand—do not ask questions! Since the days of our forefather Abraham, Jews have followed the age-old tradition of questioning God's deeds and protesting against them when they seem to step outside the bounds of ethics. As Abraham says in his critique of Divine justice at Sodom: "Far be it from You! Shall not the Judge of all the earth deal justly?" (Genesis 18:25). Moses asks, "O Lord, why did You bring harm upon this people?" (Exodus 5:22). I feel that our generation is certainly permitted to ask these kinds of questions. ...

In Tarnow, Poland, stands a tombstone erected in July 1948 by the Jewish committee of the city. Engraved on it in Hebrew, Yiddish, and Polish are these words:

> Dedicated to the memory of our dear ones.
> Here lie 800 small and broken skulls of Jewish children who were brutally murdered on
> 11 June 1942, by German executioners.

These are our children. Who more than ourselves is entitled to ask questions?

3. The Hasidic Response

How does Hasidism respond to the *Shoah* and its enigmas? A wonderful volume by Dr. Pesah [Peter] Schindler, *Responses of the Hasidim and*

Their Leaders during the Shoah in Europe, 1939–45 [New York, 1972], offers us a wealth of material enabling us to answer this question. Relying on a wide range of factual and bibliographical sources, he arrives at the following conclusion:

> In their responses, the rabbis attempted to justify God's deeds during the *Shoah*. They denied all theological distinction between judgment and mercy, good and evil. Everything that comes from God is grace, even if it is sometimes hidden from humanity's limited vision. Therefore, suffering must be accepted with love, devotion, faith, and unquestioned trust in Divine justice. (p. 2)

Dr. Schindler cites many sources in support of his conclusions. One of the more important of these is a collection of writings by Rabbi Kalonymous Kalman Shapira, the Piaseczner rebbe.

Rabbi Shapira died in the *Shoah*, but his writings were discovered in a jar in Warsaw and published as *Esh Kodesh* (*Holy Fire*) [and excerpted earlier in this volume, part I, pp. 38–47]. He reminds us that after the Romans condemned the ten martyrs to death during the Bar Kokhba rebellion, God threatened to destroy the world. The crimes of the *Shoah* undoubtedly surpass those of the Romans. . . .

Yet revolt, uprising, and protest are isolated and do not have the power to change the whole picture. Suffering comes from *Hashem*, and we must accept it with a willing spirit, with love, appreciation, happiness, and enthusiasm. Since he was dying in sanctification of the Name, *kiddush Hashem*, the rebbe of Piaseczner said that he "did not suffer at all and felt only happiness" and added, "the Omnipotent in His pure grace has taken me as a personal sacrifice" (*Esh Kodesh*, pp. 8–9).

Rabbi Ḥayyim Rabinowitz, the Rebbe of Sidlowitz, was reported to have comforted those who were packed into the cattle cars for four days without food or water on their way to the death camps: "My friends the Jews, do not fear death, for it is a great and meritorious deed to die in sanctification of the Name." . . .

Rabbi Ḥayyim Yeḥiel Rubin, the Rebbe of Dumbarova, prayed the last Sabbath service of his life with great warmth and led twenty Jews in a ḥasidic dance despite the revulsion they must have felt before falling into the graves they had dug with their own hands. . . .

I have given these examples as they are cited and do not take responsibility for their accuracy. On the contrary, I am extremely doubtful of their veracity.

4. The Rod of God

Another religious leader who tried to deal with this problem was Dr. Ignaz Maybaum. Before the war, he served as rabbi of the Berlin community, but in 1939 he fled to England where he earned a reputation as a sermonizer and writer.

One of his books was *The Face of God after Auschwitz* [Amsterdam, 1965 (excerpted in part III, pp. 402–408, below)]. In it, he asks: "God allowed this to happen; where is God?" Maybaum tried to provide both a logical and religious answer to this question. In his answer, he differentiates between *ḥurban* [total destruction] and an evil decree. An evil decree can be promulgated by humans, and it can be canceled through repentance, prayer, and charity; but *ḥurban* is from God, and from it, there is no escape. He enumerates three occurrences of such destruction in Jewish history: the First Temple, the Second Temple, and the *Shoah*. . . . "Destruction is like an operation in which God surgically cuts part of the body of humanity, thus allowing renewed, healthy life to grow" (p. 61). And further:

> God terms Nebuchadnezzar, who razed Jerusalem, "Nebuchadnezzar my servant" [Jeremiah 27:6]. Isaiah says that God Himself asked Assyria to destroy the northern Kingdom of Israel. In the Book of Job, Satan is counted among the servants and angels of the Lord. Will anyone take offense if I paraphrase the prophets, and say, "Hitler my servant"? Hitler is a servant in the sense of being a vehicle, evil and despicable as he may be, and God uses this rod or tool to cleanse, purify, and punish the world that sank in sin. The six million Jews were free of sin; they perished for the sins of others. (p. 67)

This article by a famous rabbi and sermonizer left me dumbfounded. If Hitler were a rod in the hands of God, why did the Nuremberg trials judge this "instrument" that did not sin instead of judging those others who transgressed? Why did [the State of] Israel condemn to death [Eichmann in 1961], one of these vehicles of God?

I reject Maybaum's conclusions out of hand. Yet I cannot deny that they do have a measure of consistency. . . .

It is difficult to reconcile what he proposes in his summary: to praise God and thank him for saving most of the Jewish people, and to reaffirm a sense of faith that the sacrifice of the Jews brings purification and advancement to the whole world in the future. But as much as this seems to me paradoxical and unacceptable, it is congruent with the foundations of traditional Jewish belief.

5. Our "Free" Will

The tragic simplicity of the problem makes it all the more complicated. Since ancient times, the lawmakers, prophets, and sages have struggled with the problem of evil and the question of the suffering of innocents. Theodicy, [the defense of] the righteousness of God and His judgment, existed long before Leibniz coined the term. The simplest common denominator of the problem is as follows:

God is omnipotent. If He allows evil and the suffering of innocents, then He is neither good nor righteous.

Or: God is good and righteous. If He allows evil and the suffering of innocents, then He must not be omnipotent. . . .

Another response is the admission that although God is not omnipotent, He Himself created this limitation. God gave humanity freedom of choice, the ability to choose between various courses of action. "God in His will created man as a free partner in His world," asserts Abraham Joshua Heschel in his book *Between God and Man* (New York, 1959, p. 151).

Defenders of the Holy One, blessed be He, like to emphasize the idea of a transcendent God who granted humanity freedom of choice to decide what is good and what is evil. They say that the *Shoah* has no connection to God. It is not God's decision, but rather a human act. God suffered and cried with the victims, but He can do nothing to help them. But if God gave humanity freedom of choice between good and evil, this freedom cannot be unlimited, cannot be

without fences or borders and without some measure of control. There must be rules, limitations to evil, so that even evil remains within the moral bounds of humanity and God, within borders that can be tightened and relaxed. If not, then God is made a partner to evil. If I tell my son not to jump into deep water, not to use drugs, and not to stab his friend, and I see with my own eyes that he is trying to do all those things despite my warnings, is it not my duty to stop him? Or do I leave him alone with the excuse, "I told him so"? Was it not the duty of the good and beneficent God to send His entire army of angels to the assistance of the nation with which, as it is written, He formed a covenant? Is God not guilty of breaching the important biblical rule, "You shall not stand aside while your fellow's blood is shed" (Leviticus 19:16)? Why are we angry at everyone and not at the One who is truly guilty?

Let us analyze the implications of the term "free will" in relation to the problem of the *Shoah*. Our first question is: Why did God give humanity the choice? The Torah [Hebrew Bible] teaches us that before the biblical flood, God regretted His actions and decided to destroy the human race with the flood in order to begin again. Why did He repeat his error? The Torah even teaches us [in Genesis 1:27] that the Lord created man in His form and image. Does this not mean that God Himself is able to be Korczak [head of the Warsaw ghetto orphanage] and Himmler? Why did He not make humans less God-like and more human, reducing our ability to do evil, just as He limited our ability to detect light rays to the range between ultraviolet and infrared? Why did God not create an improved version of the human creature, not necessarily a complete *tsadik* [a wholly righteous person], but just better? And why cannot God intervene with free will when it breaks through all borders? . . .

The entire concept of free will is foreign to the spirit of Judaism. The Sisyphean attempts of the sages to reconcile it with the idea of Divine providence by an omnipotent God is the main essence of Judaism; a God who is not omnipotent contradicts the very nature of religious faith. In contrast to the founding theory of Western philosophy, traditional Judaism is based on faith in God, who intervenes directly with our daily lives and manages them. Western philosophy gives humans responsibility for their actions. According to it, Eastern fatalism, religious or Marxist determinism, genetic coercion, or theories of society and environment are not considered to be factors that determine human behavior. At most, it sees them as extenuating circumstances.

The gesture that traditional Judaism makes toward free will is nothing but an exercise in evasion. This can be proved by dozens of expressions.... One has only to open a holiday prayerbook and read the *U'netaneh tokef* prayer for Rosh Hashanah (the New Year) and Yom Kippur (the Day of Atonement). The significance of these days is in the idea that God intervenes daily in earthly events and in human fate:

Let us now relate the power of this day's holiness, for it is awesome and frightening. On it Your kingship will be exalted; Your throne will be firmed with kindness and You will sit upon it in truth. It is true that You alone are the One who judges, proves, knows, and bears witness; who writes and seals; who remembers all that was forgotten. You will open the Book of Chronicles— it will read itself, and everyone's signature is in it. The great *shofar* (ram's horn) will be sounded and a still, small voice will be heard. Angels will hasten, a trembling and terror will seize them— and they will say, "Behold, it is the Day of Judgment, to muster the heavenly host for judgment!"—for they cannot be vindicated in Your eyes in judgment. All mankind will pass before You like members of the flock. Like a shepherd pasturing his flock, making sheep pass under his staff, so shall You cause to pass, count, calculate, and consider the soul[s] of all the living; and You shall apportion the fixed needs of all Your creatures and inscribe their verdict.

On Rosh Hashanah will be inscribed and on Yom Kippur will be sealed how many will pass from the earth and how many will be created; who will live and who will die; who will die at his predestined time and who before his time; who by water and who by fire, who by sword and who by beast, who by famine, who by thirst, who by storm, who by plague, who by strangulation, and who by stoning. Who will rest and who will wander, who will live in harmony and who will be harried, who will enjoy tranquillity and who will suffer, who will be impoverished and who will be enriched, who will be degraded and who will be exalted.

But repentance, prayer, and charity remove the evil of the decree.

It seems that the repentance, prayer, and charity of Miriam were not enough to cancel the evil decree. I can almost see before my eyes the judgment of the High Court on Rosh Hashanah and Yom Kippur 5702 [1941], when Miriam's sentence was decreed. The omnipotent God, merciful and compassionate, sits magnificently on a throne, the book of life and death resting open on a chair made of wishes and sighs....

This Jewish belief in heavenly bookkeeping, as it appears in the High Holy Day prayers, has always been repulsive to me. Does it mean, I asked myself, in a certain measure of naïveté, that the "vat" *Aktion* was planned, calculated, and decided by the tribunal on high about a year before it happened? One and a half million children of Israel were sentenced to death in the gas chambers by the Holy One, blessed be He, the omnipotent. What was their sin? Is there any sin that requires the punishment of Treblinka and the sacrifice of Miriam? From among all the nations, did God choose the swastika-bearing scum of the earth to carry out the sentence?

6. God's Eclipse

A decisive proof that the religious answer is not satisfactory can be found in the works of the celebrated religious thinker Martin Buber, father of the concept of dialogue and interpreter of Hasidism:

We ask and ask again: how can Jewish life continue after Auschwitz?...How can we live with God while Auschwitz is happening? The alienation is too cruel, the mystery is too deep. We can still believe in a God that allowed all this, but can anyone still speak to Him? Can anyone still hear His words? ("Diaglogue between Heaven and Earth," in *Judaism*, ed. Nahum Glatzer [New York, 1972], p.224)

Buber admits, then, that God allowed things to happen, but he felt that we could still believe in such a God. But how and why did God allow all this? Buber's answer is in what he calls God's "eclipse":

> An eclipse or failure of celestial light, an eclipse or failure of God—this characterizes the historical hour that the world is experiencing.... A solar eclipse is something that happens between our eyes and the sun, not in the sun itself. Just as during an eclipse we cannot see the sun, so we could not see God during the historical eclipse of the *Shoah*. What do we mean when we speak of an eclipse of God happening to us now? This image embraces the daring assumption that we are able to look at God with the eyes of our soul, or better, with the eyes of our being, just as we are able to lift our physical eyes to the sun. Something might rise up between us and God, just as could happen between the Earth and the sun. [The English version of this quote is found in Martin Buber, *Eclipse of God* (New York, 1952), pp. 33–34.]

It is not clear from Buber's words whether the "eclipse" means that God cannot see what is happening on earth, and the gas chambers and crematoriums are hidden from His view, or whether it was the perpetrators of evil and their victims who could not see the hand of God and His justice. (See also further excerpts from Buber, part III, pp. 372–375.)

Among the horrifying works that have come out of the *Shoah*, one book is almost peerless in its importance: *Amidst the Nightmare of Crime: Manuscripts of Members of a SonderKommando,* E.T. Kristina Michalik [Oswiecim, 1973]. Written originally in Yiddish by prisoners who worked in the gas chambers and crematoriums, these writings were discovered in the mounds of ash in Auschwitz and published by the national museum there. One of the documents tells about the *hauptstormführer,* SS Otto Mohl. He was a cold-blooded murderer who lacked all human feeling, but there was one thing he absolutely could not tolerate: the sound of a child crying. Whenever he would hear a child crying, he would throw the "culprit" into the flames of the pits where the gassed corpses were burned (pp. 55, 119). Did God not know enough to use the blackened glass that allows us to view an eclipse—a simple trick that all Mohl's

children knew? Why did He not ask one of them? Or did He prefer not to look? Buber does not have the answer, and his only comfort is that "an eclipse of God's light does not mean that it was extinguished. Whatever has hidden it can disappear the very next day" (E.T. *Eclipse of God*, p. 34).

Buber continues, "Although His next appearance will not compare to the previous ones, we will again be able to recognize our stern and merciful Lord" ("Dialogue between Heaven and Earth," p. 225).

Again we are dumbfounded by the complete helplessness of religion in offering an answer. A man of Buber's stature, one of the most respected and astute thinkers of our time, cannot conceive an answer to six million holy sacrifices, [he can] only speak about an "eclipse of God."

7. Doubting Servant of God

Job is usually presented as symbolizing piety and unquestioning faith in God, admitting his guilt with submission and humility. Nothing could be further from the truth: Job does not answer "amen" after all God's deeds, and the book does not belong to the type of theodicy that justifies everything. On the contrary, the book contains sharp criticism. Serious accusations are made against God, who is asked to explain and respond.

The story's introduction is shocking in its immorality and desecration of the sacred. Satan does not doubt Job's fear of God, nor his righteousness; rather he attacks his motivations: "Is it for nothing that Job fears God?" But is not the philosophy of reward for righteousness the foundation stone of Judaism? If so, what is wrong with Job expecting reward? Furthermore, does not God know all, including whether a person is truly God-fearing or not? Does He need to use a complex and cruel test? The rabbis wrote volumes of speculations and arguments on the question of whether a person's acts are influenced by the fact that God predetermines everything, yet they never raised a doubt about His omniscience. If so, was not the exercise of Job just a cruel jest of heartless humor?

In the first part of the book, Job's friends present the principles of traditional theodicy. If Job suffers, he must have sinned, knowingly or unknowingly, and his suffering is God's punishment. Yet Job denies this resolutely and accuses God of cruelty for its own sake. When he threatens to put God on trial, God Himself appears in the whirlwind, and we are treated to the wonderful poetry of the argument: "Where were you?" In their meeting, we expect God to tell Job that it was only a Divine trial. Yet God's sharp words are expressed in beautiful verse describing His power, the complexity of His universal reign, the wonders of nature, and His many roles....

My conclusion from all this is that the contribution of the Book of Job to a solution to our problem can be only through negation. The game is not fair. Instead of giving a direct and open answer, God casts fear on the ill, depressed, destroyed wretch; He humiliates Job, degrades his value and honor, demonstrates his insignificance and unimportance, turns him into "dust and ashes." God's answer can be summarized in one sentence: Who are you to question Me? Even if I were to explain everything to you, you would not understand, since it is beyond your comprehension, and you cannot measure Me in meager human terms. Where do you get the idea that justice is one of the foundation stones of My world and that human happiness is the first of My worries?...

Job understands this. His answer:

Behold, I am deficient; what can I answer You? I place my hand against my mouth. I spoke once and will not speak up again; as for the second, I will say no more. (40:5–6)

I had heard of You through hearsay, but now my eye has beheld You! Therefore I renounce [my words] and relent, for [I am but] dust and ashes. (42:5–6)

Do these words sound like *tzidduk hadin,* the formulation recited at a death expressing acceptance of the verdict? This seems to say, "Now I see who stands before me and what You look like. You are mighty and without mercy; before You I cannot stand, I am a worm and superficial ideas of justice have entered my head...."

Here begins the meaningless epilogue. Like a merchant, God grants Job reparations and gives him twice as much as he had previously: sheep and camels, cattle, donkeys, seven sons, and three daughters. The children are not exactly the ones he had before, but what difference does it make, Samuel or Isaac, let's not argue over petty details— seven is seven and the account is balanced. After all, Job's fate is better than ours. God in His glory has not revealed Himself to us in order to give us an answer, should we refuse to see the State of Israel as an answer and the reparations from Germany as compensation from God. As for the six million, He still owes us for them. . . .

Nevertheless, Dr. Emil L. Fackenheim rejects out of hand the conclusion that Auschwitz renders obsolete the belief in the traditional, historical Jewish God: "As believers in Judaism, we cannot separate God and the *Shoah*" (*God's Presence in History* [New York, 1970], p. 76). Despite this, we must remain faithful to the God of Israel. Why? According to Fackenheim's train of thought, there is no other way to ensure the existence of the Jewish people in the future. His conclusions are summarized in what he calls the "commanding voice of Auschwitz" or "our 614th *mitzvah* (commandment)":

What does the voice of Auschwitz command us to do?

You Jews must not grant Hitler victory after death. You must remain alive as Jews, otherwise the people of Israel will die out.

You must remember the victims of Auschwitz so that their memory will not fade.

You must not despair of man and this world, escape into cynicism or into speculations about the afterlife. If you do, you will be handing over the world to the forces that caused Auschwitz. Finally, you must not despair of the Rock of Israel, or else Judaism will be extinguished. A Jew must not respond to Hitler's attempt to destroy Judaism by aiding this destruction. . . . It would be like doing Hitler's work for him. (*God's Presence in History*, p. 84)

Fackenheim's solution is the continuation of belief in the God of Israel as a protest, as His Honor's opposition party. . . .

8. Unanswered *Kaddish* (Mourner's Prayer)

To Fackenheim, the writer Elie Wiesel is "*the* religious protester and revolutionary." Fackenheim dedicated his book *God's Presence in History* to Wiesel.

> Thirty years ago, Elie Wiesel was taken to Auschwitz from a town in Transylvania. One day when his group returned from work, he saw a boy being hanged on the camp gallows. [Wrote Wiesel:]
>
> "Where is God? Where can He be?" asked someone behind me.
>
> From within me a voice answered...: "Where is He? Here, hanging on the gallows." (p. 77; citing Wiesel's *Night* [New York, 1961], p. 78)

Elie Wiesel is one of us, he speaks in our language. For thirty years, Wiesel attempted the impossible. He dedicated his great personal charm and the adroitness of his pen to bringing God down from the gallows. He pleaded and threatened, he mourned and even profaned God. He appealed to heaven in supplication and prayer, but to no avail. The sound of his bitter lament is heartbreaking, "senseless prayers and useless tears." ...

Wiesel is torn between his traditional upbringing and the recognition that the horrors we have experienced have no explanation. He is caught in the middle between faith and rebellion, despair and the will to hold onto hope. He is aware that his work is meaningless and inconclusive. "After what happened to us, how can you believe in God?" asks Gregor in *Gates of the Forest* [(New York, 1982), p. 194]

The rebbe answers him with a smile of understanding: "How can man not believe in God after what happened?" His answer is a revolt against His Majesty, not a provocation. "In my opinion, a Jew can rebel against God, on condition that he stay with Him." ...

Wiesel cannot free himself from the shackles of his forefathers' faith, and he serves as an example of the "religious rebel," to use Fackenheim's phrase. With the strength of despair, he tries to believe in God although he knows that God does not deserve it (p. 194). ...

I seem to hear in this an echo of the victims of Stalin's purges. His tortures erased all traces of humanity, degrading and eradicating every remainder of self-respect. From a group of Stalin's

victims who stood opposite the firing squad, one could hear the cries, "Long live Stalin! Despite everything!" But why? Why must we hold onto blind, unquestioning faith in a God who betrayed His people and abandoned them in such a shameful manner? In truth, such is Jewish tradition. ...

Despite all the protest and blasphemy in Wiesel's words,

> he is deeply rooted in tradition, drawing from the theology of the Tanakh (the Hebrew Bible) that developed with Jewish literature. ... His blasphemy is the special kind of the traditional Jew. It is rooted in disappointment, not negation, and its inspiration comes from love of God and closeness to Him. (Byron L. Sherwin, "Wiesel and Jewish Theology," *Judaism* 18, no. 1 [Winter 1969]: 40)

In "My Father's Death" (from *Legends of Our Time* [New York, 1982]), the son wonders how to commemorate the *yahrzeit*, the yearly anniversary of his father's death. His first instinct is to obey tradition and follow in its footsteps. Go to the synagogue ... say the mourner's *kaddish* and before the living congregation of the people of Israel, declare the holiness and greatness of God.

But then comes a second reflection. His father died in a concentration camp, one of the six million. How can he praise God after all that happened?

> The survivors, more realistic if not more honest, are aware of the fact that God's presence at Treblinka or Maidanek—or for that matter, his absence—poses a problem which will remain forever insoluble. (p. 6)

The son concludes:

> All things considered, I think tomorrow I shall go to the synagogue after all. I will light the candles, I will say *Kaddish*, and it will be for me a proof of my impotence. (p. 7)

The *Shoah* cannot be explained within the framework of religion. Dr. Robert Gordis, a Conservative rabbi and thinker, expresses the problem in all of its severity: "A cruel God, or no God at all—is there no other option?" This is the name of his article on the significance of the *Shoah* for religion. Of course, Rabbi Gordis concludes that "it is still possible to have a living faith in the biblical God who works in history." I cannot understand how it is possible to believe in a God who allowed 1.5 million children to die in gas chambers and mass graves. No sophistry, rhetoric, or casuistry, no flood of description or poetry, no mysterious or flowery prose can answer this question. The answer is unique and as simple and final as an order to the right or left. There is no other option. Either this is the God of Treblinka— or else there is nothing. My choice is clear: There is nothing. Rabbi Eliezer Berkovits can brush aside "Auschwitz theology" and call it naive radicalism, but I do not believe in a paranoid, Stalin-like God of Israel or in His "chosen people." To believe in God after Auschwitz is an insult to our intelligence, true blasphemy, a blow to the deepest feelings of morality. Anarchy rules.

9. Voice from the Ashes

I am aware that this view raises as many questions as it attempts to answer. Recently, my seven-year-old granddaughter asked, "Mommy, what does it mean to be a Jew?" Her mother explained to her in simple terms: "A Jew has a special way of praying to God." And now I will be frank: I do not pray to God; I do not believe in God. Am I a Jew?

Yes, I am a Jew, with every bone in my body. Precisely because I am a Jew, I deny God. One and a half million children of Israel, children like Miriam and Korczack's little Yossele, Moshele, and Sherol, were murdered and butchered. For that, I will not forget nor forgive—neither humans nor God. No scholastic sophistry or wordplay can convince me that God saw the smoke of Warsaw and Auschwitz without His heart shuddering in pain, sorrow, and shame. Outbursts of complaint, bitterness, and blasphemy are ways of acknowledging Him by way of protest, and I want no part in that.

I reject Job's baseness and surrender; I reject Wiesel's sitting on the fence; I indict God without prosecuting Him. One cannot prosecute someone who does not exist. This is not a verdict; this is a statement of fact, written in blood. "Ladies and gentlemen, the emperor is naked!" . . .

What then is my Judaism, this Judaism without God? . . .

For thousands of years, Judaism and religion were synonymous. But this is no longer true in our time. Judaism and the Jewish religion are no longer one and the same. Judaism is a more inclusive term than the Jewish religion, which is only one part of Judaism. Judaism refers to the entire body of thought, emotion, and effort of the Jewish people. . . .

To me, Judaism is the most sublime concept of personal and social justice and is also a source for the ideals and noblest aspirations of all peoples throughout all history. Its tradition and wealth of legends, poetry, and song serve as a beautiful instrument for expressing this supreme living truth. Its Book of Books is full of beauty and liturgy that touches the depths of human spirit as well as the heights. "This is the record of Adam's line" (Genesis 5:1): It represents the summary of a generations-long search for God, the compendium of Israel's wisdom, its national experience and genius, the magnificent legend of the life of our people. Of all the spiritual value systems, one cannot find anything that surpasses the guidelines of Judaism that gave birth to and nourished the religious and social ideals of the Western world.

"You shall not defraud your fellow" (Leviticus 19:13); "Do not stand aside while your fellow's blood is shed" (Leviticus 19:16); "Do not do unto your fellow what you would not have him do to you" (Hillel's saying, B.T. *Shabbat* 31[a]); "Let your fellow's honor be as dear to you as your own" (Rabbi Eliezer ben Hyrkanos, *Ethics of the Fathers* 2:15). If only humanity would heed these words (and God, if He existed)! These few principles. How different this earth and its fate would be!

Abba Kovner [the Vilna partisan leader] calls us "modern alchemists trying to turn our dust into a mourner's memorial candle." Mourning, memorial services, and tears are not enough. The *Shoah* must not be a memorial of helplessness, defeatism, acceptance of fate, and moral disarmament. On the contrary, we must change it into a source of power and resolution, if not hope. We must not act as if the *Shoah* did not occur. Judaism after the *Shoah* must not be the same as before. The State of Israel must take central stage, and we must remain as strong as a rock. The *Shoah* has not become history, a literary figure of speech, a verbal image. As for me, and I am sure for many, it is still very tangible. I still see the gallows in Maidanek and the flames of the burning Warsaw ghetto. The stench of the chimneys' smoke still fills my nostrils. The clock of my life stopped in 1943 and has not yet moved from that position. Religion does not answer us; it does not comfort or strengthen us. Our God was nothing but a legend, an imaginary creature, the most beautiful of man's dreams. Nostalgia and grief remain in our hearts, along with the piercing recognition that we stand alone in our historical struggle and can rely only on ourselves.

There is no Messiah, no valley of Armageddon, no last battle in any form. The war continues daily, hourly, and within every one of us.

"What was our sin that such crimes could happen?" asks Abraham Joshua Heschel (*Man in Search of God*, p. 367). He continues by presenting the second half of the question, that is inestimably more important: "What can we do to ensure that such acts will not be repeated? Must we behave as if nothing happened, cry and mourn and then go to synagogue and praise the same God who betrayed us, and wait for the next disaster?" . . .

10. End of the Journey

About 1,700 years ago, Rabbi Yannai recognized, "It is not in our power to explain either the tranquillity of the wicked or the suffering of the righteous" (*Ethics of the Fathers* 4:19). Sisyphean

efforts have failed to bridge the gap between Divine providence and free will, between the power and goodness of God and the fact that innocents suffer. These efforts have failed shamefully, especially after the *Shoah*. I accept neither the blind faith of the ḥasid approaching death through song, nor the theory that Hitler was a tool of God, nor the naive alibis of Buber or Berkovits, nor the unfounded loyalty of Fackenheim to a God who disappointed, nor Wiesel's "nevertheless." Religion has no answer to the *Shoah*. I reject the God of Treblinka and Auschwitz, and all the attempts to avoid the problem using beautiful prose, sophistry, or casuistry. I reject the view that our fate is to disappear or to be destroyed. The *Shoah* is another turning point in Jewish history. The existence of the Jewish people and Jewish culture has entered a new age, the age of the religious revolution. . . .

I accept the basic tenets of Judaism: the affirmation of life, love, justice, freedom, and truth. I affirm life as humankind's highest value. To me, "good" is everything that contributes to life, and "bad" is anything that strangles and terminates it (see Erich Fromm, *You Should Be as God* [New York, 1966], p. 40, for an elaboration of this).

I am a Jew. I do not believe in the God of Auschwitz. I believe in rebellious, suffering, struggling humanity.

This is my faith.

This is the true voice erupting from the sacred ashes.

Moshe Unna

Moshe Unna (1902–1989) was born into a rabbinical family in Mannheim, Germany. After receiving a traditional Jewish education, he did advanced studies in agronomy in Berlin and, at the same time, received his rabbinical ordination from the famous Hildesheimer Rabbinical Seminary in Berlin in 1922. Attracted early to Zionism, he was one of the founders of a religious Zionist group in Germany known as *Baḥad* (*Brit Halutzim Dati'im* = League of Religious Pioneers). In 1927, he emigrated to the Land of Israel (then under a British mandate), settled on a kibbutz in northern Israel, and worked in the agricultural sector. In 1931, he returned to Germany as a *shaliach* (representative) of the Zionist movement and repeated this representation in 1934. On his return to pre-state Israel, he continued his activity in the religious kibbutz movement and became one of its leading figures. As a result, following Israeli independence, he was elected to the Knesset (Israel's Parliament) and served during its first six terms (1948–1963) as a representative of the National Religious party. In the Knesset, he was known especially for his support of the rights of workers and for his work on the Law Committee. Ultimately he served as the nation's deputy minister of education from 1956 to 1958. In this role he pushed hard for the support of religious education in the country. Closer to home, on his own kibbutz, Sde Eliahu, in the Bet Shean valley, he was a founder of the regional school that now serves about one thousand pupils each year.

Throughout his long life, Moshe Unna was concerned with the interconnection of religion and politics, especially in the way that these two fundamental categories were active within the rebuilt Jewish community in the Land of Israel. He expressed his views in numerous articles that dealt with, among other issues, religious education, the relationship between secular and religious Jews in the fledgling state, and the connection between the Jewish people and the State of Israel.

SELECTION

Moshe Unna's response (in *Yalkut Moreshet* 22 [1997]: 63–68) to Holocaust survivor Alexander Donat's article "Voice from the Ashes" (in *Yalkut Moreshet* 21 [June 1976]), an abridged version of which is reproduced above, pp. 275–286, seeks to defend God and Judaism in the face of Donat's "extreme expressions of defiance to the Divine." Unna, deeply offended by the extreme skepticism advocated by Donat, describes Donat's commentary as "personal, subjective testimony," which should not be allowed to "constitute guidelines in life for us." It is not, Unna argues, objective truth but the response of a broken soul. Writing from a traditional *halakhic* (religious-legal) standpoint, Unna criticizes Donat's analysis of various Jewish sources (and his use of some non-Orthodox thinkers) as mistaken and reiterates his own reading of Judaism's emphasis on freedom of choice. That is, he attempts to defend God through the classical free-will defense, which locates the cause of evil in human decisions and actions rather than in God's will and power. Furthermore, he notes that the God of Israel, as opposed to pagan nature gods, is not the "God of wonders and miracles" but rather "the God of moral accusation." Although he purportedly does not wish to delegitimize Donat's perspective as a survivor, Unna rejects his recommendation that in light of the *Shoah* we ought to exchange our faith in God for faith in the Jewish people. On both religious and utilitarian grounds, Unna objects to Donat's conclusions and cautions that following his normative prescriptions will not make the living of our daily lives any easier.

Selected Bibliography

Books and Articles by Moshe Unna

For Myself: Thought and Action (Tel Aviv, 1955) [Hebrew].
True Partnership: Essays on the Path of the Religious Kibbutz (Tel Aviv, 1962) [Hebrew].
Essays on Religious Education (Tel Aviv, 1970) [Hebrew].
Israel among the Nations (Tel Aviv, 1971) [Hebrew].
Separate Ways in the Religious Parties' Confrontation with Renascent Israel (Jerusalem, 1987) [Hebrew].
"Who Will Heal You? (Response to Alexander Donat)," *Yalkut Moreshet* 22 (1977): 63–68 [Hebrew].

Who Can Heal You?

Your devastation is as vast as the sea; who can heal you?

—Lamentations 2:13

I do not see myself as qualified to criticize Alexander Donat's article "Voice from the Ashes" (*Yalkut Moreshet* 21) in the usual manner of critics. I do not think that anyone who was not "there" should be allowed to argue with someone whose being was molded by the horrors of the death camps, or to attempt to change his views. If there is a case in which the injunction "Do not judge your fellow until you are in his place" is definitely justified, this is it. Donat's article has several extreme expressions of defiance of the Divine that I find dismaying and alarming, but I do not transform these into accusations, as I might against another person. The loss of the ability to believe, in the true meaning of the term, is to me the worst aspect of the devastation suffered by the *Shoah* survivors; therefore I do not argue with them. Despite this, if I dare to make a few comments on Donat's work, I do not intend them as a personal attack.

I would like to call the readers' attention to several aspects that I think they should consider after reading what Donat, a man of intellectual stature who is wounded to the depths of his existence, has written. I am worried that readers of his essay may draw some incorrect conclusions.

The first thing we must be aware of is that his article can be read in two ways: (1) as a revelation of truth that was hidden from the eyes of humanity and discovered at Auschwitz, or (2) as the cry of a fellow human being in whom "nothing is whole" (Isaiah 1:6), whose words shake us to the core of our souls and move us in an "intense wandering" (Isaiah 22:17) because of the humanity they evoke, and with which we identify as fellow human beings and as Jews.

There is no basis for us to accept such a personal, subjective testimony as objective truth, no matter how horrifying it may be and no matter how reliable it is as an expression of what took place within the consciousness of the writer. On the contrary, I believe that any realistic analysis must result in disqualification of such a view. This testimony cannot constitute guidelines in life for us. Would we accept as minister of foreign affairs a person with a serious war injury, one who suffered trauma and therefore judges war and peace from that personal perspective? This viewpoint is apt when we weigh Donat's words for their objective value, and it serves to guide our efforts to understand the essence of a man pulled into the swirl of tragic events. We must not divert our attention from this aspect, remaining aware of the circumstances that generated these words, especially if they direct our thought toward understanding the essence of humanity and the Jew, and are intended to influence us. (Note also that examples Donat invokes speak of this clearly, for example, when he writes, "I seem to hear the victims of Stalin's purges," who despite everything cried: Long live Stalin!)

1. Freedom of Choice Is Basic

Donat decides the position of the Jewish religion on the basis of "sources from the Jewish religion that were available to me": verses from the Bible (some of which were quoted out of context), sayings of the sages, writings of hasidic and [Reform and Conservative] rabbis (apparently the most important authorities on Judaism's position!). *Halakhah*, Jewish law, does not exist for him. However, according to any normative understanding of Judaism, *Halakhah* is what determines the Jew's actions and embodies the basics of faith. And if Donat correctly states that "the foundation of the Jewish faith is the role of God in history" [not included in the abridged essay that appears in this anthology], he is wrong in his understanding of this statement and in explaining its significance. God is not "the God of miracles and wonders" but rather *the God of moral assertion—as opposed to the pagan nature gods* [emphasis in the original]. He is completely wrong when he cites the *U'netaneh tokef* passage to prove that "the significance of holy days such as Rosh Hashanah (New Year) and Yom Kippur (Day of Atonement) is in the idea that God intervenes daily in earthly events and in human fate." Freedom of choice, one of the essential components of Judaism, "is nothing more than an exercise in evasion" to Donat.

If Donat had studied *halakhic* (religious-legal) works, he could not have arrived at this absurdity. He would understand that freedom of choice, the ability of humans to act according to their own free will, is one of the foundations of Judaism. The responsibility of humans for their actions is based on this. Without it, Judaism's entire concept of humanity and relation to the Absolute is undermined. The idea of repentance is built on these two concepts, freedom of choice and responsibility for actions. Without repentance, all would agree that Judaism cannot exist. Indeed, the significance of the High Holidays is in repentance. As Maimonides says (*Mishneh Torah: Laws of Repentance 5:1*): "The species of man is unique in the world, and there is no similar species, because he himself, in his knowledge and thought, knows good and evil, and *does everything he wants, with no one to restrain him from doing good or evil.*" To Donat, this is an "exercise in evasion" (of what?)! If he were familiar with *Halakhah*, he could not avoid Maimonides' interpretation of the verse "from the mouth of the Most High, good and evil will not issue." Donat quotes this [in the original, longer version of his essay] as a *question* and therefore it is proof that God determines everything. But Maimonides calls it a statement that "the Creator does not decide for man whether to be good and not bad," and therefore it is written after this: "we should examine ourselves, study our ways, and repent" (*halakhah* 2 in the Laws of Repentance). The essential point in this discussion is that there is a demand that a person make an effort to the best of his ability to ensure that the good or moral side prevails.

Judaism propounds the idea that God is the God of history. He does not play with people, as the pagan peoples believe about their nature gods. The basis for this lofty idea is that morality obligates humans as individuals and humanity in general, and there is a being who prosecutes any violation of that obligation. The God of the Jews is definitely not "the God of wonders and miracles" who regularly interferes in history. The opposite is true. The forty years in the desert are understood as a special period of Divine guidance; miracle stories reflect extraordinary events that do not take place every day, and therefore the sages cautioned that "we cannot count on miracles." God has the power to intervene in history, *but he does not usually do so.*

2. Beyond Comprehension

The great religious thinkers of Judaism were aware of the problem arising from the apparent conflict between "knowledge" and "choice"; between the claims of morality and justice that seem to obligate God as well as humans; between regulation of human reality by God (*hashgaḥah pratit*, or Divine providence) and human freedom of choice. The great religious Jewish thinkers considered this question and struggled with it with great honesty; they tried to find satisfactory answers, each according to his own conception, *while navigating between the two truths.* If Donat does not accept their answers, the reason could be objective (they do not stand the test of logic) or subjective (lack of understanding on his part). At any rate, this does not prove that they are incorrect. And when Donat determines that the answer does not satisfy him, without explaining his opinion ("I cannot accept" is no explanation to my mind), it seems that he is unable to contradict the basic assumptions of Judaism.

Regarding most of those whose opinion Donat cites, the main problem is not the possibility that the two principles (the human ability to mold reality, on the one hand, and Divine guidance needed to fulfill moral principles, on the other) might coexist side by side. Rather, they asked how humanity can find a way out of the dilemma posed by the conflicting principles. In this context, I would like to point out an interesting fact that should invite reflection. In 1755, a terrible earthquake shattered Lisbon, killing thousands. This event shook the faith of many. Notice that here a natural event, unconnected to human acts, caused doubts of belief and raised accusations against God and His providence; at the same time the most horrific acts of man were not considered destructive to the basis of faith.

Donat finds unsatisfactory the answer that the ways of God are beyond our understanding. The definition of God as omnipotent and omniscient is logical. Because the level of human intelligence falls short of the wisdom and understanding of God, humans must therefore understand less than

God. Maimonides attempts to ascribe this issue to the human intellect (*Mishreh Torah:* Laws of the Foundations of Torah 2:10):

> The Holy One, blessed be He, knows His own truth as it is, and does not know it as outside of Himself, like we know, since we and the known are not one. But the Creator, the known, and its existence are one, from every facet, from every corner and in every manner of His uniqueness. . . . He is at once knower, known, and knowledge itself.

Maimonides concludes this attempt to capture the ephemeral in words by saying, "The mouth has not the power to express this, nor the ear to hear it, nor can man's heart grasp this about his Creator." If this answer does not satisfy Donat, despite its logic, then perhaps we can search for the reason for this in the field of psychology: It is difficult for people in general, and Donat in particular, to accept the thought that some things are above human achievement. This refusal does not prove that such things are nonexistent.

3. Unfair Parables and Photographs

Maimonides' words on the inability of humans to express certain spiritual matters in human language lead us to another point that I cannot skip, indeed I feel that I must not pass it over. This inability to articulate ideas that we feel are crucial and the difficulty in explaining them to others leads us to the use of parables and images in order to approach the ineffable. It seems that this is inescapable; but there is also no doubt that this use of parables and images leaves an opening for misunderstanding and distorted opinion. Many argue that they cloud clear understanding as well as interpersonal relations. Those who utilize images because of the natural limits to human intelligence—and it seems that we must do so if we want to preserve the possibility of arguing about the nature of things—would do well to take care to distinguish between the image used and the idea that it is meant to express. If we treat images and parables as if they themselves are conceptual truths, we will certainly arrive at the absurd. If someone uses this warped process as a method of argument, he leaves the realm of logic. Without it, the argument becomes moot. Contempt and derision take the place of conceptual confrontation. Unfortunately, Donat has taken this path. His description of the High Court is a classic example of where this path leads.

> I can see . . . the judgment of the High Court on Rosh Hashanah and Yom Kippur 5702 [1941], when Miriam's sentence was decreed. The omnipotent God, merciful and compassionate, sits magnificently on a throne, the book of life and death resting open on a chair made of wishes and sighs.

Donat mocks one of the most serious and painful issues that humanity confronts. The image of God sitting on the throne of judgment with the books open before him is the representation of *the idea* of justice reigning in God's world. Donat's treatment of the topic is, excuse the analogy, a theological assertion à la Khrushchev, who found proof of God's nonexistence in that the astronauts did not discover him in "heaven." Donat's approach to Job [see the section of Donat's essay on "Doubting Servant of God"] is similar.

4. Failed Treatment of Wiesel and Buber

In the above, I have perhaps gone too far with the criticism I meant to avoid, and for that I apologize. But note how far Donat goes when he discusses attempts to struggle with *the* spiritual and existential dilemma of humanity! He ridicules and makes a mockery of them. He uses the following words to analyze Buber's use of the expression "eclipse of God": "Did God not know enough to use the blackened glass that allows us to view an eclipse—a simple trick that all [SS officer] Mohl's children knew? Why did He not ask one of them? Or did He prefer not to look?" In Donat's opinion, this is a "silly anecdote." Various denigrating statements can be made about Buber, but I do not believe one can say that he approaches these questions in jest. Do Buber and similar thinkers not deserve that we make an effort to fully understand them? I do not see signs of such an effort in Donat's article. It seems he has left the boundaries of discussion, transforming it into a systematic attempt at preventing honest confrontation of the questions that many believe are raised by the very nature of our humanity.

Donat's treatment of Elie Wiesel is disappointing and clearly reveals Donat's own limitations. After all, Wiesel is "one of us, he speaks in our language." Therefore Donat cannot disqualify him as he does the rest of the thinkers he quotes. But Wiesel also does not provoke any doubts in Donat, even though he is validating a viewpoint other than Donat's own. Instead of negating Wiesel's views as he does the others, Donat uses the scalpel of psychology, a known method of avoiding confrontation with an uncomfortable opinion. "Wiesel is torn between his traditional upbringing and the recognition that the horrors we have experienced have no explanation. He is caught in the middle between faith and rebellion, despair and the will to hold onto hope." "Wiesel cannot free himself from the shackles of his forefathers' faith." Donat excludes the possibility that Wiesel may have realized that he confronted the intrinsically problematic character of the human experience, torn between desires of the heart and yearning for higher values; between the freedom of choice granted to humanity (the source of its greatness and the root of its being) and the existence of "a Master of the house" to whom humanity is subordinate. A kernel of truth exists in the faith of Wiesel's forefathers, although it may be difficult, even impossible to accept as His awesomeness is revealed. It has content that is not subtracted from its existence; the reality of God is not nullified, even if there is no escape and no choice but to rebel against Him. For this reason, Elie Wiesel remains attached to this faith, but not out of the type of weakness that lacks conviction.

5. Substitute for Faith—Feeble and Frivolous

After his unbridled, undisciplined outbursts, Donat proffers his own solution. He believes, and proposes that we also believe, in "the existence of the Jewish people in the future" [see the section of Donat's essay that deals with the thought of E. Fackenheim], and concludes his essay with his belief "in rebellious, suffering, fighting humanity." He exchanges his lost belief in God for something that he does not have, for faith in the continuity of Jewry. His new "faith" does not stand up to any criticism, neither logical nor spiritual. In truth, it is the miserable antithesis of the lofty idea of a humanity filled with yearning, needing the love of the absolute God. Not all things declared as objects of faith can serve as such. Donat chose something impermanent in nature to which to attach his faith. No people has ever been created whose continuation is guaranteed to the extent that one can reasonably and substantially speak of belief in such. Yet paradoxically, there is room for faith in the continuation of the Jewish people if it directly results from faith in God and His promise. So the conundrum remains unresolved.

It seems to me that the problem that Donat presents, if we try to identify its philosophical core, is as follows: Is there an advantage to a moral system from which God is banished, and does such a system makes it easier for the Jew to accept the reality of life after Auschwitz? In other words, does the answer "anarchy rules," with which he concludes his section on the "Unanswered *Kaddish*," help restore to us the inner balance that was taken from us? Can it save us from despair, from nihilism? It seems to me that the answer to these questions is negative. Donat's

answer is an expression of despair, and nothing more. Banishing God does not add meaning to our lives, and in my opinion will not make it easier for the human soul to accept reality. Maybe people will feel their burden eased and find satisfaction and comfort in daring to rebel and destroy. Donat's words are a bitter and shocking cry, but I cannot see them as a confrontation leading to a clarification, despite the great spiritual effort invested in them.

As Donat states in dealing with his granddaughter's query about what being a Jew means, he himself "is aware that [his] view raises as many questions as it attempts to answer." In other words, he knows that what he presents to us solves nothing. Why, then, does he propose his solution? Against my will, I find myself again in the field of psychology. What pushes him, it seems to me, is the rebellion against the helplessness that he feels around him, the need to destroy the shelter that others have tried to build in order to withstand the storm of problems that have no answer in the human realm. The "destruction" in his view may be total, but it leaves no room for building. The building, in other words the proposal of his solution, is shaky; a puff of wind can knock it down.

Yehuda Bauer

Yehuda Bauer was born in Prague, Czechoslovakia, in 1926 to secular parents. After receiving his first schooling in Prague, he emigrated with his family to Palestine in 1939, just before the outbreak of World War II. After the end of the Holocaust, he left Israel to study at the University of Wales in Cardiff from 1946 to 1950. After receiving his B.A., he returned to Israel and continued his studies at Hebrew University, receiving his Ph.D. from that institution in 1960. After completing his studies, he joined the faculty of the Institute for Contemporary Jewry at Hebrew University. In 1977, he was appointed to the chair in Holocaust studies and also served as the academic chairman of the Institute for Contemporary Jewry between 1978 and 1995. He has held many additional distinguished academic positions, including serving as a visiting professor at the University of Honolulu in 1992, at Yale in 1993, and at Clark University in 2000. In 1998, he addressed the German Bundestag on Holocaust Memorial Day and in that same year received Israel's highest public academic honor, the Israel Prize. In addition, he served for many years as chair of the International Institute for Holocaust Research at Yad Vashem, Israel's national institute for remembrance and research relating to the Holocaust. He has published eleven English-language books related to the Holocaust and many additional studies on the *Shoah* in Hebrew.

SELECTION

Yehuda Bauer's "Returning to the Source of Human Morality" is a strident rebuttal of Moshe Unna's "Who Can Heal You?" which, as already noted above, was a reply to an article by Alexander Donat in which Donat, as a response to the events of the Holocaust, argued for the rejection of God. Unna, in contradistinction to Donat, defended traditional Judaism and faith in God. Now it is Bauer's turn to criticize Unna and to advance the claim that the *Shoah* has made belief in a benevolent God, or in Divine providence, impossible. Bauer contends that Unna, with his unshaken belief in a moral God, avoids the real question posed by the *Shoah* which, according to him, is: "how to believe in a God who is Satan." In addition, Bauer also takes issue with Unna's utilitarian defense of Judaism. In light of "serious dilemmas" such as the *Shoah*, truth is not a concept that can be sidestepped in order to make daily living easier. Faith in God failed because it was not based on truth; the Holocaust proved this definitively. Now, Bauer contends, we must "demand human morality for the purpose of society's existence," a task he describes as difficult but honest.

This selection first appeared in *Yalkut Moreshet* 24 (1978): 23–25.

Selected Bibliography

Books and Articles by Yehuda Bauer

From Diplomacy to Resistance (Philadelphia, 1970).
My Brother's Keeper (Philadelphia, 1974).
Flight and Rescue (New York, 1975).
The Holocaust in Historical Perspective (Seattle, 1978).
The Jewish Emergence from Powerlessness (Toronto, 1979).
American Jewry and the Holocaust (Detroit, 1982).
History of the Holocaust (Chicago, 1984).
Jewish Reactions to the Holocaust (Tel Aviv, 1988).
Out of the Ashes (Oxford, 1989).
Jews for Sale? (New Haven, Conn., 1995).
Rethinking the Holocaust (New Haven, Conn., 2001).
"Returning to the Source of Human Morality (Response to Alexander Donat and Moshe Unna)," *Yalkut Moreshet* 24 (1978): 23–25 [Hebrew].

Returning to the Source of Human Morality

In Response to Moshe Unna's "Who Can Heal You?"

Moshe Unna, as a man of faith, is justifiably shocked by Alexander Donat's article "Voice from the Ashes" (*Yalkut Moreshet* 21). Donat's words are painful, and Unna uses various techniques to ease the discomfort. His main tool is the so-called psychological method, meaning that since Donat is a *Shoah* survivor, we should try to understand him. We are dealing with a person with a bleeding psyche, and so must not take him too seriously. We should, says Unna in his opening section, relate to Donat's writing not as words of truth, but as "the cry of a fellow human being in whom 'nothing is whole' (Isaiah 1:6)" . . . "who is wounded to the depths of his existence."

Unna, therefore, rejects Donat's views out of hand. But in order to ensure that Donat's opinions cause no damage, he goes to great lengths in explaining and persuading. Yet if Donat's views are merely those of a wounded man, they are invalid as testimony on the topic they address: the theological problem of the existence of a God who remained silent while witnessing Auschwitz.

Unna's first argument relates to freedom of choice. Judaism, says Unna in the second section, teaches that humans are free to do good or evil, despite the "demand [apparently by God] that a

person make an effort to the best of his ability to ensure that the good or moral side prevails."

Unna's answer is a kind of fig leaf cover-up. No one argues that the Nazis refrained from choice, or from choosing evil; clearly, they had a choice, and choose they did. That is not the question here at all. The question is: In the *Shoah*, between 1 and 1.5 million Jewish children were murdered. Did God give them the choice between good and evil? Did they choose whether or not to go to the gas chambers? What does this have to do with freedom of choice? The Nazis had freedom of choice, not their victims.

But this question is not new at all. It already appears in Job, if not previously, because the problem is really not Job's at all. God uses Job as a toy, putting him to the test, or perhaps initiating a confrontation with Satan at Job's expense. But why are Job's wife and children victims of this confrontation? Under great duress, we can see that Job had a certain freedom of choice, not between good and evil, but between submitting or not submitting to the will of God. All would agree that Job's wife and children did not have such freedom. They are the arbitrary victims of God, who plays a cynical game with Satan. Unna's thoughts on freedom of choice, when it comes to victims of the *Shoah*, is a mockery that the mind cannot tolerate, even when the writer has the best of intentions.

I return to God's "demand" for morality. Unna's assumption is, of course, that a God exists who expresses such a demand. Donat's response is that God does not exist. There is no escape from the conclusion that Unna's underlying assumption is the object of his proof to Donat and those like him. This is a strange method of argument for a man like Moshe Unna, who trusts in the rules of logic.

It seems that Unna has also misunderstood Donat on the second issue, the religious argument that humanity cannot fully understand God's intentions. All Unna can do is to quote Maimonides' (medieval) version of the ideas Unna expresses in modern language in the previous paragraph, that humanity cannot understand God's intentions and that this follows from the definition of God. The answer to this point is also not new: I reject any answer, justification, reason, cause, or appeal to a "Divine way" that explains why the omnipotent God did not prevent the murder of a million Jewish children not yet responsible for their own actions, even according to the strictest *halakhic* (religious-legal) view. Every explanation, reason, "Divine way," rationalization, and so forth will only justify mass murder, or explain why God is a full partner in the murder of children. Such morality, which serves as the basis for a religious demand for human moral behavior, is the morality of Satan. Moshe Unna can continue to believe, and I will never protest to him. As far as I am concerned, the question remains how to believe in a God who is Satan. I prefer not to believe in Satan. The answer to Unna is not that humanity can understand the ways of God, but that humanity does not *want* to understand the ways of God, because these ways, according to the simplest logic, can only be the ways of Satan.

The rest of Unna's arguments do not really belong here. He defends Buber and Wiesel against Donat's criticism. He may be on the side of justice. But the point is not one or another interpretation of others' work. Every system of thought based on traditional Jewish foundations, even unacceptable or mistaken interpretations, must confront the idea of Divine providence and the presence of God in history. According to the theory of "the hidden face of God," He exists in history but chooses not to see or not to intervene. He cannot choose not to know, because He is all-knowing, or else religious concepts have no value. If He knows and does not intervene, hides His face, does not bring His providence to bear on millions of murder victims—it makes no difference morally. He is omnipotent and makes the free choice not to do anything. Inaction leads to mass murder. I do not want to know His motivations for this inaction; the mere fact of it is enough for me. Whatever the motivation was, it was an excuse to consent to murder. The conclusion is again the same: If there is a God, then He is Satan. If He is not Satan, then He does not exist.

Belief in the God of Israel has strengthened many Jews in their most difficult hours. Of this, there can be no doubt. Religious belief provided the basis for Jewish culture, and this is also beyond doubt. One can argue that belief in God should continue for reasons of expediency, or for nationalist reasons, or even to give higher sanction for humanitarian values. In my opinion, this is a very shaky justification for the existence of religion, but I can understand it. Yet in retrospect, we admit that belief in God in our generation has been transformed into an elementary absurdity of logic, which continues to exist for purely psychological and utilitarian reasons.

This last point stands out in Unna's attack on the logical construction of Donat's secular-nationalist solution. It is worthwhile to quote him on this issue: "It seems to me," writes Unna,

that the problem Donat presents, if we try to identify its philosophical core, is as follows: Is there an advantage to a moral system from which God is banished, and does such a system make it easier for the Jew to accept the reality of life after Auschwitz? In other words, does the answer "anarchy rules" help restore to us the inner balance that was taken from us? Can it save us from despair, from nihilism?

No, my friend Unna, that is not the question. What Unna presents is a typical utilitarian approach to the issue of religion: Does it help anyone? Is it good or bad for the Jews? Is faith better than nihilism? The question that Donat asks is completely different: Is there truth in religion or not? His answer, "anarchy rules," does not assist in confronting nihilism and does not attempt to resolve anyone's internal conflicts on the subject of religion. It merely determines that it is the truth, that is all. Now, in light of that, to which Unna has no answer, we must find ourselves a path in this cruel world. The way that Donat offers leads back to the sources of human morality. This source is not Divine, because there is no God. In the beginning, man created God, created Him in his own image, because it was convenient and good to create a higher power to which he could ascribe systems of authority, society, and morality. Human morality is a reflection of the level of interpersonal relations at which the various societies have arrived in the trajectory of their development. We must therefore demand human morality for the purpose of

society's existence. This is very difficult and raises innumerable problems. At Auschwitz, we first saw the failure of humanity juxtaposed with the nonexistence of God. Unna proposes a return to the faith that disappointed; it disappointed because at its heart was something nonexistent. Unna's manner of expression hints at the suspicion that exists in his heart as well, that basically the God to which he ascribes his moral demands is not to be found at all. Let us return to simple belief, he says, because it is more useful for us, although perhaps it is not true. The truth is really very difficult. Whoever cannot confront this truth will certainly accept Unna's solutions. Others, myself among them, cannot accept sermonizing solutions that do not provide satisfactory answers to such serious dilemmas.

Natan Alterman

Natan Alterman (1910–1970) was one of the most outstanding Hebrew poets of the twentieth century. He was born in Warsaw and emigrated to Israel in 1925 at the age of fifteen. Beginning in 1931, he began to publish the compositions that created his reputation as a modernist poet. His poetry became almost canonical in pre-state Israel as it voiced the Jewish aspiration for an end to the British mandate and the creation of an independent state. Alterman also gained fame for his contributions to Israeli culture as a dramatist (primarily in his last decade) and as a writer of folksongs, popular lyrics, and humorous pieces. In addition, Alterman translated many world classics into Hebrew. Among the works he translated were dramas by Shakespeare and Molière. Aside from his various literary pursuits, the public of his time knew Alterman as a writer of political and social verse for the daily press. He first began to publish this sort of material in the Israeli newspaper *Ha'aretz* and then, beginning in the 1940s, contributed a column called *Ha-Tur ha-shvi'i* (*The Seventh Column*) to the socialist newspaper *Davar*. During the Holocaust, he published several collections of poetry, for example, *Simach Aniyyim* (*Joys of the Poor*, 1941) and *Shirei Makkot Mizrayim* (*The Plagues of Egypt*, 1944), which addressed the first news of the *Shoah*. Later, his poetry, as in his important 1957 collection entitled *Ir ha-Yonah* (*Wailing City*), addressed the 1948 Israeli War of Independence, as well as topics on the Israeli agenda during the first twenty years of the state's existence. In 1967, after the Six Day War and Israel's occupation of territories on the West Bank of the Jordan, Alterman became one of the founders of the Movement for a Greater Israel, which promoted annexation of those areas.

SELECTION

Natan Alterman, in the essay reprinted here, tackles what he understands to be a widespread and repercussive historical misconception. The particular misconception that he wishes to address is the one which depicts the Jews who during the Holocaust fomented rebellions, for example, those responsible for the Warsaw ghetto uprising, as heroes, while the members of the *Judenräte* (the Jewish Councils, organized and tightly controlled by the Nazis, which were responsible for the daily administration of the ghettos) are seen as villains. Alterman argues that this black-and-white portrayal, this normative dichotomy, oversimplifies the roles and actions of both groups. The fact is that many Jewish Councils collectively, and many of the individuals who served on those councils, answering to their own consciences, acted justly, even heroically. Many, if not most, council members did their best under extraordinary circumstances—where the crucial issues concerning life and death were always ultimately in the hands of the Nazis—to save Jewish lives. Alternatively, those who rebelled threatened the lives of everyone around them, sometimes actually hastening the deaths of others, and created the possibility of mass reprisals by the Nazis. Given these complex realities, Alterman contends that in most situations in which Jews found themselves during the *Shoah*, the path chosen by the Jewish Councils was a better choice in terms of saving and/or prolonging Jewish lives than the option represented by outright rebellion. However, the uprisings do make sense chronologically as a "last resort" response that occurred when all other hope had disappeared. All things taken into consideration, it is not that one response was right and the other wrong, one heroic and the other cowardly. Rather, if we truly wish to learn from the Holocaust and to avoid "ready-made and prepackaged formulations [that] are the enemy of truth," we need to understand the range of actions and decisions in their proper ethical and historical contexts.

Though this selection does not directly address the theological issue of Jewish faith after the Holocaust, the editors have chosen to include it because of the profound moral questions and concerns it raises regarding Jewish behavior during the war. In that these actions are thought by many to have theological significance, this essay becomes relevant to the larger conversation of which this volume is a part.

The material here reprinted is drawn from Alterman's Hebrew *Notebooks* (Tel Aviv, 1989, pp. 13, 15, 23–25, 105–106), which were edited by Dan Laor and published posthumously. The notes to the article, also reprinted here, were supplied by Dan Laor. According to Laor, Alterman worked on these ideas relating to the *Judenräte* continuously from April to June 1954. In these reflections, as in his political poems published in his *Ha-Tur ha-Shvi'i*, Alterman expressed an extreme view shared by only a minority of the Israeli public at that time.

Selected Bibliography

Book by Natan Alterman

Two Roads: Remarks from a Notebook, edited by Dan Laor (Tel Aviv, 1989) [Hebrew].

Book about Natan Alterman

Menachem Dorman. *Natan Alterman: Chapters in His Biography* (Tel Aviv, 1991) [Hebrew].

Two Roads: Remarks from a Notebook

The Poem on the Uprisings[1]

We have taken the uprisings that took place during the *Shoah* out of context and extravagantly extolled them. By so doing, we imply that the uprisings were the correct response, while all the rest was blunder and blindness. The uprisings represented glory, while all the rest was degeneracy. It is as if the entire period were divided into two parts. We strive to stamp the entire period with the imprint of the uprising and view it as the primary symbol, or as the only

1. Refers to the poem *Yom Hazikaron Vehamordim* ["Day of Remembrance and the Rebels"], first published in "*HaTur Hashvi'i*" ["*The Seventh Column*"], *Davar*, on Holocaust Martyrs' and Heroes' Remembrance Day, 27 Nissan 5714 (30 April 1954). (The poem was reprinted with changes in *HaTur Hashvi'i* [*The Seventh Column* (Tel Aviv, 1962)], vol. 2, pp. 407–408.) The poem questions the widespread tendency to criticize and repudiate the behavior of the majority of Jews during the *Shoah*, except for the partisans and ghetto fighters, who chose the path of active resistance to the Nazis. Alterman has this viewpoint voiced in his poem through the "fighters and rebels."

symbol that can be glorified and that has significance.

This implies a distortion of the period, or emphasis on one aspect over all others. The image of the uprisings is thus distorted along with that of the whole era.

From our perspective, I say that the correct way, as opposed to the benighted and blind way, was the strategy of the community leaders and *shtadlanim* (Jewish communal intermediaries) (the *Judenrat*)[2]—not the corrupt ones but the heroes among them, *and there were heroes.* Their approach must not be labeled as blindness and blunder.

1. From the standpoint of saving Jewish lives, the course of the traditional *shtadlanim*, the community leaders and intermediaries, was *the only way.* In contrast, the leaders of the uprisings, due to the lack of time or means, could not intend to save lives, did not intend to do so, *and in fact did not do so.*
2. From the standpoint of moral authority and justification: We, the ones who revolted against the Germans, say that the *shtadlanim* used their authority and position to decide which Jews would die and which would live (for a time), killing one in order to save another. But those involved in the uprisings also asserted this authority, albeit without the justification of saving the remainder. The fighters confronted the same terrible question by deciding they had the right "to shorten the lives of the ghetto Jews by half a year" and confer upon them death in the flames without any chance of escape.

From the standpoint of intention and morality, therefore, it is a distortion to uphold the symbol of the uprising as a light in contrast to darkness and transgression.

We must view the uprising as one detail of that period which has no parallel at all, as one of the threads of Israel's history. We cannot pluck the phenomenon of the uprisings from its context in order to mold it for our own purposes as if it had an independent existence, and as if we could ignore the dark underside of the uprisings as well, being that those who chose to rebel were just as much on the edge of the abyss as those who did not.

The Dilemma of Responsibility and Privilege

The harshest accusation that the Jewish fighters' organizations fling at their Jewish opponents is that the latter arrogated to themselves the authority to expedite the sending of Jews to their death[s], in order to save whatever remnant was possible (actually, this occurred only in the final days when everything was crumbling). On this issue I will quote a selection from Ruzhka's *Lehavot BaEfer* (*Flames within the Ashes*) (*Al Hamishmar*, 30 April 1954):

> Those who were not actually inside the [Vilna] ghetto cannot comprehend how much dread the issue of collective responsibility caused.... The question whether to acquire weapons was therefore extremely difficult because of the possible dangerous concomitants. We asked ourselves: Are we truly permitted to endanger the lives of thousands of Jews? With full recognition of the responsibility that we take upon ourselves, our answer was: Yes, we are permitted, and we must![3]

2. The Nazi occupation authorities established a *Judenrat*, Jewish Council, in every Jewish community in territories under their control. Heidrich, director of the Chief Office of Reich Security, gave the order to establish the councils on 21 September 1939, a short time after the Germans occupied western Poland. According to Heydrich's explicit order, the *Judenrats* were mostly composed of public officials. He intended that they implement Nazi orders concerning the Jewish population. In actuality, the *Judenrat* functioned inside the ghettos as independent governments. They were forced to navigate the complexities of the tragic conflict between their desire to do as much good as possible for their communities and the necessity of cooperating with the German apparatus of oppression and destruction.

3. Raizl Korchak [Ruzhka] was born in 1921 in Bilsk, near Plotsk. When the Second World War began, she moved to Vilna. She was a member of *Hashomer Hatzair*, a founder of the pioneer underground in the Vilna ghetto, and active in the Jewish Fighting Organization. During the war, she joined the partisans and fought in the Rodenicki forests. After making *aliya* to the Land of Israel in 1946, she joined Kibbutz Ein Hahoresh. She recorded her wartime experiences in *Lehavot Ba'efer* [*Flames within the Ashes*], translated into Hebrew from

Afterward, this moral quandary developed into a reality that we cannot disregard. Reality did not solve the quandary but rather transformed it into fact. For the leaders of the Warsaw ghetto uprising, for example, this meant that taking up arms would lead to the complete destruction of the ghetto. In *Zmanim* of 30 April 1954, A. Rosenman[4] writes (regarding the indifference of the Polish) that "nothing touched the hearts of those surrounding the walls, not even the images of children clutching window frames for lack of courage to jump into the flames. And if by miracle someone succeeded in fleeing the inferno of the ghetto, he was immediately turned in to the Gestapo."

The Jewish fighters' organization asserted the right to force these consequences upon the ghetto Jews.

When we speak of the logic and reasoning of those who revolted, who foresaw the end that was in sight for most Jews (many Jews were blind and did not see what lay in store), we must take this into account. In the end, the rebellion led the Jews in the ghetto to the same fate as the alternative course would have led (quantitatively, the nonrevolt alternative offered greater chances of survival because it preserved the factor of *time*).

As for preserving honor, at least we can say that the rebels bought this for more than the price of their own war.

The Goal of the Uprising

... One major fallacy underlies the distortion and superficiality in the use of the term "uprising":

People associate the term with concepts associated with the classic idea of rebellion, and hold it up as a model of the heroism and honor that were extracted from a swamp of surrender and self-degradation. By doing this, we take the uprising completely out of its temporal and cultural context. The truth is that within that temporal and cultural context, surrender was not a sign of cowardice and blindness alone. That context demands that both for those who opposed the uprising as well as for those who initiated it, we look for alternative descriptors. The conditions of the time placed both of these approaches on the same plane, as true believers against true believers, or despair against despair, and not as surrender against heroism and loss of honor against saving face. The nature of this surrender is different from the nature of any other surrender, and the quality of this uprising is different from the quality of any other uprising. This is very evident in the writings of the ghetto fighters themselves, as well as in some of their speeches. Unfortunately, a florid and cliché-ridden style, originating with the Israeli activists and poets, is gradually taking root.

The term *Judenrat* has become a synonym for a pack of villains. The following quote is from *Kol Ha'am*,[5] and so apparently cannot be taken as typical of general trends, but on this issue it reflects accepted linguistic and conceptual formulations. "The *Judenrat* ... opposed the active struggle of the ghetto residents against the Nazi murderers and attempted to buy their own lives in return for service to the Nazis."

Herein we find two major points of distortion of the period: (1) generalizing that all of the *Judenrat* were totally evil, and (2) transforming the

---

the Polish manuscript by Binyamin Tannenbaum (Sifriyat Poalim, 1946). The selection quoted here is from Abba Kovner's review of the book. Ruzhka died in 1988.

4. Avraham Rosenman, editor of the journal *Zmanim*. In his article *Mered Ghetto Warsaw Beor Mesulaf* ["A Distorted View of the Warsaw Ghetto Uprising"] (*Zmanim*, 30 April 1954, p. 2), Rosenman polemicizes against the widespread tendency in Poland to present the uprising as a Polish episode (that is, a Polish revolt against the Germans) and to downplay the Jews' participation. Rosenman asserts that the Warsaw ghetto uprising was a uniquely Jewish rebellion and also maintains that most of the Polish nation was indifferent and even hostile to it.

5. See the article by M. Harkabi, *Zeh Halekakh Ve'ein Aḥer: Im Hadhiya Hanosefet Shel Mishpat Kastner-Gruenwald* ["This Is the Moral and There Is No Other: Upon the Second Postponement of the Kastner-Gruenwald Trial"], *Kol Ha'am*, 14 May 1954, p. 3. In this article, Harkabi argues against an editorial published in *Davar* (4 May 1954). He claims that the Kastner trial sheds light on "a murky issue," that of the *Judenrat*. The writer presents them as opponents to active resistance within the ghettos against the Nazi murderers, while they themselves attempted to buy their lives in return for serving the Nazis. Harkabi harshly criticizes the Zionist and *Yishuv* [Palestinian Jewish] leadership for negotiating with the Germans under their "rescue plan."

rebellion into a symbol of "active struggle," in other words, a war mandated by logic and honor. Having done this, only those who are rotten and degenerate to the core can object to the uprising.

Let us examine the so-called collaboration of the *Judenrat*. The term "collaboration" has become tainted and connotes the terrible responsibility, bordering on the criminal, for choosing those Jews who would live and those who would die.

But the reality is that during the awful darkness that descended, simple Jews as well as leaders were forced to make decisions that were outside of human ken and beyond the scope of their authority. Must we place an eternal stain on the heroes and honest individuals among those collaborators? May we forget that the epoch itself, in all its horror, forced even those who stood outside the maelstrom to make mortal decisions (although those outside belong to another category)? For example, did not the leaders of the *Yishuv*, the pre-state Jewish community in the Land of Israel, negotiate with the Nazis to exchange Jews for trains and cash? What is this negotiation if not the assertion of the same authority to decide, under which the collaborators labored? The same individuals who view negotiations conducted by the *Yishuv* as a sacred and just struggle—why should its parallel in the *Judenrat* within the innermost depths of the ghettos be defamed?

If we take this to its logical conclusion, then we must say, as does *Kol Ha'am*[6] (regarding the Kastner trial)[7] that the arbitrators of the trade negotiation are "war criminals who committed crimes against the Jewish people, against humanity" and that their rescue plan is "a traitorous plot formulated by some of our nation's very own people who have turned into destroyers and annihilators, along with the Nazi exterminators" (*Kol Ha'am*, 14 May 1954).

The thorough analysis of the uprising by Yehuda Gothalf in *Davar* (21 May 1954)[8] portrays it accurately as "a last resort." He writes that "against a depressing backdrop, the precious light of this last act shines forth. Such was the uprising of the Jewish youth, which has no parallel in its radiance, and in its tragedy."

The uprising, chronologically as well as logically (in terms of cause and effect) and with respect to its timing and the dilemmas it posed, is not one episode versus another episode, but rather a last chapter, uplifting and tragic at the same time. The satanic cunning of the enemy and internal Jewish factors (such as the sense of responsibility and mutual accountability) prevented the uprising from turning into a model that would influence the events of the entire period.[9]

The period has thus been split into two very different and opposing viewpoints—the *Shoah*

---

6. In the above-mentioned article by M. Harkabi.
7. The Kastner trial stood at the center of public interest in Israel in 1954–1955. The principal figure in the trial was Israel (Rudolph) Kastner, a journalist, public activist, and leader of Hungarian Jewry. After the occupation of Hungary in 1944, Kastner served on the rescue committee for Jewish refugees. As part of his job, he negotiated to save Hungarian Jews in return for supplying merchandise and trucks to the Germans. In reward for his activities, the Germans released about 1,700 Jews from Bergen-Belsen and allowed them to be transferred to Switzerland. Kastner made *aliya* [emigrated to Israel] in 1948. He held a senior position in the prime minister's office and in the Ministry of Trade and Industry. He served as an editor of *Oikelt*, a Hungarian newspaper, and ran for the Knesset in 1953 as a Mapai candidate. Kastner was accused by Malchiel Gruenwald of collaboration with the Nazis and assisting the release of SS officer Kurt Bachar in the Nuremberg trials. In response to the publication of these accusations, Kastner sued Gruenwald for libel. The Jerusalem District Court accepted most of Gruenwald's arguments and in June 1955 indicted Kastner for collaboration with the Nazis, indirect

responsibility for the murder of Hungarian Jews, and rescuing a Nazi criminal after the war. Kastner appealed the judgment, and the Supreme Court acquitted him of collaboration with the Nazis. In March 1957, Kastner was shot by an unidentified attacker and died from his wounds.

8. Yehuda Gothalf's article *Heshbon Yashan-Hadash* ["A New/Old Account"] (*Davar*, 21 May 1954, pp. 2 and 6) is a review of Rachel Auerbach's book *Behutzot Warsaw* [*On the Outskirts of Warsaw*, Am Oved, 5714/1954]. Gothalf agrees with Auerbach's explanation of the Jews' passive behavior during the *Shoah*, which in her analysis was unavoidable. Auerbach does not see the uprising as a practical option that the Jews could have chosen throughout the *Shoah*, but rather as a last alternative. According to Gothalf, rebellion could be implemented "only at the end, when all illusions had disappeared." In general terms, this position parallels Alterman's viewpoint as revealed in his poem "Day of Remembrance and the Rebels," quoted in Gothalf's article.

9. From the same issue of *Davar* (21 May 1954).

(by which is meant resignation) versus the *Gevurah*[10] (by which is meant the uprising), victimhood versus heroism. This results in the neglect of many other incidents that were characterized by heroic acts and by noble deeds of humanity (actions of individuals as well as groups). They are swallowed up and left unredeemed in the black hole where everything is stamped with the label *Shoah*, rather than with the (seemingly) opposite label that is "uprising."

The *Judenrat* Responsibility

The fact that some Jews in authority agreed to send Jews to their deaths is one of the most problematic aspects of this dark period. Our language, spoken and written, is inadequate and does injustice to the historical truth. It holds the *Judenrat* responsible, while exempting everyone else, and assumes that without the *Judenrat*, this phenomenon would never have taken place. This stone, if we do cast it, must not strike the *Judenrat* alone. The phenomenon [of sending Jews to their deaths] is the appalling result for which all sectors of the Jewish world must share responsibility, uprising fighters included. To say that the *Judenrat* alone were responsible is superficial and distorted. The history of blindness of our nation to encroaching dangers, the blindness of its leaders and its masses, led to indirect or direct resignation to the phenomenon by leaders, by the masses, by those in the *Yishuv*, and by those fighters who took part in uprisings. In the writings of the fighters, we find this moral accounting for dilemmas which no other nation faced. Blaming the *Judenrat* alone is a moral injustice as well as an act of contempt and superficiality regarding the history of the period, for which we must give a full and fair accounting. Whoever is seriously concerned that the nation should learn a lesson for the future from these events must object stridently to this superficiality. We must not paper over issues by using a few slogans and fancy phrases, for just as we have an obligation to study the entire period, so must we study this painful question.

At the 1974 world conference for the study of the *Shoah* and heroism, held in Jerusalem, Ben-Zion Dinur [Dinburg][11] commented:

> Our first goal is to research and know what happened in the war, to recognize it for what it was—a war against us—to understand the ways and means the war was waged, to comprehend the enemy's formula for "success," and to appreciate the myriad difficulties that confronted us. We dare not fudge unpleasant fact[s] and dare not romanticize. We must see things as they were and not take cover under clichés and hackneyed formulations. Once we have a correct and honest grasp of the national Holocaust that overtook us, we can use this as a basis for research on the whole period. We must create opportunities to conduct comprehensive studies that are well founded on solid research of all that we experienced during that period.[12]

He further declared:

> [W]e must view these things clearly. It was more than a terrible Holocaust. It was also a great national defeat. It is our duty, if we want to live as a nation, to see these things with our eyes open, to study these issues, to know them, and to understand them, because this defeat was also the spiritual and intellectual defeat of "our collective understanding."[13]

Just as he saw the necessity of obtaining a clear overview of the entire period, he also emphasized the need to gather clear and detailed information at the level of the individual events themselves. In discussing the reasons for the growing awareness of the importance of collecting material for study of the period, Dinur found that this awakening stemmed from

10. The Hebrew name for the memorial day is *Yom Hazikaron LaShoah u'LaGevurah*.

11. The lecture of Dinburg/Dinur at the conference (Organization of the Collection of Recent Material in Jewish History) was printed in *Memos on Research of the Shoah and the Uprising*, vol. 2 (Tel Aviv, 1952), pp. 11–18. Ben Zion Dinburg/Dinur [1884–1973] was a

leading Jewish historian and professor of Jewish history at Hebrew University. From 1951 to 1955, he served as minister of education and culture and from 1953 to 1959 as director of Yad Vashem.

12. *Dapim Leheker Hashoah Vehamered* [*Memos on Research of the Shoah and the Uprising*], part 2, p. 12.

13. *Dapim Leheker Hashoah Vehamered*.

the healthy instinct of a people who have experienced a tragic Holocaust. They want to know: How and why did this happen to us? Was it truly impossible for us to anticipate the evil? Was there no possibility of rescue? There is a desire to acquire as complete as possible an understanding of the events and to undertake a comprehensive study of them. There is the aspiration to gather all the material on the Holocaust in one place and to ascertain the truth about what happened and how it happened, in order to prepare for the future.[14]

The greatest enemy of this ambition to learn and know is the sentimental style of prepared formulas that claim to know all the facts already. From that point of view, those who fear the future must not recoil from protesting against the formulas that have become routine over the years.

Another point Dinur made about historical research concerns internal dissension.

The second stage in collecting material involves the issue of internal conflicts among Jews. We must know everything. We must know the degree to which one group of Jews opposed another, the mutual distrust and even betrayal; we cannot only record accounts of mutual aid, brotherly love, self-sacrifice, and acts of self-defense.... We must obtain a full and complete picture of Jewish life during this critical period in order to know and understand.[15]

It is here where the ready-made and prepackaged formulations are the enemy of truth.

14. *Dapim Leheker Hashoah Vehamered*, pp. 13, 14.

15. *Dapim Leheker Hashoah Vehamered*, p. 16.

Yehoyada Amir

Yehoyada Amir was born in Israel in 1954. He received both his undergraduate and graduate education at the Hebrew University of Jerusalem. His doctoral dissertation, written under the supervision of Professor Eliezer Schweid and completed in 1993, dealt with the relationship of a number of Israeli philosophers to the thought of Franz Rosenzweig. Since finishing his graduate studies, he has taught at Hebrew University, Ben Gurion University of the Negev, and Humboldt University in Berlin. At present, he is professor of modern Jewish thought and director of the Israel Rabbinic Program at the Hebrew Union College, Jerusalem Center. He has published two significant books: *Engendering Judaism: An Inclusive Theology and Ethics* (1998), and more recently, a Hebrew study entitled *Da'at Ma'amina* (*Reason out of Faith*; 2004), which is a detailed analysis of Franz Rosenzweig's *Der Stern der Erlösung* (*The Star of Redemption*). In addition, he has published significant essays on other nineteenth- and twentieth-century thinkers such as Nachman Krochmal, A. D. Gordon, and Hermann Cohen.

SELECTION

In the present essay, "The Concept of Exile as a Model for Dealing with the Holocaust," first delivered at a conference sponsored by the Memorial Foundation for Jewish Culture in Ashkelon, Israel, in 1999, Yehoyada Amir aims to provide a fuller definition of and a deeper understanding regarding the traditional Jewish theological concept of *Galut* (exile). Amir clearly acknowledges that the Holocaust poses a serious threat to any and all interpretations of the claimed covenantal relationship between God and the Jewish people, as well as to the traditional concept of appropriate divine reward and punishment. However, he contends that if we understand *Galut* not only or primarily as the condition of national exile, i.e., the Jewish people's exile from the land of Israel, but rather as a state of brokenness in the world, which can be remedied in part by righteous human actions, then we can still maintain hope in humankind and in its future. On this reading, "the Holocaust constitutes the cruelest and most definitive essence of exile in its widest sense." That is, we acknowledge the full horror of the death camps and *Einsatzgruppen* (Nazi murder units) and recognize that we still live in a broken, unjust world, even while we retain faith "in God and in humanity" and "in the spiritual and religious significance of human history." At the same time, we recognize that the redemption we seek involves not only divine intervention but also a human struggle in which men and women have significant responsibility for the outcome.

Selected Bibliography

Books by Yehoyada Amir

"Israeli Responses to Franz Rosenzweig" (Ph.D. thesis, Hebrew University, 1993) [Hebrew].
Program for Studies in Judaism (Tel Aviv, 1996) [Hebrew].
Knowledge and Belief: Analysis of the Thought of Franz Rosenzweig (Tel Aviv, 2004) [Hebrew].

The Concept of Exile as a Model for Dealing with the Holocaust

The issue of theodicy, which has been frequently examined from a variety of different perspectives, as in this volume, is only one aspect of the multifaceted body of thought dealing with the Holocaust. Jews and Christians, in searching for a religious vocabulary with which to deal with this question, often express their distress and dismay with the words, "Where was God during the Holocaust?" One must not deprecate the significance and profundity of this question for any monotheistic faith that seeks to see the providential God of creation as good and benevolent. But the Holocaust raises a number of other, parallel questions, in no less acute a manner: Where was humanity at that time,[1] and what are we to understand, as descendants of the actual and potential victims, on the one hand, and as part of that humanity that facilitated and executed the Holocaust, on the other hand—about ourselves, about the limits of ethical power, and about the meaning of the struggle against racism, discrimination, and xenophobia? No less relevant is the question, what light does the Holocaust shed upon the prevalent egotistical world views that often justify ignoring the suffering, poverty, and injustice inflicted upon the other?

Questions about the role played by religion during that time likewise arise, in all their severity. In recent years we have witnessed the beginning of an awakening of conscience among various Christian churches regarding their own responsibility for the human suffering that reached its climax in the Holocaust. The Roman Catholic church, under the leadership of John Paul II, has recently made several significant, positive steps in this direction.[2] It is still too early to say how far-reaching this process is and to what extent it will filter down from the church leadership to the levels of the ordinary believers. In any event, it is clear that, if the process will indeed mature to a clear and unequivocal awareness of the role played by the church in instilling both classical Jew hatred and modern anti-Semitism and of its own sins during the Holocaust, this will necessarily be accompanied by extensive theological and ideational change among the various streams in Christianity. Such a change, without which recognition of the sins of anti-Semitism and of persecution of "infidels" as such is meaningless, will necessarily upset the very foundations of Christian belief and create a new kind of religious and cultural orientation. It is still too early to say whether the Holocaust will in fact serve as a point of departure for this process, which would mark a new and revolutionary stage in the history of Christianity and in the annals of the relationship between Judaism and Christianity.

One must add that we as Jews are not merely a passive party in this process, expressing expectations

---

1. See, for example, the title of the book by the German writer Heinrich Böll, *Wo warst du Adam?* (*Where Have You Been, Adam?*). It is no coincidence that this discussion developed first of all in postwar Germany, but its applicability is not in the least limited to any one national or cultural group.
2. The tendency in various Jewish circles both in Israel and in the diaspora to take petty inventory of this

process is regrettable. Alongside just and substantial demands, such as refraining from canonizing Pope Pius XII, a certain broadness of mind and understanding of the complex contexts in which the Catholic church is operating in this issue must be shown.

and raising demands. Such a new Christian orientation, if it truly does penetrate from the periphery to the mainstreams of the different churches, will also demand of us a new approach toward our Judaism and its different principles, particularly in relation to the election of the Jewish people and the dangers of arrogance and xenophobia inherent in it.[3] Such a new perspective will require a completely different Jewish understanding of the relationship between Judaism and Christianity and Islam—a perception based on a recognition of the relative truth of the different revelations, such as alluded to in Franz Rosenzweig's philosophy.[4] It is incumbent upon us to examine the similarities and differences in the basic structure of the three faiths, to confront the issue of how we can learn from the successes and failures of the two other faiths, and to ascertain in what areas we may be able to cooperate with progressive and humanistic forces within them.

It must be emphasized that, particularly in the Christian context, this examination goes far beyond that generally implied by the aspiration for interfaith dialogue and peaceful multicoexistence with persons of different faiths. The history of problematic relationships between Judaism and Christianity and the manner in which the Holocaust poses extremely difficult questions to Christianity and Christians is likely—in the event of such profound change—to illuminate in an intimate and singular way the relationship between the two faiths. Christianity, in seeking its own Jewish roots, presents a significant challenge

for Judaism that seeks to shatter the walls of the mental ghetto in which it existed.

But even more meaningful in the Jewish context is the question of the manner in which the Jewish religion functioned for its adherents. Did Jewish faith have the power to raise their spirits and invigorate them during the most horrible crisis a person can imagine? Or did it provide false hopes, misleading and blinding its believers? To what extent did Judaism succeed in granting meaning to suffering, in helping the persecuted to endure, and in giving them a sense of direction in tumultuous times? And to what extent did it sanctify the lives of Jews living after the Holocaust—Jews who are all in principle survivors, since the grim reaper intended to get them or their parents or grandparents?

It is no accident that we do not deal overly much with these onerous questions. When we do so, it is usually most convenient for us to focus on denouncing (in itself properly) some of the ultra-Orthodox leadership, who abandoned their followers while making empty promises of imminent heavenly redemption. But this focus upon "beating the chests of others" more often than not serves as an excuse—one providing political and ideational gain—to avoid dealing in an authentic and honest way with the fundamental and painful religious and Jewish questions that emerged after the Holocaust. Such are, for example, the questions raised by Richard Rubenstein regarding the principled relationship between biblical monotheism and the concept of

---

3. The demurral from the concept of the election of the Jewish people, or at least from the exclusive interpretation that places the gentile as inferior to the Jew, is common to many modern philosophers. This demurral reached its climax in the thought of Mordecai Kaplan, who wished to totally eliminate expressions of this idea from the religious Jewish agenda. But even for a philosopher such as Rosenzweig, in whose philosophy the idea of the election plays a very central role, the concept serves to indicate a viewpoint of equal worth and necessary cooperation among the different faiths. It must be said that the idea of the "election of Israel," which devolved in Christianity to the idea of God's chosen people being embodied in the church, may turn out to be the source of much of the sanctified hatred of the other, of the readiness to ignore the other's religiosity and humanity, and of the capability not to empathize with the other or with his or her suffering.

4. In his book *The Star of Redemption*, Rosenzweig develops the concept of "man's part in truth"—an idea that provides a basis for considering religious truth, as perceived by humanity, as a subjective expression of the ultimate objective truth. He demands of each person to "experience" his or her truth and to "look" at the other's truth and recognize it. While Rosenzweig develops this concept only as a basis for mutual recognition between Judaism and Christianity, in principle it may certainly be broadened to a wider interfaith context. I deal with this issue extensively in my paper "Man's Part in Truth: On the Concept of Truth in *The Star of Redemption*" [Hebrew], in *Qolat Rabbim (Many Voices)*, *Rivka Schatz-Uffenheimer Memorial Volume*, vol. 2, edited by Rachel Elior and Joseph Dan = *Mehkarei Yerushalayim be-mahshevet Yisrael*, vols. 12–13 (1996), pp. 557–580.

genocide.[5] It also makes it possible to ignore questions regarding the meaning of faith and the significance of Jewish existence in a world in which Holocaust and genocide are among the accepted and available modes of action in various situations of tension and conflict.[6]

All these are a few aspects of the fundamental question regarding the orientation a person may adopt after the Holocaust and through confrontation with the fact of its occurrence. How can one believe in God, in humanity, in culture, or for that matter in religion, after the Holocaust? From whence can the educator or the philosopher glean the measure of optimism necessary for working in the field of education to create a new generation of productive and constructive people? In what manner can we explain both the past and the traditional interpretations of the past to make them meaningful for ourselves? Does not the fact that genocide is now a real option for human behavior—one that has recurred in various forms in the twentieth century—signify a total break in human culture, philosophy, and religion? Is it not in a sense the "crooked that cannot be made straight"?

The aim of this essay is to examine the possibility of developing a number of linguistic tools that will enable us to ask and confront some of these questions, and to a certain extent also to perhaps arrive at some answers. I make no pretension of "explaining" the Holocaust to any degree or of offering a series of "morals." I am very skeptical whether the Holocaust even gives us the option to do so. It may well be that the only explanations we can expect are historical ones that do not automatically translate into the theological or philosophical realm. As for the

"lessons" that are offered every so often, these need to be thoroughly examined to ascertain that they do not serve some political, religious, or other ideological interest, for which the Holocaust serves merely as a pretext. I prefer to explore the possibility of developing a vocabulary that will enable us to ask questions regarding the significance of our existence in view of the Holocaust and that will provide us with tools to examine what we are obligated to do as educators, as people of culture, and as Jews.

The Jewish thinker, in attempting to deal with this complex of questions while relating to the religious and national sources of one's culture, encounters already at the onset of one's perusal the special place held by history or, to be more precise, the special place held by "historical memory"[7] in shaping Jewish religious and cultural consciousness. It is well known that Jewish tradition usually regards God first and foremost as the God of history and only thus as the God of creation. The recognition that He is "the Creator of heaven and earth" is anchored paradoxically in the notion of God as "the Lord of Abraham, Isaac, and Jacob" who led the Israelites out of Egypt, the God who "sees even the lowly" in our human society[8] and who will in the future redeem us and to whom we will return. This motive reappears many times throughout Jewish prayer. Thus, for example, the worshipper, in reaffirming the fundamentals of faith in the *Shema* ["Hear O' Israel" prayer], passes naturally from the assertion that "all this is perfectly true" and that "He is the Lord of the universe" to acknowledging that "we are Israel His people" and that He has redeemed us throughout history from the hands of foes and enemies.[9] In the

5. Richard Rubenstein, *After Auschwitz: Radical Theology and Contemporary Judaism* (Indianapolis, 1966), pp. 1–58, 243–264.
6. True, the Holocaust was not the first instance of genocide in the twentieth century, and there is room to conjecture that the ease with which the genocide of 1.5 million Armenians by the Turks during World War I was accepted served as a catalyst for the idea of the attempted total annihilation of the Jewish people on the part of the Nazis. All the same, it is clear that during the second half of the twentieth century, in the wake of the Holocaust, genocide and "ethnic purging" became reasonable modes of action in different situations of

conflict, both in "Third World" countries and in the heart of Europe.
7. On the role of historical memory and its relation to historiography, see Yosef Haim Yerushalmi, *Zakhor: Jewish History and Jewish Memory* (Seattle, 1982).
8. Psalms 113:5–6.
9. Thus according to the formulation in the blessing of "redemption" in the evening prayer. The different formulas in the parallel blessing in the morning prayer point in a similar direction. Equally natural is the transition, in the *Nishmat* prayer recited on *Shabbat* and festival mornings, from the awareness that "every living soul will bless your name, O God, our Lord"

same manner the Sabbath, as mentioned in the *Kiddush* [blessing over wine] on Friday night, serves simultaneously as "a memorial of the Exodus" and "a memorial of creation," without any special spiritual or intellectual effort being required to bridge the two proclamations.

Many Jewish philosophers of the second half of the twentieth century felt that this unique manner in which we regard God and the relationship between the Jew and his or her God creates a problem affecting our manner of dealing with the Holocaust. These thinkers—such as Emil Fackenheim, Yosef Hayim Yerushalmi, Eliezer Berkowitz [Berkovits], Joseph B. Soloveitchik, Martin Buber, Eliezer Schweid, David Hartman, and Abraham Joshua Heschel—express their conviction that the intensity of the trauma caused by the Holocaust requires a deep reexamination of the fundamentals of faith, because the Holocaust redefines history and thereby also the significance of God's presence therein.

The only exception, who, so to speak, proves the rule, is Yeshayahu Leibowitz. In his view, the difficulty lies in a basic misunderstanding of the nature of Jewish religious faith. It does not in fact regard God as the "Prince of history," just as it does not regard him as the purveyor of humanity's needs. Faith in God deals only with *faith* itself and the consequent commitment to carry out the obligations of *Halakhah* (Jewish religious law). History, like all other areas of culture and civilization, is solely a human deed, and God has no part in it. From these basic axioms, it follows that the terrifying questions that arise in the face of the Holocaust need not be addressed to religion at all, but rather to humanity alone, and especially toward secular humanistic world views.

This removes not only the matter of theodicy but also the difficulty involving the possibility of faith after the Holocaust. But a very heavy price is paid. Leibowitz totally separates human reality, with its values, failures, and uncertainties, from the religious dimension of human existence. The believer can continue to believe and to fulfill the precepts, but all content is removed from it apart

from the compulsion to carry out his or her religious obligations. What Leibowitz grasps as *Torah lishema* (Torah for its own sake) is nothing other than religiosity knowingly detaching itself from every sphere of human life—from a person's spiritual aspirations and psychological needs. All of the aforementioned are abandoned to the secular sphere, at the same time that "religion" does not recognize the value of this realm and does not grant it any significance.

Hence, it is not surprising that most of the Jewish thinkers of that period based their struggles with the Holocaust on the above-mentioned notion of Jewish tradition that anchors the relationship between humanity and God first and foremost in the historical and sociological spheres and on the perception of God's providence over humanity in general and the Jewish people in particular. To be precise: not only the particular Jewish dimension is regarded by this tradition as historic but also that of humanity in general. Reading Genesis reveals that the universal level of the biblical story is also more "historic" than it is "cosmological" and "cosmogenic." Alongside the cosmogenic story of creation we encounter a "historic" tale that tells of humanity, of the divergence of the sexes, and of Adam and Eve's sin.[10] This tale, and not the first one, takes us until the flood, whose cause is social-moral. It is in this context that the central category of this history is introduced: the first covenant between God and humankind.

As an etiological story, the book of Genesis describes the status of humanity and the condition of humankind as a result of the "historic" covenant between God and those who disembarked from Noah's ark. Thus, concrete humankind, whose forefather is Noah, is not only a direct continuation of the creation and of God's mastery over the universe; it derives from the unique relationship between God and the "righteous person" who found favor in His eyes. At the core lies the covenant with the descendants of this chosen person, a covenant entailing simultaneously both promise and imperative.

---

to the idea that we, the children of Israel, wish to thank Him for "all the thousands upon thousands and myriads of good times You have granted to our forefathers and to us: You redeemed us from Egypt," etc.

10. Genesis 1:1–2:3, 2:4–3:24.

In a certain sense, a central content of this covenant is the suspension of human responsibility for the cosmic dimension. Thus, the rhythm of the seasons serves as a symbol of the order of creation—and its conversion into a constant, which is not affected by the drama that takes place on the axis between humanity and God. Humanity is obligated to carry out a number of precepts and prohibitions, first and foremost of which is the prohibition against murder. God binds Himself to this covenant by promising that, regardless of humanity's deeds and the extent to which people respond to God's decree, the natural continuity will be maintained and humanity will never again be annihilated. This is a covenant between superior and inferior, in which, paradoxically enough, it is the superior party who binds Himself irrevocably while the inferior party remains free to decide whether or not to keep the covenant.

Of course, in Jewish historical memory this covenant usually takes only a secondary and vague place, being viewed as the background for the emergence of the second covenant, that between God and His people. This latter covenant is rooted in the family history of the patriarchs, and especially in the story of the Exodus. And, just as the covenant with Noah entails the negation of the option of a second flood, so too the "redemption" in the book of Exodus is regarded as changing the existential state of the nation in an essential way.[11] From here on the nation finds itself in a direct covenant with God; it is that human community that receives the Torah and is meant to obey its laws. As such, it is subject to unique laws of providence, which transcend the overall providence of God over history and its passage.

The biblical admonitions explicitly point to the parameters of the covenant, which in turn parallel to a great extent what we have found in the covenant with Noah: The nation is obligated to obey the laws of God but maintains the ability to disobey at any time,[12] whereas God cannot be released from the covenant. According to its dicta, God is supposed to punish the nation for its sins and reward them for its good deeds; according to these very same rules, He is supposed to assure that the punishment He confers upon the nation for its sins—one that might very well be harsh and cruel—will never reach the point of total annihilation of the people. If God were to allow His people to be effaced from the face of the earth, that would be a breach of the covenant.[13]

The Bible describes a wide range of punishments that are supposed to be conferred on the people for their sins, whether these appear in the context of a prophetic admonition and a warning[14] or in the context of an explication of historic reality post factum. At the pinnacle of this list is exile (*Galut*), which serves as the counterpoint to the covenant and the liberation from Egypt. Exile, with all its horrors, is the decisive expression of the estrangement between the sinful nation and its God, an estrangement that is supposed to bring the nation to the brink of its destruction.

The primary significance of exile is explicated in Jewish tradition according to the basic liturgical formula, which gives significance to the nation's existential circumstances after the destruction of the Second Temple: "Because of our sins we have been exiled from our land." This formula not only embodies the orientation of the Jews and the possibilities available for dealing with their circumstances but also retains a deep level of hope and solace. The punishment imparted by God, who promised that we would not be obliterated off the face of the earth and that in time He

11. See for example, Exodus 14:13: "For the Egyptians whom you see today you will never see again." The Bible doesn't view the fact that the Egyptians fail to disappear from the horizon of the Israelites as nonfulfillment of this covenant, since its concern is about radical change in the status of the Israelites and the relationship between them and Egypt, and not the actual presence of the Egyptians in the field of vision of the Israelites.
12. Latter-day philosophers such as Rabbi Judah Halevi (1075–1141) thought that the nation cannot become

completely evil. This view is not anchored in the biblical statements about the covenant and establishes an "ontological holiness" for the people of Israel, perhaps as a measure of consolation in light of the nation's downtrodden status in exile.
13. See Leviticus 26:44: "Yet for all that, when they are in the land of their enemies, I will not scorn them, neither will I abhor them so as to destroy them utterly and break my covenant with them; for I am the Lord their God."
14. See, e.g., Leviticus 26:14–45; Deuteronomy 28:15–69.

would return us to our land and rehabilitate our lives—such a punishment cannot be immeasurable. The end of exile *must* come. The moment must come when it will be announced that Zion "has received from the Lord double for all its sins."[15] The suffering must end. Redemption is only a question of time and of our deeds, be these mystical, religious-*halakhic*, acute-messianic, or political-redemptive.

The Holocaust subjected this formula to a severe crisis. For many religious philosophers, its intensity and totality was too appalling for them to retain the customary formula of punishment and reward. It is true that some ultra-Orthodox circles tried to hold onto this conception despite everything, but for central elements of the Jewish religious world—Orthodox as well as non-Orthodox—a major fissure had occurred. Even the more moderate formulation of this idea—that God's actions nevertheless embody punishment and reward though we cannot comprehend His ways—is seen as inadequate. The religious philosopher who feels thus finds himself or herself in need of another explanation—one that would offer meaning to the terrible reality, and solace and hope to the life that follows in its wake.

In attempting to do so, the religious philosopher requires alternative models, to be found buried in the treasure house of Jewish religious thought. He or she must discover existing models and augment the potential inherent in others. The secular nationalist philosopher, who cannot relate to the formula "because of our sins" in its original sense, will find him- or herself burrowing in the same treasure house to examine the range of options that exists from the secular viewpoint. Such a thinker, too, will seek a rhetoric offering meaning to Jewish and human existence after the Holocaust. For both, a significant point of departure for the process might be found in a deeper consideration of the concept of exile.

The concept of exile, as developed in the Jewish tradition, presents difficulty to the discussant. On the one hand, it seems self-evident that exile, in the context of the Jewish people, refers to the

situation of existence outside the boundaries of the Land of Israel, the loss of sovereignty over the land, and dispersion among the nations. One can easily bring scores of citations from the Bible, from rabbinic and liturgical texts, and from the various strata of Jewish thought and *Halakhah*, to support this understanding of the concept. But closer investigation reveals that its full meaning is not exhausted with this explication and that there remains an additional, deeper level of meaning. Moreover, even the mundane level of this concept needs to be examined in light of this wider spiritual meaning.

In most strata of traditional Jewish thought, the meaning of exile is not exclusively, or even predominantly, the presence of an individual or of the people outside of its land or place of origin. Exile is always bound with a sense of helplessness in the face of external forces over which one has no control and which one is powerless to direct. In essence, exile is existence outside of what is considered the right place to live, under conditions considered to be defective in their decisive dimensions. Exile means living in a world in need of redemption, healing, and completion. It is bound up with the awareness that a valuable potential, which fundamentally exists in reality, is not and cannot be fulfilled until this longed-for *tikkun* (mending) takes place. Exile is defined by the consciousness that something fundamental in historical reality—and in many cases also in cosmic and divine reality—is essentially disrupted. It is always bound with yearning for the perfect reality that existed in the past and for the days "that will be renewed as in the past," in which the perfection of old that was damaged will be set aright.

The first exile described in the Bible, the expulsion from the Garden of Eden, was not explicitly identified as such, but there can be no mistake as to its nature. As an etiologic story explaining the meaning of the concrete human condition in which we live, this first "historical" tale presents human existence as one in which a dimension of exile is an inherent part. Humanity should have lived in the Garden of Eden—that is, in a reality in which people and their surroundings were in total and primeval harmony among themselves, with nature, and with God. But because of humanity's sin—however this may be

15. Isaiah 40:2.

defined—we were exiled from this existence and lost it. It is no wonder that different prophets describe the future redemption in terms that, explicitly or implicitly, suggest a return to the Garden of Eden. Thus, for example, Ezekiel prophesies, with regard to the exile in Babylon, about the day in which all those who will see the land of Israel rebuilt will say, "This land that was desolate has become like the garden of Eden; and the wasted and desolate and ruined cities are become fenced, and are inhabited."[16] The prophet of the return to Zion, in delineating the absolute change that will occur in the nature of the land upon its redemption, makes similar use of this motif, albeit in a literary and not in the literal sense: "and he will make her wilderness like Eden, and her desert like the garden of the Lord."[17]

This perception of the expulsion from Eden as exile is expressed in some of the most central exegetical works of Judaism. Thus, in [the *midrash*] *Genesis Rabba* Abba Bar Kahana describes the *Shekhinah* (Divine Presence) as being exiled from the land because of humanity's sins, primarily because of those of Adam: "The *Shekhinah* was to be found on earth. Because Adam sinned, it took off to the first heaven. Cain's sin brought it to the second ... Egypt in the days of Abraham to the seventh."[18] In the kabbalah, especially in that of Rabbi Moshe Cordovero [1522–1570] and the Lurianic school [in sixteenth-century Palestine], this motif is extensively and exhaustively developed. The sin of Eden is described there as a decisive stage in "the breaking of [the heavenly] vessels" and in the general upheaval of the divine and cosmic reality.

Thus, cosmic and human reality are touched from the very outset by a fundamental breach and impairment requiring *tikkun* and alluding to the meaning of future redemption. The story of the Garden of Eden depicts human reality as a form of exile whose meaning, according to the literal sense of the Scripture, is disruption in the life of man and in the life of woman, as well as in the relationship between them. This is a life in which death and suffering, hierarchical rule, alienation from the land, etc., are all present. Thus, all of the above are not self-evident elements of human life but represent a fundamental disruption of the laws of nature.[19]

Moreover, just as the expulsion from the Garden of Eden is not inherently considered as geographical exile but rather as exile in principle and in essence, so too geographical uprooting may not be viewed as *Galut* at all. Thus, for example, Abraham, who is commanded to leave his country, his place of origin, and his father's home,[20] is not presented as going into exile but rather as going to the land that is destined to become a homeland for him and his offspring. Similarly, Jacob and his family, who go down to Egypt to save themselves from famine, are not described in Genesis as "émigrés." Even though Egypt is not their land and their residence there is supposed to be temporary, the situation doesn't depict a sense of exile, indigence, or rupture. Only in the Book of Exodus, which describes how life in Egypt becomes one of slavery and relates the danger of annihilation that hovers over the nation, does the tale become the story of the archetypal exile. Thus, the subject of the covenant between God and the fathers is expressed here in terms of God extricating the nation from Egypt—an act that is considered as a redemption and release, one that will serve as a foundation for grasping the place of the people of Israel in history and the cognition of the covenant between them and their God.

16. Ezekiel 36:35.
17. Isaiah 51:3
18. *Midrash Genesis Rabba* 19:8 (ed. Theodor-Albeck, p. 176). The notion that seven heavens exist and that God's presence is found above the highest of those is very common in rabbinic and ancient Jewish mystical literature.
19. Maimonides proceeds in a similar direction, albeit in the context of a different world view, in setting his commentary on the story of the Garden of Eden at the beginning of *The Guide of the Perplexed*. All human political existence, including the need for law and for exhaustive treatment of human character and behavior, is no more than a consequence of the fact that human beings do not live the reality in which they were meant to. Lust and the human tendency to pursue bodily pleasures bring about "exile" from an existence in which humanity would realize its human intellectual potential to its fullest. See *Guide for the Perplexed* 1.1–2.
20. Genesis 12:1–3.

The Bible thus posits two exiles at the very onset of human history and of national history. The former, human exile, defines the condition of human existence as one of present and continuous exile; the other, national exile, defines the reality of the existence of the nation as one in which exile was negated on our behalf by God. Jews who regard themselves as having been liberated from Egypt[21] consider themselves to have been delivered from exile, as people who, following a long and arduous journey, have reached the geographical and existential place that may be presumed to be their natural home.[22] The relation between these two exiles is complex. As a person, the Jew is in the same exilic situation as that experienced by the entire human race. But within this reality of exile, the individual Jew experiences, through the formative myth of his or her people and the ever-repeated ritual, deliverance from the national exile. The life of the individual Jew is encountered with the presence of exile as well as its cancellation and the hope for full redemption.

Understandably, these initial definitions of the concept of exile serve merely as background for the principal confrontation dealing with the historical "primary experience" of the destruction of the First Temple [in 586 B.C.E.] and the Babylonian exile.[23] It is worth noting that in Jewish consciousness—as expressed in biblical literature and in its post-biblical transfiguration—the destruction of the Temple and the geographical exile from the Land of Israel combine into a single reality of total crisis in the history of the nation and in the covenant between the nation and its God. When the poet of the Book of Lamentations cries out, "Return us unto thee, O Lord, and we shall be turned,"[24] his words carry both a geographical and a theological meaning. The exile from Jerusalem and from the Land of Israel is regarded as

exile from God and loss of the sense of intimacy in the relationship between the nation and its Divine Creator. Against this light, the prophecies of consolation, which naturally bind the national redemption and the nation's return to Jerusalem and the Temple with a radical change in the cosmic reality, can be well understood. This change, as mentioned above, is often described as a symbolic return to paradise and the annulment of this primary exile. Against this background, one may also understand that the return to Zion requires making a renewed covenant in the form of the pact decreed by the people returning from Babylonia.

One may rightly argue that this viewpoint—rooted in the traditional explication of the reality of the Babylonian exile—generated in later years the consciousness of exile expressed in post-biblical literature, which in practice relates to the reality that existed after the destruction of the Second Temple and of Jerusalem. Here too the destruction is often regarded as a type of exile, despite the fact that in the historical reality of the first and second centuries C.E. it is difficult to find decisive elements of geographical exile from the Land of Israel.[25] The inability to perform sacrificial services, the exile and dismantling of the Sanhedrin[26] (as these developments are described by the *halakhic* tradition), and the so-called exile from the Land of Israel—all these are regarded as interrelated with one another and as expressing the overall reality, bound up from now on in the concept of exile.

The Jew living in this reality feels himself or herself in exile, whether living in the land of Israel or outside its borders, and whether the center of Jewish existence in his or her time is in Israel or is developing elsewhere. For exile is simultaneously a cosmic and a historic condition. It is exile of humanity and exile of the *Shekhinah*

---

21. M. *Pesahim* 10:5.
22. See Martin Buber, *On Zion: The History of an Idea*, translated by S. Goodman (Bath, England, 1973), pp. 1–29.
23. See Emil Fackenheim, *God's Presence in History* (New York, 1970), pp. 8–30; Yosef Hayim Yerushalmi, *Zakhor: Jewish History and Jewish Memory*.
24. Lamentations 5:21.
25. It is typical that the consciousness of exile is associated in classic rabbinic sources, as it is in modern Zionist historiography, with the destruction of the Second

Temple and the Great Revolt, after which Jewish settlement continued to exist in every region of the land apart from Jerusalem itself, and not necessarily with the Bar Kokhba revolt [132–135 CE], which resulted in the destruction of the Jewish settlement throughout the region of Judaea. In any event, even following the Bar Kokhba revolt, the Land of Israel remained the center of Jewish existence, and, as we know, two generations later the Jewish center in the Galilee reached the height of its influence and growth.
26. See, for example, B. T. *Rosh Hashana* 31[a–b].

[Divine Presence]. As the famous talmudic saying has it, "They were exiled to Egypt—the *Shekhinah* was with them; they were exiled to Babylonia—the *Shekhinah* was with them; they were exiled to Eilam—the *Shekhinah* is with them."[27] It is clear that this saying relates not only to the remote past of previous exiles but first and foremost to the contemporary exile and thus to the contemporary situation of the *Shekhinah* in the world. The idea that God suffers and is exiled with His people expresses the sense that the physical exile—whether regarded as a concrete experience or as a theological projection from another reality—is only an external expression of a far deeper exile that exists in the world.

The consciousness of exile would seem to reach its fullest theological significance in the talmudic dictum "From the day of the destruction of the Temple, the Holy One blessed be He has naught but the four cubits of *Halakhah* in His world."[28] This is an intentionally paradoxical saying. The world is God's world; He created it and He rules it. Nevertheless, God has, in this world, only the limited confines of *Halakhah*. From everything else—culture and history, civilization, and the beauty of nature—God Himself was, so to speak, exiled. In essence, the world no longer functions as God's world, and the *Shekhinah* is depicted as if it no longer has a place in it. Whether or not this situation is itself a result of the Divine will and could be nullified at any moment, exile is no longer portrayed exclusively as an expression of God's rule over history and the punishment that He confers on the sinning people who are His partners in a steadfast covenant but also as a cosmic and theological malfunction, which can only be mended by redemption.

Of course, alongside this meaning of the concept of exile there exists in Jewish literature the earthly one as well, which regards exile as the uprooting of the people from the Land of Israel, explained as a punishment for the people's sins. Moreover, only rarely is this view of exile as cosmic malfunction expressed in full measure. But our concern here is not with the high road of Jewish theology but rather with examining the potential concealed in byways that may seem marginal and insufficiently developed. When we pose ourselves the question as to how can one develop a religious language that will deal with the Holocaust and function in the place where the concept of "because of our sins" no longer works, it seems to me that an examination of this meaning of exile holds a certain measure of relevance.

First, it has already been observed that in its extreme, this perception of exile is expressed in the idea of *hester panim* (the hiding of God's face).[29] This idea is quite problematic. Detached from an overall context, it is of no great help in providing orientation to the faithful. As such, it only points to the fact that we have no tools to explain or to absorb reality. That is how it looks in the writings of the first philosopher to use this term with regard to the Holocaust, Martin Buber. The discussion of *hester panim* enabled him to note the problems of the issue of faith after the Holocaust, and to develop a metaphoric rhetoric to express his stubborn attachment to dialogue and revelation. His use of the term does not "explain" or "give solace."[30]

However, in the overall context of the perception of exile, it might be assigned a far broader meaning. In order to comprehend this meaning, we must first note those factors that even before the Holocaust lessened the willingness to accept the biblical formula of punishment and reward, which until the modern era delineated the parameters of Jewish historical consciousness with no little success. These factors to a great extent determine the range of options available to both Jewish religious and nonreligious cultural thought in attempting to deal with the issue of the Holocaust today.

---

27. B. T. *Megillah* 29ª.
28. B. T. *Berakhot* 8ª.
29. The motif of *hester panim*, according to which at the peak of God's punishments is the absence of His presence in history, is based on Deuteronomy 31:18; Isaiah 54:8. It is customary in rabbinic literature to refer to the story of Purim, in which God is not ex- plicitly mentioned, as an example of *hester panim*. This interpretation is based on the similarity between the name Esther and the words in Deuteronomy, *haster astir*. See, e.g., B. T. *Hullin* 139ᵇ.
30. See Martin Buber, "The Dialogue between Heaven and Earth," in *On Judaism*, ed. Nahum Glatzer (New York, 1967), pp. 221–225.

The complex of causes that brought about this weakening are related to the different meanings of the process of secularization and the new perspectives that they open to both secular and religious philosophy. It should be noted that the rise of historical consciousness and historicist views removes from this formula the very basis for its existence. First, in order to retain the classic biblical view, one's historical outlook must be decisively Judeocentric; it must ignore almost entirely the immanent context of historical developments beyond the bounds of the people of Israel, whether in the cultural, spiritual, economic, social, political, or strategic areas. Only within such a framework could the victory of Nebuchadnezzar, for example, be explained in the Bible as punishment for the sins of the people of Israel rather than as a stage in the development of the Babylonian empire. Only by almost totally ignoring the overall historic processes could the modern Jew view the reality that he or she encountered as being completely focused on the Jewish people and its destiny.[31] For many nineteenth-century philosophers such an option was nonexistent. The integration of Jews in the society and culture of the nations in which they lived made such a view of history ludicrous.

Second, the concept of history itself undergoes change. It is no longer "sacred history" in the traditional sense, but rather history that operates in accordance with human-cultural perspectives and the dynamics that govern human society and cultures. Even religious philosophers, who continue to regard this very occurrence as an expression of Divine Providence, can no longer subjugate their entire view to the protective and restrictive biblical framework of punishment and reward. Finally, it is clear that the development of historical research per se, which vastly increased our knowledge of decisive eras in the annals of the Jewish people, placed the biblical formula in a rather problematic light. It could continue to be regarded as a picturesque expression of the nation's consciousness, but it was no longer able to encompass the diverse and complex historic developments that took place in different periods of time.

Against this background, the radical changes that occurred in the explanation given for exile and its significance during the course of the modern era may be understood. Many thinkers from the latter half of the eighteenth century and during the nineteenth century tended to depict the situation of the Jewish people during the modern era in unmistakable terms: They referred to the end of exile and the beginning of a new era with clearly messianic characteristics. Emancipation, integration in general society, and the [late 18th C.] Enlightenment movement (Haskalah) were all considered signs of this process. This is not the place to elaborate in an attempt to prove this assertion. It is sufficient to note Moses Mendelssohn's [1729–1786] "Vision of the Future," which neutralized any sense of exile and which theoretically positioned the Jew within the tapestry of normal, regular life that holds neither sense of dearth nor consciousness of any vital need of redemption.[32] To the same extent it is clear that to a neo-Orthodox philosopher such as Samson Raphael Hirsch [1808–1888], who advocated the idea of "Torah and Derekh Eretz ["worldliness"; i.e., Western culture]," God's presence in His world entails much more than the four cubits of halakhah. Art, culture, the European national milieux, and scientific progress are all God's and an expression of His in-dwelling within humankind. In an even more striking manner, the cognizance of the end of exile is expressed in the Reform [movements] notion of the "mission of Israel" and the awareness that

31. Nevertheless, the idea that the concept of punishment and reward is not unique to the people of Israel and that history involves the intertwining of the destinies of nations as a consequence of their actions already appears in the Bible. Thus, for example, in the "Covenant between the Pieces," the fact that "the iniquity of the Amorite is not yet complete" (Genesis 15:16) and that therefore the land is not yet available for the nation that is to inherit it after them is used to explain the need for postponing the settlement of the Israelite nation on the land.

32. It is important to emphasize that all this does not necessarily apply to the way in which Mendelssohn understood the concrete reality in which he lived. To a great extent it could be said that his vigilance with regard to the social value of equality and his unrealized aspiration to see Judaism as a full partner in the modeling of human society augmented his sense of exile.

the integration of Jews within the surrounding societies and cultures is the highest stage in the development of Jewish "ethical monotheism" and in the realization of its full universal potential.

This consciousness of the end of exile began to show signs of fissure long before the Holocaust due to various factors. First, one must mention the rise of modern anti-Semitism, which served not only as a catalyst for the development of Zionist thought but also as the source of a sense of estrangement, insecurity, and alienation for many Jews. For many Jewish thinkers and cultural figures—whether religious, nationalist, or assimilated—it awakened a feeling that the success of emancipation per se places the Jew in a situation of exile and alienation, even if this is not necessarily apparent in the external parameters of his or her life.

Within the Zionist context as well, the significant change that occurred in the understanding of the concept of exile needs to be stressed. In Zionism, particularly of the secular variety, a special emphasis was placed on the land and its settlement, an emphasis that suppressed the other traditional dimensions of the concept of exile. The Zionist Jew living in Israel does not at all consider him- or herself as living in exile, whereas the traditional Jew who lived in that same place certainly did and governed his or her *halakhic* and social life by this premise. The earthly context of exile also defined, of course, the earthly and very concrete context of redemption.

In another sense, the overall change of atmosphere in the Western world contributed to challenging this sense of the end of exile. The concept of exile was internalized on much deeper levels of human thought and became one of the cornerstones of human consciousness, whether articulated explicitly or indirectly.[33] The understanding that one can be alienated from oneself and from one's surroundings even while living in the supposedly natural environment into which one was born and raised is of decisive significance for the manner in which we decipher human existence and give it meaning.[34]

Undoubtedly, all this is expressed inter alia in the far more limited willingness on the part of many artists, writers, and thinkers to continue to assign a classical religious interpretation to reality, to fully accept and to justify God's actions. Characteristic of this reality is Ḥayyim Naḥman Bialik's profound and distraught reaction to the pogroms in Kishinev (1905). In his famous poem *Al Hashechita* ("On the Slaughter"), the poet expressed to its fullest his inner struggle for faith. He prays to "heavens," not knowing whether they contain a God and whether there is any "path" to Him, and this while declaring that there is no longer prayer left on his lips. He sets a clear limit to his willingness to anticipate any action on the part of celestial justice, vigorously challenging heaven using insolent language.

Hence, even before the Holocaust the orientation of the modern Jew diverged in a number of directions. On the one hand, for many thinkers the classical biblical model of reward and punishment and of God directing history in response to the behavior of the people of Israel and the parameters of the covenant became very problematic. On the other hand, the consciousness of exile changed in different ways. In a certain sense, the modern Jew felt that exile was a category symbolizing a world that had passed with the destruction of the walls of the ghettos. The world is his or her own world, the culture is his or her own culture, and he or she is living in a free and well-ordered space. Even if the Jew fosters a hope for redemption, this is not necessarily connected to a sense that the present reality is essentially deficient. On the other hand, the twentieth-century Jew—like many contemporaries in other nations and cultures—may well feel that his or her own human condition is best expressed by such categories as exile, alienation, the "breaking of the [heavenly] vessels" (*shevirat ha-kelim*), and "divine hiddenness" (*hester panim*). This fact finds expression in central trends of modern art, in major works of literature—particularly those written by the generation of

---

33. See Natan Ofek, *Kafka vehakiyum hayehudi* (*Kafka and Jewish Existence*) (Jerusalem, 2002), pp. 144–166.
34. It is worthwhile to reflect on the connection between this consciousness, which usually appears as an ex- pression of the tragic state of humankind, and the motif of "for you are but resident strangers with Me" (Leviticus 25:23), which marks a central line within biblical thought.

World War I—in speculative philosophy, and in social movements.

The Holocaust constitutes the cruelest and most definitive essence of exile in its widest sense. It places humanity in an impotent position within a horror deriving from the fact that that which is good and represents the beautiful has been completely nullified, that fundamental values are shattered, and that within the world of the Holy One blessed be He, God is not even left with the four cubits of *Halakhah* intact. From the viewpoint of Jewish history, the Holocaust nullifies first and foremost the achievements of the emancipation and of the Jews' integration into society as citizens with equal rights. In the general human context, it places the values of humanism and the hopes for progress in a cruel and ludicrous light and "sanctifies" absolute evil. The Holocaust represents a world in which the remnants of goodness, beauty, and faithfulness struggle to survive while all the forces of destruction celebrate one long and murderous Walpurgis Night.

In this sense, the actual deportation to the ghettos and the transports to the concentration and death camps, as well as the death marches, are distinct symbols of an exile that has almost no redress. There is no place that can be considered a safe haven, there is no normal reality, and no measure of sanity and human values can continue and evolve. The Nazis' different modes of action were meant to destroy all elements of normal human existence for the Jews and, in so doing, managed to destroy many foundations of human existence generally. Deceit as a basic device of human behavior, the all-encompassing pressure to ignore the suffering and humanity of the other, the unrestrained looting, of whose full extent we have only become aware in recent years, as well as the manner in which it pervaded so many societies—all of the above were explicit elements of the "breaking of vessels," of a return to chaos, so to speak—in other words, an almost total embodiment of exile in the fullest sense.

With what does such an outlook provide us? It certainly does not offer comfort, and it might even increase the sense of terror. For a person contemplating the Holocaust, the events that preceded it, and its results, such an outlook does not provide any point of solace—neither in the classic sense of theodicy nor in that of a promise that it will never happen again. The covenant of the rainbow (Genesis 9:8–14) no longer seems relevant at this point; not much is left of the promise never to "eradicate" the people of Israel either. However, viewing the Holocaust as the very acme and embodiment of exile may provide one with tools for understanding that may be relevant in another sense. Our question does not pertain to the manner of dealing with the Holocaust at the time of its occurrence but rather to how we deal with the memory of the Holocaust and its significance for future generations.

We have mentioned that exile, by its very nature, is essentially a deficient situation in which the positive potential concealed within the very foundation of reality is not realized. Exile is not a self-evident situation, but a result of destruction and catastrophe. Exile is always bound with expectations of redemption and an imperative to act toward redemption. All these may be of great significance in dealing with the Holocaust. We asked at the beginning of our essay from whence the educator and thinker can secure the necessary measure of optimism and faith for working in the field of education and culture. The category of exile may provide that measure, in that it defies cruel reality and maintains that it is not self-explanatory, that it does not necessarily represent all that is intrinsic in the human race, and that it is not destined to last forever. If the prophet is allowed to envision the dissolution of exile and the return to the garden of Eden, so, too, the educator may believe in mending the world—even if this seems, at first, impossible.

Zionism adopted the slogan, which as such entails a large measure of superficiality and even estrangement, "from Holocaust to rebirth." It is easy and necessary to criticize this catchphrase, as many in Israel and the diaspora have done. True, it embodies to a great extent the arrogance of the Zionist toward the diaspora Jew who is perceived as not heeding the "warnings" and not joining the Zionist endeavor in time. It measures the immeasurable sacrifice of the victims and the survivors on the scale of establishing the state of Israel, regarding the latter as a compensation of sorts that counterbalances what took place. It too easily serves trends of politicizing the remembrance of the Holocaust.

Despite all these flaws, it contains a significant measure of truth. If we accept this slogan as expressing the awareness that the Holocaust is the extreme embodiment of exile, then we may consider it as pointing to the fact that dealing with the Holocaust must be bound with the attempt to deal with exile and to nullify it, insofar as human power is capable of doing such. The superficiality mentioned above only relates to the assumption that the establishment and thriving of a Jewish state are a full expression of such nullification of exile and the confrontation with it. But if we adopt a wider perspective on exile, such as that which stems from the sources we have cited, then our confrontation with it will also be infinitely deeper and more encompassing.

In this perspective, exile is seen as the rule of injustice in a world that ought to have been the world of the Holy One blessed be He. Hence, defeating exile is only possible by means of a constant and stubborn struggle with injustice, whether it be rendered to you or to others, whether it be done by yourself or by your political and cultural representatives, or by others. The same perspective reveals that exile is also concerned with the sense of alienation and disregard for another person's suffering, despite the fact that he or she too was created in the image of God. The struggle against exile is tantamount to the struggle against poverty, ignorance, and gratuitous suffering. The establishment of a Jewish state and the struggle for its character and ways may be a step in this direction, so long as we acknowledge that it is no more than a single limited step.

The Bible depicts both human and national existence as the result of exile and as a struggle to nullify that exile. This struggle is that which is signified by the term "redemption." The Holocaust forces us to look in the mirror and to see our world with all of its cruelty and with all of its potential for carnage and ruin. It does not enable us to feel other than in exile. But opposite this mirror one may also pose the decision to believe in the possibility of goodness, in the ability to redeem, and in the spiritual and religious significance of human history. Franz Rosenzweig, who lived and died before the Holocaust, asserted that, just as creation and revelation are the work of God, so is redemption the work of humanity. In the wake of the Holocaust this assertion seems even more essential. It does not mean that redemption will come. But it does mean that one must demand and seek—both in the religious and in the secular humanistic sense—that the redemption will come about. In this perspective, perhaps it is yet possible to believe again, despite everything, in God and in humanity, who act in history and who sanctify it.

Yosef Achituv

Yosef Achituv was born in Germany in 1933, the year Adolf Hitler came to power. His family, recognizing the danger of their situation, emigrated to Palestine, then under a British mandate, in 1935. In 1952, he became a member of the religious kibbutz Ein Tzurim. His professional career has centered around teaching, especially in the areas of religious and moral education. At present, he is a research fellow at the Shalom Hartman Institute in Jerusalem and teaches Talmud and Jewish philosophy at the Kibbutz Hadati yeshiva and in the Yaacov Herzog Center for Jewish Studies, both located in Kibbutz Ein Tzurim. He received an honorary doctorate from Bar Ilan University on 18 May 2004, "in recognition of his contributions to religious Zionism and the religious kibbutz movement, and his impact on Israel's developing Jewish, Zionist, and democratic character." He is the author of *Al Gvul Hatmura* (*On the Border of Change*; Jerusalem, 1997), a study of contemporary Jewish meanings, and has published more than 150 articles in the field of contemporary Jewish thought.

Selection

Yosef Achituv's essay "Theology and the Holocaust," first given at a conference sponsored by the Memorial Foundation for Jewish Culture held in Ashkelon, Israel, in 1999, focuses on post-Holocaust religious Zionist views regarding God's role in human history. He begins with the basic but nevertheless significant recognition that even when faced with the most daunting challenges, religious individuals and communities tend to work within their inherited traditions, or at least retain the language and themes of these traditions. This is certainly the case in Orthodox Zionist communities vis-à-vis their theological responses to the Holocaust. Thus, while a calamity as terrible and extensive as the destruction of European Jewry would seem to undermine the concept that God champions and aids the Jewish people in history, religious Zionist thinkers have maintained their inherited religious *Weltanschauung*. They have been able to do this by displaying some flexibility, and some novelty, in their theological interpretations of the meaning of the *Shoah*. Thus, for example, some Orthodox Zionist thinkers have chosen, after Auschwitz and Treblinka, to deemphasize God's direct role in history and have turned away from deterministic views of history. Alternatively, others have gone in the opposite direction. These theologians have stressed God's causal role in human affairs. For them, the Holocaust is seen as a "cruel operation" performed by God as a necessary part of His redemptive plan, with the ultimate goal of delivering the Jewish people from their long exile. Achituv, in reviewing all the possible Zionist theological options, is, to his credit, careful not to recommend one view over another. It is up to the reader to work through the various conceptual schema that are described and to decide, with all existential seriousness, which of the possible explanations appears most persuasive.

Selected Bibliography

Books by Yosef Achituv

On the Border of Change (Jerusalem, 1997) [Hebrew].

A Good Eye: Dialogue and Polemic in Jewish Culture (Tel Aviv, 1999) [Hebrew].

With Hadas Goldberg and Amichai Berholz. *A Reappraisal of the Principles of Religious Zionism and Modern Orthodoxy* (Tel Aviv, 2000) [Hebrew].

THEOLOGY AND THE HOLOCAUST

This essay will evaluate various explanations of the Holocaust offered within religious Zionist circles. It is not concerned with a comparative analysis that would elicit some criterion for judging how "successful" these explanations are. Rather, it focuses on one single issue: God's presence and His providence in human history. It will dwell on the place this issue occupies in the "theology" of religious Zionism and will examine the extent of its durability in the face of the Holocaust. I will also inquire whether it has been weakened or undermined as a result of the trauma of the Holocaust and, in addition, will explore the ways in which the Holocaust is "exploited" for the purpose of strengthening the religious Zionist identity. Finally, it will point at the process through which the religious Zionist conception that emerged from the Merkaz HaRav school (associated with R. Abraham Kook, d. 1935; and his son, R. Zvi Yehudah, d. 1982) of thought lost its hold on religious Zionism, after dominating it for over twenty years, from the end of the 1960s to the mid-1980s. This development has given rise to two opposite trends. The first sharpens and reinforces the notion of the presence of God and His providence by associating it with a particular messianic faith and a mystification of Israeli nationalism, in conformity with the Merkaz HaRav teaching. The second moderates this notion and shifts the emphasis to coping with the Holocaust on a human, ethical basis, in affinity with the nonillusionary theology that is claimed by modern Orthodox circles.

As is well known, the trauma of the Holocaust led many Jews to deny God and lose their faith.

Many were forced to rebuild themselves and their world, a world devoid of God and Torah. Those who retained their faith and still clung to the Torah and the *mitzvot* (commandments) sought the "explanation" for the Holocaust, as well as the meaning it carried—however unique and traumatic it was—within the framework of their religious world. Their modes of reaction were not, and could not have been, fundamentally revolutionary. Neither those who were satisfied with an agnostic approach nor those who preferred to keep quiet were able to create a completely new religious language. From their own religious tradition and faith-oriented world they retrieved some anchors that made it possible for them to survive as believing Jews, while shifting emphases and reorganizing the religious priorities in their lives. In other words, the most they could do was to create a variant of religious language that was absorbed in the parameters of their own traditional religious world.

History teaches us that seldom does reality uproot faith from the hearts of those it slaps in the face. Whether consciously or unconsciously, the believers mobilize all the interpretive options available to them in order to come up with adequate interpretations of the conflicting reality that threatens their world. These things are true of the individual believer. They are even more valid for a movement that invests tremendous efforts to recruit the shapers of public opinion, the educational systems, and the agents of cultural transmission for the purpose of inculcating and inseminating the principles of its faith in its followers.[1] I assume that many of you would

---

1. As Professor Dov Schwartz has noted: "There is hardly any religious Zionist thinker who has changed his views as a result of the Holocaust." *Ha-Ziyyonut ha-Datit bein Higgayon li-Meshihiyyut* (Tel Aviv, 1999), p. 134.

acknowledge this point if you considered the powerful measures taken by the ultra-Orthodox community in response to the Holocaust. Its intense indoctrinating initiative, which found its expression in numerous publications and in the introduction of ultra-Orthodox narratives of the Holocaust, is well documented in some fascinating studies that have been published in the last decades.

I would like to begin with some basic assumptions related to the issue of the presence of God and His providence in history.

1. Side by side with the belief that God revealed Himself in front of all Israel at least once in history, in the Sinai revelation, there is also a traditional religious position that God reveals Himself through history. This position is prevalent not only in Judaism but also in Christianity. According to the Christian version, the abject historical situation of the Jewish people serves as an irrefutable proof that God abandoned His covenant with the people of Israel and passed it on to those who are "Israel by spirit." Down through the ages this very notion served to oppress and humiliate the Jews. That is to say, whoever contemplates historical occurrences, at least the global ones, and is struck by the lowly, ignoble state of the Jewish people must see in it the hand of God, who speaks to us through history. In this way, the lessons taught by history fortify the Christian faith.

2. Paradoxically, another pervasive notion was that by contemplating history we come to realize that the people of Israel is not part of it. It is subject to different laws because they belong to metahistory. This is one of the formulas that was offered to counter the Christian claim. What it suggests is that the very abject situation of the Jewish people attests to its covenant with God. The people of Israel has a "different account" with God precisely because it is the Chosen People. This approach left the belief in divine providence intact. It suggested that with respect to the people of Israel, divine providence operates in a unique way, with a different kind of intensity and on a different level from the workings of His universal providence. This belief has a long and continuous tradition. Down through the ages, it assumed various forms of religious discourse, in keeping with the changing conceptual systems. Yet, essentially it did not change at all. In its traditional formulation it goes back to the talmudic saying "Israel is immune from planetary influence." What this means is that the people of Israel is not governed by the celestial systems. These are the agents of God. It is He who governs the world and Israel is subject to His direct providence. "For the Lord's portion is His people; Jacob is the lot of His inheritance" (Deuteronomy 32:9). R. Yehudah ben Asher, son of R. Asher ben Yehiel, who lived in the beginning of the fourteenth century, conveyed this idea eloquently, as follows:

> "Let us return to God for He has torn and He will heal us; He has smitten and He will bind up; after two days He will revive us; in the third day He will raise us up, and we shall live in His presence" (Hosea 6:1–2). These verses acknowledge that the punishments we suffer every day and the exile that empowers us are a matter of a profound intent and not just accidental or compelled by history. For if we trust in the blessed God in all our actions, He shall change history for us from bad to good. God forbid that we should believe in the stars, as the idolaters do, for then history will govern us and He will abandon us to the arbitrariness of the accidents. . . . For it is not the nature of heavenly spheres to drop rain over dry land and produce rain in its season and the like as a reward for observing the Torah and the *mitzvot*. The truth is that "Thine is the Kingdom O Lord" and the power over the upper worlds and everything below them. God is capable of changing nature whether positively or adversely. . . . All the more so that it is impossible for us to know His ways and how He administers the world.[2]

3. This notion recurs in a different language in various conceptual adjustments in the writings of various thinkers, ranging from R. Isaac

2. *Responsa Zikhron Yehudah*, par. 91.

Breuer of *Agudat Israel* to Franz Rosenzweig,[3] who both insisted that the people of Israel are governed by metahistorical laws. Rav Kook himself exploited the idea when he suggested that it was time for the Jewish people to resume its place in history. This was in the aftermath of the First World War, when Rav Kook was still under the innocent, euphoric impression that it was meant to be the last war on earth. He therefore proclaimed that it was now possible for the Jews to return to "world politics" and found a Jewish state.

4. Here is the place to mention that it is doubtful whether we can reckon Maimonides among those subscribing to this widespread view that God reveals Himself through history. In his *Mishneh Torah*, Maimonides states, "But how may one discover the way to love and fear Him? When man will reflect concerning His works, and His great and wonderful creatures, and will behold through them His wonderful, matchless, and infinite wisdom."[4] This statement makes no reference to the contemplation of human history. Furthermore, Maimonides' position on the issue of divine providence, as suggested in his *Guide of the Perplexed*, is far more simple. One may say that with respect to his point, he failed to make an imprint on Jewish theological thought as it developed in the course of time. In the last decade, however, some minor circles in religious Zionism invoked Maimonides in an attempt to provide religious legitimacy to their exceptional views.

5. In its extreme manifestation, this "modern deviation" suggests an awareness of the change that occurred in the traditional position in the response to "nonillusionary"[5] theology, on the one hand, and to modern notions about the nature of history and historical interpretation, on the other hand. The nonillusionary theological position corroborates the denial of any pretension to discover God through human history. Modern hermeneutics raises our awareness of the connection between the historian's system of beliefs, values, and ideology and his account of history, precise and well documented as it may be. Thus, the assumption that "the facts speak for themselves" is no longer held to be true.

For the purpose of our discussion, I am going to divide religious Zionism into three periods. The first lasted until the 1960s. During this period, religious Zionism was close in spirit to the ideals of the other pioneer movements in the Jewish *yishuv* (settlement in Palestine). This meant that, generally speaking, it perceived historical events as normal political processes. In the second period, from the 1960s up to the late 1980s, religious Zionism was dominated by the Merkaz HaRav school of thought whose intensive notion of divine providence was based on a mystical perception of Israeli nationalism. This school of thought made its imprint on, and directly influenced, the educational systems of religious Zionism, such as the high school yeshivas, the *Hesder* yeshivas, and the *Ulpanot* (seminaries). The third period, from the mid-1980s onward, is characterized by a weakening of this hegemony by a wider variety of religious Zionist ideologies and by the absorption of other, more moderate notions of divine providence.[6]

3. As he said, "Everything the Jew does, immediately leaps out of the temporal framework and becomeseternity." See Ephraim Meir, *Kokhav mi-Ya'akov*, chs. 5–6.
4. *Hilkhot Yesodei ha-Torah*, II.2.
5. On the nonillusionary belief see my "One Hundred Years of Religious Zionism," in *Ha-Ziyyonut ha-Datit*, vol. 3, edited by Avi Sagi and Yedidia Stern (Ramat Gan, 2002), pp. 17–29 [Hebrew]. This paper was written by following in the footsteps of Professor Eliezer Goldman. The nonillusionary belief denies the pretension that humans as such are capable of identifying God's intention with any measure of certainty. In addition, it removes from the concept of providence its ontological meaning and the pretension to provide a causal meaning to the course of events.

6. "Moderate concepts of providence" include a sequence represented by such figures and thinkers as R. Hayyim David Ha-Levi, Professor E. E. Urbach, and Moshe Unna, and up to Professor Eliezer Goldman and Yeshayahu Leibowitz, who denied that the belief in providence had any empirical meaning. I disagree with Professor Dov Schwartz, who excluded Goldman from the category of those worthy of being included in religious Zionism and who stated that "Goldman's thought can no longer be labeled typical religious Zionist thought and it is doubtful whether it can be ascribed to any existing religious Zionist approach whatsoever." See Dov Schwartz (supra, note 1), p. 136.

Religious Zionism is closely intertwined with the belief in the presence of God in history and His immanence. The term *Athalta di-Ge'ulah*, "the beginning of redemption," which has accompanied religious Zionism since its inception, was embraced by the precursors of Zionism as early as the beginning of the nineteenth century. It is infused with explicit mystical elements concerning the theurgic impact of normal human activity stimulated by *it'aruta di-le-tata*, the "arousal below," on *it'artua di-le-eila*, the corresponding "arousal on high." There is some misapprehension in exclusively associating this arousal with realistic acts of redemption. Thus, for Rabbi Kalisher, the clearest indication of the beginning of redemption was to be found in the land yielding its fruit. "There can be no more manifest sign of redemption than this," said R. Kalisher. About a hundred years later, in 1967, on the eve of Independence Day, R. Zvi Yehudah used almost the same words when he declared at the Merkaz HaRav yeshiva:

> The issues of redemption associated with Israel's Independence Day...are visible and explicit.... they are explicitly stated in the *Gemara* (Talmud).... There can be no more manifest sign of redemption than this. How can we recognize it? By the fact that the land of Israel produces fruit in abundance.[7]

This quasi-realistic account is nothing but a mystical formulation, no different in essence from the signs usually indicated by those who calculated the end of days and the advent of the messiah.

This term, "the beginning of redemption," gave rise to the phrase "the beginning of the emergence of our redemption." The latter was introduced into the Prayer for the Safety of the State [of Israel] in recognition of its significance, and it is in current use within all religious Zionist circles.

On the face of it, religious Zionism has its own, exclusive linguistic and conceptual tools for "explaining" the Holocaust. Generally speaking, one can say that in religious Zionism, especially from the 1960s onward, there has been a marked tendency to separate the Holocaust from the divine system of reward and punishment. Instead of attributing the Holocaust to the divine settling of scores on account of the people's sins in the past, religious Zionism views the Holocaust as an advance payment in preparation for the future, for the redemption. This transformation of the notion of the Holocaust does not transcend the limits of traditional theodicy. It is a matter of change in emphasis. In the circles of religious Zionism, the presence of God and His providence are sharply and excessively reinforced by the attempts to trace the divine redemptive moves. Henceforth I will refer to this as "an intensive notion of providence."

In order to appreciate how exaggerated this conception is, we will find it interesting to compare it to the stand taken by Rabbi Hayyim David Ha-Levi[8] toward the Holocaust. Rabbi Ha-Levi was much interested in the philosophy of history. He defined the study of history as a *mitzvah* and tended to interpret historical and topical events in terms of his own notion of providence. He used the same approach to clarify the term "the beginning of redemption" and to explore the meaning of the Holocaust and its connection with the founding of the State of Israel.

For Rabbi Ha-Levi, however, the individual's freedom of choice is a primary constituting principle. Hence, although history has a direction and a purpose, it is not deterministic. Divine providence acts in history as a "hidden hand" that offers and opens to humans "a window of opportunities" for realizing the divine purpose in the domain of history. Humans have the right to either take advantage of this opportunity or let

---

7. See Avi Ravitsky, *Ha-Ketz ha-Meguleh u-Medinat ha-Yehudim: Meshihiyyut, Ziyyonut ve-Radicalism Dati be-Yisrael* (Tel Aviv, 1993), ch. 3, particularly pp. 170–200.
8. The description of R. Ha-Levi's position is based on Zvi Zohar, "Sephardic Religious Thought in Israel: Aspects of the Theology of Rabbi Haim David Halevi," in *Critical Essays on Israeli Society, Religion, and Government*, edited by Kevin Avruch and Walter Zenner (Albany, N.Y., 1997), pp. 115–136.

it slip away. R. Ha-Levi's confidence in the possibility of fulfilling the divine intentions through human history rests on the assumption that the long course of history guarantees the necessary accumulation of appropriate human decisions.

According to Rabbi Ha-Levi, some historical periods are more "crowded" in terms of the quantitative and qualitative opportunities that unfold before us. He was convinced that the in-gathering of the exiles and the founding of the State of Israel were all part of the progress of world history. Nonetheless, he insisted on the contingency of these progressive moves. He held onto his contingent notion of history even after the Six Day War. Like many others, he was elated by the unexpected victory and the libera-tion of the occupied territories of the Land of Israel, including the Temple Mount.

R. Ha-Levi made a similar observation about the contingency of human history in reference to the period following the First World War and the Balfour Declaration. He even suggested that had the Jewish people extricated itself from the exile in those days and settled down in the Land of Israel, the Holocaust would not have taken place. God does not interfere with the free choice of human beings.

After the Six Day War, and due to a variety of factors, the preoccupation with the Holocaust gained momentum. The surging involvement with the Holocaust, in the diaspora and Israel alike, has performed a constructive role in shaping the Jewish identity of many Jews, especially those who were psychologically and mentally alienated from the *halakhic* (traditional legal-religious) way of life and the traditional Jewish culture. It is true that some interpret this phenomenon unfa-vorably. Many others share the view that it is quite possible for religious Zionism to build and shape Jewish identity without invoking the Holocaust.

Yet, if we examine the literature about the Holocaust that emerged from the circles of reli-gious Zionism, we notice that it practically swelled following the Six Day War and corre-sponding to the rising hegemony of the Merkaz HaRav school of thought. Presumably, the "manifest miracle" of the victory won in the Six Day War intensified the need to relate to the Holocaust in retrospect, while at the same time offering the opportunity to do so. In its powerful and unmatched impact, the "miraculous" vic-tory heightened the psychological awareness of the divine workings of providence, and this en-tailed an instant awareness, in retrospect, of the connection between the Holocaust and national revival. The "manifest redemption" embodied in the triumphant Six Day War has become more compelling than the fecundity of trees on the mountains of Israel. It should be noted that from a metaphysical-mystical viewpoint, the "manifest redemption" signified by the transformation of the soil is far superior because of the metaphysical standing of the land of Israel.[9] No wonder that the vigorous redemptive settlement activity, which was initiated mostly by the adherents of the Merkaz HaRav teaching and *Gush Emunin* ["the Bloc of the faithful"], began right after the Six Day War.

Thus it is no coincidence that at that time there was a breakthrough in disseminating the mystical perception of Israel nationalism, along with a detailed "providential" interpretation of the divine moves that leave their imprint on current reality. This perception originates in the teaching of R. Abraham Isaac Ha-Kohen Kook in the first decade after he settled in Israel. However, only after the Six Day War, as a result of a concurrent combination of various factors, did this latent perception emerge from below the surface and make a striking impression.[10] From 1967 onward, Rabbi Zvi Yehudah spoke of the Holocaust by using the startling image of a divine

9. According to the well-known words of R. Abba in B. T. *Sanhedrin* 98 "There can be no more manifest sign of redemption than this, viz., what is said (Ezekiel 36), 'But ye O mountains of Israel, ye shall shoot forth your branches, and yield your fruit to my people of Israel, for they are at hand to come.'"

10. See my lecture on religious Zionism, which was presented in the Van Lear Institute in honor of Pro-fessor Eliezer Schweid's seventieth birthday.

healing operation performed on the body of the nation in order to cut it off from the bonds of exile. Professor Avi Ravitsky, who was the first to comment on this image, noted that Rabbi M. M. Shneerson had preceded R. Zvi Yehudah in using it, although he did not associate it with a divine purpose of redemption. In 1971, T. Aviner wrote—apparently expressing the view for the first time—as follows:[11]

> Once again we must mention that we are not speaking here of sin and retribution.... We only speak of the fact that the people of Israel were bonded with the exile and it was necessary to sever these ties in a cruel way.... This is what my master and teacher, Rabbi Zvi Yehudah, said about this: "The truth is that all Israel, millions of individual Jews, form one single body, and when the time of redemption comes..., it is necessary to separate Israel from the exile against their will. It is then that the hand of God appears and performs a cruel operation, which brings about the separation and leads back to the land of Israel.... In fact..., the final act of severance, with all the traumatic convulsions it entails... signifies the light of the living and the revival of the holy people.... We are obligated to contemplate history, to consider the Word of God as revealed to us through the increasingly expanding channel of guidance provided by the great of Israel.... We must discern the 'sweetness' within the 'bitterness.' We must see the lights that emerged from the darkness. This light of the living is bound to intensify even as we continue to build our Holy Land and be rebuilt by it."[12]

Recently, my friend Yishai Rozen-Zvi has discussed this issue at length in a yet unpublished paper entitled Ha-Ḥoleh ha-Medumeh ["The Hypochondriac"]. He shows that the transition from justifying the ways of God to justifying the Holocaust eventually led to a decatastrophization of the Holocaust. In this explanatory system, the Holocaust does not precede redemption but ra-

ther forms an integral part of it. Rozen-Zvi further demonstrates that this idea found its way to the circles of the Merkaz HaRav school of thought. It is taught in the yeshivas and is disseminated through the publication of books, such as R. Eliyahu Bazak's last work, Medaber bi-Zedakah.[13] It should be added that in the beginning of 1999, preparations were made to set up the Zvi Yisrael Institute for studying the Holocaust in the light of faith, according to the teaching of R. Zvi Yehudah ha-Kohen Kook. The institute is presently annexed to the Ateret Kohanim yeshiva in the Old City of Jerusalem. Here is an excerpt from an interview with Rabbi Solomon Aviner that was conducted at that time:

R. Aviner: We are ordained to study history out of faith.

Question: What does it mean "out of faith"? Isn't history a sequence of objective facts? Where is the place of faith in this sequence?

R. Aviner: It all depends on what approach we adopt to relate to the facts. The starting point is that "the city is governed by a Leader," that God did not abandon the land, that He is always with us, whether in the light or in the darkness. It is not that we observe the world and accordingly we come to conclusions about the Master of the world. On the contrary, out of our faith in the Master of the world we strive to understand what is happening in this world. We even try to understand a little about the Holocaust....

Question: And how did he [i.e., R. Zvi Yehudah] understand the Holocaust?

R. Aviner: He did not explain it. He said that it was an enigma. Nonetheless, he elaborated a complete and profound system, which he himself summed up in a parable: "There is a house in the forest and it is surrounded by dangerous beasts. Mother is inside the house, preparing warm and tasty food for her child. Inside the house it is not as dangerous as outside. There is warm nourishing food. So

---

11. "Sho'ah u-Geulah," published in several publications from 1976 onward. The excerpt I cited is taken from the collection Emunah ba-Sho'ah, based on a study day on the Jewish religious meaning of the Holocaust and published by the Ministry of Culture and Educa-

tion, Department of Tarbut Toranit [Torah Culture] (Jerusalem, 1980), pp. 65–66.
12. "Sho'ah u-Geulah," p. 67ff.
13. (Jerusalem, 2000).

mother calls her child to come inside. But the child refuses. He wants to play outside. Mother is concerned about her child and so she pulls him vigorously and drags him into the house. Now he is scratched and bruised. He is bleeding all over. Yet, he is alive."

Question: Doesn't God have another way?

R. Aviner: Our master, R. Zvi Yehudah, describes the Holocaust as a divine horrible operation designed to cut Israel off from the exile. . . . The terrible destruction prepares the magnificent building. From the depth of impurity and wickedness the redeemed praise the Lord with a new song.

Once the Holocaust is explained in terms of this model of divine surgery, the intensive notion of providence is reinforced. Hence we can say that in the excerpt I quoted, the Holocaust serves to strengthen the religious Zionist conception fostered by the Merkaz HaRav teaching.

As I've already indicated, during the last decade there occurred a complex inner development within religious Zionism. This development, for which various internal and external factors are responsible, is basically characterized by the decline of the hegemony of Merkaz HaRav ideology and the rise of other ideological and religious trends. It seems plausible that the incentive to establish the Zvi Yisrael Institute came— among other things—in response to these opposite trends.

I will try to sum up those characteristics of the new trends that are relevant to this discussion. Note that by their very nature, these characteristics are diffuse rather than monolithic.

1. A contingent perception of historical events and a forecast of an open future.
2. Various concepts that moderate the intense notion of the actual role of providence in history, with the most extreme one completely denying any divine intervention in human activity and placing on humans full moral responsibility for their actions. Professor

Yeshayahu Leibowitz conveyed this position in a pointed manner when he stated:

> I am saying it as strongly as I can, notwithstanding the pain this should cause to many people, among them myself, that I cannot attach any religious meaning to the Holocaust. . . . The Holocaust was a product of a particular reality of the world. . . . This is the fate of the helpless when they are in the hands of the wicked.

3. Treating secularism as a possible alternative for understanding reality. This approach instantly rejects the redemptive messianic interpretation and the notion of divine providence. At the very least it requires a revision of traditional conventions.
4. Unwillingness to attribute to the rabbis a supreme knowledge of God and the Torah, the kind of knowledge that would enable them to explain the divine intentions underlying current historical and political moves.

In the course of a discussion I led with some members of the Religious Kibbutz Movement, I asked their opinion about the lessons of the Holocaust and whether they can point to any indications of them in the Religious Kibbutz Movement. Naturally, I got various answers, for the Religious Kibbutz Movement is not made of one piece. The following comments, however, are noteworthy: Relatively speaking, there is only a small number of written publications on this issue in the periodicals published by the religious kibbutzim. On the whole, however, the communal and ideological structure of the Religious Kibbutz Movement seems to reflect a general response to the Holocaust. This finds its expression in sensitivity to human rights; sensitivity to the use of aggressive force; a sense of duty with respect to the communal rehabilitation of the Jewish society; a principled willingness to take a critical stand toward the religious leadership; and the cultivation of modesty and humility with regard to the pretension to explain the Holocaust in religious terms.

Warren Zev Harvey

Warren Zev Harvey was born in New York in 1943. He received his B.A. from Columbia University in 1965 and his Ph.D. in philosophy from the same institution in 1973. After finishing his graduate studies, he began his teaching career at McGill University in Montreal, Canada, where he taught between 1971 and 1977. In the late 1970s, he accepted an offer from the Hebrew University of Jerusalem and has taught there ever since, working his way up the ladder from lecturer to full professor. A specialist in medieval Jewish philosophy, he is the author of *Physics and Metaphysics in Hasdai Crescas* (1998) and of numerous articles on Judah Halevi, Maimonides, Spinoza, and other medieval and modern Jewish philosophers. In addition, he has served as coeditor of *Tarbiz*, the Hebrew quarterly for Jewish studies (1992–1996), and as director of Misgav Yerushalayim, the Center for the Study of the Sephardi and Oriental Jewish Heritage (1996–2000). He has also been a visiting professor at the École Pratique des Hautes Études, Paris; the École des Hautes Études en Sciences Sociales, Paris; the University of Pennsylvania; Queens College, New York; Yeshiva University; and Yale University.

SELECTION

In the essay reprinted here, first given at a conference sponsored by the Memorial Foundation for Jewish Culture in Ashkelon, Israel, in 1999, Warren Zev Harvey seeks to defend a "rational-philosophic" approach, as compared to a "mythic-kabbalistic" approach, to the problem of evil. The mythic-kabbalistic explanatory paradigm, which has been championed, for example, by the great scholar of Jewish mysticism Gershom Scholem (d. 1982), treats evil as a real and serious problem, characterized by and explained by reference to Satan or the *Sitra Aḥra* ("the left side" in kabbalistic imagery and language). Alternatively, rationalist philosophers, like the great medieval thinker Maimonides (1135–1204), treat evil as a privation, a metaphysical nonentity. Harvey suggests that Scholem and others favor the mythic-kabbalistic view both because they find the rational-philosophic approach to be unhelpful in the face of adversity and because they understand the mythic-kabbalistic stance as advancing an explanation of reality that is more in consonance with the human experience of evil. In defense of Maimonides, Harvey explains what Maimonides means when he defines evil as a privation. Evil and evil acts occur due to an absence of knowledge by human beings. Evil acts such as "wars, oppression, terror, and murder are a result of ignorance." Thus, while it may be psychologically comforting to locate the sources of evil outside of ourselves, as is done in the mythic-kabbalistic approach, it is practically and morally more helpful to understand evil as a consequence of human behavior, that is, as something that can be combated and defeated by active strategies such as education. While the mythic-kabbalistic position encourages resignation in the face of evil, for evil is not caused by men and women but by cosmic powers, the rational-philosophic position emphasizes human responsibility for what occurs.

Selected Bibliography

Books by Warren Zev Harvey

Physics and Metaphysics in Hasdai Crescas (Amsterdam, 1998).
Edited with M. Ben-Sasson, Y. Ben-Naeh, and Z. Zohar. *Studies in a Rabbinic Family: The De Botons* (Jerusalem, 1998).

Two Jewish Approaches to Evil in History

In his classic book *Major Trends in Jewish Mysticism*, Gershom Scholem, who was not only a historian of the kabbalah but also, to use the expression of Moshe Idel, a "theoretician of the kabbalah," contrasts the approaches of kabbalah and Jewish philosophy. His contrast amounts to an appreciation of the kabbalah and a critique of Jewish philosophy. One focus of his contrast is the problem of evil in history. The theoretician of the kabbalah writes as follows:

> The fact of the existence of evil in the world is the main touchstone of [the] difference between the philosophic and the kabbalistic outlook. On the whole, the philosophers of Judaism treat the existence of evil as something meaningless in itself.... To most kabbalists... the existence of evil is... one of the most pressing problems, and one which keeps them continuously occupied with attempts to solve it. They have a strong sense of the reality of evil.... They do not, like the philosophers, seek to evade its existence with the aid of a convenient formula.[1]

Scholem often returned to this theme. In his celebrated article "Kabbalah" in the *Encyclopaedia Judaica*, he formulated it as follows:

> The question of the origin and nature of evil was one of the principal motivating forces behind kabbalistic speculation. In the importance attached to it lies one of the basic differences between kabbalistic doctrine and Jewish philos-

ophy, which gave little original thought to the problem of evil.[2]

In the alleged philosophic view that the existence of evil is "something meaningless in itself," Scholem saw a clear expression of the irrelevance of philosophy to the fundamental existential concerns of human beings. He writes, in the aforementioned discussion in *Major Trends*, about how Jewish philosophy lost touch with flesh-and-blood human beings:

> Kabbalism... did not turn its back on the primitive side of life, that all-important region where mortals are afraid of life and in fear of death, and derive scant wisdom from rational philosophy. Philosophy ignored these fears... and in turning its back upon the primitive side of man's existence, it paid a high price in losing touch with him altogether. For it is cold comfort to those who are plagued by genuine fear and sorrow to be told that their troubles are but the workings of the imagination.[3]

Scholem's accusation against Jewish philosophy is grave. By ignoring primitive human fears, the philosophers made themselves utterly irrelevant. Whereas the kabbalists had something important to say to suffering human beings, the philosophers did not: *For it is cold comfort to those who are plagued by genuine fear and sorrow to be told that their troubles are but the workings of the imagination.*

1. Gershom Scholem, *Major Trends in Jewish Mysticism* (New York, 1941), pp. 35–36.

2. *Encyclopaedia Judaica*, vol. 10 (Jerusalem, 1972), p. 583.
3. Scholem, *Major Trends*, p. 35.

The main medieval target of Scholem's comments about Jewish philosophy is the greatest of all medieval Jewish philosophers, Moses Maimonides (1135–1204). In his *Guide of the Perplexed*, part III, chapter 10, Maimonides had indeed written that evil is a "privation" or "nonexistence" (Arabic: *'adam*; Ibn Tibbon's Hebrew translation: *he'der*); and he had argued in *Guide*, part I, chapter 2, that the notions of "good" and "evil" are not objects of the intellect, and a purely rational individual could not even conceive of them. Moreover, in *Guide*, III.12, he attributes the multitude's obsession with the problem of evil to their "imagination."

If Maimonides was Scholem's main medieval target, his main target among the modern Jewish philosophers was Hermann Cohen (1842–1918), whose approach to evil may have been influenced more by Maimonides than by Kant. He quotes Cohen as stating in his *Ethics of Pure Will* that "evil is nonexistent," and "a power of evil exists only in myth."[4]

In responding to Cohen's statement of the alleged position of the Jewish philosophers, Scholem fastens onto his use of the word "myth." Myth does not have for Scholem the same negative connotations that it had for Cohen. He sees myth as being connected to "the primitive side of man's existence," that is, as being connected to the most profound human emotions, to true human life. He then addresses himself to the conflict between philosophy and myth implicit in Cohen's statement:

> One may doubt the philosophic truth of [Cohen's] statement [that a power of evil exists only in myth], but assuming its truth it is obvious that something can be said for "myth" in its struggle with "philosophy."[5]

In other words, it may or may not be true that a power of evil exists in reality; but even if it does not, the mythic approach to evil has some advantages over the philosophic approach. The main advantage, of course, is that myth addresses itself to the fears that inhabit "the primitive side of

man's existence," while philosophy is irrelevant to them. Having expressed his sympathy with myth in its struggle against philosophy, Scholem reminds us that the kabbalists are "true seal-bearers of the world of myth."[6]

I should like now to say some words about the two Jewish approaches to evil suggested in Scholem's comments: the mythic-kabbalistic approach and the rational-philosophic approach. To be sure, Scholem's distinction between "the kabbalists" and "the philosophers" is overly simplistic. Not all kabbalists fit his description of "kabbalists," and not all philosophers fit his description of "philosophers." Nonetheless, there is a heuristic advantage in this simplicity, and so I shall accept his distinction as is, without calling attention to counterexamples.

Let me begin by trying to clarify briefly what the philosophers mean by saying that evil is a privation or nonexistence. I wish to defend reason against myth, philosophy against kabbalah, Maimonides against Scholem. In our urgent search, after the Holocaust, for an understanding of the problem of evil in history, I believe that we have a need to turn to Maimonides and our other Jewish philosophers, and it is at our peril that we turn to our kabbalistic mythmakers.

Evil as a Privation versus Evil as a Power

Maimonides teaches that evil is not a power, but a privation. What about the Satan of our myths, who is admittedly mentioned in the Bible? Is not Satan the power of evil? To dispel such ideas, Maimonides cites a rabbinic dictum: "Satan, the evil inclination, and the angel of death are one and the same" (B. T. *Baba Batra* 16[a]). Satan is thus not an independent power, but a literary personification of the psychological principle known as the "evil inclination" (Hebrew: *yetzer ha-ra'*).[7] Maimonides further explains that "the imagination . . . is the evil inclination."[8] "Satan" would thus seem to be a mere metaphor for the imagination. It is

4. Scholem, *Major Trends*, p. 36. On p. 355, Scholem cites *Ethik des reinen Willens*, 2d ed. (Berlin, 1907), p. 452.
5. Scholem, *Major Trends*, p. 36.
6. Scholem, *Major Trends*, p. 36.
7. Maimonides, *The Guide of the Perplexed*, translated by S. Pines (Chicago, 1963), III.22, p. 489.
8. Maimonides, *Guide of the Perplexed*, II.12, p. 280.

not clear whether Maimonides means that Satan is the faculty of imagination, the act of imagination, or the imaginary object. He may mean that Satan is "privation" or "nonexistence," which is the object of the faculty of imagination (since what does not exist cannot be known by the intellect, but only imagined).[9] In any case, Satan is the cause of hallucinations, delusions, fantasies, irrational thoughts, and—yes—myths. The name "Satan," Maimonides reminds us, comes from the root *satoh*, meaning "to stray" or "to deviate."[10] Satan represents the psychological principle that leads us astray from the way of reason. Understood thus, Satan is not a product of myth, but myths are a product of Satan.

The identification of Satan with the privation of reason fits the following passage from *Guide*, III.11, in which Maimonides speaks about the causes of the evils that human beings wreak upon other human beings:

> The great evils that come about between the human individuals who inflict them upon one another because of purposes, desires, opinions, and beliefs, are all . . . consequent upon privation [or nonexistence]. For all of them derive from ignorance, I mean a privation of knowledge. . . . For through the cognition of truth, enmity and hatred are removed, and the inflicting of harm by people on one another is abolished.
>
> [Scripture] holds out this promise, saying, "And the wolf shall dwell with the lamb . . . ," and so on [Isaiah 11:6–8]. Then it gives the reason for this, saying that the cause of the abolition of these enmities, these discords, and these tyrannies will be the knowledge that human beings will then have concerning the true reality of the Deity. For it says: "They shall not hurt nor destroy in all My holy mountain, for the earth shall be full of the knowledge of the Lord, as the waters cover the sea" [Isaiah 11:9].[11]

Maimonides explains that the great evils human beings [have] inflict[ed] upon other human beings in history are a result of a privation or a nonexistence—the privation or nonexistence of knowledge. Wars, oppression, terror, and murder are a result of ignorance. Rational human beings know that peace and cooperation are necessary in order to fulfill their true physical and spiritual needs. Irrational human beings, motivated by their imaginary desires, by their delusions, that is, by the psychological principle personified in the Bible by Satan, do not know how to cooperate with other human beings, but quarrel with them, hurt them, oppress them, and murder them. Maimonides defines the messianic era as that time when reason, the rule of God, will be victorious over delusion, the rule of Satan.

For Maimonides, the problem of evil in history is not fundamentally a metaphysical problem, but a psychological and political one. It is a problem concerning human behavior.

If the evils human beings inflict upon each other in history are the result of the privation of knowledge, then there are measures we can take to prevent them. We can give our children a strong education in the sciences in order to develop their reason and to protect them against the delusions of the imagination. We can teach them ethics, and explain to them the importance of peace and cooperation. We can run our political communities in accordance with reason, not delusion, and we can take prudent and firm action against irrational individuals who would foment hate, strife, and violence.

Interpreting the verse "Our fathers sinned and are no more" [Lamentations 5:7], which refers to the destruction [in 586 BCE] of the First Temple by the Babylonians, Maimonides writes that our ancestors sinned in that they consulted astrologers instead of studying the art of war. Therefore, Maimonides continues, the prophets called them "fools and dolts" [Jeremiah 4:22]. Their *sin* was that they were *fools and dolts*, who thought they could defeat the invading Babylonians by astrology instead of by the art of war. Their sin was their irrationality, and their punishment was the destruction of the Temple and the

---

9. In identifying the imagination with the evil inclination, Maimonides does not use the arabic term *mutakhayyilah*, which usually denotes the imaginative faculty, but *khayy_l*, which may refer to the phantasm or the imagining.

10. Maimonides, *Guide of the Perplexed*, III.22, p. 489.
11. Maimonides, *Guide of the Perplexed*, III.11, pp. 440–441.

Babylonian captivity. The evil of the destruction and the captivity was caused by a privation, the privation of reason.[12]

The kabbalistic or mythic idea of evil in history is, as Scholem rightly observed, much different from that of the philosophers. For the kabbalists, evil is not a privation but a real entity, and Satan is not a metaphor but a cosmic power. Satan is the power of evil. He is known also as the Other Side, or *Sitra Aḥra*, that is, the rival of the Divine. As God is present in the universe by means of His ten emanations, or *sefirot*, so the Other Side is composed of ten alternative *sefirot*, which are a sort of shadow government challenging the rule of the King of the universe. Satan is so powerful that he poses a threat to God Himself.

For the kabbalists, in contrast to Maimonides, the problem of evil in history is not fundamentally a psychological or political one, but a metaphysical one.

Action versus Comfort

Scholem ridiculed the philosophic approach to evil, saying: "[I]t is cold comfort to those who are plagued by genuine fear and sorrow to be told that their troubles are but the workings of the imagination." It is presumably more comforting to be told that the evils that plague us are the workings of the *Sitra Aḥra*. There is perhaps comfort in the belief that we human beings are not primarily responsible for the evils that befall us. It is consoling to imagine that we could not have prevented them, for they were wrought by a power who can be defeated only by God. The kabbalists do say that we can assist God in his apocalyptic war against the *Sitra Aḥra* by praying and doing pious deeds. However, in the end, the belief that the *Sitra Aḥra* is the cause of the evils that afflict us leads to a severe diminution of human responsibility.

The kabbalah, like astrology, may provide comfort in the face of evil, at least in the short run. However, this comfort is achieved at the price of ignorance of the true causes of our plight

12. Maimonides, "Letter on Astrology," in *Medieval Political Philosophy*, edited by R. Lerner and M. Mahdi (Glencoe, Ill., 1963), p. 229.

and of a consequent inability to ameliorate it. By turning the problem of evil in history into a metaphysical problem, the kabbalists drew attention away from its true psychological and political causes.

The Maimonidean philosophers, unlike the kabbalists and the astrologers, were not primarily concerned about providing comfort as a response to evil. They were more concerned about *preventing* evil. They were concerned about human *responsibility*, and the awareness of human responsibility often causes discomfort, not comfort. They insisted that the source of the evils that human beings inflict upon one other is not in some external Satan, but inside the human beings themselves. Since the source of evils is human, we humans can prevent them. *We are responsible.* One can prevent evils by acting in accordance with reason. One prevents defeat in war not by consulting horoscopes or writing amulets with the names of the proper *sefirot* on them, but by studying the art of war. Maimonides and his followers sought to understand the psychological and political causes of evil in history in order to determine what *actions* need to be taken in order to prevent its recurrence.

The kabbalah and Maimonidean philosophy do represent two opposing approaches to the problem of evil in history. If the former tried to comfort the people with myth, the latter tried to improve their situation with reason.

The Holocaust

The kabbalistic approach, according to which the Holocaust was caused by the *Sitra Aḥra*, implies that the prevention of future tyranny and genocide is not primarily in the hands of us human beings. Human beings were not responsible for the Holocaust and are not responsible for preventing a future Holocaust. As opposed to the kabbalistic approach, the Maimonidean one begins with the fact that the evils of the Holocaust were perpetrated by human beings against human beings and could have been prevented by human beings. It seeks to understand the psychological and political causes of those evils, that is, to identify the privations of knowledge that made them possible. To understand how the Holocaust came about is to understand how a future Holocaust can be prevented.

It was a desire to restrain the mythical interpretation of the Holocaust that in recent years led the survivor-author Ka tzetnik to question his own powerful and unforgettable description of "the planet Auschwitz," whose laws of nature differ from those on our planet. Auschwitz, he now stressed, was run by human beings, not Satan, and was located here on earth.[13]

That regular human beings are capable of great evil is the true horror that Maimonides, unlike the kabbalists, dared to face squarely.

Arendt versus Scholem

In my comments until now, I have been responding to Gershom Scholem in the name of the Jewish philosophers. Let me now conclude by quoting a famous response to Scholem given to him in his lifetime by an important Jewish philosopher.

In the fascinating exchange of letters between Gershom Scholem and Hannah Arendt in 1963 concerning Arendt's *Eichmann in Jerusalem*, Scholem took exception to Arendt's thesis about "the banality of evil." He did not understand how Arendt, who in the past had written eloquently and eruditely about "radical evil," could now affirm the contrary thesis: Evil was not radical but banal. She replied to him as follows:

> You are quite right: I changed my mind and do no longer speak of "radical evil." ... It is indeed my opinion now that evil is never "radical," that it is only extreme, and that it possesses neither depth nor any demonic dimension. It can overgrow and lay waste the whole world precisely because it spreads like a fungus on the surface. It is "thought-defying" ... because thought tries to reach some depth, to go to the roots, and the moment it concerns itself with evil, it is frustrated because there is nothing. That is its "banality." Only the good has depth and can be radical.[14]

With these words, Arendt was responding not only to Scholem's remarks in his letter to her, but in effect also to his pro-kabbalistic and anti-Maimonidean statements about the problem of evil in *Major Trends in Jewish Mysticism* and elsewhere. Evil, she asserted, has no demonic dimension; "there is nothing." Alluding to those rare individuals who during the Nazi regime bravely acted to save Jews, she concluded: "Only the good ... can be radical."

13. See the testimony of Yeḥiel Dinur or De-Nur (Ka tzetnik) at the Eichmann trial in Jerusalem, session 68, 7 June 1961; and see his *Shivitti*, translated by E. N. De-Nur and L. Herman (New York, 1987), pp. 106–109. Ka tzetnik, who died in 2001, expressed reservations about his phrase "the planet Auschwitz" on various occasions during his last years.

14. Hannah Arendt, *The Jew as Pariah*, edited by R. H. Feldman (New York, 1978), pp. 245, 250–251.

Shalom Rosenberg

Shalom Rosenberg (b. 1937) was, until his retirement in 2005, professor of Jewish philosophy at the Hebrew University of Jerusalem. He emigrated to Israel from Argentina as a teenager and did his undergraduate and graduate studies at Hebrew University, specializing in medieval Jewish philosophy. He received his doctorate in 1974 for a dissertation on "Logic and Ontology in Jewish Philosophy in the Fourteenth Century." In addition to his regular teaching appointments at Hebrew University, he has been a visiting professor at Harvard; the Universidad Ibero-America in Mexico; the University of São Paulo, Brazil; and the Urbaniane in Vatican City, Rome. His academic research has centered around three issues: (1) the history of logic in Hebrew medieval sources; (2) the relationship between modern philosophy and Jewish thought especially as this bears on notions of revelation; and (3) the relationship between religion and ethics within the Jewish tradition. In addition, he has been involved in educational activities that seek to integrate the texts and values of medieval and modern Jewish thought into the wider Israeli cultural mainstream. He has written and edited several volumes that address this significant social issue.

SELECTION

The essay "The Holocaust: Lessons, Explanation, Meaning," first presented at a conference sponsored by the Memorial Foundation for Jewish Culture in Ashkelon, Israel, in 1999, represents a very personal response by Shalom Rosenberg to the philosophical and theological issues raised by the *Shoah*. As he understands these matters, a personal response is the only appropriate stance given what he perceives as the "sacred" character of "the memory of the Holocaust." Rosenberg feels strongly that using the Holocaust in any way, or deriving any sort of "lessons" from it, whether political, philosophical, or otherwise, constitutes a profane act.

Rosenberg contends that the Holocaust was a unique event that cannot be completely explained logically or through recourse to historical causes, nor by introducing such elements as racial theory and the concept of genocide. The Holocaust is more than an extreme manifestation of anti-Semitism which, unlike the *Shoah*, can be accounted for sociologically, psychologically, and theologically. Indeed, he holds that the destruction of European Jewry can only truly be called "an incarnation of the Devil" given what he understands to be its absurdity and the absolute evil that it represents. However, this identification of the Holocaust as demonic does not excuse those who perpetrated the deeds to which we here refer.

Rosenberg, furthermore, holds that the identification of the Holocaust as demonic entails a significant implication for Jews. The Holocaust was a war against Jews and everything or everyone identified as Jewish simply because of their Jewishness. In this, he argues, it differed from the Nazi assault against other groups. Only the Jews were selected by the Nazis as absolutely "other." As such, they must be understood as the preeminent enemy of Satan and the ally of God and the good. This distinctive interpretation of the *Shoah* still leaves us, in the face of the death camps and *Einsatzgruppen* (Nazi murder squads), in a flawed world and quite possibly without faith in divine reward and punishment on earth, but it reminds us that the Jewish people do have a "Divine mission" and a special destiny, the exact nature of which remains "the greatest riddle of our lives."

Selected Bibliography

Books and Articles by Shalom Rosenberg

"Identity and Ideology in Contemporary Jewish Thought," *Tefuzot Hagolah* 77–78 (Summer 1975): 5–15 [Hebrew].

"And Thou Shalt Walk in His Ways," in *Israeli Philosophy*, edited by Moshe Hallamish and Asa Kasher (Tel Aviv, 1983), pp. 72–92 [Hebrew].

"Ethics," in *Contemporary Jewish Religious Thought*, edited by Arthur A. Cohen and Paul Mendes-Flohr (New York, 1987), pp. 195–202.

Torah and Science (Jerusalem, 1988) [Hebrew].

Good and Evil in Jewish Thought (Tel Aviv, 1989).

"Our Generation and the Faith of Israel," *Shdemoth* 107 (1989): 85–98 [Hebrew].

Edited with Benjamin Ish-Shalom. *The World of Rav Kook's Thought* (New York, 1991).

In the Footsteps of the Kuzari (Jerusalem, 1991) [Hebrew].

Not in Heaven (Jerusalem, 1997) [Hebrew].

THE HOLOCAUST: LESSONS, EXPLANATION, MEANING

Just as standing upon sacred ground requires us to remove our shoes, while those entering the Holy of Holies must remove any golden garments, so do I feel myself obligated, when writing about the Holocaust, to so to speak remove my academic robe—and to declare that I am not speaking in the name of any academic discipline, but purely in terms of my own most intimate feelings, in the sense of "things that come from the heart."[1]

The focus of the present study is theological. But in order to present my arguments fully, I shall first need to relate to the broader context of our attitude to the Holocaust as Jews. In my opinion, an understanding of this subject requires that we confront ideological and cultural categories and frameworks. I shall divide this preliminary discussion into three foci, which I will refer to by the brief and simple rubrics of: lessons, explanation, and meaning.

Zakhor: Remember

I do not think that it would be incorrect to say that the initial religious Jewish reaction to history is to remember. Not an academic or sterile remembrance, but a free, existential remembrance, that penetrates to the innermost part of the human being. Memory sanctifies the historical dimension. Even though nature is not absent from it, the Bible teaches us the centrality of history. Nature and history are intermingled within the Jewish year. But this mingling connects two different concepts of time. Natural time is cyclical; historical time is linear and cannot be turned back. It

1. On the historian's approach, see the important interview with Professor Yehuda Bauer, "A Historian's Viewpoint," *Shoresh* 2 (Nissan 1983): 3–20 [Hebrew], and also Yehuda Bauer and Nathan Rotenstreich, eds., *The Holocaust as Historical Experience* (New York and London, 1981).

does not repeat itself; hence, it is dominated by forgetfulness. The first commandments which Israel was commanded upon leaving Egypt are thus related to the need to preserve this singular historical experience. The paschal sacrifice and the festival of unleavened bread, and in their wake the family *seder* (Passover meal) as known to us, are an attempt to preserve the historical heritage. "To remember the Exodus from Egypt" is thus the first *mitzvah* (commandment). This is the archetypal memory that influences all other remembering.

But the cause of forgetting is rooted not only in the nonrepeatable nature of time and the uniqueness of historical events, but also in the transience of human existence. One generation goes and another generation comes. Beneath the external facade of stability, the nation and the society change their essence after only a few years. Individual memory cannot be the guarantor for the possibility of collective memory. Collective memory is not a natural phenomenon, but a cultural and educational imperative.

"When your son shall ask you tomorrow" provides the surety of collective memory. But the opposite thesis—namely, that the Torah speaks of four different types of sons—indicates that memory depends upon the existential identity of the inquirer and of the one remembering. Even prior to memory there must be a certain identification that determines whether what we are remembering is in fact our own memory. In the archetypal memory, we must ask whether we are in fact the successors of that same generation which went out of Egypt. The answer is found in the call in the *Haggadah* (Passover text), "In each generation a man person must see himself as if he went out of Egypt, as is said, 'And you shall tell your son on that day, saying, Because of this the Lord did for me when I went out of

Egypt.'" The *Haggadah* emphasizes that even after many generations the father must say "for me." Memory is thus inextricably connected with the issue of identity that transcends history. I remember in the first person—both my own memories and those of my people. Before I remember I must know myself and my identity, what is mine and what is not.

One of the central elegies recited on the Ninth of *Av* [the traditional day on which the First and Second Temple were destroyed] is built upon the contrast between "when I went out of Egypt" and "when I went out of Jerusalem." "Remember what Amalek did to you" intermingles with "to remember the Exodus from Egypt." The memory of the Holocaust is another archetypal memory: "In each generation a person must see himself as if he is part of the saven remnant, in the sense of, 'You shall tell your son on that day, saying, 'The Lord did this for me when I went out of Auschwitz.' For, 'If I had been there then, I would not have been redeemed.'" Here too, as we shall see, the question of identity is a crucial issue.[2]

Memory is based upon identity, but it also creates identity. This brings us to the second component of memory. Not the "for me," but the "what." What do we need to remember? And how? We do not remember an inchoate event. Before remembering it, we need to give it a structure.

I will not go into the philosophical question of the method of "constructing" events. Nor shall I relate to the school of the classical historians, trained on and guided by scientific objectivity, nor that of the new historians who think, like Nietzsche, that "no facts exist, but only interpretations."[3] Yet for us there is no meaningful difference.[4] Even if we agree that a purely historical realm does exist, we must state that this "construction" of the historical event is in our

2. In this fact is rooted, of course, the critical difference between Jewish memory and that of the nations. The nations of the world can identify with the memory of the martyrs; in a deep sense, we are those who identify with them.
3. *The Will to Power*, trans. and ed. Walter Kaufman (New York, 1968), §481.
4. It is interesting to analyze the ideological zigzags used by the new historians in their discussions of the

Holocaust. Application to the Holocaust of the method they use with regard to Zionism would entail approval of historical revisionism and legitimization of Holocaust denial. As we shall see below, in this respect too, the Holocaust is a turning point that casts doubt upon philosophies and upon methodologies.

case problematic. This brings us to the issue of the "lessons" and their pitfalls.

Lessons and Dangers

From the outset, I must say that I "derive" a Zionist "lesson" from the Holocaust, but I am prepared to forgo it. In retrospect, I refuse in the deepest and most existential way to "derive" lessons from the Holocaust altogether. I shall attempt to explain my reasoning and arguments.

Let us begin with the initial point to which I alluded above. The lesson derived from the Holocaust is often, though not always, a function of the world view of the person deriving the lesson. However, there is no doubt that the Holocaust left behind it an imperative that is the collective lesson of the Jewish people, which is the legitimacy and need for Jewish politics. First of all [is the need for a] worldwide Jewish politics—the establishment of the Jewish state, that is, the construction of a political entity that not only returned the Jewish people to the stage of political activity, but also gave it the prerogatives of power insofar as possible. But more than that: It gave legitimacy to the Jewish politics of Jewish communities in the diaspora, wherever possible. And this, notwithstanding the danger of dual loyalty.[5]

This returns us to another claim made at times, in my opinion unjustifiably. According to this argument, we have committed a sin—sin in a certain sense, but sin nevertheless—in repressing the awareness of the Holocaust during the first years following the war. The harsh initial shock was followed by a period of repression during which any significant confrontation with the traumatic experience of the Holocaust was absent. This description is both incomplete and factually incorrect.

The *Shoah* experience in all its seriousness broke out within the life of the Jewish people. The rendering of accounts with those who served as *kapos* in the death camps and the Kastner trial (see part II, p. 214 n.15 for details) are only a few examples. But there is undoubtedly a deeper reason. The initial period after the Holocaust was guided by the awareness that we needed to devote ourselves to creating a practical answer to the Holocaust—to resolve the fundamental problem that enabled the Holocaust to take place as it did—by the establishment of the State of Israel. Precisely the thought that we were able to return to "normality" was the strongest Jewish reaction following the Holocaust. Just as the Jews in the Holocaust discovered a new significance to resisting the enemy, so did the Jewish people instinctively understand that there was meaning to the struggle for life, that biological existence bears ideological significance. Now, decades later, we can again ask about the meaning of the trauma, since we also enjoy the perspective of the State. The return to the search for meaning thus derives from both reasons.

So we stand and ponder our relationship to the Holocaust. Seemingly, matters are quite clear. The differences that separate and divide all of us, including thinkers and scholars, into different camps are erased in moments of grace, in light of the memory of the Holocaust. The Holocaust is the symbol and the event that unites all of us. All of us were candidates for Auschwitz. But we are witnesses to a terrible phenomenon: that at times the lessons of the Holocaust not only fail to unite us, but even divide us; that it is harnessed to horses that gallop in different and at times opposing directions. The respect due to the Holocaust, to the saving remnant and the memory of the martyrs, obligates us, in my opinion, to refrain from any use of this symbol in arguments and disputes having a political component and practical contemporary

5. There are those who point toward the attitude of the Jewish people toward the Jews of the Soviet Union as one of the results of the new consciousness that was born after the Holocaust. But this argument is in my opinion not valid. The process to which I refer is illustrated well by the organizations of American Jewry, albeit there one finds a fortuitous coinciding of interests. For example, the struggle on behalf of Soviet Jewry advanced the interests of the Jewish people, but since the processes against which they struggled occurred on the soil of the main political and ideological adversary of the United Sates, it was popular not only as a Jewish cause but also as suitable to the American identity of those engaged in the struggle. We can easily imagine a different scenario in which, God forbid, the meaning of the struggle would be put to a more serious test. The same holds true regarding the attitude to the State of Israel.

implications. Let us leave the lesson of the Holocaust on the individual level, as something of profound existential meaning, but refrain from drawing political conclusions, be they in the negative or the positive sense.

What is meant by refraining from this positive step? I again emphasize that, deep within my heart of hearts, I would prefer without hesitation to derive from it the Zionist lesson, primarily because Zionism spoke in a vague way of the danger of such a catastrophe from its very inception.[6] But despite all this it seems to me that, even within this Zionist context, the use of the symbol of the Holocaust demands that we engage in deeper thought. We often begin our Zionist information with the Holocaust. The visit of a foreign personality to Israel begins with a visit to Yad Vashem, or a Zionist educational film may begin with modern anti-Semitism and the horrors of the Holocaust. In my opinion, such a connection between the Holocaust and Zionism entails a certain degree of distortion of the contents, as well as a tactical error.

Distortion and error, for if the Holocaust provided a strong impetus to the struggle to establish the State, our Zionism does not begin with the Holocaust: It did not set out to solve the European Jewish problem by creating a problem in the Middle East, as is frequently emphasized by the Arab propagandists. Zionism is not sustained by the Holocaust. Moreover, even the connection between Zionism and anti-Semitism is in my eyes problematic. Zionism is none other than our generations-old struggle to return to our homeland. In light of all this, it seems to me that we are closer in our approach to the classic harbingers of Zionism than we are to the Zionism that was born in the wake of modern anti-Semitism. This was the stance of those people who felt that, just as Rome was liberated, so does Jerusalem need to be liberated. Sadly, one might also say the opposite: that we as Zionists live in the Land of Israel, and will continue to live here, notwithstanding the

fact that, in the words of the late Yeshayahu Leibowitz, the Land of Israel is evidently the most dangerous place for Jews to live.[7] Our state is not a giant refugee camp, but the birthplace of a people struggling for its national liberation who are fed up with living under foreign rule.

Thus far [I have written] regarding the positive side in the remembrance of the Holocaust. However, one may easily demonstrate that at times the consciousness of the Holocaust can be specifically negative. This may be exemplified by two illustrations. During the Lebanon war (in 1982), the identification between the Holocaust and our own destiny worked against us. Without going into a discussion of the problem per se, I may exemplify my words through two contrasting incidents that embody the problematics of which I am speaking. It seems to me that, underlying the attitude toward the Maronites (Christians) in Lebanon, there was a conscious or unconscious sense of identification: that we, as the victims who during a time of destruction did not enjoy any help from an apathetic world, may not stand aside when others find themselves in a similar situation. On the other hand, there seems no doubt that the reaction to that war of many of the nations of the world was guided by the desire to prove that, when they have the power, the children of the victims are no better than the hangmen. Sabra and Shatilla were understood as a kind of purification of the acts done at Auschwitz. The true atonement was attained through the acts of the former victim, who played the part of the hangman. By way of analogy, one might say that the traumas of the children of those saved troubles our collective "I." We are guilty for having survived. We need to be different from everyone else, purer in our politics, without any marks or stains, for if not, what right do we have to complain about the Holocaust?

But the distortion does not only derive from the outside, from the world of the nations. A striking example of this may be found, for example,

6. The comments of the late Professor Jacob Katz as to the impossibility of anticipating the Holocaust are irrelevant in this context. Jabotinsky's remarks about Bartholemew Night (August 24, 1572) were more than prophetic and were sufficient to awaken us to a Zionist lesson. The same is true of the words of other Zionist leaders. See

Jacob Katz, "Was the Holocaust Predictable?" in Bauer and Rotenstreich, eds., *The Holocaust*, pp. 23–41.
7. Leibowitz's struggle to separate Zionism from the Holocaust, even though it was in my opinion a justified struggle, prevented him from properly seeing the rebirth of anti-Semitism literally before his eyes.

in Yehoshua Sobol's play *Ghetto*.[8] Nazism was not only an external circumstance, but also an inner one. Kittel, the Nazi commander, tells Weisskopf, the organizer of the Jewish labor brigades in the ghetto, in the name of Nazism (p. 41):

> You have made yourself productive. I only created for you the proper conditions, allowing an unknown side of your Jewish nature to be revealed.... The painful, but so fruitful, combination between the German soul and the Jewish soul will yet do great things.

Another protagonist, the Nazi Dr. Poll, tells us that to "the Zionist Jews in Israel... aggressiveness... is not alien to them.... Is this the death impulse, that we have finally succeeded in infusing from our own souls into the Jewish soul?" (p. 93). And so too the Bundist (Jewish socialist), Kruk, director of the ghetto library, tells Gens, the head of the ghetto, "the true Jewish patriot and nationalist" (p. 84):

Kruk: It's a shame that Dr. Poll isn't here. They succeeded more than they imagined to themselves.
Gens: What? what are you talking about?
Kruk: Nationalism inspires nationalism.
Gens: What are you trying to suggest? That I'm influenced by the Germans?!
Kruk: Understand it as you wish.

The message conveyed by these things, in my opinion, is that a terrible process occurred in the Zionist state, whereby the victims internalized the aggression of their executioners. Such a use of the Holocaust is not new. It may have originated with [the British historian] Arnold Toynbee [d. 1975], who drew a parallel between, in his view, what the Nazis did to the Jews of Europe and what the Israelis did to the Palestinian Arabs.

Toynbee is of course aware of the quantitative difference, but this does not prevent him from drawing the parallel: While every increase in numbers brings about an increase in human suffering, it is impossible to be more than 100 percent evil. Whether I kill one man or one million, I am a murderer.

This is the decisive question. There is a clear distinction between murder and genocide, just as there is, in my opinion, a difference between genocide and the Holocaust. In any event, these remarks of Toynbee illustrate the significance of a new definition of a crime beyond the far "weaker" or "moderate" crime of murder. It is obvious that any legal or conceptual difficulty arising from such an attempt is not a rebuttal, but rather a sign of the intellectual poverty of the one who is taken aback by this difficulty. This is not only a matter of quantity creating quality, but that we find here a new, essential quality of evil and of crime revealed before our eyes.

The sophistication of such an accusation does not in any way detract from the injury and insult felt when we consider these things in our memory and in our consciousness. And to this insult is added as well a feeling of sacrilege. It is interesting to note Toynbee's response to this insult:

> I have been surprised at the vehemence of the reaction to it in the Jewish community. I have wondered myself why, if it [the comparison between the acts by the Nazis and those of the Israelis] is a preposterous suggestion, as you obviously felt it to be, you haven't said: "Here is [a] silly man, saying this silly thing. Why bother about it? If it is so silly we should leave it alone." But the reaction has not been like that. It has been, as we know, very vigorous.... I would say that, inadvertently, in this comparison I have drawn, I have given the Jewish people a piece of what psychologists call "shock treatment."[9]

Toynbee evidently forgot that, following acts of such a "crazy" coloration, we are more sensitive to dangerous stupidities and unable to ignore them. True, "shock therapy" once more presents us with the terrible dilemma in which we find ourselves. Because we have been victims of a satanic politics, we are now unable to conduct realistic politics. If it is at all permitted for us to return to history, we must live a humane or even utopian politics; anything less than that is a crime that is forbidden for us—and only for us—to perform. If we become like all the nations, we

8. The page numbers are based upon the Hebrew Or-Am edition (Tel Aviv, 1984).

9. Quoted in Yaacov Herzog, *A People That Dwells Alone* (London, 1975), pp. 26–27.

will be Nazis. It is not redundant to emphasize that, of course, international ethics obligates us as well. But the voice of this obligation is not the voice of neurotic ethics that comes from the Holocaust, but a sane voice coming from elsewhere. For us, believers [and] sons of believers, it is the voice of the Holy One blessed be He who speaks to us by means of His prophets and through our own conscience. We hear other voices from the Holocaust. The other nations, which have not been judged for their actions nor for their failures, should not be our judges and should not deal with this trauma of ours!

In light of all these things, and many others of a similar ilk, the demand, perhaps quixotic, to refrain from use of the memory of the Holocaust becomes self-evident, in any event within the context of our internal political disputes. We can learn the Zionist humanistic lessons from other pages in our long history. For the Zionist lesson it suffices to remember the Kishinev pogrom [1903], while for the humane (not humanistic!) lessons we may make use of any of the myriad examples from the history of harsh persecution which we have suffered over the course of many generations. Examination of any page in the history of totalitarianism and fascism will suffice for us to repudiate them.[10]

Nor would I wish to connect the struggle against racism with the Holocaust. I do not think that the Holocaust is identical to racism; moreover, it does not begin with racism, but long before that. It begins with the rape that takes place before our eyes in the streets; it begins with man turning his fellow man into an instrument. The Holocaust was unique in that it synthesized all the varieties of evil together and that each one of them may be exemplified from within it. But despite that it entailed something new. It was more than garden-variety evil. The very substitution of the specific noun "Holocaust" or *Shoah* by the general noun "genocide" is an unforgivable sin.

But despite my instinctive tendencies, I am almost forced to cease using the Holocaust as a weapon, that which we use almost daily to shoot at one another. I refer to the ongoing struggles between the two principal lessons derived from the Holocaust: the Zionist and the humanistic.[11]

---

10. The humanistic moral underlay the soul searching of Martin Buber conducted in 1939, in the Hebrew essay "Them and Us," one year after the riots in Germany; see his *Teudah ve-Yi'ud*, vol. 2, (Jerusalem, 1959), pp. 296ff. Buber called upon people not to "serve the god of Hitler after calling him by a Hebrew name" (p. 300), and promises in the name of a hidden providence that "he who performs the act of Hitler—will be obliterated together with him." It is interesting that Buber offers an economic explanation for what happened to our people in Europe: "The problematic of the relationship of Jews to the economy of the dominant peoples . . . whose participation therein begins, usually, not on the ground level but on the second story" (p. 298). According to him, the responsibility does not fall upon the German people but on "the German state," that is, the organization that the German people establishes for itself or agrees to, or "on those forces that it places over itself or that it suffers, and not on the German people itself" (p. 296). Again, that which may have been true regarding the stage before the war is not correct regarding the Holocaust itself. The tragedy of this moral from what occurred in Europe is that the desire to build a non-exilic society in Israel led us, without a doubt, to turn our minds away from the fact that the primary goal, cognitively, was saving Jews, in the simple literal sense.

11. I will not attempt to analyze these arguments here, but wish to emphasize one side of the problem: that there is a fundamental difference between the two lessons learned. The Zionist lesson is descriptive, while the humanitarian lesson is normative. The Zionist lesson is derived from reality itself, while the ethical lesson is concerned with norms—it engenders values. Failure to understand this difference stands out in a grotesque way when one reads the attempts made at times to prove that, because Nazi Germany was undemocratic and unethical, it failed to win the war. Before our eyes there has been woven a new theory of neo-providence that assures that the just, the ethical, and the democratic will be victorious in the final analysis: "In the final analysis the free world defeated the Nazi monster not only by power, but also by spirit." This stance is either naive or absurd. We were not freed because we were in the right, as may be seen by the vain struggle of Spartacus and the slaves who were not freed. From the Exodus we learn of the Passover, but the proper attitude to the stranger and the alien is learned not from the Exodus, but from the memory of our enslavement. The values of the good and the ethical are not instrumental, and [they] obligate us even if they are not successful from a utilitarian viewpoint. The confusion, rooted in cruel reality and which teaches us, quite rightly, that we are surrounded by wolves, requires that we also allow room for faith, in which the norm will be rooted.

These are perhaps ideological battles, but the stances of the thinkers are also reflected in the street. Against the background of social tensions, we occasionally hear such unfortunate expressions as "the job that was not finished." In certain neighborhoods, one can hear cries of "Nazi" used against the police. Advocates of certain policies are called "Judeo-Nazis" by their sharp-tongued opponents. It does not help to invoke talk about a common enemy nor descriptions of the dangers of destruction that confronted Oriental Jews. Such words simply need to be uprooted from our lexicon, for the sake of the spiritual and social hygiene of our environment.

I learned from my teacher, Professor Shoshani, of blessed memory, that the difference between objects used to perform a *mitzvah* and objects that are sacred (*tashmishei-mitzvah* and *tashmishei-kedushah*) lies in the following: that one must continue to treat sacred objects with reverence after one has used them. That is, they are not merely instrumental. By contrast, after one has used a *lulav* (palm branch) and *etrog* (citron), even reciting a blessing upon it, one may do with it as one wishes. By contrast, sacred objects must be hidden away, because they are in a certain sense an end in themselves. Unfortunately, it is clear that the politics that surrounds us on all sides will not agree to a "moratorium," to a "sabbatical year" on the instrumentalization of the memory of the Holocaust. From a religious viewpoint, I wish to say that the memory of the Holocaust is also holy in my eyes! The testimonies and experiences of the survivors, their cries and their testaments, are holy. But the studies of the experts, the theories of the thinkers, and the lessons learned by politicians are the most profane of the profane, if not less than that.

Explanation and Its Lack

Let us leave the political message and turn to the question of its religious meaning. Here too, it seems to me, a kind of moratorium on theories is called for. The various religious positions have been surveyed and analyzed any number of times, and I do not wish to add here to what has already been written. I will only say that at this stage we confront a mystery that has no theological explanation. Of course, this stance sounds apologetic by its very nature but, in my opinion, it is not so. This is so because of the thesis in which I believe and which I shall present without making any attempt to confirm it, a thesis that, notwithstanding the problematics involved, seems to me to be correct: namely, that there is no explanation for the Holocaust. Neither a religious explanation, nor a scientific explanation.

The Holocaust was a historical event, and like any historical event it requires explanation. Why did it take place, and how was it at all possible? In order to explain the above thesis, I wish to argue that we are mistaken when we offer the same explanation for anti-Semitism and for the Holocaust, as they are two entirely different phenomena. One is of course based upon the other, one is the sequel of the other, but they are not identical. For our purposes, there is a fundamental difference between them. I am able to "understand" and possibly even to agree with the psychological, sociological, economic, and even historical explanations of anti-Semitism, but I am unable to understand the Holocaust. We find ourselves confronting a unique and strange phenomenon, which has neither parallel nor explanation. Regarding this issue, we do not even have "retroactive hindsight."[12]

This is a question that thinkers and scholars—whose greatness is beyond doubt—have attempted to answer. They may have succeeded in explaining its background and the operation of its mechanism, but they have not given an explanation of the Holocaust itself, of the absurdity of the why and wherefore. The central lesson that emerges after reading their works is that many—if not the vast majority, or even all of them—have not derived any new lesson from the Holocaust,

12. I shall allow myself to state, with all due reservation and reverence, that ultimately not even fascism or Nazism are to be identified with everything that pertains to the Holocaust. See on this Saul Friedlander's article "On the Possibility of the Holocaust: An Approach to a Historical Synthesis," in Bauer and Rotenstreich, eds., *The Holocaust*, pp. 1–21.

but continue to use accepted theories and categories in order to understand it.

Because of this claim, I expose myself to harsh accusations of mystification and even mythologization of the Holocaust. I shall discuss these concepts further on but, if you wish, I accept the accusation. This is precisely my claim. And I shall formulate things even more sharply: The claim that we are dealing with an embodiment, an incarnation of the Devil in the person of Hitler, may his name be obliterated, seems more rational, and in a certain sense truer, than any other explanations that have been offered.

True, various solutions have been offered to resolve the enigma of explaining the *Shoah*. The most extreme explanation, in my opinion, is the argument that we are dealing here with a collective insanity. The use of this sort of language indicates that this presents a particularly severe problem for the psychologists, and the transition from personal pathology to collective pathology is to my mind extremely problematic. But the real problem lies elsewhere. The father of modern psychology succeeded in finding the key to understanding this "insanity" and in explaining phenomena that seemingly have no meaning whatsoever. He found reason in insanity, thereby creating a science. But the use of insanity in our context is no more than verbal manipulation. True, the term "insanity" is used in everyday language to designate phenomena that have no rational explanation. But here the talk of collective insanity serves the opposite purpose: to obscure, rather than to explain. The same holds true of other terms and concepts taken from the realm of psychology, which are likewise unsatisfactory if we do not assimilate the unique nature of the Holocaust, one that was expressed in a tragic way by the term "a different planet."

Is there in fact a historical explanation for the Holocaust? Are psychologists and sociologists able to explain the facts? My answer is negative, and I will give several examples. One striking example is to be found in the [psychological] approach of Bruno Bettelheim [d. 1990], which we may attempt to understand by way of comparison with another similar approach: the sociological position of Hannah Arendt [d. 1975].[13] The central thesis of both these thinkers may be understood as an attempt to explain the Holocaust as an episode in the struggles of authoritarian regimes to control the world. But this is not all. Bettelheim attempted to explain the camps, where he was "privileged" to live for a certain period. His position may be summarized by saying that he viewed the camps as an attempt on the part of the Nazis to find the means by which it would be possible to change and to influence the masses. Bettelheim saw himself as a laboratory animal in an experiment, in which there was tested in miniature a system which was thereafter to have been applied to the general public, a system based upon total supervision of human beings. Bettelheim thought, as did his teacher Freud, that he had found the logic within the absurd.

He lived in the camp and tried to render an account of his experiences, which belonged essentially to the initial period of Nazi rule. According to his description, an attempt was made in the camp to return the prisoner to the situation of a child, for whom others decide what is permitted and what is forbidden, regarding even the smallest details of life. The purpose of the experiment was to bring him to a state of total loss of his free will as a human being. This was a laboratory intended to accomplish the ultimate goal of Nazism—the transformation of mankind as a whole into a great automaton, who acts, without protest, according to the will of the führer.

13. We shall ignore the problematics of her approach to the Eichmann trial in her book on the subject (*Eichmann in Jerusalem: The Banality of Evil* [New York, 1963]) and the political implications of this stance, and concern ourselves here only with its philosophical implications. See on this Gershom Scholem, "Letter to Hannah Arendt" [Hebrew], in *Devarim bego* (Tel Aviv, 1976), pp. 91–95. Deserving of quotation in this context are Scholem's remarks concerning "the love of Jews, no trace of which I find in you, dear Hannah" (p. 92). Her stance derives from her own sense of identity, which included an intense hatred of Zionism. This hatred found expression in her words about Eichmann, who "became a Zionist." However, it may be that there is another, "suppressed" side to her personality, which finds expression in the testimony of her biographer [Elizabeth Young–Bruehl] concerning her reactions to the Six Day War and the Yom Kippur War.

The most important aspect of Bettelheim's interpretation is the assumption that the persecution of the Jews may be seen as one chapter in a global struggle, in which they were merely guinea pigs. This idea is particularly striking in Hannah Arendt. She sought to describe the mechanism of totalitarianism and of authoritarianism. Totalitarianism is built upon three circles, in which responsibility is confined to a very small group of people, belonging to the innermost circle. In the second circle were those people who happened to be SS members, of whom Eichmann was a prime example. Beyond them were the German people as a whole, with their masses. The paradox in this explanation is that not only were the dead martyrs victims of authoritarianism, but [so too were] the hangmen themselves, whom the system caused to lose their individuality and [who were made] into part of a mere bureaucratic system. Arendt's application of this principle to the Eichmann trial and the basic comparison she draws between the murders and the victims was deeply hurtful, in a way that was almost unforgivable. But Arendt's statements were not intended as a personal reaction to the trial, nor as a historical polemic concerning what happened, but as the application of an ideology that explains the phenomenon and why it took place. The key to her explanation lies in the fact that this was not a uniquely Jewish phenomenon, but that the Jews were merely a small and marginal factor within a far more fundamental experiment.

These explanations are not correct, in my opinion, because there is no continuity between xenophobia and anti-Semitism and the Holocaust. Moreover, that which may have been true concerning the initial expressions of Nazism experienced by Bettelheim does not necessarily hold with regard to its later manifestations. There is no single, great ideology that encompasses within it the possibility of explaining what happened in the Holocaust. It is an empirical fact that there is no narrative to the Holocaust.

Moreover, in the cases noted above, and in many others, the explanation offered is no more than a kind of misleading and "theft" of the Holocaust. This is the same theft that, in a less sophisticated manner, finds expression in monuments to the memory of the victims in which their Jewishness is not mentioned; it is the same theft as is committed by those who proclaim [the convert] Edith Stein [d. 1942] as a Christian saint, notwithstanding the fact that she died because of her being Jewish; it is the same theft that is performed by others on the ideological level.[14]

I now wish to return to the concept which I mentioned above. In the above-mentioned discussion, Professor Yehudah Bauer refers to a semantic question: " 'Mystify' is defined by the dictionary as 'to envelop in excessive secrecy; to obscure or obfuscate.' "[15] One can agree with this lexicographical comment, but there is a decisive difference between "to envelop in excessive secrecy" and "to obscure." When we seek an explanation, we find ourselves confronting an alternative. One may attack the approach of those thinkers who emphasize the unique and demonic nature of the Holocaust as "mystification," but the alternative is, in my eyes, banalization. Banalization not of the crime, but of the explanation: the marshaling of the explanation of the Holocaust to support every ideology in the world. What we have seen regarding the lesson of the Holocaust reappears in our discussion of its explanation. When we speak of uniqueness, we do not mean to deny other tragedies, nor to claim that this is the greatest human tragedy of all times. Indeed, there are more than a few examples of genocide. But no other genocide is the Holocaust. It is unique because of its nature, because of its absurdity, because of its belonging to a different planet. The perception of the Holocaust as unique is not offered in the place of scientific historiography, nor does it refuse to learn the history of the tragic events. However, it does unconditionally refuse to accept pseudo-explanations that are recruited to ideologies or scientific approaches.

There is no doubt in my mind that, as in the case of the lesson, a clear correspondence may be

---

14. The Church faced, in my opinion, two valid options: to canonize a gentile who was killed for his assisting of Jews; or to transform into a saint an "honorary" Christian, a Jew who died as a Jew. But when they canonized a Jewess who had converted, who died because of her Jewishness, they stole her after her murder. The death of Edith Stein was a central point in a play by Rolf Hochhut, *The Deputy* [1963]. His criticism, in this case, did not receive a suitable response.

15. *Hashoah: Hebetim histori'im* (Tel Aviv, 1982), p. 71.

drawn between the explanation and the guiding ideology, and even between the explanation and the Jewish identity of the one offering the explanation. In a certain strange manner, explanations of the type of Hannah Arendt's attempt to prove that the victims of the Holocaust were killed not because they were Jews, but because they represented democracy and liberalism in the eyes of those who developed a regime of dictatorship and authoritarianism. This is an inauthentic reaction, in my opinion, of people who were confronted anew by their Jewishness only by the Holocaust, in a very tragic manner, without finding any meaning to what befell them. The historical Jewish identity, and even the most fundamental categories which related to anti-Semitism and which accompanied this identity, were alien to them. We find here a phenomenon that reappears repeatedly in different guises and reincarnations: the stealing of the Holocaust. As the result of a certain identity, ideology, or philosophy, such thinkers steal the Holocaust from their Jewish brethren, and even from themselves, by erasing the victims' own identity as Jews.[16]

Meaning

The quest for the explanation of the Holocaust exposed us to the cunning of philosophy. What I say here is not intended, Heaven forbid, to cast aspersions upon the important work of scholars and researchers who have enriched our knowledge in this field. Historical science has doubtless succeeded in elevating itself to a high level of objectivity. But once we abandon the "empirical" realm and turn from knowledge of facts and processes to deep understanding and to questions of meaning and significance, we continue to read the same old philosophy of yesteryear. Indeed, in seeking the moral and [the] explanation in the third generation after the Holocaust, there appears a figure characterized not only by distortion but also by ugliness: the person who utilizes the Holocaust in order to learn a lesson and who consciously or unconsciously attempts to harness it to his own petty or "lofty" interests.

But perhaps, as we said above, a third level to our discussion also exists. The work of the Jewish psychologist Victor Frankel [d. 1997] likewise draws upon the experience of the Holocaust, and especially upon his own years in Auschwitz. He learned there, in his words, that man is capable of living even with total lack, but that if one takes away from him one fundamental thing—meaning—then he is lost and is condemned to death. But this is not included among those things that sociologists and psychologists have researched so assiduously.

The Holocaust also reveals to us man seeking meaning, who in his own private realm confronts these questions that at times "cannot be uttered by the mouth."[17] The quest for meaning

---

16. In Emil Fackenheim's thought, the Holocaust serves as a turning point, which returns the individual to his lost Jewish essence. In the earlier approach, Fackenheim emphasizes that beyond the 613 commandments, there is a 614th commandment embodied in the Holocaust—that which prohibits us from giving Hitler any posthumous victories, i.e., the disappearance of the Jewish people. [See part III, pp. 432–439, of this collection.] Such disappearance is a dangerous option that confronts us, even if it will be a "death of the kiss," through assimilation or insufficient birthrate. In his later writings, Fackenheim notes the philosophical significance of the Holocaust: The idea of the 614th commandment teaches us that the *Shoah*, which seemingly erased all meaning, in a radical way gave new meaning to the biological existence of the Jewish people per se. In the Warsaw ghetto, Zionist leader Rabbi Yitzhak Nissenbaum coined the term "sanctity of life": "Previously our enemies demanded our soul, and the Jew sacrificed his body to sanctify the holy

Name; now the enemy demands the Jewish body, and the Jew is required to protect it, to defend it." See G. Eck, *Ha-to'im bedarkei hamavet: Havai vehagut beyemei hakilayon* (Jerusalem, 1960), p. w73.

17. For a survey of personal balance sheets of this type among Holocaust survivors, see the excellent work by Reeve Robert Brenner, *The Faith and Doubt of Holocaust Survivors* (New York and London, 1980). And cf. Yehoshua Eibeschutz, *Bi-kedushah uve-gevurah* (Tel Aviv, 1976); Mordecai Eliav, ed., *Ani ma'amin: Eduyot al ḥayyeihem ve-emunatam shel anshei emunah beyemei hashoah* (Jerusalem, 1969); Rabbi E. Oshri, *She'elot u-teshuvut Mima'amakim*, 3 vols. (New York, 1949–1969); and the collection (no editor) *Emunah ba-Shoah: Iyyun be-mashma'ut ha-Yehudit datit shel ha-Shoah* (Jerusalem, 1980). The reader may find analysis and a comprehensive bibliography on this topic in the M.A. thesis of Moshe Werdiger, "The Holocaust—as Theological Turning Point" [Hebrew], Bar Ilan University, 1996.

repeatedly confronts us with the religious question.

The Holocaust in all its horrors confronts us with a world in which God's face is hidden. The last commandment in the Torah is to teach the children of Israel "The Song." A day will come, we are told there, when "I will hide My face from them, and they will be devoured; and many evils and troubles will befall them, so that they will say on that day, 'Have not these evils found us because God is not among us?'" (Deuteronomy 31:17). The song referred to there is the Song of Moses (Deuteronomy 32; known in Hebrew as *Ha'azinu*), which attempts to teach us to hold fast onto faith even in light of a reality in which "our enemies shall provoke us" and say that "the Lord has not wrought all this" (32:27). I will not enter into an analysis of this chapter, but shall merely note that it points out the consciousness of the religious problematic of history. Despite the way things seem at first glance, Jewish thought, certainly postprophetic thought, did not speak of the history of our people in categories of reward and punishment. It saw the tragedy of history subject to the hand of evil and attempted to teach that there is meaning even in the face of despair. As Rabbi J. B. Soloveitchik [d. 1993] of blessed memory, hinted in his essay "The Voice of My Beloved Knocks" [see part III, pp. 382–393 of this collection], history is a marvelous wall carpet interwoven with pictures of rare beauty, but we look at the carpet from the wrong side.

These things imply, in my opinion, a warning to whoever thinks to understand the secrets of history and of providence. But this is true not only with regard to ourselves, as believing human beings, but also with regard to science. This is so because the Holocaust does not constitute a mystery only from the religious, theological perspective alone. Scientists are also unable to explain what happened. Human understanding, to which everything is lucid and comprehensible, cannot cope with the Holocaust. We can understand evil that is done for some economic or political interest. We can "understand" the dastardly Polish peasant who betrayed a Jew because he wanted his boots. But it is impossible to understand what might be called absolute evil, the forgoing of one's own interest simply in order to do evil: evil as an end in itself. At times we hear the claim that Nazism was a collective insanity. This is precisely the confession of the litigant of the impossibility of answering the question. In this other planet, absolute evil is satanic evil!

And despite all this, the call for meaning cries out to us from hell. And precisely in the wake of this, there is something that speaks to us even from within this terrible Holocaust. One of the conflicts that arises from time to time in relation to the site of Auschwitz relates to determining the nature of the place. Here one must ask a very simple question, to which we have already alluded above. Why did the communists insist on not mentioning that those murdered at Auschwitz were Jews? Why, to this very day, do monasteries strive to establish a foothold in Auschwitz? These questions were a riddle for me, until one day I understood that perhaps the people who insist upon this themselves do not understand their own demands and their own acts.

Were we able to return to Mount Sinai and to see the *Shekhinah* [Divine Presence] descend and declaring, "You are My beloved," we would be able to say that we are the chosen people. Our souls were at Mount Sinai, but we ourselves did not merit this. However, our generation saw something else. We saw Satan descend upon earth and declare of us, the Jewish people, "You are my enemies." And the enemies of Satan are the chosen people.

This is an absurd but true jump, and it is understood by every honest and intelligent person. I have often heard directed toward me the covert or overt expression, "Too bad that the Nazis didn't finish the job." There are anti-Semites in the world, but there are also decent and ethical non-Jews, and they understand that one who was not a candidate to go to Auschwitz does not constitute a spiritual option for humanity. So one needs to invent Christian martyrs whom the Nazis murdered and their presence in the valley of destruction.

What can I tell my son, my daughter, or my students? I am not able to free you from the fears or from the nightmares that afflict me as well from time to time. I can only say that I am proud of two things. That we are the children of those who were murdered and not, Heaven forbid, the children of the murderers, or even the children of those who looked on apathetically or the collaborators. But more than that, Satan appeared and pointed to us as his enemies. Not because of our political affiliation, or because we were a threat to him. Only because we are Jews, even infants or elderly people who could not possibly do any harm. This is the unique significance of the Holocaust, which many people try to deny. Indeed, Satan properly identified his enemies. This is the voice that we hear over and beyond the tragedy and the pain: "They are loathed as absolute evil by absolute evil. In this manner they are indeed the chosen people."[18]

There is no doubt in my mind that my remarks about Satan will sound bizarre and even outlandish to rationalistic ears who will rightly demand an explanation. I do not wish to explain them. I wish the reader to relate to them at this stage not as philosophical claims, but as *aggadah* (nonlegal, more imaginative, material). I also ask of him to consider another possibility, namely, that throughout the darkness of the Holocaust, it may be that the world can be explained only by means of *aggadah* and not by philosophical systems.

The Holocaust and Philosophy

But perhaps, nevertheless, the meaning that I wish to find is no more than mystification? After all, other groups were also persecuted. But we must also take note of the difference. If we were indeed perceived as a biological danger, like the gypsies, why did they persecute Judaism? Why did they desecrate Torah scrolls and all sancta of Israel? If, indeed, the war was waged against an inhuman subspecies, how are we to understand acts of cruelty against parchment scrolls? The war was conducted against a people whose very existence was a symbol and a source of ideas that were diametrically opposed to those of Nazism. Otherwise, we cannot at all comprehend the struggle against Judaism, the ban on Jewish prayer, the war against the symbols of Judaism, against its holy books, against Jewish faces adorned with beards and *payot* (side locks). There was something there that went beyond an economic, historical, or even biological struggle.

To understand the essence of the Holocaust means, first of all, to discover our own Jewish identity "by way of negation," namely, that this was a war against Judaism. Nazism killed us because we were Jews. The Holocaust was not only a biological or political battle: It was a religious and philosophical war.

A profound attempt to deal with this confrontation may be found, in my opinion, in the sermons for *Parshat Zakhor* [Deuteronomy 25:17–19] and Purim [that commemorates the salvation of the Jews in ancient Persia] of the saintly Rabbi Kalman Kalonymus Shapira.[19] Elaborating an earlier ḥasidic idea, the Rebbe of Piaseczno relates to the conflict with philosophy. Amalek is "that which chanced upon you on the way" [Deuteronomy 25:18]—that is, which presented a path, a way of thought, that was an alternative opposed to faith. To this classic motif, another dimension is added. The alternative presented to us is that of human autonomy, namely, "the wisdoms and intellectual structures that they invented . . . from their hearts." The conflict with such autonomy finds tragic expression in the festival of Purim:

> It states in the holy [book] *Tikkunei Zohar* that Purim is compared to Yom Kippur. This may also allude to the fact that, just as on Yom Kippur [Day of Atonement], a person does not perform the fasting and repentance of that day only if he wants to do them, but whether he wants to or not, he fulfills them because such is the edict of the Holy One blessed be He, so is it the case regarding the rejoicing on Purim: not only if the person is himself in a state of joy, or in any event in a state where he is able to make himself feel joyful, must he rejoice, but even if he is in a state of lowliness and broken-heartedness, when his mind and his entire body are downtrodden, it is nevertheless the law that he must bring some spark of joy into his heart.

These things relate to what the Rebbe of Piaseczno said on *Shabbat Zakhor* concerning the confrontation of the Jews with philosophy—doubtless alluding to German philosophy, even if

---

18. In the wonderful words of Theodor Adorno and Max Horkheimer, who prophesied unknowingly. Quoted in *Yesodot ha-Antishemiut u-gevulot ha-ne'orut*, a collection from the Frankfort school (Tel Aviv, 1993), p. 279.

19. *Esh Kodesh* (Jerusalem, 1960), p. 29ff. [See, for more, part I, pp. 38–48 of this collection.]

he did not know it in its full breadth and depth. He describes Judaism as "the commandments and laws of God, whether or not a person may also understand them with his intellect. . . . One who learns it and fulfills it becomes attached to it with all his body and vitality, spirit and soul, until he also sees their goodness a little bit." The same confrontation is expressed in that between Nazism and Judaism:

> They can preach beautifully, but within themselves be filled with filth and corruption. And when they need to or simply wish to do so, just as they had previously invented wisdoms and intellectual constructions to preach about the beauty of good character, now do they invent wisdoms and intellectual constructions to preach about theft, robbery, murder, and other corrupt things, that these are good things.

The Rebbe concludes his words by saying that, just as on Yom Kippur, "the day itself atones, even if he had not completed his repentance," so too does the day of Purim have an effect upon the Jew, "even if a Jewish person was not in a state of joy as he should have been." This is an extraordinary case, the service of God in a liminal situation. The greatest test is the possibility of redeeming joy from his enslavement.

Rabbi Shapira of Piaseczno saw Nazism as the final chapter in a philosophic tradition whose central expression—we may complete his words thus by way of conjecture—was found in the teaching of Immanuel Kant. This leads us to a much broader question that is not without theological importance. What is the place of the Nazi "philosophy"? Or, to give a more specific example, do Nazism and the Holocaust, which was its sequel, constitute an offspring of Christian anti-Semitism, or do they perhaps have a different pedigree?

I do not wish to fix any rules here concerning this matter. An alternative answer to that of the Rebbe of Piaseczno may be found in various attempts—for example, in the studies of the late Jacob Talmon [1916–1980]. According to this approach, we may take a further step by understanding Nazism as a high point in the development of a certain direction in European thought. The intellectual pedigree of Nazism begins with various modern approaches, the most outstanding of which is a Social Darwinism that turned into violent and unrestrained racism.

But this explanation is only partial. I have no doubt that Nazism is to be seen as a revival of paganism in its renewed struggle against Judaism and against its influence upon the Western world. But the most striking example, albeit one based upon a number of different motifs, is to be found in the work of Richard Wagner.[20] Teutonic mythology must be the option that will bring the world to redemption from the forces that have subjugated it.[21]

One of those who anticipated this tragedy in a general way was Rabbi A. I. Kook [1864–1935], who saw the beginning of a rebellion against "the Judeo-Christian oppression." On the one hand, Rav Kook blamed Christianity for truncating and distorting healthy Judaism; on the other hand, he discerned a profound gap between the collective psychology of certain peoples and the principles of ethics, which were imposed upon them by Christianity from the outside, and to a certain extent even by the power of the sword. These peoples were not yet prepared to accept the reign of ethics. The counterrevolution was yet to break out. A poetic expression of these was given by Uri Zvi Greenberg [1896–1981] in his poem *Reḥovot Hanahar.*

And from the day that pagans of the generation
  of Abram

20. In my opinion, this brings us closer to the truth in another respect as well. Various attempts have been made, particularly in Germany, to interpret what occurred in the Nazi era as a chapter in the struggle between two Germanys: that of Lessing and Goethe, which draws upon a deep and complex culture, against that of Hitler and Goebbels, which utilizes Teutonic myth. I do not know if it is correct to see things thus, but it seems clear to me that the Holocaust gave expression to a struggle between ideologies and philosophies and was not merely a struggle for political rule or economic dominance. As we have seen, one must say here, quite simply, that there was a struggle against Judaism—but one that was not only biological.

21. From this perspective, the thought of Richard Rubenstein and his struggle to return Judaism to pagan pantheism constitutes, to use E. Fackenheim's words uttered in another context, a posthumous victory for German paganism. [Selections from Rubenstein's and Fackenheim's writings are republished in part III of this collection.]

Until the generation of the Crusade
Received from us knowledge of the One
   God. . . .
We know not any refuge from the fury of the
   nations
Their blood cries out for their primeval idol
And they return to the ancient paths
Covered with hyssop
Bringing with them our blood, as a new gift
   offering to Him.[22]

I have no doubt that Sigmund Freud, at the end of his life, also understood things in this manner. The Jewish people have been portrayed by many people, and justly so, as a kind of collective "superego," and the Holocaust as none other than an act of patricide. It seems likely that Freud's last and highly problematic book, *Moses and Monotheism* [1939], is none other than a desperate, and possibly also vain, attempt to break the connection between the image of the father and Judaism. This was accomplished by means of a theory that claims that Moses, who was really responsible for the covenantal tablets of ethics, was not a Jew and that the Jews killed him. The sin of the Jews was thus that they attempted to deny this universal sin. The gentiles took the consequences of that sin upon themselves and atoned for it by the Christian myth of the death of the son—which does not exist in Judaism.

I do not wish to enter into an analysis of the historical basis of Freud's arguments. However, the book must be catalogued not only among the works of science fiction, but also among the documents of Jewish reaction to the Holocaust. This brings me to Freud's remarks in another work when, in the wake of the First World War, he discovered that the world is dominated not only by

the libido (sexual urge), but that alongside it there also exists another force of tremendous potency—"thanatos," the death urge. Freud thought then in terms of the urge to suicide that is transformed into the murder of others. But the Second World War has taught us, to my mind, the opposite model. What was revealed then was that the impulse to murder may be transformed into that for suicide. This was the discovery of the satanic Other Side.[23]

The "Satan" thus revealed is the embodiment of evil for its own sake, and not for any political, economic, geographical, or social benefit. Not murder for the sake of desire, but the desire to murder for its own sake, as an end in itself. It is clear that this was done by human beings of flesh and blood. I do not know what is meant by "responsibility" or "justice" in a context in which all legal and ethical categories are destroyed, but I know that the final testament and command of those killed was to wage relentless war against the murderers and to bring them to justice. Recognition of the absurd, satanic quality of Nazism does not exempt the German people from responsibility for the Nazi regime. The Holocaust is not isolated from its historical context; it flourished against a particular human, social, and ideological background that bears the blame, but it cannot be explained by this background alone.[24]

But not only the Nazi "philosophy," but all philosophies stand on trial. Could they have opposed Nazism? This is the question that is being asked today, in the third generation after the Holocaust. The example of Heidegger is the most striking example. And indeed, as the Rebbe of Piaseczno thought, "Amalek" is more than just a political concept. In the words of Yossel Rakover, in a conversation with his Creator:

22. Uri Z. Greenberg, *Arba'ah Shirei Binah: Sefer ha-Idalyot veha-koaḥ* (Jerusalem and Tel Aviv, 1972), p. 32.
23. Arthur Cohen, the late American Jewish thinker, wished to see the Holocaust as an expression of the *tremendum* (attribute of judgment), in my view incorrectly. This is a central category in Rudolph Otto's philosophy of religion. Using traditional Jewish language, one might formulate things thus: In the Holocaust we did not encounter the *Sefirah* of *Gevurah* or *Middat ha-Din* (that is, the Emanation of Judgment), but the *Sitra Aḥra* (the Other Side in kabbalistic terminolgy; the satanic reality). See Arthur A. Cohen,

The Tremendum: A Theological Reinterpretation of the Holocaust (New York, 1981). [A selection from Cohen's work is republished in part III of this collection.]
24. I cannot concur with the criticism of Yermiyahu Yovel, "The Holocaust as a Component in Our Self-Image" [Hebrew], *Ha-Aretz,* 8 April 1975. The Holocaust was not "an unequivocal human event." The task of history is not measured through the creation of subjective consciousness. This is a legitimate and necessary task, but it is also called upon to explain events. In this task—that of explanation—history has failed.

God hid His face from our world and thereby brought people closer to their wild urges. I therefore think that, unfortunately, it is quite natural, at a time when urges are dominant in the world, that all those within whom there lives the godly, pure [instinct], should be its first victims. . . .

And if You are not my God—then whose God are You? The God of the murderers? If all those who exterminate me, murder me, are so dark, so evil—What am I, if not the one who carries within himself something of Your light, of Your goodness?[25]

History as Theater

One of the foci of the lifework of Yeshayahu Leibowitz was the attempt to separate Judaism from history. History is not relevant from a religious viewpoint—neither the tragedy of the Holocaust nor the heroism of the establishment of the State of Israel.

At first glance, Leibowitz's position seems opposed to the classical Judaic assumption according to which history expresses and realizes a Divine plan. There is a certain truth to this basic assumption, but it also involves no little reservation. In any event, the Divine plan does not need to be that portrayed by a certain part of classical Jewish theology, that which relies upon the principles of reward and punishment.

As we shall see below, among the approaches that negate this approach is that of the Maharal of Prague (R. Yehudah Leib, 1525–1609). In his book *Netzaḥ Yisrael*, the Maharal teaches us that, while it is indeed true that punishment was the cause of the destruction, there was also a cause for that cause, a second-level cause, which is not at all related to sin. The Maharal's approach is very radical, and we shall relate to it further on. Here I wish to briefly discuss the approach of R. Moshe Ḥayyim Luzzatto, known as the Ramḥal (1707–1747).

And this because it seems to me that the things that we have observed thus far are in a certain way close to his approach. In his mature thought,

which found expression in *Da'at Tevunot* and in *QL"H* [138] *Pitḥei Ḥokhmah*, he sees the kabbalah, in its Lurianic formulation, as a system that requires deciphering. The answer to this is found in history: the question of the sufferings of the righteous, of the unjustified suffering of the Jewish people. Luzzatto explains the entire complex system of Lurianic teaching on this basis.

Rav Yehudah Amital, for whom the Holocaust made it impossible to accept the innocent and optimistic position of Rabbenu Saadya Gaon (882–942), according to whom the rational *mitzvot* of religion are based upon the principle of gratitude, once said to me the following: "The intellect requires us to duplicate every good act."[26] That is, to repay Him good for good, whether by doing good deeds in return or by giving thanks. From this tragic comment one may infer, in my opinion, two things. The questioning of the intellectual or rational *mitzvot* expresses the fact that rationalism is lost. On the other hand, one of the central motifs in theology, the meaning of the Creation, the idea that the world was created for man's benefit, is also impossible.

Here, in my opinion, is to be found the central focal point in the Ramḥal's mature thought. The first approach, the Maimonidean, reached its full philosophical development in the generation of the Ramḥal in the thought of Leibniz. This world is the best of all possible worlds. Offhand, this approach is close to the classical rabbinic assumption according to which God builds worlds and destroys them. Those which were destroyed were destroyed, it would seem, because they were insufficiently perfect. But my teacher, Professor Shoshani, of blessed memory, taught us that Ramḥal in fact taught the exact opposite. The good worlds were rejected. The world which God chose to create was an incomplete world, not only in the absolute sense—i.e., as compared to the perfection of the Holy One blessed be He—but even relatively, in comparison to the perfection that could have been our lot. Herein lies the significance of the idea of *tzimtzum*, the act of Divine contraction (as taught by Lurianic kabbalah).

25. This text was published a number of times. See Eliav, *Ani ma'amin*, p. 302ff. [See also the text in part III, pp. 395–400, of this collection.]

26. *Emunot ve-De'ot*, III.1.

This approach of the Ramḥal indeed finds expression in the emendation that he makes to his earlier views. He now thinks that, in addition to the idea of gratitude, the idea of unity lies at the focus of the creation. God's unity must find expression in the negation of opposites. Illusions—metaphysical, religious, and moral—need to be created that seemingly negate the principle of unity.

According to Ramḥal the playwright, history is thus in fact a kind of play in a cosmic theater, a theater of the absurd, in which an illusion is created in the eyes of the viewers, but the play must end with the fact that evil itself announces its own negation.

These things are developed further in ḥasidic mysticism. The theater is not real. The most extreme expression of this view finds expression in the metaphor of the dream. One of the harshest things ever said about the Holocaust was the testimony of Ka tzetnik, who heard his neighbor groaning during a nightmare. He did not want to awaken him, because he was certain that reality was harsher than any nightmare he could be having. According to ḥasidic belief, reality itself is considered to be on the order of a dream, and redemption means that we are able to awaken from it. The words of the psalmist, "we were as dreamers," do not refer to the redemption, but rather to the exile. The exile is a nightmare, and the only answer to the question posed by the Holocaust is that at some time we shall awaken and feel that it had been no more than a nightmare.

The Ramḥal did not give reality a mystical interpretation of this sort. But he thought that history would create the possible horrors when they are needed to contradict themselves. Satan himself must announce his nullification.

History as Riddle

I have discussed the Ramḥal's approach, which touches upon history, albeit only in a fragmentary manner. Among the numerous questions connected with the discussion thus far, there remains open the question, to which I wish to relate here, which lies at the focus of the attitude to history. In my opinion, there is a basic debate within Jewish thought, whose two fundamental options are represented by the Maharal of Prague and Rav Kook.

In my opinion, the approach of the Maharal of Prague teaches us the doctrine of estrangement. The Jewish people needs to be in this world, despite the fact that it belongs to another world. In absolute contrast to Arnold Toynbee, who thought that the Jewish people are a fossilized people from the past, the Maharal views them as a representative of the future thrust into this world. But this incompatibility carries in its wake alienation and suffering. This is the meaning of exile. Of course, the redemption will ultimately take place, but it will be the result of catastrophic and apocalyptic change. The Maharal thinks that there is a kind of ontological necessity in the existence of the Jewish people in the world. It is a Divine mission, but one involving suffering and pain.

As against that, Rav Kook thought that history has significance, and it is that which will bring us to the redemption, to the world that is entirely good. Rather than the revolutionary and destructive change of which Maharal spoke, Rav Kook believed that there is a continuity to the process of redemption. R. Judah Halevi (1075–1141) had restored the historical outlook to Jewish life in exile.[27] Rav Kook continued this approach and brought it to its ultimate conclusions. Zionism is the return to history. On the face of it, this return means that we are again taking our destiny into our own hands. But this is only one stage: The return to history is guided by a more positive conception of the possibility of history and of its power.

The works of all the philosophers constitute an attempt to read the secrets of history. The rebirth of the State of Israel supported the interpretation of Rav Kook. Indeed, on the face of it, the Holocaust erased history from Jewish theology. The rise of the State of Israel restored it. This restoration was seen as significant not only for Jewry and

---

27. It seems to me that this is the root of the lack of interest in history in the world of the sages. When history does not express Divine providence, it is no longer significant: "that which was, was." These words have a

double meaning. On the one hand, it expresses the impossibility of changing the past (B.T. *Nazir* 23ᵃ), "And what could he do? That which was, was." As Rashi comments at B.T. *Yoma* 37ᵃ: "'That which

Judaism, but also for other religions. Christianity, with all its factions, is the most striking example. It is this connection that gave the Holocaust an apocalyptic character. This is the first time that apocalypse has validity and significance.[28]

But despite this, the history of the State of Israel shows that it, which was expected to bring normality to Jewish existence, lives a life of alienation, this time not on an individual but on a collective level. We have seen in our brief political history the shadows of the Holocaust, during the days of waiting prior to the (1967) Six Day War and during the opening days of the (1973) Yom Kippur War. But there too we felt that a political solution could not resolve the deeper existential questions, questions that are a function of "Jewish destiny." The meaning of that history has not yet been determined, and without doubt constitutes the greatest riddle of our lives.

In the Face of the Absurd

Thinking about the Holocaust means confronting the absurd. Do we have the strength to gamble on meaning after the absurd? I would like to conclude my remarks by quoting some things said verbally by Professor A. J. Heschel in one of his conversations, as they were recorded by Robert Alter: "A father cannot educate his son as a Jew after the Holocaust, except with the recognition that he is bringing his child into an eternal covenant with God."[29]

These are cruel words, expressing the dilemma of the Jew in certain situations, but its very presentation teaches us a great deal. First of all, that there can be destiny even without a covenant of destiny. They teach us that, beyond the covenant of destiny of the Holocaust, we need to gaze upon the horizon of the covenant of purpose. The religious perspective on the Holocaust, the question that is asked in the theological discussion of the *Shoah*, is the question of the existence of such a perspective. But perhaps it is specifically so. Perhaps even the destiny itself has meaning. A religious response to the Holocaust means faith in meaning beyond the absurd. The absurd means opening a frightening door to our own Jewish essence.

was, was'—it is already past, and it is impossible to go back." Similarly, R. Obadiah Bertinoro (Mishnah *Berakhot* 9:3) says: "One who prays concerning that which has already happened, engages in vain prayer, for that which was, was." But this concept also means that there is a past from which one cannot learn, and therefore its description is of no significance (B.T. *Yoma* 8^b): "How did he dress them? How did he dress them? That which was, was. Rather, how will he dress them in the future?" Thus the rabbis and sages spoke of a prophecy that is needed for future generations, and a prophecy that was made for its time alone.

28. I will allow myself to make use of the beautiful idiom of David Novak, in the opposite direction. Indeed, the apocalypse claims that "Post hoc ergo propter hoc."

29. Robert Alter, "Deformations of the Holocaust," *Commentary* 71, no. 2 (February 1981): 48–54.

BIBLIOGRAPHY

No author, *Amidst the Nightmare of Crime: Manuscripts of Members of a Sonderkommando*, E.T. by Kristina Michalik (Oswiecim, 1973).

Achituv, Yosef. *A Good Eye: Dialogue and Polemic in Jewish Culture* (Tel Aviv, 1999) [Hebrew].

———. *On the Border of Change* (Jerusalem, 1997) [Hebrew].

Achituv, Yosef, Hadas Goldberg, and Amichai Berholz. *A Reappraisal of the Principles of Religious Zionism and Modern Orthodoxy* (Tel Aviv, 2000) [Hebrew].

Alterman, Natan. *Two Roads: Remarks from a Notebook*, edited by Dan Laor (Tel Aviv, 1989) [Hebrew].

Amir, Yehoyada. "Israeli Responses to Franz Rosenzweig" (Ph.D. thesis, Hebrew University, 1993) [Hebrew].

———. *Knowledge and Belief: Analysis of the Thought of Franz Rosenzweig* (Tel Aviv, 2004) [Hebrew].

———. *Program for Studies in Judaism* (Tel Aviv, 1996) [Hebrew].

Bauer, Yehuda. *American Jewry and the Holocaust* (Detroit, 1981).

———. *Flight and Rescue* (New York, 1975).

———. *From Diplomacy to Resistance* (Philadelphia, 1970).

———. *History of the Holocaust* (Chicago, 1984).

———. *The Holocaust in Historical Perspective* (Seattle, 1978).

———. *The Jewish Emergence from Powerlessness* (Toronto, 1979).

———. *Jewish Reactions to the Holocaust* (Tel Aviv, 1988).

———. *Jews for Sale?* (New Haven, Conn., 1995).

———. *My Brother's Keeper* (Philadelphia, 1974).

———. *Out of the Ashes* (Oxford, 1989).

———. *Rethinking the Holocaust* (New Haven, 2001).

———. "Returning to the Source of Human Morality (Response to Alexander Donat and Moshe Unna)," *Yalkut Moreshet* 24 (1978): 23–25 [Hebrew].

Donat, Alexander. "Armageddon: Twenty Years after the Warsaw Uprising," *Dissent* 10, no. 2 (Spring 1963): 119–132.

———. *The Death Camp Treblinka: A Documentary* (New York, 1979).

———. *Holocaust Kingdom: A Memoir* (New York, 1965).

———. *Jewish Resistance* (New York, 1964).

———. *Our Last Days in the Warsaw Ghetto* (New York, 1964).

———. "Revisionist History of the Jewish Catastrophe," *Judaism* 12, no. 1 (Spring 1963): 416–435.

———. "Voice from the Ashes: Wanderings in Search of God," *Yalkut Moreshet* 21 (June 1976): 105–138 [Hebrew].

Dorman, Menachem. *Natan Alterman: Chapters in his Biography* (Tel Aviv, 1991) [Hebrew].

Fleischner, Eva, ed., *Auschwitz: Beginning of a New Era* (Hoboken, 1977).

Harvey, Warren Zev. *Physics and Metaphysics in Hasdai Crescas* (Amsterdam, 1998).

Harvey, Warren Zev, M. Ben-Sasson, Y. Ben-Naeh, and Z. Zohar, eds. *Studies in a Rabbinic Family: The De Botons* (Jerusalem, 1998).

Oppenheim, Michael. "Eliezer Schweid," in *Interpreters of Judaism in the Late Twentieth Century*, edited by Steven T. Katz (Washington, D.C., 1993), pp. 301–324.

———. "Eliezer Schweid: A Philosophy of Return," *Judaism* 37 (Winter 1986): 66–77.

———. "Paths of Return: The Concept of Community in the Thought of F. Rosenzweig and E. Schweid," in *Community and the Individual Jew: Essays in Honor of Lavy M. Becker*, edited by Ronald S. Aigen and Gershon D. Hundert (Philadelphia, 1986), pp. 66–77.

———. "The Relevance of Rosenzweig in the Eyes of His Israeli Critics," *Modern Judaism* 7 (May 1987): 193–206.

Peli, Pinchas. *Chapters in Jewish Thought in the Land of Israel* (Bet-El, 1990) [Hebrew].

———. *The Jewish Sabbath: A Renewed Encounter* (New York, 1991).

———. *Torah Today* (Washington, D.C., 1987; reprint, Austin, Tex., 2005).

Peli, Pinchas, ed. *On Repentance in the Thought and Oral Discourses of Rabbi Joseph B. Soloveitchik* (New York, 1980).

Rosenberg, Shalom. *Good and Evil in Jewish Thought* (Tel Aviv, 1989).

———. *In the Footsteps of the Kuzari* (Jerusalem, 1991) [Hebrew].

———. *Not in Heaven* (Jerusalem, 1997) [Hebrew].

———. *Torah and Science* (Jerusalem, 1988) [Hebrew].

Rosenberg, Shalom, and Benjamin Ish-Shalom, eds. *The World of Rav Kook's Thought* (New York, 1991).

Schwartz, Yoel. *Zion Today: Torah Perspective* (Jerusalem, 1986) [Hebrew].

Schwartz, Yoel, and Yitzchak Goldstein. *A Light unto the Nations*, translated by Mordecai ben Aharon and edited by Yirmeyahu Bindman (Jerusalem, 1988).

———. *Shoah: A Jewish Perspective on Tragedy in the Context of the Holocaust*, translated by Shlomo Fox-Ashrei (New York, 1990).

Schweid, Eliezer. *A History of Jewish Thought in Modern Times* (Jerusalem, 1977) [Hebrew].

———. *Israel at the Crossroads* (Philadelphia, 1973).

———. *Israel's Faith and Culture* (Jerusalem, 1976) [Hebrew].

———. "Justifying Religion in Light of the *Shoah*," *Yehadut Zmaneinu* 5 (5749): 3–24 [Hebrew].

———. *The Land of Israel: National Home or Land of Destiny* (Rutherford, N.J., 1985).

———. "The *Shoah* at the End of the Twentieth Century: A Theological and Research-Oriented Perspective," *Madei Ha-yehadut* 59 (5759): 35–49 [Hebrew].

———. *The Solitary Jew and His Judaism* (Tel Aviv, 1974) [Hebrew].

Unna, Moshe. *Essays on Religious Education* (Tel Aviv, 1970) [Hebrew].

———. *For Myself: Thought and Action* (Tel Aviv, 1955) [Hebrew].

———. *Israel among the Nations* (Tel Aviv, 1971) [Hebrew].

———. *Separate Ways in the Religious Parties' Confrontation with Renascent Israel* (Jerusalem, 1987) [Hebrew].

———. *True Partnership: Essays on the Path of the Religious Kibbutz* (Tel Aviv, 1962) [Hebrew].

———. "Who Will Heal You? (Response to Alexander Donat)," *Yalkut Moreshet* 22 (1977): 63–68 [Hebrew].

Part III

EUROPEAN AND AMERICAN RESPONSES DURING AND FOLLOWING THE WAR

INTRODUCTION

Steven T. Katz

I

The selections included in this section are drawn from European and American authors. The views expressed range across the entire theological spectrum from those that are very traditional to those that conclude that the Holocaust proves God's nonexistence. Each position is thoughtful and, in its own way, provocative. But all are open to critical interrogation and various forms of rebuttal.

The responses come mainly in two forms. The first set primarily draws upon and recycles explanatory models that have their roots in the Bible. That is, they employ explanations that were first offered in the Bible in response to the perennial questions of theodicy and human suffering. Now, in the aftermath of the Holocaust, these accounts are again appealed to, with modifications, to provide an understanding of the interaction of God and man and God and Israel. The second set of responses is composed of new answers that attempt to reconfigure the theological landscape in various original ways in light of the profound theological difficulties engendered by the existence of *Einsatzgruppen* (Hitler's murder squads in Eastern Europe) and the death camps.

Given the importance of these positions, some old, some new, it will be of help to readers, especially those just beginning their study of these issues, if each is described individually with its main conceptual features highlighted.

Let us begin with an examination of the six biblical models, starting with the famous event of the *Akedah*, "the binding of Isaac."

1. The *Akedah*: The Binding of Isaac

The biblical narrative that begins in Genesis 22:2, which reports the "binding of Isaac" by his father, Abraham, in anticipation of his being sacrificed in fulfillment of God's command, is often appealed to as a possible paradigm for treating the Holocaust. Such a theological move is well grounded in Jewish tradition, especially given its use in the medieval Hebrew martyrologies of the Crusader and post-Crusader period (late eleventh and twelfth centuries), during which the biblical event of the *Akedah* became the prism through which the horrific Jewish medieval experience became refracted and was made "intelligible" to Jews of that era. In these medieval narratives, the Jewish children of medieval Europe, and more generally all the Jews slaughtered by the Crusaders, were perceived, like Isaac of old, as martyrs to God who willingly sacrificed themselves and their loved ones in order to prove beyond all doubt their faithfulness to the Almighty.[1]

Now again, after the Holocaust, this religious model is used to describe the victims of Hitler's crusade to make the world *Judenrein*, free of Jews. The great appeal of this decipherment lies in its imputation to the dead of heroism and unwavering religious faith. Their deaths are not due to sin or to any imperfection on their part, nor are they the consequence of any violation of the covenant. Rather, they are the climactic evidence of the Jews' unwavering devotion to the faith of their fathers. Just as the Jews of medieval Europe, confronted by the Crusader bands, chose to kill their children and die themselves[2] rather than convert to Christianity and save their lives, thus affirming their belief in the truth of Judaism in the most dramatic and absolute way, so, too, the Jewish people—confronted by the satanic forces of Nazism—died as martyrs for their God. Thus, piety, not sin, is the key factor in accounting for the Holocaust. God makes unique demands upon those who love Him and whom He loves, and as with Abraham and Isaac, so too the Jewish people in our time responded with fidelity and selflessness. As such, the dreadful events become a test, the occasion for the maximal religious service "even unto death."

This response to the Holocaust is not without its intellectual and emotional appeal. Yet readers should carefully evaluate its claims, and the analogies upon which it rests, before concluding that it supplies a full "answer" to Auschwitz and Treblinka. Students need to think hard about just how exact the parallel between the *Akedah* and the Holocaust is. For example, in the *Akedah*, it is Abraham who is commanded to kill the son he loves. In the Holocaust, Hitler kills the Jews he hates. This murder creates no emotional or ethical "problem" for him; he is more than happy to carry it out.

2. Job

The biblical Book of *Job*, the best-known treatment of theodicy in the Hebrew Bible, naturally presents itself as a second possible model for decoding the Holocaust. For example, Martin Buber, Eliezer Berkovits, and Robert Gordis, all represented in this anthology, have all discussed its relevance in the context of post-Holocaust Jewish theology. That this should be the case is not surprising for Job provides an inviting paradigm in that Job's suffering is caused not by his sinfulness but rather by his righteousness—perceived by Satan as a cause for jealousy. Moreover, the tale ends on a "happy" note: Job is rewarded by God for his faithfulness with a double blessing. On a deeper level, of course, the issues are far more problematic and their meaning ambiguous. Consider that the resolution of Job's doubts is never really clear, that God's reply through the whirlwind (ch. 38) is, in important ways, no answer to his questions, and perhaps most telling, that his first wife and family are still dead through no fault of their own. It is, therefore, not surprising that the ultimate meaning of the book is unclear and much argued about and that its applicability to the Holocaust is much contested.

3. The "Suffering Servant"

One of the most influential biblical doctrines framed in response to the "problem of evil" is that of the "suffering servant."[3] Given its classic presentation in the *Book of Isaiah* (especially ch. 53), the suffering servant doctrine suggests that the righteous vicariously suffer and atone for the wicked and hence, in some mysterious way, allay God's wrath and judgment, thus making the continuation of history possible.

According to the majority of traditional *Jewish* interpreters, the suffering servant is the nation of Israel,[4] the people of the covenant, who suffer with and for God in the midst of the evil of creation. As God is long suffering with His creation, so Israel, God's people, must be long suffering. In this, they mirror the divine in their own reality and, while suffering for others, make it possible for creation to endure. Moreover, through this act of faithfulness the guiltless establish a unique bond with the Almighty. As they suffer for and with Him, He suffers their suffering, shares their agony, and comes to love them in a special way for loving Him with such fortitude and without limit.

This theme, as already evidenced in Parts I and II of this anthology, has been enunciated in Jewish theological writings emanating from the Holocaust era itself, as well as in post-Holocaust sources. One finds it in the teachings of ḥasidic rebbes as well as Conservative thinkers, such as Abraham Joshua Heschel, and Orthodox thinkers, such as Eliezer Berkovits—both of whom are represented in this anthology. In these modern sources it receives a classical exposition. For example, Berkovits writes: "God's servant carries upon his shoulders God's dilemma with man through history. God's people share in all the fortunes of God's dilemma as man is bungling his way through toward messianic realization."[5]

It should also be noted that one contemporary Jewish theologian in particular has gone beyond the traditional framework and used the suffering servant idea to construct an elaborate, very novel, reading of the Holocaust. For Ignaz Maybaum, a German Reform rabbi who survived the war in London (and whose position is represented in the selection of his writing below), the pattern of the suffering servant is the paradigm of Israel's way in history. First in the "servant of God" in *Isaiah*, then in the Jew Jesus, and now at Treblinka and Auschwitz, God uses the Jewish people to address the world and to save it: "They died though innocent so that others might live." According to this decipherment of the Holocaust, the perennial dialectic of history is God's desire that the gentile nations come close to Him, while they resist this call. Therefore, the special God-given task, the "mission" of Israel, is to foster and facilitate this relationship between God and the nations. It is they who must make God's message accessible in terms that the gentile nations will understand and respond to. But what language, what symbols, will speak to the nations? Not that of the *Akedah* in which Isaac is spared and no blood is shed but rather, and only, that of the crucifixion, i.e., a sacrifice in which the innocent die for the guilty, where some die vicariously so that others might live.

Accordingly, modern Israel repeats collectively the single crucifixion of one Jew two millennia ago, and by so doing again reveals to humankind its weaknesses, as well as the need for man to turn to Heaven for instruction and salvation. In a daring parallelism, Maybaum writes:

> The Golgotha of modern mankind is Auschwitz. The cross, the Roman gallows, was replaced by the gas chamber. The gentiles, it seems, must first be terrified by the blood of the sacrificed scapegoat to have the mercy of God revealed to them and become converted, become baptized gentiles, become Christians.[6]

For Maybaum, through the Holocaust, the world again moves morally and theologically forward and upward finally transcending the last vestiges of medieval obscurantism and intolerance, the very phenomena that produced the *Shoah*.

The theological deconstruction of the Holocaust using the suffering servant model can thus be seen to be interesting as well as challenging. Readers, however, must pause and carefully examine the plausibility of this response—and in particular Maybaum's unique rendering of this doctrine—before concluding that it supplies the needed explanation for the murder of European Jewry. And this not least because they need to ask questions about the logic of the suffering servant thesis itself. That is, they must carefully examine the notion of vicarious suffering and the issues it raises concerning God's activity in history. Would God really cause the deaths of six million people in order to make a point?

4. *Hester Panim*: "God Hides His Face"

The Bible, in wrestling with the problem of human suffering, appeals in a number of places to the notion of *Hester Panim*: "the hiding of the face of God." This concept has two meanings. The first, in Deuteronomy 31:17–18 and later in Micah 3:4, is a causal one that links God's "absence" from the unfolding historical events to human sin: God turns away from the sinner. The second sense, found particularly in a number of psalms (e.g., Psalms 44, 69, 88, and variants in, e.g., Psalms 9, 10, 13; see also Job 13:24), does not relate God's absence to sin but, instead, suggests human despair and confusion—and even protest—over His "disappearance" for no reason that can be discerned. Here mankind stands "abandoned" for reasons that are un-known and unfathomable. Thus the repetitive theme of lament sounded in the psalms: "Why" or "how long," God, will You be absent? And the putting of the bewildering question: Is it possible for God to be continually indifferent to human affairs, to be passive in the struggle between good and evil, to be unmoved by suffering and its overcoming?

In applying this unusual doctrine to the Holocaust, modern theologians—for example, Martin Buber, Joseph Soloveitchik, Zvi Kolitz, and Eliezer Berkovits, all of whom are represented in the selections that follow this introduction—are attempting to do three things: (a) to vindicate the Jewish people, i.e., the death camps are not the consequence of sin and do not represent Divine punishment; (b) to remove God as the direct cause of the evil, i.e., the Holocaust is something men did to other men, women, and children; and (c) to affirm the reality and even saving nature of the Divine despite the empirical evidence to the contrary. The first two points need no further explanation; the third does. With regard to this line of reasoning, one must understand that the notion of *Hester Panim* is not merely or only about the absence of God but rather, at least in specific contexts, entails a more complex exegesis of Divine Providence stemming from an analysis of the ontological nature of the Divine. In such instances God's absence, *Hester Panim*, is a necessary, active condition of His saving mercy. His "hiddenness" is the obverse of His "long-suffering" patience with sinners, that is, being patient with sinners means allowing sin. As Eliezer Berkovits has argued: "One may call it the divine dilemma that God's *Erek Apayim*, His patiently waiting countenance to some is, of necessity, identical with His *Hester Panim*, His hiding of the countenance, to others."[7]

Then too, within the larger mosaic of human purpose, *Hester Panim* is dialectically related to the fundamental character of human freedom without which human beings would not be the potentially majestic beings Judaism envisions them to be. (I shall return in detail to this doctrine of the absolute need for human freedom in point 6, "The Burden of Human Freedom," below.) It needs also to be recognized that this challenging notion is, at one and the same time, a proclamation of a deep religious faith. The lament addressed to God—even while He seems absent—is a sign that God is and that His manifest presence is still possible. It is an affirmation that one believes that ultimately evil will not triumph for God will not always "hide His face." In this connection, it is relevant to note that for some contemporary Jewish theologians like Emil Fackenheim, Eliezer Berkovits, Irving (Yitzchak) Greenberg, and Martin Buber—all of whom are represented in the selections below—the creation of the State of

Israel following so closely upon the Holocaust is proof of this. In the State of Israel, God again openly reveals His saving presence.

The theological claim that God hides His face undoubtedly speaks eloquently to the religious confusion of the post-Holocaust situation. But students should beware of accepting it too easily as an answer to the horror of the Nazi period for, among other reasons, it appeals to a mystery, God's hiddenness, to solve the mystery represented by the evil of the *Shoah*.

5. *Mipnei Chataeynu*: "Because of Our Sins We Are Punished"

In biblical and later Jewish (rabbinic) sources, the principal explanation for human suffering was sin. According to this view, there was a balance—established by God—in the universal order that was inescapable: Good brought forth blessing; sin brought retribution (see, for example, Deuteronomy 28). Both on the individual and the national level, the law of cause and effect, sin and grief, operated. In our time, given its undoubted theological pedigree, a number of theologians, especially those of a more traditional bent, and certain rabbinic sages, have employed this explanation to account for the Holocaust. The ḥasidic (Satmar) Rebbe, Joel Teitelbaum, for example, puts this claim forward clearly and with certitude: "[S]in is the cause of all suffering."[8]

Harsh as it is, the argument that Teitelbaum (and others who share this view) make is that Israel sinned "grievously" and God, after much patience and hope of "return," finally "cut off" the generation of the wicked. It needs to be noted explicitly that the majority of Jewish thinkers who have wrestled with the theological implications of the *Shoah* have rejected this line of analysis. Still, an important, if small, segment of the traditional religious community has consistently advanced it.

Two critical questions immediately arise in pursuing the application of this millennia-old doctrine to the contemporary tragedy of the Holocaust. The first is: What kind of God would exact such retribution? This crucial theological issue requires close and careful reflection. Second, of what sin could Israel be guilty to warrant such retribution? Here the explanations vary depending on one's perspective. For some, such as Rabbi Isaac Hutner and the aforementioned Satmar Rebbe, Yoel Teitelbaum, and his small circle of ḥasidic and extreme right-wing, anti-Zionist followers, the sin that precipitated the Holocaust was Zionism. In Zionism, Teitelbaum argued (based on a nonbinding talmudic tradition recorded in B. T. *Ketubot* 110[a]),[9] the Jewish people broke their covenant with God, which demanded that they not try to end their exile and thereby hasten the coming of the Messiah through their own means. In consequence, "we have witnessed the immense manifestation of God's anger [the Holocaust]." Rabbi Hutner, in the selection reproduced below, holding a similar theological position, links the Holocaust to the instigations of the Grand Mufti of Jerusalem who, in his view, persuaded Hitler to undertake the destruction of European Jewry. For others on the extreme right edge of the religious spectrum, the primary crime was not Zionism but Reform Judaism or, again, assimilation. In this equation, the centrality of Germany as the land that gave birth to the "Jewish Enlightenment," i.e., the movement for modernizing Jewish belief and practice, to Reform Judaism, and to Nazism is undeniable proof of this causal connection.[10] All these justifications and explanations, however, must be treated with great suspicion. Readers need to reflect on the two fundamental questions posed above when deciding whether or not this response, which blames the victims for their own destruction, is plausible.

6. The Burden of Human Freedom:
The "Free-Will Defense"

Among the theological and philosophical traditions that have been concerned to uphold God's justice despite the manifest evil in the world, none has an older or more distinguished lineage than that known as the "free-will defense." According to this argument, human evil is the ever-present possibility entailed by the reality of human freedom. If human beings are to have the potential for majesty they must, conversely, have an equal potential for corruption; if they are to be capable of acts of authentic morality, they must be capable of acts of authentic immorality. Freedom is a two-edged sword, hence its challenge and its cost. Applying this consideration to the events of the Nazi epoch, the *Shoah* becomes a case of man's inhumanity to man, the extreme misuse of human freedom. At the same time, such a position with its emphasis on human actions does not call into question God's goodness and solicitude for it is man, not God, who perpetrates genocide. God observes these events with his unique Divine pathos, but in order to allow human morality to be a substantively real thing, He refrains from intercession. Thus, at the same time that He respects human freedom and is long suffering with an evil humanity, His patience results in the suffering of others.

This defense has been advocated by a number of post-Holocaust thinkers. The two most notable presentations of this theme are found in Eliezer Berkovits's *Faith after the Holocaust* and Arthur A. Cohen's *The Tremendum;* sections from both works are excerpted below. Berkovits has employed it to defend a traditional Jewish theological position, while Cohen has utilized it to develop a Jewish "process theology" (for more on Cohen's view see part II, point 3, of this introduction, below). And in both cases—as well as in the work of other thinkers, for example, the argument of Robert Gordis in his selection below—it advances a powerful theological position. But, for all its significance, it does not fully answer the problem, for God is, in some ultimate sense, still responsible for creation. Thus, in the past He is said to have intervened in history, e.g., at the Exodus from Egypt, but this type of intervention seems altogether absent in the case of the Holocaust. (Yet, having said this, one needs to consider that Hitler was defeated; his plan totally to annihilate the Jewish people did not succeed; and after the war the State of Israel was, after 1,900 years, recreated. There are those for whom any one of these outcomes, and all of them together, may/do indicate God's active participation in history. But this is a very complex matter that requires careful and sustained theological reflection.) Again, insofar as human beings are His creation, He could have given us a stronger inclination for the good. In other words, there are many possibilities, Divine and human, that must be examined with great care before deciding to adopt this theological position as definitive.

II

The first six theological positions that have been analyzed have all been predicated upon, and are the extension of, classical Jewish responses to national tragedy. In the last four decades, however, a number of innovative, more radical responses have been proposed by contemporary post-Holocaust thinkers. Six, in particular, merit serious attention.

1. Auschwitz: A New Revelation

The first of these emerges from the work of Emil Fackenheim, who has contended that the Holocaust represents a new revelation. Rejecting any account that analyzes Auschwitz as *mipnei chataeynu* (because of our sins), Fackenheim, employing a Buberian model of dialogical revelation[11]—i.e., revelation as the personal encounter of an I with the Eternal Thou (God)—urges Israel to continue to believe despite the moral outrage of the *Shoah*. God, on this view, is always present in Jewish history, even at Auschwitz. We do not, and cannot, understand what He was doing at Auschwitz, nor why He allowed it, but we must insist that He was there. Equally, if not more significant, God commands Israel from the death camps as He did from Sinai. The essence of this commanding voice, what Fackenheim has called the "614th commandment" (there are 613 commandments in traditional Judaism) is "Jews are forbidden to hand Hitler posthumous victories." That is, Jews are under a sacred obligation to survive. After the death camps, Jewish existence itself is a holy act. Moreover, Jews are now forbidden to become cynical about the world and man, for to submit to cynicism is to abdicate responsibility for the future and to deliver the world into the hands of the luciferian forces of Nazism. And most important, Jews are "forbidden to despair of the God of Israel, lest Judaism perish." The voice that speaks from Auschwitz demands that no one assist Hitler to win posthumous victories. The Jewish will for survival is natural enough, but Fackenheim invests it with transcendental significance. Precisely because others would eradicate Jews from the earth, Jews are commanded to resist annihilation. Paradoxically, Hitler makes Judaism a necessity after Auschwitz. To say no to Hitler is to say yes to the God of Sinai; to say no to the God of Sinai is to say yes to Hitler.

To fully evaluate this interesting, highly influential response to the *Shoah* (reprinted below), a detailed analysis of a sort that is beyond our present possibilities is required. Nevertheless, it needs to be stressed that the main line of critical inquiry into Fackenheim's position—as well as that of Rabbi Jonathan Sacks, who draws his main theological argument from Fackenheim's views (see his selections below)—must center on the dialogical (Buberian) notion of revelation and the related idea of commandment, as that traditional notion is here employed. One needs to ask Fackenheim: (a) How do historical events like the Holocaust become "revelatory"? (b) What exactly does he mean by the term "commandment"? And, as a related question, one needs to ask whether one wants to make reaction to Hitler the main reason for continued Jewish existence. This latter topic is pursued, in particular, by Michael Wyschograd (see his selection below), who is highly critical of Fackenheim's attempt to respond to the Holocaust and to justify continued collective Jewish existence on grounds other than the classical doctrines of covenant and Torah.

2. The Covenant Broken: A New Age

A second contemporary thinker who has urged continued belief in the God of Israel, though on new terms, is Irving (Yitzchak) Greenberg. For Greenberg, all the old truths and certainties, all the old commitments and obligations, have been destroyed by the Holocaust. Moreover, any simple faith is now impossible. The Holocaust ends the old era of Jewish covenantal existence and ushers in a new and different one. Greenberg explains his radical view in this way. There have been three major periods in the covenantal history of Israel. The first is the biblical era. What characterizes this first covenantal stage is the asymmetry of the relationship between God and Israel. The biblical encounter may be a covenant but it is clearly a covenant in which "God is the initiator, the senior partner, who punishes, rewards, and enforces the punishment if the Jews slacken."[12] This type of understanding of the relationship between God and Israel is displayed in the crisis engendered by the destruction of the First Temple in 586 BCE. To this tragedy, Israel, through the biblical prophets and in keeping with the logic of this position, responded primarily by falling back on the doctrine of self-chastisement: The destruction of the Temple and the consequent exile of the nation were divine punishments for Israel's sinful ways.

The second phase[13] in the transformation of the covenant idea is marked by the destruction of the Second Temple by Rome in 70 CE. The meaning adduced from this event by the rabbinical sages of the era was that now Jews must take a more equal role in the covenant and become true partners with the Almighty. "The manifest divine presence and activity [were] being reduced, but the covenant was actually being renewed."[14] The destruction of 70 CE signaled the initiation of an age in which God would be less manifest though still present.

This brings us to what is decisive and radical in Greenberg's ruminations, what he has termed the "third great cycle in Jewish history," which has come about as a consequence of the Holocaust. The *Shoah* marks a new era in which the Sinaitic covenantal relationship has been shattered, and thus a new and unprecedented form of covenantal relationship—if there is to be any covenantal relationship at all—must now come into being to take its place:

> In retrospect, it is now clear that the divine assignment to the Jews was untenable. After the Holocaust, it is obvious that this role opened the Jews to a total murderous fury from which there was no escape. Morally speaking, then, God can have no claims on the Jews by dint of the covenant.[15]

What this means, Greenberg argues, is that the covenant

> can no longer be commanded and subject to a serious external enforcement. It cannot be commanded because morally speaking—covenantally speaking—one cannot order another to step forward to die. One can give an order like this to an enemy, but in a moral relationship I cannot demand the giving up of one's life. I can ask for it or plead for it—but I cannot order it.

Out of this interconnected set of considerations, Greenberg pronounces the fateful judgment: The Jewish covenant with God is now voluntary! Jews have, quite miraculously, chosen to continue to live Jewish lives and collectively to build a Jewish state, the ultimate symbol of Jewish continuity, but these acts are, after Auscnwitz, the result of the free choice of the Jewish people. "I submit," writes Greenberg, "that the covenant was broken. God was in no position to command any more, but the Jewish people [were] so in love with the dream of redemption that [they] volunteered to carry on with [their] mission."[16] The consequence of this voluntary action transforms the existing covenantal order. First, Israel was a junior partner, then an equal partner. Finally, after Auschwitz, it becomes "the senior partner in action."

In turn, Israel's voluntary acceptance of the covenant and continued will to survive suggest three corollaries. First, this acceptance points, if obliquely, to the continued existence of the God of Israel. By creating the State of Israel, by having

Jewish children, the Jewish people show that "covenantal hope is not in vain."[17] Second, and very important, in an age of voluntarism rather than coercion, living Jewishly under the covenant can no longer be interpreted monolithically, i.e., only in strict *halakhic* (traditional rabbinic) fashion. Third, any aspect of religious behavior that demeans the image of the divine or of people, for example, prejudice, sexism, and oppression of all sorts, must be purged.

Greenberg's reconstruction of Jewish theology after the Holocaust (represented in his selection below) presents a fascinating, creative reaction to the unprecedented evil manifest in the death camps. Whether his position is, finally, theologically convincing turns, however, on (a) the correctness of his theological reading of Jewish history; and (b) the meaning and status of key concepts, such as "covenant," "revelation," "commandment," and the like, in his radically revisionist theological system. For example, can the covenant made at Sinai be broken? And can a new "voluntary covenant" really take its place? Readers will have to think carefully about these issues before accepting or rejecting Greenberg's position.

3. A Redefinition of God

An influential school in modern theological circles known as "process theology," inspired by the work of Alfred North Whitehead and Charles Hartshorne, has argued that the classical understanding of God has to be dramatically revised—not least in terms of our conception of His power and direct, causal involvement in human affairs—if we are to construct a coherent theological position. According to those who advance this thesis (represented in this collection by the thoughtful work of Hans Jonas, Arthur A. Cohen, and Melissa Raphael), God certainly exists, but the old-new difficulties raised by the problem of theodicy for classical theistic positions arise precisely because of an inadequate description of the Divine, i.e., one that misascribes to Him attributes of omnipotence and omniscience that He does not possess.

Jewish theologian Arthur A. Cohen, in his *The Tremendum: A Theological Interpretation of the Holocaust*,[18] has advanced the fullest, most detailed version of this redefinitional strategy as the most appropriate way to respond to the theological challenges posed by the Holocaust. After arguing for the enormity of the *Shoah*, i.e., its uniqueness and its transcendence of any "meaning," Cohen suggests that the way out of the theological dilemma posed by the death camps for classical Jewish thought is to rethink whether "national catastrophes are compatible with our traditional notions of a beneficent and providential God."[19]

For Cohen, the answer is that they are not. Against the traditional view that asks, given its understanding of God's action in history, "How could it be that God witnessed the Holocaust and remained silent?" Cohen would pose the contrary "dipolar" thesis that "what is taken as God's speech is really always man's hearing, that God is not the strategist of our particularities or of our historical condition, but rather the mystery of our futurity, always our posse, never our acts." This means that, "if we begin to see God less as an interferer whose insertion is welcome (when it accords with our needs) and more as the immensity whose reality is our prefiguration . . . we shall have won a sense of God whom we may love and honor, but whom we no longer fear and from whom we no longer demand."[20] This redescription of God that denies that God is a direct causal agent in human affairs, coupled with a form of the free will defense (as seen in Cohen's selection below), appears to resolve much of the theological tension created by the *Tremendum*.

But this deconstruction of classical theism and its substitution by what Cohen terms theological dipolarity creates its own theological difficulties. For example, one needs to ask: Is "God" still God if He is no longer the providential agency in history? Is "God" still God if He lacks the power to enter history vertically to perform the miraculous? Is such a "dipolar" God still the God to whom one prays, the God of salvation? Students have to think through these and other religious issues raised by Cohen's redefinition of God and His role in human affairs before deciding whether to opt for or against his provocative theological revisions.

Hans Jonas's suggested redefinition of the concept of God (see his selection below) emphasizes, in contradistinction to classical theological claims that the Divine is perfect and unchanging, both that God suffers along with humankind and that through His relation with men and women He "becomes." That is, "the relation of God to the world from the moment of creation, and certainly from the creation of man on, involves suffering on the part of God." And, at the same time: "God emerges in time instead of possessing a completed being that remains identical with itself throughout eternity." God has been altered by—"temporalized" by—His relationship with others and, in the process, has become open to human suffering, which causes Him to suffer and to care. Moreover, insofar as God is not omnipotent, Jonas contends that human action is required to perfect the world. "God has no more to give: It is man's now to give to Him."

As with the ruminations of Arthur A. Cohen, Jonas's revised conception of the Divine is imaginative and provocative. Whether it sacrifices too much in its attempt to make metaphysical and ontological sense of the Holocaust is the essential question for readers to ponder.

The third redefinition of God represented in this collection is advanced by Melissa Raphael who, in an intriguing argument, suggests that during and after the Holocaust the correct way to decipher the action of the Divine is through the model of "God as mother" rather than through the inherited traditional idea of "God as father." The patriarchal notion of God as almighty and omniscient is simply incompatible with what happened in the death camps. Yet, faced with this jarring fact, one need not give up belief in God altogether. Rather, one should refashion one's understanding of God in the image of a caring, suffering, loving—but not omnipotent—mother. Calling into use the traditional rabbinic notion of God's presence in the world as being associated with feminine attributes—this divine presence being known among the rabbis and Jewish mystics as the *Shekhinah*—Raphael advances the proposal that we should continue to believe in a God who "all the while secretly sustains the world by Her care."

Raphael's proposed revision is undoubtedly suggestive, even profoundly appealing in many ways, but there remains the fundamental theological question: Will the concept of "God as mother" be able to answer all the problematic metaphysical and ethical conundrums produced by the "final solution" better, i.e., both more inclusively and more conclusively, than prior patriarchal accounts of the Divine? Or, like Cohen's and Jonas's views, does her revisionist position sacrifice too much theologically and metaphysically in order to retain some very much reduced role for God in human affairs?

4. God Is Dead

It is natural that many should have responded to the horror of the Holocaust with unbelief. How, such individuals quite legitimately ask, can one continue to believe in God when God did nothing to halt the demonic fury of Hitler and his minions? Such skepticism usually takes a nonsystematic, almost intuitive form: "I can no longer believe." However, one contemporary Jewish theologian, Richard Rubenstein, has provided a formally structured "death of God" theology as a response to the *Shoah*.

In Rubenstein's view (represented in the selections below), the only honest response to the death camps is the rejection of God, "God is dead," and the open recognition of the meaninglessness of existence. Our life is neither planned nor purposeful. History reflects no Divine will, and human affairs reveal no Divine concern. In light of the Holocaust, human beings must now reject their illusions and recognize the truth: that life is not intrinsically valuable and that the human condition reflects no transcendental purpose. All theological "rationalizations" of the Holocaust pale before its enormity and, for Rubenstein, the only reaction that is worthy is the rejection of the entire inherited Jewish theological framework: There is no God and no covenant with Israel.

Humankind must, after Auschwitz, turn away from transcendental myths and face its actual existential situation honestly. Drawing heavily upon the atheistic existentialists, Rubenstein interprets this to mean that in the face of the world's inherent nihilism, if there are to be any values, individuals must fashion and assert these values; in response to history's meaninglessness, human beings must create and project what meaning there is to be.

Had Rubenstein merely asserted the death of God, his would not be a Jewish theology. What makes it "Jewish" are the implications he draws from his radical negation with respect to the people of Israel. It might be expected that the denial of God's covenantal relation with Israel would entail the end of Judaism and so the end of the Jewish people as a meaningful collective. From the perspective of traditional Jewish theology, this would certainly be the case. Rubenstein, however, again inverts our ordinary perception and argues that with the death of God, the existence of "peoplehood," of the community of Israel, is all the more important. Now that there is nowhere else to turn for meaning, Jews need each other all the more in order to create meaning: "[I]t is precisely because human existence is tragic, ultimately hopeless, and without meaning that we treasure our religious community."[21] Though Judaism has to be "demythologized," i.e., it has to renounce all of its traditional metaphysical doctrines as well as its normative claim to a unique "chosen status," at the same time it paradoxically gains heightened importance in the process.

Rubenstein's position is certainly challenging, however it is not free of philosophical and theological difficulties. Students need, for example, to evaluate his criteria and method. That is, they have to ask whether the question of God's existence or nonexistence is subject to empirical confirmation, as Rubenstein believes. Again, if historical events like the Holocaust count against God's existence, do positive events like the creation of the State of Israel count as evidence for God's existence? (Compare, for example, the argument linking the Holocaust and the State of Israel made in the readings by Joseph Soloveitchik and Irving Greenberg.) Asking these questions, we begin to see that judging God's existence or nonexistence is no simple matter. Then, too, are Rubenstein's proposals for the need for a Jewish community in a world without God reasonable? Why, for example, should Jews not find the now-constructed meaning of their lives outside the confines of Jewish peoplehood and community?

5. An Ethical Demand

Two thinkers represented in this collection, Emmanuel Levinas and Amos Funkenstein, reject, in different ways and for different metaphysical reasons, the classical theologies and theodicies that would defend God and His justice despite the gas chambers and crematoriums. And both urge that rather than upholding theological doctrines that have been rendered "indefensible" by the Holocaust—what Levinas in a telling phrase describes as "useless suffering"[22]—the primary, absolute demand of our post-Holocaust era is the defense of the ethical obligation that human beings owe to one another. As Levinas explains:

> [T]he suffering for the useless suffering of the other person, the just suffering in me for the unjustifiable suffering of the other, opens upon the suffering the ethical perspective of the interhuman. . . . It is this attention to the other which, across the cruelties of our century—despite these cruelties, because of these cruelties—can be affirmed as the very bond of human subjectivity, even to the point of being raised to a supreme ethical principle—the only one which it is not possible to contest—a principle which can go so far as to command the hopes and practical discipline of vast human groups.

Levinas, while not denying the existence of God, stresses the obligations that one human being has *a priori* to another human being, i.e., simply by virtue of being human. Whether one is a theist or not, the fundamental human requirement after Auschwitz is caring for the other. Likewise, Funkenstein advances the primacy of the ethical as the appropriate response to the *Shoah* while arguing for a more negative theological position that denies the existence of God.

This position, i.e., the requirement that we first pay attention to ethics for, at Auschwitz, we saw what the disregard of the ethical permits, is appealing but raises, in turn, a number of deep, interrelated questions: What is the ground of the ethical? What is the source of ethical obligation? Who or what is the guarantor of the value of the ethical? Can there be truly binding ethical obligations without religious sanctions? These are very profound questions that cannot ultimately be evaded. To propound *a priori* the primacy of the ethical is merely to stipulate the conclusion, not to prove it.

6. Mystery and Silence

In the face of the abyss, the devouring of the Jewish people by the dark forces of evil incarnate, recourse to the God of mystery and the endorsement of human silence are not unworthy options. There are, however, two kinds of silence, two kinds of employment of the God of mystery. The first is closer to the attitude of the agnostic: "I cannot know," and hence all deeply grounded existential and intellectual wrestling with the enormous problems raised by the *Shoah* are avoided. The second is the silence and mystery to which the Bible points in its recognition of God's elemental otherness. This is the silence that comes after struggling with God, after reproaching God, after feeling His closeness or His painful absence. This silence, this mystery, does not attempt to diminish the tragedy by a too quick, too gauche answer, yet having followed reason to its limits, it recognizes the limits of reason. One finds this attitude more commonly expressed in the literary and personal responses to Auschwitz by survivors than in technical works of theology. For example, it is preeminent in the work of Elie Wiesel (see the final selection in this volume) and Andre Schwarzbart, as well as in the poetry of Nellie Sachs. Assuredly, there is great difficulty in ascertaining when thought has reached its limit and silence and mystery become the proper position to adopt, but, at one and the same time, there is the need to know when to speak in silence.

Still, it should be acknowledged that silence, too, can be problematic for if employed incorrectly, or too casually, or too universally, as a—or the—theological response to the *Shoah*, it removes the Holocaust from history and all post-Holocaust human experience. And by doing so, it may produce the unintended consequence of making the Holocaust irrelevant. If the generations that come after Auschwitz cannot speak of it, and thus cannot raise probing questions as a consequence of it, then it becomes literally meaningless to them.

III

One additional independent issue that should be briefly explored in an introduction to post-Holocaust Jewish theology is that of the "uniqueness" of the Holocaust. This topic, this claim (and the denial of this claim) has played a considerable role in the theological debate concerning the implications of the destruction of European Jewry. In this connection, two different concerns arise. First, there is the historical-philosophical question: Is the Holocaust unique? Second, there is the related, but separate, question: If the Holocaust is unique what, if any, theological implication(s) does this have? To answer the first question—"Is the Holocaust unique?"—we have, of necessity, to delineate the conditions that we hold make this event singular. Thus, we have to be able to show that the Holocaust is unique with respect to specific and identifiable conditions. Unless we can do this, the claim that the Holocaust is unique is either just a rhetorical assertion or a historical claim that no one need accept and which may even be false.

Having considered this issue elsewhere in detail,[23] I suggest the following way of proceeding. First, I would argue that the required individuating criteria, if there are such criteria, are not moral or metaphysical. That is, it is not the case that the Holocaust is more evil than certain other events, or that God caused the destruction in some special way. I would also eschew all questions that raise the issue of "who suffered most." There is no way to quantify and compare the suffering of, for example, Africans enslaved in the enterprise of New World slavery, Native Americans subjugated and brutally mistreated by their European conquerors and colonizers, Armenians murdered in World War I by the Turks, inmates of the Gulag, and victims in Nazi death camps. Instead, I propose that the criteria of uniqueness that we employ be phenomenological. And, on the basis of such criteria, I would argue that, in fact, "The Holocaust is phenomenologically unique by virtue of the fact that never before has a state set out, as a matter of intentional principle and actualized policy, to annihilate physically every man, woman, and child belonging to a specific people.[24] This conclusion entails that the Holocaust would not be the Holocaust if the property of "intentionally pursuing the physical annihilation of a people without remainder" were not present. Likewise, other occasions of mass death that lack this necessary intent (to murder an entire people without remainder) are not comparable to the Holocaust, at least not as regards this property. Certainly a full description and analysis of the Holocaust would include consideration of such elements as technology, bureaucracy, dehumanization, and the like in the destruction of European Jewry. But the presence of these complementary phenomena without the property of genocidal intent would not, in my view, be sufficient to establish either the character of the *Shoah* as such nor, in particular, its uniqueness. One might wish to argue with this conclusion and the criteria used to reach it but to do so one must have detailed knowledge of the historical cases to which the Holocaust is being compared, as well as sound philosophical reasons for proposing other criteria by which to measure and decide this matter.

Now I turn to our second interrelated query: Does this matter theologically? Given how I have defined the concept of "uniqueness," it is not at all clear to me that there is a direct, and preferred, theological meaning to be drawn from the exceptionality of this event. In dealing with and responding to the multiple epistemological and metaphysical issues that are here relevant, both the theological radicals, e.g., Richard Rubenstein, Arthur A. Cohen, and Irving Greenberg, and the theological conservatives, e.g., Eliezer Berkovits, Joseph Soloveitchik, Isaac Hutner, and the Satmar Rebbe, have all run ahead of the available evidence to reach conclusions that are neither epistemologically nor intellectually persuasive.

At present, almost any responsible theological position appears to me to be compatible with the singularity of the *Shoah*. Religious conservatives, who intuitively reject claims for the uniqueness of the Holocaust on the usually implicit grounds that such an unequivocal conclusion would necessarily entail ominous alterations in the inherited normative *Weltanschauung*, are simply mistaken. The fact is that the theological radicals who hold that the singularity of the *Shoah* necessarily entails religious transformations, and within Jewish parameters *halakhic* (religious-legal) changes, have not shown this to be the case. They have merely assumed it to be so, positing the "required changes" they take to be obligatory without providing either *halakhic* or philosophical justification for such innovations. The matter of whether the *Shoah* necessarily entails any religious changes regarding Jewish practices and behaviors remains an open one.

Conclusion

The death camps and *Einsatzgruppen* do challenge—even while they do not necessarily falsify—traditional Jewish theological claims. However, just what this challenge ultimately means remains undecided.

Notes

1. For more on these medieval texts, see Shlomo Eidelberg, trans., *The Jews and the Crusaders: The Hebrew Chronicles of the First and Second Crusades* (Madison, Wis., 1977). For further discussion, see Jacob Katz, *Exclusiveness and Tolerance* (London, 1961), pp. 82–92; and Moses Shulvass, "Crusaders, Martyrs, and the Marranos of Ashkenaz," in his *Between the Rhine and the Bosphorus: Studies and Essays in European Jewish History* (Chicago, 1964), pp. 1–14. For a later medieval source, see Marc Saperstein, "A Sermon on the *Akedah* from the Generation of the Expulsion and Its Implications for 1391," in *Exile and Diaspora: Studies in the History of the Jewish People Presented to Professor Haim Beinart*, edited by Aharon Mirsky et al. (Jerusalem, 1991), pp. 103–124.

2. See, for more details, Shalom Spiegel, *The Last Trial* (New York, 1967), and the medieval religious poems collected in A. M. Habermann, *Sefer Gezerot Ashkenaz Ve-Tzarfat* (Jerusalem, 1945). The Hebrew martyrologies of the Crusades era have also been translated into English by Eidelberg, *The Jews and the Crusaders*.

3. In Christian tradition, the "suffering servant" is Jesus.

4. For more on the different classical Jewish interpretations of the theme of the suffering servant in Isaiah 53, see Samuel R. Driver and Adolf Neubauer, eds., *The 53rd Chapter of Isaiah according to Jewish Authors*, 2 vols. (Oxford, 1876–1877; reprint, New York, 1969).

5. *Faith after the Holocaust* (New York, 1973), p. 127.

6. *The Face of God after Auschwitz* (Amsterdam, 1965), p. 36.

7. *Faith after the Holocaust*, p. 107.

8. *Va'Yoel Moshe*, 3 vols. (Brooklyn, N.Y., 1959, 1960, 1961), Introduction, vol. 1, p. 5 [Hebrew]. I would also note that Christian thinkers also need to reflect carefully on this question when they attribute the Holocaust to God's continuing punishment of the Jewish people for the putative crime of deicide. In a tradition that stresses divine love, is it theologically reasonable to envision a loving God punishing one million Jewish children—and six million Jews altogether—with a horrible death two thousand years after the crucifixion?

9. The text in B. T. *Ketubot* reports: "God said to the people of Israel: 'If you keep my oaths, well and good; if not I will allow your flesh to become [prey] like that of the gazelles and the hinds of the field.'" Teitlebaum interprets this text to apply to the Zionists who did not keep their "oath" to be passive in the exile that came about, in the first place, because of Israel's sins. Instead, they committed the most grievous sin of attempting to end their suffering in the lands of their dispersion through Zionism, and the Holocaust is God's punishing reply thereto. *Sefer VaYoel Moshe* (Brooklyn, N.Y., 5721/1961), p. 5 [Hebrew]. For a critique of Teitlebaum's views, see Norman Lamm, "The Ideology of *Naturei Karta* according to the Satmarer Version," *Tradition* 12, no. 2 (Fall 1971): 38–53; Allan L. Nadler, "Piety and Politics: The Case of the Satmar Rebbe," *Judaism* 31, no. 2 (Spring 1982): 135–152; and Zvi Jonathan Kaplan, "Rabbi Joel Teitelbaum, Zionism, and Hungarian Ultra-Orthodoxy," *Modern Judaism* 24, no. 2 (May 2004): 165–178. See also the critique of Rav Isaac Hutner's explanation of the Holocaust as due to Zionism offered by Lawrence Kaplan, "Rabbi Isaac Hutner's *Da'at Torah* Perspective on the Holocaust," *Tradition* 18, no. 3 (Fall 1980): 235–248. The essay by R. Hutner to which Kaplan is replying is reprinted in this collection, pp. 557–564 below.

10. For the presentation of this position, see Elhanan Wasserman, *In the Footsteps of the Messiah* (Tel Aviv, 5702/1942), p. 6 [Hebrew]; Haim Ozer Grodzinsky, *Ahiezer* (Vilna, 5699/1939) [Hebrew]; Jacob Israel Kanyevsky, *Hayyhai Olam* (Rishon Le Zion, 5732/1972) [Hebrew]. Readers should also consult the relevant material reprinted in part I of this collection.

11. This refers to Martin Buber's theory of revelation most famously presented in his classic work *I and Thou*, first published in German in 1923. For more on this, see Buber's own discussion in part 3 of *I and Thou*, translated by Walter Kaufman (New York, 1970).

12. *The Third Great Cycle of Jewish History* (New York, 1981), p. 6. Hereafter abbreviated as *TGC*.

13. To be dated approximately 150 B.C.E. to 600 C.E.

14. *TGC*, p. 7.

15. *Voluntary Covenant* (New York, 1982), p. 34.

16. *TGC*, p. 23.

17. *TGC*, p. 25.

18. (New York, 1981).

19. *The Tremendum*, p. 50.

20. Cohen, *The Tremendum*, p. 97.

21. *After Auschwitz* (Indianapolis, 1966), p. 68.

22. "Useless Suffering," in *The Provocation of Levinas*, edited by Robert Berlasconi and David Wood (London, 1988), p. 159.

23. See my full argument in Steven T. Katz, *The Holocaust in Historical Context*, vol. 1 (New York, 1994).

24. Ibid., p. 28.

Martin Buber

Martin Buber (1878–1965), the most influential Jewish philosopher of the twentieth century, was born in Vienna. From the age of three, due to his parents' divorce, he was raised in Galicia in the home of his grandfather Solomon Buber, who was a famous scholar and the editor of midrashic texts. In 1892, he returned to Lemberg to live with his father and in 1896 began his university studies at the University of Vienna. He moved to the University of Berlin to continue his academic work and received his doctorate from Berlin in 1904. He was early attracted to Herzl's Zionist movement and in 1901 became the editor of the Zionist movement's journal, *Die Welt*.

It was during the first years of the twentieth century that Buber began his study of Hasidism. In 1906 he published his first collection of hasidic material, a highly edited version (in German) of *The Tales of Rabbi Nachman*, and he followed this a year later with an edited translation of *The Tales of the Baal Shem Tov*. The exploration of Hasidism would continue to be central to his life and work for the next sixty years. In 1923, he was appointed to the first chair in Jewish studies in Germany at the University of Frankfurt, a position he held until the Nazis came to power. In the 1920s, with his great colleague Franz Rosenzweig, he began a new translation of the Hebrew Bible, which he continued to work on after Rosenzweig's death in 1929. In 1938, he emigrated to Mandate Palestine and began to teach at the Hebrew University of Jerusalem.

Buber is most famous as the author of the classic philosophical work *I and Thou*, published in German in 1923. In it, he argued that God was always available to humankind if approached in the right spirit. This association with God he defined as an *I-Thou* (as compared to an *I-It*) relationship in which one enters into an uncoerced, immediate, direct, metalinguistic, noncausal, reciprocal relation with the other. In such a relation, all matters of utility and calculation, of means and ends, disappear, and the other becomes immediately present. While it is possible to enter *I-Thou* relations with other human beings, the paradigmatic *I-Thou* relation is with God, the *Eternal Thou* who, on Buber's teaching, can never "become an It." That is, God can never be an object rather than a subject, and He cannot be described in language nor captured and explained by systems of thought.

SELECTIONS

After the Holocaust, Buber's optimism about God's continual presence and the ever-present possibility of entering into an *I-Thou* relationship with Him was severely challenged. In response, in several places, he attempted to affirm his continued faith in the reality of the God of Israel, despite the monumental evil represented by the "final solution." The two selections presented here both make the argument that while the Holocaust cannot be explained and indicates the "hiddenness of God," this hiddenness is not the same as nonexistence and that in the future God will yet reveal Himself again to the Jewish people.

The first selection is drawn from Buber's collection of essays entitled *On Judaism*, edited by Nahum N. Glatzer (New York, 1972). The second selection is from a letter Buber wrote to Ernsz Szilagyi on 29 June 1950. It has been translated by David Fromm-Barzilai and first appeared in English as appendix A in his essay "Agonism in Faith," *Modern Judaism* 23, no. 2 (May 2003): 156–179.

Selected Bibliography

Books by Martin Buber

Eclipse of God (New York, 1952).
On Judaism, edited by N. Glatzer (New York, 1972).
I and Thou, translated by Walter Kaufman (New York, 1972).

Books and Articles about Martin Buber

Schilpp, Paul, and Maurice Friedman, eds. *The Philosophy of Martin Buber* (La Salle, Ill., 1967).
Gordon, Haim, and Jochanan Bloch, eds. *Martin Buber: A Centenary Volume* (n.p., 1984).
Friedman, Maurice. *Martin Buber's Life and Work*, 3 vols. (Detroit, 1988).
Barzilai, David Fromm. "Agonism in Faith," *Modern Judaism* 23, no. 2 (May 2003): 156–179.

DIALOGUE BETWEEN HEAVEN AND EARTH

But there is, in the biblical view, a third, widest sphere of divine utterance. God speaks not only to the individual and to the community, within the limits and under the conditions of a particular biographical or historical situation. Everything, being and becoming, nature and history, is essentially a divine pronouncement [*Aussprache*], an infinite context of signs meant to be perceived and understood by perceiving and understanding creatures.

But here a fundamental difference exists between nature and human history. Nature, as a whole and in all its elements, enunciates something that may be regarded as a self-communication of God to all those ready to receive it. This is what the psalm means that has heaven and earth "declare," wordlessly, the glory of God.[1] Not so human history—not only because mankind, being placed in freedom, cooperates incessantly in shaping its course, but quite especially because, in nature, it is God the Creator who speaks, and His creative act is never interrupted; in history, on the other hand, it is the revealing God who speaks, and revelation is essentially not a continuous process, but breaks in again and again upon the course of events and irradiates it. Nature is full of God's utterance, if one but hears it, but what is said here is always that one, though all-inclusive, something, that which the psalm calls the glory of God; in history, however, times of great utterance, when the mark of divine direction is recognizable in the conjunction of events, alternate with, as it were, mute times, when everything that occurs in the human world and pretends to historical significance appears to us as empty of God, with nowhere a beckoning of His finger, nowhere a sign that He is present and acts upon this our historical hour. In such times it is difficult for the individual, and more so for the people, to understand oneself to be addressed by God; the experience of concrete responsibility recedes more and more, because, in the seemingly God-forsaken space of history, man unlearns taking the relationship between God and himself seriously in the dialogic sense.

In an hour when the exiles in Babylon perceived God's passage through world history, in the hour when Cyrus was about to release them

1. Psalm 19:2.

and send them home, the anonymous Prophet of the Exile, who like none before him felt called upon to interpret the history of peoples, in one of his pamphlets made God say to Israel: "From the beginning I have not spoken in secret" (Isaiah 48:16). God's utterance in history is unconcealed, for it is intended to be heard by the peoples. But Isaiah, to whose book the pronouncements of the anonymous prophet have been attached, not only speaks of a time when God "hideth His face from the house of Jacob" (8:17), but he also knows (28:21) that there are times when we are unable to recognize and acknowledge God's own deeds in history as His deeds, so uncanny and "barbarous" do they seem to us. And the same chapter of the Prophet of the Exile, in which God says, "Ask Me of the things to come" (45:11), states that in the hour of the liberation of peoples the masses whom Egypt put to forced labor and Ethiopia sold as slaves will immediately, with the chains of serfdom still on their bodies, as it were, turn to God, throw themselves down, and pray: "Verily Thou art a God that hideth Himself, O God of Israel, Savior!" (45:15). During the long periods of enslavement it seemed to them as though there were nothing divine any more and the world was irretrievably abandoned to the forces of tyranny; only now do they recognize that there is a Savior, and that He is one—the Lord of history. And now they know and profess: He is a God who hides himself, or more exactly, the God who hides Himself and reveals Himself.

The Bible knows of God's hiding His face, of times when the contact between heaven and earth seems to be interrupted. God seems to withdraw Himself utterly from the earth and no longer to participate in its existence. The space of history is then full of noise, but empty of the divine breath. For one who believes in the living God, who knows about Him, and is fated to spend his life in a time of His hiddenness, it is very difficult to live.

There is a psalm, the 82d, in which life in a time of God's hiddenness is described in a picture of startling cruelty. It is assumed that God has entrusted the government of mankind to a host of angels and commanded them to realize jus-

tice on earth and to protect the weak, the poor, and the helpless from the encroachments of the wrongdoers. But they "judge unjustly" and "respect the persons of the wicked." Now the Psalmist envisions how God draws the unfaithful angels before His seat, judges them, and passes sentence upon them: They are to become mortal. But the Psalmist awakes from his vision and looks about him: Iniquity still reigns on earth with unlimited power. And he cries to God: "Arise, O God, judge the earth!"

This cry is to be understood as a late, but even more powerful, echo of that bold speech of the patriarch arguing with God: "The judge of all the earth, will He not do justice?!"[2] It reinforces and augments that speech; its implication is: Will He allow injustice to reign further? And so the cry transmitted to us by Scripture becomes our own cry, which bursts from our hearts and rises to our lips in a time of God's hiddenness. For this is what the biblical word does to us: It confronts us with the human address as one that in spite of everything is heard and in spite of everything may expect an answer.

In this our own time, one asks again and again: How is a Jewish life still possible after Auschwitz? I would like to frame this question more correctly: How is a life with God still possible in a time in which there is an Auschwitz? The estrangement has become too cruel, the hiddenness too deep. One can still "believe" in the God who allowed those things to happen, but can one still speak to Him? Can one still hear His word? Can one still, as an individual and as a people, enter at all into a dialogic relationship with Him? Can one still call to Him? Dare we recommend to the survivors of Auschwitz, the Job of the gas chambers: "Give thanks unto the Lord, for He is good; for His mercy endureth forever"?[3]

But how about Job himself? He not only laments, but he charges that the "cruel" God (30:21) has "removed his right" from him (27:2) and thus that the judge of all the earth acts against justice. And he receives an answer from God. But what God says to him does not answer the charge; it does not even touch upon it. The true answer that Job receives is God's appearance

2. Genesis 18:25.

3. Psalm 106:1.

only, only this that distance turns into nearness, that "his eye sees Him" (42:5), that he knows Him again. Nothing is explained, nothing adjusted; wrong has not become right, nor cruelty kindness. Nothing has happened but that man again hears God's address.

The mystery has remained unsolved, but it has become his, it has become man's.

And we?

We—by that is meant all those who have not got over what happened and will not get over it. How is it with us? Do we stand overcome before the hidden face of God like the tragic hero of the Greeks before faceless fate? No, rather even now we contend, we too, with God, even with Him, the Lord of Being, whom we once, we here, chose for our Lord. We do not put up with earthly being; we struggle for its redemption, and struggling we appeal to the help of our Lord, who is again and still a hiding one. In such a state we await His voice, whether it comes out of the storm or out of a stillness that follows it. Though His coming appearance resemble no earlier one, we shall recognize again our cruel and merciful Lord.

A Response to a Letter from Ernsz Szilagyi, June 29, 1950

If all the signs show that the person I love is misleading me, and even if this was always the case, not in one particular aspect but in his whole being. If all the signs show me that this individual is not an angel from heaven like I saw him and accepted him, not the image of an angel that I drew based on his deception, but a demonic entity: then what?

Two possibilities arise for me.

Perhaps I shall say, "The world of the signs is the true one," and then release myself from this world. The world, either releasing myself along with it, or living without meaning the rest of my life.

Or else I shall say: "The person I love is the true one." Perhaps not so since the use of the third person in this case is meaningless, but: "You are the truth." I accepted you as the truth. I accepted you the way you are and you cannot make me doubt it. All I want is that you will be what you are and that you are what you are. My faith in you is not dependent on your doing what I see as just but in the fact that all your deeds are the just, more so, the absolute justice. And if you are a devil, then the angel should be called devil and the devil angel.

It is clear that you cannot speak in this way to a human being. But a man can only speak this way to the Almighty, השמי תבדך. And I doubt if there is any other way. If Abraham accepts Him, then he accepts Him as the one who once promised him a son, and later, when the son is grown, demands that he kill him. If someone accepts him otherwise, he accepts a statue, an idol crafted by his own hand, a "good" one who is easy to love. Truly, Abraham could not understand what he did when he accepted Him in chapter 22, verse 1, but only after he heard what he heard in the following verse, chapter 22, verse 2. Only now when he understands his deeds, when Abraham "went" the first time in chapter 12, verse 4, he "goes" anew. The ram that God sent is irrelevant: The killing of the son happened in the heart.

Otherwise Job: He protests. He said: Then in my youth when the same well-known encouragement was spread over my tent, I accepted Him as "the Justice"; but now when I got to know that His ways in the world are not just, He must reveal Himself to me to restore the situation. And God revealed Himself from the storm. He doesn't say to Job that the world is just, what Job and we will call just. He doesn't make a confession ודוי and does not reveal his secret of mercy וכחמתי. He is just there, the One who calls Himself "I am who I am," the only one called Ja'ה. And without anything further, Job said, "I am consoled רוחמתי." And only when he is being proclaimed as the servant, the "friends," the ones who were protecting God, ask him to speak for them.

So it is also in our time after Auschwitz. We cannot expect God to make a confession ודוי and explain his secrets like an idol that we make with our own hand. And we who accepted Him as the truth and learned that his creation is frightening and his deeds barbarous (Isaiah 28:21), it is not for us to imagine a state when we will be able to say ‫ומלחתי‬ [I forgive]. Because He probably will not stop being ‫אל מסתתד‬ [hidden God], when he reveals Himself anew. How will He reveal Himself? Like to Abraham when He showed him the way, like to Abraham when he demanded from him the cruelest of all demands? Like to the young, perfect, and happy Job or to the old broken Job? We don't know. We know only Him and His coming and that He is indeed coming.

How is a Jewish life after Auschwitz possible? Today I no longer know exactly what Jewish life is, and I am not sure it will be known to me in the future. But I know what it means to cling to Him. The ones who continue to cling to Him are pointing toward what could justly be called in the future Jewish life.

Abraham Joshua Heschel

Abraham Joshua Heschel (1907–1972) was born in Warsaw into a distinguished hasidic family. He was named after his famous grandfather Abraham Joshua Heschel of Apt, who had been a major figure in the hasidic movement. Raised in the very traditional Jewish environment of Poland, Heschel early showed himself to be a precocious student. In his teens, he began to study Polish and German in addition to his native Hebrew and Yiddish and then went to study at the Real Gymnasium in Vilna. After graduation, he continued his academic work in Berlin where in 1927, at the age of twenty, he enrolled in the Friedrich Wilhelm University and the Hochschule für die Wissenschaft des Judentums, a modern rabbinical seminary in which classical Jewish studies were pursued with contemporary academic methods. In 1933, he received his doctorate from the University of Berlin for a work on the phenomenology of prophecy entitled *Die Prophetie* (published in revised form in English as *The Prophets* [New York, 1962]). In the 1930s and 1940s, he published a series of papers on medieval Jewish philosophy and a biography of Maimonides (1935; translated into English and published in New York in 1982 as *Maimonides: A Biography*).

After the rise of Nazism, Heschel became active in the efforts led by Martin Buber to spread Jewish education among German Jewry as an act of Jewish resistance to Nazism. In October 1938, he was deported by the Nazis from Berlin to Poland and began teaching at the Institute for Jewish Studies in Warsaw. In April 1939, he was saved from the fate of Polish Jewry when he received an invitation to join the faculty of the (Reform) Hebrew Union College in Cincinnati, where he taught during the war years. In 1945, he moved to the (Conservative) Jewish Theological Seminary of America in New York City, where he remained for the rest of his life.

Between 1945 and his death in December 1972, Heschel published several original and important theological works, the most notable being *Man Is Not Alone: A Philosophy of Religion* (1951) and *God in Search of Man: A Philosophy of Judaism* (1956). In addition, he published two moving studies of Jewish life, *The Earth Is the Lord's: The Inner Life of the Jew in Eastern Europe* (1950) and *The Sabbath* (1951). To this list could also be added learned and influential studies on rabbinic theology, especially his magisterial Hebrew study *Torah min ha-Shamayim* (2 vols., 1962 and 1965; an English translation entitled *Heavenly Torah* appeared in 2005); on the theological significance of the Land of Israel to Judaism; and on aspects of the history of early Hasidism, among other subjects.

During his years in America, Heschel also became a friend and supporter of Martin Luther King, Jr., and worked actively in the civil rights movement. He also publicly opposed the war in Vietnam, fought for the liberation of Soviet Jewry, and opposed all forms of racism through his writings and personal example.

SELECTION

Heschel was a deeply religious person steeped in the traditional piety of the ḥasidic community of Eastern Europe, and the Holocaust challenged everything he believed about God's presence in human experience and the reality of Divine-human encounter. His most sustained response to the theological challenge posed by the Holocaust came in chapter 16 of his *Man Is Not Alone*, written while the wounds of the *Shoah*—which had claimed most of his immediate family who had remained in Poland—were still fresh. Here he turned to that most pressing of post-*Shoah* theological questions: Where is God, and how could He have allowed such a thing to happen? Rather than answering this question, however, Heschel argues that there is a basic flaw in the premise on which this question rests, i.e., humanity blaming God for what are, in truth, our own sins and failures. Heschel cites the biblical prophets' distinction between a "hidden God" (one who is absent or elusive in essence) and a "hiding God" (one who forsakes the people only *after* they turn away from Him). It is this latter term, the "hiding God," that properly describes the state of our current relationship with the deity as well as God's true nature. Man causes the tragic situation in which he finds himself by fleeing from God: Adam portrays this initial mistake, and the ensuing consequences and rejection inevitably "inaugurate eventual calamity." Our current responsibility then is "to open our souls to Him, to let Him again enter our deeds." We who have turned away from our Creator are responsible for what has subsequently befallen us, and it is now our responsibility to turn back to God, who waits longingly for our return.

Selected Bibliography

Books by Abraham Joshua Heschel

Man Is Not Alone: A Philosophy of Religion (New York, 1951).
God in Search of Man: A Philosophy of Judaism (New York, 1955).
Heavenly Torah as Refracted through the Generations, translated by Gordon Tucker and Leonard Levin (New York, 2005).
Israel: An Echo of Eternity (New York, 1969).

Books and Articles about Heschel

Borowitz, Eugene B. *A New Jewish Theology in the Making* (Philadelphia, 1968), pp. 147–160.
Kaplan, Edward K. "Language and Reality in Abraham J. Heschel's Philosophy of Religion," *Journal of the American Academy of Religion* 41 (March 1973): 94–113.
Merkle, Jonathon. *The Genesis of Faith: The Depth of Theology of Abraham Joshua Heschel* (New York, 1985).
Merkle, Jonathon, ed. *Abraham Joshua Heschel: Exploring His Life and Thought* (New York, 1985).
Kaplan, Edward, and Samuel Dresner. *Abraham Joshua Heschel: Prophetic Witness* (New Haven, 1998).
Faierstein, Morris. "Heschel and the Holocaust," *Modern Judaism* 19, no. 3 (October 1999): 255–275.
Eisen, Robert. "A. J. Heschel's Rabbinic Theology as a Response to the Holocaust," *Modern Judaism* 23, no. 3 (October 2003): 211–225.

THE HIDING GOD

For us, contemporaries and survivors of history's most terrible horrors, it is impossible to meditate about the compassion of God without asking: Where is God?

Emblazoned over the gates of the world in which we live is the escutcheon of the demons. The mark of Cain[1] on the face of man has come to overshadow the likeness of God. There has never been so much distress, agony, and terror. It is often sinful for the sun to shine. At no time has the earth been so soaked with blood. Fellow men have turned out to be evil spirits, monstrous and weird. Does not history look like a stage for the dance of might and evil—with man's wits too feeble to separate the two and God either directing the play or indifferent to it?

The major folly of this view seems to lie in its shifting the responsibility for man's plight from man to God, in accusing the Invisible though iniquity is ours. Rather than admit our own guilt, we seek, like Adam, to shift the blame upon someone else. For generations we have been investing life with ugliness and now we wonder why we do not succeed. God was thought of as a watchman hired to prevent us from using our loaded guns. Having failed us in this, He is now thought of as the ultimate Scapegoat.

We live in an age when most of us have ceased to be shocked by the increasing breakdown in moral inhibitions. The decay of conscience fills the air with a pungent smell. Good and evil, which were once as distinguishable as day and night, have become a blurred mist. But that mist is manmade. God is not silent. He has been silenced.

Instead of being taught to answer the direct commands of God with a conscience open to His will, men are fed on the sweetness of mythology, on promises of salvation and immortality as a dessert to the pleasant repast on earth. The faith believers cherish is secondhand: It is a faith in the miracles of the past, an attachment to symbols

and ceremonies. God is known from hearsay, a rumor fostered by dogmas, and even nondogmatic thinkers offer hackneyed, solemn concepts without daring to cry out the startling vision of the sublime on the margin of which indecisions, doubts, are almost vile.

We have trifled with the name of God. We have taken ideals in vain, preached and eluded Him, praised and defied Him. Now we reap the fruits of failure. Through centuries His voice cried in the wilderness. How skillfully it was trapped and imprisoned in the temples! How thoroughly distorted! Now we behold how it gradually withdraws, abandoning one people after another, departing from their souls, despising their wisdom. The taste for goodness has all but gone from the earth.

We have witnessed in history how often a man, a group, or a nation, lost from the sight of God, acts and succeeds, strives and achieves, but is given up by Him. They may stride from one victory to another and yet they are done with and abandoned, renounced and cast aside. They may possess all glory and might, but their life will be dismal. God has withdrawn from their life, even while they are heaping wickedness upon cruelty and malice upon evil. The dismissal of man, the abrogation of Providence, inaugurates eventual calamity.

They are left alone, neither molested by punishment nor assured by indication of help. The divine does not interfere with their actions nor intervene in their conscience. Having all in abundance save His blessing, they find their wealth a shell in which there is curse without mercy.

Man was the first to hide himself from God,[2] after having eaten of the forbidden fruit, and is still hiding.[3] The will of God is to be here, manifest and near; but when the doors of this world are slammed on Him, His truth betrayed, His will defied, He withdraws, leaving man to

---

1. See [Midrash] *Genesis Rabba* 22, 12, ed. Theodor, p. 219f; L. Ginzberg, *Legends of the Jews* (Philadelphia, 1968), vol. 5, p. 141.

2. Genesis 3:8.
3. Job 13:20–24.

himself. God did not depart of His own volition; He was expelled. *God is in exile.*

More grave than Adam's eating the forbidden fruit was his hiding from God after he had eaten it. "Where art thou?" Where is man? is the first question that occurs in the Bible. It is man's alibi that is our problem. It is man who hides, who flees, who has an alibi. God is less rare than we think; when we long for Him, His distance crumbles away.

The prophets do not speak of the *hidden God* but of the *hiding God.* His hiding is a function, not His essence, an act, not a permanent state. It is when the people forsake Him, breaking the Covenant which He has made with them, that He forsakes them and hides His face from them.[4] It is not God who is obscure. It is man who conceals Him. His hiding from us is not in His essence: "Verily Thou art a God that hidest Thyself, O God of Israel, the Savior!" (Isaiah 45:15). A hiding God, not a hidden God. He is waiting to be disclosed, to be admitted into our lives.

The direct effect of His hiding is the hardening of the conscience: Man hears but does not understand, sees but does not perceive—his heart fat, his ears heavy.[5] Our task is to open our souls to Him, to let Him again enter our deeds. We have been taught the grammar of contact with God; we have been taught by the Baal Shem that His remoteness is an illusion capable of being dispelled by our faith. There are many doors through which we have to pass in order to enter the palace, and none of them is locked.

As the hiding of man is known to God and seen through, so is God's hiding seen through. In sensing the fact of His hiding we have disclosed Him. Life is a hiding place for God. We are never asunder from Him who is in need of us. Nations roam and rave—but all this is only ruffling the deep, unnoticed, and uncherished stillness.

The grandchild of Rabbi Baruch was playing hide-and-seek with another boy. He hid himself and stayed in his hiding place for a long time, assuming that his friend would look for him. Finally, he went out and saw that his friend was gone, apparently not having looked for him at all,

and that his own hiding had been in vain. He ran into the study of his grandfather, crying and complaining about his friend. Upon hearing the story, Rabbi Baruch broke into tears and said: "God, too, says: 'I hide, but there is no one to look for me.'"

There are times when defeat is all we face, when horror is all that faith must bear. And yet, in spite of anguish, in spite of terror we are never overcome with ultimate dismay. "Even that it would please God to destroy me; that He would let loose His hand and cut me off, then should I yet have comfort, yea, I would exult even in my pain; let Him not spare me, for I have not denied the words of the holy One" (Job 6:9–10). Wells gush forth in the deserts of despair. This is the guidance of faith: "Lie in the dust and gorge on faith."[6]

We have heard with our ears, O God, our fathers have told us, what work Thou didst in their days, in the times of old.

How Thou didst drive out the heathen with Thy hand, and plantedst them; how Thou didst afflict the people, and cast them out.

For they got not the land in possession by their own sword, neither did their own arm save them: but Thy right hand, and Thine arm, and the light of Thy countenance, because Thou hadst a favor unto them.

Thou art my king, O God, command deliverances for Jacob.

Through Thee will we push down our enemies: through Thy name will we tread them under that rise up against us.

For I will not trust in my bow, neither shall my sword save me.

But Thou hast saved us from our enemies, and hast put them to shame that hated us.

In God we boast all the day long: and praise Thy name for ever. Selah.

But Thou hast cast off, and put us to shame; and goest not forth with our armies.

Thou makest us to turn back from the enemy: and they which hate us spoil for themselves.

Thou hast given us like sheep appointed for meat: and hast scattered us among the heathen.

4. Deuteronomy 31:16–17.
5. Isaiah 6.

6. Rabbi Mendel of Kotzk, paraphrasing Psalm 37:3.

Thou sellest thy people for nought, and dost not increase Thy wealth by their price.

Thou makest us a reproach to our neighbors, a scorn and a derision to them that are round about us.

Thou makest us a by-word among the heathen, a shaking of the head among the people.

My confusion is continually before me, and the shame of my face hath covered me:

For the voice of Him that reproacheth and blasphemeth; by reason of the enemy and avenger.

All this is come upon us; yet have we not forgotten Thee: neither have we dealt falsely in Thy covenant.

Our heart is not turned back, neither have our steps declined from Thy way.

Though Thou hast sore broken us in the place of dragons, and covered us with the shadow of death.

If we have forgotten the name of our God, or stretched out our hands to a strange god:

Shall not God search this out? for He knoweth the secrets of the heart.

Yea, for Thy sake are we killed all the day long: we are counted as sheep for the slaughter.

Awake, why sleepest Thou, O Lord? arise, cast us not off for ever.

Wherefore hidest Thou Thy face? and forgettest our affliction, and our oppression?

For our soul is bowed down to the dust; our belly cleaveth unto the earth.

Arise for our help, and redeem us for Thy mercies sake. (Psalm 44)

Joseph B. Soloveitchik

Joseph B. Soloveitchik (1903–1993), born 27 February in Pruzhan, Poland, was the scion of a great Orthodox rabbinic family connected with the teaching and tradition of R. Elijah of Vilna (the Vilna Gaon, 1720–1797). His grandfather Rav Chaim Solo-veitchik had pioneered a new method of Talmud study and his father, Rav Moshe, was an eminent talmudist and communal rabbi. Until age nineteen, Soloveitchik's education was mainly carried on under the tutelage of his father and consisted primarily of traditional talmudic studies, though in his late teens he also received the beginnings of a gymnasium-like secular education from a series of tutors. In 1925, in a bold act that remains the source of controversy and varying explanations, he left Eastern Europe and the world of the yeshiva to enroll at the University of Berlin to study philosophy. There he became a keen student of the Marburg neo-Kantian philosophy of Hermann Cohen and in 1931 received his doctorate for a thesis on Hermann Cohen's interpretation of Kant.

In 1931, after his marriage to Tonya Lewit, who held a doctorate in education, he migrated to the United States and settled in Boston, taking a post as a communal rabbi. However, his fame would derive from his position at Yeshiva University in New York City where he became professor of Talmud in the school's Rabbi Isaac Elchanan Theological Seminary. In this setting he trained generations of Orthodox rabbis and became known simply as "the Rav," the rabbinic teacher par excellence.

SELECTION

Though Soloveitchik published relatively little during his lifetime, his essays on Jewish philosophy, which combine vast rabbinic erudition with a deep knowledge of modern philosophy, became instant classics in the Orthodox Jewish world, and even beyond it. Among these essays his seminal study *Kol Dodi Dofek* ("The Voice of My Beloved Knocks"), published in 1961, represents his most sustained response to the Holocaust. Unable to explain the event itself—this always remains a mystery from the human perspective—he concentrated instead on linking the destruction of European Jewry with the creation of the State of Israel in 1948. He argued that just as the death camps appear to provide evidence against God's existence and against His special covenantal relationship with the people of Israel, the reborn State of Israel supplies powerful evidence of God's existence and His continued love affair with the Jewish people. The creation of the State of Israel is—to use an image drawn from the Song of Songs, the biblical book traditionally interpreted as a poem about the love of God for Israel—God's "knocking at the door of" the survivors.

The present selection comes from the English translation of Soloveitchik's Hebrew essay *Kol Dodi Dofek*, published in Walter Wurzburger, ed., *Fate and Destiny: From Holocaust to the State of Israel* (New York, 1961).

Selected Bibliography

Books and Articles by Joseph B. Soloveitchik

Fate and Destiny: From Holocaust to the State of Israel, edited by Walter Wurzburger (New York, 1961).

"The Lonely Man of Faith," *Tradition* 7, no. 2 (Summer 1965): 5–67.

The Rav Speaks (Jerusalem, 1983).

Halakhic Man (Philadelphia, 1983).

On Repentance (New York, 1984).

The Halakhic Mind (New York, 1986).

Out of the Whirlwind: Essays on Mourning, Suffering, and the Human Condition, edited by David Shatz, Joel B. Wolowelsky, and Reuven Ziegler (Hoboken, N.J., 2003).

Books and Articles about Joseph Soloveitchik

Lichtenstein, Aharon. "Rabbi Joseph Soloveitchik," in *Great Jewish Thinkers of the Twentieth Century,* edited by Simon Novech (New York, 1963), pp. 281–297.

Singer, David, and Moshe Sokol. "Joseph Soloveitchik: Lonely Man of Faith," *Modern Judaism* 2, no. 3 (October 1982): 227–272. ,

Borowitz, Eugene. "A Theology of Modern Orthodoxy: Rabbi Joseph B. Soloveitchik," in *Choices in Modern Jewish Thought,* edited by Eugene Borowitz (New York, 1983), pp. 218–242.

Hartman, David. *A Living Covenant* (New York, 1985), pp. 60–108, 131–159.

Angel, Marc D., ed., *Exploring the Thought of Rabbi Joseph B. Soloveitchik* (Hoboken, N.J., 1997).

Kol Dodi Dofek: THE VOICE OF MY BELOVED KNOCKS

The Righteous Who Suffers

One of the darkest enigmas with which Judaism has struggled from the very dawn of its existence is the problem of suffering in the world. Already Moses, the master of the prophets, in a moment of mercy and grace, of divine acceptance, pleaded with the Lord that He enlighten him concerning this obscure matter.[1] Moses knocked at the gates of heaven and cried out: "Show me now Thy ways, that I may know Thee, to the end that I may find grace in Thy sight.... Show me, I pray Thee, Thy glory" (Exodus 33:13, 18). Why and wherefore do afflictions and pain befall man? Why and wherefore do the righteous suffer and the wicked prosper? From that wondrous morn when Moses, the faithful shepherd, communed with the Creator of the world and sought a comprehensive solution to this question of questions, prophets and sages, through all the generations, have continued to grapple with it. Habakkuk demanded satisfaction for the affront to justice; Jeremiah, King David in his Psalms, and Koheleth [Ecclesiastes] pondered this quandary. The entire Book of Job is devoted to this ancient and mysterious query which still agitates and disturbs our world and demands an answer: Why has God allowed evil to reign over His creation?

---

1. See B. T. *Berakhot* 7a. According to R. Meir, Moses did not receive a reply to his request to comprehend the problem of suffering in the world—the righteous man who is in adversity and the wicked man who prospers. R. Yohanan in the name of R. Yose disagrees. Maimonides, in the *Guide of the Perplexed,* adopts the view of R. Yohanan in the name of R. Yose and asserts that God enlightened Moses regarding the governance of the totality of existence. See *Guide* 1:54: "This dictum—'All My goodness' (Exodus 33:19)— alludes to the display to him [Moses] of all existing things...that is, he has grasped the existence of all My world with a true and firmly established understanding."

Judaism, in its strenuous endeavor to reach a safe shore in a world torn asunder by pain and affliction, in its search for an answer to the profound dilemma posed by the evil which—apparently—reigns unboundedly, arrived at a new formulation and definition of the problem, possessed of both depth and breadth. The problem of suffering, Judaism claims, may be raised in two distinct dimensions: fate and destiny. Judaism has always distinguished between an existence of fate and an existence of destiny, between the "I" subject to fate and the "I" endowed with destiny. It is in this distinction that our teaching regarding suffering is to be found.

What is the nature of an existence of fate? It is an existence of compulsion, an existence of the type described by the Mishnah, "Against your will[2] do you live out your life" (*Avot* 4:29), a purely factual existence, one link in a mechanical chain, devoid of meaning, direction, purpose, but subject to the forces of the environment into which the individual has been cast by providence, without any prior consultation. The "I" of fate has the image of an object. As an object he appears as made and not as maker. He is fashioned by his passive encounter with an objective, external environment, as one object vis-à-vis another object. The "I" of fate is caught up in a blind, wholly external dynamic. His being is empty, lacking any inwardness, any independence, any selfhood. Indeed, an "I" of fate is a contradiction in terms. For how can "I" awareness and selfhood coexist with pure externality and objectlike being?

It is against this background that the experience of evil arises in all its terror. There are two stages to this fate-laden experience of evil. To begin with, man the object, bound in the chains of an existence of compulsion, stands perplexed and confused before that great mystery—suffering. Fate mocks him; his being, shattered and torn, contradicts itself and negates its own value and worth. The dread of annihilation seizes hold of him and crushes him, both body and soul. The

sufferer, quaking and panic-stricken, wanders in the empty spaces of a world upon which the wrath and terror of God weigh heavily. His afflictions appear shadowy and murky, like satanic forces, the offspring of the chaos and the void which pollute the cosmos that had been destined to clearly reflect the image of its Creator. In this stage of perplexity and speechlessness, of confusion of both mind and heart, the sufferer does not pose any questions about the cause and nature of evil. He suffers in silence, groaning under the weight of an agony that has stifled all complaint and suppressed all queries and inquiries.

After this psychic upheaval of the sufferer as the immediate reaction to evil has passed, there follows the intellectual curiosity which endeavors to understand the cosmos and thereby undergird man's confidence and security. In this stage, a person begins to contemplate suffering and to pose grave and difficult questions. He tracks the intellectual foundations of suffering and evil, and seeks to find the harmony and balance between the affirmation and the negation and to blunt the sharp edge of the tension between the thesis—the good—and the antithesis—the bad—in existence. As a result of the question and answer, problem and resolution, he formulates a metaphysics of evil wherewith he is able to reach an accommodation with evil, indeed to cover it up. The sufferer utilizes his capacity for intellectual abstraction, with which he was endowed by his Creator, to the point of self-deception—the denial of the existence of evil in the world.

Judaism, with its realistic approach to man and his place in the world, understood that evil cannot be blurred or camouflaged and that any attempt to downplay the extent of the contradiction and fragmentation to be found in reality will neither endow man with tranquillity nor enable him to grasp the existential mystery. Evil is an undeniable fact. There is evil, there is suffering, there are hellish torments in this world. Whoever wishes to delude himself by diverting his attention from the deep fissure in reality, by romanticizing human

---

2. The medieval authorities ([known as]*Rishonim*) already discussed the issue of a man being deprived of choice because of his being extremely steeped in sin. See Maimonides, [*Mishneh Torah*] Laws of Repentance 6:3;

and Nahmanides' *Commentary on the Torah* to Exodus 7:3, 9:12.

existence, is nought but a fool and a fantast. It is impossible to overcome the hideousness of evil through philosophico-speculative thought. Therefore, Judaism determined that man, entrapped in the depths of a frozen, fate-laden existence, will seek in vain for the solution to the problem of evil within the framework of speculative thought, for he will never find it. Certainly, the testimony of the Torah that the cosmos is very good is true. However, this affirmation may be made only from the infinite perspective of the Creator. Finite man, with his partial vision, cannot uncover the absolute good in the cosmos. The contradiction in existence stands out clearly and cannot be negated. Evil, which can neither be explained nor comprehended, does exist. Only if man could grasp the world as a whole would he be able to gain a perspective on the essential nature of evil. However, as long as man's apprehension is limited and distorted, as long as he perceives only isolated fragments of the cosmic drama and the mighty epic of history, he remains unable to penetrate into the secret lair of suffering and evil. To what may the matter be compared? To a person gazing at a beautiful rug, a true work of art, one into which an exquisite design has been woven—but looking at it from its reverse side. Can such a viewing give rise to a sublime aesthetic experience? We, alas, view the world from its reverse side. We are, therefore, unable to grasp the all-encompassing framework of being. And it is only within that framework that it is possible to discern the divine plan, the essential nature of the divine actions.

In a word, the "I" of fate asks a theoretical-metaphysical question regarding evil, and this question has no answer. It is insoluble.

In the second dimension of human existence, destiny, the problem of suffering assumes a new form. What is the nature of the existence of destiny? It is an active mode of existence, one wherein man confronts the environment into which he was thrown, possessed of an understanding of his uniqueness, of his special worth, of his freedom, and of his ability to struggle with his external circumstances without forfeiting either his independence or his selfhood. The motto of the "I" of destiny is, "Against your will you are born and against your will you die, but you live of your own free will." Man is born like an object, dies like an object, but possesses the ability to live like a subject, like a creator, an innovator, who can impress his own individual seal upon his life and can extricate himself from a mechanical type of existence and enter into a creative, active mode of being. Man's task in the world, according to Judaism, is to transform fate into destiny; a passive existence into an active existence; an existence of compulsion, perplexity, and muteness into an existence replete with a powerful will, with resourcefulness, daring, and imagination. God's blessing to the work of His hands sums up their entire purpose in life: "Be fruitful and multiply, and fill the earth and subdue it" (Genesis 1:28). Subdue the environment and subject it to your control. If you do not rule over it, it will subjugate you. Destiny bestows upon man a new rank in God's world, it presents him with a royal crown, and man becomes transformed into a partner with the Almighty in the act of creation.

As was stated above, man's existence of destiny gives rise to an original approach to the problem of evil. For so long as a person grapples with the problem of evil while still living an existence of fate, his relationship to this problem expresses itself only in a theoretical-philosophical approach. As a passive creature, the man of fate lacks the strength to struggle with evil in order to contain it or in order to utilize it to achieve an exalted goal. For the "I" subject to fate is unable to effect any matter of consequence in the sphere of his own existence. He is nourished by his external environment, and his life bears the imprint of that environment. Therefore, he relates to evil from a nonpractical standpoint and philosophizes about it from a purely speculative perspective. He wishes to deny the existence of evil and to create a harmonistic world view. The end of such an effort can only be complete and total disillusionment. Evil derides the captive of fate and his fantasy about a world which is wholly good and wholly beautiful.

However, in the realm of destiny man recognizes the world as it is and does not wish to use harmonistic formulas in order to gloss over and conceal evil. The man of destiny is highly realistic and does not flinch from confronting evil face to face. His approach is an ethico-*halakhic* [religio-legal] one, devoid of the slightest speculative-metaphysical coloration. When the man of destiny suffers he says to himself:

Evil exists, and I will neither deny it nor camouflage it with vain intellectual gymnastics. I am concerned about evil from a *halakhic* standpoint, like a person who wishes to know the deed which he shall do; I ask one simple question: What must the sufferer do so that he may live through his suffering?

In this dimension the center of gravity shifts from the causal and teleological aspect of evil (the only difference between causality and teleology being a directional one) to its practical aspect. The problem is now formulated in straightforward *halakhic* language and revolves about one's daily, quotidian tasks. The fundamental question is: What obligation does suffering impose upon man? This question is greatly beloved by Judaism, and she has placed it at the very center of her world of thought. The *Halakhah* [Jewish religious law] is concerned with this problem as it is concerned with other problems of permitted and forbidden, liability and exemption. We do not inquire about the hidden ways of the Almighty, but, rather, about the path whereon man shall walk when suffering strikes. We ask neither about the cause of evil nor about its purpose, but, rather, about how it might be mended and elevated. How shall a person act in a time of trouble? What ought a man to do so that he not perish in his afflictions?

The *halakhic* answer to this question is very simple. Afflictions come to elevate a person, to purify and sanctify his spirit, to cleanse and purge it of the dross of superficiality and vulgarity, to refine his soul and to broaden his horizons. In a word, the function of suffering is to mend that which is flawed in an individual's personality. The *Halakhah* teaches us that the sufferer commits a grave sin if he allows his troubles to go to waste and remain without meaning or purpose. Suffering occurs in the world in order to contribute something to man, in order that atonement be made for him, in order to redeem him from corruption, vulgarity, and depravity. From out of its midst the sufferer must arise ennobled and refined, clean and pure. "It is a time of agony unto Jacob, but out of it he shall be saved" (Jeremiah 30:7); i.e., from out of the very midst of the agony itself he will attain eternal salvation. The agony itself will serve to form and shape his character so that he will, thereby, reach a level of exaltedness not possible in a world bereft of suffering. Out of the negation grows the affirmation, out of the antithesis the thesis blossoms forth, and out of the abrogation of reality there emerges a new reality. The Torah itself bears witness to man's powerful spiritual reaction to any trouble that may befall him when it states: "In your distress, when all these things come upon you ... and you return unto the Lord your God" (Deuteronomy 4:30). Suffering imposes upon man the obligation to return to God in complete and wholehearted repentance.[3] Afflictions are designed to bestir us

3. The connection between trouble and repentance finds its expression in the commandment to cry out and sound the alarm with trumpets whenever trouble befalls the community. Maimonides, in [*Mishneh Torah*] Laws of Fast Days 1:1–4, states: "It is a positive scriptural commandment to cry out and sound the alarm with trumpets whenever trouble befalls the community, as it is said, 'against the adversary that oppresseth you, then ye shall sound the alarm with the trumpets' (Numbers 10:9), that is to say: Whatever is oppressing you, whether it be famine, pestilence, locusts, or the like, cry out over them and sound the trumpets. This procedure is one of the paths of repentance, for when trouble occurs and they cry out over it and sound the trumpets, everyone will know that evil has come upon them because of their evil deeds. ... On the authority of the scribes, fasting is prescribed whenever trouble befalls a community until mercy is vouchsafed to it from heaven."

There are two distinct commandments: (1) There is a positive commandment of repentance and confession for any sin that a person commits. This commandment is set forth in Numbers 5:6–7, "When a man or a woman commits any sin ... then they shall confess their sin which they have done," and Maimonides, in his [*Mishneh Torah*] *Book of Knowledge*, devoted an entire section, The Laws of Repentance, comprising ten chapters, to it. (2) There is a specific obligation of repentance during a time of trouble, as set forth in Numbers 10:9, "And when ye go forth to war in your land against the adversary that oppresseth you, then ye shall sound an alarm with the trumpets; and ye shall be remembered before the Lord your God." In terms of concrete practice, this obligation of repentance, on a scriptural level, assumes the form of sounding the trumpets, and on a scribal level, the form of fasting.

Essentially the obligation of repentance in time of trouble is connected with the suffering of the community, as the Mishnah very precisely states, "for every trouble that befalls a community—may it not happen!" (B. T. *Ta'anit* 19a), and as Maimonides emphasizes in the text we cited just above. However, the obligation of an individual in trouble to return to God also stems from this biblical passage. The fact that the

to repent, and what is repentance if not man's self-renewal and his supernal redemption?

Woe unto the man whose suffering has not precipitated a spiritual crisis in the depths of his being, whose soul remains frozen and lacking forgiveness! Woe unto the sufferer if his heart is not inflamed by the fires of affliction, if his pangs do not kindle the lamp of the Lord that is within him! If a person allows his pains to wander about the vast empty spaces of the cosmos like blind, purposeless forces, then a grave indictment is drawn up against him for having frittered away his suffering.

Judaism has deepened this concept by combining the notion of the mending and elevation of suffering with that of the mending and elevation of divine loving kindness, divine ḥesed. God's acts of ḥesed, Judaism declares, are not granted to man as a free gift. Rather, they impose obligations, they make ethico-halakhic demands upon their beneficiary. To be sure, the overflow of divine ḥesed derives from God's open, superabundant,

Halakhah accords recognition to a fast undertaken by an individual demonstrates that there is an obligation of repentance devolving upon the individual who finds himself in difficult circumstances. According to Maimonides, there is no such thing as a fast devoid of repentence. Maimonides, in Laws of Fast Days 1:19, states: "Just as a community must fast when in trouble, so an individual must fast when in trouble." Similarly, the baraita states: "Our rabbis have taught: If a city is surrounded by [hostile] Gentiles or threatened with inundation by a river, or if a ship is foundering in the sea, or if an individual is pursued by Gentiles or by robbers or by an evil spirit, [the alarm is sounded even on the Sabbath]" (B. T. Ta'anit 2b). [The bracketed phrase at the end of the quotation is the correct reading of the text, according to the Rif, Rambam, Rosh, Maharshah, and others. Translated] In all of these instances, then, it is permitted to sound the alarm (only verbally) on the Sabbath. This is also the ruling of Maimonides, as set forth in Laws of Fast Days 1:6. It follows from this that the obligation to cry out applies equally to the individual and the community. And of what value is crying out, if the cry does not issue forth from a soul that repents its sins? (It is understood that there is no law to sound the alarm with trumpets, even on a weekday, for an individual in trouble. One sounds the alarm with trumpets only for trouble which befalls a community. There are many laws, both in chapter 3 of Mishnah Ta'anit and in chapter 2 of Maimonides' Laws of Fast Days, establishing the nature of communal trouble, and none of these laws includes the individual in trouble. The only point of the baraita cited above is that an individual in trouble may cry out [according to Maimonides' explanation] even on the Sabbath.)

The difference between the general commandment of repentance and the specific obligation of repentance in time of trouble exhausts itself in one detail. Repentance for a sin is bound up with knowledge of the sin. As long as an individual is not aware of having committed any sin, he has no obligation to repent. One cannot oblige a person to seek atonement without knowledge of a sin, as it is said, "or if his sin be known to him wherein he hath sinned" (Leviticus 4:23). It is knowledge of a sin that obliges a person to bring a sin-offering. The same holds true for repentance. A person is not obliged to repent for concealed sins but only for revealed sins. However, in a time of trouble, the sufferer must examine his actions and search out his sins so that he may be able to repent for them. The very fact of suffering indicates the presence of sin and it commands a person: Find your sins and return to your Creator. This scrutinizing of one's deeds is a characteristic feature of the obligation of repentance bound up with suffering. We know that on fast days the courts would meet in session and examine the actions of the townspeople. The Talmud states: "In the morning of fast days there is a public assembly . . . and they examine the affairs of the town" (B. T. Megillah 30b). Similarly, Maimonides, in Laws of Fast Days 1:17, sets it down as a firmly established ruling that "on each fast day undertaken by a community beset by trouble, the court and the elders should meet in session at the synagogue and examine the deeds of the townspeople. . . . They should remove all of the obstacles [to righteous living] provided by transgressors and should carefully search and inquire of the extortioners and other criminals," (See B. T. Eruvin 13b: "and now that he [man] is created, let him scrutinize his [past] actions; and there are those who say: "let him be careful about his [future] actions!' "). This obligation to scrutinize one's actions refers to a time of trouble. It would seem that the special commandment of repentance on the Day of Atonement (as set forth by Maimonides in Laws of Repentance 2:7, and by Rabbenu Jonah [Gerondi] in Gates of Repentance 2:14 and 4:17) also involves, according to the ruling of the Halakhah, a special requirement of repentance for concealed sins and the obligation to scrutinize one's deeds in order to uncover and bring to the surface the degrading underside of a person's life. In this respect, the obligation of repentance on the Day of Atonement is identical with the obligation of repentance in a time of suffering. And it is with reference to such occasions that the verse states: "Let us search and try our ways, and return to the Lord" (Lamentations 3:40). [Cf. Shi'urim le-Zekher Abba Mari Z"L, vol. 1 (Jerusalem, 1983), pp. 190–192. Translator.]

and generous hand, but it is not an absolute gift, without conditions or restrictions. The bestowal of good is always to be viewed as a conditional gift—a gift that must be returned—or as a temporary gift. When God endows a person with wealth, influence, and honor, the recipient must know how to use these boons, how to transform these precious gifts into fruitful, creative forces, how to share his joy and prominence with his fellows, how to take the divine *ḥesed* that flows toward him from its infinite, divine source and utilize it to perform, in turn, deeds of *ḥesed* for others. A person who is not brought by divinely bestowed bountiful good to commit himself, absolutely and unreservedly, to God perpetrates a dire sin, and in its wake he finds himself in very difficult straits which serve to remind him of the obligation he owes to God for His gift of *ḥesed*. Our great tannaitic masters have taught us: "A man must pronounce a blessing over evil just as he pronounces a blessing over good" (B.T. *Berakhot* 9:5). In the same way that God's goodness imposes upon man the obligation to perform exalted, sublime deeds, and demands of either the individual or the community original, creative actions, so too do afflictions require of a person that he improve himself, that he purify his life—if he was previously not bestirred to action when God's countenance shined upon him, when God's *ḥesed* overflowed toward him. For there are times when a person is called upon to mend through his afflictions the flaws that he was inflicting upon creation when God "extended peace to him like a river" (cf. Isaiah 66:12). The awareness of the requirement to commit oneself entirely to God and the understanding of one's obligation to purify and sanctify oneself from precisely out of the midst of one's suffering must shine brightly in the soul of a person when he finds himself in the straits and inquires into the meaning of his very existence. At that very moment, he is obliged to mend his unfeeling heart, the moral callousness that caused him to sin while he was yet standing in the great expanses. In a word, man is obliged to resolve not the question of the causal or teleological explanation of suffering in all of its speculative complexity, but rather the question of the rectification of suffering in all of its *halakhic* simplicity.

He does this by transforming fate into destiny, elevating himself from object to subject, from thing to person.

Job

Consider: This was precisely the answer that the Creator gave to Job. As long as Job philosophized, like a slave of fate, regarding the cause of and reason for suffering, as long as he demanded of God that He reveal to him the nature of evil, as long as he continued to question and complain, asking why and wherefore afflictions befall man, God answered him forcefully and caustically, posing to him the very powerful and pointed question, "Dost thou know?"

> Who is this that darkeneth counsel by words without knowledge? Gird up now thy loins like a man; for I will demand of thee, and declare thou unto Me. Where wast thou when I laid the foundations of the earth? Declare, if thou hast the understanding. . . . Dost thou know the time when the wild goats of the rock bring forth? Or canst thou mark when the hinds do calve? (Job 38:2–4, 39:1)

If you do not even know the ABC of creation, how can you so arrogantly presume to ask so many questions regarding the governance of the cosmos? However, once Job understood how strange and inappropriate his question was, how great was his ignorance, once he confessed unashamedly, "Therefore have I uttered that which I understood not, things too wonderful for me, which I knew not" (Job 42:4), the Almighty revealed to him the true principle contained in suffering, as formulated by the *Halakhah*. God addressed him as a man of destiny and said: Job, it is true you will never understand the secret of "why," you will never comprehend the cause or telos of suffering. But there is one thing that you *are* obliged to know: the principle of mending one's afflictions. If you can elevate yourself via your afflictions to a rank that you had hitherto not attained, then know full well that these afflictions were intended as a means for mending both your soul and your spirit. . . .

Missing the Moment

Now, as well, we are living in troubled times, in days of wrath and distress. We have been the victims of vicious attacks; we have been stricken with suffering. During the last fifteen years we have been afflicted with torments which are unparalleled in the thousands of years of exile, oppression, and religious persecution. This era of suffering, this dark chapter in our history, did not come to an end with the establishment of the State of Israel. Even now, today, the State of Israel still finds itself in a crisis situation, fraught with danger, and we are all filled with fear and trembling regarding the fate of the *Yishuv*, of the struggling Jewish community in the land of Israel. We are witnesses to the rising star of the wicked and the international perversion of justice deriving from the indifference to the principles of righteousness and equity exhibited by the states of the West. Everyone flatters our enemies and adversaries, they all grovel before them in a display of hypocrisy and sycophancy of the worst order. Everyone seeks their well-being, while they treat our beleaguered and fragile *Yishuv* in the same manner as that wealthy man who stole the little ewe lamb from his poor, weak, and helpless neighbor.

The well-known metaphysical problem arises yet again and the sufferer asks: "Why dost Thou show me iniquity and beholdest mischief? . . . For the wicked doth beset the righteous; therefore, right goes forth perverted" (Habakkuk 1:3–4). However, as we emphasized earlier, God does not address Himself to this question, and man receives no reply concerning it. The question remains obscure and sealed, outside the domain of logical thought. For "Thou canst not see My face, for man shall not see Me and live" (Exodus 33:20). When the impulse of intellectual curiosity seizes hold of a person, he ought to do naught but find strength and encouragement in his faith in the Creator, vindicate God's judgment, and acknowledge the perfection of His work. "The Rock, His work is perfect; for all His ways are justice" (Deuteronomy 32:4). If we wish to probe deeply, to question profoundly during a period of nightmarish terrors, then we have to pose the question in a *halakhic* form and ask: What is the obligation incumbent upon the suf-

ferer deriving from the suffering itself? What commanding voice, what normative principle arises out of the afflictions themselves? Such a question, as we stated above, has an answer which finds its expression in a clear *halakhic* ruling. We need not engage in metaphysical speculation in order to clarify the law of the rectification of evil. "It is not in heaven" (Deuteronomy 30:12). If we should succeed in formulating this teaching without getting involved in the question of cause and telos, then we will attain complete redemption, and the biblical promise, "Take counsel together and it shall be brought to naught; speak the word and it shall not stand; for God is with us" (Isaiah 8:10), shall be fulfilled with regard to us. Then, and only then, will we rise from the depths of the Holocaust, possessed of a heightened spiritual stature and adorned with an even more resplendent historical grandeur, as it is written: "Also the Lord gave Job twice as much as he had before" (Job 42:10)—double, both in quantity and in quality.

The teaching of the rectification of suffering— when it is put into practice—demands of the sufferer both courage and discipline. He must find within himself and draw upon prodigious resources, and subject himself to a rigorous self-examination and self-evaluation, untainted by the slightest hint of partiality or self-indulgence; he must contemplate his past and envisage his future with complete and unwavering honesty. It was not easy for Job to mend his suffering. And we as well, faint-hearted and weak-willed as we are, bound in the chains of fate and lacking personal fortitude, are now called upon by divine providence to clothe ourselves in a new spirit, to elevate ourselves to the rank of the rectification of our afflictions, afflictions which are demanding of us that we provide them with their deliverance and redemption. For this purpose, we need to examine our own reflection with spiritual heroism and total objectivity. This reflection breaks through both past and present together in order to confront us directly.

If the gracious divine bounties which have been showered upon both the individual and the community obligate their beneficiary to perform special, concrete deeds, even if these bounties (like wealth, honor, influence, power, and the like, which are acquired through exhausting labor) have been bestowed upon man in a natural manner, how much more so do the divine bounties which are bequeathed in a supernatural manner, in the form of a miracle which takes place outside the context of the basic lawfulness governing the concatenation of historical events, bind the miracle's beneficiary to God? God's miraculous boon of *hesed* imposes upon man the absolute obligation to fulfill the great commandment which cries out from the very midst of the miracle itself. A transcendental commandment always accompanies a miraculous act—"Command the Israelites!" Woe unto the beneficiary of a miracle if he does not recognize the miracle performed on his behalf, if he is deaf to the imperative which echoes forth from the metahistorical event. How unfortunate is he who has enjoyed God's wonders if the spark of faith has not been kindled within him, if his conscience does not tremble and take heed at the sight of the extraordinary occurrence.

When a miracle does not find its proper answering echo in the form of concrete deeds, an exalted vision degenerates and dissipates, and the divine attribute of justice begins to denounce the ungrateful beneficiary of the miracle.

> The Almighty sought to make Hezekiah the Messiah, and Sennacherib, Gog and Magog. The attribute of justice objected, "You performed all these miracles on behalf of Hezekiah, yet he did not utter song before You. Shall You, then, make him the Messiah?"[4]

Then come times of distress; the hour of suffering makes its appearance. Suffering is the last warning wherewith divine providence alerts the man lacking any sense of appreciation for the good he has received. One must respond to this last pronouncement, arising out of suffering, with alacrity, and must answer the voice of God calling out to man, "Where art thou!" Judaism has always been very strict regarding the prohibition against missing the moment....

What is the gist of the Song of Songs if not the description of the tragic and paradoxical delay of the Shulamite maiden, drunk with love and overwhelmed with yearning, when a favorable moment, replete with awe and majesty, beckoned to her—if not her missing that great, exalted, and momentous opportunity that she had dreamed about, fought for, and sought so passionately? The tender and delicate Shulamite maiden, impelled by longing for her bright-eyed beloved, roamed during sun-drenched days through the bypaths of vineyards and over the crests of mountains, through fields and gardens, and during pale, magical moonlit nights, during pitch-black nights, between the walls, searching for her beloved. One cold and rainy night she returned to her tent, tired and worn out, and fell fast asleep. The sound of quick and light footsteps could be heard in the silence of the tent. On that strange and mysterious night, suddenly the beloved emerged from out of the dark and knocked on the door of his darling, who had intensely yearned for and awaited him. He knocked and pleaded with her to open the door of her tent. "It is the voice of my beloved that knocketh. 'Open to me, my sister, my darling, my dove, my undefiled; for my head is filled with dew, my locks with the drops of the night' " (Song of Songs 5:2). The great moment that she had looked forward to with such impatience and longing materialized unexpectedly. Her elusive, self-concealing beloved, tired of wandering and hardships, appeared with his curly hair, black eyes, powerful build, and radiant countenance. He stood by her door, stretched his hand in through the hole in the latch, sought refuge from the damp of night, and wished to tell her about his powerful love, about his desires and yearnings, about a life of companionship, filled with delight and joy, about the realization and attainment of their aspirations and hopes. Only the slight movement of stretching out her hand and turning the latch intervened between her and her beloved, between the great dream and its complete fulfillment. With a single leap the Shulamite maiden could have obtained her heart's longings—"Draw me, we will run after thee ... we will be glad and rejoice in thee" (Song of Songs 1:4). But the heart is deceitful, and who can discern it? Precisely on that very night, a strange, stubborn indolence overcame her. For a brief moment the fire of longing that had burned so brightly was dimmed, the fierce passion ebbed, her emotions were stilled, her dreams extinguished.

4. B. T. *Sanhedrin* 94a.

The maiden refused to descend from her bed. She did not open the door of the tent to her handsome beloved. A cruel madness swept her into an abyss of oblivion and indifference. The maiden proved stubborn and lazy and rained down a multitude of excuses and rationalizations to account for her peculiar behavior: "I have put off my coat; how shall I put it on? I have washed my feet; how shall I soil them?" (Song of Songs 5:3). The beloved knocked again and again, and the more insistent his knocks, the louder they grew, the more her icy, defiling madness increased in intensity. As the whispered entreaties of the beloved pierced the silence of the night, the heart of his darling became harder and harder—like stone. The beloved continued to knock, pleading patiently, and together with his knocks the clock sounded the minutes and hours. The maiden paid no heed to the voice of her beloved; the door to her tent remained shut up tight. The moment was lost; and the vision of an exalted life faded away. It is true that after a brief delay the maiden awoke from her slumber and, confused and startled, leaped from her bed to welcome her beloved: "I rose up to open to my beloved" (Song of Songs 5:5); but she arose too late. Her beloved had stopped knocking and vanished into the darkness of the night—"My beloved had turned away and gone" (Song of Songs 5:6). Her life's joy was fled; her existence—a desolate wilderness, an empty waste. The saga of her passionate quest began anew. She is still wandering amidst the shepherds' tents—searching for her beloved.

Six Knocks

Eight years ago, in the midst of a night of terror filled with the horrors of Maidanek, Treblinka, and Buchenwald, in a night of gas chambers and crematoria, in a night of absolute divine self-concealment (*hester panim muḥlat*), in a night ruled by the satan of doubt and apostasy which sought to sweep the maiden from her house into the Christian church, in a night of continuous searching, of questing for the Beloved—in that very night the Beloved appeared. "God who conceals Himself in His dazzling hiddenness" suddenly manifested Himself and began to knock at the tent of His despondent and disconsolate love, twist-

ing convulsively on her bed, suffering the pains of hell. *As a result of the knocks on the door of the maiden, wrapped in mourning, the State of Israel was born!*

How many times did the Beloved knock on the door of the tent of His love? It appears to me that we can count at least six knocks.

First, the knock of the Beloved was heard in the political arena. No one can deny that from the standpoint of international relations, *the establishment of the State of Israel, in a political sense, was an almost supernatural occurrence.* Both Russia and the Western countries jointly supported the idea of the establishment of the State. This was perhaps the only proposal where East and West were united. I am inclined to believe that the United Nations organization was created specifically for this purpose—in order to carry out the mission which divine providence had set for it. It seems to me that one cannot point to any other concrete achievement on the part of the UN. Our sages, of blessed memory, already expressed the view that at times "rain" descends "for a single person," or for a single blade of grass. I do not know whom the journalists, with their eyes of flesh and blood, saw sitting in the chairman's seat during that fateful session when the General Assembly decided in favor of the establishment of the State. However, someone who at that time observed matters well with his spiritual eye could have sensed the presence of the true chairman who presided over the discussion—i.e., the Beloved! It was He who knocked with His gavel on the podium. Do we not interpret the verse "That night the sleep of the king fled" (Esther 6:1) as referring to "the sleep of the King of the universe" (B.T. *Megillah* 15ᵇ)? Were it Ahasuerus alone who could not sleep, it would have been of no consequence, and the salvation of Israel would not have blossomed forth on that night. However, if it is the King of the universe Who, as it were, does not slumber, then the redemption will be born. If it had been John Doe who called the session of the United Nations to order, the State of Israel would never have come into being—but if the Beloved knocked on the chairman's podium, then the miracle occurred. It is the voice of my Beloved that knocketh!

Second, the knocking of the Beloved could be heard on the battlefield. *The small Israeli Defense*

Forces defeated the mighty armies of the Arab countries. The miracle of "the many in the hands of the few" took place before our very eyes. And an even greater miracle occurred at that time. God hardened the heart of Ishmael and enjoined him to do battle against the State of Israel. Had the Arabs not declared war against the State, and, instead, agreed to the Partition Plan, the State of Israel would have lacked Jerusalem, a large part of the Galilee, and several areas of the Negev. Had Pharaoh, thousands of years ago, allowed the Israelites to depart from Egypt immediately, in accordance with Moses' original request, Moses would have been bound to keep his promise and would have had to return after three days. However, Pharaoh hardened his heart and did not hearken to Moses. The Almighty took the Israelites out of Egypt with a strong hand and an outstretched arm. Consequently, Moses' pledge that they would return to Egypt was no longer binding. A bilateral contract cannot bind one party if the other party refuses to fulfill his obligations. It is the voice of my Beloved that knocketh!

Third, the Beloved began to knock as well on the door of the theological tent, and it may very well be that this is the strongest knock of all. I have often emphasized, when speaking of the land of Israel, that all the claims of Christian theologians that God deprived the Jewish people of its rights in the land of Israel, and that all the biblical promises regarding Zion and Jerusalem refer, in an allegorical sense, to Christianity and the Christian church *have been publicly refuted by the establishment of the State of Israel and have been exposed as falsehoods*, lacking all validity. It requires a comprehensive knowledge of Christian theological literature, from Justin Martyr down to contemporary theologians, to properly appreciate the great miracle which so clearly invalidated this central premise of Christian theology. We ought to take note of the "learned" explanation of our secretary of state, Mr. [John Foster] Dulles, who also serves as an elder in the Episcopal church, at a meeting of a Senate committee, that the Arabs hate the Jews because the Jews killed the founder of their religion. This "explanation" possesses profound, hidden symbolic significance. I am not a psychologist and certainly not a psychoanalyst; however, I do have some acquaintance with the

Talmud, and I remember well what our sages said about Balaam: "From his blessing...you may learn what was in his heart" (B.T. *Sanhedrin* 105[b]; cf. Rashi on Numbers 24:6). When a person speaks at length, the truth may, at times, slip out. When one of the senators asked the secretary of state: "Why do the Arabs hate the Jews?" he really wanted to reply: "I myself, as a Christian, don't bear any great love for them, for they killed our Messiah and, as a result, lost their share in the inheritance of Abraham." However, an angel intervened or a bit was placed in the secretary's mouth (as happened to Balaam, according to the sages' interpretation of the verse "and He put a word into his mouth" [Numbers 23:16; cf. Rashi ad loc. and B. T. *Sanhedrin* 105[b]), and instead of uttering the words "our Messiah" and "I myself," alternative terms slipped out of his mouth, and he said "the Arabs" and "Muhammad." In his subconscious he is afraid of the "terrible" fact that the Jewish people rule over Zion and Jerusalem. I find special pleasure in reading articles about the State of Israel in Catholic and Protestant newspapers. Against their will they have to use the name "Israel" when they report the news about Zion and Jerusalem which are now in our hands. I always derive a particular sense of satisfaction from reading in a newspaper that the response of the State of Israel is not as yet known, since today is the Sabbath and the offices of the ministries are closed, or from reading a news release from the United Press on Passover eve that "the Jews will sit down tonight at the *Seder* table confident that the miracles of Egypt will recur today." It is the voice of my Beloved that knocketh!

Fourth, the Beloved is knocking in the hearts of the perplexed and assimilated youths. The era of self-concealment (*hastarat panim*) at the beginning of the 1940s resulted in great confusion among the Jewish masses and, in particular, among the Jewish youth. Assimilation grew and became more rampant, and the impulse to flee from Judaism and from the Jewish people reached a new height. Fear, despair, and sheer ignorance caused many to spurn the Jewish community and board the ship "to flee unto Tarshish from the presence of the Lord" (Jonah 1:3). A raging, seemingly uncontrollable, torrent threatened to destroy us. Suddenly, the Beloved began to knock on the doors of the hearts of the perplexed, and *His knock, the rise of the State of Israel*, at the very least slowed the process of flight. Many of those who, in the past, were alienated from the Jewish people are now tied to the Jewish state by a sense of pride in its outstanding achievements. Many American Jews who had been semi-, demi-, or hemi-assimilated are now filled with fear and concern about the crisis overtaking the state of Israel, and they pray for its security and welfare, even though they are still far from being completely committed to it. Even those who are opposed to the State of Israel—and there are such Jews—are compelled to defend themselves, without let-up, against the strange charge of dual loyalty, and they loudly proclaim, day in [and] day out, that they have no share in the Holy Land. It is good for a Jew not to be able to hide from his Jewishness, but to be compelled to keep on answering the question "Who art thou? And what is thine occupation?" (cf. Jonah 1:8), even if, overcome by cowardice, he lacks the strength and courage to answer proudly: "I am a Hebrew; and I fear the Lord, the God of heaven" (Jonah 1:9). This persistent question, "Who art thou?" binds him to the Jewish people. The very fact that people are always talking about Israel serves to remind the Jew in flight that he cannot run away from the Jewish community with which he has been intertwined from birth. Wherever we turn we encounter the word "Israel"; whether we listen to the radio, read the newspaper, participate in symposia about current affairs, we find the question of Israel always being publicly discussed.

This fact is of particular importance for Jews who are afflicted with self-hatred and wish to escape from Judaism and flee for their lives. They, like Jonah, seek to hide in the innermost part of the ship and wish to slumber, but the shipmaster does not allow them to ignore their fate. The shadow of Israel pursues them unceasingly. Buried, hidden thoughts and paradoxical reflections emerge from the depths of the souls of even the most avowed assimilationists. And once a Jew begins to think and contemplate, once his sleep is disturbed—who knows where his thoughts will take him, what form of expression his doubts and queries will assume? It is the voice of my Beloved that knocketh!

The fifth knock of the Beloved is perhaps the most important of all. For the first time in the history of our exile, divine providence has surprised our enemies with the sensational discovery that *Jewish blood is not free for the taking, is not hefker* [without value or ownership]! If anti-Semites wish to describe this phenomenon as "an eye for an eye," so be it; we will agree with them. If we wish to heroically defend our national–historical existence, we must, at times, interpret the verse "an eye for an eye" (Exodus 21:24) literally. How many eyes did we lose during the course of our bitter exile because we did *not* return blow for blow? The time has come for us to fulfill the law of "an eye for an eye" in its plain, simple sense. I am certain that everyone who knows me knows that I am a believer in the Oral Law and, consequently, that I do not doubt that the verse refers to monetary compensation, in accordance with the *halakhic* interpretation. However, with regard to Nasser or the Mufti[5] I would demand that we interpret the phrase "an eye for an eye" in a strictly literal sense—as referring to the removal of the concrete, actual eye. Pay no attention to the fine phrases of well-known Jewish assimilationists or socialists, who continue to adhere to their outworn ideologies and think that they are living in the Bialystok, Minsk, or Brisk of 1905, and who publicly declaim that it is forbidden for Jews to take revenge at any time, any place, and under all circumstances. Vanity of vanities! Revenge is forbidden when it serves no purpose. However, if by taking revenge we raise ourselves up to the plane of self-defense, then it becomes the elementary right of man qua man to avenge the wrongs inflicted upon him. . . .

[I]n general, how absurd it is to demand of a people that it be completely dependent upon the good graces of others and that it relinquish the ability to defend itself. The honor of every community, like the honor of every individual, resides in the ability to defend its existence and honor.

[5. Rav Soloveitchik is here referring to Gamal Abdul Nasser, President of Egypt during the Six Day War between Israel & Egypt in 1967 and to Haj Amin el-Husseini, The Grand Mufti of Jerusalem who, during World War II, was an ally of Hitler's and who sought the annihilation of the Jewish community in Palestine.]

A people that cannot ensure its own freedom and security is not truly independent. The third phrase in God's promise of redemption is: "And I will redeem you with an outstretched arm *and with great judgments*" (Exodus 6:7). *Blessed be He who has granted us life and brought us to this era when Jews have the power, with the help of God, to defend themselves!*

Let us not forget that the venom of Hitlerian anti-Semitism, which made the Jews like the fish of the sea to be preyed upon by all, still infects many in our generation who viewed the horrific spectacle of the gassing of millions with indifference, as an ordinary event not requiring a moment's thought. The antidote to this deadly poison that envenomed minds and benumbed hearts is the readiness of the State of Israel to defend the lives of its sons, its builders. It is the voice of my Beloved that knocketh!

The sixth knock, which we must not ignore, was heard when the gates of the land were opened. A Jew who flees from a hostile country now knows that he can find a secure refuge in the land of his ancestors. This is a new phenomenon in our history. Until now, whenever Jewish communities were expelled from their lands, they had to wander in the wilderness of the nations and were not able to find shelter in another land. Because the gates were barred before exiles and wanderers, many Jewish communities were decimated. Now the situation has changed. If a particular people expels the Jewish minority from its midst, the exiles can direct their steps unto Zion, and she, like a compassionate mother, will gather in her children. We have all been witness to Oriental Jewry's settling in the land of Israel in the past few years. Who knows what might have befallen our brethren in the lands in which they had settled had not the land of Israel brought them by boats and planes to her? Had the State of Israel arisen before Hitler's Holocaust, hundreds of thousands of Jews might have been saved from the gas chambers and crematoria. The miracle of the State came just a bit late, and as a result of this delay thousands and tens of thousands of Jews were murdered. However, now that the era of divine self-concealment (*hester panim*) is over, Jews who have been uprooted from their homes can find lodging in the Holy Land. Let us not view this matter lightly! It is the voice of my Beloved that knocketh!

Zvi Kolitz

Zvi Kolitz (1919–2002) was born into a rabbinical family in Alyta, Lithuania. He received a traditional yeshivah education and studied at the famous Slobodka yeshiva, though he was also early inspired by the Zionist movement then taking hold in the Land of Israel. In 1936, at the age of seventeen, Kolitz left Lithuania due to its growing anti-Semitism and migrated to Italy where he studied at the University of Florence and the Naval Academy at Civitavecchia. After four years in fascist Italy he again moved, this time to Palestine. At first interned by the British, he eventually was freed from imprisonment and joined the British army fighting the Nazis in North Africa. At the end of the war he went to work as an emissary for the World Zionist Organization and, clandestinely, recruited soldiers for the radical Jewish underground organization known as the Irgun, led by Menachem Begin, which sought to force the British out of Palestine and to create a Jewish state in the land of Israel. After the establishment of the State of Israel, he held various official positions in Israel. In addition, he began to produce films, including the first full-length Israeli film, *Hill 24 Doesn't Answer* (1954). Later in life he emigrated one final time, now to the United States, where he became involved in a variety of Jewish and cultural activities, including, in 1964, coproducing Rolf Hochbuth's important and controversial play *The Deputy,* about the behavior of Pope Pius XII during World War II. He also taught Jewish philosophy at Yeshiva University for many years; published several works of fiction; produced several nonfiction studies, including *The Teacher: An Existential Approach to the Bible* (Northvale, Calif., 1982) and *Confrontation: The Existential Thought of Rabbi J. B. Soloveitchik* (New York, 1993); and wrote a weekly column for the Yiddish newspaper the *Algemeiner Journal.*

SELECTION

Asked to contribute a piece to a special *Yom Kippur* (Day of Atonement) issue of a Yiddish newspaper in Buenos Aires after the Holocaust, Kolitz wrote his famous Holocaust theological dialogue, *Yossel Rakover's Appeal to God.* In this piece, set in the Warsaw ghetto during the war, a Holocaust victim addresses God with his doubts and accusations but, ultimately, remains faithful to God despite all that has happened to him and his people. "I believe in the God of Israel, even when he has done everything to make me cease to believe in him." Though not a technical, philosophical argument nor analysis of the problem of theodicy, *Yossel Rakover* expresses a profound, faithful, Jewish response to the Holocaust, and the piece has become a classic work, especially among Orthodox Jews. For many years, because it appeared in English and Hebrew without Mr. Kolitz's name as the author, *Yossel Rakover* was misidentified as a work actually composed during the Holocaust rather than a work of fiction written after the war.

Selected Bibliography

Book by Zvi Kolitz

Yossel Rakover Talks to God (New York, 1999).

YOSSEL RAKOVER TALKS TO GOD

In the ruins of the ghetto of Warsaw, among heaps of charred rubbish, there was found, packed tightly into a small bottle, the following testament, written during the ghetto's last hours by a Jew named Yossel Rakover.

Warsaw, 28 April 1943

I, Yossel, son of David Rakover of Tarnopol, a ḥasid of the rabbi of Ger and a descendant of the great and pious families of Rakover and Meisel, inscribe these lines as the houses of the Warsaw ghetto go up in flames. The house I am in is one of the last unburnt houses remaining. For several hours an unusually heavy artillery barrage has been crashing down on us, and the walls are disintegrating under the fire. It will not be long before the house I am in is transformed, like almost every other house of the ghetto, into a grave for its defenders. By the dagger-sharp, unusually crimson rays of the sun that strike through the small, half-walled-up window of my room through which I have been shooting at the enemy day and night, I see that it must now be late afternoon, just before sundown, and I cannot regret that this is the last sun that I shall see. All of our notions and emotions have been altered. Death, swift and immediate, seems to us a liberator, sundering our shackles, and beasts of the field, even if their freedom exceeds their gentleness, seem to me to be so lovable and dear that I feel deep pain whenever I hear the evil fiends that lord it over Europe referred to as beasts. It is untrue that the tyrant who rules Europe now has something of the beast in him. Oh, no! He is a typical child of modern man; mankind as [a] whole spawned him and reared him. He is merely [the] frankest expression of its innermost, most deeply buried instincts.

In a forest where I once hid, I encountered a dog one night, sick and hungry, his tail between his legs. Both of us immediately felt the kinship of our situation. He cuddled up to me, buried his head in my lap, and licked my hands. I do not know if I ever cried so much as that night. I threw my arms around his neck, crying like a baby. If I say that I envied the animals at that moment, it would not be remarkable. But what I felt was more than envy. It was shame. I felt ashamed before the dog to be a man. That is how matters stand. That is the spiritual level to which we have sunk. Life is a tragedy, death a savior; man a calamity, the beast an ideal; the day a horror, the night—relief.

When my wife, my children—six in all—and I hid in the forest, it was the night and the night alone that concealed us in its bosom. The day turned us over to our persecutors and murderers. I remember with the most painful clarity the day when the Germans raked with a hail of fire the thousands of refugees on the highway from Grodno to Warsaw. As the sun rose, the airplanes zoomed over us and the whole day long they murdered us. In this massacre, my wife with our seven-month-old child in her arms perished. Two of my five remaining children also disappeared that day without a trace. Their names were David and Yehuda, one was four years old, the other six.

At sunset, the handful of survivors continued their journey in the direction of Warsaw, and I, with my three remaining children, started out to comb the fields and woods at the site of the massacre in search of the children. The entire night we called for them, but only echoes replied. I never saw my two children again, and later, in a dream, I was told that they were in God's hands.

My other three children died in the space of a single year in the Warsaw ghetto. Rachel, my daughter of ten, heard that it was possible to find scraps of bread in the public dump outside the ghetto walls. The ghetto was starving at the time, and the people who died of starvation lay in the streets like heaps of rags. The people of the ghetto were prepared to face any death but the death of hunger. Against no death did they struggle so fiercely as against death by starvation.

My daughter Rachel told me nothing of her plan to steal out of the ghetto, which was punishable by death. She and a girlfriend of the same age started out on the perilous journey. She left home under cover of darkness, and at sunrise she and her friend were caught outside the ghetto walls. Nazi ghetto guards, together with dozens of their Polish underlings, at once started in pursuit of those two Jewish children who dared to venture out to hunt for a piece of bread in a garbage can. People witnessing the chase could not believe their eyes. It was unusual even in the ghetto. It looked like a pursuit of dangerous criminals. A horde of fiends run amok in pursuit of a pair of starved ten-year-old children did not endure very long in the unequal match. One of them, my child, running with her last ounce of strength, fell exhausted to the ground and the Nazis put a bullet through her head. The other child saved herself, but, driven out of her mind, died two weeks later.

The fifth child, Yacob, a boy of thirteen, died on his Bar Mitzvah day of tuberculosis. The last child, my fifteen-year-old daughter, Chaya, perished during a *Kinderaktion*—a children's operation—that began at sunrise last Rosh Hashanah and ended at sundown. That day, before sunset, hundreds of Jewish families lost their children.

Now my time has come. And like Job, I can say of myself, nor am I the only one who can say it, that I return to the soil naked, as naked as the day of my birth.

I am forty-three years old, and when I look back on the past I can assert confidently, as confident as a man can be of himself, that I have lived a respectable, upstanding life, my heart full of love for God. I was once blessed with success, but never boasted of it. My possessions were extensive. My house was open to the needy. I served God enthusiastically, and my single request to Him was that He should allow me to worship Him with all my heart, and all my soul, and all my strength.

I cannot say that my relationship to God has remained unchanged after everything I have lived through, but I can say with absolute certainty that my belief in Him has not changed by a hair's breadth. Previously, when I was happy and well off, my relation to God was as to one who granted me a favor for nothing, and I was eternally obliged to Him for it. Now my relations to Him are as to one who owes me something, too, who owes me very much in fact, and since I feel so, I believe I have the right to demand it of Him. But I do not say like Job that God should point out my sin with His finger so that I may know why I deserve this; for greater and saintlier men than I are now firmly convinced that it is not a question of punishing sinners: something entirely different is taking place in the world. It is, namely, a time when God has veiled His countenance from the world, sacrificing mankind to its wild instincts. This, however, does not mean that the pious members of my people should justify the edict, saying that God and His judgments are correct. For to say that we deserve the blows we have received is to malign ourselves, to desecrate the Holy Name of God's children. And those who desecrate our name desecrate the Name of the Lord; God is maligned by our self-deprecation.

In a situation like this, I naturally expect no miracles, nor do I ask Him, my Lord, to show me mercy. May He treat me with the same indifference with which He treated millions of His people. I am no exception, and I expect no special treatment. I will no longer attempt to save myself, nor flee any more. I will facilitate the work of the fire by moistening my clothing with gasoline. I have three bottles of gasoline left after having emptied several scores over the heads of the murderers. It was one of the finest moments of my life when I did this, and I was shaken with laughter by it. I never dreamed that the death of people, even of enemies—even such enemies—could cause me such great pleasure. Foolish humanists may say what they choose. Vengeance was and always will be the last means of waging just battles and the greatest spiritual release of the oppressed. I had never until now understood the precise meaning of the expression in the Talmud which states that vengeance is sacred because it is mentioned between two of God's names: A God of vengeance is the Lord. I understand it now. I know now, moreover, why my heart is so overjoyed at remembering that for thousands of years we have been calling our Lord a God of vengeance: A God of vengeance is our Lord! We have had only a few opportunities to witness true vengeance. When we did, however, it was so good, so worthwhile, I felt such profound happiness, so terribly fortunate—that for a moment it seemed an entirely new life was springing up in me. A tank had suddenly broken in our street. It was bombarded with flying bottles of gasoline from all the embattled houses. They failed to hit their target, however, and the tank continued to approach. My friends and I waited until the tank was almost upon us. Then, through the half-bricked-up window, we suddenly attacked. The tank soon burst into flames, and six blazing Nazis jumped out. Ah, how they burned! They burned like the Jews they had set on fire. But they shrieked more. Jews do not shriek. They welcome death like a savior. The Warsaw ghetto perishes in battle. It is going down shooting, struggling, blazing, but not shrieking!

I have three more bottles of gasoline. They are as precious to me as wine to a drunkard. After pouring one over my clothes, I will place the paper on which I write these lines in the empty bottle and hide it among the bricks filling the window of this room. If anyone ever finds it and reads it, he will, perhaps, understand the emotions of a Jew, one of millions, who died forsaken by the God in whom he believed unshakably. I will let the two other bottles explode on the heads of the murderers when my last moment comes.

There were twelve of us in this room at the outbreak of the rebellion. For nine days we battled against the enemy. All eleven of my comrades have fallen, dying silently in battle, including the small boy of about five—who came here only God knows how and who now lies dead near me, with his face wearing the kind of smile that appears on children's faces when dreaming peacefully—even this child died with the same epic calm as his older comrades. It happened early this morning. Most of us were dead already. The boy scaled the heap of corpses to catch a glimpse of the outside world through the window. He stood beside me in that position for several minutes. Suddenly he fell backwards, rolling down the pile of corpses, and lay like a stone. On his small, pale forehead, between the locks of black hair, there was a spattering of blood.

Up until yesterday morning, when the enemy launched a concentrated barrage against this stronghold, one of the last in the ghetto, every one of us was still alive, although five were wounded. During yesterday and today, all the rest fell, one after the other, one on top of the other, watching and firing until shot to death. I have no more ammunition, apart from the three bottles of gasoline. From the floors of the house above still come frequent shots, but I can hold out no more hope for them, for by all signs the stairway has been razed by the shell fire, and I think the house is about to collapse. I write these lines lying on the floor. Around me lie my dead comrades. I look into their faces, and it seems to me that a quiet but mocking irony animates them, as if they were saying to me, "A little patience, you foolish man, another few minutes and everything will become clear to you too." This irony is particularly noticeable on the face of the small boy lying near my right hand as if he were asleep. His small mouth is drawn into a smile exactly as if he were laughing, and I, who still live and feel and think—it seems to me that he is laughing at me. He laughs with that quiet but eloquent laughter so characteristic of the wise speaking of knowledge with the ignorant who believe, as ignorants always do, they know everything. Yes, he is omniscient now. Everything is clear to the boy now. He even knows why he was born, but had to die so soon—why he died only five years after his birth. And even if he does not know why, he knows at least that it is entirely unimportant and insignificant whether or not he knows it, in the light of that Godly majesty which shines over him in the better world he now inhabits, and in the arms of his murdered parents to whom he has returned. In an hour or two I will make the same discovery. Unless my face is eaten by the flames, a similar smile may rest on it after my death. Meanwhile, I still live, and before my death I wish to speak to my Lord as a living man, a simple, living person who had the great but tragic honor of being a Jew.

I am proud that I am a Jew not in spite of the world's treatment of us, but precisely because of this treatment. I should be ashamed to belong to the people who spawned and raised the criminals who are responsible for the deeds that have been perpetrated against us or to any people who tolerated these deeds.

I am proud to be a Jew because it is an art to be a Jew. It is no art to be an Englishman, an American, or a Frenchman. It may be easier, more comfortable to be one of them, but not more honorable. Yes, it is an honor, a terrible honor to be a Jew!

I believe that to be a Jew means to be a fighter, an everlasting swimmer against the turbulent human current. The Jew is a hero, a martyr, a saint. You, our evil enemies, declare that we are bad. I believe that we are better and finer than you, but even if we were worse, I should like to see how you would look in our place!

I am happy to belong to the unhappiest of all peoples of the world, whose precepts represent the loftiest and most beautiful of all morality and laws. These immortal precepts which we possess have now been even more sanctified and immortalized by the fact that they have been so debased and insulted by the enemies of the Lord.

I believe that to be a Jew is an inborn trait. One is born a Jew exactly as one is born an artist. It is impossible to be released from being a Jew. That is our Godly attribute that has made us a chosen people. Those who do not understand this will never understand the higher meaning of our martyrdom. If I ever doubted that God once designated us as the chosen people, I would believe now that our tribulations have made us the chosen one[s].

I believe in You, God of Israel, even though You have done everything to stop me from believing in You. I believe in Your laws even if I cannot excuse Your actions. My relationship to You is not the relationship of a slave to his master but rather that of a pupil to his teacher. I bow my head before Your greatness, but I will not kiss the lash with which You strike me.

You say, I know, that we have sinned, O Lord. It must surely be true! And therefore we are punished? I can understand that too! But I should like You to tell me whether *there is any sin in the world deserving of such a punishment as the punishment we have received?*

You assert that You will yet repay our enemies? I am convinced of it! Repay them without mercy? I have no doubt of that either! I should like You to tell me, however—*is there any punishment in the world capable of compensating for the crimes that have been committed against us?*

You say, I know, that it is no longer a question of sin and punishment, but rather a situation in which Your countenance is veiled, in which humanity is abandoned to its evil instincts. But I should like to ask You, O Lord—and this question burns in me like a consuming fire—*what more, O, what more must transpire before You unveil Your countenance again to the world?*

I want to say to You that now, more than in any previous period of our eternal path of agony, we, we the tortured, the humiliated, the buried alive and burned alive, we the insulted, the mocked, the lonely, the forsaken by God and man—we have the right to know *what are the limits of Your forbearance?*

I should like to say something more: Do not put the rope under too much strain, lest, alas, it snaps! The test to which You have put us is so severe, so unbearably severe, that You should—You must—forgive those members of Your people who, in their misery, have turned from You.

Forgive those who have turned from You in their misery, but also those who have turned from You in their happiness. You have transformed our life into such a frightful, perpetual ordeal that the cowards among us have been forced to flee from it; and what is happiness but a place of refuge for cowards? Do not chastise them for it. One does not strike cowards, but has mercy on them. Have mercy on *them,* rather than *us,* O Lord.

Forgive those who have desecrated Your name, who have gone over to the service of other gods, who have become indifferent to You. You have castigated them so severely that they no longer believe that You are their Father, that they have any Father at all.

I tell You this because I do believe in You, because I believe in You more strongly than ever, because now I know that You are my Lord, because after all You are not, You cannot possibly be after all the God of those whose deeds are the most horrible expression of ungodliness!

If You are not *my* Lord, then whose Lord are You? The Lord of the murderers?

If those who hate me and murder me are so benighted, so evil, what then am I if not he who reflects something of Your light, of Your goodness?

I cannot extol You for the deeds that You tolerate. I bless You and extol You, however, for the very fact of Your existence, for Your awesome mightiness!

The murderers themselves have already passed sentence on themselves and will never escape it, but may You carry out a doubly severe sentence on those who are condoning the murder.

Those who condemn murder orally, but rejoice at it in their hearts. . . . Those who meditate in their foul hearts: It is fitting, after all, to say that he is evil, the tyrant, but he carries out a bit of work for us for which we will always be grateful to him!

It is written in Your Torah that a thief should be punished more severely than a brigand, in spite of the fact that the thief does not attack his victim physically and merely attempts to take his possessions stealthily.

The reason for this is that a robber by attacking his victim in broad daylight shows no more fear of man than of God. The thief, on the other hand, fears man, but not God. His punishment, therefore, is greater.

I should be satisfied if You dealt with the murderers as with brigands, for their attitude toward You and toward us is the same.

But those who are silent in the face of murder, those who have no fears of You but fear what people might say (Fools! They are unaware that the people will say nothing!), those who express their sympathy with the drowning man but refuse to rescue him though they can swim—punish them, O Lord, punish them, I implore You, like the thief, with a doubly severe sentence!

Death can wait no longer. From the floors above me, the firing becomes weaker by the minute. The last defenders of this stronghold are now falling, and with them falls and perishes the great, beautiful, and God-fearing Jewish part of Warsaw. The sun is about to set, and I thank God that I will never see it again. Fire lights my small window, and the bit of sky that I can see is flooded with red like a waterfall of blood. In about an hour at the most I will be with the rest of my family and with the millions of other stricken members of my people in that better world where there are no more questions.

I die peacefully, but not complacently; persecuted, but not enslaved; embittered, but not cynical; a believer, but not a supplicant; a lover of God, but no blind amen-sayer of His.

I have followed Him even when He rejected me. I have followed His commandments even when He castigated me for it; I have loved Him and I love Him even when He hurls me to the earth, tortures me to death, makes me an object of shame and ridicule.

My rabbi would frequently tell the story of a Jew who fled from the Spanish Inquisition with his wife and child, striking out in a small boat over the stormy sea until he reached a rocky island where a flash of lightning killed his wife; a storm rose and hurled his son into the sea. Then, as lonely as a stone, naked, barefoot, lashed by the storm, and terrified by the thunder and the lightning, hands turned up to God, the Jew, setting out on his journey through the wastes of the island, turned to his Maker with the following words:

God of Israel, I have fled to this place in order to worship You without molestation, to obey Your commandments and sanctify Your name. You, however, have done everything to make me stop believing in You. Now lest it seem to You that You will succeed by these tribulations to drive me from the right path, I notify You, my God and the God of my father, *that it will not avail You in the least!* You may insult me, You may castigate me, You may take from me all that I cherish and hold dear in the world, You may torture me to death—I shall believe in *You,* I shall love You no matter what You do to test me!

And these are my last words to You, my wrathful God: nothing will avail You in the least. You have done everything to make me renounce You, to make me lose my faith in You, but I die exactly as I have lived, a *believer!*

Eternally praised be the God of the dead, the God of vengeance, of truth and of law, who will soon show His face to the world again and shake its foundations with His almighty voice.

Hear, O Israel, the Lord our God the Lord is One.

Into your hands, O Lord, I consign my soul.

Ignaz Maybaum

Ignaz Maybaum (1897–1976) was born in Vienna on 2 March 1897. His father had a modest tailoring business in the city. After receiving his secular education and serving in the Austrian army in World War I, achieving the rank of lieutenant, he enrolled in the Reform Theological Seminary (Hochschule für die Wissenschaft des Judentums) in Berlin and was ordained as a Reform rabbi in 1926. In addition, during these years, he studied at the University of Berlin and received his doctorate from that institution in 1925. After receiving his doctorate and his rabbinical degree, he served as a rabbi in Bingen (1926–1928), then Frankfurt on the Oder (1928–1936), and then in 1936 was called to Berlin, where he remained in this rabbinical position until 1939. Fortunately, despite his arrest in 1935 by the Gestapo and imprisonment in Berlin for comments critical of Hitler, he was able to leave Nazi Germany for England in 1939 thanks to the sponsorship of Chief Rabbi J. H. Hertz of London. His mother and sisters were not so fortunate and died in Theresienstadt and Auschwitz, respectively. In England, after being unemployed for ten years and being supported by the Chief Rabbi's Emergency Council, he became the rabbi of the Edgeware Reform Synagogue, a position he held until his retirement in 1966. Also, beginning in 1956, he began to lecture at the Reform Leo Baeck Theological College in London. In the 1950s and 1960s, he was also a regular participant in ecumenical conferences in Germany and was an active member of the English Council for Christians and Jews. A devoted disciple of Franz Rosenzweig, he published a number of theological works beginning with his 1935 German *Parteibefreites Judentum* and continuing, in English, with a number of studies, the most important of which was *The Face of God after Auschwitz*, published in 1965.

SELECTION

The present selection is taken from Maybaum's *The Face of God after Auschwitz*. In this work he attempts to explain the Holocaust by invoking, in a unique way, the classical theology of the "suffering servant" preached by the prophet Isaiah (ch. 53), which has been central to both classical Jewish theology and the Christian understanding of the death of Jesus on the cross. That is to say, Maybaum here argues that in order for the Jewish people to fulfill its mission "as a light unto the gentiles," it had to become—by way of the Holocaust—a vicarious atonement for the nations in the image of the "suffering servant." In this context, Maybaum stresses that, insofar as Christian civilization thinks theologically in terms of the crucifixion, i.e., that the death of the righteous brings salvation to others, this modern crucifixion of the Jewish people was required in order for Judaism to communicate with and effect a change in the character of Christian civilization.

Precisely what teaching, what elevation, has this monumental sacrifice of six million—this modern Golgotha—achieved? Maybaum would have us recognize in it the decisive end of the medieval epoch, by which he means the termination of the era of religious authoritarianism, religious persecution, and theocratic oppression. Nazism was the final manifestation of the medieval world view, and the cataclysmic event of the Holocaust was the means whereby the world moved with finality from medievalism to modernity.

Selected Bibliography

Books by Ignaz Maybaum

Man and Catastrophe, translated by Joseph Leftwich (London, 1941).
Synagogue and Society: Jewish-Christian Collaboration in the Defense of Western Civilization, translated by Joseph Leftwich (London, 1944).
The Sacrifice of Isaac: A Jewish Commentary (London, 1959).
Jewish Existence (London, 1960).
The Faithful of the Jewish Diaspora (London, 1962).
The Face of God after Auschwitz (Amsterdam, 1965).

Article about Ignaz Maybaum

Katz, Steven T. "The Crucifixion of the Jews: Ignaz Maybaum's Theology of the Holocaust," in Steven T. Katz, *Post-Holocaust Dialogues: Critical Studies in Modern Jewish Thought* (New York, 1983), pp. 248–267.

The Face of God after Auschwitz

Why did Hitler single out the Jew as his chief enemy? I am not satisfied with the answer: "Hitler was a maniac." Nor do I accept as an explanation the racial myth in which Hitler believed. The Jewish people consists of various racial components. Yet there is a reason why the Jew was seen as *the* enemy of Nazism.

The reason is that after millennia of a varied history the election of the Jewish people still existed as a living and strong factor. We need only compare the role of the Christian church with the role of the Jewish people in Hitler's empire. True, every church tower in the German landscape was a finger pointing in warning to the realm which was ignored and whose existence was denied by pagan man. The churches were not burned like the synagogues, they still adorned the landscape of Nazi Germany, they still gave grandeur to their cities. But pagan man bypassed them. The churches were silent. A concordate even legalized noninterference by the Roman Catholic church. Hitler could trust the Vatican. Roman Catholic diplomacy accommodated itself

to the Third Reich. The Evangelical Confessional church at least attempted opposition. The Vatican never tried. The only authority left in Nazi-occupied Poland was the church. The churches in Nazi-occupied Poland were thronged with people. A single word by a bishop would have saved Jews. This word was not spoken. Thus it was easier to save a thousand Jews in the occupied West than a single Jewish child in Poland. Any child who strayed into the countryside, after his father and mother were shot by the Nazis, was handed over to the Gestapo by the peasants: the Jews had killed Christ. A doctrine of the medieval church did most efficiently the work which Nazi ideology also had as its aim.

The only one who never had the faintest possibility of any Munich with Hitler, the only one who was stigmatized as the irreconcilable opponent of Nazism was the Jew. Hitler knew, as we know, that not every Jew is just, merciful, and truthful. But Hitler also knew that the Jew, historically and existentially, even without any personal choice, stands for justice, mercy, and truth.

He stood for everything which made every word of Hitler a lie. The Jew, without opening his mouth to utter a single word, condemned Hitler. The Jew walking his way in Hitler['s] Germany, even before he was compelled to wear the Star of David, did what the church did not do: he tore up the land into two realms which were without any communication; the Jew walked outside the realm which was that of Baal. Doing nothing, the Jew created by his mere existence a situation in which Germany was visible as a land of Baal. Nobody can tell and should even ask how many Jews would have liked to conform to Hitler's ideology in order to save their lives. This is an irrelevant question. Jews are human beings like other men, weak or strong, cowardly or heroic. But they proved to be what others, what millions were not: they were chosen. In the apocalyptic hour of modern mankind the Jews did not bow before the Moloch. God did not let them. They were His people. Their election was still valid. Again it was demonstrated that to be chosen means to have no choice. God chooses. The Jewish people was again chosen to be not like the gentiles.

Our post-medieval situation makes it necessary to demythologize many traditional aspects not only of Christianity but also of Judaism. When demythologized, the doctrine of the election of the Jewish people shows that group life in which the Jewish people is chosen to live. Besides his political and spiritual existence man has a third possibility: his existence in privacy. In the state man moves in public or is condemned to anonymity, wields power or is subjected to power. In the church a similar dichotomy prevails, that between spiritual and secular life, between clergy and laymen. In the family alone man is allowed to be "whole" man, and it is the family which constitutes Jewish life. Freedom is there where the state does not interfere. Where the Jew can live as a Jew, everybody else is happy, too, has access to the good life. The totalitarian state persecutes the Jew, because he contradicts the view that only tragic life is noble life. The church, if still rooted in its Jewish origin, cannot be blind to the fact, visible for all to see, that the Jew can comprehend and appropriate holiness without aspiring to a spiritual status. Thus the Jew represents what neither state nor church represent:

the human situation. Man remaining in the human situation and yet being a witness of God exists in the election in which the Jew lives. The Jewish people are chosen to worship God in the human situation.

The Christian story of a deicide throws its dark shadow on the history of man; through this very story, history is explained as a place where people kill and are killed. Will the process of demythologizing the New Testament reach the story of the deicide itself? Will the Christian theologians have the courage to continue the work which they have only begun? Matthias Gruenewald, the most German and most medieval painter, shows Christ's sufferings on the cross in a realism mercilessly displaying the dislocated bones of the hanging body. One of the tortures which the SS inflicted on their victims was to hang them with their hands on their backs, a process which had the effect of slow death; they suffered the very pain which Gruenewald shows on the dying Christ. Is there a connection between the bestiality of the SS and Gruenewald's anatomic realism in the picture of the deicide? No lesser man than Goethe demands for the sake of the saner education of youth that we should "draw a veil over this suffering" (*Wilhelm Meister's Wanderjahre*, book 2, ch. 2).

The Greek and Latin Fathers of the church performed the gigantic work of explaining with the methods of the philosophers that the doctrine of the Trinity is not a lapse into a heathen polytheism. But the myth of the deicide was no embarrassment to them. There were still Jews living around them. Did not these Jews make the myth a historical fact? Thus the medieval Fathers who demythologized the polytheism of the Christian narrative through their philosophical doctrine of the Trinity left the deicide unchanged. The Christian church remains a medieval institution as long as the doctrine "The Jews killed Christ" is upheld. It was the medieval church, not Christianity, which provoked Voltaire's *écrasez l'infâme!* A church upholding the doctrine "the Jews have killed Christ" is the medieval institution which had in torture and Inquisition the prerequisites of church government. The story of the deicide makes redemption inaccessible to the history of man: if a god has been killed—a story told by Semitic and Greek mythology—man cannot complain at being involved in this terrible business of killing and being killed; this business makes history a pagan place from which Christianity is unable to expel cruelty and bloodshed.

After 1945 the attention of the Jewish people was turned to the heroic fight of the new Maccabees in what was at that time still Palestine under British Mandate. A preacher who expounded in the synagogue the holiness of martyrdom, the holiness of the martyrdom of the six million Jews, faced a congregation which wanted to hear of the heroism of the new Maccabees in what was to become the State of Israel.

I have praised the new Maccabees as I have always praised the Maccabees of old. I shall continue to sing this praise. But I shall not allow the character of the Jewish people to be changed. We remain the people which has forged its swords into plowshares. The *Akedah*, the story that Isaac was not sacrificed at Moriah (Genesis 22), reveals the heart of Judaism just as the Cross erected at Golgotha is the great symbol of Christianity. The *Akedah* pronounces that Isaac can grow up to manhood, marry, and have children; the cross tells those standing in mourning around it that the sacrifice was necessary and meaningful. The *Akedah* brings good tidings: There is a way to justice and peace without the sacrifice of the sons on the battlefields. Progress without heroic tragedy is possible. Judaism is the way to the good life.

The Cross of Christianity is the symbol that the sacrifice of life is meaningful. A soldier who dies on the battlefield dies that others may live and be safe. The Cross contradicts the *Akedah*: Isaac *is* sacrificed. The two thousand years of Christianity were two thousand years of wars, nation fighting nation; the soldier wielding the sword, fighting, shedding blood, and killing was imbued with spiritual splendor as the Christian warrior. Christianity possessed its dogmatic adjustment to the phrase *dulce et decorum est pro patria mori*. As the atom bomb makes wars impossible, the message of the *Akedah* will at last be understood by the Christian gentiles. The good life is a religious concept. The *Akedah* preaches Judaism, and Judaism is the way to the good life. A word, summarizing everything that Judaism stands for, is: peace, *shalom*.

When praising the Maccabees in a sermon, I had a responsive congregation. But I had—

during the Israeli war—difficulty in convincing a section of my congregation of the need to see the holiness of martyrdom. *Genug schon gelitten* (we have suffered enough); with this phrase from a Yiddish folksong the *Palmach* [Israeli] fighters went to battle and wiped away the specter of the recent and past chapters of martyrdom. Haunted by terrible personal experience, they were surviving victims of Nazi persecution who became our new Maccabees.

The Maccabee is a Jewish figure. He becomes truly visible as a Jewish figure if compared with the Christian figure of the Crusader. The Maccabees, the old and the new Maccabees, fight in defense of freedom; man must be free. The freedom of worship makes man free. The freedom which creates man's political, economic, and cultural form of life is derived from the freedom of worship. The Maccabee becomes a warrior in defense of human rights against an aggressor. All the Allied soldiers who fought the tyranny of our time can look to the Maccabees as their example....

Christianity and the cult of Mithras were once in a competition which made the outcome a fifty-fifty chance. Both appealed equally to the Roman soldier who had to fight the endless wars of the Roman Empire. The cross won, because of its message to a world of constant war. The message to the living was: somebody had to die that others may live. In the symbol of the tomb of the unknown soldier, the Cross is revived in modern form. The Christian consolation unites noble tragedy and martyrdom in the symbol of the Cross. To the world of antiquity which saw noble tragedy as the propriety of the hero, the *Akedah* has another message. In the *Akedah* Isaac is *not* sacrificed. The good life is "higher" life and yet not heroic. "God will wipe away the tears from off all faces" is the prophetic message to the mothers of heroes and martyrs: But God is most merciful when He does not allow tears to stain faces. God appears in the *Akedah* in his unlimited mercy, granting happiness to man. The Cross is not a picture of happiness; it is a symbol created to combine the holiness of martyrdom with the nobility of the tragic hero....

The Eichmann trial [in Israel in 1961] and after it Hochhuth's play *The Representative* forced the world to ask: how could Auschwitz happen after two thousand years of Christianity—or better—in spite of two thousand years of Christianity?

It is a fact, perhaps a strange fact, that the Eichmann trial impressed the world's conscience to a greater degree than the Nuremberg trial. At Nuremberg the crime against humanity was on trial together with the crimes against Jews. In the Eichmann trial the crime against the Jewish people was on trial—more visibly than in Nuremberg—as a crime against humanity. The judges, both in Nuremberg and in Jerusalem, were fair, without mean impulses of revenge; they were true servants of justice. But in Jerusalem the judges were Jews; they showed before the eyes of the world the noble spectacle of an immaculate judiciary; they were as Jews themselves implicated in the greatest tragedy of their people. For the first time in history Jews sat in judgment over a crime against Jews, dealing with it as what it always was: a crime against humanity.

I used the word *ḥurban* for the first time in print in my book *The Jewish Mission* (1949). The catastrophe which befell Jewry in the years 1933–1945 is now throughout the Jewish world called the third *ḥurban*. The first *ḥurban* destroyed the Temple of Solomon, the second *ḥurban* the Temple of Herod. The catastrophe of the expulsion from Spain or the massacre of Ukrainian Jews through the hordes of Chmelnitzki were not called *ḥurban* but *gezeirah* (evil decree). The meaning of *ḥurban* is that of a catastrophe which makes an end to an old era and creates a new era. This meaning is "awful" in the sense of the old English word and in the sense of the Hebrew word *nora*. The *ḥurban* is a day of awe, of awe beyond human understanding. Having, like others, used the word *ḥurban*, I had begun to see that this word had a meaning which was not at once obvious but implicit and frightening: *ḥurban* implied progress. The *Akedah* had the message: progress is possible without sacrifice. The *ḥurban*, on the other hand, is the progress achieved in a history in which the gentiles are the chief actors, or better, perpetrators. The *ḥurban* is progress achieved through sacrifice.

Which kind of progress can the third *ḥurban* have created? Pondering about these questions in the pulpit in fear and trembling, I preached: the Middle Ages have come to an end. Although my answer is the outcome of theological inquiry, it could first be given only in the form of a confessing sermon. Only in the exalted atmosphere of the pulpit could I dare to say that *ḥurban* and progress are connected: the Jewish people, although having its Ashkenazi and Sephardi diaspora widened to a world diaspora, has now its sole existence within the West; it is committed to a dialogue with the free democracies and is free to emancipate itself socially and culturally from all that which existed before the French Revolution. With this new commitment we can say farewell to our own Middle Ages. By preaching that *ḥurban* and progress are connected, I did not say anything more than did the rabbis who preached that the Messiah to come was born on the day when Jerusalem was destroyed. One of them, in the apocalyptic exuberance of his comment to Amos's "Day of the Lord" (5:18) even said:

> When the Messiah is to come, the house of learning will be a place of fornication, Galilee will be devastated, people will wander from town to town but find no compassion, the wisdom of the rabbis will decay, the pious will be despised, chastity will not be found, and truth will be absent. (*Mishnah Sota* 14)

What a terrible indictment of nineteenth-century positivism which viewed progress as a line leading upward with mathematical necessity!

I am not satisfied with explaining this passage as meaning: it must become worse before it can become better. This passage is a warning against the political messianism as it existed in the circles of Jewish and Christian zealots. But the profound meaning of this passage is really sensed in the following exposition: when man fails to provide a place for justice, civilization decays and eventually collapses in an apocalyptic upheaval, and the historic change occurs like an earthquake or like any other catastrophe in nature.

The medieval society which had survived in Europe is crushed today. Hitler, Lenin, and Stalin did what should have been done by kinder and wiser men but, alas, was not done by them. On the contrary, the old order had its defenders. We Jews could not do anything. Even the only outlet, emigration to America, was no longer a relieving measure possible to Eastern European Jews after 1918.

Eastern European Jewry was exterminated in the gas chambers. Two-thirds of the Jewish people survived Auschwitz, in great measure owing to their residence outside Hitler's reach. But after Auschwitz an Eastern European Jewry exists no longer. The historic time in which Eastern European Jewry lived was of medieval pattern.

Jews who left this pattern of life during the last two hundred years and entered the Western stage enriched the New World because they transferred what was best in the Middle Ages into the new era. Jews who have become Westernized Jews are not secularized Jews. Jews are able to move from one historic time to another; it is nonsensical to speak of a secularized Jewry. A church can become secularized. By being secularized the church gives free rein to her political components and is, in fact, a state outwardly displaying the insignia of a church.

The gentiles hailing from the church, the secularized Christian gentiles, far from being innocent gentiles, become demonic gentiles, pagans who retain the principles of faith, sacrifice, obedience, and hope, but serve with them the Moloch. The secularized offspring of the medieval church practiced medieval politics in the twentieth century. "The SS were the dominicans of the technical age" (Hochhuth), the Fuehrer principle represented papal infallibility, Auschwitz was the place where the directors of the Inquisition did their work in the midst of the twentieth century. The guilt of the Roman Catholic church was that it was a medieval church in the twentieth century.

In the Middle Ages lord and vassal were bound together by the authoritarian principle. Fascism rejecting democracy and choosing the authoritarian principle was political medievalism. In the Middle Ages the hierarchical principle created a social pyramid in which not equality but inequality was the socially binding force. The man at the top was unique. The Caesar as pope or as emperor made the Middle Ages the heir of Roman imperialism. In the Christian Middle Ages there was no place for the Jews; they were those who had killed Christ and who were, therefore, according to the Christian dogma providentially destined to be persecuted. Hitler could be viewed by the Vatican as a Crusader; the change came late: a pope of the 1960s expunged—

a century and a quarter after the French Revolution—the phrase *perfidiis Judaeis* from the Easter liturgy. The Middle Ages are over today; as late as that. Nazism was the last chapter of the Middle Ages. Jews and Christians are driven to reform lest their historic role dies with the dying Middle Ages.

The reform visualized now by all Christian churches demands first of all the rejection of the doctrine which regards the Jew as an anti-Christian. Jews are non-Christians whom Christians have to acknowledgde in their importance for themselves. That Jesus had a Jewish mother is a philosemitic statement but carries only weight within a dialogue in which both partners accept Christian imagery. The Jew does not do this; he has done for two thousand years what the Protestant professor of theology Rudolf Bultmann began to do only recently; he has "demythologized" the New Testament images. Jews are non-Christians; in this gentile world in which they are bidden by God to live as a dispersed people, Jews have a history to which the servant-of-God texts of the Book of Isaiah provide the pattern. In Auschwitz, I say in my sermons—and only in sermons is it appropriate to make such a statement—Jews suffered vicarious death for the sins of mankind. It says in the liturgy of the synagogue in reference to the first and second *hurbans*, albeit centuries after the events: "because of our sins." After Auschwitz Jews need not say so. Can any martyr be a more innocent sin-offering than those murdered in Auschwitz! The millions who died in Auschwitz died "because of the sins of others." Jews and non-Jews died in Auschwitz, but the Jew hatred which Hitler inherited from the medieval church made Auschwitz the twentieth-century Calvary of the Jewish people.

The fact that a liberal pope expunged an offensive phrase about the Jews from Christian liturgy should not be reported in a condescending way. It is a small matter and should only be a beginning. The reform through which the church will emancipate herself from her medieval blindness in regard to the synagogue will have to mean much more. Judaism is the seed, and Yehuda Halevi and Maimonides taught: out of this seed grows the tree, the church. The Golgotha of modern mankind is Auschwitz. The Cross, the Roman gallows, was replaced by the gas chamber. The gentiles, it seems, must first be terrified by the blood of the sacrificed scapegoat to have the mercy of God revealed to them and become converted, become baptized gentiles, become Christians.

Abraham saw the ram in the thicket and sacrificed it as ransom, whereas the gentiles of his time deemed it necessary to bring their human sacrifice to the Moloch. Abraham is above the belief of the gentiles. The Christian message contradicts the belief of the gentiles. But in the Christian contradiction the gentile belief survives. The message of the Cross contradicts the gentiles by telling them: your atoning sacrifice has been brought, it is there on the Cross, do not kill any more. Thus speaks the Cross to the gentiles who argue that the sacrifice is necessary, the sacrifice on the altar of the Moloch. The Jewish message is: atonement is necessary but is possible without sacrifice. What about our sins? On the Day of Atonement the Jewish liturgy announces: "All the people did it—*bish' gagah*—in error." Never can God's love be better preached than in the message of His forgiveness which we receive without having to buy it by any sacrifice. The great sermon of the love of God is unsurpassably preached in the *Akedah*, the 22nd chapter of Genesis, in the book which the church calls the "Old" Testament.

Besides the *Akedah* we read in the Old Testament of the "servant of God." The expression the "suffering servant of God" does not occur in the Hebrew text and is already a Christian exegesis of this text. Abraham, the patriarch, the happy husband and father, the figure which seems to Christian eyes a "bourgeois" figure, any prophet, that prophet, too, who has no other name than "servant of God," each one of them is a human person and no more, but also no less. None of them offers himself as a mediator between God and man. Each one of them invites man himself to meet God, in happiness like Abraham or, in the hour of martyrdom, like the "servant" of the Book of Isaiah. Of the martyr-servant it is written: "Behold, My servant shall succeed, he shall be exalted and lifted up, and shall be very high" (52:13). Happiness surrounded Abraham when he left Moriah. Those who died in the gas chambers are also granted—happiness. Leo Baeck when he came out from the hell of Terezin whence the trainloads of Jews

moved to Auschwitz brought with him a message in which he interpreted the Book of Daniel. In this book the author, a Jew who lived at the time of the religious persecution through Antiochus, asked: what happens to those who die and will not see the liberation, soon and surely to come? The answer was we do not die into the grave, we die into the eternity of God.

The church interpreted mankind's history by introducing the Year One. Before that year the old era, after that, the new era. The philosopher Karl Jasper doubted the justification of such division. He found the eighth century before the Christian Year One more important, because at this juncture mankind awakened simultaneously at different places of the globe to its greatest height: prophecy in Palestine, philosophy in Greece, and Buddhism in India. Compared with the impact of this great awakening the Year One concerns only an event within the Hellenistic syncretistic movement bringing Athens and Jerusalem together. There were others who established a new era with a Year One: the men of the French Revolution and Lenin.

In Jasper's critical attitude to the Christian Year One is a positive element which is more important than anything else he says in this connection. By bringing to our consciousness the power of Buddhism he speaks in fact not so much of what he calls the "axial period" of the pre-Christian eighth century but of our modern situation. In our post-Auschwitz situation Jew and Christian—and for that matter Muslim, too,—have a new partner to face: the Buddhist. Europe is no longer the cultural entity without connection with Asia. Exhausted after two world wars and after the impact of the cold war, Europe is open to the danger of Asiatic nihilism. In this situation it must be remembered that the only radical antithesis to Buddhism is prophetic Judaism.

We deceive ourselves when we plan for the future without admitting that it leads away from all our yesterdays. The frame of our mind is shaped by two events for which there is no comparison in the whole past of mankind's history: Auschwitz and Hiroshima.

After Auschwitz the human imagination is not what it was before. After Auschwitz a new era begins which will lead either away from everything which led to Auschwitz or will continue in the vein of Auschwitz. We must ask whether European man, having now in his vocabulary the word Auschwitz, is still the same man who looked at the world with the imagination so far typical for him. We must ask whether European man with the word Auschwitz in his vocabulary now has an experience which makes him prone to Asian thinking, to a skepticism and nihilism which only Buddha can cure. Man "saved" by Buddha is no longer a European, he is not a Jew and not a Christian. With Auschwitz a dam has burst in Europe, and Asia can gush forward. Christianity's battle of Stalingrad was fought in Auschwitz, and Christianity was not the victor. In this great Christian defeat, Judaism is not involved; we lost six million of our people, but the teaching of the prophets and rabbis was not found wanting.

Kant said after the French Revolution: "The world is no longer what is was before." After Auschwitz and Hiroshima we must face a hitherto unknown element of human existence. We have looked into an abyss which we know now to be very close to us. We can only save mankind through a greater charity and a greater responsibility than shown so far by civilized man. The globe itself populated with numerous races must become our concern. The whole earth can become devastated by "the bomb," and entire races can be wiped out by barbarism. Only the biblical view regarding the world as the creation of God and every human being as created in the image of God can save us from the catastrophe looming on the horizon of a civilization alienated from God "the Creator of heaven and earth."

Richard Lowell Rubenstein

Richard Rubenstein was born into an assimilated Jewish family in New York City in 1924. After difficult teen years in which he suffered directly and physically from anti-Semitism—despite his not having a Bar Mitzvah because of his family's complete disinterest in Judaism—he flirted with the idea of becoming a Unitarian minister. Drawn back to Judaism, he enrolled in September 1942 as a rabbinical student at Hebrew Union College, the Reform movement's rabbinical seminary in Cincinnati, and spent three years there. During these years he also studied at the University of Cincinnati and in 1945–1946 he received a B.A. in philosophy from the university. After the end of the war, in the wake of the Holocaust and the creation of the State of Israel, he returned to his rabbinical studies. However, he was unhappy at HUC and with the help of Abraham Joshua Heschel, who had made a similar move, and the well-known Orthodox rabbi Isaac Hutner, at whose yeshiva he had begun to study in New York City, he transferred in 1948 to the Conservative Jewish Theological Seminary in New York City. He was ordained at JTS in 1952. He then did graduate work at Harvard, worked as a Conservative rabbi in Brockton, Massachusetts, and served as the Hillel director at Wellesley College between 1958 and 1960. In 1960 he received his doctorate from Harvard for a thesis in which he applied Freudian analysis to rabbinic *aggadah* (the nonlegal sections of the traditional rabbinic texts).

After receiving his doctorate, and while serving as the Hillel director at the University of Pittsburgh, Rubenstein became involved in the incipient theological debate about the Holocaust and the so-called death-of-God movement among Christian theologians. In consequence, he published his own version of a Jewish death-of-God theology in his highly influential 1966 collection, *After Auschwitz: Radical Theology and Contemporary Judaism*. This provocative work caused great offense in many Jewish establishment quarters and, in consequence, he was essentially "exiled" from the Jewish community.

In the late 1960s and 1970s, Rubenstein continued to publish a series of important books: *The Religious Imagination* (1968); *Morality and Eros* (1970); *My Brother Paul* (1972); *Power Struggle: An Autobiographical Confession* (1974); and *The Cunning of History* (1975). In 1970, he moved to a full-time professorship in religion at Florida State University. In this new role he published his challenging study of modernity as an age of genocidal violence, *The Age of Triage: Fear and Hope in an Overcrowded World* (1983). In 1977 he was honored as Distinguished Professor of the Year at Florida State University, the university's highest honor. In 1995, at age seventy-one, he became president of the University of Bridgeport, a position from which he retired on 31 December 1999. He has been awarded honorary doctorates by the Jewish Theological Seminary of America (1987) and Grand Valley State University (1999).

SELECTIONS

The three selections from Rubenstein's work are all drawn from the first edition of *After Auschwitz*. The first of these explains the basic theological problem he was both wrestling with and seeking to overcome, namely, classical Christian anti-Semitism and the idea of Jewish guilt which, for the Christian, is connected most specifically and acutely to the accusation of deicide. Rubenstein was shocked by the employment of this traditional theology by a leading German Christian theologian as an explanation of the Holocaust, i.e., God is punishing Jews for the crime of deicide through the instrument of Hitler. The second selection attempts to explain why Rubenstein holds fast to the importance of Judaism and Jewish community while also attempting to redefine the notion of God, now as Nothingness, as a consequence of the death camps. The third excerpt makes the interesting argument that even though Judaism no longer carries its historic and normative ontological content, it still provides valuable and much-needed human meaning in a world otherwise devoid of meaning. In a world in which "God is dead," Judaism (and other religions) become all the more relevant as the source of human caring and solidarity.

Selected Bibliography

Books by Richard Rubenstein

After Auschwitz: Radical Theology and Contemporary Judaism (Indianapolis, 1966; 2d ed., Baltimore, 1992).
The Religious Imagination: A Study in Psychoanalysis and Jewish Theology (Indianapolis, 1968).
My Brother Paul (New York, 1972).
Power Struggle: An Autobiographical Confession (New York, 1974).
The Age of Triage: Fear and Hope in an Overcrowded World (Boston, 1983).

Books and Articles about Richard Rubenstein

Katz, Steven T. "Richard Rubenstein, the God of History, and the Logic of Judaism," in Steven T. Katz, *Post-Holocaust Dialogues* (New York, 1983), pp. 174–204.
Hellig, Jocelyn. "Richard Rubenstein," in *Interpreters of Judaism in the Twentieth Century*, edited by Steven T. Katz (Washington, D.C., 1993), pp. 249–264.
Braiterman, Zachary. *(God) after Auschwitz* (Princeton, 1998).

THE DEAN AND THE CHOSEN PEOPLE

The more one studies the classical utterances of Christianity on Jews and Judaism, while at the same time reviewing the terrible history of the Nazi period, the more one is prompted to ask whether there is something in the logic of Christian theology, *when pushed to a metaphysical extreme,* which ends with the justification of, if not the incitement to, the murder of Jews. Though there is an infinitude of pain in the exploration of this question, neither the Christian nor the Jew can avoid it.

Given the question of the relationship between Christianity and the Holocaust, I considered myself very fortunate when, during the summer of 1961, while I was on a visit to West Germany, the *Bundespresseamt,* the Press and Information Office of the German Federal Republic, made it possible for me to visit and interview Dr. Heinrich Grüber, Dean of the Evangelical Church in Berlin, at his home in Berlin-Dahlem. It was my third visit to Germany in thirteen months. The first two visits were private and unofficial. On this occasion the Press and Information Office was extremely helpful in making it possible for me to come to understand something of the complex reality that is present-day West Germany.

Thousands of Germans could have testified against Eichmann [at his trial in Jerusalem in 1961] and offered relevant testimony. Only one actually made the trip to Jerusalem to testify. Dean Grüber is a Protestant clergyman with a very long and heroic record of opposition to the Nazis on Christian grounds, and of friendship and succor for Nazism's chief victims. In the end, his courage brought him to Dachau and near-martyrdom. His resistance was especially meritorious because it incurred the possibility of great danger to his wife and children as well as to himself.

Since the war Dean Grüber has devoted himself to the work of healing and reconciliation. He has been instrumental in creating the Heinrich Grüber Haus in Berlin-Dahlem, an old-age residence for victims of the Nuremberg Laws. These included Germans who had married Jews, Jews who had converted to Christianity, and a few old Jews who, in spite of the fury which had disrupted their lives, wanted to end their days in Berlin. With public and government support, a very spacious and attractive home has been built for these people who were the very special concern of the Dean.

In addition to testifying at the Eichmann trial, Dean Grüber has been instrumental in fostering the work of reconciliation between Germany and Israel on the political level, and between German Christianity and Judaism at the religious level. At his suggestion, on his seventieth birthday his German friends and admirers contributed well over one hundred thousand marks for the planting of a forest in his honor in Israel. He rejected all gifts. He insisted instead that the money be given to build Israel. He is also active in a German-Israeli organization devoted to the exchange of visits between the youth of the two countries. He has visited Israel three times.

The Dean is over seventy, but there is a healthiness and a heartiness to his person which are noticeable immediately. He has a very attractive and spacious home, something very rare in Berlin today where, of necessity, apartment-house living

is all that most people can hope for. He met me at the door and brought me to his study, which was lined with books, a rather attractive oil copy of Rembrandt's *Flora,* and all sorts of relics and souvenirs of a long and distinguished career. In one corner, there was also a very impressive sculpture of the Dean's head.

After many sessions of interviewing Germans in all walks of life, I had learned to expect the interviewee to undergo a warm-up period before the initial reserve wore off. In the case of the Dean, this was unnecessary. There was an admirable bluntness and candor to his manner which revealed that the man means exactly what he says. This thoroughgoing honesty was present to the point of pain throughout the interview. It was not a quality the Nazis valued.

The most obvious point of departure for the conversation was the Eichmann trial. He explained that he went to Jerusalem with the greatest reluctance, and only after his name had come up so frequently that he felt he had no decent alternative. He also asserted that he went as a German, a member of the people who had perpetuated the injustice, and a member of the Christian church which had remained silent before it.

"Did testifying cause you any harm with your own people?" I asked.

He replied that it had not and went on to say that he did not really see much difference between himself and Eichmann, that he too was guilty, that, in fact, the guilt was to be shared by all peoples rather than by Eichmann alone.

"If there had only been a little more responsibility all around, things would have been different."

He complained bitterly of how the governments of practically every civilized country turned their backs on the Jews, making it impossible for them to leave. He spoke of his own efforts to secure immigration visas and complained of how seldom he succeeded.

I asked him about the Heinrich Grüber Haus. He explained that he had helped hundreds of people, many of whom were victims of the Nuremberg Laws, to leave Germany. In recent years some wanted to return. Originally he had founded his home for twenty people, most of whom were Christians who had lost Jewish relatives during the persecutions. He felt that these people deserved a more comfortable life in their remaining years than most old people. It was also extremely difficult to place them successfully in the average German old-age home as many German old people were still bitterly anti-Semitic and would have objected. To meet these problems, he had built, with much public support, this very unique and very beautiful home.

Without being asked, the Dean informed me that he had never converted Jews and did not want to do so now. On the contrary, he wanted Christians to become better Christians and Jews to become better Jews. I quickly learned that the Dean had very decided ideas on what Jews ought to be and how they ought to behave.

Again continuing without being questioned on the matter, the Dean informed me that Germany's Jews today were in great danger. He said that once again Jews are influential in the banks, the press, and other areas of public interest. This surprised me, as I had been informed that there are only eight thousand employed or self-employed Jews in a nation of fifty million.

"The problem in Germany is that the Jews haven't learned anything from what happened to them," he informed me. "I always tell my Jewish friends that they shouldn't put a hindrance in the way of our fight against anti-Semitism."

In view of his long-established friendship for the Jewish people, I asked him to clarify his statement. He replied that many of the brothels and risqué nightclubs, for example, are now in Jewish hands, especially those in close proximity to the army camps.

"For hundreds of years, there has been a virulent tradition of anti-Semitism among the Germans. Hitler exploited that tradition for his own ends. It is very difficult for us to wipe it out. After the Eichmann trial, this is one of my tasks. I am involved in one or two meetings a week to help end anti-Semitism, but it is very difficult because of the Jews in prominent positions and those who are engaged only in seeking money no matter what they do."

In reply, I told the Dean of the feelings of many Israelis that one of the most wonderful things about Israel is that there Jews have the right to be anything they want without relating it to the Jewish problem. I put the problem to him in terms of the freedom of every man to make his own life choices and to pay the price for his personal decisions.

"Look, I don't understand why you are so troubled about a pitifully small number of Jews in shady positions or being interested in making money rather than following edifying pursuits. It seems to me that every person pays a price for the kind of life he leads. Why should Germans be upset about the life decisions of these Jews unless they are unduly envious or neurotically involved in other people's lives? Must every Jew make himself so pale, so inconspicuous, even invisible, that he will give no offense? Is that the lesson Jews must learn from the death camps, that they must prove to the Germans their preeminent capacity for virtue? Wouldn't it seem a far better solution for all Jews left in Germany to leave and go where they could be anything they wished, without worrying about what the Germans thought or felt about them? After what has happened, why should any Jew remain and worry about attaining the approbation of the German people?"

The Dean was not prepared to let go. He was disturbed at the thought of the few remaining Jews leaving Germany. He felt that I was correct that Jews had as much right to be anything they pleased as the Germans, but he also felt that, after what had happened, they ought not to do these things, as it made the work of ending anti-Semitism so much harder. It was evident that in his mind there was an objective relationship between Jewish behavior and anti-Semitism.

Having asserted that the Jews had as much right to produce scoundrels or scalawags as any other people, the Dean quickly retracted. He spoke of the ancient covenant between God and Israel and how Israel as the chosen people of God was under a very special obligation to behave in a way which was spiritually consistent with Divine ordinance.

"I don't say this about Israel; God says this in the Bible and I believe it!" he insisted with considerable emotion.

The Dean was not the first German clergyman who had spoken to me in this vein concerning Israel. I had previously met a number of others in Berlin and Bonn. All insisted that there was a very special providential relationship between

Israel, what happened to it, and God's will, that this had been true in the time of the Bible and that the *Heilsgeschichte* [sacred history] of the Jewish people had continued to unfold to this very day. In fairness to them, it should be pointed out that this belief has been shared by the vast majority of religious Jews throughout history. The theological significance of the Zionist movement and the establishment of the State of Israel lay largely in the rejection of *Heilsgeschichte* and the assertion that Jewish misfortune had been made by men and could be undone by men. For the pastors the conviction remained—it should be said that the conviction has been strengthened—that nowhere in the world were the fruits of God's activity in history more evident than in the life and the destiny of the Jewish people. In each instance I very quickly rejoined that such thinking had as its inescapable conclusion the conviction that the Nazi slaughter of the Jews was somehow God's will, that God really wanted the Jewish people to be exterminated. In every instance before meeting Dr. Grüber, I was met by an embarrassed withdrawal.

Countess Dr. von Rittberg, the representative of the Evangelical church to the Bonn government, a charming and learned lady, was one of the German religious personalities with whom I discussed this issue. She had offered the customary interpretation of Israel's destiny as being guided by a special Divine concern, but she partially withdrew it in the face of my objection.

"Theologically this may be true, but humanly speaking and in any terms that I can understand, I cannot believe that God wanted the Nazis to destroy the Jews," she said.

Her reluctance to follow the logic of her theology to its hideous conclusion, which made the Nazis the accomplices of God, was, humanly speaking, most understandable. I found a similar reluctance in the other clergymen with whom I spoke, though, because I was a rabbi and a guest, there is a distinct possibility that I did not get a random sampling of theological opinion.

The same openness and lack of guile which Dean Grüber had shown from the moment I met him was again manifest in his reaction to my question concerning God's role in the death of the six million, a question which I believe is decisive for contemporary Jewish theology.

"Was it God's will that Hitler destroyed the Jews?" I repeated. "Is this what you believe concerning the events through which we have lived?"

Dr. Grüber arose from his chair and rather dramatically removed a Bible from a bookcase, opened it, and read: "*Um deinetwillen werden wir getotet den ganzen Tag* . . . for Thy sake are we slaughtered every day" (Psalms 44:22).

"When God desires my death, I give it to him!" he continued. "When I started my work against the Nazis I knew that I would be killed or go to the concentration camp. Eichmann asked me, 'Why do you help these Jews? They will not thank you.' I had my family; there were my wife and three children. Yet I said, 'Your will be done even if You ask my death.' For some reason, it was part of God's plan that the Jews died. God demands our death daily. He is the Lord, He is the Master, all is in His keeping and ordering."

Listening to the Dean, I recalled Erich Fromm's descriptions of the authoritarian personality in *Escape from Freedom*.[1] All the clergymen had asserted the absolute character of God's Lordship over mankind and of mankind's obligation to submit unquestioningly to that Lordship, but none had carried the logic of this theology as far as the Dean did.

The Dean's disturbing consistency undoubtedly had its special virtues. No consideration of personal safety could deter the Dean from total obedience to his heavenly Master; this contrasted starkly with too many of his fellow countrymen who gave lip-service to a similar ideal but conveniently turned the other way in the crisis. Nevertheless, there was another side to this stance which was by no means as pleasant. Eichmann also had served his master with complete and utterly unquestioning fidelity. Even sixteen years after the close of hostilities, not only Eichmann, but apparently his defense counsel, seemed to feel that such servitude was self-justifying. Furthermore, in both the Dean and his demonic antagonist, the will of the master, in the one case God, in the other case Hitler, was unredeemed by a saving empiricism. Neither man preferred an inconsistency in logic to the consistency of accepting the

1. (New York, 1941).

gratuitous murder of six million. In neither individual was there even a trace of personal autonomy.

When Dr. Grüber put down his Bible, it seemed as if, once having started, he could not stop himself. He looked at recent events from a thoroughly biblical perspective. In the past, the Jews had been smitten by Nebuchadnezzar and other "rods of God's anger." Hitler was simply another such rod. The incongruity of Hitler as an instrument of God never seemed to occur to him. Of course, he granted that what Hitler had done was immoral and he insisted that Hitler's followers were now being punished by God.

"At different times," he said, "God uses different peoples as His whip against His own people, the Jews, but those whom He uses will be punished far worse than the people of the Lord. You see it today here in Berlin. We are now in the same situation as the Jews. My church is in the East sector. Last Sunday (13 August, the day of the border closing) I preached on Hosea 6:1 ('Come, and let us return unto the Lord: For He hath torn, and He will heal us; He hath smitten, and He will bind us up'). God has beaten us for our terrible sins; I told our people in East Berlin that they must not lose faith that He will reunify us."

I felt a chill at that instant. There was enormous irony in the Dean's assertion that the Germans had become like Jews. I was listening to a German clergyman interpret German defeat as the rabbis had interpreted the fall of Jerusalem almost two thousand years before. For the rabbis, Jerusalem fell because of the sins of the Jewish people. For Dean Grüber, Berlin had fallen because of the sins of the German people. When he sought words of consolation with which to mollify the wounding of his imprisoned church he turned to the very same verses from Hosea which had consoled countless generations of Israel.

He pursued the analogy between Germany and Israel: "I know that God is punishing us because we have been the whip against Israel. In 1938 we smashed the synagogues; in 1945 our churches were smashed by the bombs. From 1938 we sent the Jews out to be homeless; since 1945 fifteen million Germans have experienced homelessness."

The feeling of guilt was very apparent; so too was the fact that for him German suffering appeased and ameliorated this feeling. Everything he said reiterated his belief that God was ultimately responsible for the death of the Jews. It may have been a mystery to him, but it was nevertheless taken as unshakable fact.

The Dean has asserted that God had been instrumental in the Holocaust. He had not asserted the nature of the crime for which God was supposed to have smitten the Jews. During the Eichmann trial, Dr. Servatius, the defense counsel, had offered the suggestion that the death of the six million was part of a "higher purpose," and in recompense for an earlier and greater crime against God, thereby joining the modern trial in Jerusalem with one held twenty centuries before. Time was running short. I did not have the opportunity to question Dean Grüber concerning the nature of the enormous crime for which six million Jews perished. His thinking was so thoroughly drenched in New Testament and prophetic categories that there is little reason to think that he would have disagreed with Dr. Servatius. Stated with theological finesse it comes to pretty much the same thing as the vulgar thought that the Christ-killers got what was coming to them. . . .

It would seem that as long as there is Christianity, Jews will be the potential objects of a special and ultimately pernicious attention which can always explode in violence. Even were all the textbooks "corrected," there would still be the Gospels, and they are enough to assure the ever-present threat of a murderous hatred of Jews by Christians. Even when Christians assert that all men are guilty of the death of the Christ, they are asserting a guilt more hideous than any known in any other religion, the murder of the Lord of Heaven and Earth. On the Jewish side, we would say that not only are the Jews not guilty of this deicide, but that no man is guilty because it never happened. Here again there is an unbridgeable wall. The best that Christians can do for the Jews is to spread the guilt, while always reserving the possibility of throwing it back entirely upon the Jews. This is no solution for the Jews, for they must insist that this dimension of guilt exists for no man in reality, although they might be willing to admit that it exists for every man in fantasy.

SYMPOSIUM ON JEWISH BELIEF

I am convinced that the problems implicit in "death of God" theology concern Judaism as much as Christianity. Technically death-of-God theology reflects the Christian tradition of the passion of the Christ. As such, the terminology of the movement creates some very obvious problems for Jewish theologians. Nevertheless, I have, almost against my will, come to the conclusion that the terminology is unavoidable. The death-of-God theologians have brought into the open a conviction which has led a very potent underground existence for decades. Death-of-God theology is no fad. It is a contemporary expression of issues which have, in one way or another, appeared in embryo in scholastic philosophy, medieval mysticism, nineteenth-century German philosophy, and in the religious existentialism of Martin Buber and Paul Tillich.

No man can really say that God is dead. How can we know that? Nevertheless, I am compelled to say that we live in the time of the "death of God." This is more a statement about man and his culture than about God. The death of God is a cultural fact. Buber felt this. He spoke of the eclipse of God. I can understand his reluctance to use the more explicitly Christian terminology. I am compelled to utilize it because of my conviction that the time which Nietzsche's madman said was too far off has come upon us. There is no way around Nietzsche. Had I lived in another time or another culture, I might have found some other vocabulary to express my meanings. I am, however, a religious existentialist after Nietzsche and after Auschwitz. When I say we live in the time of the death of God, I mean that the thread uniting God and man, heaven and earth, has been broken. We stand in a cold, silent, unfeeling cosmos, unaided by any purposeful power beyond our own resources. After Auschwitz, what else can a Jew say about God?

When Professor William Hamilton associated my theological writings with the death-of-God movement in his article on radical theology in *The Christian Scholar*,[1] I was somewhat dubious about

his designation. After reflection, I concluded that Professor Hamilton was correct. There is a definite style in religious thought which can be designated death-of-God theology. I have struggled to escape the term. I have been embarrassed by it. I realize its inadequacy and its Christian origin. I have, nevertheless, concluded that it is inescapable. I see no other way of expressing the void which confronts man where once God stood.

I am acutely aware of the fact that Christian death-of-God theologians remain fully committed Christians as I remain a committed Jew. As Professor Hamilton has suggested, Christian death-of-God theologians have no God, but they do have a Messiah. Christian death-of-God theology remains Christocentric. I affirm the final authority of Torah and reject the Christian Messiah, as Jews have for two thousand years. Professor Thomas J. J. Altizer welcomes the death of God. He sees it as an apocalyptic event in which the freedom of the Gospels is finally realized and the true Christian is liberated from every restraint of the Law. I do not see that awful event as a cosmic liberation. I am saddened by it. I believe that in a world devoid of God we need Torah, tradition, and the religious community far more than in a world where God's presence was meaningfully experienced. The death of God leads Altizer to a sense of apocalyptic liberation; it leads me to a sad determination to enhance the religious norms and the community without which the slender fabric of human decency might well disappear. In the time of the death of God, Christian theologians still proclaim the Gospel of the Christ; Jewish theologians proclaim the indispensability of Torah.

I believe the greatest single challenge to modern Judaism arises out of the question of God and the death camps. I am amazed at the silence of contemporary Jewish theologians on this most crucial and agonizing of all Jewish issues. How can Jews believe in an omnipotent, beneficent God after Auschwitz? Traditional Jewish theology maintains that God is the ultimate, omnipotent actor in the historical drama. It has interpreted every major catastrophe in Jewish history as God's

1. William Hamilton, "The Death of God Theology," *Christian Scholar* 48 (Spring 1965).

punishment of a sinful Israel. I fail to see how this position can be maintained without regarding Hitler and the SS as instruments of God's will. The agony of European Jewry cannot be likened to the testing of Job. To see any purpose in the death camps, the traditional believer is forced to regard the most demonic, antihuman explosion in all history as a meaningful expression of God's purposes. The idea is simply too obscene for me to accept. I do not think that the full impact of Auschwitz has yet been felt in Jewish theology or Jewish life. Great religious revolutions have their own period of gestation. No man knows the hour when the full impact of Auschwitz will be felt, but no religious community can endure so hideous a wounding without undergoing vast inner disorders.

Though I believe that a void stands where once we experienced God's presence, I do not think Judaism has lost its meaning or its power. I do not believe that a theistic God is necessary for Jewish religious life. Dietrich Bonhoeffer has written that our problem is how to speak of God in an age of no religion. I believe that our problem is how to speak of religion in an age of no God. I have suggested that Judaism is the way in which we share the decisive times and crises of life through the traditions of our inherited community. The need for that sharing is not diminished in the time of the death of God. We no longer believe in the God who has the power to annul the tragic necessities of existence; the need religiously to share that existence remains.

Finally, the time of the death of God does not mean the end of all gods. It means the demise of the God who was the ultimate actor in history. I believe in God, the Holy Nothingness known to mystics of all ages, out of which we have come and to which we shall ultimately return. I concur with atheistic existentialists such as Sartre and Camus in much of their analysis of the broken condition of human finitude. We must endure that condition without illusion or hope. I do not part company with them on their analysis of the human predicament. I part company on the issue of the necessity of religion as the way in which we share that predicament. Their analysis of human hopelessness leads me to look to the religious community as the institution in which that condition can be shared in depth. The limitations of finitude can be overcome only when we return to the Nothingness out of which we have been thrust. In the final analysis, omnipotent Nothingness is Lord of all creation.

The Symbols of Judaism and the Death of God

Finally, there is the problem of God after the death of God. The focus of the synagogue upon the decisive events and seasons of life gives us a clue to the meaning of God in our times. At one level, it is certainly possible to understand God as the primal ground of being out of which we arise and to which we return. I believe such a God is inescapable in the time of the death of God. The God who is the ground of being is not the transcendent, theistic God of Jewish patriarchal monotheism. Though many still believe in that God, they do so ignoring the questions of God and human freedom and God and human evil. For those who face these issues, the Father-God is a dead God. Even the existentialist leap of faith cannot resurrect this dead God after Auschwitz.

Nevertheless, after the death of the Father-God, God remains the central reality against which all partial realities can be measured. I should like to suggest that God can be understood meaningfully not only as ground of being but also as the *focus of ultimate concern*. As such He is not the old theistic Father-God. Nor is He reconstructionism's "power that makes for salvation in the world." He is the infinite measure against which we can see our own limited finite lives in proper perspective. Before God, it is difficult for us to elevate the trivial to the central in our lives. The old Hebraic understanding of the meaning of idolatry is important for an understanding of the meaning of God as the focus of ultimate concern. Idolatry is the confusion of a limited aspect of things with the ground of the totality. This is not the occasion to catalog the idolatries of our time. That task has been well done by others. If an awareness of God as the ground of being does nothing more than enable us to refrain from endowing a partial and limited concern with the dignity and status reserved for what is of ultimate concern, it will have served the most important of all tasks. The ancient Hebrews regarded idolatry as a special form of enslavement. Nothing in our contemporary idolatries makes them less enslaving than their archaic counterparts. God can truly make us free.

We live in a culture which tends to stress what we can do rather than what we can become. A few examples will suffice to illustrate the encouragements to idolatry and self-deception with which our culture abounds. We are forever encouraged to deny the passing of time in our overestimation of the importance of both being and looking young. One of our greatest needs is to acknowledge our temporality and mortality without illusion. By so doing, we are not defeated by time. We establish the precondition of our *human* mastery over it. As the focus of ultimate concern the timeless God reflects our seriousness before our human temporality.

Another decisive contemporary need is to learn how to dwell within our own bodies. That is not so easy as it may seem. Fewer capacities come harder to Americans than the capacity to dwell within their own bodies with grace, dignity, and gratification. We become caricatures of our human potentialities when we fail to acquire this wisdom. By coming to terms with the biological nature of the timetable of life, we experience an enormous liberation yet develop the capacity for equally great renunciations when necessary. In the presence of God as the focus of ultimate concern, we need no deceptive myths of an immortal soul. We are finite. He is eternal. We shall perish. He remains ever the same. Before Him we confront our human nakedness with truth and honesty. In this venture, our voyage of self-discovery is enormously aided by Judaism's insistence through ritual and tradition on our continuing awareness of where we are in the biological timetable of life. The ancient Gnostics disparaged the God of the Jews as the God of this world. They asserted that all of His commandments were concerned with the conduct of life in this perishing cosmos. They correctly understood Judaism in their hostility. Unlike Gnosticism, Judaism refused to turn the regard of Jews away from the only life they will ever know, the life of the flesh in this world. God as the focus of ultimate concern challenges us to be the only persons we realistically can be, our authentic, finite selves in all of the radical insecurity and potentiality the life of mortal man affords.

One cannot pray to such a God in the hope of achieving an I-Thou relationship. Such a God is not a person over against man. If God is the ground of being, He will not be found in the meeting of I and Thou but in self-discovery. That self-discovery is not necessarily introspective. The whole area of interpersonal relations is the matrix in which meaningful and insightful self-discovery can occur. Nor can the I-Thou relation between God and man be achieved through prayer. This does not do away with worship. It sets worship in proper perspective. Even Buber admits, in his discussion of the eclipse of God, the contemporary failure of personal prayer. While prayer as address and dialogue has ceased to be meaningful, the burden of this paper has been to suggest some of the ways in which religious ritual has retained its significance. Ritual is more important today than prayer save as prayer is interwoven with ritual. Our prayers can no longer be attempts at dialogue with a personal God. They become aspirations shared in depth by the religious community. As aspiration there is hardly a prayer in the liturgy of Judaism which has lost its meaning or its power. Worship is the sharing of ultimate concern by the community before God, the focus of ultimate concern.

Paradoxically, God as ground does everything and nothing. He does nothing in that He is not the motive or active power which brings us to personal self-discovery or to the community of shared experience. Yet He does everything because He shatters and makes transparent the patent unreality of every false and inauthentic standard. God, as the ultimate measure of human truth and human potentiality, calls upon each man to face both the limitations and the opportunities of his finite predicament without disguise, illusion, or hope.

There remains the question of whether the religion of God as the source and ground of being, the God after the death of God, is truly a religion. Can there be a religion without a belief in a theistic, creator God? Pagan religions have never celebrated such a God. As I have suggested elsewhere, in the time of the death of God a mystical paganism which utilizes the historic forms of Jewish religion offers the most promising approach to religion in our times.

Judaism no longer insists on the affirmation of a special creed. It has long since ceased rejecting its communicants because of ritual neglect. This does not mean that Judaism has descended to the level of a tribal herd bound together by a primitive and externally enforced we-feeling. No religion can exist without a meaningful form of sacrifice. Though it is not always apparent, contemporary Judaism does have its form of sacrifice. It is just as meaningful and in some ways more demanding than the older forms. This form of sacrifice is peculiarly appropriate to our new understanding of the meaning of God and the power of symbols in contemporary Judaism. Our sacrifice is not philanthropy. Nor is it the renunciation of personal autonomy which some traditions demand. The sacrifice required of those who would participate in the community of ultimate concern is perhaps one of the most difficult in today's society. It is the sacrifice of that pride through which we see our individual roles, status, attainments, or sophistications as in any way more significant than that of any other human being with regard to the decisive events in the timetable of life. We share in the synagogue what we experience in common from birth to death. These events which we celebrate with the traditions of Judaism are the really decisive events. We can succeed in the world of affairs yet, humanly speaking, be wretched failures in the business of

life if we fail to put a goodly measure of energy and attention on the decisive events. The traditions and ritual of the synagogue call upon us for this kind of concentration. That is why the sacrifice of pride in attainments which are not central to the business of life is so essential. I do not wish to disparage worldly attainment or professional competence; I want to suggest the wisdom of Judaism in insisting upon its essential emptiness when the business of life is ignored. Each of us before God as the focus of ultimate concern must regard the real challenges of his personal existence as essentially the same as those of any other human being. Whether we are intellectuals, merchants, or laborers, we are born in the same way, need the same love, are capable of the same evil, and will die the same death. Concentration on what is of genuine significance in the business of life is the contemporary form of the renunciation of idolatry.

The religious symbol and the God to whom the religious symbol points were never more meaningful than they are today. It is no accident that the twentieth century is characterized by theological excitement and renewal. Our myths and rituals have been stripped of their historic covering. No man can seriously pretend that the literal meanings given to our traditions before our time retain much authority today. Happily, in losing some of the old meanings we have also lost some of the old fears.

God stands before us no longer as the final censor but as the final reality before which and in terms of which all partial realities are to be measured.

The last paradox is that in the time of the death of God we have begun a voyage of discovery wherein we may, hopefully, find the true God.

Emil Fackenheim

Emil Fackenheim (1916–2003) was born into a distinguished, Jewishly identified, religiously "Liberal"[1] family in Halle, Germany. His father was a successful attorney in the city. He received a typical secular education but was drawn to Jewish study and therefore enrolled as a rabbinical student at the Hochschule für die Wissenschaft des Judentums in Berlin. On *Kristallnacht*, the "Night of Broken Glass," in Germany (10 November 1938), when Jewish businesses and synagogues were attacked by the Nazis, he was arrested and sent to Sachsenhausan concentration camp. After several months he had the good fortune to be released and upon his release was able to secure a visa for entry into Scotland. After a short stay in Scotland he was sent, in 1940, to an internment camp in Canada where he remained for eighteen months. After his release he served as a Reform rabbi in Hamilton, Ontario (1943–1948) and at the same time, he also enrolled at the University of Toronto, where he specialized in eighteenth- and early nineteenth-century German philosophy, receiving his Ph.D. in 1948. That year, Fackenheim also received a permanent position at the University of Toronto and advanced through the usual academic ranks to become eventually a full professor in the Department of Philosophy. His expertise in German philosophy led to a number of significant publications, including *Metaphysics and Historicity* in 1961 and his highly influential *The Religious Dimension in Hegel's Thought* in 1968.

In the late 1960s, stirred especially by the Six Day War in Israel in 1967 and its aftermath, he emigrated to Israel and settled in Jerusalem where he became a Fellow of the Institute of Contemporary Jewry at the Hebrew University of Jerusalem. He passed away in Jerusalem at the age of eighty-seven in 2003.

SELECTIONS

Fackenheim began to reflect publicly on the Holocaust in the mid-1960s. Energized by the debate that was created by Richard Rubenstein's *After Auschwitz*, and even more by the 1967 Six Day War in Israel, Fackenheim tried to think through the meaning of the Holocaust in a way that, contrary to the "death of God" theologians, would affirm the existence of God despite the death camps and, even more, would affirm the present role of God in Jewish history through the "salvific" existence of the State of Israel. In the first three selections from his work, drawn from his Deems Lectures given at New York University in 1968, he begins to sketch his own post-Holocaust theological position. Drawing on the I-Thou philosophy of Martin Buber, he affirms God's presence in the here and now despite Auschwitz and insists that Auschwitz provided a form of revelation that addresses Israel out of the Holocaust. God's new revelation now is: "Jews are forbidden to hand Hitler posthumous victories. They are commanded to survive as Jews, lest the Jewish people perish" (*God's Presence in History*, p. 84; in this collection as "The Commanding Voice of Auschwitz," p. 434).

In the fourth and fifth selections reproduced here, drawn respectively from his collection of essays entitled *The Jewish Return into History: Reflections in the Age of Auschwitz and a New Jerusalem* (1978) and from his 1982 study *To Mend the World: Foundations of Future Jewish Thought,* Fackenheim spells out more fully what Jewish life, especially in light of the creation of the State of Israel following the Holocaust, now means. In particular, in the fifth selection he is trying to provide reasons for thinking that even after Auschwitz it is possible, through our actions, to "repair the world" in some way. (He uses the Hebrew expressions *Tikkun* = to repair and *Tikkun Olam* = to repair the world in order to try and convey his meaning.) The State of Israel is for him the clearest evidence that some form of *Tikkun,* however "fragmentary," is possible.

Notes

1. "Liberal" in this context means a modernized form of Judaism somewhat akin to American Conservative Judaism today.

Selected Bibliography

Books by Emil Fackenheim

God's Presence in History: Jewish Affirmation and Philosophical Reflections (New York, 1970).

Encounters between Judaism and Modern Philosophy: A Preface to Future Jewish Thought (New York, 1973).

The Jewish Return into History: Reflections in the Age of Auschwitz and a New Jerusalem (New York, 1978).

To Mend the World: Foundations of Future Jewish Thought (New York, 1982).

What Is Judaism: An Interpretation for the Present Ages (New York, 1987).

Jewish Philosophy and Jewish Philosophers, edited by Michael Morgan (Bloomington, 1996).

Books and Articles about Emil Fackenheim

Wyschogrod, Michael. "Faith and the Holocaust," *Judaism* 20 (Summer 1971): 286–294.

———. "Auschwitz: Beginning of a New Era?" *Tradition 17,* no. 1 (Fall 1977): 63–78.

Katz, Steven T. "Emil Fackenheim on Jewish Life after Auschwitz," in Steven T. Katz, *Post-Holocaust Dialogues* (New York, 1983), pp. 205–247.

Morgan, Michael. Introduction to *The Jewish Thought of Emil Fackenheim* (Detroit, 1987), pp. 13–18.

———. "The Central Problem of Fackenheim's *To Mend the World,"* *Journal of Jewish Thought and Philosophy* 5 (1996): 297–312.

Braiterman, Zachary. *(God) after Auschwitz* (Princeton, N.J., 1998).

The Structure of Jewish Experience

Root Experiences

It would be incongruous for us to reject, as misleading, any beginning with abstract notions of history-in-general, and yet ourselves begin with Jewish history-in-general. We must rather begin with particular events within the history of the Jewish faith, or, more precisely, with epoch-making events.

Even this term is not yet precise or radical enough. In its millennial career the Jewish faith has passed through many epoch-making events, such as the end of prophecy and the destruction of the First Temple, the Maccabean revolt, the destruction of the Second Temple, and the expulsion from Spain. These events each made a new claim upon the Jewish faith and, indeed, would not be epoch-making if it were otherwise. They did not, however, produce a new faith. What occurred instead was a confrontation in which the old faith was tested in the light of contemporary experience. Jewish history abounds with such confrontations between past and present. At least until the rise of the modern world, these have all one common characteristic. The strain of confrontation may often have come near a breaking point, yet present experience, however new, unanticipated, and epoch-making, never destroyed the past faith. Its claims upon the present survived. But—and this is crucial—this past faith had not come from nowhere but had *itself* originated in historical events. These historical events, therefore, are more than epoch-making. In the context of Judaism, we shall refer to them as root experiences.[1]

What, considered abstractly, are the characteristics of a root experience in Judaism? What are the conditions without which a past event cannot continue to make a present claim—the claim that God is present in history? According to Rabbi Eliezer, . . . the maidservants at the Red Sea saw what even Ezekiel did not see. This means, on the one hand, that Rabbi Eliezer himself does *not* see and, on the other hand, that he *knows* that the maidservants saw, and he does not. If he himself saw, he would not defer to their vision—his own being superior or equal to theirs and in any case a present standard by which to measure the past. If he did not know that they had seen, their past vision would be of no present relevance and, indeed, would be wholly inaccessible. Only because of this dialectical relation between present and past can a past experience legislate to the present. *This is the* first *condition of a root experience in Judaism.*

By itself, however, this condition (as yet far from fully intelligible) is far from sufficient as well. According to Rabbi Eliezer, this condition

would apply to Ezekiel's vision as much as to the maidservants' at the Red Sea. Yet Ezekiel's vision is not a root experience in Judaism. It is the experience of an isolated individual and may legislate to isolated individuals after him—those few to whom the heavens are accessible. At the Red Sea, however, the whole people saw, the lowly maidservants included, and what occurred before their eyes was not an opening of heaven but a transformation of earth—a historic event affecting decisively all future Jewish generations. These future generations, on their part, do not, like the maidservants at the Red Sea, see the presence of God. But to this day they recall twice daily in their prayers the natural-historical event through which that presence was once manifest, and the Passover Seder is wholly dedicated to it. Indeed, according to some rabbis, so profoundly legislating is this past event to future times that it will continue to be remembered even in the messianic days.[2] *Its public, historical character is the* second *condition of a root experience in Judaism.*

Still missing is a third condition, and this will turn out to be the crucial one. The vision of the maidservants at the Red Sea may be analyzed into two components. First, they experienced impending disaster at the hands of the pursuing Egyptian army and then salvation through the division of the Red Sea; that is, they experienced a natural-historical event. But they also experienced the presence of God. Subsequent generations, on their part, recollect the natural-historical event, but they do not see what the maidservants saw. Both points are not in question in the midrashic account. What is in question is whether, and if so how, *subsequent generations have access to the vision of the maidservants—to the presence of God.*

If they have no such access, then the event at the Red Sea cannot be a root experience in Judaism. A skeptic would in any case deny that the natural-historical event even happened, or else view it as a mere fortunate coincidence. What matters here is that even a believer would have

1. For this concept I am indebted to Irving Greenberg's concept of "orienting-experience." I here prefer the term "root experience" because I wish to analyze the intrinsic characteristics of the experience before considering its historical efficacy. It would be desirable to

find a word uniting both connotations, but I have not been able to find such a word.
2. *Mechilta de-Rabbi Ishmael*, edited by J. Z. Lauterbach (Philadelphia, 1949), I.135ff. The passage refers to the commemoration of the Exodus as a whole.

little cause for remembering it. For the "miracle" remembered would be for him, not a past event of divine Presence, but merely one particular effect of a general—and remote—divine cause. And, if his concern were with the general divine cause, no particular effect would stand out in importance; and, if it were with particular effects, it should be with *present* effects, not with the dimly remembered past. In connection with a discussion of the religious relevance of history, Hegel somewhere wryly quotes a proverb to the effect that with the passage of time the past loses its truth. If later generations of Jewish believers have no access whatever to the vision of the maidservants, this proverb would be applicable to the event at the Red Sea.

Such proverbs cease to apply, however, if the past vision of the maidservants is somehow still presently accessible; for in that case a divine Presence, manifest in and through the past natural-historical event, could not fail to legislate to future generations. (This is true at least if, as the Midrash states, the Divinity manifest is not a finite, tribal deity but the universal "Creator of the world." The past presence of such a God can continue to legislate even in the messianic days.) *This accessibility of past to present is the* third *and* final *characteristic of a root experience in Judaism.*

This characteristic is clearly if implicitly asserted by Jewish tradition. Thus the pious Jew remembering the Exodus and the salvation at the Red Sea does not call to mind events now dead and gone. He reenacts these events *as a present reality*: only thus is he assured that the past saving God saves still,[3] and that He will finally bring ultimate salvation. We have already stressed that Rabbi Eliezer knows that the maidservants saw the divine Presence at the Red Sea; we must now add that *he could not have this knowledge unless he had somehow himself access to their vision.*

But how shall we understand this access when Rabbi Eliezer—and the pious Jew during the Passover Seder—does not see what the maidservants saw? Indeed, how shall we understand the original event itself—a divine Presence which is manifest *in* and *through* a natural-historical event, not in the heavens beyond it?

An understanding is given in a remarkable passage in Martin Buber's *Moses*—one so remarkable and relevant to our purpose that we shall return to it again and again. . . . Buber writes:

> What is decisive with respect to the inner history of Mankind . . . is that the children of Israel understood this as an act of their God, as a "miracle"; which does not mean that they interpreted it as a miracle, but that they experienced it as such, that as such they perceived it. . . .
>
> The concept of miracle which is permissible from the historical approach can be defined at its starting point as an abiding astonishment. The . . . religious person . . . abides in that wonder; no knowledge, no cognition, can weaken his astonishment. Any causal explanation only deepens the wonder for him. The great turning-points in religious history are based on the fact that again and ever again an individual and a group attached to him wonder and keep on wondering; at a natural phenomenon, at an historical event, or at both together; always at something which intervenes fatefully in the life of this individual and this group. They sense and experience it as a wonder. This, to be sure, is only the starting point of the historical concept of wonder, but it cannot be explained away. Miracle is not something "supernatural" or "superhistorical," but an incident, an event which can be fully included in the objective, scientific nexus of nature and history; the vital meaning of which, however, for the person to whom it occurs, destroys the security of the whole nexus of knowledge for him, and explodes the fixity of the fields of experience named "nature" and "history." . . .
>
> We may ascribe what gives rise to our astonishment to a specific power. . . . For the

---

3. In the Passover *Haggadah* we find the following statement:

> It was not one only who rose against us to annihilate us, but in every generation there are those who rise against us to annihilate us. But the Holy One, blessed be He, saves us from their hand.

It is only a small exaggeration for me to say that whether, and if so how, the contemporary religious Jew can still include this sentence in the Passover *Seder* liturgy is the paramount question behind my entire investigation.

performance of the miracle a particular magical spirit, a special demon, a special idol is called into being. It is an idol just because it is special. But this is not what historical consideration means by miracle. For where a doer is restricted by other doers, the current system of cause and effect is replaced by another.... *The real miracle means that in the astonishing experience of the event the current system of cause and effect becomes, as it were, transparent and permits a glimpse of the sphere in which a sole power, not restricted by any other, is at work.*[4]

Buber's modern terms may be applied to the ancient Midrash in every particular. First, they remove a false understanding. Second, they make sense of a divine Presence manifest in and through a natural-historical event. Third, they explain how Rabbi Eliezer, while unable to see what the maidservants saw, nevertheless has access to their experience. Let us consider these three points in turn.

Those present at the Red Sea do not *infer* their God from the natural-historical event in an attempt to *explain* that event. A god of this kind would not be "Creator of the world" or "sole Power" but only a "magical spirit." He would not be "immediately recognized" but at most would be a probable hypothesis. And he would not be present but, rather, necessarily absent. As for the abiding astonishment, this would be dissipated by the explanation. This much would be true even of the original witnesses at the Red Sea. As for subsequent believers (who already possess this or some other explanation), they would not be astonished at all. And the past would be a dead past without present relevance. So much for the first point. What of the second?

The "sole Power" is immediately present *at the Red Sea,* in and through *the natural-historical event* for *the abiding astonishment of the witnesses.* All three terms introduced by Buber are needed, and they are intelligible only in their relation. (a) Except for the immediate presence of the sole Power the natural-historical event would not be a miracle but rather a strange incident in need of explanation; and the astonishment would only be

curiosity or, in any case, not abide, for it would vanish when the explanation is given. (b) Except for the abiding astonishment, the sole Power would not be present or, in any case, not be *known* to be present; and the miracle would, once again, be a mere incident to be explained. (c) Except for the natural-historical event, the sole Power, if present at all, would either be present in the heavens beyond history, or else dissolve all historical particularity by its presence within it; and the abiding astonishment would be equally historically vacuous. But the salvation at the Red Sea is not historically vacuous. It has "intervene[d] fatefully" in the history, if not of all mankind, certainly of Israel.

To come to the third point, how then is Rabbi Eliezer (and the pious Jew during the Passover *Seder*) related to the maidservants at the Red Sea? *In reenacting the natural-historical event, he reenacts the abiding astonishment as well, and makes it his own.* Hence the sole Power present then is present still. Hence memory turns into faith and hope. Hence the event at the Red Sea is recalled now and will continue to be recalled even in the messianic days. Thus the reenacted past legislates to present and future. Thus, in Judaism, it is a root experience.

Saving and Commanding Divine Presence

We have thus far used one particular root experience in Judaism in an attempt to elicit the characteristics of all such experiences. We must now turn, however briefly, to one other such experience—the commanding Presence at Sinai. Not only is every attempt to understand Judaism without Sinai impossible, it is also the case that, except for a commanding Presence, any divine Presence in history remains, for Jewish experience, at best fragmentary.

The divine Presence thus far considered is a saving Presence. Salvation is not here, however, what it might be in a different religious context. It occurs *within* history, not in an Eternity beyond it, nor for a soul divorced from it, nor as an apocalyptic or messianic event which consummates history. It therefore points necessarily to *human action.* In the biblical account Moses cries unto God, but is told to bid his people go for-

4. Martin Buber, *Moses* (New York, 1958), pp. 75–77 (italics added).

ward (Exodus 14:15). The Midrash dwells on this thought and affirms that no salvation would have occurred had Israel shrunk in fear from walking through the divided sea.[5] And it exalts one Naḥshon Ben Amminadab who, in the midst of universal hesitation, was first to jump into the waves.[6] *A commanding Voice is heard even as the saving event is seen; and salvation itself is not complete until the Voice is heeded.*

The astonishment abides as the commanding Voice is heard: this becomes clear when that Voice comes on the scene in its own right to legislate to future generations—in the root experience of Sinai. The structure of that experience is reflected in the following Midrash:

> Rabbi Azaryiah and Rabbi Aḥa in the name of Rabbi Yoḥanan said: When the Israelites heard at Sinai the word "I" [i.e., the first word of the Ten Commandments], their souls left them, as it says, "If we hear the voice . . . any more, then we shall die" (Deuteronomy 5:22). . . . The Word then returned to the Holy One, blessed be He and said: "Sovereign of the Universe, Thou art full of life, and Thy law is full of life, and Thou has sent me to the dead, for they are all dead." Thereupon the Holy One, blessed be He, sweetened [i.e., softened] the Word for them.[7]

The Midrash affirms that at Sinai, as at the Red Sea, the whole people saw what Ezekiel and the other prophets never saw.[8] Yet because the divine Presence is here a *commanding* Presence, the astonishment has a different structure. A commandment effected by a distant divine cause would be divine only by virtue of its external sanction and inspire no abiding astonishment. If the astonishment abides, it is because Divinity is *present in* the commandment. Because it is a *commanding* rather than a *saving* Presence, however, the abiding astonishment turns into deadly terror. Indeed, such a Presence is, in the first instance, nothing short of

paradoxical. For, being *commanding*, it *addresses human freedom*. And being *sole Power*, it *destroys* that freedom because it is only human. Yet the freedom destroyed is also required.

Hence the divine commanding Presence can be divine, commanding, and present only if it is *doubly* present; and the human astonishment must be a *double* astonishment. As *sole* Power, the divine commanding Presence *destroys* human freedom; as *gracious* Power, it *restores* that freedom, and indeed *exalts* it, for human freedom is made part of a covenant with Divinity itself. And the human astonishment, which is *terror* at a Presence at once divine and commanding, turns into a *second* astonishment, which is *joy*, at a Grace which restores and exalts human freedom by its commanding Presence.[9]

According to the Midrash all generations of Israel were present at Sinai, and the Torah is given whenever a man receives it.[10] A man can receive it only if he reenacts the double astonishment. If he remains frozen in stark terror, he cannot observe the commandments at all. And, if he evades that terror, he may observe the commandments, but he has lost the divine commanding Presence. Only by reenacting both the terror and the joy can he participate in a life of the commandments which lives before the sole Power and yet is human.

Dialectical Contradictions

But threats arise to the reenactment of the root experiences of Judaism from two main quarters. One quarter is history itself. Since the reenactment does not occur in a historical vacuum, each historical present, or at any rate each epoch-making historical present, makes its own demands over against the past and its reenactment; and, since each epoch-making present must be taken seriously in its own right, it is not possible to

---

5. See *Mechilta*, I.216:

> Rabbi Eliezer says, The Holy One, blessed be He, said to Moses: "Moses, My children are in distress. The sea forms a bar and the enemy pursues. Yet you stand and say long prayers! Why do you cry unto Me?" Rabbi Eliezer was wont to say, there is a time to be brief in prayer, and a time to be lengthy.

6. *Mechilta*, I.237.
7. *Midrash Rabbah*, Song of Songs, 16 §3, translated by Maurice Simon (London, 1961), p. 252ff.
8. *Mechilta*, II.212.
9. On this subject, see further my *Quest for Past and Future*, ch. 14.
10. See, e.g., *Midrash Tanḥumah*, Yitro.

anticipate the outcome.... Another type of threat, however, may be dealt with at once, for it is general, unchanging, and abstractable from history. This is the threat posed by reflective, philosophical thought.

The root experience itself is an immediacy, and so is its reenactment by subsequent believers. It is the potential object, however, of *philosophical reflection;* and the moment such reflection occurs it reveals the root experience to be shot through with at least three all-pervasive, dialectical contradictions.

The first of these is between divine transcendence and divine involvement. The sole Power present at the Red Sea and Mount Sinai manifests a *transcendent* God, for involvement would limit His Power; it manifests an *involved* God as well if only because it *is* a Presence. As will be seen, this contradiction exists even in the case of the saving Presence. In the case of the commanding Presence it is unmistakable.

This contradiction is logically first, but no more significant than the other two—respectively, between divine Power and human freedom, and between divine involvement with history and the evil which exists within it.

Divinity would not contradict human freedom if it were either present but finite, or infinite but absent—confined, so to speak, to heaven and leaving to man the undisputed control of earth. An infinite divine Presence, in contrast, is a present sole Power, which "explodes the fixity of nature and history," rendering "transparent" the causal nexus constituting both; and this negates the self and its freedom.

At the same time, the divine Presence *requires* the self and its freedom in the very moment of its presence. There is no abiding astonishment unless men exist who can be astonished; moreover, the divine Presence—saving as well as commanding—remains incomplete unless human astonishment terminates in action. Conceivably Ezekiel's selfhood dissolved in the moment in which the heavens were opened. This is impossible when, as at the Red Sea, salvation occurs to a flesh-and-blood people; or when, as at Sinai, the divine Presence gives commandments for human performance.

The third contradiction arises because a God revealed as sole Power in *one* moment of history

is revealed, in that very moment, as the God of *all* history[11] ... [W]e have rejected, as alien to the dynamic of the Jewish faith, all abstract doctrines concerning God-in-general, Providence-in-general, or man-in-general, which are only accidentally "applied" to the historical particular. It now emerges, however, that universality is implicit *in* the particular. A God present in one historical moment would not be sole Power if He were *confined to* that moment. He who fought at the Red Sea on Israel's behalf would not be Creator of the world if, having once fought, He could fight no more. Nor could the event of His presence be subsequently reenacted. But, if the God present in one moment of history is the God of all history, He is in conflict with the evil which is within it.

This must be listed as a third contradiction over and above that between divine Power and human freedom, if only because not all evil in history is attributable to human sin; and, still more decisively, because sin cannot be viewed as an act of freedom which, real from a human standpoint, is, from the standpoint of divine Providence, either an unreal shadow or an instrument to its purposes. These views are ruled out by the root experiences of Judaism—by the fact that the divine Presence occurs *within* history, not as its consummation or transfiguration. Salvation at the Red Sea is real only because the prior threat of catastrophe is real; as will be seen, it is incomplete even when it occurs; and—to put it mildly—when in subsequent ages this root experience is reenacted salvation is not always a present reality. Similarly, the freedom to reject the divine commanding Presence at Sinai exists at the very moment of presence, and this Presence cannot, as it were, play games with itself when it allows that possibility; moreover—again to put it mildly—subsequent generations of Israelites have not always matched the faithfulness of the generation of Sinai.

Such are the contradictions in the root experiences of Judaism insofar as they concern our present purpose. Philosophical reflection, on becoming aware of these contradictions, is tempted

11. On this point, see Buber's treatment of "moment gods," *Between Man and Man* (Boston, 1955), p. 15.

to remove them, and to do so by means of a retroactive *destruction of the root experiences themselves*. At this point, however, Jewish theological thought exhibits a stubbornness which, soon adopted and rarely if ever abandoned, may be viewed as its defining characteristic. Negatively, this stubbornness consists of resisting all forms of thought which would remove the contradictions of the root experiences of Judaism at the price of destroying them. Positively, it consists of developing logical and literary forms which can preserve the root experiences of Judaism despite their contradictions.

Jewish theological thought resists, first, a God who is sole Power but *without involvement*, withdrawn from history and demanding a like withdrawal from history on the part of His human worshippers. There has always been room for mysticism within Judaism, but never for an otherworldly mysticism which abandons salvation *in* and commandments for history, thus retroactively destroying the events at the Red Sea and Sinai.

Jewish theological thought resists, second, a sole Power which *overwhelms* history, allowing no room for either freedom or evil and manifesting itself as fate. To be sure, it may seem at times that "all is in the hands of Heaven except the fear of Heaven." Even at such times, however, the fear of Heaven, far from a "small thing,"[12] is what makes history to the extent to which human freedom then can make it. To embrace fatalism would be retroactively to destroy the freedom manifest at both Sinai and the Red Sea, and thus these root experiences themselves.

Jewish theological thought resists, finally, any notion of a God who is not, after all, sole Power or Creator of the world—*a god as finite as the idols*. Such a notion, to be sure, is not rejected simply, i.e., at the price of belittling or denying either human freedom or evil. But neither is it simply acceptable. Instead, a dialectical tension develops, and this points to a future in which evil is vanquished by divine Power and human freedom, and in which divine Power and human freedom are reconciled. This future, a necessity for theo-logical thought, is a necessity for immediate experience as well, and indeed rivals in significance the root experiences of the Red Sea and Sinai. It is not, however, itself a root experience, for it is a future anticipated rather than a past reenacted. If nevertheless it is as basic as these root experiences, it is because, without that anticipation, any reenactment of the root experiences of Judaism remains incomplete. Indeed, these experiences themselves remain incomplete. The messianic faith arose at a relatively late date in Jewish history. As will be seen, it is implicit in Judaism ever since the Exodus.

The Midrashic Framework

Negatively, Jewish theological thought resists the dissipation of the root experiences of Judaism. Positively, it aims at preservation. It succeeds in its aim by becoming midrashic. In the preceding pages we have already made much use of midrashic thinking. We must now pause briefly to consider its nature.

Five characteristics will suffice for the present purpose:

i. Midrashic thinking reflects upon the root experiences of Judaism, and is not confined to their immediate—e.g., liturgical—reenactment.

ii. For this reason midrashic, like philosophical, reflection becomes aware of the contradictions in the root experiences of Judaism.

iii. Unlike philosophical reflection, however, it a priori refuses to destroy these experiences, even as it stands outside and reflects upon them. For it remains inside even as it steps outside them, stubbornly committed to their truth. In two midrashim, Rabbi Eliezer and Rabbi Yohanan both *reflect*, respectively, upon the events at the Red Sea and Sinai and *remain* immediately *at* the Red Sea and *before* Sinai.

iv. Midrashic thought, therefore, cannot resolve the contradictions in the root experiences of Judaism but only express them. This expression (a) is fully conscious of the contradictions expressed; (b) is fully deliberate in leaving them unresolved; (c) for both reasons

---

12. B. T. *Berakhoth* 33[b]. Rabbi Hanina, the author of this statement, adds that "God has in His storehouse nothing but the fear of heaven."

combined, is consciously fragmentary; and (d) is insistent that this fragmentariness is both ultimate for human thought and yet destined to an ultimate resolution. *Midrashic thought, therefore, is both fragmentary and whole.*

v. Seeking adequate literary form, the midrashic content can find it only in story, parable, and metaphor. Were they projected into the modern world, Rabbi Eliezer and Rabbi Yoḥanan might follow our present example and engage in a second-order philosophical reflection designed to explore the ontological and epistemological status of their midrashim. However, this would not replace their first-order reflection which would remain committed to the truth of the root experiences of the Red Sea and Sinai even as it reflected upon them. Unless we shall find cause to judge otherwise, to this day their stance remains normative for the Jewish theologian. Having engaged in a second-order reflection upon Midrash as a whole, he must himself retell the old Midrash—or create a new.

The Logic of Midrashic Stubbornness

We shall illustrate the above abstract contentions by a few concrete examples and confine these to the events at the Red Sea and Sinai.

We begin with a verse in the biblical song sung at the Red Sea: "YHVH is a man of war, YHVH is His name" (Exodus 15:3). Why, the first of the two midrashim we shall cite asks, are the seemingly superfluous words "YHVH is His name" added? Lest the idolatrous nations have an excuse for believing in many gods. For at the Red Sea He "appeared . . . as a mighty hero doing battle. . . . at Sinai He appeared as an old man full of mercy." The words "YHVH is His name" are added, then, to teach that, while a God manifest *in* history manifests Himself differently according to the exigencies of the historical moment, He is, nevertheless, manifest *in each* moment as the *one* sole Power of every moment. "It is He who was in the past and He who will be in the future. It is

He who is in this world and He who will be in the world to come."[13]

But our second Midrash shows that this universal revelation at the Red Sea would be wholly pointless if, in the case of the idolatrous nations, it fell on wholly deaf ears. However, it did not fall on deaf ears. All the nations joined in the words "Who is like unto Thee, O Lord, among the gods" (Exod. 15:11)?

> As soon as the nations of the world saw that Pharaoh and his hosts perished in the Red Sea and that the kingdom of the Egyptians came to an end, and that judgments were executed upon their idols, they all renounced their idols, and opened their mouths and, confessing God, said: "Who is like unto Thee, O Lord among the gods?" You also find that in the future likewise the nations of the world will renounce their idols.[14]

The universality of the sole Power manifest in a unique saving event demands a correspondingly universal human *recognition* of its universality, thus inspiring the poetic truth of the universal abolition of idolatry. We have cited two Midrashim: they must be taken together.

But if taken together they reveal a contradiction. This appears even in the first Midrash taken by itself: a God who, by Himself, was, is, and shall be, yet must be present *differently* if His presence is to be *within* history. A contradiction is more evident in the second Midrash taken by itself: the nations forsake idolatry only poetically, and even then only for a moment, a fact which makes a messianic reference necessary. The contradiction is altogether inescapable when the two Midrashim are taken together. The God who is Lord of history was, is, and shall be sovereign as sole Power. Yet, even in a supreme (albeit pre-messianic) manifestation of His power, He stands in need of human glorification; and the fact that this glorification is momentarily given by all the nations reveals more poignantly the paradox of a subsequent relapse into idolatry by the nations, Israel herself included. Confronting this contradiction and commenting upon the verse "I will glorify Him" (Exod. 15:7), Rabbi Yishmael asks: "Is it possible for a

13. *Mechilta*, II.31ff.

14. *Mechilta*, II.59ff.

man of flesh and blood to add to the glory of His Creator?"[15]

Rabbi Yishmael's question is radical. If the event of divine saving Presence is complete without glorifying human recognition, then man, his abiding astonishment included, has lost all significance for the Divine; and the Divine is sole Power, either because It is indifferent to history or because It overwhelms history. And if human glorification is required, then even a saving divine Presence—not to speak of a commanding Presence—is incomplete without it. No wonder Rabbi Shim'on Bar Yoḥai seeks to avoid the dilemma when he comments on the same Biblical verse as follows: "When I praise God, He is lovely; and when I do not praise Him, He is, so to speak, lovely in Himself."[16]

Rabbi Shim'on's answer does not, however, escape from the dilemma. How can human praise add to the divine glory and yet human failure to give praise not diminish it? Other rabbis (and Shim'on Bar Yoḥai himself in a different context) admit that human failure to give praise, so to speak, weakens the Power on high.[17]

Rabbi Yishmael himself answers his own question as follows: "'I will glorify Him' means: I shall be beautiful before Him in obeying the commandments."[18] This answer, however, only serves to reproduce the dilemma in a still more ultimate form. A saving divine Presence may require only human recognition; a commanding divine Presence requires human action. The saving Presence may conceivably (if only momentarily) overwhelm human freedom. The commanding Presence cannot do likewise without becoming an intrinsic impossibility. Hence, as the midrashic writers turn from the first to the second, they are forced to face up to an unmitigated paradox: "'Ye are My witnesses, saith the Lord, and I am God' (Isa. 43:12). That is, when ye are My witnesses, I am God, and when ye are not My witnesseses, I am, as it were, not God."[19]

"When the Israelites do God's will, they add to the power of God on high. When the Israelites do not do God's will, they, as it were, weaken the great power of God."[20]

Taking all the cited Midrashim together, we find that the contradictions between divine transcendence and divine involvement and between divine Power and human freedom are not resolved but only expressed; and, indeed, that the expression could not be more frank, open, and conscious.

However, the Midrash holds fast to the truth of these contradictory affirmations even as it expresses their contradictoriness. In rabbinic theology, the term "as it were" (Kivyachol) is a fully developed technical term, signifying, on the one hand, that the affirmation in question is not literally true but only a human way of speaking; and, on the other hand, that it is a truth nonetheless which cannot be humanly transcended. The rabbinic thinker both reflects upon his relation to God and yet stands directly before Him, and his theology is consciously and stubbornly fragmentary.

But this does not exhaust the stubbornness of rabbinic thought. Conceivably one might speculate that the contradictions between divine transcendence and divine involvement and between divine Power and human freedom, all too real from the standpoint of man, are nevertheless transcended from the standpoint of God. And such speculation might (as, for example, in Kant)[21] take the form of a mere experiment of thought, or (as notably in Hegel)[22] that of a bold, actual ascent of thought to Divinity. In either case speculation might entertain the idea that history in the sight of God is other than history in human experience. For man, history is shot through with sin and suffering, only rarely lit up by the divine Presence; for God, it is transparent in the light of divine Power, and all darkness consists of insubstantial shadows. What is grimly real for human experience is, in the ultimate perspective, a cosmic game.[23]

15. Mechilta, II.25.
16. Sifre Deuteronomy, Berakhah §346.
17. Ibid.; Sifre Deuteronomy, Ha'azinu §319.
18. Mechilta, II.25.
19. Midrash Rabbah, Psalms, on Psalms 123:1.
20. Midrash Rabbah, Lamentations, on Lamentations 1:6.
21. See his Critique of Judgment, §76.

22. See my The Religious Dimension in Hegel's Thought (Bloomington, 1968), especially chs. 5 and 6.
23. Hegel rejects and possibly is able to avoid this conclusion. But if he can avoid it, it is because his rise in thought to Divinity is a Christian or post-Christian possibility.

Rabbinic thought stubbornly rejects a God playing such games and stubbornly holds fast to the reality of human history—even in the sight of God. To do otherwise would be, in the final analysis, to be unfaithful to the root experiences of Judaism—to a God present in history. How could Divinity be actually present as commanding unless obedience and disobedience made a real, ultimate difference? How could even a saving Divinity be actually present if the human perception of salvation were a matter of irrelevance?

All problems and dilemmas might resolve themselves if the saving divine Presence transfigured history. The divine saving Presence at the Red Sea, however, occurs in history and does not end or transfigure it. A much-quoted Midrash relates that when the ministering angels beheld the destruction of the Egyptians at the Red Sea they wanted to break out into song. God, however, reproved them, saying, "My children lie drowned in the Red Sea, and you would sing?"[24] This Midrash is much quoted, for it encourages moralistic sermons concerning a God endowed with universal benevolence. The real content of the Midrash, however, is otherwise. *Even in the supreme but premessianic moment of His saving presence God cannot save Israelites without killing Egyptians.* Thus the infinite joy of the moment—a moment in which even the maidservants saw what no prophet saw—is mingled with sorrow, and the sorrow is infinite because the joy is infinite. Thus the root experience in Judaism is fragmentary and points to a future consummation because of its fragmentariness. Thus God and man in Judaism pay each their price for the stubbornness with which they hold fast to actual—not "spiritual"—history.

The Divine Presence and Catastrophe

But one may hold fast to history and yet do so not very seriously. Seriousness is tested in self-exposure to crisis situations. Rabbinic faith and

thought were uniquely tested when, in 70 C.E., the Temple was destroyed by Titus, and still more so when, after the Bar Kochba revolt, Hadrian transformed Jerusalem into a pagan city (135 C.E.). Rarely in all the subsequent centuries was there to be a comparable clash between the root experiences of Judaism and present historical realities, and the well-nigh inescapable temptation of the times was to flee from history into either gnostic individualism or apocalyptic otherworldliness. The rabbis, however, remained *within* the midrashic framework, and indeed, responded to the radical crisis with the most profound thought ever produced within that framework. This was because they both faced the present with unyielding realism and held fast to the root experiences of Judaism with unyielding stubbornness.[25]

Never before had the conflict between past and present been so radical. It is true that the God of past history, revealed as the God of all history at the Red Sea and Sinai, could often seem to be in conflict with present history. But one obvious response to this apparent conflict had always been to view suffering as deserved punishment, and in the earlier books of the Bible—notably Judges—this response had seemed totally adequate. To be sure, this was no longer so in the later books of the Bible. But the Book of Job questions this response only on behalf of the individual; and while the prophet Jeremiah protests against the prosperity of the wicked (Jeremiah 12:1) he is also able to view the destruction of the First Temple as a divinely willed punishment and the tyrant Nebuchadnezzar as the rod of God's anger and His instrument (Jeremiah 25:9, 27:6, 43:10).

No rabbi described Titus as God's instrument. No rabbi understood the paganization of Jerusalem as an event which was divinely willed. To quote N. N. Glatzer, the rabbis

> could still understand a destroyed Jerusalem in terms of a divine plan for history, not, however, a pagan Jerusalem. Only because of despair of the realization of the kingdom of God on earth did the protest against Rome in the form of an armed national insurrection come to include the

---

24. B. T. *Megillah* 10[b].

25. This is comprehensively expounded and documented by N. N. Glatzer, *Untersuchungen zur Geschichtslehre der* *Tannaiten* (Berlin, 1933). The present section . . . is greatly indebted to Glatzer's masterful work.

Tannaitic rabbis, who had hitherto not required that form, guided as they had been by the idea of a divine plan. Only thus can one understand the fact that Rabbi Akiba, who had hitherto shown great... patience vis-à-vis Rome, was now gripped by the national impatience and agreed with Bar Kochba.[26]

It is true that in their catastrophic present the rabbis did not fail to explore and deepen already familiar lines of response. Thus the second destruction of the Temple, like the first, was viewed as a case of deserved punishment; and the punishment then, as before, became bearable because repentance would end the exile even as sin had caused it. And yet, the vast Roman Empire was absurdly out of proportion to the sins of a handful of Jews; and to the repentance of that handful, ludicrously world-historical consequences had to be ascribed. Taken by itself and made absolute, then, this response was totally inadequate; it was bound to produce the view that God had destroyed His sanctuary without adequate cause, and that He was now distant and uncaring. "The concept of sin was insufficient to explain the course of events."[27]

Another long-familiar response, too, if taken by itself and made absolute, was bound to lead to despair. In catastrophe the psalmist had lamented that there was now a hiding of the divine face and yet could hope that God's presence would again be manifest. The rabbis too spoke of a divine self-concealment. But was this enough? And was there any imminent hope? Not the second as far as one could anticipate. Not the first if the brute present realities were the evidence. According to Rabbi Shim'on Ben Gamliel, to write of the sufferings of the time was beyond all human power.[28] Rabbi Akiba, more full of hope than any other rabbi after the Temple had been destroyed,[29] was cruelly put to death by the tyrant Rufus after the Bar Kochba revolt [132–135 CE]. Was this how God "judged

the righteous through the wicked"?[30] No wonder Rabbi Eleazar lamented that, ever since the destruction of the Temple, the gates of prayer were closed, and only those of tears were still open.[31] In earlier Jewish experiences the divine self-concealment had only been partial and temporary. Now it seemed otherwise. Now Rabbi Eleazar was forced to say: "Since the day of the destruction of the Temple, a wall of iron separates Israel from her Father in heaven."[32]

Had the rabbis staked all on the response of a divine self-concealment they would have lost the divine Presence in history in the time of Hadrian. Neither the past saving Presence nor the past commanding Presence could have continued to be reenacted. The past saving Presence would have been overwhelmed by the present catastrophe. Even the past commanding Presence would have vanished; there would have remained only obedience to commandments performed in God's absence. This being the case, what hope for a messianic divine Presence could have remained in an age of so total a divine self-concealment?

In this extreme crisis the rabbis struck out boldly in a new direction. Far from being unconcerned or concealed, God, so to speak, cried out every night in bitter lament, as with a lion's voice.[33] Rather than judge the righteous through the wicked, He, as it were, lamented His own decision; in causing His Temple to be destroyed and His people to be exiled, either He could not act otherwise or had grievously erred.[34] Here as elsewhere Rabbi Akiba is bolder than any other rabbinic theologian:

> Were it not expressly written in Scripture, it would be impossible to say it. Israel said to God, "Thou hast redeemed Thyself," as though one could conceive such a thing. Likewise, you find that whithersoever Israel was exiled, the *Shekhinah* [immanent Divine Presence], as it

26. Glatzer, *Untersuchungen*, p. 5.
27. Glatzer, *Untersuchungen*, p. 106.
28. B. T. *Shabbath* 13[b].
29. Once four rabbis—Gamliel, Eleazar Ben Azaryah, Joshua, and Akiba—walked by the ruins of the Temple. Suddenly they saw a fox emerging from the place which had once been the Holy of Holies. The others wept. Akiba, however, laughed, for he saw this event as confirming a prophecy of doom and was thus

strengthened in his faith in another prophecy which promised redemption (*Midrash Rabbah*, Lamentations, III:18).
30. *Midrash Rabbah*, Lamentations, III:17.
31. B. T. *Berakhoth* 32[b].
32. B. T. *Berakhoth* 32[b].
33. B. T. *Berakhoth* 3[a].
34. B. T. *Berakhoth* 3[a].

were, went into exile with them. When they went into exile to Egypt, the *Shekhinah* went into exile with them, as it is said, "I exiled Myself unto the house of thy fathers when they were in Egypt" (1 Samuel 2:27). When they were exiled to Babylon, the *Shekhinah* went into exile with them, as it is said, "For your sake I ordered Myself to go to Babylon" (Isaiah 43:14). When they were exiled to Elam, the *Shekhinah* went into exile with them, as it is said, "I will set My throne in Elam" (Jeremiah 49:38). When they were exiled to Edom, the *Shekhinah* went into exile with them, as it is said, "Who is this that cometh from Edom" (Isaiah 63:1). And when they return in the future, the *Shekhinah*, as it were, will return with them, as it is said: "That then the Lord thy God will return with thy captivity" (Deuteronomy 30:3). Note that it does not say, "The Lord will bring back" (*veheshib*), but it says, "He will return" (*ve-shab*).[35]

What an altogether breath-taking turn of thought! The thought is breath-taking, for it is as if Rabbi Akiba had looked ahead to an exile unequaled in length and depth of misery and then taken the only turn of thought which could have saved Jewish faith during that millennial trial. The Jew would be in exile, but not cut off from the divine Presence. He could still hold fast to history, for the God who had been present in history once was present in it still and would in the end bring total redemption. Thus for nearly two millennia the Jew—mocked, slandered, persecuted, homeless—held fast to the God of history with a faith which, if not in principle unshakable, remained in fact unshaken.

But Rabbi Akiba's turn of thought raises one all-important question. A God in exile still commands, for He continues to be present. His presence still comforts, for it holds out hope for a future salvation as His past saving acts are remembered. But where, we must ask, is the sole Power or the Creator of the world?

As if in reply to this question, Rabbi Joshua ben Levi taught a century after Rabbi Akiba:

The men of the Great Assembly are given this title because they restored God's crown to its former state. For Moses had said, "the great, powerful, and awe-inspiring God." Then came Jeremiah and said, "The gentiles are destroying His Temple: where then is the fear of Him?" Hence he omitted[36] the adjective "awe-inspiring." Then came Daniel and said, "The gentiles are enslaving His children: where then is His power?" Hence he omitted[37] the adjective "powerful." Then, however, came the men of the Great Assembly and said: "On the contrary, this is His power, that He controls His anger and is long-suffering to evildoers; and this is His fear—how could one nation exist among the nations of the world without the fear of the Holy One, blessed be He?"

Why did these sages alter what Moses had ordained? Rabbi Eleazar replied: "They knew of the Holy One, blessed be He, that He is truthful, and would say nothing untrue about Him."[38]

We conclude, then, that the rabbis remained true to the catastrophic historical present, even as they remained faithful to the saving and commanding past. They remained stubborn witnesses to the nations that all history both stands in need of redemption and is destined to receive it.

Spurious and Genuine Contemporary Criticism

This must suffice as an account of God's presence in history, as it is affirmed in Jewish tradition. At the outset we noted that this faith is the object of criticism, but also raised doubt as [to] whether it falls prey to easy and obvious criticisms.

The account now concluded has confirmed these initial doubts. Thus, on one side, philosophical reflection soon discovers contradictions between divine Power and human freedom and between divine Providence over history and the evil which is within it; and, finding these contradictions insoluble, is apt to disconnect God from history speedily and without further thought. Such speed, we have

35. *Mechilta*, I.114ff. See Lauterbach's notes which make it clear that the scriptural proof-texts must be given a special interpretation in order to bear out Rabbi Akiba's Midrash.

36. In Jeremiah 32:16ff.
37. In Daniel 9.
38. B. T. *Yoma* 69[b].

now seen, is ill advised. It would in any case be strange if Judaism and Christianity (both of which stand or fall with God's presence in history) had failed to note these contradictions in their long careers. We have found reasons for insisting that far deeper philosophical criticisms are necessary if they are to strike the mark.

What is true of much general philosophical criticism offered on one side is also true of much specifically Jewish theological criticism offered on the other side. At the present time we are told, at one extreme, that Auschwitz is punishment for Jewish sins, and this is slander of more than a million innocent children in an abortive defense of God.[39] At the opposite extreme, we are told that precisely because this slander is inadmissible the God of history is impossible: a God concerned with Auschwitz must have decreed Auschwitz, and such a God is dead.[40]

We need not go beyond the ancient rabbis to reject both these theological doctrines. When the tyrant Rufus martyred Rabbi Akiba the rabbis did not slander either Akiba or his saintly contemporaries. And when Hadrian made Jerusalem

a pagan city they, as it were, made God weep over it.

But it would be theological smugness of the gravest kind to dismiss all contemporary philosophical and theological criticisms along with these spurious ones. The ancient rabbis remained within the midrashic framework; ever since the rise of the modern world, Jewish theological thought has confronted the challenge of secularism—that of stepping outside that framework and of calling it into question from outside. Moreover, ever since the Nazi Holocaust, Jewish theology has faced the necessity of questioning the midrashic framework from inside as well. The rabbis confronted Titus and Hadrian; they were spared the necessity of confronting Hitler. In the present age in which Jewish existence is uniquely embattled, the Jewish faith in God's presence in history is no less uniquely embattled. The Jewish theologian would be ill advised were he, in an attempt to protect the Jewish faith in the God of history, to ignore contemporary history. For the God of Israel cannot be God of either past or future unless He is still God of the present.

The 614th Commandment

In groping for authentic responses to our present Jewish crisis, we do well to begin with responses which have already occurred. I believe that there are two such responses: first, a commitment to Jewish survival; and second, a commitment to Jewish unity.

I confess I used to be highly critical of Jewish philosophies which seemed to advocate no more

---

39. Z. M. Schachter writes:

> In response to Nazi hostilities, we judged *all* Germans to be inhuman, predatory beasts, and the Germans returned the compliment. They were the stronger, and we, by definition, the vermin to be exterminated. In short, *the Holocaust was partially caused by Jews who did not think it worthwhile, or even possible, to reprove the Germans.* (*The Religious Situation,* edited by D. R. Cutler [Boston, 1968], p. 81.)

The only excuse for Schachter's statement is a desperate desire to exonerate God. (i) It is false that Jews (Schachter himself included) judged all Germans to be beasts; the fatal Jewish error, if any, was the opposite—an inability to believe, until it was too late, that Jews were destined for wholesale murder. (ii) It is absurd to believe that any Jewish "reproving" of Nazis might

have had a beneficial effect; the exact opposite would have occurred. Schachter is not alone among the religiously minded to fall prey to this error, Martin Niemoeller is reported to have said recently that he sinned in failing to attempt to convert Hitler. Perhaps the attempt was his Christian duty. But can he seriously believe that he might have succeeded?

40. See R. L. Rubenstein, *After Auschwitz* (Indianapolis, 1966); also "Homeland and Holocaust Issues in the Jewish Religious Situation," in *The Religious Situation,* pp. 39–64, 102–111. For my own fragmentary attempts to cope with the Holocaust, see "Jewish Values in the Post-Holocaust Future: A Symposium," *Judaism* (Summer, 1967): 266–299. [Selections from Richard Rubenstein's work are republished above, pp. 410–418.]

than survival for survival's sake. I have changed my mind. I now believe that, in this present, unbelievable age, even a mere collective commitment to Jewish group survival for its own sake is a momentous response, with the greatest implications. I am convinced that future historians will understand it, not, as our present detractors would have it, as the tribal response mechanism of a fossil, but rather as a profound, albeit as yet fragmentary, act of faith, in an age of crisis to which the response might well have been either flight in total disarray or complete despair.

The second response we have already found is a commitment to Jewish unity. This, to be sure, is incomplete and must probably remain incomplete. Yet it is nonetheless real. Thus, the American Council for Judaism is an anachronism, as is, I venture to say, an Israeli nationalism which would cut off all ties with the diaspora. No less anachronistic is a Jewish secularism so blind in its worship of the modern secular world as wholly to spurn the religious resources of the Jewish past; likewise, an Orthodoxy so untouched by the modern secular world as to have remained in a premodern ghetto.

Such, then, are the responses to the present crisis in Jewish history which we have already found in principle, however inadequately in practice. And their implications are even now altogether momentous. Whether aware of what we have decided or not, we have made the collective decision to endure the contradictions of present Jewish existence. We have collectively rejected the option, either of "checking out" of Jewish existence altogether or of so avoiding the present contradictions as to shatter Jewish existence into fragments.

But the question now is whether we can go beyond so fragmentary a commitment. In the present situation, this question becomes: can we confront the Holocaust, and yet not despair? Not accidentally has it taken twenty years for us to face this question, and it is not certain that we can face it yet. The contradiction is too staggering, and every authentic escape is barred. *For we are forbidden to turn present and future life into death, as the price of remembering death at Auschwitz. And we are equally forbidden to affirm present and future life, at the price of forgetting Auschwitz.*

We have lived in this contradiction for twenty years without being able to face it. Unless I am mistaken, we are now beginning to face it, however fragmentarily and inconclusively. And from this beginning confrontation there emerges what I will boldly term a 614th commandment: *the authentic Jew of today is forbidden to hand Hitler yet another, posthumous victory.* (This formulation is terribly inadequate, yet I am forced to use it until one more adequate is found. First, although no anti-Orthodox implication is intended, as though the 613 commandments stood necessarily in need of change, we must face the fact that something radically new has happened. Second, although the commandment should be positive rather than negative, we must face the fact that Hitler did win at least one victory—the murder of six million Jews. Third, although the very name of Hitler should be erased rather than remembered, we cannot disguise the uniqueness of his evil under a comfortable generality, such as persecution-in-general, tyranny-in-general, or even the demonic-in-general.)

I think the authentic Jew of today is beginning to hear the 614th commandment. And he hears it whether, as agnostic, he hears no more, or whether, as believer, he hears the voice of the *metzaveh* (the commander) in the *mitzvah* (the commandment). Moreover, it may well be the case that the authentic Jewish agnostic and the authentic Jewish believer are closer today than at any previous time.

To be sure, the agnostic hears no more than the *mitzvah*. Yet if he is Jewishly authentic, he cannot but face the fragmentariness of his hearing. He cannot, like agnostics and atheists all around him, regard this *mitzvah* as the product of self-sufficient human reason, realizing itself in an ever-advancing history of autonomous human enlightenment. The 614th commandment must be, to him, an abrupt and absolute *given*, revealed in the midst of total catastrophe.

On the other hand, the believer, who bears the voice of the *metzaveh* in the *mitzvah*, can hardly hear anything more than the *mitzvah*. The reasons that made Martin Buber speak of an eclipse of God are still compelling. And if, nevertheless, a bond between Israel and the God of Israel can be experienced in the abyss, this can hardly be more than the *mitzvah* itself.

The implications of even so slender a bond are momentous. If the 614th commandment is binding upon the authentic Jew, then we are, first, commanded to survive as Jews, lest the Jewish people perish. We are commanded, second, to remember in our very guts and bones the martyrs of the Holocaust, lest their memory perish. We are forbidden, thirdly, to deny or despair of God, however much we may have to contend with him or with belief in him, lest Judaism perish. We are forbidden, finally, to despair of the world as the place which is to become the kingdom of God, lest we help make it a meaningless place in which God is dead or irrelevant and everything is permitted. To abandon any of these imperatives, in response to Hitler's victory at Auschwitz, would be to hand him yet other, posthumous victories.

How can we possibly obey these imperatives? To do so requires the endurance of intolerable contradictions. Such endurance cannot but bespeak an as yet unutterable faith. If we are capable of this endurance, then the faith implicit in it may well be of historic consequence. At least twice before—at the time of the destruction of the First and of the Second Temples—Jewish endurance in the midst of catastrophe helped transform the world. We cannot know the future, if only because the present is without precedent. But this ignorance on our part can have no effect on our present action. The uncertainty of what will be may not shake our certainty of what we must do.

Today, the distinction between religious and secularist Jews is superseded by that between unauthentic Jews who flee from their Jewishness and authentic Jews who affirm it. This latter group includes religious and secularist Jews. These are united by a commanding Voice which speaks from Auschwitz.

The Commanding Voice of Auschwitz

What does the Voice of Auschwitz command?

> Jews are forbidden to hand Hitler posthumous victories. They are commanded to survive as Jews, lest the Jewish people perish. They are commanded to remember the victims of Auschwitz lest their memory perish. They are forbidden to despair of man and his world, and to escape into either cynicism or otherworldliness, lest they cooperate in delivering the world over to the forces of Auschwitz. Finally, they are forbidden to despair of the God of Israel, lest Judaism perish. A secularist Jew cannot make himself believe by a mere act of will, nor can he be commanded to do so.... And a religious Jew who has stayed with his God may be forced into new, possibly revolutionary relationships with Him. One possibility, however, is wholly unthinkable. A Jew may not respond to Hitler's attempt to destroy Judaism by himself cooperating in its destruction. In ancient times, the unthinkable Jewish sin was idolatry.

1. "Jewish Faith and the Holocaust," *Commentary* 46 (August 1968): 32.

Today, it is to respond to Hitler by doing his work.[1]

Elie Wiesel has compared the Holocaust with Sinai in revelatory significance—and expressed the fear that we are not listening. We shrink from this daring comparison—but even more from not listening. We shrink from any claim to have heard—but even more from a false refuge, in an endless agnosticism, from a Voice speaking to us. I was able to make the above, fragmentary statement (which I have already previously made and here merely quote) only because it no more than articulates what is being heard by Jews the world over—rich and poor, learned and ignorant, believing and secularist. I cannot go beyond this earlier statement but only expand it.

1. The First Fragment

In the murder camps the unarmed, decimated, emaciated survivors often rallied their feeble remaining resources for a final, desperate attempt at revolt. The revolt was hopeless. There was no hope but one. One might escape. Why must one escape? To tell the tale. Why must the tale be told when evidence was already at hand that the world would not listen?[2] Because not to tell the tale, when it might be told, was unthinkable. The Nazis were not satisfied with mere murder. Before murdering Jews, they were trying to reduce them to numbers; after murdering them, they were dumping their corpses into nameless ditches or making them into soap. They were making as sure as was possible to wipe out every trace of memory. Millions would be as though they had never been. But to the pitiful and glorious desperadoes of Warsaw, Treblinka, and Auschwitz, who would soon themselves be as though they had never been, not to rescue for memory what could be rescued was unthinkable because it was sacrilege.[3]

It will remain a sacrilege ever after. Today, suggestions come from every side to the effect that the past had best be forgotten, or at least remain unmentioned, or at least be coupled with the greatest and most thoughtless speed with other, but quite different, human tragedies. Sometimes these suggestions come from Jews rationalizing their flight from the Nazi Holocaust. More often they come from non-Jews, who rationalize their own flight, or even maintain, affrontingly enough, that unless Jews universalize the Holocaust, thus robbing the Jews of Auschwitz of their Jewish identity, they are guilty of disregard for humanity.[4] But for a Jew hearing the commanding Voice of Auschwitz the duty to remember and to tell the tale, is not negotiable. It is holy. The religious Jew still possesses this word. The secularist Jew is commanded to restore it. A secular holiness, as it were, has forced itself into his vocabulary.

2. The Second Fragment

Jewish survival, were it even for no more than survival's sake, is a holy duty as well. The murderers of Auschwitz cut off Jews from humanity and denied them the right to existence; yet in being denied that right, Jews represented all humanity. Jews after Auschwitz represent all humanity when they affirm their Jewishness and deny the Nazi denial. They would fail if they affirmed the mere *right* to their Jewishness, participating, as it were, in an obscene debate between others who deny the right of Jews to exist and Jews who affirm it.[5] Nor would they deny the Nazi denial if they affirmed merely their humanity-in-general, permitting an anti-Semitic split between their humanity and their Jewishness, or, worse, agreeing to vanish as Jews in one way, in response to Hitler's attempt to make them vanish in another. The commanding Voice of Auschwitz singles Jews out; Jewish survival is a commandment which brooks no compromise. It was this Voice which was heard by the Jews of Israel in May and June 1967 when they refused to lie down and be slaughtered.

Yet such is the extent of Hitler's posthumous victories that Jews, commanded to survive as Jews, are widely denied even the right. More precisely— for overt anti-Semitism is not popular in the post-Holocaust world—they are granted the right only on certain conditions. Russians, Poles, Indians, and Arabs have a natural right to exist; Jews must earn that right. Other states must refrain from wars of aggression; the state of Israel is an "aggressor" even if it fights for its life. Peoples unscarred by Auschwitz ought to protest when any evil resembling Auschwitz is in sight, such as the black ghettos or Vietnam. The Jewish survivors of Auschwitz have

---

2. See especially Elie Wiesel, "A Plea for the Dead," *Legends of Our Time* (New York, 1968), pp. 174–197.
3. See especially Yuri Suhl, *They Fought Back* (New York, 1967).
4. Wiesel is dismayed to discover that some critics of Nelly Sachs's poetry try to minimize its Jewishness and contrast a "universal vision" with a merely Jewish one. He comments:

   Her greatness lies in her Jewishness, and this makes it belong to all mankind. It is perhaps only natural that there are those who try to remove her, if not to

estrange her, from us. But this will never happen. She has many Jewish melodies left to sing. . . . What disturbs me is that strangers have stolen them. ("Conversation with Nelly Sachs," *Jewish Heritage* [Spring 1968]: 33)

5. In recent years some North American TV stations and university groups have seen fit to furnish American Nazis and German neo-Nazis with a forum, and even invited Jews to debate with them, apparently utterly oblivious to the obscenity of such invitations.

no right to survive unless they engage in such protests. Other peoples may include secularists and believers. Jews must be divided into bad secularists or Zionists, and good—albeit anachronistic—saints who stay on the cross.

The commanding Voice of Auschwitz bids Jews reject all such views as a monumental affront. It bids them reject as no longer tolerable every version—Christian or leftist, gentile or Jewish—of the view that the Jewish people are an anachronism, when it is the elements of the world perpetrating and permitting Auschwitz, not its survivors, that are anachronistic. A Jew is commanded to descend from the cross and, in so doing, not only to reiterate his ancient rejection of an ancient Christian view but also to suspend the time-honored Jewish exaltation of martyrdom. For after Auschwitz, Jewish life is more sacred than Jewish death, were it even for the sanctification of the divine Name. The left-wing secularist Israeli journalist Amos Kenan writes: "After the death camps, we are left only one supreme value: existence."[6]

3. The Third Fragment

But such as Kenan, being committed and unrepentant lovers of the downtrodden, accept other supreme values as well, and will suspend these only when Jewish existence itself is threatened or denied. Kenan has a universal vision of peace, justice, and brotherhood. He loves the poor of Cuba and hates death in Vietnam. In these and other commitments such left-wing secularists share the ancient Jewish religious, messianically inspired refusal to embrace either pagan cynicism (which despairs of the world and accepts the status quo) or Christian or pseudo-Christian otherworldliness (which despairs of the world and flees from it). The commanding Voice of Auschwitz bids Jews, religious and secularist, not to abandon the world to the forces of Auschwitz, but rather to continue to work and hope for it. Two possibilities are equally ruled out: to despair of the world on account of Auschwitz, abandoning the age old Jewish identification with poor and persecuted humanity; and to abuse such identification as a means of flight from Jewish destiny. It is precisely because of the uniqueness of Auschwitz, and in his Jewish particularity, that a Jew must be at one with humanity. For it is precisely because Auschwitz has made the world a desperate place that a Jew is forbidden to despair of it.[7] The hero of Wiesel's *The Gates of the Forest* asserts that it is too late for the Messiah—and that for exactly this reason we are commanded to hope.

4. The Fourth Fragment

The Voice of Auschwitz commands the religious Jew after Auschwitz to continue to wrestle with his God in however revolutionary ways; and it forbids the secularist Jew (who has already, and on other grounds, lost Him) to use Auschwitz as an additional weapon wherewith to deny Him.

The ways of the religious Jew are revolutionary, for there is no previous Jewish protest against divine Power like his protest. Continuing to hear the Voice of Sinai as he hears the Voice of Auschwitz, his citing of God against God may have to assume extremes which dwarf those of Abraham, Jeremiah, Job, Rabbi Levi Yitzhak. (You have abandoned the covenant? We shall not abandon it! You no longer want Jews to survive? We shall survive, as better, more faithful, more pious Jews! You have destroyed all grounds for

---

6. "A Letter to All Good People—To Fidel Castro, Sartre, Russell, and All the Rest," *Midstream*, October 1968 (this article originally appeared first in *Yediot Aḥaronot* and was republished in *The New Statesman*). Here and in the following, I single out this article, not only because of its excellence, but also (a fact doubtless largely accounting for this excellence) because its author is a left-wing secularist (who cannot and will not abandon his universalistic ideals) and an Israeli (who cannot and will not condone collective Jewish suicide).

7. I distinguish with the utmost sharpness between (a) the view that because of Auschwitz the justification of Jewish existence depends on Jews behaving like superhuman saints toward all other peoples ever after and (b) the view that because of Auschwitz Jews are obligated to (i) Jewish survival as an end which, less than ever, needs any justification [and] (ii) work for oppressed and suffering humanity everywhere. I accept the second view, and (as will be seen) the inevitably painful conflicts that go with it. The first view is totally unacceptable.

hope? We shall obey the commandment to hope which You Yourself have given!) Nor is there any previous Jewish compassion with divine power-lessness like the compassion required by such a powerlessness. (The fear of God is dead among the nations? We shall keep it alive and be its witnesses! The times are too late for the coming of the Messiah? We shall persist without hope and rec-reate hope—and, as it were, divine Power—by our persistence!) For the religious Jew, who re-mains within the midrashic framework, the Voice of Auschwitz manifests a divine Presence which, as it were, is shorn of all except commanding Power. *This* Power, however, is inescapable.

No less inescapable is this Power for the secu-larist Jew who has all along been outside the midrashic framework and this despite the fact that the Voice of Auschwitz does not enable him to return into that framework. He cannot return; but neither may he turn the Voice of Auschwitz against that of Sinai. For he may not cut off his secular present from the religious past: the Voice of Auschwitz commands preservation of that past. Nor may he widen the chasm between himself and the religious Jew: the Voice of Auschwitz com-mands Jewish unity.

As religious and secularist Jews are united in kinship with all the victims of Auschwitz and against all the executioners, they face a many-sided mystery and find a simple certainty. As regards the minds and souls of the victims of Auschwitz, God's presence to them is a many-sided mystery which will never be exhausted either by subsequent committed believers or by subsequent committed unbelievers, and least of all by subsequent neutral theorists—psychological, sociological, philo-sophical, theological—who spin out their theories immune to love and hate, submission and rage, faith and despair. As regards the murderers of Auschwitz, however, there was no mystery, for they denied, mocked, murdered the God of Israel six million times—and together with Him four thousand years of Jewish faith. For a Jew after Auschwitz, only one thing is certain: he may not side with the murderers and do what they have left undone. The religious Jew who has heard the Voice of Sinai must continue to listen as he hears the commanding Voice of Auschwitz. And the secularist Jew, who has all along lost Sinai and now hears the Voice of Auschwitz, cannot abuse that Voice as a means to destroy four thousand years of Jewish believing testimony. The rabbis assert that the First Temple was destroyed because of idola-try. Jews may not destroy the Temple which is the tears of Auschwitz by doing, wittingly or unwit-tingly, Hitler's work.

5. The Clash between the Fragments

Such is the commanding Voice of Auschwitz as it is increasingly being heard by Jews of this gen-eration. But how can it be obeyed? Each of the four fragments described—and they are mere fragments, and the description has been poor and inadequate—is by itself overwhelming. Taken together, they seem unbearable. For there are clashes between them which tear us apart.

How can the religious Jew be faithful to both the faith of the past and the victims of the present? We have already asked this question, but are now further from an answer than before. For a recon-ciliation by means of willing martyrdom is ruled out by the duty to Jewish survival, and a recon-ciliation by means of refuge in otherworldly mys-ticism is ruled out by the duty to hold fast to the world and to continue to hope and work for it. God, world, and Israel are in so total a conflict when they meet at Auschwitz as to seem to leave religious Jews confronting that conflict with nothing but a prayer addressed to God, yet spoken softly lest it be heard: in short, with madness.

But the conflict is no less unbearable for the secularist Jew. To be sure, the space once occu-pied by God is void for him or else occupied by a question mark. Only three of the four fragments effectively remain. Yet the conflict which re-mains tears him asunder.

Søren Kierkegaard's "knight of faith" was obliged to retrace the road which led Abraham to Mount Moriah, where Isaac's sacrifice was to take place.[8] A Jew today is obliged to retrace the road which led his brethren to Auschwitz. It is a road of pain and mourning, of humiliation, guilt, and despair. To retrace it is living death. How suffer this death and also choose Jewish life which, like all life, must include joy, laughter, and childlike

---

8. See *Fear and Trembling* (Garden City, N.Y., 1954).

innocence? How reconcile such a remembrance with life itself? How dare a Jewish parent crush his child's innocence with the knowledge that his uncle or grandfather was denied life because of his Jewishness? And how dare he not burden him with this knowledge? The conflict is inescapable, for we may neither forget the past for the sake of present life, nor destroy present life by a mourning without relief—and there is no relief.

Nor is this all. The first two fragments above clash with each other: each clashes with the third as well. No Jewish secularist today may continue to hope and work for mankind as though Auschwitz had never happened, falling back on secularist beliefs of yesterday that man is good, progress real, and brotherhood inevitable. Yet neither may he, on account of Auschwitz, despair of human brotherhood and cease to hope and work for it. How face Auschwitz and not despair? How hope and work, and not act as though Auschwitz had never occurred? Yet to forget and to despair are both forbidden.

Perhaps reconciliation would be possible if the Jewish secularist of today, like the Trotskys and Rosa Luxembourgs of yesterday, could sacrifice Jewish existence on the altar of future humanity. (Is this in the minds of "progressive" Jews when they protest against war in Vietnam but refuse to protest against Polish anti-Semitism? Or in the minds of what Kenan calls the "good people" of the world when they demand that Israel hand over weapons to those sworn to destroy her?) This sacrifice, however, is forbidden, and the altar is false. The left-wing Israeli secularist Kenan may accept all sorts of advice from his progressive friends, but not that he allow himself to be shot for the good of humanity. Perhaps he has listened for a moment even to this advice, for he hates a gun in his hand. Perhaps he has even wished for a second he could accept it, feeling, like many of his pious ancestors, that it is better to be killed than to kill. Yet he firmly rejects such advice, for he is commanded to reject it; rather than be shot, he will shoot first when there is no third alternative. But he will shoot with tears in his eyes. He writes:

Why weren't the June 4 borders peace borders on the fourth of June, but will only become

so now? Why weren't the UN Partition Plan borders of 1947 peace borders then, but will become so now? Why should I return his gun to the bandit as a reward for having failed to kill me?

I want peace peace peace peace, peace peace peace.

I am ready to give everything back in exchange for peace. And I shall give nothing back without peace.

I am ready to solve the refugee problem. I am ready to accept an independent Palestinian state. I am ready to sit and talk. About everything, all at the same time. Direct talks, indirect talks, all this is immaterial. But peace.

Until you agree to have peace, I shall give back nothing.

And if you force me to become a conqueror, I shall become a conqueror. And if you force me to become an oppressor, I shall become an oppressor. And if you force me into the same camp with all the forces of darkness in the world, there I shall be.[9]

Kenan's article ends:

[I]f I survive..., without a god but without prophets either, my life will have no sense whatever. I shall have nothing else to do but walk on the banks of streams, or on the top of the rocks, watch the wonders of nature, and console myself with the words of Ecclesiastes, the wisest of men: For the light is sweet, and it is good for the eyes to see the sun.[10]

The conclusion, then, is inescapable. Secularist Jewish existence after Auschwitz is threatened with a madness no less extreme than that which produces a prayer addressed to God, yet spoken softly lest it be heard.

Madness and the Commanding Voice of Auschwitz

The Voice of Auschwitz commands Jews not to go mad. It commands them to accept their singled-out condition, face up to its contradictions, and endure them. Moreover, it gives the power of endurance, the power of sanity. The Jew of today

---

9. Kenan "A Letter to All Good People," p. 35.

10. Kenan, "A Letter to All Good People," p. 36.

can endure because he must endure, and he must endure because he is commanded to endure.

We ask: whence has come our strength to endure even these twenty-five years—not to flee or disintegrate but rather to stay, however feebly, at our solitary post, to affirm, however weakly, our Jewishness, and to bear witness, if only by this affirmation, against the forces of hell itself? The question produces abiding wonder. It is at a commanding Voice without which we, like the Psalmist (Psalms, 119:92), would have perished in our affliction.

ISRAEL AND THE DIASPORA: POLITICAL CONTINGENCIES AND MORAL NECESSITIES; OR, THE *Shofar* OF RABBI YITZHAK FINKLER OF PIOTRKOV

The Termini of Jewish History

We all recall the great, terrifying biblical tale of Abraham's sacrifice of Isaac. In Jewish tradition that tale assumes world-historical significance, and is referred to as the "binding" of Isaac, to indicate that there was a reprieve, that in this particular case the shedding of Jewish blood was averted, and a ram sacrificed in Isaac's stead.

Not surprisingly, the ancient rabbis think highly of that ram. Concerning one of them, Rabbi Hanina Ben Dosa, there is a current scholarly controversy as to whether or not he lived to see that great shedding of Jewish blood—the destruction of the Jerusalem Temple in the year 70 C.E. Rabbi Hanina told a story, a Midrash, about that ram. It was so holy that no part of it went unused. Its ashes subsequently became part of the inner altar of the Temple. Its sinews were made into strings of David's harp; its skin, into the girdle of Elijah's loins. Finally there were the horns. What about those ram's horns? One of them—so Rabbi Hanina Ben Dosa concluded his Midrash— was used at Mount Sinai. And the other, somewhat larger, will be blown in the End of Days, so as to fulfill the saying of the prophet Isaiah, "And it shall come to pass in that day that a great horn will be blown" (Isaiah 27:13).[1]

In Jewish historical tradition and religious imagination the ram's horn, or *shofar*, has many uses. Its best known and most regular use, during the Rosh Hashanah festival and at the end of Yom Kippur, is to arouse the worshippers to repentance. But it is also used to warn of danger and to arouse to battle, just as it is an expression of grateful relief when the danger has passed. Sometimes it is used to arouse men; at other times, to arouse God. Only one thing is always the same: *the shofar always arouses*, or as Maimonides in a rare flight into poetry put it, it is meant to awaken the sleepers from their sleep.[2]

What then of those two horns of the ram that was sacrificed in Isaac's stead? The left blown at Sinai, ushered in Jewish history, whereas the right—somewhat larger—will mark its eschatological end. The Jewish people exist between these two termini and are defined by them, and in 1921 the greatest theological work within the Judaism of this century, Franz Rosenzweig's *Star of Redemption*, was still able to assert that nothing decisive has happened or can happen between these two poles.

Rosenzweig died in 1929. Less than four years after, events began to take their course which, though most people today pretend that they are over and done with, continue to have world-historical effects. As for the Jewish people, to attempt to forget would be to attempt the impossible. And so distant has Rosenzweig's vision become from us that is impossible for the Jew of today to hear authentically either the *shofar* of Sinai or the *shofar* of the End of Days without also hearing yet a third

---

Originally delivered as Yaacov Herzog Memorial Lecture at McGill University, Montreal, on 27 November 1974, and subsequently published as a pamphlet by the sponsors.

1. *Pirke Rabbi Eliezer* 31, quoted in S. Y. Agnon, *Days of Awe* (New York, 1965), p. 67.

2. [*Mishneh Torah*] Laws of Repentance III.4, quoted by Agnon, *Days of Awe*, p. 72ff.

shofar—the *shofar* of Rabbi Yitzḥak Finkler of Piotrkov. *Whatever the political contingencies of history between Sinai and the End, there exists now a new moral necessity, for the Jewish people and indeed for the world.*

Piotrkov

Let me tell you about the city of Piotrkov. I look at the map, and find that it is located some hundred miles to the south of Warsaw. I look next at the recently published Jewish encyclopedia, for I want to know about the Jewish population, and I find some very precise statistics. In 1917 the Jewish population of Piotrkov was 14,890. Four years later it had dropped, for reasons one may guess, to 11,630. And then a sentence leaps at you from the pages—on 28 October 1939, the first Nazi-established ghetto was set up in Piotrkov. Thereafter the Jewish population began to rise, for reasons which are only too obvious. By April 1942, it had risen to 16,469: the statistics are still quite precise. In October of the same year it had risen dramatically: it had leaped to 25,000. The figure is no longer precise. There was no longer time to worry about statistics, and a few hundred Jewish lives more or less no longer mattered so much. And then a second sentence leaps at you— in a single week in October 1942, 22,000 Jews were deported to Treblinka, to be murdered.

I look at my atlas to find out about Piotrkov today. It tells me that its population is roughly 58,000. There is no mention of Jews in Piotrkov. It is not necessary. After the Nazi murders and a vicious post-Nazi Polish anti-Semitism, which persists to this day, it would be surprising if there were a single Jew left in Piotrkov.

Rabbi Yitzḥak Finkler

Let me tell you about Rabbi Finkler. I find out about him in a memorial book. After the great catastrophe, reverent survivors all over the world composed a large number of memorial books to commemorate the saintly victims who otherwise would be as though they had never been. The memorial book about Piotrkov tells me that Rabbi Finkler was a man of conscience. When the Nazis came and said to the Jewish community

council, "Register young Jews for work, it will be good for them—they will get more food," Rabbi Finkler said, "No, you do not have the right to make such decisions for someone else!"

Then the Nazis asked for volunteers and said to Jews, "You, you, and you—report for work, it will be good for you!" And Rabbi Finkler said, "Let *no one* go voluntarily! Do anything, everything. Disappear, hide, lie down, anything—but don't volunteer!" Thus Rabbi Finkler is credited by his chronicler not only with great moral integrity but with a political shrewdness and uncanny foresight that are almost superhuman.

One therefore wonders whether in this case, as in so many others, the chroniclers in their pious anguish do not exaggerate the virtues of their dead—until one comes to a passage which has the ring of utter authenticity: the piety of Rabbi Finkler. Throughout the ordeal he studied and prayed, a source of comfort and strength to all. More seriously, he obeyed the commandments. This is more serious, at a time of such hunger, observing the dietary laws. So we find it quite plausible and indeed inevitable that during the one and a half years which he spent in a forced-labor camp before Treblinka, he suffered more than others, not only spiritually but physically, because of the unaccustomed labor—and above all, the hunger.

The Third Shofar

Then came Rosh Hashanah, and Rabbi Finkler and his followers were deeply worried because they did not have a *shofar*. A *shofar* which to blow, so as to let it arouse them to penitence for their sins. So they sold their bread for money, gave the money to a Polish gentile who had access to the labor camp, and asked him to buy a *shofar* outside. The Pole made a mistake and came back with a calf's horn, the only kind of horn not permitted, reminiscent as it is of the golden calf and the time of Israel's great sin. By then Rabbi Finkler and his pious ones were full of anxiety, for Rosh Hashanah was already near, but they sent out the good-natured Pole again and he finally came, just in time, with a genuine ram's horn. And, thus, the chronicler finishes: "They blew the ram's horn on Rosh Hashanah and a prayer rose heavenward, together with the sound of the *shofar*. It threw itself before the throne of Divinity saying 'tear up the evil decree.' "[3] But alas, the evil decree was not torn up—*and this is why the shofar of Rabbi Yitzhak Finkler still resounds on earth and in heaven, and will never be silenced until the End of Days.*

Anyone who knows Jewish liturgy understands the reference of the chronicler. Of all the prayers of the awesome festival, the most awesome is one supposedly composed by a medieval martyr, the *Untanne Tokef.* It projects what might happen in the year to come. Who will grow richer, who poorer? One does not know. Who will live and who will die? It is unknown. Who will die at his time, and who before his time, and among the latter who will die of hunger and who of thirst, who by fire, by the sword, by strangulation or the plague? And, after all this, the grim but utterly realistic catalog ends with the tremendous affirmation that "repentance, prayer, and good works will tear up the evil decree."

Try to picture Rabbi Yitzhak Finkler in his last days, his last hours, in the last minute of horrified recognition which surpassed all possible foresight. There can be no question as to how he behaved. Most assuredly he said to himself and to his pious ones: If the evil decree was not torn up in our case, although it surpasses all evil decrees ever, it is because we did not repent enough, because we did not pray enough, because we did not do enough good works. That is what *he* said. But it cannot possibly be what *we* can say. We must cry out to God and men: if not for him and his like, then for whom? If not for these righteous ones and these saintly ones—then when will the evil decree ever be torn up? And this is why for all those who come after and hear that *shofar*—be they Jews, be they gentiles, be they diaspora Jews or Israeli Jews—there is now a new moral necessity amidst all the contingencies of human existence, that *the course of history, or in any case the course of Jewish history, must be so altered that such as Rabbi Yitzhak Finkler will never again be the helpless victims of the great hatred.*

Of Those Who Did Not Hear

We ask: who listened then; who listened at the time when Rabbi Finkler blew his *shofar?* I will forbear today to ask questions about God. There are too many questions about man. And the first statement to be made may seem to be a ridiculous statement, a redundant statement, a totally superfluous statement: the Nazis did not listen to that *shofar.*

Of course they did not listen. We all know that. But then a question must be asked. The human species, supposedly created in the image of God, includes SS men. It includes Himmler and Heydrich, Eichmann and Hitler. The question therefore is *why* they did not listen.

We do not know.[4] However, we know very well how they would have behaved if by chance they literally had heard Rabbi Finkler blow his *shofar.* If any member of the Nazi apparatus had been physically present, he might have murdered Rabbi Finkler on the spot for the unforgivable crime of practicing Judaism on holy Aryan ground. As an alternative, he might have called in a few comrades for some fun and games. Some of the Nazis were familiar with Jewish theology. They knew that the *shofar* is supposed to avert the evil decree. Let's put this to a little test. Come Rabbi Finkler, blow the horn! Blow it, let us say, twelve times, and we'll have twelve Jewish babies and a little target practice after every sound! Or maybe, to vary things, throw a baby here and there up into the air, and catch him with a bayonet! Amusement and theology, all in one!

Contrary to traditional Jewish practice, we must dwell on the deeds of the wicked ones in order to emphasize that not only was Nazism evil, it was an evil unprecedented under God's sun, and that its central target was *both* the Jewish people and the Jewish faith. Moreover, its shadow is still over us. When the ancient Syrians attacked the Maccabees on the Sabbath, it was a case of pragmatic cynicism; unwilling to fight on the Sabbath,

3. *Piotrkov Trybunalski, Sefer Zikaron,* published by the Landsmanschaften of Piotrkov in Israel, the United States, Great Britain, France, and Argentina, n.d., pp. 55–61.
4. The mountainous literature attempting to answer this question confirms this statement. Accounts which *do* give explanations of Nazi behavior are either offensively glib or unconsciously circular (such as in the use of the unexplained terms mania, madness, psychosis, and the like). And those accounts which inch closer to an understanding succeed by virtue of a deep sense of shock, horror, and intellectual humility.

the Jews were caught unawares. When the Nazis customarily rounded up Jews on their holiest days—Jews whom they could equally have rounded up on any other day—it was, so to speak, a case of diabolical idealism. It served no practical end. It was desecration for desecration's sake. And if this point needs to be made with great emphasis, it is because since that time we have become more and more accustomed to desecration for desecration's sake, particularly if its victims are Jews. UNESCO never raised any questions about the desecration of Jewish cemeteries and synagogues when Jordan occupied the Old City. (Now, when there is no desecration whatever in the Old City, UNESCO expels Israel, after the Jordanian desecrators have joined with the Polish anti-Semites to sponsor the motion.) When the Yom Kippur War was launched almost no one really asked—almost no one to this day really asks—why it was launched on Yom Kippur. Indeed, I myself believed at first that it was comparable to the case of the ancient Syrians, a case of pragmatic cynicism: the Jews got caught unawares. But then one realizes that this is the one day on which Israeli soldiers can easily be reached: in the synagogue. More important still, more significant to anyone who knows Israel's highways, it is the one day in the year on which the highways are clear and not crowded with traffic. So why is it that to this day no one is really bothered, let alone appalled, by the date on which the Egyptians and the Syrians attacked? No, the Nazis did not listen to the *shofar* of Rabbi Finkler of Piotrkov, and the effect is still with us.

Did the world listen? Let us consider the testimony of that most gentle of Zionist statesmen, Chaim Weizmann. He visited the United States in 1940 when that country, in his words, was "violently neutral" and any mention of the Jewish tragedy was associated with "war mongers." He writes: "It was like a nightmare which was all the more oppressive because one had to maintain silence. To speak of such things [as the danger to European Jewry] in public was 'propaganda'."

In 1943, Weizmann came to New York again, and to speak of war then was no longer propaganda. In Madison Square Garden he made this statement:

When the historian of the future assembles the bleak record of our days, he will find two things unbelievable; first, the crime itself, second, the

reaction of the world to the crime. . . . He will be puzzled by the apathy of the civilized world in the face of the systematic carnage of human beings. . . . He will not be able to understand why the conscience of the world had to be stirred. Above all, he will not be able to understand why the free nations, in arms against a resurgent, organized barbarism, required appeals to give sanctuary to the first and chief victims of that barbarism. Two million Jews have already been exterminated. The world can no longer plead that the ghastly facts are unknown or unconfirmed.[5]

Among the two million already dead was Rabbi Yitzhak Finkler of Piotrkov.

Of Some Who Heard

Let us turn to some who listened. It is a relief, it is a great joy; under the circumstances one might almost say it is a miracle, to be able to report that some *did* listen. In 1946 David Ben-Gurion appeared before the Anglo-American Committee of Inquiry, a committee composed of men who, after the tragedy had been revealed, took seriously the possibility that there might have to be a Jewish state. Ben-Gurion tried to explain why Jews had come to Palestine. He spoke, of course, of those who came because of persecution. But he also asked why some came who were not persecuted. Why did some come from friendly, free countries? Ben-Gurion replied in part as follows:

They came because they felt it was unendurable that they should be at the mercy of others. Sometimes the others are excellent people, but not always, and then there is discrimination, and they did not like it. As human beings with human dignity, they did not like it, and they did not see how they can change the whole world, so they decided to return to their own country and be masters of their own destiny. I want to give you an example of moral discrimination. Gentlemen, I do not know in Europe a more tolerant, a more liberal, a more fair-minded

5. Quoted in Walter Laqueur, *A History of Zionism* (London, 1972; New York, 1976), pp. 550, 551.

people than the English people in their own country. . . . There was recently in the House of Lords . . . a debate on the Jewish problem. . . . It was on the seventh of December 1945, and in that debate the Archbishop of York in very strong language condemned anti-Semitism as un-Christian. . . . He also expressed deep concern over the sufferings of the Jewish people. . . . He then began talking about the Jewish attacks on or criticism of the policy of His Majesty's Government in Palestine, meaning the White Paper policy of 1939, and the attacks being made by Jews on both sides of the Atlantic, and he said these significant words: "It [meaning, this criticism] is being resented and may easily lead to a most dangerous reaction." Well, Jews are not the only people who are criticizing or attacking the White Paper policy. In 1939, the White Paper policy was described, not by a Jew, but an Englishman, a pure Englishman, a gentile, as a "mortal blow to the Jewish people." The name of that Englishman, gentlemen, is Winston Churchill. We agree with this description. It was and is a mortal blow.

Well, gentlemen, when a people receives a mortal blow from somebody, would anybody ask them to lie down and take it silently—*a mortal blow?* Would anybody resent this criticism, this attack on the mortal blow? This was said by Mr. Churchill in 1939 when our people in Europe were still alive. Since then tens of thousands of human beings, of babies—after all, Jewish babies are also babies—have met their death because of that policy. . . . Is it surprising that we as human beings should criticize or attack this policy? I am sure His Grace understands that. He is a great personality, he knows the mind of his people, and said this may lead to a most dangerous reaction. We receive a mortal blow; we must be silent. If not, it may lead to a dangerous reaction. Where? Not in Poland, but in that most liberal and tolerant country—I say this with the greatest respect—England.[6]

This is what Ben-Gurion said in 1946. And there were men and women throughout the world then who listened and understood. They

understood that, whatever the political contingencies of the world (then very uncertain, perhaps far more uncertain than today), *there were certain moral necessities that had gradually but inescapably become clear in the development of the Zionist movement from Theodor Herzl to David Ben-Gurion; and that among these was a Jewish state.*

The State of Israel as a Moral Necessity

The most obvious factor that had made a Jewish state necessary was, of course, the Holocaust. But in view of worldwide, well-oiled Arab and communist propaganda it is necessary to remind ourselves at this time that this was by no means the only factor. The well-known [literary] critic Robert Alter lists the following additional factors. First, there was the series of murderous assaults by armed Arab mobs on the Jewish populace of Palestine beginning in 1921, long before a Jewish state existed when, except for organized Arab terror, there might well have gradually developed a binational state, a secular democratic state, and all the rest that we hear of today. Second, there was the British mandatory abrogation of even the humanitarian aspects of the national home by cutting off Jewish immigration at the precise time that Hitler was preparing the gas chambers. Third, there was an absolute refusal on the part of the Arabs to cooperate politically with Palestinian Jewry or to consider any binational alternative. Fourth (if one had been in the United Nations in November 1974 and listened to Yassir Arafat's address and the Assembly's reaction, one would have thought this had never happened) there was the total unwillingness of the Arabs of Palestine to agree even to the admission of a hundred thousand survivors of the gas chambers, coupled with the promise that those would be the last Jews to be admitted.

These are the facts, or some of the facts, that made a Jewish state a moral necessity. What is more, that state has become a moral necessity, not only for the Jews of Israel but for all Jews throughout the world, or at least for those who remember, understand, and are lent courage by their duty. For no matter where they live, *it has become a duty for Jews in this century not to tolerate "moral discrimination"* any longer. They owe this

6. Quoted in *Israel through the Eyes of Its Leaders*, edited by Naamani-Budavsky-Katsh (Tel Aviv, 1971), p. 7ff.

duty to the memory of their martyrs. They also
owe it to the countries in which they live, lest
these countries have even the slightest resemblance to the Nazi criminals. However, they shall
find the strength to fulfill this duty only because of
the heroic example of the State of Israel. This
means no less than that the State of Israel has become the spearhead of the whole Jewish people.
(All attempts to separate Israel and the diaspora are
attempts either of self-hating or cowardly Jews, or
of our enemies.) It may even be said that, after
what has happened in this century, in a certain
respect the State of Israel is a spearhead of all
mankind. The world is somewhat less dark today
because after the Holocaust there arose a State of
Israel, a state in which Jews are "masters of their
own destiny." There were many who understood
this at the time. Among them were Winston
Churchill, Harry Truman, and our own Lester
Pearson. . . .

Israel and the Diaspora

Under the grim circumstances just described it is
not surprising that the Jews of the diaspora should
be gripped by a certain failure of nerve. They too
have become uncertain as to where in this world
of political contingencies moral necessities lie. I
am not referring to assimilationist, let alone self-
hating Jews, who never did perceive any moral
necessity unless it was related to people other than
Jews themselves. The trauma of today is that there
is a failure of nerve among some of the most
committed. Ever since the Yom Kippur War we
have heard statements such as "we in Canada or
the United States cannot be vicarious Israelis" and
"Israel is not all of Judaism." Also, there has been
a flurry of spiritual activities, even including the
creation of new journals.

In themselves, such statements and activities are
unexceptionable. What must cause surprise and
suspicion is their timing. Could it be that what is at
work here is, so to speak, a spiritual hedging of
bets, purportedly for the sake of Judaism?[7] If so, let

it be said loudly and clearly that this is not the time
for the diaspora to back away from what continues
to be the spearhead of the Jewish people and a
spearhead of all mankind—the embattled State of
Israel. Are there today, once again, good Jews,
devoted Jews, who try to hear the *shofar* either of
Sinai or of the End of Days, but at the same time
wish to reassert the view that nothing decisive has
happened or can happen between these two termini of Jewish history? Are there Jews, too, who
no longer hear the *shofar* of Rabbi Yitzhak Finkler
of Piotrkov, or even seek to silence it? If so, the
attempt must fail.

Israel and Judaism

Let us consider the present state of Jewish eschatological expectation. On the liberal and left wing
this is now as always thought of in terms of a this-
worldly messianic universalism, a future condition
in which every people is free, just, and fulfilled.
However, Rabbi Finkler's *shofar* arouses one to
the realization that, unless something new and
particular is added to this "universalism" in this
projected fulfillment of all the peoples, the *Jewish*
people alone will either have disappeared or else,
once again, be at the mercy of others. Thus this
form of left-wing or liberal theological internationalism reveals itself as a form of escapism.

A different form of escapism is found on the
Orthodox right. An American Jewish theologian
asserts that nothing evil happened to the children
of Auschwitz, that they are all happy with God in
heaven. This is not a use of traditional Jewish
belief in the world to come, but rather an abuse.
And it is apt to make Marxists of us all. For Marx,
religion was the opiate of the people. Here we
have a religious opiate of the Jewish people after
the Nazi Holocaust.

In search of a stern realism one does well to
ask how the ancient rabbis thought of the *shofar* at
the End of Days. According to the Midrash, who
will blow the final *shofar*? Elijah, the prophet who
has seen all, knows all, and yet has retained the
strength to wait for the End. At his first blow,
the primal light which shone before the week of
the creation will reappear. (A great cosmic
event!) At his second blow, the dead will rise and
assemble around the Messiah from all corners of

7. See my article in *The Yom Kippur War: Israel and the
Jewish People*, edited by Moshe Davis (New York,
1974), pp. 107–123.

the earth. (After this, what more?) At his third blow, the *Shekhinah*, the Presence of God, will become visible to all. (For the pious of many faiths the ultimate, unsurpassable consummation!) What, one may ask by way of a lapse into eschatological humor, can Elijah do for an encore? He can perform one climactic task. Indeed, only after all the preceding works are accomplished is it possible for him to perform it: he will slay Samael, the evil angel.[8] So utterly serious is the midrashic eschatological expectation about the necessity to confront evil. So far removed is it from all escapism.

What of the other *shofar*, blown at Sinai and ushering in Jewish history? We read in Exodus:

> And it came to pass on the third day, when it was morning, that there were thunder and lightnings and a thick cloud upon the mount, and the voice of a horn exceeding loud.... Now Mount Sinai was altogether on smoke, because the Lord had descended in fire, and the smoke thereof ascended as the smoke of a furnace and the whole mountain quaked greatly.... And the voice of the horn waxed louder and louder. (Exodus 19:16, 18–19)

Two questions arise, Who blew? We are not told. Was it God to arouse men? Or men to arouse God? Or, as one who does not believe in God might say, was it one man who blew, to arouse both himself and all others? We are not told, and perhaps it does not matter. Perhaps what matters is not who blows but whether the sound is heard. This is the first question.

The second question is raised by the Midrash, and answered as follows: "Ordinarily the more the sound of a voice is prolonged the weaker it becomes. But here the longer the voice lasted the stronger it became. And why was it weaker at first? That the ear might get it in accordance with its capacity of hearing."[9]

There is now in process a great, hidden spiritual conflict concerning the Holocaust. It is hidden, for it is rarely articulated, and more rarely still in the right terms. It is great because it is meant by all or most of the articulated conflicts and discussions—between believers and secularists, Israel and the diaspora, the Jewish people and the world. It is the great unspoken subject. Is the *shofar* of Rabbi Yitzhak Finkler of Piotrkov *wholly unlike* the *shofar* of Sinai? Does its sound grow ever dimmer with the passage of time so that even now it has perhaps ceased to be audible? Or is it, on the contrary, *wholly like* the *shofar* of Sinai? Is its sound waxing louder and louder, so that its sound mingles with the sound of Sinai, and no effort to silence it can ultimately prevail? All kinds of men try to silence that *shofar* which sounded a generation ago. Some do so innocently. Others are far from innocent. Some simply cannot bear to remember the crime. Others are heirs of the criminals. Others still are bystanders now as they were bystanders then. But the truth will not be silenced.

Epilogue

One morning, at the outset of the Yom Kippur War, an Israeli tank driver in the Golan Heights perceived a scene which he subsequently compared to a scene from a bad Italian movie. Wave upon unending wave of Syrian tanks appeared on the horizon, and between these thousand or more vehicles and the Israeli heartland there were a mere seventy-odd Israeli tanks. So, as he told the story to our friend Professor Yehuda Bauer, there was nothing to do but shoot until the ammunition gave out, rush for more ammunition, and come back to shoot again. The possibility of *not* returning to that hell, Professor Bauer commented when he told us of the incident, never occurred to this tank driver. The specter of a violent and total end of Jewish history, begun at Sinai, must have appeared before his mind but was immediately rejected. This secularist Israeli heard the shofar of Rabbi Yitzhak Finkler—and, mingled with it, the shofar of Sinai.

Another friend, Professor Pinchas Peli, edits an Israeli magazine called *Panim El Panim*. One day, in a German paper, he saw a picture of two soldiers in the Sinai during the Yom Kippur War, gun in hand, and dressed in the traditional phylacteries and prayer shawl. The picture of the

---

8. L. Ginzberg, *The Legends of the Jews* (Philadelphia, 1954), vol. 4, p. 234ff.

9. *Mechilta de-Rabbi Ishmael*, edited by J. Z. Lauterbach (Philadelphia, 1949), vol. 2, p. 223.

older man reminded him of another picture of a Jew dressed in the same traditional garments. Where had he seen that face before? Soon he remembered a well-known picture of a pious Jew praying for his dead lying at his feet whom the Nazis had murdered, and he was surrounded by the murderers, jeering, laughing, and enjoying the fun. (One of them had photographed the scene, and this is how we have the picture.) So Professor Peli decided to write an article, and with this he printed the two pictures side by side.

Next week he received a letter from a hospital, saying something like this:

> I am the other man in the picture in the Sinai, and the day it was taken I was shot. I am not writing for sympathy; indeed, I wish to remain anonymous. I am writing to tell you something. All my life I have thought of the generation murdered in the Holocaust as being collectively my father and mother. However, being collective, my relation to them was vague. Now it is no longer vague. I have seen that picture of the old man, praying for his dead, mocked and

jeered at by the murderers of his people. And as long as I live, I will think of *this* man as my father.

This Israeli soldier heard the shofar of Sinai and, mingled with it, the shofar of Rabbi Yitzhak Finkler of Piotrkov.

Some may consider my citing these two cases as reflecting a vicarious Israeli chauvinism and militarism. It would be in keeping with the spirit of the times. Yet those uttering such condemnations would in fact condemn themselves. After Arafat's speech, Israeli Ambassador Tekoah gave verbal expression to the horn of Sinai when at the U.N. he reminded the world of the prophetic promise that the nations would beat their swords into plowshares. Even as he spoke most of those present walked away. Yet with the shofar of Sinai was mingled the shofar of Rabbi Yitzhak Finkler of Piotrkov, calling ever louder, ever more inescapably, to Israel, to the Diaspora, to the nations of the world, and indeed to God himself: "I shall not die but live, and declare the works of God."

Historicity, Rupture, and *Tikkun Olam* (Mending the World)

What is a Jew? Who is a Jew? After this catastrophe, what is a Jew's relation to the Jewish past? We resume our original question as we turn from one rupture in post-Holocaust Jewish existence— of the bond with the gentile world—to the other—of the bond with his own past history, past tradition, past God.

After all previous catastrophes ever since biblical times, a Jew could understand himself as part of a holy remnant. Not that the generation itself was holy, a presumptuous view, and one devoid of any real meaning. The generation was rather heir to holy ones—not to the many who had fallen away but rather to the few that, whether in life or the death of martyrdom, had stayed in fidelity at their singled-out Jewish post. Was there ever a self-definition by a flesh-and-blood people that staked so much—staked *all*—on fidelity? It is the deepest definition of Jewish identity in all Jewish history.

It cannot, however, be the self-definition of this Jewish generation for, except for an accident,

we, the Jews of today, would either have been murdered or never born. *We are not a holy remnant. We are an accidental remnant.* However we may wish to evade the grim fact, this is the core definition of Jewish identity today.

The result is that we, on our part, cannot consider ourselves heir to the few alone. (For the religious among us, the martyrs and their prayers; for the secularists, the heroes and their battles.) We are obliged to consider ourselves heir to the whole murdered people. We think of those made into *Muselmänner* by dint of neither virtue nor vice but some "banal incident." We think of the children; their mothers; of the countless saints, sinners, and ordinary folk who, unsuspecting to the end, were gassed in the twinkling of an eye. And what reaches us is nothing so much as *the cry of an innocence that shakes heaven and earth; that can never be stilled; that overwhelms our hopes, our prayers, our thought.* Maimonides is said to have ruled that any Jew murdered for no reason other than being a Jew is to be considered holy. Folk tradition, already existing, cites Maimonides to this effect and views all the Jewish victims of the Holocaust as *kedoshim*—as holy ones. Only in this and no other sense are we, the accidental remnant, also a holy remnant. *In this sense, however, our holiness is ineluctable and brooks no honest escape or refusal.*

This circumstance places us into a hermeneutical situation that, after all that has been said about a post-Holocaust *Tikkun*, is new and unique still. Indeed, the dilemma in which we are placed is so extreme, so unprecedented, so full of anguish as to seem to tear us in two; and as to cause us to wonder whether, at the decisive point where all comes to a head, a post-Holocaust *Tikkun* of any kind is not seen, after all, to be impossible.

The dilemma is as follows. If (as we must) we hold fast to the children, the mothers, the *Muselmänner*, to the whole murdered people and its innocence, then we must surely despair of any possible *Tikkun*; but then we neglect or ignore the few and select—those with the opportunity to resist, the will and strength to resist, deriving the will and strength we know not whence—whose *Tikkun* (as we have seen) precedes and makes mandatory our own. And if (as also we must) we hold fast to just these select and their *Tikkun*, then our *Tikkun*, made possible by theirs, neglects and ignores all those who performed no heroic or saintly deeds such as to merit holiness and who yet, murdered as they were in utter innocence, must be considered holy. Not accidentally, "Holocaust theology" has been moving toward two extremes—a "God-is-dead" kind of despair, and a faith for which, having been "with God in hell," either nothing has happened or all is mended.[1] However, post-Holocaust thought—it includes theological concerns but is not confined to them—must dwell, however painfully and precariously, between the extremes, and seek a *Tikkun* as it endures the tension.

The *Tikkun* emerging from this tension is composed of three elements: (a) a recovery of Jewish tradition—a "going back into possibilities of [Jewish] *Dasein* that once was *da*";[2] (b) a recovery in the quite different sense of recuperation from an illness; and (c) a fragmentariness attaching to these two recoveries that makes them both ever-incomplete and ever-laden with risk. Without a recovered Jewish tradition—for the religious Jew, the Word of God; for the secular Jew, the word of man and his "divine spark"—there is no Jewish future. Without a recuperation from the illness, the tradition (and hence the Jewish future) must either flee from the Holocaust or be destroyed by it. And without the stern acceptance of both the fragmentariness and the risk, in both aspects of the recovery, our Jewish *Tikkun* lapses into inauthenticity by letting theirs, having "done its job," lapse into the irrelevant past.

To hold fast to the last of these three elements is hardest but also most essential. Once Schelling and Hegel spoke scathingly about theological contemporaries who were momentarily awakened from their dogmatic slumber by the Kantian philosophy but soon used that philosophy as a soporific: every old dogma, bar none, could become a "postulate of practical reason." Jewish thought today is in a similar danger. We remember the Holocaust; we are inspired by the martyrdom and the resistance: and then the inspiration quickly degenerates into this, that every dogma, religious or secular, is restored as if nothing had happened. However, the unredeemed anguish of Auschwitz must be ever-present with us, even as it is past *for* us. *Yom Ha-Shoah cannot now, or ever after, be assimilated to the ninth of Av.*

The attempt, to be sure, is widely made; but it is impossible. The age-old day of mourning is for catastrophes that are punishment for Jewish sins, vicarious atonement for the sins of others, or in any case meaningful, if inscrutable, divine decrees. The new day of mourning cannot be so

1. The most influential expression of the first extreme is Richard Rubenstein's *After Auschwitz* (Indianapolis and New York, 1966). A poignant expression of the second is Eliezer Berkowitz [Berkovits], *With God in Hell* (New York, 1979). As is clear from his *Faith after the Holocaust* (New York, 1973), Berkowitz does not assert either that nothing has happened or all is mended. He does, however, affirm a *faith* for which this is true, i.e., one which, though deeply shaken by the Holocaust, is not altered in consequence. [For more see the Berkowitz selections below, pp. 463–489.]
2. An allusion to the German Philosopher Martin Heidegger.

understood, for it is for the children, the mothers, the *Muselmänner*—the whole murdered people in its utter innocence. Nor has the *Yom Ha-Shoah* [Holocaust Remembrance Day] ceremony any such content, for it commemorates not Jewish sin but innocent Jewish suffering; not sins of others vicariously atoned but such as are incapable of atonement; not an inscrutable decree to be borne with patience but one resisted then, and to be resisted ever after. As for attempts to find a ninth-of-Av [the day commemorating the destruction of the First & Second Temple] meaning in the Holocaust—punishment for the sins of Zionism; or of anti-Zionism; or a moral stimulus to the world—their very perversity confirms a conclusion reached earlier . . . *Galut* [exilic] Judaism, albeit most assured not *Galut* [exile] itself, has come to an end.

Even so the attempt to assimilate *Yom Ha-Shoah* to the ninth of Av must be viewed with a certain sympathy. The cycle of the Jewish liturgical year—Rosenzweig described it sublimely—is an experience anticipating redemption. The ninth of Av, though a note of discord, fits into this cycle: but does *Yom Ha-Shoah*? The ninth of Av does not touch Yom Kippur—the Jewish "experience" of the "end" not through "dying" but living. *Yom Ha-Shoah* cannot but touch it; indeed it threatens to overwhelm Yom Kippur. Martin Buber has asked his post-Holocaust Jewish question—not whether one can still "believe" in God but whether one can still "speak" to Him. Can the Jew still speak to God on Yom Kippur? If not how can he speak to Him at all? The Jewish fear of *Yom Ha-Shoah*—the wish to assimilate it to the ninth of Av—is a fear, in behalf not only of *Galut* Judaism but also of Judaism itself.

"Judaism and the Holocaust" must be the last, climactic question not only of the present exploration but also of this whole work. Meanwhile we ask what ways of Jewish *Tikkun* there could be even if the climactic question had to be indefinitely suspended. These ways are many; their scope is universal. (The task is *Tikkun Olam*, to mend the world.) Yet they would all become insubstantial without one *Tikkun* that is a collective, particular Jewish response to history. This *Tikkun* may be said to have begun when the first Jewish "DP" gave a radical response to what he had experienced. Non-Jewish DPs, displaced

though they were, had a home to which to return. This Jewish DP did not—and even so was barred by bayonets and laws from the land that had been home once and that Jewish labor was making into home once again. Understandably, many of his comrades accepted these facts with a shrug of centuries, and waited for someone's charity that would give them the blessings of refuge, peace, and oblivion. (They waited in camps, often the very places of their suffering—and for years.) This Jewish DP took his destiny in his own hands, disregarded the legal niceties of a world that still classified him as Pole or German, still without Jewish rights, and made his way to the one place where there would be neither peace nor oblivion but which would be, without ifs and buts, home.

The *Tikkun* that is Israel is fragmentary. This fact need not be stressed, for it is reported almost daily in the newspapers. The power of the State is small, as is the State itself. It can offer a home to captive Jews but cannot force captors to set them free. Limited abroad, it is limited at home as well. It cannot prevent strife. It cannot even guarantee its Jewish citizens a culture or a strong Jewish identity. *Galut* Judaism may have ended; but there is no end to *Galut* itself, inside as well as outside the State of Israel.

If the *Tikkun* is fragmentary, the whole enterprise is laden with risk. (This too the papers report assiduously.) Within, *yerida*—emigration of Israelis—threatens to rival or overtake *aliyah*, the in-gathering. Without, for all the talk of a comprehensive peace, implacable enemies remain; and while enemies elsewhere seek to destroy a regime, or at most conquer a state, these enemies seek destruction of a state—and renewed exile for its Jewish inhabitants.

What then is the *Tikkun*? It is Israel itself. It is a state founded, maintained, defended by a people who—so it was once thought—had lost the arts of statecraft and self-defense forever. It is the replanting and reforestation of a land that—so it once seemed—was unredeemable swamps and desert. It is a people gathered from all four corners of the earth on a territory with—so the experts once said—not room enough left to swing a cat. It is a living language that—so even friends once feared—was dead beyond revival. It is a city rebuilt that—so once the consensus of mankind had it—was destined to remain holy ruins. And it is in and through all this, on behalf of the accidental remnant, after unprecedented death, a unique celebration of life.

It is true—so fragmentary and precarious is the great *Tikkun*—that many want no share of it, deny it, distort it, slander it. But slanders and denials have no power over those who are astonished— ever again astonished—by the fact that in this of all ages the Jewish people have returned—have been returned?—to Jerusalem. Their strength, when failing, is renewed by the faith that despite all, because of all, the "impulse from below" will call forth an "impulse from above."

Epilogue

Simha Holzberg is an Orthodox Jew and a Hasid. He fought in the Warsaw ghetto uprising. He survived, made his way to Israel, and prospered.

Holzberg, in short, was fortunate. But he was also haunted and without peace, rushing from school to school, kibbutz to kibbutz, synagogue to synagogue, always urging Jews to do more, to mourn more deeply, to remember more profoundly. It was not enough. It could not have been enough. Then came the Six Day War, and with it its widows and orphans, and Simha Holzberg made the deepest commitment of his life. He became the adoptive father of orphans, vowing to care for them until they were married.

Holzberg has remained a man of anguish. The great wound is not healed nor can it be healed. The unprecedented rupture is not "overcome" or reduced to a "problem" about to be "solved" or already solved. But this Israeli Jew has ceased to be haunted. He has even found a measure of peace. When last heard of by this writer, he was already the adoptive grandfather of more than a hundred grandchildren.

Emmanuel Levinas

Emmanel Levinas (1906–1996) was born in Kovno (now Kaunas), Lithuania, on 12 January. He grew up in the intensely Orthodox Jewish atmosphere of that city. His first languages were Hebrew and Yiddish while he learned Russian from a tutor. During World War I, when Kovno was occupied by German forces, the Levinas family moved to Kharkov in the Ukraine and here Levinas was one of the few Jewish children admitted to the Russian *Gymnasium*. In 1923 he began his university studies, concentrating in philosophy, at the University of Strasbourg (France). In 1927, he received his first degree in philosophy. He then continued his studies at the University of Freiburg in Germany where he attended seminars given by both Edmund Husserl and Martin Heidegger. He then returned to Strasbourg where he completed his doctoral studies by writing his thesis on *The Theory of Intuition in Husserl's Phenomenology*, which was published in Paris in 1930.

Levinas then began his teaching career at the *Alliance Israélite Universelle* in Paris. During the 1930s, he published a wide variety of essays on philosophical and topical issues and became a well-known younger member of Paris's extraordinary intellectual community, which included individuals such as Jean-Paul Sartre and Gabriel Marcel. In 1939, the threat of war saw Levinas drafted into the French army. In June 1940, he was taken as a prisoner of war and sent to a military prisoners' camp. There, the Jewish prisoners were separated from the others and made to wear special uniforms with the word *Jud* on them. His wife and young daughter were hidden in Paris by friends and then by the sisters of a Vincentian convent outside Orleans. Both survived the war and were reunited with Levinas in 1945 at the liberation of France.

Levinas now became the director of the École Normale Israélite Orientale (ENIO), supported by the Jewish community. In this role he also took responsibility for teaching Talmud and Rashi (d. 1105; the great Jewish medieval Bible and Talmud commentator) to the students. In the late 1940s, he also began to publish a long list of major philosophical studies, as well as his lectures on Talmud and other Jewish themes, publications that began to distinguish him among his peers. In 1964, he was appointed professor of philosophy at the University of Poitiers, while continuing on as director of the ENIO. In 1967, he was appointed professor at the new University of Paris, Nanterre. As his publications were translated into English and other languages, his fame grew, and he was awarded a number of honorary doctorates by American, Dutch, Belgian, German, Swiss, and Israeli universities. In 1973, he was appointed professor of philosophy at the Sorbonne. He continued to teach at the Sorbonne until his retirement and went on writing important philosophical works until his death.

SELECTION

The present selection "Useless Suffering," considers, in Levinas's understated way, the problem of theodicy—defending God and His justice in a world in which there is evil—after Auschwitz. For Levinas, the effort to defend God's justice is made impossible by the murder of European Jewry, during which he lost most of his close family who still lived in Kovno, Lithuania, when the Nazis arrived. Instead, Levinas would have us understand Auschwitz and the Holocaust as paradigms of the universal problem of evil—he explicitly refers to other events of mass death such as the Gulag and "the genocide of Cambodia"—that demand an ethical rather than a theological response in which causing or allowing the suffering of the Other becomes unpardonable. Levinas's essential argument is this: If we each cared, as we should, for the Other, there would have been no Holocaust, no Cambodia, and no Rwanda. This obligation, rather than metaphysical efforts to justify the Divine, is the real need of the present hour.

Selected Bibliography

Books by Emmanuel Levinas

Totality and Infinity: An Essay in Exteriority, translated by Alphonso Lingris (Pittsburgh, 1979).
Otherwise Than Being; or, Beyond Essence, translated by Alphonso Lingris (The Hague, 1981).
Collected Philosophical Papers, edited and translated by Alphonso Lingris (Dordrecht, 1987).
The Levinas Reader, edited by Sean Hand (Cambridge, Mass., 1990).
Difficult Freedom: Essays on Judaism, translated by Sean Hand (Baltimore, 1990).
Nine Talmudic Readings, translated by Annette Aronowitz (Bloomington, 1990).
In the Time of the Nations, translated by Michael B. Smith (Bloomington, 1994).

Works about Emmanuel Levinas

Wyschogrod, Edith. *Emmanuel Levinas: The Problem of Ethical Metaphysics* (The Hague, 1974).
Cohen, Richard A., ed., *Face to Face with Emmanuel Levinas* (Albany, N.Y., 1986).
Bernasconi, Robert, and Simon Critchley and David Wood, eds., *The Provocation of Levinas: Rethinking the Other* (London, 1988).
———. *Re-Reading Levinas* (Bloomington, 1991).
Cohen, Richard A. *Elevations: The Height of the Good in Levinas and Rosenzweig* (Chicago, 1994).
Critchley, S., and Robert Bernasconi, eds., *The Cambridge Companion to Levinas* (Cambridge, 2002).

USELESS SUFFERING

Theodicy

"He that increaseth knowledge increaseth sorrow," says Ecclesiastes (1:18), where suffering appears at the very least as the price of reason and of spiritual refinement. It would also temper the individual's character. It would be necessary to the teleology of community life, where social unrest awakens a useful attention to the health of the collective body. The social utility of suffering is necessary to the pedagogic function of Power in education, discipline, and repression. Is not fear of punishment the beginning of wisdom? Is it not believed that sufferings, submitted to as sanctions, regenerate the enemies of society and man? This political teleology is founded, to be sure, on the value of existence, on the perseverance of society and the individual in being, on their successful health as the supreme and ultimate end.

But the unpleasant and gratuitous nonsense of pain already pierces beneath the reasonable forms which the social "uses" of suffering assume.

452 PART III EUROPEAN AND AMERICAN RESPONSES DURING AND FOLLOWING THE WAR

These, in any case, do not make the torture which strikes the psychically handicapped and isolates them in their pain any less scandalous. But behind the rational administration of pain in sanctions distributed by human courts, immediately dressing up dubious appearances of repression, the arbitrary and strange failure of justice amidst wars, crimes, and the oppression of the weak by the strong, rejoins, in a sort of fatality, the useless sufferings which spring from natural plagues as if effects of an ontological perversion. Beyond the fundamental malignity of suffering itself, revealed in its phenomenology, does not human experience in history attest to a malice and a bad will?

Western humanity has nonetheless sought for the meaning of this scandal by invoking the proper sense of a metaphysical order, an ethics, which is invisible in the immediate lessons of moral consciousness. This is a kingdom of transcendent ends, willed by a benevolent wisdom, by the absolute goodness of a God who is in some way defined by this supernatural goodness; or a widespread, invisible goodness in nature and history, where it would command the paths which are, to be sure, painful, but which lead to the Good. Pain is henceforth meaningful, subordinated in one way or another to the metaphysical finality envisaged by faith or by a belief in progress. These beliefs are presupposed by theodicy! Such is the grand idea necessary to the inner peace of souls in our distressed world. It is called upon to make sufferings here below comprehensible. These will make sense by reference to an original fault or to the congenital finitude of human being. The evil which fills the earth would be explained in a "plan of the whole"; it would be called upon to atone for a sin, or it would announce, to the ontologically limited consciousness, compensation or recompense at the end of time. These suprasensible perspectives are invoked in order to envisage in a suffering which is essentially gratuitous and absurd, and apparently arbitrary, a signification and an order.

Certainly one may ask if theodicy, in the broad and narrow senses of the term, effectively succeeds in making God innocent, or in saving morality in the name of faith, or in making suffering—and this is the true intention of the thought which has recourse to theodicy—bearable. By underestimating its temptation one

could, in any case, misunderstand the profundity of the empire which theodicy exerts over humankind, and the *epoch-making* character—or the *historical* character, as one says today—of its entry into thought. It has been, at least up to the trials of the twentieth century, a component of the self-consciousness of European humanity. It persisted in watered-down form at the core of atheist progressivism, which was confident, nonetheless, in the efficacy of the Good which is immanent to being, called to visible triumph by the simple play of the natural and historical laws of injustice, war, misery, and illness. As providential, nature and history furnished the eighteenth and nineteenth centuries with the norms of moral consciousness. They are associated with many essentials of the deism of the age of Enlightenment. But theodicy—ignoring the name that Leibniz gave to it in 1710—is as old as a certain reading of the Bible. It dominated the consciousness of the believer who explained his misfortunes by reference to the Sin, or at least by reference to his sins. In addition to the Christians' well-established reference to Original Sin, this theodicy is in a certain sense implicit in the Old Testament, where the drama of the diaspora reflects the sins of Israel. The wicked conduct of ancestors, still nonexpiated by the sufferings of exile, would explain to the exiles themselves the duration and the harshness of this exile.

The End of Theodicy

Perhaps the most revolutionary fact of our twentieth-century consciousness—but it is also an event in Sacred History—is that of the destruction of all balance between the explicit and implicit theodicy of Western thought and the forms which suffering and its evil take in the very unfolding of this century. This is the century that in thirty years has known two world wars, the totalitarianisms of Right and Left, Hitlerism and Stalinism, Hiroshima, the Gulag, and the genocides of Auschwitz and Cambodia. This is the century which is drawing to a close in the haunting memory of the return of everything signified by these barbaric names: Suffering and evil are deliberately imposed, yet no reason sets limits to the exasperation of a reason become political and detached from all ethics.

Among these events the Holocaust of the Jewish people under the reign of Hitler seems to us the paradigm of gratuitous human suffering, where evil appears in its diabolical horror. This is perhaps not a subjective feeling. The disproportion between suffering and every theodicy was shown at Auschwitz with a glaring, obvious clarity. Its possibility puts into question the multimillennial traditional faith. Did not the word of Nietzsche on the death of God take on, in the extermination camps, the signification of a quasi-empirical fact? Is it necessary to be surprised, then, that this drama of Sacred History has had among its principal actors a people which, since forever, has been associated with this history, whose collective soul and destiny would be wrongly understood as limited to any sort of nationalism, and whose *gesture,* in certain circumstances, still belongs to revelation—be it as apocalypse—which "provokes thought" from philosophers or which impedes them from thinking?[1]

Here I wish to evoke the analysis which the Canadian Jew the philosopher Emil Fackenheim of Toronto has made of this catastrophe of the human and the divine in his work, and notably in his book *God's Presence in History*:

> The Nazi genocide of the Jewish people has no precedent within Jewish history. Nor . . . will one find a precedent outside Jewish history. . . . Even actual cases of genocide, however, still differ from the Nazi Holocaust in at least two respects. Whole peoples have been killed for "rational" (however horrifying) ends such as power, territory, wealth. . . . The Nazi murder . . . was annihilation for the sake of annihilation, murder for the sake of murder, evil for the sake of evil. Still more incontestably unique than the crime itself is the situation of the victims. The Albigensians died for their faith, believing unto death that

God needs martyrs. Negro Christians have been murdered for their race, able to find comfort in a faith not at issue. The more than one million Jewish children murdered in the Nazi Holocaust died neither because of their faith, nor despite their faith, nor for reasons unrelated to the Jewish faith [but] because of the Jewish faith of their great-grandparents [who brought] up Jewish children.[2]

The inhabitants of the Eastern European Jewish communities constituted the majority of the six million tortured and massacred; they represented the human beings least corrupted by the ambiguities of our world, and the million infants killed had the innocence of infants. Theirs is the death of martyrs, a death given in the torturers' unceasing destruction of the dignity which belongs to martyrs. The final act of this destruction is accomplished today in the posthumous denial of the very fact of martyrdom by the would-be "revisers of history." This would be pain in its undiluted malignity, suffering for nothing. It renders impossible and odious every proposal and every thought which would explain it by the sins of those who have suffered or are dead. But does not this end of theodicy, which obtrudes itself in the face of this century's inordinate distress, at the same time in a more general way reveal the unjustifiable character of suffering in the other person, the scandal which would occur by my justifying my neighbor's suffering? So that the very phenomenon of suffering in its uselessness is, in principle the pain of the Other. For an ethical sensibility—confirming itself, in the inhumanity of our time, against this inhumanity—the justification of the neighbor's pain is certainly the source of all immorality. Accusing oneself in suffering is undoubtedly the very turning back of the ego to itself. It is perhaps thus; and the for-the-other—

1. Maurice Blanchot, who is known for his lucid and critical attention to literature and events, notes somewhere: "How philosophize, how write in the memory of Auschwitz, of those who have said to us sometimes in notes buried near the crematories: 'Know what has happened,' 'do not forget,' and, at the same time, 'You will never know'?" I think that all the dead of the Gulag and all the other places of torture in our political century are present when one speaks of Auschwitz. [Blanchot's words appear in his article "Our Clandestine Companion," translated by David Allison, in *Face to Face with Levinas,* edited by Richard Cohen (Albany, N.Y., 1986), p. 50: translator's addition.]

2. Emil Fackenheim, *God's Presence in History: Jewish Affirmations and Philosophical Reflections after Auschwitz* (New York, 1970), pp. 69–70. [This work has been translated into French by M. Delmotte and B. Dupuy (Lagrasse, 1980): translator's note.] [For additional writings by Emil Fackenheim see pp. 420–449 above in this volume.]

the most upright relation to the Other—is the most profound adventure of subjectivity, its ultimate intimacy. But this intimacy can only be discreet. It could not be given as an example, or be narrated as an edifying discourse. It could not be made a predication without being perverted.

The philosophical problem, then, which is posed by the useless pain which appears in its fundamental malignancy across the events of the twentieth century, concerns the meaning that religiosity and the human morality of goodness can still retain after the end of theodicy. According to the philosopher we have just quoted, Auschwitz would paradoxically entail a revelation of the very God who nevertheless was silent at Auschwitz: a commandment of faithfulness. To renounce after Auschwitz this God absent from Auschwitz—no longer to assure the continuation of Israel—would amount to finishing the criminal enterprise of National Socialism, which aimed at the annihilation of Israel and the forgetting of the ethical message of the Bible, which Judaism bears, and whose multimillennial history is concretely prolonged by Israel's existence as a people. For if God was absent in the extermination camps, the devil was very obviously present in them. From whence, for Emil Fackenheim, comes the obligation for Jews to live and to remain Jews, in order not to be made accomplices of a diabolical project. The Jew, after Auschwitz, is pledged to his faithfulness to Judaism and to the material and even political conditions of its existence.

This final reflection of the Toronto philosopher, formulated in terms which render it relative to the destiny of the Jewish people, can be given a universal signification. From Sarajevo to Cambodia humanity has witnessed a host of cruelties in the course of a century when Europe, in its "human sciences," seemed to reach the end of its subject, the humanity which, during all these horrors, breathed—already or still—the fumes of the crematory ovens of the "final solution" where theodicy abruptly appeared impossible. Is humanity, in its indifference, going to abandon the world to useless suffering, leaving it to the political fatality—or the drifting—of the blind forces which inflict misfortune on the weak and conquered, and which spare the conquerors, whom the wicked must join? Or, incapable of adhering to an order—or to a disorder—which it continues to think diabolic, must not humanity now, in a faith more difficult than ever, in a faith without theodicy, continue Sacred History, a history which now demands even more of the resources of the *self* in each one, and appeals to its suffering inspired by the suffering of the other person, to its compassion which is a non-useless suffering (or love), which is no longer suffering "for nothing," and which straightaway has a meaning? At the end of the twentieth century and after the useless and unjustifiable pain which is exposed and displayed therein without any shadow of a consoling theodicy, are we not all pledged—like the Jewish people to their faithfulness—to the second term of this alternative?[3] This is a new modality in the faith of today, and also in our moral certainties, a modality quite essential to the modernity which is dawning.

3. We said above that theodicy in the broad sense of the term is justified by a certain reading of the Bible. It is evident that another reading of it is possible, and that in a certain sense nothing of the spiritual experience of human history is foreign to the Scriptures. We are thinking here in particular of the Book of Job which attests at once to Job's faithfulness to God (2:10) and to ethics (27:5 and 6), despite his sufferings without reason, and his opposition to the theodicy of his friends. He refuses theodicy right to the end and, in the last chapters of the text (42:7), is preferred to those who, hurrying to the safety of Heaven, would make God innocent before the suffering of the just. It is a little like the reading Kant makes of this book in his quite extraordinary short treatise of 1791, *Uber das Misslingen aller philosophischen Versuche in der Theodicee* [*On the Failure of All the Philosophical Attempts at a Theodicy*], where he demonstrates the theoretical weakness of the arguments in favor of theodicy. Here is the conclusion of his way of interpreting what "this ancient book expresses allegorically": "In this state of mind Job has proven that he did not found his morality on faith, but his faith on morality; in which case faith, however weak it may be, is nonetheless one of a pure and authentic kind, a kind which does not found a religion of solicited favors, but a well-conducted life" (*welche eine Religion nicht der Gunstbewerbung, sondern des guten Lebenswandels grundet*).

Michael Wyschogrod

Michael Wyschogrod was born in Berlin in 1928 into an Orthodox family. As a child, he received a traditional Jewish education. In 1939, he and his family were fortunate to escape from Nazi Germany and to find refuge in the United States. After his high school education in both public schools and Yeshiva Torah Vaadath in New York City, he entered City College where he majored in philosophy. After receiving his B.A., he went on to do graduate work in philosophy at Columbia University and received his Ph.D. in 1953. Professor Wyschogrod has studied with the distinguished Jewish thinker R. Joseph B. Soloveitchik (also represented in this anthology) and with perhaps the most famous Protestant theologian of the twentieth century, Karl Barth.

Professor Wyschogrod spent most of his academic career at Baruch College (part of the City University of New York). In 1957–1958 he was also a visiting professor at Bar Ilan University in Israel. Late in his career he moved, with his wife, Edith Wyschogrod, who is also a distinguished philosopher, to Rice University. His major philosophical interests have centered on twentieth-century European existentialism and especially on the work of Martin Heidegger, one of the most influential thinkers of the age. In addition, he has been an important contributor to contemporary discussions and debates in the areas of Jewish philosophy and theology and Jewish-Christian relations.

SELECTION

In his essay "Faith and the Holocaust," Michael Wyschogrod levels a critique against Emil Fackenheim's response to the Holocaust. Fackenheim argues for the continued existence of Judaism and the Jewish people as a direct response to Hitler's efforts. Wyschogrod finds the logic of Fackenheim's "The 614th Commandment" (reprinted in this anthology) to be faulty, and he rejects what he views as the use of the Holocaust as a *justification* for continued Jewish life. Furthermore, he feels that Fackenheim's assertion that the Holocaust is a unique event in history undermines his own secular, universalist position. The essence of Wyschogrod's critique of Fackenheim lies in his argument that Fackenheim's "negative natural theology," as Wyschogrod labels it (which, parallel to natural theology's positive argument-by-design for the existence of God, commands Jewish survival through the "Voice of Auschwitz"), is unconvincing and overreaches itself. Wyschogrod asserts that it is more limiting but more honest to acknowledge a fixation on the Holocaust, as distinct from other human atrocities, simply "because Israel is the elect people of God through whom God's redemptive work is done in the world" (p. 461 below). Accordingly, the Jewish people occupy a special place in the world as God's emissaries/representatives, and thus the Jewish plight is of particular significance theologically. Wyschogrod acknowledges that this viewpoint is not accessible to "nonbelievers," as Fackenheim's viewpoint attempts to be, but, alternatively, Wyschogrod understands his argument as being a plausible perspective on, and a response to, the Holocaust from within the "circle of faith."

The present selection, "Faith and the Holocaust," is reprinted from *Judaism* 20 (Summer 1971): 286–294.

Selected Bibliography

Works by Michael Wyschogrod

Kierkegaard and Heidegger: The Ontology of Existence (London, 1953).
"Israel, the Church, and Election," in *Brothers in Hope,* edited by John Oesterreicher (New York, 1970), pp. 79–87.
"Faith and the Holocaust," *Judaism* 20 (Summer 1971): 286–294.
"Some Theological Reflections on the Holocaust," *Response* 25 (Spring 1975): 65–68.
"Buber's Evaluation of Christianity: A Jewish Perspective," in *Martin Buber: A Centenary Volume,* edited by Hayim Gordon and Jochanan Bloch (Tel Aviv, 1981), pp. 403–417 [Hebrew]; pp. 457–472 [English].
"Symposium: The State of Orthodoxy," *Tradition* 20 (Spring 1982): 80–83.
"A New Stage in Jewish-Christian Dialogue," *Judaism* 31 (Summer 1982): 355–365.
The Body of Faith: Judaism as Corporeal Election (Minneapolis, 1983).
Abraham's Promise: Judaism and Jewish-Christian Relations (Grand Rapids, 2004).

Article about Michael Wyschogrod

Blumenthal, David. "Michael Wyschogrod," in *Interpreters of Judaism in the Late Twentieth Century,* edited by Steven T. Katz (Washington, D.C., 1993), pp. 393–405.

Faith and the Holocaust

Speaking of the Holocaust, Emil Fackenheim writes in *God's Presence in History: Jewish Affirmations and Philosophical Reflections*[1]: "Silence would, perhaps, be best even now, were it not for the fact that among the people the flood-gates are broken, and that for this reason alone the time of theological silence is irretrievably past."

The flood-gates are, indeed, broken and silence no longer surrounds the Holocaust. Whether it was the people who broke the flood-gates or whether it was a small number of Jewish writers who, in recent years, have not permitted the people to forget what many have very much wanted to forget, remains an open question. From their side, the Holocaust thinkers (Fackenheim, Elie Wiesel, and one or two others) have been driven above all by the terror that the people will

forget, that the Holocaust will cease to be the central event of contemporary Jewish existence and become, instead, one memory among the many others that make up Jewish history. The people, for their part, have been ambivalent. On the one hand, they have certainly wanted to forget: Jewish life, after all, has not been transformed by the Holocaust, business continues as usual, and time has shown once again that it heals all wounds—a fact for which men cannot help thanking God while recognizing the horror of the process when such wounds as the Holocaust are involved. On the other hand, the Jewish public has also wanted to remember: The reception accorded the writings of Elie Wiesel demonstrates the point. Whoever addresses Jewish audiences with any frequency can testify to the kind of charge generated when the Holocaust is mentioned. This is the one common experience of the Jewish people today, believing and unbelieving, learned and simple, young and old. Not

1. Emil L. Fackenheim, *God's Presence in History* (New York, 1970).

to be addressed by the Holocaust is the one sure sign of exclusion from the Jewish people; it is the great divide that separates those in from those out. It is this ambivalence of forgetting and remembering that characterizes, it seems to me, the attitude of the people.

It was the philosopher Ludwig Wittgenstein who announced that concerning those matters of which we cannot speak we ought to remain silent. While, of course, he had nothing like the Holocaust in mind, it is difficult, as Fackenheim well understands, not to apply the rule of silence to it. The peril is blasphemy. In fact, it seems to me that nothing but blasphemy can be the result if we view the Holocaust from the human point of view. If we find ourselves continuing to believe in the biblical God after the Holocaust, we can neither forgive Him nor love Him. Or, following Richard Rubenstein, we blaspheme by denying the existence of the God of history and are driven into some form or other of atheism.

Fackenheim, for his part, has little sympathy for Rubenstein. He speaks (p. 71) of "the view of a 'radical' Jewish theologian who asserts that...the midrashic framework is shattered by Auschwitz; the God of history is dead." Without mentioning Rubenstein's name in the body of the text (though he is identified in a footnote), Fackenheim calls him to task for having the temerity to speak: "What assures him [Rubenstein] of his capacities to deal with the trauma—or stills his fear that some other mechanism may cause him to utter words which should have never been spoken?" Fackenheim's lack of sympathy for Rubenstein's total rejection of the "for our sins are we punished" theology would make good sense if Fackenheim could see his way to embracing this standpoint, a standpoint which is, after all, not unhallowed by Jewish history. The fact of the matter, however, is that Fackenheim, too, finds it impossible to embrace the theology of "for our sins are we punished." As a response to Auschwitz, this doctrine, according to Fackenheim, "becomes a religious absurdity and even a sacrilege" (p. 73). Fackenheim buttresses this contention by reference to the work of N. N. Glatzer who had claimed in his *Untersuchungen zur Geschichtslehre der Tannaiten* that the "for our sins are we punished" view was

rejected by the ancient rabbis, "perhaps not in response to the destruction of the Temple by Titus, but in response to the paganization of Jerusalem by Hadrian" (Fackenheim, p. 73). This being so, what is so dreadfully wrong with Rubenstein's rejection of the biblical God once he found himself rejecting the view that, in Hitler, Israel was once more feeling the scourge of God?

In the section of the book entitled "The Midrashic Framework and the Holocaust" (pp. 69–79), Fackenheim examines the various standpoints that attempt to deal with the Holocaust from within the circle of faith and finds them all lacking. He then examines "Jewish Secularism and the Holocaust" (pp. 79–84) and finds that Jewish secularism, in stubbornly persisting in its Jewish identity after the Holocaust, is also involved in a profound contradiction, because the logic of its position would dictate assimilation, a solution that would seem to be indicated by the cost of Jewish survival, especially in the twentieth century, but which the Jewish secularist nevertheless refuses to embrace. The two frameworks, the theological and the secular, from which the Holocaust can be approached are, therefore, rejected by Fackenheim, and this explains his dissatisfaction with Rubenstein to the extent that he reads Rubenstein as simply representative of the secular option. It should, however, be kept in mind that Fackenheim rejects with equal firmness the standpoint of simple faith, be this in the "for our sins are we punished" form or perhaps an even more simple faith which refers to the inscrutability of God's will. All these are inadequate. What then, is adequate?

Only obedience to the Voice of Auschwitz. This Voice, as heard by Fackenheim, commands the survival of Jews and Judaism. Because Hitler was bent upon the destruction of both, it is the duty of those Jews who survived Hitler to make sure that they do not do his work, that they do not, by assimilation, bring about the disappearance of what Hitler attempted but ultimately failed to destroy. For the religious Jew, this means that he must go on being religious, however inadequate Auschwitz has shown his frame of reference to be. And for the secular Jew, the Voice of Auschwitz commands not faith, which even the Voice of Auschwitz cannot command, but preservation of Jews and Judaism. Speaking of the significance of the Voice of Auschwitz for the secular Jew, Fackenheim writes:

> No less inescapable is this Power for the secularist Jew who has all along been outside the midrashic framework and this despite the fact that the Voice of Auschwitz does not enable him to return into this framework. He cannot return; but neither may he turn the Voice of Auschwitz against that of Sinai. For he may not cut off his secular present from the religious past: The Voice of Auschwitz commands Jewish unity. (pp. 88–89)

The sin of Rubenstein is, therefore, that he permits Auschwitz further to divide the Jewish people at a time when survival is paramount if Hitler is not to be handed a posthumous victory, and survival demands unity. Because this is so, Rubenstein should presumably soft-pedal his doubts so as not to threaten the Jewish people at a time when everything must be secondary to the issue of survival.

What can be said about all this?

Since all criticism proceeds from a point of view, it would be best for me to state mine. I do not think that a voice can be extracted from the Holocaust which will speak to believer and nonbeliever alike. I do not think that the question of faith can be circumvented by means of Auschwitz. Finally, I do not think that Judaism can be given a new hold on life by means of Auschwitz. For me, the Holocaust was a totally destructive event which makes my remaining a Jew infinitely more difficult than it has ever been. I can only marvel at Fackenheim's effort to extract a positive result from the Holocaust, a kind of negative natural theology with the survival of the people, rather than the existence of God, as the conclusion.

Let us first examine the contention that the Voice of Auschwitz speaks to the secular Jew and commands him to adhere to his Jewishness so as not to hand Hitler a posthumous victory. At the risk of drawing simplistic analogies, it is necessary to examine the logic of the argument. Let us imagine that there arises a wicked tyrant who sets as his goal, for his own depraved and psychotic reasons, the extermination of all stamp collectors in the world. It is clear that it would be the duty of every decent person to do everything in his power to frustrate the scheme of that tyrant. Let us further imagine, however, that before the tyrant is made harmless, he succeeds, in fact, in murdering a large proportion of the world's stamp collectors. Does it now follow that subsequent to the tyrant's demise it becomes the duty of the remaining stamp collectors not to lose interest in their stamp collecting so as not to hand the tyrant a posthumous victory? Isn't there all the difference in the world between exterminating persons who wish to be stamp collectors just because they wish to be stamp collectors and the right of individuals or groups to lose interest in something they no longer wish to remain interested in? Would it be a posthumous victory for the tyrant were stamp collecting to disappear from the world as long as this disappearance is due, not to force, but to free choice? I cannot see why, if I am a secular, nonbelieving Jew, it is incumbent upon me to preserve Judaism because Hitler wished to destroy it. What was incumbent upon me was to destroy Hitler, but once this is accomplished, the free choice of every individual is restored, and no further Hitler-derived burdens rest on the nonbelieving Jew.

It is, of course, true that there are secularist Jews who insist on remaining Jews even after the Holocaust. Fackenheim seems to be convinced that, if not for the Voice of Auschwitz, these secularist Jews would have every reason to embrace assimilation in light of the price that Jewish existence extracts. The desire of some secularist Jews to remain Jews may be due, however, to the fact that they find positive value in remaining Jews independently of the Holocaust. Jewish secularism, with its national and ethnic identification, existed long before the Holocaust, when surely no Voice from Auschwitz could be heard. In such circles, assimilation was resisted, partly because of a genuine and deep pride in the historic contribution of the Jewish people to civilization and, partly, I would think, because assimilation was never quite as possible as Fackenheim seems to think it was and is. And finally, there is the possibility that there is something slightly irrational about the desire to perpetuate Jewish existence when this desire is combined with secularist premises. To the believer, this can be taken to demonstrate that Jews remain in the service of God even in their state of disbelief and that forces deeper than those known to the individuals concerned shape Jewish existence. But all this is a far cry from turning this state of affairs into an ideology, which is precisely what Fackenheim attempts to do.

I have already termed Fackenheim's enterprise "negative natural theology," a phrase which deserves brief explanation. Traditionally, natural theology has been the enterprise whereby the existence of God is demonstrated on the basis of some rational evidence, without recourse to faith or revelation. Most commonly, the point of departure for such an attempt was some "positive" feature of the world as it appears to man: its order, its beauty, or its harmony. It was then argued that such characteristics could not be the result of pure chance and that it was, therefore, necessary to posit some all-powerful and rational being as the author or creator of a universe possessing the respective positive characteristics. Such an argument was presumably persuasive to the nonbeliever and could force him to concede the existence of an intelligent creator, all without having to leave the framework of reason with which we started.

Fackenheim's point of departure is, of course, the opposite of the "positive." Instead of being the order, beauty, harmony, or justice of the universe, it is a totally unique crime, unparalleled in human history. But once we get over this initial difference, similarities appear. In the positive version, a positive characteristic of the universe is noted, and it is argued that no natural explanation for it is adequate. In negative natural theology, an evil is pointed out for which also, it is alleged, no natural explanation is possible. Of course, the conclusion in negative natural theology cannot be identical with that of positive natural theology, inasmuch as the problem of theodicy cannot here easily be ignored. Nevertheless, the conclusion which Fackenheim draws, the sacred duty to preserve the Jewish people, is the functional equivalent of the existence of God in positive natural theology, inasmuch as it becomes a total foundation for the continued existence of Judaism, a foundation as fully serviceable to the secularist as to the believer. One is almost driven to the conclusion that in the absence of the Holocaust, given Fackenheim's profound understanding of the irreversibility of the secular stance, no justification for the further survival of Judaism could have been found. With the Holocaust, amazing as this may appear, Judaism has gotten a new lease on life.

Because the Holocaust becomes, for Fackenheim, the fulcrum of his negative natural theology, he apparently finds it necessary to claim that it was, and remains, a unique event in human history. Strictly speaking, this is not necessary, since any sufficiently terrible negative event can become the foundation of a negative natural theology so long as it can be argued that it is not amenable to natural explanation. Nevertheless, it is understandable that an overwhelmingly terrible event such as the Holocaust would be even more useful if it could be demonstrated that in addition to everything else it was totally unique. Now this is precisely what Fackenheim maintains. According to him, the uniqueness of the Holocaust consists of the fact that there was no "rational" purpose in the crime. "Whole peoples," writes Fackenheim "have been killed for 'rational' (however horrifying) ends such as power, territory, wealth, and in any case supposed or actual self-interest. No such end was served by the Nazi murder of the Jewish people" (p. 70). In a footnote, he adds:

> I feel constrained to stress once again that I assert only that the Nazi genocide of the European Jews is unique, not that it is a greater or more tragic crime than all others. Thus, for example, the fate of the gypsies at the hand of the Nazis (itself an "ideological" project) is at least in one sense more tragic—that no one seems to bother to commemorate them. Even this example of genocide, however, though itself a product of Nazi ideology, still differs from the Nazi genocide of European Jewry: no comparable hate propaganda was directed by the Nazis against the gypsies. Whence this groundless, infinite hate, indiscriminately directed against adults and children, saints and sinners, and so relentlessly expressed in action. (p. 100)

What are we to make of this claim?

It would be rather beside the point, though not without logical force, to argue that, in one sense, all events are unique, since there can be no event which does not have at least one characteristic not shared by any other event—if only its exact place and time of occurrence. In another sense of the word "unique," no event is unique for there is no event which does not share at least one characteristic with at least one other event—if only the fact that both are events. This being so, it might not be altogether unreasonable to expect some discussion of the sense of the word "unique" in such a vehement claim by a philosopher of the uniqueness of an event. Even so, the issue far transcends such relatively technical considerations. The crux of the matter is a moral one.

Although, as we have seen, Fackenheim restricts himself to the claim that the Holocaust was a unique crime and not that it was a greater or more tragic crime than all the others, the claim of uniqueness reflects an existential fact: that for Fackenheim the focus of his life is the destruction of European Jewry and not the extermination of the gypsies or of the residents of Hiroshima in World War II, the Armenians in World War I, or the illiterate peasants of Vietnam in the recent past. In some way, the fate of European Jewry is for Fackenheim in a class by itself, having an existential significance for him that these other horrors do not have. We will soon have to ask why this is so or, perhaps more to the point, what justification Fackenheim can offer for this being so. It is not to be expected that the obvious reply, namely, that since Fackenheim is a Jew he is more reached by the fate of Jews than by that of others, will satisfy either Fackenheim or his critics. Fackenheim's insistence on the uniqueness of the Holocaust indicates that he feels constrained to justify his preoccupation on grounds other than simple ethnic or national partiality. And he feels constrained to justify his preoccupation because he senses an accusation in the air, an accusation emanating from those who present themselves as equally reached by the death of any child, be he in Warsaw or Biafra, in 1943 or 1970. To this sensibility such dwelling on a catastrophe of the past is an evasion of the crimes—as they see it— being committed today about which something can still be done but about which Fackenheim does not write books and articles. For such people, the ultimate object of reverence is man wherever he appears, rather than just "one's own," which is the light in which they see Fackenheim's enterprise.

It is at this point that Holocaust theology as practiced by Fackenheim finds itself on the defensive. At this point, it is essential to be scrupulously honest. It is necessary to admit that we are fixated on the Holocaust to an extent quite unacceptable in a universalistic framework. The moral force of those who cannot share this fixation must be recognized. It is, I believe, necessary to abandon the attempt to find "objective" criteria in accordance with which such a fixation on the Holocaust will be made plausible, simply because any and all such criteria bestow uniqueness on the Holocaust at the expense of diminishing the other occasions of human suffering. To argue that one is asserting only the uniqueness of the Holocaust and not that it is a greater or more tragic crime than all others, simply won't do because the uniqueness which is asserted ("groundless, infinite hate indiscriminately directed against adults and children, saints and sinners, and so relentlessly expressed in action") turns out to be morally decisive and not just an attribution of abstract uniqueness. It is necessary to recognize that, from any universally humanistic framework, the destruction of European Jewry is one notable chapter in the long record of man's inhumanity against man, a record which compels the Holocaust to resign itself to being, at most, a first among equals.

If we therefore remain fixated on the Holocaust, it must be for another reason. It is true that the Holocaust is *our* catastrophe and one is entitled to mourn more intensely for the death of a relative than for that of another. But this consideration cannot have ultimate significance. On the psychological plane such partiality is understandable; on the final, moral plane, all men enjoy the same dignity as my relatives, and it therefore follows that crimes against them cannot be qualitatively different from those against others.

To justify Emil Fackenheim's and my fixation with the Holocaust, I must resort to theology. To make clear my meaning, I must recount an episode that I witnessed quite recently.

A devout Catholic philosopher of my acquaintance returned from mass one Sunday morning in a state of agitation. Some progressive members of the parish had removed the crucifix from its usual position and substituted for it a contemporary crucifix on which, instead of the suffering Jesus, there was affixed a collage depicting suffering Vietnamese men, women, and children. My friend was outraged. "How can they," he asked, "equate human suffering with the suffering of the Incarnate Son, a person of the Godhead?" I had no doubt of his deep and genuine compassion for the suffering of man, wherever and whenever it occurs. But it was only the suffering of the Son of God at Golgotha that, he argued, redeemed the sins of the world and healed the suffering of man. To substitute the suffering of man for this saving event was to confuse man with God, something that benefits neither.

Must we not say something at least somewhat similar if we are to remain really honest? The fate of Israel is of central concern because Israel is the elect people of God through whom God's redemptive work is done in the world. However tragic human suffering is on the human plane, what happens to Israel is directly tied to its role as that nation to which God attaches His name and through which He will redeem man. He who strikes Israel, therefore, engages himself in battle with God and it is for this reason that the history of Israel is the fulcrum of human history. The suffering of others must, therefore, be seen in the light of Israel's suffering. The travail of man is not abandoned, precisely because Israel suffers and, thereby, God's presence is drawn into human history and redemption enters the horizon of human existence.

Can we deny that all this must be a scandal in the eyes of nonbelief? Can we expect the nonbeliever to concede that somehow the fate of Israel is more central, more decisive, more important than the fate of any other people? We cannot and must not expect this; we must learn to live with the knowledge that there is an abyss between belief and nonbelief, that for nonbelief Auschwitz is a member of a large and tragic class of human evil whose voice, if it commands anything, commands men to struggle against evil and injustice wherever perpetrated. When we observe the Holocaust fading from the consciousness of men, as it inevitably will, when we observe it fading to some extent even from the consciousness of our young, we must be neither surprised nor outraged. To remember is not, after all, the really natural inclination of man.

Were this not so, the Torah would not find it necessary to command the remembering of the Amalekite assault on Israel. [Deuteronomy 25:17–19]. The Torah commands it precisely because it is natural for man to forget, for memories to fade, for emotions to be calmed, and for wounds to heal. The Torah commands remembering because only a believing community can transcend time, can fixate on events of very limited "historic" significance (how "significant" was the Exodus to the ancient world whose records never mention it?) and find in them the significance of a redemption history apparent only to the eyes of faith. For believing Israel, the Holocaust is not just another mass murder but, perhaps, the final circumcision of the people of God. But how else, except by the power of God, can anyone believe that?

One final word about the theology of Emil Fackenheim. Israel's faith has always centered about the saving acts of God: the election, the Exodus, the Temple, and the Messiah. However more prevalent destruction was in the history of Israel, the acts of destruction were enshrined in minor fast days while those of redemption became the joyous proclamations of the Passover and Tabernacles, of Hanukkah and Purim. The God of Israel is a redeeming God; this is the only message we are authorized to proclaim, however much it may not seem so to the eyes of nonbelief. Should the Holocaust cease to be peripheral to the faith of Israel, should it enter the Holy of Holies and become the dominant voice that Israel hears, it could not but be a demonic voice that it would be hearing. There is no salvation to be extracted from the Holocaust, no faltering Judaism can be revived by it, no new reason for the continuation of the Jewish people can be found in it. If there is hope after the Holocaust, it is because to those who believe, the voices of the prophets speak more loudly than did Hitler, and because the divine promise sweeps over the crematoria and silences the Voice of Auschwitz.

Eliezer Berkovits

Eliezer Berkovits (1908–1992) was born into an Orthodox Jewish family in Transylvania, which then was part of the Austro-Hungarian empire and which today is
located in northern Romania. As a young man he received a traditional Jewish
education, and this prepared him to continue his studies at the Hildesheimer Rabbinical Seminary in Berlin, Germany. After completing his rabbinical studies, he
moved on to the University of Berlin and received his doctorate in philosophy in
1933. He then began his rabbinical career and held pulpits in Berlin (1934–1939);
Leeds, England (1940–1946); Sydney, Australia (1946–1950); and finally Boston
(1950–1958). In 1958, he gave up the communal rabbinate to assume the chairmanship of the Department of Jewish Philosophy at the Hebrew Theological College
in Skokie, Illinois, where he became an outstanding teacher to generations of rabbinical students. He published a series of significant works on subjects ranging from
the Bible to modern Jewish thought. These publications include his influential study
God, Man, and History, published in 1959; his wide-ranging study of other major
twentieth-century Jewish thinkers, *Major Themes in Modern Philosophies of Judaism,*
published in 1974; and his three well-known works on the Holocaust, *Faith after the
Holocaust* (1973), *Crisis and Faith* (1975), and *With God in Hell: Judaism in the Ghettos
and Camps* (1979).

SELECTIONS

The first and longer of the two Berkovits selections reproduced here is drawn from his
Faith after the Holocaust. In this thoughtful work, Berkovits seeks to defend God after
Auschwitz. Beginning with the premise that the Holocaust is not unique, that the
Jewish people have "had innumerable Auschwitzes," he returns to classical responses
to the "problem of evil" and, while acknowledging that the Holocaust was "an
injustice countenanced by God," nevertheless seeks to explain the Holocaust by
combining two classical arguments. The first appeals to the notion of *Hester Panim,* the
hiding of God's face, i.e., there are times when God mysteriously and inexplicably—
and without any obvious human cause such as sin—turns His face away from man.
The second argument recycles the seminal doctrine of "free will."

Berkovits argues that God's hiddenness is required in order for man to be a moral
creature. God's hiddenness brings into being the possibility for ethically salient human action, for by "absenting" Himself from history He creates the reality of human freedom, which is necessary for moral behavior. Moreover, for human morality
to be a real possibility, God has to respect the decisions of mankind and be bound by
them. He has to abstain from reacting immediately to evil deeds if our actions are to
possess value. Yet, just as moral humanity requires freedom, freedom is always open
to abuse.

The second selection, drawn from Berkovits's *Crisis and Faith,* gives expression to his profound conviction that God, after the Holocaust, has returned to an identifiable role in human history, primarily through the ending of the long night of Jewish exile and the creation of the State of Israel. For Berkovits, the State of Israel is nothing short of an act of Divine Providence in response to the death camps.

Selected Bibliography

Books by Eliezer Berkovits

Faith after the Holocaust (New York, 1973).
Major Themes in Modern Philosophies of Judaism (New York, 1974).
Crisis and Faith (New York, 1975).
With God in Hell: Judaism in the Ghettos and Death Camps (New York, 1979).

Works about Eliezer Berkovits

Fox, Marvin. "Berkovits' Treatment of the Problem of Evil," *Tradition* 14, no. 3 (Spring 1974): 116–124.
Katz, Steven T. "Eliezer Berkovits's Post-Holocaust Jewish Theodicy," in Steven T. Katz, *Post-Holocaust Dialogues: Critical Studies in Modern Jewish Thought* (New York, 1983), pp. 268–286.
Raffel, Charles M. "Eliezer Berkovits," in *Contemporary Jewish Thinkers*, edited by Steven T. Katz (Washington, D.C., 1993), pp. 1–16.
Braiterman, Zachary. *(God) after Auschwitz* (Princeton, N.J., 1998).

FAITH AFTER THE HOLOCAUST

The Hiding of the Face

The problem thus raised by the prophets and the teachers of the Talmud is of course the age-old problem of the theodicy. The manner of its formulation testifies to the fact that there was a full realization in biblical and Talmudic times that there is indeed undeserved suffering in history.[1] This, of course, requires a modification of the concept of *mipnei hataeinu,* "Because of our sins." No doubt it does demand great strength of character of an individual—and how much more of an entire people—to acknowledge that one's misfortunes are due to one's own failings and to accept responsibility for them.[2] At the same time, looking at the entire course of Jewish history, the idea that all this has befallen us because of our sins is an utterly unwarranted exaggeration. There is suffering because of sins; but that all suffering is due to it is simply not true. The idea that the Jewish martyrology through the ages can be explained as divine judgment is obscene. Nor do we for a single moment entertain the thought that what happened to European Jewry in our generation was divine punishment for sins committed by them. It was injustice absolute; injustice countenanced by God.

In biblical terminology, we speak of *hester panim,* the Hiding of the Face, God's hiding of his countenance from the sufferer. Man seeks God in his tribulation but cannot find him. It is, however, seldom realized that "The Hiding of

---

1. This is true, notwithstanding the attempt by some talmudic teachers to interpret the phenomenon as an appropriate balancing of justice between this world and the world to come. See, for instance, B.T. *Kiddushin,* 39 b. Medieval Jewish philosophers often follow the same inadequate argument.

2. Not to be confused with the Christian interpretation of Jewish history. The Jew says: because of our sins. The Christian maintains: Because of your sins.

the Face" has two meanings in the Bible, which are in no way related to each other. It is generally assumed that the expression signifies divine judgment and punishment. We find it indicated, for instance, in Deuteronomy 31:17–18 in the words:

> Then My anger shall be kindled against them in that day, and I will forsake them, and I will hide My face from them, and they shall be devoured, and many evils and troubles shall come upon them;..., And I will surely hide My face in that day for all the evil which they shall have wrought, in that they are turned unto other gods.

But the Bible also speaks of the Hiding of the Face when human suffering results, not from divine judgment, but from the evil perpetrated by man. Even the innocent may feel himself forsaken because of the Hiding of the Face. A moving example of this form of *hester panim* is the Forty-Fourth Psalm, from which we have already quoted a short passage. One should study the entire psalm: we shall recall here only its closing verses:

> All this is come upon us; yet have we not
>   forgotten Thee,
> Neither have we been false to Thy covenant.
> Our heart is not turned back,
> Neither have our steps declined from Thy
>   path;
> Though Thou hast crushed us into a place of
>   jackals,
> And covered us with the shadow of death.
> If we had forgotten the name of our God,
> Or spread forth our hands to a strange god;
> Would not God search this out?
> For he knoweth the secrets of the heart.
> Nay, but for Thy sake are we killed all the
>   day;
> We are accounted as sheep for the slaughter.
> Awake, why sleepest Thou, O Lord?
> Arouse Thyself, cast not off for ever.
> Wherefore hidest Thou Thy face,
> And forgettest our affliction and our
>   oppression?
> For our soul is bowed down to the dust;
> Our belly cleaveth to the earth.
> Arise for our help,
> And redeem us for Thy mercy's sake.

The Hiding of the Face about which the Psalmist complains is altogether different from its meaning in Deuteronomy. There it is a manifestation of divine anger and judgment over the wicked; here it is indifference—God seems to be unconcernedly asleep during the tribulations inflicted by man on his fellow. Of the first kind of *hester panim* one might say that it is due to *mipnei ḥataeinu*, that it is judgment because of sins committed, but not of the second kind. It is God hiding himself mysteriously from the cry of the innocent. It is the divine silence of which the rabbis spoke in the Talmud.

The Affirmation

Not only had the problem already been raised in all seriousness and full intellectual honesty in biblical and talmudic times, it was also fully realized that at stake was God's presence in history. There was full awareness that the seriousness of the problem was apt to lead many a Jew to what is today called radical theology or the rejection of divine concern with human destiny. Ezekiel reported about the reaction of some people to the catastrophe of the destruction of the Temple and the loss of independence. He quotes their words: "...The Lord seeth us not, the Lord hath forsaken the land."[3] Like Ivan Karamazov, they too maintained that since God has absented himself, all was permissible. These were the early radical theologians in ancient Israel. The prophet Malachi, too, knew them. It is to them that he lets the words of God be addressed:

> Your words have been all too strong against
>   Me,
> Saith the Lord.
> Yet ye say: "Wherein have we spoken against
>   Thee?"
> Ye have said: "It is vain to serve God;
> And what profit is it that we have kept His
>   charge,
> And that we have walked mournfully
> Because of the Lord of hosts?

3. Ezekiel 8:12.

And now we call the proud happy;
Yea, they that work wickedness are built up;
Yea, they try God, and are delivered.[4]

"To walk mournfully because of the Lord" is not to walk like Ivan Karamazov, not to consider everything permissible, but to live obeying the laws of God. It is, however, useless to do so. God is not really concerned or, perhaps, he cannot do much about it anyway. For do not the wicked prosper and are not the proud happy? Is not evil successful? How may it be reconciled with God's providential presence?

Such were the radical theologians of old Israel. There is at least one outstanding figure known to us in talmudic times who belongs in the same category. He was Elisha ben Abuyah, at one time the teacher of the great Rabbi Meir. He lost his faith because he could find no solution to the problem of the theodicy. In view of the suffering of the innocent, he questioned God's justice and providence. He found no answer and became *Aḥer,* a changed person. According to one opinion he witnessed the accidental death of a young boy who was engaged in a work by which he was fulfilling a biblical commandment and also obeying the will of his father, thus honoring him as also required by the Bible. According to another version, he saw how the tongue of the martyred Hutspith, the Interpreter, was dragged along by a pig. He exclaimed at the sight: "The mouth from which issued wisdom like pearls should lick the dirt!" At that, "he went cut and sinned."[5] There were others like him, less distinguished. Inevitably, in the course of Jewish history, the quest and the questioning continued. We even have a prayer for the radical theologian on record. According to one interpretation, in the abridged form of the *Amidah* we pray "For those who in this long exile are critical of God, believing that He has forsaken them. May they experience God's providential care, His mercy and grace."[6]

If Judaism rejected its radical theologians through the ages, it was not because of lack of sensitivity to the seriousness of the problem that they raised. The men of faith in Israel knew very well of the problem. They experienced it in their own lives on their own bodies. How often did they cry out in their agony over the terrible experience of God's absence! The Psalms, for example, are replete with the experience and the cry. Who could have felt the absence of God more crushingly than the man who exclaimed:

Awake, why sleepest Thou, O Lord?
Arouse Thyself, cast not off forever.
Wherefore hidest Thou Thy face,
And forgettest our affliction and our
    oppression?
For our soul is bowed down to the dust;
Our belly cleaveth unto the earth.
Arise for our help,
And redeem us for Thy mercy's sake![7]

It was the excruciating experience of divine indifference that caused the psalmist to plead:

How long, O Lord, wilt Thou forget me for
    ever?
How long wilt Thou hide Thy face from
    me?[8]

The intensity of the experience comes to most moving expression in the phrase: "wilt Thou forget me for ever?" No one ever has an everlasting experience. The phrase tells of the long wait for divine help that was all in vain; it conveys the idea of utter hopelessness, of radical abandonment by God. The words would not have been inadequate for the agony of the death camps.

It is because of the apparent divine unconcern that the psalmist has to cry out:

Arise, O Lord: O God, lift up Thy hand;
Forget not the humble.
Wherefore doth the wicked condemn God,
And say in his heart: "Thou wilt not re-
    quire"?[9]

Such passages, and numerous others of the same kind, give expression to the struggles of men of faith against the demonic in history. They

4. Malachi 3:13–15.
5. B.T. *Kiddushin,* 39 b.
6. According to Rabbenu Yona, quoted in *Kesef Mishne,* Maimonides, [*Mishneh Torah*] *Hilkhot Tefilla,* 2, 2.
7. Psalms 44:24–27.
8. Ibid., 13:2.
9. Ibid., 10:12.

are the questioning, searching, yes! even the accusing cry of faith induced by God's silence in the face of evil. It is also the lament of Isaiah, when he declares:

> But Zion said: "The Lord hath forsaken me,
> And the Lord hath forgotten me."[10]

Obviously, to feel that one is forgotten by God is not a realization that one is being punished for one's sins. Whom God punishes is not forgotten by God. Zion's plight of being abandoned and forgotten is the experience of divine unconcern, of God's indifference toward human destiny. Through the ages, men of faith knew that human suffering was not to be explained by divine punishment alone, as expiation for guilt and divine justice done. They knew well that the poor and the weak were the victims, that wickedness and evil often held the upper hand, that God was often silent in history.

The experience of God's "absence" is not new: Each generation had its Auschwitz problem. Neither is the negative response of resulting disbelief new in the history of Jewish spiritual struggle: Each generation had its radical theology. Yet, the men of faith in Israel, each facing his own Auschwitz, in the midst of their radical abandonment by God, did not hesitate to reject the negative resolution of the problem. Notwithstanding the fact that so much in their experience tended to lead to the conclusion that there is "neither judgment nor a Judge," they insisted: "Still there is judgment and there is a Judge." Significantly, the formulation is Rabbi Akiba's, himself—as we saw—the saintly giant of Jewish martyrdom.[11]

However, if the problem were seen so clearly, how was it met? Needless to say, what we have called the simplistic theory of history that wishes to explain it all by the principle of "because of our sins," the idea that if a man does the will of God and lives uprightly all will be well with him and that if he suffers his very suffering testifies against him, was indeed rejected. But the rabbis spoke of the silence of God as a historical fact, not of His absence. The one who is silent may be so

called only because He is present. Somehow they are able to hold onto both ends of the dilemma. It is not an either-or proposition for them. Indeed the same may be said of the nature of the problem as it is originally raised in the Bible. The same Jeremiah who contends with God because the way of the wicked prosper, also refers to God as "the righteous judge who examines the reins and the heart."[12] He predicts the destruction of Jerusalem because of the sins of her people. Habakkuk, too, in the very same context in which he complains about God's standing by as the wicked swallow up the righteous also speaks of the scourge of the Chaldeans, "that bitter and impetuous nation" that is sent out by God "for a judgment and established for a correction."[13] In the same breath, he holds onto the theory of God's worldwide historic providence of justice as well as to the facts of history which seem to contradict it. This dramatic grasping at once both horns of the dilemma finds its most moving expression in Job, when he exclaims:

> Though he slay me, yet will I trust in Him;
> But I will argue my ways before Him.[14]

There is trust in God to the end; yet there is contest with Him, because the facts of human experience seem to assail that trust. How was it possible for these men to retain their faith in the God of history, in His justice and providence, notwithstanding the fact that their own historical experience seemed to contradict the faith and the trust?

Much more astounding, however, is the fact that even though the Jewish people were fully aware of the conflict between history and teaching, yet they staked their very existence on the original biblical proposition that life and the moral good were identical, as were death and evil; on the view that all history was ultimately under divine control, that all depended on doing the will of God, on living in accordance with His Torah. Flying in the face of all historical experience, they organized their own existence in history on the proposition that "the Eternal is nigh unto all of them that call

---

10. Isaiah 49:14.
11. [*Midrash*] *Bereshit Rabba,* 29, 14.
12. Jeremiah 11:20.

13. Habakkuk 1:12.
14. Job 13:15.

upon Him, to all that call upon Him in truth."[15] Nor did they do it naively, childishly, not realizing the full implication of their undertaking. After Jeremiah, Habakkuk, Job, and the divine silence actually experienced in their history, how could they affirm three times daily in their prayers that "the Eternal is good to all and His tender mercies are over all His works"[16] without a great deal of sophistication! A quality of this sophistication I find in a midrash that deals with our subject. It is a comment on the words of the psalmist "The Eternal preserveth the faithful."[17] Playing on the Hebrew *emumin* (faithful) and its association *amen* (an exclamatory affirmation) and *emunah* (faith, trust), it is maintained in the typical midrashic style: "The faithful," these are those who answer with *Amen* in complete trust (*emunah*). What does this mean? They say: "Blessed be the One who quickens the dead." It has not yet come about, nevertheless they believe in God, that He does quicken the dead. They say: "Blessed be the Redeemer of Israel." But He has not redeemed them, except for a very short period, after which they became once more oppressed; yet, they believe that "I shall redeem them.... O for the faithful whom God preserves."[18] One can almost see the sad smiles on the faces of the rabbis who left us with this comment. "God preserves the faithful?" God the Redeemer, the Resurrector? Indeed? Yes, indeed. Nevertheless, and in spite of it all, it is so. We adorn God with a great many attributes which mean to describe His actions in history even though they are contradicted by the facts of history. Fully aware of the facts, with open eyes, we contradict our experience with our affirmations. Yes, all these attributes of God in history are true; for if they are not true now, they will yet be true.

The Explanation

It would seem to us that what the just-quoted midrash wishes to convey is the idea that God is what Judaism believes Him to be. True enough,

many of His attributes are not manifest in history, but they will yet be revealed. On what grounds could such a statement have been made?

We have discussed earlier the two different forms of *hester panim*, of the "hiding of the face": one as judgment, the other as apparent divine indifference toward the plight of man. We may glean a hint of the theological significance of such apparent divine indifference from a passage in Isaiah. The prophet says of God:

Verily Thou art a God that hidest Thyself,
O God of Israel, the Savior.[19]

In this passage God's self-hiding is not a reaction to human behavior, when the hiding of the face represents God's turning away from man as a punishment. For Isaiah, God's self-hiding is an attribute of divine nature. Such is God. He is a God who hides Himself. Man may seek Him and He will not be found; man may call to Him and He may not answer. God's hiding His face in this case is not a response to man, but a quality of being assumed by God on His own initiative. But neither is it due to divine indifference toward the destiny of man. God's hiding Himself is an attribute of the God of Israel, who is the Savior. In some mysterious way, the God who hides Himself is the God who saves. Thus, Isaiah could also say:

And I will wait for the Lord that hideth His face from the house of Jacob and I will hope for Him.[20]

One may well wait and hope for the God who hides His face, if the God who hides Himself is the Savior. But how may the hiding of the face assume this second meaning and become a divine attribute in such close association with God's self-revelation as the Savior? An analysis of a talmudic passage may lead us to an appreciation of this second—and more fundamental—meaning of the concept of the hiding of the face. It is no mere coincidence that it happens to be a discussion between Rabbi Meir and his quondam teacher Elisha ben Abuyah, who became *Aḥer*,

15. Psalms 145:18.
16. Ibid., 145:9.
17. Ibid., 31:24.

18. *Midrash Tehillim*, 31.
19. Isaiah 45:15.
20. Ibid., 8, 17.

"another," because of the problem of evil on earth. It is said that after *Aher* had turned into the "path of licentiousness," he asked Rabbi Meir: "What is the meaning of the saying that 'God hath also made the one over against the other'?"[21] Answered the former disciple: "Whatever the Holy one, blessed be He, created in his world, he also created its opposite. He created mountains and He created hills; He created oceans and He created rivers." To which *Aher* countered: "Not like this spoke your master Rabbi Akiba. But said he: God created the righteous and He created the wicked; he created Gan Eden [Paradise] and He created Gehenna."[22]

The dating of the discussion as having taken place "after *Aher* had turned into the path of licentiousness" is an indication that the subject of the discussion has some bearing on *Aher*'s problem and heresy. What is it they are discussing? It would seem to us that the subject of their discussion is the dialectical principle, which is seen as a principle of creation, incorporated in the functioning of the universe. Rabbi Meir expresses it in general terms. Whatever God created, He also created its opposite. It could not be otherwise. There could be no mountains without valleys. A thing is defined by its limits. It is recognizable for what it is by the contrast to its opposite. A is A because it is limited by non-A; it has selfhood because it is encumbered, because it is denied by non-A. Rabbi Akiba seems to express the same dialectical principle, but he gives it a limited ethical application. The dialectics of creation is responsible for the opposites: the righteous and the wicked, good and evil. Without good, no evil; without evil, no good! Why then did Aher oppose the general formula of the dialectical principle, holding onto the manner of its specifically ethical application by Rabbi Akiba? There is a vast distinction between Rabbi Meir's grasp of the dialectics of creation and the way *Aher* wants it to be understood. The example in the case, on which *Aher* insists, is adequate to illustrate the dialectics. However, it must have been noted that Rabbi Meir's example is some-

what gauche. The dialectical contrast would have to be between mountains and valleys, oceans and continents, not between mountains and hills nor between oceans and rivers. Yet, in his opening comment, Rabbi Meir invokes the dialectics of creation. It would seem to us that in Rabbi Meir's opinion the dialectics in creation does not represent pure opposites. The contrast is not absolute but relative. There is no absolute valley as there is no absolute mountain; the highest mountain is only a high hill and the lowest valley is really a bit of a hill. So too with the opposites of water and land. Neither the oceans nor the continents are absolutely alien to each other. The difference is only a relative one, like the one between oceans and rivers, like that between more and less. There is neither absolute depth to which to sink, nor absolute heights to which to rise. *Aher* cannot accept it, for the former disciple really discusses the problem and case of his sometime master. If the opposites of creation are absolutes, then good and evil too are absolutes; the Creator is then directly responsible for both. He is then really beyond good and evil, for He is equally involved in both or, as one might also say, He is indifferent to ethical considerations. If so, *Aher* is right; there is neither judgment nor a Judge. It is for this reason that he insists on citing Rabbi Akiba whose formulation seems to suggest this kind of divine irresponsibility or indifference. The opposites, according to this version, are the *tsadik* (righteous) and the *rasha* (wicked). God himself created both, is *Aher*'s interpretation of Rabbi Akiba's statement. The *tsadik* is what he is and the *rasha* is what he is; the one is not to be praised, the other, not to be condemned. God Himself created them that way. They are part of a universe that has no partiality for either of them. And once again, *Aher* himself is vindicated. It is exactly this kind of interpretation that Rabbi Meir wishes to obviate by his "bad" example of the dialectics. The opposites are not absolutes, which means they are not categories of creation. Rabbi Meir is not in disagreement with Rabbi Akiba. It is *Aher* who insists on an interpretation of Rabbi Akiba's

21. Ecclesiastes 7:14. More in keeping with the Hebrew original, and in conformity with the manner in which the verse was understood by the rabbis in the Talmud,

we depart somewhat from the rendering of the verse in the R. V.
22. B.T. *Hagiga*, 15 a.

statement that was never intended by its author. Rabbi Akiba never meant to say that God actually creates the *tsadik* and the *rasha,* that good and evil are indifferently incorporated in the universe. His whole life contradicts this kind of a teaching. Nor is it likely that *Aḥer* was unaware of it. It is with tongue in cheek that he reminds his former disciple: "Not like this did your master Rabbi Akiba explain it." Rabbi Meir spoke in general terms; he did not expatiate on the dialectics of good and evil, of the righteous and the wicked. Out of tact and consideration for the feelings of his former teacher, he did not pursue the implications for ethics and morality of a dialectics that does not recognize absolutes as ontological categories of creation. *Aḥer* understood him well. One imagines the impishly appreciative smile on his face as he was saying: "Not like this did your master explain it." Indeed, not like this; yet, exactly like this.

Rabbi Akiba expresses in ethical terms the significance of the dialectics of Rabbi Meir. God does not determine in advance that one person be a *tsadiq,* and another a *rasha.* But unless the possibility existed for a man to be a *rasha,* if he so desires, one could not only be a *rasha,* one could not be a *tsadiq* either. For one can only be a *tsadiq* as a result of responsible choices made in the freedom of available alternatives. Where the choice is nonexistent, where the possibility of becoming a *rasha* is not open to man, the possibility of becoming a *tsadiq* too has been excluded. The ethical significance of Rabbi Meir's "bad" dialectics is that being a *tsadiq* is conditioned by man's freedom to choose the way of wickedness, just as being a *rasha* presupposes his freedom to turn into the path of righteousness. The *tsadiq* is defined by the *rasha* as the *rasha* is defined by the *tsadiq.* That which is good is so because of the possibility of evil and vice versa. If, now, the dialectical principle is at work in the universe yet the opposites are not to be understood as absolute categories of creation and being, then God's creating the *tsadiq* and the *rasha* means that God created both possibilities for man, to be a *tsadiq* or to be a *rasha.* We have quoted Isaiah's statement earlier that God forms the light and creates darkness, makes peace and creates evil. Isaiah of course did not mean to say that God actually does evil. Rejecting Manichaean dualism, the prophet maintains that God alone is the Creator. He created evil by creating the possibility for evil; He made peace by creating the possibility for it.[23] He had to create the possibility for evil, if He were to create the possibility for its opposite: peace, goodness, love.

In a sense, God can be neither good nor bad. In terms of His own nature He is incapable of evil. He is the only one who *is* goodness. But since, because of His very essence, He can do no evil, He can do no good either. God, being incapable of the unethical is not an ethical being. Goodness for Him is neither an ideal, nor a value; it is existence, it is absolutely realized being. Justice, love, peace, mercy are ideals for man only. They are values that may be realized by man alone. God is perfection. Yet because of His very perfection, He is lacking—as it were—one type of value, the one which is the result of striving for value. He is all light; on just that account, He is lacking the light that comes out of the darkness. One might also say that with man the good is axiology; with God, ontology. Man alone can strive and struggle for the good; God is Good. Man alone can create value; God is Value. But if man alone is the creator of values, one who strives for the realization of ideals, then he must have freedom of choice and freedom of decision. And his freedom must be respected by God Himself. God cannot as a rule intervene whenever man's use of freedom displeases Him. It is true, if He did so the perpetration of evil would be rendered impossible, but so would the possibility for good also disappear. Man can be frightened; but he cannot be bludgeoned into goodness. If God did not respect man's freedom to choose his course in personal responsibility, not only would the moral good and evil be abolished from the earth, but man himself would go with them. For freedom and responsibility are of the very essence of man. Without them man is not human. If there is to be man, he must be allowed to make his choices in freedom. If he has such freedom, he will use it. Using it, he will often use it wrongly; he will decide for the wrong

---

23. See our discussion of the quotation from Isaiah and the concept of creation connected with it in our book, *God, Man and History* (New York, 1959), ch. 9.

alternative. As he does so, there will be suffering for the innocent.

The question therefore is not: Why is there undeserved suffering? But, why is there man? He who asks the question about injustice in history really asks: Why a world? Why creation? To understand this is of course far from being an answer to our problem. But to see a problem in its true dimension makes it easier for us to make peace with the circumstances from which it arises. It is not very profitable to argue with God as to why He created this world. He obviously decided to take His chance with man; He decided for this world. Given man, God Himself could eliminate moral evil and the suffering caused by it only by eliminating man, by recalling the world of man into nothingness.

These theological concepts have found their more intimate expression in the language of religious affirmation. We are familiar with biblical passages that speak of God's mercy with the sinner. We readily appreciate pronouncements like the one in Ezekiel that declares:

> As I live, saith the Lord God, I have no pleasure in the death of the wicked, but that the wicked turn from his way and live.[24]

In keeping with deep-rooted biblical tradition, the rabbis in a homily interpreted the plural form of the Hebrew expression that describes God as "long-suffering" as meaning that God is long-suffering in numerous ways. He is long-suffering with the wicked as well as with the righteous. We have great understanding for the fact that God is merciful and forgiving, that He does not judge man harshly and is willing to have patience with him. God is waiting for the sinner to find his way to Him. This is how we like to see God. This is how we are only too glad to acknowledge Him. But we never seem to realize that while God is long-suffering, the wicked are going about their dark business on earth and the result is ample suffering for the innocent. While God waits for the sinner to turn to Him, there is oppression and persecution and violence among men. Yet, there seems to be no alternative. If man is to be, God must be long-

suffering with him; He must suffer man. This is the inescapable paradox of divine providence. While God tolerates the sinner, He must abandon the victim; while He shows forbearance with the wicked, He must turn a deaf ear to the anguished cries of the violated. This is the ultimate tragedy of existence: God's very mercy and forbearance, His very love for man, necessitates the abandonment of some men to a fate that they may well experience as divine indifference to justice and human suffering. It is the tragic paradox of faith that God's direct concern for the wrongdoer should be directly responsible for so much pain and sorrow on earth.

We conclude then: He who demands justice of God must give up man; he who asks for God's love and mercy beyond justice must accept suffering.

One may call it the divine dilemma that God's *erek apayim* His patiently waiting countenance to some, is, of necessity, identical with His *hester panim,* His hiding of the countenace, to others. However, the dilemma does find a resolution in history. If man is to be, God Himself must respect his freedom of decision. If man is to act on his own responsibility, without being continually overawed by divine supremacy, God must absent Himself from history. But man left to his freedom is capable of greatness in both—in creative goodness and destructive evil. Though man cannot be man without freedom, his performance in history gives little reassurance that he can survive in freedom. God took a risk with man and He cannot divest himself of responsibility for man. If man is not to perish at the hand of man, if the ultimate destiny of man is not to be left to the chance that man will never make the fatal decision, God must not withdraw His providence from His creation. He must be present in history. That man may be, God must absent Himself; that man may not perish in the tragic absurdity of his own making, God must remain present. The God of history must be absent and present concurrently. He hides His presence. He is present without being indubitably manifest; He is absent without being hopelessly inaccessible. Thus, many find Him even in his "Absence"; many miss Him even in His presence. Because of the necessity of His absence, there is the "hiding of the face" and suffering of the innocent; because of the necessity of His presence,

24. Ezekiel 33:11.

evil will not ultimately triumph; because of it, there is hope for man.

Mighty and Awesome

In other words, God's presence in history must remain—mostly—unconvincing. But, perhaps, this is a mere theory, unsupported by experience? After all, how can one prove an unconvincing presence convincingly? There is another passage in the Talmud that leads us to a deeper grasp of our problem and its possible solution. Ezra, the great rejuvenator of Judaism at the time of the return from Babylon, and his associates in his endeavors were known as the "Men of the Great Assembly." The Talmud discusses the question of this honorific title. How did they deserve it? The answer is given. They were so called because they restored the old glory of the divine crown. The "crown" was described by Moses when he called God: "the great God, the mighty and the awful."[25] But Jeremiah, in the light of the experiences of his generation, could not accept this description. He was perplexed. Strangers mock Him in His sanctuary! Where is His awesomeness? No longer did he say of God, as did Moses, that He was "awful." Then came Daniel. His charge was: Strangers subjugate His children! Where are His mighty deeds? He stopped saying of God that He was mighty. But then came Ezra and his assembly and they explained: "That indeed is His mightiness that He subdues His inclination and grants long-suffering to the wicked. And this in itself is a proof of His awesomeness; for were it not for the fear of Him, how could one people (i.e., Israel) survive among the nations."[26] One might say that as a challenge to faith the problems of Jeremiah and Daniel were not different in essence from the problem of the present post-Auschwitz generation of Jews. The vulgarity that God might have died did not enter the mind of Jeremiah or Daniel. But they were perplexed by their God. How was He to be understood? What were His attributes in view of the manner of His functioning in history? If God's enemies feared Him, they would not dare mock Him. If God were mighty, He would use His might to protect His people.

Most noteworthy in this discussion of our problem is the complete antithesis in the position of the side that raises the question and the one that offers the solution. The question as to God's presence in history is raised on the assumption that the fear of God ought to subdue the enemies of God and the power of God ought to protect God's people. The answer is based on a radical redefinition of the concepts of the fear and the might of God. The mightiness of God is shown in His tolerance of the mocking of His enemies; it is revealed in His long-suffering. This is in keeping with the interpretation of the words of the psalmist that we quoted earlier: "Who is like unto You among the mighty?"—enduring insults and remaining silent. The awesomeness of God is revealed in the survival of Israel. The meaning of the redefinition of the concept of the divine power is twofold. First of all, it means that it is impossible for God to be present in history by using His physical omnipotence. If God had meant to rule the world of man by material might He might well have given up the thought at its very conception. Man can only exist because God renounces the use of His power on him. This, of course, means that God cannot be present in history through manifest material power. Such presence would destroy history. History is the arena for human responsibility and its product. When God intervenes in the affairs of men by physical might as, for instance, in the story of Exodus, we speak of a miracle. But the miracle is outside of history; in it history is at a standstill. However, beyond that we are introduced to a concept of divine mightiness that consists in self-restraint. For the omnipotent God to act powerfully would indeed be a small matter. The rabbis in the Talmud saw the mightiness of the Almighty in that He controls His inclination to judge and to punish and behaves in history as if He were powerless. To curb the use of power where infinite power is at hand, to endure the mocking of one's enemies when one could easily eliminate them, that is true strength. Such is the mightiness of God. God is mighty, for He shackles His omnipotence and becomes "powerless" so that

25. Deuteronomy, 10, 17.
26. B.T. *Yoma*, 69 a. For the references to Jeremiah, Daniel, Ezra, cf. Jeremiah, 32, 18; Daniel, 9, 4; Nehemiah, 9, 32.

history may be possible. In spite of His infinite power, He does not frighten man but lets him find his own way, extending to him his long-suffering. God is mighty in the renunciation of His might in order to bear with man.

Yet He is present in history. He reveals His presence in the survival of His people Israel. Therein lies His awesomeness. God renders Himself powerless, as it were, through forbearance and long-suffering, yet He guides. How else could His powerless people have survived! He protects, without manifest power. Because of that, Israel could endure God's long silences without denying Him. Because of the survival of Israel, the prophets could question God's justice and yet believe in Him. The theology of a God unconvincingly present in history alone might not have sufficed. The dilemma cannot be resolved on the intellectual level alone. And, indeed, neither Jeremiah, nor Habakkuk, nor even Job, were given an intellectually valid answer. The talmudic conclusion was correctly reached: God was silent. Yet, the dilemma was resolved, not in theory, but, strangely enough, in history itself. Now, historical facts that conflict with a philosophy of history *eo ipso* refute that philosophy. But historical facts, however numerous, cannot refute another historical fact however irregular and solitary. It is indeed true, as was seen by Jeremiah, Habakkuk, and others, that a great deal of the historical experience contradicts some essential Judaic propositions of a just and benevolent providence; the way of the wicked often succeeds, God is much too often silent. But it is even more true that seen in the light of the generally observed facts and processes of history, the very idea of a people of God, of constituting a people on the basis of a commitment to do the will of God and to the belief that life and death are determined by the ethical categories of good and evil, was a fantastic proposition. All history advised against it. From the very beginning, all the powers and processes that determine the course of history were poised to render its materialization impossible. Indeed, had it all been only an idea, a theology or philosophy, the testimony of the facts of history would have rendered the concept of a people of God and the propositions on which it was to be based ridiculously absurd. However, this fantastic concept became itself a fact of history. The people

of God did come into being; it entered history, it became itself a historical reality, exercising great historical influence and demonstrating mysterious survival power. It has all been quite irregular. It is all in conflict with the rest of historical experience, yet itself a fact of history.

There is this difference between a fact and an idea. The more irregular an idea is, i.e., the less it is in harmony with the generally prevailing principles relevant to it, the less the likelihood that it is valid and true. The same may be said of a philosophy of history: The more it is contradicted by historical experience, the less tenable it is. But a fact obeys the opposite rule. The more irregular it is, the more unique it is, the less in keeping with what is generally observed and experienced, the greater is its significance. The more intensely a unique historical reality is disavowed and challenged by the overwhelming force of a universal historical experience, and yet is able to maintain itself and to survive all conflicts and all challenges, it has by its very staying power proved its unique vitality as well as the validity of the principle which it proclaims. Such a unique and absurdly irregular historic fact has been the people of God. But because it is a historic fact of inexplicable surviving power, the more it is challenged by the facts of universal history, the more is it confirmed in the unique stands which it takes, simply because it does take that stand and survives in spite of it all. Jeremiah could face with complete intellectual honesty the unpleasant fact that the way of the wicked does prosper, without embracing it as an ultimate truth in history upon which to base a Machiavellian type of philosophy. He could do that because the reality of Israel, notwithstanding all its contemporary misery, pointed as a fact in the opposite direction. The rabbis of the Talmud could speak of the silence of God at the time of the destruction of the Temple and the state and yet remain true to His word, because notwithstanding the *ḥurban* Israel survived, remained historically viable, full of future expectation.

This, however, means that a Jewish philosophy of history is not to be based on the teachings alone. The teaching, as such, is contradicted by a great deal of historical experience. But neither should Jews allow such conflicting evidence to sway them in determining their outlook on history, for such evidence itself is contradicted by their own existence, by the historic reality of Israel, by the place of the Jewish people in history, by the survival of the people of God; yes, by the fact that once again this people of God is back in its ancient homeland, in Zion and Jerusalem.

It would seem to us that there are two histories: one, that of the nations and the other, that of Israel. The history of the nations is self-explanatory. It is naturalistic history, explainable in terms of power and economics. It is exactly on those terms that the history of Israel remains a sealed secret: It defies that kind of interpretation. The history of Israel alone is not self-explanatory; it testifies to a supranatural dimension jutting into history. Now, if the two could have been neatly divided and separated from each other, things might have worked out quite nicely. There would not have been either anti-Semitism or pogroms, either ghettos or crematoria. But unavoidably, both histories take place in the same time dimension and occupy the same space; together they form the history of mankind. Of necessity, the two histories interpenetrate. Thus, in the naturalistic realm occasionally the Voice is heard and a glimpse is gained of the presence of the supranatural in this world. On the other hand, the wild unbridled forces of the naturalistic realm ever so often invade—and wreak havoc in—the this-worldly domain in which sustenance of meaning and purpose is drawn from the supernatural dimension.

Jews are confused in our times because they imagine that the problem of Jewish faith arises from the conflict between Jewish teaching and Jewish or general historical experience. In fact, the conflict takes place between two histories. There are two realms: the realm of the Is and that of the Ought. The history of the nations is enacted mainly in the realm of the Is. It is naturalistic history, essentially power history. The history of Israel belongs chiefly in the realm of the Ought; it is faith history, faith that what ought to be, what ought to determine and guide human life, should be and will be. Faith history is at cross-purposes with power history, but history it is. As long as Israel lives the Ought holds onto reality, be it only by the skin of its teeth. As long as this is the case, the Ought has proved its vitality as a this-worldly possibility; it has found admittance into the realm

of the Is. As long as Israel is, the Ought too is; the supernatural has acquired a footing in the natural. As long as this is so there is hope for both—for there is hope for the ultimate merger of the two realms, when the Ought will be fully real and the real will be convincingly identified as the life which is the Good. In the meantime the conflict obtains, not between ideas and philosophies, which is easily bearable, but between fact and fact; between the powerful reality of the Is and the meaningful and mysterious reality of the Ought. Since it is a conflict between fact and fact, history and history, reality and reality, the conflict is clash, a battle accompanied by untold human suffering.

Why has it been so arranged by the God of history? We may not find an explanation. Decisive is, however, the realization that no matter what our solution may be to our specific problems, it must not abandon the truth to which the reality of Israel testifies. No matter how silent God may every so often be, we have heard His voice and because of that we know His word; no matter how empty of God vast tracts of the wastelands of history may appear to be, we know of His presence as we stand astounded contemplating our own existence. True, these are contradictory experiences which present the mind with a serious dilemma. But no matter how serious the dilemma, it cannot erase the fact of the enduring reality of Israel. Even if no answers could be found we would still be left with the only alternative with which Job too was left, i.e., of contending with God while trusting in Him, of questioning while believing, inquiring with our minds yet knowing in our hearts! And even as we search for the answer, praising Him as the rabbis of old did: Who is like You our God, mighty in silence!

The Witness

God's unconvincing presence in history is testified to through the survival of Israel. All God's miracles occur outside of history. When God acts with manifest power, history is at a standstill. The only exception to the rule is the historic reality of Israel. That faith history has not been erased from the face of the earth by power history, notwithstanding the incalculable material superiority of the forces arrayed against it all through history, is the ultimate miracle. Since, however, it has been accomplished without manifest divine intervention, it remains within history, the only miracle that is a historic event, the miracle of the viability of faith history. It is for this reason that Isaiah could say of Israel on behalf of God: "Therefore ye are My witnesses, saith the Eternal, and I am God."[27] Rightly do the rabbis add the comment: If you are my witnesses, I am God; if you do not witness, I am—as it were—no God.[28] There is no other witness that God is present in history but the history of the Jewish people. God's own destiny in history is joined to the history of Israel. Great empires do not testify to divine presence in history. Whatever they are and accomplish is fully explicable in terms of their material resources. They have their self-explanatory place in power history. Half a billion Christians all over the world prove nothing about God's presence in history. They are too many, too influential, too pervasive. They are a this-worldly power in the context of power history. The same is true of any other of the great world religions. They have too many followers, control too much territory, too many resources of influence and power to prove anything. God is a mere adjunct to their position in history. Their religious affirmatives are incidental to their position in history. They all function in power history. Only a small people whose very existence is forever assailed by the forces of power history and yet survives and has an impact on world history, completely out of proportion to its numbers and its material power, proves the validity of another dimension of reality and testifies to God's "powerless" guidance in the affairs of men. God's own destiny in history is linked to the history of Israel. Only by means of Israel may His, of necessity, unconvincing presence in history be surmised.

This is the ultimate significance of the idea of the chosen people. God needs a small and relatively weak people in order to introduce another dimension into history—human life—not by might nor by power but by His spirit. "The Eternal did not love you nor choose you because you were more numerous than any other peo-

ple";[29] He could not associate His cause with the mighty and the numerous. It is not through them that a God who renders Himself "powerless" in history, for the sake of man, can advance His purpose for man. Only a nation whose presence in and impact on history testify to God's presence may be God's people. God's relation to human history is such that He needs a chosen people. The chosen people satisfies a need for divine concern for all men. Why the Jews? No matter whom He would have chosen, they would have to become Jews. This idea of the divine need comes to expression in the passage in Isaiah to which we had occasion previously to refer. The concept of the witness is also stated in the following manner:

Ye are My witnesses, saith the Eternal,
And My servant whom I have chosen;
That ye may know and believe Me, and
    understand
That I am He;
Before Me there was no God formed,
Neither shall any be after Me.[30]

A careful reading of the text will show that Israel does not witness, nor was it chosen, because it knows, believes, and understands. On the contrary, it has been made the witness and has been chosen, so that it may know, believe, and understand. Out of his chosenness, from his own history he should learn to know, to believe, and to understand. He is the witness, whether he knows it or not, whether he consciously testifies or refuses to testify. His very existence, his survival, his impact, testifies to God's existence. That he is here, that he is present, bears witness to God's presence in history. He has been chosen for this purpose and he should have the moral courage to draw the consequences from his own function in history. Then he will know and he will learn to believe, and through faith will learn to understand.

Jewish survival has confounded Israel's enemies and opponents and has been a source of disquieting puzzlement in the affairs of men. It is the

---

27. Isaiah 43:12.
28. *Sifrei.*

29. Deuteronomy 7:7.
30. Isaiah 43:10.

great mystery of world history. The survival of a people that has lived without power is inexplicable in a world that lives essentially by reliance on power. A people without a country, without an organized government, without any of those resources of material power that alone seem to count in human history—whence its staying power, whence its stamina to preserve its identity? In the Christian Dark and Middle ages, the mystery of Israel's survival was explained as the work of the Devil: The Jew was in alliance with the Adversary, the Jew was satanic or Satan himself. Given the Christian premise, this was in a sense "logical." The Jew lived and endured by a strength unrecognized in Christendom. It was a strength unknown in Christian lands and therefore hidden and mysterious. If it was not of God, surely it must come from the Adversary. Given the Christian premise, there was some truth in the argument. Israel endured in the midst of Christendom in a manner that defied all the "Christian" requirements for survival in history. To discern in the features of the Jew the face of Satan was a Christian necessity of the Dark and Middle ages. It was the tragic recognition of God's people by the medieval Christian psyche. In more modern times, the "explanation" was not readily acceptable. The Satan of Christendom was replaced by the secret international conspiracy of the elders of Zion. This idea, however fantastic, also has a certain logic of its own. It acknowledges the fact that Israel's survival is not explicable in terms of the historical dimensions within which people normally live. It rightly surmises that there is a secret to which the mysterious survival power of this powerless nation is due. It is wrong in the identification of that secret. That, too, is understandable. For the secret is God's hidden presence in history. There is indeed a "secret world government" at work in history. It consists of God's power-divested guidance in history. Because it is "powerless" it is hidden; yet its reality is intimated in the inexplicable survival of God's people.

The most tragic testimony to this presence-in-absence is provided by the Nazi crime of Germany against Israel. The ferocity with which this crime was perpetrated represents the ultimate of irrationality. The conscious and radical removal of every vestige of moral restraint on subhuman passions, the limitless inhumanity, the calculated reversal of all human values and the extirpation of all human feelings, the ideology of hate and the religion of brutality pursued and practiced by the Germans was not "of this world." It had a quality of the transcendental about it; it was metaphysical barbarism. It was not just inhuman; it was satanic. Many millions perished at the hand of the Germans, but the satanic hatred of Nazi Germany was reserved for the Jews exclusively. In terms of "this world" the hatred is inexplicable. Nazi Germany was, indeed, afraid of Israel. The fear was utterly unjustified in terms of material or political power. Nothing could be more ridiculous than to imagine that there was any rational foundation for one of the great military powers of history to be afraid of the might of "world Jewry." Nothing could be further from the truth than the mad suspicion of a Jewish conspiracy against Germany. Yet, the fear was real, more real than any fear human beings may have of superior material or political forces that may be arrayed against them. It was a metaphysical fear of the true mystery of God's "powerless" presence in history as "revealed" in the continued survival of Israel. It was a well-justified fear. For the presence of the "powerless" God in history indeed spelled the doom of the Nazi-German rebellion against all universal human values from the very beginning. The rebellion had to be satanic because it was to dethrone God. The "hiding" God of history was a repudiation of everything Nazi Germany stood for. He was to be eliminated for all times. There lies the origin of the satanic idea of the "final solution." If the symbol of this presence-in-absence were eliminated, if the witness were destroyed, God himself would be dead. The metaphysical quality of the Nazi-German hatred of the Jew as well as the truly diabolical, superhuman quality of the Nazi-German criminality against the Jew are themselves testimonies to the dark knowledge with which a nazified Germany sensed the presence in history of the hiding God. God is revealed in the midst of the hiddenness in the suffering of his people. At times, his enemies sense his hidden presence more actuely than those who are of his people. . .

The fear that so many different civilizations have of the Jew, the suspicion with which he is met, is utterly irrational, yet it has its justification. It is utterly irrational, because it has no basis in the behavior of the Jew or in his character. It is a form of international madness when it is founded on a belief in Jewish power and Jewish intention to hurt, to harm, or to rule. Yet it has its justification as a metaphysical fear of the staying power of Jewish powerlessness. The very existence of the Jewish people is suggestive of another dimension of reality and meaning in which the main preoccupations of the man of power history are adjudged futile and futureless in the long run. Israel's survival has a corollary in the judgment that is, sooner or later, executed in history notwithstanding God's silence. While God is long-suffering, he is not so forever. That would not be divine mercy, but divine indifference. Were there no judgment in history over power history, faith history would have no chance of survival. Israel has survived because of the world judgment that is also found in world history.

According to Jewish tradition, God originally planned to create the world according to his attribute of justice. But he saw that a world ruled by a just God could not exist. He, therefore, let his attribute of mercy precede and, thus, he associated mercy with justice and created the world.[31] What is not stated in the teaching but is implied, is the equally true thought that although it is sure that the world will not stand by divine justice, it is at least extremely doubtful that it could survive by unlimited divine mercy. For it is God's love and mercy that gives men the opportunity for satanic self-assertion and rebellion against God himself. Because of God's long-suffering, man may indulge in hubris and get away with it. But hubris too, if it remains unchecked, will destroy man. A world ruled by divine justice would perish because of God's justice; a world ruled by divine mercy would perish because of human hubris. A world of justice could not endure the divine wrath; a world of pure divine long-suffering could not endure man's wrath. There is judgment, but mercy precedes it. Judgment is delayed by divine mercy and forebearance. Because mercy delays judgment, man may indulge in rebellion and become guilty of hubris. Because God is forebearing, man may get away with it for a while. But judgment is only delayed. The man of hubris does not escape

nemesis. There is judgment and there is a Judge in world history. The manner of Israel's survival testifies to the long-suffering Judge of history.

Galut

Galut, exile, seems to be the dominant feature of Jewish history. The Jewish people have lived longer in exile than in their homeland in *Eretz Yisrael*, yet *Galut* is considered an abnormal condition both politically and spiritually. The Jew in the *Galut* is fenced in on all sides, politically, socially, economically; his very life is continually in jeopardy. The area too in which Judaism may grow and live is narrowly circumscribed—it is largely limited to the synagogue and the home. How did Jews understand their exile? How did they explain it to themselves? They looked upon it as part of the great dialogue between God and Israel. In the Books of Moses, and later on by the prophets, they already were warned that if they did not keep their covenant with God, the land would "spew" them out and they would be scattered among the nations. Indeed there exists a deep-rooted tradition that *Galut* is a punishment for sins. It is the old *mipnei hataeinu* (Because of our sins) idea that we discussed earlier. It was not easy to maintain such an idea. Exile has gone on much too long; the suffering was often too heavy to bear. The questions were unavoidable: Are we so much worse than the others? Are our transgressions so much more grievous? A great deal of ingenuity was spent in order to justify the idea of punishment. If one would wish not to lose faith in the merices of the Almighty, one could take recourse in the talmudic teaching that God is exacting of the righteous "up to a hair-breadth." The righteous are judged much more strictly, because they ought to know better. One could also take refuge from the searching questions of threatening disbelief by recalling the words of Amos (3:2):

> You only have I known of all the families of
> the earth;
> Therefore I will visit upon you all your iniquities.[32]

---

31. Cf. Rashi's commentary on Genesis 1:1.

32. Amos 3:2.

Although, as we saw earlier, even in the Bible and the Talmud it was not accepted as the only satisfactory explanation, Jews through the ages clung to it stubbornly. It is understandable; there was solace in it. One could preserve one's self-respect and also retain ones faith in God's justice. Israel's very closeness to God explained Israel's destiny in exile.

Such ideas were supported by another trend in Jewish thought—the positive value of suffering. Rightly endured, suffering purifies and deepens the human personality. It induces man to turn inward; to foreswear the superficial pleasures of the passing moment and to concentrate on the enduring values of human existence, perhaps to seek ultimate meaning where alone it may be found—in a realm beyond time and space. The ideas were often helpful in the darkest hours of the *Galut*. They enabled the Jew to carry on, to move from catastrophe to catastrophe without surrendering either faith or hope. Indeed, after each catastrophe his spirit revived in faith, sure that suffering was the necessary phase preceding the coming of the Messiah. Jews could believe it because through suffering they had atoned for their sins, they were purified, they were tested and stood the test. Because of suffering they were ready for the Messiah, worthy of him. The periods of great crisis and persecution were usually the hour of the false Messiah. If the Messiah did not come, there was always an explanation. Somehow, Jews failed again. The explanation was not always convincing. The *Galut* had gone on too long, it was too cruel. In the numerous penitential prayers of the synagogue, the *S'liḥot*, the question for the reason of it all, is recurring continually. It was summed up in a famous passage: "All exiles come to an end, only mine increases; all questions are answered, but my question returns ever to the place from which it came."[33]

Is there nothing but punishment, purification, and waiting only to be disappointed? Needless to say, in the light of all that has been said earlier in this essay there is also another approach to the problem, more valid and equally well rooted in the teaching. Exile as a single event may well be punishment. But exile as an enduring condition, and entailing survival in spite of it, belongs to a fundamentally different category. Usually, exile is understood as a sequence, an abnormal phase following upon a normal one. *Galut*, the specifically Jewish form of exile, is rather different: it does not follow; it is at the beginning. Jewish history begins with God's words to Abraham: "Get thee out of thy country, and from thy kindred, and from thy father's house, unto the land which I will show thee."[34] The history of Judaism commences with *Galut*. If exile is at the very start then there must be something in the nature of Judaism, in God's plan for the Jewish people, which is inseparable from it. Abraham, in order to become the patriarch of Israel, had to leave his father's house and the land of his birth. He embraced his destiny in a world which was alien to him, to his faith, to his values, to his truth. He went into exile, because in the world as it existed then, Abraham could not find a home. He had the choice: either to be true to himself and become a stranger, or wanderer, or to become one with his surroundings and remain at home. He chose himself, his own personal destiny; but in order to do that he had to go into exile. Even before they were born, it was decreed concerning his descendants that they would be strangers in a land that was not theirs, where they would be oppressed and afflicted for four hundred years.[35] Obviously this could not have been a punishment. The children of Israel, whom the natural course of events had taken to Egypt, could have merged with the Egyptian people and have been completely absorbed by Egypt's civilization. But if they were to remain Jews and loyal to the obligations of their descent, they had to remain apart. Again, like their father Abraham, they had a choice: to surrender their identity and submerge in the majority or to remain true to themselves and become strangers and live in exile.

What is the significance of *Galut* as a starting point? One might generalize and say: There are certain ideals that are not easily absorbed by the order of the world; there are values that are re-

---

33. Quoted from *Galut* by Yitzhak F. Baer (New York, 1947), p. 26.

34. Genesis 12:1.
35. Ibid., 15:13.

pulsed by the laws of power history; ideas and values that are strangers among men and are of tragic necessity forced into exile. Such a stranger in history is the idea represented by the Jewish people in the history of mankind. The history of a people of God, a people that enters on the scene of history on the strength of a covenant with God, that sees its responsibility as a people to obey God's word and to do his will, must begin in a condition of *Galut*. As Abraham did not fit into the local world of his birthplace so do his children not fit into the universal world of the nations to the extent that it is dominated by materialistic self-interest and ambitions of power. We say in our prayers, "Because of our sins we have been exiled from our land," but the truth is that during the period of the Second Temple the Jewish people had already completely given up every form of idolatry. It was the period of the great teachers of the Mishnah. During that time Israel was probably closer to God than in any previous phase in its history. Yet, this generation was overtaken by the catastrophe of the *ḥurban*, the destruction of the Temple and the state and the scattering of the people into the four corners of the world. There was no metaphysical reason for this. What happened was quite natural. For in the world as it existed then, a world ruled by the Roman Empire, there was indeed no room for the people of the prophets, the people of a Hillel and a Rabban Gamliel.

There are many passages in Talmud and Midrash that describe God as weeping over the exile of his children.[36] This is in keeping with our earlier analysis that God, having created man, rendered himself "powerless" in a sense. Why should exile involve the kind of suffering Israel had to endure? It is taken for granted that a minority scattered all over the world that attempts to retain its identity will be oppressed and persecuted. But this can only be taken for granted because there is something very wrong with man and with the world. Whenever a minority is persecuted, justice, humanity, decency are all in a state of exile from the affairs of men. The case of the Jew is, of course, aggravated by the fact that, not by what he does, but by what he is, indeed by

the fact that he is, represents a challenge to the principle by which nations "normally" live. And God himself is "powerless." He could crush man and destroy man's world. But if He desires man, He must take the risk with him and wait for him until man becomes what he ought to be. This, of course, means that exile is a cosmic condition. God Himself is a refugee in the world. This is the final meaning of the Jewish concept of *sh'khinta b'Galuta,* the Divine Presence in exile in the world. The *Galut* of the Jewish people is a specific case of this cosmic condition and a necessary outcome of it.

In spite of the suffering involved there is also majesty in exile, the majestic loyalty of a people that in an unprecedented and unparalleled manner has kept faith with an ideal. Even Jews are often inclined to look upon their *Galut* as a phase of passivity in which the Jewish people are a mere object for the butt end of history. The truth is that their condition was a matter of choice. But for the Nazi period, Jews could always escape persecution through apostasy, by conversion, through assimilation and complete surrender of identity. The arms of Christianity, especially, were always spread out invitingly toward the Jew. Because of the daily pressures and persecutions, every day that the Jew endured and remained loyal to his God or to his identity was a day of choice and decision. To accept the day-by-day challenge and not to surrender, no matter what the consequences, has been a deed of the spirit that for intensity, duration, and willingness for self-sacrifice remains unique in the history of mankind.

The Suffering Servant of God

If God is "powerless," God's people, too, will be powerless. To be God's people is more than acknowledging God; it means accepting God's world in all its consequences for those who acknowledge Him. God's people may cry out in their agony: How long still, O God! but will put up with God's long-suffering, with His questionable experiment, man. To be chosen by God is to be chosen for bearing the burden of God's long-suffering silences and absences in history. It is for this reason that at the beginning of Israel's

36. Cf. f. i., B.T. *Berakhot,* 59 a.

history stands the *Akeidah*, the binding of Isaac. Abraham was not guilty, nor was the sacrifice desired of him punishment. It was initiation into the sacrificial way of the Chosen Ones. What was revealed to the patriarch was repeated as his children were led onto the path that they were to take through history: "Know of a surety that thy seed shall be a stranger in a land that is not theirs, and shall serve them, and they shall afflict them four hundred years."[37] It was all decided before the child, destined to become father to the nation, was even born. It was repeated innumerable times later. God's chosen ones suffer guiltlessly. It is what is called in Hebrew terminology *gezeira*, an inscrutable divine decree. The decree is not that there be human suffering; the decree is that there be divine long-suffering with man in spite of man's criminal turpitude; indeed, the decree is that there be this world of man which could not stand without divine forbearance. Suffering of the guiltless is the indirect result of the decree of creation. The thought finds its moving expression in the awesome solemnity of the liturgy of the "Ten Martyrs," which is recited on the Day of Atonement. The very angels in heaven cried out bitterly: "Is this then the Torah? And this its reward?" Whereupon a heavenly voice was heard: "If I hear another sound, I shall turn the world back to water and My throne's footstool [i.e., the earth[38]] to *tohu vᵃ'bohu* [primordial chaos] . This is a decree [*gezeira*] from before Me. Accept it ye who find your pleasure in the Law, which precedes the creation." Why did they not utter that one sound, that protesting No to the abomination, euphemistically called "the footstool of His throne"? If such is the footstool, by all means let it go crashing down into its primordial *tohu vᵃ'bohu!* The martyrs, Rabbi Akiba and his saintly friends, did not speak that condemning No. They knew that the real issue was not their suffering; at stake was God's act of creation, His freedom and authority to say, "Let there be!" The chosen ones know that the choice is between *tohu vᵃ'bohu* of nonexistence and their acceptance of the yoke of the divine experiment of creation. Without their acceptance, the world would indeed have to be turned back into nothingness. Only when the chosen ones choose to accept "the decree' does the world acquire the moral right to continue to exist. As they accept the yoke, God may go on being long-suffering with the rest of mankind. The world is sustained by the suffering of the guiltless.

God's chosen people is the suffering servant of God. The majestic fifty-third chapter of Isaiah is the description of Israel's martyrology through the centuries. The Christian attempt to rob Israel of the dignity of Isaiah's suffering servant of God has been one of the saddest spiritual embezzlements in human history. At the same time, the way Christianity treated Israel through the ages only made Isaiah's description fit Israel all the more tragically and truly. Generation after generation, Christians poured out their iniquities and inhumanity over the head of Israel, yet they "esteemed him, stricken, smitten of God, and afflicted." At the same time, they misunderstood the true metaphysical dignity of the suffering of God's servant. What is the weight of one sacrifice compared to the myriads of sacrifices of Israel? What is one crucifixion beside a whole people crucified through centuries? But, it is maintained, the one crucified was a god, whereas the untold millions of Jewish men, women, and children were only human beings. Human beings only! As if the murder of an innocent human being were a lesser crime than the killing of a god. A god after all does not have to die. If he is killed, it is because he offers himself freely as a sacrifice. A god chooses to be killed; he knows what he is doing and why he is doing it. And when he dies, he does not suffer as a god. As a "very man" he suffers the agony of a single man. But the little boy who at the door of the gas chamber says to his mother: "But, Mama, I was a good boy!"[39] that is something quite different. That is crucifixion! Or the little boy of eleven pressed into the indignity of a cattle truck on its way to Treblinka. The

37. Genesis 15:13.
38. Cf., Isaiah 66:1.
39. This is a quote from André Schwarz-Bart's, *The Last of the Just* [E.T., New York, 1960] . The next episode is described in a letter by the father of the child, published in *Kiddush Hashem*, ed. S. Niger (New York, 1946/7). The last episode referred to is recorded in *Notes from the Warsaw Ghetto* trans. Jacob Sloan (New York, 1958), the Journal of Emanuel Ringelblum.

endless journey in the heat of a burning summer. There is hardly any room to stand. Occasionally, one steps on a corpse who only moments ago was a neighbor, a friend, a loved one. There is no air, no water, no sanitary facilities; ultimate darkness and doom! The father beside him. "My little boy, whom I was holding by the hand was almost suffocating from lack of air and thirst. His legs were giving way under him; he was sagging to the floor. I had to support him. He spoke in his fever: Daddy! We are going to Mama. Aren't we? I do see her. Hie! Open the doors! Shoot us! An end! Let there be an end to it!" This too is something quite different. This is what I call crucifixion. Or the eight-year-old in the refugee center in the Warsaw ghetto. The child is by now mad and runs around screaming: "I want to steal, I want to rob, I want to eat, I want to be a German." Such is crucifixion. And it has been suffered not by gods, but by human beings, endured again and again on innumerable occasions all through Jewish history in Christian lands. That deicide is the greatest of human crimes is among the most dangerous fallacies ever taught to man. The truth is that the capital crime of man is not deicide, but homicide. To torture and to kill one innocent child is a crime infinitely more abominable than the killing of any god. Had Christianity, instead of being preoccupied with what it believed to have been a deicide, concentrated its educative attention on the human crime of homicide, mankind would have been spared much horror and tragedy. There would have been much less suffering and much less sorrow among all men; nor could there have been either Auschwitz or Treblinka. Unfortunately, the teaching of deicide became an excuse, and often a license, for homicide. Pity any god thus caricatured by his devotees!

God suffers not on account of what man does to Him. What could man do to God? He suffers because of what man does to himself and to his brother. He suffers the suffering of His servant, the agony of the guiltless. In all their affliction, He is afflicted.[40] In the liturgy of the High Holy Days, God is referred to as the one who suffers, as He averts His eyes from the rebellious. He is long-suffering with man and suffers with the

victims of man who carry the burden of His long-suffering patience and mercy. How He must love those who suffer innocently because He cannot but bear even with those of His creatures who have failed Him! God's servant carries upon his shoulders God's dilemma with man through history. God's people share in all the fortunes of God's dilemma as man is bungling his way through toward messianic realization. The status of the dilemma at any one moment in history is revealed by the condition of Israel at that moment. God's people is God's challenge to man. God, who leads man "without might and without power" sent His people into the world without the might of power. This is the essence of the confrontation between Israel and the world. It was in this confrontation that Western man had to prove himself. God has pushed Israel right across the path of Christianity. Israel was God's question of destiny to Christendom. In its answer, the Christian world failed him tragically. Through Israel God tested Western man and found him wanting. This gruesome failure of Christianity has led the Western world to the greatest moral debacle of any civilization—the Holocaust.

The Witness after the Holocaust

1

Does all this justify God's silence during the European Holocaust of the Jewish people or does it even explain it? As we have already stated it is not our intention to explain it, and certainly not to justify it. We have tried to show what is implied in Judaism's faith in the God of history independently of our contemporary experience. The question is, of course, well grounded: Can such faith still be maintained in the face of the destruction of European Jewry? People of our day are often apt to give quick and mainly emotional answers to the question. This is understandable. We have been too close to the catastrophe, too deeply and personally involved. However, notwithstanding our deep emotional involvement, it is essential first of all to gain a clear intellectual grasp of the problem.

The Jewish, radical theologian[s] of our day— and the numerous less sophisticated people whose

40. Cf. Isaiah, 63:9.

preoccupation with the problem of Auschwitz does not let them reach any other solution but the negative one—do not understand the true nature of the quandary of faith that confronts us. The problem of faith here is a problem of theology in the broadest sense of the word. What becomes questionable is the manner in which God relates Himself to the world and to man. Strictly speaking, the questioning of God's justice in His relation to history has little to do with the quantity of undeserved suffering. The enormity of the number of martyrs of our generation—six million—is not essential to the doubt. As far as our faith in an absolutely just and merciful God is concerned, the suffering of a single innocent child poses no less a problem to faith than the undeserved suffering of millions. As far as one's faith in a personal God is concerned, there is no difference between six, five, four million victims or one million. Naḥmanides expressed the thought clearly in his *Sha'ar Ha'gmul* in the following words:

> Our quest [regarding theodicy] is a specific one, about [the plight of] this particular man. . . . This problem is not reduced if those who fall are few in number; nor does it become more serious if their number increases. For we are not discussing [the ways of] man. . . . Our arguments concern the Rock, whose work is perfect and all His ways just; there is nothing perverse or crooked in them.[41]

Nothing is easier than to miss, for emotional reasons, the decisive importance of such a statement. How can one compare the suffering of a few to that of a multitude? How dare one raise the problem over the death of one innocent child as one must over that of a million and a half innocent Jewish children slaughtered by the Germans! One cannot and one dare not—as long as one judges man. There is a vast difference between less injustice and more injustice, between less human suffering and more. One human tragedy is not as heartbreaking as the same tragedy multiplied a millionfold. A man who murders one person is not as guilty as a mass murderer. The German

crime of the ghettos and concentration camps stands out in all human history as the most abominable, the most sickening, and the most inhuman. But justice and injustice, guilt and innocence are matters of degree only for man. When one questions the acts of an absolute God, whose every attribute, too, is absolute by definition, the innocent suffering of a single person is as incomprehensible as that of millions, not because the suffering of millions matters as little as those of one human being, but because with Him the suffering of the one ought to be as scandalous as that of multitudes. An absolute just God cannot be a tiny bit unjust. The least injustice in the Absolute is absolute injustice. An infinitely merciful God cannot be just a little bit unconcerned about innocent suffering. The least amount of indifference in the Infinite is infinite indifference. With Elisha ben Abuyah, to have witnessed one case of undeserved suffering of the innocent was sufficient to raise the problem and cause him to lose faith. Such was also the insight of Camus. One compares the two sermons of the priest in *The Plague*. The first is a fire-and-brimstone preachment about the divine judgment that descended upon the sinful city; the second one is the mild acknowledgment of an impenetrable mystery. What happened between the two preachings? The priest had to witness the agony of a single child dying of the plague. One case was sufficient to change the man, who ultimately dies of the sickness of the incomprehensible.

Once the problem of evil is understood in its valid dimensions, the specific case of the Holocaust is not seen to be essentially different from the old problem of theodicy.

It is still the old problem of Epicurus that confronts us. If God desires to prevent evil but is unable, He is not omnipotent. If He is able to prevent evil, but does not desire to do so, He is malevolent. If He is able and desires to prevent it, whence evil? The problem has been discussed by all thinking and believing people through the ages. It is one of the themes in Plato's *Statesman*. Already in those days there were those who from the presence of evil in the world concluded that God must be absent from history. He had to be far removed from the earthly scene; He could have no knowledge of man. If He did, how could He tolerate the evil that was done under the sun!

41. *Shaar Ha'gmul* in Ḥiddushei Ha'Ramban, Part I., p. 193 (Benei Brak, 5719)

This consideration was also one of the reasons for the assertion in later Aristotelianism that God had no knowledge of "singulars" and thus, divine providence was in no way concerned with the plight of the individual being or creature. These were the early forms of what in our day likes to call itself radical theology.

Once the questioning of God over the Holocaust is motivated by the vastness of the catastrophe, the questioning itself becomes ethically questionable. It is of course more human to query God about the suffering of the many rather than the few, but it is certainly not more humane. On the contrary, it is more ethical, and intellectually more honest and to the point, to question God about the life and happiness of which even a single soul is being cheated on this earth than to base one's doubts and quest on the sacrificial abandonment of millions. With God the quantity of injustice must be immaterial. To think otherwise is itself a sign of callous indifference toward injustice and human suffering. To suggest that one could put up with less evil and less injustice, but not with so much, is cruelly unethical. Indeed, the Holocaust was only possible because mankind was quite willing to tolerate less than the Holocaust. This was the decisive aspect in the guilt of man in our times. It is important to understand the true nature of the problem if one involves God in it, questioning His ways with man and the world. It is the precondition for developing the attitude that may enable us to live meaningfully with the problem, even though its ultimate solution may forever escape us. Understood in its vastest intellectual dimension and its radical ethical relevance, the question is not why the Holocaust, but why a world in which any amount of undeserved suffering is extant. This, of course, means that the question is tantamount to, why man? Why a world of man? For, indeed, if man is to be as a being striving for value realization, God must

tolerate and endure him as a failure and an accusation.

How long is he to be tolerated as a failure, how long to be endured by God as an accusation of God? Who is to say! In order to answer the question, one ought to know the heart of God. How long God is willing to endure His creation even as a failure is the secret of creation itself. God's dominion over the world is not a dominion of justice.[42] In terms of justice, He is guilty. He is guilty of creation. But is He guilty of indifference or is He guilty of too much long-suffering? How vast is the infinitude of His mercy, His patience with man? When is it the moment for His justice to intervene and to call a halt to misused human freedom? Can we gauge the reach of His love even for the wicked, be they even those of His creatures who choose to become His failures? According to midrashic teaching, at the time of the drowning of the hosts of Pharaoh in the Red Sea the angels in heaven, as is their wont, were preparing to chant the daily hymn in praise of the Almighty. But God silenced them with the words: "The works of My hands are drowning in the sea and you sing My praises!"[43] It is not an easy matter for God to execute judgment over the guilty. Even "His failures" are the works of His hands.

2

The question after the Holocaust ought not to be, how could God tolerate so much evil? The proper question is whether, after Auschwitz, the Jewish people may still be witnesses to God's elusive presence in history as we understand the concept. What of the nemesis of history and what of Jewish survival?

The Nazi crime of the German people attempted to eradicate the last vestiges of a possible innate sense of humanity, it sought the conscious extirpation from human nature of the last re-

42. We are not unaware of the biblical verse that asserts that "all His ways are justice." (Deut. 32:4) Obviously, the midrashic statement we have quoted in our text about the creation of the world by mercy and justice is not in keeping with such a reading. However, the Hebrew Bible does not have: "all His ways are justice." But, "all His ways are *Mishpat*." I have shown in

a recent work how misleading it is to translate the biblical *Mishpat* as "justice" in the sense of Western civilization. See the chapter, "The Biblical Meaning of Justice," in my *Man and God Studies in Biblical Theology* (Detroit, 1969).
43. B.T. *Sanhedrin*, 39 b.

minder of the fear of God in any form. It was the ultimate rebellion of nihilism against all moral emotion and all ethical values. However, this up to now mightiest and most morbid manifestation of human hubris too was overtaken by its complete and inescapable nemesis. In every field the very opposite of its goals has been accomplished. "Das Tausendjährige Reich," the empire for a millennium, was in ashes after twelve terrible years. Instead of the much-heralded "Gross Deutschland" there is a divided Germany with greatly reduced frontiers. The nemesis is not limited to Nazi Germany alone, it has overtaken Western civilization itself. The Holocaust is not exclusively the guilt of Germany; the entire West has a goodly share in it. One of the most tragic aspects of the world catastrophe of Nazism is to be seen in the fact that it was able to assume its vast dimensions of calamity mainly because of the tolerance and "understanding" that it enjoyed in the world community of nations for many years. During the period of favorable international climate, Nazified Germany was able to create one of the most powerful war machines in all history, to poison the minds of vast sections of the world's population, and to corrupt governments and public officials in many lands. This was possible partly because, with the help of the anti-Semitic heritage of the West, Nazi Germany was able to bring about the moral disintegration of many peoples with diabolical efficiency and speed and partly—and not altogether independently of it— because of the cynical calculations of worldwide power politics. Germany was meant to become the bulwark of the West against the threat of Russian communism. To this end many were willing to ignore the German-Nazi challenge to elementary justice and humanity. After all, its worst venom was directed against the Jews only. Even after the Second World War had already pursued its horrifying course in Europe for several years, there were still influential forces in the high seats of power, and even on the throne of so-called spiritual grandeur, that hoped for a rapprochement between Nazi Germany and the Western powers. They thought it politically wise to go slow on Nazi-German criminality, piously hoping to bring off the brotherly alliance that would enable them to launch the greatest of all crusades, that against Soviet communism. Thus

they became accomplices in the criminality of Auschwitz and the gas chambers. Nothing of what they had hoped for has been achieved. Instead of a curbing of communism, for which Germany and her sympathizers hoped, communism has reached its widest penetration the world over. This is not stated with any partiality for communism, but solely from the point of view of an observer who tries to detect the functioning of [a]nemesis in history. Nazi Germany could have been stopped early in its track had there been less indifference toward the plight of the Jews and a better understanding of the demoralizing power of anti-Semitism. But anti-Semitism had long been a respectable trait in Western civilization. Thus, the Second World War became inevitable, as a result of which all the formerly great powers of Europe have been reduced to second and third rank. And even Russia and the United States, who came out of the war as superpowers dwarfing all others, what have they gained if, as a result of their overwhelming might, they render each other's future, as well as that of all mankind, rather questionable? It is no mere coincidence that having countenanced the "final solution" to the Jewish problem, partly with glee and partly with equanimity the world is now confronted with the serious possibility of a "final solution" to the entire problematic existence of man on this planet. Every one of the ambitions that the forces of power history have been pursuing have been weighed and found wanting. Had the nations and their churches not been silent and indifferent to what was recognizably afoot in the early days of Nazism, world history would have taken an entirely different course and mankind would not now be balancing on the very edge of the thermonuclear abyss. This post-Holocaust era is charged with the nemesis of history. This is the ignoble twilight hour of a disintegrating civilization.

It is true the Jewish people had to pay a terrible price for the crimes of mankind and today, too, as part of mankind, they are themselves deeply involved in the crisis of the human race, yet the "final solution" intended for them is far from being final. Though truncated, Israel survived this vilest of all degradations of the human race. Not only has it survived, but rising from one of its most calamitous defeats, it has emerged to new dignity and historic vindication in the State of Israel.

The most significant aspect of the establishment of the State of Israel is the fact that Jews through the ages knew that it was to come. They were waiting for it during their wanderings for long and dark centuries. There was little rational basis for their faith in the eventual return to the land of their fathers. Yet they knew that one day the faith would be translated into historical reality. They lived with that faith in the sure knowledge of divine concern. For the Jew, for whom Jewish history neither begins with Auschwitz nor ends with it, Jewish survival through the ages and the in-gathering of the exiles into the land of their fathers after the Holocaust proclaim God's holy presence at the very heart of His inscrutable hiddenness. We recognized in it the hand of divine providence because it was exactly what, after the Holocaust, the Jewish people needed in order to survive. Broken and shattered in spirit even more than in body, we could not have been able to continue on our Jewish way through history without some vindication of our faith that the "Guardian of Israel neither slumbers nor sleeps." The State of Israel came at a moment in history when nothing else could have saved Israel from extinction through hopelessness. It is our lifeline to the future.

3

Confronting the Holocaust, the relevant consideration is the full realization that it does not preempt the entire course of Jewish history. One dare not struggle with the problem of faith as if the Holocaust were all we knew about the Jew and his relation to God. There is a pre-Holocaust past, a post-Holocaust present, and there is also a future, which is, to a large extent, Israel's own responsibility. Auschwitz does not contain the entire history of Israel; it is not the all-comprehensive Jewish experience. As to the past, we should also bear in mind that the Jew, who has known so much of the "hiding of the face," has also seen the divine countenance revealed to him. Notwithstanding Auschwitz, the life of the patriarchs is still with him; the Exodus did not turn into a mirage; Sinai has not come tumbling down; the prophets have not become charlatans; the return from Babylon has not proved to be a fairy tale. It is, of course, possible for people to

secularize the history of Israel and deny the manifestation of a divine presence in it. However, such secularization is independent of the Holocaust. It is not very meaningful to interpret the entire course of Jewish history exclusively on the basis of the death-camp experience of European Jewry. If the believer's faith in Israel's "encounters" with God in history is false, it must be so not on account of Auschwitz, but because the "encounters" just did not happen. On the other hand, if these manifestations of the divine presence did occur, then they are true events and will not become lies because of the Holocaust.

For the person who does not recognize the presence of God in the Exodus, at Sinai, in the words of the prophets, in innumerable events of Jewish history, Auschwitz presents no problem of faith. For him God is forever absent. Only the Jew who has known of the presence of God is baffled and confounded by Auschwitz. What conclusions is he to draw from this terrifying absence of divine concern? Is God indifferent to human destiny? But the Jew knows otherwise. He knows of the most intimate divine concern. Has God, perhaps, died? Is it possible that once upon a time there was a God who was not indifferent toward Israel, but that now something has happened to Him, He has gone away, He is no longer? This is plain silly. It is possible for a human being to lose faith in God. But it is not possible for God to die. He either is and therefore will ever be; or He is not and therefore never was. But if God who was, is, and will ever be, is it possible that at Auschwitz He rejected Israel, He turned away from Israel as a punishment for its sins? To believe this would be a desecration of the Divine Name. No matter what the sins of European Jewry might have been, they were human failings. If the Holocaust were a punishment, it was a thousandfold inhuman. The only crime of man for which such punishment might be conceivable would be the Nazi crime of Germany, and even there, one would hesitate to impose it.

The Jew of faith is thus left with the perplexing duality of his knowledge of God. He knows of the numerous revelations of the divine presence as he knows of the overlong phases of God's absence. Auschwitz does not stand by itself. Notwithstanding its unique position as perhaps the most horrifying manifestation of divine silence, it has its place in Jewish history beside the other silences of God together with the utterances of His concern. The Jew was called into being by the revelation of the divine in history. It is because God allowed His countenance to shine upon man that he is what he is. Only because of that does he know of the absence of God. But thanks to that, he also knows that God's absence, even at Auschwitz, is not absolute. Because of that it was possible for many to know God even along the path to the gas chambers. There were many who found Him even in His hiding. Because of the knowledge of God's presence, the Jew can find God even in His absence.

No, the Holocaust is not all of Jewish history, nor is it its final chapter. That it did not become the "final solution" as was planned by the powers of darkness enables the Jew who has known of the divine presence to discern intimations of familiar divine concern in the very midst of his abandonment. This, too, is essentially an old Jewish insight.

Yet all this does not exonerate God for all the suffering of the innocent in history. God is responsible for having created a world in which man is free to make history. There must be a dimension beyond history in which all suffering finds its redemption through God. This is essential to the faith of a Jew. The Jew does not doubt God's presence, though he is unable to set limits to the duration and intensity of His absence. This is no justification for the ways of providence, but its acceptance. It is not a willingness to forgive the unheard cries of millions, but a trust that in God the tragedy of man may find its transformation. Within time and history that cry is unforgivable. One of the teachers of the Talmud notes that when God asks Abraham to offer Him his son Isaac as a sacrifice, the exact rendering of the biblical words reads: "Take, I pray thee, thy son."[44] In the view of this teacher the "binding of Isaac" was not a command of God, but a request that Abraham take upon himself this most exacting of all God's impositions. In a sense, we see in this a recognition that the sacrificial way of the innocent through history is not to be vindicated or justified! It remains unforgivable. God Himself has to ask an Abraham to favor Him by accepting the imposition of such a sacrifice. The divine request accompanies all those through history who suffer for the only reason that God created man, whom God Himself has to endure. Within time and history God remains indebted to His people; He may be long-suffering only at their expense. It was hardly ever as true as in our own days, after the Holocaust. Is it perhaps what God desires—a people, to whom He owes so much, who yet acknowledge Him? Children, who have every reason to condemn His creation, yet accept the Creator in the faith that in the fullness of time the divine indebtedness will be redeemed and the divine adventure with man will be approved even by its martyred victims?

CRISIS AND FAITH

Normally, we think of *Galut* as a phenomenon of Jewish history. It is, however, vital that we understand what *Galut* has meant in the foundation and formation of Judaism. *Galut* did not start with the destruction of Jerusalem and the dispersion of the Jewish people to the four corners of the world. It stands at the very beginning of the road. Even before there was a Jewish people there was already Jewish exile. It all started with the call to Abraham: "Get thee out of thy country, and from thy kindred, and from thy father's house, unto the land that I will show thee." This is how the path of the first Jew began—exile and promise. When the father of the nation-to-be was still childless, it was already decreed and revealed to him: "Know of a surety that thy seed shall be a stranger in a land that is not theirs, and shall serve them; and they shall afflict them four hundred years; and afterwards shall they come out with great substance"

44. Ibid., 89 b.

(Genesis 15:13). Once again, even before there was a Jewish people there was already exile and the promise of redemption. Not only did this exile not destroy the sovereignty of the Jewish people but, on the contrary, it was through exile that Abraham became the father of Israel and it was in exile that the children of Jacob became the people of Israel, the children of Israel of history. It happened in Egypt that they were for the first time referred to as a people, when Pharaoh said of them: "Behold, the *people* of the children of Israel are too many and too mighty for us." In our Egyptian exile we became a nation. What is the significance of all this?

There are two kinds of exiles. There is a national exile which begins with Ḥurban, with the destruction of the sovereignty of the people and their dispersion into alien lands. However, prior to national exile, and more fundamental and universal, there is cosmic exile. National exile is a phenomenon in the history of nations; cosmic exile bespeaks the spiritual quality of the universal human condition at any one time in history.

What do we mean by "cosmic exile"? God has His plan for the world. The entire creation is infused with a divine purpose that longs for and seeks its realization in the cosmos in general and in human history in particular. Since, however, mankind has its own goals such as passion for power, desire for domination, for possessions and pleasures, such egotistic human drives deny the divine purpose in the creation of man. As a result, God's own purpose finds itself in exile in the history of mankind. So long as the divine plan remains unrealized in history, the history of mankind tells the story of—what Jewish tradition calls—Galut haShekhinah, the exile of the Divine Presence. God Himself is, as it were, a refugee in the world of men. It is this exile that is prior to, and at the root of, every national exile. It is on account of this that the history of the Jewish people begins with exile. The call that went out to Abraham was a call for identification with the divine plan in history. This, however, compelled him to leave everything behind and to join the exile of the Divine Presence in history. But by way of this identification with the divine purpose and the divine Galut, he became Abraham, the father of a "multitude of nations." The Egyptian exile was of similar significance for his descendants. Egypt was

one of the phases of the exile of the divine plan in history. To have been in *Galut* at the very beginning of their way meant that the starting point of the way was identification of the children of Jacob with the exile of the Divine Presence. Yet it was through this identification that they became the people of Israel, *Am Eḥad*, one people in the world. The association of the children of Israel with the cosmic *Galut,* sharing in it right from their beginnings, made them the Jewish people.

However, precisely on this account, exile is not only misery and disaster, but also challenge and responsibility with life-giving and life-sustaining meaning. The symbol of the Roman occupation in ancient Israel was the city of Caesarea. Comparing the symbol of Caesarea with that of Jerusalem, the Talmud says: If they tell you Caesarea and Jerusalem both are settled or that both are destroyed, do not believe it. But if they say Caesarea is settled and Jerusalem destroyed or Jerusalem is settled and Caesarea destroyed, believe it. For when one is safely established, the other cannot be so. (T.B., *Megillah,* 6a). In this manner, the Talmud expressed the confrontation between two principles in history. In the world of triumphant Caesarea there is little room for Jerusalem, the Holy City, just as in the world of established Jerusalem, there is no place for the Caesarea of the Caesars. At the time just preceding the destruction of the second Jewish commonwealth, there was a very real choice before the people: either find a place in the world order of the Roman Empire which was wide open to them, or identify themselves with the destiny of the *Shekhinah*, of the Divine Presence, with the divine exile that was unavoidable within the *pax romana*. The Jewish people chose between these two possibilities. The result of their choice was the Ḥurban, the destruction of their state and their dispersion. But it is only because of that choice that the people of Israel are still the people of Israel and are still around in the world of men.

In other words, this Ḥurban was not just disaster. It was choice! We chose to side with the divine plan for man, which was denied in the world of Caesar. The destruction of Jerusalem and of the state was not a disaster that overwhelmed the Jewish people with the blind force of a natural catastrophe. What happened was the result of a free choice of unparalleled heroism in human history. True, it brought exile down upon our heads. Yet this consciously determined embracing of Jewish destiny granted us our eternal share in life. The source of our suffering has also been the source of our survival. And so, too, has it been to this day, the source of our timelessness.

There is this difference between national and cosmic exile. National exile—the dispersal of an entire people from its homeland—is stagnation, loss of vitality, decline, and, ultimately, disappearance. This is the law in the world of Caesar. But in the cosmic exile of the divine purpose there is never stagnation, never irreversible stagnation. The realization of the divine purpose may be again and again tragically delayed, but it cannot be defeated. This exile is forever a process—often one of roundabout paths beyond immediate human understanding—towards its realization. As the Kabbalists would say, the fall is often the prerequisite for the rise. The Exile of the Divine Presence in history is a continuous progression toward Redemption. Because we have identified ourselves from the very beginning with the cosmic exile, which indeed constitutes the essence of our being, we have been able to find the certainty of our redemption—and often a measure of its fruition in anticipation—at the very heart of our various exiles. This is the secret of Israel eternal.

Our Exile, then, is twofold: national and universal, the exile of the people, and the exile of the *Shekhinah* in which we share. Because of that, Jewish messianism is also twofold. The Talmud teaches that the only difference between the present world and the days of the Messiah is the freedom from alien subjugation. But Isaiah prophesied: A nation will not raise the sword against another, nor will they learn the art of war any longer. Both are right; both redemptions are needed; national redemption for the national exile, universal redemption for *Galut haShekhinah,* for the exile of God in human history. Jewish history seeks redemption in a twofold drive. It drives for national redemption among the nations, as well as universal redemption for all the nations. For this reason every from of national redemption can only be *Athalta deGe'ulah,* the beginning [of redemption]. Only universal redemption may be acknowledged as *Ge'ulah She-*

lemah, redemption completed and time fulfilled. No separation between the two is possible. Jewish history has been moving on a double track. At times, we are warned "not to force the end"; at others, as at the time of the return from Babylon, we are punished for not having "gone up like a solid national phalanx."

The phase of the exile in our times has to be recognized as total crisis because of the radically new event—the total threat—that entered Jewish history. It is usually referred to as the *Sho'ah,* the Holocaust. This is probably not the right term. In our exiles, we have experienced numerous holocausts—during the Crusades, the Black Death [1348–1349], the Chmelnicki pogroms [1648–1649], the massacres in the Ukraine at the end of the First World War, etc., etc. This catastrophe, however, was different from all of them, not just in degree, but in kind, in its essential quality. The proper name for it is not *Sho'ah,* but Ḥurban, annihilation. For the first time in our history, the exile itself was destroyed. After every other national catastrophe, there was still enough strength left in the Jewish people to continue, to rebuild and to recuperate. As we have indicated earlier, something of the awaited redemption was present in every one of our exiles. This time what happened was radically new. In our generation, the generation of Nazism, of humanity's betrayal of all the values without which life itself becomes absurd indeed, the *Galut haShekhinah* (the exile of the Divine Presence) reached its nadir, its most tragic intensification in history. Since Jewish existence interlocks with the *Galut haShekhinah,* we too were forced down to the depth of suffering and martyrdom and at the end of it we were left completely exhausted. Even that spark of *Ge'ulah* which was present before in every *Galut* and which alone enabled us to continue, to rebuild and to create anew, was extinguished this time. Our faith was shaken to its foundations.

At this fateful hour in Jewish history there was only one remedy left for the destruction of the *Galut,* and it had to be as radical and revolutionary as the destruction itself: national redemption in the sight of all men through the restoration of Israel's sovereignty in the land of Israel. Redemption was long overdue. It had to come. Without it, we would not have been able to continue. The rise of the State of Israel, after two millennia of such exile and at the moment when it occurred, has become the reviving force, calling back to life the "dry bones" of the shattered *Galut*. Divine Providence had no choice but to grant us a measure of national redemption to meet the national *Ḥurban*. However, therein lies too the cause for this new phase of the total crisis that has broken over us since the Yom Kippur War. The national redemption, *because it had to come* for the sake of Jewish survival, was running ahead of *Galut haShekhinah*, of the redemption of the Divine Presence from its exile in the affairs of men and nations. The national redemption of the Jewish people came without a corresponding measure of universal redemption. This is the root of Israel's present problem. In our days, a civilization that has been drifting ever since its spiritual and moral collapse in the era of Nazism is once again being tested. What a degradation of the dignity of man that formerly proud nations can be treated today by oriental potentates like big daddy treats his little children to whom he grants pocket money according to whether they please him or displease him! Is a darker eclipse of human values imaginable than when the conscience and the standard of values of formerly great nations are determined by the amount of oil Arabia is willing to allow to reach them? What a demoralization of international order, what a derision of international justice! International cynicism is eating away the last shreds of the moral fibers of human society, already sickened by the universal catastrophe of Nazism. Mankind is on the road to universal chaos. As in the days of Nazism, with the selling out of the Jewish people to Hitlerism, the world was moving fast toward the Second World War, so today with the cynical willingness of formerly great nations to sell the State of Israel and the Jewish people for a barrel of oil, the world is approaching the day of reckoning, the hour of the thermonuclear Armageddon.

We concede this is indeed a metaphysical interpretation of Jewish existence. But Jewish survival testifies to the fact that we are a "metaphysical" people. As in the time of triumphant Nazism, so today the plight of the *Shekhinah* in human history is dramatically reflected in the destiny of Israel. If

it were otherwise we would not be Jews. Because our destiny has been linked to *Galut haShekhinah*, to the exile of the Divine Presence, once again in this hour of the total demoralization of the international order the crisis is total. Once again everything seems to be in the balance. But just because the crisis is total, the promise too is total. God's own destiny in human history is linked to our own destiny. He needs us no less than we need Him. This is probably the deepest meaning of the idea of being "a chosen people." God has joined His fortunes among men to our fortunes, as we have joined our destiny to Him on this earth. He let it be said by the mouth of His prophet, "Ye are My witnesses, saith God." And the rabbis commented: "If you are My witnesses, I am God; if not, I am not God." But since God will be, so must the witness too. This is the source of our suffering, the source of our dignity, the guarantee of our survival till the end of days. We have reached a juncture in world history when the existence of the Jewish people cannot be separated from the existence of the State of Israel. And the future of the people of Israel is inseparable from *Ge'ulat haShekhinah,* from the redemption of God Himself from His man-created exile. Because of that, Israel will still dwell in Zion and Jerusalem long after the wells of Arabia have been forced to surrender their last drop of oil.

The question, of course, is: What is our function, the function of the Jewish people, in such a scheme of history? It would seem to us that no matter what our reaction to the scheme may be, we shall remain the witnesses. What God has started with us He will complete. Too much remains unfinished; too much awaits its justification; too much waits for its redemption. God will not die in His exile. As far as we are concerned the question is: Shall we just endure our destiny or willingly embrace it? We shall not escape it. This is the lesson that we must learn from the Yom Kippur War. The State of Israel has been forced back into Jewish history. If the tragedy of the Yom Kippur War will bring home to us the futility of our desire to become a "normal" people and will induce us to recover the ethos of the Jewish stance in history in the context of *Galut* and *Ge'ulah*, it may yet be turned into a triumph of our struggle for survival within the messianic wave of world history. Only in that context can it be said that the

State of Israel has come to stay. Of course, it is going to stay. The attempt to break out of that context has failed. It is going to fail again and again. The God of history will not let us go. We are not being asked. There is no escape for Israel from the historic destiny of Israel. The question again is: Shall we only endure it, or shall we find the ultimate meaning of our human existence in it by embracing it with resolute determination and dedication? There has hardly ever been a more worthwhile moment in history to be a Jew in the classical context of *Galut* and *Ge'ulah* [redemption] than at this time of moral and spiritual exhaustion of the human race.

Robert Gordis

Robert Gordis (1908–1992) was born in New York. He received his rabbinical ordination from the Jewish Theological Seminary of America in 1932. A year earlier, in 1931, he had already begun to serve as the rabbi of Temple Beth El in Far Rockaway, New York, and he served in this position until 1968. In addition, a lifelong student of the Hebrew Bible, he began to teach biblical studies at the Jewish Theological Seminary in 1940, and then taught at Columbia University beginning in 1948, at Union Theological Seminary beginning in 1960, and finally, at Temple University from 1967 to 1974. He also served as editor of the influential journal *Judaism,* as the president of the Conservative movement's Rabbinical Assembly, as president of the Synagogue Council of America, and as a consultant to the Center for the Study of Democratic Institutions. His main area of scholarly expertise was the so-called wisdom literature of the Bible, e.g., *Ecclesiastes* and *Job,* and he wrote valuable studies of both of these biblical books. In addition, he wrote several books on Jewish theology, intended for the wider Jewish community as well as for scholars, that established his reputation as a theologian.

SELECTION

The present essay was first published in the journal *Judaism* 21, no. 3 (Summer 1972): 277–284. In it Gordis, responding primarily to Richard Rubenstein's "death of God" theology, attempts to present an alternative, more traditional, theological posture based on a cluster of fundamental biblical ideas. Though these biblical views are suggestive, they are not argued for in a tight philosophical or theological way. Nevertheless, this essay provides a set of basic theological notions of which students need to be aware when discussing the difficult issues of Jewish faith after the Holocaust.

Selected Bibliography

Books by Robert Gordis

Koheleth: The Man and His World (New York, 1951).
Judaism for the Modern Age (New York, 1955).
Faith for Moderns (New York, 1960).
God and Man: A Study of Job, (New York, 1965).

A CRUEL GOD OR NONE: IS THERE NO OTHER CHOICE?

"Give a dog a bad name and hang him" has always been good hard-headed advice. In our day there is no dirtier word in the language than "the establishment." Pin the label on a cause or an idea and it is damned beyond recovery. It is, therefore, natural, though regrettable, that even scholars and thinkers have not been able to resist the temptation to discredit opposing viewpoints by using the device of guilt by epithet.

Thus, Richard Rubenstein, in his zeal to propagate his version of "nontheistic religion," declares that contemporary Jewish theologians fall into two opposing categories that he calls "establishment" and "academic," the former representing the hidebound outworn doctrines of the past, the latter the relevant, vital ideas of the present. It is an interesting contrast he draws, even if a little less than convincing.

Undoubtedly, the great watershed in contemporary Jewish thought is the Holocaust, the brutal extermination by the Nazis of six million Jewish men, women, and children. To this, the most monstrous program of bestiality in history, the free world, with only a few exceptions, reacted with passivity and indifference. The mountain of human misery created by the Nazi Holocaust poses a major problem for the traditional biblical faith that God works in history, and for its corollary that His righteousness is manifest in human affairs.

How can the Holocaust be justified? Only one response, Rubenstein declares, is possible for the conventional "establishment" thinkers—the Holocaust was a Divine visitation on a sinful generation. Where there is sin, there must be suffering; hence, the massive suffering of our age implies massive sin. This "justification" Rubenstein rightly regards as monstrous. He therefore rejects the traditional faith in God as no longer possible in the post-Hitler era. He insists that the Nazi campaign of mass murder cannot be categorized as merely another instance of man's propensity for evil differing in degree, but not in kind, from the wars and massacres that have disfigured

human history through the ages. On the contrary, we are told, the technological processes of destruction utilized by Hitler, his sophisticated techniques of propaganda, and the efficiency of the operation make the Nazi Holocaust totally different from any other event in history. Hence, the only possible conclusion for modern man is that "the belief in God as the Lord of history must be rejected." Rubenstein believes passionately that "Jewish paganism is the most viable religious option available to contemporary Jews." In a recent article (*New York Times*, 4 March 1972) he urges Christians as well as Jews to adopt "nontheistic forms of religion often based on ancient pagan or Asian models." He himself opts for the "ancient earth gods and the realities to which they point," because they alone offer men the opportunity to "celebrate" what he, following in the footsteps of Sartre, Camus, and Genet, regards as the human condition "entirely enclosed within the fatalities of an absurd earthly existence." In brief, modern man has only two choices—either a cruel God or none. For Rubenstein there is no God and Israel is His witness.

Before we examine, however briefly, both the negations and the affirmations of the old-new paganism, we should examine its psychological roots. The measureless immensity of the moral catastrophe of Nazism is undoubtedly the mainspring for this and similar approaches to the perennial issue of man's place in the world. But more mundane factors help to attract attention, if not assent, for such views in our time. Deeply rooted in human nature is the desire for novelty, be it in content or in form. The wish to assert one's identity in opposition to accepted views, to attack the "establishment" without knowing precisely what the "establishment" is, the all-but-universal impulse to "do one's thing"—these elements play an important role today. To tell the truth, this "modern" tendency is no modern invention. The prophet Jeremiah, himself a supreme rebel in his generation, twenty-six centuries ago declared:

Two wrongs My people have committed,
    they have forsaken Me,
the fountain of living waters,
    and hewed out cisterns for themselves,
broken cisterns,
    that can hold no water. (2:13)

However, as Emerson, perhaps overoptimistically, reminded us, there is a law of compensation operating in the world. Two centuries ago, Voltaire delivered himself of the ironic observation that "the Bible is more celebrated than known." The statement is truer today than when first made. Yet even this sorry state of affairs is not a total loss. With the Bible virtually an unknown to modern men, they may perhaps be willing to approach it with an unjaded gaze. They may then discover that a viable faith in the biblical God operating in history is still possible—that it is, in fact, far superior to the newly packaged religions that "celebrate" the "absurdity" of human existence.

It may prove helpful to restate in modern terms some of the biblical insights on which our generation can build a modern faith that will sustain the spirit without demanding the abdication of the mind. Before doing so, it is important to point out that a peculiar form of moral blindness inheres in positions such as Rubenstein's. At which point does a sin become monstrous: at six million victims, or at five million, or three or one? Is it not true that the suffering and death of a single child is an infinite calamity before the throne of God? Are the conventional theologians, therefore, wrong in regarding the Nazi Holocaust as morally on a par with the mass deaths perpetrated by the builders of the Egyptian pyramids, or the palaces of Babylon, or the roads and bridges of the Roman Empire? Do Dachau and Auschwitz and Bergen-Belsen differ in quality from the massacres of the Crusades and of Chmiel, the tortures of the Inquisition, the pogroms of czarist Russia? What about the conscious and systematic starvation of millions in the early years of Soviet Russia and Communist China, or the thousands of deaths in Biafra or in Bangladesh? Is the statistical yardstick to be employed in determining the dimensions of human suffering and the challenge it poses to faith in God?

If, on the other hand, the problem does not arise for the first time with twentieth-century Nazism, we have a moral and intellectual duty to examine the insights at which men arrived in earlier periods of agony and wrath. Perhaps, after all, the Bible deserves its reputation! It deserves better than the simplistic approach of "revolutionary" theologians who offer little more than a caricature of biblical prophecy, wisdom, and faith.

We suggest that there are five biblical ideas upon which modern men, like their predecessors, may draw in constructing a view of human life and destiny capable of sustaining them in the face of the evils of existence. These fundamentals, set down here in outline, need to be fleshed out in order to become truly alive:

The glory of life and the goodness of God. This basic principle of Jewish theology has become familiar to many moderns in the presentations of Ḥasidism offered by Martin Buber in the previous generation and by Elie Wiesel in ours. Unfortunately, these brilliant reinterpretations of Ḥasidism are highly personal. Thus, Elie Wiesel declares, "Man owes it to himself to reject despair.... There is no alternative. *One must impose a meaning on what perhaps has none* and draw ecstasy from nameless, faceless pain" (italics ours). Neither Israel Ba'al Shem Tov, the founder of Ḥasidism, nor his great successors, nor their disciples would have agreed that they were imposing a meaning on life where there was none. Unlike Buber and Wiesel, the ḥasid had a source for triumphant affirmation of life, going back to the opening chapter of Genesis: "God saw all that He had made and behold, it was very good." The rabbis in the Talmud, by a word-play on the Hebrew *tov me'od*, "very good," pronounced as *tov mot*, declare that even death is good, because the world has its source in the God of Life.

Man's right and duty to confront evil in the world. Biblical faith does not interpret man's cruelty, which reaches its apex in the Holocaust, as a "punitive visitation" by God that must be borne in submission. Far from accepting evil in the world, Jewish religious thought challenges God and demands His adherence to the moral law. Many of the most moving tales in Hasidic lore picture Rabbi Levi Yitzḥak of Berditchev confronting God in the name of his suffering, poverty-stricken brothers.

Here, too, the roots are centuries older than Ḥasidism. The Book of Job is a great existentialist protest against injustice visited upon God's creatures. The final judgment of the book is not that Job is wrong or blasphemous in challenging his Maker. On the contrary, it is the conventional defenders of God who stand in need of forgiveness: "For you have not spoken the truth about Me, as has My servant Job" (42:7). In a striking ironic utterance, God declares that it is Job who must plead that his antagonists be forgiven. The Hebrew prophets were not only God's spokesmen to men, but of men challenging God. "You are righteous, therefore do I contend with You," Jeremiah declares. "Why do the wicked prosper and the treacherous succeed?" This strand of biblical faith the Bible traces back to the patriarch Abraham in Genesis. When the Lord decides to destroy the sinful cities of Sodom and Gomorrah, Abraham bargains for the lives of the sinners and hurls the challenge: "Must not the Judge of all the earth act justly?"

The core of mystery in evil. To be sure, biblical and post-biblical religion offer many positive answers to the problem of evil. We are reminded of a truth easily forgotten, that evil is not always triumphant—that, on the contrary, wickedness often does bring disaster in its wake. The psalmists underscore the need for men's patience and faith, because the process of retribution is slower at times than we would wish, often extending over generations. Experience teaches, too, that suffering may turn out to be a blessing in disguise.

Yet no matter how valid these insights may be, the presence of the Book of Job, the profoundest work in the Bible, has always prevented the acceptance of these conventional manmade answers as final and complete explanations, for Job prevents men from forgetting that a core of mystery in evil remains. In the words of Rabbi Yannai in the *Ethics of the Fathers,* "We do not know the reason either for the suffering of the righteous or the prosperity of the wicked"—or the death of a child or the devastation of an earthquake. The disastrous Lisbon earthquake of 1755 led to Voltaire's brilliant novella *Candide,* which satirized Leibniz's philosophical optimism then fashionable. But Voltaire's masterpiece did not reckon with the profound insight of biblical religion that, after all legitimate explanations are advanced, an irreducible element of mystery still

inheres in the world. Voltaire urged his readers, "let us cultivate our own gardens," while the "tough-minded" in every age are willing to follow the sage Ben Sira's advice given nineteen centuries earlier, to "have no concern with mysteries." "The tender-minded," as William James called them, continue to confront the perennial issues of existence in which the mystery of evil is central.

But the Book of Job goes beyond the position of *ignoramus,* "We do not know." Granted that a total answer to the problem of evil is denied us, yet a basic response is available in the "Speeches of the Lord" (chs. 38–41), expressed, not explicitly, but by implication. The poet presents triumphant affirmation of the glory of the natural order often transcending human standards of beauty. He thus suggests, persuasively, that the moral order also has pattern and meaning, even when it is veiled from men, for both aspects of reality are the creation of the one God, who is both Lord of nature and God of history. These Speeches of the Lord out of the whirlwind do not demand mere submission to God on the ground that man's understanding of the natural world is limited. With power and passion, they call for recognition of the reality of a pattern in the moral sphere as well. As against bitter atheism or sad agnosticism, Job offers a reasonable and hopeful faith in the structure of the world and human experience. Within this larger framework supplied by Job, more specific insights are to be found in such biblical masterpieces as Genesis, Deuteronomy, and Isaiah.

Man's freedom. Basic to the biblical view of man is the conviction, stated three times in the Book of Deuteronomy and implicit everywhere else, that man is morally free: "Behold, I place before you this day life and death, the blessing and the curse." Every individual, every generation, every nation, every society is endowed with this fateful and perilous privilege of freedom in the moral sphere. It has been the great achievement of modern science, of biology, psychology, economics, sociology, and other disciplines, to reveal the pressure and limitations to which man is subjected by virtue of his biological constitution, his sexual drives, his economic needs, his cultural background. But as all human experience demonstrates, no man is wholly *determined* by these factors—even the degrees to which he is *conditioned* by them differs with each individual. That man is morally free is reaffirmed by the talmudic statement—"Everything is in the hands of God except the fear of God" (B.T. *Berakhot* 33b).

The basis for this conviction lies in the biblical doctrine in Genesis that man is created "in the image of God." This profound metaphor, the implications of which are far-reaching, declares that man partakes, on a small and imperfect scale, of the preeminent attributes of God. The "image" has been identified variously with the gift of immortality, the capacity for love, the love of righteousness, the power of creation. Above all, it has been interpreted as the power of reason. Now, what is reason in the intellectual sphere is freedom of will in the moral area, and this, in turn, is the basis for responsibility in the social arena, for without freedom there is no possibility of holding a man responsible for his actions, and the fabric of society must dissolve into anarchy.

Once man, unlike any other creature known to us, has been endowed with the fateful power of freedom of choice, he can, and all too often does, choose evil, including the monstrous evil of Nazism. The freedom of man is not only indispensable to religion—without it no society can long endure. The major ills afflicting human life—war, poverty, and, in large measure, disease—are not the will of God but the act of man, the bitter fruits of the freedom he has abused. Consequently, not God, but man, can stamp them out by the exercise of intelligence and the moral will.

But even if the reality of man's freedom—and man's responsibility—is granted, an excruciating question remains. Why is it possible for some men to sin—and cause others to suffer? The agonizing cry, "Why do the wicked prosper and the righteous suffer?" will continue to reverberate as long as men live. Here, too, we have no total answer, but some light may be found in an insight of the unknown prophet of the Babylonian Exile, whose words are embedded in the Book of Isaiah. Basic to his world view, but permeating biblical and rabbinic thought as a whole, is the concept of the interdependence of mankind.

The interdependence of mankind is no pleasant Sunday school platitude, but a hard reality of the human condition. The Rabbis were once asked to cite the greatest verse in the Bible. As might be expected, one quoted the Golden Rule in Leviticus (19:18), "Thou shalt love thy neighbor as thyself." The other, more surprisingly, cited the prosaic opening verse in the genealogies in Genesis (5:1), "This is the book of the generations of Adam; in the day that God created Adam it was in the image of God that He created him" (*Sifra, Kedoshim* 4.12). The verse embodies two fundamental truths about man—the dignity of each human being created in the Divine image, and the unity of all men derived from a single ancestor. The biblical law giver, prophet, and sage all emphasize the thought that the entire human race is a unit, both "horizontally" through space and "vertically" through time. All the members of a single generation in space have a common destiny they cannot escape, and the various links in a family through time are also insolubly joined together, both for good ("the merit of the fathers") and for ill ("the sins of the fathers upon the children").

This concept of the interdependence of mankind was not permitted to remain a pious abstraction. It became an indispensable weapon for survival in the critical period of the Babylonian Exile. After the burning of the First Temple and the destruction of the Jewish state, the exiled Jews not only sat weeping by the rivers of Babylon, but agonized over their tragic lot. Some lost heart and, deciding that "God is dead," were assimilated to the triumphal paganism all about them. Others, of sterner stuff, vigorously challenged the justice of God that made them lowly and oppressed aliens while the heathen conquerors ruled the world. In response to this situation, Deutero-Isaiah enunciated the doctrine that this uprooted and degraded people was the "servant of the Lord." The prophet believed that Israel was suffering contumely and misery at the hands of the nations, not because of its sins, but because of its role in the world as the teacher and witness to God's law of justice, freedom, and peace. When the nations outgrow their moral immaturity and achieve insight and understanding, they will accept the Divine law of righteousness. They will cease to despise and attack Israel, and, on the contrary, accord it a place of dignity and honor within the family of mankind.

It should be noted that, contrary to widespread opinion, the prophet is not enunciating the concept of vicarious atonement, which is a theological doctrine, but the reality of vicarious suffering, which is a fact of life, a datum of human experience that every mother and, indeed, every parent, knows at firsthand. When one loves another human being, one is bound to suffer with and for the loved one. Even when conscious love is absent— even when there is indifference or hatred—the fate of all men is inexorably intertwined, for we are all brothers in a merciless, as well as in a merciful, sense. As a graphic parable of the Rabbis puts it, we are all in the same boat and one man cannot bore a hole in it with the excuse that it is only under his own seat that he is making the hole.

That man's baleful actions take place on a more colossal scale today than in the past, does not render the truth of the prophetic insight irrelevant. For each soul is of infinite worth and all human suffering is on an infinite scale, so that six thousand crucified by Alexander Jannaeus in the second century BCE is qualitatively no less grievous than six million exterminated by Hitler, nor more heinous than three men nailed to a cross by the Romans.

When we become aware of the perilous nature of human freedom and of each man's interdependence and involvement with his fellows, and when we recognize the reality of vicarious suffering, we are no longer compelled to regard suffering as meaningless, life a horror, and the world an absurdity. It becomes possible, even in the most brutal of centuries, to believe that there is meaning and plan in the universe, even if it is far less neat and pleasant than we would wish.

To be sure, the horrors spawned by twentieth-century technological man are far more extensive than those of his medieval forebears or his ancient ancestors, but equally enlarged are his capacities for good. Perhaps the most important moral advance in the modern age is man's refusal to accept most forms of suffering as ineluctable elements of the human condition. Modern man denies that war is ineradicable, that poverty will always be with us, that racial injustice and social oppression are eternal. Perhaps the citadel of death cannot be stormed, but disease can be controlled and minimized. As against the major sins of which modern man is guilty, we must set the major virtue of his refusal to acquiesce in evil as inevitable.

In the past, only the prophets of Israel had the vision and the faith to believe that war would cease, that poverty could be destroyed and oppression be uprooted. Even Plato, the noblest of the Greeks, in sketching the outlines of the ideal commonwealth in his *Republic,* regarded war as a permanent condition of man and ordained a standing army to protect the republic against the barbarians without the gates. It was the Hebrew prophets who declared that world peace was the inevitable goal of human history. But the prophetic contribution went even further. Isaiah underscored the truth that world peace does not require the transformation of men and nations into angels, but, rather, the establishment of the moral law as sovereign above individual and group interests. What Plato could not conceive, and even the prophets could envision only for the distant future, our age regards as entirely realizable, and since it seems remote in the present, we blame the "enemy" on the other side. The chaos and conflict, even the impatience and violence of our age point, not to the absurdity of the human condition, but to its potential for good.

The faith that derives from the Bible recognizes that the messianic age of justice, freedom, and peace will not be ushered in without pain and destruction. Armaggedon remains the prelude to a new heaven and a new earth. The Rabbis spoke of "the birth pangs of the messiah." Some of them went so far as to say, "Let the Messiah come and I not be there to see him." Nevertheless, the messianic hope remains the capstone in the arch of biblical religion and in a viable faith for modern men. As Martin Buber pointed out, even the Greeks had no conception of "the whole earth" and of "the end of days." That mankind was one family and that history was moving to a great consummation was the contribution of the Hebrew prophets.

Undoubtedly, many men today, their spirits crushed by the world they see, will be unable to muster this confidence in the meaning of life.

They will prefer one or another of the unfaiths that shock and fascinate so many of our contemporaries. But for many other men who are neither enslaved by nostalgia for the past nor overwhelmed by the evils of the present, biblical faith is a rich resource that can speak to the mind as well as the heart. When reinterpreted with insight and perspective on the one hand, and with sympathy and concern for the human condition on the other, the biblical faith emerges, not as a collection of platitudes, but as a revolutionary manifesto calling men to life, to hope, and to action.

Irving (Yitzchak) Greenberg

Irving Greenberg was born in 1933 in Brooklyn, New York. His father was the rabbi of the *Chevra Shas* (a talmudic study group) in Boro Park. As a child, he received an Orthodox day school education that was enriched by active involvement in the Zionist youth movement *Hashomer Hadati* (known today as *Bnai Akiva*). He continued his Jewish education at the Beth Joseph Rabbinical Seminary and his secular education at Brooklyn College. In 1953, he received his B.A. in history from Brooklyn College and continued on to a doctoral program in intellectual history at Harvard. He received his Ph.D. from Harvard in 1960. Eschewing an academic career, he became a communal rabbi in Boston where he came under the influence of Rabbi Joseph B. Soloveitchik. This encounter caused a change of career plans, and Greenberg began to teach Jewish history at Yeshiva University in New York City. In 1961–1962, he was a Fulbright scholar at Tel Aviv University and while in Israel turned to deep reading about both the Holocaust and the State of Israel. Upon his return to the United States, he became involved in Holocaust education which, in turn, led him to leave Yeshiva University in 1965 in order to accept a rabbinical position in Riverdale, New York. After seven years in this post, he once again entered academic life, accepting the chairmanship of the Department of Jewish Studies at the City University of New York. In 1979 he made another turn, leaving the university to become the director of CLAL, the National Jewish Center for Learning and Leadership, an organization that aimed to bring intense, advanced, Jewish education to the wider Jewish community. During the 1970s, Greenberg also teamed with Elie Wiesel and others to create the U.S. Holocaust Memorial Museum, and from 2000 to 2002 he served as chairman of the museum's council.

Through all these turns and changes, there has been one constant in Greenberg's adult career: his profound concern with the theological and sociopolitical implications of the Holocaust for both contemporary Jews and Christians. This is most clearly displayed in his list of publications on these themes, which includes the papers "Cloud of Smoke, Pillar of Fire: Judaism, Christianity, and Modernity after the Holocaust"; "The Interaction of Israel and American Jewry after the Holocaust"; "The Third Great Cycle of Jewish History"; and "Voluntary Covenant." This concern also permeates all of his other mature publications on Jewish thought and on Jewish-Christian dialogue.

SELECTIONS

The first selection from Greenberg's work is taken from his essay "Cloud of Smoke, Pillar of Fire: Judaism, Christianity, and Modernity after the Holocaust." This essay was first presented in 1973 as a lecture at a major ecumenical conference on the

Holocaust at the Cathedral of St. John the Divine in New York City. After setting out the theological problem created by the Holocaust, Greenberg attempts to create a new category of dialectical faith, defined as "moment faiths," that recognizes the power of evil in our world but still has the courage not to give up on the belief in God. History provides evidence both for and against God, and thus some form of faith, however fragile and insecure, is not absurd. For Greenberg, the coming into being of the State of Israel after the Holocaust is, from a Jewish theological perspective, particularly strong evidence for God's existence. Importantly, Greenberg also draws ethical consequences from this post-Holocaust faith, the most important being "the self-criticism and review of every cultural or religious framework that may sustain some devaluation or denial of the absolute and equal dignity of the other."

The second selection is taken from Greenberg's deconstruction of the meaning of Jewish history in "The Third Great Cycle of Jewish History." In this thoughtful essay, he attempts to understand the post-Holocaust era as the "third era" in Jewish history in which, following the biblical and rabbinic eras (identified as eras one and two), the Holocaust has changed everything. Within the Jewish world, the very nature of the covenantal relation between God and Israel and the obligations it entails have been transmuted.

The third selection, "Voluntary Covenant," carries forward the theme of a radical post-Holocaust third era in Jewish history. Most dramatically, Greenberg now pronounces the fateful judgment: *The covenant is now voluntary!* After Auschwitz, Jews have, miraculously, chosen to continue to live Jewish lives and collectively to build a Jewish state, the ultimate symbol of Jewish continuity, but these acts are now the result of the free choice of the Jewish people:

> I submit that the covenant was broken but the Jewish people, released from its obligations, chose voluntarily to take it on again and renew it. God was in no position to command any more but the Jewish people were so in love with the dream of redemption that they volunteered to carry on with their mission.

The consequence of this voluntary action transforms the existing covenantal order. First, Israel was a junior partner, then an equal partner, and now, after Auschwitz, it becomes "the senior partner in action. In effect, God was saying to humans: You stop the Holocaust. You bring the redemption. You act to ensure: never again. I will be with you totally in whatever you do, wherever you go, whatever happens, but you must do it."

Selected Bibliography

Books and Articles by Irving (Yitzchak) Greenberg

"Cloud of Smoke, Pillar of Fire: Judaism, Christianity, and Modernity after the Holocaust," in *Auschwitz: Beginning of a New Era?*, edited by Eva Fleischner (New York, 1977), pp. 7–55, 441–446.

"The Interaction of Israel and American Jewry after the Holocaust," in *World Jewry and the State of Israel,* edited by Moshe Davis (New York, 1977), pp. 259–282.

"The Third Great Cycle of Jewish History," *Perspectives* (September 1981).

"Voluntary Covenant," *Perspectives* (October 1982).

The Jewish Way: Living the Holidays (New York, 1993).

Living in the Image of God: Jewish Teachings to Perfect the World (Northvale, Calif., 1998).

For the Sake of Heaven and Earth: The New Encounter between Judaism and Christianity (Philadelphia, 2004).

Works about Irving Greenberg

Wyschogrod, Michael. "Auschwitz: Beginning of a New Era? Reflections on the Holocaust,"
    Tradition 17 (Fall 1978–Spring 1979): 63–78.

Singer, David. "The New Orthodox Theology," *Modern Judaism* 9, no. 1 (1989): 35–54.

Katz, Steven T. "Voluntary Covenant: Irving Greenberg on Faith after the Holocaust," in
    Steven T. Katz, *Historicism, the Holocausts and Zionism: Critical Studies in Modern Jewish
    Thought and History* (New York, 1992), pp. 225–250.

————. "Irving (Yitzchak) Greenberg," in *Interpreters of Judaism in the Late Twentieth Century*,
    edited by Steven T. Katz (Washington, D.C., 1993), pp. 59–89.

Levenson, Jon D. "Chosen Peoples: A Review of *For the Sake of Heaven and Earth*,"
    Commonweal 131, no. 9 (5 November 2004): 49–53. Reply by Irving Greenberg, "Do
    Jews and Christians Worship the Same God?" *Commonweal* 132, no. 2 (28 January 2005):
    12–13; with a response by Jon D. Levenson, p. 13.

Cloud of Smoke, Pillar of Fire: Judaism, Christianity, and Modernity after the Holocaust

To the memory of my father, Rabbi Eliyahu Chaim Greenberg,
1894–1975

I. Judaism and Christianity: Religions of Redemption and the Challenge of History

Both Judaism and Christianity are religions of redemption. Both religions come to this affirmation about human fate out of central events in history. For Jews, the basic orienting experience has been the Exodus. Out of the overwhelming experience of God's deliverance of His people came the judgment that the ultimate truth is not the fact that most humans live nameless and burdened lives and die in poverty and oppression. Rather, the decisive truth is that man is of infinite value and will be redeemed. Every act of life is to be lived by that realization.

For Christians, the great paradigm of this meaning is the life, death, and resurrection of Jesus Christ. By its implications, all of life is lived.

The central events of both religions occur and affect humans in history. The shocking contrast of the event of salvation come and the cruel realities of actual historical existence have tempted Christians to cut loose from earthly time. Yet both religions ultimately have stood by the claim that redemption will be realized in actual human history. This view has had enormous impact on the general Western and modern view that human liberation can and will be realized in the here and now.

Implicit in both religions is the realization that events happen in history which change our perception of human fate, events from which we draw the fundamental norms by which we act and interpret what happens to us. One such event is the Holocaust—the destruction of European Jewry from 1933 to 1945.

Work on this article was supported by a fellowship from the National Endowment for the Humanities in 1974–1975 and research support from the Meinhardt Spielman Fund for the Department of Jewish Studies, City College, CUNY. The author wishes to thank Professor Alvin Rosenfeld of Indiana University for his most helpful close reading and extensive editorial comments on this text as well as for a series of conversations in Jerusalem which affected the final content of this essay.

The Challenge of the Holocaust

Both religions have always sought to isolate their central events—Exodus and Easter—from further revelations or from the challenge of the demonic counterexperience of evil in history. By and large, both religions have continued since 1945 as if nothing had happened to change their central understanding. It is increasingly obvious that this is impossible, that the Holocaust cannot be ignored.

By its very nature, the Holocaust is obviously central for Jews. The destruction cut so deeply that it is a question whether the community can recover from it. When Adolf Eichmann went into hiding in 1945, he told his accomplice Dieter Wisliceny that if caught, he would leap into his grave laughing. He believed that although he had not completed the total destruction of Jewry, he had accomplished his basic goal—because the Jews could never recover from this devastation of their life center. Indeed, Eichmann had destroyed 90 percent of Eastern European Jewry, the spiritual and biological vital center of prewar world Jewry. Six million Jews were killed—some 30 percent of the Jewish people in 1939; but among the dead were over 80 percent of the Jewish scholars, rabbis, full-time students, and teachers of Torah alive in 1939.[1] Since there can be no covenant without the covenant people, the fundamental existence of Jews and Judaism is thrown into question by this genocide. For this reason alone, the trauma of the Holocaust cannot be overcome without some basic reorientation in light of it by the surviving Jewish community. Recent studies by Professor Simon Herman, an Israeli social psychologist, have indicated that the perception of this event and its implications for the Jews' own fate has become a most widespread and powerful factor in individual Jewish consciousness and identity.[2]

The Holocaust as Radical Countertestimony to Judaism and Christianity

For Christians, it is easier to continue living as if the event did not make any difference, as if the crime belongs to the history of another people and faith. But such a conclusion would be and is sheer self-deception. The magnitude of suffering and the manifest worthlessness of human life radically contradict the fundamental statements of human value and divine concern in both religions. Failure to confront and account for this evil, then, would turn both religions into empty, Pollyanna assertions, credible only because believers ignore the realities of human history. It would be comparable to preaching that this is the best of all possible worlds to a well-fed, smug congregation, while next door little children starve slowly to death.

Judaism and Christianity do not merely tell of God's love for man, but stand or fall on their fundamental claim that the human being is, therefore, of ultimate and absolute value. ("He who saves one life it is as if he saved an entire world"—B. T. *Sanhedrin* 37[a], "God so loved the world that He gave His only begotten son"—John 3:16.) It is the contradiction of this intrinsic value and the reality of human suffering that validates the absolute centrality and necessity of redemption, of the messianic hope. But speak of the value of human life and hear the testimony of S. Szmaglewska, a Polish guard at Auschwitz, about the summer of 1944. The passage (from the Nuremburg trial record) deserves commentary:

---

1. Dieter Wisliceny, affidavit dated November 29, 1945, printed in *Nazi Conspiracy and Aggression* (Washington, D.C., Government Printing Office, 1946), 8:610; he quotes Eichmann as follows: "I laugh when I jump into the grave because of the feeling I have killed 5,000,000 Jews. That gives me great satisfaction and gratification." Rudolf Höss, the head of Auschwitz, reports Eichmann's joy grew out of his conviction that he had landed a fatal blow by devastating Jewry's life center. In Höss's responses to Dr. Jan Sehn, the examining judge, printed as appendix 3 in Höss's autobiography, *Commandant of Auschwitz* (London: Weidenfeld & Nicolson, 1959), p. 215. The estimate of Jewish scholars, rabbis, and full-time students killed is by Rabbi M. J. Itamar (Wohlgelernter), formerly secretary general of the chief rabbinate of Israel. Heydrich, the original

head of the "final solution" project and its driving force until his death by assassination, instructed the *Einsatzgruppen* that in killing the Jews of Eastern Europe, they would be killing the "intellectual reservoir of the Jews."

2. Simon Herman, *Israelis and Jews: A Study in the Continuity of an Identity* (New York, 1970), pp. 78–80, 175, 186, 191, 203–4, 211–13; idem, lecture given at the annual meeting of the Memorial Foundation for Jewish Culture in Geneva, July 9, 1974, published in 1975 *Proceedings of the Memorial Foundation for Jewish Culture*; idem, "Ethnic Identity and Historical Time Perspective: An Illustrated Case Study: The Impact of the Holocaust (Destruction of European Jewry) on Jewish Identity," mimeographed (Jerusalem, 1972); idem, research in progress.

Witness: . . . women carrying children were [always] sent with them to the crematorium. [Children were of no labor value so they were killed. The mothers were sent along, too, because separation might lead to panic, hysteria—which might slow up the destruction process, and this could not be afforded. It was simpler to condemn the mothers too and keep things quiet and smooth.] The children were then torn from their parents outside the crematorium and sent to the gas chambers separately. [At that point, crowding more people into the gas chambers became the most urgent consideration. Separating meant that more children could be packed in separately, or they could be thrown in over the heads of adults once the chamber was packed.] When the extermination of the Jews in the gas chambers was at its height, orders were issued that children were to be thrown straight into the crematorium furnaces, or into a pit near the crematorium, without being gassed first.

Smirnov [Russian prosecutor]: How am I to understand this? Did they throw them into the fire alive, or did they kill them first?

Witness: They threw them in alive. Their screams could be heard at the camp. It is difficult to say how many children were destroyed in this way.

Smirnov: Why did they do this?

Witness: It's very difficult to say. We don't know whether they wanted to economize on gas, or if it was because there was not enough room in the gas chambers.[3]

A word must be said on the decision to economize on gas. By the summer of 1944, the collapse of the eastern front meant that the destruction of European Jewry might not be completed before the advancing Allied armies arrived. So Hungarian Jewry was killed at maximum speed—at the rate of up to ten thousand people a day. Priority was given to transports of death over trains with reinforcements and munitions needed for the Wehrmacht. There was no time for selections of the healthy, of young Jews for labor, or even for registering the number of victims. Entire trainloads were marched straight to the gas chambers.

The gas used—Zyklon B—causes death by internal asphyxiation, with damage to the centers of respiration, accompanied by feelings of fear, dizziness, and vomiting. In the chamber, when released,

> the gas climbs gradually to the ceiling, forcing the victims to claw and trample upon one another in their struggle to reach upward. Those on the top are the last to succumb. . . . The corpses are piled one on top of another in an enormous heap. . . . at the bottom of the pile are babies and children, women, and old people.[4]

The sheer volume of gas used in the summer of 1944 depleted the gas supply. In addition, the Nazis deemed the costs excessive. Therefore, in that summer, the dosage of gas was halved from twelve boxes to six per gassing. When the concentration of the gas is quite high, death occurs quickly. The decision to cut the dosage in half was to more than double the agony.

How much did it cost to kill a person? The Nazi killing machine was orderly and kept records. The gas was produced by the Deutsche Gesellschaft fur Schadlingsbekampfung m.b.H. (German Vermin-Combating Corporation, called DEGESCH for short). It was a highly profitable business, which paid dividends of 100 percent to 200 percent per year (100 percent in 1940 and 1941; 200 percent in 1942, 1943) to I. G. Farben, one of the three corporations which owned it.[5] The bills for Zyklon B came to 195 kilograms for 975 marks = 5 marks per kilogram. Approximately 5.5 kilograms were used on every chamberload, about fifteen hundred people. This means 27.5

3. S. Szmaglewska, in *Trial of the Major War Criminals before the International Military Tribunal* (Nuremberg, 1947–49), 8:319–20, quoted in Erich Kulka and Uta Kraus, *The Death Factory* (Oxford, 1966), p. 114. (In the IMT record she is listed as Shmaglevskaya.) Cf. also Höss, *Commandant of Auschwitz*, pp. 149–51.
4. S. Szmaglewska, *Trial of the Major War Criminals.*
5. Raul Hilberg, *The Destruction of the European Jews* (Chicago, 1966); Hilberg, ibid., p. 569, fn. 65, cites

5.28 RM per kg. for TESTA's price from DEGESCH before resale to Gerstein, the chief disinfection officer in the office of the hygienic chief of the Waffen-SS, for use in Auschwitz. However, a photograph of an invoice from DEGESCH to Kurt Gerstein dated March 13, 1944, published in *La Deportation* (n.d., n.p., published by Fédération Nationale des Déportés et Internis Resistants et Patriots), p. 138, clearly shows a price of 5 RM per kg. (210kg. for 1,050 RM).

marks per fifteen hundred people. With the mark equal to 25 cents, this yields $6.75 per fifteen hundred people, or forty-five hundredths of a cent per person. In the summer of 1944, a Jewish child's life was not worth the two-fifths of a cent it would have cost to put it to death rather than burn it alive. There, in its starkest form, is the ultimate denial.

In short, the Holocaust poses the most radical countertestimony to both Judaism and Christianity. Elie Wiesel has stated it most profoundly:

> Never shall I forget the little faces of the children, whose bodies I saw turned into wreaths of smoke beneath a silent blue sky.
>
> Never shall I forget those flames which consumed my faith forever.
>
> Never shall I forget that nocturnal silence which deprived me, for all eternity, of the desire to live.
>
> Never shall I forget those moments which murdered my God and my soul and turned my dreams to dust.
>
> Never shall I forget these things, even if I am condemned to live as long as God Himself. Never.[6]

The cruelty and the killing raise the question whether even those who believe after such an event dare talk about God who loves and cares without making a mockery of those who suffered.

Further Challenge of the Holocaust to Christianity: The Moral Failure and Complicity of Anti-Semitism

Unfortunately, however, the Holocaust poses a yet more devastating question to Christianity: What did Christianity contribute to make the Holocaust possible? The work of Jules Isaac,

Norman Cohn, Raul Hilberg, Roy Eckardt, and others poses this question in a number of different ways. In 1942, the Nietra Rebbe went to Archbishop Kametko of Nietra to plead for Catholic intervention against the deportation of the Slovakian Jews. Tiso, the head of the Slovakian government, had been Kametko's secretary for many years, and the rebbe hoped that Kametko could persuade Tiso not to allow the deportations. Since the rebbe did not yet know of the gas chambers, he stressed the dangers of hunger and disease, especially for women, old people, and children. The archbishop replied:

> It is not just a matter of deportation. You will not die there of hunger and disease. They will slaughter all of you there, old and young alike, women and children, at once—it is the punishment that you deserve for the death of our Lord and Redeemer, Jesus Christ—you have only one solution. Come over to our religion and I will work to annul this decree.[7]

There are literally hundreds of similar anti-Semitic statements by individual people reported in the Holocaust literature. As late as March 1941—admittedly still before the full destruction was unleashed—Archbishop Grober (Germany), in a pastoral letter, blamed the Jews for the death of Christ and added that "the self-imposed curse of the Jews, 'His blood be upon us and upon our children' had come true terribly, until the present time, until today."[8] Similarly the Vatican responded to an inquiry from the Vichy government about the law of 2 June 1941, which isolated and deprived Jews of rights: "In principle, there is nothing in these measures which the Holy See would find to criticize."[9]

---

6. Elie Wiesel, *Night* (New York, 1960), pp. 43–44.

7. Michael Dov Weissmandl, *Min Hametzar* (1960; reprint ed., Jerusalem, n.d.), p. 24. See also Weissmandl's report of his conversation with the papal nuncio in 1944. He quotes the nuncio as saying: "There is no innocent blood of Jewish children in the world. All Jewish blood is guilty. You have to die. This is the punishment that has been awaiting you because of that sin [deicide]." Dr. Livia Rotkirchen of Yad Vashem has called my attention to the fact that the papal nuncio tried to help save Jews and used his influence to do so. Weissmandl's quote appears to be incompatible with that image. Dr. Rotkirchen speculates that Weissmandl, in retrospect, attributed the statement

to the wrong person. In any event, this judgment that the Jews deserved their fate as punishment for deicide or rejecting Christ is a strong and recurrent phenomenon. On the papal nuncio's work, see Livia Rotkirchen, "Vatican Policy and the Jewish 'Independent' Slovakia (1939–1945)," *Yad Vashem Studies* 6 (1967): 27–54.

8. Pastoral letter of March 25, 1941, A. B. Freiburg, no. 9, March 27, 1941, p. 388; quoted in Günter Lewy, *The Catholic Church and Nazi Germany* (New York, 1964), p. 294.

9. Saul Friedlander, *Pius XII and the Third Reich: A Documentation* (New York, 1966), p. 97. Cf. the whole discussion of the decrees by the Vatican, ibid., pp. 92–99.

In general, there is an inverse ratio between the presence of a fundamentalist Christianity and the survival of Jews during the Holocaust period. This is particularly damning because the attitude of the local population toward the Nazi assault on the Jews seems to be a critical variable in Jewish survival. (If the local population disapproved of the genocide or sympathized with the Jews, they were more likely to hide or help Jews, resist or condemn the Nazis, which weakened the effectiveness of the killing process or the killers' will to carry it out.) We must allow for the other factors which operated against the Jews in the countries with a fundamentalist Christianity. These factors include Poland and the Baltic nations' lack of modernity (modernity = tolerance, ideological disapproval of mass murder, presence of Jews who can pass, etc.); the isolation and concentration of Jews in these countries, which made them easy to identify and destroy; the Nazis considered Slavs inferior and more freely used the death penalty for any help extended to Jews; the Nazis concentrated more of the governing power in their own hands in these countries. Yet even when all these allowances are made, it is clear that anti-Semitism played a role in the decision not to shield Jews—or to actually turn them in. If the teaching of contempt furnished an occasion—or presented stereotypes which brought the Nazis to focus on the Jews as the scapegoat in the first place; or created a residue of anti-Semitism in Europe which affected the local populations' attitudes toward Jews; or enabled some Christians to feel they were doing God's duty in helping kill Jews or in not stopping it—then Christianity may be hopelessly and fatally compromised. The fact is that during the Holocaust the church's protests were primarily on behalf of converted Jews. At the end of the war, the Vatican and circles close to it helped thousands of war criminals to escape, including Franz Stangl, the commandant of the

most murderous of all the extermination camps, Treblinka, and other men of his ilk. Finally in 1948, the German Evangelical Conference at Darmstadt, meeting in the country which had only recently carried out this genocide, proclaimed that the terrible Jewish suffering in the Holocaust was a divine visitation and a call to the Jews to cease their rejection and ongoing crucifixion of Christ. May one morally be a Christian after this?[10]

Even some Christians who resisted Hitler failed on the Jewish question. Even the great Christians— who recognized the danger of idolatry and resisted the Nazi government's takeover of the German Evangelical church at great personal sacrifice and risk—did not speak out on the Jewish question.[11] All this suggests that something in Christian teaching supported or created a positive context for anti-Semitism, and even murder. Is not the faith of a gospel of love, then, fatally tainted with collaboration with genocide— conscious or unconscious? To put it another way: If the Holocaust challenges the fundamental religious claims of Christianity (and Judaism), then the penumbra of Christian complicity may challenge the credibility of Christianity to make these claims.

Is the wager of Christian faith lost? There is yet a third way in which this problem may be stated. In its origins, Christianity grew out of a wager of faith. Growing in the bosom of Judaism and its messianic hope, Jesus (like others) could be seen either as a false messiah or as a new unfolding of God's love and a revelation of love and salvation for mankind. Those who followed Jesus as the Christ, in effect, staked their lives that the new orientation was neither an illusion nor an evil, but yet another stage in salvation and a vehicle of love for mankind. "The acceptance . . . of Jesus as the

10. "Ein Wort zur Judenfrage, der Reichsbruderrat der Evangelischen Kirche in Deutschland," issued on April 8, 1948, in Dietrich Goldschmidt and Hans-Joachim Kraus, eds., *Der Ungekundigte Bund: Neue Begegnung von Juden und christlicher* (Stuttgart, 1962), pp. 251–54. The extent to which Vatican circles helped Nazi war criminals escape is only now becoming evident. See on this Gitta Sereny, *Into That*

Darkness (London, 1974), pp. 289–323. See also Ladislav Farago, *Aftermath: Martin Bormann and the Fourth Reich* (New York, 1974).

11. Cf. memorandum submitted to Chancellor Hitler, June 4, 1936, in Arthur C. Cochrane, *The Church's Confession under Hitler* (Philadelphia, 1962), pp. 268–79; J. S. Conway, *The Nazi Persecution of the Churches* (London, 1968), pp. xx, xxiii, 84–85, 261–65.

Messiah means beholding him as one who transforms and will transform the world."[12] As is the case with every vehicle, divine and human, the spiritual record of this wager has been mixed—comprising great inspiration for love given and great evils caused. The hope is that the good outweighs the evil. But the throwing into the scales of so massive a weight of evil and guilt raises the question whether the balance might now be broken, whether one must not decide that it were better that Jesus had not come, rather than that such scenes be enacted six million times over—and more. Has the wager of faith in Jesus been lost?

II. The Challenge to Modern Culture

The Breaking of Limits

The same kinds of questions must be posed to modern culture as well. For the world, too, the Holocaust is an event which changes fundamental perceptions. Limits were broken, restraints shattered, that will never be recovered, and henceforth mankind must live with the dread of a world in which models for unlimited evil exist. Premodern man thought there were limits. But consider Einsatz Commando A, Strike Commando 3, which reported its daily activities as follows:[13]

[*Executions*]

8/23/41	Panevezys	1312 Jewish men, 4602 Jewish women, 1609 Jewish children	7,523
8/18 to 22/41	Rasainiai District	466 Jewish men, 440 Jewish women, 1020 Jewish children	1,926
8/25/41	Obelisi	112 Jewish men, 627 Jewish women, 421 Jewish children	1,160
8/25 and 26/41	Seduva	230 Jewish men, 275 Jewish women, 159 Jewish children	664
8/26/41	Zarasai	767 Jewish men, 1113 Jewish women, 1 Russian communist woman, 1 Lithuanian communist, 687 Jewish children	2,569
8/26/41	Pasvalys	402 Jewish men, 738 Jewish women, 209 Jewish children	1,349
8/26/41	Kaisiadorys	All Jews (men, women, and children)	1,911
8/27/41	Prienai	All Jews (men, women, and children)	1,078
8/27/41	Dagda and Kraslawa	212 Jews, 4 Russian prisoners of war	216
8/27/41	Goniskis	47 Jewish men, 165 Jewish women, 143 Jewish children	355
8/28/41	Wilkia	76 Jewish men, 192 Jewish women, 134 Jewish children	402
8/28/41	Kedainiai	710 Jewish men, 767 Jewish women, 599 Jewish children	2,076
8/29/41	Rumsiskis and Ziezmariai	20 Jewish men, 567 Jewish women, 197 Jewish children	784
8/29/41	Utena and Moletai	582 Jewish men, 1731 Jewish women, 1469 Jewish children	3,782
9/1/41	Mariampole	1763 Jewish men, 1812 Jewish women, 1404 Jewish children, 109 mental patients, 1 female German national who was married to a Jew, 1 Russian woman	5,090

. . .

12. A. Roy Eckardt, *Elder and Younger Brothers* (New York, 1967), p. 107.

13. Raul Hilberg, *Documents of Destruction* (Chicago, 1973), pp. 50–51.

III. The Holocaust as Orienting Event and Revelation

Not to Confront Is to Repeat

For both Judaism and Christianity (and other religions of salvation—both secular and sacred), there is no choice but to confront the Holocaust, because it happened, and because the first Holocaust is the hardest. The fact of the Holocaust makes a repetition more likely—a limit was broken, a control or awe is gone—and the murder procedure is now better laid out and understood. Failure to confront it makes repetition all the more likely. So evil is the Holocaust, and so powerful a challenge to all other norms, that it forces a response, willy-nilly; not to respond is to collaborate in its repetition. This irony of human history, which is already at work, is intensified by the radical power of the Holocaust. Because the world has not made the Holocaust a central point of departure for moral and political policy, the survivors of the Holocaust and their people have lived continually under the direct threat of another Holocaust throughout the past thirty years. Muslims who feel that the event is a Western problem and that Christian guilt has been imposed on them have been tempted to try to stage a repeat performance. They lack the guilt and concern, and that in itself leads to guilt.

The nemesis of denial is culpability. Pope John XXIII, who tried strongly to save Jews in the Holocaust (he made representations and protests, issued false baptismal papers, helped Jews escape), felt guilty and deeply regretted the Catholic church's past treatment of Jews. This pope did more than any other pope had ever done to remove the possibility of another destruction (through the Vatican II Declaration, revising Catholic instruction and liturgy with reference to the Jews, dialogue, etc.).[14] Pope Paul VI, who denied the complicity or guilt of Pius XII in the Holocaust, was tempted thereby into a set of policies (he watered down the Declaration, referred to Jews in the old Passion story terms, refused to recognize Israel's de jure political existence, maintained silence in the face of the threat of genocide), which brings the dreadful guilt of collaboration in genocide so much closer.

This principle applies to secular religions of salvation as well. Thus, the German Democratic Republic (East Germany) has denied any responsibility for the Holocaust, on the grounds that it was carried out by fascist and right-wing circles, whereas East Germany is socialist. As a result, it has allowed Nazis back into government with even more impunity than West Germany. Whereas West Germany has given back billions of dollars of Jewish money in the form of reparations (it is estimated that many more billions were directly stolen and spoiled), the GDR, having no guilty conscience, has yielded up none of the ill-gotten gains of mass murder. In fact, East Germany and its "socialist" allies have pursued policies which have kept the genocide of the Jewish people in Israel a live option to this day. Thus, failure to respond to the Holocaust turns a hallowed ideology of liberation into a cover for not returning robbed goods and for keeping alive the dream of another mass murder.

This is not to say that all-out support for Israel is the only way to avoid complicity in attempted genocide. The communist world could have pursued a pro-Arab policy on its merits. Had they felt as guilty as they should have—as they actually were—they would have made a sine qua non the giving up of all genocidal hopes and talk by the Arabs. In actual fact, the opposite occurred. Several times, when such extreme possibilities were

---

14. Writing under a pseudonym, a priest who had served as ghost writer for Pope John published a report on Vatican II which stated that John had composed a prayer about the Jews. The text, to be read in all Catholic churches, said: "We are conscious today that many centuries of blindness have cloaked our eyes so that we can no longer see the beauty of Thy chosen people.... We realize that the mark of Cain stands on our foreheads. Across the centuries our Brother Abel has lain in blood which we drew, or shed tears we caused, forgetting Thy love. Forgive us for crucifying Thee a second time in their flesh. For we knew not what we did."[15] While the prayer is apocryphal (no trace of it has been found in John's papers), widespread acceptance of its attribution reflects John's known regret and concern.

15. F. E. Cartus [pseud.], "Vatican II and the Jews," *Commentary* (January 1965): 21.

about to be dropped by the Arab world, Russian intervention, with no such policy conditions attached (or with tacit encouragement of destructive goals), restored this abominable option.

The Holocaust cannot be used for triumphalism. Its moral challenge must also be applied to Jews. Those Jews who feel no guilt for the Holocaust are also tempted to moral apathy. Religious Jews who use the Holocaust to morally impugn every other religious group but their own are the ones who are tempted thereby into indifference at the Holocaust of others (cf. the general policy of the American Orthodox rabbinate on U.S. Vietnam policy). Those Israelis who place as much distance as possible between the weak, passive diaspora victims and the "mighty Sabras" are tempted to use Israeli strength indiscriminately (i.e., beyond what is absolutely inescapable for self-defense and survival), which is to risk turning other people into victims of the Jews. Neither faith nor morality can function without serious twisting of perspective, even to the point of becoming demonic, unless they are illuminated by the fires of Auschwitz and Treblinka.

The Dialectical Revelation of the Holocaust

The Holocaust challenges the claims of all the standards that compete for modern man's loyalties. Nor does it give simple, clear answers or definitive solutions. To claim that it does is not to take burning children seriously. This surd will—and should—undercut the ultimate adequacy of any category, unless there were one (religious, political, intellectual) that consistently produced the proper response of resistance and horror at the Holocaust. No such category exists, to my knowledge. To use the catastrophe to uphold the univocal validity of any category is to turn it into grist for propaganda mills. The Nazis turned their Jewish victims into soap and fertilizer after they were dead. The same moral gorge rises at turning them into propaganda. The Holocaust offers us only dialectical moves and understandings—often moves that stretch our capacity to the limit and torment us with their irresolvable tensions. In a way, it is the only morally tenable way for survivors and those guilty of bystanding to live. Woe to those so at ease that they feel no guilt or tension. Often this is the sign of the

death of the soul. I have met many Germans motivated by guilt who came to Israel on pilgrimages of repentance. I have been struck that frequently these were young people, too young to have participated in the genocide; or, more often, persons or the children of persons who had been anti-Nazi or even imprisoned for resistance. I have yet to meet such a penitent who was himself an SS man or even a train official who transported Jews. Living in the dialectic becomes one of the verification principles for alternative theories after the Holocaust.

Let us offer, then, as working principle the following: No statement, theological or otherwise, should be made that would not be credible in the presence of the burning children. In his novel *The Accident*, Elie Wiesel has written of the encounter of a survivor with Sarah, a prostitute who is also a survivor. She began her career at twelve, when she was separated from her parents and sent to a special barracks for the camp officers' pleasure. Her life was spared because there were German officers who liked to make love to little girls her age. Every night she reenacts the first drunken officer's use of a twelve-year-old girl. Yet she lives on, with both life feeling and self-loathing. And she retains enough feeling to offer herself to a shy survivor boy, without money. "You are a saint," he says. "You are mad," she shrieks. He concludes:

> Whoever listens to Sarah and doesn't change, whoever enters Sarah's world and doesn't invent new gods and new religions, deserves death and destruction. Sarah alone has the right to decide what is good and what is evil, the right to differentiate between what is true and what usurps the appearance of truth.[16]

In this story Wiesel has given us an extraordinary phenomenology of the dialectic in which we live after the Holocaust. Sarah's life of prostitution, religiously and morally negative in classic terms, undergoes a moral reversal of category. It is suffering sainthood in the context of her life and her ongoing response to the Holocaust experience. Yet this scene grants us no easy Sabbatianism, in which every act that can wrap itself in the garment of the Holocaust is justified and

16. Elie Wiesel, *The Accident* (New York, 1962), p. 91.

the old categories are no longer valid. The ultimate tension of the dialectic is maintained, and the moral disgust which Sarah's life inspires in her (and Wiesel? and us?) is not omitted either. The more we analyze the passage the more it throws us from pole to pole in ceaseless tension. The very disgust may, in fact, be the outcome of Sarah's mistaken judgment; she continues to judge herself by the categories in which she was raised before the event. This is suggested in the narrator's compassion and love for her. Yet he himself is overcome by moral nausea—or is it pity?—or protest?—until it is too late and Sarah is lost. There is no peace or surcease and no lightly grasped guide to action in this world. To enter into Sarah's world in fear and trembling, and to remain there before and in acting and speech, is the essence of religious response today, as much as when normative Judaism bids us enter into the Exodus, and Christianity asks we enter into Easter and remain there before and in acting or speaking. The classic normative experiences themselves are not dismissed by Wiesel. They are tested and reformulated—dialectically attacked and affirmed—as they pass through the fires of the new revelatory event.[17]

Resistance to New Revelation: Jewish and Christian

Much of classic Jewish and Christian tradition will resist the claim that there have been new revelatory events in our time. Judaism has remained faithful to the covenant of Sinai and rejected this claim when expressed in the life of Jesus as understood by St. Paul and the Christian church, or in the career of Sabbatai Zvi [1626–1676] and others.[18] There are precedents for a reformulation of the covenant in the light of great events, such as the developments which followed the destruction of the Temple, especially the Second Temple.[19] It took, however, a major flowering of Judaism and extraordinary spiritual leadership to articulate and restructure the tradition and it was a painful, soul-searching, and highly conflictual process.[20] The very quality of faithfulness to the covenant resists acceptance of new revelation—as it should. Human nature's love for the familiar conspires with faithfulness to keep new norms out. But no one said that the Holocaust should be simply assimilable. For traditional Jews to ignore or deny all significance to this event would be to repudiate the fundamental belief and affirmations of the Sinai covenant: that history is meaningful, and that ultimate liberation and relationship to God will take place in the realm of human events. Exodus-Sinai would be insulated from all contradictory events—at the cost of removing it from the realm of the real—the realm on which it staked its all—the realm of its origin and testimony. However much medieval Judaism was tempted to move redemption to the realm of eternal life, it never committed this sacrilege. It insisted that the messianic Kingdom of God in this world was not fulfilled by the salvation of the world to come.[21] Even after the expulsion from Spain [in 1492] and the spread of kabbalah, messianic expectation was not totally spiritualized. There is an alternative for those whose faith can pass through the demonic, consuming flames of a crematorium: It is the willingness and ability to hear further revelation and reorient themselves. That is the way to wholeness. Rabbi Nachman of Bratzlav [1772–1810] once said that there is no heart so whole as a broken heart. After Auschwitz, there is no faith so whole as a faith shattered—and re-fused—in the ovens.

17. Elie Wiesel, "The Death of My Father," in *Legends of Our Time* (New York, 1968), pp. 2, 4, 5, 6, 7; idem, *The Gates of the Forest* (New York, 1966), pp. 194, 196, 197, 198, 224, 225–26.

18. Gershom Scholem, *Sabbatai Sevi: The Mystical Messiah* (Princeton, N.J., 1973).

19. Jacob Neusner, *A Life of Rabban Yohanan ben Zakkai* (Leiden, 1962); idem, *Fellowship in Judaism in the First Century* (New York, 1972). But see also idem, "Judaism in a Time of Crisis: Four Responses to the Destruction of the Temple," *Judaism* 21, no. 3 (Summer 1972): 313–27. See Peter R. Ackroyd, *Exile and Restoration* (Philadelphia, 1968); and Yehezkel Kaufmann, *The Religion of Israel* (Chicago, 1960), epilogue; see also Salo W. Baron, *Social and Religious History of the Jews* (New York, 1952), vol. 1, chs. 4, 5, on the impact of the destruction of the First Temple.

20. See Irving Greenberg, *Crossroads of Destiny* (New York, [1975]), and any of the standard history books, such as Salo W. Baron, *Social and Religious History*, vol. 2, chs. 11, 12, et seq.

21. Cf. Maimonides, *Commentary on the Mishnah, Sanhedrin*, ch. 10, mishnah 1.

Since this further revelation grows in the womb of Judaism, it may be asked whether it speaks only to Jews, or to Christians also. Classic Christianity is tempted to deny further revelation after Easter. Christianity testified and built itself on the finality of revelation in Christ's life and teaching. Yet, at its core, Christianity claims that God sent a second revelation, which grew out of the ground of acknowledged covenant, superseded the authority of the first revelation, and even supplied a new, higher understanding of the first event. Christian polemic has mocked and criticized the people of Israel for being so blinded by the possession of an earlier revelation and by pride in its finality that Israel did not recognize the time of its visitation. However unjust the polemic against Judaism was (as I believe it was), it ill behooves Christianity to rule out further revelation a priori—lest it be hoist by its own petard. Rather, it should trust its own faith that God is not owned by anyone and the spirit blows where it "likes"? The very anguish and harsh judgments which the Holocaust visits on Christianity open the possibility of freeing the Gospel of Love from the incubus of evil and hatred.

The desire to guarantee absolute salvation and understanding is an all too human need which both religions must resist as a snare and temptation. Just as refusal to encounter the Holocaust brings a nemesis of moral and religious ineffectiveness, openness and willingness to undergo the ordeal of reorienting by the event could well save or illuminate the treasure that is still contained in each tradition.

There are Jews who have sought to assimilate the Holocaust to certain unreconstructed tradi-

tional categories, to explain destruction as a visitation for evil.[22] To account for the Holocaust as God's punishment of Israel for its sins is to betray and mock the agony of the victims. Now that they have been cruelly tortured and killed, boiled into soap, their hair made into pillows and their bones into fertilizer, their unknown graves and the very fact of their death denied to them, the theologian would inflict on them the only indignity left: that is, insistence that it was done because of their sins. As Roy Eckardt wrote, this is the Devil's work. God comforts the afflicted and afflicts the comforted, whereas the Devil comforts the comforted and afflicts the afflicted.[23] A great Jewish scholar sought to account for the Holocaust in terms of Jewish sin. He was led by the logic of his position, first to blame the Zionists rather than the Nazis for the evil; then, to join the enemies of the Jewish state sworn to destroy the Jewish people in common ground of hatred and denunciation of Israel—in effect, collaborating in providing the setting for attempted genocide.[24] By the gracious irony of God, this satanic denouement was happily frustrated by the strength and exploits of those he maligned and excoriated. It is a sobering demonstration that failure to respect the dialectic of the Holocaust can dialectically turn faithfulness into demonism.

IV. Jewish Theological Responses to the Holocaust

A Critique

There have been some notable Jewish theological responses that have correctly grasped the

22. Cf. the moving article by Immanuel Hartom, "Hirhurim al Ha Shoah," Deot 18 (Winter 5720 [1961]): 28–31; and the responses of Isachar Jacobson, "HaChashiva HaMikrait V'HaShoah," Deot 21 (Spring 5722 [1962]): 26–28, and David Chomsky, "Hirhurim al HaShoah v'al Tekumat Yisrael," ibid., pp. 28–39, and Jacob Rothschild, "Od L'Inyan Darkei HaHashgachah V'HaArachat HaShoah," Deot 20 (Summer 5722 [1962]): 39–40. Compare this to the ugly work of R. Yoel Teitelbaum, Al HaGeulah v'al Hatemurah (Brooklyn, N.Y., Jerusalem Publishing, 1967).
23. A. Roy Eckardt, "Is the Holocaust Unique?" Worldview (September 1974): 21–35. See also idem. "The

Devil and the Yom Kippur War," Midstream (August–September 1974): 67–74.
24. Teitelbaum, Al HaGeulah v'al Hatemurah, pp. 6, 11, 18, 29, 77, 84, 88. This is foreshadowed in Teitelbaum's earlier work, VaYoel Moshe (Brooklyn, N.Y., 1962), pp. 6–8, 122–24, 140, and passim. Cf. New York Times, April 1967, seriatim. A news account in Ha'aretz, February 16, 1975, reported that a meeting between Neturei Karta representatives (allied with R. Joel Teitelbaum against Israel) and PLO representatives was held. The Neturei Karta delegates identified with the PLO's commitment to destroy the present state of Israel and replace it with a "secular, democratic" Palestine.

centrality of the Holocaust to Jewish thought and faith. The two primary positions are polar. One witness upholds the God of history. Emil Fackenheim has described the commanding Voice of Auschwitz, which bids us not to hand Hitler any posthumous victories, such as repudiating the covenant and retrospectively declaring Judaism to have been an illusion. Eliezer Berkovits has stressed that Jewish survival testifies to the Lord of history. The other witness affirms the death of God and the loss of all hope. Richard Rubenstein has written: "We learned in the crisis that we were totally and nakedly alone, that we could expect neither support nor succor from God nor from our fellow creatures. Therefore, the world will forever remain a place of pain, suffering, alienation, and ultimate defeat."[25] These are genuine important responses to the Holocaust, but they fall afoul of the dialectical principle. Both positions give a definitive interpretation of the Holocaust which subsumes it under known classical categories. Neither classical theism nor atheism is adequate to incorporate the incommensurability of the Holocaust; neither produces a consistently proper response; neither is credible alone—in the presence of the burning children.

Rubenstein's definitiveness is part of this writer's disagreement with him. Rubenstein concluded that "Jewish history has written the *final chapter* in the terrible story of the God of History," that "the world will *forever* remain a place of pain . . . and *ultimate defeat*," and that the "pathetic hope [of coming to grips with Auschwitz through the framework of traditional Judaism] *will never be realized*" (italics supplied).[26] After the Holocaust, there should be no final solutions, not even theological ones. I could not be more sympathetic to Rubenstein's positions, or more unsympathetic to his conclusions. That Auschwitz and the rebirth of Israel are normative; that there are traditional positions which Auschwitz moves us to repudiate (such as "we were punished for our sins") is a profoundly, authentically Jewish response. To declare that the destruction closes out hope forever is to claim divine omniscience and to use the Holocaust for theological grist. Contra Rubenstein, I would argue that it is not so much that any affirmations (or denials) cannot be made, but that they can be made authentically only if they are made after working through the Holocaust experience. In the same sense, however, the relationship to the God of the covenant cannot be unaffected.

Dialectical Faith, or "Moment Faiths"

Faith is living life in the presence of the Redeemer, even when the world is unredeemed. After Auschwitz, faith means there are times when faith is overcome. Buber has spoken of "moment gods": God is known only at the moment when Presence and awareness are fused in vital life. This knowledge is interspersed with moments when only natural, self-contained, routine existence is present. We now have to speak of "moments when Redeemer and vision of redemption are present, interspersed with times when the flames and smoke of the burning children blot out faith—though it flickers again. Such a moment is described in an extraordinary passage of *Night*, as the young boy sentenced to death but too light to hang struggles slowly on the rope. Eliezer finally responds to the man asking, "Where is God now?" by saying, "Here He is—He is hanging here on this gallows."[27]

This ends the easy dichotomy of atheist-theist, the confusion of faith with doctrine or demonstration. It makes clear that faith is a life response of the whole person to the Presence in life and history. Like life, this response ebbs and flows. The difference between the skeptic and the believer is frequency of faith, and not certitude of position. The rejection of the unbeliever by the believer is literally the denial or attempted suppression of what is within oneself. The ability to live with moment faith is the ability to live with pluralism and without the self-flattering,

25. Berkovits, *Faith after the Holocaust*; Emil Fackenheim, *God's Presence in History* (New York, 1970); Richard Rubenstein, *After Auschwitz* (Indianapolis, Ind., 1966), especially pp. 128–29.

26. Richard Rubenstein, "Homeland and Holocaust," in *The Religious Situation 1968* (Boston, 1969), pp. 39–111.

27. Wiesel, *Night*, p. 71.

ethnocentric solutions which warp religion, or make it a source of hatred for the other.

Why Dialectical Faith Is Still Possible

The persistence of Exodus. Of course, the question may still be asked: Why is it not a permanent destruction of faith to be in the presence of the murdered children?

One reason is that there are still moments when the reality of the Exodus is reenacted and present. There are moments when a member of the community of Israel shares the reality of the child who was to have been bricked into the wall but instead experienced the liberation and dignity of Exodus. [The reference here is to the rabbinic legend that in Egypt, Jewish children were bricked into a wall if their parents did not meet their daily quota of bricklaying.] This happens even to those who have both literally and figuratively lived through the Holocaust. Wiesel describes this moment for us in *The Gates of the Forest,* when Gregor "recites the Kaddish, the solemn affirmation . . . by which man returns to God his crown and his scepter."[28] Neither Exodus nor Easter wins out or is totally blotted out by Buchenwald, but we encounter both polar experiences; the life of faith is lived between them. And this dialectic opens new models of response to God, as we shall show below.

The Breakdown of the Secular Absolute. A second reason is that we do not stand in a vacuum when faith encounters the crematoria. In a real sense, we are always choosing between alternative faiths when we make a decision about ultimate meaning. In this culture the primary alternative to religion is secular man in a world closed off from any transcendence, or divine incursion. This world grows out of the intellectual framework of science, philosophy, and social science, of rationalism and human liberation, which created the enterprise of modernity. This value system was— and is—the major alternative faith which Jews and Christians joined in large numbers in the last two centuries, transferring allegiance from the Lord of history and revelation to the Lord of science and humanism. In so many ways, the Holocaust is the direct fruit and will of this alternative. Modernity fostered the excessive rationalism and utilitarian relations which created the need for and susceptibility to totalitarian mass movements and the surrender of moral judgment. The secular city sustained the emphasis on value-free sciences and objectivity, which created unparalleled power but weakened its moral limits. (Surely it is no accident that so many members of the *Einsatzgruppen* were professionals.) Mass communication and universalization of values weakened resistance to centralized power, and served as a cover to deny the unique danger posted to particular, i.e., Jewish, existence.

In the light of Auschwitz, secular twentieth-century civilization is not worthy of this transfer of our ultimate loyalty. The victims ask that we not jump to a conclusion that retrospectively makes the covenant they lived an illusion and their death a gigantic travesty—a product of their illusions and gentile jealousy of those pathetically mistaken claims.[29] It is not that emotional sympathy decides the validity or invalidity of philosophic positions. The truth is sometimes very unpleasant, and may contradict cherished beliefs or moral preferences. But the credibility of systems does rise or fall in the light of events which enhance or reduce the credibility of their claims.[30] A system associated with creating a framework for mass murder must be very persuasive before gaining intellectual assent. The burden of the proofs should be unquestionable. Nothing in the record of secular culture on the Holocaust justifies its authority claims. The victims ask us, above all, not to allow the creation of another matrix of values that might sustain another attempt at genocide. The absence of strong alternative value systems gives a moral monopoly to the wielders of power and authority. Secular authority unchecked becomes absolute. Relative values thus become the seedbed of absolute claims, and this is idolatry. This vacuum was a major factor in the Nazi ability to concentrate power and carry out the destruction without protest or resistance. (The primary sources of

28. Wiesel, *The Gates of the Forest,* pp. 225–26.
29. Rubenstein, *After Auschwitz,* pp. 9–101.
30. Anthony Flew and Alistair MacIntyre, *New Essays in Philosophical Theology* (London, 1958), pp. 103–5, 109–30.

resistance were systems of absolute alternative values—the Barmen Conference in the Confessional church, Jehovah's Witnesses, etc.)[31] After the Holocaust it is all the more urgent to resist this absolutization of the secular. As Emil Fackenheim has pointed out, the all-out celebration of the secular city by Harvey Cox reflected the assimilation of Christian values to a secular civilization given absolute status.[32] It is potential idolatry, an idolatry to which we more easily succumb if we have failed to look at the Holocaust.

If nothing else sufficed to undercut this absolute claim of nonaccessibility of the divine, it is the knowledge that the absence of limits or belief in a judge, and the belief that persons could therefore become God, underlay the structure of *l'univers concentrationnaire*. Mengele and other selectors of Auschwitz openly joked about this. I will argue below that the need to deny God leads directly to the assumption of omnipotent power over life and death. The desire to control people leads directly to crushing the image of God within them, so that the jailer becomes God. Then one cannot easily surrender to the temptation of being cut off from the transcendence, and must explore the alternatives. Surely it is no accident that in the past forty years language analysts like Wittgenstein, critics of value-free science and social sciences, existentialists, evangelical and counterculture movements alike, have fought to set limits to the absolute claims of scientific knowledge and of reason, and to ensure the freedom for renewed encounter with the transcendental.

The Logic of Post-Holocaust and, therefore, PostModern faith. A third reason to resist abandoning the divine is the moral urgency that grows out of the Holocaust and fights for the presence of the Lord of history. Emil Fackenheim has articulated this position in terms of not handing Hitler posthumous victories. I prefer an even more traditional category, and would argue that the moral necessity of a world to come, and even of resurrection, arises powerfully

out of the encounter with the Holocaust. Against this, Rubenstein and others would maintain that the wish is not always father to the fact, and that such an illusion may endanger even more lives. To this last point I would reply that the proper belief will save, not cost, lives (see below). It is true that moral appropriateness is not always a good guide to philosophic sufficiency; but the Holocaust experience insists that we best err on the side of moral necessity. To put it more rationally, sometimes we see the narrower logic of a specific argument rather than the deeper logic of the historical moment or setting. This could make the narrower logical grounds formally consistent and persuasive, yet utterly misleading, since they may start from and finish with the wrong assumptions.

Moral necessity validates the search for religious experience rather than surrender to the immediate logic of nonbelief. Thus, if the Holocaust strikes at the credibility of faith, especially unreconstructed faith, dialectically it also erodes the persuasiveness of the secular option. If someone is told that a line of argument leads to the conclusion that he should not exist, not surprisingly the victim may argue that there must be alternative philosophical frameworks. Insofar as the Holocaust grows out of Western civilization, then, at least for Jews, it is a powerful incentive to guard against being overimpressed by this culture's intellectual assumptions and to seek other philosophical and historical frameworks. (Cf. Wiesel's more mystical version of this argument—Gyula's comment in *The Accident*: "Lucidity is fate's victory, not man's. It is an act of freedom that carries within itself the negation of freedom. Man must keep moving, searching, weighing, holding out his hand, offering himself, inventing himself.")[33]

The point to keep in mind is that currents of thought and popular assumptions are so ubiquitous that they appear to be self-evident and beyond cavil. It has been pointed out that the opposing positions within one civilization (such

31. Cf. Höss, *Commandant of Auschwitz*, pp. 88–91; Saul Friedlander, *Counterfeit Nazi: The Ambiguity of Good* (London, 1969), pp. 21–22, 36, 59, 64.

32. Emil Fackenheim, "On the Self-Exposure of Faith to the Modern Secular World," reprinted in his *Quest for Past and Future* (Boston, 1968), pp. 289 ff.

33. Wiesel, *The Accident*, p. 118.

as religion and secularity) may have more in common with each other than their presumed associated positions across civilizational lines. Thus modern religion and secularity may have more in common with each other than with their respective official analogues—medieval religion and secularity. The flaws, the hidden assumptions that turn out to be questionable, often do not become obvious until the whole climate of opinions and range of assumptions has changed as a new civilization emerges. The moral light shed by the Holocaust on the nature of Western culture validates skepticism toward contemporary claims—even before philosophic critiques emerge to justify the skepticism. It is enough that this civilization is the locus of the Holocaust. The Holocaust calls on Jews, Christians, and others to absolutely resist the total authority of this cultural moment. The experience frees them to respond to their own claim, which comes from outside the framework of this civilization, to relate to a divine other, who sets limits and judges the absolute claims of contemporary philosophic and scientific and human political systems. To follow this orientation is to be opened again to the possibilities of Exodus and immortality.

This is a crucial point. The Holocaust comes after two centuries of Emancipation's steadily growing domination of Judaism and the Jews. Rubenstein's self-perception as a radical breaking from the Jewish past is, I think, misleading. A more correct view would argue that he is repeating the repudiation of the God of history and the chosen that was emphasized by the modernizing schools, such as Reconstructionism. This position had become the stuff of the values and views of the majority of Jews. "Being right with modernity" (defined by each group differently) has been since 1750 the dominant value norm of a growing number of Jews, as well as Christians. Despite the rear-guard action of Orthodox Judaism and Roman Catholicism (until the 1960s) and of fundamentalist groups, the modern tide has steadily risen higher. The capacity to resist, criticize, or break away from these models is one of the litmus tests of the Holocaust as the new orienting experience of Jews and an indication that a new era of Jewish civilization is under way. This new era will not turn its back on many aspects of modernity, but clearly it will be freer to reject

some of its elements, and to take from the past (and future) much more fully.

The revelation in the redemption of Israel. I have saved for last the most important reason that the moment of despair and disbelief in redemption cannot be final, at least in this generation's community of Israel. Another event has taken place in our lifetime which also has extraordinary scope and normative impact—the rebirth of the State of Israel. As difficult to absorb in its own way and, like the Holocaust, a scandal for many traditional Jewish and Christian categories, it is an inescapable part of the Jewish historical experience in our time. And while it is a continuation and outgrowth of certain responses to the Holocaust, it is at the same time a dialectical contradiction to many of its implications. If the experience of Auschwitz symbolizes that we are cut off from God and hope, and that the covenant may be destroyed, then the experience of Jerusalem symbolizes that God's promises are faithful and His people live on. Burning children speak of the absence of all value—human and divine; the rehabilitation of one-half million Holocaust survivors in Israel speaks of the reclamation of tremendous human dignity and value. If Treblinka makes human hope an illusion, then the Western Wall asserts that human dreams are more real than force and facts. Israel's faith in the God of history demands that an unprecedented event of destruction be matched by an unprecedented act of redemption, and this has happened.[34]

This is not simply a question of the memories of Exodus versus the experience of Auschwitz. If it were a question of Exodus only, then those Jews already cut off from Exodus by the encounter with modern culture would be excluded and only "religious" Jews could still be believers.

But almost all Jews acknowledge this phenomenon—the event of redemption and the event of catastrophe and their dialectical interrelationship—and it touches their lives. Studies show that the number of those who affirm this phenomenon as central (even if in nontheological categories) has grown from year to year, that its impact is now almost universal among those who

34. Cf. I. Greenberg, *The Rebirth of Israel: Event and Interpretation* (forthcoming).

will acknowledge themselves as Jews, and that its force has overthrown some hierarchies of values that grew as modernity came to dominate Jewish life.[35] In fact, the religious situation is explosive and fermenting on a deeper level than anyone wishes to acknowledge at this point. The whole Jewish people is caught between immersion in nihilism and immersion in redemption—both are present in immediate experience, and not just historical memory. To deny either pole in our time is to be cut off from historical Jewish experience. In the incredible dialectical tension between the two we are fated to live. Biblical theology already suggested that the time would come when consciousness of God out of the restoration of Israel would outweigh consciousness of God out of the Exodus. In the words of Jeremiah:

> The days will come, says the Lord, when it shall no longer be said: "as God lives who brought up the children of Israel out of the land of Egypt" but "as God lives who brought up the children of Israel from the land of the north and from all the countries whither He had driven them," and I will bring them back into their land that I gave to their fathers. (Jeremiah 16:14–15)

Despite redemption, faith remains dialectical. But if Israel is so redeeming, why then must faith be "moment faith," and why should the experience of nothingness ever dominate?

The answer is that faith is living in the presence of the Redeemer, and in the moment of utter chaos, of genocide, one does not live in His presence. One must be faithful to the reality of the nothingness. Faith is a moment truth, but there are moments when it is not true. This is certainly demonstrable in dialectical truths, when invoking the truth at the wrong moment is a lie. To let Auschwitz overwhelm Jerusalem is to lie (i.e., to speak a truth out of its appropriate moment); and to let Jerusalem deny Auschwitz is to lie for the same reason.

The biblical witness is that a permanent repudiation of the covenant would also have been a lie. "Behold, they say: our bones are dried up and our hope is lost; we are cut off entirely" (Ezekiel 37:11). There were many who chose this answer, but their logic led to dissolution in the pagan world around them. After losing hope in the Lord of history, they were absorbed into idolatry—the faith of the gods of that moment. In the resolution of the crisis of biblical faith, those who abandoned hope ceased to testify. However persuasive the reaction may have been at that time, every such decision in Israel's history—until Auschwitz—has been premature, and even wrong. Yet in a striking talmudic interpretation, the rabbis say that Daniel and Jeremiah refused to speak of God as awesome or powerful any longer in light of the destruction of the Temple.[36] The line between the repudiation of the God of the covenant and the Daniel-Jeremiah reaction is so thin that repudiation must be seen as an authentic reaction even if we reject it. There is a faithfulness in the rejection; serious theism must be troubled after such an event.

This points to another flaw in interpreting the Holocaust through the traditional response, which declares, "We were punished for our sins." Blaming Israel is an attempt to be faithful to the Holocaust and to the tradition, as well as to the Exodus experience. But it lacks the combination of imagination and faithfulness of the rabbis and the honesty of Daniel and Jeremiah. It justifies God, not man. Yet surely it is God who did not keep His share of the covenant in defending His people in this generation. It is the miracle of the people of Israel that they persist in faith. Surely it is they who should be justified. The Talmud teaches that if one suffers personally, it is meritorious to say, "I am suffering for my sins," and thereby be motivated to repentance. But if someone else is suffering and cannot help himself, and one tells him he is suffering for his sins, it is considered abuse with words. The Talmud calls it *onaat devarim*, literally, "to exploit or abuse with words." Since, in fact, even if the sufferer repented, he would continue to suffer, explanations

---

35. Compare and contrast Marshall Sklare (with Joseph Greenblum), *Jewish Identity on the Suburban Frontier* (New York, 1967), especially pp. 214–49, 322–26, with T. I. Lenn and Associates, *Rabbi and Synagogue in Reform Judaism* (Hartford, Conn., 1972), especially ch. 13, pp. 234–52. Note especially the younger age shift on p. 242. Cf. also how low Israel rates in the "essential" category of being a good Jew, in respondents in Sklare, p. 322.

36. Cf. B. T. *Yoma* 68[b].

of the agony that charge him with guilt are mockery and abuse.[37]

Moreover, summon up the principle that no statement should be made that could not be made in the presence of the burning children. On this rock, the traditionalist argument breaks. Tell the children in the pits they are burning for their sins. An honest man—better, a decent man—would spit at such a God rather than accept this rationale if it were true. If this justification is loyalty, then surely treason is the honorable choice. If this were the only choice, then surely God would prefer atheism. In this context, the Darmstadt Conference's statement that the Holocaust is God's call for a Jewish *mea culpa* which leads to Christ may have totally compromised the legitimacy of the cross as a religious symbol for any decent human being.

VI. The Central Religious Testimony after the Holocaust

Recreating Human Life

In the silence of God and of theology, there is one fundamental testimony that can still be given—the testimony of human life itself. This was always the basic evidence, but after Auschwitz its import is incredibly heightened. In fact, it is the only testimony that can still be heard.

The vast number of dead and morally destroyed is the phenomenology of absurdity and radical evil, the continuing statement of human worthlessness and meaninglessness that shouts down all talk of God and human worth. The Holocaust is even model and pedagogy for future generations that genocide can be carried out with impunity—one need fear neither God nor man. There is one response to such overwhelming tragedy: the reaffirmation of meaningfulness, worth, and life—through acts of love and life-giving. The act of creating a life or enhancing its dignity is the countertestimony to Auschwitz. To talk of love and of a God who cares in the presence of the burning children is obscene and incredible; to leap in and pull a child out of a pit,

to clean its face and heal its body, is to make the most powerful statement—the only statement that counts.

In the first moment after the Flood, with its testimony of absurd and mass human death, Noah is given two instructions—the only two that can testify after such an event. "Be fruitful and multiply and replenish the earth" (Genesis 9:1–7), and "but your life blood I will hold you responsible for"—"who sheds man's blood, shall his blood be shed; for in the image of God made He man" (Genesis 9:5–6). Each act of creating a life, each act of enhancing or holding people responsible for human life, becomes multiplied in its resonance because it contradicts the mass graves of biblical Shinar—or Treblinka.

Recreating the Image of God

This becomes the critical religious act. Only a million or billion such acts can begin to right the balance of testimony so drastically shifted by the mass weight of six million dead. In an age when one is ashamed or embarrassed to talk about God in the presence of the burning children, the image of God, which points beyond itself to transcendence, is the only statement about God that one can make. And it is human life itself that makes the statement—words will not help.

Put it another way: The overwhelming testimony of the six million is so strong that it all but irretrievably closes out religious language. Therefore the religious enterprise after this event must see itself as a desperate attempt to create, save, and heal the image of God wherever it still exists—lest further evidence of meaninglessness finally tilt the scale irreversibly. Before this calling, all other "religious" activity is dwarfed.

But where does one find the strength to have a child after Auschwitz? Why bring a child into a world where Auschwitz is possible? Why expose it to such a risk again? The perspective of Auschwitz sheds new light on the nature of childrearing and faith. It takes enormous faith in ultimate redemption and meaningfulness to choose to create or even enhance life again. In fact, faith is revealed by this not to be a belief or even an emotion, but an ontological life force that reaffirms creation and life in the teeth of overwhelming death. One must silently assume redemption in order to have the

37. B.T. *Baba Mezia* 58[b].

child—and having the child makes the statement of redemption.

There is a Jewish tradition that unashamedly traces the lineage of the Messiah to Lot's two daughters (Genesis 19:30ff.), the survivors of the brimstone-and-fire catastrophe of Sodom. Lot and the two daughters believed that they were the only survivors of another world catastrophe (Genesis 31). What is the point, then, of still conceiving? What possible meaning or value can there be to life? The answer to absurd death is unreasoning life; it is *chesed*—loving kindness that seeks to create an object of its love, that sees that life and love can overcome the present reality, which points to and proves a new creation and final redemption. So the daughters stopped at nothing—getting their own father drunk, seducing him, committing drunken incest—yet conceiving the Messiah. (Jewish tradition traces the Messiah from Moab to Ruth, to David, to the final Redeemer.)[38] It is quite a contrast to the Immaculate Conception, but it is truer to human reality and redemption out of the human condition. In the welter of grubby human reality, with evil and death rampant, with mixed human motives and lusts, the Redeemer comes out of the ground of new creation and hope. "On the day the Temple was destroyed, the Messiah was born."[39] After the war, one of the highest birth rates in the world prevailed in the displaced-persons camps, where survivors lived in their erstwhile concentration camps.

The reborn State of Israel is this fundamental act of life and meaning of the Jewish people after Auschwitz. To fail to grasp that inextricable connection and response is to utterly fail to comprehend the theological significance of Israel. The most bitterly secular atheist involved in Israel's upbuilding is the front line of the messianic life force struggling to give renewed testimony to the Exodus as ultimate reality. Israel was built by rehabilitating a half-million survivors of the Holocaust. Each one of those lives had to be rebuilt, given opportunity for trust restored. I have been told of an Israeli Youth Aliyah village

settled by orphaned children from the European camps, which suffered from an infestation of mice for a long time. There were children in this village who had lived through the shattering effect of the total uprooting and destruction of their reality, of the overnight transition from affluence to permanent hunger. Ten years after the Holocaust, some of these children would still sneak bread out of the dining room and hide it in their quarters. They could not believe that this fragile world of love would not again be shattered at any time. They were determined not to be caught without a supply of bread. And neither reassurances nor constant searches could uncover the bread; it was hidden in ever more clever caches—only to bring the mice. Yet these half a million—and the eight hundred thousand Jewish refugees from Arab countries—were absorbed and given new opportunity and dignity. (They found enough strength to live under the shadow of another genocide aimed at themselves for more than twenty-five years.)

The Context of an Image of God

In a world of overpopulation and mass starvation and of zero population growth, something further must be said. I, for one, believe that in the light of the crematoria, the Jewish people are called to recreate life. Nor is such testimony easily given. One knows the risk to the children.

But it is not only the act of creating life that speaks. To bring a child into a world in which it will be hungry and diseased and neglected is to torment and debase the image of God. We also face the challenge to create the conditions under which human beings will grow as an image of God, to build a world in which wealth and resources are created and distributed to provide the matrix for existence as an image of God.

We also face the urgent call to eliminate every stereotype discrimination that reduces—and denies—this image in the other. It was the ability to distinguish some people as human and others as

---

38. Cf. [*Midrash*] *Bereshith Rabba, Seder VaYera*, parsha 50, par. 16; also ibid., parsha 51, par. 10; B.T. *Yevamot* 77[a]; see Z. Y. Lipovitz, *Commentary on the Book of Ruth* (Tel Aviv, 1959) [Hebrew].

39. J.T. *Berakhot* 15[b] (ch. 2, *halakhah* 4); [*Midrash*] *Eichah Rabba*, parsha 1, sec. 51.

not that enabled the Nazis to segregate and then destroy the "subhumans" (Jews, Gypsies, Slavs). The ability to differentiate the foreign Jews from French-born Jews paved the way for the deportation first of foreign-born, then of native, French Jews. This differentiation stilled conscience, stilled the church, stilled even some French Jews. The indivisibility of human dignity and equality becomes an essential bulwark against the repetition of another Holocaust. It is the command rising out of Auschwitz.

This means a vigorous self-criticism, and review of every cultural or religious framework that may sustain some devaluation or denial of the absolute and equal dignity of the other. This is the overriding command and the essential criterion for religious existence, to whoever walks by the light of the flames. Without this testimony and the creation of facts that give it persuasiveness, the act of the religious enterprise simply lacks credibility. To the extent that religion may extend or justify the evils of dignity denied, it becomes the Devil's testimony. Whoever joins in the work of creation and rehabilitation of the image of God is, therefore, participating in "restoring to God his scepter and crown." Whoever does not support—or opposes—this process is seeking to complete the attack on God's presence in the world. These must be seen as the central religious acts. They shed a pitiless light on popes who deny birth control to starving millions because of a need to uphold the religious authority of the magisterium; or on rabbis who deny women's dignity out of loyalty to divinely given traditions.

VII. Religious and Secular after the Holocaust

The end of the secular-religious dichotomy. This argument makes manifest an underlying thrust in this interpretation. The Holocaust has destroyed the meaning of the categories of "secular" and "religious." Illuminated by the light of the crematoria, these categories are dissolved and not infrequently turned inside out.

We must remember the many "religious" people who carried out the Holocaust. There were killers and murderers who continued to practice organized religion, including Christianity. There were many "good Christians," millions of respectable people, who turned in, rounded up, and transported millions of Jews. Some sympathized with or were apathetic to the murder process, while perceiving themselves as religiously observant and faithful—including those who did an extra measure of Jew-hunting or betrayal because they perceived it as an appropriate expression of Christian theology. Vast numbers of people practiced religion in this period, but saw no need to stand up to or resist the destruction process. As Camus said:

> I continue to struggle against this universe in which children suffer and die.
>
> ... For a long time during those frightful years I waited for a great voice to speak up in Rome. I, an unbeliever? Precisely. For I knew that the spirit would be lost if it did not utter a cry of condemnation when faced with force. It seems that that voice did speak up. But I assure you that millions of men like me did not hear it and that at that time believers and unbelievers alike shared a solitude that continued to spread as the days went by and the executioners multiplied.
>
> It has been explained to me since that the condemnation was indeed voiced. But that it was in the style of the encyclicals, which is not at all clear. The condemnation was voiced and it was not understood! Who could fail to feel where the true condemnation lies in this case and to see that this example by itself gives part of the reply, perhaps the whole reply, that you ask of me.[40]

To add a final, more obscene note on the domestication of God and the denaturing of religion: Heinrich Himmler, overall head of the kingdom of death, told Felix Kersten, his masseur, "some higher Being...is behind Nature...If we refused to recognize that we should be no better than the Marxists....I insist that members of the SS must believe in God."[41]

40. Albert Camus, *Resistance, Rebellion, and Death* (New York, 1961), p. 71.

41. Quoted in Roger Manvell, *S.S. and Gestapo* (New York, 1969), p. 109.

(Whenever I reread this passage, I swear that the name of God must be hidden away in absolute silence and secrecy for so long that all the murderers and bystanders will have forgotten it. Only then can it be brought out and used again.)

If "all is permitted," what is the "fear of God"? The Holocaust is overwhelming witness that "all is permitted." It showed that there are no limits of sacredness or dignity to stop the death process. There were no thunderbolts or divine curses to check mass murder or torture. The Holocaust also showed that one can literally get away with murder. After the war a handful of killers were punished, but the vast majority were not. Catholic priests supplied disguises and passports for mass murderers to help them escape punishment. German and Austrian officials cleared them of guilt—or imposed a few years of prison for killing tens of thousands. Men in charge of legally ostracizing Jews and clearing them for destruction became secretaries to cabinet ministers. Men who owned gas-producing companies, those who had built crematoria, were restored to their full ownership rights and wealth. Thirty years later, an anti-Nazi woman was imprisoned for seeking to kidnap and deliver for extradition a mass murderer, while he went free. Austrian juries acquitted the architects of the Auschwitz gas chambers. If all is permitted, why should anyone hold back from getting away with whatever one can? The prudential argument, that it is utilitarian not to do so, surely is outweighed by the reality that one can get away with so much. And the example of millions continually testifies against any sense of reverence or dignity to check potential evil.

I would propose that there is an explanation; a biblical category applies here. Whoever consistently holds back from murder or human exploitation when he could perpetrate it with immunity—or any person who unswervingly devotes himself to reverence, care, and protection of the divine image which is man, beyond that respect which can be coerced—reveals the presence within of a primordial awe—"fear of God"—which alone evokes such a response.

The biblical category suggests that fear of God is present where people simply cannot do certain things. It is, as it were, a field of force that prevents certain actions. The midwives feared God (Exod. 1:21), and therefore they simply could not kill newborn babies. When fear of God is not present, then there are no limits. Amalek could attack the weak and those who lagged behind because Amalek did not "fear God" (Deut. 25:18). A man can be killed in order to be robbed of his fair wife in a place where there is no fear of God (Gen. 20:11). We posit that this presence is a shield. This is why people cannot kill human beings in the "image of God"—they must first take them outside the pale of uniqueness and value before they can unleash murder. They must first be convinced that there is no divine limit. In the glare of the fires, by their piercing rays, we now can see clearly who has this fear of God and who does not.

It makes no difference whether the person admits the presence of God. From the biblical perspective, the power of the limit reveals that the divine presence's force is operating. (This is the meaning of Rabbi Akiva's statement in the Talmud, that in the moment that the thief steals, he is an atheist. Otherwise, how could be disobey the divine voice that says: Thou shalt not steal.)

Religious and secular self-definition in light of Auschwitz. Nor can we take self-definitions seriously. During the Holocaust, many (most?) of the church's protests were on behalf of Jews converted to Christianity. Consider what this means. It is not important to protest the murder of Jews; only if a person believes in Jesus Christ as Lord and Savior is there a moral need to protest his fate.[42] Can we take such self-definitions of religious people as reflection of belief in God?

---

42. J.S. Conway, *The Nazi Persecution of the Churches*, pp. 261–65; Saul Friedlander, *Counterfeit Nazi*, pp. 37, 38, 145–49; Falconi, *Silence of Pius XII*, p. 87; Friedlander, *Pius XII and the Third Reich*, pp. 92–102, but see also p. 114 ff.; Gitta Sereny, *Into That Darkness*, pp. 276 ff., 292–303. See also Weissmandl, *Min Hametzar*, pp. 21– 22, 23–24. Cf. also Karl Barth's *mea culpa* on the Jewish issue in a letter to Eberhard Bethge, quoted in E. Bethge, "Troubled Self-Interpretation and Uncertain Response in the Church Struggle," in Littell and Locke, *German Church Struggle*, p. 167.

When, in May and June 1967, it appeared that another Holocaust loomed, men of God remained silent. Pope Paul VI, moved by all sorts of legitimate or normal considerations (concern for Christian Arabs, concern for holy places, theological hang-ups about secular Israel) remained silent. A self-avowed atheist, root source of much of modern atheism, Jean-Paul Sartre, spoke out against potential genocide—even though he had to break with his own deepest political alliances and self-image in his links to Arabs and Third World figures to do so. He knew that there is one command: Never another Holocaust. Which is the man of God, which the atheist? By biblical perspective? By Auschwitz perspective? Are title, self-definition, official dress, public opinion—even sincere personal profession—more significant than action?

If someone were to begin to strangle you, all the while protesting loudly and sincerely: "I love you!" at what point would the perception of that person's sincerity change? At what point would you say, "Actions speak louder than words"? As you turn blue, you say, "Uh . . . pardon me, are you sure that I am the person you had in mind . . . when you said, 'I love you'?"

One must fully respect the atheist's right to his own self-definition. But from the religious perspective, the action speaks for itself. The denial of faith has to be seen as the action of one determined to be a secret servant, giving up the advantages of acknowledged faith, because at such a time such advantages are blasphemous. Perhaps it reveals a deeper religious consciousness that knows there must be a silence about God—if faith in Him is not to be fatally destroyed in light of the Holocaust and of the abuse of faith in God expressed by a Himmler. Thus, the atheist who consistently shows reverence for the image of God, but denies that he does so because he is a believer in God, is revealed by the flames to be one of the thirty-six righteous—the hidden righteous, whom Jewish tradition asserts to be the most righteous, those for whose sake the world exists. Their faith is totally inward and they re-

nounce the prerequisites of overt faith; and for their sake the world of evil is borne by God.[43]

The State of Israel: A study in secularity and religion after Auschwitz. By this standard, the "secular" State of Israel is revealed for the deeply religious state that it is. Both its officially nonreligious majority as well as its official and established religious minority are irrelevant to this judgment. The real point is that after Auschwitz, the existence of the Jew is a great affirmation and an act of faith. The re-creation of the body of the people, Israel, is renewed testimony to Exodus as ultimate reality, to God's continuing presence in history proven by the fact that his people, despite the attempt to annihilate them, still exist.

Moreover, who show that they know that God's covenant must be upheld by re-creating his people? Who heard this overriding claim and set aside personal comfort, cut personal living standards drastically, gave life, health, energy to the rehabilitation of the remnants of the covenant people? Who give their own lives repeatedly in war and/or guard duty to protect the remnant? Surely the secular Jews of Israel as much as, or more than, the religious Jew, or non-Jews anywhere.

The religious-secular paradox goes deeper still. Instead of choosing to flee at all costs from the terrible fate of exposure to genocide, instead of spending all their energy and money to hide and disappear, Jews all over the world—secular Jews included—renewed and intensified their Jewish existence and continued to have and raise Jewish children. Knowing of the fate to which this choice exposes them (a fate especially dramatically clear in Israel, where year after year the Arabs have preached extermination); aware of how little the world really cared, or cares, and that the first time is always the hardest—what is one to make of the faith of those who made this decision and who live it every day, especially in Israel? The answer has been given most clearly by Emil Fackenheim. To raise a Jewish child today is to bind the child and the child's child on the altar,

43. Cf. Irving Greenberg, "A Hymn to Secularists (Dialogue of Irving Greenberg and Leonard Fein at the General Assembly in Chicago)," November 15, 1974 (cassette distributed by Council of Jewish Federations and Welfare Funds, New York, 1975).

even as father Abraham bound Isaac. Only, those who do so today know that there is no angel to stop the process and no ram to substitute for more than one and one-half million Jewish children in this lifetime. Such an act then, can only come out of resources of faith, of ultimate meaningfulness— of Exodus trust—on a par with, or superior to, father Abraham at the peak of his life as God's loved and covenanted follower. Before such faith, who shall categorize in easy categories the secular and the devout Israeli or Jew?

A classic revelation of the deeper levels can be found in the "Who is a Jew" controversy, and in the Israeli "Law of Return," which guarantees every Jew automatic admittance into Israel. This law has been used against Israel, in slogans of "racism," by those who say that if Israel only de-Zionizes and gives up this law she would have peace from her Arab neighbors, and by Christians and other non-Jews who then assess Israel as religiously discriminatory. All these judgments cost the secular Israelis a great deal—not least because any weakening of public support means a heightened prospect of genocide for themselves and their children. In turn, the secular Israeli is bitterly criticized by observant Jews for not simply following the traditional definition of who is a Jew. In 1974 this issue even disrupted attempts to form a government, at a time when life-and-death negotiations hung in the balance. Why, then, has the law been stubbornly upheld by the vast majority of secular Israelis?

It reveals the deepest recesses of their souls. They refuse to formally secularize the definition of "Israeli" and thereby cut the link between the covenant people of history and the political body of present Israel—despite their own inability to affirm, or even their vigorous denial of, the covenant! They see Auschwitz as revelatory and commanding, normative as great events in covenant history are, and they are determined to guarantee automatic admission to every Jew— knowing full well he is always exposed (by covenantal existence) to the possibility of another Holocaust with no place to flee. The lesson of Auschwitz is that no human being should lack a guaranteed place to flee again, just as the lesson of the Exodus was that no runaway slave should be turned back to his master (Deut. 23:16). (Needless to say, there is self-interest involved also—

more Jews in Israel strengthen the security of Israel. But the admixture of self-interest is part of the reality in which religious imperatives are acted upon by all human beings.)

In light of this, Zionism, criticized by some devout Jews as secular revolt against religion and by other observant Jews for its failures to create a state that fully observes Jewish tradition, is carrying out the central religious actions of the Jewish people after Auschwitz. Irony piles upon irony! The re-creation of the state is the strongest suggestion that God's promises are still valid and reliable. Thus the secularist phenomenon gives the central religious testimony of the Jewish people today. In the Holocaust many rabbis ruled that every Jew killed for being Jewish has died for the sanctification of the name of God. In death as in life, the religious-secular dichotomy is essentially ended.

Dialectical Reflections on the End of the Secular-Religious Difficulty

Contra humanism. Once we establish the centrality of the reverence for the image of God and the erosion of the secular-religious dichotomy after Auschwitz, then the dialectic of the Holocaust becomes visible. Such views could easily become embodied in a simple humanism or a new universalist liberation that is totally absorbed in the current secular option. To collapse into this option would be to set up the possibility of another idolatry. True, it would be more likely a Stalinist rather than a fascist idolatry; but it reopens the possiblity of the concentration of power and legitimacy which could carry out another Holocaust. We are bidden to resist this temptation. Indeed, there is a general principle at work here. Every solution that is totally at ease with a dominant option is to be seen as an attempt to escape from the dialectical torment of living with the Holocaust. If you do escape, you open up the option that the Holocaust may recur. A radical self-critical humanism springing out of the Holocaust says no to the demons of Auschwitz; a celebration of the death of God or of secular man is collaboration with these demons.

Contra protean man. The fury of the Holocaust also undercuts the persuasiveness of another modern emphasis—the sense of option and choice of existence. This sense of widespread freedom to choose identity and of the weakening of biological or inherited status is among the most pervasive values of contemporary culture. It clearly grows out of the quantum leap in human power and control through medicine and technology, backed by the development of democratic and universalist norms. It has generated a revolt against inherited disadvantage, and even genetic or biological limitations. The freedom of being almost protean is perceived as positive—the source of liberation and human dignity. In light of the Holocaust, we must grapple with the question anew. Is the breaking of organic relationships and deracination itself the source of the pathology which erupted at the heart of modernity? Erich Fromm has raised the issue in *Escape from Freedom.* Otto Ohlendorf—the head of D Einsatzgruppe, and one of the very few war criminals willing to admit frankly what he did and why—stressed the search for restored authority and rootedness (e.g., the failure to conserve the given as well as the freely chosen in modern culture) as a major factor in the scope and irrationality of the Nazis' murderous enterprise. Since the attack started against the people of Israel, but planned to go on to Slavs and other groups, it poses a fundamental question to the credibility of modern culture itself. There has not been enough testing and study of this possibility in the evidence of the Holocaust yet, but it warrants a serious study and an immediate reconsideration of the persuasiveness of the "freedom-of-being" option in modernity. The concept is profoundly challenged by the Jewish experience in the Holocaust.[44] For the demonic assault on the people of Israel recognized no such choice. Unlike the situation that prevailed in medieval persecutions, one could not cease to be a Jew through conversion. In retrospect, liberation turned out to be an illusion that weakened the

victims' capacity to recognize their coming fate or the fact that the world would not save them—because they were Jews.

Contra the superiority of the spirit over the flesh. This insight also reverses the historical, easy Christian polemic concerning the "Israel of the flesh" versus "Israel of the spirit." After all, is not Israel of the spirit a more universal and more committed category, a more spiritually meaningful state, than the status conferred by accident of birth? Yet the Holocaust teaches the reverse. When absolute power arose and claimed to be God, then Israel's existence was antithetical to its own. Israel of the flesh by its mere existence gives testimony, and therefore was "objectively" an enemy of the totalitarian state. By the same token neither commitment to secularism, atheism, or any other faith—nor even joining Christianity—could remove the intrinsic status of being Jewish, and being forced to stand and testify. Fackenheim, Berkovits, Rubenstein, and others have spoken of the denial of significance to the individual Jew by the fact that his fate was decided by his birth—whatever his personal preference. But classical Jewish commentators had a different interpretation. The mere fact that the Jew's existence denies the absolute claims of others means that the Jew is testifying. The act of living speaks louder than the denial of intention to testify, as I have suggested in my comments on fear of God above. During the Holocaust, rabbis began to quote a purported ruling by Maimonides that a Jew killed by bandits—who presumably feel freer to kill him because he is a Jew—has died for the sanctification of the Name, whether or not he was pressured before death to deny his Judaism and his God.[45] This testimony, voluntarily given or not, turns out to be the secret significance of "Israel of the flesh." A Jew's life is on the line and therefore every kind of Jew gives testimony at all times.

44. Cf. Erich Fromm, *The Fear of Freedom* (American title, *Escape from Freedom*), 1st ed. (London, 1942). See George Stein, *The Waffen SS* (Ithaca, N.Y., 1970); for Ohlendorf's testimony, see *Trials of War Criminals before the Nuremberg Military Tribunals under Control Council Law No. 10, October 1946–April 1949* (Washington, D.C., 1952), vol. 4; *United States of America* v. *Otto Ohlendorf et al.*, case no. 9, pp. 384–91.

45. The purported Maimonides ruling is quoted in Rabbi Simon Huberband's essay on *Kiddush Hashem* (Sanctification of God's name), found in the collection of his Holocaust writings printed under the title *Kiddush Hashem* (Tel Aviv, 1969), p. 23. Rabbi Menachem Ziemba, the great rabbinical scholar of Warsaw, is quoted as citing the same Maimonides ruling in Hillel Seidman, *Yoman Ghetto Varsha* (New York: Jewish

Israel of the spirit testifies against the same idolatry and evil. Indeed, there were sincere Christians who stood up for their principles, were recognized as threats, and sent to concentration camps. However, Israel of the spirit only has the choice of being silent; with this measure of collaboration, it can live safely and at ease. Not surprisingly, the vast majority chose to be safe. As Franklin Littell put it, when paganism is persecuting, Christians "can homogenize and become mere gentiles again; while the Jews, believing or secularized, remain representatives of another history, another providence.[46] It suggests that from now on one of the great keys to testimony in the face of the enormously powerful forces available to evil, will be to have given hostages, to be on the line because one is inextricably bound to this fate. The creation of a forced option should be one of the goals of moral pedagogy after the Holocaust. It is the meaning of chosenness in Jewish faith. The Christian analogy of this experience would be a surrender of the often selfdeceiving universalist rhetoric of the church and a conception of itself as people of God—a distinct community of faith with some identification—that must testify to the world.

VIII. Final Dialectic: The Dialectic of Power

There is yet another dialectic we must confront. To do so we must encounter the Holocaust once more, in a scene from Tadeusz Borowski's account of life at Auschwitz. Says Borowski:

> They go, they vanish. Men, women, and children. Some of them know.

Here is a woman—she walks quickly but tries to appear calm. A small child with a pink cherub's face runs after her and, unable to keep up, stretches out his little arms and cries: "Mama! Mama!"

"Pick up your child, woman!"

"It's not mine, sir, not mine!" she shouts hysterically and runs on, covering her face with her hands. She wants to hide, she wants to reach those who will not ride the trucks, those who will go on foot, those who will stay alive. She is young, healthy, good-looking, she wants to live.

But the child runs after her, wailing loudly: "Mama, mama, don't leave me!"

"It's not mine, not mine, no!"

Andrei, a sailor from Sevastopel, grabs hold of her. His eyes are glassy from vodka and the heat. With one powerful blow he knocks her off her feet, then, as she falls, takes her by the hair and pulls her up again. His face twitches with rage.

"Ah, you bloody Jewess! So you're running from your own child; I'll show you, you whore!" His huge hand chokes her, he lifts her in the air and heaves her on to the truck like a heavy sack of grain.

"Here! And take this with you, bitch!" and he throws the child at her feet.

"*Gut gemacht*, good work. That's the way to deal with degenerate mothers," says the S.S. man standing at the foot of the truck. *"Gut, gut, Russki."*[47]

We have to comprehend that mother. We know from hundreds of accounts that Jews went to their death because they wanted to stay with their families. We know of mothers who gave themselves up to transport when their children were seized. We know of parents who declined to go to the forests or to the Aryan side because their children could not go. Imagine, then, this mother. She had voluntarily gone on the train to be with her child; she had declined to escape. She

---

Book, 1959), p. 221. An exhaustive search of Maimonides' work (including consultation with Dr. Haym Soloveitchik, who has edited a mimeographed collection of Maimonides' writings on *Kiddush Hashem* for the Hebrew University) makes clear that there is no such ruling in Maimonides. The acceptance during the Holocaust of the view that Maimonides issued such a ruling—even by scholars of Maimonides such as Ziemba—only shows the urgency of the need for such a ruling. The rabbis instinctively recognized that every Jew was making a

statement when killed in the Holocaust—the very statement that the Nazis were so frantically trying to silence by killing all the Jews. This is contra Richard Rubenstein's comments in "Some Perspectives on Religious Faith after Auschwitz," in Littell and Locke, *German Church Struggle*, p. 263.

46. Franklin H. Littell, *The German Phoenix: Men and Movements in the Church in Germany* (Garden City, N.Y., 1960), p. 217.
47. Tadeusz Borowski, *This Way for the Gas, Ladies and Gentlemen* (New York, 1967), p. 87.

522 PART III EUROPEAN AND AMERICAN RESPONSES DURING AND FOLLOWING THE WAR

arrives at Auschwitz after a stupefying trip, described by another as follows:

> When I climbed in, the carriage was half-full. The smell of chlorine hit my nose. The walls and the floor were white and everything was covered with disinfectant-powder. Immediately experienced a dryness and a queer burning in my mouth and throat. Thirst began to torture me.... The heat grew worse all the time. Moisture which had condensed from the vapours began to drip from the ceiling. People began to unbutton their coats to get relief from the heat and the stuffiness.... The heat in the carriage became worse every moment, and so did our state. We were dazed: half sane, half mad. The will-to-live became independent of the person and uncontrollable.... Manners and conventions which everyone observed up till now are no longer seen. They evaporate in the heat. The will-to-live has taken the floor. Women of all ages remove their coats. They tear their dresses from themselves. They stand half naked. Someone relieves himself. Everything is overturned and uprooted; a mist fogs one's consciousness.[48]

In this state, when she suddenly understood where she was, when she smelled the stench of the burning bodies—perhaps heard the cries of the living in the flames—she abandoned her child and ran.

Out of this wells up the cry: Surely here is where the cross is smashed. There has been a terrible misunderstanding of the symbol of the crucifixion. Surely, we understand now that the point of the account is the cry: "My Lord, my Lord, why have You abandoned me?" Never again should anyone be exposed to such one-sided power on the side of evil—for in such extremis not only does evil triumph, but the Suffering Servant now breaks and betrays herself. Out of the Holocaust experience comes the demand for redistribution of power. The principle is simple. No one should ever have to depend again on anyone else's good will or respect for their basic security and right to

exist. The Jews of Europe needed that good will and these good offices desperately—and the democracies and the church and the communists and their fellow Jews failed them. No one should ever be equipped with less power than is necessary to assure one's dignity. To argue dependence on law, or human goodness, or universal equality is to join the ranks of those who would like to repeat the Holocaust. Anyone who wants to prevent a repetition must support a redistribution of power. Since this, in turn, raises a large number of issues and problems with regard to power, we will not analyze it here. But the analysis of the risks of power and the dialectic of its redistribution is a central ongoing task of religion and morality, and a vast pedagogical challenge to all who are committed to prevent a second Auschwitz.

IX. Living with the Dialectic

The dialectic I have outlined is incredibly difficult to live by. How can we reconcile such extraordinary human and moral tensions? The classical traditions of Judaism and Christianity suggest: by reenacting constantly the event which is normative and revelatory. Only those who experience the normative event in their bones—through the community of the faith—will live by it.[49] I would suggest, then, that in the decades and centuries to come, Jews and others who seek to orient themselves by the Holocaust will unfold another sacral round. Men and women will gather to eat the putrid bread of Auschwitz, the potato peelings of Bergen-Belsen. They will tell of the children who went, the starvation and hunger of the ghettos, the darkening of the light in the Mussulmen's eyes. To enable people to reenact and relive Auschwitz there are records, pictures, even films—some taken by the murderers, some by the victims. That this pain will be incorporated in the round of life we regret; yet we may hope that it will not destroy hope but rather strengthen responsibility, will, and faith.

48. A. Carmi, "The Journey to Eretz Israel," in *Extermination and Resistance* (Kibbutz Loḥamei Hagetaot, Israel, 1958), 1:87–101, especially pp. 94–96.
49. *Haggadah* of Pesach; Exodus 12:13, 20:1–14, 22:21; Leviticus 11, esp. v. 45, 19:33–36, 23:42–43, 25:34–55; Deuteronomy 4:30–45, 5:6–18, 15:12–18, 16:1–12, 26:1–11, Joshua 24; Judges 2:1–5, 11–12; Jeremiah 2:1–9, 7:22–27, 11:1–8, 16:14–15, 22:7–8, 31:3–33, 32:16–22, 34:8–22; Ezekiel 20; Nehemiah 9.

After Auschwitz, one must beware of easy hope. Israel is a perfect symbol for this. On the one hand, it validates the right to hope and speak of life renewed after destruction. On the other hand, it has been threatened with genocide all along. At the moment it is at a low point—yet prospects for a peace also suddenly emerge. Any hope must be sober, and built on the sands of despair, free from illusions. Yet Jewish history affirms hope.

I dare to use another biblical image. The cloud of smoke of the bodies by day and the pillar of fire of the crematoria by night may yet guide humanity to a goal and a day when human beings are attached to each other; and have so much shared each other's pain, and have so purified and criticized themselves, that *never again will a Holocaust be possible*. Perhaps we can pray that out of the welter of blood and pain will come a chastened mankind and faith that may take some tentative and mutual steps toward redemption. Then truly will the Messiah be here among us. Perhaps then the silence will be broken. At the prospect of such hope, however, certainly in our time it is more appropiate to fall silent.

THE THIRD GREAT CYCLE OF JEWISH HISTORY

Judaism is a midrash on history. Its fundamental assertion is that human life and history are rooted in the divine, an infinite source of life and goodness. History, therefore, is moving toward a final perfection. At the end, human life will be redeemed and every human will attain his or her fullest expression as a creature created in the image of God. In that age, the infinite value, equality, and uniqueness of every human being will be upheld by the socio economic realities of the world; there will be no oppression or exploitation; there will be adequate resources to take care of every single life appropriately. The physical, emotional, and relational aspects of the individual's life will be perfected. Judaism dreams that life will win out so that eventually even sickness and death will be overcome. Judaism affirms that this incredible perfection will be attained in this world, in actual human history. God, the ultimate source of life and energy, has made that promise. In return, the Jews pledged to live their lives in obedience to the divine mandate and as witnesses to the promised final perfection. This mutual pledge constitutes the covenant of the Jewish people.

The meaning of redemption that is central to Jewish tradition grew out of and is validated by an event in Jewish history: the Exodus, the freeing of the Hebrew slaves from bondage in Egypt. The lessons of the Exodus—that there is a redeeming God, that human power is not absolute and will not be permitted to oppress people indefinitely, and that freedom and dignity are the inherent rights of all individuals—will be universalized at the onset of the messianic age, which will be the culmination of history. Judaism has been guided by the Exodus as its orienting event since biblical times. This orientation has set the basic direction, goal, and operating methods of Judaism in history.

Since the religion is committed to the proposition that the final realization of the Exodus will take place in actual history and not in some other world or reality, the credibility and persuasive power of the promise of redemption rises and falls under the impact of historical events. History apparently confirms or denies the basic teaching. Jewish triumphs or rescues from evil traditionally have been perceived as confirmations of the promise of history. Occasionally, historical events were of such magnitude that they profoundly affected the understanding of the central model—one could not go on affirming the central message without taking the new event into account. Such events became orienting events themselves and were incorporated into the religion and way of life of the Jewish people.

Why should the vicissitudes of Jewish history affect divine teaching so much? According to the Bible, the Jewish people are the carriers of the message of redemption to the world. This people models moments of perfection, testifies to the future redemption, and witnesses to the divine concern and presence which will bring it all about. Because God is infinite and beyond human comprehension, the news of God's presence and promise is communicated through the Jewish people. Therefore, the persuasiveness of the message is directly correlated to Jewish existence and Jewish life. The ultimate message of the infinite has been turned over to a flesh-and-blood people to deliver to others and to incarnate in its own life. While Jewish sociology and Jewish theology are not identical, they are profoundly interrelated.

The Jews are all too human. Even the heroes and great religious figures of Jewish history are flawed, as are all humans. This fallibility is built into the divine assumptions; the sociological dynamics and personal needs of the people which are bound to shape, if not distort, every teaching are allowed for in the divine strategy of redemption. It follows that events which are everyday history in other people's annals become part of the sacred history of the Jewish people. Furthermore, the triumphs and tragedies of the Jews have direct effects on the believability and the understanding of the central message of redemption. For this reason, again, great events in Jewish history do not only affect the sociological or geographical condition of the Jews but directly influence their theological and cultural self-understanding. Consequently such events powerfully affect the legitimacy and credibility of Jewish institutions and that of Jewish leadership groups.

Classical Jewish theology holds that God continually calls into existence the leadership needed to guide the people and replaces or rejects those who do not measure up. But one need not even accept the notion of divine agency to see how powerfully sociology confirms this tendency. Leadership—especially political leadership—is primarily tested by its ability to ensure the basic needs of security and livelihood. When the Jews ruled their own land, kings could stay in power by meeting these needs, even if they diverged from the higher purposes and values of the Jewish covenant. But the land of Israel was never insulated from outside cultures. In the final analysis, Jews were a minuscule minority. Only a mission of universal significance made it essential in their eyes that they go on living and testifying as Jews. The price of surrendering meaningful differences between Jewish and non-Jewish culture was the

bleeding away of the Jews. Whenever the legitimacy of institutions or the persuasiveness of the content of Jewish testimony was shaken by events, the leadership quickly lost its following unless it could convincingly explain the events and make sense of the Jewish condition. It had to incorporate the event into the Jewish way and harmonize or correlate it with Jewish destiny. If it could not do so, the leadership itself gave up or lost its hold on the people. Leadership passed to any group that could again correlate the Jewish purpose and Jewish condition.

Because of the fragility of Jewish existence and the incredible breadth of [the] Jewish claim to significance, Jewish history has been harsh to Jewish leadership. There is a continuous pressure which sweeps clean and ensures the survival of the fittest. In the short run "the fittest" are not necessarily measured by a values standard; given the pressure which must be met, "fittest" is clearly defined by survival itself, not by the highest ideals of Judaism. In the long run, though, leaders who merely ensured survival while ignoring, repudiating, or excessively diluting the religion's ultimate redemptive message would typically lose their effectiveness as Jews assimilated or as conditions changed again.

There need not be a fundamental transformation in the understanding of the redemption paradigm after each event. Given the power of inertia, the desire for the familiar, and the power of cultural homeostasis, new evidence and developments are assimilated to the existing structures. Important changes may lead to the coexistence of newer institutions and leadership with the old. For example, the growth of prophecy in the monarchical period of biblical history from the tenth to the sixth century B.C.E. did not overthrow the centrality of king and priest, or of the monarchy and the Temple, as the cultic center. The Temple retained its force because there the same God who spoke through prophets could be contacted and would speak to the masses through the priest. However, sometimes an event is so shattering or so transforms the basic Jewish condition that it cannot be simply assimilated to the central Jewish paradigm. Either the paradigm is changed or new institutions, theology, and, consequently, new leadership are needed to make the whole amalgam cohere once again.

In retrospect, we can see that in all of Jewish history, there have been two grand fusions of basic condition, theological message, institutional performance, and leadership group. Despite continuing shifts in local situations, institutions, practices, and self-understanding, these four elements were so coherent that one may characterize the overall era as a unity. In each case, it took a fundamental change in condition to motivate the kind of transformation which led to a new synthesis. Yet the resolution was seen as a continuation of the previous pattern and the new Jewish equilibrium that emerged was perceived as a station on the way to the final goal. These two historical syntheses correspond to the biblical and the rabbinic eras. Each era oriented the Jewish way in the light of a major event. In the biblical age, the event was one of great redemption, the Exodus; in the rabbinic age, it was an event of great tragedy, the destruction of the Temple. Remarkably enough, in this age the emergence of a new synthesis is taking place before our very eyes. The third era is beginning under the sign of a great event of destruction, the Holocaust, and a great event of redemption, the rebirth of the State of Israel.

The Biblical Era

Historians and scholars, traditionalists and critics argue about the actual historical character of the Exodus and about how and in what sequence biblical understandings flowed from it. Such arguments are important but they reflect the ideological agenda of modern culture, primarily the concern that the divine authority of the Bible would be challenged by different versions of its origins or by showing outside cultural parallels to its teachings. But, all this is a moot point from the perspective of the overall synthesis of the biblical era. Whether the monotheism exemplified by the Exodus applies to all people immediately or centuries later; whether freedom from slavery initially applies only to Jews and later is generalized; whether the Exodus is the miraculous departure of more than a million Jewish slaves and families or the flight from Egypt of a small group of tribes and fellow travelers is secondary in light of the overarching unity of the biblical period. Out of

the Exodus, directly and through interpretation, by revelation and by generalization, comes the teachings which revolutionized Jewish fate and humanity's history. Central to biblical thought are the ideas that there is an ultimate power that cares about humanity; that there is a fundamental human right to freedom and dignity; that the covenant makes the divine commandments binding on both ruler and ruled; and that there are basic laws by which human behavior should be guided as exemplified in the Ten Commandments.

According to biblical teaching, whatever happens to Jews to form Jewish values also shapes the destiny of the world. It follows from the Exodus that, sooner or later, the entire world will be perfected. This concept implies that until that perfection is attained, one should not settle for anything less. Telling and retelling the Exodus story and its underlying event has been the Jewish religious vocation. Out of this soil grew the Christian teaching of salvation that passed over to other nations and changed the values of half the world. Centuries later, in secularized form, the redemption paradigm was the seed for Marxism's insistence that the dispossessed must revolt and that all institutions will be overthrown until a final equality is reached. Millenarian movements in earlier centuries and liberation theology in the twentieth century have turned this idea toward the political and economic spheres while preserving its religious ground with explosive effects on the status quo. Alfred North Whitehead, the great British philosopher, has argued that the biblical idea of an orderly created universe whose laws can be discovered combined with the idea of perfecting the world gave rise to Western culture in which science, treating nature lawfully yet instrumentally, can grow.[1] Hence, Jewish values and culture have shaped political behavior, shaken the local culture of billions of people in the modern period, and stimulated some of the great dynamic thrusts of Western culture.

The great internal struggle of the biblical era lay in coping with the challenge of Jewish sovereignty and statehood while trying to live up to

---

1. Alfred North Whitehead, *Science and the Modern World* (New York, 1926).

covenantal values. The land of Israel was located at a highly strategic crossroads of the world, along the invasion routes between Europe, Asia, and Africa. Thus, every world empire sooner or later marched its armies on the road to Jerusalem. The vulnerability and fragility of Jewish existence in the land was exacerbated by the relatively small Jewish population and the continual magnetism of foreign cultures. International pressure made a central ruler an inescapable necessity, so the monarchy was instituted over the opposition of tribal loyalties, religious objections, and other centrifugal forces. But the monarchs and ruling classes into whose hands Jewish fate was consigned were continually forced or drawn into active contact with outside powers which only increased the cultural vulnerability of the Hebrew religion. It was difficult to live up to covenantal values of dignity for the weak or freedom for Hebrew slaves when comfort, power, and the need for defense conspired to legitimize self-interest and the rule of might makes right. The dialectic of power and covenantal values was fought out in confrontations between prophets and kings, even as the need for legitimacy and religious guidance unified kings, priests, and court prophets.

How noble to us, but how naive to their contemporaries, the prophets appeared as, in the name of God, they made their demands for absolute righteousness and immediate freedom for the slaves. I recall how moved I was as a child by *Jeremiah*, chapter 34, in which the prophet chastises the kings and nobles for their failure to live up to the covenant and free the Hebrew slaves after six years. How powerful the message and how unequivocal! The nobility had not kept the covenant and God would therefore give the people into the hands of the Babylonians as slaves. When I grew up and became an administrator, my perspective changed. I envisioned the king and nobility desperately trying to build defenses as the mighty armies of Babylonia drew near. It was hard enough to build fortresses under the best of conditions. Now they had to use all the labor—both free and slave—they could get. Without adequate defenses, the people of God

could well be crushed and destroyed! Yet, at the moment of gravest danger, the prophet—that wild man—walks in and says: "Let the slaves go free!" Obviously, kings cannot depend on the insubstantial words of prophets for national security. Government must defend its people or fail totally. The prophet speaks with all the idealism of a man who never met a payroll in his life!

Of course, the "realist" version is likewise incomplete. If pure political calculation was to win out, the sense of Jewish calling would dissipate, leaving Israel and Judea totally vulnerable to disintegration and assimilation. Fortunately, in biblical times, periodic phases of religious renewal maintained some balance of values and power. Nevertheless, in the biblical period, the prophets did not, by and large, succeed with the masses. Their uncompromising demands, coming from a source beyond the people, were too far away from the equivocal realities of everyday life. Later the rabbis, operating out of the people's reality, compromised and improved matters, step by step. They educated the people, and finally uplifted them to the point where they accepted the prophets as normative and saw prophetic ethics as within reach.

During the biblical era, the covenantal relationship itself was marked by a high degree of divine intervention. God's manifest presence in the Temple was the cultic counterpart of prophecy. Even as God spoke directly to Israel through prophets, so at Jerusalem the divine could be contacted. The awe and power of the place demanded that Israelites go through careful ritual purification before entering. Unauthorized encounters with the divine presence led to instant death.[2]

The same overt divine intervention expressed itself in the events of biblical history. When Israel obeyed the Lord, it was victorious. When it strayed, it was defeated. Defeat, itself, was the best proof that disobedience had taken place. Thus, the setback to Joshua's invading army at Ai—coming as it did after the great victory at Jericho—was quickly traceable to the sacrilegious taking of booty by a man named Achan.[3] "Stand and see the salvation of the Lord," says Moses.

---

2. Cf. Leviticus 10:10; 2 Samuel 6:6ff.

3. Joshua 7.

"God will fight for you and you will hold your peace."[4] These words precede the splitting of the Red Sea, the triumphal moment of the Exodus when divine power finally and completely shattered Pharaoh's human might, underscoring the ultimate weakness and relativity of all human power. This overwhelming divine might was the best proof of God's presence and God's existence. Human power denied God's might.[5] At this moment of divine triumph, Israel saw the great hand, feared the Lord, and believed.[6] The covenant may be a partnership but it is very clear that God is the initiator, the senior partner, who punishes, rewards, and enforces the partnership if the Jews slacken. In the stinging words of Ezekiel, "You say, we will be as the nations.... As I live, says the Lord God, with a strong hand and an outstretched arm and with poured out fury...I will rule over you."[7]

In sum, during the biblical period, the way of redemption is marked by a growing sense of mission; both manifest divinity and holiness are expressed in cult and prophecy. The primary institutions of Temple, priests and prophets, and the Jewish leadership reflect the active intervention of the divine in Jewish life as well as the struggle to live with the tensions between the covenant and realpolitik. This entire complex was first challenged and then transformed in the aftermath of the Temple's destruction and the people of Israel's exile.

The Rabbinic Era

The destruction of the Second Temple and the succeedingly crushing defeats of the Jews in 70 and 135 C.E., after wars that bled Judea white, generated a major crisis of faith and meaning in the Jewish people. The massive loss of life, the sale of tens of thousands of Jews into slavery, and the triumph of Rome despite the conviction of Jewish zealots that God alone should rule Israel, deepened the questions. Was there not God? Had God been overpowered by the Roman gods? Had God rejected the covenant with Israel and allowed His people and Holy Temple to be destroyed? Were the traditional channels of divine love, forgiveness, and blessing now closed to the Jewish people?

Today it is hard to recapture the monumental importance of those questions in the first century. It is now 1900 years after the Rabbis resolved the crisis of faith that followed the Temple's destruction. We are the beneficiaries of the Rabbis' achievement and of the ways they responded to the questions. Their responses are so entrenched in the tradition as to blur the importance of the questions they answered. In that powerful and undermining crisis of faith, at least one group of Jews concluded that Judaism was finished following the destruction. Christian Jews until then had operated within the covenant of Judaism, praying in synagogues and regarding Jesus as the fulfillment of the messianic promises within Judaism. The polarizing effect of the Roman wars, the spread of Christianity primarily among gentiles but not Jews, and the destruction of the Temple convinced them that they had misread the signs. The razing of the sanctuary meant that the old channels of atonement and connection with God, which they initially thought were being paralleled in Jesus, were in fact blotted out by the destruction. They concluded that Jesus was not a continuation of the Jewish way but a *new* channel of salvation. The Gospels were a *New* Testament, not a section of the Old; Jesus' life was the occasion of a new covenant, not merely a renewed one. The destruction meant that Jesus' sacrifice must have replaced the Temple and Judaism. This reinterpretation of Jesus' life was to guide them over the next section of the road to final perfection. Paradoxically, the Christian Jews were very Jewish in their thinking when they concluded that the Temple's destruction was a great historical event that held a religious message for them.

The Christian analysis was shared by other Jews. The Sadducees, especially the court nobility and the priests, could not envision Judaism without a Temple. When they proved unable to rebuild the sanctuary, the Sadducees could not

---

4. Exodus 14:13–14.
5. Exodus 10:1–2.

6. Exodus 14:31.
7. Ezekiel 20:32–33.

cope with the Jewish people's situation and religious needs and so faded from the scene. Indeed, many Pharisees and Rabbis shared the Sadducees' analysis and poured enormous efforts into trying to rebuild the Temple. Some declared they would have no children and no celebrations—they would allow no normal life—until the Temple was restored. Although Rabbi Akiba reassured the Jews that even without the Temple, it was possible to obtain atonement directly from God, he nonetheless gave all-out support to Bar Kochba's desperate attempt to recapture independence and rebuild the Holy Sanctuary [132–135 CE]. Akiba went so far as to endorse Bar Kochba as the Messiah. It was all in vain. The Romans were too powerful. Had the Temple-centered view triumphed, the Jews would have put all their effort into regaining Jerusalem, a policy that would have spelled frustration, spiritual exhaustion, and, finally, devastation.

Another effect of the destruction and exile was the increased exposure of Jews to the external culture. By destroying the major lodestone of Jewish life and, through geographic dispersion, immersing more Jews in Greek culture, the destruction exposed Jews to the extraordinary magnetism of Hellenism. Hellenism was a cosmopolitan, sophisticated culture led by an affluent and pleasure-seeking elite that had already drawn many followers from the Jewish leadership. The loss of the Jewish land brought Hellenism to the masses, as well. In fact, Jewry could not have maintained itself in the face of this competition but for the Rabbis' development of a more learned and more internalized Jewish practice and value system.

The Rabbis responded with what became the first public education system for adults. If the direct connection to the Temple were lost, then Torah study would enable the Jews to internalize the teachings and values of God's way. This would allow them to confront the challenge of Hellenism and the more open society in which they lived following the dispersion. Study was glorified as the ultimate *mitzvah* in the saying "Talmud Torah [study of Torah] equals them

all."[8] The *Beit Knesset* (house of assembly/synagogue) was made into a *Beit Midrash* (house of study). Opportunities for study were built into the services and the home liturgies. All aspects of life could be suffused with Jewish values and the meanings taught through actions and words.

The Rabbis' fundamental theological breakthrough was a kind of secularization insight. The manifest divine presence and activity were being reduced but the covenant was actually being renewed. God had not rejected the Jews, but rather had called them to a new stage of relationship and service. From where did the rabbis draw the authority to take charge of Jewish religion and destiny, to expand required observance in every area of life, to shape new institutions, and to legitimize the use of their minds and reason as the key source for deriving knowledge of "what does the Lord require of thee?" The unspoken, oft-used axiom is the unfolding of the covenantal model. The Jewish people, the passive partner in the biblical covenant, is being urged to assume a new level of responsibility by its divine counterpart. If Israel's phylacteries praise God as the *echad,* the unique one, its God also wears phylacteries which contain the praise of Israel: "Who is like Your people, Israel, one unique nation in the earth?" The Divine Partner becomes more restrained, more hidden, more intimate in relationship to the Jews.

In the biblical period, God's presence was manifest by splitting the Red Sea and drowning the Egyptians. In the Second Temple siege, God did not show up, like the cavalry in the last scene of a western movie, to save the day. God had, as it were, withdrawn, become more hidden, so as to give humans more freedom and to call the Jews to more responsible partnership in the covenant. Rabbi Joshua ben Levi said that God's might, shown in biblical times by destroying the wicked, is now manifest in divine self-control. The *Ethics of the Fathers* says: "Who is mighty? He who exercises self-restraint."[9] God allows the wicked to act without being cut off immediately.[10] The great biblical praise of God as "great, mighty, and awesome" found in Deuteronomy[11]

8. Mishnah *Peah* 1:1.
9. *Ethics of the Fathers* 4:1.
10. B.T. *Yoma* 69[b].
11. Deuteronomy 10:17.

is used as the model of divine praise for the opening of the central rabbinic prayer, the *Amidah*, the standing, silent prayer, *but the meaning is reversed*. God's might is expressed in allowing human freedom instead of punishing the wicked.

Although the central biblical idea of covenant implies a treaty between two sides, nowhere in the Bible is the term "partner" or "partnership" used. Divine intervention is so overwhelming that the term partnership is hardly appropriate. One of the Rabbis' most powerful ideas is that the people Israel and the individual Jew become partners of God through religious activity. "He who prays on the eve of Sabbath and chants *Vayechulu* ['And the heavens and the earth were complete,' Genesis 2:1] becomes, as it were, *a partner* to the Holy One, blessed be He, in the work of creation" (italics supplied).[12] A judge who gives true judgment[13] and one who observes the holy days[14] become partners with God.

A world in which God is more hidden is a more secular world. Paradoxically, this secularization makes possible the emergence of the synagogue as the central place of Jewish worship. In the Temple, God was manifest. Visible holiness was concentrated in one place. A more hidden God can be encountered everywhere, but one must look and find. The visible presence of God in the Temple gave a sacramental quality to the cultic life of the sanctuary. Through the high priest's ministrations and the scapegoat ceremony, the national sins were forgiven and a year of rain and prosperity assured. In the synagogue, the community's prayers are more powerful and elaborate than the individual's but the primary effect grows out of the individual's own merits and efforts. One may enter the synagogue at all times without the elaborate purification required for Temple entrance because sacredness is more shielded in the synagogue. In the Temple era God spoke directly, through prophecy or through the *urim and tumim* breastplate [Exodus 28:30]. In the synagogue, God does not speak. The human-divine dialogue goes on through human address

to God.[15] Prayer, which we view today as a visibly sacred activity, was, by contrast with Temple worship, a more secular act. Prayer became the central religious act because of the silence of God.

The classic expression of the broadening and diffusion of holiness is the rabbinic application of Temple purity standards to the home and other nonsacred settings, a process that started before the destruction. Indeed, Jacob Neusner suggests that the Oral Torah—the Rabbis' primary document—existed from Sinai as a Torah for the world outside the cult, paralleling and completing the written Torah which was written for the cult. However, the "worldly" Torah won out when rabbinic leadership won out in the aftermath of the Temple's destruction. The rabbinic interpretation and intertwining of the two Torahs shaped the understanding which became dominant for those who survived as Jews. Temple holiness was metaphysically applied to everyday acts of life. By washing hands ritually before the meal and by learning Torah at the meal, the table becomes an altar. The *Shekhinah*, the divine presence, is there when people eat together and exchange words of Torah, or when even one person studies Torah. "The *Shekhinah* is at the head of the bed when one visits the sick."[16] "When husband and wife are loving and worthy, the Divine Presence is between them."[17] Blessings to express gratitude and the awareness of God were articulated for every moment of life from awakening to going to sleep, from feeling or flexing muscles to urination or defecation. In effect, the blessings help the individual discover the divine that is hidden in the everyday secular society.

The Rabbis were a more secular leadership than priests or prophets. Priests were born to holiness and were bound to ritually circumscribed lives. The rabbis won their status through learning and were not bound to sacramental requirements different from the average Jew. Prophets spoke the unmediated word of God: "Thus, saith the Lord." By contrast, the rabbi

12. B.T. *Shabbat* 119[b].
13. B.T. *Shabbat* 10[a].
14. B.T. *Pesikta Zutarti Pinchas*.
15. Joseph B. Soloveitchik, "The Lonely Man of Faith," *Tradition* 7, no. 2 (Summer 1965): 37.

16. B.T. *Shabbat* 12[b].
17. B.T. *Sota* 17[a].

judged what God asks of us by the best exercise of his judgment, guided by his knowledge of the past record of God's instruction—the biblical models and the legal precedents. The Rabbis stated that prophecy had ended with the destruction and the exile. In fact, however, biblical prophets such as Ezekiel had prophesied during the Babylonian exile. What the Rabbis really meant then, was prescriptive. After the second destruction, there can be no prophecy. If God has withdrawn, then prophecy is inappropriate. Prophecy is the communicative counterpart of splitting the Red Sea! Rabbinic guidance is the theological counterpart of a hidden God.

The prophets gave clear, unambiguous instruction from God. If two prophets disagreed about the divine mandate, one of the two was a false prophet. But if human judgment is the new source of understanding, then two rabbis can come to different conclusions. The Talmud captures the uneasiness caused by this departure from the old certainty by stating that when the students of Hillel and Shammai did not serve their teachers properly, disagreements as to the law multiplied. People feared that the two schools' opposing views could not coexist and therefore, one school's view must be false. After three years of anxiety, prayer, and seeking divine guidance, a heavenly voice told them that "both views are the words of the living God."[18] Since humans are being given more responsibility for leading Israel on its redemptive way, then it is right that there be more than one path to follow. For practical reasons, the majority decides which of the two paths shall be followed but the views of the minority are *not* wrong. The authority for this transition comes from the old source, a heavenly voice, but one which can only speak to confirm the new rabbinic responsibility.

The famous rabbinic story of Rabbi Eliezer ben Hyrkenus's refusal to accept a majority vote against this legal ruling takes on new meaning in light of his analysis. Rabbi Eliezer evokes three divine miracles and a heavenly voice to prove that his view of the divine will was correct but he was still overruled.[19] The story is not merely an ex-ample of the democratic assertion of human authority. Rather, it shows the Rabbis in action, willing to face the consequences of divine withdrawal. If the human power is to be more responsible, then God cannot intervene in the legal process with miracles and heavenly voices such as Rabbi Eliezer had invoked. The majority of the rabbis must rule. It is surely no coincidence that Rabbi Eliezer was a part of the first generation of students of Rabbi Yohanan ben Zakkai, the great leader of the rabbinic response to the Temple destruction. Rabbi Eliezer's excommunication for his refusal to accept the majority opinion also makes sense. It is a harsh penalty but it is asserted in a generation which is struggling to affirm the calling of the Jews to responsibility. The Rabbis' own hesitations and inner divisions about assuming the authority to interpret the divine mandate create the need to punish disobedience.

The Rabbis recognized that God's withdrawal and their own new authority meant that an event such as the Exodus in which God directly intervened would not occur again. This led them to postulate a new central redemptive event for their age. The Rabbis saw Purim [described in the biblical Book of Esther] as the redemptive paradigm for the post-destruction world. In the Purim story the Jewish people in exile after the first destruction are threatened with genocide. The nation is saved by the actions of Esther and Mordecai. Operating as fallible and flawed human redeemers, the two manage, by court intrigues and bedroom politics, to save the Jewish people and win permission for the Jews to fight off their enemies. The Rabbis point out that the story of Esther marks the end of redemptive miracles; it is not a miracle, it is a natural event. In justifying the new holiday of Purim, the Rabbis connect Esther's name to the biblical verse "I [the Lord] will hide [*asteer* in Hebrew, closely resembling the word *Esther*] My face on that day."[20] God's name does not appear in the Book of Esther, yet this hidden presence is the redemptive force which the people acknowledge. In an incredibly bold analogy, the Rabbis go one step beyond comparing Purim to Sinai as a

---

18. B.T. *Eruvim* 13[b].
19. B.T. *Baba Metzia* 59[b].

20. Deuteronomy 31:18.

moment of covenant acceptance. They say acceptance of the covenant at Sinai was "coerced" by the manifest miracles of God and would not be legally binding today. However, on Purim the Jewish people reaccepted that covenant by recognizing God's presence and salvation in the guise of the secular redemption.[21] This acceptance was binding because it occurred in the context of a world in which God does not split the sea but works in mysterious ways through human redeemers. Thus, the reacceptance of the covenant is legally the equivalent of the Jewish people's maturation and the acknowledgment of their new responsibilities.

Of course there are no neat dividing lines in history. People are too conditioned by their habitual modes of thinking to make total breaks in response to any event. The kernel of the synagogue and of the major rabbinic theological themes existed before the destruction and were available for development.[22] "God prepares the medicine before the sickness comes," said the Rabbis. And the Rabbis were neither consistent nor total secularizers. They invoked divine intervention through miracles throughout this era. But God's intervention was perceived in more limited forms and without *manifest* participation in major historical events. The shift in Judaism is a percentage shift but the effect—in terms of theological understanding, the perception of the Jewish people's role, and the development of new centers—is a new era. Having successfully interpreted and coped with the new Jewish condition, the new cadre of rabbis replaced the biblical leadership groups.

This argument is not meant to suggest that the Rabbis won strictly on the theological merits. In all historical situations, sociology and theology interact. Jacob Neusner has pointed to the Rabbis' link-up with the Babylonian ruling authorities. Their role as civil servants undergirded their spiritual role with political power and legitimacy.[23] Still the Rabbis' ability to interpret the meaning of Jewish fate, to give assurance that

the covenant was not broken, to broaden holiness and make it available everywhere, and to teach their values to disciples and the masses made their victory possible. Indeed, they were most suited to interpret the meaning of the new Jewish condition of powerlessness and exile. Their teaching and *halakhic* [religious-legal] developments gave sustenance to a people that had lost the power of policy making and of deciding its own fate.

Although the long exile led to many dispersions, persecutions, and changing cultural conditions, there was enough flexibility and dynamism in the system to adjust to new conditions. Some of the crises generated major new developments. The Spanish expulsion [in 1492] brought kabbalah [Jewish mysticism] to the fore as a means of interpreting and overcoming the disaster. Kabbalah gave new inner content and theological models to the rabbinic system. The Sabbatai Zvi false messianic movement in the seventeenth century shook and divided rabbinic leadership. Later, [18th C.] social estrangement and spiritual isolation in Eastern Europe brought Ḥasidism into being, replacing rabbis with rebbes. Yet all these developments can be seen as articulations or modifications of the rabbinic synthesis. The basic unity of a condition of relative political powerlessness; of a hidden or more withdrawn God; of synagogues as institutional centers; and of rabbinic leadership gave coherence to the second era of Jewish history.

The rabbinic synthesis was continuous with the biblical. The carrier people of salvation was the same: Israel. The covenantal goal was the same: redemption. The covenantal partner was the same: God. However, the level of Jewish participation was transformed. The Rabbis were aware of their role in transforming Judaism. Yet they insisted that their teachings were derived directly from Sinai. One rabbinic legend captures this dialectic superbly: Moses, visiting Rabbi Akiba's academy, was totally unable to comprehend the form and details of the Torah study there and he grew faint at the shock of his ignorance. He was revived and reassured when a

21. B.T. *Shabbat* 88ª.
22. See on this, Jacob Neusner, *Early Rabbinic Judaism* (Leiden, 1975): "Emergent Rabbinic Judaism in a Time of Crisis: Four Responses to the Destruction of

the Second Temple," pp. 34–49. See also Neusner, *A Life of Yochanan Ben Zakkai* (Leiden, Brill, 1962).
23. Jacob Neusner, *There We Sat Down: Talmudic Judaism in the Making* (Nashville, Tenn., 1971).

master told his disciple that the Torah he was teaching was from Moses at Sinai.[24]

Finally, it should be pointed out that the influence of the rabbinic synthesis did not stop with the Jewish people. Despite the relative isolation and pariah status of the Jews and despite their outsider status in Christian and, often, in Muslim societies, rabbinic Judaism affected the world. Islam was formed under the influence of rabbinic Judaism. Medieval Christianity was influenced by Judaism. One might also argue that the tremendous rabbinic expansion of the law and articulation of the covenant played an important role in shaping the parameters of Western constitutional thought and its focus on the law. Thus did Jewry and Judaism—being truthful to themselves and sharing their story with the outside world—play the role of witness and source of blessing in the second era. Yet, that era too has come to an end in the twentieth century.

The Third Era That Wasn't

Judaism's first confrontation with modernity can be analyzed as an initial attempt to enter a third era. In the late eighteenth and nineteenth centuries, drawn by the dynamic modern culture, Jews were pulled from rural and premodern ghettos into the cities and the frontiers of the new world aborning. The remarkable flowering of ideals—democracy, liberalism, socialism, revolution, to mention only a few—seemed to many Jews to offer the possibility of a basic transformation of the Jewish condition from outsider to full participant, from pariah to equal citizen of the nation or of the world. To many Jews, fundamental theological transformations were dictated by the new culture. For some, God could be dispensed with as men took charge of human fate. For others, the concepts of God and Judaism were transformed by rational or evolutionary criteria. The result was the (re)casting of Judaism into more universal, rational forms by Reform Judaism; into modern, more folk-oriented criteria by Conservative Judaism and later by reconstructionism; or by secular standards ranging from Zionism to Ethical Culture.

New leadership emerged in the Jewish community, its authority validated by a superior relationship with the modern culture's authorities. Thus, in the early modern period access to gentile ruling circles bestowed leadership on people whose lifestyle and involvement had moved them out of the traditional community. Affluence, political links, philanthropy, and competence in modern culture became keys to Jewish community leadership. Access to modern culture became a more important power source than access to traditional culture. One can trace the growing modernity in Eastern Europe by a shift in the alliances between riches and learning when rabbinic students were replaced by university-educated beaux as preferred matches for daughters of wealthy families.

New organizations arose to represent Jewish interests and care for Jewish redemption. The Zionists felt that a basic change in the Jewish condition could only come about by reestablishment of Jewish sovereignty. For others, the basic change took the form of citizenship in a host country or in some worldwide humanitarian movement. Reform Jews spoke freely of the end of rabbinic Judaism. Nowhere is the dynamic of the new era captured as well as in American Reform's Pittsburgh Platform of 1886 which speaks of "the modern era" as "the approach of the realization of Israel's great Messianic hope for the establishment of the kingdom of truth, justice and peace among all men." Of course, to the rabbis in Pittsburgh, the fundamental change in the Jewish condition was the giving up of nationhood and attaining full participation in the world, as a religious community.

In retrospect, we see that this initial attempt to enter a third era of Judaism was stillborn and did not change the fundamental Jewish condition. The Holocaust showed that Jewish powerlessness had not changed in the modern period. As the catastrophe revealed, the real change was that the oppressive power that could be brought to bear on the Jews had been enormously multiplied by the unfolding technology and bureaucracy of modern culture. The theological transformations induced by modernity ultimately came under review and fire. No new leadership cadres and institutions totally won out in Jewish life, although they did begin to develop. Still, modernity had an

24. B.T. *Menachot* 29[b].

enormous impact on Jews and Jewish culture, primarily by universalizing Judaism or substituting universalisms for Judaism and Jewish identity. But modernity was an outside force. Using it as the touchstone for the emergence of a third era constitutes the imposition of external categories on Jewish history. In any event, for many Jews this cut-to-measure Judaism has been overturned by the Holocaust and the rebirth of Israel. The Holocaust posed a radical challenge to all the hopes and assertions of modernity as it did to Jewish existence itself. And Israel reborn cast its own spell on Jews, drawing them to the central significance of redemption and the nature of Jewish life in our time. For those Jews who will remain Jewish, these events do impact Jewish history—they neutralize and even shatter the magnet of modernity. Future ages will recognize that in these two events of destruction and redemption the third era of Jewish history was born.

Modernity is not likely to be rejected by the Jews. The Holocaust assured modernity's triumph by killing off 90 percent of the Jewish groups that still actively resisted modern culture. But modern values are likely to be filtered and recast in the Jewish categories of existence. The earlier overwhelming rush to modernity will be seen as a temporary jiggle on the graph of Jewish history and destiny. The question that must be posed is this: If the biblical era, under the sign of the Exodus, produced a Bible which has been a central values force in Western culture; and if the rabbinic era, under the sign of the Second Temple's destruction, produced a Talmud and many other treasures that also affected humanity; then what will be the outcome of an era that grows out of both an event of destruction unparalleled in Jewish history and an event of redemption that rivals the Exodus?

The Third Era

About 6,000,000 Jews were killed in the Holocaust, approximately one-third of the world's Jewish population. But the Holocaust cut even deeper. It is estimated that more than 80 percent of the rabbis, Judaica scholars, and full-time Talmud students alive in 1939 were dead by 1945.

Ninety percent of Eastern European Jewry—the biological and cultural heartland of Jewry—was decimated.

The Nazis sought to wipe out Judaism, not just Jews. Before they were killed, Jews were denied access to synagogues, *mikvehs* [ritual baths], and kosher food. They were stripped of Jewish learning, opportunities, and cultural resources. Parents were forced to choose between their own survival or their children's, and children were told to sacrifice elderly parents or face their own deaths. Nazi round-ups and *aktionen* were systematically scheduled for Shabbat and Jewish holidays to poison reverence and depress Jews on those days. In persecution, as in life, Jewish existence and faith were inseparable. Theologically speaking, the decision to kill every last Jew was an attempt to kill God, the covenantal partner known to humanity through the Jewish people's life and history. As the frenzy of mass killing unfolded, the murderers sought to make Jewish life less worthy of care and respect, ever cheaper to eliminate. The total assault on the value and dignity of the Jew—an absolute contradiction of the Jewish belief in the infinite value of human life—reached a stunningly successful climax in the summer of 1944 when thousands of Jewish children were thrown into the burning pits while still alive in order to economize on the two-fifths of a cent's worth of Zyklon B it would have taken to gas them first. This triumph of murder and oppression was and still is countertestimony to the Jewish witness that life will triumph over death and that redemption is the fate of humanity. The Nazi assault shattered the covenant of redemption.

Thus, the third era opens with a crisis of faith and meaning that dwarfs the earlier ones. The burning children challenge the faith in a God who cares; the meanness and cruelty of the deaths of 6,000,000 Jews and the apathy and indifference of the world toward their deaths make the dream of perfection appear to be an illusion.

Those who seek to minimize the religious significance of the Holocaust argue that there have been other catastrophes in Jewish life and that there is nothing especially decisive about this one. Actually, the opposite is closer to the truth. Lesser disasters had a profound impact on Judaism. The kabbalah's spread and triumph in Jewish life was made possible and even necessary by the need for consolation and redemptive hope and meaning after the expulsion from Spain. And both the Shabbatai Zvi false messianic movement and Hasidism's growth owed a great deal to the search for meaning after the Chmelnitzki mass pogroms of the seventeenth century.

The Nazi decision to kill every last Jew and their near success raised the crisis to a whole new level. When Richard Rubenstein wrote that after Auschwitz "we live in the time of the death of God," he meant that hope of redemption was destroyed. Rubenstein quotes an Isaac Bashevis Singer character who states that "Death is the Messiah." He concludes that "the world will forever remain a place of pain...and ultimate defeat."[25] Rubenstein thus expresses the dimensions of the crisis well, although his response is not representative of the Jewish people and I do not believe that his views will prevail. What is under way is an enormous communal and theological effort by the Jewish people to confront the challenges of the Holocaust and to integrate this unassimilable surd into the Jewish midrash on history. That response is shaping the third era.

At the same time, the redemption inherent in the rebirth of Israel puts it on a par with the Exodus. Three hundred thousand survivors were taken from hunger, psychic wounding, and memories of terror from statelessness and marginality, and given a chance for a renewed and dignified life in the state of Israel. The ascent from the depths of the slavery and genocide of Auschwitz or Sobibor to the heights of Jerusalem reborn surpasses the climb from the slavery and slaying of children in Egypt to Mount Sinai. In addition, 800,000 Jews came to Israel from Arab lands where most had lived as second-class citizens, many in a state of premodern poverty and illiteracy. While the Sephardim's integration into Israeli society has been less than perfect, the net improvement in their lives has been enormous. The same can be said of Soviet Jewry and other groups of immigrants. The restoration of Jewish sovereignty after 1900 years and the reunification

of Jerusalem only confirm Israel's rebirth as a redemptive event of historic magnitude.

The Holocaust and the rebirth of Israel are profoundly linked yet dialectically opposed to each other, deepening the power of these events over Jewish self-understanding. Does the Holocaust disprove the classic Jewish teaching of redemption? Does Israel validate it? Does mass murder overwhelm the divine concern? How should we understand the covenant after such a devastating and isolating experience? Can the Jewish condition be the same after sovereignty is regained? These questions are being answered by the lives of the Jewish people. Already the basic condition of the Jewish people has changed. New institutions have grown up. New leadership is emerging that offers credible visions of Jewish purpose and methods of coping with the challenge of Jewish existence. That this is not clear stems from the fact that, by contrast with the past, today there are no universally accepted interpretations—or interpreters—of Jewish life. The lack of clarity is a historical optical illusion. Only in retrospect do the prophets stand out as the authoritative interpreters of the biblical experience. Only in hindsight, and after their rivals have faded from Jewish history, do the Rabbis clearly appear to give the correct understanding of Jewish life's transformation after the destruction. Yet one cannot sit out history and wait for an official guideline. Most people react to a new situation by trying to act as they did before the orienting event occurred or by using their inherited models as best they can to respond to the new challenge. However, if we study Jewish behavior since 1940, we can discern the outlines of an emerging new synthesis in Jewish life and culture.

The Hiddenness of God; or, Holy Secularity

The key rabbinic insight that led to the transformation of the covenant after the destruction was the understanding that God had become more hidden. God's withdrawal respected human freedom and was a call to Jews to assume a more responsible partnership in the covenant. If God was more hidden after the destruction of the

25. Richard Rubenstein, *After Auschwitz* (Indianapolis, 1966).

Temple, how much more hidden must God be in the world after the Holocaust? Thus, religious activity itself must be profoundly immersed in the secular, where God is hidden. In fact, this has been the primary thrust of Jewish activity since 1945.

There are good theological reasons that there be less talk about God now. Faith is living life in the presence of the Redeemer, even when the world is unredeemed. After Auschwitz, there are moments when the Redeemer and the vision of redemption are present and moments when the flames and smoke of burning children blot out faith.[26] But even when faith reasserts itself, the smoke of Auschwitz obscures the presence of God.

Heinrich Himmler, the man in charge of the "final solution," told Felix Kersten that he insisted members of the SS believe in God, otherwise "we should be no better than the [atheistic] Marxists." Many of the defense affidavits introduced at the trial of *Einsatzgruppen* (shooting squads) leaders spoke of their religiosity. In December 1941, the commander of the German eleventh Army in the Crimea told the head of the *Einsatzkommando* in Simferopol to finish killing the Jews *before* Christmas (so killing on the day itself would not spoil the holiday spirit). The Vatican and other churches protested the deportation of Jews converted to Christianity but not of Jews who were still Jews. In light of such behavior, it is incumbent on religious people to hide the divine presence until the murderers and the indifferent will have forgotten about God and released God's name from the grip of evil.

Elsewhere I have suggested that "no statement, theological or otherwise, should be made that would not be credible in the presence of burning children."[27] This suggests that we are entering a period of silence in theology—a silence that corresponds to profound hiddenness. The fundamental religious act is the reaffirmation of faith, redemption, and meaningfulness through acts of love and life giving. Indeed, creating life is only possible out of enormous faith in ultimate redemption and a willingness to risk the worst suffering to keep the covenantal chain going. In an age when one is ashamed or embarrassed to talk about God in the presence of burning children, the creation of an image of God—viz., a human being of infinite value, equality, and uniqueness—is an act that speaks even louder than words. This image points beyond itself to transcendence. The human vessel imprinted with the image of God testifies by its very existence to the source of that image. Perhaps this testimony is the only statement about God we can make.

The religious enterprise is an all-out, even desperate attempt to create, save, and heal the image of God. Every departure from the standard of human beings' infinite value, equality, and uniqueness becomes a confirmation of the Holocaust's denial of God. Thus, past acceptance of the inequality of the other, and residual denigration of the infinite value of another, become intolerable in an age when the entire religious witness is all but overwhelmed by the mass weight and countertestimony of six million dead. Indeed, creating life is only possible where there is enormous faith in the meaningfulness of ultimate redemption. Yet, the very acts of love and conception, justice and equality, concern and respect of uniqueness are generally viewed as secular activities. Hence, the paradox that in the third era, the primary scene of religious activity must be the secular.

The Talmud asked: If God is profoundly hidden after the destruction, how do we know God's presence? How do we know God is awesome? The answer is: The ongoing existence of the Jewish people testifies to it. How else can the Jewish people, one nation alone in a world of hostile or apathetic nations, like a sheep among seventy wolves, survive? How else but that there is a hidden force field, the divine, that is with it?![28] Thus the physical presence of the Jewish people—and that existence is made possible by secular Israelis as well as religious Jews—is the best testimony to the divine.

To restore the credibility of redemption, there must be an extraordinary outburst of life and

---

26. Irving Greenberg, "Cloud of Smoke, Pillar of Fire," in *Auschwitz: Beginning of a New Era?* edited by Eva Fleishchner (New York, 1977), p. 27.

27. Greenberg, "Cloud of Smoke," p. 23.
28. B.T. *Yoma* 69[b].

redeeming work in the world. The State of Israel, including its rehabilitation of more than a million survivors and Oriental Jews, is the Jewish people's fundamental act of life and meaning after Auschwitz. The great biblical sign of the ongoing validity of the covenant—the affirmation of God and hope—is the restoration of Jewry to Israel.[29] Yet, the State shifts the balance of Jewish activity and concern to the secular enterprises of society building, social justice, and human politics. The revelation of Israel is a call to secularity; the religious enterprise must focus on the mundane.

This secularism must not be confused with atheism or the celebration of the death of God. The claims of absolute secular humanism have been shattered in the Holocaust. The absence of limits or belief in a Judge led directly to the belief that humans can become God and can hold the ultimate power of life and death. Mengele and other selectors at Auschwitz openly joked about this, especially when they scheduled selections for Yom Kippur—the day when, according to Jewish tradition, God decides who shall live and who shall die. A world in which humans are grounded in the infinite is a world in which humans have infinite value. If we have human, finite gods, then the image of God must be reduced proportionately as it was reduced in Auschwitz to "an anonymous mass...non-men who march and labor in silence, the divine spark dead within them...on whose face and in whose eyes not a trace of thought is to be seen."[30] At the heart of this new secular effort to recreate the infinite value of the human being is a hidden relationship to God's presence in history and a loving kindness that, out of faith in redemption, defies death and evil. The old categories of secular and religious are undone. Religion is as religion does; all the rest is talk.

Here we come to the paradox of the Rabbis' insight. After the destruction, God was more hidden but the divine presence could be found in more places. If the divine presence resided on Jerusalem's holy mount, then the hidden God could be found everywhere. So synagogues could be located anywhere. By this logic, the God who, after the Holocaust, is even more profoundly hidden must be found everywhere. The divine is experienced neither as the intervening, commanding One of the Bible, nor the law-giving partner of the rabbinic experience but as the ever-present presence of our era. "I [God] am with him in trouble" (Psalms 91:15) means that where Israel suffers, God is present, suffering with God's people.[31] The answer to the question "Where was God at Auschwitz?" is: God was there starving, beaten, humiliated, gassed, and burned alive, sharing the infinite pain as only an infinite capacity for pain can share it.

A presence need not formally command. Indeed, it does not command if a command means an order in words from the outside. The fact that I relate to the presence of God means that I sense more clearly the expectations, I feel more obligation and motivation, and I am more deeply moved than any words or formalized commands can express. If God did not stop the murder and the torture, then what was the statement made by the infinitely suffering Divine Presence in Auschwitz? It was a cry for action, a call to humans to stop the Holocaust, a call to the people Israel to rise to a new, unprecedented level of covenantal responsibility. It was as if God said: "Enough, stop it, never again, bring redemption!" The world did not heed that call and stop the Holocaust. European Jews were unable to respond. World Jewry did not respond adequately. But the response finally did come with the creation of the State of Israel. The Jews took on enough power and responsibility to act. And this call was answered as much by so-called secular Jews as by the so-called religious. Even as God was in Treblinka, so God went up with Israel to Jerusalem. Says the Talmud: "Wherever Israel was exiled, the Shekhinah was with them...in Egypt, in Babylon. Even so, when they will be redeemed in the future, the Divine Presence will be with them, as it is said, 'the loving God, your Lord shall come back with your captivity.'"[32] It does not say "shall bring

---

29. See Isaiah 41, 42, 45, 48, 49, 50; Jeremiah 16:9–15 and 30, 31, 32, 33.

30. Primo Levi, *Survival in Auschwitz* (New York, 1961), p. 82.

31. [*Midrash*] *Exodus Rabba, Mishpatim* 30:24.

32. Deuteronomy 30:3.

back" but rather "shall come back" which teaches that the Holy One, blessed be He, comes back with them from the exile.[33] This is the answer to Richard Rubenstein's argument that God cannot be absolved of the Holocaust yet credited with the rebirth of Israel. God is involved with both events in the same way.

Thus, we are at the opening of a major new transformation of the covenant in which Jewish loyalty and commitment manifests itself by Jews taking action and responsibility for the achievement of its goals. This is not a radical break from the past. In retrospect, this move is intrinsic in the very concept of covenant. Says Rabbi Joseph Soloveitchik, "[God] . . . became a partner in this community. . . . He joins man and shares in his covenantal existence. Finitude and infinity, temporality and eternity, creature and creator become involved in the same community. They bind themselves together and participate in a unitive existence." Soloveitchik explains, "the whole concept of 'I shall be with him in trouble' can only be understood with the perspective of the covenantal community which involves God in the destiny of His fellow members."[34]

To see the divine everywhere, the Jewish people must be attuned to covenant. The people's religious receptors must be developed. The divine is more present than ever, in street and factory, media and stage, but the catch is that one must look and be open to the encounter. One is reminded of the story of [the 19th-century ḥasidic rebbe] Mendel of Kotzk who asked: "Where is God?" And he answered: "Wherever you let God in." If Jewry fails to deepen its insight, it runs the risk that it will continue to cling to existing concepts of ritual and denigrate the new activity instead of relating to it with its *halakhic* structures. It may mistakenly define the new activity as secular and cut off from the covenant instead of being grounded in it. The incredible effort on behalf of Israel has fallen afoul of both risks. In America, particularly as Jewish observance and the power of the synagogue have declined and that of federations has risen, there has been a growing, almost petulant, dismissal

of UJA [United Jewish Appeal] and the work for Israel as "checkbook Judaism," "civil Judaism," "vulgarization," etc. Israel has been dismissed as a vicarious inauthentic myth, an instrument for the ignorant, nonobservant nouveaux riches to assert mastery over the community without living Jewishly. Even more dangerously, too many practitioners of philanthropy have accepted the definition of secularity and ruled out Federation involvement in religious or personal Jewish education. Both views are incorrect. The focus on philanthropy, the creation of a society, and the restoration of the dignity of Jewish life have been the profoundest religious responses of the Jewish community to the Holocaust. The Nazis said, "Jewish life is not worth one-half a cent to put it out of its misery." Somebody else came along and said, "Have you anything to say that contradicts the Nazi testimony, other than the cheap and easy way of saying a prayer?" And one Jew, and another and then another said, "I say a Jewish life is worth a million dollars!" That became the power and testimony of UJA [United Jewish Appeal] and Israel!

The focus on life and even materialism in Israel, and elsewhere, is part of the reaffirmation of all of life's sacredness. Biblical Judaism emphasized the unity of body and soul and stressed that the real world is where God's love and man's redemption is realized. Over the course of the exile, the separation of the spiritual from the material deeply penetrated Judaism as it did Christianity. Now body and soul will come together again in the sacred significance of the secular.

The synagogue and the tradition have been weakened by their failure to fully grasp this situation. They have clung so strongly to the inherited model of the covenant that they have been unable to respond adequately to its renewal. This failure has encouraged laypeople to continue to neglect the tradition and to succumb to modernity's temptations. As long as the present model persists, the synagogue will continue to lose ground. Indeed, the synagogues' dilemma is comparable to that of the Temple and prophecy after the destruction. Even when prophecy spoke

33. B.T. *Megillah* 29ᵃ.
34. Joseph B. Soloveitchik, "Lonely Man of Faith," p. 28. See also B.T. *Sanhedrin* 46ᵃ, J.T. *Sukkah* 4:3. N.B. I

deal with this question more fully in "Voluntary Covenant." [See below, pp. 543–555.]

it was not listened to after the destruction. The Temple was too sacramental and prophecy too manifest in light of the more hidden Presence of God; the synagogue which functions as if nothing has changed is also too sacramental in light of the even more hidden God of the post-Holocaust era. Today, the most successful synagogues are those that have moved to a more *havurah*-like [participatory] approach, a more secular style that reaches out into the home, street, etc.

But the greatest danger of misunderstanding may lay in the opposite direction. The religious devotion required to faithfully carry out secular activity—the sacrificial giving work and soldiering—may not develop if the secular Jews fail to see the profound religious context out of which they grow. The rising incidence of emigration from Israel is the first warning of what can happen when religious and cultural deracination goes unchecked and materialistic values triumph. Much of the recent *yeridah* [emigration from Israel] has been among Sephardic Jews cut off from the life of Israeli society in part by the deliberate, politically motivated actions of past Labor governments. Among them are many who still accept the traditional categories. They have now tasted the erosive affluence of modern culture and can neither renounce materialism nor relate it to tradition. The pity is that the exploration of affluence's religious dimensions may well be one of the special aspects of the call to secularity. After rehabilitation and liberation, the next stage is the imbuing of daily life and affluence with meaning and values. Just as the move from powerlessness to power calls on the Jews to stop the suffering, so the move to secularity is a call to explore the religious dimensions of pleasure and the material. A more secular *Halakhah* [Jewish law] would go from denial to directed enjoyment. Thus, the religious challenge is not merely to give up work on Shabbat in testimony to creaturehood but to explore work as a sacred means of perfecting creation all week long.[35]

The religious challenge of sexuality is met not only in disciplining it through relationships and fidelity or occasionally giving it up through the *mikveh* [ritual bath] ritual but in "making oneself holy in the permitted," making sexuality the expression of a loving relationship and discovery of the uniqueness of the body and soul of another. Affluence becomes the experience of leisure to develop oneself; the increased opportunity for sharing; and the giving of direction to pleasure through blessings.[36]

The same issue underlies the continuing conflict over autopsies in Israel. The sacramental notion of the sacredness of the body, which is not to be exploited or instrumentally used after death, has blinded many rabbis to the holiness of using human power to gain medical insight and thereby save lives, giving more holiness and dignity to life. The secular notion of scientific power has blinded many doctors to the importance of not making autopsy a routine procedure. Using dead patients instrumentally can lead to a breakdown of reverence for the human being, a loss of values often expressed in excessive medical use of patients, both living and dead.

Finally, the Rabbis' secularizing insight following the destruction led them to the concept of a renewed covenant based on a further event of redemption. Saying that the covenant of Sinai was coercive and less binding in a world where the Romans triumphed, the Rabbis put forth Purim, with its hidden, human agency and flawed redemption, as *the* new redemptive model to which the Jews gave assent in upholding the covenant. Today we can say that the covenant validated by Purim is also coercive, for then the genocide was foiled, and it is less binding in a world that saw Hitler's murder of six million Jews. The redemptive event which evokes Jewish assent in upholding the covenant after the Holocaust is a new one: the recreation of the State of Israel. It is more flawed, because Israel has many social problems; more secular in that God's role and presence are even more hidden; and more vulnerable as it is challenged and assaulted by Arabs, Russians, etc. Paradoxically, Israel's flaws and shortcomings are the best proof that this is he true, appropriate hidden redemption for this era. Anything more manifest would be inappropriate for this age and would not be heard. Note, too,

---

35. Irving Greenberg, *Guide to Shabbat* (New York, 1981), section II.

36. I will deal with this question in a future essay in this series, "Toward a Holy Secularity."

that the religious group that does see Israel in manifestly messianic terms, *Gush Emunim* [The Bloc of the Faithful], has, in fact, shaken support for Israel among a wide spectrum of American Jews and non-Jews of a more liberal, secular stripe. Only a hidden messianism can be fully credible—once it is discerned.

History suggests that even as Purim renewed the covenant of redemption, upholding the Exodus and bringing its traditions into the rabbinic era, so the rebirth of Israel must uphold the Exodus and Purim, bringing them with it into the third era. The contemporary task, therefore, is to find new meaning in the tradition, a process that has already started with the "Judaization" of Federation and UJA circles and the explosion of Torah study in Israel.

Franz Rosenzweig [1886–1929] once suggested that some day, as religious insight broadened, a mother's recipe for gefilte fish would be passed on in the family, bearing with it the same sense of tradition as do formal commandments or customs. Every act of social justice, every humane or productive factory, every sport contest in community centers, every act of human socializing and dignity will become a secularized *Halakhah* as Jewish religious insight deepens and the sacred dimensions of the profane are uncovered. The classic memories and religious models of the Jewish people will have to be brought closer to daily life in order to influence and shape it. Nowhere is this more focused than in the State of Israel and the exercise of Jewish power everywhere. This is, at once, the transformation of the Jewish condition and the test of the ongoing validity of Jewish tradition and culture.

From Powerlessness to Power: Secularity Applied

The most decisive change in the Jewish condition and in the shift of focus from the realm of the sacred to the realm of the secular is the move from powerlessness to power. The creation of Israel is an act of restoration and redemption and is the affirmation of the covenant through worldly effort. It is the key application of religion to actuality and as such it is the classic expression of hiddenness and the new holy secularity.

Attaining sovereignty brought a major shift in the allocation of Jewish resources, energy, and spirit as it became necessary to create a society and build the infrastructure of power. The bulk of the activity in society and state is secular by pre-Holocaust standards. In itself this assures the relative centrality of secular activity in the third era. But this activity is also central to the defense of Jewish existence and therefore is life affirming and gives religious testimony. The real power of the secular is that it combines natural and spiritual paths in an indissoluble way. Similarly, relating to and backing the state become socially and theologically compelling activities, providing legitimacy and importance to fundraising, political activity, and other secular activities while also giving great emotional and spiritual moment to prayer and the synagogue. The secular organizations, however, have been frankly designed to serve this purpose, while the synagogue has been slower and more reluctant to respond, further tilting the balance in Jewish life toward the secular realm.

As the state, or the exercise of Jewish power elsewhere, becomes central to Jewish life, the litmus test of the classic ideas increasingly becomes whether they work in real life and whether a society can be shaped by them. In similar fashion, the ability to generate moral or responsible exercises of power and a sense of purpose and meaning in personal activity becomes critical to the State's ability to hold its own Jews and to attract others. Incompetence in daily functions or loss of moral and ethical standards will quickly be translated into loss of participation. Thus, every act of daily performance takes on transcendent meaning in completing the redemption of the Jewish people. Building the earthly Jerusalem becomes the basis for reestablishing the heavenly Jerusalem. The ability and willingness to perform daily actions faithfully and meticulously will also make or break the State physically and spiritually.

The key to performance and ethical excellence will be the systematic reconciliation of Jewish covenantal ideas and historical memory to the contemporary lives and activities of the Jewish people. Since power is results-oriented, more pragmatic and even more amoral than ideals, the capacity of the tradition to supply power with values and direction will be tested to the limit. Purists will recoil and dream of a purer religious reality or will offer a spiritual critique of the grubby Israeli reality. Yet the assumption of power is inescapable if Jewish existence is to continue. This secularity is a matter of life or death. Thus, the Holocaust and Israel come together, compelling the assumption of full responsibility for Jewish fate through the everyday activities of the Jewish state and of the Jewish society. There is a steady flow of Jewish energy, wealth, and talent as well as continuing reorganization of the community in Israel and abroad to deal with the exercise of power.

The reasons for this are *historically inescapable*.[37] The Holocaust made it overwhelmingly clear that Jewish powerlessness was no longer compatible with Jewish survival.[38] The Nazis' extraordinary success was made possible by Jewish powerlessness. Had the Jews ruled their own land, millions could have been saved. In the crunch, even decent countries like the United States of America failed to open their doors to Jewish refugees. It is no accident that the PLO [Palestine Liberation Organization] continually attacks the Law of Return which guarantees every Jew the automatic right to become a citizen of Israel. The right to unlimited immigration means more than recruitment of the population that Israel needs. At the present time, the immigration rate is insufficient for this purpose. Despite the continuing attack on the law as racist, the Law of Return is staunchly upheld by Israelis because it is the most sensitive indicator that Jews are masters in their own land, that they exist by right and not by sufferance or by tolerant good will. Before the Holocaust, Zionism was a mass movement only in countries of Jewish persecution and Western Jewry was neutral or negative toward it. Since the Holocaust, However, Jews have become overwhelmingly Zionist because they have learned the lesson. Dig beneath the surface and you will discover that even Jews who prefer to live in the lands of the diaspora have learned the lesson of the Holocaust. Even if you believe that it won't hap-

pen here, you can never again say it can't happen here. Only the Jews who reject the significance of the Holocaust and live as if it never happened, such as *Neturei Karta* (Guardians of the city) or all-out assimilationists, now deny this truism.

Jewish powerlessness is also immoral. It tempts anti-Semites into evil behavior.[39] Had there been no Jewish army or air force there would have been another Holocaust or two since 1945 and the singling out of Jews for imprisonment or destruction such as almost happened at Entebbe would have gone unchecked. Since the kind of power needed for self-defense in the modern period is only available to sovereign states, the Jewish consensus has raised the obligation for Jews to assume power to the level of sacred principle. Thus, the experience of the Jews in the Holocaust demands that Jews take power and the recreation of the Jewish state in Israel responds to this demand. Any principle that is generated by the Holocaust and to which Israel responds, any action which is confirmed by the revelation in both of the two great events of this era, becomes overwhelmingly normative for the Jewish people. The shift from powerlessness to power becomes the necessary change in the fundamental Jewish condition in the third era. This recognition explains Arthur Hertzberg's inspired observation that the only sin for which the organized Jewish community decrees excommunication is the sin of denying Israel.[40] However, arguing about how the power is used is acceptable, especially inside Israel where it is not threatening to the Jewish possession of power. How to use the power is the new *Halakhah*, but denial or endangering the power is considered the unforgivable sin. In this era, which orients by the Holocaust and Israel, such a denial is the equivalent of the excommunicable sins of earlier eras: denying the Exodus and the God who worked it in the biblical age or denying the Rabbis and separating from Jewish fate in the rabbinic era. I believe that the community has been too fearful of discussion or criticism in this matter and would

37. Yehuda Bauer, *The Jewish Emergence from Powerlessness* (Buffalo, N.Y., 1971).
38. This idea is expanded in Chapter III, "Power and Politics," in the full version of this essay.
39. Manes Sperber, *Than a Tear in the Sea*. Introduction by Andre Malraux, translated by Constantine Fitzgibbon (New York, 1967).
40. Arthur Hertzberg, *Being Jewish in America* (New York, 1978).

benefit by expanding the margins of discussion. However, a famous Yiddish proverb is operating here: "If you burn your tongue once on hot soup, in the future you blow first, even on cold soup." Having tasted the bitter cup of powerlessness to its dregs, the community overreacts to any perceived threat or undermining of the power it has.

Yet, there is a great deal of confusion regarding assumption of power as a basic change in the Jewish condition. Some scholars argue that, far from ending the threat to Jews, Israel itself is threatened and that far from ending Jewish ghetto existence, Israel is a kind of national ghetto in the Middle East. These observations only prove that Jews do not yet have enough power to remove the active threat to their existence. In the world we live in, no nation has enough power totally to ensure its safety. In the case of the Jews, the relative balance of strength and threat is still too close for comfort. But there is a fundamental difference between the two situations. A threatened ghetto in Eastern Europe could only wait for its enemies to act, hope to sustain bearable losses, and live on by sufferance. When it was destroyed or expelled, the ghetto's wealth and achievement enriched its enemies. By contrast, Israel has a major voice in its own fate, indeed it has decided its own fate repeatedly in the past decades. And, while Israel's wartime losses have been devastating, with their lives the Jewish soldiers bought dignity, freedom, and a measure of security for the Jewish people in Israel. Many times more Jews died in the Crusades, pogroms, or the Holocaust, but their deaths made the Jews more vulnerable and more persecuted than before. The difference is noteworthy and in the kind of world we live in, no small accomplishment. It is a basic measure of human dignity that my life is not cheap and that I give it for my purposes, values, and benefit, that I choose for whom it shall be given; and my family and friends, not my enemies, inherit me. Thus power upholds the covenantal statement of Jewish dignity and the sacredness of life.

It is not just a matter of choices about death. It is the application of life's efforts, as well. Ninety years of building in the Land of Israel have created a remarkable Jewish infrastructure containing school systems teaching Judaism and Jewish history; media, art, literature, and scholarship in Hebrew; a firm foundation of agricultural and industrial productivity, all taxed and utilized for the benefit of Jewish life and Jewish people everywhere. The priorities of Jewish fate and purpose determine everything from national park preserves and museums to phone systems and garbage dumps. One need not deny Israel's many problems or faults to realize what a treasure of life and human sustenance has been built there. Just as in biblical times, such activity was perceived as holy, despite its flaws, and was blessed, prayed for, and nourished by the sacred cult and system, so will this activity today become suffused with religious symbolism and purpose.

Indeed the model is so impressive and catching that, despite their minority status, American Jewry, French Jewry, and others have become increasingly politically active. Partly out of the lessons of the Holocaust and the example of Israel and partly out of desire to prevent another Holocaust and to preserve Israel, they have moved from invisibility in the political system to active involvement in it.[41] These Jewries may stay in diaspora but psychologically they are coming to the end of exilic Judaism. In exile the Jews' destiny was in the hands of others. As a marginal community the Jews could only take the political order as a given and seek to accommodate to it or serve it. Individuals, especially marginal ones, could revolt but the collective could not. The community did not have the power nor could it afford the moral luxury of judging the system. Of course, one must recognize that Jewish power is still limited. However, the change that has occurred has made all the difference in the world.

In the exilic phase, the great task of religion was to give dignity to the powerless, to show that one also serves by standing and waiting. Martyrdom was the highest sanctification of God's name. Since the condition itself could not be changed, the stress on exile as punishment for Israel's sins was a way of asserting control over the Jews' fate, a way of reclaiming moral dignity. If only Jews would repent enough, they would be delivered so they can perform morally responsible actions. The dignity of suffering, the

---

41. For more on this see chapter III of the original version of this essay.

hope for the world to come, the moral heroism of ascetism, penitential prayer—thousands of religious values and practices were conditioned to heal and uphold powerless Jewry.

The emergence of the State of Israel constituted the taking of power into Jewish hands so that Jews could shape their own destiny and affect or even control the lives of others. It represented a revolutionary, 180-degree moral turn in the religious situation. The dilemmas of power are far different from the temptations and problems of powerlessness. Jews have been fond of contrasting Christian persecution of Jews or Christianity's failure to crusade for social justice in the medieval world with Jewish behavior. It remains to be seen whether Judaism did not act similarly merely because it was powerless and whether it will not repeat or do worse in a situation of power. Will Judaism be able to function in a situation of power without becoming an established religion which interferes with the freedom of others, both Jews and non-Jews?

Ideally speaking, both Jewish religion and Jewish values can now actually do what they have always wanted to do. The assumption of power will now force them to put up or shut up. Spinning out ideal values will now be seen as empty blather if those values cannot be realized in daily life. If Israeli society fails, the credibility of Judaism drops. Jewish values will be seen, at best, as glittering generalities that do not work in the real world. Yet, all the ambiguities of power and reality will still operate. The recalcitrance of the real to receive the ideal; the frequent lack of a pure good or pure bad side in the real world; the demonic and ironic elements in human nature and history; the exhausting tension between the ideal and the real; the sheer contrast between what can be realized and what can be dreamed will all test the inner fiber of the Jewish people and Jewish culture.

Work in real power situations is closer to the rabbinic, *halakhic* process than to prophetic stances. It involves the capacity to judge specific situations and to reconcile shifting claims and facts. This probably spells the end of the traditional Jewish tilt toward the radical end of the political spectrum, a phenomenon that reflected lack of policy-making responsibility. Policy choices involve compromise and conservation as

well as reform and perfection. Ultimate ends and proximate means must be linked in a continual process, something which can only be done through involvement, guilt, and partial failures. Power inescapably corrupts yet its assumption is inescapable. The test of morality then is relative reduction of evil and better mechanisms of self-criticism, correction, and repentance. There is a danger that those who have not grasped the full significance of the shift in Jewish condition will judge Israel by the ideal standards of the state of powerlessness, thereby not only misjudging but unintentionally collaborating with attempted genocide. Ideal moral stances applied unchanged to real situations often come out with the opposite of the intended result.

Yet how can we utilize power without becoming the unwitting slaves of bloodshed or an exploitative status quo? The National Religious Party and *Gush Emunim*'s [The Block of the Faithful] largely jingoistic position is a warning both of the unsuitability of older models and the overwhelming pull of the new situation. Exercise of power must be accompanied by strong models and constant evocation of the memory of historic Jewish suffering and powerlessness. It is so easy to forget slavery's lessons once one is given power, but such forgetfulness leads to the unfeeling infliction of pain on others. The memory of the Holocaust has enabled Israel to be a responsible and restrained conqueror. Memory is the key to morality.

The historical record of every group shows that even subtle participation in the realm of the possible can lead to acceptance of the status quo unless judgment is continually refreshed through exposure to prophetic norms. Jews will have to learn to reconcile prophetic idealism with the compromise of policy making and to incorporate conserving and healing roles in Judaism to deal with tragedies and defeats which are the inescapable consequences of the human condition. The shock and depression of the Israelis following the Yom Kippur War [of 1973] only prove how human they are and how important religious values are in this era of power. But unless religion develops greater openness to other groups' criticism and greater sensitivity to other groups' needs, it may offer a morally deadening moral rearmament. It may also become guilty of idolatry, if it fails to critique even as it affirms the State.

The use of power also mandates the occasional use of immoral strategies to achieve moral ends. The acceptance of the guilt inherent in such actions calls for people of exceptional emotional range and strong orientation both to absolute norms and relative claims, both to judgment and to mercy.

Many inherited models will have to be reversed to function properly today. After Auschwitz, martyrdom is morally offensive. The command is to live and to testify. Power must be widely distributed to ensure that it will not be abused. This sets up a dialectic of power which must be applied to Israel as well as to all power-wielding nations. The ideal would be maximum self-government for Palestinians and Arabs as a check on Jewish abuse. But such self-government can only be accepted if it does not threaten the existence and security of the Jewish people. To yield autonomy without overwhelming proof of Palestinian desire to live in peace is to invite martyrdom and morally reprehensible death by genocide. The Palestinians will have to earn their power by living peacefully and convincing Israel of their beneficence or by acquiescing to a situation in which Israel's strength guarantees that the Arabs cannot use their power to endanger Israel.

The same principle applies to internal Jewish society. One of the ironic and unintended side effects of Israel's 1967 victory was an economic boom that left many Sephardim behind, trapped in poverty. The morally and religiously erosive effects of ill-distributed affluence must be challenged by the application of covenantal values and the political redistribution of power in Israel. While many American Jews are unhappy with the present [right-wing] Likud government and its perceived conservatism, clericalism, and even jingoism, they fail to see how much of its support comes from Sephardic Jewry. The redistribution of power caused by Likud's victory in 1974 brought new people into government, including many who did not know how to function effectively due to lack of experience. The opposition came to power after thirty years of Labor governments and it must be given time to develop competence. This is all part of the normal back-and-forth shifting in the course of learning to exercise power and, despite the fumbling, it is a healthy development. The exaggerated and even apocalyptic talk of the breakdown of Israel now ripe among American Jews as well as Israelis is a reflection of the relative immaturity of the new Jewish culture of power. People who live by ideal principles believe that everything will crumble once there is failure. Politicians know that there are cycles of victory, defeat, competence, and ineffectiveness. But in a democracy, there are mechanisms for correction which will eventually bear fruit. Obviously, it is nerve-wracking to watch this ineffectiveness against the background of the continuing Arab and Soviet bloc hostility toward Israel. As Jews grow used to the exercise of power, however, the apocalyptic tone should modulate to a prodding, patient awareness of an involvement with the State of Israel. The ability of Jews to reconcile realities and covenantal ideals; the ability to generate the human, moral, and religious resources to carry on the struggle; and the ability to set about perfecting the world, however modestly, will be the test of Judaism in the third era.

Voluntary Covenant

The Age of the Voluntary Covenant

The Shattering of the Covenant

When the Nazis came to power, they began a devastating assault on the Jewish people. As other nations and peoples failed to resist, the attack broadened. An unprecedented decision was taken to kill every last Jew in the world—for the crime of being. In 1941 the phase of mass murder began.

As the attack developed, the Nazis unleashed all-out violence against the covenant as well. The values and affirmations of the covenant were totally opposed, indeed reversed, even as the covenant people were killed. Jewish holy days were violated with round-ups, *Aktionen,* selections, and evil decrees. The Warsaw ghetto was enclosed on Yom Kippur 1940. Deportations from Warsaw to Treblinka death camp at the rate of 6,000, then 10,000 a day were begun on Tisha B'Av 1942. The final destruction of the ghetto was scheduled for Passover 1943. Public prayer was prohibited in Warsaw in 1940. Keeping the Sabbath became impossible because forced labor was required on that day. Education was forbidden; newspapers were closed; libraries confiscated.

The assault on Jewish life and values became total. *Einsatzgruppen* (murder squads) were deemed too slow, too costly, too problematic. The search for cheaper, swifter killing methods led to use of Zyklon B gas, an insecticide, in the Auschwitz gas chambers. To bring the cost down, the amount of gas used was cut in half [in] the summer of 1944. This doubled the time of agonizing death, a death marked by asphyxiation, with damage to the centers of respiration, accompanied by feelings of fear, dizziness, and vomiting. Jews were impressed into service to round up other Jews for transport. The alternative was death or being sent themselves. Parents were pitted against children and children against parents for survival. A food ration of 800 calories per day was established in the ghettos, in a climate where working people need 3,000 calories per day. But the amount of food needed to supply even the official caloric standard was never delivered. Kosher slaughter was banned.

The degree of success of this attack constitutes a fundamental contradiction to the covenant of life and redemption. In Kovno, pregnancy was prohibited on pain of death. In Treblinka and Auschwitz, children were automatically selected for gassing upon arrival (except for some twins and others selected for medical experimentation). The Jewish covenant pledges that human life is of infinite value. As the killing frenzy intensified, thousands of Jewish children were thrown directly into the crematoria or burning pits in Auschwitz to economize on gas. Still another time, the gas chambers were full of adults, so several thousand children were gathered and burned alive. The *sonderkommando* prisoner testified about this as follows:

> When one of the SS sort of had pity on the children, he would take a child and beat the head against a stone before putting it on the pile of fire and wood, so that the child lost consciousness. However, the regular way they did it was by just throwing the children onto the pile. They would put a sheet of wood there, then sprinkle the whole thing with petrol, then wood again, and petrol and wood and petrol—and then they placed the children there. Then the whole thing was lighted.[1]

"Could there be a more total despair than that generated by the evil of children witnessing the murder of other children...being absolutely aware that they face the identical fate.... there is now a Godforsakenness of Jewish children that is the final horror."[2] Does not despair triumph over hope in such a moment?

Since there can be no covenant without the covenant people, is not the covenant shattered in this event? In Elie Wiesel's words: "The Jewish people entered into a covenant with God. We were to protect His Torah, and He in turn assumes responsibility for Israel's presence in the world.... Well, it seems, for the first time in history, this very covenant is broken."[3] Or as Jacob Glatstein put it: "We received the Torah at Sinai / and in Lublin we gave it back / Dead men don't praise God / The Torah was given to the Living."[4] In response to the destruction of the Temple, the talmudic Rabbis said: *Mi Kamocha ba'ilmim HaShem?* ("Who is like you among the silent, O God?") instead of *Mi Kamocha ba'elim HaShem?* ("Who is like You among the mighty, O God?")[5] Today would they not say what Glatstein said?

1. See my "Lessons to Be Learned from the Holocaust," paper presented at the Hamburg Conference, 1975.
2. A. Roy Eckardt, "The Recantation of the Covenant," in Alvin Rosenfeld and Irving Greenberg, eds., *Confronting the Holocaust: The Work of Elie Wiesel* (Bloomington, 1980), p. 163.
3. Elie Wiesel, "Jewish Values in the Post-Holocaust Future," *Judaism* 16, no. 3 (Summer 1967): 281.
4. Jacob Glatstein, "Dead Men Don't Praise God," in *Selected Poems of Jacob Glatstein*, translated by Ruth Whitman (New York, 1972), pp. 68–70.
5. B.T. *Gittin* 56[b]. This is a commentary/critique based on Exodus 15:11.

By every logical standard, Weisel and Glatstein are right. The crisis of the covenant runs deep; one must consider the possibility that it is over. Had the Holocaust stood alone, would not affirmations of the covenant of redemption appear to be mockery or illusion?

A. Roy Eckardt has pointed to yet another dimension of the crisis. In retrospect, the divine assignment to the Jews was untenable. In the covenant, Jews were called as witness to the world for God and for a final perfection. In light of the Holocaust, it is obvious that this role opened the Jews to a murderous fury from which there was no escape. Yet the Divine could not or would not save them from this fate. Therefore, morally speaking, God must repent of the covenant, i.e., do *teshuvah* for having given His chosen people a task that was unbearably cruel and dangerous without having provided for their protection.[6] Morally speaking, then, God can have no claims on the Jews by dint of the covenant.

The fundamental shift in the nature of the covenant can be put yet another way. It can no longer be commanded. Covenantally speaking, one cannot *order* another to step forward to die. One can give an order like this to an enemy, but in a moral relationship, one cannot demand the giving up of the other's life. One can *ask* such a sacrifice, but one cannot order it. To use another image of Elie Wiesel's: when God gave us a mission, that was all right. But God failed to tell us that it was a suicide mission.[7] One cannot *order* another to go on a suicide mission. Out of shared values, one can only ask for volunteers. Similarly, God can no longer enforce or educate for the covenant by punishment. The most horrifying of the curses and punishments threatened in the Torah for failing to live up to the covenant pale by comparison with what was done in the Holocaust. All Jews now know that by being Jewish they expose not only themselves but their children and even grandchildren to ultimate danger and agony.[8] No divine punishment can enforce the covenant, for there is no risked punishment so terrible that it can match the punishment risked by continuing faithfulness to the covenant. If the Jews keep the covenant after the Holocaust, then it can no longer be for the reason that it is commanded or because it is enforced by reward or punishment.

The Assumption of the Covenant

But do the Jews keep the covenant? There were a significant number of suicides among survivors who so despaired that they could not live on without their lost loves, lost families, lost faith. Still others converted or ran away from the Jews to assimilate and pass among the gentiles and so tried to shake off the danger and pain of being a Jew. But the overwhelming majority of survivors, far from yielding to despair, rebuilt Jewish lives and took part in the assumption of power by the Jewish people. For many of them, refusal to go anywhere but Israel meant years of waiting in DP camps, or a miserable risky trip in crowded, leaky, and unseaworthy boats to Israel or internment in refugee camps in Cyprus and Mauritius. Was there ever faith like this faith?

The Jewish people overwhelmingly chose to recreate Jewish life, to go on with Jewish testimony after the Holocaust. What is the decision to have children but an incredible statement of hope, of unbroken will to redemption, of belief that the world will still be perfected—so that it is worth bringing a child into this world. When there was no hope, as in Kovno or Warsaw in 1943–1944 the birth rate dropped precipitously to a ratio of less than one to forty deaths. Logically, assimilated Jews should have gone even further with assimilation once they heard about the Holocaust for thus they could try to rid

---

6. Cf. Eckardt, "Recantation," pp. 164–165.
7. In a public lecture, Wiesel has used the image that, in light of the evil revealed in the Holocaust, the risk in the Jewish mission to the world can be compared to a collective suicide mission. Conversation with author, 12 May 1982.
8. Note that by Nazi decree grandchildren of people who were Jewish but had converted to Christianity or assimilated were also identified as Jews and killed. Cf. Emil Fackenheim, "Jewish Faith and the Holocaust," *Commentary* (August 1967); E. Fackenheim, *God's Presence in History* (New York, 1970), pp. 70–71. Compare Irving Greenberg, *Confronting the Holocaust and Israel* (New York, n.d.), pp. 16–17, 20–22.

themselves of the dangers of being Jewish. Instead, hundreds of thousands of them opted to become more Jewish. Committed Jews have responded by the largest outpouring of charity and concern for other Jews in history. Observant, learned Jews have recreated *yeshivot* [places of traditional learning] and Torah study so that today more people study *Torah / Talmud* full time than ever before in Jewish history, and that includes the Golden Age of Spain and the heyday of Eastern European Jewry.

By every right, the Jews should have questioned or rejected the covenant. If the crisis of the first destruction was whether God had rejected the covenant, then the crisis that opens the third stage of the covenant is whether the Jewish people would reject the covenant. In fact, the bulk of Jews, observant and nonobservant alike, acted to recreate the greatest biblical symbol validating the covenant, the State of Israel. "The reborn State of Israel is this fundamental act of life and meaning of the Jewish people after Auschwitz.... The most bitterly secular atheist involved in Israel's up-building is the front line of the messianic life force struggling to give renewed testimony to the Exodus as ultimate reality."[9]

What then happened to the covenant? I submit that its authority was broken[10] but the Jewish people, released from its obligations, chose voluntarily to take it on again. We are living in the age of the renewal of the covenant. God was no longer

in a position to command, but the Jewish people was so in love with the dream of redemption that it volunteered to carry on its mission.

When the Jewish people accepted the covenant, they had no way to measure what the cost might be. The *Midrash* repeatedly praises the Israelites' response to the offer of the covenant, "We will do and we will listen,"[11] as amazing. As the cost of faithfulness increased, the Jews might have withdrawn and cut their losses. In fact, in this era, their faithfulness proved unlimited. Their commitment transcended all advantages of utilitarian considerations. They had committed their very being.[12]

In Rav Soloveitchik's words, the covenant turned out to be a covenant of being, not doing.[13] The purpose of the Jewish covenant is to realize the total possibility of being. It is not like a utilitarian contract designed to achieve limited ends where, if the advantage is lost, the agreement is dropped. The Jewish covenant is a commitment, out of faith, to achieve a final perfection of being. Faith sees the risks but knows that without the risks the goal can never be realized. Covenanted living, like marriage or having children, is an open-ended commitment, for the risks are great and one never knows what pain, suffering, danger, or loneliness one is taking on. Faith in the final perfection involves seeing what is, but also what could be, precisely because

9. I. Greenberg, "Cloud of Smoke, Pillar of Fire: Judaism, Christianity, and Modernity after the Holocaust," in Eva Fleischner, ed., *Auschwitz: Beginning of a New Era* (New York, 1977), p. 43.
10. The term "broken covenant" must be properly understood. A broken covenant may still exercise a powerful magnetism. While its brokenness reflects the wound inflicted on the covenantal people and the damage done to the credibility of hope and redemption, paradoxically the shattering also witnesses to the profound bond between the covenant and the Jewish people. The covenant shares Jewish fate; the Torah is not insulated from Jewish suffering. Thus its brokenness makes the covenant more adequate insofar as it relates more totally to the human condition. This helps account for the extraordinary pull it exerts on this generation of Jews. Elsewhere, I have cited Rabbi Nachman of Bratslav's famous dictum that "nothing is so whole as a broken heart" and I argued that, after the Holocaust, "no faith is so whole as a broken faith." By this logic, no covenant is so complete as a broken covenant.
11. Exodus 24:7. The Jews' response—*na'aseh v'nishmah* ["we will do and we will listen"]—implies commitment before hearing all the risks.
12. The Talmud tells a story which illuminates the faith underlying the response. An opponent once saw Raba so engrossed in learning that he ignored a wound in his hand. The Sadducee exclaimed: "You rash people [You Jews], you put your mouths ahead of your ears! And you still persist in your recklessness. [You continue to make incredible commitments!] First you should have heard out [the covenant terms in detail]. If it is within your powers, then accept. If not, you should not have accepted." Raba answered: "We walked [with God] with our whole being. [Rashi: We walked ... as those who serve [God] in love. We relied on Him not to burden us with something we could not carry. Of us it is written, The wholeness of the righteous shall guide them (Proverbs 11:3)." B.T. *Shabbat* 88[a–b].
13. Joseph B. Soloveitchik, "The Lonely Man of Faith," *Tradition* 7, no. 2 (1965): 23, 24, 27, 28–30, 33ff.

life is rooted in the ground of the Divine and we do have a promise of redemption. Out of this faith comes the courage to commit.

The crisis of the Holocaust was that not in their wildest dreams did Jews imagine that this kind of pain and destruction was the price of the covenant. Nor did they realize that the covenant might unfold to the point where God would ask them to take full responsibility and unlimited risks for it. Yet, in the ultimate test of the Jews' faithfulness to the covenant, the Jewish people, regardless of ritual observance level, responded with a reacceptance of the covenant, out of free will and love. For some, it was love of God; for others, love of the covenant and the goal; for others, love of the people or of the memories of the covenantal way. In truth, it hardly matters because the three are inseparable in walking the covenantal way.[14]

If the covenant is not over, then what does the Holocaust reveal about the nature of the covenant? What is the message to us when the Divine Presence was in Auschwitz, suffering, burning, starving, yet despite the most desperate pleas, failing to stop the Holocaust?

The Divine Presence need not speak through prophets or rabbis. The Presence speaks for Itself. If the message of the destruction of the Temple was that the Jews were called to greater partnership and responsibility in the covenant, then the Holocaust is an even more drastic call for total Jewish responsibility for the covenant. If after the Temple's destruction, Israel moved from junior participant to true partner in the covenant, then after the Holocaust, the Jewish people are called upon to become the senior partner in action. In effect, God was saying to humans: You stop the Holocaust. You bring the redemption. You act to ensure that it will never again occur. I will be with you totally in whatever you do, wherever you go, whatever happens, but you must do it. And the Jewish people heard this call and responded by taking responsibility and creating the State of Israel. Thereby, the people took power into their hands to stop another Holocaust as best they could.

The decision to create a Jewish state is also a decision to create a society and social reality in which Jews and Jewish values direct the fundamental decisions. For two thousand years, the Jewish witness to the world could only operate on the verbal level, indirectly influencing the forces which moved the world such as Christianity, Islam, Western culture. Now Jewish actions can directly affect the historical destiny of the world. Now Jews can construct a society that can affect others by example. Israel, as a Jewish-run reality, can exemplify the joint process of human liberation and redemption. For example, Israel represents an agricultural society that utilizes limited resources, transforming desert into fertile, productive land, thus offering the way for the world to overcome poverty and hunger. Israel serves as a model of an open, educational society taking a population from premodern poverty and passivity and creating from it a people that assumes responsibility and increases its dignity without losing its past and its values. This is what Israel has done in part with its Oriental Jewish immigration. Both these models are particularly significant for the Third World where the bulk of humanity struggles with the problems

---

14. Michael Berenbaum has powerfully and convincingly argued that, in his writings, Elie Wiesel has developed a doctrine of "an additional covenant forged at Auschwitz, a covenant that renews Israel's mission despite the void . . . [a covenant] between Israel and its memories of pain and death, God and meaning." Berenbaum finds three elements in Wiesel's additional covenant doctrine: solidarity, witness, and the sanctification of life. See Michael Berenbaum, "The Additional Covenant," in Rosenfeld and Greenberg, *Confronting*, pp. 169, 171ff. Berenbaum has placed these reflections in the context of his important and comprehensive analysis of Wiesel's and others' Holocaust theology in *The Vision of the Void: Theological Reflections on the Works of Elie Wiesel* (Middletown, Conn., 1979). While I differ somewhat from Berenbaum's assessment as to how much Wiesel comes down on the side of [a] theological void after the Holocaust and while my thesis of the voluntary reassumption of the covenant differs from the additional covenantal model, I am indebted to Michael Berenbaum for opening my eyes to the concept of an additional covenant in Wiesel's writings. Eckardt's concept of divine repentance at giving the covenant (see footnote 52) particularly, and Berenbaum's formulation of the additional covenant as well, were fruitful intellectual stimulants at the time that I was struggling to articulate this paradigm of the voluntary covenant.

of poverty, fatalism, and renewal of social institutions.

Of course, the politics of oil and world rivalries have isolated Israel and reduced its influence. Also, Israel itself is far from perfect and has only partially succeeded in these models. However, these limitations are congruent with the shift from powerlessness and ideal existence to exercise of power and the conquest of reality. Reality is recalcitrant and flawed, and all triumphs are partial and equivocal. It is also true that many Israelis accept the call to prevent another Holocaust, but do not accept the commitment to create a redemptive model society. In a situation of voluntary covenant, there cannot be one goal imposed from above. Rather, those who accept the calling must persuade and influence the others to take part in the process.

The Jewish tradition itself has been less helpful than it could be because traditionalists have not fully taken up the challenge of the new covenantal role for Israel. Religious leaders have spent much energy trying to rebuild the pre-destruction reality rather than sanctifying the new every day. Sometimes people say that they would respond if only they were to receive clear prophetic instruction.[15] But the revelation of our lifetime is so veiled and ambiguous that there is little certainty and few clear, unassailable responses. This very lack of clarity is consistent with the voluntary nature of the covenant and the new maturity of the people Israel. Anything clearer might be coercive. The redemption will become obvious only retrospectively when the Jewish people recognize it as such. Jews must take a more active role in discerning the covenant's presence and in realizing its goals. Then will the Jewish people truly have come of age in the covenant.

Was the Holocaust Necessary?

The recognition that consciousness of the voluntary covenant grows out of the experience of the Holocaust may lead to misunderstanding. This insight may be interpreted as an affirmation of the Holocaust.[16] Some have argued: Without the catastrophe, there would have been no State of Israel. Therefore, the Holocaust is a necessary sacrifice or blood-letting that paves the way for redemption. Similarly, some may think that since the maturation of the covenant comes out of the Holocaust, the disaster was necessary. Some may also believe that this unfolding of the covenant is an explanation of why the Holocaust happened or even some rationale for it. I reject these possibilities.

There can be no rationale for the Holocaust. If anyone offers such, you may be sure that the explanation has domesticated or denatured the Holocaust. The explanation is no explanation but rather some plausible tale about a sanitized and selected version of the Holocaust which has little to do with its reality.[17] There can be historical or sociological or military explanations of how the Holocaust actually operated and what factors enabled the Nazis to carry out the mass murder so successfully. Such explanations are necessary if for no other reason than the need to prevent a recurrence. But that is a far cry from explaining the "why" or the essence of the event.

The same must be said about the development of the voluntary covenant. In retrospect, the voluntary stage is implicit in the covenantal model from the very beginning. Once God self-limits out of respect for human dignity, once human free will is accepted, the ultimate logic is a voluntary covenant. As Soloveitchik writes: "The very validity of the covenant rests upon the *Juridic-Halakhic* principle of *free negotiations,* mutual assumption of duties, and full recognition of the "*equal rights of both parties* concerned with the covenant"[18] (italics added). The full dignity of the human partner can only emerge when that partner takes full responsibility. Any state less than that is encouragement to dependence out of weakness. Residual punishment is coercive and

15. See Michael Wyschogrod's review of Eva Fleischner, ed., *Auschwitz: Beginning of a New Era* (New York, 1977), in *Tradition* 17, no. 1 (Fall 1977): 63–78.

16. "Out of the fierce, came forth sweetness," Judges 14:14.

17. One may offer the analogy of talk about God. Any explanation or description of God may be useful or

valid as long as it recognizes its metaphoric essence and its inability to portray the Divine exhaustively or even in its actual essence. Any portrait that "captures" the Divine is an idol, not a representation of God.

18. Cf. Soloveitchik, "The Lonely Man of Faith," p. 29.

erodes the moral insight of the human partner. In a voluntary covenant, there is a deeper dependence—that of relationship, love, self-expectations based on the model of the other—but it is a dependence out of strength. The ultimate logic of parenting is to raise children to meet life's challenges, but to sustain them with a continuing presence and model, not with continual interference or rescue from problems. Further analysis suggests that in every covenantal relationship, the partners must ultimately choose between equality and force. True love can only exist when the imbalance of power has been overcome by redistribution of power or, in God's case, by a binding renunciation of using the imbalance.[19]

This redistribution of power was the underlying thrust behind modern culture's empowering of the human being. In retrospect, this is what Zionism sought to do to the Jewish covenant starting in the nineteenth century. Thus there were positive reasons and forces operating before the Holocaust to bring Jews and humanity a higher level of responsibility for redemption, just as there were "secularizing" trends preceding the destruction of the Temple. Nevertheless, most traditionalists and modernists failed to see this new dynamic of power as operating within the covenantal framework. Many concluded that the true purpose of modern culture was to reject the covenant or slay the covenantal partner for the sake of human liberation. In significant measure, this misconstruction is directly implicated in the emergence of pathological forms of total human power unleashed in the modern forces which reach a climax in the Holocaust itself. In a counterpart error which was the mirror image of that of modern total secularists, religious groups interpreted the covenant to demand human subservience or passivity and opposed the emergence of the new level of human responsibility. However, now that the Holocaust has occurred, it is no longer possible to delay the emergence of the new level.

There is no good in the Holocaust, only a tragedy which forces us to face up to an issue and a responsibility which was long coming. The Jewish response to the Holocaust, as to the destruction of the Temple, is the act that crystallizes and energizes this transition. The Holocaust is not a necessary *quid pro quo* for anything. It is the shock that almost destroys the covenant. It continues to degrade God and educate humans to savagery and destruction. However, thanks to the power of human love and faith that will not yield the dream of redemption, the Holocaust can be fought, and perhaps its effects can be overcome in history. This is the struggle that is now going on.

Implications of the Voluntary Covenant

The Promise of Pluralism

The total assault on Judaism and on the Jewish people was an attempt to stamp out the covenant, the witness, and, ultimately, the presence of God who is the ground of life and the covenantal hope. Therefore, the very existence of the Jewish people is a fundamental statement that the covenant is ongoing. The survival of the Jewish people in a world full of enemies, where the model of the Holocaust is circulating, is in itself testimony to the existence of a hidden God whose awesome, if invisible, force is evidenced in the ongoing life of the Jewish people.[20] The renewal of Jewish living through having children and restoring human dignity constitute the creation of images of God.[21] These images point to the God of whom they are the image; they are the best, most indelible testimony to God in a world where total evil has triumphed in recent times. Such witness could not be given without profound wells of faith and hope to draw upon by the individual Jews who live this way. Finally, the Jewish people, by recreating the State of Israel and rebuilding the land, have given the witness which shows the

19. When the Rabbis said: "Do not be like servants who serve the Master for the sake of reward, but be like servants who serve the Master not for the sake of reward" (*Ethics of the Fathers* 1:3), they were more prophetic than was realized at the time. Continual

divine rewards (or punishments) are in tension with the goal of a relationship based on love.
20. Based on Rabbi Joshua ben Levi's views in B.T. *Yoma* 69[b].
21. Cf. I. Greenberg, "Cloud of Smoke," p. 41ff.

world that God lives and the covenantal hope is not in vain.[22] All Jews who elect to live as Jews make these statements whatever their self-definition and official behavior.

It makes no essential difference if the Jews involved consciously articulate the covenantal hope or express a belief in the God who is the ground of the covenant. The witness is given by their actions. Actions speak louder than words. People who profess God but gas men, women, and children or burn them alive are atheists whatever their words may be. People who profess to be atheists or to be without hope yet who actively uphold the covenant, even at the cost of their lives, betray their true position by their actions. If anything, their denials only add to the hiddenness of the Divine. Therefore, their theological language is the appropriate one for this time, more appropriate than those who go on speaking as if God were visible and fully performing under the previous terms of the covenant.

In the age of voluntary covenant, every person who steps forward to live as a Jew can be compared to a convert insofar as a convert, one who voluntarily opts to be a Jew, must make certain commitments and express certain beliefs. Then the classic conversion ceremony may guide us to contemporary Jews' proper affirmations. Through the conversion process, the convert testifies that although the Jews are driven, tormented, and persecuted to this very day, the convert still wants to be a Jew, that is, wants to offer the testimony of hope anyway. The convert learns the unity of God and the denial of idolatry; the analogue in our time is the affirmation of God's presence which is witnessed by Jewish existence itself.

The convert must affirm some of the weighty commandments/obligations of a Jew and some of the lighter ones. In this generation, all who opt to live as Jews automatically state their readiness for martyrdom, not only for themselves but for their children and grandchildren as well. There can be no "weightier" commitment than this. A decision to live in Israel and to a lesser extent, a commitment to support it, constitutes acceptance of the

mitzvah [religious obligation] to witness, to build a redeeming social reality, even to bring the Messiah. The appropriate range of "lighter" commandments/obligations to be undertaken can be explored or debated between the denominations. But morally speaking, the simple observance of all the classical *mitzvot* can hardly be the only option offered under the covenantal definition.[23]

While the covenant is now voluntary, birth into it remains an important statement. By being born a Jew, a person summons up all the associations and statements implicit in Jewish existence, including the Jewish testimony to a God who cares. One may opt out by refusing to live as a visible Jew, by trying to escape the fate of a Jew, by trying to deny. However, if one chooses to continue living as a Jew, one makes all the fundamental affirmations implicit in Jewish existence. This is true even if one does not use the officially articulated ways of making one's statements such as bearing witness to creation through Shabbat observance or expressing the messianic hope through prayers such as *Aleinu* ["It is our duty…"].

As long as the covenant was involuntary, it could be imposed from above in a unitary way. This corresponds with the image and role of revelation in the biblical period, which includes unequivocal command and visible reward and punishment for obedience and disobedience. With the shift in covenantal relationship which characterizes the rabbinic era, the revelation becomes more hidden, more subject to pluralist interpretation. Focus on reward and punishment shifts from the worldly toward the otherworldly hidden realm.

In the new era, the voluntary covenant is the theological base of a genuine pluralism. Pluralism is not a matter of tolerance made necessary by living in a non-Jewish reality, nor is it pity for one who does not know any better. It is a recognition that all Jews have chosen to make the fundamental Jewish statement at great personal risk and cost. The present denominations are paths for the covenant-minded all leading toward the final goal. The controversy between them

---

22. That resettlement of the land is proof of the ongoing validity of the covenant is a central theme in Isaiah, Jeremiah, and other prophetic books.

23. For the format of the classical ceremony of conversion, see B.T. *Yevamot* 47[a–b].

will not be whether God has commanded these ways. Conservative, Reform, and secular Jews can freely concede the dimensions of past commandments, but insist nevertheless that these are no longer effective or optimal ways of achieving the goals. Orthodox Jews, even the ultra-Right who uphold every past observance or *minhag* (custom), will recognize that their commitment to observe the entire tradition constitutes a voluntary acceptance, one which can be modeled but cannot be *demanded* of all. Thus, they can be faithful to the full authority of the *Halakhah*, accepting the challenge of modeling it and making it credible and persuasive to *Klal Yisrael*, [the people of Israel] while respecting the *incredible* other types of commitment and contributions which other Jews are making. Such an admission would only confirm the phenomenology of Jewish life as it is now being lived. It would be morally and humanly liberating without yielding the hope of moving *Klal Yisrael* into the classic paths of *Halakhah*. Of course, the psychology of Orthodoxy currently will not be receptive to this approach, but such an obstacle is not a problem of principle or integrity. Rather, it is a function of human limitations, community and political needs, all of which can be dealt with tactically.

It would be unreasonable and, considering the varieties of religious experience and sociological circumstance, unwise to expect total religious unity. There can still be ongoing controversies and policy differences among the denominations. But the members of all the groups have committed their total being to be witness to the covenant by living as Jews. The recognition of this overarching unity enables us to adjudge these controversies as being "for the sake of heaven."[24] In the Talmud, the school of Shammai and the school of Hillel often gave diametrically opposite rulings. Yet they affirmed that both views are "the words of the living God,"[25] precisely because they recognized the underlying unity of their common assumptions about the nature of God and revelation. The unity which was destroyed in the modern period is restored in the common recognition of the voluntary covenant.

Groups can go on judging and trying to persuade each other to change, but the criteria for resolution of the conflict will be the ability to reach the goals of the covenant, including contemporary effectiveness and transmissibility. Orthodoxy might concede that a particular practice is not effective today. However, they continue to accept it as binding out of respect for past generations and their role in the covenant. Out of the sense that this generation is only a way station on the long covenantal road, they can accept temporary ineffectiveness of a practice in one moment in order to have the resource available in another. The definition of being Orthodox might be: accepting the models of the past as binding out of recognition of the incredible, divine power in them, and being bound by the process of the covenant, a process seen as inseparable from its goals and content. Then the differences with non-Orthodox Jews are tactical, and others' faithfulness to God and to the covenant can be admitted without undermining Orthodox affirmations. Once the validity of the others is recognized, the shortcomings or faults in the *halakhic* system can be admitted and, to the extent possible, corrected. As long as the legitimacy of the others is not recognized, many problems will be denied and possible solutions rejected on the grounds that to change would give aid and comfort to the "enemy."

By the same token, Reform, Conservative, and secular Jews would waive the modernist criteria that justify their positions. This means that every part of the tradition may present itself for serious consideration to be judged by the same criteria of consistency with the covenant, transmissibility, and effectiveness. Any new approaches developed by these movements will also be reviewed by the same criteria. Some changes may be judged as concessions legitimated by the need to successfully negotiate the covenantal paths, and they are subject to repeal or redirection if the situation changes. New paths or models may be as sacred or more sacred than the inherited ones if they are deemed closer to the covenantal values or more effective in attaining them. It follows from this, however, that both reform and tradition are

---

24. Cf. "Every controversy for the sake of heaven will have a lasting result." *Ethics of the Fathers* 5:20.

25. B.T. *Eruvin* 13[b].

aligned along a continuum of attempts to live by the covenant. Reform behavior is not antinomian, but is distinguished from traditional Judaism by the giving of different weights to different covenantal values. The increased "heavier" role of women in Reform is an affirmation of the covenantal promise of redemption and ultimate dignity for women as well as men, rather than a rejection of the commandments or roles for males in tradition. Feminist corrections of the *Halakhah* are an attempt to move more urgently toward the covenantal goal of humankind being in the image of God, which implies equality for women, rather than a rejection of the concept of obligation or of the traditional feminine positive roles.[26]

Once disagreements take place within the bounds of the common risk and dream of Jewish existence, the groups might take on or set aside a common practice for the sake of unity, beyond the merits of the practice itself. Each group would be committed to use all its resources and methods to reach out and enable the others to live in good conscience with the same model or at least not to disrupt or shatter the others' ways where they differ. At least all groups would recognize the element of risk and creativity in trying to be faithful to the covenant at a moment when new roles and new institutions are emerging. Since whatever models of service are offered tend to be projections of past experience, there is a tendency in transition times to offer the familiar even when something new or original may be needed. At moments of transformation there is the risk of a faithfulness that misdirects, even as there is a risk of excessive novelty and betrayal of the tried and true methods of the covenant. Each group should welcome the insights and criticisms of the others as necessary correctives, sources of perspective in a fluid and unformed situation in which all want to do the right thing but fear falling short.

Human Co-creativity in the Covenant

Although obedience is the natural response in an involuntary covenant, nevertheless the principle of mutual obligation stimulated the Jews to engage in controversies with God throughout history. The greater the degree of human partnership, the more frequent and profound is the role of humans in challenging God to live up to the covenant. In an age of voluntary covenant, humans have all the more right and obligation to represent the covenantal goals and values to God. Humans must take responsibility, both for the goals and the consistency of the means with the goals. Since humans are being called to take full responsibility in action for the realization of the covenant, they cannot escape the responsibility to judge the means and methods available to pursue the goals. Those who are entrusted with a task, and who take full responsibility for its realization, must be allowed discretion to achieve the goal. This delegation of authority is all the more justified in light of the Jewish faithfulness to the covenant, exemplified by the voluntary reassumption of the covenant in this generation despite the obvious risks involved.

The urgency of closing any gap between the covenantal methods and goals is greater in light of the overwhelming countertestimony of evil in this generation. The credibility of the covenant is so weakened and so precariously balanced that any internal element that disrupts or contravenes its affirmations must be eliminated. So savage was the attack on the image of God that the counterresponse of reaffirmation must be extraordinary. Any models or behavior patterns within the tradition that demean the image of God must be cleansed and corrected at once. The hope of breakthrough toward perfection is higher in a generation which feels the obligation to match the extraordinary outburst of evil with a countervailing upsurge of good. Therefore, there is motivation and sufficient authority even among the Orthodox to correct the tradition or move it toward its own goals of perfection. The authority to change grows out of loyalty to the tradition and to the covenantal goals.

Part of the response must be to identify covenantal values and make judgments on the relative weight to be assigned to each. In the past, it has been argued that any judgment in conflict with established tradition is improper. Since the word of God is self-validating, change, by definition, must be based on appeal to outside criteria

---

26. See "The Theoretical Basis of Women's Equality in Judaism," in Blu Greenberg, *On Women and Judaism* (Philadelphia, 1981), pp. 39–55.

and is therefore invalid. With increased human responsibility and greater hiddenness of God and of revelation, the exercise of judgment not only by rabbis but by a wider variety of people becomes urgent. One cannot pass the buck to tradition. The responsibility for getting to the final perfection is squarely on this generation. It must exercise the responsibility with humility and self-criticism, but faithfulness requires that judgments be made.

Since the State of Israel is the central vehicle of Jewish power, self-defense, and redemption building, its needs should be given greater religious weight, perhaps rated as a matter of life or death. Some will object that this runs the risk of idolatry vis-à-vis the state. Both traditionalist and liberal Jews might conclude that the danger of idolatry is the overriding concern. Other traditionalist and liberal Jews might pursue a policy stressing the State's needs while taking action to avoid idolatry. Either decision would be good, particularly as it grows out of a wrestling with the actual situation, rather than out of the routine party lines of conflicting forces in modernity and tradition. The treatment of women, of the handicapped, and of gentiles in the tradition are other examples where Jewish utopian values are in conflict with the present reality. These value concessions to reality must now be challenged even if we agree that they are divinely normative. The challenge, the defense, and the final resolution should not follow present party lines, but should explore the best ways of advancing the covenantal goals. Indeed, side-by-side experiments may be the right prescription until we sort out the best ways. In an experimental situation, either a more traditional or a more innovative modus operandi becomes a creative and helpful foil for the other position, so that pluralism becomes a source of strength.

Messianic Time

Classically, great destruction so challenges the affirmations of the covenant that it creates an urgent anticipation of a countervailing achievement of redemption. Nothing less can restore the credibility of the way. An event as massively devaluing as the Holocaust needs an event of messianic proportions to restore the balance. Voluntarily taking up the covenant, then, means taking up the challenge of messianic breakthroughs. The expectation of great redemption is further nurtured by the incredible nature of the creation of Israel, which is heralded in the tradition as the harbinger and necessary condition for the messianic fulfillment.

Why, then, has this generation hesitated to speak in messianic terms? Partly it is due to the need to speak modestly after such a triumph of evil; partly the hesitation is due to the triumph of modernity and its rational, limiting style which has a chilling effect on messianic expectations.[27] And why has the messianic principle, when applied, been such a poor guide to action? The invocation of messianic associations for David Ben Gurion [Israel's prime minister, 1948–1953] was essentially a political trick to gain new immigrant votes for the very people who were proceeding to strip the Sephardim of their traditional values and give them the short end of the social stick. In the case of *Gush Emunim*, the messianic models have led to a devaluation of security and other realistic considerations and sometimes to a downgrading of the dignity of Arab concerns and needs on the West Bank.

I submit that these ills grow out of a failure to grasp the nature of the messianic in the era of voluntary covenant. A messiah who is triumphant and does it all for Israel would be utterly inappropriate in such an age. The arrival of such a messiah would be morally outrageous, for the Messiah would have come at the wrong time. As Elie Wiesel has written, if any Messiah were going to redeem us by divine strength, then the time to have come was during the Holocaust. Any Messiah who could have come and redeemed us, and did not do so then but chooses to come now is a moral monster. Wiesel is right: It is too late for the Messiah to come.[28] *Therefore we will have to bring the Messiah.* Bringing the Messiah is the crowning response to the divine call for humans to take full responsibility in the covenant. A messiah who

27. Cf. I. Greenberg, "Toward Jewish Religious Unity," *Judaism* 15, no. 2 (Spring 1966): 135.

28. Cf. Elie Wiesel, *Gates of the Forest* (New York, 1966) pp. 41ff., 215; cf. 42–43 and 223.

needs to be brought can only be partial, flawed, hidden.[29] Such a model of the Messiah may dampen the dangerous tendency to excessive utopianism, not to mention antinomianism, implicit in the end time. At the same time, the model assigns new urgency to achievements of justice and peace, to coming closer to vegetarianism[30] and the full dignity of other humans, to witnessing more openly and more universally even as we prepare to become one with the world.

Responding

In a situation of fundamental transformation, playing it safe is tempting, but dangerous. The familiarity of the response gives consolation and a false sense of security in a bewildering vortex of change. However, there is a real risk of acting like the Sadducees at the destruction of the Temple. Upholding the familiar, insisting that it is the only authoritative way, may leave one totally invested in recreating the status quo. When the status quo does not return, exhaustion and death of the spirit follow.

The alternative is to incorporate the new events and the new situation, first into understanding and then into the covenantal way. This process may lead to mistaken judgments ranging from premature messianism to present-mindedness to loss of a coherent sense of the past. Taking action is risky; not taking action is risky. The appropriate response is to act, with anxiety, with conflict, with fear, but to act nonetheless. The first step is to incorporate the new event into the traditional way of life and into Jewish memory. *Yom HaShoah* [Holocaust Memorial Day] and *Yom Ha-Atzmaut* [Israeli Independence Day] must become central holy days of the Jewish calendar. Their "secular" nature and grassroots origins are appropriate to the new era of holiness in which humans take responsibility for sanctification and redemption. The ambiguity of the days, and the fact that their sanctity is open to challenge, is an expression of the hiddenness of the Divine in the new era.

Many other commandments emerge from the new reality. The model/*mitzvah* of pilgrimage, both to the scenes of the Holocaust and to Israel, and the telling of the tale in secular settings, including film, books, and other media, are the new secular liturgical acts. A range of acts of justice and restored dignity, which flow from these events (you were slaves, you were in ghettos, you were in camps, therefore you . . . ; you were freed, you were outsiders and taken to the promised land, therefore you . . .), are the ethical counterparts of this liturgical development. Both types of acts are part of the expansion of the covenantal round of life to incorporate the new experiences. The accounts of these events and the lives and the models that grow out of them constitute a new Scripture and a new Talmud.

The redemption event of this era, Israel, the Scriptures which are being written, the spiritual leadership of this new age will be even more secular, more "naturalistic," more flawed than in the rabbinic era, as is appropriate given the greater hiddenness of God. Every act of life becomes potentially holy, the locus of the hidden Divine Presence. Not only are special days such as Shabbat and prohibition of work ways of sanctification, but work itself properly done is a religious act Work as the expression of the commandment/*lashevet*—to settle the world—work as the creation of an infrastructure for human dignity, work as the exercise of the human capacity for power and control which are part of the image of God will become a *halakhically* holy enterprise.[31] Thus, every day and not just one out of seven can become a holy day.

The holiness of sexuality can be expressed not only in its prohibition or in *mikveh*, but in the acts of love themselves. Sexuality as communication, as the revelation of the image of God in me, as the discovery of the image of God in the other, as affirmation of the pleasure of life, as a joyous vehicle of creating life becomes the continual expression of holiness. The Torah commands the Jewish people: *kedoshim tih'yu* (Be holy).[32] In a classic commentary, Nachmanides defines

---

29. Elsewhere I have suggested that this is a messiah who limps even as Jacob did after his struggle with the Angel of the Night left him wounded—but unbowed.
30. I. Greenberg, "Jewish Tradition and Contemporary Problems," in *Relationship between Jewish Tradition and*

Contemporary Issues (New York, n.d.), p. 11; and Samuel Dresner and Seymour Siegel, *The Jewish Dietary Laws* (New York, 1959), pp. 21–30.
31. See *Guide to the Shabbat* (New York, 1981), pp. 8–12.
32. Leviticus 19:2.

holiness above and beyond specific ethical and ritual commandments as fulfillment of the talmudic dictum *kadesh atzmecha b'mutar* lach.[33] (Sanctify yourself in the areas which are permitted), go beyond the letter of the law and exercise restraint in those areas which are permitted.[34] The concept of a secular sanctification suggests that holiness in the permitted is achieved not only by extending prohibition, but by directing action and spirit toward the covenantal goal.

Much of the expression of holiness can be accomplished using the existing models of *b'rachah* (blessing), selection, and sharing. Some of this expansion may come from heightened consciousness and developing inner attitudes and perceptions of holiness. Thus the voluntary covenantal model reaches a climax. In such moments, it begins to approximate Jeremiah's promise of a new covenant written on the heart.[35] However, this renewed covenant does not reject law or form, nor does it repudiate or supersede the original covenant. The voluntary covenant is built on the involuntary covenant; it continues and moves toward the final goal.

Contemporary Jews will have to explore the liturgical sources and models that can nurture a holiness that is at once more subtle and more elusive. The great covenantal symbol, circumcision, reflects the involuntary nature of the covenant. It also "excludes" women and makes their representative function relatively less central.[36] In the new era, the symbol of the voluntary covenant may well be the revival, side by side with circumcision, of the *brit bayn habetarim*, the covenant between the pieces.[37] This was the original covenant ceremony, the conversion ritual of Abraham, the first non-Jew to become a Jew. He entered this covenant voluntarily before he became circumcised and permanently marked. Women can enter into the covenant between the pieces equally with men. This ceremony symbolizes that in the era of the voluntary covenant, all are bound equally, i.e., all have voluntarily committed themselves to this incredible and dangerous task.[38]

Modern history has shown that democracies can ask for and elicit more total sacrifices from their citizens than even the great tyrannies can dare demand of their people. This encourages us to hope that the age of voluntary covenant will be marked by more encompassing religious life, greater commitment to justice, and an overall higher level of spiritual achievement by the Jewish people. The age has already started with unprecedented spiritual heroism in the response to the Holocaust. One may pray that we be worthy— and that the best is yet to come.

33. The talmudic phrase is found in B.T. *Yevamot* 20ᵃ.
34. See Nachmanides' analysis in his commentary on Leviticus 19:2 d.h. *kedoshim tih'yu.*
35. Jeremiah 31:30.
36. The rabbinic analogue to this concept is the ruling that one who is commanded and performs the act is at a higher level than one who is not commanded but does the act. Cf. B.T. *Kiddushin* 31ᵃ. This distinction comes to serve as an obstacle to the admission of women into liturgical roles. Cf. Blu Greenberg, *On Women and Judaism*, pp. 82–85.
37. Genesis 15:5–18.
38. The third era analogue to this concept may be that "greater is the one who is not commanded but voluntarily comes forward than the one who acts only out of command."

Isaac Hutner

Rabbi Hutner (1906–1980) was born into a traditional ḥasidic family in Warsaw, Poland. His father was a disciple (a "ḥasid") of the Kotzker ḥasidic tradition, a form of Ḥasidism known for its eccentricity and intellectualism. Provided with a traditional Orthodox Jewish education as a youngster, Isaac Hutner was soon recognized as a precocious student and was sent to study at the great Lithuanian yeshiva in Slobodka. This yeshiva was the crown jewel in what were known as *musar* yeshivot, meaning they combined intensive rabbinic study—for which their students were famous—with a concern for inner spirituality and ethical sensitivity. (The *Musar* movement was created in the mid-nineteenth century by the sage R. Israel Salanter.)

After completing his studies in Lithuania, Rabbi Hutner went on to study in Palestine, then under the British mandate, in the yeshiva in Hebron. There he was influenced both by the mystical, Zionist Chief Rabbi of Palestine R. Abraham Kook and by the anti-Zionist circles of R. Joseph Ḥayyim Sonnenfeld. In 1929, following the anti-Jewish riots in Hebron, R. Hutner returned to Warsaw and then went to study at the University of Berlin, which was at that time, just prior to the rise of Hitler to power, a major academic center for Orthodox young men from Eastern Europe. (This included Joseph Soloveitchik, Eliezer Berkovits and Abraham Joshua Heschel.) In 1935, R. Hutner came to America where he founded and led the yeshiva *Mesivta R. Ḥayyim Berlin*. In later years, he also began a similar institution in Jerusalem and headed both institutions, commuting each year between New York and Jerusalem. In America, he became one of the most influential ultra-Orthodox rabbis and a leader of the *Agudat Yisrael* (ultra-Orthodox) organization. Between 1951 and his death, R. Hutner published his collected lectures, which eventually came to total eight volumes and which was entitled *Pachad Yitzchak (The Banner of Isaac)*.

SELECTION

The present selection is drawn from the ultra-Orthodox English journal the *Jewish Observer* (October 1977): 3–9. Rabbi Isaac Hutner, one of the most revered ultra-Orthodox rabbinical figures in world Jewry, speaks from, as he describes his position, "a Torah view of the world." Accordingly, he examines Jewish history, including the Holocaust, from a distinctive, Orthodox religious perspective. From this angle of vision he sees in modernity "promises of [Jewish] equality made and then broken." But these frustrating and corrupting events are already anticipated in the Torah, which warns the Jewish people what will happen if they succumb to "the lure of strange nations and trust in them." That is to say, the tragedy of the Holocaust can be understood within the parameters of the classical interpretations of the concepts of reward and punishment, now applied to the experience of the Jewish people in the twentieth century. Understood accordingly, the Holocaust is a divine punishment for Israel's sins, especially the sins of assimilation, religious nonobservance, and the efforts to rebuild a Jewish state through human effort as embodied in secular Zionism. Thus, what we must now do, Hutner urges, is repent, disavow our "earlier infatuation with gentile ways," and turn back to Torah. Moreover, suffering, Hutner reminds us, is already spoken of in the Torah as a punishment for disobedience. Thus, what we need to do is acknowledge the true significance of this recent *Shoah*—whose uniqueness he explicitly denies—so that we can act correctly as "Torah Jews," i.e., act as those who fear God, keep His commandments, and work for the coming of the Messiah in obedience with His transcendental plan.

Selected Bibliography

Works by Isaac Hutner

"Holocaust," *Jewish Observer* (October 1977): 3–9.
Pachad Yitzchak . . . [*The Banner of Isaac: Torah Discourses on Matters of Faith and the Duties of the Heart*], 8 vols. (Brooklyn, N.Y., 1965–1982) [Hebrew].

Articles about Isaac Hutner

Goldberg, Hillel. "Rabbi Isaac Hutner," in *Between Berlin and Slobodka: Jewish Transition Figures from Eastern Europe* (Hoboken, N.J., 1989), pp. 63–87.
———. "Rabbi Isaac Hutner: A Synoptic Interpretive Biography," *Tradition* 22 (Winter 1987): 18–46.
Kaplan, Lawrence. "Rabbi Isaac Hutner's '*Da'at Torah* Perspective' on the Holocaust," *Tradition* 18, no. 3 (Fall 1980): 235–248.
Schwarzschild, Steven S. "An Introduction to the Thought of R. Isaac Hutner," *Modern Judaism* 5 (Fall 1985): 235–277.
———. "Two Lectures of R. Isaac Hutner," *Tradition* 14 (Fall 1974): 90–109.
———. "Isaac Hutner," in *Interpreters of Judaism in the Late Twentieth Century*, edited by Steven T. Katz (Washington, D.C., 1993), pp. 151–165.
Sefer haZikkaron . . . [*Memorial Volume on the Late Author of "Pachad Yitzchak"*], edited by J. Buksboim (Brooklyn, N.Y., 1984) [Hebrew].

HOLOCAUST

1. Is the term *Shoah* (lit. Holocaust) acceptable in describing the destruction of European Jewry during World War II?
2. Should the "Holocaust" be taught separately as many schools are now doing or planning to do, or incorporated into regular courses on Jewish history and taught as part of the studies on this particular time period?
3. If the latter, where indeed does the Holocaust "fit in" with the rest of Jewish history?

Yeshiva and day school principals from across the nation posed the above questions to Rabbi Yitzchok [Isaac] Hutner, head of the Yeshiva Rabbi Chaim Berlin-Aryeh and a member of the *Moetzes Gedolei HaTorah* (Council of Torah Sages) of *Agudat Israel* or America.

In response, Rabbi Hutner delivered a discourse to a gathering of approximately one hundred educators assembled at the yeshiva. In it, he focused on significant aspects of the *ḥurban* (destruction) that were hitherto either little known or studiously avoided.

I.

In order to determine the appropriateness of any term, one must first thoroughly understand what one is trying to define. Clarity of expression depends upon clarity of perception. Therefore, before we attempt to designate a name for the shattering events of 1939–1945, we must examine the significance of those events in their historical context. For our present purpose of identification only, we shall refer to the term "Holocaust" when we discuss the Nazi destruction of European Jewry during World War II. As we shall see, this in no way signifies the acceptability of this term.

It should be made clear at the outset that we shall not merely discuss history this evening. Our orientation toward Jewish history must reflect an attitude toward *kedusha* [holiness]—approaching that which is most holy and sacred. This sanctity stems from the fact that "the Jewish people and the Torah are one" (*Zohar, Acharei Mos*, 73), thus intimately relating the proper study of Jewish history with the study of Torah. Yet, unfortunately, just as in the study of Torah itself, we are familiar with the phenomenon of those who distort and misinterpret the meaning of Torah (see *Pirke Avot* [Ethics of Fathers] 3:11), so is there an even subtler danger from those who distort the meaning of Jewish history. It will be our task this evening to untangle the web of distortions about recent Jewish history, which has already been woven, and uncover the Torah perspective which has been hidden from us.

To be sure, it will not be easy to regain this perspective. The thoughts which we will explore this evening will be difficult to digest because of our long subsistence upon the forced diet of public opinion. The creators of the powerful force of public opinion are beyond the realm of our control and the mind-numbing results of their influence are largely out of our hands. In order to achieve any hold upon the truth, we will first have to free ourselves from the iron-clad grip of their puissance and open our minds and hearts to the sometimes bitter pill of truth.

II. The Origins of the Term

As in all quests for the truth, we must return to origins. The term *Shoah* was coined by the founders of *Yad V'Shem* [the Israeli Holocaust Memorial] in Jerusalem, since they were convinced that the tragedy of European Jewry was so unique in its proportions and dimensions that no previous phrase could encompass its meaning. Undoubtedly, to a certain degree they were correct, for indeed the destruction of hundreds of thousands of Jewish communities *was* unique in its proportions and dimensions. Yet by singling out the quantitative differences of this particular *ḥurban*, those who sought a new terminology for these events missed the essence of their uniqueness. It is not just the proportions and dimensions of the Holocaust which define its quintessence, but its establishment of a new and significant pattern in Jewish history. Yet at the same time it must be stressed that this pattern, far from coincidental, is intricately related to the basic pattern of Jewish history itself and profoundly affects our entire vision of recent history and indeed current events.

By placing the Holocaust in its historical perspective we shall uncover two new directions in recent Jewish history in reference to the gentile persecution of Jews. Whereas our entire history has been replete with various instances of persecution by different civilizations, empires, and nations—varying only in intensity, means, and ferocity—recent history has shifted dramatically in two new areas.

III. The Era of Disappointment

The first of these epochal changes involves the shift from generations of gentile mistreatment of Jews which, if unwelcome, were nevertheless expected and indeed announced our oppressors—to an era where promises of equality were made and then broken, rights were granted and then revoked, benevolence was anticipated, only to be crushed by cruel malevolence.

This change in our historical pattern, although it has hitherto gone largely unnoticed, is nevertheless a seminal movement in our progress toward the inevitable culmination of history in absolute redemption. The recent examples of these disappointments may be readily brought to mind, and indeed some are yet fresh with the pain of unfulfilled anticipation. The French Revolution, in that first eighteenth-century burst of dedication to equality and freedom, had granted equal rights to Jews *as citizens*, although nothing to Jews *as Jews*. The Treaty of Versailles [June 28, 1919] had gone even further and granted rights to minorities *as minorities*, including Jews *as Jews*. Of course, these promises were later nullified or retracted, and heard from no more. In Russia, too, Lenin had signed in 1917 the Soviet Minority Rights Law, granting a kind of Jewish self-government in the form of a Jewish soviet. This, too, was soon abolished in the 1920s by Stalin, dashing those bright hopes that had been kindled. England, too, entered the twentieth century by revoking a promise made to Jews in the form of the Balfour Declaration. In November 1917, Jews danced in the streets because Britain had declared that "His Majesty's Government views with favor the establishment in Palestine of a national home for the Jewish people." The declaration was accepted at the Conference of San Remo in 1920. Yet by June 1922, Winston Churchill, then British colonial secretary, was qualifying that the declaration did not mean the "imposition of a Jewish nationality upon the inhabitants of Palestine as a whole, but further development of the existing Jewish community." Of course, a long, bitter period followed where a British hand held the gun of the age-old oppressor of Israel.

Thus it becomes clear that the trend of the anti-Jewish phenomena of the first half of the twentieth century was characterized, not so much by persecutions and pogroms as in the past, but by the legalized retraction of existing laws granting sundry privileges. Although these reversals are

dramatic and telling enough of themselves, they pale in the face of the retractions and total turnabouts made by the Germans in the 1920s and 1930s. On March 11, 1812, Prince Karl August von Hardenberg had issued his famous edict emancipating Prussian Jews, but in 1919, as supplement to the German translation of the so-called *Protocols of the Elders of Zion*, Gottfried Zur Beek (Ludwig Miller) used Hardenberg's definition of a Jew in drafting proposals for anti-Jewish legislation. These proposals culminated in 1935 in the so-called Nuremberg Laws which legitimized anti-Semitism and legalized anti-Jewish bigotry. These *Rassengesetz* [racial laws], which forbade marriage between Germans and Jews and disenfranchised non Aryans, exactly paralleled earlier rights and privileges legally granted to Jews. Thus the cycle was diabolically complete. What had been given legally was taken away, leaving the Jewish people with a growing and ultimately inexorable disillusionment with the promises and even legal enactments of the gentile world.[1]

Let us restate clearly the pattern we have discovered in recent Jewish history. Jews have always been beaten by gentiles; only the means and instruments of torment have varied. The innovation of recent times has been that for long periods, Jews were deluded into trust in the gentiles by a series of laws and regulations in their behalf, only to have trust shattered by the rescission of those very laws. This historical period culminated in the Holocaust, the largest-scale annihilation of a people in history, yet resulting not from lawless hordes but flowing directly from legalized and formal governmental edicts. The end result of this period for the Jewish psyche was a significant—indeed, crucial—one. From trust in the gentile world, the Jewish nation was cruelly brought to a repudiation of that trust. In a relatively short historical period, disappointment

1. Of course many works have been devoted solely to the German anti-Jewish legislation which preceded and legalized the murder which was to follow. An idea of the vastness of the literature may be gotten from the fact that *Die Gesetzebung Adolf Hitlers* (*Hitler's Legislation*) takes up 33 volumes (edited by Werner Hoche, 1933–1939). As early as 27 May 1924, the Nazis introduced a motion to place all members of the Jewish race under special legislation (*sonderrecht*). And from then on, every

bit of terror perpetrated against the Jews was, with German thoroughness, preceded by meticulously worded legislation. It is perhaps significant that where anti-Jewish violence broke out in German streets before the laws had been enacted to that effect, Wilhelm Frick, minister of the interior, and Reichsbank president Hjalmar Schacht condemned and ordered a stop to the "illegal actions" (see Lucy S. Dawidowicz, *The War against the Jews* [New York; 1976], p. 83).

in the non-Jewish world was deeply imprinted upon the Jewish soul.

IV. Torah Source for the New Era

As we delve more deeply into the Torah view of these awesome events, we shall find that they certainly are not coincidental, but reflect the greater cosmic plan of the Creator of the universe. If we find in world history an era where Jews move from the expectation of persecution by gentiles to a period of disappointment in those very people, this change must be reflected in the Torah. As we said earlier, since the Jewish people and the Torah are one, what happens in one must have a counterpart in the other. Therefore, let us study together the [biblical] passage where the monumental turn of events is reflected:

> And the Lord said to Moses: Behold you will soon pass on and this nation will arise and fall prey to the lure of strange nations and trust in them.... And I will hide My face from them and they will become as food for their enemies and great evils and troubles will come upon them. Then shall they declare: it is because my God has not been in my midst that these evils have befallen me. (*Deuteronomy* 31:1–17)

We must first establish what is meant by the Hebrew words in the passage. It should be noted that we translated it as "the lure of strange nations and trust in them," and not as the "worship of strange gods." This interpretation follows *Onkelos* [the ancient Aramaic translator of the Hebrew Bible], who translates the Hebrew literally as "the temptation of the nations." This translation, rather than the more obvious one of "idol worship" reflects the sense of passage, for we know (B. T. *Yoma* 69^b) that the *yeitzer hara*—the evil inclination—for idolatry has long been eliminated by the *Anshei Knesses Hagadola*—the Men of the Great Assembly [circa 4th C. BCE]. We can only appreciate the gravity of the sin of straying after "the lure of strange nations" when we realize that only here does the Torah mention the terrifying punishment of becoming consumed by our enemies. Even the two *tochachos*—the portions of the Torah where God rebukes His nation for its sins and warns of the terrible consequences of evil (see, e.g., Deuteronomy 28)—do not allude to such dire punishment. The "great evils and troubles" which are the direct result of trusting and relying upon the gentile world signify the impetus for the next immediate stage in Jewish history, a unique point in the *teshuva* [repentance] process: "Then shall they declare: it is because my God has not been in my midst that these evils have befallen me."

When we now carefully study the Torah passages quoted, we will be struck by the Jews' response to the great "evils and troubles" which befall them. We know that the *viduy*—[confession and] the enumeration of sins—associated with true repentance necessitates the declaration that "I have sinned" in addition to the specifics of the transgression. Here, there seems to be *teshuva*, yet no real admission of wrongdoing has been made. In effect, what we encounter in this passage, unique in the Torah, is a kind of *teshuva*/non-*teshuva*, a leaning toward (but not completion of) the complete penitence required by the Torah.

The Ramban [Rabbi Moses ben Naḥman, d. 1270], in his explication of this passage, grants us the key to this paradox. He explains that it reflects the very first stirrings of *teshuva* in its nascency. The lowest rung of evil is the disavowal of wrongdoing. Thus, as Ramban quotes, "Behold I do judgment with you for saying, 'I have not sinned'" (*Jeremiah* 2:35) because this is the total rejection of guilt. We know that the essence of *teshuva* is *viduy*—admission of wrongdoing and enumeration of sins. Yet, the prophet proclaims that punishment will not come because one has said, "I have not sinned," but because—infinitely worse—one has declared, "I have not sinned." Once the repudiation of innocence has been accomplished, the *teshuva* process has begun. Even if one has not yet arrived at the positive point of *viduy* the implicit significance of no longer claiming innocence is that the road to repentance has been cleared and one is ready for formal acceptance of guilt and positive commitment to the future. This, then, is a stage of *teshuva*, a kind of *teshuva*-readiness that *Knesses Yisroel* [the community of Israel] will reach in future days before it achieves total repentance.

This stage of *teshuva* will come about as a direct result of the "great evils and troubles" which—as we interpreted according to *Onkelos*—come upon them because of their trust in the nations. The effect of the great calamities of those days, far from merely being a punishment for wrongdoing, will be to correct the previously misplaced trust and prepare the way for true *teshuva*. As we have seen, the "great evils and troubles" did indeed come upon us from those very gentile nations which had gained our confidence and trust.

Thus, there is revealed to us both the chronology and the impetus of the *teshuva* of *Acharis Ha Yamim* (the End of Days). The very first step will be reached by *Klal Yisroel* [the people of Israel] through their repudiation of their earlier infatuations with gentile ways. In our terms, this is when the Jewish people move toward repentance because of disappointment in the gentiles. This can only come about through promises rescinded, rights revoked, and anticipation aborted. The plan and anguish at the time of these shattered illusions is all too real and tragic; yet the events themselves serve to bring us to the recognition that "it is because my God has not been in my midst that these evils have befallen me." This the Ramban sees as the necessary prerequisite to the final step of *teshuva* when they will add to their earlier regret the complete confession and total penitence.

Our new understanding of the essence of our era allows us some comprehension of the phenomenon of our "age of *baalei-teshuva*" [those who have returned to the tradition]. It has often been noted that *teshuva* seems to "be in the air," and indeed the many movements currently succeeding to an unprecedented degree in bringing Jews closer to Judaism are but a reflection of the fact that the very climate is permeated with a kind of *teshuva*-readiness. This climate is the result of the disappointment in gentiles which demolished the first stumbling block to *teshuva* and forced the recognition that "it is because my God has not been in my midst" that the awesome events of recent times have occurred. Of course, this is not to say that each individual *baal teshuva* [penitent] has experienced a personal disappointment in gentiles. There are characteristics and trends common to an entire epoch which eventually affect each individual in his own way.

I had an occasion to elaborate on this point, when by a combination of circumstances I found myself in *Eretz Yisroel* [the Land of Israel] in the company of a group of extreme leftists on [the former prime minister David] Ben Gurion's

yahrzeit [anniversary of his death]. I was asked to say a few words in honor of the day and felt it worthwhile to relate the following to them.

Ben Gurion often used to tell people that now was not the proper time to resolve controversy between the religious and antireligious. When the opportunities arose for resolving such issues, he made sure they were tabled until a future time. Undoubtedly, his reasoning—conscious or subconscious—was that time was on the side of secularists. The experience of Ben Gurion's generation was that the number of observant Jews was steadily decreasing and a Judaism empty of Torah seemed on the ascent.

In so calculating, Ben Gurion made a grave error. In that group of leftists, there were representatives of many prewar cities from various types of Jewish communities all over Europe. I asked each of the assembled in turn, "Do you recall *Meḥalel Shabbos*—a nonobservant Jew—in your city who had a son who became *Shomer Shabbos* [Sabbath observant]?" Each of them answered with the same emphatic "No." Yet, I pointed out to them, today there are thousands of *baalai teshuva* [formerly nonobservant Jews who have now returned to the religious tradition] whose parents knew virtually nothing of their faith. Ben Gurion, in his time, seemed to be correct, but he could only calculate chronological time and knew nothing of [the] eschatological movement of generations. The era of disappointment tore a generation from the clutches of "the temptation of the nations" and prepared the way for an era of true *teshuva*.

So much for the first direction in Jewish history in relation to gentile persecutions.

V. Public Opinion versus Truth

Before we explore the second of the new directions in detail, it is important to establish a clear distinction between any common approach to world events and *daas Torah*—a Torah view of the world. "Public opinion" and any but the Torah approach is by definition colored by outside forces, subjective considerations, and the falsehood of secular perspective.

An example of how public opinion can be molded—indeed, warped—at the whim of powerful individuals can be taken from a study of Russian history textbooks published during the respective reigns of Lenin, Stalin, and Khrushchev. During each period, the textbooks hailed the then-current leader to the exclusion of all his predecessors as the savior of Russia and hero of his people. Undoubtedly, "public opinion" during each period, once children's minds had been suitably molded, reflected the thinking and wishes of the state. While more subtle in form, this ability to direct public opinion exists in democratic countries as well. Thus, we already pointed out at the beginning that we must make every effort to free ourselves from the powerful grip of public opinion and must be ever on our guard that our opinions of the true nature of world events be shaped only by Torah views through Torah eyes.

Sadly, even in our own circles, the mold for shaping public opinion lies in the hands of the State of Israel. An appropriate example of this dangerous process of selectively "rewriting" history may be found in the extraordinary purging from the public record of all evidence of the culpability of the forerunners of the State [of Israel] in the tragedy of European Jewry and the substitution in its place of factors inconsequential to the calamity which ultimately occurred.

To cover its own contribution to the final catastrophic events, those of the State [of Israel] in a position to influence public opinion circulated the notorious canard that *Gedolei Yisroel* [great Jewish sages] were responsible for the destruction of many communities because they did not urge emigration. This charge is, of course, a gross distortion of the truth and need not be granted more dignity than it deserves by issuing a formal refutation. However, at the same time as the State [of Israel] made certain to include this charge as historical fact in every account of the war years, it successfully sought to omit any mention of its own contribution to the impending tragedy. What the [leaders of the] State [of Israel] omitted in its own version of history is the second of the above-mentioned new directions in recent Jewish history. It is the phenomenon which we must now examine.

VI. East and West Meet

For centuries, indeed millennia, gentile persecution of Jews took one of two forms, but the two never worked simultaneously. Either Jewry had to contend with the *Yishmael* [Ishmaelite, i.e., Muslim] nations of the East or was persecuted and expelled by the nations of the West. Never in our history did the nations of the Occident join forces with those of the East for the purpose of destroying Jews.

With World War II, this long epoch was brought to a crude and malevolent close. In 1923 Hitler wrote *Mein Kampf* spelling out his belief that the Jewish people should be wiped out. This was read by Haj Amin el-Husseini, the Grand Mufti of Jerusalem, who [together with Hitler] formed one of the most significant alliances of modern times. There is ample documentation that not only did the Mufti visit Hitler and his top aides on a number of occasions, but indeed with Adolf Eichmann, he visited the Auschwitz gas chamber incognito to check on its efficiency.[2]

The extent of the Mufti's influence upon the Nazi forces may be seen in a crucial decision made by Hitler at the height of the war. Railroad trains were much in demand by the Axis, and Hitler's troops badly needed reinforcements in Russia. Yet, soon after he landed in Berlin in November 1941, the Mufti demanded all available resources be used to annihilate the Jews. The choice: *Juden nach Auschwitz* [Jews to Auschwitz] or *Soldaten nach Stalingrad* [German soldiers to Stalingrad] was resolved his way. Two months later (20 January 1942) at the Wannsee Conference, the formal decision was made to annihilate all Jews who had survived the ghettos, forced labor, starvation, and disease.

Of course, the Mufti was serving his own perverted fears, which were the influx of millions of Jews into Palestine and the destruction of the

---

2. Detailed documentation of the Mufti's activities may be found in Simon Wiesenthal's *The Grand Mufti* (London, 1993) (who relates that Haj Amin also visited Maida- nek); Maurice Pearlman's *Mufti of Jerusalem* (New York, 1965), and Joseph B. Schechterman's *The Mufti and the Fuehrer* (New York, 1965).

Mufti's personal empire. Yet, there can be no doubt that through their symbolic relationship, Hitler and the Mufti each helped the other accomplish his own evil goal. Eichmann simply wanted to kill Jews; the Mufti wanted to be sure they never reached Palestine. In the end, the "final solution" was the same. At one point, Eichmann even seemed to blame the Mufti for the entire extermination plan, when he declared, "I am a personal friend of the Grand Mufti. We have promised that no European Jew would enter Palestine any more."[3]

The Mufti's trip to Berlin was the first ominous step in the joining of the anti-Jews of the East with those of the West to accomplish their diabolic design. This second of the new directions in Jewish history reached a climax of sorts last year [1975] when Yassir Arafat, avowed destroyer of the State of Israel, stood before the United Nations and received a standing ovation by the nations of the East and West alike.

For the purely secular historical viewpoint, there is no connection between the two directions we have discussed. The Muslim world never granted privileges which it later retracted and, thus, never disappointed the Jews in its midst. What, then, joins the two trends which seem to have coincided so significantly in our generation? A passage from the Torah can give us the answer:

> And Eisav [Esau] went unto Yismael [Ishmael] and took Machlas the daughter of Yishmael [Ishmael], Abraham's son, the sister of Nevayos, in addition to his other wives, for a wife. (*Genesis* 28:9)

Since the actions of the patriarchs are a sign of what would happen later to the children and every action in the Torah is eternally significant, we may learn from this passage that it was inevitable for the forces of Esau and Ishmael to combine. We are now living in the midst of that pivotal moment in Jewish history.

It should be manifest, however, that until the great public pressures for the establishment of a Jewish state, the Mufti had no interest in the Jews of Warsaw, Budapest, or Vilna. Once the Jews of Europe became a threat to the Mufti because of their imminent influx into the Holy Land, the Mufti in turn became the *Malah ha-Mavet*, the incarnation of the Angel of Death. Years ago, it was still easy to find old residents of Jerusalem who remembered the cordial relations they maintained with the Mufti in the years before the impending creation of a Jewish state. Once the looming reality of the State of Israel was before him, the Mufti spared no effort in influencing Hitler to murder as many Jews as possible in the shortest amount of time. This shameful episode, where the founders and early leaders of the State [of Israel] were clearly a factor in the destruction of many Jews, has been completely suppressed and expunged from the record. Thus it is that our children who study the history of that turbulent era are taught that *Gedolei Yisroel* share responsibility for the destruction of European Jewry and learn nothing of the guilt of others who are now enshrined as heroes.

VII. Coming to Terms

We may now return to the original questions. "Is the term *Shoah* acceptable?" The answer is *clearly not*. The word *Shoah* in Hebrew, like "Holocaust" in English, implies an isolated catastrophe, unrelated to anything before or after it, such as an earthquake or tidal wave. As we have seen, this approach is far from the Torah view of Jewish history. The *hurban* of European Jewry is an integral part of our history, and we dare not isolate and deprive it of the monumental significance it has for us.

In truth, the isolation of one part of Jewish history from another has caused much of the inability to deal with events such as the *Hurban* Europe. Much of our education has been permeated with the "sunny side of Judaism," resulting from a cowardice and failure of will to deal with the misfortunes of *Klal Yisroel*. Yet, here is one of the sources of our uniqueness. We are happy to teach our children of our "chosenness" in *mitzvos* (commandments) and our closeness to God. Yet, at our peril, we ignore the fact that there are three different portions of *tochacha*—rebuke and promise of punishment in the Torah (*Behukosai [Leviticus 26]*, *Ki Savo [Deuteronomy*

3. Quoted by Pearlman, *Mufti of Jerusalem*, pp. 71–72, and Schechterman, *The Mufti and the Fuehrer*, p. 158.

[26:1–29:8], and *Nitzavim-Vayeileh [Deuteronomy [29:9–31:30]]*. We must learn these parts of the Torah with our children as well as the "sunnier" portions. These portions must become as much a part of the Jewish psyche as the *mitzvos* we strain so hard to imbue. Thus, when a Jewish child—or indeed, adult—hears for the first time of *Yiddish tzaros*—the suffering of the Jewish people—he will not be shocked by a contradiction to what he has learned but will see the living proof of the Torah he has absorbed.

Thus we have exposed graphically the mistake of the founders of *Yad V'Shem* who felt compelled to find a new term for the destruction of European Jewry because of its proportions and dimensions. Ironically, the artificially contrived term they finally applied empties the *hurban* of its profound meaning and significance. In appropriating a term which signifies isolation and detachment from history, they did not realize that the significance of the "Holocaust" is precisely in its intricate relationship with what will come after. The pattern of Jewish history throughout the ages is *Hurban—Galut—Geula* (Destruction—Exile—Redemption), and no event requires new categories or definitions. The answers to questions 2 and 3 are therefore obvious and need no further elaboration.

VIII. *Tochacha* versus Specific Guilt

It should be needless to say at this point that since the *hurban* of European Jewry was a *tochacha* phenomenon, an enactment of the admonishment and rebuke which *Klal Yisroel* carries upon its shoulders as an integral part of being the *Am Hanivchar*—God's chosen ones—we have no right to interpret these events as any kind of *specific punishment for specific sins*. The *tochacha* is a built-in aspect of the character of *Klal Yisroel* until *Mosh-*

iach (the Messiah) comes and is visited upon *Klal Yisroel* at the Creator's will and for reasons known and comprehensible *only to Him*. One would have to be a *Navi* or *Tanna* [a prophet or a sage of the mishnaic era, ending in 200 c.e.], to claim knowledge of the specific reasons for what befell us; anyone on a lesser plane claiming to do so tramples in vain upon the bodies of the *kedoshim* (holy martyrs) who died *al Kiddush ha-Shem* ("*for the Sanctification of God's name*") and misuses the power to interpret and understand Jewish history.

For other reasons, too, one must be careful of sudden popular "awakenings" to different aspects of Jewish history such as "Holocaust studies." Nachum Goldmann, head of the only international secular Jewish organization not directly subservient to the Jewish state, has stated that the weakening of sympathy for the State [of Israel] was the result of the lengthy period of time after the Holocaust having passed and the resultant forgetting by the world at large. Undoubtedly, the State, taking advantage of the arbitrary figure of thirty years, sought to reawaken interest in what it now termed the *Shoah* to regain some of the lost sympathy of the late 1940s and 1950s.

This aspect of the current widespread interest in the World War II years should only serve to alert us once more to the often duplicitous sources of public opinion. Of course, this in no way impugns the motives of those who have genuinely dedicated their lives to the study of this epochal time—especially the *She'aris Hapleita* [survivors of the Holocaust] who feel the scars on their own bodies and who cry out in pain to the world not to forget. It does, however, give us an idea of the tremendous pitfalls of the road to a clear understanding of the true patterns of Jewish history. Only through a rededication to the sole use of the Torah as a guide through the byways of history will we be sure to arrive at the truth we all seek.

Arthur A. Cohen

Arthur A. Cohen (1928–1987) was born into an affluent Jewish family in New York City. A gifted student, he received his B.A. from the University of Chicago in 1946 and his M.A. three years later from the same institution. At Chicago he began to take a serious academic interest in Jewish thought and therefore he enrolled, in 1950, to do a master's degree in medieval Jewish philosophy at the Jewish Theological Seminary of America in New York City. After two years at the Seminary, he made a life-altering decision that his future lay outside academic life and in the world of publishing. Accordingly, in 1951 he founded Noonday Press; in 1956 he created Meridien Books; and from 1960 to 1974 he founded and ran the Ex Libris Publishing Company. He also served as editor in chief of Holt, Rinehart and Winston. During all this time, however, his interest in Jewish thought remained strong, and in 1962 he published his significant study of modern Jewish philosophy, *The Natural and Supernatural Jew,* in which he declares himself a decidedly "supernatural" Jew. In addition, he began to write novels, many with a Jewish theme. Over a period of sixteen years he published *The Carpenter Years* (1967), *In the Days of Simon Stern* (1973), *A Hero in His Time* (1976), *Acts of Theft* (1980), and *An Admirable Woman* (1983), which won a National Jewish Book Award. Near the end of his life he also returned directly to Jewish thought through his work in connection with the valuable collection of essays on Jewish theology that he co-edited with Paul Mendes Flohr, *Contemporary Jewish Religious Thought.* The book appeared just after his death in 1987.

SELECTION

The present reading from Arthur Cohen is drawn from his book *The Tremendum: A Theological Interpretation of the Holocaust,* published in 1981. In this work, Cohen sets out to show why the Holocaust, which he prefers to call the *tremendum,* undermines classical Jewish theology, which believes in a personal, omniscient, and omnipotent deity. Instead of this biblical idea of the deity, Cohen proposes a radically revised understanding of God that "reduces" His traditional attributes and removes Him from active participation in human history. There is a divine being but He does not enter into, or direct, human affairs. At the same time, however, Cohen advances a revised version of the "free will defense" of God according to which the Holocaust was not God's doing but, rather, the consequence of the misuse of human freedom. Indeed, in a world in which God does not interfere regularly and directly in human history, the actions and decisions of men and women become all the more consequential and decisive.

Selected Bibliography

Books and Articles by Arthur Cohen

The Natural and Supernatural Jew (New York, 1962).

Editor of *Arguments and Doctrines: A Reader of Jewish Thinking in the Aftermath of the Holocaust* (New York, 1970).

The Tremendum: A Theological Interpretation of the Holocaust (New York, 1981).

"On Theological Method: A Response on Behalf of the *Tremendum*," *Journal of Reform Judaism* 31, no. 2 (Spring 1984): 56–65.

Article about Arthur Cohen

Katz, Steven T. " 'The Tremendum': Arthur Cohen's Understanding of Faith after the Holocaust," in Steven T. Katz, *Historicism, the Holocaust, and Zionism* (New York, 1992), pp. 251–273.

The *Tremendum*

I call the death camps the *tremendum*, for it is the monument of a meaningless inversion of life to an orgiastic celebration of death, to a psychosexual and pathological degeneracy unparalleled and unfathomable to any person bonded to life. And of the nations and cultures of the West, is there any so totally committed to life, to the choice of life and its enlargement as a system of conduct and behavior, as that of the Jews? The Jew may well be the ideal victim because his mere persistence, his sheer endurance, his refusal to die throughout four millennia until the *tremendum*, was a celebration of the tenacity of life. Every Jew who has left Judaism for Christianity has invariably—and the literature is astonishing in its confirmation of this insistence from Paul of Tarsus to Boris Pasternak—argued that the old Jew is dead, that Judaism has no more life to speak, no more novelty to contribute, nothing vital and energetic any longer to transmit to the species. The Jew is, in such literature, construed as though dead, whereas no less clearly it is necessary to mortify Judaism in order to rationalize and excuse its abandonment. The living Jew must become the dead Jew in order that the non-Jew be saved.

Martin Buber has written in a passage often cited that there is no caesura in the history of the Jews, no midpoint, no intermediation, no gap to be filled by the Holy Spirit, no descending dove of grace, no yawning time waiting for the divine incursion. Most specifically, in this teaching, Buber was addressing the absence of penultimate messianic moments. "In our view," Buber wrote:

> redemption occurs forever, and none has yet occurred. Standing, bound and shackled, in the pillory of mankind, we demonstrate with the bloody body of our people the unredeemedness of the world. For us there is no cause of Jesus; only the cause of God exists for us.

Buber tried to deal with the *tremendum* on several occasions, always obliquely. He spoke of our times as the eclipse of God, times when between men and God a veil had been dropped, a veil of confusion, obstinacy, or demonism through which the Word of God could not penetrate. He believed until the end of his life that God continued to speak but that no man heard. Moreover, he continued to believe that God's speech was his action and that not hearing that speech was, in effect, to destroy the efficacy of God. God spoke and created the world; God spoke and the people covenanted themselves to his service. Six million died and God's speech was not heard. Not enough. Moving rhetoric, but unfortunately not theology, not thinking. It has to be tougher than that. It has to be more than the eclipse of God. It has to be more than the death of God. It has to be more even than Nietzsche's madman proclaiming, "we have slain him." Not enough. And we know that now.

Buber's assertion that there is no caesura in Jewish history is accurate insofar as it concerns the eschatological vision of the perfecting and redemption of history, but wrong insofar as it misses the underside of history, the corrupting caesura, the abyss rather than the heavens of the historical. For the holy there may be no caesura, but for the unholy its name is caesura. The discontinuity of the abyss is precisely what ensures that it is both caesura and *tremendum*. The abyss of history is in this view, also a gap in normal time, no less a gap, no less a decisive gap than would be the messianic redemption. In the time of the human *tremendum*, conventional time and intelligible causality is interrupted. In that time, if not redemption, then the demonic tears the skein of events apart and man (and perhaps God no less) is compelled to look into the abyss. The Jews, for reasons no longer curious, have looked into the abyss several times in their long history. Tradition accounts the destruction of the Temple and the obliteration of the Jewish settlement in ancient Palestine as one abyss. There was a caesura. The abyss opened and the Jews closed the abyss by affirming their guilt, denying the abyss, and taking upon themselves responsibility for the demonic. Not "beyond reason," but "within providence" became the satisfactory explanation. The expulsion of the Jews from Spain is accounted another. There was a caesura. The abyss opened and the Jews closed the abyss once again not only by reaffirming their guilt, but more by transforming the event into an end time of ordinary history and the beginning time of mystic gnosis in which a new heaven was limned and the unseen order became transparent to mystical understanding. The death camps of the modern world is a third. There was another caesura of the demonic. This time the abyss opened and one-third of the Jewish people fell in.

The Natural and Supernatural Jew

Beyond the easy book of 1962, I have tried several times to describe the purview and method of Jewish thinking in the aftermath of the *tremendum*. *The Myth of the Judeo-Christian Tradition* (1970) was a self-stripping, an argument of divestment, putting distance between myself and Christianity,

by allowing myself the opportunity—giving myself indirect permission, so to speak—to despise Christianity and Christendom in the open. I made clear then (and I repeat now) that never persons but ideologies bore the weight of my enmity as I believe not Jews but Judaism should receive the intent of Christian enmity. Enmity does not mean enemies, if persons have the courage to risk articulating their sense of destiny and the possibility of history as ongoing; as long as they dream to themselves, dreams turn to ash and fury, but when they speak openly their dreams of faith, it is possible to know the ground on which human beings stand. It is then that enmity becomes its opposite, as fundamental a source of hope as love. Beyond *The Myth*, I worked between a poorly constructed fiction, *The Carpenter Years*, which set forth some of the premises of Jewish anti-Christianity (what I have elsewhere referred to as "envy of the gentiles"), and *In the Days of Simon Stern*, an obsessive, maddened novel of Jewish rage, Jewish enmity, and Jewish hope. But of the *tremendum* as such I spoke not at all. For nearly a generation I could not speak of Auschwitz, for I had no language that tolerated the immensity of the wound: I worked around the abyss and I made of it imaginings and nightmares, but only once, in the lecture "Thinking the *Tremendum*," did I approach the matter. Even then I found myself driven to recoil, not because the vision was untrue, but rather because the vision remained vision. That lecture succeeded in limning the parameters of the abyss but found them beyond compass and containment. It was a probing that left me dry with rage and without hope. Whatever its merits, the argument remained locked within the terms of historical inquiry, a marking out of terrain, replete with markers and the surveyor's annotation of sightings, but without an overall scheme that encouraged the colonization of its barren landscape.

The analysis that I propose now engages the issues raised by the earlier topographic abstract: The questions are no longer those of historical and literary identification but rather the reality of evil and the existence of God, the extremity of evil and the freedom of man, the presentness of evil and the power of God. My thinking is, as will be evident, dialectical, although the dialectic is neither a sufficient nor a persuasive method of proceeding. However, dialectical inquiry is appropriate to the spoken word where all depends upon the audible yes and no, leaving the power of the copulative conjunction, the indispensable link, to emerge from the ontological annotation that succeeds dialectic. The whole to which my argument will press is a unity which sustains the rhythm of each affirmation and negation, in which, I hope, negativity will emerge as no longer necessarily evil and evil will be perceived to be not simply negative, but no less an argument in which the God who emerges as possible to thought beyond the *tremendum* is no longer the God of traditional theology, while remaining nonetheless the divinity of whom Thales of Miletus [6th C. BCE] observed, "God is the oldest of beings."

To suggest that the future of Jewish theology in the time beyond the *tremendum* be explored is to assume that there is a possible connection between thought and the *tremendum*; moreover, it is to conjure the possibility that if the *tremendum* has more than a tangential or accidental impact upon Jewish thought (and hence, ultimately, upon the content of Jewish belief), then it is something that can be compassed and interpreted by thought. Is thought then commensurate or incommensurate with the *tremendum*? That is to say, can an intellectual aptitude encompass the *tremendum* as a historical event or is the *tremendum as historical event* of such complexity that, at best, the tools of historical retrieval can succeed only in the development of intermediate judgments of social, political, psychological origin. Thought may describe the limit implications of the *tremendum*, but its ability to pierce the borders of historical determination and caprice to assertions about general significance and meaning may be regarded by some as hopeless, given the unavoidable narrowness of the single thinker's viewpoint or the denigration of thought itself as too cool or too dispassionate a procedure for estimating such historical immensity. Obviously, for those who disrespect thinking or find its methods and attenuations too slow and plodding when the earth cries out for justice, I have no contention. They are right to set thought aside, although they run the risk that by ignoring its deliberations, real evil will neither have the confinement of under-standing nor the prospect which I hold—that it have its portion before a real God. Again, I understand their point of view. No God is worth a single child's life. How much more so untold children? I would agree with this caveat as well, if I also agreed that life can be winnowed with such equivalences, with such an overwhelming dramaturgy, for history nowhere presents such symmetrical historical options as God or your babe.

The antagonism to deliberative scrutiny of the *tremendum* has a variety of origins, not the least relevant of which is Kai Erikson's observation about the psychological condition of its survivors, who, having outlived its destructiveness, are prone forever after to overestimate "the perils of their situation, if only to compensate for the fact that they underestimated those perils once before." The mentality of the survivor—and Judaism is a tradition which has apostrophized the miracle of survival from its very beginnings, underscoring in each generation the sign of the Exodus and its symbolic adumbration in each historical searing—consists in a continuous self-rebuke, wherein the past is repeatedly examined for danger signs overlooked and the future is read without the normal ability, in Erikson's phrase, to "screen out the signs of danger" from the line of sight. But more than such psychological resistance is the pervasive popular conviction that theology, with its unavoidable eccentricity of language and its insistence upon pinning down the reality in focus, makes the *tremendum* into an object—a mere object—when it is regarded by survivors and memorialists alike to be so charged a reality as to require that the extremities of subjectivity and passion be engaged in its evocation.

It is out of regard, therefore, for these sensibilities that I have adopted the term *tremendum*. The term is allusive; it encourages the awareness of alien immensity, acknowledging the anguish of the survivors and their ongoing apprehensiveness, while refusing to foreclose the possibility that it is, at one and the same time, a destructive event that uniquely occurred (and therefore a proper object of study), as well as a reality that endures and continues to make assaultive claim upon subjective, impassioned, even unconscious awareness.

If we stand on the contention that thought is essentially incapable of compassing the *tremendum*, that it must fall silent and dumb before its monstrousness, there are additional consequences which extend far beyond the matter of personal decision, emotional tolerance, and consciousness. The first and most pressing is that the past that pressed against us before the *tremendum* is annihilated; by implication, those who would make thought ineffectual or the event unthinkable succeed not only in obliterating the past as the legacy of continuity and instruction but also destroy the past-oriented purview of historical consciousness itself. If the *tremendum* is an event unparalleled, unique in every characteristic dimension of uniqueness, and if, as is signaled by our language, *tremendum* means historical immensity for which there is neither a satisfactory analogue nor historical model, the history of the past becomes irrelevant.

The judgment that thought is inadequate to the *tremendum* is, in one sense, based upon a logical fallacy, for it is never suggested that thought can number six million particularities or, for that matter, the hundred million slain in this century's wars of skill and ideology. The fact that the mind cannot contain such particularity is not a mark of the incommensurability of thought, but only of memory's inability to particularize each loss. The containment of the numbers is not the issue nor even the diabolic planning and imagination which devised these holocausts, but rather (as Erich Kahler observed in his premonitory *Man the Measure* [1943]) the triumph of technics by which procedures of dehumanization and distanciation were brought to their perfection. The evil is remarked less in its passion than in its coldness. Indeed, if the *tremendum* cannot be thought, more than the past would have been lost and loss of the past would be loss enough.

If the Holocaust is allowed to stand as a *mysterium*, indeed, a mysterious *tremendum* unavailable to thought, unsusceptible of any intellectual seizure and identification, the profound risk is run that a historical event is made absolute and therefore necessary, overturning all other historical events whose occurrence is contingent and whose meaning is tributary. Or the Holocaust is allowed to stand as a *mysterium*, indeed, a *mysterium tremendum* precisely because it is not historical and derives its force and arbitrariness from the metaphysical structure of the universe, no less

absolute and necessary, overtur[ning] other metaphysical structures [...] whose existence is claimed by cl[...] alone absolute and necessary. In [...] holocaustal *tremendum* is necessa[...] evil in contradiction and negation of God (who traditionally is alone thought to be necessary) or coeval and coexistent with God, since it enjoys a metaphysical identity accorded no other reality besides God. If the project of absolutizing the Holocaust is pushed much further than it has been already, it is made twin of the divine, indeed, a function of the divine (or the divine a function of evil's naturalness) and a partner of its relation to the world. Such a radical extension of the argument from holocaustal ontologies ends by making the *tremendum* no different than divine and divine truth.

The extremities of the argument are implicated, on the one hand, by those who have expressed the hope that the Holocaust had no meaning, that is to say, conveyed no historical judgment, that it was an emptiness, a void ("meaning" to be understood in such usage as significant, interpretive truth, bearing insight from past to future). In such a view the Holocaust is neither philosophically nor theologically relevant, except as exemplifying the void before which we gape in disbelief. But on the other side, there are those who suggest that the Holocaust—far from being without meaning—contains absolute meaning. Indeed, the Holocaust is regarded as a decisive event by which the whole of the past and the future is henceforth to be marked out and scanned.

Implicit in either the denial of meaning or the absolutization of meaning is a reflection upon the historical reality to which the Holocaust adhered. The Holocaust in fact may have been of history, but its reading and significance may be transhistorical and its metaphysical truth may be transcendent of history. We begin however by retracing the evisceration of the transcendent from history.

Historical existence has been stripped of sacral implication for more than two centuries. This is not to hold a brief for the modalities of its improper sanctification, for my interest is not in the investment of the historical with sacerdotal sanctities but rather with the uncompromised openness of the historical to both the sacred and

...ie ordinary. The profane has passed its judgment; whether church or synagogue manipulate the saeculum, not the holy but the profane triumphs, not the believing people but their authoritative powers are victorious. The church year, for example, which Rosenstock-Huessy elaborated, or calendrical holiness, which Franz Rosenzweig described, had not only a visionary prospect but a didactic annotation of the historical past at issue. The human in the human being counts for little. Submitted to anonymous, manipulative, depersonalized control, the individual and his free imagination are flayed raw. Within a stripped and naked saeculum the Holocaust can be only relatively situated. A historical order without prevenient limits set by the holy is, at most, relatively disastrous; absolute disaster to be meaningful occurs only within a perspective that continues to acknowledge the absolute. Otherwise employed, lacking the texture of being, absolute "anything" is always rhetorical language, since the affirmed absolute is absolute only in relation to the lesser, remaining relative in relation to the superior and true absolute whose presence and power have been lost from view. In short, then, given a historical vision or social doctrine which allows of no transcendence, no openness before absolute claim, no nexus between the human and the divine, what has occurred as *tremendum* is, at best, a malign fortuity which, as its sufferers, we force upon the world's attention as though it were of significance to everyone or, abashed, we deny it meaning, hoping from the benign indifference of secular toleration that the accident will not become normative. The dialectic of the dilemma suggests that whichever side is espoused we are endangered: If we describe the *tremendum* as the inevitable product of a stripped saeculum, unconstrained by the limits conscience sets to the demonic imagination, the Holocaust is rendered an absolute relative, that is, an event marked by perfect relativity, relativity of value, meaning, truth, precisely as its conception and machinery effect the total humiliation of man. It is absolute because it serves as the model—comprehensive, logical, obsessively organized and consummated. On the other hand, if it is hastily transformed into a theological repudiation of God, a defiance flung before divinity, a historical rebellion against His silent intimacy, it emerges as

a relative absolute, since it makes the contention that God is incomplete, inadequate, impotent before the domain of history and, therefore, given its assertion of providential solicitude and concern, no longer God.

What is common to both viewpoints is the immense seriousness with which history is regarded. History is treated as though it were self-interpreting, as though the adduction of history carries with it the force of clarification and proof. Constantly counseled to consult the historical to chasten optimism or reprove despair, history becomes for us the advisor of the secular imagination, indeed, the new divinity of events to be set beside biological, physical, cosmological contentions. Clearly, however, the inability of historical description and analysis to compass the Holocaust is one of the central reasons for the assertion of its incommensurability to thought. The Holocaust cannot be thought because it cannot be exhausted by historical narration. It remains elusive, uncontained, a putative mystery because the categories by which such immensities are grasped seem inadequate and trivial.

Before this century, intellectual projects seemed well scaled and hence possible. Even where God was set forth as a problem of mind, the God in view was easily reduced to the scale of mind. *Our* history, however, is one apparently without a canon, without reliable *docta* of exegesis, without even an ideology of national *hubris* supplying its rationale and interpretation. We have neither a contemporary Hegel nor a Marx; however much we make appeal to them, our discourse of longing or rage consists in knocking upon their closed doors beseeching that our categories be admitted. Instead, our times turn to revisionist instruction about history, accumulating the information dropped from previous renditions, obscured as they were by clouds of ideology and interests. Revisionist history (written with no less passion than those of national self-interpretation and excuse) has the purpose of filling the foreground with visible events so large (and yet without previous advocacy) that they could be ignored in the nineteenth century's rush to national exaltation.

Our predicament at the borders of the *tremendum* and in its aftermath is that the familiar disciplines of interpretation seem compromised or ineffective: Philosophic thought appears debarred, the social consensus seems dehumanized, historical identification and description seem lacking in theoretical grandeur and comprehensiveness. . . .

I am no longer persuaded, as I once was, that Martin Buber was correct in his contention that there are no caesuras in Jewish history. Clearly, Buber's stand against historical caesura grew out of his polemical interpretation of Christianity. Buber regarded salvation out of incarnation and the empty tomb as an arbitrary insertion of the plumb line of eternity into the vortex of time, with the result that history was broken open to the pre-Christ and the post-Christ and the marking off within Judaism of prophetic figurations and posterior stubbornness. Buber's insistence therefore that Judaism has no midpoints, that Jewish history is cantilevered from its moorings in creation toward an unfixed end time, was part of his intellecual momentum *contra Christiana* and, as such, is unexceptionable. And yet, although I feel impelled by the logic of my own argument to validate caesura, I do so with much hesitation and uncertainty.

Caesura was intended by Buber to describe a vertical insertion of the divine into history, a breaching of the historical by the eternal, a setting forth within history of a divine exposition as incarnational God-man. But caesura need not be only the descent of the dove; it can be a raising up and release of chthonic instinctualism as well, the terrestrial fission of caprice and the passivity of nature. Caesura in such a reversal can emerge from below, a verticality as infernal as incarnation may be divine. But what matters in caesura is not its content, but its rupture.

The content of the *tremendum* is always historical—its cruelties and murders; the caesura, however, is that the *tremendum* marks off and breaks. The caesura is the formal definer of Holocaust, what makes it special, separable, ontic.

The *tremendum* is more than historical. It is an elaboration of the most terrible of Jewish fears—that the eternal people is not eternal, that the chosen people is rejected, that the Jewish people is mortal. If there is one incontestable article of the Jewish unconscious, it has been the mythos of indestructibility and the moral obligation of tenacity. Six years, nonetheless, nearly concluded

three millennia of endurance. Is it a wonder that Jews should regard the *tremendum* as a caesural fissure that acquires with each decade a more and more profound metahistorical station as the counterevent of Jewish history, the source of its revisionist reconsideration and self-appraisal. No accounting, even in the most dreadful apocalyptic readings of modern history, adumbrated a structure of convergent causalities that might have yielded an event of such catastrophic destructiveness. The break is in our reading of the historical—that we are obliged to insert into the history of salvation, alongside ancient martyrologies (individual saints and heroes whose deaths provided two millennia with models of courage and steadfastness), a litany of faceless numbers that declare to us nothing but monstrousness.

And yet, however much it all seems clear, the wish to transform the *tremendum* into an event without analogue or historical echo, without forecastings or preludes, to make of it not only the paradigm of theological ultimacy but historical ultimacy may be called a rush to ontologize history. The Holocaust is surely ours; against its background, we can verify no other event of comparable magnitude. The destruction of the Temple and the exile of Israel have already found their portion in the liturgic imagination, and there is no doubt that for classic Judaism it was a shattering and defining event that marked off a Judaism of the beforehand and the after, determining the end of a cult of silent acts and the beginning of a synagogue of prayer and study. For their consciousness it was caesura; but the insistence of the rabbis that the continuity be underscored, and the eternal life of Torah planted in their midst be tended without interruption, neutralized caesura and recast it as an instructive historical eruption. In our eyes, therefore, the destruction of the Temple in 70 C.E. was no caesura because the tradition took up the frayed ends of time and knotted them. It was no less with the catastrophic destruction of Sephardic [Spanish] Judaism, begun in 1391 and completed beyond the expulsion. Once again, a world came to an end and, once again, a mythos of incorporation and consolation emerged with which to supply a nexus and continuity, where previously only despairing caesura had been palpable. What is read as judgment, and received as the passion of the Jewish people, is transmuted, the agony of history lifted up into a reading that allowed to God vastly more complexity and interior movement than had been envisaged by the negative theologies that preceded it.

Historical extremity has compelled the tradition to rethink. Neither arguments over doctrine nor conflicts between theology and philosophy nor combat between religion and science moved Jewish thought to reformulate, but rather the aftermath of shattering historical events. Judaism has always been content to overhear the disputes of others and file the reconciliations they devise. What Judaism combats, the battlefield of its proper *agon*, is the historical. . . .

It is necessary to take up once again the argument set forth previously. If the *tremendum* marks off and separates, if it is caesura, how does one speak of God? God is, of course, in some sense, most immediately, presentness. He may be spoken of anew as if for the first time, our minds a *tabula rasa* from which the *tremendum* has erased memory and historical reflection. And surely this is not rhetorical formulation, although a methodological erasure of this magnitude is inevitably flawed by rhetoric. The force of the question is, however, that the *tremendum*, not alone as event of history, but as event that annihilates the past of hope and expectation, confronts us as an abyss. As abyss, the *tremendum* transforms everything that went before into distance and remoteness, as though an earthquake had overturned the center of a world, obliterating mountains that had once been near at hand and that we had formerly dreamed of scaling. The *tremendum*, by definition an ontological immensity, cuts through and parts our perception of the real and the principles we had inherited for its parsing and description. We can and do continue to perform old routines—like arms that instinctively reach out to grasp and hold although the hand has been severed—but we know that all is changed. The most optimistic and hopeful of peoples is certainly—despite the fantastic emergence of the Jewish state—a people of anxiety, confronting with nervousness the impingement of the great annihilation.

But what has all this to do with theology and thinking about God? Everything.

The *tremendum* as abysmal evil, as the ultimate negative historical configuration, is regarded by

some as no less [a] paradigm than the giving of Torah on Sinai. To make, however, the *tremendum* even the symbolic equivalent of Sinai is false. The claim of Sinai is that God spoke only to Israel, revealing his name to this one among the seventy nations of the world. But did the *tremendum* speak only to Jews? If only to the Jews then is all the rest of mankind exempted from hearing its meaning? If it is equivalent to Sinai as paradigm, intending that what the Jews heard on Sinai they should speak and witness to all the nations, a further disproportion is disclosed, for the people who attended at Sinai were addressed that they might hear and do, but the imperative of the *tremendum* is [a] final solution for much more than Jews and Judaism. The unexpressed urgency of the symmetry of Sinai and the Holocaust is that neither may be forgotten, that the indelible inscription of the one must be matched by the immemoriality of the other, the revelation at Sinai paralleled by the disclosure of the *tremendum*. But is the symmetry structural or polemical, real or hortatory? There are two responses that may be made: The first is that God's self-revelation at Sinai is not only ultimate *in our regard*, but ultimate in God's as well (everything that Sinai commands exhibits the involvement of God in the particularity of our lives—it is a measure of God's immanentism that his transcendence can speak its name to the people and evidence that it is he himself who speaks that name in thunder and in lightning), whereas everything that the Holocaust reveals is ultimacy *in our regard* without the complementarity of God's authentication. Man speaks at and toward God in the *tremendum*, but God's voice is really silent (which is other than the implicit criticism so often made of God's silence at Auschwitz, which entails a formal repudiation of his omnipotence and providence). The second response is that forming the symmetry of Sinai and the *tremendum* contradicts the *tremendum* as transforming caesura. If the Holocaust is a monumentality structurally identical with or structurally complementary to or structurally indispensable as Sinai, it cannot be caesura. The one characteristic of the historical event as *tremendum* is that is annihilates for us the familiar categories by which we have read and decoded our past. The revelation at Sinai must be read differently after the *tremendum* because the *tremendum* disallows traditional memory, obliging it to regard all settled doctrine[s] anew, all accepted principle[s] afresh, all closed truths and revelations as open. Quite the contrary, therefore, the formulation must be that Sinai and the *tremendum* are nonsymmetrical, indeed, incommensurable and that our obligation to relate them follows not from their ontological resemblance or continuity, but from the extreme discontinuity that the *tremendum* inserts into Jewish history. We speak about them in the same breath because their relation is negative, the contrary of internality, sundering connection rather than effecting it. The only contact that Sinai and the *tremendum* make is the Jewish people.

The Jewish people is the reality that sustains both Sinai and Holocaust. If the Jewish people is only of history (that is, if it has no God—and the silent God is treated by some of His critics as though speech were the only mark of affect or miracle the only modality of caring; hence silence is ineffectuality and the equivalent of the "not-God"), then Sinai and *tremendum* are shibboleths, for no amount of memorialization remembers and no amount of revelation persuades, the event at Sinai or at Auschwitz passing as history passes and memory fades. But if the Jewish people is an ontological structure, convoked and held in the maelstrom of immanence by the immeasurable concern of God, the matter comes out differently. One can slay God or declare the *tremendum* a running amok, a historical "out-of-hand" which, like a madman's speech, has no truth to disclose other than about the nature of madness; but if one wishes meaning, structure is implied, and if one wishes truth, each reality must be considered in itself, and if one wishes interconnectedness, history cannot be the medium.

I take the view that to propose the symmetry of Sinai and the *tremendum* is an instance of overwhelming theological terrorization and evidence of a panic so deeply felt that its manifest coherence and consistency are taken as sufficient marks of truth. But coherence and consistency may be characteristic of obsessional disorder no less than of true perception. It is not that I could not bear to be persuaded that the solicitous God of Sinai is the malign God of the *tremendum*, and in convincing me, the love and compassion that I feel for God's lonely magnificence would die away within me, but to assert God's death in the interest of self-liberation seems to me a trifling narcissism and God's death only a memento of an already well-established irrelevance.

The irrelevance of God is, of course, a commonplace response of some modern thinkers not only to religion and its familiar forms but also to the apparent inadequacy of religious language and imagery to speak intelligently or clearly about the brutal facts of modern historical life. I have made the *tremendum* as crucial as I have precisely because it seems to me that the judgment upon traditional religious philosophy in Judaism and the theology of Torah reflect the considered opinion of the Jewish people that the classic tradition and the *tremendum* are not yet squared, that the traditional God has no connection with the Holocaust despite the palpable fact that the immensity of the *tremendum* implies a judgment upon God. Jewish religious thinking that would seek, in a time as riven by ontic structures of evil as ours, the clarification of conceptual language in order to make its form and content coherent with advanced formulations of linguistic theory, philosophic analysis, and phenomenological hermeneutics, without reopening consideration of its fundamental theological presuppositions, is idle, cowardly, finally worthless.

The challenge of the *tremendum* to Judaism is not that traditional Jewish reality cannot survive the scrutiny of its teaching, that it will be found archaic or outmoded, that its inherited custom is insupportable, but rather that its view of its own depths will be found shallow, insufficiently deep and flexible enough to compass and contain the *tremendum*. Jewish reality must account for the *tremendum* in its view of God, world, and man; it must constellate Jewish facts of practice and belief in such a way as to enable them to endure meaningfully in a universe that endures the *tremendum* and withstands it and a God who creates a universe in which such destructiveness occurs. If either side goes, the whole collapses. If such a universe cannot withstand the *tremendum*, then it is not only ultimate but final. If God is creator of the *tremendum* he cannot be accounted good as classical theism requires.

It is time now to build a bridge over the abyss of the *tremendum*. It is a bridge that spans the abyss but does not obscure it. Wayfarers upon the bridge, however its moorings in the past of the Jewish people and its future in the prospect of its ongoing life, cannot neglect the obligation to look over into the chasm beneath. They know the abyss but, since they pass along the bridge, they know equally that they do not have their being in its depths; however much the ineffaceable abyss informs them, their own being and proper life is elsewhere—on the bridge, in fact, over the abyss.

The Bridge over the Abyss: Schemas of Construction

The *tremendum*, as an ontological gathering of evil, is a watershed reality that casts doubt upon the formulations of traditional Jewish theism and requires, if it is not to be final as well as ultimate, a response in its aftermath that takes account of the profound challenge of its negativity.

I have tried, in what has preceded, to make clear the theological relevance of the holocaustal caesura. As well, I have undertaken a brief account of historical theology as it worked through the materials of traditional theism up to the borders of the Holocaust, indicating something of its argument and difficulties. By the time of the *tremendum* of this century, the suppositions of classical theism had already passed through the testing fires of radical criticism that left them depleted. Only by recourse to a precipitous rush to mystery could the assertion of an absolute and monarchic God, whose relations to creation were at best formal and external, be reconciled with the scriptural disclosure of a loving, merciful, and just God. The God of classical theism, in no way constituted by His creatures or affected by the trials and alarums of creation, has disappeared finally into the folds of mystery, where reason cannot make meaningful the relativity implicit in God's involvement with creation and faith cannot make cogent the remoteness and impassivity that God's absoluteness requires.

The *tremendum* forces a resolution of this conflict, not alone as an obligation placed upon reason to account for its occurrence in a universe fashioned by a presumptively omnipotent, omniscient, and providential ruler, but even more as an obligation it places upon our humanity—as creatures without presuppositions—to account

for the *tremendum*, to justify and redeem, if that is possible, the surpassing suffering of its victims and the unbearable guilt of its perpetrators. This is nothing more nor less than our obligation to account for the reality of God in the aftermath of the *tremendum*. The task entails (beyond the work of constructive theology that makes clear and meaningful the nature of God and his relation to the historical *scenum*) the translation of that constructive language into terms that will renew the meaning of creation and authenticate—as more than this century's groans for liberation—the promise of redemption.

What I undertake—and perforce within the abbreviated compass of this discussion it must be schematic—is a redefinition of the reality of God and His relations to the world and man, but as well a reinvestment of the passive receptiveness of the world and the active freedom of man with significant meaning.

The thinker has no choice but to stand precariously within his own limitation when he tries to speak, without subjectivity, about the nature of God and to stand firmly in his own freedom when he tries to speak, without detachment, about the actions of man in history. He must hold firmly to his freedom when he addresses the absolute God. But no less, when he describes the God of creation and redemption, he must contain the certitude of God's comprehensive perfection. It is a dialectical precariousness in which the absolutely existent (that abstract ground of all), remote and distant, parsed in the classical tradition by negative arguments that winnowed divinity of all admixture, is commingled with the divine concrete and caring, the presentness and immediacy that validates our own human individuality, the particularity of our destiny, and the futurity of our personal history.

The philosophic critique of classical theism (its insistence upon the irreconcilability of a God of absolute monopolarity and the scriptural evocation of an engaged and available God) obliged neo-Orthodox theologians of earlier decades of this century to center the debate upon a different terrain. The God of medieval philosophy, sequestered within His forbidden supremacy, was bespoken in our world by a series of paradoxical formulations which guaranteed His absoluteness while assuring us of our freedom. The neo-Orthodox formulations to which among Jews, Abraham Joshua Heschel and Will Herberg, with varying degrees of emphasis and assent, gave themselves, will blunt the epistemological inquiry by grounding the recognition of God as the preeminent object of wonder and the existential situation of the believer as one of faithful transcendence of philosophic question to trust in the generosity of the divine person. The negative theology of medieval Judaism gave way to assertions of paradox, too quickly passing from the difficulties of formulating cogent theology to the positing of ultimate mystery.

The varieties of neo-Orthodoxy (and I suppose my own work prior to recent years would be classifiable among them) have had the effect of making the _tremendum_ an event alongside historical events, neither of history nor of teleology, and hence beside the point of theological labor. Neo-Orthodoxy does not cope adequately since it situates the _tremendum_ as the dialectic counter of an absent or hidden God, enabling the immensity of the one to pass the mystery of the other in the dark night of this century without compelling them to their dreadful confrontation.

Any constructive theology after the _tremendum_ must be marked by the following characteristics: First, the God who is affirmed must abide in a universe whose human history is scarred by genuine evil without making the evil empty or illusory nor disallowing the real presence of God before, even if not within, history; second, the relation of God to creation and its creatures, including, as both now include, demonic structure and unredeemable events, must be seen, nonetheless, as meaningful and valuable despite the fact that the justification that God's presence renders to the worthwhileness of life and struggle is now intensified and anguished by the contrast and opposition that evil supplies; third, the reality of God in His selfhood and person can no longer be isolated, other than as a strategy of clarification, from God's real involvement with the life of creation. Were any of these characteristics to be denied or, worse, proved untrue and unneeded, as strict and unyielding Orthodox theism appears to require, creation disappears as fact into mere metaphor or, in the face of an obdurate and ineffaceable reality such as the _tremendum_, God ceases to be more than a metaphor for the inexplicable.

The _tremendum_ as ultimate oppository immensity obliges us to bring together two vectors of modern theological thinking, to join them by compelling their formulation in complementarity. There is, on the one side, the view enforced by Gershom Scholem's reading of the kabbalistic counterhistory of Judaism that God, in the immensity of His being, was trapped by both its absoluteness and necessity into a constriction of utter passivity which would have excluded both the means in will and the reality in act of the creation. Only by the spark of nonbeing (the interior apposition of being, the contradiction of being, the premise of otherhood, the void that is not vacuous) was the being of God enlivened and vivified. Within such a cosmogonic mythology of a divine complex, gestational stages are described whereby God focused the nexus of nonbeing and being, withdrawing from nonbeing within Himself to extrude nature from the void. The cosmogony of the kabbalah entails scaled emissions of being which derive their nature and vitality from divine nature and life, emerging from lowest to highest, linked by the complexity of their own structure to the divine structure, by their own simplicity to the divine univocality, imperfect according to the portion of waste within the divine contraction, perfect according to the formal adhesion to the divine image.

This cosmogonic tradition, abhorred by historical Judaism for its seeming concession to the power of gnostic imagery, its no less palpable irrationality and mythic imagery, its involvement with neo-Platonic and later Christian emanationist doctrines, its devolution into magical and heterodox practice, has preserved its life as a hermetic teaching which, precisely because its texts were not critically edited, its canonic scholarship inchoate, its antimodernism apparent, its fancifulness and obscurity part of its intellectual charm, has not emerged to light until the present day. It has come now to the forefront not least because of Scholem's superlative advocacy, but surely more because the times require it, calling forth from other quarters and persuasions considerations that demand revisionism since they, too, cannot abide the formulations of inherited Orthodoxy.

The tradition cannot deal with the _tremendum_ as it is presently understood, but the cosmogonic imagination of the kabbalah does define a trope that indeed addresses it and can compass its oppository immensity. No less than the kabbalah is a tradition of Western thought—heartily Christian in its auspices, but gnostic-kabbalistic in its origins, a tradition that runs from Joachim of Fiore [113?–1201] through Schelling [1775–1854] to Franz Rosenzweig [1886–1929]. Briefly summarized it is an interpretation that takes the formulation of the Johannine Gospel as metaphysical instruction and mediates [on] its significance.

"In the beginning was the Word." The divine word is the origin of the creation out of the void (which, although empty, is not nothing; put more precisely, is nothingness, although not nothing). The Gospel according to John opens with a gloss of the original assertion of the Book of Genesis: "In the beginning God created heaven and earth." Clearly not with hands, as a craftsman or master builder, did God make the heavens and the earth; but as absolute and necessarily existent being, classic theism affirms.

The only instrument of creation dephysicalized—the breath of being—is speech. The divine being speaks and creates. So much for the creation. The tradition of transcendental idealism that has its origins in Joachim's typological correspondences of the ages of the church and the persons of the Trinity and Nicholas of Cusa's [1401–1464] mathematical correlation of the minima of the world with the maxima of the creator through Jakob Boehme's [1575–1624] mysticism of the plenteous nothingness of God's supernal ground to the Schellingian doctrine of the indispensable and informing contradiction—all these supply the logical trope of Franz Rosenzweig's *The Star of Redemption* [1921]. Schelling and Rosenzweig concur out of their sources that within God and before creation there is the working out of the parts of divine speech. The divine speech-grille, or rules of divine language, is not to be taken as only a metaphor for the anthropomorphism of divine speech. Obviously, it was easier to say that "God made" than that "God spoke." The creation that follows from the ambiguous making could retain its abstractness, pressed by negative theology, back to the fashioning out of nothing that need not speak its means. The Gospel was for Hebrew ears a corrupt anthropomorphism, for the Psalmist contradicts the idolatrous imputation of divine speech, hearing, smell, handling; but the issue is not speech as such, but *logos* and *onoma* (name and language) which in Stoic teaching are linked as the interior archetype and its external formation. Philo of Alexandria [1st C. CE] is, of course, close to the Gospel in his use of *logos*, but for us the issue is not one of tracing historical proof-citations, but rather the suggestibility of certain conceptions of the creation.

Logos and speech are signs that direct us to aspects of God that may offer a way out of the dilemma of the absolute and necessary existent who is God and the miraculous fiat of *creatio ex nihilo*, by using the image of speech to describe a movement within God that occurs in his eternal instant and in our time for everlasting. The varieties by which Schelling describes this turning inward within God, whose consequence is the turning outward of creation, are, as Jehudah Halevi [1075–1141] remarked, apparently complex because they are so simple. Most briefly described, Schelling's argument may be summarized in this way: "What is necessary in God," Schelling begins, "is God's nature," His "ownness." Love—that antithetic energy of the universe—negates "ownness" for love cannot exist without the other, indeed, according to its nature as love, it must deny itself that the other might be (contracting itself that the other might be, setting limits to itself). However, since the divine nature as *esse* cannot have personality without the outpouring, the self-giving of love to define those limits, it must be postulated that within God are two directions (not principles, as Schelling says): one which is necessary selfhood, interiority, self-containment, and another, vital, electric, spontaneous that is divine *posse*, the abundant and overflowing. There arises from all this the dialectic of necessity and freedom, the enmeshment of divine egoity and person, divine self-love and free love, divine narcissism and the created image, the sufficient nothing of the world and the creation of being. The human affect is toward the overflowing, the loving in God; His containment, however, the abyss of His nature, is as crucial as is His abundance and plenitude. These are the fundamental antitheses of the divine essence without which the abyss would be unknown or all else would be regarded as plenitude.

Another means of imagining this dialectic is through that of language and silence (the logos of revelation), for clearly the quiet God is as indispensable as the revealing God, the abyss as much as the plenitude, the constrained, self-contained, deep divinity as the plenteous and generous.

This is as perfunctory as I would dare to make the speculation of Schelling in *The Ages of the World* [1811–1815] and book 1 of Rosenzweig's *The Star of Redemption*, which is built upon its foundations. Both together, Schelling for Johannine Christianity and Rosenzweig for the Jews, suggest the foundation of revisionist theism. Both share a common vision that only by assuming that human natures are created and, therefore, in reality dependent upon the operative analogue of divine nature can statements be made about the nature of human and divine life. Both would argue that only when we transcend our natural categories, mired as they are in finitude and limitation, extending the lines of the creative process, refining them of gross physicalities and pantheistic dependency, rendering them truly abstract because absolute and not abstract for the sake of absoluteness, is it possible to understand why creation follows from God as *His event of speech and love* rather than as an event mysteriously unfathomable and unaccountable. As God's being is full and plenteous, creation is an overflowing—the cosmogonic reading. As God's nature is abundant, what is plenitude for God is seen by His creatures as love—a religioethical reading. As the whole of the divine nature is enlarged by the presence of nonbeing, by the depths of the divine made manifest, so creation is necessity within God and free act to man.

The divine essence is dipolar in its nature and in its manifestation: Movement within God is the premise of His nature and the plenitude of God (the manifold richness of His essence) is devised by us as the variousness of creation. Creation is already the gloss of wonder that makes the silent speech of plenitude vocal, naming it as creation without naming God, determining its irradiance without the sureness to confirm its origin. The divine nature *eo ipso* always overflows, that is, always creates, for the world is from the standpoint of the divine nature always in the beginning, never at its end. To be finished and concluded, to regard

seven days literally, is mythic encapsulation that we employ as finite creatures (metaphysical language conserved as liturgical language), six days' work and Sabbath rest are devices of symbolization that recall a metaphysical description that is in turn time-language recalling the divine word (all that was heard) that is for everlasting the beginning in God's eternity.

If what is absolute in God (that His nature is necessarily existent) is seen by us under the aspect of His plenitude, it must be said that God's relation to Himself is different from God's relation to us; or, put otherwise, if the divine essence is the form of perfection and the divine egress from self and entrance into creation is the multifariousness of His potential for the creation of form, it would follow that God does not renew the work of creation daily, but rather that each day we acknowledge what passes ceaselessly within God, namely, that *our novelty* is a rehearsal of God's eternal plenitude. New forms, new beginnings, new creation for us are forms already within God, creations already predicated of God's armory of possibility, beginnings eternally begun within God. The dipolar God—the God of absolute being and internal involvement with the created—must be paralleled by bipolar vision, that we draw distinctions but maintain them in synchronicity, recognizing the difference between essence and creation, between Being and being, between the absolute rest of God and the engagement of His plenitude, between His eternity and His "in the beginning."

The world that the word made is silent for its logos has no throat. Within plastic nature, the freedom of God's interior negation elaborates the formal configurations of *physis* or nature—their drama of attraction and repulsion, charge and static field, penetration and seeming void. The world is the divine *scenum*, the mime theater where only the passivity of God's essence is displayed, hum of growth according to law, instinct, numb order, every irregularity altering the inadequacy of old formulations, demanding newer and more comprehensive readings, endlessly complex and ramified in its panoply, but in its essence as simple and monologic as silence itself.

The world (which is the passivity of God) is complemented by man whose essential character is freedom. It is not reason that makes man little lower than angels, but freedom and speech. Reason is facultative necessity, not unlike the passive necessity of God's nature which moves along the tried ridges and grooves of His unchallenged being. It is freedom, however, and the linguistic imagination that marks the attraction of nonbeing for the rationality of man. The implosion of the divine nature which, in its act, is devised as creation is no less recognized in our own existentiality. Man is a creature whose freedom tempts his reason. Otherwise formulated out of Schelling, nonbeing has in freedom the contradiction of being, for freedom is naked caprice before it is measured and bounded by the rational aspect of our being. There is in man an enduring strife and tension, enlarged and made threatening by our finitude, in which freedom enhances when it is marked and contained by reason, but when reason fails to find language, freedom is destructively cut loose or bends toward untruth or succumbs to sheer willfulness.

Reason orders the energy of caprice into freedom; being sets limits to the surge of nonbeing. Man reconciles and contains his contradiction, repressing madness and evil. This is the optimism and hope of being created in the image of God: His plenitude is always in the beginning of our ends and our true end—that God describes the limits but man sets them, that God engenders possibility but that man enacts them, that God's freedom to be eternally open to His own nature is our freedom to speak and enact in time.

We had thought at the conclusion of the nineteenth century that reason and universal telos had become one, that a single mind and energy ordered the universe, that reason was abundant, that progress and enlightenment represented the best and most beneficent humanizing of the races of mankind. Our innocence was deceptive and our trust naive or deceitful. The age was withered by the criticism of Marx [1818–1883] who discerned the corrupt self-interest of institutions and the conversion of free energy into instrumental and manipulated power. Freud [1856–1939], no less a critic of the age, projected a pessimism of the limitless caprice and the insatiable id that was either to be chastened by the superego with the guilt of bonded service or else chastised in the hope of containing its limitless ambition. The Marxist critique devolved beyond

the *tremendum* to an analysis of secular messianism that reintroduces hope as the measure and containment of social disruption. Post-Freudian critics are ready to recognize that Freud's attack on mythological religion was more an attack on unsuccessful repression than a debunking of the humanizing function of the sacred. Indeed, from the vanguard of the most radical opponents of historical religion may come forth interpreters who make vital again the essential appeal of a transcendent claim. Both Marx and Freud were prophets who have not been adequately heard. The machinery of society enlarged and reason withdrew, the dreams of disorder became habitual and the tyrannical machinery of repression failed. By 1945 the old world of hope was crushed forever and what stood forth, isolate, marked by grim parameters and horrendous reminders, never to be effaced as dreams become nightmares, was the *tremendum* of this century.

The bridge that I have, not casually but I fear insubstantially, cast over the abyss is one that sinks its pylons into the deep soil of human freedom and rationality, recognizing no less candidly now than before that freedom without the containment of reason returns to caprice, and reason without the imagination of freedom is supineness and passivity. Since all of our world here below is marked by coming to be and passing away, birth and death, all human projects toward the world and its settlement are traded off against the selfishness of our preoccupation with our own finality. To engage man beyond the self, to win his free reason and his reasonable freedom requires beyond the life of the single man the containment of his community, where the freedom of all is open to the prophetic recall of the one. The life of man through God, both as imitation and as real presentation, is not surety enough unless enacted within community, where not only numbers maintain guard but also where collective language makes audible the silent speech of creation.

What the single man of being and nonbeing, passivity and affirmation, reason and caprice assembles as the creature of instructed freedom is, before the plenitude of God's engagement to the world, as silent in his gratitude as God is silent in creation. The word of God is God's flesh. It is only when man begins to speak that he enfleshes the forms of creation, naming their substantiality, devising their discrimination and identity, denominating their selfhood. Human grammar is divine, but divine speech is human. Or otherwise affirmed, what creation is for God is revelation for man, the silence of God becoming the speech of man. When God is denied, nothing can be named; when God is speculated, God remains the Something sought whose name is unknown; when God is affirmed, the name of God is given; and when life is lived in community with God, God's name is spoken as continuous presentness, the ongoing *koh 'amar* ("Thus says the Lord") of creation answered by the response of revelation, *hinneni* ("Here I am").

The *tremendum* remains *tremendum*, neither diminished nor explained, but nonetheless limned by interpretation. As I have proposed, it has at least one interpretation that allows the enterprise of human community to endure, that encourages human struggle to persevere, that obliges trust to assert once again its claim upon the future. If the *tremendum* of evil was the dissolution of the fragile human integration of energetic caprice and orderly reason, the union of nonbeing and being, and, as if by some monstrous reversal, the structure of being was dislocated, order rather than reason machining caprice and the energy of caprice immolating reason, it is no wonder that the searing fire of Holocaust would burn out Europe. How such a reversal of integration, such a dissolution of structure occurred, how the historical explosion was prepared is work enough for a century of historians, psychologists, and memorialists.

The *cri de coeur* of the memorialists of the *tremendum* is the silence of God. How could it be that God witnessed the Holocaust and remained silent, that within the providential plan of God the Holocaust should figure among its details, that God is vaunted presentness but was absent, that God is highest manifest reality but recondite and hidden? What, in truth, does the cry contend and require? Nothing less than the interruptive miracle, that the sea open and the army of the enemy be consumed? This is surely what all of us might have dreamed for the miracle of ransom. The ancient model, embedded as the scheme of our redemption from the land of Egypt, is the prefiguration of modern hope. The interruptive God, however, is not ever interruptive even were the sea to part and close or the earth of Auschwitz to open and the murderers to fall in. The presupposition upon which such a view of divine miracle depends is that the creation we take to be real is not an emergence beyond God's being. Such a view of the miracle—to be coherent—must assert either that the created world is never independent of God, that it is, at most, the extension of God and that what appears as God's interruption is the logical trope of his own reflexivity. Such a pantheism, retracing its ground in Spinoza [1632–1677], makes suffering and evil unclarity and inadequate perception; or else, if not pantheism, it must return to the naive grounds of fundamentalist theism that considers God respondent to extremity, the greater the human need the greater the certainty of His assistance, with the result that human life denies its essential freedom, returning to ethical passivity and quietism in which everything is compelled to be God's direct work.

The most penetrating of post-*tremendum* assaults upon God has been the attack upon divine silence. Silence is surely in such a usage a metaphor for inaction: passivity, affectlessness, indeed, at its worst and most extreme, indifference and ultimate malignity. Only a malign God would be silent when speech would terrify and stay the fall of the uplifted arm. And if God spoke once (or many times as Scripture avers), why has He not spoken since? What is it with a God who speaks only to the ears of the earliest and the oldest and for millennia thereafter keeps silence and speaks not. In all this there is concealed a variety of assumptions about the nature and efficacy of divine speech that needs to be examined. The first is that the divine speech of old is to be construed literally, that is, God actually spoke in the language of man, adapting speech to the styles of the patriarchs and the prophets, and was heard speaking and was transmitted as having spoken. God's speech was accompanied by the racket of the heavens so that even if the speech were not heard by more than the prophetic ear, the marks and signals of divine immensity were observed. As well, there is the interpretive conviction that God's speech is action, that God's words act. Lastly, and most relevantly to the matter before us, God's speech enacts and therefore confutes the projects of murderers and tyrants—He saves

Israel, He ransoms Jews, He is forbearing and loving. God's speech is thus consequential to the historical cause of justice and mercy. Evidently, then, divine silence is reproof and punishment, the reversal of His works of speech, and hence God's silence is divine acquiescence in the work of murder and destruction.

Can it not be argued no less persuasively that what is taken as God's speech is really always man's hearing, that God is not the strategist of our particularities or of our historical condition, but rather the mystery of our futurity, always our *posse*, never our acts. If we can begin to see God less as the interferer whose insertion is welcome (when it accords with our needs) and more as the immensity whose reality is our prefiguration, whose speech and silence are metaphors for our language and distortion, whose plenitude and unfolding are the hope of our futurity, we shall have won a sense of God whom we may love and honor, but whom we no longer fear and from whom we no longer demand.

Steven T. Katz

Steven T. Katz was born in Jersey City, New Jersey, on August 24, 1944, into an orthodox Jewish family. He received a traditional yeshiva education in his youth and then went on to receive his B.A. from Rutgers University (New Jersey) in 1966, his M.A. from New York University in 1967, and his Ph.D. from Cambridge University, England, in 1972. He began his teaching career at Dartmouth College in 1972. In 1984 he moved to Cornell University where he chaired the Department of Near Eastern Studies and directed the Jewish Studies Program. In 1996 he was invited to become the director of the Judaic Studies Program at Boston University, a position he still holds. He has also been a visiting professor at, among other universities, Yale, the Hebrew University, and the University of Pennsylvania.

His scholarly work has been concentrated in three areas: (a) modern Jewish thought; (b) Holocaust studies; and (c) comparative mysticism. In the first he has published, among other studies, two collections of essays, *Post-Holocaust Dialogues: Critical Studies in Modern Jewish Thought* (New York, 1983) and *Historicism, the Holocaust, and Zionism: Critical Studies in Modern Jewish Thought and History* (New York, 1992). In the area of Holocaust studies he is the author of a multivolume study entitled *The Holocaust in Historical Context*, volume 1 of which appeared in 1994 and volumes 2 and 3 of which will appear shortly. In the area of comparative mysticism, Katz has edited and contributed to four collections of original essays, as well as an anthology of mystical sources, all published by Oxford University Press.

Katz is also the founder and editor of the prize-winning journal *Modern Judaism* and the editor of volume 4 of the *Cambridge History of Judaism* (Cambridge, 2006). He was awarded the Lucas Prize by the University of Tubingen, Germany, in 2000 and won an NEH Fellowship in 2004, among many other awards.

SELECTIONS

The selections here reproduced are from two collections of Steven Katz's essays. The first three selections are drawn from his *Post-Holocaust Dialogues*. Selections four and five are republished from his *Historicism, the Holocaust, and Zionism*. All the selections reflect a close, critical reading of the work under review and have been selected specifically because they reflect upon earlier book reprinted in this anthology. Katz, as is clear from his writings, is appreciative of the diverse intellectual efforts that have been made to decipher and respond to the theological challenges posed by the Holocaust, but, ultimately, he finds each of the positions he reviews logically and philosophically unpersuasive, hence the need to continue this vital theological conversation.

Selected Bibliography

Works by Steven T. Katz

Historicism, the Holocaust, and Zionism: Critical Studies in Modern Jewish Thought and History (New York, 1992).
The Holocaust in Historical Context, vol. 1 (New York, 1994).
Post-Holocaust Dialogues: Critical Studies in Modern Jewish Thought (New York, 1983).
Editor, *The Impact of the Holocaust on Jewish Theology* (New York, 2005).

Richard Rubenstein, the God of History, and the Logic of Judaism

In the last fifteen years or so, Jewish thinkers of all persuasions have begun to consider the theological and historical ramifications of the Holocaust as they bear upon Jewish existence and identity in the post-Holocaust age.[1] The competence, appeal, and richness of these differing reflections have varied widely but none has been more radical than that of Richard Rubenstein. In response to Auschwitz, Rubenstein has taken the extreme theological position of denying God's existence. If his thesis is correct, then all other less radical responses to the Holocaust, which are predicated on some continued affirmation of the existence of God, are not viable.

Rubenstein's position can be summed up in three words: "God is Dead." The logic that has driven him to utter these three extraordinarily powerful words can be put in the following syllogism: (1) God, as He is conceived of in the Jewish tradition, could not have allowed the Holocaust to happen; (2) the Holocaust did happen. Therefore, (3) God, as He is conceived of in the Jewish tradition, does not exist.

This seemingly straightforward argument is the basis upon which Rubenstein has felt compelled to reject the God of history and hence the God of Jewish tradition. The radical negation represented by this position is of the utmost seriousness for modern Jewish (and non-Jewish) thought and, even if one finally demurs, one must grapple with it rather than merely dismiss it as out of place in a Jewish context, as some naive critics have done.[2] It does raise a real, if frightening, possibility about the "meaning of Auschwitz," i.e., that there is *no* meaning to history, for history is a random, arbitrary series of events that are unrelated either to a transcendental order or to a context of absolute meaning or value. In *After Auschwitz*,[3] Rubenstein stated this contention articulately:

---

1. For a fuller account of all these approaches see S. Katz, *Jewish Philosophers* (New York, 1975), pp. 223–224; and S. Katz, "Jewish Faith after the Holocaust: Four Approaches," in my *Post-Holocaust Dialogues* (New York, 1983), pp. 141–173. The Judaica journals such as *Judaism, Tradition, Reform Judaism, The Reconstructionist* and *Conservative Judaism* have all contained articles and treatments of this theme; see their indexes since 1965. The *Journal of the American Academy of Religion* and similar general theological journals have carried important articles touching directly and indirectly on this theme. Selections from Rubenstein's work appear above pp. 410–418.

2. It should be mentioned at the start of this paper, in the clearest possible terms, that my criticism of Rubenstein is intended to be *strictly* philosophical and *not ad hominem*. I wish to dissociate myself *totally* from those critics

who, rather than discuss Rubenstein's ideas, have abused the man. No instances of such abuse will be singled out for citation here, but those familiar with the literature will recognize this as an all-too-prevalent, and odious, element in the critical response to Rubenstein's position. Let me add for this reprinting of the present essay that Professor Rubenstein has taken the criticism offered by me in a most generous spirit and has, since its appearance, become a valued friend.

3. *After Auschwitz* (Indianapolis, 1966). This is Rubenstein's earliest and most important collection of material dealing with the Holocaust and its implications. This paper will primarily deal with Rubenstein's views as presented in this work, which I take to be his most significant statement on the theological implications of this theme. Hereafter this work is cited as *AA*.

When I say we live in the time of the death of God, I mean that the thread uniting God and man, heaven and earth has been broken. We stand in a cold, silent, unfeeling cosmos, unaided by any purposeful power beyond our own resources. After Auschwitz what else can a Jew say about God?...I see no other way than the "death of God" position of expressing the void that confronts man where once God stood.[4]

Philosophically this challenge to belief, generated from the consideration of the implications of Auschwitz, is both interesting and more problematic than it at first appears. Of course, the "Death of God" is not a new challenge, being already *very* familiar in modern philosophical literature since the proclamation to this affect by Nietzsche's madman in *The Gay Science*. More recently, its appeal has been expressed most forcefully in the extremely influential French atheistic existentialist school associated with the names of Camus and Sartre. Alternatively, what is novel in Rubenstein's employment of this notion is his use of this idea in a Jewish theological context. Many modern Jews since the *Haskalah* [the "Jewish Enlightenment" dating from the mid-eighteenth century onward] have spoken in more or less muted terms of this "event," but no one until Rubenstein's reflections on the Holocaust thought to use it as the basis for a Jewish theology of history.

In order to expose both the merits and the insufficiencies of this stance as a Jewish theology let us take a closer, more rigorous, look at its structural character. Nine primary logical-philosophical topics will be considered in turn.

1. To begin on the positive side, one must recognize at the outset what is perhaps the most important underlying reason for the adoption of this position as a way of dealing with the "cause" and "meaning" of the Holocaust. Traditional theology has had to deal with the "problem of evil" for millennia and in reaction has given a variety of "answers" ranging from the most

dominant traditional Jewish response, namely that evil is a punishment for sin, *mi-penei hata'einu* in the classical Hebrew phrase, to the notion that suffering is an "affliction of love," *yissurin shel ahavah.*[5] All of these solutions and their concommitant theodicies are found inadequate to deal with the reality of the death camps by the "Death of God" theologian—and I believe he is absolutely correct in this judgment. He, in alliance with almost all Jewish theologians of whatever persuasion, is especially adamant that the destruction of European Jewry cannot be *mi-penei hata'einu*—for what sins could Israel have committed to justify such evil and what kind of God would punish *even* a sinful Israel with such fury? Similarly, the classical Christian account of Jewish suffering, which views it as deserved punishment for Israel's guilt for its alleged role in the death of Jesus—even if seen as deicide in classical Christian terms—which is used by some Christian theologians to "justify" the Holocaust, needs to be reconsidered by Christians.[6] Is there not something fundamentally wrong with the image of a God of love wreaking such vengeance on a million children after two thousand years?

Rather than accept either Israel's sinfulness as the justification for the Holocaust or see it as some inscrutable act of Divine wrath or fiat, the vision of which appears to blaspheme against the loving God of the Jewish tradition and the entire meaning of Jewish convenantal existence, the radical theologian takes the difficult step of denying both poles of the Divine–human dialectic, thereby destroying the traditional theological encounter altogether. There is no God and there is no covenant with Israel.

> If I believed in God as the omnipotent author of the historical drama and Israel as His Chosen People, I had to accept [the]...conclusion that it was God's will that Hitler committed six million Jews to slaughter. I could not possibly believe in such a God nor could I believe in Israel as the chosen people of God after Auschwitz.[7]

---

4. *AA*, p. 49.
5. On the nation of "yissurin shel ahavah" see, for example Saadiah Gaon, *Emunot ve' Deot,* V:3. Alternatively, Maimonides rejects this notion; see *Guide for the Perplexed* 3:24.

6. I hope to deal with this material in a future paper.
7. *AA* p. 47.

2. The second element emerging out of, as well as essential to, the "Death of God" view putatively grounded in the Holocaust experience is more problematic. It concerns nothing less than how one views Jewish history, its continuities and discontinuities, its "causal connectedness" and interdependencies. By raising the issue of how one evaluates Jewish history and what hermeneutic of historic meaning one need adopt, I mean to bring into focus the fact—and it is a fact—that the radical theologian sees Jewish history too narrowly, i.e., focused solely in and through the Holocaust. He takes *the* decisive event of Jewish history to be the death camps. But this is a distorted image of Jewish experience, for there is a pre-Holocaust and post-Holocaust Jewish reality that must be considered in dealing with the questions raised by the Nazi epoch. These questions extend beyond 1933–1945 and touch the present Jewish situation as well as the whole of the Jewish past. One cannot make the events of 1933–45 intelligible in isolation. To think, moreover, that one can excise this block of time from the flow of Jewish history and then by concentrating on it, extract the "meaning" of *all* Jewish existence, is more than uncertain,[8] no matter how momentous or demonic this time may have been.

Jews went to Auschwitz, suffered and died at Auschwitz, through no specific fault of their own: their crime was their Jewishness. The Nuremberg laws extracted from the 1933–45 generation the price of their parents', grandparents' and great-grandparents' decision to have Jewish children. This, if nothing else, forces us to widen our historic perspective when we try to comprehend what happened in Nazi Germany. When one tries to understand the "grand-parents" of the death camp generation one will find that their actions are likewise unintelligible without following the historic chain that leads backwards into the Jewish millennial past. The same rule also applies in trying to fathom the historic reality of the murderers and their inheritance. The events of 1933–45 were the product of the German and Jewish past; to decode this present we must enter into that past.

This recognition of a pre-Holocaust and post-Holocaust Israel forces two considerations upon us. The first is the very survival of the Jewish people *despite* their "sojourn among the nations." As Karl Barth once said, "the best proof of God's existence is the continued existence of the Jewish people." Without entering into a discussion of the metaphysics of history, let this point just stand for further reflection, i.e., that the Jews survived Hitler and Jewish history did not end at Auschwitz. Secondly, and equally if not more directly significant, is the recreation after Auschwitz of a Jewish state, the Third Jewish Commonwealth in the Land of Israel.[9] This event, too, is remarkable in the course of Jewish existence. Logic and conceptual adequacy require that if in our discussion of the relation of God and history we want to give theological weight to the Holocaust then we *must* also be willing to attribute *theological* significance to the State of Israel. Just what weight one assigns to each of these events, and then again to events in general, in constructing a theological reading of history is an extraordinarily complex theoretical issue, about which there is the need for much discussion, and which allows for much difference of view. However, it is clear that any final rendering of the "meaning of Jewish history" that values in its equation *only* the negative factors of the Nazi Holocaust or it and previous Holocausts, is, at best, arbitrary. If one wants to make statements about God's presence (or in this case absence) in Jewish history as a consequence of Auschwitz then one must also, in all theological and existential seriousness, consider the meaning of His presence (or absence) in Jewish history as played out in Jerusalem. If it makes sense to talk theologically at all—an open question—about God's presence and absence, His existence and nonexistence, and to judge these matters on the basis of what happened to the Jews of Europe in some sort of negative

8. Those who would deal with the Holocaust need to master not only Holocaust materials but also the whole of Jewish history. This point has been well made by E. Berkovits in his *Faith After the Holocaust* (New York, 1973). To obtain some idea of what is involved in such a mastery of Jewish history readers are referred to Salo

Baron's magisterial *A Social and Religious History of the Jews* (New York, 1951–ongoing; 17 volumes have so far appeared), and especially to his extraordinary notes.

9. On Rubenstein's appreciation of the state of Israel see, for example, his essay on "The Rebirth of Israel in Jewish Theology" in *AA*.

natural theology, then it is equally meaningful—*and logically and theologically necessary*—to consider what the events in *Eretz Yisroel* since 1945 tell us about His reality and ours. To his credit, Rubenstein does appreciate that the State of Israel is of consequence, even momentous consequence, but he insists on treating it as *theologically* independent from Auschwitz so that no positive linkage in some larger rendering of Jewish experience is possible; nor can we posit what in traditional idiom would be termed "redemptive" significance to this national rebirth. Rather, the renaissance of Jewish life in its ancestral homeland is seen by Rubenstein, consistent with his own procedure, as the clearest manifestation of the post-1945 rejection of the God of history by Jews and their return to a natural, land-related, nontheistic life. However, despite Rubenstein's interesting working through of this event in his own terms, his interpretation of the situation will not do, for it is clear that from a logical point of view it is methodologically improper to construct a phenomenology of historical reality that gives weight only to the negative significance of "evil" without any attempt to balance it against the positive significance of the "good" we encounter in history. History is too variegated to be understood only as good or evil; the alternating rhythms of actual life reveal the two forces as interlocked and inseparable. For our present concerns, the hermeneutical value of this recognition is that one comes to see that Jewish history is neither conclusive proof for the existence of God (because of the possible counterevidence of Auschwitz), nor conversely, for the nonexistence of God (because of the possible counterevidence of the State of Israel as well as the whole three thousand-year historic Jewish experience). Rubenstein's narrow focus on Auschwitz reflects an already decided theological choice based on certain normative presuppositions and a compelling desire to justify certain conclusions. It is not a value-free phenomenological description of Jewish history.

Before leaving this argument it should be made absolutely clear that it is not being asserted that the State of Israel *is* compensation for Auschwitz, nor that Auschwitz is the "cause," in a theological or metaphysical sense, of the creation of the Jewish state, as many simplistic historical and theological accounts, offered for all kinds of mixed reasons, have done. Whatever relation does exist between Holocaust Europe and the State of Israel is far more ambiguous and many-sided than a simple causal or compensatory schema would explain. The argument as presented, however, is a reminder that the State of Israel is an event—one might, I think, even legitimately say a "miracle," if that term means anything at all—at least equal to if not more important than Auschwitz in Jewish theological terms; it must be respected as such.

3. There is an unspoken but implied, highly influential, premise in Rubenstein's argument concerning the relation of God and history. This hidden premise relates to what is well known as the "empiricist theory of meaning" made famous by A. J. Ayer in *Language, Truth and Logic* and then given a more particularly significant theological twist by Anthony Flew in his "falsifiability challenge." This was first expressed in the widely discussed "University Discussion" reprinted in *New Essays in Philosophical Theology*.[10] Space prohibits an extended review of this most aggressive challenge to religious belief, which in any case is familiar enough if not always completely understood, but its implicit use in the "Death of God" argument must at least be called into the open, for it is the employment of this thesis that provides much of the initial rigor of the radical theologian's challenge. I am not sure whether Rubenstein's employment of this notion is intentional or indirect but its presence and significance for Rubenstein is nonetheless real. He at least tacitly accepts the basic premise of the "empiricist falsifiability thesis,"[11] i.e., that propositions about God are to be straightforwardly confirmed or disconfirmed by appeal to empirical events in the world. It is only the result of the at

10. See A. Flew's essay in *New Essays in Philosophical Theology* (London, 1964). For a useful introduction to the enormous literature generated by this issue see R. Heimbeck's *Theology and Meaning* (London, 1969), especially his bibliography and notes.
11. On the "verification principle" see the sources given in R. Heimbeck, *Theology and Meaning.*

least implicit adoption of this empirical principle, or something very close to it, that allows Rubenstein to judge that "God is dead," for it is only on the basis of some such norm that the conditions of the Holocaust can become the empirical test case for the existence or nonexistence of God. In effect Rubenstein argues: if there is too much evil in the world (putting aside the problem of how one would measure this for the moment and recognizing that this subject is never dealt with by Rubenstein) then God, as conceived in the Jewish tradition, cannot exist. At Auschwitz there was such evil and God did not step in to stop it; thus God does not exist. Hence the traditional theological notions based upon such a belief in God are decisively falsified by an appeal to this empirical evidence.

Respecting this challenge as an important one that is often too lightly dismissed by theologians, and respecting Rubenstein's employment of it as an authentic existential response to an overwhelming reality, it nonetheless needs to be suggested that the empirical falsifiability challenge is not definitive one way or the other in theological matters and thus can not provide Rubenstein (or others) with an unimpeachable criterion for making the negative theological judgments that he seeks to advance regarding the nonexistence of God. The "falsifiability" thesis neither allows one *decisively* to affirm nor disaffirm God's presence in history, for history provides evidence both for and against the nonexistence of God on empirical-verificationist grounds, i.e., there is both good and bad in history. Moreover, the very value of the empirical criteria turns on the one hand on what one considers to be empirical-verificationist evidence, i.e., on what one counts as empirical or experiential, and on the other, on whether the empirical-verificationist principle is, in itself, philosophically coherent, which it appears not to be. Again, here too the State of Israel is a crucial "datum" (and solidly empirical) for the radical theologican to consider when framing his falsifiability equation, for the Jew (or others) might

challenge the critic with this counterclaim: "Yes, the assertion of God's existence *does* depend on what happens in history. Among the events of history is not only Auschwitz but also the creation of the State of Israel. Whereas the former event is evidence against the 'God-Hypothesis' the latter is evidence in its favor." Neither position is decisively provable—but both are equally meaningful,[12] as well as equally unprovable.

Again, the Jew (or a Christian like Barth) might respond to the falsifiability challenge by returning to the first historical argument discussed above (as point 2), i.e., Auschwitz is not decisive evidence for or against God's existence, and meet the empiricist critic head-on by rephrasing the nature of the empiricist challenge itself. That is, he could argue that he accepts the challenge in general terms but offers different specific empirical conditions by which to decide the matter one way or the other. For example, he stipulates as the decisive falsifying condition the complete elimination of Jews from history which was, in fact, Hitler's goal through his "Final Solution." Here we have a straightforward, if theologically enormous, claim: the existence of God is inseparably related to the existence of the Jewish people (a claim not too distant from that actually made in at least some classical Jewish sources). If the Jewish people are destroyed then we will agree that God does not exist. This is certainly a falsifiable proposition, or at least, it is hoped, only an *in principle* falsifiable thesis, i.e., the Jewish people *logically* are removable from history. What happens to the empiricist challenge at this point? This question seems especially challenging given that the hypothetical argument constructed can be construed, at least according to a certain quite respectable theological ideology, as a close analog to what actually transpired in twentieth-century Europe.

What this second counterexample, as well as the argument advanced above, suggest is that Rubenstein has too easily accepted some form of the empiricist theory of meaning and verification.

---

12. Readers must not confuse "verification" and "meaning"—the essential error made by A. J. Ayer. Nor should they confuse "meaning" and "falsification," which is a common distortion of Karl Popper's

extremely interesting and widely influential views. See Popper's own discussion of this matter in his *Conjectures and Refutations* (London, 1963).

Though this theory is obscure at best and probably ultimately philosophically indefensible, Rubenstein has made this, or something like it, a foundation stone of his entire enterprise without a sufficient degree of epistemological self-consciousness regarding its philosophical accuracy or logical adequacy. In his invocation of this procedure, he has sought to adopt a clear and indisputable method of reaching theological conclusions, the appeal of such clarity and decisiveness being obvious. But the seductiveness of this strategem is more illusory than real, for the empirical-verificationist criterion achieves its putative precision and rigor only by illegitimately reducing the complex to the simple and the ambiguous to the transparent. Thus its results are a caricature of the situation.

Before moving on it should be registered that despite our criticism of Rubenstein's formulation of the empiricist issue as logically inadequate, his intentions are well directed, namely, he wants to find nonapologetic, nonhomiletical, nonsubjective ways to talk meaningfully about convenantal existence, or rather, its nonexistence, after the Holocaust and in light of what the Holocaust has to teach us. But, alternatively, what also needs to be recognized is that his frontal assault on the questions involved, using various forms of empiricist-verificationist instruments, is not successful; other ways to get at the root of the problem need to be found.

4. In addition to the unsatisfactory way in which Rubenstein handles the matter of falsifiability and its corollary, the linkage of empirical evidence to "God-language," there is a still larger, even more fundamental, weakness of a meta-physical sort that needs to be confronted. One might describe it as a paucity of metaphysical imagination. This conceptual limitation manifests itself in the sharp disjunctions and black-white dichotomies with which Rubenstein works, which are not true to the richness and variety of human experience, nor, as indicated above, to the ambiguity of history, nor again to the possible varieties of *metaphysical* accounts of reality that might be employed to deal with history in general and Auschwitz in particular, nor finally, in Rubenstein's case, to the notion of "God" and its corollaries, which he treats very simplistically.[13] A close reading of Rubenstein's work[14] suggests that he has given insufficient attention to metaphysical considerations. He is, of course, unhappy with traditional metaphysical schemata in general and this is one of the contributing reasons why he has become a "Death of God" theologian,[15] but this unhappiness, even if justified, is not in itself a license to dismiss metaphysics altogether. What is required is a new and better metaphysics—either with or without God, as the facts of the case turn out to warrant—rather than the erroneous, and ultimately self-defeating, disregard for all serious metaphysical investigation.

If one speculates, as Rubenstein does, on the teleological character of history, the existence or nonexistence of God, the interdependence or otherwise of God and man, and the presence or absence of "meaning" in both the cosmos and human life, among many other issues, metaphysical imagination is a *sine qua non*. The author of *After Auschwitz* seems genuinely unaware that his is a substantial *metaphysical* speculation rather than either a set of empirical propositions or a

13. I hasten to add that the existential-historical complexity and ambiguity referred to is not a plea for the obscurantism of much contemporary thought, especially in existentialist circles, but is a reminder to beware the facile oversimplification of much that appears as clarity and rigor in analytic philosophical circles, especially as regards the understanding of history and philosophical anthropology, two areas in which the analytic tradition has been particularly sterile. On these issues there is almost nothing of any real significance that has been produced by the analytic school of philosophy. On the issue of philosophical anthropology there is not even one work to single out as being of outstanding quality.

14. *After Auschwitz* (Indianapolis, 1966), *The Religious Imagination* (Indianapolis, 1968), *Eros and Morality* (New York, 1970), *My Brother Paul* (New York, 1972), *The Cunning of History* (New York, 1975), and *Power Struggle* (New York, 1974).

15. See also on this issue: T. Altizer's *Gospel of Christian Atheism* (Philadelphia, 1966); *Towards a New Christianity: Readings in the Death of God Theology* (Philadelphia, 1967); and *Mircea Eliade and the Dialectic of the Sacred* (Philadelphia, 1963). Also, G. Vahanian's *The Death of God* (New York, 1961); *No Other God* (New York, 1966); and *The God Is Dead Debate* (New York, 1976).

phenomenological description of a straightforward kind (if any such phenomenological descriptions there be at all). To justify his account, therefore, metaphysical considerations become centrally relevant, especially those which try to wrestle with the meaning and logical implications of themes such as God's freedom and creative power and His creation of men as free beings.

The acknowledged indebtedness of Rubenstein to his existentialist predecessors is of importance, especially here.[16] Like them, Rubenstein thinks that criticism and purposeful eschewing of metaphysics is a suitable substitute for metaphysical enterprise and imagination. However, just as this lack has proved a singularly negative factor in existentialist thought, so too does it manifest itself here. Rather than working through the logic of his position for himself, Rubenstein has chosen to adopt as true the antimetaphysical existentialist credo which has been in circulation at least since Kierkegaard's anti-Hegelian polemic immortalized this approach. This choice, however, embodies a significant error for at least two reasons. First, the inherited existentialist position is itself inadequate *per se*. While claiming to be antimetaphysical in the name of "existence," this very claim is itself a metaphysical assertion. Space prevents more than the bare presentation of this fact, which is now widely recognized to obtain. Secondly, the wholesale application of this existentialist attitude to Judaism, to the Holocaust and to the post-Holocaust Jewish situation, is dubious, for it fails to recognize that Judaism has its own *internal* metaphysical understanding of events and reality whose perspective can only be mastered from within Judaism in the first instance.[17] For example, Judaism has its own account of the meaning of the terms "God", "history" and "covenant," to cite only three cardinal concepts in Rubenstein's schema.

5. The first four topics so far touched upon have been of a broader nature, probably relevant not only to a consideration of Rubenstein's reconstructions, but also to the efforts of all thinkers

who have tried (or will try) to construct a "Death of God" theology on the basis of the Holocaust experience. There are, however; two additional subjects which I should like to engage that are particular to Rubenstein's now de-mythologizing now re-mythologizing vision. The first concerns Rubenstein's interesting, if curious, advocacy of the value of Jewish community despite, or even more precisely, because of the Holocaust. The second turns on his prescription that the Jew after Auschwitz should substitute a mystical, pagan, nature-religion for traditional Jewish theology.

As to the importance of Jewish community after the Holocaust, Rubenstein argues as follows. After the traumatic experiences of recent Jewish history, the community of Israel, the social solidarity of one Jew for another, is all the more called for because now, after the "Death of God," there is nowhere else for man to turn for the meaning of human life. Certainly, according to Rubenstein, no transcendental revelatory Absolute exists which will or could infuse our life with significance; all pious traditional nostalgia of this sort is to be recognized as the false, and no longer efficacious, opiate that it is. Alternatively, however, in the face of the abyss that threatens to engulf us, Jews must and can create that "meaning" which there is to be, and they do this primarily in community: "It is precisely because human existence is tragic, ultimately hopeless, and without meaning that we treasure our religious community."[18] Although, according to Rubenstein, post-Holocaust Judaism has to be vigorously "demythologized," that is, it has to recognize the emptiness of the historic claims ("myths") of Israel to be a uniquely "chosen people" and to be God's beloved, at the same time Judaism, as an existential reality, paradoxically gains heightened immediacy in this very process of contemporary redefinition. It does so because despite the Jew's new reflective self-consciousness, which coincides with his dismemberment of the "mythic" structure of traditional Judaism and the ideology by which the Jewish

16. As noted, Rubenstein's procedure here is not uncommon in modern existentialist literature. Buber, for example, favors such an argument as well. Buber, however, only once again shows the weakness of such a gambit. See here my "Dialogue and Revelation in

the Thought of Martin Buber," in *Religious Studies*, Vol. 14, 1 (March, 1978), pp. 47–48.
17. For more on the Jewish understanding of these two notions see my *Jewish Concepts and Ideas* (New York, 1978).
18. *AA,* p. 68.

people has traditionally understood its experience, he is still a Jew and as such carries with him the "shared vicissitudes of history, culture and psychological perspective"[19] that define a Jew. Jews, like all human beings, are rooted in concrete life situations. As such, for a Jew, only Jewish experience can be authentic; only in its traditional forms of life can he best and most completely express his aspirations and ideals, only here can the Jew participate in a "community of shared predicament and ultimate concern."[20]

Before analyzing Rubenstein's understanding of the "demythologizing" of Judaism and its subsequent sociological and psychological role in contemporary Jewish life, I want to call attention to Rubenstein's indebtedness to the atheistic existentialist program of creating values through human resources and needs alone. We cannot rehearse, in detail, the limits of this position here[21] but only offer that if Rubenstein's adoption of this scenario is correct then the whole notion of "value"—human or otherwise—is more than dubious, being, if not self-contradictory, at best hollow. Morality and commitment, authenticity and responsibility, as well as all the other "value" words in our philosophical and theological lexicon—and in Rubenstein's—actually become empty. They continue, however, to be used by Rubenstein with some semblance of intelligibility and normative density because it is not recognized that their employment is parasitic on the very traditional metaphysical and axiological notions that have been overtly rejected. This self-contradictory parasitism is essential to Rubenstein's program though, of course, its identification makes the entire systematic structure implausible.

We can now consider the existential, social-psychological context Rubenstein wants to emphasize. Those familiar with modern Jewish thought will recognize Rubenstein's demythologized sociological rendering of Judaism and its stress on Jewish community and shared history as close to, if not identical with, the sentiments articulated by Mordecai Kaplan in his 1934 classic, *Judaism as a Civilization,* and styled by him as "Reconstructionism." This version of Judaism has been correctly subjected to many criticisms[22] and we have no wish to re-iterate the majority of them here. Only one demands comment: the thesis that traditional Jewish forms of life can continue to play an enriching psychological and existential role in the lives of Jews even if they are divorced from their more traditional theological content. We can most precisely express our concern in the interrogative: can the socio-religious rituals, customs, liturgical activities, as well as the wide range of *mitzvot* (religious commandments and obligations) continue to provide "meaning," even if only this-worldly and existential, for Jews and Judaism in the new, naturalistic, pagan context envisioned by Rubenstein?

Rubenstein's argument, to his credit, raises fundamental semantic questions about "meaning" and its relation to the notions of "form" and "content." What Rubenstein is insinuating is that one can keep the "form(s)" of Jewish life but radically change their "content" and thereby still make it possible to maintain the social and psychological "value" or "meaning" of these Jewish activities. This is a highly suggestive, psychologically sophisticated, thesis. Unfortunately, it is untenable because it is based on a misunderstanding of the interrelation of "form," "content," and "meaning," paying insufficient attention to the indissoluble link between the three concepts and the complex structural interdependance that obtains between them. That is to say, if you thoroughly and consistently change the "content," even if you try to maintain the "form," you will necessarily change the "meaning." In effect, the schematic weakness arises because Rubenstein undervalues the formal linkage of "content" and "meaning" (existential, social, and psychological

19. *AA,* p. 119.
20. *AA,* p. 119.
21. For criticism of the atheistic existentialist position see, for example, Edith Kern, ed., *Sartre: A Collection of Critical Essays* (Englewood Cliffs, N.J., 1962); and Mary Warnock, ed., *Sartre: A Collection of Critical Essays* (New York, 1974).

22. For criticism of Kaplan's views, see E. Fackenheim, "A Critique of Reconstructionism," *CCAR Journal* (June, 1960), pp. 51–59; E. Berkovits, "Reconstructionist Theology," *Tradition,* Vol. 2 (Fall, 1959), pp. 20–66. For my own views on Kaplan see S. Katz, "Mordecai Kaplan: A Philosophical Demurrer," *Sh'MA* (November 1, 1974), pp. 156–57.

"meaning" in Rubenstein's sense, not semantic, ontological, or logical "meaning"). In general, Rubenstein's contrary view is not supported by any arguments and in fact contradicts the psychological, sociological, and philosophical grammar of the situation.

A clearer conception of what is at stake can be obtained if we examine Rubenstein's own examples of how this transformed post-Auschwitz situation functions in terms of "form," "meaning," and "content." He has, and for this he is to be applauded, tried to give specific illustrations of how certain classic modes of personal and group Jewish behavior can continue to be adhered to, i.e., can continue to provide "meaning," at the same time that their underlying justifying ideology is radically modified. Thus, for example, he argues that in the new, now demythologized post-Holocaust Judaism he envisions, bar mitzvah, while continuing to be celebrated, should not be understood as the public acceptance of the Torah's obligations by the now religiously "adult" boy but rather as a puberty rite, a *rite de passage,* which signals the public acceptance of the young man of thirteen as sexually adult in the eyes of the community.[23] However, this case (and others) lacks compelling force, for it seems reasonable to expect that rather than continuing to perform bar mitzvahs, albeit for a new purpose, it is more likely that not only will the specific occasion of bar mitzvah fall into disuse but the entire fabric of Judaism as a socially cohesive, "meaning-giving" entity will disintegrate, as indeed has happened in assimilated Jewish circles in the past where the cement of classical Jewish theology was rejected. What reason is there to think that celebrating a boy's "sexual maturity" will serve *in a Jewish context* to enhance Jewish communal identity? Rubenstein's reasoning here, of course, borrows from anthropological sources wherein such sexual *rites de passage* are reported to function as prominent socially cohesive factors in certain other non-Jewish group behavior. But what grounds are there for suggesting that Judaism can be, or should be, so readily transposed or "re-

duced" to these non-Jewish patterns of meaning? No evidence has been offered to demonstrate that what functions in one way in a specific context will function in a similar way in another, quite different, cultural and theological setting. The web of social solidarity is so fine that one marvels at the optimism that believes it could withstand such a shock as is involved in this social transubstantiation without irreparable dissolution. In addition, there is the question to be asked of why these non-Jewish patterns of signification should be considered meaningful at all, especially in the face of the "Death of God." Then, too, one can be forgiven for being puzzled about why one should try to maintain Jewish forms of life, Rubenstein's psychological explanation notwithstanding, if we are going, of necessity, to have to give them non-Jewish content(s). What *Jewish* import can derive from this procedure? If celebration of sexual maturity can give life a purpose why worry about Judaism at all? Why not either convert to groups that already perform these rites, or just celebrate them in "non-religious" ways? The modern post-Emancipation history of Jewry has amply shown that Jews are an adaptable people who can assimilate themselves to alien designs both of form and of content—something Rubenstein's psychological premises seem committed, incorrectly, to denying. In light of this consideration, Rubenstein's desire to retain Jewish "forms" seems little more than well-meant but misplaced nostalgia. Now, nostalgia is an essential quality in traditional religion, integral as it is to that notion of tradition which is so key an element in Judaism, but can nostalgia serve as the sufficient foundation for the social structure and group dynamics of Rubenstein's radically reconstructed Jewish community? For a *halachah* without God?

Another factor that should also be taken account of is the extreme selectivity of Rubenstein's examples of how his restructured Judaism would work. Thus, bar mitzvah is used as a key example—but in traditional rabbinic calculations there are 613 *mitzvot.* How many of these would be "translatable" into Rubenstein's new naturalistic paganism? For example, to choose some widely practiced *mitzvot* at random, what happens to all the rules of purity? Or *kashruth*? Or Sabbath? Or

23. *AA,* pp. 244 ff. See also Rubenstein's discussion in *The Religious Imagination.*

Succoth, lulav and *esrog* (the palm waved on *Succoth*)? Or *tephillin* (phylacteries)? Or *mikva* (ritual bath)? Or *matzo* and *chometz* (leaven)? On Rubenstein's account we would no doubt have a sharply reduced list of *mitzvot*. But the question that then arises is whether in such altered circumstances we would even have the "form" of Judaism—to say nothing of its social solidarity and "meaning." Reform Judaism has already lived through (and is living with) this problem and not to its (or anyone else's) satisfaction. The serious crisis in contemporary Reform Judaism is witness to the limitations of this view while the return to more traditional forms and the reinclusion of more *mitzvot* into Reform Judaism is evidence of the at least tacit admission that the "translation" technique by which Judaism is translated into non-Jewish ideologies, and Jewish authenticity is measured by non-Jewish criteria, has negative consequences both for the quality of one's Jewish life as well as for Jewish survival. Judaism as a community of shared values dies, as recent history indicates, under these procedures.

As a consequence of the historical and theoretical considerations advanced, it seems reasonable to contend that—whether for good or bad, logical or irrational reasons—the entire world history of the Jewish people, as well as the psychosocial history of the individual Jew *qua* Jew, is very closely associated with, one might even say defined by, the notion of linear, teleological history and the God of such history.[24] It, therefore, would appear more reasonable to argue that the rejection of the God of history will eventuate in the elimination of Judaism rather than be the basis for its transmutation. Though it has been history that has subjected the Jew to so much, at one and the same time his belief in the Lord of History has allowed him to endure this very adversity and survive.

6. This brings us face to face with Rubenstein's advocacy of a pagan naturalism. Rubenstein waxes eloquent on the virtues of this paganism, urging the Jew to return to the cosmic rhythms of nature.[25] His statement of this reversal is so extraordinary that I quote it at length:

> In the religion of history, only man and God are alive. Nature is dead and serves only as the material of tool-making man's obsessive projects. Nature does not exist to be enjoyed and communed with; it exists to be changed and subordinated to man's wants—the fulfillment of which brings neither happiness nor satisfaction. In the religion of nature, a historical, cyclical religion, man is once more at home with nature and its divinities, sharing their life, their limits, and their joys. The devitalization of nature, no matter how imposing, has as its inevitable concomitant the dehumanization of man with its total loss of *eros*. Herbert Marcuse states the issue extremely well when he speaks of the subordination of the logic of gratification to the logic of domination. Only in man at one with nature is *eros* rather than eroticism possible. Historical man knows guilt, inhibition, acquisition, and synthetic fantasy, but no *eros*. The return to the soil of Israel promises a people bereft of art, nature, and expansive passion, a return to *eros* and the ethos of *eros*. In place of the Lord of history, punishing man for attempting to be what he was created to be, the divinities of nature will celebrate with mankind their "bacchanalian revel of spirits in whom no member is drunk."[26]

The Jew, Rubenstein argues, must now reinterpret his traditional, normative categories in naturalistic rather than linear and historical terms. He must recognize that both salvation in the here and now, as well as the future and final redemption, will not be, as traditionally conceived, the conquest of nature by history but rather the reverse. As a consequence of this inversion of the priority and relation of nature and history Jews have to rediscover the sanctity of natural life. They have to learn to enjoy their bodies, rather than follow the classical, but now recognized as self-destructive, paths of sublimation and transformation. Above all, they have to

24. See Salo Baron, *A Social and Religious History of the Jews,* Vol. I, chapters 1 and 2. See also Yehezkial Kaufmann, *Golah ve Nekhar* (Tel Aviv, 1929–32), on the centrality of religion in Jewish history.

25. *AA*, pp. 131–42 and pp. 227–43.
26. *AA*, pp. 136–37.

reject the futile transcendentalizing (historicizing) of these phenomena.

Rubenstein sees in the renewal of Zion and the rebuilding of the land of Israel, with its return to the soil by the Jew, a harbinger of this movement. This regression to the earth points towards the Jews' final escape from the negativity of history to the vitality of self-liberation through the rediscovery of one's primal being. He writes:

> The result of the attainment of the goal of Jewish history must inevitably be that the people of Israel will cease to see gratification as a future hope and will learn to live their lives so that each generation takes its fair share of life's joys and sorrows, knowing that it will be succeeded by other generations who will repeat the cycle rather than improve upon it. Nor does Zionism mean an end to life's inevitable insecurities. It merely means an end to the interpretation of insecurity as guilt, with its psychic impediments to those joys which are realistically available. Sooner or later Israel's Jews will come to understand that they have no need of distant utopias or far-off lands, that their task is to enjoy the fullness of being in the present. This is, in principle, a decisive turning of world-historical significance. The deliberate turning of the people of the religion of history to the religion of nature is a moment of *kairos* fully in keeping with the twentieth century's return to primal origins and primal circularities.[27]

This striking passage shows the imprint of much modern nature-romanticism as well as of Nietzsche and his heirs, and an iconoclastic, though dubious mixture of Freudianism, paganism, naturalism, and eroticism. Space prevents extended analysis of this syncretism but four theses require comment in the context of the Holocaust. The first is that Rubenstein misunderstands the innermost character of Zionism. Certainly the Jew, through this decisive Zionist act, breaks out of the narrow parameters of his exilic existence and "break(s) with bourgeois existence as the characteristic form of Jewish social organization,"[28] (though to a more limited extent). But to

equate these Zionist realities with the "resurrection of the divinities of Israel's earth"[29] is sheer mythography.

Secondly, what is the "cash-value" of this return to nature à la Rubenstein? After one reads through it all there seems no actual program on which to build a life either for the individual or for the national community. The point seems to be that in some Freudian sense (as represented in Norman Brown's writings, for example, which Rubenstein specifically commends) men will be "happy" (i.e., not neurotic). But there is no clear sense of what this "happiness" really consists of either in Freud or in Brown—or in Rubenstein. Does Rubenstein, who, in his long opening essay in *After Auschwitz*, entitled "Religion and the Origin of the Death Camps," concentrates on anality as the key to decoding the Holocaust, really want to suggest that three thousand years of Jewish history—or even that of 1933–45—can be explained primarily by reference to toilet training and anal satisfaction and that all Israel's suffering now leads it to the "promised land" of sexual gratification above all else? "A new Jewish contribution [to mankind]," he tells us, may come from Zion, "the example of self-liberation and self-discovery, of mankind returned and restored to its only true hearth—the bosom of mother earth. . . ."[30] But what does this self-liberation and self-discovery amount to, consist of, lead towards? Nothing—for the article ends here—and nowhere in any of Rubenstein's writings is the missing answer supplied. Moreover, one would have thought that even in this new "natural" environment of the kibbutz and Zion, neuroses would not disappear altogether, given the sorts of beings we are, but rather new neuroses would replace the old ones, as indeed has happened on kibbutzim and in Israel generally.

Even if one were willing to grant Freudianism (or psychoanalysis more broadly defined) some limited therapeutic value, there is no evidence to suggest that it is able to provide a structural program for that reconstruction of society that would be equivalent in character to that utopian fulfillment envisioned by Rubenstein. Furthermore, let

27. *AA*, p. 136.
28. *AA*, p. 138.

29. *AA*, p. 142.
30. *AA*, p. 142.

us remember that Freudianism is not only as metaphysical and nonconfirmable as any traditional Jewish theology, allowing nothing to count against it and explaining all possible counterevidence away, but it also lacks any firm hermeneutical base or methodological rigor. That is to say, it is not even a particularly attractive metaphysical doctrine and thus its adoption as a basic truth is no particular strength or touchline to reality.[31] To think that psychoanalysis is the key to the unraveling the course of history, Jewish or otherwise, manifests a gross reductionism that fails to grasp or to grapple with the multifaceted ontological skeleton of reality. It should be noted, if I understand Rubenstein's more recent work (*The Cunning of History*, 1975) aright, that he has also come to see the real limitations of psychoanalysis as the main interpretive tool for excavating history and now would prefer a wider, more sociological, approach.

Third, this late in the history of philosophy it is odd to find someone extolling the values of nature per se. Nature is morally neutral; it will not provide the basis for any new comradeship of man with man. The return to nature, its deification and worship, is a blind idolatry without recompense. The dehumanization Rubenstein lays at the door of history, which is to be redeemed by the forces of nature, is in fact the very product of an incipient, if not explicit, naturalism, not its antithesis. Certainly the way to God (if He exists) and moral value must be *through* the world, the real world, the natural world. Assuredly no excessive asceticism, no illicit selfish escapism, no pitting of God against world, no Kierkegaardian either/or that tears God asunder from His creation, is to be allowed. Rubenstein, I believe, is aware of this, though he may see it only "through a glass darkly." Yet his solution to this ever-present threat of Manicheanism, which is to immerse man into nature without remainder, may well be his most consequential error. For out of nature can come no overcoming of the contradictoriness of existence, no lessening of the "absurdity" which surrounds us; rather it portends what it has always

portended: the cruel, amoral, "meaningless" drudgery of natural selection and survival.

In this connection let me say too that Rubenstein's forceful naturalistic imagery carries one along primarily because of its illicit anthropomorphizing and spiritualizing of blind forces. Only thus is nature equated with Spirit, or again with the demonic. However, this anthropomorphizing rests on philosophical improprieties rather than on phenomenological astuteness. This is not to deny that Rubenstein's mystification of nature is not powerfully evocative; rather, it is to assert that for all its appeal the mystical seductiveness attributed to nature is inapplicable.

Fourth, and perhaps most important, is an issue already hinted at: was it not precisely a mystical pagan naturalism that Nazism extolled? Was it not in the name of the pagan deities of primal origins that Europe was enjoined to shed the yoke of the Jewish God—"conscience is a Jewish invention," Himmler reminded the SS—and thus liberate itself to do all that had heretofore been "forbidden." Was it not the rejection of the taboos of good and evil associated with the God of the Covenant, a rejection now made possible by His "death," which made real the Kingdom of Night? Was it not that very romanticism of blood and land so deeply ingrained in German culture that Hitler appealed to when he spoke of the extermination of the Jew? Was it not in the name of "self-liberation" and "self-discovery" that six million Jews, and upwards of thirty million others, died? After Auschwitz, the very title of Rubenstein's most well-known work, is it not time to be afraid of naturalism and paganism and sceptical in the extreme about the purported health-restoring, life-authenticating, creative, organic, and salvific qualities claimed for them?

Conclusion

Rubenstein's deconstructive proposals are certainly to be reckoned with. They are provocative, intelligent, and thoughtful in many ways and my

31. On Freudianism as metaphysics see F. Cioffi and R. Borger, eds., *Explanation in the Behavioural Sciences* (Cambridge, 1970). See also the relevant essays in R. Wollheim, ed., *Freud: A Collection of Critical Essays* (New York, 1974). See as well the study by B. A. Farrell entitled *The Standing of Psychoanalysis* (Oxford, 1981).

serious reservations about them should not obscure these facts. They force us, as few other challenges do, to rethink our assumptions and our acceptance of the theological commonplace. However, as we have shown, his suggestions and substitutions for classical theology are deficient. Then again, there are those curious self-contradictions in his work that are both so interesting and yet so limiting. Perhaps the most striking of these is found at the end of the first essay in *After Auschwitz* which, in conclusion, I cite against Rubenstein himself. Speaking of the Nazis he wrote: "The final lesson may very well be that there is more realistic pleasure in the disciplines and norms of the Living God than in all the freedoms of the Dead God."[32]

The Crucifixion of the Jews: Ignaz Maybaum's Theology of the Holocaust

Elsewhere[1] we have described the quite extraordinary theological exposition of the Holocaust advocated by Ignaz Maybaum. Weaving together elements of traditional Jewish belief, Reform Jewish ideology, and Franz Rosenzweig's philosophy of history, Maybaum has suggested that the *Sho'ah* be understood through the application of Christological categories, especially that of the Crucifixion. Like Jesus of old, the Jews are an innocent vicarious sacrifice through which God elevates humankind to a new level of spiritual maturity. In support of this reading of recent Jewish history he has marshalled considerable Jewish learning and philosophical intelligence and has blended them together, not least because of his own deep belief both in God's reality and in His goodness. Yet this synthesis is not free of fundamental weaknesses and it is with an analysis of these limitations that the present essay will deal.

I

Let us begin by considering Maybaum's fundamental contention that Jewish history must work itself out in ways intelligible to the nations. This thesis is both correct and incorrect. It is correct insofar as it properly stresses the *contextual* character of Jewish history and the organic development of Judaism as a concrete phenomenon that proceeds in interdependence with the larger unfolding of world history. The all too common attempt to treat Jewish history as if it had existed at any period in a hermetically sealed ghetto is mistaken.[2] The inpenetrable ghetto exists only in the imagination of certain scholars. Yet alternatively, there is a valid distinction to be acknowledged between that internal Jewish history which is *not* totally reducible to, or even primarily intelligible through, an analysis of Judaism's external relations to the nations and its extrinsic history in which the nations play the dominant role. That is, there *is* a dimension of the Jewish past and present that is best understood as an autonomous socio-religious reality. In this mode Judaism and the Jewish people of course adopt and reshape external ideas and materials and, of necessity as well as choice, respond to outside events, but in these instances the choices are made according to an independent Jewish value system and inherent, particular rhythms.

32. *AA*, p. 44.
 1. See my essay "Jewish Faith After the Holocaust: Four Approaches," in my *Post-Holocaust Dialogues* (New York, 1983), pp. 141–173. (And now see the Maybaum selection above, pp. 402–408.)
 2. See, for example, the work of the great Jewish historian Salo Baron, *Social and Religious History of the Jews* (New York, 1952 on), who makes this point abundantly clear. See also Simon Dubnow's *World History of the Jewish People* (South Brunswick, New Jersey, 1967–1973). However, Dubnow's approach is not free of the weakness we are here discussing as is obvious when it is compared, for example, to the method adopted by David Pipes's essay on "Catherine the Great and the Jews," *Soviet Jewish Affairs*, Vol. 1, No. 3 (1972), pp. 20–40. See also Jacob Talmon's remarks on this issue in *The Unique and the Universal* (New York, 1965), pp. 64–90.

It is no easy matter to isolate and describe this special Jewish *Weltanschauung*, for as Jacob Talmon has correctly noted, "Jewish impulses and reactions, attitudes and sensitiveness, Jewish modes of feeling and patterns of behavior call for the intuition of the artist, and indeed can only be intimated by symbols, conjured up by the poetic incantation, and communicated by the art of the novelist."[3] Yet to deny this reality is to be ignorant of authentic Jewish life *as lived from within the tradition*. It is to reduce Judaism and the Jew to that set of external relations into which they enter either by choice or fate, while denying them any essential being that is truly their own. Moreover, it is to forget that it is simply irrelevant, for example, whether the non-Jewish world grasps the meaning of most halachic actions or the inner spirituality of *Ish ha-Halachah*[4] (Halachic man) for the Jewish significance of such behavior is not dependent on non-Jewish understanding. And yet the core of Jewish historical existence, certainly until very recently, was inseparable and unintelligible aside from such halachic behavior and its meta-halachic metaphysical justification which created the uniquely Jewish relationship to the world-historical. Conversely, if the nations of the world, as happened under Hitler, decide that Judaism has no more "meaning" for them, are Jews to willingly disappear? The world, of course, will have its way with Israel and it will understand Jewish life and its significance as it likes, but this perception is not all-inclusive and monopolistic, for at all times and places the Jew has his own perception of events and his own schematization of reality and its meaning. To fail to appreciate this two-sidedness of Jewish historical existence, as Maybaum does, is to fail to do justice to both the logic of the historiographical circumstance as well as the theological and ontological character of Jewish being in history. In respect of this interpretive limitation

Maybaum is a victim of his inheritance; that is, of those earlier modernizing attempts which sought to evaluate and interpret Judaism primarily through alien standards and for largely apologetic purposes, i.e., defending the continued vitality of Judaism as an authentic religious posture in post-Enlightenment, liberal Christian, European circles on the basis of an appeal to non-Jewish norms and structures.

This hermeneutic, this method of validating Judaism through the prism of norms not her own, is of considerable historical and philosophical significance. It is, of course, the major interpretive element in nineteenth- and much twentieth-century Jewish historiography and philosophy in which the criteria used to evaluate Judaism were drawn especially from Kantian, Hegelian, and Romantic schools of thought. The clearest expression and manifestation of this exercise is certainly to be seen in Reform Judaism, whose checkered nineteenth-century career we need not and cannot recount here. Maybaum is a direct heir of these ideological influences and, in particular, of their underlying philosophical assumptions. While this is a rich inheritance one must also be sensitive to its darker underside and to the negative consequences that flow from this methodological procedure if it is not balanced by other countervailing and complementary considerations. But Maybaum attacks this critical self-consciousness and as a result he fails to recognize the major danger which this approach inevitably entails when unadulterated by other values, namely, that Judaism loses all internal integrity. What is considered authentic and worth preserving in Judaism is dictated by the outsider (even if then internalized by Jews), e.g., those elements assimilable to Kantian morality in classical Reform theology and now in Maybaum's theology those phenomena which can be reinterpreted through reference to the

3. Jacob Talmon, op. cit., p. 70. Though I think Talmon essentially correct here and hence quote him approvingly he does get a bit carried away by his own rhetorical and "poetic" eloquence.

4. This is the title of Rabbi Joseph Soloveitchik's famous essay in *Talpiot* (1944) pp. 651–734 (in Hebrew). I have given a summary of Soloveitchik's views in my *Jewish*

Philosophers (New York, 1975), pp. 215–221. On Soloveitchik's position regarding *Halachah* see also David Singer and Moshe Sokol's article: "Joseph Soloveitchik: Lonely Man of Faith," *Modern Judaism* Vol. 2, no. 3 (September, 1982); and Rachel Shihor, "On the Problem of Halakhah's Status in Judaism," *Forum* (Spring–Summer, 1978), pp. 146–153.

Crucifixion and related Christian theological categories.[5]

We must ask Maybaum, did God enter into covenantal relation with Abraham and his heirs only so as to crucify them? Does being Jewish mean primarily, essentially, being a "lamb for the slaughter?" Is there not something intrinsic, essential, about the Jewish relationship to God which is the Jews' alone? Some inner reality, some special holiness, some particular "priestliness" that is not dictated by the needs of the nations but rather by the intimacy of covenantal existence. One feels the need to insist that Judaism does embody truth in its own unique fashion, that it does possess its own logic and substantiality, its own creativity and normativity, its own facticity, its own internal meaning which connects it to God as well as to the nations, and that these relationships are truly dialectical and predicated on a mutual integrity, so that Judaism will not ultimately be negated altogether. Were it otherwise, were Judaism of worth only insofar as it measured up to the prescriptive ideals of others, then there would be nothing valuable about Judaism per se, nor, and here is the rub, would its decline or even disappearance matter except for atavistic or nostalgic reasons. Moreover, and to rephrase and expand a point made parenthetically above, were Judaism to exhaust its "meaning" for the non-Jewish world either according to its internal calculus or, as seems more likely, in the equation of the nations, does this require by some inner logic that Judaism evacuate all realms of self-meaning and obligate Jews to commit collective ideological suicide in some form of mass assimilation? Or rather, is it not possible, indeed actual, for Judaism to be value-laden and life-enriching for its adherents in *irreplaceable* ways on

bases altogether other than those dictated by the needs of the nations?

It is here, and only now, that we can enter into dialogue with Maybaum's adoption of *Churban*[6] (unavoidable national tragedy) and hence "Crucifixion" as the master code which must be applied to Jewish history to make it intelligible *even to Jews.* Offered as a Jewish theology of history, this thesis is a particularly extreme example of interpreting Judaism in non-Jewish, or, more narrowly still, Christian terms.[7] This Christocentric orientation is, of course, taken over, with modification, from Maybaum's great mentor Franz Rosenzweig, but this does not make it true; it merely makes it an error with a pedigree. It will be recalled that Rosenzweig, after his near conversion to Christianity, fashioned a remarkable Jewish vision that in effect accepted the Christian account of Western history and its interpretation of the roles of Israel and the Church in the world. But having accepted this portrayal, he departed from the Christian script by transforming Judaism's ahistoricity into a virtue.[8] History, Rosenzweig affirmed, does belong to Christianity but this is not a sign of the Divine rejection of Israel but of Israel's immediate and eternal meta-historic relation to God. Through this inversion Rosenzweig transmuted Jewry's unenviable this-worldly circumstance into a blessing and Jewish oppression into a mark of transcendental love.

Even in Rosenzweig's pre-Holocaust form this argument met with great resistance; few Jewish thinkers, despite the near-universal homage paid to Rosenzweig's memory, are Rosenzweigians in this respect. In Maybaum's sharpened post-*Sho'ah* version, emphasizing the role of vicarious victim, of the six million as the Christ of our age, the

---

5. This use of the "Crucifixion" by German (and other Western) Jewish intellectuals to express their deepest sense of tragedy is an important index of their assimilation. They lack a fully Jewish, Jewishly formed and saturated, imagination.

6. Maybaum's use of this notion and its significance is explained in the essay "Four Responses," cited in n. 1.

7. The same substitution has, of course, been made in the name of Marxism, Socialism, Humanism, etc. in the modern era.

8. See on this F. Rosenzweig, *Stern der Erlosung (Star of Redemption,* New York, 1971). See also A. Altmann,

"Franz Rosenzweig on History" in A. Altmann, ed., *Between East and West* (London, 1958), pp. 194–214. See also Maybaum's comments on Rosenzweig in *Face of God After Auschwitz* (Amsterdam, 1965), pp. 170 ff. For the details of Rosenzweig's near conversion to Christianity, see N. Glatzer, *Franz Rosenzweig* (New York, 1953); and A. Altmann's and D. Emmett's edition of the letters of Eugen Rosenstock Huessey and Franz Rosenzweig which appeared under the title *Judaism Despite Christianity* (New York, 1969).

thesis is still more problematic. And it is problematic not least because Maybaum misunderstands the ontological and theological circumstances that allow Christian theology to affirm that "Christ died for the sins of mankind." Christians are able to make this declaration for (at least) two cardinal reasons. The first and most weighty is that Christ is believed to be God Incarnate, the Second Person of the Trinity; the Crucifixion is God taking the sins of mankind *on Himself.* He is the vicarious atonement for mankind. There is thus no terrible cruelty or unspeakable "crime" but only Divine Love, the presence of unlimited Divine Grace. Secondly, the human yet divine Christ, the Hypostatic Union of man and God, mounts the Cross voluntarily. He willingly "dies so that others might live." How very different was the *Sho'ah.* How very dissimilar its victims (not martyrs) and their fate. The murdered, including the million Jewish children, were not Divine— they were all too human creatures crushed in the most unspeakable brutality. If God was the cause of *their* suffering how at odds from the traditional Christian picture, for here God purchases life for some by sacrificing others, not Himself. Here Grace, if present, is so only in a most paradoxical way, and certainly not in the reality of the victims. Here there is only Golgotha, Crucifixion, Death; there is no Easter for the crucified ones. Furthermore, the Jews were singled out "unwillingly," they were *not* martyrs in the classical sense though we may wish to so transform their fate for *our* needs. There were of course those who willingly died for *Kiddush Ha-Shem*[9] (dying as martyrs for the "sanctification of the Divine Name"), but they were a small, very special minority. The majority of Jews died otherwise.

The *disanalogy* of the Holocaust and Good Friday would yet reveal something more. According to Maybaum the symbol of the Crucifixion is that of vicarious atonement. But given the circumstances of this vicarious sacrifice, of

Auschwitz and Treblinka, of *Einsatzgruppen* and gas chambers, is it not the case that the nature of the atonement is far more criminal and infinitely more depraved than the sins for which it atones? What sort of reconciliation can the work of Himmler and the SS have been? What sort of *kohanim* (priests) were these and what sort of sacrifice can they bring? Can one truly envision God, the God of Israel, making such vicarious expiation? And who makes amends for the Nazis? Are their sins not beyond all reparation? Is the world not forever darkened by the ashes of the crematoriums and the screams of the murdered millions? Is not reality more alienated from God as a consequence of the Holocaust than ever it was before it? To equate "Planet Auschwitz" with atonement, or in Maybaum's special typology of *Churban* with progress, seems, in this light, an absurdity. For this reason one feels obligated to raise against Maybaum's thesis the same objection one raises against the Free-Will Defense when it is employed in a Holocaust context,[10] namely, that if the Holocaust is the price of freedom, or in this case of progress and expiation, then better to do without such evolution and reconciliation—the price is just too high. It is morally and theologically unacceptable. To insist on it is to turn God, *kivyachol*[11] ("as if one could say this"), into a moral monster.

An impossible irony also discloses itself as a corollary of Maybaum's suggestion that God used Hitler for His purposes. If the *Sho'ah* is God's Will, if Hitler is "My servant," then to resist Hitler is to resist God; to fight the Nazis is to fight the Lord. As such the Warsaw ghetto resisters, the inmates who rebelled at Treblinka, the "righteous of the nations" who risked death, and more often than not died, to save Jewish lives, all these were rebels against the Almighty. The SS were God's angels of death while the Jews and their precious few allies were enemies of Heaven. This entailment, however, is offensive

9. Eliezer Berkovits' several works on the Holocaust emphasize such behavior. See for example his *Faith After the Holocaust* (New York, 1973); *Crisis and Faith* (New York, 1976); and *With God in Hell* (New York, 1979). Emil Fackenheim's newest book dealing with the Holocaust, entitled *To Mend the World* (New York, 1982), also gives such behavior a more prominent place than heretofore.

10. See my exegesis and critique of Eliezer Berkovits' response to the Holocaust in this anthology, pp. 601–608.
11. This is the traditional rabbinic phrase used to qualify what seem overly anthropomorphic statements about the Divine.

in every way: it requires an inversion of all sanity, all morality, and all that is theologically authentic. As such it must be rejected and rejected totally.

II

Necessarily allied to the doctrine of vicarious atonement in Maybaum's exegesis of Crucifixion is the notion of progress, i.e., Crucifixion interpreted as vicarious atonement makes progress possible. As one reflects upon this metaphysical presupposition, however, it becomes ever less compelling. To begin with it is not the universal historical explanatory category Maybaum presumes. While it does work suggestively, if not examined too closely, as an "explanation" of the *Sho'ah* it does not seem to fit the historical realities appertaining to the destruction of the First or Second Temples as Maybaum suggests.[12] Christianity did not exist in 586 BCE and was only a splinter group within Judaism in 70 CE; there is therefore no justification for conveying the meaning of 586 or 70 to the Babylonians or Romans in terms of the essentially Christian idea that "progress is achieved through sacrifice." They would have found this Christological idea, along with the modern notion of progress, unintelligible.[13] The ancients certainly utilized sacrifice as the main means of relating to the gods, but this relationship was not based on an understanding of history as progressive. Rather sacrifice was seen as expiatory and appeasing. Similarly from the Jewish side, the events of 586 and 70 were not seen as moments of spiritual ascent but of spiritual descent; the Exile of the *Shechinah* (Divine Presence) as well as of Israel. Exile is not a desirable state of spiritual exaltation, it is a mark of sin and alienation. Jews mourn on *Tisha b'Av*, they do not celebrate. Of course, Maybaum might contend in reply that "God's ways are a mystery" and therefore that it matters little, if at all, that the ancients did not grasp the significance, the prog-

ress, embedded in the events in which they participated and to which they gave witness. But this reply will not do, for the essence of Maybaum's claim is that progress is possible only through sacrifice because this is all the nations comprehend, i.e., God has to speak to them, has to rouse them, in their language. But if, as we would contend, the ancients, including the Jews, did not perceive matters this way at all, did not assimilate this sign-language in this manner, then the entire argument collapses under the weight of its own internal premises. Alternatively, if Maybaum still insists that God brought about progress nonetheless and even without the understanding of the contemporary participants then the argument has shifted in character and destruction now becomes something required by God, not man, for progress to occur. Thus the Holocaust, too, is a Divine, not a human, prerequisite. But if so then God is simply, as far as we can fathom, immoral. What else can we say of a God who executes an undeserved Holocaust for His requirements?

But let us move beyond these more cosmic considerations and turn to the application of the Maybaumian thesis to the Holocaust. The issue then becomes: What progress has resulted from the *Sho'ah*? What advance has been achieved because of Auschwitz? The world as a whole is unequivocally not an appreciably better place. Since 1945 mass murder has occurred in Uganda, Biafra, Vietnam, Cambodia, Rwanda, Yugoslavia, Sudan, Burundi, India, Pakistan, and parts of Central and South America.[14] The "nations" have been slow to learn any ethical imperative from the *Sho'ah*.

III

The subject of Zionism, the re-establishment of a Jewish state in Israel, demands another word. With regard to an attempt to fashion either a Jewish philosophy of history or a philosophy of

---

12. *Face*, p. 32 and elsewhere.
13. See on this, for example, Robert Nisbet's *History of the Idea of Progress* (New York, 1980).
14. For more on these mass murders see Leo Kuper, *Genpcide* (New Haven, 1982); and Jack Nusan Porter (ed.), *Genocide and Human Rights* (Washington, D.C., 1982). Both of these volumes contain helpful summaries of these events.

Jewish history, the State of Israel is as significant, if not more significant, than the Holocaust, and yet it is an event, a reality, that escapes if it does not altogether negate Maybaum's categories. For the meaning of Jewish history as disclosed through the State of Israel is the antithesis of the Crucifixion mentality. Jews have now declared (seemingly with God's permission): we have suffered enough, died enough, been put upon enough; we wish to reject forever our state of powerlessness! We wish to live in the Land of the Covenant in peace with man and God. In this way the flow of Jewish history itself has provided the most telling of all objections to Maybaum's theodicy insofar as Maybaum revels in Jewish powerlessness and the lack of a public Jewish dimension. The tragic paradox in all this, of course, is that the State of Israel is the most significant evidence of "progress" that Maybaum could appeal to—but ironically, even bizarrely, it is a datum that he must reject because of the larger metaphysical construct to which his theory of progress is tied.

Here two metaphysical systems mix and reinforce each other. The first is the a-Zionist,[15] ahistorical Rosenzweigian perspective that views Jewish settlement outside of Israel as part of the cosmic design for the Jewish people which has now fulfilled its historic mission and is, in Rosenzweig's language, "with God" while the "nations," immersed as they are in history, are still on their way, through Christianity, to this end. The second is Reform Judaism's reconstruction of the idea of the "Jewish mission to the gentiles" which positively values Jewish life "among the nations." From both perspectives the Diaspora is a "consummation devoutly to be wished" rather than a state whose end is longed for night and day. But in reaction we must say that whatever validity this outlook may

have had pre-1933 it has almost none today, certainly not as an anti-Zionist apologetic. Martin Buber already in the 1930s had written to the anti-Semitic theologian and Bible scholar, Gerhard Kittel, who had asserted that the Jews were true to their vocation only as aliens:

> Authentic Jewry, you say, remains faithful to the symbol of the restless and homeless alien who wanders the earth. Judaism does not know of such a symbol. The "wandering Jew" is a figure of Christian legend, not a Jewish figure.[16]

Properly modified Buber's rebuke is also a reply to Maybaum's enthronement of the Diaspora as the "goal" of Jewish life.

Another quotation from Buber from a not unrelated context is also apposite. In 1939 no less a figure than Mahatma Gandhi argued against Zionism. In reply Buber wrote:

> Dispersion is bearable; it can even be purposeful. If there is somewhere an ingathering, a growing home center, a piece of earth where one is in the midst of an ingathering and not in dispersion, and whence the spirit of the ingathering may work its way into all the places of the dispersion. When there is this, there is also a striving common life, the life of a community which dares to live today because it may hope to live tomorrow. But when this growing center is lacking, dispersion becomes dismemberment.[17]

Buber's answer to Gandhi may also serve as a response to Maybaum, for he too would turn what Judaism always held was the temporary, negative, status of *galut* (exile) into a cardinal blessing.[18]

The State of Israel has, of course, to be understood aright in this connection. It is not only a political reality—though there is nothing wrong with a "mere" Jewish political reality, nor is there

---

15. Maybaum is an ideological anti-Zionist, not an active physical opponent of the State of Israel as, for example, are Satmar Hasidim and members of Naturei Karta. See *Face*, pp. 28 ff., and elsewhere.

16. Translated and reprinted in F. Talmage, ed., *Disputation and Dialogue* (New York, 1975), p. 53. I cite this particular passage not to equate Maybaum and Kittel but because his position is directly related to the Christian-Rosenzweigian reading of post-70 C.E. Jewish history.

17. Martin Buber to Gandhi, translated in W. Herberg, ed., *The Writings of Martin Buber* (New York, 1958), p. 28.

18. Even in *galut* Jews controlled their own immediate "space." This was one of the remarkable features of Jewish communal life through all the various stages of the Exile as represented by various *Kehilla* organizations and structures. See, for example, Salo Baron's *Jewish Community*, 3 volumes (Philadelphia, 1942); and Louis Finkelstein's *Jewish Self-Government in the Middle Ages* (New York, 1924). See also Yitzchak Baer, *Galut* (New York, 1961).

anything "mere" about it—but it is also a primary theological datum, for Christians no less than for Jews. For Jews the reason is transparent if not self-evident:[19] this is an act of redemption, if the God of Israel lives. For Christians Zionism must also be a theological commitment after Auschwitz because, as Emil Fackenheim has recently described it:

> No less than Jews themselves, Christians must wish Jewish existence to be liberated from dependence on charity. On behalf of their partners in dialogue, they must wish independence from charity-in-general. On behalf of their own Christianity, they must wish it from Christian charity-in-particular. The post-Holocaust Christian must repent of the Christian sin of supersessionism. One asks: How can he trust in his own repentance—that it is both genuine and complete? There is only one answer: If he supports firmly and unequivocally the Jewish search for independence not only from the power of its enemies but also from that of Christian friends. Without Zionism—Christian as well as Jewish—the Holy Spirit cannot dwell between Jews and Christians in dialogue.[20]

IV

One last matter of consequence remains, Maybaum's conception of God. Put more exactly, what persists as an occasion for astonishment as well as perplexity is Maybaum's willingness to affirm not only that God was present in the Holocaust but that Hitler was His agent. In advancing this claim Maybaum follows the logic of his commitment to God's presence in the here and now further, more radically, and more consistently than do others who likewise want to locate the Almighty in history but who, at one and the same time, are unwilling to draw this consequence from the common premise. As the prophet Jeremiah saw Nebuchadnezzar, the destroyer of Jerusalem, as the "servant of God" (Jer. 27:6) so Maybaum is willing to consciously paraphrase

Jeremiah's idiom and give expression to the terrifying paradox: "Hitler, My servant!"[21]

> Hitler was an instrument... God used this instrument to cleanse, to purify, to punish a sinful world; the six million Jews, they died an innocent death; they died because of the sins of others.[22]

Yet what does this "explanation" entail vis à vis the 'Lord of Hosts'? What kind of Divinity would use the murder of six million Jews and countless others for purposes of purification? Would use the SS as His instruments of purification? What kind of Diety would employ vicarious atonement as experienced at Auschwitz for any reason whatsoever? The moral equation of means and ends must enter into the picture here and now. It is not enough to declare:

> How terrible that we paid for this progress with the death of six million martyrs. Can you understand it? I cannot. You cannot. It is not for us to understand. For us it remains to praise the works of God.[23]

Suggestive as such faith is Maybaum owes us more than this, because he has ventured to go beyond faith to understanding through his typology of *Churban* and the meaning it imputes to the Jewish victims of Nazism. This contended meaning requires that we comprehend that God willingly, indeed causally, created the "Kingdom of Night" and purposefully consigned the Jews to be consumed in it. But if this hell is the means then what can be its end? That there is a Creator can still be affirmed. But can one, does one care to, pray to this Being? Has not the God of Israel, of the Covenant, of redemption, become another casualty of the *Sho'ah*?

Maybaum seeks to use the Holocaust as a medium of communication between Heaven and earth, but could the Maker of all things not speak to the world in a less horrific way? That is to say, it is one thing to attribute the Holocaust to men, as

19. It is not self-evident as there are groups like the *Naturei Karta* and Satmar Hasidim who deny the State of Israel positive theological meaning. I believe they are wrong, fundamentally and inexcusably wrong, in this regard, but this is another matter.

20. Emil Fackenheim, *To Mend the World* (New York, 1982), p. 297.
21. *Face*, p. 67.
22. *Face*, p. 67.
23. *Face*, p. 64.

many do,[24] but once one attributes it directly—causally—to God, it becomes impossible to understand or to justify, for an omnipotent, omniscient Being must be able to instruct His creation and to lead it where He will in ways other than Auschwitz. If He cannot then He is not the all-encompassing Absolute of Maybaum's metaphysics. If He does not then He is not the moral Deliverer of Judaism. Thus, while Maybaum is willing to follow the logic of omnipotence to its seemingly logical end, i.e., that God must be the real cause of the Holocaust, he totally fails to grapple with the deeper dilemma posed by theodicy, namely, the defense of God's attributes of love and justice. If there is only Divine Power to contend with there is no problem of theodicy to begin with—an all-powerful Deity could indeed do what Maybaum contends. But could an *El melech channun ve rachamim* (a "long-suffering and merciful God") do so? Could the Lord of the Covenant truly employ a "Hitler, My servant!" Once we juxtapose these complementary Divine attributes of mercy and love against Divine might, it becomes impossible to accept either Maybaum's logic or his ontology.

Conclusion

Admirable as Maybaum's refreshing willingness to draw difficult conclusions from his premises is, in the final analysis his "explanations" do not explain the theological dilemmas posed by the Holocaust. Rather, they merely push them one step further back, where they reappear with a new vigor. Thus, at best, Maybaum's attempt merely shifts, while it does not solve, the problem of continued Jewish belief after Auschwitz. At worst, it makes it impossible to be a "believing Jew," for who wants to believe in, to pray to, a God who would use the likes of a Hitler as His instrument against innocent men, women and children?[25] Then too, even the blessing and sustenance that is the State of Israel is denied by Maybaum's curious ontological presuppositions. If this is where Maybaum's theology leads us it is time to transcend it and open ourselves once again to the living reality of Judaism and the Jewish people. Hence, Maybaum's account can only be judged an unacceptable, if not uninteresting, response to the theological crisis of our time.

ELIEZER BERKOVITS'S POST-HOLOCAUST JEWISH THEODICY

There is much that is moving, even eloquent in Eliezer Berkovits's discussion of the implications of the Holocaust for Jewish faith. Two factors in particular shine through: his devotion to and great love for the People Israel—what tradition calls *ahavat yisroel* (love of Israel)—and his mastery of the world of traditional Jewish learning. The latter, in particular, separates him from most of the other philosophers and theologians who have publicly responded to the theological challenge posed by the Holocaust and the difference in tone and the depth of resonance as a consequence of this rabbinical erudition is striking. In addition, Berkovits's nonradical, more traditional response along the lines of classical theodicy has much intellectual force, certainly more than some of the

---

24. As, for example, do three other "Holocaust theologians," R. Rubenstein, Emil Fackenheim, and Eliezer Berkovits, whose work appears above.

25. Certain Orthodox thinkers also hold that Hitler was God's agent, but with an important difference. For them Hitler was an instrument used to mete out Divine Punishment for various "sins" committed by the Jewish people. See here, for example, R. Joel Teitelbaum (the Satmar Rebbe), *Va'Yoel Moshe*, 3 volumes (Brooklyn, 1959–1961) (in Hebrew); and R. Chaim Eleazar of Munkacs (the Munkacer Rebbe),

Divrey Torah (Munkacs, 1929) (in Hebrew). This still puts God in a terrible light as far as I can see for what sin could Israel have committed to merit such a "punishment." (The Satmar Rebbe identified the "sin" as Zionism, others identify it as "Reform Judaism.") But it does transform the equation in certain basic ways and is certainly more in keeping with traditional Jewish thought, if also, in Teitelbaum's hands and others of his ilk, a perversion of it. See also the essay by Rav I. Hutner reprinted above, pp. 557–564.

novel alternatives. It also has the advantage of calling attention to important elements that need to be considered in any adequate post-Auschwitz theology, elements that other thinkers of a more radical persuasion ignore or underplay. Yet, in the final analysis, neither the rabbinical learning nor the dependence upon and reference to the great Western tradition of theodicy is fully adequate to the issue of the *Sho'ah*.[1]

I

The premise of Berkovits's position is his contention that the *Sho'ah* is not historically unique and therefore does not raise original issues for Jewish theology. This denial of uniqueness, and its concomitant conclusion that the Holocaust does not force Judaism into new and unprecedented reactions and transformations, is what distinguishes Berkovits from the other major theologians[2] who have wrestled with this issue. According to Berkovits, Auschwitz is unique in the magnitude of its horror but *not* in the dilemma it presents to religious faith. "From the point of view of the problem," he writes, "we have had innumerable Auschwitzs."[3] With this declaration we are provided with the basic axiom of Berkovits's entire response to the Holocaust. If Auschwitz is only the repetition of an ancient pattern then the entire nature of the challenge it poses is altered; or perhaps still more accurately, one might say that the magnitude of the Holocaust makes no difference theologically. For the theological conundrum, as Berkovits sees it, is the same whether one Jew or six million are slaughtered. Each raises the question: How could God permit it? How does this

action square with God's providential presence and moral perfection?

> While in absolute terms the horrors of the German death camps by far surpassed anything that preceded it, in terms of subjective experience the impact of the catastrophe on the major tragic occasions of Jewish history was no less intense than the impact of the horrors of our own experience. The problem of God's providential presence is always raised in relationship to man's subjective experience of His presence. The objective quantitative magnitude of the tragedy has little to do with it. It is for this reason that while the holocaust is unique in the objective magnitude of its inhumanity, it is not unique as a problem of faith resulting from Jewish historical experience. Indeed, one might say that the problem is as old as Judaism itself.[4]

This conclusion, however, cuts two ways. On the one hand, my own research[5] quite clearly confutes Berkovits's simple assimilation of the Holocaust to previous national catastrophes in the history of the Jewish people. Historically speaking, the *Sho'ah* does represent a *novum* in Jewish history, a *novum* whose essential distinctiveness is captured by the need for a new word to describe it—genocide.[6] Hence I disagree with Berkovits' historical analysis of the Holocaust as it presents itself as a theological datum. The Holocaust does require that we rethink (this does not mean change!) our traditional theological modalities, that we test our inherited "categories" against its novelty. Not to do so is not to recognize the full magnitude and character of the *Sho'ah*; it is to hide from a full frontal confrontation with Auschwitz.

1. Berkovits has written three books that deal with the Holocaust. They are: *Faith After the Holocaust* (New York, 1973); *Crisis and Faith* (New York, 1976); and *With God in Hell* (New York, 1979). The first of these sets out his overall theological position vis à vis the challenge posed by Auschwitz in its most extended form. Our remarks, while drawing on all three works, will thus concentrate on this work. Selections from Berkovits appear above, pp. 463–489.
2. Ignaz Maybaum, the German-English theologian, also denied the uniqueness of the Holocaust. For the details of his position see his *The Face of God After Auschwitz* (Amsterdam, 1965). See selections above, pp. 402–408.

3. *Faith After the Holocaust*, p. 90 (hereafter referred to as *Faith*).
4. Ibid., p. 90. This is also Jacob Neusner's conclusion in his "The Implications of the Holocaust," in the *Journal of Religion* Vol. 53, No. 3 (1973), pp. 293–308, and now reprinted in his *Stranger at Home* (Chicago, 1981), pp. 65–81.
5. See my *The Uniqueness of the Holocaust*, (New York, 1994), Vol. I for more on this issue. Volumes 2–4 of this project are forthcoming.
6. The first use of the word to describe the *Sho'ah* is usually credited to Raphael Lemkin, *Axis Rule in Occupied Europe* (Washington, D.C., 1944), pp. 79–95.

Alternatively, this does not mean as Berkovits seems to feel, that on the basis of such a re-examination one will necessarily conclude that the tradition is inadequate or in need of revision. For the connection between historical uniqueness and the need for theological change in not self-evident. Thus, the proper procedure is to investigate the historical structure of the *Sho'ah* and then to ask, as a second step, what theological consequences, if any, flow from one's judgment regarding the historical events. Berkovits, however, does not follow this course. He fails to do the former because he knows in advance what he wants to protect vis à vis the latter. But this avoidance of the root issue leaves his conclusions even when correct, open to criticism, for it appears that they are cheaply won, predicated on a failure to face what happened to the Jewish people in the twentieth century. Contra Berkovits it needs to be recognized that the historical query concerning "uniqueness" is one thing, and the theological understanding of what this might mean, though related, is another. One's preconceived conclusions regarding theological matters should not dictate one's answers to historical questions.

II

One could pick at the edges of Berkovits' position at length but the center of his argument turns on his advocacy of a traditional "free will" theodicy. Therefore one can cut to the heart of the matter by turning directly to a scrutiny of his presentation of this defense. Taking his cue from the biblical doctrine of *hester panim* ("the Hiding Face of God"), Berkovits claims that God's hiddenness is required for man to be a moral creature. God's hiddenness brings into being the possibility for ethically valent human action, for by "absenting" Himself from history He creates the reality of human freedom which is necessary for moral behavior. For human good and human evil to be real possibilities God has to respect the decisions of mankind and be bound by them. Among the necessary corollaries of this ethical autonomy is that God has to abstain from reacting immediately to immoral deeds, and cer-

tainly from acting in advance to suppress them. But it is just here that the fundamental paradox emerges: for a moral humanity to exist freedom must exist, yet it is the nature of freedom that it is always open to the possibility of abuse.

The corollary of this, as Berkovits understands the situation, is that "while He [God] shows forbearance with the wicked, He must turn a deaf ear to the anguished cries of the violated."[7] Consequently, the paradoxical reality that flows from this Divine Circumstance is that humanity is impossible if God is strictly just, while if God is loving beyond the requirements of strict justice there will be human suffering and evil.

> One may call it the divine dilemma that God's *erek apayim*, His patiently waiting countenance to some is, of necessity, identical with His *hester panim*, His hiding of the countenance, to others.[8]

Auschwitz is a paradigmatic instantiation of this truth.

What is one to say to this argument? The first thing is, I think, that in the face of the *Sho'ah* this millennial-old theodicy is as coherent as any of those, new or old, that has been proposed, even if not fully convincing. The second thing is that Berkovits reveals his mature theological intuition by opting for this gambit as his "response." The third is that the many dramatic, intensely moving, examples of Jewish heroism in the face of Nazism that Berkovits cites in his studies do help advance a case for the existence of evil as a possibility which must be allowed by God in order for there to be true human freedom; and also for the reality of evil as an ingredient in the generation of certain "goods," for example, love and compassion, fidelity and courage. Granting all this, however, two pressing difficulties remain. With regard to human autonomy and while recognizing its two-sidedness all the more because of Berkovits's discussion of Jewish heroism in the camps and elsewhere, an ancient enquiry reasserts itself: "Could not God, possessed of omniscience, omnipotence, and absolute goodness, have created a world in which there was human freedom but no evil?" And secondly, "Even if certain 'goods' are generated by overcoming or in re-

7. *Faith*, p. 106.

8. Ibid., p. 107.

sponse to evil, couldn't God either have allowed the production of these goods without so much evil, or, more radically still, wouldn't it be preferable if there were no such goods given the evil (and suffering) needed to produce them?" Let us examine each of these questions in turn.

The issue as to whether God could have created a world in which men always freely choose to do the good has been given a particularly tight formulation by J. L. Mackie. In a well-known article in *Mind* he commented:

I should query the assumption that second order evils are logically necessary accompaniments of freedom. I should ask this: if God has made men such that in their free choices they sometimes prefer what is good and sometimes what is evil, why could he not have made men such that they always freely choose the good? If there is no logical impossibility in a man's freely choosing the good on one, or on several, occasions, there cannot be a logical impossibility in his freely choosing the good on every occasion. God was not, then, faced with a choice between making innocent automata and making beings who, in acting freely, would sometimes go wrong: there was open to him the obviously better possibility of making beings who would act freely but always go right. Clearly, his failure to avail himself of this possibility is inconsistent with his being both omnipotent and wholly good.[9]

Many theologians and philosophers have replied to Mackie's challenge, the most cogent counter being Alvin Plantinga's. For our present purposes, I am prepared to admit his general conclusion, which I cite at length.

THE FREE WILL DEFENSE VINDICATED

Put formally, the Free Will Defender's project is to show that

(1) God is omniscient, omnipotent, and wholly good is consistent with

(2) There is evil.

What we have seen (in a previous argument) is that

(3) It was not within God's power to create a world containing moral good but no moral evil

is possible and consistent with God's omnipotence and omniscience. But then it is clearly consistent with (1). So we can use it to show that (1) is consistent with (2). For consider

(1) God is omnipotent, omniscient, and wholly good

(3) It was not within God's power to create a world containing moral good without creating one containing moral evil

and

(4) God created a world containing moral good.

These propositions are evidently consistent— i.e., their conjunction is a possible proposition. But taken together they entail

(2) There is evil.

For (4) says that God created a world containing moral good; this together with (3) entails that He created one containing moral evil. But if it contains moral evil, then it contains evil. So (1), (3), and (4) are jointly consistent and entail (2); hence (1) is consistent with (2); hence set A is consistent. Remember: to serve in this argument (3) and (4) need not be known to be true, or likely on our evidence, or anything of the sort; they need only be consistent with (1). Since they are, there is no contradiction in set A; so the Free Will Defense appears to be successfull.[10]

9. J. L. Mackie, "Evil and Omnipotence," originally published in *Mind*, Vol. 44, No. 254 (1955). Reprinted in L. Urban and D. Walton (eds.), *The Power of God* (New York, 1978), pp. 17–31. This quote is from p. 27. A similar position has also been advanced by A. Flew, "Divine Omnipotence and Human Freedom," in *New Essays in Philosophical Theology* (New York, 1955), ch. 8. A counter argument has been provided by, among others, Ninian Smart, "Omnipotence, Evil and Su-

permen," in *Philosophy* Vol. 36, No. 137 (1961). Smart's position has in turn been criticized by H. J. McCloskey, *God and Evil* (The Hague, 1974), pp. 103–105.

10. A. Plantinga, *God, Freedom and Evil* (New York, 1974), pp. 54–55. I have revised the numbering of the various propositions in this argument. Plantinga's numbering being different because part of a larger thesis, e.g., my number (2) is his (3), my (3) his (35), my (4) his (36).

Berkovits provides nothing logically comparable to Plantinga's reasoning, but I am willing[11] to allow Plantinga's analysis to stand in defense of Berkovits's championing of the "free will" position, recognizing that Berkovits would endorse both Plantinga's procedure and conclusion.

However, this vindication pushes us another step and here I demur from Plantinga's and Berkovits's position. For the problem now becomes: "Could not God have created a world in which there was human freedom but *less* evil (as compared to no evil)?" Again Plantinga (and by inference Berkovits) answers "no" to this question[12] for, according to his analysis of the Free Will Defense, given genuine freedom, God cannot control the amount of evil in the world. But this "no" is not convincing, for the quantity of sheer gratuitious evil manifest during the Holocaust goes beyond anything that seems logically or metaphysically necessary for the existence of human freedom and beyond the bounds of "toleration" for an omnipotent, omniscient, and just God. One has only to recognize that given the belief in miracles, which Berkovits shares,[13] one miracle, even a "small" one, could have reduced some of the tragedy of the *Sho'ah* without cancelling the moral autonomy of the murderers. Thus it is logically conceivable and requires no great feat of the imagination to imagine a world in which there was less evil.

As to the second question, it increasingly seems to me that it would have been preferable, morally preferable, to have a world in which "evil" did not exist, at least not in the magnitude witnessed during the *Sho'ah*, even if this meant doing without certain heroic moral attributes or accomplishments. That is to say, for example, though feeding and caring for the sick or hungry is a great virtue it would be far better if there were no sickness or hunger and hence no need for such care. The price is just too high. This is true even for the much exalted value of freedom itself. For we recognize the need to limit freedom where evil consequences are concerned, for example, we allow convicts to be incarcerated so that they will not cause further evil, we limit the right to cry "fire" in a crowded theatre, we curtail the right to molest children, and the list goes on. That is to say, we recognize, as these examples indicate, that freedom is properly subordinated to the prevention of suffering and other undesirable consequences. In respect of the *Sho'ah* such a limitation on freedom would have clearly been preferable to the results of freedom run riot, whatever limited instances of good the evil of Auschwitz engendered.

At this juncture some might want to object that my refutation of the Free Will thesis and its attendant call to limit freedom in the face of the Death Camps has not confronted the truly radical implication of my own contention regarding autonomy and its restraints. This is because to suggest controlling Free Will would not mean only overriding the rights of individuals to do certain particular things, as in the examples just given, but also overcoming the basis for freedom altogether. This clarification rightly recognizes that Free Will is not equivalent to liberty of action being more fundamental and at the same time a necessary condition of morality. In reply, however, it seems cogent to advance the reservations introduced above, if with modification. Better to introduce limits, even limits on that freedom of the will requisite to moral choice, than to allow Auschwitz. Here it is salient to recognize that Free Will is not, despite a widespread tendency to so understand it, all of one piece. One can limit Free Will in certain aspects, that is with respect, for

---

11. I have technical philosophical reservations regarding Plantinga's argument. Given our present concern, however, we need not take them up here. For the sorts of issues that are relevant to a discussion of Plantinga's views see: J. E. Tomberlin and F. McGuiness, "God, Evil and the Free Will Defense," in *Religious Studies*, Vol. 13 (1977), pp. 455–475, which is critical of Plantinga's position. This paper has, in turn, been replied to by Del Ratzsch, "Tomberlin and McGuiness on Plantinga's Free Will Defense," *International Journal for the Philosophy of Religion*, Vol. 12, No. 4 (1981),

pp. 75–95; and by Robert Burch, "The Defense of Plenitude against the Problem of Evil," *International Journal for the Philosphy of Religion*, Vol. 12, No. 1 (1981), pp. 29–38. And idem., "Plantinga and Leibniz's Lapse," *Analysis*, Vol. 39, No. 1 (January, 1979), pp. 24–29. This should be taken as only a sample of the extensive secondary literature generated by Plantinga's important, if not fully convincing, work.

12. Ibid., pp. 55 ff.

13. On this issue of miracles and its relevance see the argument below.

example, to specific types of circumstances, just as one constrains action in particular ways. For example, a person can have a phobia about X which does not impair his unrestrained power of decision in regard to Y. Such a case reveals that the call to limit Free Will does not necessarily mean its total elimination but rather its powerful curtailment by, in our present context, a Divine Intelligence under conditions such as those that reigned supreme during the Holocaust. Consider, too, that God could have created a humankind that, while possessing Free Will, nonetheless also had a proportionately stronger inclination for the Good and a correspondingly weaker inclination to evil. He could also have endowed us with a greater capacity for moral education. Neither of these alterations in the scheme of things would have obviated the reality of Free Will though they would have appreciably improved humankind's moral record, perhaps even to the point of significantly reducing the moral evil done to the innocent by a Hitler.

Much of my disquiet with this whole line of defense lies in my somewhat different mode of reasoning about morality. In contradistinction to the habitual way of conceiving the problem of freedom's relation to morality, that is, no volitional autonomy no morality, one can and should turn the issue around and argue that if one has no, or smaller amounts of, evil to contend with, Free Will is less necessary because those virtues generated through its exercise, e.g., concern, love, etc., are not required in the same way. Macrocosmically, morality is a good not least because it helps us make our way in an evil world; eliminate or lessen the evil we encounter and the need for morality declines correspondingly.

From this angle of vision it becomes clear that the Jobian thesis usually developed in this connection, that is, the view that suffering creates higher goods and in addition trains one's character, requires another look. It has been asserted that:

> The value-judgment that is implicitly being invoked here [in the Jobian thesis] is that one who

has attained to goodness by meeting and eventually mastering temptations, and thus by rightly making responsible choices in concrete situations, is good in a richer and more valuable sense than would be one created *ab initio* in a state either of innocence or of virtue. In the former case, which is that of the actual moral achievements of mankind, the individual's goodness has within it the strength of temptations overcome, a stability based upon an accumulation of right choices, and a positive and responsible character that comes from the investment of costly personal effort.[14]

This contention is not without interest as long as Job stays alive. But as a response to Auschwitz Job is not the right model for unlike Job of old the Jews in the death camps were not protected from destruction. Therefore, the Jobian defense of tragedy, of suffering as the occasion for growth and overcoming, has little relevance to the Holocaust.

The incremental conception is simply too naive, too optimistic. It emphasizes the positive value of evil as an aid to the growth and manifestation of goodness, but it ignores altogether the more telling fact that wickedness of the magnitude and quality unloosed by Nazism not only, or even primarily, increased our opportunities to display courage and love but even more—and essentially—destroyed forever such possibilities for six million Jews, including the all too many Jewish children whose youthful potential was never to be realized. Still more, the logic of this incremental thesis leads, if followed to its end, to an untenable conclusion. It suggests that good comes from, or in response to, evil, and that without evil there would be no heroism, no forgiveness, no love. The greater the malevolence the greater the heroism. The significance of Berkovits's constant invocation of instances of truly extraordinary moral heroism in the face of Nazi brutality turns on this contention. Yet the irony here is this: if an increase in the diabolic is defended by recourse to the greater good it produces, i.e., more heroism is generated by Nazism than by a lesser plague, then the proper goal to be

14. J. Hick, *Evil and the God of Love* (London, 1966), pp. 255–256. A similar argument is advanced by Gordon Kaufman in his *God The Problem* (Cambridge, 1972), pp. 171–200. Berkovits is explicitly sensitive to the

disanalogy involved in the Job metaphor per se (see *Faith*, pp. 67–70), though he uses the same argument in a more general way.

desired is a still greater Holocaust (God forbid) which would, by this line of reasoning, make for still more courage and fortitude. Thus if killing six million Jews caused a corresponding amount and kind of virtue, killing twelve million will produce, say, twice the amount and a still higher quality of moral nobility. But surely this is all wrong. The recognition of its absurdity forces us to acknowledge the inherent deficiency of the incremental thesis as exposed by the reality of the *Sho'ah*.

There is still another moral objection to this incremental line of reasoning. One can contend that selfless love or forgiveness, or faith and fortitude, are unavailable without that corruption to which they are a reaction, but even if one makes this case, which in itself is not an easy case to make, it does not justify the evil per se. To argue the contrary is to suggest that the Nazis were helping Jews be virtuous, and were assisting Jews in their ethical development. Likewise, is it morally acceptable to suggest that Jewish children should suffer disease and starvation, death by fire and by gas, so that others might have an opportunity to care for or comfort them? As to the children themselves, what sort of standard is involved? What moral improvement was achieved when Janus Korczak's orphans, and countless others like them, died in the ghettos and crematoriums? Their death contradicted that very freedom and moral autonomy that are at the base of the "Free-Will" defense. God's goodness is also impugned in the face of such barbarities. He, so the position contends, gave mankind freedom because He is gracious and compassionate, loving and concerned—but here His care for Nazis and for their freedom meant a total absence of solicitude for their victims.

III

The "free will" position becomes still more difficult to maintain when employed as a Jewish theodicy. The reason for this increase in complexity is the necessity of relating the "free will"

defense, as drawn in a more general philosophical way, with the God-idea of Judaism, i.e., the God of the Bible who is known to perform miracles in the face of overwhelming evil. Thus, it is not only a case of trying to decipher the world God set out to create in some theologically neutral sense but rather of understanding Jewishly why, given the exaggeratedly high cost of human freedom, God did not once again, as He had in the past, step into the flow of events and say "enough."

Berkovits is theologian enough to be aware that this is a serious objection and he tries to meet it:

> Man can only exist because God renounces the use of his power on him. This, of course, means that God cannot be present in history through manifest material power. Such presence would destroy history. History is the arena for human responsibility and its product. When God intervenes in the affairs of men by physical might as, for instance, in the story of Exodus, we speak of a miracle. But the miracle is outside of history; in it history is at a standstill.[15]

But this is an evasion, for the critical challenge simply needs to be rephrased: why, if God performed a miracle and entered history at the Exodus, did He show such great self-restraint at Auschwitz? Wasn't Auschwitz far worse than Egypt, Pharoah far more humane than Hitler? Given that history did not end because of the miracles connected with the Exodus why would a miracle at Auschwitz now "destroy history?" Given Berkovits's biblically rooted faith this line of defense is not plausible.

Then, too, if God did not intervene in the *Sho'ah*, even if one might still thereafter be able to defend His power by recourse to a Berkovits-like argument regarding Divine self-restraint, what happens in such an equation to God's love? Is a God who allows such total freedom, who does not act when human freedom takes on an apocalyptic character of frenzied sadism, still worthy of respect and admiration? Of being worshipped? In aid of the "Free Will" defense Berkovits might be able to argue with cogency that "God cannot

---

15. *Faith*, p. 109. Berkovits's preference for the term "miracle" is both correct and misleading. That is, we can grant the term and the correctness of its usage but this does not solve anything. The issue merely becomes why God did not perform a miracle.

608   Part III European and American Responses during and following the War

as a rule intervene whenever man's use of free-dom displeases him."[16] But surely Auschwitz is not a mere "whenever;" it was a time that de-manded just such interference.

IV

A further corollary of Berkovits's teaching is also worthy of mention. He recognizes that for all its logical suggestiveness the "Free Will" counter is not convincing.[17] Thus he feels compelled to add:

> all this does not exonerate God for all the suf-fering of the innocent in history . . . there must be a dimension beyond history in which all suffering finds its redemption through God. This is essential to the faith of a Jew.[18]

This well-worked proposal is tantamount to a confession that human freedom extorts too high a price; thus the traditional "crutch" of an afterlife is introduced without any justification to bolster the classical metaphysical and moral structure under pressure.

This other-worldly appeal, however, is less than adequate to the task. Besides the elemental difficulty of the absence of any legitimation being given for this belief in the Hereafter, the fact is that what this suggestion translates into is an appeal for compensation. God wrongs mankind and then tries to make up to it for the unjustifiable evil done. But just as we reject such compensatory actions as lesser goods in human relations, how much more so does it seem unworthy of God. It is this moral disquiet that makes the conclusion of

the Book of Job so unsatisfactory and which makes it more unsatisfactory still in the case of victims of the *Sho'ah*. God may "redeem" the suffering but it seems morally preferable that there should be no evil to redeem. Berkovits is right; this argument does not exonerate God.

There is also a deep irony in all this relating to the heart of the "free will" thesis. If there is a Heaven where one resides in bliss without the tensions and difficulties caused by freedom of choice, why did God not create such an Earth without freedom of choice and all of its terri-ble consequences? That is, if Heaven is better than earth with or without human autonomy why wouldn't a similarly structured earth, one in which Auschwitz would be impossible, be likewise good? And if so, the whole "free will" defense falls.[19]

Conclusion

Of the major thinkers who have had the courage to deal with the "meaning" and reality of the *Sho'ah*, Eliezer Berkovits has articulated the most conservative and traditional position. This conservatism has paid important dividends. For despite the lacunae in his work, he has gi-ven one of the most theologically and Jewishly convincing "responses" of all those who have taken part in the discussion. Thus, while his views cannot be accepted as the final word on the matter, he has pointed us in the direction of important truths that need further reflection and development.

---

16. Ibid., p. 105.
17. In his most recent book, *With God in Hell*, Berkovits elaborates on this weakness at some length. In addition to the appeal to a "Hereafter" he refers to three other Jewish "responses" to buttress the "free will" argu-ment. They are: the *Akedah*, the "Exile of the She-chinah," and the "Suffering Servant" motif. I shall not discuss Berkovits's treatment of these themes as they do not seem to me to advance appreciably the logic of the argument. Readers are referred to *With God in Hell*, pp. 124 ff., for Berkovits's presentation.
18. *Faith*, p. 136. This, of course, is a standard proposal often made in the past by theists. See, e.g., Kant's moral

theism as developed in a number of his works, and C. A. Campbell's *On Selfhood and Godhood* (London, 1959), among many other instances of this defense.
19. The possible counterargument some might advance, that Heaven is good because it is earned by good deeds, would not be relevant in the case I present. This because the causal mechanism whereby one gets to heaven does not account for, and is a different matter from, Heaven's intrinsic goodness. Heaven is good per se not because this is where righteous souls ascend to. Rather, righteous souls ascend to heaven because it is good.

"Voluntary Covenant": Irving Greenberg
on Faith after the Holocaust

One of the most widely discussed recent theological responses to the Holocaust is to be found in Irving (Yitz) Greenberg's challenging and provocative writings on this theme.[1] In this essay I would like to review and critique Greenberg's analysis of this difficult matter.

Critique

As the critical remarks that I am now about to offer are meant to be suggestive rather than exhaustive I shall present them *seriatim*.

(1) In responding to the many genuinely interesting philosophical and theological positions Greenberg has advanced there is, to begin, a certain unease that one has not quite captured his meaning completely. The source of this disquiet lies not only in the limits of one's own understanding but also in Greenberg's imprecise use of essential terms and ideas. Such elemental terms as "revelation," "messianic," "messianism," "history," "redemption," "real," "secular," "religious," are all used in a multiplicity of ways, aimed at a spectrum of differently informed listeners, and all are employed (perhaps in part intentionally) without any precising definitions being offered. Then again, his work suffers from a certain lack of logical rigor. This is evident both in the construction of particular arguments as well as in certain underlying architectonic features of Greenberg's thought as a whole. The most notable of these lapses, which is present so consistently that it should be seen as a structural flaw, is located in his hermeneutical overemployment of the notions "dialectic" and "dialectical" and in his unsatisfactory usage of the interrelated notion of "paradox." Merely holding, or claiming to believe, two contradictory

propositions simultaneously is *not* a fruitful theological procedure.

(2) Greenberg offers two seminal criteria of verification for theological discourse in our time. The first criterion is strikingly powerful in its directness and simplicity. It states: "No statement, theological or otherwise, should be made that would not be credible in the presence of burning children."[2] The second criterion, more philosophically sculpted and no doubt shaped in response to the Positivist verificationist challenge, reads as follows:

Faith is not pure abstraction, unaffected or unshaken by contradictory events; it is subject to "refutation." Yet it is not simply empirical either. A purely empirical faith would be subject to immediate refutation, but in fact the people of Israel may continue to testify in exile and after defeat. It may see or hope beyond the present moment to the redemption which will inevitably follow. Thereby, it continues to testify despite the contradiction in the present moment. In fact, when the redemption comes, it will be all the greater proof of the assertions of faith and of the reliability of God's promises because it will overcome the present hopeless reality. On the other hand, if redemption never came or if Israel lost hope while waiting for redemption, then the status quo would win and Jewish testimony would come to an end. Thus, faith is neither a simple product of history nor insulated from history. It is a testimony anchored in history, in constant tension with it, subject to revision and understanding as well as to fluctuation in credibility due to the unfolding events.[3]

While modern Jewish philosophers have tended to ignore the all-important challenge raised by requests for verification, here Greenberg,

1. See the selections of his work above, pp. 499–555.
2. Irving Greenberg, "Cloud of Smoke, Pillar of Fire: Judaism, Christianity, and Modernity after the Holocaust," in E. Fleischner, ed., *Auschwitz: Beginning of a New Era?* (New York, 1977), p. 23.

3. "Judaism and History: Historical Events and Religious Change," in Jerry V. Dillen, ed., *Ancient Roots and Modern Meanings* (New York, 1978), pp. 47.

astutely as well as courageously, meets it head-on. The question to be put to him, however, is whether his two formulations are adequate as principles of verification. Begin with the first formulation. It does not set out a straightforward empirical criterion. Empirical evidence will neither simply confirm it, nor as it is phrased in the negative, simply disconfirm it. There is no empirical statement E with which it is incompatible. That is, it is not, finally, a statement of an empirical sort. But this need not matter *decisively*, for it is not put as an empirical criterion; rather, its appeal is to the broader category of "credibility" and many things are credible that are not empirical. In this way, the task before us transforms itself into showing that "credible" is not used trivially, but this is a far more ambiguous and uncertain task than at first appears to be the case. Consider, for example, the remarks of the German Protestant Pastor Dean Grüber that had such a profound impact on Richard Rubenstein.[4] The Dean honestly held that Jewish children died for the crime of deicide committed by their First Century ancestors. Such "good" Christian theology was obviously "credible" to the Dean in the face of the Holocaust. Likewise, Satmar Hasidim and other right-wing orthodox Jews who continue to account for the Holocaust through recourse to the doctrine of "for our sins we are punished" (*mipnei chata'eynu*), remembering, for example, the terrible fate of the children of Jerusalem of old recounted in Lamentations which is credited to "our sins," also believe that their propositions are "credible." It thus becomes evident that *credible* is not a self-explanatory category of judgment. What is credible to Dean Grüber and the Satmar Rebbe is *incredible* to Greenberg—and the dispute between them is not resolved by appeal to the criterion Greenberg has established, as it would be were it a viable criterion. It turns out that what is "credible" depends on one's prior theological commitments, the very issue at stake. Accordingly, the argument becomes circular.

Consider now the second, more formal, criterion. It is attested to be falsifiable, "subject

to refutation," yet it is not, at the same time, a "simply empirical" proposition. The two conditions of "refutation" established are: (a) "Redemption never comes"; or (b) "if Israel lost hope while waiting for redemption, then the status quo would win." The first criterion appears, at least in what has been called a "weak" sense, to be empirically verifiable—i.e., it states a specific empirical condition under which it would, in principle, be disconfirmed. However, the established thesis is inadequate as a criterion because it turns on the temporal notion "never comes." Logically, we could not make any use of this norm until world history ended, in redemption or otherwise. At any time prior to the end of history an appeal could be made to "wait a minute more," hence putting off the empirical disconfirmation indefinitely. It certainly is not, *contra* Greenberg, a "testimony anchored in history..." in any strong sense, as immediate and available historical evidence, e.g., the obscene reality of the Death Camps, is deflected by appeal to the end that never is.

The second condition offered is of more interest. But it, too, is not sufficient for two reasons. First, the continued and continuing status of Israel's faith *qua* subjective affirmation is not a logical or ontological warrant for any proposition regarding "God's mighty Acts in History," Greenberg's claim to the contrary notwithstanding. What is disconfirmed "if Israel loses hope" is, of course, Israel's faith—i.e., the strength of its commitment—but the ontological content of the commitment is unaffected. Propositions such as "there is a God," or "God Redeems," or "History reveals a loving Providence," are neither confirmed by Israel's faith nor disconfirmed by Israel's apostasy.

Given the weak verification procedures proposed by Greenberg, his advocacy of faith in God after the *Shoah* would seem compatible with any empirical set of conditions. That is, there seems no empirical state of affairs that is actually incompatible with theism, especially Greenberg's particular exposition of theism.

(3) What is the relationship, if any, between the *Shoah* and *halachah* (Jewish law)? Does the *Shoah* justify *halachic* (religious-legal) transvaluations? Here one needs to go slowly. As a preliminary conclusion subject to revision it appears

4. On the details of this encounter see R. Rubenstein's article in *After Auschwitz* (Indianapolis, 1966), pp. 47–58.

to me that the *Shoah* does *not* legitimate either wholesale *halachic* change or a transformation in the fundamental structures of the *halachic Weltanschauung*.[5] Greenberg's extremely well-intentioned call for widespread and dramatic *halachic* innovation, for a *voluntary covenant* and the rest, even if made with enormous *ahavat Yisroel*, "love of Israel," may well be misguided. In any case, there seems no certain methodological or metaphysical bridge between Auschwitz and *halachah*, between Nazis killing Jews and the need for a Jewish-re-definition of *halachah*.

To avoid any misunderstanding let me repeat that this conclusion is not based on the denial of the 'uniqueness' of the Holocaust as is usually the case with more *halachic* orientations. Indeed I am convinced of the historical uniqueness, both in Jewish and in world-historical terms, of the *Shoah*.[6] However, having come to this conclusion, which I share, for various reasons, with Greenberg and the other post-Holocaust theologians such as Richard Rubenstein and Emil Fackenheim, I do not see any compelling logical or theological reason for equating this historical judgment with a mandate for *halachic* change. Historical uniqueness is one thing, the legitimating criteria for *halachic* change are something else and I am yet to see, or to have been shown, the bridge from one to the other.

(4) Revelation is a technical and awe/ful term. A term not heard often enough today even in theological circles yet, ironically, at times overused and almost always employed too loosely and imprecisely in contemporary discourse. These several thoughts are sparked by Greenberg's recurring, often imprecise or ambiguous theological employment of this theme, especially as it becomes decisive in relation to claims made by him for the putative revelatory character of the *Shoah* and the reborn State of Israel. From a narrowly Jewish theological perspective nothing

rivals these assertions in importance, for no category is as elemental as revelation. All that Judaism is flows from revelatory claims, is predicated on a specific understanding of what revelation is and is not. The structure as well as the content of Judaism presumes a delimited and defined hermeneutic of the revelatory event as well as of the way the content of revelation is unfolded, expounded, applied. Because the stakes are so high, insisting, *contra* Greenberg, on a careful employment of this term is required lest the possibility arise that any claim might be advanced as a revelatory one.

(5) The structure of Greenberg's three covenantal eras, his many propositions about a "saving God," his talk of revelation and redemption, and his radical proposition that the Almighty is increasingly a "silent partner" in Jewish and world history, all these ideas cannot be advanced without pondering their consequences for the "God of Abraham, Isaac and Jacob."

To put it directly, what happens to the God of Judaism in Greenberg's theology? *Prima facie* the God of all the traditional omni-predicates does not fit easily with a "God" who is a "silent partner." This may not be a telling criticism, though I think it is, because Greenberg is free to redefine "God" for the purposes of theological reflection. But having redefined "God" however he feels it appropriate, Greenberg must attend to the myriad metaphysical and theological consequences of such an action. It is therefore incumbent to require that whatever Greenberg's "God-idea," its character and implications be explained fully and carefully. On the one hand, this means that the ontological entailments of treating God as a "silent partner" have to be spelled out. On the other hand, the implication of such a metaphysical principle (God as a "silent partner") for such traditional and essential Jewish concerns as covenant, reward and punishment, morality, Torah, *mitzvot*, redemption, and

5. Here a clarification made by Dr. Greenberg, in response to this criticism, deserves citing. He replies to my argument as follows:

It is not that Holocaust validates halachic change but that it makes more urgent the accomplishment of the redemptive goals; it calls for a "messianic" breakthrough in this generation. This expresses itself in coming closer to the ideal norms of the tradition

in such areas as women, Gentiles, etc.... This is not to be confused, however, with faddishness or trying to be on the right side of currently trendy values and issues. (Private communication from Dr. Greenberg, January 3, 1989).

6. I have made a detailed study of this central issue in volume 1 of my *The Holocaust in Historical Context*, (New York, 1994).

other eschatological matters, have to be attended to. For example, is a God who is a "silent partner" capable of being the author and guarantor of moral value both in human relations as well as in history and nature more generally? Or is the axiological role traditionally occupied by God largely evacuated?[7] Likewise, is there a possibility of sin, in a substantive and not merely a metaphorical sense, in this perspective? Again, is God as a "silent partner" capable of being the God of salvation both personal and historic? And lastly, is God as a "silent partner" the God to whom we pray on Yom Kippur and to whom we confess our sins and ask forgiveness? If my skepticism regarding the ability of Greenberg's "God-idea" to answer to these challenges is misplaced, this has to be demonstrated. For it would appear that while this revised "God-idea" allows him to unfold the logic of the "Third Era" as he desires, it in turn generates more theological problems than it solves.

(6) This brings us to the most dramatic, most consequential, of Greenberg's affirmations—his espousal, in our post-Holocaust era, of a "voluntary covenant." According to Greenberg, as seen in his work presented above (pp. 543–555), the Sinaitic covenant was shattered in the *Shoah*. As a consequence he pronounces the fateful judgment: *the Covenant is now voluntary!* Jews have, quite miraculously, chosen after Auschwitz to continue to live Jewish lives and collectively to build a Jewish State, the ultimate symbol of Jewish continuity, but these acts are, post-*Shoah*, the result of the free choice of the Jewish people.

Logically and theologically the key issue that arises at this central juncture, given Greenberg's reconstruction, is this: if there was ever a valid covenant[8] i.e., there is a God who entered into such a relationship with Israel, then can this covenant be "shattered" by a Hitler? Or put the other way round, if Hitler can be said to have "shattered" the covenant, was there ever such a

covenant, despite traditional Jewish pieties, in the first place? The reasons for raising these repercussive questions are metaphysical in kind and are related to the nature of the biblical God and the meaning of His attributes and activities, including His revelations and promises, which are immune, by definition, from destruction by the likes of a Hitler. If Hitler could break God's covenantal promises, God would not be God and Hitler would indeed be central to Jewish belief.

Conclusion

The nature of this analysis, and the character of my critique, reflect the seriousness with which I believe one must take Greenberg's theological position. Its sensitivity to the right issues, its commitment to the Jewish people, its learning and intelligence, its concerns with the interfacing of *halachah* and history, its profound affirmation of the meaning of the State of Israel, are all attributes that recommend it to those truly concerned with the present condition of the people Israel and the viability of Jewish belief in the post-Holocaust age. Alternatively, however, much of its argumentation is unconvincing, its use of sources open to question, and its "method" often lacking in method. Paradoxes are admitted too easily, and the notions of dialectic and dialectical are far too casually employed, often to avoid facing real and pressing logical contradictions. For these reasons, Greenberg's work must be judged unfinished, still in the stage of development and completion. A judgment Greenberg himself would agree with. This conclusion, however, should not be misunderstood. It does not negate the value of Greenberg's provocative conceptual efforts, but rather challenges all of us to re-engage still more deeply the rudimentary theological matters that he has the courage to address.

---

7. Here a further nuance must be noted. Greenberg insists that though God is intentionally more self-limited in the "Third Era," this should not be misunderstood as positing either God's absence or weakness. God is still active, though He is more hidden. In a private correspondence Greenberg argued that in his view God is still seen as possessing, at least, the following four clas-

sical attributes of "calling," "accompanying," "judging," and "sustaining" men and women, as well as of the world as a whole. Whether Greenberg has a right to maintain these attributes for his "God-idea," given the other characteristics of his theology, is open to question.

8. An open question on independent philosophical grounds.

"The Tremendum": Arthur Cohen's Understanding of Faith after the Holocaust

Among the most sustained recent Jewish theological discussions of the *Sho'ah* is Arthur A. Cohen's *The Tremendum: A Theological Interpretation of the Holocaust.*[1] Though a relatively short book, 110 pages in all, it attacks this immense conceptual issue with all of Cohen's customary verve and intelligence. No school theologian, either in the dogmatic or systematic sense, Cohen here makes a prodigious effort to strike out in a new, more radical metaphysical direction as a necessary response to the Event with which he deals.

I

Four highly ramified theses lie at the root of Cohen's philosophical reflections. They are: (1) the Holocaust is unique and this uniqueness entails particular theological concomitants; (2) thought is unable to grasp the reality of Auschwitz; (3) no "meaning" is to be found in this genocidal carnage; and (4) evil is more real, more consequential, than Cohen had heretofore allowed. These four intellectually radical presuppositions lead Cohen to recognize the need to return, with a new uncertainty, to the traditional questions of theology. To ask again concerning "the reality of evil and the existence of God, the extremity of evil and the freedom of man, the presentness of evil and the power of God."[2] To ask still more concretely if "like our ancestors we are obliged to decide whether (national) catastrophes are compatible with our traditional notions of a beneficent and providential God. The past generations of Israel decided that they were. The question today

is whether the same conclusion may be wrung from the data of the *tremendum.*"[3]

If this is, and I agree that it is, the essential question, what is Cohen's answer? If "there is no end until the end is final. Until that moment, it is only caesura and new beginning,"[4] what is the substance of the new, post-*tremendum* beginning? Cohen presents the following schematic formulation of its defining and necessary characteristics:

> Any constructive theology after the *tremendum* must be marked by the following characteristics: first, the God who is affirmed must abide in a universe whose human history is scarred by genuine evil without making the evil empty or illusory nor disallowing the real presence of God before, even if not within, history; second, the relation of God to creation and its creatures, including, as both now include, demonic structure and unredeemable events, must be seen, nonetheless, as meaningful and valuable despite the fact that the justification that God's presence renders to the worthwhileness of life and struggle is now intensified and anguished by the contrast and opposition that evil supplies; third, the reality of God in his selfhood and person can no longer be isolated, other than as a strategy of clarification, from God's real involvement with the life of creation. Were any of these characteristics to be denied or, worse, proved untrue and unneeded, as strict and unyielding orthodox theism appears to require, creation disappears as fact into mere metaphor or, in the face of an obdurate and ineffaceable reality such as the *tremendum,* God ceases to be more than a metaphor for the inexplicable.[5]

1. Published in New York in 1981. See the selections from this work above, pp. 566–580.
2. Ibid., p. 38.
3. Ibid., p. 50.
4. Ibid., p. 58.
5. Ibid., p. 86. It should be noted that Cohen is very, and rightly, critical of liberal theology after the *tremendum,* see pp. 45 and 46. He is also correct in his critical

judgment of what he terms "the varieties of neo-orthodoxy" (p. 55) which he scores as follows: "Neo-orthodoxy does not cope adequately since its situates the *tremendum* as the dialectic counter of an absent or hidden God, enabling the immensity of the one to pass the mystery of the other in the dark night of this century without compelling them to their dreadful confrontation" (Ibid., pp. 85–86).

What these three theological requirements entail for Cohen is the bringing together of two seemingly opposite traditional theological strategies. One is that "of the kabbalistic counter history of Judaism"[6] by reference to which Cohen intends to call attention to the kabbalistic doctrine of the *Eyn Sof* (God beyond all attributes) and the related doctrine of creation in which:

"God, in the immensity of his being, was trapped by both its absoluteness and necessity into a constriction of utter passivity which would have excluded both the means in will and the reality in act of the creation. Only by the spark of nonbeing (the interior apposition of being, the contradiction of being, the premise of otherhood, the void that is not vacuous) was the being of God enlivened and vivified."[7]

And this cosmogonic speculation has now to be linked to a second cosmological tradition, that associated with [Schelling] and [Rosenzweig]. This Cohen describes as follows:

"What is necessary in God," Schelling argues, "is God's nature," his "own-ness." Love—that antithetic energy of the universe—negates 'own-ness' for love cannot exist without the other, indeed, according to its nature as love, it must deny itself that the other might be (contracting itself that the other might be, setting limits to itself). However, since the divine nature as *esse* cannot have personality without the outpouring, the self-giving of love to define those limits, it must be postulated that within God are two directions (not principles, as Schelling says): one which is necessary selfhood, interiority, self-containment and another, vital, electric, spontaneous that is divine *posse,* the abundant and overflowing. There arises from all this the dialectic of necessity and freedom, the enmeshment of divine egoity and person, divine self-love and free love, divine narcissism and the created image, the sufficient nothing of the world and the creation of being. The human affect is toward the overflowing, the loving in God; his containment, however, the abyss of his nature, is as

crucial as is his abundance and plenitude. These are the fundamental antithesis of the divine essence without which the abyss would be unknown or all else would be regarded as plenitude.... the quiet God is as indispensable as the revealing God, the abyss as much as the plenitude, the constrained, self-contained, deep divinity as the the plenteous and generous.[8]

What the synthesis of these kabbalistic and Schellingian conceptions means for Cohen is that: (a) there is an elemental side of God that is necessarily hidden, but still necessary, in the process of creation and relation; (b) conversely, reciprocally, creation, which is continuous and ongoing, is a necessary outcome of God's loving nature; (c) God's nature requires our freedom; and lastly, (d) we require a "dipolar"[9] theological vision which admits that things and events look different from God's perspective, and to God as He is in Himself, than they do from our vantage point and vis-à-vis our relation to the transcendent.

On the basis of these complex theological foundations Cohen goes on to fashion what in fairness can be called a new, if dramatic, version of the "Free-Will defense," i.e., an articulated theodicy that turns on the necessity for, as well as on the abuse of, human freedom in creation. Framed in Cohen's unique idiom, this ambitious defense is described as "an enduring strife and tension (in man), enlarged and made threatening by our finitude, in which freedom enhances when it is marked and contained by reason, but when reason fails to find language, freedom is destructively cut loose or bends toward untruth or succumbs to sheer willfulness."[10]

What this means as specifically applied to the *Sho'ah* is, Cohen argues, that we require a new understanding of God's work in the world that insistently differs elementally from that taught by traditional theism. The understanding of the traditionalists issues forth in the putatively "unanswerable" question: "How could it be that God witnessed the holocaust and remained silent?"[11] Alternatively, Cohen's recommendation would free us of this causal understanding of the need

6. Ibid., p. 86.
7. Ibid., pp 86f.
8. Ibid., pp 89f.

9. Cohen's term, ibid., p. 91.
10. Ibid., p. 92.
11. Ibid., p. 95f.

for direct Divine intervention and allow us to see: "that which is taken as God's speech is really always man's hearing, that God is not the strategist of our particularities or of our historical condition, but rather the mystery of our futurity, always our *posse*, never our acts."[12]

If we can acquire this alternative understanding of what divine action allows—as well as of what it does not allow—we will "have won a sense of God whom we may love and honor, but whom we no longer fear and from whom we no longer demand."[13] This argument, with its redefinition of God and its emphasis on human freedom, emerges as the center-piece of Cohen's revisionist "response" to the *tremendum*.

Exegesis of Cohen's position, however, would not be complete without brief comment on one further aspect of his argument, his critique of Zionism. Whereas most of the other major thinkers[14] who have discussed the *Sho'ah* in theological terms have embraced the re-creation of the State of Israel as a positive event, even while understanding its value in a variety of ways, e.g., in terms of Richard Rubenstein's naturalism or Irving (Yitzchak) Greenberg's incipient messianism, Cohen remains wedded to a non-Zionist (which must be scrupulously distinguished from an anti-Zionist) theological outlook. Cohen's reservation stems from his continuing understanding, indebted as it is to Franz Rosenzweig, of the Jewish people's "peculiar" role in history, or rather, as Cohen describes it, "to the side of history."[15]

> It may well be the case that the full entrance of the Jewish people into the lists of the historical is more threatening even than genocide has been, for in no way is the Jew allowed any longer to retire to the wings of history, to repeat his exile amid the nations, to disperse himself once again in order to survive. One perceives that when history endangers it cannot be mitigated. This we know certainly from the *tremendum,* but we know it no less from the auguries of nationhood, that every structure of history in which an eternal people takes refuge is ominous.[16]

This reserve, this mooted pessimism as regards the State of Israel is the product of Cohen's transcendental theology coupled, it must be said, with a not inconsiderable degree of historical realism. While I do not agree with his formulation of the meaning of Israel among the nations, nor his explication of Israel's mission, nor again his reserve about the return to Zion as positive theological fact, I do recognize a certain real wisdom in his caution, for the Jewish people and the Jewish State have not yet arrived at the *eschaton*. At most, we are at "the beginning of the dawn of our redemption," as the prayer for the State of Israel composed by the Israeli Chief Rabbinate has phrased it. Perhaps even more accurately, if sceptically, one ought to refer to "the hope that this is the beginning of the dawn of our redemption," and reserve further judgment. In any case, however, Cohen's a-Zionist dogmatics raise an important, if unfashionable, issue for consideration. We ignore his challenge at great cost to ourselves.

II

There is much to agree with in Cohen's novel formulation of the theological implications of the *tremendum*. One is impressed by his bold attempt to shift the angle of vision for the discussion as a whole, as well as of individual elements within the whole. And one is even more impressed by his willingness, even passion, to do theology—a rare passion-flower in this a-theological era. Cohen is correct in his belief that Jewish thinkers cannot, ultimately, eschew theology. Then again, his willingness to strike unpopular positions, e.g., his stance on the theological, or one might more accurately say the non-theological, significance of the State of Israel, is commendable, even if one seriously disagrees with it, for theologians should not theologize to win friends but for the sake of Truth. Lastly, one recognizes in Cohen's difficult style, for all its obscurity, authentic theological seriousness that is being stretched on the rack of the most intractable, the most basic, theological

---

12. Ibid., p. 97.
13. Ibid., p. 97.
14. Ignaz Maybaum tried haltingly to deal positively with the State of Israel though he was unable to do much

with it theologically because of the nature of his thought as a whole.
15. Ibid., p. 103. This is Cohen's phrase.
16. Ibid., p. 101.

issues. Having oneself experienced the need to seek out new, more elastic resources in language in order to address these matters, one recognizes that Cohen is trying to say what seems *a fortiori* unsayable. In short, there is a good deal to be learnt, if most notably of a deconstructive sort, from Cohen.

Acknowledging all this, and much else of value in Cohen's work, I remain unpersuaded by his main theological claims, his most essential doctrinal affirmations. Indeed, where theological fundamentals, or rather *the* theological fundamental— namely God—is at issue, I am in basic disagreement with what Cohen has described as "dipolar" theism and its implications for thinking about, and responding to, the *Sho'ah*. In what remains of this chapter I would like to set out my particular reservations and the reasons that lie behind them.

(1) Let us begin our critique where Cohen begins his constructive theological endeavor, i.e., with his invoking and employment of the theological systems of the Kabbalah and Schelling. Cohen argues for the need to rediscover the value of each of these "counter-history" traditions and then to bring them together in a larger, original theological synthesis. However, even before proceeding to Cohen's exegesis of the substantive content of these respective systems a seminal fact needs to be recognized about their structure and context and it is this: neither account stands independently of a broader intellectual environment. For Kabbalah this larger environment is the Jewish halachic tradition in all its breadth and diversity as well as certain gnostic trends which it adapted and re-worked according to its own genius. For example, its doctrine of *tzimtzum*, Divine Contraction, to which Cohen appeals for the initial half of his *dipolar* theism, is inseparably part and parcel of a larger "mythos" (not myth in the pejorative sense) that was grounded, in particular, in the then (medieval) shared traditional Jewish dogma regarding the

absoluteness and literalness of the Sinaitic revelation. Added to this were a wide range of metaphysical and theological concepts and beliefs, for example, the belief in the ontic status of the Hebrew alphabet, or again, very specific theories of emanation drawn from neo-Platonism, and a host of notions regarding creation. It was only out of, and on the grounds of, these seminal propositions that the Kabbalists could offer their celebrated cosmogonic speculations—and believe them.[17] But Cohen, especially as becomes clear in his technical discussion of miracles,[18] and his sharp critique of what he calls fundamentalism[19]— something which all the classical Kabbalists were in that sense of the term which he criticizes—does not share any of these primal beliefs and therefore it is hard to see how he can recommend and defend the theory of *tzimtzum* (Divine Contraction) torn out of its original context. Gershom Scholem's work, and his deserved prestige, referred to by Cohen in this connection does not alter this fact for Scholem is a historian of Kabbalah not its advocate.[20] One simply cannot base a contemporary theological reconstruction on Scholem's work without additional argument that moves the creative discussion from the historical and descriptive to the theological and prescriptive—but this additional, independent link has not been supplied.

While the theory of Divine Contraction sounds plausible in its kabbalistic context, the grounds of its plausibility in a modern non-kabbalistic philosophical setting need to be worked through and argued for. Here it is explicitly to be recognized that Cohen would certainly not subscribe to the traditional kabbalistic gnosis, interlaced with neoplatonic metaphysical premises, cum *halachah* (Jewish law), that gives the original doctrine it conceptual foundation and hence one would think that for Cohen the doctrine should lose its coherence even in its uniquely kabbalistic modality. Cohen ignores

---

17. On the significance of these issues see Steven T. Katz, "The Conservative Character of Mystical Experience," in Steven T. Katz, ed., *Mysticism and Religious Traditions* (New York, 1983); and my more recent essay "Mystical Speech and Mystical Meaning," in Steven T. Katz, ed., *Mysticism and Language* (New York, 1992).

18. See *The Tremendum*, p. 95ff.
19. See ibid., p. 96f.
20. David Biale's suggestion that Scholem is also something of a Kabbalist himself is hard to accept; see Biale's comments in his *Gershom Scholem* (Cambridge, MA, 1979).

altogether the fact that the kabbalistic account also seeks to assure the continued and direct interaction between above and below, between God as *Eyn Sof* after the act of *tzimtzum* and the emanated world, through the action of the *sefirot* (divine pleroma). This is a necessary, unbreakable, causal connection rooted in the metaphysics and logic of emanation. This link is of the essence for the *mekubbalim* (the mystics), for it is this relationship that allows the entire dialectical process of the system to function, including the ultimate aims of *devekut* (personal adhesion to God in mystical relation), and *tikkun olam* (repairing the world) by the messianic action of reversing the downward and negative flow of reality, i.e., raising the *nitzozot* (the sparks of holiness) in things and thereby restoring the broken primordial harmony in the upper realm. It is this ontic reciprocity that also gives Torah and *mitzvot* their cosmological status and power—*mitzvot* are the lever by which the Jew moves the world, uniting even God Himself in the process (*kivyachol*, as if we can say this). Cohen's metaphysics, built putatively on this kabbalistic (and Schellingian) tradition, and on which more below, explicitly denies, and is designed so as to deny, just such causal ontological relationships. Alternatively, if Cohen wishes to eschew this claimed kabbalistic inheritance and to argue instead for the more open-ended thesis that creation requires some limitation of God, he can do so just as well, probably even better, without invoking technical kabbalistic notions whose meaning has been negated by the negation of their context. Such a non-kabbalistic doctrine of Divine limitation would, of course, still require justification but it would now come to us on independent grounds for assessment and verification. And it would not raise all sorts of historic and ideological associations and meanings Cohen wishes to have no part of. In such revised circumstances it would certainly lack the prestige of Kabbalah, that emo-

tional and exotic seductiveness that Kabbalah has come to acquire in our time thanks in large part to Scholem's work,[21] but it would also come to us in a more accurate way.

A similar demurral must also be voiced against Cohen's recourse to Schelling as the grounds for his argument for the di-polarity of God. For again, Schelling's thought comes to us from a context that is a murky admixture of misunderstood Enlightenment natural science, doses of gnosticism and mythology, and overwhelming quantities of German Idealism, even if an Idealism in tension with the reigning Idealist conception of Hegel and earlier of Fichte. Hence it *means* in a very particular context—but can this idealist-cum-gnostic context be defended today? Or rather, has it not been thoroughly discredited, making appeal to it less than convincing. While Schelling, for all his contradictoriness and tendency to the obscure, is a thinker of genius, and Cohen's use of him is, in places, theologically intriguing, one is hard pressed to credit the introduction of his theism *per se* as providing any substantive part of a contemporary theology. Certainly one cannot merely adopt segments, fragments, of his world-view without finding convincing ways to defend them on more secure and independent philosophical grounds than Schelling himself provided. However, Cohen does not enter into such a protracted and technical transcendental discussion, nor does he provide such autonomous legitimating grounds. Rather, he naively assumes, and I choose this characterization with great care, the usefulness of Schelling's account and employs it accordingly. But all this is too direct, too unconvincing a procedure under the intellectual circumstances.

There is also a second, even more telling, hermeneutical difficulty connected with Cohen's reliance on Kabbalah, Schelling and Rosenzweig, and it is this. The *caesura* marked by the *tremendum* has, on Cohen's own definitions of *caesura* and *tremendum,* broken the continuity of Jewish and

---

21. The influence of Martin Buber's hasidic work is also a seminal, if more oblique factor, here tied up as it is with the widespread interest in "mysticism" in our time. In fact, Gershom Scholem credits Buber with being the first modern Jewish thinker to take mysticism seriously as an integral part of Judaism and hence opening the kabbalistic tradition as a legiti- mate resource for others, including himself. See G. Scholem, "Martin Bubers Auffassung des Judentums," in *Eranos-Jahrbuch* XXV (Zurich, 1967), pp. 9–55. Available in an English translation as "Martin Buber's Conception of Judaism," in G. Scholem, *On Jews and Judaism in Crisis* (New York, 1976), pp. 126–171.

world history into *pre-tremendum* and *post-tremendum* epochs. The philosophical and theological systems that served to make sense of the world before Auschwitz—understanding "system" here in its broadest sense—are no longer viable after Auschwitz. The Holocaust has changed everything. This being so, indeed it is the primal assumption of Cohen's whole mode of reflection, how can either the *pre-tremendum* mythos of the Kabbalah or the *pre-tremendum* idealism, or anti-idealism if you wish,[22] of Schelling or Rosenzweig, be retrievable as the appropriate structural bases for the post–*Sho'ah* moment. It is true that these exemplary intellectual and spiritual traditions can be classed as subterranean and proclaimed, with some justification, as "counter-history," but by what inventive logic do we say that the *tremendum* invalidated only the orthodoxies of the *pre-tremendum* era. Surely, if Cohen's explicit root premise is correct, then it forces drastic revision, if not outright rejection, of all *pre-tremendum* thinking, whether such thought is diagnosed as mainline or underground, acclaimed or suppressed, history or "counter-history." One would think, given what has here been assumed *a priori*, that Kabbalah and Schelling-Rosenzweig are outdistanced no less so than other *pre-tremendum* theologies. Alternatively, if this is not the case, then a convincing argument for the unique retrievability of just this specific material must be provided.

David Tracy in his Foreword to the work before us described Cohen's intended procedure as follows:

—To understand any tradition after the *tremendum* is to retrieve its genius through a retrieval that is also a suspicion. Through that kind of hermeneutics, we may find hidden, forgotten, even repressed aspects of the tradition for thought now. A hermeneutical enterprise like this occurs in the powerful theological reflections of the final chapter of this work. There the reader will find Arthur Cohen's own constructive rethinking of the reality of God in a post-*tremendum* age. Unless I misread him, Arthur

Cohen moves in this section through a powerful hermeneutics of suspicion to an equally powerful hermeneutics of retrieval. By that dangerous route he retrieves for thought the deconstructive mode of thinking of the Jewish kabbalistic tradition historically retrieved by Scholem, the negative theology in the gnostic-kabbalistic tradition from Boehme through Schelling, and, above all, the unthought that must now be thought in the mystic epistemology and ontology of the incomparable Franz Rosenzweig.

Cohen does not allow himself simply to "repeat" the solutions of his chosen classics, those defamiliarizing trajectories of the tradition. The choice of these particular classics is both liberating and courageous. For precisely these classic modes of deconstructive thought, let us recall, were and are still often despised when not altogether forgotten or repressed by both Jewish and Christian theologians in favor of some "clearer" or "more orthodox" aspect of the traditions. As Cohen's creative rethinking of the position of Franz Rosenzweig makes especially clear, he understands this subterranean tradition of negative deconstructive theological reflection on God only by understanding it differently. He must so understand it for Cohen understands it post-*tremendum*. Traditional deconstruction must itself now be deconstructed in order to be retrieved at all.[23]

Here Tracy indicates his theological and methodological sophistication. He knows that all *pre-tremendum* theology, even that of a "negative deconstructive" sort, can only be retrieved, if retrievable at all, *differently* than in the past because it is now retrieved *post-tremendum*. If Cohen had accomplished through his analysis what Tracy attributes to it, it would indeed be of the greatest importance and our present critical remarks would be in error. However, while the conscious design behind the work might be as Tracy describes it, it is difficult to discern any real "deconstruction" of Kabbalah and very little of Schelling in the actual working out of its argument. There is some in respect of Rosenzweig,

---

22. Debates about the historical and philosophical nature of Schelling's and Rosenzweig's relation to idealism need not detain us here.

23. *The Tremendum*, "Foreward" (by David Tracy), pp. x–xi.

though not of Rosenzweig's account of creation but rather, in a modest way, of his view of history and the Jewish presence in, or in Cohen's phrase "on the side of" history. At the same time, the explication of a radical hermeneutics of suspicion is not provided beyond the banal assertion of traditional theology's inadequacy in the face of the Death Camps while the deeper, more substantive retrieval desired through the deconstruction of the deconstructive tradition is very little advanced. There are, at best, only intimations of what could be adjudged a thorough deconstructive exploration prior to any mature theological retrieval. Therefore, we ought to characterize Cohen's presentation as a *stipulated* hermeneutics of suspicion followed by a *stipulated* retrieval for, in its generality, the "unthought that now must be thought" has not been thought. As a consequence, Cohen's conclusions never progress beyond the level of assertions.

(2) This first preliminary observation concerning method brings into focus a related epistemological question that Cohen does not address. What is the *status* of his radical theological remarks? Are his theological recommendations, drawn from Kabbalah, Schelling and Franz Rosenzweig, to be understood as *hypotheses,* and if so, how are they to be tested and against what and how? Are they *proofs* à la Anselm or Aquinas? Are they tautologies? Are they necessary *a priori* synthetic propositions? Are they first principles as in a mathematical-deductive system? If so, what governs their confirmation and possible revision? These are questions to which Cohen supplies no answers.

(3) Let us now move to the very center of Cohen's response to the *tremendum,* his dipolar account of God. The subtle intention that lies behind this transformative re-description of God is two-fold. On the one hand it seeks to assure the reality of human freedom and hence to facilitate a simultaneous re-employment of a sophisticated version of a "Free-Will" theodicy. On the other hand, and reciprocally, it redefines the transcendent nature of God's being such that He is not directly responsible for the discrete events of human history and hence cannot be held responsible for the *Sho'ah* or other acts of human evil. This is a very intriguing two-sided ontological strategy. Our question therefore must

be: does Cohen defend it adequately? If so, at what theological price?

Let us explore these questions by deciphering first Cohen's second thesis as to God's re-defined role in history. The clearest statement of Cohen's revised God-idea in respect of Divine accountability for the *Sho'ah* comes in his discussion of God's putative silence and what Cohen takes to be the mistaken tradition-based expectation of miraculous intervention.

> The most penetrating of post-*tremendum* assaults upon God has been the attack upon divine silence. Silence is surely in such a usage a metaphor for inaction: passivity, affectlessness, indeed, at its worst and most extreme, indifference and ultimate malignity. Only a malign God would be silent when speech would terrify and stay the fall of the uplifted arm. And if God spoke once (or many times as scripture avers), why has he not spoken since? What is it with a God who speaks only to the ears of the earliest and the oldest and for millennia thereafter keeps silence and speaks not. In all this there is concealed a variety of assumptions about the nature and efficacy of divine speech that needs to be examined. The first is that the divine speech of old is to be construed literally, that is, God actually spoke in the language of man, adapting speech to the styles of the Patriarchs and the Prophets, and was heard speaking and was transmitted as having spoken. God's speech was accompanied by the racket of the heavens so that even if the speech was not heard by more than the prophetic ear, the marks and signals of divine immensity were observed. As well, there is the interpretive conviction that God's speech is action, that God's words act. Lastly, and most relevantly to the matter before us, God's speech enacts and therefore confutes the projects of murderers and tyrants—he saves Israel, he ransoms Jews, he is forbearing and loving. God's speech is thus consequential to the historical cause of justice and mercy. Evidently, then, divine silence is reproof and punishment, the reversal of his works of speech, and hence God's silence is divine acquiescence in the work of murder and destruction.[24]

24. Ibid., p. 96f.

As opposed to this older view Cohen recommends an alternative:

> Can it not be argued no less persuasively that what is taken as God's speech is really always man's hearing, that God is not the strategist of our particularities or of our historical condition, but rather the mystery of our futurity, always our *posse,* never our acts. If we can begin to see God less as the interferer whose insertion is welcome (when it accords with our needs) and more as the immensity whose reality is our prefiguration, whose speech and silence are metaphors for our language and distortion, whose plenitude and unfolding are the hope of our futurity, we shall have won a sense of God whom we may love and honor, but whom we no longer fear and from whom we no longer demand.[25]

In response to this reconstruction of the God-idea four critical observations are in order. First, it need not be belabored that there is truth in the proposition that "what is taken as God's speech is really always man's hearing."[26] But at the same time, it is only a half-truth as stated. For our hearing the word of revelation does not create "God's speech"—this would be illusion and self-projection. Certainly we can *mis*hear God, or not hear what there is to hear at all—but these qualifications do not erase the dialogical nature of Divine speech, i.e., the requirement that there be a Speaker as well as a Hearer. And if revelation requires this two-sidedness, then we have to reject Cohen's revisionism because it fails to address the full circumstance of the reality of revelation and God's role in it. Alternatively, if Cohen's description is taken at face value, revelation as such disappears, in any meaningful sense, from the theological vocabulary, for what content can we ultimately give to "man's hearing" as revelation? And specifically from a Jewish point of view, anything recognizable as *Torah* and *mitzvot* (commandments) would be negated altogether.

Secondly, this deconstruction of classical theism and its substitution by theological di-polarity

fails to deal with the problem of Divine attributes. Is God still God if He is no longer the providential agency in history? Is God still God if He lacks the power to enter history vertically to perform the miraculous? Is such a dipolar Absolute still the God to whom one prays, the God of salvation? Put the other way round, Cohen's divinity is certainly not the God of the covenant,[27] nor again the God of Exodus-Sinai, nor yet again the God of the Prophets and the *Ḥurban Bayit Rishon* (Destruction of the First Temple) and the *Ḥurban Bayit Sheni* (Destruction of the Second Temple). Now, none of these objections, the failure to account for the very building blocks of Jewish theology, count *logically* against Cohen's theism as an independent speculative exercise. However, they do suggest that Cohen's God is *not* the God of the Bible and Jewish tradition and that if Cohen is right, indeed, particularly if Cohen is right, there is no real meaning left to Judaism and to the God-idea of Jewish tradition. Cohen's deconstruction in this particular area is so radical that it sweeps away the biblical and rabbinic ground of Jewish faith and allows the biblical and other classical evidence to count not at all against his own speculative metaphysical hypotheses.

The dipolar ontological schema is certainly logically neater and sharper than its "normative" biblical and rabbinic predecessor, but one questions whether this precision has not been purchased at the price of adequacy, i.e., an inadequate grappling with the multiple evidences and variegated problems that need to be addressed in any attempt, however bold, to fashion a defensible definition and description of God and His relations to humankind. Logical precision must not be achieved here too easily, nor given too high a priority, in the sifting and sorting, the phenomenological decipherment and re-arranging, of God's reality and our own.

Third, is the dipolar, non-interfering God "whom we no longer fear and from whom we no longer demand" yet worthy of our "love and honor?"[28] This God seems closer, say, to Plato's

25. Ibid., p. 97.
26. Ibid., p. 97.
27. Cf. here my comments on Yitzchak Greenberg's redefinition of God and his notion of a "volun-

tary covenant" in the previous selection in this collection.
28. Ibid., p. 97.

Demiurgos or perhaps closer still to the innocuous and irrelevant God of the Deists. Such a God does not count in how we act, nor in how history devolves or transpires. After all "God is not," Cohen asserts, "the strategist of our particularities or of our historical condition." But if this is so, if God is indeed so absent from our life and the historical record, what difference for us between this God and no God at all? Again, is such a God who remains uninvolved while Auschwitz is generating its corpses any more worthy of being called a "God whom we may love," especially if this is His metaphysical essence, than the God of tradition?[29] A God who we can only see as the "immensity whose reality is our prefiguration" while rhetorically provocative, will not advance the theological discussion for it provides negations and evasions just where substantive analysis is required.

In this connection let me add a relevant historical observation. In the medieval era Jewish theologians and philosophers conducted a constant and ongoing debate with Platonists and Aristotelians regarding creation. The "deep structure" of the debate turned on the desire of Jewish thinkers to defend God's will, i.e., to defend creation as an act of God's will rather than as a result of the necessity of His nature, which they recognized was essential to the maintenance of Judaism, for only a God with a will could make covenants and give the Torah. The *locus*

classicus of this view is found in Maimonides' [1135–1204] *Guide for the Perplexed* II:25. Here Maimonides argues as follows:

> Know that with a belief in the creation of the world in time, all the miracles become possible and the Law becomes possible, and all questions that may be asked on this subject, vanish. Thus it might be said: Why did God give prophetic revelation to this one and not to that? Why did God give this Law to this particular nation, and why did He not legislate to the others? Why did He legislate at this particular time, and why did He not legislate before it or after? Why did He impose these commandments and these prohibitions? Why did He privilege the prophet with the miracles mentioned in relation to him and not with some others? What was God's aim in giving this Law? Why did He not, if such was His purpose, put the accomplishment of the commandments and the nontransgression of the prohibitions into our nature? If this were said, the answer to all these questions would be that it would be said: He wanted it this way; or His wisdom required it this way. And just as He brought the world into existence, having the form it has, when He wanted to, without our knowing His will with regard to this or in what respect there was wisdom in His particularizing the forms of the world and the time of its

---

29. It is worth comparing Cohen's present description and understanding of the Divine as dipolar with his comments made in conversation with Mordecai Kaplan over the idea of God in Kaplan's reconstructionism and printed in the volume entitled *If Not Now, When?* (New York, 1973). There Cohen offered:

     I think it also implies a rather fundamental distinction within the tradition between God as creator and God as revealer. One of the things that I particularly love in Rosenzweig's discussion of the reality of God in his *The Star of Redemption* is the recognition that the distinction between God the creator and God the revealer is rather too sharp in traditional theology. The assumption that the creating God is not also a revealing God and that the revealing God is not also a creating God at one and the same time is mistaken. The God who brought the people of Israel out of the land of Egypt to be their God was not only revealing himself to the people and calling the people to himself, convoking the people as the object of the act, but at the same time was exhibiting an undis-

   closed aspect of himself. The notion in classical theology (which I dislike as much as you do) that God is *being* alone, *ens entissimus*, and that history is somehow oppositive to the divine nature; that God concedes to history, condescends himself to it, seems to me meaningless and defeating.

     God needs history. God needs his creatures. God as creator requires as much the thing that he creates as does the capacity to create.

     The creation of the universe and the giving of the Torah are part of the same continuum of self-expression. God's nature demands self-expression as profoundly as his creatures demand it.

   Cohen's presentation here seems more satisfying and closer to the reality of Jewish views of God than his statement in his new work. It is instructive to follow the whole of Cohen's debate with Kaplan. Also of interest is a comparison of his present views as to the nature of God with those voiced in his earlier, *The Natural and the Supernatural Jew* (New York, 1962).

creation—in the same way we do not know His will or the exigency of His wisdom that caused all the matters, about which questions have been posed above, to be particularized. If, however, someone says that the world is as it is in virtue of necessity, it would be a necessary obligation to ask all those questions; and there would be no way out of them except through a recourse to unseemly answers in which there would be combined the giving the lie to, and the annulment of, all the external meanings of the Law with regard to which no intelligent man has any doubt that they are to be taken in their external meanings. It is then because of this that this opinion is shunned and that the lives of virtuous men have been and will be spent in investigating this question. For if creation in time were demonstrated— if only as Plato understands creation—all the overhasty claims made to us on this point by the philosophers would become void. In the same way, if the philosophers would succeed in demonstrating eternity as Aristotle understands it, the Law as a whole would become void, and a shift to other opinions would take place. I have thus explained to you that everything is bound up with this problem. Know this.[30]

Ironically, Cohen's present metaphysical suggestion for redescribing the nature of God again raises this same issue of Divine volition. That is, its determinate account of creation as a necessity of God's nature à la Schelling, rather than as an act of God's free will, makes it impossible, now for yet another reason, to sustain Torah and Covenant, i.e., Judaism.

Lastly, this proposed metaphysical reconstruction is not founded upon any direct phenomenological procedure per se. Though fashioned in response to the Sho'ah, belief in such a dipolar God requires just as great a "leap of faith"—maybe even greater as it lacks the support of the Jewish past—as do the theistic affirmations of the tradition. Phenomenologically, it is difficult to discern why one would move in the direction of dipolar theism, given the negativity of the Sho'ah, unless one were committed at a minimum to theism, if not dipolar theism, to start with. Cohen is correct that both Schelling and Rosenzweig begin "by *assuming* that human natures are created and therefore dependent upon the operative analogue of divine nature."[31] But why should we, or he, begin with this assumption? Especially given his negation of much of the theistic inheritance that both Schelling and Rosenzweig retained, even if not always consciously. It is surely not enough to introduce this as an argument from authority, i.e., to hold this view on the claimed authority of Schelling and Rosenzweig; some better reason(s) for even introducing the dipolar God into the present conversation is required—but remains always absent.

(4) The second major aspect of Cohen's account turns on what I have called his revised "Free-Will" theodicy. He advances the familiar thesis that God gave mankind freedom as an integral part of creation and, of necessity, this freedom can be variously misused, *ergo* the *tremendum*.

> The bridge that I have, not casually but I fear insubstantially, cast over the abyss is one that sinks its pylons into the deep soil of human freedom and rationality, recognizing no less candidly now than before that freedom without the containment of reason returns to caprice and reason without the imagination of freedom is supineness and passivity.[32]

In response to this proposal two reservations must be entered. The first is evoked by the particular form that the reconstructed Cohenian version of this classic theodicy takes. The second concerns itself with the "Free-Will" defense in its generality.

(a) It is not clear why we need dipolar theism to produce the "Free-Will" defense; or that the "defense" is any more or any less sound in a dipolar than a traditional theistic context. That is, given Cohen's metaphysical dependence on Kabbalah and Schelling it is hard to see why or how their thinking makes any effective difference to the correctness, or otherwise, of the "Free-Will" position.

30. Maimonides, *Guide of the Perplexed*, English translation by S. Pines (Chicago, 1963), II, 25.
31. *The Tremendum*, p. 90. The emphasis of "assumed" is supplied by me.
32. Ibid., p. 94.

Cohen, in attempting to justify recourse to these sources in this context, i.e., in relation to the reality of authentic human freedom, criticizes traditional theism, what he chooses to call "fundamental theism," for holding that:

> God (is) respondent to extremity, the greater the human need the greater the certainty of his assistance, with the result that human life denies its essential freedom returning to ethical passivity and quietism in which everything is compelled to be God's direct work.[33]

But this criticism is inaccurate and establishes a "straw man" to be demolished by Cohenian dipolarity. "Fundamentalist" theologians have championed the "Free-Will" defense as vigorously and as "successfully" as Cohen; see, for example, Eliezer Berkovits' recent theological response to the Holocaust.[34] *Contra* Cohen, the pressing, gnawing problematic for the "fundamentalist" does not arise from the side of human freedom but rather from the belief in a Saving God, a belief radically challenged by the Holocaust. That is to say, the "fundamentalist" knows the evil of humankind to be a striking challenge to its elemental doctrine(s) regarding the character of the Creator. In comparison, Cohen's position is specifically structured in such a way so as not to have to grapple with this extreme difficulty. Indeed, this is the very reason for his particular theological reconstruction, i.e., the world's evil does not, cannot, impinge in a dipolar system upon God's being or status. But while this metaphysical redescription succeeds in solving, or dissolving, certain tensions—not allowing the evil of the world to count against God—it raises others of equal or greater force, especially regarding the Divine attributes, in particular, those relating to the categories of omnipotence and omniscience. Of course, Cohen wants to redefine these cardinal attributes, this is, if I understand his call for a renewal of a kabbalistic-Schelling model of Creation-Revelation ar-

ight, exactly what he intends. But in so doing does his dipolar God still remain God-like? Or has Cohen actually capitulated to those critics who deny God's meaningful reality, by whatever name, while attempting to make a virtue of this covert capitulation.

Then, too, the moral dimension of theodicy remains to be dealt with even after Cohen's ontological reconstructions, if for something of a new reason. For the moral, or rather, amoral corollary of the dipolar schematization of God is deeply disquieting. Cohen's dipolar God appears, of necessity, morally indifferent to human suffering and historical acts of evil,[35] factors of no small consequence for, in the end, the most sensitive as well as the most telling objections to theodicy arise from the side of the ethical.

(b) Elsewhere (in my *Post-Holocaust Dialogues* [New York, 1983], pp. 270–283 [reprinted above pp. 603–608]) I have analyzed the logical weaknesses inherent in attempting to meet the theological problems raised by the *Sho'ah* through recourse to the "Free-Will" argument. Though this analysis needs to be modified in certain specific respects given the total construction of Cohen's theodicy, he general negative conclusion there argued—that this defense is inadequate to the immense task at hand—applies in the case of *The Tremendum* as well. Rather than setting out my views again in full here let me add just one additional summary comment. Of all the "moves" made in the theodicy debate, the "Free-Will" gambit is as sober, intelligent and persuasive as any proposed alternative. However, it is, on the one hand, altogether too emaciated an "explanation" of the experience of the *victims*, while on the other hand, it vindicates God's morality, in Cohen's system God's indifference, too easily. Insofar as this argument has real strengths, and it does have such strengths, I think Cohen's employment of it shares in these residual virtues,[36] while insofar as it

---

33. Ibid., p. 96.
34. Compare in particular Eliezar Berkovits, *Faith after the Holocaust* (New York, 1973), and *With God in Hell* (New York, 1978). See also my critical discussion of Berkovits' views in *Post-Holocaust Dialogues* (New York, 1983), pp. 268–286. Selections from Berkovits' work appear above, pp. 463–489. My criticism of Berkovits is reprinted in this volume, pp. 603–608.

35. For more on the issue of the relation of God and History see section (5) below.
36. Cohen's reliance on this argument attests to his theological sensibilities.

remains incomplete, Cohen's version of the argument does not materially improve it or remedy its incompleteness.

(5) Cohen recognizes that his programmatic reconstruction impacts upon the fundamental question of God's relation to history. In explicating his understanding of this vexing relationship he writes:

> God and the life of God exist neither in conjunction with nor disjunction from the historical, but rather in continuous community and nexus. God is neither a function nor a cause of the historical nor wholly other and indifferent to the historical.[37]

If God then is unrelated to the historical in any of these more usual ways, as "neither a function nor a cause," how then is He present, i.e., not "wholly other and indifferent," and what difference does He make in this redefined and not wholly unambiguous role:

> I understand divine life," Cohen tells us, "to be rather a filament within the historical, but never the filament that we can identify and ignite according to our requirements, for in this and all other respects God remains God. As filament, the divine element of the historical is a precarious conductor always intimately linked to the historical—its presence securing the implicative and exponential significance of the historical— and always separate from it, since the historical is the domain of human freedom.[38]

But this advocacy of an "implicit" but non-causal nexus will not do.

In the final reckoning, this impressionistic articulation of the problem must collapse in upon itself for at some level of analysis the reciprocal notions of "causality" and "function" cannot be avoided. One can talk lyrically of God as a "filament" and a "conductor" in history as if these were not causal or connective concepts but upon deeper probing it will be revealed that they are. For talk of God as "filament" and "conductor" to retain its coherence, for it not to evaporate into empty metaphor, we have to know what it means to refer to God as a "filament," as a "conductor," no matter how precarious. To rescue these instrumental concepts from complete intellectual dissolution we need also to know something of how God is present in the world in these ways—what evidence can we point to in defense of these images.[39] For example, and deserving of a concrete answer, is the question: What of God is conducted? His love? Grace? Salvation? And if so, how? Wherein, against the darkness of the tremendum, do we experience His love, His grace, His salvation? To anticipate this objection as well as to attempt to deflect it by arguing that God is a "filament" but "never the filament that we can identify..."[40] is a recourse to "mystery"[41] in the obfuscatory rather than the explanatory sense. For as explanation it means simply: "I claim God is somehow present or related to history but don't ask me how." Alternatively, to come at this thesis from the other side, the analogies of "filament" and "conductor" are disquieting as analogs of the relation of God and history because they so strongly suggest passivity and inertness. If they are the proper analogs for God's activity or Presence in history, all our earlier concrete concerns about maintaining the integral vitality of Judaism re-surface. For the God of creation, covenants, Sinai and redemption is altogether different, i.e., qualitatively, metaphysically and morally other, than a "conductor" or "filament."

Given the dispassionate, disinterested, amoral nature of Cohen's deity, it is not surprising that the conclusion drawn from this descriptive recasting of God's role in "community and nexus" is, vis-à-vis the Sho'ah, finally, trivial (in the technical sense).

> Given these assumptions, it would follow that the tremendum does not alter the relation of God to himself, nor the relation in which God exists to the historical, nor the reality of creation to the process of eternal beginning within God, but

37. Cohen, The Tremendum, p. 97.
38. Ibid., pp. 97–98.
39. Here, that is, we raise issues as to meaning and related, but separate, questions as to verification, i.e., not conflating the two but asking about both.
40. Ibid., p. 97f.
41. See my paper on the "Logic and Language of Mystery," in S. Sykes and J. Clayton, eds., Christ, Faith and History (Cambridge, England, 1972), pp. 239–262, for a fuller criticism of this common theological gambit.

it does mean that man—not God—renders the filament of the divine incandescent or burns it out. There is, in the dialectic of man and God amid history, the indispensable recognition that man can obscure, eclipse, burn out the divine filament, grounding its natural movement of transcendence by a sufficient and oppository chthonic subscension. It is this which is meant by an abyss of the historical, the demonic, the *tremendum*.[42]

That the Holocaust makes no difference to God's relation to Himself we can grant *in principle* for the purposes of this analysis. And, logically and structurally, i.e., ontologically, we can allow for the purposes of argument Cohen's conclusion that "the *tremendum* does not alter the relation in which God exists to the historical." But, having granted both these premises it is necessary to conclude, *contra* Cohen, that the *tremendum* is not, and *in principle* could not be, a theological problem. It is, on its own premises, irrelevant to God's existence, irrelevant to God's relation to history and, on these criteria, irrelevant to God's relation to mankind— whatever mankind's relation to God.

The *tremendum* is seen by Cohen to be crucially relevant to man's recognition of a Creator, but this is anthropology for it perceives the *tremendum* only as human event with *no* consequences for God other than our indifference to Him. And our indifference does not appear to matter in any transcendental sense, for God apparently does not make any response to it. This is the logic of the "Free-Will" position driven to its "nth" degree. To a degree that makes God all but irrelevant. This remarkable implication flows, ironically, from Cohen's consummate attempt to redefine and reconstruct the theological landscape in order to *protect the viability of some* (not the traditional) *God-idea* in the face of the *tremendum*. An end it accomplishes through the total disconnection of God and the *tremendum*.

Talk of God's involvement in history in terms of "community"[43] after the manner of Cohen becomes unintelligible at this juncture. When God joins in the classic covenantal community of Israel He speaks of being together with His people, *Emo anochi B'tzarah* ("I will be with them in their troubles"),[44] i.e., God shares in the suffering of Israel. This doctrine is the root of the haunting midrashic image of the "Exile of the Shechinah" (*Galut ha-Shechinah*) that expresses the idea that the Divine Presence wanders along with exiled Israel.[45] However, in Cohen's projected "community" such an image of God's participation, as any representation of active participation on His part, is disallowed and unavailable. But then what sort of community can be said to exist between God and Israel, especially in light of the Death Camps—when six million of one's community are murdered, and it makes no difference to one's essential self, "God's relation to Himself," or to one's relations with the decimated community, "God's relation to the historical." Community is not an apt analogy or description of such unrelatedness.

(6) The a-Zionism[46] which is the complement of this ontology is logically consistent. If God is not the causal agent of Auschwitz He is not the causal agent of the Return to the Land. Hence Zionism becomes, if not theologically problematic, then certainly theologically irrelevant. And yet Cohen's formulation of his view is so gnomic, so sibylline, that I think, in fairness, it should be quoted rather than paraphrased.

Earlier in this discussion I expressed a provisional pessimism. I spoke darkly in the language of history about the Jewish people taking up the arms of history to come before it. For those who caught my gloom, it may well have sounded like the trope of one who stood outside not only the Jewish State but also *propter hoc* outside the Jewish people. Not at all. In fact, at this juncture, quite the contrary. Outside the Jewish State, any

42. Cohen, *The Tremendum*, p. 98.
43. This is the term Cohen uses to describe the relation of God to history, see ibid., p. 97. I have quoted this passage above.
44. Rav Joseph Soloveitchik has emphasized this text and its meaning for an understanding of covenantal existence and relationship in his classic article, "The

Lonely Man of Faith," in *Tradition*, Vol. 7, No. 2 (Summer, 1965): pp. 5–67.
45. Eliezer Berkovits has also expanded upon and utilized this notion in connection with the *Sho'ah*; see, for example, his *With God in Hell*, final chapter.
46. Stated in Cohen, *The Tremendum*, p. 101ff.

state for that matter, but never outside the Jewish people. Indeed, it is precisely because the Jewish people constitutes the eternal speaking of revelation to the Jew of history, the turn of that people into the winds of history, its taking up of the arms of the nations, is a turning of its guardianship of the word towards the nations, rather than its traditional posture as merely concerned observer. The being of the Jewish people is always behind the becoming of the nations, its reformulation as State coming at a moment when the states of the nations are weary and declining, but this is the way of Being—imponderable slowness, because its renewals and conservations are outside life and death, but always changes rung on eternal scales.[47]

In these cryptic remarks about the relation of Israel's Being to the "becoming" of the nations, Cohen seems to want to say something positive about the importance, theologically rendered, of the State of Israel, but does not know how and so falls back on a Rosenzweigian-like vocabulary and ideology. Yet, this will not do. Neither its obscurity nor its espousals recommend it. Indeed, its positive ideology claims too much given Cohen's stringent earlier ontological commitments while, on the other hand, it clearly does not dare enough, from a Jewish theological perspective, where the State of Israel is concerned. And this not least because after Auschwitz, and after more than forty years of the existence of the State of Israel, one

cannot so easily dissociate the nature and fate of the Jewish people from that of the Jewish State in which about thirty percent of the Jewish people now live, an ever-increasing percentage, and in which more than forty percent of Jewish infants world wide are born. A theology in which this does not matter, as the *Sho'ah* does not matter theologically, cannot speak meaningfully to the Jewish condition after Auschwitz.[48]

III

The Tremendum is an important work, though at times stylistically and theologically infuriating. Important because it forces us to do theology, a rare occurrence in modern Jewish circles; important because it is saturated with and grows out of an intense concern with the people of Israel; important because it knows, despite its intellectual roots, its conceptual dogmatics, that something has happened in the *tremendum* (and in the State of Israel) that stretches us to the limits as human beings as well as theologians. We therefore need to learn those things that Cohen can teach us. And then having learnt them, we need to go beyond them, beyond Cohen's deeply problematical dipolar theism and its profoundly unsatisfactory corollaries, in search of a more comprehensive, more Jewishly satisfying response to the problematics of Jewish life and thought after, and in the face of, the *tremendum*.

47. Ibid., p. 109.
48. The single exception to this generalization is to be found in right-wing ultra-orthodox circles, e.g., Satmar Ḥasidism and among the *Naturei Karta* of Jerusalem, who can carry on a meaningful Jewish existence because of their profound commitment to traditional Torah observance and study. Outside of these very small, very specially constituted groups, however, my judgment stands.

Hans Jonas

Hans Jonas (1903–1993) was born in a small town in Germany. In the 1920s, he studied philosophy and theology at the University of Freiburg under the world-famous philosopher Martin Heidegger and the well-known theologian Rudolf Bultmann. In 1928, he received his doctorate *summa cum laude* from the University of Marburg. In 1933, with the accession of Hitler to power, he left Germany and found his way to mandate Palestine, where he began to lecture on philosophy and the history of religions. With the beginning of World War II, he joined the British army and fought in the North African campaign. After the end of the war, he returned to his academic studies while also serving in Israel's army, with the rank of lieutenant, during Israel's War of Independence in 1948–1949. In 1949, he left Israel for a teaching position at McGill University in Montreal, Canada. This was followed by a one-year appointment at Carleton College in Ottawa, and a more permanent position at the New School for Social Research in New York City. He chaired the Department of Philosophy at the New School from 1957 to 1963 and served as Alvin Johnson Professor of Philosophy at the New School between 1966 and his retirement in 1976.

His first important scholarly monograph, dealing with early Christian doctrine, was published in German in 1930 under the title *Augustin und das paulinische Frei-heitsproblem*. It clearly shows the influence of Heidegger's existentialism and Bult-mann's "demythologizing" hermeneutic. This was followed by his most well known work, *Gnosis und spaetaniker Geist* (1934–1935), which originally appeared in two volumes in German. Again, Jonas worked to demythologize early gnosticism and give it a this-worldly interpretation. The study was translated into English in 1958 and has remained influential ever since.

Late in life, Jonas became interested in a wide range of ethical issues, including those raised by medicine, medical practice, and modern biology. He voiced his views on these issues in a book entitled *The Phenomenon of Life* (1982) and again in *The Imperative of Responsibility* (1984).

SELECTION

This selection was originally Hans Jonas's speech on the occasion of receiving the Leopold Lucas Prize from the University of Tübingen in 1984. In it, theologizing under the long shadow cast by the reality of the Nazi death camps, he attempted, like Arthur A. Cohen and others, to rethink the meaning of the idea of God. In place of the biblical notion of the deity, Jonas proposes a conception of God that emphasizes God's "becoming" and His lack of omnipotence. "For the sake of any viable theology," he tells his reader, "we cannot uphold the time-honored (medieval) doctrine of absolute, unlimited divine power." Jonas argues that this major concession regarding our idea of

God is required if the concept of the divine is not to lose all intelligibility and result in what he terms "complete divine inscrutability."

Selected Bibliography

Works by Hans Jonas

Philosophical Essays (Chicago, 1980).
The Phenomenon of Life (New York, 1982).
The Imperative of Responsibility (Chicago, 1984).

THE CONCEPT OF GOD AFTER AUSCHWITZ: A JEWISH VOICE

After Auschwitz, that is to say, after the Holocaust for whose widely dispersed reality that single name serves as a blindingly concentrating lens, the Jew can no longer simply hold onto the time-honored theology of his faith that has been shattered by it. Nor, if he wills Judaism to continue, can he simply discard his theological heritage and be left with nothing. "Auschwitz" marks a divide between a "before" and an "after," where the latter will be forever different from the former. For the sake of this after, and in the somber light of the dividing event, we must rethink the concept of God entrusted to us from the past. And even if not to the future, do we owe it to the fast-receding shadows of the victims that their long-gone cry to a silent God be not left without some sort of an answer if we can possibly find one for them and for us.[1] So we must try.

What I have to offer is a piece of frankly speculative theology. Whether this behooves a philosopher is a question I leave open. Immanuel Kant has banished everything of the kind from the territory of theoretical reason and hence from the business of philosophy; and the logical positivism of our century, the entire dominant analytical creed, even denies to the linguistic expressions such reasonings employ for their purported subject matters this very object-significance itself, that is, any conceptual meaning at all, declaring already—prior to questions of truth and verification—the mere speech about them to

be nonsensical. At this, to be sure, old Kant himself would have been utterly astounded. For he, to the contrary, held these alleged nonobjects to be the highest objects of all, about which reason can never cease to be concerned, although it cannot hope ever to obtain a knowledge of them and in their pursuit is necessarily doomed to failure by the impassable limits of human cognition. But this cognitive veto, given the yet justified concern, leaves another way open besides that of complete abstention: Bowing to the decree that "knowledge" eludes us here, nay, even waiving this very goal from the outset, one may yet meditate on things of this nature in terms of sense and meaning. For the contention—this fashionable contention—that not even sense and meaning pertain to them is easily disposed of as a circular, tautological inference from first having defined "sense" as that which in the end is verifiable by sense data or from generally equating "meaningful" with "knowable." To this axiomatic fiat by definition only he is bound who has first consented to it. He who has not is free, therefore, to work at the *concept* of God, even knowing that there is no *proof* of God, as a task of understanding, not of knowledge; and such working is philosophical when it keeps to the rigor of concept and its connection with the universe of concepts.

But of course, this epistemological *laissez-passer* is much too general and impersonal for the matter

1. In the opening paragraph of the German address [given on the occasion of receiving the Lucas Prize at the University of Tübingen], I had noted that Dorothea Lucas, mother of the endower of the prize, perished in Auschwitz as did my mother, and that this fact moved me irresistibly to the choice of my topic.

at hand. As Kant granted to the practical reason what he denied to the theoretical, so may *we* allow the force of a unique and shattering experience a voice in the question of what "is the matter" with God. And there, right away, arises the question, What did Auschwitz add to that which one could always have known about the extent of the terrible and horrendous things that humans can do to humans and from times immemorial have done? And what has it added in particular to what is familiar to us Jews from a millennial history of suffering and forms so essential a part of our collective memory? The *question of Job* has always been the main question of theodicy—of general theodicy because of the existence of evil as such in the world, and of particular theodicy in its sharpening by the riddle of election, of the purported covenant between Israel and its God. As to this sharpening, under which our present question also falls, one could at first invoke—as the prophets did—the covenant itself for an explanation of what befell the human party to it: The "people of the covenant" had been unfaithful to it. In the long ages of faithfulness thereafter, guilt and retribution no longer furnished the explanation but the idea of "witness" did instead—this creation of the Maccabean age, which bequeathed to posterity the concept of the martyr. It is of its very meaning that precisely the innocent and the just suffer the worst. In deference to the idea of witness, whole communities in the Middle Ages met their death by sword and fire with the *Sh'ma Jisrael,* the avowal of God's Oneness, on their lips. The Hebrew name for this is *Kiddush-hashem,* "sanctification of the Name," and the slaughtered were called "saints." Through their sacrifice shone the light of promise, of the final redemption by the Messiah to come.

Nothing of this will still serve us in dealing with the event for which "Auschwitz" has become the symbol. Not fidelity or infidelity, belief or unbelief, not guilt and punishment, not trial, witness, and messianic hope, nay, not even strength or weakness, heroism or cowardice, defiance or submission had a place there. Of all this, Auschwitz, which also devoured the infants and babes, knew nothing; to none of it (with rarest exceptions) did the factory-like working of its machine give room. Not for the *sake* of faith did the victims die (as did, after all, "Jehovah's Witnesses"), nor *because* of their faith or any self-affirmed bend of their being as persons were they murdered. Dehumanization by utter degradation and deprivation preceded their dying, no glimmer of dignity was left to the freights bound for the "final solution," hardly a trace of it was found in the surviving skeletal specters of the liberated camps. And yet, paradox of paradoxes: It *was* the ancient people of the "covenant," no longer believed in by those involved, killers and victims alike, but nevertheless just this and no other people, who under the fiction of race had been chosen for this wholesale annihilation—the most monstrous inversion of election into curse, which defied all possible endowment with meaning. There does, then, in spite of all, exist a connection—of a wholly perverse kind—with the god seekers and prophets of yore, whose descendants were thus collected out of the dispersion and gathered into the unity of joint death. And God let it happen. What God could let it happen?

Here we must note that on this question the Jew is in greater theoretical difficulty than the Christian. To the Christian (of the stern variety) the world is anyway largely of the devil and always an object of suspicion—the human world in particular because of original sin. But to the Jew, who sees in "this" world the locus of divine creation, justice, and redemption, God is eminently the Lord of *history,* and in this respect Auschwitz calls, even for the believer, the whole traditional concept of God into question. It has, indeed, as I have just tried to show, added to the Jewish historical experience something unprecedented and of a nature no longer assimilable by the old theological categories. Accordingly, one who will not thereupon just give up the concept of God altogether—and even the philosopher has a right to such an unwillingness—must rethink it so that it still remains thinkable; and that means seeking a new answer to the old question of (and about) Job. The Lord of history, we suspect, will have to go by the board in this quest. To repeat then, What God could let it happen?

For a possible, if groping, answer, I fall back on a speculative attempt with which I once ventured to meet the different question of immortality but in which also the specter of Auschwitz already played its part. On that occasion, I resorted to a *myth* of my own invention—that vehicle of imaginative but credible conjecture that Plato allowed for the sphere beyond the knowable. Allow me to repeat it here:

In the beginning, for unknowable reasons, the ground of being, or the Divine, chose to give itself over to the chance and risk and endless variety of becoming. And wholly so: entering into the adventure of space and time, the deity held back nothing of itself; no uncommitted or unimpaired part remained to direct, correct, and ultimately guarantee the devious working-out of its destiny in creation. On this unconditional immanence the modern temper insists. It is its courage or despair, in any case its bitter honesty, to take our being-in-the-world seriously: to view the world as left to itself, its laws as brooking no interference, and the rigor of our belonging to it as not softened by extramundane providence. The same our myth postulates for God's being in the world. Not, however, in the sense of pantheistic immanence: if world and God are simply the same, the world at each moment and in each state represents His fullness, and God can neither lose nor gain. Rather, in order that the world might be, and be for itself, God renounced His being, divesting Himself of his deity—to receive it back from the odyssey of time weighted with the chance harvest of unforeseeable temporal experience: transfigured or possibly even disfigured by it. In such self-forfeiture of divine integrity for the sake of unprejudiced becoming, no other foreknowledge can be admitted than that of *possibilities* which cosmic being offers in its own terms: to these, God committed His cause in effacing Himself for the world.

And for eons His cause is safe in the slow hands of cosmic chance and probability—while all the time we may surmise a patient memory of the gyrations of matter to accumulate into an ever more expectant accompaniment of eternity to the labors of time—a hesitant emergence of transcendence from the opaqueness of immanence.

And then the first stirring of life—a new language of the world: and with it a tremendous quickening of concern in the eternal realm and a sudden leap in its growth toward recovery of its plenitude. It is the world accident for which becoming deity had waited and with which its prodigal stake begins to show signs of being redeemed. From the infinite swell of feeling, sensing, striving, and acting, which ever more varied and intense rises above the mute eddyings of matter, eternity gains strength, filling with content after content of self-affirmation, and the awakening God can first pronounce creation to be good.

But note that with life together came death, and that mortality is the price which the new possibility of being called "life" had to pay for itself. If permanence were the point, life should not have started out in the first place, for in no possible form can it match the durability of inorganic bodies. It is essentially precarious and corruptible being, an adventure in mortality, obtaining from long-lasting matter on its terms—the short terms of metabolizing organism—the borrowed, finite careers of individual selves. Yet it is precisely through the briefly snatched self-feeling, doing, and suffering of *finite* individuals, with the pitch of awareness heightened by the very press of finitude, that the divine landscape bursts into color and the deity comes to experience itself. . . .

Note also this, that with life's innocence before the advent of knowledge, God's cause cannot go wrong. Whatever variety evolution brings forth adds to the possibilities of feeling and acting, and thus enriches the self-experiencing of the ground of being. Every new dimension of world response opened up in its course means another modality for God's trying out His hidden essence and discovering Himself through the surprises of the world adventure. And all its harvest of anxious toil, whether bright or dark, swells the transcendent treasure of temporally lived eternity. If this is true for the broadening spectrum of diversity as such, it is even truer for the heightening pitch and passion of life that go with the twin rise of perception and motility in animals. The ever more sharpened keenness of appetite and fear, pleasure and pain, triumph and anguish, love and even cruelty—their very edge is the deity's gain. Their countless, yet never blunted incidence—hence the necessity of death and new birth—supplies the tempered essence from which the godhead reconstitutes itself. All this, evolution provides in the mere lavishness of its play and the sternness of its spur. Its creatures, by merely fulfilling themselves in pursuit of their lives, vindicate the divine venture. Even their suffering deepens the fullness of the symphony. Thus, this side of good and evil, God cannot lose in the great evolutionary game.

Nor yet can He fully win in the shelter of its innocence, and a new expectancy grows in Him in answer to the direction which the unconscious drift of immanence gradually takes.

And then He trembles as the thrust of evolution, carried by its own momentum, passes the threshold where innocence ceases and an entirely new criterion of success and failure takes hold of the divine stake. The advent of man means the advent of knowledge and freedom, and with this supremely double-edged gift the innocence of the mere subject of self-fulfilling life has given way to the charge of responsibility under the disjunction of good and evil. To the promise and risk of this agency the divine cause, revealed at last, henceforth finds itself committed; and its issue trembles in the balance. The image of God, haltingly begun by the universe, for so long worked upon—and left undecided—in the wide and then narrowing spirals of prehuman life, passes with this last twist, and with a dramatic quickening of the movement, into man's precarious trust, to be completed, saved, or spoiled by what he will do to himself and the world. And in this awesome impact of his deeds on God's destiny, on the very complexion of eternal being, lies the immortality of man.

With the appearance of man, transcendence awakened to itself and henceforth accompanies his doings with the bated breath of suspense, hoping and beckoning, rejoicing and grieving, approving and frowning—and, I daresay, making itself felt to him even while not intervening in the dynamics of his worldly scene: For can it not be that by the reflection of its own state as it wavers with the record of man, the transcendent casts light and shadow over the human landscape?[2]

Such is the tentative myth I once proposed for consideration in a different context. It has theological implications that only later unfolded

to me. Of these I shall develop here some of the more obvious ones—hoping that this translation from image into concept will somehow connect what so far must seem a strange and rather willful private fantasy with the more responsible tradition of Jewish religious thought. In this manner I try to redeem the poetic liberties of my earlier, roving attempt.

First, and most obviously, I have been speaking of a *suffering God*—which immediately seems to clash with the biblical conception of divine majesty. There is, of course, a Christian connotation of the term "suffering God" with which my myth must not be confounded; it does not speak, as does the former, of a special act by which the deity at one time, and for the special purpose of saving man, sends part of itself into a particular situation of suffering (the incarnation and crucifixion). If anything in what I said makes sense, then the sense is that the relation of God to the world *from the moment of creation,* and certainly from the creation of man on, involves suffering on the part of God. It involves, to be sure, suffering on the part of the creature too, but this truism has always been recognized in every theology. Not so the idea of God's suffering with creation, and of this I said that, prima facie, it clashes with the biblical conception of divine majesty. But does it really clash as extremely as it seems at first glance? Do not we also in the Bible encounter God as slighted and rejected by man and grieving over him? Do not we encounter Him as ruing that He created man, and suffering from the disappointment He experiences with him—and with His chosen people in particular? We remember the prophet Hosea, and God's love lamenting over Israel, His unfaithful wife.

Then, second, the myth suggests the picture of a *becoming God.* It is a God emerging in time instead of possessing a completed being that remains identical with itself throughout eternity. Such an idea of divine becoming is surely at variance with the Greek, Platonic-Aristotelian tradition of philosophical theology that, since its medieval incorporation into the Jewish and Christian theological tradition, has somehow

2. Hans Jonas, "Immortality and the Modern Temper," first printed in *Harvard Theological Review* 55 (1962): 1–20; now in H. Jonas, *The Phenomenon of Life* (Chicago, 1982), pp. 262–281.

usurped for itself an authority to which it is not at all entitled by authentic Jewish (and also Christian) standards. Transtemporality, impassibility, and immutability have been taken to be necessary attributes of God. And the ontological distinction that classical thought made between "being" and "becoming," with the latter characteristic of the lower, sensible world, excluded every shadow of becoming from the pure, absolute being of the godhead. But this Hellenic concept has never accorded well with the spirit and language of the Bible, and the concept of divine becoming can actually be better reconciled with it.

For what does the becoming God mean? Even if we do not go so far as our myth suggests, that much at least we must concede of "becoming" in God as lies in the mere fact that He is affected by what happens in the world, and "affected" means altered, made different. Even apart from the fact that creation as such—the act itself and the lasting result thereof—was after all a decisive change in God's own state, insofar as He is now no longer alone, His continual *relation* to the creation, once this exists and moves in the flux of becoming, means that He experiences something with the world, that His own being is affected by what goes on in it. This holds already for the mere relation of accompanying knowledge, let alone that of caring interest. Thus if God is in any relation to the world—which is the cardinal assumption of religion—then by that token alone the Eternal has "temporalized" Himself and progressively becomes different through the actualizations of the world process.

One incidental consequence of the idea of the becoming God is that it destroys the idea of an eternal recurrence of the same. This was Nietzsche's alternative to Christian metaphysics, which in this case is the same as Jewish metaphysics. It is indeed the extreme symbol of the turn to unconditional temporality and of the complete negation of any transcendence that could keep a memory of what happens in time to assume that, by the mere exhaustion of the possible combinations and recombinations of material elements, it must come to pass that an "initial" configuration recurs and the whole cycle starts over again, and if once, then innumerable times—Nietzsche's "ring of rings, the ring of eternal recurrence." However, if we assume that

eternity is not unaffected by what happens in time, there can never be a recurrence of the same because God will not be the same after He has gone through the experience of a world process. Any new world coming after the end of one will carry, as it were, in its own heritage the memory of what has gone before; or, in other words, there will not be an indifferent and dead eternity but an eternity that grows with the accumulating harvest of time.

Bound up with the concepts of a suffering and a becoming God is that of a *caring God*—a God not remote and detached and self-contained but involved with what He cares for. Whatever the "primordial" condition of the godhead, He ceased to be self-contained once He let Himself in for the existence of a world by creating such a world or letting it come to be. God's caring about His creatures is, of course, among the most familiar tenets of Jewish faith. But my myth stresses the less familiar aspect that this caring God is not a sorcerer who in the act of caring also provides the fulfillment of His concern: He has left something for other agents to do and thereby has made His care dependent on them. He is therefore also an endangered God, a God who runs a risk. Clearly that must be so, or else the world would be in a condition of permanent perfection. The fact that it is not bespeaks one of two things: that either the One God does not exist (though more than one may), or that the One has given to an agency other than Himself, though created by Him, a power and a right to act on its own and therewith a scope for at least codetermining that which is a concern of His. This is why I said that the caring God is not a sorcerer. Somehow He has, by an act of inscrutable wisdom or love or whatever else the divine motive may have been, forgone the guaranteeing of His self-satisfaction by His own power, after He has first, by the act of creation itself, forgone being "all in all."

And therewith we come to what is perhaps the most critical point in our speculative, theological venture: This is not an omnipotent God. We argue indeed that, for the sake of our image of God and our whole relation to the divine, for the sake of any viable theology, we cannot uphold the time-honored (medieval) doctrine of absolute, unlimited divine power. Let me argue this first, on a purely logical plane, by pointing out the paradox in the idea of absolute power. The logical situation indeed is by no means that divine omnipotence is the rationally plausible and somehow self-recommending doctrine, while that of its limitation is wayward and in need of defense. Quite the opposite. From the very concept of power, it follows that omnipotence is a self-contradictory, self-destructive, indeed, senseless concept. The situation is similar to that of freedom in the human realm: Far from beginning where necessity ends, freedom consists of and lives in pitting itself against necessity. Separated from it, freedom loses its object and becomes as void as force without resistance. Absolute freedom would be empty freedom that cancels itself out. So, too, does empty power, and absolute, exclusive power would be just that. Absolute, total power means power not limited by anything, not even by the mere existence of something other than the possessor of that power; for the very existence of such another would already constitute a limitation, and the one would have to annihilate it so as to save its absoluteness. Absolute power then, in its solitude, has no object on which to act. But as objectless power it is a powerless power, canceling itself out: "All" equals "zero" here. In order for it to act, there must be something else, and as soon as there is, the one is not all-powerful any more, even though in any comparison its power may be superior by any degree you please to imagine. The existence of another object limits the power of the most powerful agent at the same time that it allows it to be an agent. In brief, power as such is a *relational* concept and requires relation.

Again, power meeting no *resistance* in its relatum is equal to no power at all: Power is exercised only in relation to something that itself has power. Power, unless otiose, consists in the capacity to overcome something; and something's existence as such is enough to provide this condition. For existence means resistance and thus opposing force. Just as, in physics, force without resistance—that is counterforce—remains empty, so in metaphysics does power without counterpower, unequal as the latter may be. That, therefore, on which power acts must have a power of its own, even if that power derives from the first and was initially granted to

it, as one with its existence, by a self-renunciation of limitless power—that is, in the act of creation.

In short, it cannot be that all power is on the side of one agent only. Power must be divided so that there be any power at all.

But besides this logical and ontological objection, there is a more theological, genuinely religious objection to the idea of absolute and unlimited divine omnipotence. We can have divine omnipotence together with divine goodness only at the price of complete divine inscrutability. Seeing the existence of evil in the world, we must sacrifice intelligibility in God to the combination of the other two attributes. Only a completely unintelligible God can be said to be absolutely good and absolutely powerful, yet tolerate the world as it is. Put more generally, the three attributes at stake—absolute goodness, absolute power, and intelligibility—stand in such a logical relation to one another that the conjunction of any two of them excludes the third. The question then is, Which are truly integral to our concept of God, and which, being of lesser force, must give way to their superior claim? Now, surely, goodness is inalienable from the concept of God and not open to qualification. Intelligibility, conditional on both God's nature and man's capacity, is on the latter count indeed subject to qualification but on no account to complete elimination. The *Deus absconditus,* the hidden God (not to speak of an absurd God) is a profoundly un-Jewish conception. Our teaching, the Torah, rests on the premise and insists that we can understand God, not completely, to be sure, but something of Him—of His will, intentions, and even nature—because He has told us. There has been revelation, we have His commandments and His law, and He has directly communicated with some—His prophets—as His mouth for all men in the language of men and their times: refracted thus in this limiting medium but not veiled in dark mystery. A completely hidden God is not an acceptable concept by Jewish norms.

But He would have to be precisely that if together with being good He were conceived as all-powerful. After Auschwitz, we can assert with greater force than ever before that an omnipotent deity would have to be either not good or (in His world rule, in which alone we can "observe" Him) totally unintelligible. But if God is to be intelligible in some manner and to some extent (and to this we must hold), then His goodness must be compatible with the existence of evil, and this it is only if He is not *all* powerful. Only then can we uphold that He is intelligible and good, and there is yet evil in the world. And since we have found the concept of omnipotence to be dubious anyway, it is this that has to give way.

So far, our argument about omnipotence has done no more than lay it down as a principle for any acceptable theology continuous with the Jewish heritage that God's power be seen as limited by something whose being in its own right and whose power to act on its own authority He Himself acknowledges.[3] Admittedly, we have the choice to interpret this as a voluntary concession on God's part, which He is free to revoke at will—that is, as the restraint of a power that He still and always possesses in full but, for the sake of creation's own autonomous right, chooses not fully to employ. To devout believers, this is probably the most palatable choice. But it will not suffice. For in view of the enormity of what, among the bearers of His image in creation, some of them time and again, and wholly unilaterally, inflict on innocent others, one would expect the good God at times to break His own, however stringent, rule of restraint and intervene with a saving miracle.[4] But no saving miracle occurred. Through the years that Auschwitz raged God remained silent. The miracles that did occur came forth from man alone: The deeds of those solitary, mostly unknown "just of the nations" who did not shrink from utter sacrifice in order to help, to save, to mitigate—even, when nothing else was left, unto sharing Israel's lot. Of them I shall speak again. But God was silent. And there I say, or my myth says, not because He chose not to, but because He *could* not intervene did He fail to intervene. For reasons decisively prompted by contemporary experience, I entertain the idea of a God who for a time—the time of the ongoing world process—has divested Himself of any power to interfere with the physical course of things; and who responds to the impact on His being by worldly events, not "with a mighty hand and outstretched arm," as we Jews on every Passover recite in remembering the exodus from Egypt, but with the mutely insistent appeal of his unfulfilled goal.

In this, assuredly, my speculation strays far from oldest Judaic teaching. Several of Maimonides' [1135–1204] Thirteen Articles of Faith, which we solemnly chant in our services, fall away with the "mighty hand": the assertions about God ruling the universe, His rewarding the good and punishing the wicked, even about the coming of the promised Messiah. Not, however, those about His call to the souls,[5] His inspiration of the prophets and the Torah, thus also not the idea of election: For only to the physical realm does the impotence of God refer. Most of all, the *Oneness* of God stands unabated and with it the "Hear, O Israel!" No Manichaean dualism is enlisted to explain evil; from the hearts of men alone does it arise and gain power in the world. The mere permitting, indeed, of human freedom involved a renouncing of sole divine power henceforth. And our discussion of power as such has already led us to deny divine omnipotence, anyway.

The elimination of divine omnipotence leaves the theoretical choice between the alternatives of either some preexistent—theological or ontological—*dualism*, or of God's *self*-limitation

---

3. The same principle has been argued, with a slightly different reasoning, by Rabbi Jack Bemporad, "Toward a New Jewish Theology," *American Judaism* (Winter 1964–1965): 9ff.

4. An occasional miracle, i.e., extramundane intervention in the closed causality of the physical realm, is not incompatible with the general validity of the laws of nature (rare exceptions do not void empirical rules) and might even, by all appearances, perfectly conform to them—on this question, see H. Jonas, *Philosophical Essays* (Chicago, 1980), pp. 66–67, and, more extensively, my Rudolf Bultmann Memorial address of 1976 at Marburg University, "Is Faith Still Possible? Memories of Rudolf Bultmann and Reflections on the Philosophical Aspects of His Work," *Harvard Theological Review* 75, no. 1 (January 1982): 1–25, esp. 9–15; see also the relevant pages of this address for a statement of the religious objection against thinking of God as "Lord of history."

5. For more about this inalienable postulate of revealed religion—the possibility of revelation itself, i.e., of God's speaking to human *minds* even if debarred from intervening in physical *things*—see Jonas, "Is Faith Still Possible?" pp. 18–20.

through the creation from nothing. The dualistic alternative in turn might take the Manichaean form of an active force of evil forever opposing the divine purpose in the universal scheme of things: a two-god theology; or the Platonic form of a passive medium imposing, no less universally, imperfection on the embodiment of the ideal in the world: a form-matter dualism. The first is plainly unacceptable to Judaism. The second answers at best the problem of imperfection and natural necessity but not that of positive evil, which implies a freedom empowered by its own authority independent of that of God; and it is the fact and success of deliberate evil rather than the inflictions of blind, natural causality—the use of the latter in the hands of responsible agents (Auschwitz rather than the earthquake of Lisbon [1755])—with which Jewish theology has to contend at this hour. Only with creation from nothing do we have the oneness of the divine principle combined with that self-limitation that then permits (gives "room" to) the existence and autonomy of a world. Creation was that act of absolute sovereignty with which it consented, for the sake of self-determined finitude, to be absolute no more—an act, therefore, of divine self-restriction.

And here let us remember that Jewish tradition itself is really not quite so monolithic in the matter of divine sovereignty as official doctrine makes it appear. The mighty undercurrent of the kabbalah, which Gershom Scholem [1897–1982] in our days has brought to light anew, knows about a divine fate bound up with the coming-to-be of a world. There we meet highly original, very unorthodox speculations in whose company mine would not appear so wayward after all. Thus, for example, my myth at bottom only pushes further the idea of the *tzimtzum,* that cosmogonic center concept of the Lurianic kabbalah.[6] *Tzimtzum* means contraction, withdrawal, self-limitation.

To make room for the world, the *En-Sof* (Infinite; literally, No-End) of the beginning had to contract Himself so that, vacated by Him, empty space could expand outside of Him: the "Nothing" in which and from which God could then create the world. Without this retreat into Himself, there could be no "other" outside God, and only His continued holding-Himself-in preserves the finite things from losing their separate being again into the divine "all in all."

My myth goes further still. The contraction is total as far as power is concerned; as a whole has the Infinite ceded His power to the finite and thereby wholly delivered His cause into its hands. Does that still leave anything for a relation to God?

Let me answer this question with a last quotation from the earlier writing. By forgoing its own inviolateness, the eternal ground allowed the world to be. To this self-denial all creation owes its existence and with it has received all there is to receive from beyond. Having given Himself whole to the becoming world, God has no more to give: It is man's now to give to Him. And he may give by seeing to it in the ways of his life that it does not happen or happen too often, and not on his account, that it "repented the Lord"[7] to have made the world. This may well be the secret of the "thirty-six righteous ones" whom, according to Jewish lore, the world shall never lack[8] and of whose number in our time were possibly some of those "just of the nations" I have mentioned before: Their guessed-at secret being that, with the superior valency of good over evil, which (we hope) obtains in the noncausal logic of things there, their hidden holiness can outweigh countless guilt, redress the balance of a generation, and secure the peace of the invisible realm.[9]

All this, let it be said at the end, is but stammering. Even the words of the great seers and

6. Originated by Isaac Luria (1534–1572).
7. Genesis 6:6–7.
8. B.T. *Sanhedrin* 97[b]; B.T. *Sukkah* 45[b].
9. The idea that it is we who can help God rather than God helping us I have since found movingly expressed by one of the Auschwitz victims herself, a young Dutch Jew, who validated it by acting on it unto death. It is found in Etty Hillesum, *An Interrupted Life: The Diaries of Etty Hillesum, 1941–1943* (New York, 1983). When the deportations in Holland began, in 1942, she came forward and volunteered for the Westerbork concentration camp, there to help in the hospital and to share in the fate of her people. In September 1943 she was shipped in one of the usual mass transports, to Auschwitz and "died" there on 30 November 1943. Her diaries have survived but were only recently published.

adorers—the prophets and the psalmists—which stand beyond comparison, were stammers before the eternal mystery. Every mortal answer to Job's question, too, cannot be more than that. Mine is the opposite to the one given by the Book of Job: This, for an answer, invoked the plenitude of God's power; mine, His chosen voidance of it. And yet, strange to say, both are in praise. For the divine renunciation was made so that we, the mortals, could be. This, too, so it seems to me, is an answer to Job: That in him God Himself suffers. Which is true, if any, we can know of none of the answers ever tried. Of my poor word thereto I can only hope that it be not wholly excluded from what Goethe [1749–1832], in "Testament of Old Persian Faith," thus put into Zarathustra's mouth:

> All that ever stammers praising the Most
> High
> Is in circles there assembled far and
> nigh.[10]

I quote from Neal Ascherson ("In Hell," *New York Review of Books* 31, no. 13 [19 July 1984]: 8–12, esp. 9):

> She does not exactly "find God," but rather constructs one for herself. The theme of the diaries becomes increasingly religious, and many of the entries are prayers. Her God is someone to whom she makes promises, but of whom she expects and asks nothing. "I shall try to help You, God, to stop my strength ebbing away, though I cannot vouch for it in advance. But one thing is becoming increasingly clear to me: that You cannot help us, that we must help You to help ourselves. . . . Alas, there does not seem to be much You Yourself can do about our circumstances, about our lives. Neither do I hold You responsible. You cannot help us, but we must help You and define Your dwelling place in us to the last."

Reading this was to me a stunning confirmation, by a true witness, of my so much later and sheltered musings—and a consoling correction of my sweeping statement that we had no martyrs there.

10. "Und was nur am Lob des Höchsten stammelt, / Ist in Kreis' um Kreise dort versammelt"; Goethe, "Vermächtnis altpersischen Glaubens."

Amos Funkenstein

Amos Funkenstein (1937–1995) was, at the time of his death, professor of Jewish studies at the University of California at Berkeley. He previously held appointments at UCLA and at Tel Aviv and Stanford universities. He came from a very Orthodox religious home in Jerusalem and received a traditional Jewish education in some of the best Orthodox schools in the city. However, as a teenager, he already declared his lack of belief in God. He continued his advanced studies for one year at the Hebrew University of Jerusalem and then, in 1958, went to Germany where he received his B.A. and, in 1965, his doctorate in philosophy from the Free University of Berlin for a dissertation entitled *Heilsplan and natürliche Entwicklung*. He then came to America to begin his teaching career at UCLA in 1967.

His two major intellectual interests were the emergence of modern science and its impact on modern philosophy, as analyzed especially in his important 1986 study, *Theology and the Scientific Imagination,* and Jewish philosophy in all its forms in both the medieval and modern periods. He wrote a substantial book on Maimonides, the greatest of the medieval Jewish philosophers, as well as important studies of the major medieval Jewish biblical commentator and kabbalist Moses ben Naḥman (Naḥmanides). He felt very strongly that knowledge of this medieval tradition was required in order to fully understand modern Jewish thought. At the same time, his long years of study in Germany made him especially familiar with and sympathetic to the long line of modern Jewish philosophers from Moses Mendelssohn to Martin Buber and Franz Rosenzweig, though he did not share their religious beliefs. In addition, he had deep interests in the philosophy of history, Jewish history, and the history of biblical exegesis. A polymath, his work ranges over a wide variety of eras and subjects.

SELECTION

In his essay "Theological Interpretations of the Holocaust," which first appeared in *Unanswered Questions: Nazi Germany and the Genocide of the Jews,* edited by François Furet (New York, 1989), pp. 275–303, Amos Funkenstein questions the very premise of viewing the significance of the Holocaust from a theological rather than an anthropological perspective. To make the case for doing the latter, he begins with a telling critique of various influential ultra-Orthodox views, e.g., those of R. Yoel Teitelbaum, the Satmar Rebbe, who saw the cause of the Holocaust in the Zionist attempt to bring salvation through human effort, thus, in his view violating God's will, and the Israeli followers of *Gush Emunim* (Bloc of the Faithful), who see the cause of the Holocaust in exactly the opposite way, i.e., as a result of Israel's passivity and lack of initiative in leaving the exile and reclaiming the Land of Israel. Funkenstein then moves on to critically evaluate a group of theologians whom he identifies as being "more courageous" and who use the Holocaust as a justification for atheism or the loss of faith, such as Karl Rahner, Gregory Baum, and Richard L. Rubenstein. Funkenstein sees the root of these theologies in Heidegger's famous work *Sein und Zeit [Being and Time]*, in which Heidegger "distinguishes two modes of human existence, the inauthentic and the authentic." Authentic existence is defined as the life that is "capable of asking the question-of-being, the question to which there is *ipso facto* no answer." Conversely, inauthentic existence is defined as being "alienated from itself, lost in the world in such a manner that it uses things in the world and is absorbed in it." Now, even though, as Funkenstein notes, Heidegger intended that this distinction regarding alternative forms of human existence should carry no moral corollaries, such implications are unavoidable since, "from an ethical point of view, *every life is authentic.*" That is, "life, the life of each individual, must be taken to be always meaningful in and of itself." In other words, Heidegger's distinction is dangerous from the perspective of ethical judgments because it inevitably results in prizing "authentic" existence and devaluing "inauthentic" existence. This, then, in effect, amounts to an intrinsic "assault on the *dignitas hominas*, the integrity and worthiness of each concrete individual life, however lived."

Driving and underlying all of Funkenstein's critiques of the various theological responses to the Holocaust is his concern that they represent abstract theories and beliefs rather than being centered around concrete, accountable human actions. Those who are focused on "religious questions" have, he argues, a "commitment to values higher than human life and human integrity," which can (and has) undermined human ethical behavior. Funkenstein suggests that what we ought to do in light of the Holocaust is turn our focus from God to man. Then we can study and learn the really pressing and fundamental lessons from what is, in fact, an "eminently human event."

Selected Bibliography

Books and Articles by Amos Funkenstein

"Anti-Jewish Propaganda: Ancient, Medieval, and Modern," *Jerusalem Quarterly* 19 (Spring 1981): 56–72.

Maimonides: Nature, History, and Society (Tel Aviv, 1983) [Hebrew]. Translated into French as *Maimonides: Nature, histoire, et messianisme* (Paris, 1988)

Theology and the Scientific Imagination from the Middle Ages to the Seventeenth Century (Princeton, N.J., 1986).

"Job without Theodicy," in *Perceptions of Jewish History: from Antiquity to the Present* (Tel Aviv, 1991), pp. 35–40 [Hebrew].

"Collective Memory and Historical Consciousness," *History and Memory* 1 (1989): 5–26.

Medieval and Biblical Exegesis: A Short Introduction (Tel Aviv, 1990) [Hebrew].

"An Escape from History? Franz Rosenzweig and the Destiny of Judaism," *History and Memory* 2 (1990): 117–135.

Perceptions of Jewish History from Antiquity to the Present (Tel Aviv, 1991) [Hebrew].

Perceptions of Jewish History (Berkeley, Calif., 1993).

"The Incomprehensible Catastrophe: Memory and Narrative," *Narrative Study of Lives* 1 (1993): 21–29.

Article about Amos Funkenstein

Myers, David, et al., eds., Amos Funkenstein's Perceptions of Jewish History: An Evaluation of His Works by His Students," special issue of *Jewish Social Studies* 6, no. 1 (1999).

THEOLOGICAL INTERPRETATIONS OF THE HOLOCAUST

The Meaning of Meaning

That the extermination of the Jews in Europe ought to arrest the attention of theologians seems obvious. That it has actually done so, especially in the last decade, and continues to do so, is a fact. But what we *mean* when we ask about the theological "meaning" of the Holocaust is far from obvious. For some it means the meaning of the catastrophe in inherited theological terms: an attempt to salvage a theodicy from the rubble left by the eruption of evil as an apparently autonomous force. For others it means the meaning of the catastrophe *for* theology: either in a polemical vein, when they address the failure or even complicity of rival theologies; or critically, when they question the legitimacy of their own theological heritage in the shadow of the systematic destruction of human life and dignity. I shall call these trends, in turn, the direct, the polemical, and the critical-reflexive modes of theologizing about the Holocaust. And I shall argue that the first is offensive, the second hypocritical, and the third not radical enough even in its most radical manifestations.

The Holocaust as Punishment and Signal

One of the few who dare to state that the Holocaust is perfectly comprehensible in traditional theological terms shall serve as our starting point. From the extreme case we may learn something about seemingly more reasonable attempts in the same direction.

Shortly after the foundation of the State of Israel, there appeared a book with the typical rabbinical title *And It Pleased Moses (Vayo'el Moshe).*[1] Its author, R. Yoel Teitelbaum, was the leader of an ultra-Orthodox, anti-Zionist, cohe-

sive movement whose branch in Israel is known as the "Guardians of the City" (*Neturei Karta*). It summarizes all traditions in support of passive messianism—I shall explain the term immediately—and concludes that the Holocaust was an inevitable consequence of, and punishment for, a formidable sin: the transgression of the divine warning not to seek redemption by one's own hands, through human initiative. His argument is as follows:

"Because of our sins we have been exiled from our land." The dispersion and oppression of the Jewish nation in the diaspora has a punitive-cathartic function, and only God can call an end to the punishment. Those who wish to "precipitate the end" and force God's hand through human action are, whether or not they know it, rebels. Three times the Song of Songs repeats an oathlike formula: "I put you under oath, the daughters of Jerusalem, in the name of the deer and the gazelles of the field, not to hasten nor to precipitate love until it desires." An old exegetical tradition justified the inclusion of such eminently secular love songs in the canon of sacred Scriptures on the grounds that it ought to be read *only* allegorically, as a dialogue between God and the spirit of Israel (or in other quarters, the *ecclesia*). The three oaths, we are taught in the tractate *Ketubot* of the Babylonian Talmud, have a particular allegoresis.[2] The threefold repetition of the formula refers to three oaths imposed on Israel and on the nations of the world after the destruction of the Temple. Israel was held by oath not to rebel against the nations among which it is held as a "prisoner of war," and not to try and "hasten the end." In return, the nations of the world were held by the third oath not to oppress Israel *too* much.

From these premises Teitelbaum draws an outrageous conclusion. Because, in the course of

1. Yoel Teitelbaum, *Va'Yoel Moshe*, 3 vols. (New York, 1952; 2nd ed., 1957).
2. B.T., *Kelubot* 111ᵃ; *[Midrash] Song of Songs. Rabba* 2.7. Literally, the formula is an oath, but a playful imitation of one, where the invocation of God (*el Shaddai,*

el Tseva'ot) is replaced by a phonetical simile (*aylot ha'sade tsviot*). Cf. R. Gordis, "The Song of Songs," in Mordecai M. Kaplan, ed., *Jubilee Volume* (New York, 1953), pp. 281–397, esp. 308–309.

the Zionist movement, an ever growing number of Jews broke the oath and took their fate into their own hands—they wished to turn, in Herzl's words, "from a political object into a political subject"—the nations of the world, in turn, likewise felt themselves free of the oath not to oppress Israel too much, and oppress they did. Why did they? Teitelbaum assumes, as a matter of course, that "Esau always hates Jacob," inherently and incessantly. The Holocaust is the inevitable consequence of the Jewish spontaneous drive toward sovereignty or even autonomy. It is not even the last catastrophe: The perpetration of the sin continued with the foundation of the State of Israel. A catastrophe is imminent, after which only a few, the "remnants of Israel," will survive to witness the true redemption. Indeed, Teitelbaum's whole argument is embedded in the apocalyptical premise that the true redemption, through divine miracle, is very close at hand. The times preceding it are, in the traditional imagery, times of extreme wars and tribulations, times replete with false hopes and false messiahs.

In a curious way Teitelbaum shares the belief that the messianic days are at the threshold with his Orthodox adversaries, the "Bloc of the Faithful" (*Gush Emunim*).[3] They too assume that hatred against Jews is inherent in the nations of the world because the choice of God fell upon Israel, or, in the more secular version of U. Z. Greenberg, because Israel is "the race of Abraham, which had started on its way to become master."[4] They regard the Holocaust and the subsequent formation of the State of Israel and its wars as a divine signal for an active preparation in "the dawn of our redemption." Since our time is the time of the messianic war, and redemption has already started, it is incumbent upon Jews to conquer and hold to the promised borders of

their holy land, to shape it into a *civitas dei*. For Teitelbaum the Holocaust came because Jews were too active; for the *Gush Emunim*, because Jews were too passive; for both it is a portent of the Messiah.

Two distinct traditions of Jewish messianism clash here in their exaggerated forms: the passive-utopian messianic tradition as opposed to active-realistic messianism. The former has been by far the predominant tradition, an antidote of the rabbinical establishment against dangerous messianic eruptions; the latter, although a minority tradition, has had a continuous career and some notable authorities on its side: Maimonides, Jacob Berab, Zvi Kalisher. Maimonides, to whom world history is a continuous history of the monotheization of the world guided by God's *List der Vernunft*—i.e., "miracles of the category of the possible"—saw also in the messianic days a period within history without change in cosmic or human nature.[5] He believed that there were some ways to precipitate them through human initiative, as by the reconstruction of the old court system in the Land of Israel. Jacob Berab, who tried to implement this plan through the attempt to renew the pristine ordination, was rebuked by the Jerusalemite head of the court, who insisted that the messianic days can come only as a package deal: No element of them can be taken out of its miraculous context to be implemented now.[6] Kalisher, in the nineteenth century, devoted his life to encouraging settlement in Israel or even the renewal of some sacrifices in the present for the very same reasons. Note that this active messianism is not a precursor of Zionism. On the contrary: Zionism started with an antimessianic claim, a desire for sovereignty irrespective of messianic expectations. Both Teitelbaum and the *Gush Emunim* represent pre-Zionistic mentalities. Both are, in

---

3. Menachem M. Kasher, *Hatekufa hagdola* (Jerusalem, 1969); it contains explicit polemics also against Teitelbaum.

4. U. Z. Greenberg, *Rehovot hanabar, Safer hailiot veha'koah* (Tel Aviv, 1957), p. 7; "father of the superior race, p. 31 and passim. *Geza* is the accepted modern Hebrew term for "race"; a racial ideology will be called *torat geza*. In 1957 it had other connotations than in 1920, when Jabotinsky promised: "With blood and with sweat/A

race will be formed for us / proud, magnanimous, and cruel."

5. A. Funkenstein, "Maimonides: Political Theory and Realistic Messianism," *Miscelanea Medievalia* 2 (1977): 81–103.

6. R. Levi ben Habib, *Responsa* (Venice, 1565), appendix (*Kuntres hasmicha*); on the ideological background cf. J. Katz, "Mahloket hasmicha ben Yaakov-Berab veha Ralbah," *Zion* 6 nos. 3–4 (1951): 34ff; Funkenstein, "Maimonides," p. 102.

different ways, fossils of the past, albeit poisonous fossils.

The ideology of passive messianism, to which Teitelbaum is an heir, should not be confused with the myth of the physical passivity of diaspora Jewry. Why did Jews not offer resistance in the face of their extermination? Raul Hilberg, in the introduction to his monumental book,[7] refers to the alleged two thousand years of mental conditioning in appeasement. Passivity, he believes, was an intrinsic mental feature of diaspora Jewry. This is a myth as widespread as it is dangerous; dangerous it is because it suggests an artificial gap between the passive diaspora mentality and the active, healthy mentality of the new species of Jew in Israel. Neither in antiquity nor in the Middle Ages did Jews abstain from physical resistance in the face of persecution, whenever feasible. They resisted during the Crusaders' pogroms, the Chmelnitzki pogroms, and modern pogroms. Resistance during the Nazi occupation was no less than among most other occupied population. At best, one could ask why German Jews were not more active in the resistance movement until 1939, or why there was more cooperation than necessary later. But if there was passivity, it was not a heritage of diaspora mentality but rather of modern vintage. To the modern European Jew, who identified himself with the state he lived in, resistance against his state seemed outside the universe of discourse; nor could he conceive of a state acting against the *raison d'état*. The pre-emancipation Jew, by contrast, always saw himself as an alien, as a "prisoner of war," and was always on the alert. The legal principle, "the law of the kingdom is valid law," which was quoted by some reformers of the nineteenth century to prove the priority of state law even in Jewish terms, originally meant the opposite. It pertained to property only and delineated a *Widerstandsrecht:* Only if a ruler acts in accord with the law of the land is one obliged to obey him.[8] The ideology of passive messianism is the only true nucleus of the myth of passivity: It served to emphasize the lack of acute political aspiration. In a way, then, the political emancipation and acculturation of Jews in Europe opened the way for two extreme new possibilities: total passivity and total self-assertion. In the language of Sartre, the post-emancipation Jew may be said to live in a constant "situation" of *être-vu*[9]: He shunned it by identifying with the aggressor, or defined it by becoming Zionist.

At best, passive messianism was an ideology not a legally binding position. It was prevalent once, but is obsolete today even among the Orthodox. Why then dignify Teitelbaum's insult to common sense and decency with a detailed discussion? Because in theology, as in the law, much can be learned from extreme-limit cases. An overt absurdity is better than a covert one. Jewish theologians who are less extreme than either Teitelbaum or the *Gush Emunim*, such as E. Fackenheim or E. Berkovits,[10] admit that they can see no theological rationale to the Holocaust. The Holocaust is incomprehensible, they say, and defies all theodicies. But they do find a theological meaning in the survival: the survival of each man or the survival of the nation and the rebirth of the state. In both they find a confirmation of the divine presence and a promise to preserve Israel.

Even these diluted versions of a theodicy are offensive. Having survived while others—close family and friends—have not is a terrible burden to many survivors. Haunted by excruciating memories, many of them refused to talk or reminisce in the years following internment; some of them do so only now, fearing that true memories will be lost within their generation. It may well be that the State of Israel too owes its establishment in part to the Holocaust; but this also is a terrible burden, not a sign of chosenness or divine grace. Similar perceptions may have moved George Steiner in his recent book, tasteless as it

7. R. Hilberg, *The Destruction of the European Jews* (Chicago, 1967). We elaborated some of the following remarks elsewhere (*The Passivity of Diaspora Jewry Myth and Reality*, Aran Lecture 11, Tel Aviv, 1982).
8. B.T. *Nedarim* 28[a]; B. T. *Gittin* 10[b]; B.T. *Baba Kama* 111; B.T. *Baba Batra* 54[b]–55[a]; Cf. Sh.

Shnoh, *Dina demalchuta dina* [Hebrew] (Jerusalem, 1974).
9. J.-P. Sartre, *Réflexions sur la question juive* (Paris, 1947).
10. E. Fackenheim, *God's Presence in History* (New York, 1970); *The Jewish Return into History* (New York, 1978). E. Berkovits, *Faith after the Holocaust* (New York, 1973).

may otherwise be.[11] There is only one instance of theologizing in Primo Levi's account of his survival in Auschwitz. It reads:

> Now everyone is busy scraping the bottom of his bowl with his spoon so as not to waste the last drops of the soup; a confused, metallic clatter, signifying the end of the day. Silence slowly prevails and then, from my bunk on the top row, I see and hear old Kuhn praying aloud, with his beret on his head, swaying backwards and forwards violently. Kuhn is thanking God because he has not been chosen.
>
> Kuhn is out of his senses. Does he not see Beppo the Greek in the bunk next to him, Beppo who is twenty years old and is going to the gas chamber the day after tomorrow and knows it and lies there looking fixedly at the light without saying anything and without even thinking any more? Can Kuhn fail to realize that the next time it will be his turn? Does Kuhn not understand that what has happened today is an abomination, which no propitiatory prayer, no pardon, no expiation by the guilty, which nothing at all in the power of man can ever clean again?
>
> If I was God, I would spit at Kuhn's prayer.[12]

The Dialectical Theology of Meaninglessness

To the most courageous among recent theologians, the very meaninglessness of the Holocaust constitutes its theological meaning. To lose faith in the face of the Holocaust is itself, they say, a manner of faith, a positive religious act. When, in the eleventh century, Anselm of Canterbury advanced his ontological proof of God's existence, he also gave a new meaning to the psalm's verse: "The fool [wicked] hath said in his heart: there is no God." Since God's existence is necessarily implied by His very concept, whoever thinks of God yet denies His existence cannot but be foolish (wicked). The modern theologians I have in mind—Rahner, Baum, Rubenstein, and others—turned Anselm on his head.

A person deeply troubled by the Holocaust and made unable to affirm God's presence is caught in an essentially religious question and hence already under the influence of God's grace. If a person were shallow, or wholly pragmatic, or egotistical, or only concerned about protecting his own interests, he would not be troubled at all. He is troubled because he is religious.[13]
Even atheists, Vatican II reminds us, may be touched by grace.

The admission that God—or ethical theism—died in Auschwitz because Auschwitz defies all meaning calls, we are told, for a radical change of the most fundamental premises.

> What has emerged in our theological reflection based on Karl Rahner is a rather different religious imagination. Here God is not conceived of as a lord ruling history from above, but as the vitality at the core of people's lives making them ask the important questions and moving them toward their *authentic* existence. God is conceived here as the *ground* of human existence, as the summons operative in their lives, and as the *horizon* toward which they move. God is not so much lord of the universe as heart of the world. What is emphasized in this theology is what theologians call Divine immanence, which in ordinary [!] language means God's being *in-and-through the world*. . . . God's presence to people changes them, severs them from destructive trends, and moves them towards a more creative future. . . . But the in-and-throughness of God does not leave the world as it is; it judges the world and *summons* it to new life.[14]

Yet even here, where theologians are most courageous, false tunes are unavoidable. The key phrases underlined by us point unmistakably to a definite philosophical source. Exchange "God"

11. George Steiner, *The Portage to St. Christobel of A. H.* (New York, 1982).
12. Primo Levi, *Survival in Auschwitz* (orig title *Se questo è un uomo*), translated by S. Woolf (New York, 1961), pp. 151–152.
13. G. G. Baum, *Christian Theology after Auschwitz* (Robert Waley Cohen Memorial Lecture) (London, 1976), esp. pp. 7–15.
14. Baum, *Christian Theology*, p. 19.

for "being" (*Sein*); the rest of the vocabulary is Heidegger's. Seemingly without ethical judgments, Heidegger distinguishes two modes of human existence, the inauthentic and the authentic. So does the quoted passage. *Dasein*, "being-there" or existence, is the only form in which the elusive *Sein*, "being" (in contrast to *Seiendes*, "entities") is concerned with itself: "[*Das Dasein ist ein Seiendes*], *dem es in seinem Sein um dieses Sein selbst geht.*"[15] Yet in its first and average occurrence it is alienated from itself, lost in the world (*In-der-welt-sein*) in such a manner that it uses things in the world (*Zuhanden-sein*) and is absorbed in it. With every man are inseparably others with whom he shares the concern (*Sorge*) with the mundane. *Dasein* is inauthentic in that state, it is "man"—everyone—characterized by *Seinvergessenheit*, disconcern with its true self-being. It flees fear (*Angst*) rather than facing it, facing its basic feature as *Geworfen-sein*, being "thrown into" (as well as "projected into": *geworfen*) the world. Only the authentic self, in contrast to the inauthentic "everyone" (*man*), and moved by fear and trembling (*Angst*), is capable of asking the question-of-being (*Daseinfrage*), the question to which there is ipso facto no answer because its answer is for that particular being to be no more. Here too the meaninglessness of the question constitutes its very meaning. Here too it is the characteristic of the authentic self which is not "lost in trivial concerns" to ask such questions to which there is no answer. Rather than the "chatter" (*Gerede*) of "everyone" (*man*), the authentic self lets Being, which is in itself, speak for itself through his very futile question of being.

Few who read Heidegger's *Sein und Zeit* failed to be caught by its spell. The fascination with Heidegger's thought is similar in many ways to the fascination with Spinoza's *Ethics;* both have a uniquely comforting power. In both, the ultimate meaning of everything that is resides in itself only. Spinoza's *Deus sive natura* reifies the logic of the Megarians to the utmost: Only that which is, is possible; that which is not is impossible, even meaningless. Like Spinoza's God, Heidegger's being is always expressed through beings (*Seiende*),

and is never capable of expressing "itself" immediately and without them; it illuminates without being seen, just as (if one may borrow a metaphor from Wittgenstein) a picture never points at itself. In contrast to Spinoza's substance, however, Heidegger insists on the necessary temporal structure of being. The acquiescence with the total immanence of the meaning of the world—including, for Heidegger, the temporality of being—means that there is no more to the life of a subject than itself; it cannot be endowed with a transcendent meaning or value; when it comes to its individual end, its meaning will be no more nor less than *that* and *what* it was. Annihilation does not deprive that which is from having meaning; it rather constitutes an integral part of that meaning.

This having been said, we turn back to the call for authenticity which some of the more courageous theological reflections on the Holocaust borrowed from Heidegger.

It is precisely at this point, namely, with the distinction between authentic and inauthentic existence, that the ethical critique—a critique from the vantage point of ethics—must commence. Heidegger promises us that no moral judgment is implied in that distinction.[16] In an almost Hegelian manner, he even sees in the alienation of *Sein* in *Dasein* from itself through the flight into unauthentic existence a necessary stage for its return (*Kehre*) unto itself. Yet consider the further attributes of inauthenticity. Only the authentic self can be said to possess conscience or even to be capable of "sinning." The anonymous "everyone" lives in a continuous degeneration and fall (*Verfall des Daseins*), a fall "into the world" (*in die Welt verfallen*). "Everyone" is, literally, interchangeable with everyone else.

Without entering a sustained discussion about the nature of moral speech, let me assume that we ought to start with some "concrete absolutes" in an ethical discourse if we wish to navigate between relativization and empty, formal abstractions. Let me also assume that human life and human dignity are such absolutes—be it in a cognitive or axiomatic-thetic, descriptive or normative

---

15. M. Heidegger, *Sein und Zeit* (Tübingen, 1957), p. 12.

16. Heidegger, *Sein and Zeit*, p. 175: "Der Titel [Das Verfallen, etc.], der keine negative Bewertung ausdrückt."

sense. They command our relentless respect; they are the "infinite right" of each subject. We may conceive of situations, such as the necessity of self-defense, in which we would be justified in violating them: It would be an evil act, even when justifiable.

Human life and the incommensurable value of each individual were assaulted in infinite ways in Nazi Europe. An ethical perspective of this sort cannot avoid being extremely narrow-minded, rigorously one-sided. It can make no concessions to higher gods and higher values, and it cannot permit any distinction between individuals based on higher values. Life, the life of each individual, must be taken to be always meaningful in and of itself. The everyday reality of Heidegger's "everyone," the person who never attends to the question of being but is "lost unto the world," must be endowed from the one-sided vantage point of ethics with as much dignity and intrinsic value as the life of the searcher for fundamental existential truths. The man who cultivates his garden and does all the things in the way he is supposed to cannot be called inauthentic except by his author. From an ethical point of view, *every life is authentic,* a value in and of itself, not interchangeable with any other human life, a mode *sui generis.* Once discrimination is permitted even in theory, its consequences are difficult to foretell. If the person of "everyone" is interchangeable with everyone else, let alone if he is classified a nonperson—that is, without personality—then he is less valuable. And if less valuable, then perhaps also dispensable. Or again: is not crisis—say, war and destruction—beneficial in Heidegger's terms, because it "calls" man to his true self? Heidegger himself drew such conclusions after 1933.

But, you may object, the possible or even real abuses of a theory (even by its promoter) need not be held against it: In part, this has been my own argument. My critique, however, goes deeper than that. The very distinction between authentic and inauthentic existences, not only its possible career, is an intrinsic assault on the *dignitas hominis,* the integrity and worthiness of each concrete individual life, however lived. The latter attitude, with its difficulties and paradoxes, must constitute the absolute center of humanistic ethical theories, even at the cost of subscribing to a one-dimensional, flat philosophical anthropology. At best, Heidegger's distinction diverts from this focus; at the worst, it undermines it.

I do believe, however, that much of the force of Heidegger's insistence on the immanence of being, of which we spoke earlier, can be saved without redundant discriminations. An ethical monadology is conceivable in which the life of each is a unique and significant point of view of human possibilities for better and worse; each situation, individual and collective, is such that it is significant and something can be learned from it about man; and, should all human history have, finally, come to pass and leave behind no record, its meaning will be that and what it was, as replete with good and evil, the beautiful and the ugly, as it then will have been.

Mutatis mutandis, the flaws in the thought of Heidegger are also the flaws in those dialectical theologies which speak in Heidegger's idiom. Why is the person who "asks important questions," say, concerning God's presence in the face of massive evil, "more authentic" than the person who does not? And why are the questions of the *homo religiosus,* however broadly we define him, more important than the purely human questions asked by others about their experience in the concentration camps? Consider, for example, the most moving and reflective account written about the experience of Auschwitz, Primo Levi's *Se questo è un uomo* (published in English as *Survival in Auschwitz*). It asks many questions, but none of them theological. It refuses to see the concentration camp as meaningless: "We are in fact convinced that no human experience is without meaning or unworthy of analysis, and that fundamental values, even if they are not positive, can be deduced from this particular world which we are describing." Indeed, the religious-theological questions, were he to ask them, would distract from the power of Levi's reflections, which are centered around man, not around God.

As against the distinction between the begraced and those who lack grace, between authentic and inauthentic existences, the reality of the concentration camps taught Levi other distinctions, distinctions which are purely homocentric, such as the distinction between "the drowned and the saved."

We do not believe in the most obvious and facile deduction: that man is fundamentally brutal, egotistic and stupid in his conduct once every civilized institution is taken away, and that the *Häftling* is consequently nothing but a man without inhibitions. We believe, rather, that the only conclusion to be drawn is that in the face of driving necessity and physical disabilities many social habits and instincts are reduced to silence.

But another fact seems to us worthy of attention: there comes to light the existence of two particularly well-differentiated categories among men—the saved and the drowned. Other pairs of opposites (the good and the bad, the wise and the foolish, the cowards and the courageous, the unlucky and the fortunate) are considerably less distinct, they seem less essential, and above all they allow for more numerous and complex intermediary gradations.

This division is much less evident in ordinary life; for there it rarely happens that a man loses himself. A man is normally not alone, and in his rise or fall is tied to the destinies of his neighbours; so that it is exceptional for anyone to acquire unlimited power, or to fall by a succession of defeats into utter ruin. Moreover, everyone is normally in possession of such spiritual, physical and even financial resources that the probabilities of a shipwreck, of total inadequacy in the face of life, are relatively small. And one must take into account a definite cushioning effect exercised both by the law, and by the moral sense which constitutes a self-imposed law; for a country is considered the more civilized the more the wisdom and efficiency of its laws hinder a weak man from becoming too weak or a powerful one too powerful.

But in the *Lager* things are different: here the struggle to survive is without respite, because everyone is desperately and ferociously alone. If some *Null Achtzehn* [one without a name] vacillates, he will find no one to extend a helping hand; on the contrary, someone will knock him aside, because it is in no one's interest that there be one more "mussulman" dragging himself to work every day; and if someone, by a miracle of savage patience and cunning, finds a new method of avoiding the hardest work, a new art which yields him an ounce of bread, he will try to keep his method secret, and he will be esteemed and respected for this, and will derive from it an exclusive, personal benefit; he will become stronger and so will be feared, and who is feared is, ipso facto, a candidate for survival. . . .

They crowd my memory with their faceless presence, and if I could enclose all the evil of our time in one image, I would choose this image which is familiar to me: an emaciated man, with head dropped and shoulders curved, on whose face and in whose eyes not a trace of thought is to be seen.

If the drowned have no story, and single and broad is the path to perdition, the paths to salvation are many, difficult and improbable.[17]

Among the "saved" then are both the noble (such as his friend Alberto) and the ignoble, the cunning and the less cunning. Levi employs the theological idiom ironically: as if to say that being saved is not of a theological or other transcendental character; it is a most basic human property. Out of the experience of the concentration camp, Levi crystallized the building blocks of a true philosophical anthropology, more genuine and accurate than either Heidegger's or any recent theologian's. The power of his reflections, I repeat, lies in that they are centered around the concrete man, not around a chimera of the authentic self nor around God.

Indeed, religious questions may even be detrimental to ethical human concerns. They are detrimental, I believe, in the following sense. The assumption is made by even the most self-critical theologians that there exists a particular virtue in the commitment to values higher than human life and human integrity, that the person who lives his life *veluti pecora*, without asking existential-religious questions, lacks "grace." But the table may be turned as follows. A commitment to higher values above the sanctity of the individual not only distracts from the study of man, but can and did lead to abuses and crimes of much greater extent than selfish self-interest ever perpetrated. Concededly, this is not a *necessary* consequence of commitments to absolutes, but it has often enough been so. Now it matters little whether the higher values were transcendent or immanent, God, fatherland, race, or the ideal

17. Primo Levi, *Survival in Auschwitz*, pp. 100–103.

society of the future. In the name of all of them crusades were fought, genocides committed, persons degraded. No major religion I know of was immune. Perhaps then dialectical theologians are not radical enough. Perhaps theology itself is one source of that very danger which they contemplate. William of Ockham [1287–1347], whose ethical theory recognizes very clearly the need for a concrete absolute if one wishes to navigate between the Scylla of relativization and the Charybdis of empty, formal abstractions, claimed it is wrong to say that God wants that which is good. Rather, it is good because God wanted it. The God of the Bible wanted, as it were, a genocide against the Amalekites, including women, children, and cattle. A more refined God of later centuries wanted heretics to be "compelled to enter" or be abolished. An even more refined God may demand the self-sacrifice of the believer so as to sanctify the name of God. A secular age translated such demands into world-immanent terms, among them race. *Tantum religio potuit suadere malorum*. [To what evils is religion capable of leading men to.]

Again, I do not argue that religious commitments do, of necessity, lead to abuse. But neither should it be argued that because of lack of religiosity (so to say, as an "outburst of paganism") concentration and extermination camps became possible. I rather argue that the focus on the religious-theological implications of the Holocaust is intrinsically the wrong focus. The question of what it teaches us about God or any other higher norms and values is insignificant beside the question of what it teaches us about man, his limits, his possibilities, his cruelty, his creativity, and his nobility. In human terms the Holocaust was not meaningless. To say that it was seems as offensive as to say that it had a theological meaning, that is, a divine purpose.

For similar reasons we ought to object to the characterization of the Holocaust as "incomprehensible." It is one of the most prevalent predicates in the theological literature about the Holocaust—and not only in the theological literature. On the contrary: Historians, psychologists, sociologists, and philosophers ought to make every effort to comprehend the catastrophe, and they ought to be guided by the reasonable expectation that they can comprehend it. The crime

committed by the Nazis was of immense proportions: The horror and the suffering transgress our capacity of imagination, but it is possible to understand them rationally. Even if the perpetrators of the crime were madmen who lost all touch with reality, a reconstruction of their mentality and patterns of action would be possible. But they were not madmen, at least not in the clinical sense of the word: If madness entails loss of the sense of reality, then no society can be called mad, because reality is a social construct through and through. The prehistory of the genocide, its necessary conditions, can be illuminated more and more. The mental mechanisms by which Nazi ideology justified mass murder can be followed step by step. Germany stood fast in its illusion of apocalyptic "total war." The Jews, they were certain, are not only an inferior race on the order of Slavs and blacks, they are even more dangerous, because they are a universal, destructive parasite which (unlike other races) cleverly adapts to become almost indistinguishable from the host society in order to destroy the healthy texture of that society from within. Their extermination was spoken of in terms of hygienic medicine: Jews were labeled a dangerous bacteria. *Entlausung* (delousing) was the terrible realization of an ideological metaphor in the concentration camps. By degrading the inmates of the camps, by robbing them of their personalities, the victims were supposed to turn into that which the Nazi ideology claimed they had always been: subhuman. It was a mechanism which functioned to concretize, to visualize, the rationale for extermination. Nor is it true that the extermination of the Jews was carried out at the cost of the war effort, as Hilberg and others once believed. We cannot excuse ourselves from the obligation to understand the Nazi mentality if we want to condemn it, let alone if we want to prevent similar crimes from being committed again.

Theologians seem to emphasize the "incomprehensibility" of the Holocaust and the "madness" of those who caused it because they cannot find any theological meaning in it. Perhaps also it is because they hardly dare to say that if one were to believe in transcendent forces, the Holocaust would prove the autonomy of evil, an evil manifested not only or primarily by the number of its victims but by its sheer inexhaustible inventiveness, by the almost infinite number of methods found for systematic killing and degradation. If, however, we turn from God to man, the Holocaust is neither incomprehensible nor meaningless. It was neither bestial nor indeed pagan. It was, instead, an eminently human event in that it demonstrated those extremes which *only* man and his society are capable of doing or suffering. It pointed at a possibility, perhaps unknown before, of human existence, a possibility as human as the best instances of creativity and compassion.

Melissa Raphael

Melissa Raphael (b. 1960) is professor of religious studies at the University of Gloucestershire, England. She received her B.A. from Oxford University in 1983 and her Ph.D. from King's College, University of London, in 1990. She is an honorary research scholar at the University of Wales, Lampeter, and sits on the international board of *The Journal of Feminist Studies in Religion*. She is also a member of the European Society for Women in Theological Research and an associate member of the Centre for Comparative Studies in Religion and Gender, Bristol University. Since 2004, Professor Raphael also serves as a delegate of the British government on the International Task Force for Cooperation on Holocaust Education, Remembrance, and Research.

Professor Raphael has written extensively on the issues of gender and feminist theology as well as modern Jewish thought, especially on the Holocaust. She is now engaged in writing a new book on *Judaism and the Visual: A Post-Holocaust Theology of Jewish Art.*

SELECTION

Melissa Raphael, in her interesting and provocative study *The Female Face of God in Auschwitz,* constructs a theology that she argues both "saves" God in the post-Holocaust world and also combats the "masculinization of theology," a phenomenon that does a disservice not just to women but to all humanity. Beginning with the fact that many post-Holocaust theologies focus on the absence or even death of God, Raphael examines the question of just what kind of God, i.e., what conception of God, was invalidated by Auschwitz since, "while there is only one God, there is more than one model of God" to be refuted or supported. She concludes her investigation of this fundamental issue with the proposal that it is a patriarchal, hierarchical notion of the Divine that the Holocaust threatens. However, this conception, this model, is a sort of paper tiger, for that slain deity is, she posits, "an omnipotent God-king who was never there in the first place." While this "impassible," i.e., unchanging, perfect, all-powerful "God of Jewish philosophers" falls to the wayside, a different "God-She" emerges as neglected but present.

Raphael, drawing on the work of Buber and Levinas, then goes on to explore the notion of a relational God whom she associates with the feminine in-dwelling *Shekhinah* [Divine Presence] (of traditional rabbinic and kabbalistic thought) who suffers with humanity. Raphael finds evidence of the *Shekhinah* in the testimonies about the compassionate maternal love women showed one another during the horrific conditions of the Holocaust. This aspect of divinity, Raphael notes, while representative of women's unique perspective toward theology, is not exclusively biologically female; she cites a Ḥasidic rebbe's "maternal" attitude toward his followers as an example of immanent, divine love. However, the attributes of the "maternal *Shekhinah*" are traditionally associated with women and thus provide an element of theology that has been overlooked in male-run theologies and Holocaust studies and "set outside the precincts of the holy for most of Jewish history."

In her research into women's Holocaust experiences, Raphael found that "the presence of a caring other . . . made the living/dying (only just) survivable." This relational God, made visible through the acts of the "caring other," may not be omnipotent but she is omnipresent and redemptive in her unconditional love. Raphael asks not why did God not intervene during the Holocaust (since that is a question for a masculinized theology), but rather "how could and can we protect God's presence as it is this which makes it possible to know God in the other and for God to know God-self in creation." Our responsibility is to find and bring the *Shekhinah* into human lives, to bring God out of hiding through our own redemptive acts.

Selected Bibliography

Books and Articles by Melissa Raphael

"Feminism, Constructivism, and Numinous Experience," *Religious Studies* 30 (1994): 551–526.
Theology and Embodiment: The Post-Patriarchal Reconstruction of Female Sacrality (Sheffield, England, 1996).
Rudolf Otto and the Concept of Holiness (Oxford, 1997).
"Goddess Religion, Postmodern Jewish Feminism, and the Complexity of Alternative Religious Identities," *Nova Religio* 1 (1998): 198–214.
Introducing Thealogy: Discourse on the Goddess (Sheffield, England, 1999).
" 'I Am Who I Will Be': The Representation of God in Postmodern Jewish Feminist Theology and Contemporary Religious Education," *British Journal of Religious Education* 21 (1999): 69–79.
"When God Beheld God: Notes towards a Jewish Feminist Theology of the Holocaust," *Feminist Theology* 21 (1999): 53–78.
"Is Patriarchal Theology Still Patriarchal: Reading Theologies of the Holocaust from a Jewish Feminist Perspective," *Journal of Feminist Studies of Religion* 18 (2002): 105–113.
"Holiness in Extremis: Jewish Women's Resistance to the Profane in Auschwitz," in *Holiness Past and Present*, edited by S. Barton (Edinburgh, 2002).
The Female Face of God in Auschwitz: A Jewish Feminist Theology of the Holocaust (London, 2003).
"The Price of (Masculine) Freedom and Becoming: A Feminist Critique of the Use of the Free Will Defence in Post-Holocaust Jewish Philosophy," in *Feminist Philosophy of Religion: Critical Perspectives*, edited by Pamela Sue Anderson and Beverley Clack (London, 2003), pp. 136–150.
"From History to Theology: Gender and Ethics in the Production of Holocaust Theology from Women's Memoirs of Auschwitz," in *Religion and Gender: New Perspectives*, edited by Ursula King and Tina Beattie (London, 2003), pp. 101–112.

THE FEMALE FACE OF GOD IN AUSCHWITZ

Presence, Absence, and Gender

Terhri Utriainen's anthropological study of female presence and the dying found that her research subjects needed no more than for the other to be *there*. Presence is the key to a good death. *In extremis*, passive presence (rather than the efforts of doctors or other skilled practitioners) covers the spiritual and material nudity of death and dying. This mode of being and holding is a significant part of the practice and iconography of mothering for the mother is a liminal figure mediating both life and death. Women take care of the intimate processes of dying and death where men, at a distance, govern the rituals that publicly sanctify death.[1] Of course, in the camps it was a matter of the dying caring for the dying. The dying were not watched over in grieving tranquillity from the bedside. But the point remains that the trope of divine hiddenness from suffering may fail to engage women's experience of holocaustal (or any other) death. Women would be more likely to postulate the presence of God over and above God's power over life and death. As the memoir literature repeatedly testifies, it was only the presence of a caring other (herself in acute need of care) who made the living/dying (only just) survivable.

The problem with theologies dependent on the trope of hiddenness is that while there is only one God, there is more than one model of God. By nature of their attributions, some of these conceptual models allow God's presence to withstand Auschwitz and others do not. For example, contrary to those who believe him to have turned his face, the excessively patriarchal god called God could have been—as numen—very much present in Auschwitz. In that apocalyptical place of fire and smoke, of terror and ultimacy, of the *tremendum*, where the Bible's most severe prophetic warnings of desolation and abomination were realized, the patriarchal God was indeed almost at home. Auschwitz was *his place* insofar as the conditions of numinous horror were graphic illustrations of his threats to bring punitive disaster upon the house of Israel. But this (sometimes, not always) vindictive, savage God of Joshua whose conquest drives all before him, is but a scarecrow, a paper tiger, a Wizard of Oz. This God of smoke and consuming fire before whom all but his technicians cower is merely one aspect of an idolatrous projection of patriarchal hubris, cast in the likeness of its own aspiration.

The tradition also proposes very different non-anthropomorphic models of God and, by con-

trast, these would be too transcendental in form and quality for him to make any incursion into history. Traditional Jewish philosophy—which in its negative theological turn refuses to allow anything to be predicated to God except his (at least grammatical) masculinity—would be loath to countenance the possibility of divine presence within the conditions of finitude. The God of Jewish philosophical theology, to whom George Steiner refers as an "unbearable," "immeasurable absence," "blank as the desert air,"[2] has not given much ground for hoping that he will take his suffering people to his bosom. He is already absent and silent. The God of Jewish philosophers is one who,

> despite happy anthropomorphisms and intimacies, is construed as a God of immense distance and immaculate isolation, without qualities drafted from the observation of nature, bereft of any attributes of diminution or constraint, without limit or condition, without temporality and affect. A supreme and awesome integer of abstract grandeur and magnificence is our God.[3]

But this metaphysical diremption of God and world is far from the whole of Jewish theology. Most believing Jews have devoted their lives to making the world fit for the divine presence and many have espoused a prophetic theology where Jewishness is above all expressed in a commitment to social justice. Moreover, not all Judaism is as aniconic as its more austerely philosophical practitioners would intend it to be. While the impassible God is a legacy of medieval Jewish anti-anthropomorphism and the negative theologies that drove an ontological wedge between divine and humanity, Jewish tradition has always enjoyed a bipolar theology where God is at once suprapersonal and transcendent and personal and immanent in the world. So that, in tension with the wholly inaccessible God "without temporality and affect," is what [Arthur A.] Cohen calls "the incarnate God of study": a guardian and participant of Jewish learning and *halakhic* (religious legal) argumentation. This God, he claims, was

---

1. "The Modern Pietà: Religious Imagery in the Construction of Gendered Embodiment," a paper given at the Annual Conference of the British Sociological Association, Sociology of Religion Study Group, Plater College, Oxford, 11 April 2001. Utriainen's book, whose title can

be translated as *Present, Naked, Pure: A Study of the Anthropology of Religion on Women by the Side of the Dying* (Helsinki, 1999), is shortly to appear in English.
2. *In Bluebeard's Castle* (London, 1971), p. 38.
3. *The Tremendum* (New York, 1993), p. 77.

destroyed by the Holocaust, leaving only "the extreme monopolarity of Jewish theism."[4]

This is not quite right. God's intimate presence is not only accessible to learned men and the conditions of God's presence were not destroyed by the Holocaust. To the contrary, ... the conditions by which Cohen's "incarnate God" could be present were maintained by women's relational labors that are themselves a part of Jewish history and therefore of the tradition. It was the "supreme and awesome integer of abstract grandeur and magnificence" who disappeared during the Holocaust because he never could have appeared.[5] That God's inaction or hiddenness in the Holocaust was not so much a sign of his betrayal as a sign of his nonexistence, though his nonintervention was such as to make little or no practical difference whether he existed at all.[6]

I want to suggest that if God is one who abandons us and is silent in the face of our suffering (as in Psalms 22:2–3) there can be little to experientially distinguish this God's silence from his nonexistence. God's silence in Auschwitz was the silence of an omnipotent God-king who was never there in the first place, but was one who reigned in the minds of those who required divine sanction for their own hierarchical rule. He was not hidden in Auschwitz; he was simply deposed and, abjected, had fallen from view. The Psalmist cries out that God has turned his face from him and he is "numbered with those go down into the pit"; he is "abandoned among the dead, like bodies in the grave of whom [God is] mindful no more" (Psalms 88:5–7). In Auschwitz, the patriarchal God was numbered with those in the pit for in those "darkest places, in the depths" evoked by the Psalmist, God's patriarchal face disappeared and his power was extinguished.

But the metapatriarchal God was also, differently, numbered with those in the pit for she never left their side. What is perceived as divine absence may, then, approximate more closely the displacement of a particular model of God which, being only fictive, had only fictive power. Robert Jan van Pelt, the Dutch architectural historian once referred to "the singular, numinous and kerygmatic reality of Auschwitz."[7] Could the kerygma of Auschwitz proclaim the disgrace, dispossession, and exile of God by patriarchy itself?

Theological discourse on Auschwitz turns on the presence or absence, silence or speaking of God, but I have indicated that the meaning of these turn on whose God and which God we are speaking of[8] Gender difference in women's and men's experience of Judaism may produce difference in the way they construe the characteristic dialectic of God's presence/absence on which post-Holocaust theology turns. The history of Jewish marital relationships (on which Israel's relationship with God has been so often modeled) could, for example, suggest that women may have had lower expectations of a divine interventionary presence during the Holocaust period than men. In prewar Eastern Europe in particular, Orthodox Jewish life was homosocial in character. There were large numbers of men who, freed by their wives or parents-in-law from economic responsibilities in order to pursue their religious studies, would "abandon" their families on a daily basis, sitting in the bath and study houses, discussing matters of religious and political interest for most of the day and long into the night. Such husbands might often spend long periods with their Rebbe, often at some distance from their wives and children.[9] A form of masculine desertion, then, was already integral to many Jewish women's lives.

4. Ibid.
5. This is not to renounce the central moment and idea of Jewish salvation history: the Exodus and its revelation of an accompanying God of liberation from oppression.
6. The Holocaust was, of course, to play a significant role in the American 'death of God' theological movement of the 1960s. See further, Stephen R. Haynes and John K. Roth, eds., *The Death of God Movement and the Holocaust: Radical Theology Encounters the Shoah* (Westport, Conn., 1999), esp. Thomas J. J. Altizer, "The Holocaust and the Theology of the Death of God," pp. 17–23.
7. Cited in Gillian Rose, *Judaism and Modernity: Philosophical Essays* (Oxford, 1993), p. 244.
8. Some believe that the entire post-biblical period is a time of the silence of God since that of the direct prophetic encounter with God has passed (M. Wyschogrod, *The Body of Faith* [New York, 1983], p. 85).
9. Naomi Seidman, "Theorizing Jewish Patriarchy *in Extremis*," in M. Peskowitz and L. Levitt, eds, *Judaism since Gender* (New York, 1997), p. 45. Seidman is using Bluma Goldstein's research here.

Without dismissing the strengths and virtues of Jewish marriage, it is possible that during the Holocaust many Jewish women would have perceived God's apparent desertion and punishment for unknown sins differently than men. Perhaps the hurt was less. They were used to coping without male presence and were sometimes familiar with male violence. The assumption of the masculinity of God had further acclimatized them to experiencing him at one remove. In the creation story in which woman was fashioned by God from the body of man and then given back to him as a gift (Genesis 2:18–24),[10] the almost ineradicable marks of gendered separation and subordination Judaism bears had been, from the very beginning, cosmologically inscribed.

Some women's sense of exclusion from the immediate presence of God was also already affected by their exemption-turned-exclusion from the study of Torah. Orthodox women of the Holocaust period would not have enjoyed the same sort of proximity to and intimacy with the male God of the Torah as would have the men who daily communed with him in study and prayer. Conversely, boys' achievement of spiritual maturity in *cheders* and seminaries at the expense of separation and ever-greater distance from maternal care could have contributed to some Jewish men's sense of God's presence in the camps and ghettos as a disciplinary power not entirely discontinuous with that exercised by those administering (often punitively) the childhood religious education of the period.[11]

That women may have a sense of living to the side of divine presence, of living with male attention trained elsewhere, is not uncommon in female Orthodox circles today. As one woman tellingly remarked in a discussion group: "You see I'm very happy with the woman's role in the home. I don't need the spiritual side, but I'm very lucky that I haven't had a crisis when I've needed to turn to God."[12] If experience of God's presence/absence is gendered, who, in the holocaustal situation, is hiding who from whom? If the face of the monarchical God was turned from Israel, might the face of an-Other God have been turned toward it, even if it were one Israel could not recognize? Rabbi Barukh of Mezibizh told that God hides himself, but no one wants to seek him. Similar could be said of God-She.[13]

Israel, Present to God

There has been too much asking "*where* was God in Auschwitz?" and not enough "*who* was God in Auschwitz?" An answer to the second question is also an answer to the first. Jewish feminism has been asking "who is God?" for several decades and much of the movement wants to name the God of their experience *Shekhinah*.[14] The *Shekhinah* traditionally marks Judaism's faith in God's immanence. As the attribute of presence, *Shekhinah*'s does not make God identical with the world. God's transcendence ensures that the divine will and purpose are unconditioned by human evil, while God's immanence ensures that humanity can become God's partner (*shuttaf*) in bringing God's purposes to fulfillment in the immanent realm.[15] [Michael] Wyschogrod is right that "if there is no need for sacrament in Judaism, it is because the people of Israel in whose flesh the presence of God makes itself felt in the world becomes the sacrament." Without in any sense deifying Israel, it can be said that it is "the collective existence of the Jewish people that is the dwelling place of Hashem."[16] If, wherever they may be, the people of Israel are presentative of God

10. See further Hyman E. Goldin, *The Jewish Woman and Her Home* (New York, 1978), pp. 235, 239.
11. See Theo Richmond, *Konin: A Quest* (London, 1996) pp. 37–40. Girls did not normally go to *cheder* at an early age. Older girls could, however, receive a rudimentary Jewish education premised on their domestic and familial religious responsibilities.
12. Adrienne Baker, *The Jewish Woman in Contemporary Society: Transitions and Traditions* (London, 1993), p. 90.
13. Martin Buber, *Tales of the Hasidim: Early Masters* (New York, 1947), p. 97.
14. Jewish feminists who wish to make *Shekhinah* less an attribute of God than a name of God tend to omit the definite pronoun before *Shekhinah*'s name.
15. See Isidore Epstein, *Judaism: A Historical Presentation* (Harmondsworth, 1959), pp. 137–38.
16. *The Body of Faith*, pp. 25, 212, 103. "Hashem" (literally, the Name) is a reverent circumlocution most often used by hasidic and other ultra-Orthodox Jews.

we can begin to see that God is not only or even predominantly a God who conceals God-self.

The *Shekhinah* is a manifestation of God defined by her presentness. While the conditions in Auschwitz were wholly nonordinary, God-She may have been so "ordinarily" present among women whose personhood was getting ever less perceptible that she was herself imperceptible. But that is not to say that she had deliberately hidden *herself*. If she seemed hidden it was by virtue of the nonnuminousness of the medium of her presence, the depth of evil into which she was plunged, and her very soft tread. It may then be the case that God's presence in the camps was hidden only in that it was not ordinarily perceptible. In a religious feminist context the phrase *hester panim* could connote not so much the hiding of the face as its disguise, and one which brought God deep into the broken heart of Auschwitz. She remained among us, perhaps unknown and unknowable, but not hidden. (Much as in the women's camp at Auschwitz-Birkenau when one of Charlotte Delbo's friends has pulled her safely from the flailing clubs and lashes of the SS, Delbo is asked "Who were you with?" "With me, we were together," (interjects Yvonne. Delbo says, "She had never stopped being by my side. I had not seen her."[17])

While some women had to turn their faces from others' suffering because they were too horrified to watch or too exhausted and numbed by their powerlessness to stop it,[18] *Shekhinah* did not hide her face; they—the desecrators—hid her face just as they hid women's behind the accretion of filth that was integral to the holocaustal assault. But even from the pit, among the dead of whom the patriarchal God seemed mindful no more, she could still see and hear Israel because she loves and knows Israel like a mother loves and knows her children from near and far; she is, as parents are, moved by their affliction to the point where she would willingly suffer it for them. God was among us, not as us, but as the figure of our assembly. The *Shekhinah* indicates the real presence of a suffering God but, not herself a person, is not a quasi-Christian incarnation of God crucified in Auschwitz.[19] Jürgen Moltmann, in a Christian depiction that is close but not identical to this one, characterizes the *Shekhinah* or the spirit of God as one who "wanders with Israel through the dust of the streets and hangs on the gallows of Auschwitz."[20] In Jewish understanding, the suffering of the *Shekhinah* is that of one who, being among us, suffers with us, but does not suffer vicariously *for* us.

The argument, then, is this: that the divine presence *is* the assembly of Israel. And in that the assembly of Israel was there and no longer there God's presence was continuous with her absence. The face of *Shekhinah* was hidden only insofar as the Jewish faces that imaged her were de-faced by their profanation, burned and dispersed as ash. Insofar as God had been turned away because Jewry had been turned away by Christian Europe, God could not see us and if God could not see us, still less could we see God. Yet in women's care for the other—emblematized in the wiping of filth from a face—God's face was revealed as present and visible to the eye of spiritual perception in the facing image. But this is a God whose face is *already* partially hidden, not because she chooses to withdraw for the sake of our freedom, but because the full revelation of the Jewish God whose oneness makes God both masculine *and* feminine in character—not half a God—has been eclipsed by the masculinization of theology and worship. This God has been profaned twice over: by the profanization of the

---

17. *Auschwitz and After*, p. 37.
18. E.g. Delbo writes of a young woman who, literally dying of thirst, breaks rank during a roll-call to eat snow from a ditch and is stranded there, too skeletally weak to move and only moments from her death at the jaws of an SS dog: 'I no longer look at her. I no longer wish to look. If only I could change my place in order not to see her. . . . Why does she stare at us? Isn't she pointing at me? Imploring me? I turn away to look elsewhere. Elsewhere' (*Auschwitz and After* [New Haven, 1995], p. 26).

19. Wyschogrod helps us to elucidate the nature of God's presence. God is not incarnated in Israel, "No, that would be going too far. . . . But God certainly dwells in the midst of his people in some special way. Perhaps it would be best to say that he does not dwell *in* the people of Israel but among or alongside them." God's immanence is akin to how a person dwelling in a city has not actually fused with its walls (*The Body of Faith*, p. 11).
20. Trans. R.A. Wilson and J. Bowden, *The Crucified God: The Cross of Christ as the Foundation and Criticism of Christian Theology* (London, 1974), p. 274.

female face in Auschwitz and by the profanization of her own face—that aspect of God that has
been set outside the precincts of the holy for most
of Jewish history.

If God is, as it were, completed by the creation of humanity in God's image and restored by
the human recreation of humanity in God's image, perhaps, for some, it was less a question of
how God might have been present to Jewry in the
Holocaust, but how Jewry might have been present to God. Etty Hillesum, aware of the dangers
of what she calls "heroic illusions," writes in the
midst of catastrophe: "I shall merely try to help
God as best I can and if I succeed in doing that,
then I shall be of use to others as well." On
another occasion she writes, "And if God does
not help me to go on, then I shall have to help
God."[21] Hillesum is as much present to God as
God, through the reciprocities of love and service, is present to her. It is she who, close to her
end, reassures God with the words "believe me, I
shall always labor for You and remain faithful to
You and I shall never drive You from my presence."[22] Buber also regards God's fate as a human
responsibility. We must offer ourselves to God as
his "helpers and companions." Buber addresses
his reader: "Don't you know also that God needs
you, in the fullness of His eternity, you? How
would man exist if God did not need Him, and
how would you exist?"[23] There is an old and
fragile narrative thread running through the tradition of a God whose heart will break if we do
not mend it, if we do not take some of God's
burden from him. If a nonomnipotent God

weeps for his exiled children B.T. *Berakhot* 59[a],
how can we *not* comfort God? Later Jewish mysticism is founded upon doctrines of creation and
redemption where at creation God empties God-
self of God so as to enter into a relationship with
the world which will not absorb it into the totality of Godhead. And this God's creation will
only be redeemed by the mutuality of divine and
human labor; the world is mended not solely
from above but also from below.

Insofar as God is made present as much by our
beckoning as by the initiative of God, the theme
of hiddenness may not be entirely dispensable.
In this sense post-Holocaust theology is right in
observing that the conditions of presence and absence in Auschwitz must have coexisted in dialectical relation to one another. If the theme of
God's apparent absence is to be of assistance to a
feminist theology it may be more fruitful to look
to narratives of divine hiddenness other than
those of scripture where it is at worst a punishment and at best distressingly inexplicable.

In particular, the Ashkenazic legend of the
Lamedvovnik, or Just Man, suggests a preferable
model of divine presence-in-absence than that of
Berkovits's admittedly more distinguished, scriptural theology.[24] The Jewish legend of the *Lamed
Vav Zaddikim*, or thirty-six hidden saints, tells of
the Just Men concealed in every generation upon
whom the fate of the world depends. Without
their shouldering the terrible burden of human
suffering God's tears would drown the world.[25]
Among one of them might be the Messiah but he
is unknown and unrevealed because the people

21. *Etty: A Diary* (London, 1985), pp. 193, 192.
22. Ibid. p. 198.
23. *I and Thou*, trans. Walter Kaufmann (New York, 1970), p. 130.
24. See further my article, "The Face of God in Every Generation: Jewish Feminist Spirituality and the Legend of the Thirty-Six Hidden Saints," in Ursula King, ed., *Spirituality and Society in the New Millennium* (Brighton, 2001), pp. 234–6, from which some of the present discussion of the Just Man is drawn.
25. The legend of the Just Man (in Yiddish, the *Lamedvovnik*) originates in the Babylonian Talmud (*Sanhedrin* 97[b]; *Sukhah* 45[b]) and is accredited to the fourth-century teacher Abbaye. The Just Man is not to be confused with the Suffering Servant of Isaiah 53

who, though similarly despised, suffers sacrificially and intercessively for Israel's sin. The legend of the Just Man has gained currency only among Ashkenazic Jews where it is found in kabbalistic and hasidic folklore and, in the early twentieth century, in the Yiddish and Hebrew literature of modernist writers such as I. L. Peretz and Moyshe Kulbak. Orthodoxy has expressed some reservations about the twentieth-century literary evolution of the legend—particularly that of André Schwartz-Bart's characterization of his fictional Ernie Levy as the last of a dynasty of Just Men. Schwartz-Bart's renowned *The Last of the Just*, trans. Stephen Becker (London, 1962), may, in Orthodoxy's view, owe more to Schwartz-Bart's imagination and to Christian theological influence than to the original Jewish sources of the legend.

are not worthy to recognize him. Some Just Men are not even aware of their being of the chosen thirty-six. Often held in contempt, these men live without honor in humble anonymity; the essence of their saintliness lies precisely in such. Mysteriously, silently, appearing and disappearing, they journey through the *shtetls* (small towns and villages) of European Jewry, painfully singled out to see the face of God, to receive the Divine Presence. They disappear so that God can appear.

Mystical Judaism has seen God in the unassuming disguise of the Just Man. Like the *tsadiq* (holy man) who, disguised as a humble pretzel seller, cured the blind daughter of a ḥasid of the Rabbi of Rizhyn,[26] the Just Man's secret care for the sick is a miracle of modest piety. Such stories will raise a wry smile among women. Since they are expected to conform to the codes of feminine modesty, their care for others is not a particular sign of the holy; it does not have to be carried out in secret; it is merely normal, public, and assumed. Humility and anonymity are prerequisite for ordinary virtue in a woman but supererogatory, indeed, redemptive, virtues in a man. Orthodox women, then, can hardly assume the redemptive role of the ḥasidic *nistar*, or hidden saint, when their discursive and religious "hiddenness" is that of required modesty or, in effect, their erasure from the public religious sphere.

While the discursive and religiosocial hiddenness of Orthodox women can be an affront to their intellectual and spiritual abilities, female hiddenness may bear different theological meaning in the holocaustal situation. For here God-She may have been known in, and her grief carried by, the many anonymous female "saints" described in the memoir literature who appear and disappear on their own short journeys of erasure through Auschwitz and the other camps and ghettos of the Holocaust.

I have asked elsewhere whether Jewish tradition has made a Just Man of God by hiding the female face of God behind the male face of God and in doing so left God's female aspect nameless.[27] God too is cast out; like the *Lamedvovnik* she wanders through Jewish history, all the while secretly sustaining the world by her care. And it is not only God, but the women created in her image who are, as it were, the other Just "Men," the hidden of the hidden. For in the *shtetls*, it was they, not men, who lived in ill-educated anonymity by virtue of their sex, not just their class. Women enjoyed none of the public honors of the religious life; as women their domestic and mercantile labors went on unremarked and screened off from the world of public religious devotion. Yet, . . . from a post-Holocaust perspective, their labors, like that of the Just Men, carried the world through Auschwitz, redeeming it from chaos, and, declaring a Sabbath on its grinding cycle of destruction, returned to the world a sense of the renewed, cleaned dimension of its creation.

Contrary to the received view that the Jewish God is unrepresentable, God's face is visible and his love figurable as it passes across the face of the Just Man or (nontraditionally) Just Woman. Her modest care tells us something else about what is beloved of God and about the locus of Jewish revelation, namely, that revelation may sometimes consist precisely in what is unrevealed, unnoticed, and intellectually despised. If the Jewish God has long been a humble God of care got up in the heavy robes of monarchical patriarchy, then, stripped of its office, the underface of this Other God may be revealed in the faces of women who, in every generation, have labored to bear the exiled *Shekhinah* to wherever their exile has taken them, including the death and concentration camps. Here, without the supernatural finery of omnipotence, God can only do her restorative work in and with those whose care—even unknowingly—invokes, meets, and labors alongside her.

In Bergen-Belsen, in the first months of 1945, Bertha Ferderber-Salz remembers listening to an old Hungarian woman softly intoning a Sabbath prayer as she lay in utter dereliction in the darkness and stench of a filth-sodden bunk. The dying woman then wished Ferderber-Salz "A good week! A good week to you, to the family, and to all the House of Israel. Amen!" When asked if she had been praying, the old woman replied "in a

26. Martin Buber, *Tales of the Hasidim: Later Masters* (New York, 1961), p. 65.

27. "The Face of God in Every Generation," p. 239.

weak, barely audible voice," "It is our duty to praise God at all times and in every place. God hears our prayers even when they are said from the deepest pit. And even if He does not come to our aid, there are other Jews in the world for whom we should request a good week."[28]

Had Ferderber-Salz not recorded this Just Woman's words in her memoir no one would ever know of that moment of God's hearing, at the bottom of "the deepest pit" where she lay dying among the dying (compare again Psalm 88). The old woman's prayer was not for God to intervene on her own behalf and she does not decry her abandonment by God. She affirms her own and God's love of Israel. God's hearing in the pit allowed the woman to die celebrating and mediating the obligations of a divine love upon which she made no personal demand. It may even be that the prostrate God *could not* come to our aid and the old woman blesses Israel in God's stead.

Giuliana Tedeschi's memoir yields another such female hierophany (though she would not describe it as such). One night in Auschwitz, in a "state of spiritual prostration an overwhelming desperation" took hold of Tedeschi. Cast out as a punishment from the barrack block into the freezing night wearing only a thin sleeveless nightshirt, in physical pain, her human dignity violated, forcibly separated from her husband and children, and with the flaming crematoria before her, she had never before had "such a strong feeling of being a grain of sand alone in the universe." Prostrate on the freezing ground she wept. It was then that she felt two hands lay a garment around her shoulders:

> I recognized her in the glow from the flame. A Frenchwoman, quite old, who worked in the *Schuhkommando* [mending shoes], one of those dull creatures, without life or intelligence, who in normal circumstances barely manage to get by, and who in the camps seemed mad and moronic. I threw my arms around the neck of this companion in punishment, while to console me she whispered: *"Ça va finir, mon petit, ça va finir; bientôt!"*[29]

Both of these narratives owe something to the European tradition of wise women: crones who, bent over by age, appear on the path from nowhere to guide and protect the good who are lost in the metaphorical forest. Of course the "crones" recalled by Ferderber-Salz and Tedeschi are themselves the objects of Nazi fury and can protect no one. Abjection is not the condition of spiritual and ethical virtue. But while their protection is not deliverance, it is protection of a kind. I am reminded of a now almost iconic nameless old woman with "hair white as snow" who is remembered for holding in her arms a motherless one-year-old child as she stood at the edge of the communal pit, about to be shot with the rest of her village by Nazi troops. The old woman sang to the child and tickled him under the chin until he laughed with joy. Then they were shot.[30]

These women's (disappearing) faces bear traces of the female face of God, dimly glowing as when the face of the moon is eclipsed by passing clouds in the night sky. And when there was no one at all, inanimate natural objects could take on the functions of divine presence for women. Victor Frankl remembers a young woman in Auschwitz who, as she lay dying, told Frankl (who at first thought she was hallucinating) that she could see one almost bare branch of a chestnut tree from the window of her block. There were two blossoms on the branch. The girl told Frankl that the tree was the only friend she had in her loneliness and that she often talked to it. When asked by Frankl if the tree replied she answered, "It said to me, 'I am here—I am here—I am life, eternal life.'"[31] If God has chosen Israel as God's vehicle of self-revelation then the suffering of Israel must tell us something about the nature and posture of God's presence among us. It may seem little more than a tree stripped of its leaves by an untempered wind....

In women's memoirs of Auschwitz relationships with men generally become *textually* incidental. Relatively little reference is made by their authors to absent or dead husbands and fathers. This is not, of course, because men and women

28. *And the Sun Kept Shining* (New York, 1980) pp. 143–44.
29. *There Is a Place* (London, 1994), p. 86.
30. Cited by Eliezer Berkovits, *With God in Hell* (New York, 1979), p. 19.
31. *Man's Search for Meaning* (Boston, 1962), p. 69.

were indifferent to each others' fate or because varying degrees of sexual segregation were already a feature of women's lives by virtue of the economic and religious demands made on men and women's time. It is rather that in the immediacy of the crisis women were very often forced to manage and survive on their own. The capacity of the mother/daughter relation to withstand the catastrophe often becomes the most important story to be told of their holocaustal experience. In the many women's memoirs of the Holocaust published in recent years (one thinks of those of, say, Trudi Birger, Sara Tuvel Bernstein, Rena Kornreich Gelissen, Kitty Hart, Clara Isaacman, and Schoschana Rabinovici)[32] it is the author's relation with her mother (whether living or dead) which gives meaning, purpose, and substance to her survival and thence to the narration of her experience. Sisters, especially in the absence of a mother, similarly anchor meaning and hope. (Kornreich's memoir, for example, is shaped by the promise she made to her mother to protect her sister Danka, who, the physically weaker of the two, also helps Kornreich herself to survive Auschwitz.) It is as if within the story of Israel's relationship with the male Father/King God, is another (untold) story: the story of the female bond of protective love between the Mother-God and the daughters of Israel *in extremis.* If love is stronger than death (Song of Songs 8:6) then so is maternal presence—a phenomenalizing of divine and human love. . . .

Because classical theology generally postulates an omnipotent God who subjects history to the mysterious purposes of his will, Holocaust theology to date does not (and perhaps *cannot* in the counterevidential light of bottomless human suffering) take the love of God as its determining theme. To imagine a Mother-God in Auschwitz is to envision a different covenant of divine/human love. Here the love of God for Israel is no longer, as in prophetic tradition, likened to a patriarchal marriage where the husband's physical and social power renders him a violent or loving master according to whim or circumstance. This God is not the Lord of Hosts (or armies). Rather, God's maternal love for Israel can be figured by women as that countermand to wanton destruction which comes of bearing the increasing weight of their creation within their own bodies, suffering to bring it safely from the tight darkness into light and air, and knowing its absolute dependence on their protective presence. The face-to-face relation of the mother and newborn child is the first form and moment of presence. And more than that, feminist spirituality and the maternalist epistemology it commonly proposes has insisted that the motherhood of God bespeaks a commonality between divine and female personality. It is this maternal commonality that redefines our trust (*emunah*) in the loving presence traditionally ascribed to God but which in post-Holocaust theology, betrayed by the desertion of its Father-God, has been substantially lost. Irving Greenberg, for example, argues that after God allowed the Holocaust and withheld his protection from Jewry he can have no moral claim on Jews' covenantal allegiance; it must now be voluntary. The covenant can no longer be commanded or enforced by reward and punishment.[33]

Israel too is the child for whom the Mother-God is covenanted to take responsibility and to share or take away its pain. But Israel is also, like all children, covenanted through the reciprocities of love to take increasing responsibility for the world given it by God. The Holocaust imposed a complex set of maternal responsibilities. We have already seen that maternal obligations often had

32. Trudi Birger and Jeffrey M. Green, *A Daughter's Gift of Love: A Holocaust Memoir* (Philadelphia, 1992); Sara Tuvel Bernstein et al., *The Seamstress: A Memoir of Survival* (New York, 1997). This memoir tells of how Bernstein survived Ravensbrück by banding together with her sister Esther and two friends. See also Rena Kornreich Gelissen, *Rena's Promise* (Boston, 1996), Kitty Hart, *Return to Auschwitz* (St. Alfans, 1983), Schoschana Rabinovici et al, trans. Shoshanah Rabinovits, *Thanks to My Mother* (London, 2000). This book describes how Rabinovici's mother enabled her and many other women to survive the camps. See further, Brana Gurewitsch and Leon J. Weinberger, eds., *Mothers, Sisters, Resisters: Oral Histories of Women Who Survived the Holocaust* (Tuscaloosa, 1999), and Roger A. Ritvo and Diane M. Plotkin, *Sisters in Sorrow: Voices of Care in the Holocaust,* (Austin, 1998).

33. "Voluntary Covenant," in S. L. Jacobs, ed., *Contemporary Jewish Religious Responses to the Holocaust* (Lanham, Md., 1993), pp. 92–93 and *passim.*

to be reciprocated by children prematurely matured by danger and need. Mothers had responsibilities not only to their children but also to their elderly parents. This traditional duty of daughterly care further endangered women's lives; had it not been that women felt that they could not leave their parents to an unknown fate, many could have escaped before emigration became impossible. Lucie Adelsberger, for example, refused to leave her elderly mother in Germany. Although offered a visa for the United States for herself, she could not obtain one for her mother.[34]

Women's friendships could also entail mothering. Mothers mothered mothers in Auschwitz. Lying in her bunk and in great distress, Giuliana Tedeschi's friend Zilly held Tedeschi's hand in her own "small, warm hand." Zilly pulled the blanket around Tedeschi's shoulders and in a "calm, motherly voice" whispered in her ear, "Good night dear—I have a daughter your age!" Sleep then "crept slowly into [her] being along with the trust that hand communicated, like blood flowing along the veins."[35] Or again, Charlotte Delbo used to hold her friend Germaine's hand in Auschwitz to help her get to sleep. Germaine later says: "Do you recall how you used to say, in Auschwitz, 'Let me hold your hand so I'll fall asleep. You have my mother's hands.' Do you remember saying that, Charlotte?"[36] Once voiced in the promise of Ruth to her mother-in-law, Naomi, that she will go where Naomi goes, where Naomi dies she shall die, that nothing but death shall part her from Naomi (Ruth 1:16–17), it may be that maternal presence in its multiple forms and surrogates offers a different means to trust in God than those to which tradition has accustomed us.

This is not to lapse into cliché: mothers are often bored, irritated, and angered by their chil-

dren. Not all mothers and children like one another. Some children are frightened of their mothers. Nor are mothers and their children immunized by love. During the Holocaust, maternal power (more a fancy of nineteenth-century social and religious rhetoricians than a political force) could become an ever more necessary fiction, a way of suspending disbelief. Clara Isaacman's memories of hiding from the Nazis in occupied Belgium are illustrative of my point. During their two and a half years in hiding, Isaacman's mother would hold and comfort her, speaking confidently and with conviction of their future. It was only when the war was over that Isaacman wondered whether her mother had ever really believed her own reassurances.[37] Isaacman recalls how the expression of love had become ritualized, almost a performance of sympathetic magic. Mothers would hold their children before the latter went out on dangerous errands, willing that if nothing else, their love would protect them.[38] Sometimes the "strong wishing" worked and children might often not have survived were it not for the love and proximity of their parents.[39] And even when, in the great majority of cases, children did not survive, their end could be eased by a fiction that maternal or quasi-maternal presence would be their redemption.[40]

When God calls to Abraham, Jacob, and Moses they answer *hinneni*, "I am here" or "here I am,"[41] For Levinas this "I am here" is the meaning of love.[42] This is also the meaning of love between God and persons. Therefore to ask the question of God's presence during the Holocaust is not only to ask "how was God made present to us?" but also, and inseparably from that, "how did we make ourselves present to God?" There is no divine presence without human presence—the *hinneni* or "here I am." Presence is transitive; God

34. L. Adelsberger, *Auschwitz: A Dictors Story* (London, 1996), p. 12.

35. *There Is a Place*, pp. 9–10.

36. *Auschwitz and After*, p. 510.

37. C. Isaacman, *Clara's Story* (Philadelphia, 1984), p. 37. Cf. Hanna Mortkowicz Olczakowa's account of Korczak's assuring his children of a future in which he does not believe ("Janosz [sic] Korczak's Last Walk," in Jacob Glatstein et al., eds., *Anthology of Holocaust Literature* (New York, 1985), p. 135).

38. See, e.g., Isaacman, *Clara's Story*, p. 60.

39. See, e.g., ibid., p. 97.

40. Cf. André Schwartz-Bart's fictional account of this phenomenon in his novel, *The Last of the Just,* trans. Stephen Becker (London, 1962), pp. 337–45.

41. See Genesis 22:1, 31:11, 46:2; Exodus 3:4. See also Isaiah 6:8 Cf. Cohen *The Tremendum*, p. 95.

42. E. Levinas, *Otherwise than Being*, trans. by A. Lingis (The Hague, 1981), pp. 113, 147.

cannot be present to nothing and nowhere. Just as a mother murmurs, "Mummy's here," when her child cries out in the night or when he is afraid because he cannot see her, to say "her I am" is to say here with you *I am*; my being human is to find and be present to you, here, in a place, answering you.

It was not uncommon for children in the ghettos to be orphaned or to be rounded up from the streets and deported without their parents. In such an environment of sudden disappearances, the threat of maternal absence to modify children's behavior—"Mummy won't be with you on the transport"[43]—would have been peculiarly terrifying. But more positively, the promise of maternal or quasi-maternal presence soothed children's terror. Maternal love could take on the function and attribute of divine love. For the Warsaw ghetto orphans in Janusz Korczak's care, "Whatever would happen, they were to know that it would not matter as long as he, the doctor, would be with them. All he asked was that they remain together.... And so the children set out on their journey [to the death camp, Treblinka].... Nothing mattered, as long as the doctor was with them."[44]

The redemptive loading of maternal presence is now, and was at the time, not limited to biological mothers or even a female object. Korczak refused offers of rescue from the ghetto and of a personal reprieve at the time of his deportation. He chose to accompany the children and, on his now legendary "last walk" from the orphanage to the freight wagons, he is reputed to have carried the two smallest children in his arms—this, despite his failing health, swollen feet, and the children who walked close to his side.[45] A similarly "maternal" attitude can be found among ḥasidic men, the physical presence of whose Rebbe offered not only religious teaching, but calming words, counsel, consolation, and a practical support that was reciprocated by his followers. Among numerous possible examples is the Komarner Rebbe, Rabbi Baruch Safrin, who refused two offers of rescue, insisting that he remain with his followers in their distress. The Paizesner Rebbe also refused to abandon his ḥasidim, stating: "Wherever my ḥasidim are, there I shall be as well." The Slonimer Rebbe knew that he might have been mistaken in refusing to leave Barenowich, but said "What can I do when my little children [his ḥasidim] are dependent upon me?"[46]

Primarily, though, accounts of those who told themselves and others stories about the almost miraculous power of maternal relationships to withstand terror and annihilation are characteristic of the women's memoir literature. Eva Weiss, a Jewish nurse herself selected for death on account of her scarlet fever, attempted to calm and comfort those women around her who were terrified by their suspected fate. Knowing that they would indeed all be taken in an ambulance directly to the crematorium, she promised them that they were to be transferred to a larger hospital where some of them might find their mothers.[47] The children's sense that everything will be all right as long as they are with their mother, and even if it is not, they can hold onto her and she will not let go of their hand, was emblematized in the mass graves of Auschwitz. Ferderber-Salz and other women had to remove corpses from the graves and burn them before the liberating army reached the camp. There they sometimes found two bodies: "a mother and a child, locked in an eternal embrace, since the mother had tried to protect the child with her body. The murderers' bullets had passed through the mother's body and entered her child's, killing both of them together."[48]

43. Etty Hillesum, *Letters from Westerbork*, trans. by A. J. Pomerans (London, 1985), p. 121.
44. Aaron Zeitlin, "The Last Walk of Janusz Korczak," trans. Hadassah Rosensaft and Gertrude Hirschler, in Janus Korczak, *Ghetto Diary*, trans. by J. Bachrach & B. Kezyurcka (New York, 1978), pp. 56–7.
45. Hanna Mortkowicz Olczakowa, "Janosz [sic] Korczak's Last Walk," in Jacob Glatstein, et al., eds., *Anthology of Holocaust Literature* (New York, 1985), p. 135.

46. Pesach Schindler, *Hasidic Responses to the Holocaust* (Hoboken, 1990), pp. 74–9.
47. Olga Lengyel, *Five Chimneys* (New York, 1995), p. 64. This moment is, I hope, unrepeatable, and ungeneralizable. It is not presented here as a means of advocating that women should be spared difficult knowledge.
48. Ferderber-Salz, *And the Sun Kept Shining*, p. 102.

Contemporary Jewish feminist liturgy widely expresses the faith that "The Lord is warmth / She will cradle me. The Wings of the Lord will cover me. Her breath will soothe me."[49] There are, in short, important intertextual connections to be made among scriptural words, these contemporary words, and women's words about Auschwitz where the meaning and purpose of Jewish motherhood was to be destroyed and where pregnancy—motherhood of an unborn child—could not be declared. Much Jewish feminism has insisted that the motherhood of God is the undeclared, untold story still unborn from the body of Israel, and it seems necessary to bring these narratives of maternal disappearance together and to reflect upon them without confusing their reasons.

A Dying and Deathless God

Narratives of maternal presence and disappearance thread their way through women's Holocaust memoirs, whether they write as mothers of hidden children, of children struggling to survive, of dead children, or whether they write as daughters with, or longing for, their mothers. As I read it, this narrative corpus is both a historical and theological commentary on presence and absence, appearance and disappearance. In these stories and fragments of stories, the face of *Shekhinah* shines dimly, almost imperceptibly, through the smoke clouds of Auschwitz. Hers was a countenance figured by the *tremendum* of divine maternal wrath at the despoliation of her love, Israel, and the *fascinans* of her divine longing, seeking, and calling to what was disappearing—literally going up in smoke—before her. And it was this resistant love which *Shekhinah*, God-in-relation-to-the-world, could mediate to those who still inhabited the relational structures (namely, those of family or its surrogates) to receive and express it.

It would seem that for many mothers, grief predominated over rage. Rage was impotent, but

grief held a woman to the object of her love rather than to her grief's hated cause. Women in Auschwitz sang songs redolent of peace and safety in a place which could supply neither of these. Among other survivors, Bertha Ferderber-Salz remembers how even the memory of singing lullabies to children now dead helped mothers release their grief. Women who were forced to sew in the workshops would cry as they sewed, remembering how they would once sing lullabies to their children. Other young mothers continued to sing lullabies even though their children were dead because by doing so they remained close to their children: "That's how I used to sing to my Sarahle when I was putting her to bed."[50] Jacob Neusner has theorized Torah as God's song; Israel sings responsively to God. Yeshiva scholars sing to one another in sing-song chanting speech that is song when the ear is attuned to its rhythms. In answer, God's is not the voice of thunder but the thin urgent voice that pierces the silence.[51] Neusner's thesis points toward a way of calling to God and being called to by God that is well known to mothers, even mothers who, in Auschwitz, sang to the silence. Their mother-songs were songs of the *Shekhinah*, whose own song is the maternal song that soothes the good to sleep/death; in the tradition, the death of the righteous comes by the kiss of the *Shekhinah*.

As mother, *Shekhinah* intercepted, suffered, and was extinguished by violence. As God-present-among-us she was bound by the conditions of immanence, namely, by the kenosis of the transcendental divinity whose absolute incommensurability would have made her unknowable even while it would have kept her from the consequences of immanence. It is possible for the love between a mother and child to approximate the absorptive love described by Jewish mystics as *devekuth*—a cleaving to God. And when God is alongside us, it is this form of love which best describes the anguished love God bears for us, her creation, when we are not what we were created and born(e) into this world to

---

49. Maggie Wenig, cited in David Blumenthal, *Facing the Abusing God* (Louisville, KY, 1993), p. 79.
50. *And the Sun Kept Shining*, pp. 122, 117; See also Sada Nomberg-Przytyk, *Auschwitz*, trans. by R. Hirsch,

E. Pfefferkow and D. Hirsch (Chapel Hill, 1985), p. 181, n. 17.
51. Jacob Neusner, *Judaism's Theological Voice: The Melody of the Talmud*, (London and Chicago, 1995), pp. 13, 1.

be. (Thus Lewinska on the man she saw in Auschwitz being dragged by his legs, his dead body "tracing a great furrow in the black mire": "If you had seen your child so, oh mother, or you, wife, if you had seen your love and joy in such a state.")[52] Both God and human persons suffer with what we have created because, as its creator, our love, will, and personality are in it. So too, where Israel loved and suffered for its children its face was transparent to the face of its God. God suffered in Auschwitz because Israel, the bearer of her creative love, lay s(p)oiled and mortally wounded in the fathomless holocaustal pit, taken beyond her consolatory touch, but not beyond her love. In that place, God was diminished by the hemorrhaging of that human and divine creative love—that which makes persons, persons, and God, God. But this is not to imply a Rubensteinian or Nietzschean death of God. As *Shekhinah*, God suffers the conditions of finitude. But as God, she endures forever.

That God was both dying and deathless in Auschwitz was attested in the maternal love that was a manifestation of God's love. Like God's, the maternal love of the dying mother was also sometimes experienced as deathless and therefore as an antidote to death. Isabella Leitner remembers how her mother, facing imminent death on her way to Auschwitz, reassured her son and five daughters: "And wherever I'll be, in some mysterious way, my love will overcome my death and will keep you alive. I love you."[53] Long after liberation, with children of her own, Leitner promises her mother, "I will tell them to make what is good in all of us our religion, as it was yours, Mother, and then you will always be alive and the housepainter [Hitler] will always be dead."[54] Analogically, God's immanence as the maternal *Shekhinah* was both infinitely strong as the presence of unconditional love and also *thereby* infinitely vulnerable to harm. . . .

It may be asked what purpose was served by the maternal, grieving presence of *Shekhinah* if it could not offer actual deliverance from evil *then*,

not in a time to come. But within the logic of the model of God I am proposing it is not meaningful to ask why God did not protect us at that time because it is not the nature or function of God to be reduced to that of a fortification against particular suffering. God is not a supernatural arsenal. Rather, it should be asked how we could and can protect God's presence as it is this which makes it possible to know God in the other and for God to know God-self in creation. And it is in this mutual knowing that both God and humanity will come to experience the blessings consequent upon the reconciliation within self and world traditionally described as *tikkun*. Because women are made in the image of God, *Shekhinah* suffered in the suffering of women. So that what has been called the "gender wounding" of Jewish women in the death and concentration camps was also a wounding of God. But conversely, when women's acts of care restored in one another that profaned spark of the divine which rendered them a reflection of God, they also restored God to God. In this sense, the redemption of both women and God from patriarchy was occurring as together they fell into the holocaustal pit.

The human face turned toward the other summoned the excluded, profaned God from her place by the gates—each redeemed spark lighting God's way back into the world, a God who, once having entered into the conditions of the world is not of a nature to alter them by fiat. Here she was shut out and shouted down, and against this was simply, silently, *there*. It may be that there are places of individual powerlessness and despair where, finally, all the other can do is to stand (spiritually if not physically) immovably by, like the women in black who have stood patiently in front of the government buildings of oppressive regimes holding up images of their dead or missing children. As Mother, God could not be cut off from Israel, her child. She could not remain outside the gates of the city of death while her children were within.[55] In an early

---

52. Pelagia Lewinska, "Twenty Months at Auschwitz," in C. Ruther & J. Roth, eds., *Different Voices* (New York, 1993), p. 87.
53. Isabella Leitner, *Fragments of Isabella*, p. 17.
54. Ibid., p. 95.

55. Cf. Isaiah 63:9: 'In all their troubles He was troubled, and the angel of His Presence delivered them. In His love and pity He Himself redeemed them, Raised them, and exalted them all the days of old.'

seventeenth-century letter, Shlomo Dresnitz recorded a dream of Rabbi Abraham Halevi. While in Jerusalem, Halevi dreamed that he saw the *Shekhinah* standing with her back to him, above the Wailing Wall. She was half-naked and the reader infers that she has been raped. Halevi was distraught at seeing her thus, but she turned and touched his face and wiped away his tears, comforting him with words of a better future.[56]

God hides her glory and comes hidden in the rags and filth of her suffering. She is, as it were, smuggled into Auschwitz: this is, or what should be, meant by the hiddenness of God. And yet, within its gates, she is also held aloft by the women who carry other women, who lift them up. It is not that the *tremendum* of her presence is deferred by her abjection; *in* her abjection she comes as eschatological comforter, witness, and judge.

To hold up another woman, to raise her face from the ground, as has been recorded of women in Auschwitz,[57] was to raise God's standard in Auschwitz. To drag or carry another along was not only to save her from death; it was to carry *Shekhinah* through the camp as she went in her ragged, blood- and mud-spattered tent on her way to Jerusalem. According to tradition, where there is peace, *Shekhinah* returns to Jerusalem. These women lifted up the face of God and carried it as a sign of peace. They bound up her wounds (a definitive act of *tikkun* [mending or repair]) and sent her on her way. Although Auschwitz can never be justified as its instrument, relationality constituted a redemptive moment of human presence: a *staying there* against erasure. It is that staying there that signals toward the liberation of God from the demonic attempt to remove or disappear the human(e) and the divine in the establishment of its own space, supremacy, and possession. If anything about female moral practice in Auschwitz was messianic, it was this. As Levinas proposes, where the suffering self is given over to the other's demand, then the self, in breaking through the violence of history to another way of being, is him- or herself the Messiah.[58]

---

56. Cited without a reference in Helen Freeman, "Chochmah and Wholeness," in Sybil Sheridan, ed., *Hear Our Voice* (London, 1994), p. 187.
57. See, e.g., Lewinska, "Twenty Months at Auschwitz," pp. 87–8.
58. E. Levinas *Difficile liberté* (Paris, 1963), pp. 122, 123.

It should be noted that Levinas insists that the moral law of the face does not promise a happy ending; faith is believing in responsibility and love without victory or reward. See also Raoul Mortley, *French Philosophers in Conversation* (London, 1991), p. 21.

Jonathan Sacks

Jonathan Sacks was born in London in 1949. He received a modern Orthodox education before going up to Cambridge University in 1968. At Cambridge he studied philosophy and graduated with highest honors. After graduation he pursued his rabbinical studies and received an Orthodox rabbinical ordination from both Jews' College, London, and London's Yeshiva Etz Chaim. He began his career as rabbi of the Golders Green synagogue and then moved on to become rabbi of the Marble Arch synagogue in London. He also served as Principal of Jews' College, London. In 1991 he was appointed Chief Rabbi of the United Hebrew Congregations of the British Commonwealth. While serving as Chief Rabbi, he has also been a visiting professor of philosophy and theology at a number of British universities and at the Hebrew University of Jerusalem. Rabbi Sacks holds honorary doctorates from seven universities and was awarded the doctor of divinity degree by the Archbishop of Canterbury in 2001 in recognition of his first ten years in the office of Chief Rabbi. He has published thirteen books, several of which have won major international awards and prizes, and is a regular, monthly contributor to the *Times of London* where he writes a column entitled "*Credo.*"

SELECTIONS

The two selections reprinted here are taken from Jonathan Sacks's *Tradition in an Untraditional Age: Essays in Modern Jewish Thought* (1990) and his 1992 book entitled *Crisis and Covenant: Jewish Thought after the Holocaust*. In the first of these selections, Sacks essentially reviews the main responses to the problem of evil given in the Jewish tradition over the centuries, including a review of the theological positions regarding the Holocaust of a number of significant recent thinkers—all of whom are represented in the present collection. In the second selection, while Sacks again reflects on the theological ruminations of several other contemporary thinkers, he attempts to provide his own theological argument, which turns out to be, despite his philosophical reservations regarding Fackenheim's general theological response to the *Shoah,* a version of Fackenheim's claim for the 614th commandment, i.e., that after Auschwitz, "the authentic Jew of today is forbidden to hand Hitler yet another, posthumous victory." The distinctive twist that Sacks gives this "commandment" arises from his interpretation of the high birth rate in the Orthodox, and especially the ultra-Orthodox, Jewish community since the Holocaust. This birth rate testifies, according to the reading here given it, to trust in God. It is, Sacks argues, a modern version of the vision of the biblical prophet Ezekiel in which God says to Israel: "O My people, I am going to open your graves and bring you up from them" (*Ezekiel* 37:12). Sacks sees in the birth of young Jews after the Holocaust, "a kind of rebirth ... and with it the start of the 'mending' of a broken world."[1]

Selected Bibliography

Books by Jonathan Sacks

Tradition in an Untraditional Age: Essays in Modern Jewish Thought (London, 1990).
Persistence of Faith (London, 1991).
Arguments for the Sake of Heaven (London, 1991).
Crisis and Covenant: Jewish Thought after the Holocaust (London, 1992).
One People? (London, 1993).
The Politics of Hope (London, 1997; 2d ed., 2000).
Radical Then, Radical Now (London, 2001), published in America as *A Letter in the Scroll* (New York, 2000).
Dignity of Difference (London, 2002).

The Holocaust in Jewish Theology[1]

The Holocaust is a mystery wrapped in silence. For almost twenty years afterward, little was said, still less written about it. Like many others of the post-Holocaust generation, I was reluctant to presume on so unfathomable a subject. The questions insist on being asked: How could one dare to speak? And how could one dare not to speak? The conflict itself is part of the continuing presence of the Holocaust, so it is here that I begin.

First, I and others of my generation are too far away from that time. Which of us who were born after the Holocaust, which of us who did not lose family in the Holocaust, can speak about the Holocaust? The Book of Lamentations speaks about the destruction of Jerusalem with the authority of an eyewitness: *Ani ha-gever ra'ah oni:* "I am the man who has seen affliction."[2] The books written, the films made about the destruction of European Jewry speak to us precisely in the measure that they are *edut:* testimony or witness. And the task of the post-Holocaust generation has been not to speak but to listen and record.

We are too far away to speak. But second, in an important sense we are also too close. Just as we now ask questions about the Holocaust, so tradition tells us that we would ask questions about the exodus from Egypt and the events that preceded it. The [Passover] *Haggadah* speaks of four questions asked by four children, the *rasha, tam, she'eno yodea lish'ol,* and *chakham,* the wicked, the simple, the inarticulate, and the wise. If we examine the Bible, we find that three of the four questions—those of the wicked, the simple, and the inarticulate—appear clustered together in the Book of Exodus,[3] set at the time of the event itself. The fourth question—that of the *chakham,* the wise son—does not appear until the Book of Deuteronomy,[4] at a point in time forty years later. We will not go far wrong if we say that the biblical time scale applies to the Holocaust too: we should expect it to take forty years even to find the right question, let alone expect an answer.

Third, just as we resist looking too long at the sun for fear of being blinded, we resist looking too long at the blinding darkness of Auschwitz for fear of being driven to despair. Consider. After the destruction of the First Temple, the author of Lamentations was driven to say: *Haya hashem ke-oyev,* "God has become like an enemy." *Bila Yisrael:* "He has swallowed up Israel."[5] After the destruction of the Second Temple, the Talmud states that *din hu shenigzor al atzmenu shelo le'echol basar velo lishtot yayin:* "by rights we

---

1. This chapter is a revised draft of a lecture delivered under the auspices of the Yad Vashem Committee on 26 November 1986. I have, as far as possible, left the original form intact, hence the frequent signs of an oral presentation.

2. Lamentations 3:1.
3. Exodus 12:26, 13:8, 13:14.
4. Deuteronomy 6:20.
5. Lamentations 2:5.

should decree that no Jew should ever again eat meat or drink wine."[6] There should never again be Jewish rejoicing. Indeed we never forget those tragedies; we ruled that even in the midst of celebration there should be a *zekher le-churban,* a pause to weep for the destruction.[7] What then would it be like fully to integrate into our lives a *zekher le-shoah,* a weeping for the Holocaust? Would it not overwhelm us?

The Talmud itself envisages just such a possibility. It gives the following parable of what Jewish history would eventually be like. It is like a man who was traveling on a road and met a wolf and escaped. And he would then tell people of his deliverance from the wolf. But then he met a lion and escaped. And he would then speak of his deliverance from the lion. But then he met a snake and escaped. And so he forgot the wolf and the lion and would speak only of the snake. So with Israel. *Tzarot achronot meshakhot et ha-rishonot:* "the later sufferings eclipse all the earlier ones."[8]

The revelation of evil contained within the Holocaust is blinding indeed. Elie Wiesel has insisted that we call it a revelation, a demonic counterpart of Sinai.[9] Which of us can look at it for long? If turning to look on the destruction of the wicked turned Lot's wife into stone, how much more so looking upon the destruction of the innocent and righteous?

These then are the three reasons why I and many others, confronted by the Holocaust, respond as did the Israelites at Sinai: *Vayar-ha-am vayanu'u vaya'amdu merachok:* "they saw and trembled and stayed at a distance."[10] This feeling will govern what I have to say, but cannot altogether inhibit it. Because theology must perform the dual task, of respecting such sentiment on the one hand and wrestling with it on the other.

To respect it is to admit that we are not yet in sight of the time when the Holocaust is intelligible within the classic terms of Jewish history. We are not yet ready to say where it belongs in the drama between God and His people. We will shortly encounter theologies which deny this, which say that it is perfectly clear what the Holocaust means. About such theories I will argue that they are not just premature, but false.

But theology must wrestle with these feelings, and for a simple reason. The Bible is full of commands to remember: "Remember that you were a slave in the land of Egypt."[11] "Remember what Amalek did to you."[12] "Beware lest you forget."[13] Yosef Hayyim Yerushalmi, in his recent study of Jewish history and Jewish memory, has written that "Only in Israel and nowhere else is the injunction to remember felt as a religious imperative to an entire people."[14] "Memory," he says, is "crucial to its faith and ultimately to its very existence."[15] The word *zakhor* in its various forms occurs in the Bible no less than 169 times. And the command to remember is directed to Israel specifically of episodes which we had every reason to wish to forget.

Nor are they acts of memory alone in any simple sense. They are also acts of reliving and acts of redemption. We remember the exodus by reliving the exodus, as if we ourselves had been among those to leave.[16] We redeem our slavery in Egypt by never allowing ourselves to be the victims or perpetrators of another enslavement.[17] All these are commands which apply with equal force to the Holocaust as well. Not least because this is what was asked of us by the victims themselves.

There is a moment in Claude Lanzmann's film *Shoah* in which one survivor talks of watching his friends go to their deaths in the ovens. They refused to obey the order to undress, and they

6. B. T. *Baba Batra* 60[b].
7. B. T. *Sotah* 49[a]; B. T. *Baba Batra* 60[b]; Maimonides, *Mishneh Torah Taaniyot* 5:12–15; *Shulchan Arukh, Orach Chayyim* ch. 560.
8. B. T. *Berakhot* 13[a].
9. I owe the reference to Wiesel to Emil Fackenheim, *The Jewish Return into History* (New York, 1978), p. 53.
10. Exodus 20:15.
11. Deuteronomy 5:15, 15:15, 16:12, 24:18, 24:22.
12. Deuteronomy 25:17.
13. Deuteronomy 6:12, 8:11.
14. Yosef Hayyim Yerushalmi, *Zakhor: Jewish History and Jewish Memory* (Seattle, Wash., 1982), p. 9.
15. Yerushalmi, *Zakhor,* p. 9.
16. Mishnah, *Pesachim* 10:5.
17. On the role of the exodus in providing reasons for the commandments in the Bible itself, see David Weiss Halivni, *Midrash, Mishnah, and Gemara* (Cambridge, Mass., 1986), pp. 9–17.

stood and sang first the Czech national anthem and then the "Hatikva." He, who was not scheduled to die, ran in to join them, knowing for certain that having seen what he had seen he could not continue to live. But they thrust him out, telling him: You must live and bear witness to our suffering.

To live and *bear witness* to their suffering, to live and *give meaning* to their suffering is a command by which all post-Holocaust Jews stand bound. For we fail in our covenantal duty to the past if we allow the Holocaust to be forgotten. And we fail in our covenantal duty to the future if we allow the Holocaust so to haunt the Jewish condition that Hitler's ghost meets us at every turn. How we map a path between these unacceptable alternatives is the task of theology. To this I now turn.

One thinker at least was in no doubt as to the meaning of the Holocaust. It is important to confront him seriously and not immediately to dismiss his proposition as an outrage. For it belongs to a central tradition.

One of the great moments of Jewish theological self-definition came in the years leading up to the destruction of Jerusalem and the kingdom of Judah by the Babylonians in 587 B.C.E. Throughout the precarious history related in the Books of Kings, disaster had often threatened but had always somehow been averted. For the first time, now, no miracle happens. No escape takes place. The kingdom and the Temple are destroyed and the people taken into exile. It could have been interpreted as the defeat of a people and its God. But the prophet Jeremiah took the opposite alternative: it was the defeat of a people *by* its God.[18] It was, in short, a Divine punishment. The Babylonians, though they were the enemies of God, were unwittingly the instruments of God, agents of His retribution. As Jeremiah himself put it: "And when your people say, 'Why has the Lord our God done all these things to us?' you shall say to them, 'As you have forsaken Me and served strange gods in your land, so you shall serve strangers in a land that is not yours.' "[19]

This is the biblical response to catastrophe: to see it in terms of Divine action and Providence, Divine justice and punishment. It should not surprise us therefore to discover that someone saw the Holocaust in just these terms. It was a punishment. The Jewish people had sinned. God was present at Auschwitz, and the Third Reich was the instrument of his anger. This was the thesis propounded and argued with prophetic fervor by the late Rabbi yoel Teitelbaum, the Satmarer Rebbe.[20] What was the sin that merited the destruction of one-third of the Jewish people? The sin was: Zionism.

Only one sin could have been punished measure for measure by the near destruction of diaspora Jewry, and that was the premature attempt by Jewry itself to put an end to diaspora, to exile. The Jewish people had, according to the Talmud, taken an oath not to rebel against the nations of the world in their dispersion. They had promised not to hasten the end by an attempt to regain possession of the Land of Israel. So long as they lived submissively and passively in exile, the nations too were bound by an oath not to oppress Israel excessively.[21]

The Zionist movement, according to the Satmarer, was a rebellion of unprecedented dimensions against God. First it was worse than idolatry. It was an avowedly secular movement which denied Providence and believed that politics and the exercise of power could achieve what the will of God had evidently not yet decreed. Second, it was a contagion, luring into its ranks

---

18. For a provocative treatment of this aspect of Jewish spirituality, see Dan Jacobson, *The Story of the Stories* (London, 1982).

19. Jeremiah 5:19.

20. The thesis is propounded in two books: Yoel Teitelbaum, *Vayel Moshe*, 3 vols. (New York, 1959); *Al ha-Ge'ulah ve'al ha-Temurah* (New York, 1967).

21. B. T. *Ketubot* III[a] according to which there were three oaths: "One, that Israel shall not go up [to the land of Israel all together as if surrounded] by a wall; the second, that whereby the Holy One, blessed be He, adjured Israel that they shall not rebel against the nations of the world; and the third is that whereby the Holy One, blessed be He, adjured the idolaters that they shall not oppress Israel too much."

even religious Jews like those of *Mizrachi*. Third and most important, it broke the very terms of Jewish existence in the diaspora, the tacit agreement between Jews and their host cultures, whereby Jews might negotiate or pray their way to safety but would never become activist, politically organized, or organize public protests. Zionism was the work of Satan. The Jewish people had been tempted and succumbed. And judgment was duly visited upon them.

I should add at this point that the Satmarer Rebbe, though he was an extremist, was also a scholar and intellect of great distinction. Nor was he speaking from a position of comfort: he was himself rescued from Bergen-Belsen. And this very disturbing line of argument becomes more disturbing still if I add another voice. Rabbi Teitelbaum's views represent the ideology of *Neturei Karta,* the ultra-Orthodox opponents of the State of Israel. But in 1977, a member of *Agudat Yisrael, not* an opponent of the state, offered an explanation of the Holocaust. He was the late Rabbi Yitzchak [Isaac] Hutner, one of the most revered yeshivah leaders in America. His argument went as follows.[22]

We are wrong to think of the Holocaust as solely the product of Christian Europe. A major part in the decision to annihilate European Jewry was played by the Grand Mufti of Jerusalem, Haj Amin al-Husseini. The "final solution" was agreed on in January 1942, a mere two months after the Mufti's arrival in Berlin for talks with von Ribbentrop and Hitler. The Mufti himself was not an avowed enemy of the Jews until pressure began to be applied for the creation of a Jewish state. Hence Zionism brought about for the first time a collaboration between the Christian West and the Muslim East to destroy the Jewish people. Zionism was the cause of the Holocaust. It is reported that this view now prevails in mainstream yeshivah circles in America.

No comment on these views is necessary, because there is another conclusion about the Ho-

locaust to be drawn from exactly the same premise, namely, that when tragedy strikes the Jewish people it is always a Divine punishment for sin. In 1962 an Orthodox rabbi in Israel, Menachem Immanuel Hartom, asked just this question.[23] What sin could have been so grave? What sin could have evoked, measure for measure, the annihilation of European Jewry?

His answer is this. The quintessence of biblical Judaism is that the worst punishment that can befall the Jewish people is *Galut*, exile. Throughout the long second exile Jews believed just that: that they were in exile, that this was dislocation, a not-being-at-home; and they longed for a return to their land. Until the Emancipation. Then, with the end of the ghetto and the granting of civil equality, for the first time Jews argued that this was where they belonged, in an emancipated Europe. Assimilated Jews, Reform Jews, even Orthodox Jews, found positive meaning in German, Austrian, or French identity. Some abandoned the hope for a return to Israel altogether. Others deferred it to a metaphysical end of days. They became Germans of the Jewish persuasion. For the first time in history Jews *ceased* to be Zionists.

And for this they were punished. The retribution was precise. Having wished to make their permanent home in a strange land they were shown that there is no home for Jews in any land but their own. And the country that sought to make the world *Judenrein* [free of Jews] was none other than Germany, the country above all others that had been worshipped by its Jews as the epitome of civilization, the cultural utopia.

This view is shared by most secular Zionists. A. B. Yehoshua, for example, calls the Holocaust the final decisive proof of the failure of diaspora existence.[24] But Rabbi Hartom is not a secular Zionist. He is a religious Jew seeking an explanation of the Holocaust in terms of Divine Providence. And his case is stronger than he himself makes it, because—though he does not

22. I am indebted, for this presentation, to Lawrence Kaplan, "Rabbi Isaac Hutner's *Daat Torah* Perspective on the Holocaust: A Critical Perspective," *Tradition* 18:3 (Fall 1980): 235–248. [See also Hutner's full essay above, pp. 557–563.]

23. Menachem Immanuel Hartom, "Hirhurim al ha-Shoah," *Deot* 18 (Winter 5720/1961): 28–31.
24. A. B. Yehoshua, *Between Right and Right,* translated by Arnold Schwartz (New York, 1981), p. 12.

mention it[25]—there is a precise biblical prooftext in the twentieth chapter of the Book of Ezekiel. The prophet says:

> You say, "We want to be like the nations, like the peoples of the world...." But what you have in mind will never happen. As surely as I live, declares the Sovereign Lord, I will rule over you with a mighty hand and an outstretched arm and with fury poured out. I will bring you from the nations and gather you from the countries where you have been scattered—with a mighty hand and an outstretched arm and with fury poured out.[26]

Ezekiel predicts a time when the desire for assimilation will overtake the Jewish people and the return to Zion will be forgotten. At that time there will be a day of judgment, and the Jewish people will be turned into Zionists against their will.

So there is clear and decisive proof for Rabbi Teitelbaum that the Holocaust was a punishment for Zionism. And there is clear and decisive proof for Rabbi Hartom that the Holocaust was a punishment for anti-Zionism.

But I have to do more than show that this line of thought leads to contradiction. For there was a third group which saw the Holocaust in terms of Providence and Divine punishment. We must have the honesty to see clearly where this form of theology leads.

In 1948, a mere three years after the *Shoah,* a German Evangelical Conference met at Darmstadt. It proclaimed that Jewish suffering in the Holocaust was the work of God. It issued a call to Jews to cease their rejection and ongoing crucifixion of Jesus.[27] Genocide was the punishment for deicide.

Again I make no comment, except to say this. The idea that Jews were killed for their obstinacy in not becoming Christians was not restricted to Christians who were active collaborators with or passive accomplices of the Nazis. It is to be found even among Christians who were opponents of Hitler. Perhaps the greatest Christian theologian of this century, Karl Barth, himself an opponent of the Nazi regime, wrote during the Holocaust that the Jews were serving as witnesses of the sheer stark judgment of God. "This," he wrote, "is how Israel punishes itself for its sectarian self-assertion."[28]

One might well conclude that the attempt to find Divine meaning in the *Shoah* leads only to madness. This was precisely the conclusion drawn by the most radical of Jewish theologians, Richard Rubenstein, in his book *After Auschwitz.*[29] His argument is this. Believing in the Jewish God of history entails that we see the Holocaust as an act of God and an act of punishment for sin. But no sin could be sufficient to justify the inhuman evil of the Holocaust. No *tzidduk ha-din,* no "vindication

---

25. Since this lecture was delivered a new book has appeared which takes Ezekiel's text as its title: Bernard Maza, *With Fury Poured Out: A Torah Perspective on the Holocaust* (Hoboken, N.J., 1986). Maza's thesis is that the Holocaust was the work of Providence. Torah-true communities were on the wane, suffering from the impact of Emancipation, secularization, and Zionism. The Holocaust has driven Jews back to their millennial vocation, the study of Torah.

> Decades have passed since the Holocaust, and effects of the Holocaust have come into view. We have seen the resurgence of Torah in the east and in the west since the Holocaust. We know that by sacrificing their lives they made it come to be. It may therefore be that it was the will of Hashem [God] that they gave their lives so that the Torah and the Jewish people who live by it shall live. (p. 226)

This is a teleological restatement of the Holocaust-as-punishment thesis, and is open to the objections raised against such views by Maimonides, *Guide for the Perplexed,* III.24.

26. Ezekiel 20:32–34.
27. I owe this reference to Irving Greenberg, "Cloud of Smoke, Pillar of Fire: Judaism, Christianity, and Modernity after the Holocaust," in Eva Fleischner, ed., *Auschwitz: Beginning of a New Era?* (New York, 1977), p. 13, n. 10.
28. Karl Barth, "The Judgment and the Mercy of God," in F. E. Talmage, ed., *Disputation and Dialogue* (New York, 1975), p. 43. See also Richard L. Rubenstein, "The Dean and the Chosen People," in his *After Auschwitz: Radical Theology and Contemporary Judaism* (Indianapolis, Ind., 1966), pp. 47–58. [Reprinted above, pp. 410–414.] One Christian theologian to have reflected deeply on the implications of the Holocaust for Christianity is A. Roy Eckardt. See his *Elder and Younger Brothers* (New York, 1967); *Long Night's Journey into Day* (with Alice L. Eckardt) (Detroit, 1982); *Jews and Christians: The Contemporary Meeting* (Bloomington, 1986).
29. Rubenstein, *After Auschwitz,* esp. pp. 61–81.

of the ways of Providence," is sufficient to explain the death of the righteous and the innocent, the million and a half children slaughtered. Therefore there is no God of history. Traditional Jewish belief has been shattered. Quoting the rabbinic phrase for heresy, he concludes: *leit din ve-leit dayan:*[30] "There is no justice and there is no Judge."

I have to add that Rubenstein is both a theologian and a rabbi, although a rabbi of a kind unfamiliar in British Jewry. He is a Reconstructionist and believes that the only kind of Judaism possible after the Holocaust is a secular, even pagan one, which recognizes God in nature but not in history. History is meaningless, and in his words, "Omnipotent nothingness is Lord of all creation."[31]

What do these four approaches have in common? They assumed that a theology of the Holocaust must consist in understanding the Holocaust from the point of view of Providence. The Jewish view of history, and the Christian view of Jewish history, are that great tragedies are always acts of God, and therefore acts of justice, and therefore acts of punishment. So an anti-Zionist rabbi sees the *Shoah* as punishment for Zionism, and a Zionist rabbi sees it as punishment for anti-Zionism. A Christian theologian sees it as punishment for the Jewish rejection of Christianity. And Rubenstein concludes that a God who would punish in such a way cannot exist.

We could dismiss all four as simply canceling each other out. Or we could say that when they claim to be talking about the Holocaust they are really only talking about themselves. We could say, as most of us would, that though we have the faith that somehow, despite the concentration camps, there is Divine justice, we will never be able to understand it: *Ki lo machshevotai machshevotechem,* "For My thoughts are not your thoughts, nor My ways your ways, saith the Lord."[32]

We have, though, to go further than this. It is a striking fact that though the prophets evince an intense interest in the revelation of Divine purpose in the specificities of Jewish history, the rabbis do not.[33] In contrast to the apocalyptic literature that flourished from 200 B.C.E. to 100 C.E. the Mishnah is remarkable for its "utter silence" on the "tremendous issues of suffering and atonement, catastrophe and apocalypse."[34] History is no longer the primary locus of the Divine act. To some of the sages the Divine Presence had retreated to heaven. "When [the Temple] was burned, the Holy One, blessed be He, said: I no longer have a seat upon earth. I shall remove my *Shekhinah* [Divine Presence] from there and ascend to My first habitation."[35] To others, the Divine Presence was itself

---

30. [Midrash] *Leviticus Rabbah* 28:1. The statement is attributed to Cain in *Targum Jonathan* to Genesis 4:8.

31. The final words of his contribution to the symposium The State of Jewish Belief *Commentary,* August 1966, pp. 132–135. See also his *The Religious Imagination: A Study in Psychoanalysis and Jewish Theology* (Indianapolis, 1968), esp. pp. 171–183. Alasdair MacIntyre has distinguished two kinds of atheism. One is "speculative atheism which is concerned to deny that over and above the universe there is something else, an invisible intelligent being who exists apart from the world and rules over it." The other, in the tradition of Feuerbach and Marx, goes further and claims that "Religion is misunderstood if it is construed simply as a set of intellectual errors; it is rather the case that in a profoundly misleading form deep insights, hopes, and fears are being expressed.... Religion needs to be translated into nonreligious terms and not simply rejected." Alasdair MacIntyre, *Against the Self-Images of the Age* (London, 1971), pp. 12–13. Rubenstein is an atheist in the second sense.

32. Isaiah 55:8.

33. Yerushalmi notes that it is "remarkable that after the close of the biblical canon the Jews virtually stopped writing history.... It is as though, abruptly, the impulse to historiography had ceased.... More sobering and important is the fact that the history of the Talmudic period itself cannot be elicited from its own vast literature" (*Zakhor,* pp. 16–18). Jacob Neusner has similarly argued that "The Mishnah's framers' deepest yearning is not for historical change but for ahistorical stasis" (*Judaism: The Evidence of the Mishnah* [Chicago, 1981], p. 27), and "The Talmud contains virtually no reference to the most important events of the age in which it took shape and reached closure" (*Our Sages, God, and Israel* [New York, 1984], p. xix). One significant moment is captured in the displacement of the historical account of the events surrounding the festival of Chanukkah and the exclusion from the canon of the Books of Maccabees in favor of the supernatural narrative of the oil that burned for eight days, B. T. *Shabbat* 21[b]. That the process is incomplete, however, can be seen in the fact that the military victory is retained in the liturgy in the *Al ha-Nissim* [On the Miracles] prayer, *Singer's Prayer Book,* pp. 53–54.

34. Neusner, *Judaism,* p. 37.

35. [Midrash] *Lamentations Rabbah,* Proem 24. See also B. T. *Rosh Hashanah* 31[a].

in exile: "Wherever Israel went into exile, the *Shekhinah,* as it were, was exiled with them."[36] But the lucid presence of God in history which is of the essence of the prophetic literature is at an end, to be recovered only in the messianic future.

A new emphasis enters the rabbinic response to national tragedy. There are indeed places where the rabbis speak of the Roman destruction of the Temple in the classic terminology of sin and punishment.[37] But in a daring stroke they see God as weeping over the fate of his people. He suffers with them. He mourns as they do.[38] The concept of *kiddush ha-shem* (sanctification of the Divine name) is developed to embrace the death, as well as the life, of the righteous. Alongside martyrdom, never allowing it peace as a sufficient explanation, is the countervailing force of the reiterated question: "Is this the Torah and is this its reward?"[39] Job-like arguments with the ways of Providence are revived and audaciously placed in the mouths of the patriarchs, Moses, even the angels.[40] The aggadic literature contains reflections saved only from blasphemy by their searing pathos: "Were it not explicitly stated in Scripture, it would be impossible to say so, but...the Holy One, blessed be He, lamented, saying: Woe to the King who succeeded in His youth but failed in His old age."[41] To be sure,

these motifs are present in the Bible,[42] but now they begin to dominate.

Why the sudden change? The answer was given in different ways by [the medieval thinkers] Judah Halevi,[43] Maimonides,[44] and Naḥmanides,[45] but they converge on a common, if understated, conclusion. Divine Providence governs the affairs of Israel when the Jewish people exist as a sovereign people in the land of Israel. Then there is reward and punishment and prophecy. But exile, diaspora, *Galut* precisely means being removed from the mercy of God and placed at the mercy of the nations. It means the withdrawal of Providence, what the Bible calls *hester panim,* the "hiding of the face" of God, what Maimonides calls being left to chance.[46]

Levi ben Gershom (Gersonides, 1288–1344) instructs us to distinguish between tragedies like the destruction of Sodom, which are the *work* of Providence, and tragedies like the defeat of the Israelites at Jericho, which are the result of the *withdrawal* of Providence.[47] The difference may be slight, but it is all the difference in the world. If God destroys, then He destroys the guilty. If God withdraws, and then man destroys, the innocent suffer as well.[48]

In rabbinic times and throughout the Middle Ages there were great catastrophes of which Jews

36. *Mekhilta de-Rabbi Ishmael, Massekhta de-Pisha,* xii See E. E. Urbach, *The Sages* (Jerusalem, 1975), pp. 37–65.
37. B. T. *Yoma* 9[b], B. T. *Shabbat* 119[b], B. T. *Baba Metzia* 30[b].
38. See, e.g., B. T. *Berakhot* 3[a], and many examples in [*Midrash*] *Lamentations Rabbah.*
39. B. T. *Berakhot* 61[b], B. T. *Menachot* 29[b].
40. See, for a striking example, [*Midrash*] *Lamentations Rabbah,* Proem 24.
41. [*Midrash*] *Lamentations Rabbah,* Proem 24.
42. That Divine pathos is at the heart of prophetic consciousness is the argument of A. J. Heschel, *The Prophets* (Philadelphia, 1962). The argument with God over the ways of Providence is to be found in several key passages. See, e.g., Genesis 18: 17–32; Exodus 5:22, 32:12, 32:12; Jeremiah 12:1; Habakkuk 1:1–4.
43. See, e.g., *Kuzari* II.14, 29–44; V.22–23.
44. See, e.g., *Mishneh Torah, Ta'aniyot* 1:1–3; *Guide for the Perplexed,* II.36.
45. See, e.g., Commentary to Leviticus 18:25. And see, on the general subject, Y. Baer, *Galut* (New York, 1947).
46. See, e.g., Deuteronomy 31:18; Isaiah 8:17, 64:6; Ezekiel 39:23–24; Maimonides, *Mishneh Torah, Ta'aniyot* 1:3; *Guide for the Perplexed,* III.36.

47. See *Perush Ralbag* [*Gersonides Commentary*] to Joshua 7:1. See also Commentary of Abarbanel ad loc.:

There is a distinction between punishment which comes about by [a Divine] action and punishment which comes about through removal of providence. When God punishes by direct action. He does not punish the person who has not sinned on account of him who has. . . . Not so the punishment which comes about by chance as a result of God's withdrawing His providence. For this befalls the community in its entirety in that, because there are sinners amongst them, God hides His face from them all. . . . All of them become exposed to the workings of chance and accident, so that occasionally the person who has not sinned is also smitten when he is exposed to danger, and the sinner, who may not have been there, escapes unharmed.

48. This is also the sense of the talmudic statement (B.T. *Baba Kamma* 60[a]) that "Once permission has been granted to the Destroyer, he does not distinguish between the righteous and the wicked."

were the victims. There were the Hadrianic persecutions, the murder of Jews in the Crusades, the blood libels, the Inquisition, the pogroms. All of them were faithfully recorded in Jewish memory, written down and recited in *kinot,* elegies which we say to this day. In each case the rabbis and poets tried to find religious meaning in tragedy. But rarely if ever did they find that meaning in terms of sin and punishment.[49] Already the opinion had been voiced in the early rabbinic literature that reward and punishment were reserved for the world to come and that "There is no reward for the precepts in this world."[50] The poets of catastrophe during the Crusades related their sufferings to the binding of Isaac,[51] to the tragedy of Job,[52] to the suffering servant of Isaiah:[53] all the cases in the Bible where suffering is *not* related to sin.[54]

Several centuries later, in the wake of the Spanish expulsion [in 1492], Solomon Ibn Verga asks: "Tell me the reason for the fall of the Jews since ancient times.... for behold, I have found their fall to be neither in a natural way, nor due to divine punishment. For we have seen and heard of many nations that have transgressed and sinned more than they and were not punished."[55] *Galut* means exile from history in the prophetic sense of the intimate reciprocity of deed and fate. It means risk, exposure, and a faithful waiting.

Understood in this way, the Holocaust does not tell us about God but about man. It tells us not about Divine justice but about human injustice. And this is not radical theology but the whole weight of Jewish tradition in relation to *Galut.*[56] Rabbi Teitelbaum and Rabbi Hartom are wrong in what they assert. Richard Rubenstein is wrong in what he rejects. Significantly wrong. For they have mistaken the nature of the Jewish tradition and blasphemed against the memory of the dead. God forbid that we should add to their death the sin of saying that it was justified.[57] And God forbid that we should follow Rubenstein and add

49. See Yerushalmi, *Zakhor,* pp. 31–52; David G. Roskies, *Against the Apocalypse* (Cambridge, Mass., 1984), pp. 15–52. Yerushalmi writes: "The catastrophe [at Mainz] simply could not be explained by the stock notion of punishment for sin, for the Ashkenazic communities of the Rhineland were holy communities, as their own response to the crisis had demonstrated" (*Zakhor,* p. 38). Hence the invocation of the binding of Isaac as the dominant explanatory image for Jewish suffering in the Middle Ages.

50. B.T. *Kiddushin* 39[b], B.T. *Chullin* 142[a]. And see Urbach *The Sages,* pp. 436–444.

51. See Shalom Spiegel, *The Last Trial* (New York, 1979), for a detailed study of the development of the interpretation of the binding of Isaac as an image for Jewish suffering during the Crusades.

52. See, e.g., the *kinah* [the lament], "I said: Look away from me," composed by Kalonymous b. Judah of Mayence, dedicated to the victims of the second Crusade (Abraham Rosenfeld, *The Authorised Kinot for the Ninth of Av* [London, 1965], p. 140). This invokes Job's famous affirmation, "Though He slay me, yet I will trust in Him" (Job 13:15).

53. This is invoked by Judah ha-Levi, *Kuzari* II.34–41: "Israel amidst the nations is like the heart amidst the organs of the body."

54. There is frequent reference in the *kinot* to the sinlessness of the victims. "My thoughts are dismayed, shuddering and distraughtness take hold of me; [because] of one single [good deed] did Scripture find for King Abijah hope and expectation.... [Yet] those who were perfect in all their deeds submitted themselves to slaughter out of fear of the [enemy's] army: to them even burial was not granted" (*Kinah* by Kalonymous b. Judah, Rosenfeld, *Authorised Kinot,* p. 141). Rosenfeld himself continues the tradition in the *kinah* he composed for the victims of the Holocaust: "Distinguished scholars sit on the ground in stunned silence. 'What, Oh what, was their guilt?' they ask, And why was the decree issued without mercy?" (Rosenfeld, *Authorised Kinot,* p. 173).

55. Solomon Ibn Verga, *Shevet Yehudah,* cited in Yerushalmi, *Zakhor,* p. 55.

56. That we should see the Holocaust in terms of the "hiding of the face" of God has been argued by Rav Soloveitchik, and recently by Norman Lamm. See Abraham Besdin, *Reflections of the Rav* (Jerusalem, 1979), p. 37: "The Holocaust ... was *hester panim* [God hiding His face]. We cannot explain the Holocaust but we can, at least, classify it theologically.... The unbounded horrors represented the *tohu va-vohu* [chaos and void] anarchy of the pre-*yetzirah* [formation] state. This is how the world appears when God's moderating surveillance is suspended." See also Norman Lamm, *The Face of God: Thoughts on the Holocaust* (New York, 1986).

57. Irving Greenberg argues that this would be to "inflict on them the only indignity left"; "Cloud Of Smoke, Pillar of Fire," p. 25. The classic statement against "criticizing the Jewish congregation" is to be found in Maimonides' *Epistle on Martyrdom,* translated in A. Halkin and D. Hartman, *Crisis and Leadership: Epistles of Maimonides* (Philadelphia, 1985), pp. 15–34. See also B.T. *Pesachim* 87[a]–[b].

to the death of six million Jews the death of the Jewish God. . . .

Which brings me to the final thinker I want to consider, and the one who, to my mind, most accurately embodies an authentic Jewish response, namely, Eliezer Berkovits.[58] Berkovits disputes the central argument of Fackenheim, that the Holocaust is unique. It may indeed be unique from some perspectives, but not in a way that is relevant to faith.

The problem of *tzaddik ve-ra lo*, the "righteous who suffers," is one as old as Abraham. *Hashofet kol ha'aretz lo ya'aseh mishpat:* "Shall the judge of all the earth not do justice?"[59] The answer given by tradition applies to the Holocaust too. God, in giving man the freedom to choose to be good, at the same time necessarily gives him the freedom to be evil. God teaches us what goodness is. But He does not intervene to force us to be good or to prevent us from being wicked. This is the extraordinary Jewish conception of the power of God. God is powerful not through His interventions in history but through His self-restraint.

Berkovits quotes the extraordinary interpretation of the verse "Who is a mighty One like You, O Lord?" (Psalms 89:9), given by the Tannaitic teacher Abba Hanan. "Who is like You, mighty in self-restraint? You heard the blasphemy and the insults of that wicked man [Titus], but You kept silent!" In the school of R. Ishmael the verse "Who is like You, O Lord, among the mighty [*elim*]" (Exodus 15:11) was amended to read, "Who is like You, O Lord, among the silent ones [*illemim*]"—since He sees the suffering of His children and remains mute.[60] The central religious paradox is that God leaves the arena of history to human freedom, and therein lies His greatness.

So when human beings perpetrate evil it is human beings who are to blame, not God. But then the crucial question arises: Where do we witness God in history? Berkovits answers: God reveals His presence in the survival of Israel. Not

in His deeds, but in His children.[61] There is no other witness that God is present in history but the history of the Jewish people.

Hence the demonic character of the Nazi project. The "final solution," says Berkovits, was an attempt to destroy the only witnesses to the God of history. The in-gathering of exiles after the Holocaust and the creation of the State of Israel revealed God's presence at the very moment when we might have despaired of it altogether. The rebirth of the State came at a moment in history when nothing else could have saved Jews from extinction through hopelessness. The miracle that testifies that God exists is that the people of Israel exist. Though they walked through the valley of the shadow of death, *am yisrael chai,* the people Israel lives.

The only meaning to be extracted from the Holocaust is that man is capable of limitless evil. The religious meaning of six million deaths is no more and no less than that they, as other Jews had done before them, died *al kiddush hashem,* for the sanctification of God's name, suffering, as Isaiah saw the servants of God would always suffer, until the world finds it in its heart not to afflict the children of God. We find meaning not in the Holocaust but in the fact that the Jewish people survived the Holocaust. The existence of the State of Israel does not explain the *Shoah,* but it gives us faith despite the *Shoah.*

That is perhaps as near as we will come to a theology of the Holocaust. It helps to explain why Orthodox Judaism has been reluctant to create a new fast for *Yom Ha-Shoah,*[62] and why thinking about the Holocaust has played a less prominent part in Orthodox circles than elsewhere. Not because Orthodoxy has felt it less acutely than others: on the contrary, no other group lost so much as the worlds of the yeshivah and the hasidim. Rather it was because the traditional Jewish response has been *not* to sanctify suffering but instead to rebuild what was broken. Indeed it is the ultra-Orthodox groups in par-

58. Eliezer Berkovits, *Faith after the Holocaust* (New York, 1973). See also his *With God in Hell* (New York, 1979). [See selections above, pp. 463–489.]

59. Genesis 18:25.

60. *Mekhilta* 42[b]; B.T. *Gittin* 56[b]; *Faith after the Holocaust,* p. 94.

61. *Faith after the Holocaust,* pp. 109–127.

62. See, for example, Sir Immanuel Jakobovits, "More from the Chief Rabbi's Correspondence Files," *L'Eylah* (Spring 5745/1985): 32–33.

ticular that have tacitly insisted that the one command to come from Auschwitz was: Let there be more Jewish children. Who is to say that this is not the deepest response of all?

One writer about the Holocaust records that he met a rabbi who had been through the camps, and who, miraculously, seemed unscarred. He could still laugh. "How," he asked him, "could you see what you saw and still have faith? Did you have no questions?" The rabbi replied:

Of course I had questions. But I said to myself: If you ever ask those questions, they are such good questions that the Almighty will send you a personal invitation to heaven to give you the answers. And I preferred to be here on earth with the questions than up in heaven with the answers.

This too is a kind of theology.

We have not reached the end of thinking about the Holocaust, and in a sense we have hardly begun. The proof is that the most compelling writing about the Holocaust today is done not by rabbis, philosophers, or theologians, but by novelists like Elie Wiesel. A novel is a vehicle for unresolved tension and ambiguity, and is evidence that a problem still disturbs and bewilders us.[63]

Manifestly, we have not yet learned how to integrate the Holocaust into Jewish consciousness as we once integrated the exodus or the destruction of the Temples. The reason is clear. The Holocaust does not point anywhere but everywhere.[64] We have considered just a few examples. For some it confirms their faith, for others it confirms their lack of faith. For some it has proved that it is impossible to escape from Jewish identity, for others it has made it all the more urgent to do so. For some it has made it imperative to live in Israel, for others it has made it imperative that Jews be scattered everywhere, that a remnant shall always remain. The reason is not to be sought in the Holocaust itself but in something that preceded and still survives it. Namely, that since the Emancipation, there is no such thing as a common Jewish consciousness for any Jewish experience to be integrated into. Each of us relates to the Holocaust in our own way; but there is no longer a collective way, as there was when *Tisha b' Av* [the ninth of the month of Av, the day of commemoration for the first & second Temples] was instituted. We are no less fragmented after Auschwitz than we were before it.

This, it seems to me, is the central issue to be addressed. Rav Soloveitchik has spoken of the two covenants which bind Jews to one another and to God. There is the *brit goral* and the *brit ye'ud,* the covenant of a shared history and the covenant of a shared destiny.[65] The Holocaust has immeasurably deepened the *brit goral,* the covenant of shared history. The sentence of death was over each of us in some way that we can understand, whether we are secular or religious, Zionist or diasporist. What has not been deepened is the *brit ye'ud,* the covenant of shared destiny, of a common future.

In a remarkable passage the Talmud says that though the Torah was accepted at Sinai, it was only fully accepted on Purim.[66] It was on Purim [as narrated in the Book of Esther] that the Jewish people had stood under the decree directed "to destroy, massacre, and exterminate all the Jews, young and old, children and women, on a single day,"[67] the first warrant for genocide. It was only after Purim, says the Talmud, that *kiyemu ve-kiblu ha-yehudim,* that the covenant made at Sinai was fully entered into. The covenant of shared history was turned into a covenant of shared destiny.

In our day this has not yet happened. Yet the Holocaust still asks this question of us: If Jews were condemned to die together, shall we not struggle to find a way to live together? To find

---

63. See Yerushalmi's perceptive comments on the contemporary divorce of Jewish history from Jewish memory in *Zakhor,* pp. 81–103.
64. See A. B. Yehoshua, *Between Right and Right* (New York, 1981) pp. 1–21. And see D. J. Silver, "Choose Life," *Judaism* 35:4 (Fall 1986): 458–466:

The Holocaust cannot and does not provide the kind of vitalizing and informing myth around which American Jews could marshal their energies and construct a vital culture. Martyrs command respect, but a community's sense of sacred purpose must be woven of something more substantial than tears.

65. The distinction is made in the essay *Kol Dodi Dofek,* in J. D. Soloveitchik, *Divrei Hagut ve-Ha'arakhah* (Jerusalem, 1981), pp. 7–55. [This essay is reprinted above, pp. 382–393.]
66. B.T. *Shabbat* 88ª.
67. Esther 3:13.

a way of bringing the fragmented, splintered, shrinking Jewish world into a common future is the monumental task facing rabbis and theologians today. On their success will hinge the answer to the question: Was the Holocaust a tragedy or a turning point for the Jewish people?

The Valley of the Shadow

Judaism has its silences, Elie Wiesel once said, but we don't speak about them. After the Holocaust, the *shoah,* there was one of the great silences of Jewish history.

A third of world Jewry had gone up in flames. Entire worlds—the bustling Jewish townships of Eastern Europe, the talmudic academies, the courts of the Jewish mystics, the Yiddish-speaking masses, the urbane Jews of Germany, the Jews of Poland who had lived among their gentile neighbors for 800 years, the legendary synagogues and houses of study—all were erased. A guard at Auschwitz, testifying at the Nuremberg trial, explained that at the height of the genocide, when the camp was turning 10,000 Jews a day into ashes, children were thrown into the furnaces alive. When the destruction was over, a pillar of cloud marked the place where Europe's Jews had once been; and there was a silence that consumed all words.

More had died in the "final solution" than Jews. It was as if the image of God that is man had died also. We know in retrospect that Jews—both victims and survivors—simply could not believe what was happening. Since the Enlightenment they had come to have faith that a new order was in the making. The age-old teachings of contempt for the chosen-or-rejected people were at an end, they believed, and in their place would come a rational utopia.

It is hard in retrospect to imagine that sense of almost religious wonder which German Jews felt for the country of Goethe, Beethoven, and Immanuel Kant. That Christian anti-Judaism might mutate into the monster of racial anti-Semitism; that a Vatican might be silent as the covenantal people went to its crucifixion; that chamber music might be played over the cries of burning children; that the rational utopia might be *Judenrein* [free of Jews]: these, for the enlightened Jews of Europe, were the ultimately unthinkable thoughts. Since the early nineteenth century, humanity had seemed to many Jews a safer bet than God; and it was that faith that was murdered in the camps. Where was man at Auschwitz?

But where, too, was God? That He was present seemed a blasphemy; that He was absent, even more so. How could He have been there, punishing the righteous and the children for sins, their own or someone else's? But how could He *not* have been there, when, from the valley of the shadow of death, they called out to Him?

Jewish faith sees God in history. But here was a definitive, almost terminal, moment in Jewish history, and where was God's hand and His saving, outstretched arm? It seemed as if the *shoah* must have, yet could not have, religious meaning.

Wiesel has written of that time: "Never shall I forget those moments which murdered my God and my soul and turned my dreams to dust. Never shall I forget these things, even if I am condemned to live as long as God Himself." But to whom could one speak of these things so much larger than man, if not to God? It was a crisis of faith without precedent in the annals of belief. If God existed, how was Auschwitz possible? But if God did not exist, how was humanity after Auschwitz credible?

Covenant and Refutation

There is a line of theological reasoning which argues that a single moment of innocent suffering is as inexplicable as attempted genocide. Abraham, faced with the proposed destruction of the cities of the plain, had prayed, "Far be it from You to do such a thing, to bring death upon the innocent as well as the guilty, so that innocent and guilty fare alike. Far be it from You! Shall not the Judge of all the earth deal justly?"[1] Abraham began his famous dialogue with the possibility that there might be fifty innocent individuals; he stopped short at ten. But logic would pursue the argument further. The death of one child is [as] much a crisis for religious belief as the *Shoah*.

That is true. But it is to miss an essential feature of Jewish belief. There is theology, but beyond that there is covenant, the bond between God and a singular people. The Torah—the Hebrew Bible—reveals a single universal God who created the world and sits in judgment over the whole of human history. But with Abraham and the exodus and the revelation at Sinai, God chooses to associate His name with the fate of a particular extended family: the seed of Abraham, the children of Israel, the Jewish people. It is through them that His presence would be peculiarly manifest. Their way of life would set them apart as a holy nation. Their history would seem to be more than the morally indifferent play of cause and effect. It would read as a succession of commentaries to the covenant. Its deliverances and exiles, sufferings and salvations, its sheer improbable persistence, would invite the adjective "miraculous." The people of Israel would, in its own existence, bear testimony to the existence of God.

So the eternity of God is mirrored in the eternity of the Jewish people. The frightening sequence of curses at the end of the Book of Leviticus ends with the verse, "Yet in spite of this, when they are in the land of their enemies, I will not reject or abhor them so as to destroy them completely, breaking My covenant with them."[2] The prophet Jeremiah declared,

> This is what the Lord says, He who appoints the sun to shine by day, who decrees the moon and the stars to shine by night, who stirs up the sea so that its waves roar—the Lord Almighty is His name: "Only if these decrees vanish from My sight," declares the Lord, "will the descendants of Israel ever cease to be a nation before Me."[3]

The faith of Israel cannot be summarized in a set of theological statements which might be true whatever happened in space and time. It is peculiarly tied to the physical existence of the people of Israel. Theological propositions normally resist falsification. They are ways of interpreting events; hence they are not given to refutation by events. But the central premise of Judaism carries with it the risk of refutation. If there were no Jews, Judaism would have proven to be false. The survival of the Jewish people is the promise on which the entire covenant rests. An early rabbinic commentary put the point audaciously: " 'You are My witnesses, says the Lord, and I am God' (Isaiah 43:12)—that is, if you are My witnesses, I am God, and if you are not My witnesses, I am, as it were, not God."[4]

Jews had faced inquisitions and pogroms before. They had even, in the Book of Esther, known what it was to be condemned by Haman's decision "to destroy, kill, and annihilate all Jews—young and old, women and children—on a single day."[5] But redemption had always come, or if not redemption, refuge. In the Holocaust there was neither. Jews came face to face with a systematic program of extinction.

The demonic character of the "final solution" was not missed by Jewish thinkers. George Steiner has traced the intellectual progression from Nietzsche's "death of God" to the planned death of the people of God.[6] Josef Mengele, the doctor of Auschwitz, openly joked that he had replaced God as the judge of "who shall live and who shall die." Franz Stangl, the Treblinka *Kommandant*, insisted that pious Jews be made to spit on Torah scrolls, and that when they ran out of spittle more should be supplied by spitting into their mouths. In the ghettos and camps, Jewish sabbaths and festivals were singled out for special actions of cruelty and extermination.

Emil Fackenheim has argued convincingly that the Holocaust eclipses all previous trials of faith.

---

1. Genesis 18:25.
2. Leviticus 26:44.
3. Jeremiah 31:35–36.
4. *Midrash Tehillim* to Psalm 123:1.

5. Esther 3:13.
6. George Steiner, *In Bluebeard's Castle* (London, 1971), pp. 29–48.

The children of Auschwitz were tortured and murdered, not because of their faith nor despite their faith nor for reasons unrelated to the Jewish faith. The Nazis, though racists, did not murder Jews for their "race" but for the Jewish faith of their great-grandparents.... At some time in the mid-nineteenth century, European Jews, like Abraham of old, brought a child sacrifice; but unlike Abraham they did not know what they were doing—and there was no reprieve. It is as if Satan himself had plotted for four thousand years to destroy the covenant between God and Israel, and had at last found the way.[7]

The *Shoah,* then, did not simply raise six million times over the traditional question of theodicy: Why do the innocent suffer? It raised the ultimate question of Jewish existence. The covenant had promised that though individuals might be lost, the people as a whole would eternally survive. A *Judenrein* universe, a world free of Jews, would have refuted the ground of all Jewish hope from the days of Abraham. Not only the present and future, but the Jewish past too would have died.

So, for many years after the *Shoah,* the silence outweighed words. The questions were too painful to ask. It was as if, like Lot's wife, turning back to look on the destruction would turn one to stone....

Survival and Redemption

There is one...theme in Jewish thought whose invisible presence is crucial to an understanding of post-Holocaust Jewish history. In this case, though, let us approach it obliquely through a dialectical encounter between modern theology and a historic moment.

It was in 1967, in the weeks surrounding Israel's Six Day War, that an extraordinary transformation took place in Jewish sensibilities. In the anxious weeks before the war, with Israel surrounded and apparently abandoned, facing the threat of being driven into the sea, it seemed as if a second Holocaust was in the making. It was

then that the memory of the first, so traumatic for two decades, broke through with terrible force, in the form of an imperative: *never again.*

Israel's sudden victory released a flood of messianic emotion. For some it seemed as if the beginning of redemption had arrived. When the mood subsided a deeper sense began to form: that the State of Israel was a powerful Jewish affirmation of life, a determination never again to suffer the role of victim. Virtues which had long been at the heart of Judaism in exile—powerlessness, passivity, martyrdom, trust—had been overthrown. They now seemed, in retrospect, to be unwitting compliance in genocide. A quite new way of speaking about the Holocaust began to emerge.

Its most articulate spokesman was Emil Fackenheim, and he gave the mood of the moment its most famous expression. The *Shoah* was not to be understood. But it was to be responded to. Auschwitz yielded a command. Fackenheim invoked the traditional concept of the 613 commandments that constituted biblical Judaism. There had now been added a 614th command: "The authentic Jew of today is forbidden to hand Hitler yet another, posthumous victory."[8]

The imperative was Jewish survival as such. He explained:

I confess I used to be highly critical of Jewish philosophies which seemed to advocate no more than survival for survival's sake. I have changed my mind. I now believe that in this present, unbelievable age, even a mere collective commitment to Jewish group survival for its own sake is a momentous response, with the greatest implications.

It was, he said, "a profound, albeit as yet fragmentary, act of faith in an age of crisis to which the response might well have been either flight in total disarray or complete despair."[9]

Fackenheim spoke to a new Jewish consciousness. There was a sense, shared by many, that the universalist vision that had driven Jews of the nineteenth century to "normalize" the Jewish situation was over. Jews had been singled out by the "final solution," not for what they did or what

---

7. Emil Fackenheim, *The Jewish Return into History* (New York, 1978), p. 47.

8. Fackenheim, *The Jewish Return into History,* p. 22. [See selections above, pp. 420–454.]

9. Fackenheim, *The Jewish Return into History,* pp. 21–22.

they believed but for what they were. Israel itself had become isolated in the Middle East. A biblical phrase first uttered by the prophet Balaam suddenly came to seem an inexorable fate. Israel was "a people that dwells apart, not reckoned among the nations."[10]

Only after 1967 could this be seen as something other than a tragic fate. The State of Israel's victory, her determination to survive and the intense involvement of Jews everywhere in her fate, all combined to place Jewish peoplehood and survival at the center of the religious drama. It was as if, by reentering history and exercising power, Jews had exorcised the ghosts of powerlessness. Successfully emerging from a second trauma they could at last articulate their thoughts about the first.

But there was a further stage in the dialectic. In the twenty years since Fackenheim's commandment to survive, it has become clear that not all sectors of the Jewish world have heeded its call. In the diaspora, Jewish birth rates have fallen to below-replacement levels. The momentum of assimilation has accelerated. Intermarriage rates have risen. Frustrating Hitler has failed as an effective rationale for Jewish survival.

One group of Jews, though, has obeyed Fackenheim's command to the letter. They have had children in great numbers. They have rebuilt their lost worlds. They have proved themselves the virtuosi of survival. The irony is that they are a group that would deny the entire basis of Fackenheim's thought. They are the ultrareligious, for whom piety, not peoplehood, is the dominant value, and to whom secular survival is not Jewish survival at all.

There is a point at which theology has direct bearing on demography. Fackenheim has written poignantly about what it means to have Jewish children after the Holocaust. More than a million children died, not because of who they were but because of who their grandparents were. "Dare we *morally* raise Jewish children," asks Fackenheim, "exposing our offspring to a possible second Auschwitz decades or centuries hence? And dare we *religiously not* raise Jewish children, completing Satan's work on his behalf?" He adds, "My soul is aghast at this impossible choice, unprecedented in the annals of faith anywhere."[11]

But in this last statement Fackenheim is significantly mistaken. The Talmud records that just such a dilemma was faced by Jews in the second century C.E., having experienced the destruction of the Temple, the brutal suppression of the Bar Kochba rebellion [132–135 CE] and the Hadrianic persecutions [between 117 and 135 CE]. A statement in the name of Rabbi Ishmael reads:

> From the day that a government has come to power which issues cruel decrees against us and forbids us to observe the Torah and its commands . . . we ought by rights to bind ourselves not to marry and beget children, with the result that the seed of Abraham our father [the Jewish people] would come to an end of its own accord.[12]

This haunting passage tells us that there were profoundly religious Jews like Rabbi Ishmael who believed that on rational grounds one should not bring Jewish children into a world which had experienced nightmare. But Rabbi Ishmael added that were this to be issued as a ruling it would not be obeyed, for the faith of ordinary Jews transcends logic.

Does this mean that it is an irrational faith? The rabbis implicitly posed the question elsewhere in the form of a projected dialogue between two biblical figures, Amram and his daughter Miriam, at the time of Pharoah's decree that every male Israelite child should be cast into the river and drowned.[13] Amram and the other Israelite men, according to rabbinic tradition, thereupon divorced their wives and refused to have children. Amram's daughter protested. The decision, she said, was worse than Pharaoh's decree. It condemned both boys and girls. It deprived them of both this world and the next. Amram relented and he and his wife had a son: Moses. The implication is clear. From faith comes redemption. Trust in the future is neither rational nor irrational. Rather it is, in crisis, the critical test of religious courage.

---

10. Numbers 23:9.
11. Fackenheim, *The Jewish Return into History*, p. 48.
12. B.T. *Baba Batra* 60[b].
13. B.T. *Sotah* 12[a].

Against the backdrop of falling Jewish marriage and birth rates Orthodox Jews, in particular those of the ḥasidic and *yeshiva* communities, have dedicated themselves after the Holocaust to having large families. This is surely not unrelated to the fact that they, above all, adhere strenuously to the traditional tenets of Jewish faith. They deny absolutely Fackenheim's claims that the Holocaust is a *novum* in Jewish history, that it reveals a new 614th command, and that after the *Shoah* Jews are bidden to survive for survival's sake. Precisely because the dilemmas raised by the Holocaust are not unprecedented, they invite the classic response of Jewish faith, namely, to have trust in the future and to bring it into being.

Again we are reminded of the Book of Job. Job, having heard God in the whirlwind, recovers faith, though it is a faith without answers. The book then ends with a concluding chapter in which Job's fortunes are restored. At the beginning Job's sons and daughters died. At the end, he has new sons and daughters. To some readers this epilogue had seemed unconvincing, as if Job's sufferings could be unwritten by a happy ending. To a post-Holocaust generation the epilogue is disclosed in its full profundity. Job has no answers, but he has been lifted beyond his personal tragedy by the knowledge that he can still speak and be spoken to by God. This gives him the strength to go on living and have children after catastrophe.

That is the kind of faith manifest in traditionalist responses to the Holocaust. Rather than engaging in theological reflection on the Holocaust, the survivors of the ḥasidic and *yeshiva* communities of Eastern Europe concentrated on having children to replace a lost generation and rebuilding their shattered townships and institutions in Israel and America, as if to say that death is redeemed only in new life.

The word "redeemed" brings us finally to the concept that has lain just beneath the surface of our discussion: the resurrection of the dead. Early rabbinic Judaism did not formulate principles of Jewish faith. Its energies went into the articulation of law, not dogma. Nonetheless a Mishnah rules that one who denies the resurrection of the dead has no share in the world to come.[14] This was, for the rabbis, an indispensable requirement of belief. Necessarily so, for Judaism was predicated on the idea of divine justice, yet the sages lived in a world from which it seemed to be absent. *Halakhah* [Jewish religious law] rejected the mystical idea that evil, stripped of our veil of ignorance, would turn out to be good in disguise. To be sure, this idea is present in Judaism. But Jewish law rules that though one must pronounce a blessing over evil as well as over good, they are not the same blessing.[15] The fact of evil could not be denied. If there was justice, it lay in the future. But the existence of divine justice was the faith on which Judaism staked its very being. Therefore if anything were certain, it was that a time would come—in the form of the messianic age or the resurrection of the dead—in which the moral dislocation of the world would be righted. The past would be redeemed.

Whether we speak of the individual birth of Jewish children or the collective rebirth of Israel as a nation, the strongest metaphor to emerge in the wake of the Holocaust is that of resurrection. Rabbi Elhanan Wasserman's dying words have not ceased to reverberate, that "The fire which burns our bodies will be the fire that restores the Jewish people." Another rabbi, Yissachar Shlomo Teichtal [Yissakhar Taykhtahl], shortly before his murder in Auschwitz in 1944, wrote in a similar vein.

> Now if we shall arise and ascend to Zion we can yet bring about a *tikkun* ["mending," restitution] of the souls of the people Israel who were murdered as martyrs since it is on their account that we are being stimulated to return to our ancestral inheritance. . . . Thus we bring about their rebirth.[16]

To the biblical paradigms of the "suffering servant" of Isaiah and the Book of Job must therefore be added the vision of Ezekiel who witnessed a valley of dry bones and saw them come to life again:

---

14. Mishnah, *Sanhedrin* 10:1. The Mishnah goes further and rules that one who denies that the resurrection of the dead is *derived from the Torah* has no shre in the world to come.

15. Mishnah, *Berakhot* 9:2, 5.

16. Quoted in Fackenheim, *To Mend the World* (New York, 1982), p. 255. [See also selections in part I above, pp. 28–36 and 75–82.]

Then He said to me: Son of man, these bones are the whole house of Israel. They say, Our bones are dried up and our hope is gone; we are cut off. Therefore prophesy and say to them, This is what the Lord God says: O My people, I am going to open your graves and bring you up from them; I will bring you back to the land of Israel.[17]

This too has been part of the Jewish experience after the Holocaust. The messianic age has not come. The past has not been redeemed. The cries of the victims still haunt the Jewish imagination. But a kind of rebirth has taken place, nonetheless, and with it the start of the "mending" of a broken world.

Renewing the Covenant

An analysis of contemporary Jewry and Judaism must begin with the Holocaust because in it, the covenantal people came face to face with the possibility of its own extinction. It took several decades before theologians felt able freely to articulate their thoughts about it. In some circles, silence is still felt to be the best, perhaps the only, response.

The Holocaust reveals to the full the problematic nature of the religious interpretation of history. It has not yielded a single meaning but a vast multiplicity, of which only a narrow range has been touched on here. In the absence of prophecy there are no such things as events which carry with them their own interpretation. And yet Judaism must continue to wrestle with the problem. For one of its primary expressions is narrative: telling the story of the covenantal people through time. Judaism is not simply a faith. It is a faith embodied in a particular people, the way of life it lives, and the path it takes through the complex map of history.

Reflection on the *Shoah* reveals two significant facts about contemporary Jewish existence. The first is the absence of a shared set of Jewish meanings which alone might have allowed the Holocaust to be incorporated into collective Jewish memory. For the religious believer, the Holocaust confirms his faith; for the unbeliever it

confirms his lack of faith. For the radical it creates a *novum* in history; for the traditionalist it recalls earlier catastrophes. For the pietist it testifies to God's suffering presence in the world; for the secularist it proves His absence. These variant readings have shown no tendency to converge over time.

The fundamental divide is between those who see the Holocaust as an unprecedented event which shatters our previous understanding of the covenant, and those who insist that the covenant survives intact even in the valley of the shadow of death. Those who take the first view see *Yom Ha-Shoah*, Holocaust Memorial Day, as a seminal addition to the Jewish calendar, a turning point in history. Those who take the second see the Holocaust as a new dimension in an ancient grief, such as that expressed on the ninth of Av, the day of mourning for the destruction of the Temples.[18]

It is important to understand that the ambiguity of the Holocaust is not a feature of the event itself. It is a feature of the pre-understandings that different thinkers bring to it. For many centuries, from the destruction of the Second Temple to the threshold of European Emancipation, Jews shared a broad framework of belief that allowed them to understand their present situation, why it had come about and to what it eventually would lead. They were in exile because of their sins, and one day they would return to their land. That shared framework, which experienced stresses from the Spanish expulsion onward, finally collapsed in the nineteenth century. Those who held to traditional beliefs were now not Jews *tout court,* but a subsection of the community known to their critics as "Orthodox" Jews. The multiplicity of responses to the Holocaust testifies to the still fragmented nature of Jewish consciousness, which lacks a common language through which a people might reflect on its fate. This preceded the Holocaust itself and has persisted since.

But the second fact is in sharp contradistinction to the first. For the *Shoah* confronted Jews with an inescapable reminder that though they might not share a common language, they shared

---

17. Ezekiel 37:11–12.

18. For a discussion of this controversy, see Irving Greenberg, *The Jewish Way* (New York, 1988), pp. 314–372.

a common fate. The "final solution" made no distinctions between Jews. The assimilated half- or quarter-Jew from Vienna or Berlin was cast into the same camp with the pious talmudist from Vilna and the bearded mystic from Berditchev. Jews had different self-definitions. But they were subject to the same other-definition. They might not see themselves, but they were seen by others, as members of the same people.

That fact has significantly shaped post-Holocaust Jewish awareness. The sense of being a people apart and alone, held together in a collective destiny and exercising collective responsibility, has grown. Its focus is the land and State of Israel, symbol and reality of the Jewish determination never again to be homeless, powerless victims. Israel, the land and state, has brought in its wake intractable problems, political, military, and ethical; and over these, too, Jews have been divided. But this does not detract from its centrality in Jewish life worldwide. Nor is this a political proposition only. It is in its own right a theological proposition, albeit a controversial one. For the Bible and all subsequent Jewish thought had seen in the return of Jews to their land a new chapter—perhaps the ultimate one— in the covenantal story.

Jewish responses to the Holocaust, then, reveal not only the divisions that still exist in Jewish thought but also a new impetus toward unity: toward a clear and collective sense of peoplehood. For what is striking is that Jews of all kinds, religious and secular, have responded to their threatened destruction with a fierce determination to survive. "I will not die, but I will live," says the psalm,[19] and that has been the Jewish response to the journey through the valley of the shadow of death. There may be no common understanding of the Jewish destiny, but there is a common conviction that it must be continued. Faced with its eclipse, the Jewish people has reaffirmed its covenant with history. The story of contemporary Jewry begins with what in retrospect is a not unremarkable fact: that the people Israel lives and still bears witness to the living God.

19. Psalms 118:17.

Elie Wiesel

Elie Wiesel was born into a ḥasidic family in Sighet, a small town in Romania, in 1928. As a child, he received a traditional Jewish education. In 1944, when Wiesel was fifteen, the Nazis deported the Jews of Sighet to the death camps of Poland. Wiesel and his family were sent to Auschwitz, where his mother, father, and little sister were murdered. After the war, he settled in Paris, and from 1948 to 1951 he attended the Sorbonne. Eventually he became a journalist writing for both French and Israeli newspapers. It was also in Paris that he wrote his most famous book, *Night* (*La Nuit*, 1958). Its first, longer version was in Yiddish, and this was then followed by a shorter version in French. In this work, in the form of a novel, Wiesel described his experiences during the Holocaust.

In the 1960s, he moved to New York where he continued to work both as a journalist and as a novelist. In 1972, he also began to teach at the City College of New York. In 1976, he became Andrew Mellon Professor of the Humanities at Boston University, a position he has held ever since. Over the past four decades, he has become not only a world-famous author but also a highly influential statesman and humanitarian, working both for Jewish causes, such as the liberation of Soviet Jewry in the 1970s and the State of Israel, and for international humanitarian causes, such as the protection of the native peoples of Central and South America and the victims of war in Yugoslavia. He was the founding chairman of the U.S. President's Commission on the Holocaust in 1979–1980, which created the U.S. Holocaust Memorial Museum in Washington, D.C. In 1986, he received the Nobel Peace Prize. He has also been the recipient of dozens of honorary degrees and major international literary and humanitarian awards. In addition to this extraordinary public career, he has continued to publish a long series of significant novels and essays, most of which deal with the universal meaning of the modern Jewish experience. He has also published two volumes of autobiography, *All Rivers Run to the Sea* (1995) and *And the Sea Is Never Full* (1999).

SELECTION

The present selection, drawn from Elie Wiesel's autobiographical memoir *All Rivers Run to the Sea* is a thoughtful, challenging, mature reflection on the theological significance of the Holocaust. It contends that God suffers along with the Jewish people, that "what happens to us touches God." Yet this fundamental, ontological fact does not lighten the suffering of human beings, though it attributes to it a deeper metaphysical dimension, nor does it justify—for nothing could "justify"—Auschwitz. Instead, this awareness ultimately adds further overwhelming complexity and uncertainty to the human situation and this, in turn, leads to the raising of profound questions about what it is to be human and what sort of world we live in, although it provides no convincing theological answers. Thus, Wiesel's striking and provocative meditation on the problem of evil leaves us with still-unanswered questions and a profound sense of the mystery of being.

Selected Bibliography

Books by Elie Wiesel

Night (New York, 1960): new translation by Marion Wiesel (New York, 2005).

Dawn (New York, 1961).

The Jews of Silence: A Personal Report on Soviet Jewry (New York, 1966; 2d ed., New York, 1973).

Legends of Our Time (New York, 1968).

Souls on Fire: Portraits and Legends of Hasidic Masters (New York, 1972).

With others, *Dimensions of the Holocaust* (Bloomington, Ind., 1977).

Four Hasidic Masters and Their Struggle against Melancholy (Notre Dame, Ind., 1978).

Against Silence: The Voice and Vision of Elie Wiesel, 3 vol., edited by Irving Abrahamson (New York, 1985).

The Trial of God (As It Was Held on February 25, 1649, in Shamgorod): A Play in Three Acts (New York, 1995).

All Rivers Run to the Sea: Memoirs (New York, 1995).

And the Sea Is Never Full: Memoirs 1969– (New York, 1999).

After the Darkness (New York, 2002).

Works about Elie Wiesel

David, Colin. *Elie Wiesel's Secretive Texts* (Gainesville, Fla., 1994).

Lazo, Caroline Evensen. *Elie Wiesel* (New York, 1994).

Rosenfeld, Alvin. *Confronting the Holocaust* (Bloomington, 1978).

Sibelman, Simon P. *Silence in the Novels of Elie Wiesel* (New York, 1995).

Stern, Ellen Norman. *Elie Wiesel: A Voice for Humanity* (Philadelphia, 1996).

God's Suffering: A Commentary

Here is what the Midrash tells us. When the Holy One, blessed be His name, comes to liberate the children of Israel from their exile, they will say to him: "Master of the Universe, it is You who dispersed us among the nations, driving us from Your abode, and now it is You who bring us back. Why is that?" And the Holy One, blessed be His name, will reply with this parable: One day a king drove his wife from his palace, and the next day he had her brought back. The queen, astonished, asked him: "Why did you send me away yesterday only to bring me back today?" "Know this," replied the king, "that I followed you out of the palace, for I could not live in it alone." So the Holy One, blessed be His name, tells the children of Israel: "Having seen you leave my abode, I left it too, that I might return with you."

God accompanies his children into exile. This is a central theme of midrashic and mystical thought in Jewish tradition. Just as the people of Israel's solitude mirrors the Lord's, so the suffering of men finds its extension in that of their Creator. Though imposed by God, the punishment goes beyond those upon whom it falls, encompassing the Judge himself. And it is God who wills it so. The Father may reveal Himself through His wrath; He may even sharpen His severity, but He will never be absent. Present at the Creation, God forms part of it. *Let atar panui minei* is the key phrase of the Book of Splendor, the *Zohar*: No space is devoid of God. God is everywhere, even in suffering and in the very heart of punishment. Israel's sadness is bound to that of the divine presence, the *She'ḥina*: together they await deliverance. The waiting of the one constitutes the other's secret dimension. Just as the distress of the *She'ḥina* seems unbearable to the children of Israel, so Israel's torments rend the heart of the *She'ḥina*.

What happens to us touches God. What happens to Him concerns us. We share in the same adventure and participate in the same quest. We suffer for the same reasons and ascribe the same coefficient to our common hope.

Now, this community of suffering presents certain difficulties. Its purpose is ambiguous. Does it aim to make our human ordeal easier or more difficult to bear? Does the idea that God also suffers—that He suffers with us and therefore on our account—help us to bear our grief, or does it simply augment its weight? Surely we have no right to complain, since God, too, knows suffering; nevertheless, we can say that the suffering of the one does not cancel out the other; rather, the two are added together. In this sense, divine suffering is not consolation but additional punishment. We are therefore entitled to ask of heaven, "Do we not have enough sorrow already? Why must You add Yours to it?"

But it is not our place to make decisions for God. He alone has discretion in the thousands of ways of joining His suffering to ours. We can neither elicit nor reject them, but can only seek to be worthy of them, even without understanding. Where God is concerned, all is mystery.

We know that God suffers, because He tells us so. We know of His role as an exile, because He offers us vivid descriptions. Yet we do not even know His name. When Moses asked Him [in Exodus 3], He replied: "*Eh yeh asber eh yeb*," I shall be who I shall be—in other words, I do not define Myself in the present; My name itself is a projection into the future. "And on that day," says the prophet, "God will be one and His name will be one." Does that mean that now, in exile, God has more than one name? Let us say that His ineffable name has been disseminated in more than one place, taking on more than one identity. But this ineffable name eludes us. It is not the Tetragrammaton, but something else. It is the name the High Priest used to pronounce but once a year, during the Yom Kippur service, in the Holy of Holies of the Temple, in Jerusalem.

Since the Temple no longer exists and its servants were massacred, God seems to have retaken His name, causing it to escape our awareness. But how, then, are we to speak to Him? God has no need of a name to be present. He is present in our request and its fulfillment alike. He is both question and answer. For us mortals, He is at once link and sundering, pain and healing, injury and peace, prayer and pardon. He is, and that must be enough for us.

I confess, however, that sometimes it is not enough for me. Nothing is enough for me when I consider the convulsions our century has endured. God's role is important in that context. How did God manage to bear His suffering added to our own? Are we to imagine the one as justification for the other? Nothing justifies Auschwitz. Were the Lord Himself to offer me a justification, I think I would reject it. Treblinka erases all justifications and all answers.

The barbed-wire kingdom will forever remain an immense question mark on the scale of both humanity and its Creator. Faced with unprecedented suffering and agony, He should have intervened, or at least expressed Himself. Which side was He on? Isn't He the Father of us all? It is in this capacity that He shatters our shell and moves us. How can we fail to pity a Father who witnesses the massacre of his children by his other children? Is there a suffering more devastating, a remorse more bitter?

This is the dilemma confronted by the believer late in this century: by allowing this to happen, God was telling humanity something, and we don't know what it was. That He suffered? He could have—should have—interrupted His own suffering by calling a halt to the martyrdom of innocents. I don't know why He did not do so and I think I never shall. Perhaps that is not His concern. But I find myself equally ignorant as regards men. I will never understand their moral decline, their fall. There was a time when everything roused anger, even revolt, in me against humanity. Later I felt mainly sadness, for the victims.

Commenting on a verse of the prophet Jeremiah according to which God says, "I shall weep in secret," the Midrash remarks that there is a place called "secret" and that when God is sad, He takes refuge there to weep.

684 Part III EUROPEAN AND AMERICAN RESPONSES DURING AND FOLLOWING THE WAR

For us this secret place lies in memory, which possesses its own secret.

A Midrash recounts: When God sees the suffering of His children scattered among the nations, He sheds two tears in the ocean. When they fall, they make a noise so loud it is heard round the world. It is a legend I enjoy rereading. And I tell myself: Perhaps God shed more than two tears during His people's recent tragedy. But men, cowards that they are, refused to hear them.

Is that, at last, an answer?

No. It is a question. Yet another question.

BIBLIOGRAPHY

Angel, Marc D., ed. *Exploring the Thought of Rabbi Joseph B. Soloveitchik* (Hoboken, N.J., 1997).

Barzilai, David Fromm. "Agonism in Faith," *Modern Judaism* 23, no. 2 (May 2003): 156–179.

Berkovits, Eliezer. *Crisis and Faith* (New York, 1975).

———. *Faith after the Holocaust* (New York, 1973).

———. *Major Themes in Modern Philosophies of Judaism* (New York, 1974).

———. *With God in Hell: Judaism in the Ghettos and Death Camps* (New York, 1979).

Bernasconi, Robert, and Simon Critchley, eds. *Re-Reading Levinas* (Bloomington, Ind., 1991).

Bernasconi, Robert, and David Wood, eds. *The Provocation of Levinas: Rethinking the Other* (London, 1988).

Blumenthal, David. "Michael Wyschogrod," in *Interpreters of Judaism in the Late Twentieth Century*, edited by Steven T. Katz (Washington, D.C., 1993), pp. 393–405.

Borowitz, Eugene B. *A New Jewish Theology in the Making* (Philadelphia, 1968).

———. "A Theology of Modern Orthodoxy: Rabbi Joseph B. Soloveitchik," in *Choices in Modern Jewish Thought*, edited by Eugene B. Borowitz (New York, 1983), pp. 218–242.

Braiterman, Zachary. *(God) after Auschwitz* (Princeton, N.J., 1998).

Buber, Martin. *Eclipse of God* (New York, 1952).

———. *Ich und Du* (Leipzig, 1923).

———. *I and Thou*, translated by Walter Kaufman (New York, 1970).

———. *On Judaism*, edited by N. Glatzer (New York, 1972).

Cohen, Arthur A. *The Natural and Supernatural Jew* (New York, 1962).

———. "On Theological Method: A Response on Behalf of the *Tremendum*," *Journal of Reform Judaism* 31, no. 2 (Spring 1984): 56–65.

———. *The Tremendum: A Theological Interpretation of the Holocaust* (New York, 1981).

Cohen, Arthur A., ed. *Arguments and Doctrines: A Reader of Jewish Thinking in the Aftermath of the Holocaust* (New York, 1970).

Cohen, Arthur & Paul Mendes Flohr, eds., *Contemporary Jewish Religious Thought* (New York, 1988).

Cohen, Richard A. *Elevations: The Height of the Good in Levinas and Rosenzweig* (Chicago, 1994).

Cohen, Richard A., ed. *Face to Face with Emmanuel Levinas* (Albany, 1986).

Cohen, David, *Elie Wiesel's Secreting Texts* (Gainesville, 1994).

Critchley, Simon, and Robert Bernasconi, eds. *The Cambridge Companion to Levinas* (Cambridge, 2002).

Eidelberg, Shlomo, trans. *The Jews and the Crusaders: The Hebrew Chronicles of the First and Second Crusades* (Madison, Wis., 1977).

Eisen, Robert. "A. J. Heschel's Rabbinic Theology as a Response to the Holocaust," *Modern Judaism* 23, no. 3 (October 2003): 211–225.

Fackenheim, Emil. *Encounters between Judaism and Modern Philosophy: A Preface to Future Jewish Thought* (New York, 1973).

———. *God's Presence in History: Jewish Affirmation and Philosophical Reflections* (New York, 1970).

———. *Jewish Philosophy and Jewish Philosophers*, edited by Michael Morgan (Bloomington, Ind., 1996).

———. *The Jewish Return into History: Reflections in the Age of Auschwitz and a New Jerusalem* (New York, 1978).

———. *To Mend the World: Foundations of Future Jewish Thought* (New York, 1982).

———. *What Is Judaism: An Interpretation for the Present Ages* (New York, 1987).

Faierstein, Morris. "Heschel and the Holocaust," *Modern Judaism* 19, no. 3 (October 1999): 255–275.

Fox, Marvin. "Berkovits' Treatment of the Problem of Evil," *Tradition* 14, no. 3 (Spring 1974): 116–124.

Friedman, Maurice. *Martin Buber's Life and Work*, 2 vols. (Detroit, 1988).

Funkenstein, Amos. "Anti-Jewish Propaganda: Ancient, Medieval, and Modern," *Jerusalem Quarterly* 19 (Spring 1981): 56–72.

———. "Collective Memory and Historical Consciousness," *History and Memory* 1 (1989): 5–26.

———. "An Escape from History? Franz Rosenzweig and the Destiny of Judaism," *History and Memory* 2 (1990): 117–135.

———. "The Incomprehensible Catastrophe: Memory and Narrative," *Narrative Study of Lives* 1 (1993): 21–29.

———. "Job without Theodicy," in Perceptions of Jewish History: From Antiquity to the Present (Tel Aviv, 1991), pp. 35–40 [Hebrew].

———. *Maimonides: Nature, History, and Society* [Hebrew] (Tel Aviv, 1983). Translated into French as *Maimonides: Nature, histoire, et messianisme* (Paris, 1988).

———. *Perceptions of Jewish History* (Berkeley, 1993).

———. *Theology and the Scientific Imagination from the Middle Ages to the Seventeenth Century* (Princeton, N.J., 1986).

Goldberg, Hillel. *Between Berlin and Slobodka: Jewish Transition Figures from Eastern Europe* (Hoboken, N.J., 1989).

———. "Rabbi Isaac Hutner: A Synoptic Interpretive Biography," *Tradition* 22 (Winter 1987): 18–46.

Gordis, Robert. *Faith for Moderns* (New York, 1960).

———. *God and Man: A Study of Job* (New York, 1965).

———. *Judaism for the Modern Age* (New York, 1955).

———. *Koheleth: The Man and His World* (New York, 1951).

Gordon, Haim, and Jochanan, Bloch, eds. *Martin Buber: A Centenary Volume* (n.p., 1984).

Greenberg, Irving (Yitzchak). "Cloud of Smoke, Pillar of Fire: Judaism, Christianity, and Modernity after the Holocaust," in *Auschwitz: Beginning of a New Era?* edited by Eva Fleischner (New York, 1977), pp. 7–55, 441–446.

———. "The Interaction of Israel and American Jewry after the Holocaust," in *World Jewry and the State of Israel*, edited by Moshe Davis (New York, 1977), pp. 259–282.

———. "The Third Great Cycle of Jewish History," *Perspectives* (September 1981).

———. *For the Sake of Heaven and Earth: The New Encounter between Judaism and Christianity* (Philadelphia, 2004).

———. *The Jewish Way: Living the Holidays* (New York, 1993).

———. *Living in the Image of God: Jewish Teachings to Perfect the World* (Northvale, Calif., 1998).

———. *The Third Great Cycle of Jewish History* (New York, 1981).

———. "Voluntary Covenant," *Perspectives* (October 1982).

Habermann, A. M., *Sefer Gezerot Ashkenaz Ve-Tzarfat* (Jerusalem, 1945) [Hebrew].

Hartman, David. *A Living Covenant* (New York, 1985).

Hellig, Jocelyn. "Richard Rubenstein," in *Interpreters of Judaism in the Twentieth Century*, edited by Steven T. Katz (Washington, D.C., 1993), pp. 249–264.

Heschel, Abraham J. *God in Search of Man: A Philosophy of Judaism* (New York, 1956).

———. *Heavenly Torah as Refracted through the Generations*, translated by Gordon Tucker and Leonard Levin (New York, 2005).

———. *Man Is Not Alone: A Philosophy of Religion* (New York, 1951).

Hutner, Isaac. "Holocaust," *Jewish Observer* (October 1977), pp. 3–9.

———. *Pachad Yitzchak . . . [The Banner of Isaac: Torah Discourses on Matters of Faith and the Duties of the Heart*]; 8 vols. (Brooklyn, N.Y., 1965–1982) [Hebrew].

———. *Sefer haZikkaron* [*Memorial Volume on the Late Author of "Pachad Yitzchak"*], edited by J. Buksboim (Brooklyn, N.Y., 1984) [Hebrew].

Jonas, Hans. *The Phenomenon of Life* (New York, 1982).

———. *Philosophical Essays* (Chicago, 1980).

———. *The Imperative of Responsibility* (Chicago, 1984).

Kaplan, Edward K. "Language and Reality in Abraham J. Heschel's Philosophy of Religion," *Journal of the American Academy of Religion* 41 (March 1973): 94–113.

Kaplan, Edward, and Samuel Dresner. *Abraham Joshua Heschel: Prophetic Witness* (New Haven, 1998).

Kaplan, Lawrence. "Rabbi Isaac Hutner's 'Da'at Torah Perspective' on the Holocaust," *Tradition* 18, no. 3 (Fall 1980): 235–248.

Kaplan, Zvi Jonathan. "Rabbi Joel Teitelbaum, Zionism, and Hungarian Ultra-Orthodoxy," *Modern Judaism* 24, no. 2 (May 2004): 165–178.

Katz, Jacob. *Exclusiveness and Tolerance* (London, 1961).

Katz, Steven T. "The Crucifixion of the Jews: Ignaz Maybaum's Theology of the Holocaust," in Steven T. Katz, *Post-Holocaust Dialogues: Critical Studies in Modern Jewish Thought*, (New York, 1983), pp. 248–267.

———. "Emil Fackenheim on Jewish Life after Auschwitz," in Steven T. Katz, *Post-Holocaust Dialogues*, (New York, 1983), pp. 205–247.

———. "Irving (Yitzchak) Greenberg," in *Interpreters of Judaism in the Late Twentieth Century*, edited by Steven T. Katz (Washington, D.C., 1993), pp. 59–89.

———. "Richard Rubenstein, the God of History, and the Logic of Judaism," in Steven T. Katz, *Post-Holocaust Dialogues*, (New York, 1983), pp. 174–204.

———. "'The Tremendum': Arthur Cohen's Understanding of Faith after the Holocaust," in Steven T. Katz, *Historicism, the Holocaust, and Zionism* (New York, 1992), pp. 251–273.

———. *The Holocaust in Historical Context*, vol. 1 (New York, 1994).

———. "Voluntary Covenant: Irving Greenberg on Faith after the Holocaust," in Steven T. Katz, *Historicism, the Holocaust and Zionism: Critical Studies in Modern Jewish Thought and History* (New York, 1992), pp. 225–250.

Kolitz Zvi. *Yossel Rakover Talks to God* (New York, 1999).

Lazo, Caroline, *Elie Wiesel* (New York, 1994).

Levenson, Jon D. "Chosen Peoples: A Review of [Irving Greenberg's] *For the Sake of Heaven and Earth*," *Commonweal* 131, no. 9 (5 November 2004): 49–53. With a reply by Irving Greenberg, "Do Jews and Christians Worship the Same God?" *Commonweal* 132, no. 2 (28 January 2005): 12–13; with a response by Jon D. Levenson, p. 13.

Levinas, Emmanuel. *Collected Philosophical Papers*, edited and translated by Alphonso Lingris (Dordrecht, 1987).

———. *Difficult Freedom: Essays on Judaism*, translated by Sean Hand (Baltimore, Md., 1990).

———. *In the Time of the Nations*, translated by Michael B. Smith (Bloomington, Ind., 1994).

———. *The Levinas Reader*, edited by Sean Hand (Cambridge, Mass. 1989).

———. *Nine Talmudic Readings*, translated by Annette Aronowitz (Bloomington, Ind., 1990).

———. *Otherwise Than Being; or, Beyond Essence*, translated by Alphonso Lingris (The Hague, 1981).

———. *Totality and Infinity: An Essay in Exteriority*, translated by Alphonso Lingris (Pittsburgh, 1979).

———. "Useless Suffering," in *The Provocation of Levinas*, edited by R. Berlasconi and D. Wood (London, 1988).

Lichtenstein, Aharon. "Rabbi Joseph Soloveitchik," in *Great Jewish Thinkers of the Twentieth Century*, edited by Simon Noveck (New York, 1963), pp. 281–297.

Maybaum, Ignaz. *The Face of God after Auschwitz* (Amsterdam, 1965).

———. *The Faithful of the Jewish Diaspora* (London, 1962).

———. *Jewish Existence* (London, 1960).

———. *Man and Catastrophe*, translated by Joseph Leftwich (London, 1941).

———. *The Sacrifice of Isaac: A Jewish Commentary* (London, 1959).

———. *Synagogue and Society: Jewish-Christian Collaboration in the Defense of Western Civilization*, translated by Joseph Leftwich (London, 1944).

Merkle, Jonathon. *The Genesis of Faith: The Depth of Theology of Abraham Joshua Heschel* (New York, 1985).

Merkle, Jonathon, ed. *Abraham Joshua Heschel: Exploring His Life and Thought* (New York, 1985).

Morgan, Michael. "The Central Problem of Fackenheim's *To Mend the World*," *Journal of Jewish Thought and Philosophy* 5 (1996): 297–312.

———. Introduction to *The Jewish Thought of Emil Fackenheim* (Detroit, 1987), pp. 13–18.

Myers, David, et al., eds. "Amos Funkenstein's Perceptions of Jewish History: An Evaluation of His Works by His Students," special issue of *Jewish Social Studies* 6, no. 1 (1999).

Nadler, Allan L. "Piety and Politics: The Case of the Satmar Rebbe," *Judaism* 31, no. 2 (spring 1982): 135–152.

Raffel, Charles M. "Eliezer Berkovits," in *Contemporary Jewish Thinkers*, edited by Steven T. Katz (Washington, D.C., 1993), pp. 1–16.

Raphael, Melissa. *The Female Face of God in Auschwitz: A Jewish Feminist Theology of the Holocaust* (London, 2003).

———. "Feminism, Constructivism, and Numinous Experience," *Religious Studies* 30 (1994): 511–526.

———. "From History to Theology: Gender and Ethics in the Production of Holocaust Theology from Women's Memoirs of Auschwitz," *Religion and Gender: New Perspectives*, edited by Ursula King and Tina Beattie (London, 2003), pp. 101–112.

———. "Goddess Religion, Postmodern Jewish Feminism, and the Complexity of Alternative Religious Identities," *Nova Religio* 1 (1998): 198–214.

———. "Holiness in Extremis: Jewish Women's Resistance to the Profane in Auschwitz," in *Holiness Past and Present*, edited by S. Barton (Edinburgh, 2002).

———. "'I Am Who I Will Be': The Representation of God in Postmodern Jewish Feminist Theology and Contemporary Religious Education," *British Journal of Religious Education* 21 (1999): 69–79.

———. *Introducing Theology: Discourse on the Goddess* (Sheffield, England, 1999).

———. "Is Patriarchal Theology Still Patriarchal: Reading Theologies of the Holocaust from a Jewish

Feminist Perspective," *Journal of Feminist Studies of Religion* 18 (2002): 105–113.

———. "The Price of (Masculine) Freedom and Becoming: A Feminist Critique of the Use of the Free Will Defence in Post-Holocaust Jewish Philosophy," in *Feminist Philosophy of Religion: Critical Perspectives*, edited by Pamela Sue Anderson and Beverley Clack (London, 2003), pp. 136–150.

———. *Rudolf Otto and the Concept of Holiness* (Oxford, 1997).

———. *Theology and Embodiment: The Post-Patriarchal Reconstruction of Female Sacrality* (Sheffield, England, 1996).

———. "When God Beheld God: Notes towards a Jewish Feminist Theology of the Holocaust," *Feminist Theology* 21 (1999): 53–78.

Ravitsky, Aviezer. *Messianism, Zionism, and Jewish Religious Radicalism*, translated by Michael Swirsky and Jonathan Chipman (Chicago, 1996).

Rosenfeld, Alvin, *Confronting the Holocaust* (Bloomington, 1978).

Rubenstein, Richard. *After Auschwitz: Radical Theology and Contemporary Judaism* (Indianapolis, 1966; 2d ed., Baltimore, Md., 1992).

———. *The Age of Triage: Fear and Hope in an Overcrowded World* (Boston, 1983).

———. *My Brother Paul* (New York, 1972).

———. *Power Struggle: An Autobiographical Confession* (New York, 1974).

———. *The Religious Imagination: A Study in Psychoanalysis and Jewish Theology* (Indianapolis, 1968).

Sacks, Jonathan. *Arguments for the Sake of Heaven* (London, 1991).

———. *Crisis and Covenant: Jewish Thought after the Holocaust* (London, 1992).

———. *Dignity of Difference* (London, 2002).

———. *One People?* (London, 1993).

———. *Persistence of Faith* (London, 1991).

———. *The Politics of Hope* (London, 1997; 2d ed., London, 2000).

———. *Radical Then, Radical Now* (London, 2001), published in America as *A Letter in the Scroll* (New York, 2000).

———. *Tradition in an Untraditional Age: Essays in Modern Jewish Thought* (London, 1990).

Saperstein, Marc. "A Sermon on the *Akedah* from the Generation of the Expulsion and Its Implications for 1391," in *Exile and Diaspora: Studies in the History of the Jewish People Presented to Professor Haim Beinart*, edited by Aharon Mirsky et al. (Jerusalem, 1991), pp. 103–124.

Schilpp, Paul, and Maurice Friedman, eds. *The Philosophy of Martin Buber* (La Salle, Illinois, 1967).

Schwarzschild, Steven S. "An Introduction to the Thought of R. Isaac Hutner," *Modern Judaism* 5 (Fall 1985): 235–277.

———. "Isaac Hutner," in *Interpreters of Judaism in the Late Twentieth Century*, edited by Steven T. Katz (Washington, D.C., 1993), pp. 151–165.

———. "Two Lectures of R. Isaac Hutner," *Tradition* 14 (Fall 1974): 90–109.

Shulvass, Moses. "Crusaders, Martyrs, and the Marranos of Ashkenaz," in his *Between the Rhine and the Bosphorus: Studies and Essays in European Jewish History* (Chicago, 1964), pp. 1–14.

Sibelman, Simon P. *Silence in the Novels of Elie Wiesel* (New York, 1995).

Singer, David, and Moshe Sokol. "Joseph Soloveitchik: Lonely Man of Faith," *Modern Judaism* 2, no. 3 (October 1982): 227–272.

———. "The New Orthodox Theology," *Modern Judaism* 9, no. 1 (1989): 35–54.

Soloveitchik, Joseph B. *Fate and Destiny: From Holocaust to the State of Israel*, edited by Walter Wurzburger (New York, 1961).

———. *Halakhic Man* (Philadelphia, 1983).

———. *The Halakhic Mind* (New York, 1986)

———. "The Lonely Man of Faith," *Tradition* 7, no. 2 (Summer 1965): 5–67.

———. *On Repentance* (New York, 1984).

———. *Out of the Whirlwind: Essays on Mourning, Suffering, and the Human Condition*, edited by David Shatz, Joel B. Wolowelsky, and Reuven Ziegler (Hoboken, N.J., 2003).

———. *The Rav Speaks* (Jerusalem, 1983).

Spiegel, Shalom. *The Last Trial* (New York, 1967).

Stern, Ellen Norman, *Elie Wiesel: A Voice for Humanity* (Philadelphia, 1996).

Teitelbaum, Joel. *VaYoel Moshe*, 3 vols. (Brooklyn, N.Y., 1959, 1960, 1961).

Wasserman, Elhanan. *In the Footsteps of the Messiah* (Tel Aviv, 5702/1942) [Hebrew].

Wyschogrod, Edith. *Emmanuel Levinas: The Problem of Ethical Metaphysics* (The Hague, 1974).

Wyschogrod, Michael. *Abraham's Promise: Judaism and Jewish-Christian Relations* (Grand Rapids, 2004).

———. "Auschwitz: Beginning of a New Era?" *Tradition* 17, no. 1 (Fall 1978): 63–78.

———. *The Body of Faith: Judaism as Corporeal Election* (Minneapolis, 1983).

———. "Buber's Evaluation of Christianity: A Jewish Perspective," in *Martin Buber: A Centenary Volume*, edited by Hayim Gordon and Jochanan Bloch (Tel Aviv, 1981), pp. 403–417 [Hebrew]; pp. 457–472 [English].

———. "Faith and the Holocaust," *Judaism* 20 (Summer 1971): 286–294.

———. "Israel, the Church, and Election," in *Brothers in Hope*, edited by John Oesterreicher (New York, 1970), pp. 79–87.

———. *Kierkegaard and Heidegger: The Ontology of Existence* (London, 1953).

———. "A New Stage in Jewish-Christian Dialogue," *Judaism* 31 (Summer 1982): 355–365.

———. "Some Theological Reflections on the Holocaust," *Response* 25 (Spring 1975): 65–68.

———. "Symposium: The State of Orthodoxy," *Tradition* 20 (Spring 1982): 80–83.